Human Factors in Computing Systems

Common Ground

CHI 96

CHI 96 CONFERENCE PROCEEDINGS

EDITORS

Michael J. Tauber

Victoria Bellotti, Design Briefings
Robin Jeffries, Papers
Jock D. Mackinlay, Papers
Jakob Nielsen, Design Briefings

TECHNICAL PROGRAM CO-CHAIRS

Bonnie Nardi
Gerrit C. van der Veer

Sponsored by ACM's Special Interest Group
on Computer-Human Interaction (SIGCHI)

Conference on Human Factors in Computing Systems

APRIL 13–18, 1996

VANCOUVER, BRITISH COLUMBIA, CANADA

The Association for Computing Machinery, Inc.
1515 Broadway
New York, NY 10036

...In proceedings of the CHI '96, 1996 (Vancouver, BC, Canada, April 13-18, 1996) ACM, New York, 1996, pp. 23-35.

Ordering Information

Nonmembers
Nonmember orders placed within the U.S. should be directed to:

Addison-Wesley Publishing Company
Order Department
Jacob Way
Reading, MA 01867
Tel: +1 800 447 2226

Addison-Wesley will pay postage and handling on orders accompanied by check. Credit card orders may be placed by mail or by calling the Addison-Wesley Order Department at the number above. Follow-up inquiries should be directed to the Customer Service Department at the same number. Please include the Addison-Wesley ISBN number with your order:

A-W ISBN 0-201-94687-4

Nonmember orders from outside the U.S. should be addressed as noted below:

Europe/Middle East

Addison-Wesley Publishing Group
Concertgebouwplein 25
1071 LM Amsterdam
The Netherlands
Tel: +31 20 6717296
Fax: +31 20 6645334

Germany/Austria/Switzerland

Addison-Wesley Verlag Deutschland GmbH
Hildachstrasse 15d
Wachsbleiche 7-12
53111 Bonn
Germany
Tel: +49 228 98 515 0
Fax: +49 228 98 515 99

UK/Ireland/Africa

Addison Wesley Longman Ltd.
Edinburgh Gate
Harlow, Essex CM20 2JE
United Kingdom
Tel: +44 1279 623623
Fax: +44 1279 431059

Asia

Addison-Wesley Singapore Pte. Ltd.
No. 11 Cantonment Road
Singapore 089736
Tel: +65 223 8155
Fax: +65 223 7155

Japan

Addison-Wesley Publishers Japan Ltd.
Nichibo Building
1-2-2 Sarugakucho
Chiyoda-ku, Tokyo 101
Japan
Tel: +81 33 291 4581
Fax: +81 33 291 4592

Australia

Addison Wesley Longman Australia Pty. Ltd.
95 Coventry Street
South Melbourne, VIC 3205
Australia
Tel: +61 3 9697 0666
Fax: +61 3 9699 2041

New Zealand

Additon Wesley Longman
New Zealand Ltd.
46 Hillside Road
Glenfield
Auckland 10
New Zealand
Tel: +64 9 444 4069
Fax: +64 9 444 4957

Latin America

Addison-Wesley Iberoamericana S.A.
Boulevard de las Cataratas #3
Colonia Jardines del Pedregal
Delegacion Alvaro Obregon
01900 Mexico D. F.
Tel: +52 5 660 2695
Fax: +52 5 660 4930

Canada

Addison-Wesley Publishing
(Canada) Ltd.
26 Prince Andrew Place
Don Mills, Ontario M3C 2T8
Canada
Tel: +416 447 5101
Fax: +416 443 0948

ACM Members
A limited number of copies are available at the ACM member discount. Send order with payment in US dollars to:

ACM Order Department
P.O. Box 12114
Church Street Station
New York, N.Y. 10257

OR

ACM European Service Center
108 Cowley Rd. Oxford
OX4/JF, UK
Tel: +44 1865 382338
Fax: +44 1865 381338
email:acm_europe@acm.org

Credit card orders from U.S.A. and Canada:
+1 800 342 6626

New York Metropolitan Area and outside of the U.S.:
+1 212 626 0500
Fax +1 212 944 1318
Email:acmhelp@acm.org

Please include your ACM member number and the ACM Order number with your order.

ACM Order Number: 608960
ACM ISBN: 0-89791-777-4

Papers: Color and Transparency

THURSDAY, APRIL 18—11:30 AM TO 1:00 PM

SESSION CHAIR
Don Gentner, *SunSoft*

Papers: Information Structure

THURSDAY, APRIL 18—2:30 PM TO 4:00 PM

SESSION CHAIR
Scott Hudson, *Georgia Institute of Technology*

Papers: Usability Issues

THURSDAY, APRIL 18—2:30 PM TO 4:00 PM

SESSION CHAIRS
Richard I. Anderson, *Usability/Design Adventures*
John Karat, *IBM T.J. Watson Research Center*

Design Briefings: Small Objects of Desire

TUESDAY, APRIL 16—2:30 PM TO 4:00 PM

SESSION CHAIR
Karen Bedard, *Hyundai Electronics America*

Design Briefings: Design for Communication and Communication for Design

WEDNESDAY, APRIL 17—9:00 AM TO 10:30 AM

SESSION CHAIR
Allan MacLean, *Rank Xerox Research Centre*

Design Briefings: User Interfaces for Large Markets

WEDNESDAY, APRIL 17—11:30 AM TO 1:00 PM

SESSION CHAIR
Daniel Rosenberg, *Oracle Corporation*

Invited Contribution

TUESDAY, APRIL 16—11:30 AM TO 1:00 PM

SESSION CHAIR
Judy Hammond, *University of Technology, Sidney*

Invited Contribution

TUESDAY, APRIL 16—2:30 PM TO 4:00 PM

SESSION CHAIR
Terry Winograd, *Stanford University*

Invited Contribution

THURSDAY, APRIL 18—2:30 PM TO 4:00 PM

SESSION CHAIR
Ian McClelland, *Philips Corporate Design*

환영 **Benvinguts** *Soyez le bienvenu* **Velkommen** ようこそ Bien Venido dobro nam došli **Välkommen** **KALOS IRTHATE** 歓迎

Welcome from the ACM SIGCHI Chair and Executive Vice-Chair

On behalf of the Executive Committee of ACM's Special Interest Group on Computer-Human Interaction (ACM SIGCHI), welcome to CHI 96, SIGCHI'S annual conference on Human-Computer Interaction. Each CHI conference offers a snapshot of the HCI field as it grows and evolves, of the people who define the HCI field, and of the people who collectively form SIGCHI. These proceedings provide a history of the growth and evolution of HCI. As HCI has evolved, so have these proceedings evolved as an experiment in electronic publishing. The CHI 96 Proceedings will be available on the world wide web several months after the conference. We are grateful to the CHI 96 committee for taking this step and look forward to using what they learn this year in evolving proceedings in future years.

We also welcome you to participate in SIGCHI, a global society of over 5,000 people with a common interest in HCI. While the CHI conference is the most visible activity of SIGCHI, we also:

- support conferences in computer-supported cooperative work (CSCW), multimedia (MM), user interface software and technology (UIST), designing interactive systems (DIS), and intelligent user interfaces (IUI).
- distribute the highly-respected quarterly SIGCHI Bulletin to members and others.
- supported the "birth" and continue to support the evolution of two new publications—Transactions on Computer-Human Interactions (TOCHI), a member of the ACM Transactions series, and interactions, ACM's first magazine devoted to HCI practitioners.
- provide support to a number of activities proposed by our members that provide benefit both to SIGCHI and the field of HCI. The SIGCHI Development Fund supports many of these activities and Calls for Proposals are distributed at this conference and appear frequently in the SIGCHI Bulletin.

SIGCHI is a vibrant and growing community and we invite your continued participation. This conference is one of the forums that SIGCHI provides for people to meet, both formally and informally, to exchange views, to share experiences, and to learn. These forums are not just attended by SIGCHI members, they are defined by SIGCHI members. We invite you to join and stay involved in this community and to define the forums of the future. We also invite you to join with other volunteers in providing SIGCHI's leadership.

Finally, on behalf of ACM/SIGCHI, we thank and congratulate the conference committee and all the volunteers who make this conference possible and who ensure a valuable experience for all of us. Thanks for a job well done!

Welcome to CHI 96 and to SIGCHI.

Mike Atwood | ACM SIGCHI Chair

Guy Boy | ACM SIGCHI Executive Vice-Chair

Bine aţi venit **Welkom** Добро пожаловать Benvenuto **Üdvözölve** vítáme Vás **Ongi ettori** **Willkommen** ***Witamy***

환영 **Benvinguts** *Soyez le bienvenu* **Velkommen** ようこそ Bien Venido dobro nam došli Välkommen KALOS IRTHATE 歡迎

Welcome from the Conference Co-Chairs

The use of computer technology is no longer the privilege of an elite few. Rapid technological progress in fields such as Multimedia, Telecommunications, Computer Graphics and Networking is pushing the development of personal and ubiquitous computing. Computers are becoming increasingly part of everyone's life. Research and development in these fields focus on the design and implementation of advanced technologies. However, they are not primarily concerned with how their creations influence, determine, constrain, or enhance the way people think, act, work, and collaborate.

In the light of these rapid changes in technology, it is a continuous challenge for the field of Human-Computer Interaction (HCI) to keep its collective eyes on the humans using the technology, and understand and design the way that people interact with and via computers.

Since several different fields and cultures currently see themselves as advocates for a human-centered view, we are increasingly aware of the trend toward diversification within HCI. As these CHI 96 Proceedings and Companion show, we have contributions from

• different research fields (e.g. Computer Science, Psychology, Social Science, Graphics Design, Architecture)

• different sub-fields (e.g. Multimedia, Computer Graphics, Virtual Reality, User Interface Technology, CSCW)

• universities, research laboratories, big and small companies

• different application fields (e.g. E-Mail, News, World Wide Web, Telephones)

• different work cultures (e.g. academia, industry; software engineers, graphic designers, movie makers, researchers)

• different parts of the world (North America, Asia, Australia, Europe)

focusing at

• different markets (specialized and small, large), and

• different user groups (e.g. children, everyone, special jobs, special needs)

Common Ground is the theme for CHI 96, emphasizing the need for identifying and experiencing the commonality between the different views, fields, and cultures involved in HCI. In his opening address, Herb Clark discusses the important role of a common ground to facilitate communication between people, as well as between people and machines. A common ground needs to be built and maintained in order to keep communication alive. The same holds for the field of Human-Computer Interaction.

Many contributions to CHI 96 address the issue of a common ground in HCI. We encourage the reader of these CHI 96 Proceedings and Companion to do the same: to explore the Common Ground between the different fields and cultures forming the discipline of Human-Computer Interaction. The challenge is to see beyond the obvious differences to an underlying core of shared beliefs and experiences. This is the Common Ground that allows us to exchange ideas and learn from each other.

Kevin M. Schofield | **Michael J. Tauber**

CHI 96 General Co-Chairs

Bine aţi venit **Welkom** Добро пожаловать Benvenuto **Üdvözölve** vítáme Vás **Ongi ettori** **Willkommen** ***Witamy***

SPECIAL THANKS

The CHI 96 conference would not be possible without the efforts of the conference committee volunteers. Thanks to all these individuals and the following institutions whose support has made their participation possible:

- 3M Hardgoods and Electronic Support Division
- AT&T
- Apple Computer, Inc.
- Bank of Montreal
- Bowling Green State University
- CNUCE-C.N.R
- Design Technologies, Inc.
- EDS Technical Consulting Program
- Hewlett-Packard
- Hitachi Denshi, Ltd.
- IBM
- LGI-IMAG
- Lawrence Livermore National Laboratory
- Lockheed AI Center
- Lotus Development Corporation
- Microsoft
- National University of Singapore
- Philips
- Simon Fraser University
- SunSoft, Inc.
- The University of Huddersfield
- U S WEST
- University of British Columbia
- University of Guelph
- University of Maryland
- University of Massachusetts Lowell
- University of Minnesota
- University of New Mexico
- University of Paderborn
- University of Queensland
- University of Technology Loughborough
- University of Technology Sidney
- University of Toronto
- University of Vienna
- University of Washington
- Vrije Universiteit Amsterdam
- Xerox

CHI 96 acknowledges the conference corporate sponsors for their generous support:

- Apple
- AT&T Bell Labs
- Bellcore
- Canon
- IBM
- Intel
- Microsoft
- NORTEL/BNR
- NYNEX
- Oracle
- Philips
- SunSoft
- U S WEST

Rent-a-Computer

CHI 96 thanks Rent-a-Computer, Philips, and John Wiley and Sons for their support for CHIkids

CHI 96 is sponsored by the ACM Special Interest Group on Computer-Human Interaction (ACM SIGCHI).

Cooperating Societies

- ACM Special Interest Group on Computer Graphics (ACM SIGGRAPH)
- ACM Special Interest Group on Computers and the Physically Handicapped (ACM SIGCAPH)
- ACM Special Interest Group on Office Information Systems (ACM SIGOIS)
- Association for Artificial Intelligence of Russia (RAAI)
- Association Française des Sciences et Technologies de l'Information et des Systèmes (AFCET)
- Association pour la Recherche Cognitive (ARC)
- Austrian Computer Society (OCG)
- Belgian Ergonomics Society (BES)
- British HCI Group (B-HCI-G, BCS)
- Chinese Society of Multimedia Technology
- CHISIG, Australia (CHISIGAU)
- CHISIG, New Zealand (CHISIGNZ)
- Cognitive Science Society
- Czech Society for Cybernetics and Informatics
- The Division of Applied Experimental and Engineering Psychologists of the American Psychological Association (Div. 21 of APA)
- Dutch Computer Society (NGI)
- Eurographics
- European Association of Cognitive Ergonomics (EACE)
- Gesellschaft für Informatik, Fachgruppe Softwareergonomie (GI)
- Hongkong Chapter of the ACM
- Human Factors and Ergonomics Society (HFES)
- Human Interface (SICE-HI Japan)
- IEEE Computer Society
- IEICE, Human Communication Engineering Group, Japan
- Information Processing Society of Japan, SIGGroupware and SIGHI (IPSJ)
- Italian Association for Artificial Intelligence (AIIA)
- Italian Computer Society (AICA)
- Italian Ergonomics Society (SIE)
- Japanese Society for Artificial Intelligence
- Slovak Society for Cybernetics and Informatics
- Software Psychology Society (Potomac Chapter)
- Swedish Interdisciplinary Interest Group for Human-Computer Interaction (STIMDI)

Senior Management Team

Conference Co-Chairs
Kevin M. Schofield
Microsoft (USA)

Michael J. Tauber
University of Paderborn (Germany)

Technical Program Co-Chairs
Bonnie Nardi
Apple Computer, Inc. (USA)

Gerrit C. van der Veer
Vrije Universiteit Amsterdam, University of Twente (The Netherlands)

Technology Support Chair
Steve Guest
Loughborough University (UK)

Treasurer
Bob Gallup
Microsoft (USA)

SIGCHI CMC Liaison
Gene Lynch
Design Technologies, Inc. (USA)

ACM Liaison
Diane Darrow, CAE
ACM (USA)

Technical Program

Basic Research Symposium
Alan Dix
The University of Huddersfield (UK)

Francesmary Modugno
University of Washington (USA)

Demonstrations
Gurminder Singh
National University of Singapore (Singapore)

Dan Venolia
Apple Computer, Inc. (USA)

Design Briefings
Victoria Bellotti
Apple Computer, Inc. (USA)

Jakob Nielsen
SunSoft, Inc. (USA)

Doctoral Consortium
Tom Carey
University of Guelph (Canada)

Simon Kaplan
University of Queensland (Australia)

Organization Overviews
Lisa Neal
EDS Technical Consulting Program (USA)

Gerd Szwillus
University of Paderborn (Germany)

Panels
Joelle Coutaz
LGI-IMAG (France)

Steve Whittaker
AT&T Research Laboratories (USA)

Papers
Robin Jeffries
SunSoft, Inc. (USA)

Jock D. Mackinlay
Xerox PARC (USA)

Short Papers and Interactive Posters
Michael J. Muller
U S WEST Advanced Technologies (USA)

Manfred Tscheligi
University of Vienna (Austria)

Social Action Interactive Posters
Pamela Burke
AT&T (USA)

Andrea Mosher
Xerox (USA)

Tutorials
Mark W. Altom
AT&T Bell Laboratories (USA)

Marian G. Williams
University of Massachusetts Lowell (USA)

Videos
Mark Chignell
University of Toronto (Canada)

Catherine Plaisant
University of Maryland (USA)

Workshops and SIGS
Ellen Issacs
SunSoft, Inc. (USA)

Vicki O'Day
Xerox PARC (USA)

Operations

Audio Visual Support
Curt Stevens
Apple Computer, Inc. (USA)

Childcare
Allison Druin
University of New Mexico (USA)

Commons
Lyn Bartram
Simon Fraser University (Canada)

Computing Support
Jon Dukes-Schlossberg
Lockheed AI Center (USA)

Exhibits
Joe Konstan
University of Minnesota (USA)

Janelle Kozak
3M Hardgoods and Electronics Support Division (USA)

Hypermedia Support
Keith Instone
Bowling Green State University (USA)

Industry Liaison
Ian L. McClelland
Philips Corporate Design (The Netherlands)

Cathleen Wharton
U S WEST Advanced Technologies (USA)

Local Arrangements
Mark A. Leonard
Hewlett-Packard (Canada)

Publications
Ralf Bilger
University of Paderborn (Germany)

Jane Dailey
Microsoft (USA)

Bob Mack
IBM (USA)

Collin Page
Microsoft (USA)

Registration
Steve Anderson
Lawrence Livermore National Laboratory (USA)

Chris Ghinazzi
Lawrence Livermore National Laboratory (USA)

Student Volunteers
Robert Fein
U S WEST Advanced Technologies (USA)

Kori Inkpen
University of British Columbia (Canada)

Survey and Evaluations
Lorraine Borman
(USA)

International Relations

Americas
Mary Lytwyn
Bank of Montreal (Canada)

Asia
Hirotada Ueda
Hitachi Denshi, Ltd. (Japan)

Australia
Judy Hammond
University of Technology, Sidney (Australia)

Europe
Fabio Paterno
CNUCE-C.N.R. (Italy)

Professional Staff

Conference Management
Paul Henning
Conference and Logistics Consultants (USA)

Public Relations Consultant
Rosemary Wick Stevens
Ace Public Relations (USA)

Conference Administrator
Patty Scarbro
Conference and Logistics Consultants (USA)

Registration Services
Registration Systems Lab (USA)

Publications Design
Mo Viele
Mo Viele, Inc. (USA)

Papers Committees

Meta-Reviewers
Richard I. Anderson
Usability / Design Adventures (USA)

Rachel Bellamy
Apple Computer, Inc. (USA)

Susan T. Dumais
Bellcore (USA)

Steven Feiner
Columbia University (USA)

Scott Hudson
Georgia Institute of Technology (USA)

Bonnie E. John
Carnegie Mellon University (USA)

John Karat
IBM T.J. Watson Research Center (USA)

Laura Leventhal
Bowling Green State University (USA)

Satoshi Matsuoka
University of Tokyo (Japan)

Jim Miller
Apple Computer, Inc. (USA)

Thomas P. Moran
Xerox PARC (USA)

Dan R. Olsen Jr.
Brigham Young University (USA)

Judith S. Olson
The University of Michigan (USA)

Peter Pirolli
Xerox PARC (USA)

Robert Rist
University of Technology, Sydney (Australia)

Teresa L. Roberts
University of Colorado (USA)

Paulien Strijland
Apple Computer, Inc. (USA)

Piyawadee "Noi" Sukaviriya
IBM T.J. Watson Research Center (USA)

John C. Tang
SunSoft, Inc. (USA)

Bill Verplank
Interval Research (USA)

Colin Ware
University of New Brunswick (Canada)

Catherine G. Wolf
IBM T.J. Watson Research Center (USA)

Nicole Yankelovich
Sun Microsystems Laboratories (USA)

Jürgen E. Ziegler
Fraunhofer Institute IAO (Germany)

Reviewers

Gregory Abowd
Georgia Institute of Technology (USA)

Klaus H. Ahlers
European Computer-Industry Research Centre (ECRC) GmbH (Germany)

Bengt Ahlstrom
UI Design AB & Royal Institute of Technology (Sweden)

Motoyuki Akamatsu
National Institute of Bioscience and Human-Technology (Japan)

Nerio Allamanno
Olivetti (Italy)

Robert (Bob) B. Allen
Bellcore (USA)

James Lenton Alty
Loughborough University of Technology (UK)

Matthew Anderson
IBM Software Solutions (USA)

Mark Apperley
University of Waikato (New Zealand)

Barry Arons
Speech Interaction Research (USA)

Stacey Ashlund
Lotus Development Corporation (USA)

Remi Bastide
Universite Toulouse I (France)

Thomas Baudel
Alias Wavefront (Canada)

Michel Beaudouin-Lafon
Université de Paris-Sud (France)

Vivienne S. Begg
Cadence Design Systems Inc. (USA)

Matt Belge
Vision & Logic (USA)

Lucy Berlin
Taligent, Inc (USA)

Randolph G. Bias
IBM Corporation (USA)

Meera M. Blattner
University of California, Davis, and Lawrence Livermore Nat. Lab. (USA)

Jeanette Blomberg
Xerox PARC (USA)

Sara A. Bly
Consultant (USA)

Heinz-Dieter Böcker
German National Research Center for Information Technology (Germany)

Guy A. Boy
European Institute of Cognitive Sciences and Engineering, EURISCO (France)

Paul Brennan
NORTEL (Canada)

Jerome Broekhuijsen
Novell Corporate R&D (USA)

Ruven Brooks
Schlumberger Austin Product Center (USA)

Maddy D. Brouwer-Janse
Philips Research Laboratories - IPO (The Netherlands)

Marc H. Brown
DEC Systems Research Center (USA)

Richard Catrambone
Georgia Institute of Technology (USA)

Chaomei Chen
Glasgow Caledonian University (UK)

Gilbert Cockton
MARI Computer Systems and Universities of Glasgow and Newcastle (UK)

Maxine S. Cohen
IBM Corporation (USA)

Penny Collings
University of Canberra (Australia)

Al Corbett
Carnegie Mellon University (USA)

Maria Francesca Costabile
Universita' di Bari (Italy)

William Cowan
University of Waterloo (Canada)

Allen Cypher
Apple Computer, Inc. (USA)

Mary Czerwinski
Microsoft Corporation (USA)

Clare Davies
De Montfort University (UK)

Alan Dix
University of Huddersfield (UK)

Paul Dourish
Rank Xerox Research Centre (UK)

Elizabeth Dykstra-Erickson
Apple Computer, Inc. (USA)

Kate Ehrlich
Lotus Development Corp. (USA)

George Engelbeck
U S WEST Advanced Technologies (USA)

Tom Erickson
Apple Computer, Inc. (USA)

Stephanie Everett
US Naval Research Laboratory (USA)

Sidney Fels
Virtual Technologies (USA)

Bob Fields
University of York (UK)

Robert S. Fish
Bellcore (USA)

James Foley
Georgia Institute of Technology (USA)

Peter Forbrig
Universität Rostock (Germany)

George W. Furnas
University of Michigan (USA)

Bill Gaver
Royal College of Art (UK)

Don Gentner
SunSoft (USA)

David J. Gilmore
University of Nottingham (UK)

Andreas Girgensohn
NYNEX Science & Technology (USA)

Robert J. Glushko
Passage Systems, Inc. (USA)

Louis M. Gomez
Northwestern University (USA)

Michael D. Good
SAP America, Inc. (USA)

Peter Gorny
University of Oldenburg (Germany)

Rich Gossweiler
Silicon Graphics Inc. (USA)

Mark Green
University of Alberta (Canada)

Saul Greenberg
University of Calgary (Canada)

Masami Hagiya
University of Tokyo (Japan)

Judy Hammond
University of Technology, Sydney (Australia)

Marti Hearst
Xerox PARC (USA)

Bill Hefley
Carnegie Mellon University (USA)

Austin Henderson
Apple Computer, Inc. (USA)

Scott Henninger
University of Nebraska-Lincoln (USA)

Harry M. Hersh
Fidelity Investments (USA)

Tom Hewett
Drexel University (USA)

Ken Hinckley
University of Virginia (USA)

Debby Hindus
Interval Research (USA)

H. Ulrich Hoppe
University of Duisburg (Germany)

Steve Howard
Swinburne University of Technology (Australia)

Keith Instone
Bowling Green State University (USA)

Ellen Isaacs
SunSoft (USA)

Robert J.K. Jacob
Tufts University (USA)

Christian Janssen
Fraunhofer Institute IAO (Germany)

Pertti Jarvinen
University of Tampere (Finland)

Brian Scott Johnson
Synopsys, Inc. (USA)

Chris Johnson
University of Glasgow (UK)

Anker Helms Jørgensen
Copenhagen University (Denmark)

Susanne Jul
University of Michigan (USA)

Clare-Marie Karat
IBM TJ Watson Research Center (USA)

Paul Kearney
Sharp Laboratories of Europe Ltd. (UK)

Reinhard Keil-Slawik
University of Paderborn (Germany)

Wendy A. Kellogg
IBM T.J. Watson Research Center (USA)

David Kieras
University of Michigan (USA)

Takayuki Dan Kimura
Washington University in St. Louis (USA)

Muneo Kitajima
National Institute of Bioscience and Human-Technology (Japan)

Hideki Koike
University of California at Berkeley (USA)

Joseph A. Konstan
University of Minnesota (USA)

Christopher Koster
Bell Communications Research, Bellcore (USA)

Srdjan Kovacevic
U S WEST Advanced Technologies (USA)

Larry Koved
IBM Research (USA)

David Kurlander
Microsoft Research (USA)

Masaaki Kurosu
Shizuoka University (Japan)

Hideaki Kuzuoka
University of Tsukuba (Japan)

James Landay
Carnegie Mellon University (USA)

Alison Lee
NYNEX Science & Technology, Inc. (USA)

John R. Lee
University of Edinburgh (UK)

Mark Linton
Vitria Technology (USA)

Jerry Lohse
The Wharton School of the University of Pennsylvania (USA)

Ishantha Lokuge
Silicon Graphics, Inc (USA)

Jonas Löwgren
Linköping University (Sweden)

Wendy Mackay
University of Paris (France)

Christine L. MacKenzie
Simon Fraser University (Canada)

Allan MacLean
Rank Xerox Research Centre (UK)

Ghassan A. Al-Qaimari, MACS
Royal Melbourne Institute of Technology (Australia)

David Maltz
Carnegie Mellon University (USA)

Munir Mandviwalla
Temple University (USA)

Toshiyuki Masui
Sony Computer Science Laboratory Inc. (Japan)

Kevin A. Mayo
Thomson Electronic Information Resources (TEIR) (USA)

Marshall R. McClintock
Microsoft Corporation (USA)

Jean McKendree
University of York (UK)

Cliff McKnight
Loughborough University (UK)

William W. McMillan
Eastern Michigan University (USA)

John F. Meech
University of the West of England (UK)

Hans van der Meij
University of Twente (The Netherlands)

Naomi Miyake
Chukyo University (Japan)

Tom Moher
University of Illinois at Chicago (USA)

Anders Morch
University of Oslo (Norway)

Sougata Mukherjea
C&C Research Lab, NEC (USA)

Michael J. Muller
U S WEST Advanced Technologies (USA)

Alice M. Mulvehill
The MITRE Corporation (USA)

Brad A. Myers
Carnegie-Mellon University (USA)

Beth Mynatt
Xerox PARC (USA)

Frieder Nake
University of Bremen (Germany)

Jocelyne Nanard
University Montpellier (France)

William Newman
Rank Xerox Research Centre (UK)

Erik Nilsen
Lewis & Clark College (USA)

Lorraine F. Normore
Chemical Abstracts Service, Research Unit (USA)

Else Nygren
Uppsala University (Sweden)

Gary M. Olson
University of Michigan (USA)

Scott P. Overmyer
University of Maine (USA)

Sharon Oviatt
Oregon Graduate Institute of Science and Technology (USA)

Philippe Palanque
LIS-IHM, University Toulouse I (France)

John F. Patterson
Lotus Development Corporation (USA)

Ken Pier
Xerox PARC (USA)

Philippe Piernot
Interval Research (USA)

Andrea Polli
Robert Morris College (USA)

Peter G. Polson
University of Colorado (USA)

Kari-Jouko Raiha
University of Tampere (Finland)

Ramana Rao
Xerox PARC (USA)

Matthias Rauterberg
Swiss Federal Institute of Technology (ETH) (Switzerland)

Michael J Rees
Bond University (Australia)

Brian Reilly
Apple Computer, Inc. (USA)

Chris R. Roast
Sheffield Hallam University (UK)

Scott Robertson
U S WEST Advanced Technologies (USA)

Elizabeth Rosenzweig
Eastman Kodak Company (USA)

Steven Roth
Carnegie-Mellon University (USA)

Peter Rowley
Ontario Institute For Studies in Education (Canada)

Dick Rubinstein
Sun Microsystems, Inc. (USA)

Carrie Rudman
U S WEST Advanced Technologies (USA)

Alexander I. Rudnicky
Carnegie Mellon University (USA)

Pamela Samuelson
Cornell Law School (USA)

Anthony Savidis
Institute of Computer Science, FORTH (Greece)

Dominique L. Scapin
INRIA (France)

Mark Schlager
SRI International (USA)

Egbert Schlungbaum
University of Rostock (Germany)

Franz Schmalhofer
DFKI GmbH (Germany)

Chris Schmandt
MIT Media Laboratory (USA)

Jean Scholtz
Intel Corporation (USA)

Andrew Sears
DePaul University (USA)

Dore'e Duncan Seligmann
AT&T Bell Laboratories (USA)

Brian Shackel
HUSAT Research Institute Loughborough University (UK)

Donald P. Sheridan
Auckland University (New Zealand)

Frank M. Shipman III
Texas A&M University (USA)

John L. Sibert
The George Washington University (USA)

Liz Sonenberg
The University of Melbourne (Australia)

John Stasko
Georgia Institute of Technology (USA)

Karl Steiner
Ameritech (USA)

Constantine Stephanidis
Institute of Computer Science, FORTH (Greece)

Joseph W. Sullivan
FX Palo Alto Laboratory, Inc. (USA)

John Sullivan
General Magic (USA)

Alistair Sutcliffe
City University, London (UK)

Pedro Szekely
USC/ISI (USA)

Gerd Szwillus
University of Paderborn (Germany)

Haruo Takemura
Nara Institute of Science and Technology (Japan)

Yuzuru Tanaka
Hokkaido University (Japan)

Masayuki Tani
Hitachi Ltd. (Japan)

Michael J. Tauber
University of Paderborn (Germany)

Loren Terveen
AT&T Research (USA)

Linda Tetzlaff
IBM T.J. Watson Research Center (USA)

John C. Thomas
NYNEX Science and Technology (USA)

Peter Thomas
University of the West of England, Bristol (UK)

Greg Trafton
Naval Research Laboratory (USA)

Manfred Tscheligi
University of Vienna (Austria)

Thomas S. Tullis
Fidelity Investments (USA)

Charles van der Mast
Delft University of Technology (The Netherlands)

Gerrit C. van der Veer
Vrije Universiteit (The Netherlands)

Bradley T. Vander Zanden
University of Tennessee (USA)

Robert A. Virzi
GTE Laboratories Incorporated (USA)

Yvonne Waern
Linköping University (Sweden)

Gerhard Weber
University of Stuttgart and F.H.Papenmeier GmbH (Germany)

Anette Weisbecker
Fraunhofer Institute IAO (Germany)

Alan Wexelblat
MIT Media Lab (USA)

Steve Whittaker
Lotus Development Corporation (USA)

Susan Wiedenbeck
University of Nebraska (USA)

Terry Winograd
Stanford University (USA)

G. Bowden Wise
Rensselaer Polytechnic Institute (USA)

Dennis Wixon
Digital Equipment Corporation (USA)

Polle Zellweger
Xerox PARC (USA)

Ronald J. Zeno
Documentum, Inc. (USA)

Shumin Zhai
University of Toronto (Canada)

Design Briefings Review Committee

Karen Bedard
Hyundai Electronics America (USA)

Brenda J. Burkhart
Bellcore (USA)

Ellen C. Campbell
Silicon Graphics, Inc. (USA)

Paul Dourish
Rank Xerox Research Centre (UK)

Thomas Erickson
Apple Computer, Inc. (USA)

Anatole Gershman
Andersen Consulting (USA)

Michael Harris
AT&T Human Interface Technology Center (USA)

Austin Henderson
Apple Computer, Inc. (USA)

Masaaki Kurosu
Hitachi Ltd. (Japan)

David Leffler
General Magic, Inc. (USA)

Dan Ling
Microsoft (USA)

Arnold M. Lund
Ameritech (USA)

Ian McClelland
Philips Corporate Design (The Netherlands)

Michael McDevitt
Microsoft (USA)

Allan MacLean
Rank Xerox Research Centre (UK)

Mark Malamud
Microsoft (USA)

Naomi Miyake
Chukyo University (Japan)

Mike Mohageg
Silicon Graphics, Inc. (USA)

Rolf Molich
Kommunedata (Denmark)

Osamu Morikawa
National Institute of Bioscience and Human Technology (Japan)

Shogo Nishida
Osaka University (Japan)

Kimberly Donner O'Brien
SunSoft (USA)

Ron Oosterholt
Philips Corporate Design (The Netherlands)

Kara Pernice
Interleaf, Inc. (USA)

Daniel Rosenberg
Oracle Corporation (USA)

Gitta Salomon
IDEO Product Development (USA)

Sara Sazegari
Taligent, Inc. (USA)

Lauren S. Schwartz,
Microsoft (USA)

Tim Shea
Vivid Design (USA)

Tim Skelly
Microsoft (USA)

Desiree Sy
A. Rockley Consulting Associates (Canada)

Jose Carlos Teixeira
Universidade de Coimbra (Portugal)

Maria G. Wadlow
Transarc Corporation (USA)

Annette Wagner
SunSoft Inc. (USA)

Ellen A. White
Bellcore (USA)

Irene Wong
Apple Computer, Inc. (USA)

Kristina Hooper Woolsey
Apple Computer, Inc. (USA)

Common Ground is the theme of CHI 96. For the technical program this means creating a common base of understanding between all CHI participants. Practitioners and researchers need to appreciate each other's work and motives. Students of HCI and educators should be able to speak a common language. CHI participants from different cultures and continents should understand one another's concerns for a humane way to design and use information technology. Users and designers should share a common concern for usability.

We are very proud of our CHI 96 plenary speakers, Dr. Herb Clark, a psycholinguist at Stanford University and Dr. Betty Edwards, Director of the Center for Educational Applications of Brain Hemisphere Research, California State University, Long Beach, California. We also have a new event this year, Invited Contributions, which come from outside the traditional HCI disciplines. In the spirit of reaching out to find common ground with new disciplines, we have contributions from cognitive neuroscience, library science, and modern dance. We also have a report from the CHIKids' experience with creative childcare. Dr. Andrew Magpantay of the American Library Association, Dr. Boris Velichkovsky of Dresden University, Dr. Allison Druin of the University of New Mexico and Ms. Sang Mah of Simon Fraser University participated in our invited contributions.

Another CHI 96 innovation is a Preconference Events Retrospective. Workshops, the Doctoral Consortium and the Research Symposium report highlights of their events.

This year we provided mentoring help to those not familiar with CHI traditions. We had some successes with accepted papers! We hope the mentoring program will become a regular part of CHI.

We are working toward making CHI a global conference. We have international coordinators from four continents, a highly international conference committee and review committees. The accepted submissions are more international than ever before.

This year we updated and freshened the publications format. The templates are easier to use. We have already had another conference ask our permission to use our new format, proving once again that imitation is the sincerest form of flattery (and that news travels fast on the Web).

In the Technical Program, there are thirteen different types of activities (in addition to the Plenary talks and the Invited Contributions). Full papers are published in the Proceedings. The Conference Companion contains Short Papers, Interactive Posters, Social Action Posters, Workshops, SIGs, Demos, Videos, Design Briefings, Panels, Organization Overviews, Research Symposium and Doctoral Consortium.

Workshops take place prior to the main conference. They bring together people with a very focused shared interest. Special Interest Groups (SIGs) provide short meetings during the conference, again centered around a focused shared interest.

Demonstrations enable participants to view systems in action and discuss them with the people who created them.

Design Briefings present notable user interface designs with special emphasis on conceptual issues embodied in the designs.

Panels allow speakers and the audience to reflect on and discuss provocative HCI issues.

Organization Overviews provide briefings on the work of organizations engaged in HCI research and practice.

The Research Symposium, held prior to the main Conference, considers a range of research issues in HCI.

The Doctoral Consortium, held prior to the main Conference, allows doctoral students in the final stages of their research projects to interact with more experienced researchers.

It has been a pleasure and a privilege to work with our dedicated, talented Technical Program area chairs. They make this complicated and diverse conference a reality. Our most heartfelt thanks to them for their creativity, hard work, tact, and good cheer.

Bonnie A. Nardi | Gerrit C. van der Veer

Technical Program Co-Chairs

Self Disclosure on Computer Forms: Meta-Analysis and Implications

Suzanne Weisband
Department of Management Information Systems
University of Arizona
Tucson, Arizona 85721 USA
Tel: +1-520-621-8303
E-mail: sweisband@bpa.arizona.edu

Sara Kiesler
HCI Institute &
Department of Social and Decision Sciences
Carnegie Mellon University
Pittsburgh, PA 15213 USA
Tel: +1-412-268-2848
E-mail: kiesler@andrew.cmu.edu

ABSTRACT

Do people disclose more on a computer form than they do in an interview or on a paper form? We report a statistical meta-analysis of the literature from 1969 to 1994. Across 39 studies using 100 measures, computer administration increased self-disclosure. Effect sizes were larger comparing computer administration with face-to-face interviews, when forms solicited sensitive information, and when medical or psychiatric patients were the subjects. Effect sizes were smaller but had not disappeared in recent studies, which we attribute in part to changes in computer interfaces. We discuss research, ethical, policy, and design implications.

Keywords

computer forms, computer interviews, electronic surveys, measurement, disclosure, response bias, electronic communication.

INTRODUCTION

As computer and computer-based telecommunications technologies improve, assessment increasingly is being accomplished using these technologies. Previously existing mental health questionnaires, personality scales, job attitude scales, cognitive selection tests such as the Graduate Record Examination, and training inventories are among the many kinds of forms that have been converted to computerized administration [24]. Computer-administered employment, medical intake, and blood donor forms are being developed to replace face-to-face interviews, and electronic surveys administered from remote sites already are being used to gather personnel, medical, and consumer information, as well as in social science research [20, 29].

The possibility that people would tell an impartial machine personal or embarrassing things about themselves, without fear of negative evaluation, has been raised since the first uses of computers for communication [27]. One of the first applications of the computer for assessment was the computerized psychiatric interview [32]. Researchers reported that patients not only responded positively to computer interviews but also gave honest answers [13]. Subsequently, medical, marketing, personnel, and social science researchers have explored computer administration as a means for reducing social desirability biases [9] and obtaining more sensitive information from respondents than could be obtained using more traditional formats. A belief that computer administration encourages self-disclosure has led to the development of important applications, such as computer interviews to detect risk conditions and behaviors of blood donors [2, 23].

If existing interviews and forms are converted to computer forms, or if forms are administered by computer and also in other formats, then increased self-disclosure by those using the computer version raises psychometric and ethical questions. Increased self-disclosure might lead to nonequivalence of scores on measures in which respondents are asked to reveal personal or sensitive information. The computerized form might even be measuring a different underlying construct.

Among the reasons offered as to why people disclose when using a computer are that computer interfaces as compared with traditional formats create in respondents an inattention to audience, immersion in the immediate task along with a sense of invulnerability to criticism, an illusion of privacy, the impression that responses "disappear" into the computer, or other misattributions that cause respondents to be careless about their responses. For example, people can be induced to behave as if computers are human, suggesting that human-computer interaction is fundamentally social [25]. If so, perhaps informed consent statements should warn respondents about these misattributions. Perhaps computer forms that simulate a face-to-face interview should include a representation of the interviewer. These speculations are moot if respondents, in fact, do not in fact respond differently to computers than to other formats, as some researchers have concluded [6].

META-ANALYSIS

Researchers' mixed conclusions about self-disclosure in computer forms led to our examination of the literature using statistical meta-analysis. The main hypothesis we tested was that responses to a computer form, as compared with its face-to-face or paper-and-pencil counterpart, would be more self-disclosing. We did not use the meta-analytic procedure to examine the reasons for this difference. However, we derived plausible predictions based on two arguments: (1) that computer interfaces lack social context cues, which in turn causes reduced evaluation anxiety, feelings of safety or invulnerability, and less concern with looking good, and (2) that people lack experience with computers and therefore are not aware of the risks of self-disclosure of personal information to a computer. We explored these hypotheses indirectly by comparing characteristics across and within studies that should predict self-disclosure if these arguments were valid. For example, with respect to the impact of computer experience, since the general public has become more computer literate in each decade, effect sizes should decline with year of study. Predictors such as the year of publication were assessed in models of effect sizes [15].

Sample

Our sample consisted of 39 published experimental studies of self-disclosure in standardized and unstandardized interviews, questionnaires, tests, and scales that solicited socially undesirable, personally relevant, or sensitive information.[1] We included studies in the social science, computer science, and medical literature. We adopted a broad definition of self-disclosure in forms in order to consider all relevant studies. For example, we not only included studies of questionnaires that solicited highly sensitive information such as a person's criminal record but also studies of forms on which consumers were asked to disclose their complaints. However, for a study to be included it had to investigate a form; we did not include studies of free group discussion by computer [19], studies of computerized skill or cognitive ability or achievement, such as the GRE [24], or any studies in which some kind of self-disclosure was not measured. Our sample does not include several published studies of disclosure that employed no comparison or control group or otherwise seriously violated normal standards of experimental design.

Variables Coded

The following variables were coded from each study: (a) experimental design (between subjects, within subjects); (b) comparison form (face-to-face interview, paper-and-pencil form, test, or questionnaire); (c) sensitivity of information presented to subjects; (d) subject population (student, psychiatric or medical patient, other adult); (e) sex of sample (male, female, both) based on the percentage of males; (f) presence of others (e.g., other subjects) during computer administration (alone, not alone); (g) whether subjects responded to a standardized form; and (h) date of publication. Operationalization of these variables was straightforward except in the case of categorizing measures as sensitive. We coded a measure as sensitive if it seemed to ask for information not normally discussed among casual acquaintances or colleagues, such as about one's medical status, mental health, criminal record, use of drugs, and so forth. Two raters discussed disagreements and resolved them. Many of the measures coded as sensitive were psychiatric tests. We assume such measures are more sensitive than measures such as those assessing product or job satisfaction, for instance.

Calculation of Effect Size

The effect size (g) for each study was calculated as the mean of disclosure in the computer-administered form condition minus the mean of disclosure in the "traditional" or comparison condition (face-to-face interview or paper-and-pencil form), divided by the pooled standard deviation. Effect sizes reported are positive when there was more disclosure with the computer form and negative when there was more disclosure with the traditional format. We used Johnson's DSTAT upgrade computer program to analyze the results [17]. The g s were converted to d s by correcting them for sample size bias in small studies. Each d was weighed by the reciprocal of its variance to put greater weight on effect sizes estimated from large sample sizes. We performed two sets of meta-analyses. One analysis was based on effect sizes that were collapsed across repeated measures so that each study could be represented by one effect size. We did this because meta analytic techniques assume independent effect sizes. The second analysis was based on multiple effect sizes when needed to test particular hypotheses. For example, Koson et al. [21] administered two comparison instruments, one, a face-to-face interview, and the other, a paper-and-pencil questionnaire. We hypothesized that disclosure in computer instruments as compared with face-to-face interviews versus paper surveys. In cases like this, a separate effect size was computed for each relevant instrument.

RESULTS

With each study contributing a single effect size (n = 39), the mean was .33, indicating greater self-disclosure in computer administered tests. The 95% confidence interval for this mean was, CI = .28 to .39, which differs significantly from 0, Z =11.76, p <.001. The hypothesis of homogeneity was rejected, Q (38) = 339.73, p < .001, which indicates that the effect size derived in this analysis does not describe the entire dataset. We performed an outlier analysis to obtain homogeneity of variance. Six outliers (15%) were removed such that Q (32) = 48.90, p = .06. The resulting mean effect size was .21 (CI = .15 to .27), Z = 6.85 (p < .001).

Categorical Models

We tested a series of hypotheses by applying categorical models to the 39 studies plus any within-study effect sizes that were present after the studies were partitioned on the basis of the attribute under investigation. For example, 33

[1] Due to space limitations, the studies included in the meta-analysis are not referenced in this paper. A full reference list is available from the authors.

of the 39 studies in our dataset used either a face-to-face or paper-and-pencil comparison condition and 6 studies used both. Hence. we computed 45 (33+(6*2)) separate effect sizes in the categorical model comparing face-to-face and paper-and-pencil cases. A summary of the categorical models are presented in Table 1.

Tests of Social Context Cue Hypotheses

Interviews versus Questionnaires

An absence of social context cues can increase perceived privacy, or reduce evaluation anxiety or perceived risk. We hypothesized that studies comparing computer forms with face-to-face interviews (which have many social context cues) will show a larger effect size (increased self-disclosure in the computer condition) than studies comparing computer forms with paper-and-pencil forms. The 15 computer vs. face-to-face cases showed a much stronger effect size (d = .62) than the 30 computer vs. paper-and-pencil cases (d =.20), $Q_B(1) = 49.4$, $p < .0001$. The mean effect size for each comparison deviated significantly from zero, indicating that self disclosure was higher in the computer condition, albeit less so in comparison to paper-and-pencil questionnaires.[2]

Sensitive Information

The presence or absence of social context cues will matter more when the information being elicited from respondents is sensitive. Therefore, we hypothesized that studies comparing computer forms with other formats will show a larger effect size (increase in self-disclosure in the computer condition) when the measure elicits sensitive, personal, or otherwise risky information than when the measure elicits more impersonal information. We divided study measures according to whether or not they solicited sensitive information (e.g., mental health measures, measures of illegal activity). As seen in Table 1, the effect size in favor of computer administration when the measure elicited sensitive information was significantly stronger (d = .35) than when the measure did not elicit sensitive information (d = .16), $Q_B(1) = 14.55$, $p < .001$.

Vulnerable Populations

Prisoners, patients, and others whose lives are heavily influenced by others' decisions may feel particularly vulnerable to the consequences of self-disclosure, and therefore might be more sensitive to differences in administration. We hypothesized that studies in which the subjects were medical or psychiatric patients would show larger effect sizes. The comparisons shown in Table 1 are of 39 cases in which the subjects were students, patients, or other adults. Consistent with the significant between-classes effect, the mean for the patient effect size differed significantly from the means of both students and other adults, $\chi^2(1)=25.8$ and $\chi^2(1)=42.4$, respectively, $ps<.001$. This result gives additional support to the argument that computer responding increases the sense of privacy, although many alternative explanations can be generated (e.g., patients probably have lower socio-economic status, less knowledge of computers, and more experience with traditional tests).

Gender

Since females are reputed to be more sensitive to social context and tend to be more disclosing [10], we hypothesized that studies comparing computer forms with other formats will show a larger effect size (increased self-disclosure in the computer condition) when the subjects are female. Table 1 shows studies categorized by whether the investigators' sample was all male, all female, or a mixed sample. The effect size for the 3 studies with all-female samples (d =.47) was much larger than the effect size for the 9 studies with all-male samples (d = .22), though due to the small number of studies with all-female samples, the difference did not reach significance, $\chi^2(2) = 3.3$, p =.19. The effect size for mixed sample studies (d = .40) was not different from the effect size for all-female sample studies ($\chi^2(2) = 0.3$, p =.84), but it was significantly different from the effect size for all-male sample studies ($\chi^2(2) = 5.8$, $p < .05$). We also ran a continuous model using the percentage of males in the sample to predict effect size. Seven cases were removed because the authors did not say what percent of the subjects were male. The effect (in the direction of more disclosure when the sample had fewer males) was not significant ($Z = -1.43$, p =.15).

Presence of Others

The presence of other persons when one is completing a form provides social context cues to the nature of the test environment. We hypothesized that studies comparing computer forms with other formats would show a larger effect size (increased self-disclosure in the computer condition) when respondents in the computer condition were alone while they completed the form. Of the 29 studies where information was available, 19 of them (66%) were those in which subjects were alone at the computer when completing the questionnaire. The effect size and confidence intervals show that self disclosure was increased in the studies where subjects were alone (d =.26) as compared to when subjects were not alone (d =.15), $Q_B(1) = 2.67$, p =.10, though the difference is marginal.

Tests of Technological Change Hypotheses

When a technology is first introduced, people might not be aware of its risks. Lack of computer experience and knowledge might lead people to be careless about the information they give to a computer. Also, the technology may have design deficiencies that are corrected later. For example, early computer-administered questionnaires often prevented respondents from editing or undoing their responses as they could with paper questionnaires. This constraint might have led them to accidentally disclose information they would have deleted if this were possible.

---

[2]Outlier analyses were performed when cases within categories were not homogeneous. The procedure involves removing outliers until homogenity is obtained (when p > .05 for the Q_W statistic). Due to space limitations, these analyses are not reported but can be obtained from the authors. None of these analyses change the main results of this study.

Table 1. Categorical Effects for Study Characteristics

Class	Between-classes Effect (Q_B)	k [a]	Mean-weighted Effect Size (d_{i+})	95% CI Lower	95% CI Upper	Q_{wi} [b]
Comparison group	49.37, p <.0001					
Face-to-Face		15	.62	0.52	0.73	258.41**
Paper and Pencil		30	.20	0.15	0.27	56.50*
Sensitive information	14.55, p <.001					
Sensitive		29	.35	0.29	0.41	315.63**
Not Sensitive		20	.16	0.08	0.24	48.04**
Sample	53.22, p <.0001					
Patient		13	.66	0.54	0.77	254.12**
Student		19	.29	0.20	0.37	28.82
Other		7	.16	0.07	0.26	12.53
Sex of sample	6.86, p <.05					
Male		9	.22	0.10	0.34	7.02
Female		3	.48	0.23	0.72	1.56
Both		20	.40	0.32	0.48	204.62**
Tested alone[c]	2.67, p =.10					
Alone		19	.26	0.17	0.36	67.35**
Not Alone		10	.15	0.06	0.24	28.00*
Standardized tests	3.24, p =.07					
Yes		28	.39	0.31	0.45	337.82**
No		14	.28	0.20	0.37	18.22
Year published[d]	32.69, p <.0001					
1969 – 1982		10	.63	0.48	0.78	62.35**
1983 – 1986		10	.28	0.17	0.38	51.69**
1987 – 1991		10	.44	0.34	0.54	177.37**
1992 – 1994		9	.15	0.05	0.25	15.62

Note. Effect sizes are positive for differences in the computer direction and negative for differences in the comparison condition direction. k = number of effect sizes; ES = effect size; CI = confidence interval for the mean weighted effect size; L = lower limit; U = upper limit.

[a] The sample size for each analysis was based on the total number of studies represented by the measure. Of the 39 studies used for these analyses, one study employed more than one design, and 15 studies employed more than one measure. Thus, k varies by category.

[b] Homogeneity within each class; significance indicates rejection of the hypothesis of homogeneity.

[c] For this category, there were 12 missing cases.

[d] The 39 studies used for this analyses were grouped arbitrarily into quartiles.

**p<.01,*p<.05.

Precomputer Standardized Tests
Standardized tests, such as the MMPI, were developed for traditional forms of communication. People are used to seeing them in traditional formats and may not pay them as much respect, or realize their personal consequences, when these instruments are displayed on a computer screen. Therefore, we hypothesized that studies comparing computer administration with other forms of administration might show larger effect sizes (increased self-disclosure in the computer condition) in studies using standardized tests as compared with unstandardized formats (some of which were developed specifically for computer administration). The hypothesis was supported marginally. The effect size for cases where the researcher used standardized tests was somewhat higher (d =.39) than the effect size for cases in which the measure was not a standardized test (d = .28), $Q_B(1) = 3.24$, p =.07.

Students
Since high school students and undergraduates are likely to be more familiar with computers than today's adults, and more knowledgeable about computers than others, we hypothesized that studies comparing computer forms with other formats would show larger effect sizes (increased self-disclosure in the computer condition) in studies using subjects other than students. There were 19 cases in which the subjects were students, and as we showed in Table 2, the effect size for computer administration in these cases (d=.29) was not smaller than the effect size in studies using other adults as subjects (d =.16), $c^2(2) = 3.47$, p =.18. So, there is not strong support for this hypothesis.

Years
We hypothesized that effect sizes would decrease over the years, as people became more familiar with computers and what could be done with them. We first ran a continuous model on the year of publication for the 39 studies. The model showed a strong effect for year, in that effect sizes did get smaller over the years (Z = 2.6, p < .01.) We next divided the 39 studies into quartiles. Consistent with the continuous model, Table 1 shows that studies published in the most recent years (1992–1994) had a significantly lower effect size than studies published in two of the earlier periods, 1969–1982 (d =.63, $\chi^2(3) = 26.9$, p <.001), and 1987–1991 (d =.44, $\chi^2(3) = 15.5$, p <.001). Also, studies published in the earliest period (1969–1982) had a significantly higher effect size (d =.63) as compared to the studies published in the next period (1983–1986; d =.28), $\chi^2(3) = 14.1$, p <.01.

The year effect might be an artifact due to a change investigators use of study characteristics associated with disclosure (such as whether sensitive information was solicited). We evaluated the impact of any study characteristic used differently over time on the effect size within quartile periods. One significant change in the studies over the years was that in earlier years investigators used more measures we had coded as soliciting sensitive information. However, considering only studies that used sensitive measures, there remained an effect of year ($Q_B(3)$ = 18.8, p < .01). Another manner in which studies changed over the years was in the use of patients as subjects, another variable that strongly predicts disclosure in a computer instrument. Within studies using patients as subjects, however, there remained a significant effect of year of study ($Q_B(3) = 101.8$, p < .01). These analyses indicate that the impact of computer administration has declined over the years and that this decline is not explained fully by changes in the use of various study characteristics in evaluation studies. Despite this decline, the effect of computer administration did not disappear.

DISCUSSION

Research Issues
Our meta-analysis gives support to the main hypothesis that computer administration elicits more self-disclosure than traditional forms of administration do. In recent years, the disclosure effect has declined significantly due, perhaps, to increasing public knowledge of computers, increasing public computer literacy, or even people's reduced awe of the computer. (The credibility of the instrument is important because it affects the degree to which respondents believe the questions have a legitimate purpose and are not simply voyeuristic or commercial, or have criminal intent [7].) Our indirect analysis, however (for example, comparing students to other adults), did not support explanations related to public knowledge of computers.

An unresolved research issue is that changes in computer technology have made it possible for a computer instrument to have the "look and feel" of a paper-and-pencil questionnaire, typed form, or printed test. Forms now look more like paper questionnaires, forms, or tests than they did in earlier years, and allow for more stereotypical questionnaire-type responses using radio buttons and fill in blanks (as compared with typed commands). These changes might have increased respondents' sense of the computer interaction as a evaluation or test situation and consequently reduced their disclosure. Unfortunately, we were unable to evaluate this idea in the meta-analysis because few investigators described their computer interfaces in sufficient detail. Possibly researchers did not realize computer interfaces would change so much. In any case, the idea that differences in the interface can affect disclosure has not been investigated yet.

A related issue is the belief by many that answering questions on a computer changes respondents' perceptions of the test environment. For example, working on a computer could create a sense of privacy or anonymity. Some investigators have reported a strong relationship between anonymous and identified computer responding [6, 8]. However, research is needed to examine directly whether perceptual and motivational changes mediate the linkage between the administration of computer forms and responses to those forms.

Ethical Issues
If people have a false illusion of privacy or otherwise let down their guard when they respond to a computer, the world has discovered an easy, cheap way to obtain sensitive information from people. Other methods of eliciting sensitive information, such as the polygraph [4], bogus pipeline [26], or telephone interviews [22] are difficult or expensive. Researchers, therapists, marketers, developers of World Wide Web sites and others will be drawn to use computers to obtain sensitive information, and increasingly they will do this remotely, so their instructions and consent forms (if any) also are completed by computer. Currently, the American Psychological Association Guidelines for Research on Human Participants, as well as most research organizations' codes of research conduct are silent with regard to such topics as how to obtain informed consent electronically (and whether it is legitimate to do so), how much to reveal about remote sites of data collection, and about electronic forms in general.

Stronger admonishments in instructions, policy statements, and informed consent statements might be required for computer forms to obtain the same level of risk as traditional formats. However, simply changing the wording or format of conventional warnings might not be effective. An unpublished study by Kiesler, Sieff, and Geary[3] showed that a small picture of the interviewer on the screen did not inhibit disclosure in a computer interview as did a real interviewer's presence. Moreover, that computer scientists disclose even more than others in a computer instrument [18] suggests that responses to known risks and warnings can habituate.

Policy Issues
To our knowledge, the use of computer forms has not proved to be a source of social disagreement in the way computerized monitoring and informal electronic communications like email have [30]. Our review suggests that more cases will arise like that of the six William Morris assistants who were fired when their candid email correspondence about their bosses and how to avoid additional duties was mistakenly sent to an administrator.[4] Many companies and universities are embedding forms in their World Wide Web pages to take surveys, orders, and collect personal information about potential applicants.

The legal situation is presently unstable. Many organizations consider any information sent through, or held on, company computers to be in the organization's domain. Few people know that they can be held legally accountable for information they type into a computer and send to others, or that they might be disciplined by a company for information that they access on a computer form. Unlike telephone calls, electronic forms (and forms sent by email) can be treated in the courts as documents that can be used as legal evidence without a court order. Many public and private organizations take the position that they have a right to randomly monitor communications on "their" networks, and to use computers to collect data about employees or customers, on the grounds that such access is necessary to properly administer the computer system, or to implement business goals [1]. To the degree that people believe or perceive their communications through computers to be safe, current organizational and legal policies may be inappropriate.

Design Issues
As the power and speed of computers continues to increase, researchers and technologists have responded by improving the readability and ease of response in computer forms, interviews, surveys, and tests. For example, respondents can use radio buttons to select choices from a table rather than type commands. Advances in computer interfaces also have increased the variety, credibility, and salience of social information in forms, for example, through animated characters or icons. Will new computer interface designs induce people to act more like they would using a paper questionnaire or in an interview with another person? A study by Sproull et al. [28] compared the impression management concerns of subjects who answered questions in one of two computer interview conditions. In one condition, subjects interacted with a computer "counselor" embodied in a talking face on the screen; in other condition, subjects interacted with the counselor by typing and reading text on the screen. The subjects revealed less to the talking face than to the text and evaluated her less well. This study suggests that social interfaces will reduce self disclosure in computer forms, perhaps because they remind the user of a face-to-face interview.

However, increasing the amount of social information in a computer display or device does not guarantee that the distribution of social information will be like that in an ordinary social setting. Weisband, Schneider, and Connolly [31] have shown that when a narrow set of social information about members' relative group status is salient in electronic communication, this information overdetermines people's responses to others. Computer interfaces that partially mimic social situations may offer a distorted version of these situations, and change people's responses unexpectedly.

An important point that emerges from consideration of how computer design is evolving is that "computer interview" or "computer survey" should no longer be treated as a single, unidimensional category of administration by either researchers or practicioners. Computer forms are multidimensional, increasingly so as interfaces incorporate speech and speech recognition [16], auditory and kinesthetic feedback [12], social intelligence [5], emotional response [11], directed animation [3, 14], talking to people on the screen [28] or even virtual reality [33]. To understand how design affects disclosure in new computer instruments, we

---

[3]Manuscript available from S. Kiesler, Carnegie Mellon, Pittsburgh, PA, 15213.

[4]Thompson, Anne. (1992). Forget doing lunch—Hollywood's on E-mail. *The New York Times*, September 6. F-23.

will have to investigate which features of computer forms affect people's perceptions and responses. It will be interesting to see how much users disclose when the computer form is delivered by an animated cartoon character.

ACKNOWLEDGMENTS

This work was supported in part by NSF grant #IRI-9309133 to the first author, and a NIMH scientist development award and grant from the Carnegie Mellon University Information Networking Institute to the second author. The authors thank Melissa Wingert, who assisted in collecting, organizing, and coding the studies.

REFERENCES

1. Aiello, J. R. (1993). Computer-based work monitoring: Electronic surveillance and its effects. *Journal of Applied Social Psychology, 23*, 499-507.

2. American Institutes for Research. (1993, July 30). *Increasing the safety of the blood supply by screening donors more effectively*. Final Report, Vol I. AIR, 3333 K St. Washington, DC 20007.

3..Ball, E., Ling, D. T., Pugh, D., Skelly, T., Stankosky, Thiel, D. (1994). ReActor: A system for real-time, reactive animations. *Conference Companion: Demonstrations*, CHI '94, Boston, Mass., April 24-28.

4. Bashore, T. R., & Rapp, P. E. Are there alternatives to traditional polygraph procedures? *Psychological Bulletin, 113*, 3-22.

5. Binik, Y. M., Servan-Schreiber, D., Freiwald, S., & Hall, K. S. (1988). Intelligent computer-based assessment and psychotherapy: An expert system for sexual dysfunction. *Journal of Nervous and Mental Disease, 178*, 387-400.

6. Booth-Kewely, S., Edwards, J. E., & Rosenfeld, P. (1992). Impression management, social desirability, and computer administration of attitude questionnaires: Does the computer make a difference? *Journal of Applied Psychology, 77*, 562-566.

7. Catania, J. A., Gibson, D. R., Chitwood, D. D. & Coates. T. J. (1990). Methodological problems in AIDS behavioral research: Influences on measurement error and participation bias in studies of sexual behavior. *Psychological Bulletin, 108*, 339-362.

8. Connolly, T., Jessup, L. M., & Valacich, J. S. (1990). Effects of anonymity and evaluative tone on idea generation in computer-mediated groups, *Management Science, 36*, 689-703.

9. Crowne, D., & Marlowe, D. (1964). *The approval motive*. New York: Wiley.

10. Dindia, K. & Allen, M. (1992). Sex differences in self-disclosure: A meta-analysis. *Psychological Bulletin, 112*, 106-124.

11. Elliott, C. (1994). Research problems in the use of a shallow artificial intelligence model of personality and emotion (pp. 9-15), *Proceedings of the Twelfth National Conference on Artificial Intelligence,*.

12. Gaver, W. W. (1986). Auditory icons: Using sound in computer interfaces. *Human-Computer Interaction, 2*, 167-177.

13. Greist, J. H., Gustafson, D. H., Stauss, F F., Rowse, G. L., Laughren, T. P & Chiles, J. A. (1973). Computer interview for suicide-risk prediction. *American Journal of Psychiatry, 130*, 1327-1332.

14. Hayes-Roth, B., Sincoff, E., Brownston, L., Huard, R., & Lent, B. (1995). Directed improvisation with animated puppets (pp. 79-80). In *Human Factors in Computing Systems: CHI '95 Conference Companion* (Proceedings document). May 7-10, Denver.

15. Hedges, L V., & Olkin, I. (1985). *Statistical methods for meta-analysis*. San Diego: Academic Press

16. Itou, K. S., Hayamizu, S. & Tanaka, H. (1992). Continuous speech recognition by context-dependent phonetic HMM and an efficient algorithm for finding N-best sentence hypotheses. *Proceedings of ICASSP*. IEEE Press.

17. Johnson, B. (1989). *Software for the meta-analytic review of research literatures*. Hillsdale, NJ: Erlbaum. (Upgrade documentation, 1993)

18. Kiesler, S., & Sproull, L. S. (1986). Response effects in the electronic survey. *Public Opinion Quarterly, 50*, 402-413.

19. Kiesler, S. & Sproull, L. (1992). Group decision making and communication technology, *Organizational Behavior and Human Decision Processes*, 96-123.

20. Kiesler, S., Walsh, J., & Sproull, L. (1992). Computer networks in field research. In F. B. Bryant , J. Edwards, S. Tindale, E. Posavac, L. Heath, E. Henderson, & Y. Suarez-Balcazar, (Eds.), *Methodological Issues in Applied Social Research* (pp. 239-268). New York: Plenum.

21. Koson, D., Kitchen, M., Kochen, M, & Stodolsky, D. (1970). Psychological testing by computer: Effect on response bias. *Educational and Psychological Measurement, 30*, 803-810.

22. Locander, W., Sudman, S. & Bradburn, N. (1976). An investigation of interview method, threat and response

distortion. *Journal of the American Statistical Association, 71*, 267-275.

23. Locke, S. E., Kowaloff, H. B., Hoff, R. G., Safran, C., Popovsky, M. A., Cotton, D. J., Finkelstein, D. M., Page, P. L., & Slack, W. V. (1992). Computer-based interview for screening blood donors for risk of HIV infection. *The Journal of the American Medical Association, 268*, 1301-1305.

24. Mead, A. D. & Drasgow, F. (1993). Equivalence of computerized and paper-and-pencil cognitive ability tsts: A meta-analysis. *Psychological Bulletin, 114*, 440-458.

25. Nass, C., Moon, Y., Fogg, B. J., Reeves, B., & Dryer, D. C. (1995). Can computer personalities be human personalities? *International Journal of Human-Computer Studies, 43*(2), 223-239,

26. Roese, N. J. & Jamieson, D. W. (1993). Twenty years of bogus pipeline research: A critical review and meta-analysis. *Psychological Bulletin, 114*, 363-375.

27. Smith, R E. (1963). Examination by computer. *Behavioral Science, 8*, 76-79.

28. Sproull, L., Walker, J., Subramani, R., Kiesler, S., & Waters, K. (in press). When the interface is a face. *Human-Computer Interaction.*

29. Synodinos, N. E., & Brennan, J. M. (1988). Computer interactive interviewing in survey research. *Psychology and Marketing, 5*, 117-137.

30. Weisband, S. P. & Reinig, B. A. (1995). Understanding users' perceptions of electronic mail privacy. *Communications of the ACM , 38* (12), 40-47.

31. Weisband, S. P., Schneider, S. K., & Connolly, T. (1995). Computer-mediated communication and social information: Status salience and status awareness. *Academy of Management Journal, 38*, 1124-1151.

32. Weizenbaum, J. (1976). *Computer power and human reason.* San Francisco: Freeman.

33. Welch, R. B., Blackmon, T. T., Liu, A., Mellers, B. A., & Stark, L. W. (in press). The effects of pictorial realism, delay of visual feedback, and observer interactivity on the subjective sense of presence. *Presence: Teleoperators And Virtual Environments.*

The Design and Long-Term Use of a Personal Electronic Notebook: A Reflective Analysis

Thomas Erickson
Advanced Technology, Apple Computer, Inc.
1 Infinite Loop, 301-4UE
Cupertino CA 95014 USA
Tel: +1-408-974-3767
E-mail: thomas@apple.com

ABSTRACT
This article describes the design and use of a personal electronic notebook. The findings provide a useful data point for those interested in the issue of how to design highly customizable systems for managing personal information. After a description of the notebook's interface and the usage practices that have co-evolved with the interface, I discuss some of the features which have made the notebook useful over the long term, and trends in the evolution of its design.

Keywords
Electronic notebooks, personal information management, customization, tailoring, longitudinal study, reflective analysis, co-evolution of design and practice

INTRODUCTION

Notebooks are a well known tool for those involved in practices which involve observation, reflection, analysis, and synthesis. John-Steiner, in her wide-ranging study of "experienced thinkers" [6], observes that one of the central challenges of creative work is the capture of images and other forms of "condensed thought," and the development of this private language into public, expressive language. She notes the frequent use of notebooks for this purpose, not only by writers and scientists, but by painters, composers, and choreographers.

Given the well recognized role of such personal notebooks in intellectual and artistic endeavors, it is rather surprising that there are only a few examples of computer-based applications that are designed specifically to act as personal notebooks. These include Notes [9], a physician's notebook [1], a prototype of a biologist's notebook [10] and NoteCards [5]. If the constraints are relaxed to allow collaborative systems, other examples appear, such as the Virtual Notebook System™ [4, 11], and Lotus Notes® [3]. We will not consider systems tailored to support specific tasks, such as capturing and elaborating on design rationale (e.g., [2, 13]); their degree of structure and formality make them quite different from systems directed towards the easy capture, management, and transformation of personal information which is our focus of interest. The term notebook is also applied to some types of hardware. Indeed, "notebook" serves as the new generic term for laptop computer, with "sub-notebook" being used to describe the new, smaller generation of laptops. However, in both cases the primary connotation of the name seems to be that of size—such systems exhibit no particular specialization for personal information management. Perhaps a better fit are personal digital assistants (PDA's)—exemplified by the Apple Newton® and the Sharp Wizard®—hand held devices that are explicitly aimed at helping users manage their personal information.

Personal electronic notebooks pose an interesting challenge for designers and developers. A general design problem is discovering how to make something useful, as opposed to just usable. This problem is particularly acute for systems like electronic notebooks that support the capture, use, and management of personal information. Unlike conventional applications such as word processors or spreadsheets, a notebook is very personal: it only becomes useful over time—months or years—as it becomes the repository of more and more personally relevant information. While it is straightforward to study usability—that is, how easy it is to learn and use various features of the notebook—it is much more of a challenge to understand which features, and which modes of use, would make such a notebook useful.

Very little evaluation of the use of notebook-like applications or devices has been done. Typically, if evaluation has been done at all, it is at the level of usability testing, and is rarely described in detail. The only example of longitudinal evaluation that I can find is NoteCards [12]. NoteCards has undergone considerable evaluation, including longitudinal studies of use over periods up to seven months [7, 8]. However, at least in the longitudinal studies, NoteCards was used to support the collection and organization of research notes and the production of a particular paper, rather than as a more general system for managing personal information. Clearly, there is much more to be learned.

Proteus

Several years ago I participated in a project that involved the design of a working prototype of a personal notebook. As noted above, while it is easy to study the usability of such a notebook, it is more difficult to understand which features would contribute to its usefulness over the long term. In this case, fragility of both the software and hardware prototypes frustrated any attempts at longitudinal evaluation.

One approach is to study how people manage their personal information today. In fact, we began our project by looking at how people used artifacts such as notebooks, calendars, post-it notes, and computers. This proved to be a rich source of ideas, and particularly drove home the point that different people did very different things. But it doesn't fully address the question. An electronic device for managing personal information will have properties that are very different from those of paper-based artifacts, and will therefore be used in different ways. So, the question remains: how can we learn about the ways in which an electronic personal information manager will really be used over a long period of time?

My response was to build my own electronic notebook, which I refer to as Proteus. My original intent was to force myself to use it on a daily basis for two months, keep track of how it evolved to support my work practices, and to make note of its benefits and drawbacks. Proteus turned out to be sufficiently useful that little discipline was required to accomplish this. As of this writing I've been using Proteus on a daily basis for three years. The occasional periods when I am forced to do without it because of mechanical or logistical problems reveal that it has become the primary tool by which I manage my work and professional life.

In more objective terms, Proteus is a HyperCard®-based application that is designed for use on a PowerBook®. In terms of content, Proteus consists of approximately 1500 pages of personally meaningful information, collected over the course of five years (some preexisting information was imported into Proteus). In terms of technology, Proteus is a collection of 9 HyperCard stacks taking up about 6 megabytes of disk space; it consists of about 80 handlers, and a few commonly available X-commands.

A Note on Method

While I have drawn upon a number of sources of data for this account—a change diary I kept about modifications to Proteus and the rationale behind them, archives of notebook versions and their contents, and an automatically-generated log of notebook commands—the fact remains that this is essentially a subjective account of my experience. Where possible, I have used analysis of portions of the notebook contents and the command log to confirm basic facts such as the approximate frequency of usage. But this has not revealed any surprises. The most interesting aspects of this account—claims about why certain features succeeded or failed, what accounts for the notebook's usefulness, the co-evolution of work practice and functionality—can not be verified by analyzing command logs or content.

Objections to this approach to exploring design issues include concerns about subjectivity, and the lack of generality of any findings. While I do not contest these objections—indeed, they are quite reasonable—I would note that no method is so sound as to allow designers to confidently proceed from the findings of one or even a few studies done within its scope. I believe that the sort of reflective analysis exemplified by this paper is well-suited to the inherently personal nature of this topic. Reflective analysis can yield much of value if it is carried out carefully, and if designers also draw upon other methodologies to inform their work.

What's Next?

I begin with an overview of the Proteus interface, and then discuss the ways in which I actually use Proteus. Finally I describe some of the lessons I've learned from this experience. Throughout this paper I maintain a deliberately casual, first-person style, as a reminder that the findings being described are based on a population of one.

AN OVERVIEW OF THE INTERFACE

It is difficult to describe Proteus because it has changed over time. What I'll do is describe the interface as it was in June 1994; at that time, most of the features discussed had been stable for about a year.

Proteus can be thought of as a series of notebooks. There is a primary notebook called the "working notebook" that is almost always open. In addition, a "bookshelf" menu gives access to secondary notebooks (e.g., a notebook of reading quotations, working notes for 1993, etc.) and reference stacks (e.g., a company phone directory).

Notebooks contain two types of pages: content pages where notes are made, and table of contents (TOC) pages which provide structural overviews of the notebook.

Content Pages

A content page contains four areas (figure 1):

- Header area. The top portion of the page has several fields for header information such as the name of the notebook section and subsection, the date the page was started, and so on.
- Content area. This is a single scrolling field where almost all information is entered.
- Page-Specific Controls. Below the content field is a

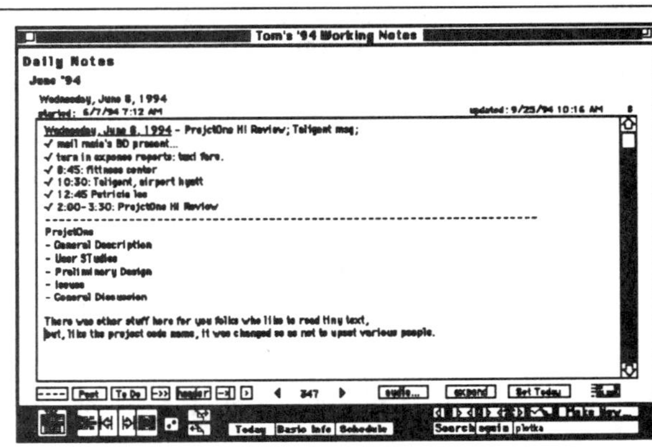

Figure 1. A content page. The large scrolling field is where the content is entered. The area at the top of the page is for various types of header information. And at the bottom of the page are page-specific and global controls (on light and dark backgrounds, respectively).

series of buttons for commands which apply to the content area. The page-specific controls appear to be on the same background as the content and header areas.

- Global Controls. Below the page-specific controls, on a darker graphic background, are controls which support global commands—primarily commands for navigating around the notebook.

Table of Contents (TOC) Pages

The other type of page is the table of contents page (TOC)—it provides structural overviews of the notebook or parts of the notebook. The structure of the notebook is quite simple: it is divided into sections, the sections are divided into subsections, and the subsections consist of pages. Each level of hierarchy has its own TOC page. That is, there is a global TOC for the whole notebook, and there are separate TOCs for each section and for each subsection. Typically, a TOC will only show the next lower level in the hierarchy, although this can be overridden. The TOC for a subsection will show the first line from the content area of each of its content pages.

The Global TOC

The global TOC (figure 2) has browser-like properties: selecting a section name from one of the upper panes in the window will show a list of its subsections (and sometimes subsection contents) in the lower pane. Clicking on any item in the lower pane will take you to that page.

Section and Subsection TOCs

The section and subsection TOCs are simply lists of their contents. The section TOC contains a list of subsections, and the subsection TOC contains a list of pages (where each page is represented by the first line of its contents). Clicking on any item in the TOC will take you to the appropriate page. Figure 3 shows an example of a subsection TOC (the "May '94" subsection of the "Daily Notes" section). (Over time a convention has evolved of summarizing a content page's important entries on its first line, enabling the TOC page to function as a sort of abstract or summary of its subsection.)

Accessing Functionality

Most of the functionality of Proteus is accessed through page-specific and global controls arrayed along the bottom of the page. Page-specific controls (see figure 1) typically act on the contents of a page, and are used for common actions such drawing a dashed line to separate entries, prepending selected lines of text with >'s (for preparing responses to email), and turning selected lines of text into an email message.

Global controls are for navigating around the notebook, or for altering the notebook's structure. Examples of global controls include buttons for jumping to the global TOC, today's notes page, and the next section, as well as buttons searching, creating stamps, and making new pages.

Other mechanisms for accessing functionality include a "Bookshelf" menu for navigating between notebooks, and key shortcuts for commonly done actions (e.g., hide notebook; jump to Finder; go to next page).

HOW I USE PROTEUS

Proteus evolved to support me, and therefore it is appropriate to say a few words about my inclinations and activities before describing how I use Proteus. As with the interface description, I focus on the period centered on June, 1994, when my job had been stable for about a year, and my commuting situation had been stable for about three months.

Context

My work situation in June, 1994, was that I was part of a small, 3 person group located in Cupertino, California. My activities involved communicating closely with my colleagues, and with groups scattered across the organization. I was involved—at least at a peripheral level—in many tasks at once. In general, my roles included acting as a researcher, designer, strategist, and consultant.

I commute to my California office from Minnesota, flying in for one week a month. The week that I'm in town is focused on meetings—approximately a dozen formal (scheduled) meetings, and lots of informal visits and

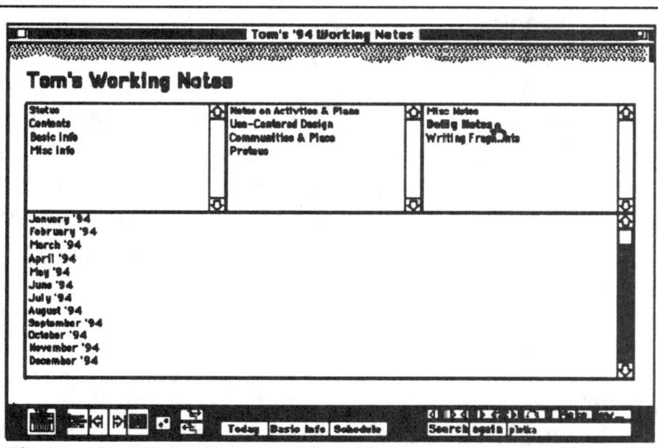

Figure 2. The global table of contents permits users to browse the contents of sections. Here, the "Daily Notes" section (in the upper right field) is selected, and its subsections displayed in the lower pane.

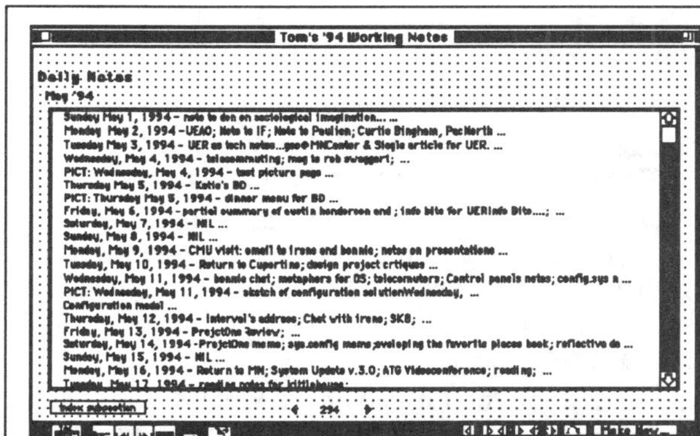

Figure 3. An example of a subsection TOC. Each entry is the first line of the content field of the page; clicking on an entry takes you to that page.

hallway conversations. When I work from my Minnesota office, I attend one or two meetings a week by phone, but focus more on tasks like reading, writing, and analysis. At the time being discussed, I sent perhaps 10 email messages a day, and received about 30 (the majority not personally addressed to me), regardless of geographic location.

In general, I am a very text-oriented person with a variety of interleaved, on-going activities. I read a lot, and write a lot. Writing includes papers, email, and notes about meetings, projects and design issues. In a very real sense writing is my way of thinking about things: I work out ideas and their implications in the process of making notes, writing email, and authoring papers.

Daily Use as a Work Diary
The principle function of Proteus is as a work diary. I use it to maintain a To Do list, to keep notes on meetings, to compose and send email, and as a repository for information (e.g., email messages) on which I want to reflect or act later on. I keep all the information for a day on one page in a long scrolling field (see figure 4).

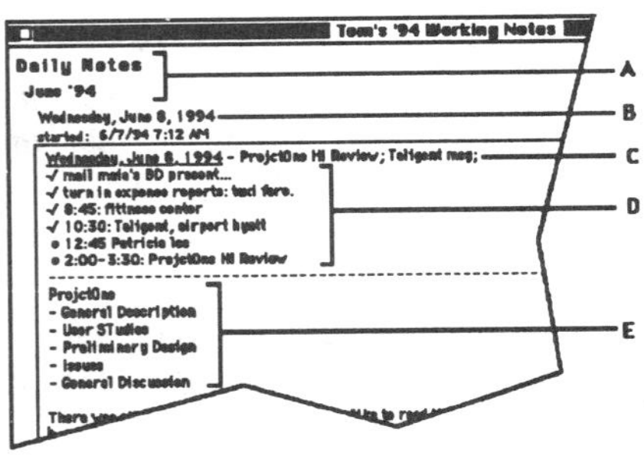

Figure 4. Detail of a content page:
A: Section and Subsection titles.
B: Page date (daily notes section only).
C: First line of contents field (appears in tables of contents).
D: To Do list
E: Beginning of notes for first meeting.

I've developed a fairly consistent daily routine for using Proteus:

- I begin by going to the page of the day.
- I update the To Do list at the top of the page (usually, the To Do list for that day has already been started).
- I switch out of Proteus and check my email and calendar. This may result in further additions to the To Do list. Email that has content that I want to save or that I want to reflect on and answer later, may be pasted into the content area.
- As the day goes on I usually have Proteus near at hand. I will use Proteus to update my To Do list, to jot brief notes (e.g. telephone messages; thoughts), and to compose and send email. When in meetings, I will usually make notes in Proteus; if the meeting is fairly large and is covering matters that don't concern me, I'll make notes on other things, update my To Do list, or do email, while monitoring what's going on in the meeting.

So, in summary, frequent uses of Proteus (ranging from once or twice a week to many times a day) include:

- Managing my tasks (To Do'ing)
- Recording meeting notes
- Messaging
- Serving as a repository for information

Occasional Use for Reference and Summaries
I use Proteus for a number of other tasks, although their frequency is in the range of from once a week to once a month. These include:

- Reference. I use the search command to search through Proteus for information several times a month—occasionally a particular quotation from something I've read, more often notes from a particular meeting.
- Summarization. Once a month I do a report on my activities; this involves browsing the last month's worth of Proteus entries. Occasionally, I need to produce a summary of the results of a series of meetings, and will search for notes relevant to particular projects.
- Diagramming. A couple times a month I will use Proteus to draw diagrams or models relevant to meetings or projects in which I'm evolved. (This is a completely unanticipated use: I hadn't imagined that anyone—let alone me—would want to draw with a track ball!)
- Capturing Reading Notes. If I read something useful, I'll often transcribe quotations from it into a special section of Proteus. This activity occurs in bursts—with several months intervening between bursts.

Ways in Which I Don't Use Proteus
It is interesting to note that I do not use Proteus in the way I originally thought I would. The motivation behind transforming Proteus from a stack of quotations into a full-featured electronic notebook was the vision of being able to make notes for a paper, and link the notes to the relevant quotations. However, after finishing the work of programming Proteus, I quickly abandoned this use. I found that jumping to the quotations caused a disruptive context shift, and that the functionality provided by HyperCard text fields was insufficient. What I really wanted (and soon switched to) was an outliner into which I could copy my quotations, and where I could interleave them with notes and writing fragments. In general, I do not use Proteus to author structured documents.

Usage of Proteus versus Paper Notebooks
Before Proteus I was a heavy user of paper notebooks. As with Proteus, I used paper notebooks as a sort of work diary: I started each day on a new page, kept a To Do list, meeting notes, and used it as a repository for other information. However, there are couple of striking differences (besides the obvious one that I didn't use it for

composing email). First, I find that I make many more notes in Proteus—in part this is because I find typing easier and faster than writing, and in part because of synergetic effects I describe in the next section. Second, I rarely looked back through my paper notebooks—and when I did, I only tended to look at recent entries. In contrast, I re-read entries in Proteus frequently. There are several reasons for this: it is easier to search and browse; the content is more legible; and when I find something useful it can be copied and re-used.

LESSONS LEARNED

Contributions to Usefulness

Although there are many ways in which Proteus is quite useful, two are so important as to make it an essential part of my work activity.

Synergy

Probably the most significant impact of Proteus is a sort of synergy among the activities of note making, reference, and messaging. Messaging drives this synergy. I write notes more often—and my notes are of higher quality—because I know that I am more likely to email them to others. Because the quality of my notes is higher, I reference (and reuse) them more when I'm writing a relevant message or paper. Also, the increased quality means that I am more likely to understand them when I look back at them after six months. In turn, the increased frequency of reference also drives note making and messaging: the more use I get out of them, the more effort I'm willing to put into them. Thus, there is a curious sort of ambiguity when writing in Proteus: my proximate goal may be keeping notes on an interesting meeting, but I also know in the back of my mind that they may also turn into a message or serve as grist for a future paper.

Context Independence

The other major aspect of Proteus' usefulness has to do with its portability, and with the amount of personally relevant information in it. I typically carry Proteus with me and so I always have a variety of tasks of various sizes that I can work on. If I arrive at a meeting early, I can compose a message, review notes, or update my To Do list while waiting for others to arrive.

This has changed my behavior. I am more willing to go to large meetings where some or all of the content is of unknown relevance: if the meeting is relevant, I pay attention and take notes; if parts are irrelevant, I can work on other things while keeping half an ear on the meeting. I have had extremely productive work sessions when 'stuck' in the middle of a row in the auditorium. While this may sound like a small thing, the degree to which it alleviates irritation at late-starting meetings, and anxiety about being stuck in irrelevant meetings, makes a significant difference in my life.

Finding Things

Although note making, messaging, and activity management are the primary uses of Proteus, information storage and retrieval plays an important role in supporting these tasks, as well as being useful independently. Proteus supports a variety of ways of searching for things. One can use text search, browse using the section and subsection TOCs, or search for items that have been specially marked in various ways.

Text Search

One of the putative benefits of an electronic notebook is that you can use text search. This is not as useful as it might seem. There are three problems: First, a fact of life for me, and I suspect for most electronic notebook users, is that notes are written hastily, and hence contain frequent misspellings, typos, and abbreviations. Thus, standard keyword searches are not very effective in finding words which have been mistyped or hastily abbreviated. Second, I use many words much more frequently than I'm aware of. Words like object, metaphor, interface, and communications are so frequent as to not be worth searching for, as are common project names. In this respect the use of To Do lists is a drawback, as important projects and items tend to recur in To Do lists and generate hit after hit when searching. Finally, the limitations of HyperCard's search mechanism (it takes you to the card, and shows only the first word of the first instance that matches) exacerbates the above problems. A search mechanism that would generate a list of fuzzy hits (so that when searching for PowerTalk, you'd also get PowerTlk, and PwerTalk), shown with surrounding context, would be far more useful.

As a consequence of this, text search in Proteus is primarily useful when: 1) trying to put together a summary of what has happened on a project (i.e., many hits are just what you want); 2) when searching for a relatively unique target that is probably spelled correctly (e.g., part of an email address string such as "boombox"; or 3) when the approximate location of the item is known, so that the search can be limited to that neighborhood.

Marking

A second strategy for finding is to mark things when you think you may want to find them later. Proteus provides two mechanisms for this: stamps and dog-ears. A stamp is a way of providing a sort of topic-specific book mark—Proteus had stamps for addresses, reference citations, and 'interesting items.' The user can select a type of stamp and can then jump from one stamp to the next. Dog-ears are similar to stamps except a bit simpler: they are the analog of folding over the corner of a page. Like stamps, the user can jump from one dog-ear to the next.

I use dog-ears several times a month; however, I rarely use stamps. One reason for this has to do with overhead. While stamps are easy to use, requiring no more than a click to stamp something, if I'm engaged in my current activity I don't think about the desirability of stamping the item, or if I do, I often don't want to interrupt my flow of activity. If I do decide to interrupt myself, I still tend not to use stamps. Stamps are primarily a way of deferring actions until later: I stamp addresses so I can enter them in my address file; I stamp citations so I can put those in a special place; and so on. If I decide to interrupt my activity, I typically just go ahead and do the whole thing.

However, this doesn't explain why dog-ears are used so much more frequently than stamps, since they are logically and functionally equivalent, both requiring a click to create, and both requiring clicking a button to search for. I believe that the explanation is that stamping something seems to require more cognitive overhead. In stamping something, the user is basically making the decision to apply a particular label to a particular piece of content. In contrast, marking a page with a dog-ear is simply saying 'I may want to look at something on this page again.' Dog-ears are more light weight than stamps.

Browsing
Proteus succeeds best at search by browsing. That is, a common strategy for finding something—if its approximate location is known—is to browse the appropriate table of contents. I may recognize what I'm searching for, and can then jump directly to it. Or I may see something which reminds me of the context, and thus generates more cues about what I'm searching for. The decision to include the first line of each content page in the subsection TOCs turned out to be a good one.

(Of course, it should be noted that TOCs were not designed with this use in mind. TOCs evolved in the context of the original quotations stack (see next subsection), and the idea of using the first line of each page was derived from an analogy to the indices of poetry and quotation anthologies.)

Evolution of the Design
One interesting facet of Proteus is that it has changed considerably over time, both in terms of its underlying structure and function, and in how it was used.

The Pre-History of Proteus
Proteus did not spring into existence as an electronic notebook, or as a vehicle for exploring issues about customization and long term usefulness. Rather, it went through a gradual evolution.

Proteus began as a stack of quotations and notes (my practice is to copy down quotes from favorite books or articles). After a year or so, I had enough entries that using them became cumbersome, and so I added a table of contents that could be recompiled when new quotations were added. As more cards were added it became desirable to break it into subsections and to have a hierarchical table of contents.

About this time, I realized that with 'just a little more work' I could have an electronic notebook that would allow me to explore on a personal level some of the frustrating issues already described. I also had a concrete task in mind for Proteus: I had been wanting to write a paper that drew upon a number of the quotations I had collected in the stack, and I thought it would be very useful to be able to outline the paper, and link parts of it to relevant quotations.

From Linking/Authoring to Messaging and Note Making
Personal electronic notebooks have a paradoxical aspect to them: they really don't become useful until considerable material has been entered, and yet how many people will exert the effort needed to enter material, before the utility is evident? I call this the start up problem. While it is dangerous to generalize from a population of one, the case of Proteus suggests an interesting answer to the start up problem.

Initially, Proteus tried to solve the start up problem by cheating, in that it began with a large number of quotations that had been gradually built up over a couple of years. However, this failed, in that the initially envisioned authoring/linking use for Proteus didn't pan out: it was too cumbersome. Instead, what saved Proteus from being abandoned was its use as a diary, and that in turn was driven by the incorporation of messaging functionality. Messaging added collaborative value to the note making functionality of Proteus, and permitted it to be useful (and encouraged the entry of information), until there was enough information to make Proteus useful for reference purposes.

(As in the case of TOCs, the full importance of messaging was not anticipated. Messaging was originally incorporated in Proteus only because it was easy to add. I already had an X-command and script for messaging that I had used in another stack, the electronic edition of a newsletter I edit. Ironically, messaging was a failure in *that* context; fewer than a dozen people ever made use of it.)

Increasing Structure
When working on the predecessor to Proteus (the original, working prototype of an electronic notebook), I had a running debate with another designer over how much structure people wanted in an electronic notebook. What I wanted, I claimed, was something very simple: just a temporally-ordered set of pages. People remember things by time, I said, and if you allow them to move pages around, and create sections, they'll just start losing things, and we'll have to introduce all sorts of functionality for organizing and navigating the notebook.

As Proteus evolved, it quickly became apparent that I was wrong. While I don't find it surprising when my intuitions about what other people want are wrong, I was surprised to discover that my intuitions about what I wanted were wrong. But it's incontestable. The most obvious trend in the evolution of Proteus is the gradual addition of more and more layers of structure. Proteus started out as one notebook; after a bit it was broken into sections, each with their own table of contents. After a bit longer subsections and subsection TOCs were added. And finally major sections of the notebooks were broken apart into separate notebooks which can be accessed through a bookshelf menu.

At the same time, it is important to note that at the beginning I neither wanted nor needed the structure. It was only as time went on, and I added more and more information, and begin to develop specialized ways of interacting with it, that the increased structure became useful for supporting access and browsing, and for segregating functionality.

Increasing Specialization
This brings us to the next trend in the evolution of Proteus: the increasing degree of task-specific specialization. As I

began using Proteus in new ways, after a while I would develop functionality that support the new mode of use. For example, the use of Proteus as a diary started out fairly simply: text was simply entered onto a blank, unspecialized content page. But as time went on I developed various conventions, and then eventually implemented functionality to support and reinforce those conventions. Some instances:

- The diary page begins with the date. Initially the date was entered manually. After a while, I created a "header" button to automatically generate the date for the day. As of this writing, the working notebook for a new year is generated, with the diary pages having the date embedded in them.
- As the To Do list became more heavily used, buttons that supported particular operations on it appeared (e.g., a 'procrastinate button', that moves selected To Do items to tomorrow's page; a 'to do button' that copies selected text (usually from notes), and inserts it in the To Do list.)
- A convention of separating different items with dashes was codified with the "---" button, which automatically drew a line of dashes.

These are all minor things. However, they do use up significant amounts of the limited space for controls, and contribute to the transformation of pages in the "daily notes" section from generic content pages to diary-specific pages. The appearance of task-specific controls also increased the pressure to split off the diary portion of the notebook into its own notebook. Perhaps most importantly, the appearance of task-specific functionality resulted in new structural features of the notebook which could then be used to support the development of more task-specific functionality. For example, once the "---" button for separating items was implemented, it was easy to create a button to jump from one item to the next because the system could tell that a new item was marked by the appearance of a particular number of dashes; prior to that, when dashed separators were generated manually and might have any number of dashes, the task of writing a script to distinguish separators from other uses of dashes was more work than seemed justified.

Similar stories can be told about other uses of Proteus. The quotation reference section of Proteus became more specialized, and was split off into its own notebook. A section of Proteus that started out to support scheduling, gradually became more complex and specialized, until it was replaced with links to an external, calendar application. The global Table of Contents began as a regular TOC (as in figure 3), and only gradually developed the browser-like structure shown in figure 2. Again and again there was a move from generality and simplicity towards specialization and complexity. And while there are many instances of periods of simplification (e.g., the removal of unused functionality), these simplifications were often triggered by the desire to make room for new functionality.

From Generic & Usable to Arcane & Useful

When I began using Proteus, I had a relatively simple application that was easy to use and to explain to others. Now, Proteus is much more complex; it has quite a few features that are useful only to me, and that make the interface more complex and difficult to learn for anyone else. In the process of being customized for my purposes, Proteus has shifted from being usable (by anyone) to being useful (to me).

This raises some interesting questions. How general is this tradeoff between simplicity and usability on the one hand, and specialization and complexity on the other? Will technologies like OpenDoc, which promise to support customization, manifest this trend? Or, less generally, suppose that three years ago I had been magically given Proteus as it is structured today: would I have found it either usable or useful? I suspect the answer is no. My guess is that my work practices had to gradually evolve in consonance with the structure and function of Proteus. That is, rather than this being a process of me gradually customizing Proteus to my needs, it feels more like a process of co-evolution in which the electronic notebook and my work practices have mutually conditioned one another. For example, as previously noted, the use of Proteus resulted in me being more willing to attend large meetings, and in turn, more frequent use of Proteus in large meetings resulted in various adaptations for more effective use in such situations (e.g., an easy way to turn the sound off).

On Customizability

It's important to note that Proteus evolved only because HyperCard provided such a flexible and readily-customizable environment. Three things seem of importance. First, the ability to change small things—graphics, buttons, handlers—made Proteus feel like a truly malleable environment. It got me into the habit of tweaking things. Another important factor was the availability of modules of functionality that could be imported from elsewhere. Scripts created both by myself and by others were often incorporated into Proteus. This greatly decreased the overhead involved in adding functionality, and made it much easier to experiment. For example, it took me less than twenty minutes from conception to working implementation to add voice notes into Proteus (and this is fortunate because I never used them). Finally, the aforementioned context independence provided by Proteus also applied to its customization. That is, at any time I encountered a problem or thought of a way Proteus could be tuned to better support my practices, I could do it. A number of small but important features were implemented while waiting for people to show up, or while 'stuck' in large meetings. This practice was so prevalent during the early stages of developing Proteus, that I built in a special command key combination to jump into the HyperTalk Reference stack.

CONCLUDING REMARKS

There are a number of reasons Proteus is a useful tool for me. One is simply that it supports the representations with which I work. Proteus is good at dealing with text, and many of the ways in which I reflect, communicate, and act, are entwined with textual representations. A person for whom other representations of information were more critical, would probably not find Proteus a useful tool.

A less obvious point is that Proteus is useful because of the synergy between note making and messaging. As noted, the messaging built into Proteus increases the potential utility (and quality) of note making, and the note making in turn provides grist for messages and other re-uses of content. Re-use of content is facilitated, in its turn, by the malleable nature of text, and by the support for browsing provided by the subsection tables of contents. And browsing itself is made easier because the normally ephemeral information that is captured — To Do lists, email messages, notes — provide more cues about what is being searched for. Interestingly, the synergy I've observed between note making and messaging resonates with John-Steiner's [6] characterization of paper notebooks as a means of capturing "condensed thought", and as an aid to transforming it into public language. (It is humbling to note that two of the more critical features in supporting this synergy—messaging, and the subsection tables of contents—were developed with different applications in mind, and without any suspicion of their ultimate usefulness.)

Finally, the fact that the portability of Proteus enables me to perform many tasks—reflection, communication, activity management—anywhere, has proved to be very useful. While this result was by no means unanticipated, the second order effects such as my increased willingness to attend large meetings were not expected.

Proteus is also interesting as an illustration of evolution through customization. Over the course of three years Proteus exhibited consistent trends towards specialization, task-specific functionality, and greater complexity. In addition, there was a pronounced tendency for Proteus and my work practices to co-evolve—it seems doubtful that starting out with the final version of Proteus would have been useful.

Finally, there are striking parallels between the design of Proteus, and design in the large. Common beliefs about designing products for users—that designers' intuitions aren't to be trusted, that designers are poor at predicting how a technology will be used, that iteration is an inherent part of design, that features will be used in unanticipated ways, that users are poor at articulating what they really need—carry over even to the case where the designer and the user are one.

ACKNOWLEDGMENTS

Thanks to a number of anonymous reviewers for suggestions and comments.

HyperCard, Newton, and PowerBook are registered trademarks of Apple Computer. The Virtual Notebook System is a trademark of Baylor College of Medicine and the ForeFront Group. Lotus Notes is a registered trademark of Lotus Development Corporation. Wizard is a registered trademark of Sharp.

REFERENCES

1. Assimacopoulos, A., Revillard, C., Herrmann, F., Borst, F., Paschoud, N. and Scherrer, J. R. An Electronic Notebook for Problem Oriented Patient Progress Notes: Testing a Concept. *Proceedings of the 6th Annual Conference on Medical Informatics* (1989), pp. 813-817.
2. Conklin, J. and Begeman, M. L. gIBIS: A Hypertext Tool for Exploratory Policy Discussion. *Proceedings of CSCW '88*, (1988), ACM Press.
3. Dejan, D. and Dejan, S. B. *Lotus Notes at Work.* Lotus Books, New York, 1991.
4. Fowler, J., Baker, D. G., Dargahi, R., Kouramajian, V., Gilson, H., Long, K. B., Petermann, C., and Gorry, A. G. Experience with the Virtual Notebook System: Abstraction in Hypertext. *Proceedings of CSCW '94.* (1994). ACM Press, pp. 133-143.
5. Halasz, F., Moran, T. P., and Trigg, R. H. NoteCards in a Nutshell. *Proceedings of CHI + GI 1987* (1987), ACM Press, pp. 45-52.
6. John-Steiner, V. *Notebooks of the Mind: Explorations of Thinking.* Harper & Row, New York, 1985.
7. Monty, M. L. *Issues for Supporting Notetaking and Note Using in the Computer Environment.* (1990) Unpublished Dissertation, Department of Psychology, University of California, San Diego.
8. Monty, M. L. and Moran, T. P. A Longitudinal Study of Authoring Using NoteCards. *SIGCHI Bulletin 18,* 2 (1986), pp. 59-60.
9. Neuwirth, C., Kaufer, D., Chimera, R., and Gillespie, T. The Notes Program: A Hypertext Application for Writing from Source Texts: Experiences and Writing. *Proceedings of the Hypertext '87 Conference,* (1987), ACM Press, pp. 121-141

10 Schnase, J. L. and Leggett, J. J. Computational Hypertext in Biological Modeling Applications. *Proceedings of the Hypertext '89 Conference,* (1989), ACM Press, pp. 181-197.

11 Shipman, F. M., Chaney, R. J., and Gorry, G. A.. Distributed Hypertext for Collaborative Research: The Virtual Notebook System. *Proceedings of the Hypertext '89 Conference,* (1989), ACM Press, pp. 129-135.

12 Trigg, R. H. and Irish, P. M. Hypertext Habitats: Experiences of Writers in NoteCards: *Proceedings of the Hypertext '87 Conference,* (1987), ACM Press, pp. 89-108

13 Twidale, M., Rodden, T., and Sommerville, I. The Designers' Notepad: Supporting and Understanding Cooperative Design. *Proceedings of the Third European Conference on Computer-Supported Cooperative Work* (1993), pp. 93-107.

Technomethodology: Paradoxes and Possibilities

Graham Button and Paul Dourish
Rank Xerox Research Centre
Cambridge Laboratory (EuroPARC)
61 Regent Street
Cambridge CB2 1AB
United Kingdom
+44 1223 341500
button@europarc.xerox.com, dourish@europarc.xerox.com

ABSTRACT

The design of CSCW systems has often had its roots in ethnomethodological understandings of work and investigations of working settings. Increasingly, we are also seeing these ideas applied to critique and inform HCI design more generally. However, the attempt to design from the basis of ethnomethodology is fraught with methodological dangers. In particular, ethnomethodology's overriding concern with the detail of practice poses some serious problems when attempts are made to design around such understandings. In this paper, we discuss the range and application of ethnomethodological investigations of technology in working settings, describe how ethnomethodologically-affiliated work has approached system design and discuss ways that ethnomethodology can move from design critique to design practice: the advent of *technomethodology.*

Keywords

Ethnography, ethnomethodology, design practice, methodology, accounts, abstraction.

ETHNOMETHODOLOGY AND DESIGN

There has been much discussion within the HCI community about a "turn to the social" (e.g. [23], [38]). Particularly within CSCW, but also within HCI, many of those who are considering such a move have been attracted to ethnomethodology [18] as a favoured sociological position. Ethnomethodology turns away from the structures and theorising of traditional sociology, concentrating instead on the details of the practices through which action and interaction are accomplished. In this respect, designers have found ethnomethodology a richer resource for insights about the organisation of work than other, more theoretically oriented, sociological positions.

More or less ethnomethodologically-oriented investigations are now regularly presented at CSCW conferences (e.g. [1], [5], [7], [8], [30], [37], [39]) and increasingly at HCI conferences, ([6], [13], [26]). Ethnomethodology is being used to inform design through:

1. fieldwork investigations that develop an understanding of work and organisations from the "inside", providing innovative insights into the organisational situatedness of work and the methods and practices through which work activities and interactions are assembled and which may be used in the design of technology to support work; and
2. developing an understanding of the temporal organisation of activities and interactions, revealing them to be a moment-by-moment organisation, and in so doing furnishing new concepts around which to generally consider the design of technology.

There are a number of inter-related reasons why some within the design community are taking up these two sets of issues.

First, Lucy Suchman's book "Plans and Situated Actions" [43], which articulated an argument that has significantly influenced many designers, was partly founded in the work of ethnomethodology. Her analysis emphasised a perspective on purposeful human action as situated in (and organised around) the context of particular circumstances, and, in doing so, provided a forceful critique of the user modelling and plan-based approaches common in both HCI and AI. Suchman's book has had considerable influence upon HCI research and design, becoming almost an icon of a concern in HCI with work settings and the detail of everyday working practices; and, as relevant parts of the design community have taken on board Suchman's arguments they have also taken on, perhaps unwittingly, an ethnomethodological influence.

Second, there has been a strong and vocal group within HCI who have consistently argued that the requirements for technology should be developed around the work situations of users, most particularly in the Participatory Design movement (e.g. [22]). Ethnomethodology is generally concerned with the "detailed and observable practices which make up the incarnate production of ordinary social facts" [35] which means that its studies of work domains contain rich descriptions of work practices. This may suggest to those who are already concerned with the relationship between work and design that they have an analytic ally who may be readily turned to as a resource to draw upon either for methodological sustenance or even empirical descriptions.

Third, for a variety of reasons that we will not go into here, ethnography as a method of enquiry has been attracting a great deal of attention from some within CSCW and HCI, (see e.g. [2], [31]). Like some other positions within sociology, ethnomethodology uses ethnographically generated material in its studies, though the analyses that it develops from these can vary significantly from those produced by other types of sociology. It is often difficult for those in the design community to apprehend the difference between competing sociological arguments, and the relevance for so doing might even be questionable. Ethnomethodology may, as a consequence, be basking in the sun of ethnography in general, some in design equating an interest in ethnography with an interest in ethnomethodology[1].

Fourth, Grudin [23] has argued that HCI has passed through a number of stages and is currently moving from the fourth stage which focused upon a dialogue with the user to a fifth stage of focusing the interface not around the individual but the work setting. Ethnomethodology may thus be, for some, a port in the storm of transition, for ethnomethodologists' emphasis upon not only work practice but also upon the organisational situatedness of work may offer candidate solutions to problems of incorporating the work settings, as well as work practice, into design.

However, the experience has been that the attempt to incorporate ethnomethodological understandings into design—either specific artifacts, or the design process in general—has been problematic. The models, assumptions, processes and sensitivities of the various groups involved have been sufficiently different as to present problems for their integration. This paper, indeed, follows in a tradition of introspection and analysis on the integration of our disciplines, and the respective roles played by each (e.g. [31], [41]), and this reflection mirrors similar issues in the integration of other theoretical approaches to the human sciences into HCI design (e.g. [3]). In this paper we want to unpack the issues surrounding the application of ethnomethodological accounts of working situations, and, critically, of ethnomethodology itself, not only to situations which involve technology, but to the design and introduction of advanced technologies. Our goal is primarily to understand and develop the relationship between ethnomethodology and technological design; secondarily, we hope that this might address some issues in the relationship of the human sciences to HCI practice more widely.

Having reviewed the basis for the current interest in ethnomethodology within HCI, we will next examine the contributions that have so far been made for technological support for socially-organised activity which have come from an ethnomethodological perspective—what we'll call "technomethodology".

1.Although we cannot develop the point, note that ethnography and ethnomethodology are not the same thing. Loosely, ethnography can thought of as a collection of techniques for gathering and organising field materials, while ethnomethodology is an analytic study policy which may draw upon ethnographic materials.

ASPECTS OF TECHNOMETHODOLOGY

Ethnomethodologically affiliated studies have been conducted across a wide range of work situations that involve technology: the work of air traffic controllers [25], city stockbrokers [30], software engineers [12], designers [36], print shop workers [8], municipal transport controllers [27], as well as the users of menu-driven computer systems [29], multimedia technologies [28] and photocopiers [43].

These studies fall into two related areas of enquiry: investigations of the organisation of social action and interaction; and investigations of the organisation of work and work settings.

The Organisation of Social Action and Interaction

One direction of research has been into the ways in which people organise and manage everyday social activity. In particular, Conversation Analysis, a branch of ethnomethodology, has developed an extensive corpus of findings about the ways in which people generally build up their social actions and interactions with one another and more recently, a conversation analytic sensibility has been extensively used in studies of the ways in which people interact with one another through or around technology. An obvious contender for such scrutiny are technologies that provide for access between persons who are geographically distributed, and attention has been paid to video-mediated communication, (e.g. [28]). The thrust of this work is to furnish descriptions of the ways in which persons normally organise their actions and interactions and then compare this to what is possible or not possible using the technology. However, it is not just video-mediated communication that has been the subject of such examinations but also other work settings in which technology is used, such as control suites [27]; the doctor's consulting room [21], and stock dealing rooms [30].

The Organisation of Work

A second major thrust in the work of ethnomethodology has been the examination of the practices and methods through which people accomplish their work. In particular, it has been concerned with how it is organised in such a way as to make it recognisable to others as uniquely the work it is. Ethnomethodologically affiliated studies of work have been made of technologically rich work settings. Suchman has, over a number of studies (e.g. [45]), developed descriptions of the practices through which particular types of work-settings are organised as centres of co-ordination. A team of researchers at Lancaster University in the UK have, again over the course of a number of studies (e.g. [25]), developed detailed descriptions of the work of air-traffic controllers. There has also been a series of studies of the work of engineers (e.g. [42]). In addition to these examples of sustained enquires into domains of work there have been numerous one-off studies of work and the role of technology. These mainly involved studies of the organisation of the work prior to the introduction of technology and the subsequent effects that the technology had, e.g. Button and Harper's [11] examination of the introduction of an accountancy package into the furniture industry and Bowers, Button and

Sharrock's [8] description of the impact of a Management Information System on the work practices involved in the organisation of a flow of work on the shop-floor in the print industry.

Ethnomethodological Critiques of Technology

We have been describing two main themes in ethnomethodological work, the organisation of social action and interaction and the organisation of work, and how these have been applied by those who claim an ethnomethodological affiliation to the study of social action, interaction and work involving technology. Taken together, ethnomethodologically affiliated studies have produced a strong critique of the design of technology at work for they have displayed that technology, at best, often fails to support the work it is designed for, or at worst, does not allow people to actually engage in their work, because the technology is not aligned to the practices through which they organise their actions, interactions and work. Heath et al summarise this conclusion for CSCW in the following: "Despite impressive technological developments in CSCW, it is widely recognised that there are relatively few examples of successful applications in real world settings. [...] it is suggested that the lack of success of CSCW systems derives not so much from their technological limitations, but more from their insensitivity to the organisation of work and communication in real work environments" [30].

We will content ourselves with two examples to make this point. First, based in part upon Conversation Analysis and the work of its founder Harvey Sacks, Lucy Suchman [44] has challenged speech act theory upon which systems such as Winograd and Flores' "THE COORDINATOR" are based. The thrust of her criticism in this respect is that conversation analysis has demonstrated that meaning and intention are interactionally contingent, something that is not accounted for in speech act theory. Consequently, this is a feature of ordinary action and interaction which cannot be supported by THE COORDINATOR, indeed a feature of social action and interaction that is violated in the stipulative organisation imposed by the system.

Second, Bowers, Button and Sharrock [8] examined the work of printers on the shop-floor and described how, in being faced with the uncertainties of orders which could result in either periods of high demand which stretched operators and machinery or in periods of low demand when operators and machinery were idle, operators would use ad hoc practices not found in the formal representation of the work-flow of the print room, to "even out" the flow of work. However, when a technology designed to organise the flow of work on the shop-floor was introduced, it utilised a formal model of work flow which prevented the operators from utilising their ad hoc practices. The result was that the printing work was seriously disrupted with order deadlines being missed and significant over-time having to be done. Quite simply, the technology was not designed with knowledge of the methods and practices through which the work it was designed to organise was done, the methods and practices being revealed through ethnomethodological study.

Critique and Design—Two Paradoxes

As we have seen, then, ethnomethodological analyses have been used in a range of circumstances to critique technological design in particular working settings and situations. Ethnomethodology, in attending in particular to the details of everyday action and work practice, has been able to expose an unfortunate paradox in the design of technologies for collaborative activity (or socially-constructed action). This is the *paradox of system design*—that the introduction of technology designed to support "large-scale" activities while fundamentally transforming the "small-scale" detail of action can systematically undermine exactly the detailed features of working practice *through which* the "large-scale" activity is, in fact, accomplished. It points, fundamentally, to the interdependence of minute practice and grand accomplishment.

However, in so doing, ethnomethodology finds itself caught in a second paradox—the *paradox of technomethodology*[1]. Given the concern with the particular, with detail, and with the moment-by-moment organisation of action, how can ethnomethodology be applied to the design of new technologies? Certainly, ethnomethodologists have urged that designers take into account the methods and practices through which social action, interaction and categories of work are organised; but in the face of the unavoidably transformational nature of technology and system design in working settings, it would seem that ethnomethodology becomes relatively powerless. Its tradition is in analysing practice, rather than "inventing the future". Even Heath and Luff's observations of the relative impotence of gaze and gesture in video-mediated communication are, to an extent, undermined by accounts of the active transformation of visual conduct in video-mediated interaction by which the same communicative *accomplishments* are reconstructed; reconstructed, ironically enough, out of the *lived detail* of video interaction [17].

Ethnomethodologists interested in technology and design have thus so far, and after much effort, managed to make the first step from the study of the use of technology to the critique of technology. The next step however is yet to be taken and will be more problematic which is to move from critique to design. How can design now productively learn from ethnomethodology?

LEARNING FROM ETHNOMETHODOLOGY

We have outlined two related forms of "technomethodological" enquiry. Operating across these, however, are fundamental issues about how to incorporate findings and insights from ethnomethodology into the process of design. This integration is at the heart of technomethodology, and raises some of the most important questions for both ethnomethodologists and designers. To explore the issues, we set out three ways in which this relationship can operate. Two caveats should be noted. First, actual practice will tend to draw, to some extent, on elements of each; but a pedagogical separation helps frame the discussion. Second, for the

1. Taken together, these paradoxes produce what Grudin and Grinter [24] have called the "ethnographers' dilemma".

CHI audience, we present these largely in terms of design *learning from* the ethnomethodological perspective; in practice, of course, the relationship is bidirectional.

Learning from the Ethnomethodologist

Arguably, to date, the most widespread and successful approach to incorporating ethnomethodological input into the design process is for the design process and designers to *learn from the ethnomethodologist.* In this model, the ethnomethodologist goes into the field to study a work setting. While the results may be written up as an ethnomethodological account of the work, it is not this account, but rather the ethnomethodologist, who will be the primary resource for the design process. Fresh from the field, brimming with detailed observations and an analytical framework within which to organise them, the ethnomethodologist works closely with the designers from the earliest points in the process. From the designers' perspective, the ethnomethodologist serves as a proxy for the users in the field—or, perhaps more accurately, a proxy for the *field setting* itself. Design ideas can be "bounced off" the ethnomethodologist, who draws on field observations both to evaluate and to contribute to aspects of the design.

Where is the locus of the ethnomethodology, in this model? Primarily, it is in the ethnomethodologist's head. From the perspective of the designers, the ethnomethodologist is almost indistinguishable from any other fieldworker, and ethnomethodology, itself, is not crucial as input. Ethnomethodologists will presumably use their analytical perspective in shaping a story about the field setting, and in evaluating and contributing to the design. However, it is primarily the ethnomethodologist—as a trained field worker—who acts as a channel between the designers and the users.

Learning from Ethnomethodological Accounts

A second approach is to organise the design around *specifically* ethnomethodological analysis. In particular, the second approach involves *learning from ethnomethodological accounts of work settings.* Like the first approach, this will probably involve the close collaboration of ethnomethodologist and designer; however, the primary difference is that the designer is working with a specifically ethnomethodological analysis of the work situation, rather than with an ethnomethodologist who might use his training and judgement to respond to design specifics.

The locus of ethnomethodology is in the account—and that's a key distinction, because now it is an explicit part of the communication between field and design. In many ways, this is a much more satisfactory way to proceed; one which proceeds from an understanding that ethnomethodology is an analytical perspective, a form of "writing up" rather than a form of data collection [2]. However, it's harder to do, and it's certainly less common. The first approach, after all, does not require the designers to be sufficiently well-versed in ethnomethodology to be able to read an ethnomethodologist's account of a working situation. What's more, the first approach more directly reflects the feeling that design must "engage the user"; the feeling which has lead to the emergence of User-Centred Design as a movement, and to the increasing use of ethnographic field techniques in design in the first place! Connection between designers and users is valued and sought out, so the "disconnection" implied by mediation through an ethnomethodological analysis rather than through a person is, consequently, to be avoided. However, the second approach more adequately builds on ethnomethodological understanding (rather than simply any field observation); and so, if we are to take seriously a turn towards ethnomethodology *in particular,* then we must similarly understand how this second approach proceeds.

Learning from Ethnomethodology

In the first approach, design was organised directly around the contribution or involvement of an ethnomethodologist. In the second approach, it was organised around an ethnomethodological analysis of a working situation; a more explicit basis in ethnomethodological investigation, rather than simply on field observation and commentary. The third approach is to make the connection at a deeper level yet. Here, the design process *learns from ethnomethodology.* That is, we consider the implications which foundational ethnomethodological principles—those insights and perspectives which characterise the discipline—hold for both the artifacts and processes of design. In this approach, design does not take on board ethnomethodological analysis and insights, but takes on board the very study policy of ethnomethodology.

This approach differs significantly from the first two, in that it regards the relationship between ethnomethodology and system design as a theoretical matter. Again, this theoretical orientation is why we have been concentrating on ethnomethodology, rather than qualitative methods in general. So, rather than have systems design and ethnomethodology "reach" towards each other and "meet" at a design, we instead look to forge more foundational relationships, and then approach design from this new position. This foundational relationship is one in which design adopts the analytic mentality of ethnomethodology, and ethnomethodology dons the practical mantle of design. We look forward, through this approach, to what Garfinkel has often referred to as the emergence of a "hybrid" discipline from out of ethnomethodological studies of other disciplines.

This approach is as radical for ethnomethodology as it is for system design. On the one hand, it deals directly with the generally operative social processes which are the currency of ethnomethodology; elements such as situatedness, practical action and representation, achievement and mechanism, phenomena of order, and accountability. On the other hand, it deals with the fundamental, almost implicit, aspects of system design—generalisation and abstraction, configuration, data and process, fixedness and mutability. So rather than ask, "what are the implications of this ethnomethodological account of the work of hotel receptionists for the design of a booking system?", we might ask, "what are the implications of the operation and use of member categorisations for questions of individuality and grouping in software systems?". This is a quite different order of question.

To make this more concrete, let's consider a specific example. In recent work, we have been concerned with issues of abstraction and representation in system design. In particular, we have looked at the contrast between, on one hand, the traditional role of abstraction in systems design and, on the other, the practical aspects of representations of activity from an ethnomethodological perspective. From this we have developed of a notion of "accounts" [16]; computational representations which systems continuously offer of their own behaviour and activity, as a resource for improvised and contextualised action[1]. Accounts draw on recent research on software architectures and "open implementations" [33], which introduce the idea of a "causal connection" which maintains the correspondence between representations and the systems they represent. In the accounts model, this causal connection provides for the continual *accountability* of the account; the backing in its relationship to the action of the system which lends it legitimacy. Just as ethnomethodology has shown how social activity is accountable, i.e. performed in such a way as to reveal its organisation, so our notion of computational accountability relates interface activity to the structure of what lies below. Interface activity is organised within an account of the system's action, so that it can become a resource for the ongoing management of user activity and interaction.

The notion of accounts and accountability as a basis for system-building constitutes a significant reorientation of abstraction in system design. Computational abstractions provide modularity and separation. The abstraction "stands for" the behaviour of the code which implements it. Abstraction barriers are opaque; on the one hand, they hide the complexity of what lies behind, and on the other, they present it for use in some rationalised way. So system design traffics in abstractions, rather than in meanings, interpretations or behaviours.

Accounts begin to capture some of the flavour of the social. This alternative view is less concerned with what the abstraction (or representation) *is*, in itself, focusing instead on what it can do and how it can be made to work. They place the emphasis on where the abstraction came from, how and why it was produced, by whom and for whom. The representation exists only by dint of its being maintained and supported, being made acceptable to the parties on either side for some set of purposes and actions. So when we begin to design systems with a model of "abstractions as accounts", the action isn't in the abstraction, but in how the abstraction can be *worked*—in the notions of accountability which make it useful.

Accounts illustrate the investigation of an aspect of system design with respect to an aspect of ethnomethodology as a body of knowledge. As such, they exemplify our third approach to system learning—from ethnomethodology itself, rather than from particular ethnomethodological investigations, or from the ethnomethodologist as a proxy of the working situation. The success of the first two approaches in the development of CSCW systems and technologies is testament to their value; however, the deeper connection between ethnomethodology and system design as disciplines, seems crucial to the progression from study and critique to design.

1. We present this work only as an example of the relationship between fundamental concepts from the disciplines; a fuller description—an "account of accounts"—is outwith the scope of this paper.

HUMAN SCIENCES AND DESIGN PRACTICE

The general problem which we have addressed here—on the relationship between a body of disciplinary knowledge and the practice of HCI or CSCW design—is hardly a new one to the HCI community. Over the past ten years or so, many analyses have focused on the relationship between a range of scientific understandings and HCI design (see, for example, [3], [34]); a range of design approaches drawing on different levels of theoretical input have been developed and explored (e.g. [14], [15], [32]); and attempts have been made to integrate multiple theoretical and practical approaches to HCI design (e.g. [4], [9]).

In many ways, some of the distinctions which we have presented in this paper—especially our separation between the three modes of incorporation of ethnomethodological understandings into design efforts—mirror these analyses of (primarily) cognitive science and human factors knowledge into the HCI design process. In much the same way as we describe designers learning from ethnomethodologists as work-setting proxies, so human factors specialists have been introduced into design teams. Similarly, by analogy with our second form of collaboration, attempts have been made to inform system design on the basis of cognitive models of human activity. And finally, our third approach can be thought as being related to more radical attempts to restructure the design process around a cognitive "science base". Even in particular, restricted areas of research investigation, we can see these various approaches operating at once—consider, for example, the range of ways in which research on mental models has been incorporated, more or less directly, into the design of interactive systems.

In this way, then, our concerns here relate to a larger set of concerns within the HCI community. As such, we hope that our perspective can also shed light on those general issues. However, there are a number of aspects of our position which differ from these approaches in significant ways, some of them based on the nature of the particular theoretical perspective, ethnomethodology, which concerns us. We will address three here.

The first reason to explore these issues was discussed in the first section of this paper—the prevalence of ethnomethodological perspectives in the design of collaborative systems. Collaborative systems open up new sets of issues for theoretical exploration, and we have increasingly found those issues work their way back to more traditional areas of HCI. So, just as the various approaches to the incorporation of cognitive and psychological approaches to HCI design reflect the particular details of the various approaches—indeed, different approaches appear to be most fruitfully applied in different ways and at different points in the process—so a focus on ethnomethodology, simply as a new discipline, opens up these issues to further scrutiny.

The second important point to be made is that the third level of connection between ethnomethodology and system design which we have advocated, and described with the example of the "accounts" work, is *not* a link between theory and practice; it's a link between theory and theory. An important understanding which underpins our attempt to identify fruitful relationships of this sort is that it is not simply enough to consider the implications which a theoretical orientation has for the way in which we design systems; rather, it is critical that we consider the implications for the *nature of the systems we design*. A respectfulness for the notion of improvised action, or for the social production and use of representations, forces a reorientation of perspective which reaches deeper than the design process itself.

The third issue has to do with the very nature of ethnomethodological understandings; and in particular, with ethnomethodology's overriding attentiveness to the detail of practice. Ethnomethodology itself set out to respecify issues arising from the application of models, theories and structures in traditional sociology, and hence ethnomethodology's position on the relationship between practice and generalisation is itself a slippery one, forcing us to look in new ways at how to incorporate ethnomethodological understandings in system design. So this relationship between the abstract and the particular is the crux of any relationship we might try to derive between ethnomethodology and design.

ABSTRACTION AND PARTICULARITY

> *"... the reported phenomena are only inspectably the case. They are unavailable to the arts of designing and interpreting definitions, metaphors, models, constructions, types or ideals. They cannot be recovered by attempts, no matter how thoughtful, to specify an examinable practice by detailing a generality."*
> *—Harold Garfinkel [19]*

The roots of ethnomethodology—and, in particular, its radical respecification of the issues of sociological analysis—are firmly grounded in a primary concern with the particulars of everyday, practical action. System design, on the other hand, is fundamentally about the creation, manipulation and use of abstractions. So, as ethnomethodology has encountered systems design, it has sometimes, perhaps unfairly, been seen as exclusively concerned with detail and specifics—the "excruciatingly particular"—and unwilling, or unable, to trade in generalisations.

However, this is a short-sighted criticism. It is important to note that many of the social "mechanisms" that ethnomethodology has described are found across many different social circumstances. For example, Garfinkel and Sacks [20] describe "cohort independence" phenomena, by which they mean social phenomena that are not tied to the scenic features of their production. Thus, for example, the model for turn-taking in conversation [40] is, in some crucial respects, cohort independent in that it operates across local circumstances such as gender, ethnicity, race, occupational identity, etc. It is these sorts of generally operative social processes, explicated by ethnomethodology, which we turn to in our third approach to technomethodology. These processes are, in Sacks et al's terms, "context free, yet context sensitive".

Since we are advocating the use in design of general processes arising from a discipline concerned with the particular, there are some issues to be clarified. We will make two points here.

The first is to emphasise that the generally operative social processes to which we make appeal are incontrovertibly grounded in practice. They arise from, and are employed in, the specifics of everyday action. Their generality does not lie in any "abstracting away" of detail; it lies, instead, in their general *operativeness,* the wide range of actions and interactions which they underpin.

The second observation is that ethnomethodologists and system designers will typically put the generalisations of their disciplines to work in very different ways. On one hand, the ethnomethodologist's generalisations tend to be *analytic* characterisations—categories and descriptions of action employed to delineate, describe and explicate action. On the other hand, the abstractions of software engineering are *generative*; they not only characterise system action but, themselves, give rise to it. Abstractions in computer programs produce behaviour; indeed, all behaviour is generated through some set of abstractions (embodied in software systems, programming languages and instruction sets). As a result, ethnomethodologists and system designers have, traditionally, had very different ideas of the scope, form, nature and use of generalisations.

Understanding the place of abstraction and generalisation in ethnomethodological accounts of work is critical to making the move between the three forms of learning, because it represents a move towards the abstract. In particular, the move represents an attempt to work with a set of *sensibilities* rather than with the details of specific activity, even though, of course, those sensibilities arise out of the discipline's very concern with the grounded and specific experience of everyday activity. In other words, the third approach to technomethodology attempts to align system design not so much with the details of *specific working practices*, as with the details of the *means by which such working practices arise and are constituted.*

This distinction is critical to the successful interworking of systems design and ethnomethodology, as is the recognition—and, subsequently, the *working*—of the difference in models of abstraction.

Consider an example to illustrate this distinction. In recent years, there has been an interest in utilising the insights of ethnomethodology for the development of dialogical interfaces. Attempts have been made to build in the *specifics* of Sacks et al's turn-taking model, such as the rules associated with speaker transfer, into computer interfaces. However, our argument is that the value of the turn-taking model described by Sacks et al is in the way it which it shows how the abstractions of conversational flow are *sustained*, rather than rote procedures by which they might be *enacted* [10]. It is this notion of the ongoing management of conversation, rather than the specifics of any human dialogue, which provides an abstraction for design. When we fail to make the distinction, we fall foul of the paradox of technomethodology.

So, the two paradoxes which we described—the paradox of system design, and, particularly, the paradox of technomethodology—are based in large part in the differing forms and uses of generalisation in the two disciplines. The third approach of technomethodology—one which attempts to work with generally operative processes from ethnomethodology as resources for design—is a starting-point in attempting to resolve some of these difficulties.

SUMMARY

The design of both single-user and multi-user interactive systems on the basis of ethnomethodological studies of working settings and work practice has been relatively successful, but nonetheless problematic. The force and tellingness of these accounts of work is testament to their utility, but aspects of ethnomethodology's project pose problems for design practice. The paradox of technomethodology lies in the attempt to design novel technological solutions based on an analytical perspective with a specific orientation towards the existing detail of practical action. We have discussed three approaches to working with ethnomethodology in system design; and in particular, we have proposed a model which applies not simply to the process of design but, crucially, to the nature of computational artifacts in working settings. Our intention is to identify ways in which ethnomethodology and system design can be combined in ways which are respectful of both as bodies of knowledge and practice; and, in so doing, we have pointed in particular to fundamental differences in the nature and use of generalisations and abstractions in the two disciplines. Our ongoing project is the investigation and exploitation of precisely these relationships in the pursuit of technological support for everyday activity and working practice.

ACKNOWLEDGMENTS

We would like to acknowledge many colleagues who have helped us develop these ideas, especially Annette Adler, Bob Anderson, Victoria Bellotti, John Bowers, Christian Heath, Beki Grinter, Wes Sharrock, and Lucy Suchman. May they still talk to us. John Tang and the CHI reviewers provided valuable feedback on an earlier draft of this paper.

REFERENCES

[1] Anderson, R., Button, G. and Sharrock, W., "Supporting the Design Process Within an Organisational Context", Proc. European Conf. Computer-Supported Cooperative Work ECSCW'93, Milano, Italy, September 1993.

[2] Anderson, R., "Representation and Requirements: The Value of Ethnography in System Design", Human-Computer Interaction, 9, pp. 151–182, 1994.

[3] Barnard, P., "Building Bridges Between Basic Theories and the Artifacts of Human-Computer Interaction", in Caroll (ed.), *"Designing Interaction: Psychology at the Human-Computer Interface"*, Cambridge University Press, New York, 1991.

[4] Bellotti, V., Buckingham-Shum, S., MacLean, A. and Hammond, N., "Multidisciplinary Modelling in HCI Design... In Theory and Practice", Proc. ACM Conference on Human Factors in Computing Systems CHI'95, Denver, Colorado, May 1995.

[5] Bentley, R., Rodden, T., Sawyer, P., Sommerville, I., Hughes, J., Randall, D. and Shapiro, D., "Ethnographically-Informed Systems Design for Air Traffic Control", Proc. ACM Conference on Computer-Supported Cooperative Work CSCW'94, Toronto, Canada, November 1992.

[6] Bowers, J. and Pycock, J., "Talking Through Design: Requirements and Resistance in Cooperative Prototyping", Proc. ACM Conference on Human Factors in Computing Systems CHI'94, Boston, Mass., May 1994.

[7] Bowers, J., "The Work to Make a Network Work: Studying CSCW In Action", Proc. ACM Conference on Computer-Supported Cooperative Work CSCW'94, Chapel Hill, North Carolina, October 1994.

[8] Bowers, J., Button, G. and Sharrock, W., "Workflow from Within and Without", Proc. European Conf. Computer-Supported Cooperative Work ECSCW'95, Stockholm, Sweden, September 1995.

[9] Buckingham-Shum, S. and Hammond, N., "Delivering HCI Modelling to Designers: A Framework, and Case Study of Cognitive Modelling", Interacting with Computers, in press.

[10] Button, G. and Sharrock, W., "On Simulacrums of Conversation", in Thomas (ed), *"The Social and Interactional Dimensions of Human-Computer Interfaces"*, Cambridge University Press, Cambridge, 1995.

[11] Button, G. and Harper, R., "Taking the Organisation into Accounts", in Button (ed), *"Technology in Working Order"*, Routledge, London, 1993.

[12] Button, G. and Sharrock, W., "Occasioned Practices in the Work of Software Engineers", in Jirotka and Goguen (eds.) *"Requirements Engineering: Social and Technical Issues"*, Academic Press, London, 1994.

[13] Button, G. and Sharrock, W., "Ethnomethodology and HCI", presentation at the CHI'95 Research Symposium, Denver, Colorado, May 1995.

[14] Carroll, J. and Kellogg, W., "Artifact as Theory-Nexus: Hermeneutics Meets Theory-Based Design", Proc. ACM Conference on Human Factors in Computing Systems CHI'89, Austin, Texas, 1989.,

[15] Carroll, J., Kellogg, W. and Rosson, M.B., "The Task-Artifact Cycle", in Carroll (ed), *"Designing Interaction: Psychology at the Human-Computer Interface"*, Cambridge University press, New York, 1991.

[16] Dourish, P., "Accounting for System Behaviour: Representation, Reflection and Resourceful Action", Proc. Computers in Context CIC'95, Aarhus, Denmark, August 1995.

[17] Dourish, P., Adler, A,. Bellotti, V. and Henderson, A. , "Your Place or Mine? Learning from Long-Term Use of Video Communication", to appear in Computer-

Supported Cooperative Work: An International Journal.

[18] Garfinkel, H., *"Studies in Ethnomethodology"*, Prentice-Hall, Englewood Cliffs, New Jersey, 1967.

[19] Garfinkel, H., "Respecification", in Button (ed), *"Ethnomethodology and the Human Sciences"*, Cambridge University Press, Cambridge, 1991.

[20] Garfinkel, H. and Sacks, H., "On Formal Structures of Practical Actions", in McKinnley and Tiryakian (eds), *"Theoretical Sociology"*, pp. 338–366, Appleton Century Crofts, New York, 1970.

[21] Greatbatch, D., Luff, P., Heath, C. and Campion, P., "Interpersonal Communication and Human-Computer Interaction: An examination of the use of computers in medical consultations", Interacting with Computers, 5, pp. 193—216, 1993.

[22] Greenbaum, J. and Kyng, M., *"Design at Work: Cooperative Design of Computer Systems"*, Laurence Erlbaum Associates, Hillsdale, New Jersey, 1991.

[23] Grudin, J., "The Computer Reaches Out: The Historical Continuity of Interface Design", in Proc. ACM Conference on Human Factors in Computing Systems CHI'90, Seattle, Washington, April 1990.

[24] Grudin, J. and Grinter, R., "Ethnography and Design", Computer-Supported Cooperative Work 3(1), pp. 55–59, 1995.

[25] Harper, R. and Hughes, J., "What A F-ing System! Send 'em all to the same place and then expect us to step 'em hitting: Making technology work in air traffic control", in Button (ed), *"Technology in Working Order"*, Routledge, London, 1993.

[26] Heath, C. and Luff, P., "Disembodied Conduct: Communication through video in a multi-media environment", Proc. ACM Conf. Human Factors in Computing Systems CHI '91, New Orleans, Louisiana, 1991.

[27] Heath, C. and Luff, P., "Collaboration and Control: Crisis Management and Multimedia Technology in London Underground Line Control Rooms", Computer Supported Cooperative Work, 1(1–2), pp. 69–95, 1992

[28] Heath, C. and Luff, P., "Media Space and Communicative Asymmetries: Preliminary Observations of Video-Mediated Interaction", Human-Computer Interaction, 7(3), pp. 315–346, 1992.

[29] Heath, C. and Luff, P., "System Use and Social Organisation", in Button (ed.), *"Technology in Working Order"*, Routledge, London, 1992.

[30] Heath, C., Jirotka, M., Luff, P. and Hindmarch, J., "Unpacking Collaboration: The Interactional Organisation of Trading in a City Dealing Room", Proc. Third European Conference on Computer Supported Cooperative Work ECSCW'93, Milano, Italy, September 1993.

[31] Hughes, J., Randall, D. and Shapiro, D., "From Ethnographic Record to System Design: Some Experiences from the Field", Computer Supported Cooperative Work, 1(3), pp. 123–141, 1993.

[32] Keiras, D., "Towards a Practical GOMS Model Methodology for User Interface Design", in Helander (ed), *"Handbook of Human-Computer Interaction"*, Elsevier, New York, 1988.

[33] Kiczales, G., "Towards a New Model of Abstraction in Software Engineering", Proc. IMSA'92 Workshop on Reflection and Metalevel Architectures, Tokyo, Nov 4–7, 1992.

[34] Long, J. and Dowell, J., "Conceptions of the Discipline of HCI: Craft, Applied Science and Engineering", in Sutcliffe and Macaulay (eds.), *"People and Computers V"*, Cambridge University Press, Cambridge, 1989.

[35] Lynch, M., Livingstone, E. and Garfinkel, H., "Temporal Order in Laboratory Work", in Knoll-Centina and Mulkay (eds), *"Science Observed"*, Sage, London, 1983.

[36] Rogers, Y., "Coordinating Computer-Mediated Work", Computer Supported Cooperative Work, 1(4), pp. 295–315, 1993.

[37] Rogers, Y., "Exploring Obstacles: Integrating CSCW in Evolving Organisations", Proc. ACM Conference on Computer-Supported Cooperative Work CSCW'94, Chapel Hill, North Carolina, October 1994.

[38] Rogers, Y., Bannon, L. and Button, G., "Rethinking Theoretical Frameworks for HCI", SIGCHI Bulletin, 26(1), 1994.

[39] Rouncefield, M., Hughes, J., Rodden, T. and Viller, S., "Working with Constant Interruption: CSCW and the Small Office", Proc. ACM Conference on Computer-Supported Cooperative Work CSCW'94, Chapel Hill, North Carolina, November 1994.

[40] Sacks, H., Schegloff, E. and Jefferson, G., "A simplest systematics for the organisation of turn-taking in conversation", Language, 50(4), pp. 696–735, 1974.

[41] Shapiro, D., "The Limits of Ethnography: Combining Social Sciences for CSCW", Proc. ACM Conference on Computer-Supported Cooperative Work CSCW'94, Chapel Hill, North Carolina, October 1994.

[42] Sharrock, W., Button, G. and Anderson, R., "Inside Design", Hillsdale, N.J. Lawrence Erlbaum, forthcoming

[43] Suchman, L., *"Plans and Situated Actions: The problem of human-machine communication"*, Cambridge University Press, Cambridge, UK, 1987.

[44] Suchman, L., "Do Categories have Politics? The language/action perspective reconsidered", Computer-Supported Cooperative Work, 2(3), pp. 177–190, 1994.

[45] Suchman, L., "Centers of Coordination: A case and some themes", in Resnick (ed), *"Discourse, Tools and Reasoning"*, forthcoming.

Does Animation in User Interfaces Improve Decision Making?

Cleotilde Gonzalez
Universidad de las Americas-Puebla
Computer Engineering Department
Apartado Postal 100, Cholula 72820, Puebla, Mexico.
(52) (22) 29 20 29
cleo@uldapvms.pue.udlap.mx

ABSTRACT

This paper reports a laboratory experiment that investigated the relative effects of images, transitions, and interactivity styles used in animated interfaces in two decision making domains. Interfaces used either realistic or abstract images, smooth or abrupt transitions, and parallel or sequential interactivity. Results suggest that decision making performance is influenced by the task domain, the user experience, the image, transition, and interactivity styles used in animated interfaces. Subjects performed better with animated interfaces based on realistic rather than abstract images. Subjects were more accurate with smooth rather than abrupt animation. Subjects were more accurate and enjoyed more the animation with parallel rather than sequential interactivity. Implications on the design of animated interfaces for decision making are provided.

Keywords: Animation, Decision Making.

INTRODUCTION

The conventional wisdom is that animation makes interfaces easier to use, more enjoyable, and understandable [15], [2]. However, inconsistent empirical results indicate that there is not enough theoretically-based evidence to guide the design of animated interfaces to improve human performance. Very little is known about the design and effective use of animation in user interfaces [17], [2], [13]. Managers have traditionally relied on static displays and textual or tabular data representations to make decisions. How should animated interfaces be designed to improve decision making performance? This is the main question this research addresses.

The uncertainty surrounding the use and effectiveness of animation starts with its definition. A definition of animation in HCI seems unclear [17]. Most definitions found in the literature are based on the classical notion that movement is the essence of animation, involving a change in the positioning of the objects on a screen [2]. However, computer animation seems to be quite different from classical animation [5]. Specifically, appropriateness of the user's/decision-maker's mental model and interactivity must be explicitly considered if computer-based animation is going to be an effective decision-support tool [7].

To account for appropriateness and interactivity, animation in HCI can be defined as: *a series of varying images presented dynamically according to user actions in ways that help the user to perceive a continuous change over time and develop a more appropriate mental model of the task [7].* A task is generally considered a meaningful unit of work performance, and interactivity is usually defined by the visible or motor actions the user performs on the interface.

This paper summarizes previous empirical research on animation and reports a laboratory study conducted to evaluate the decision making effectiveness of different types of images, transitions, and interactivity styles used in animated interfaces. The paper concludes with implications and recommendations concerning the design of animated interfaces for supporting decision making.

LITERATURE REVIEW OF EMPIRICAL RESEARCH OF ANIMATION INTERFACE DESIGN

Empirical research on interfaces for decision making has largely focused on comparisons of textual information, table-based information, and static 2D charts [8] [9]. Relatively little empirical research has investigated the effectiveness and appropriateness of animation in HCI [13], [17]. Computer-Based Instruction (CBI) is probably the area that provides more information about animation effectiveness, but yet in this area there is a small number of studies concerning the empirical evaluation of animation [13]. The few serious attempts to empirically investigate animation in instructional studies have reported inconsistent results [14]. Reviews of selected empirical investigations from the literature in Education, Psychology, and HCI suggest that animation may make interfaces easier, more enjoyable, and understandable [7]. However, there is limited theoretically-based empirical evidence to design, use, and evaluate animation for improving human performance.

The inconsistency in the results of empirical studies of animation may be due to several factors. First, most studies involve the comparison of static textual information versus graphical dynamic presentations. Since it has been found that textual versus graphical symbols in static form have different effects on performance [4], differences in performance may be due to the use of different representations, not to the dynamic nature of the presentation of graphics. Second, most studies use animation to show obvious movements of graphical objects in demonstrating a computer task. When animation is used to demonstrate tasks that the user already knows or when the user does not feel mentally engaged in processing the task, animation will probably show no positive effects. Therefore, inconsistent results in animation may be caused by an inadequate selection of the tasks to be animated. Third, most studies use animation as a presentation technique rather than as an interactive technique. Passive environments and inconsistent allowance of user's interactivity may cause conflicting conclusions of animation effectiveness.

In summary, little or no work has been done to study the effect of animation on decision making. Most current studies suggest the need for theory and theory-based data to support animation design.

EMPIRICAL APPROACH

The empirical approach investigates the theoretical propositions developed in an Animation User Interface Design (AUID) Framework [7]. The AUID framework predicts that the task domain and structure, individual differences such as visual abilities and experience, and characteristics of the animated interface such as image realism, continuity of the transitions, and correspondence between the interactivity style and the form of presentation affect decision making performance. To investigate these propositions, a 2 (Image) X 2 (Transition) X 2 (Interactivity) X (2 (Task) X S(89)) mixed four-factor within-subjects design was used. Eight animation user interface prototypes were constructed to provide all combinations of two types of images, transitions, and interactivity styles in two task domains. The eight animated interfaces for each task varied by the type of image (Realistic, Abstract), the type of transitions (Gradual, Abrupt), and the type of interactivity (Parallel, Sequential). These prototypes created eight treatment conditions (Table 1) that were administered to eighty nine undergraduate students that participated voluntarily in the experiment. All subjects received course credit for their participation and an extra incentive of $5 cash based on both, accuracy and time performance. Subjects performed one task in each of two different domains. To reduce the possible practice effects, the tasks were presented randomly in a balanced order across the subjects.

Treatment	Image	Transition	Interactivity	Code
1	Realistic	Gradual	Parallel	1RGP
2	Realistic	Gradual	Sequential	2RGS
3	Realistic	Abrupt	Parallel	3RAP
4	Realistic	Abrupt	Sequential	4RAS
5	Abstract	Gradual	Parallel	5AGP
6	Abstract	Gradual	Sequential	6AGS
7	Abstract	Abrupt	Parallel	7AAP
8	Abstract	Abrupt	Sequential	8AAS

Table 1. Eight treatment conditions

Decision making performance was determined by objective and subjective measures. Objective measures of performance (time and accuracy) were determined during the execution of the tasks with the animated interfaces. Decision time constituted the minutes spent to make a choice. Decision accuracy was the closeness between the user's response and the objective. Only one correct answer existed for a given task. Subjective measures of performance (ease of use and enjoyability) were gathered by an instrument consisting of questions from previous satisfaction MIS questionnaires [7].

Task Environment

Each subject performed one decision making task in each of two domains: a real estate problem called "Home Directory" (HomeD) and a Physics problem called "Bolt in the Boat" (BinB). Finding a home has been considered a laborious task, usually performed by manual search on paper directories and used as an example in the development of dynamic queries systems [1]. Physics problems of classical mechanics such as the comparison of sunken and floating objects have been considered extremely difficult in perception and cognition experiments [10]. These two domains involved choice tasks with multiple alternatives corresponding to two common decision strategies: linear (based on alternative processing) and majority of confirming dimensions (based on attribute processing) [9]. In the selection and design of the tasks issues such as appropriateness and attractiveness of the tasks, facility to represent and implement the tasks graphically, minimization of differences among subjects, and possibility to evaluate and measure performance were considered.

The HomeD graphically described hypothetical places (houses and apartments) available to rent in a small southwestern city. The HomeD required the subjects to evaluate and select a place to rent from a set of twenty alternatives, based on the value of eleven fixed non-prioritized attributes. The alternatives and their attributes were obtained from real estate guides of the city. The user's objective was to select a place to rent among the alternatives that most closely met the attributes of a predefined ideal place. The attributes of the ideal place were explicitly given to the subjects in a pre-experimental description of the task.

The BinB graphically described alternative scenarios of fluid displacement levels caused by sunken and floating objects. The BinB required the subjects to compare, evaluate, and select a water level from a set of five scenarios. The base for the comparison was a realistic scenario: a heavy metal bolt placed into a boat floating on water within a container caused the water level to rise from level zero to a new level. Five different scenarios in which the same bolt was sunk into the water producing different changes in the water level were the predefined alternatives for this task [10]. The user's objective was to select the water displacement level that appeared less artificial and better predicted what would happen in real life.

Animation User Interface Prototypes

Sixteen animation user interface prototypes were constructed, eight different prototypes for each task domain according to the manipulation of the variables: image, transition, and interactivity. The prototypes were prepared in a PowerMac computer for a 13-inch color monitor using Macromedia Director version 4.0. The prototypes were embedded into an application to control the execution of the tasks and to store the information about the users' performance. The screen layout was divided into three

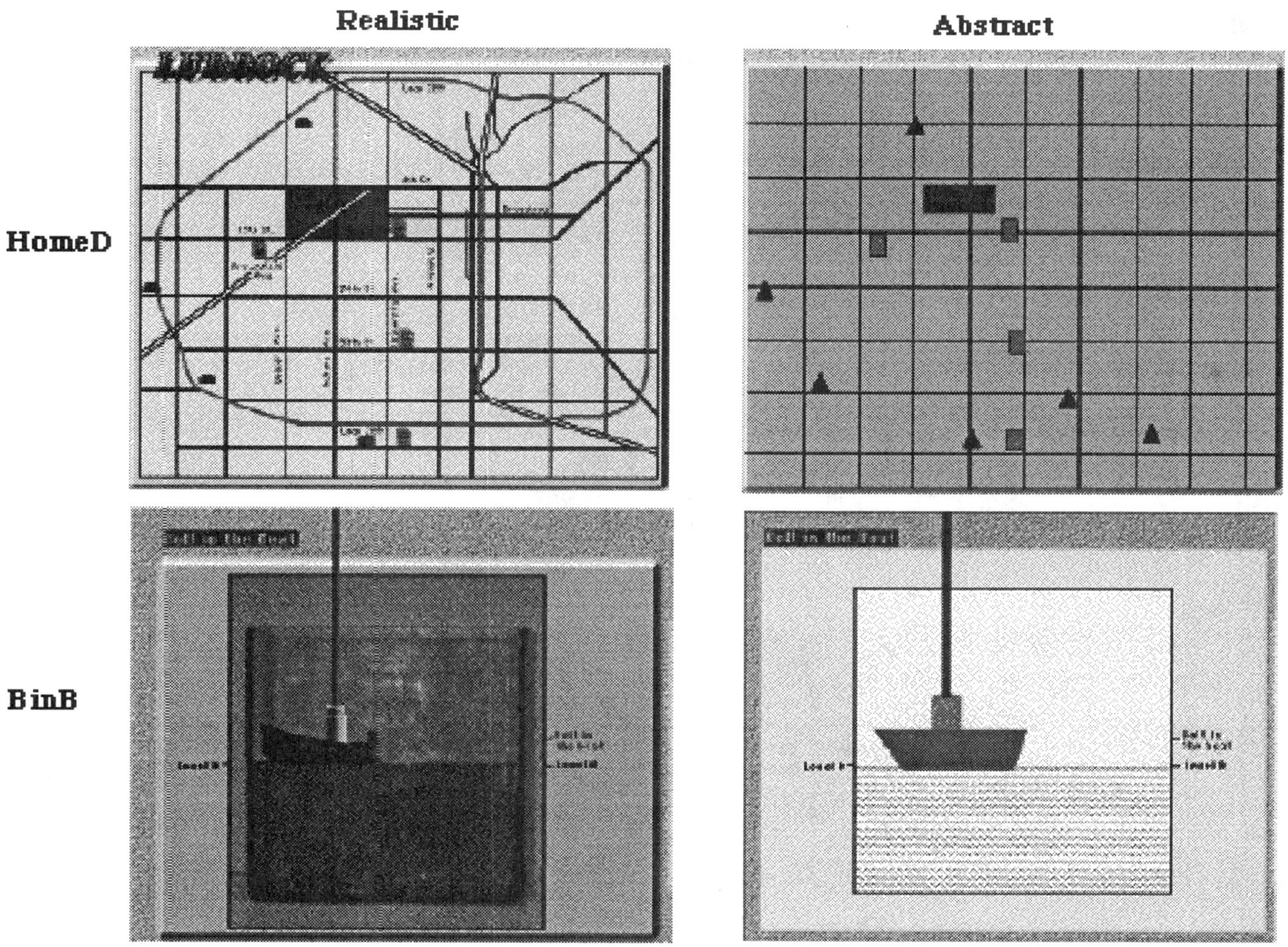

Figure 1. The Manipulation of Images as Realistic and Abstract in Two task Domains

functional areas: the images area, the interactivity area, and the messages area. Because it has been suggested that the addition of sound to animation improves the operation and understanding of interfaces [6], sound effects (i.e., mouse clicks) and music were added. These characteristics were constant for all prototypes. The eight prototypes for each task were designed to last the same time without any user interactivity.

Design of Images

Figure 1 summarizes the manipulation of images. In the HomeD, realistic images were based on the image of a city map. A map of the city was scanned and edited to provide shadows and colors with realistic effects. Graphical icons represented houses or apartments, and variations in the size of icons represented the number of bedrooms (small = 1 bedroom, medium = 2 bedrooms, large = 3 bedrooms). Abstract images in the HomeD were based on a starfield display (two-dimensional scatterplot) [1]. Geometric shapes were used to represent houses (triangles) and apartments (squares). As with realistic images, different sizes were used to represent the number of bedrooms.

In the BinB, realistic images were digital pictures taken from a real model constructed for this purpose. The model was constructed using a transparent glass container and a small toy boat. Pictures of the realistic model were taken with a digital camera and imported to Macromedia Director. A 3D representation of a metallic colored bolt was constructed using Macromedia MacroModel. Abstract images in the BinB were 2D geometric representations constructed using Director's drawing tools. A square represented a container, a trapezoid represented a boat, and a rectangle represented a bolt. The graphical elements in the abstract images were designed in the same sizes and colors as those in the realistic images, but no shadows or depth cues were included.

Design of Transitions

Gradual transitions were implemented by providing transition effects between the display of two consecutive alternatives and by assuring the minimum change between two consecutive frames. The dissolve "bits fast" effect provoked the fade-out of an image superimposed on the fade-in of the next. Besides transition effects, gradual transitions involved the change of only one element in each display frame of the animation. In the HomeD, icons representing

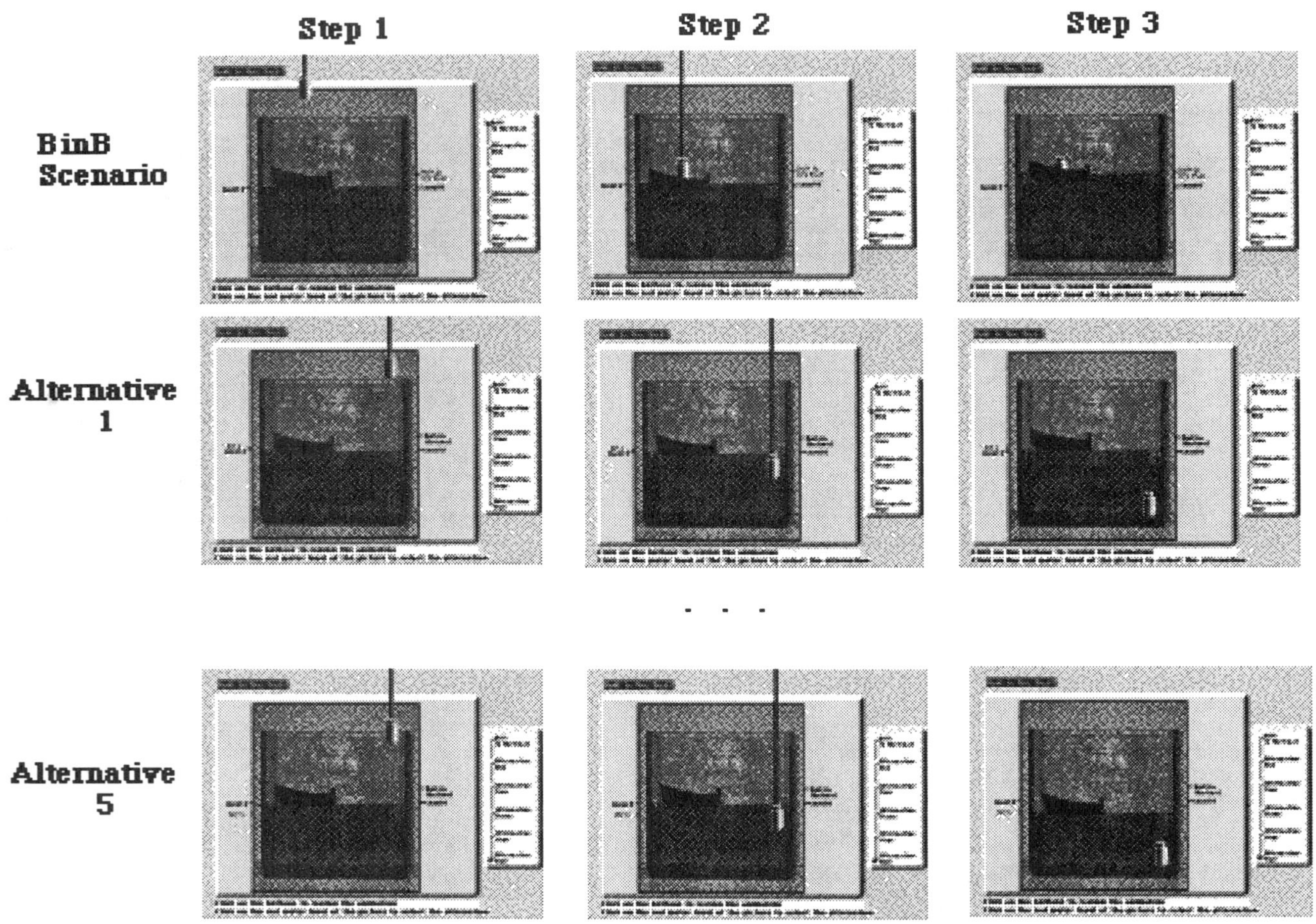

Figure 2. Example of Frames Used in the Animation of the BinB Problem

the alternative places appeared one at a time, instead of all together in one display frame. In the BinB, gradual transitions involved a small change of position in the objects between two consecutive frames. The movement of the bolt placed into the boat or the water and the movement of water and the boat to reach the new water level, were implemented by small changes on the positions of the elements between two display frames.

The treatments involving abrupt transitions used no transition effects, providing a relatively instantaneous change between animation frames. Also, the change provoked between one display frame and the next was considerably large compared to the gradual transitions. In the HomeD, abrupt transitions showed all the icons representing the alternatives that met one attribute in one display frame. In the BinB, abrupt transitions showed the change in position of the graphical elements in three screens. In one screen the bolt is shown out of the water, in the next one, the bolt is shown right above the water, and in the last screen the bolt is shown into the water. Figure 2 shows an example of some of the frames used in the BinB animation. The first three frames show the realistic scenario used for comparison; the next three frames show the first alternative continuing until the fifth alternative is presented.

Design of Interactivity

Icons representing buttons for direct manipulation were the interactivity style used for all prototypes. Figure 3 summarizes the manipulation of interactivity. Parallel interactivity provided the user with buttons to illustrate a segment of the task in any order. In the HomeD, parallel interactivity allowed the user to choose attributes to observe the alternatives. The user was allowed to click on any button of the interactivity panel at any time, and the system responded by showing the alternatives that met the attribute selected. In the BinB, parallel interactivity allowed the user to choose any alternative scenario in any order. The user was allowed to click on any button of the interactivity panel at any time, and the system responded by showing the animation of the scenario selected.

Sequential interactivity provided the user with buttons to navigate through the animation in the same order. The buttons included those normally found in any device for sequential manipulation: play, step forward, stop, step backward, and play backward. The user was allowed to click on any of these buttons at any time, and the system responded by showing the corresponding sequence of the animation (play forward and play backward buttons), stopping (stop button), or showing the next or previous step and stopping (step forward and step backward buttons).

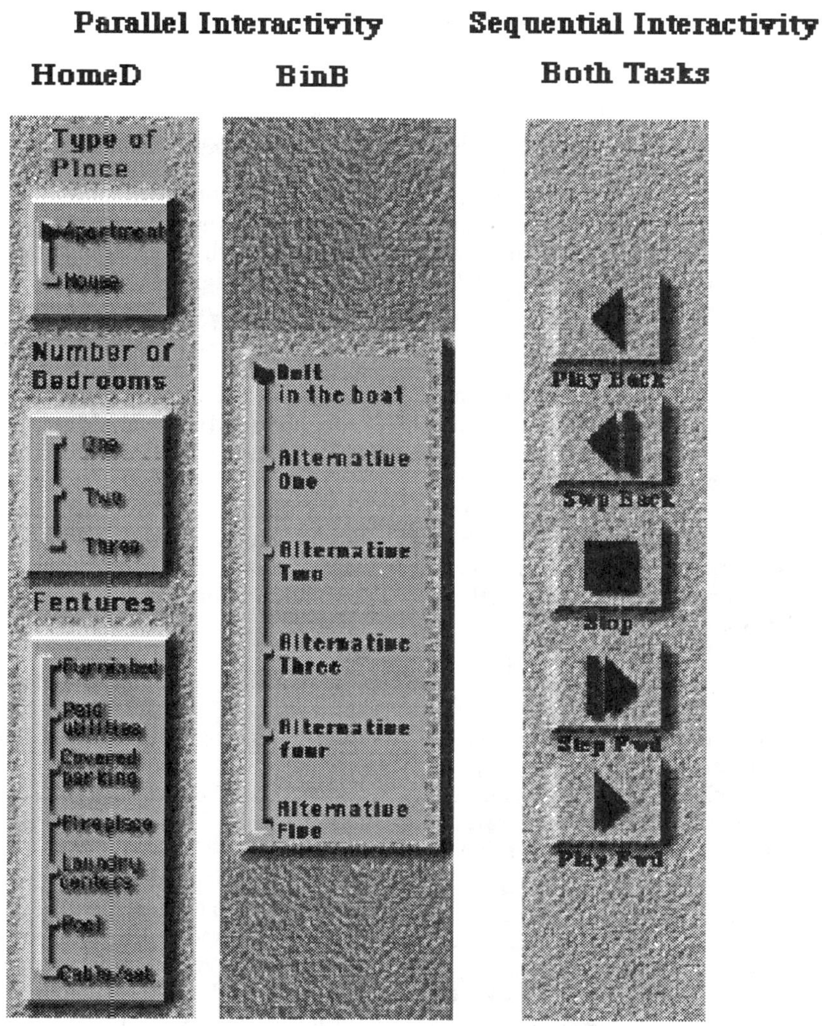

Figure 3. The Manipulation of Interactivity as Parallel and Sequential

In both types of interactivity, the user selected one alternative by pointing and clicking on the graphical elements in the image's area of the screen. These actions caused a movable window to appear on the screen from which the user could select or cancel the alternative. This technique was used to reduce the complexity of the display, and to allow the user to focus on detailed information [1].

Other Experimental Materials

The user's visual abilities and experience were gathered by two post-experimental questionnaires. The Vividness of Visual Imagery Questionnaire (VVIQ) as formulated by Marks [11] was used in this research to obtain data concerning the quality of the mental images formed by the subjects and to explain possible differences in performance due to subjects' visual ability differences. To determine user's experience, a questionnaire containing the three main dimensions suggested by Nielsen [12] was developed in this research. The questionnaire contained five factors explaining the user's experience in computers in general, experience with the two task domains, and experience with animation use and development [7].

Experimental Procedure

Subjects were tested in groups of eight during five days. Each session of the experiment lasted from 30 to 40 minutes. Before the session started, headphones were attached to the eight computers and run-time versions of the prototypes were pre-loaded. By using a dialog box, the researcher input the user information: the number, the starting task, the file on which to store the information, and the treatment number.

A set of instruments consisting of written instructions, task descriptions, and questionnaires were prepared for each subject before the experimental session. To ensure that the instructions were delivered to the subjects consistently and clearly, both written instructions and verbal instructions via videotape were provided. After receiving the instructions, the subjects started the laboratory work.

The computers used were Power Macintosh configured with 13-inch color monitor and 8 MB of RAM. The computer process began with a Welcome screen. Wearing headphones, the users started the execution of the first task by clicking on the button at the right-hand side corner of the screen. After executing the first task, a screen indicated the end of it and a subjective ratings questionnaire pertaining to that task was completed. The user started the execution of the second task by clicking on the button at the right-hand side corner of the screen. After executing the second task, a screen indicated the end of the session and a subjective ratings questionnaire pertaining to that task was completed. The user then clicked on the button at the right-hand side corner of the screen to find out about the extra monetary prize shown on a message box. Subjects answered the VVIQ and experience questionnaires at the end of the session.

DATA ANALYSIS AND RESULTS

The mean values of accuracy, time, ease of use, and enjoyability for the two types of images, transitions, and interactivity styles indicated that realistic images, gradual transitions, and parallel interactivity produced better decisions. The statistical significance of these observations was investigated using StatView 4.0 for Macintosh and SAS for Vax. The principal statistical procedure was the General Linear Model (GLM) to perform repeated measures analyses of variance (repeated ANOVAs) evaluated with the F-statistic at a .05 level. Statistical assumptions, practice effects, and interaction effects were verified. Partial correlations between visual abilities (VisualA), total experience (TotExp), and time over the dependent measures (accuracy, time, ease of use, and accuracy) were investigated to determine the inclusion of these variables as covariates. Statistical models including these variables as covariates were used in the analyses. Table 2 provides an overview of the main significant main effects found in this study.

	Decision Making Performance			
	Accuracy	Time	Ease of Use	Enjoyability
Task			■	■
User				
TotExp		■		
Interface				
Image	■	■	■	■
Transition	■			
Interactivity	■			■

Table 2. Overview of Main Significant Effects

Interface Main Effects

The analyses of accuracy showed that in both tasks, the use of realistic images provided more accurate responses than the use of abstract images in animated interfaces. A repeated measures ANOVA showed that the difference in accuracy caused by the use of realistic versus abstract images was significant across tasks (F(1,78)=10.29, p<.05). The analysis of time showed that in both tasks, subjects exposed to animation with abstract images took longer to make a decision than subjects exposed to realistic images. A repeated measures ANOVA showed a significant difference in time between realistic and abstract images across tasks (F(1,78)=7.13, p<.05). The analysis of ease of use showed that in both tasks, subjects using animation with realistic images perceived the systems more easily than those using animation with abstract images. The difference in ease of use caused by the use of realistic versus abstract images was significant across tasks, as showed by a repeated measures ANOVA (F(1,80)=4.41, p<.05). The analysis of enjoyability showed that animation with realistic images was more enjoyable than animation with abstract images in both tasks. These observations were confirmed with a repeated measures ANOVA (F(1,80)=17.14, p<.05).

Observations of accuracy data indicated that animation with gradual transitions produced more accurate responses than animation with abrupt transitions. These observations were statistically significant across tasks (F(1,78)=5.84, p<.05). The analyses of time for gradual and abrupt transitions showed no significant differences between gradual and abrupt transitions at the .05 level. The analyses of ease of use showed a significant interaction between the transition manipulation (Gradual, Abrupt) and the order in which the tasks were presented for the ease of use measure (F(1,81)=4.77, p<.05). No main effects of the transition factor on ease of use can be claimed due to this significant interaction. Observations of the enjoyability data indicated that gradual transitions caused subjects to enjoy the animation more than abrupt transitions; however, these observations were not statistically significant at the .05 level.

The analyses of accuracy data showed that in both tasks, subjects were more accurate in their decisions when they used animation with parallel interactivity than when they used sequential interactivity. A repeated measures ANOVA showed that the difference in accuracy caused by the use of parallel versus sequential interactivity was significant across tasks (F(1,78)=12.70, p<.05). The interactivity types did not make a significant difference in the decision making time for any of the two tasks at the .05 level. The analyses of the ease of use data showed a significant interaction between the interactivity type (parallel, sequential) and the task domain (HomeD, BinB) (F(1,80)=4.49, p<.05). This interaction was further investigated with two separate ANOVAs by task. The results showed a significant difference in the user's perception of ease of use for parallel versus sequential interactivity only for the BinB (F(1,88)=4.83, p<.05). Observations of enjoyability data indicated that parallel interactivity caused the subjects to enjoy more the animation than sequential interactivity in both tasks. The results from the repeated measures ANOVA showed that the difference in enjoyability caused by the use of parallel versus sequential interactivity was significant across tasks (F(1,80)=4.37, p<.05).

Task and User Effects

Observations of the ease of use and enjoyability data indicated that the HomeD task was considered easier and more enjoyable than the BinB task. The repeated measures ANOVA analyses showed significant effects of the task domain for accuracy (F(1,78)=6.53, p<.05), time (F(1,78)=8.88, p<.05), ease of use (F(1,80)=8.57, p<.05), and enjoyability (F(1,80)=6.51, p<.05).

The investigation of the visual abilities and experience as covariates showed some correlations (>.10) between VisualA and the subjective measures of performance, and between TotExp and the objective measures of performance. The users' visual abilities, however, did not have a significant effect on any of the dependent measures at the .05 level. The users' total experience appeared significant across tasks only for the time measure ($F(1,78)=7.43$, $p<.05$). More experienced users finished the tasks faster than novice users.

DISCUSSION OF THE RESULTS

The results from this study provide evidence for the effects of different animation design elements, task characteristics, and user characteristics on the performance of decision making tasks.

Interface Effects

This research showed that decision making accuracy, time, ease of use, and enjoyability in animated interfaces are influenced by the form of image representation, the transition effects, and the form of interactivity.

The findings of this study provide additional support for pursuing realism in the representation of information. Previous studies have demonstrated the positive effects of image realism by using 3D wireframe versus 3D shaded static images for mental rotation tasks [3]. The benefits of using 3D versus 2D images, however, are controversial. This study demonstrates the positive effects of image realism in comparing 2D geometrical representations versus 2D maps and photo-realistic pictures in animated interfaces. The accuracy and time of the decision, and the subjective perception of ease of use and enjoyability improve when cues of realism are added to the images in animated interfaces. The effects of realistic versus abstract images, however, may be stronger or weaker, according to the task domain. In the HomeD the user may be less aware of his/her manipulation of the mental model than in the BinB [16]. Therefore, cues for realism may be more important for domains that require making value judgments than for problem solving in Physics.

The findings in this study provide theory-based data that support the design of smooth animation to increase the accuracy of the decisions. Although smoothness is considered a basic principle of animation design [17], the effects of smooth presentations have not always shown to be effective. This research isolated the transition effects from the effects of images and interactivity, and showed that smooth animation has positive effects over abrupt animation in the accuracy of the decisions across two decision making domains. Subjects using animation with gradual transitions were more accurate than subjects using animation with abrupt transitions. The effects of transitions, however, seem to be more important for Physics problems (BinB) than for problems requiring value judgments (HomeD). Making value judgments is a more discrete domain than problem solving in Physics [16]. The HomeD did not involve changes of the objects' position (movement) but involved the appearance/disappearance of objects, while the BinB required mainly the transformation of the objects' positions on the screen. It seems that when the visualization of the movement of the objects is critical to understand the task, gradual transitions are more important to ensure accurate responses than in situations that do not require the objects' movement.

Finally, this study provides additional support for animation as an interactive technique rather than as a presentation technique. Animation has been considered in two states: passive (classical animation) and completely interactive (real-time animation). This research used animation in an intermediate type of interactivity. Differences in performance due to different interactivity techniques have not been studied. This research showed that interactivity per se is important for the accuracy and enjoyability of decision making tasks in animated environments. Subjects using parallel interactivity were more accurate in their decisions and enjoyed more the animation than subjects using sequential interactivity, regardless of the type of image and the animation smoothness. The effects of different interactivity techniques on the perception of the ease of use of animation, however, may depend on the task structure. The interdependent attributes in the HomeD may have caused a better processing with sequential than with parallel interactivity. Besides, the interactivity panel for the HomeD was organized by attribute while the panel for the BinB was organized by alternative. The organization by attribute may have caused an insignificant difference between parallel and sequential interactivity in the HomeD.

Task and User Effects

The results from this empirical investigation indicate that the task domain is a significant factor of decision making performance in animated interfaces. This research found no significant effect of the user's visual abilities on any of the measures of decision making performance, and significant effects of the user's experience only on decision making time. In this study, however, the user's visual abilities and experience scores were used as statistical ways to reduce the experimental error rather than as experimental means. The data collected from the user's visual abilities and experience revealed that on average, the subjects that participated in this experiment were novices and good visualizers.

CONCLUSIONS

This research supports the idea that to be an effective decision support tool, animation must be smooth, simple, interactive and explicitly account for the appropriateness of the user's mental model of the task. The theory-based data indicated that:

a) To ensure more accurate decisions, with which the subjects feel satisfied, designers should base their animation on realistic graphical representations rather than on abstract images.

b) To ensure more accurate decisions, animation designers should determine the required changes on images and transition effects that would make the animation smoother. They should also determine changes in graphical objects according to the type of visual characteristics, and define transition effects according to the task structure.

c) To ensure more accurate decisions and more enjoyable interactions, the designer should allow the user to manipulate directly different segments of the animation in a parallel

rather than sequential order. Animation designers should provide parallel interactivity if the successive steps in the task structure can be executed in any order.
d) To ensure faster decisions, animation designers should take into consideration the subjects' experience with computers in general, with the task and with animation use and development.
e) The design of animated interfaces should be based on both the characteristics of the task domain and the structure of the task(s) the user performs. Knowing the characteristics of the task domain, the designer may define the best decomposition, representation, and retrieval of the task. By defining the structure of the task, the designer is better able to decompose the task into animation segments and understand the sequence and type of interactivity that would allow the design of more comprehensible animation, thus supporting the user's awareness of the events and accounting for human memory capabilities. These characteristics would determine particular design decisions of the visual representations, the order of the presentation of alternatives, and the type of interactivity allowed.

The results of this study show that decision making performance is highly contingent on the properties of the animation user interface such as image realism, transition smoothness, and interactivity style, and also sensitive to the task domain and the user's experience. However, many other issues need to be investigated in the effective use of animated interfaces for decision making. First, further development of interactive animation design theories is required in HCI. Second, the development of a formal taxonomy of interactivity styles would be extremely important in the research of interactivity in animated interfaces. Third, further empirical investigation of the propositions of the AUID framework is required to objectively evaluate its predictive potential. Fourth, knowledge on differing task environments is very important to improve the use of animation in decision making and to guide animation interface design. Finally, the use of animation in more realistic and complex environments is required to support the external validity of these findings.

REFERENCES

1. Ahlberg C., Shneiderman B. Visual Information Seeking: Tight Coupling of Dynamic Query Filters with Starfield Displays. In *Proc. of CHI'94* (April 24-28, Boston, MA). ACM/SIGCHI, NY, 1994, pp. 313-317.

2. Baecker R., Small I. Animation at the Interface. In Laurel B. (Ed.) *The Art of Human-Computer Interface Design.* Addison-Wesley Pub. Co., Inc., 1990.

3. Barfield W., Sandford J., Foley J. The Mental Rotation and Perceived Realism of Computer-generated Three-dimensional images. *International Journal of Man-Machine Studies.* Vol. 29, No. 6, Dec. 01, 1988. pp. 669.

4. Booher, H. R. Relative comprehensibility of pictorial information and printed words in procedural instructions. *Human Factors.* Vol. 17, 1975, pp. 266-277.

5. Chang B., Ungar D. Animation: From Cartoons to the User Interface. In *Proc. of UIST '93* (November 3-5, Atlanta, GA). ACM/SIGGRAPH, SIGCHI, NY, 1993, pp. 45-55.

6. Clanton C., Young E. Film Craft in User Interface Design. In *Tutorial notes of CHI'94.* CHI'94 (April 24-28, Boston, MA). ACM/SIGCHI, NY, 1994.

7. Gonzalez C. Animation in User Interface Design for Decision Making: a Research Framework and Empirical Analysis. Dissertation. Texas Tech University. December, 1995.

8. Ives B. Graphical Interfaces for Business Information Systems. *MIS Quarterly/Special Issue in Graphical User Interfaces.* 1982, pp. 15-47.

9. Jarvenpaa S. The Effect of Task Demands and Graphical Format on Information Processing Strategies. *Management Science*, Vol. 35, No. 3, 1989, pp. 285-303.

10. Kaiser M. K., Proffitt D. R., Whelan S. M., Hecht H. Influence of Animation on Dynamical Judgments. *Journal of Experimental Psychology: Human Perception and Performance.* Vol. 18, No. 3, pp. 669-690, 1992.

11. Marks D. F. Visual Imagery Differences in the Recall of Pictures. *British Journal of Psychology.* Volume 64, No. 1, pp. 17-24, 1973.

12. Nielsen J. *Usability Engineering.* Academic Press, Inc., 1993.

13. Palmiter S. The effectiveness of Animated Demonstrations for Computer-based Tasks: a Summary, Model and Future Research. *Journal of Visual Languages and Computing.* Vol. 4, 1993, pp. 71-89.

14. Rieber L. P. Animation in Computer-Based Instruction. *Educational Technology Research and Development,* Vol. 38, No. 1, 1990, pp. 77-86.

15. Robertson G. G., Card S. K., Mackinlay J. D. Information Visualization Using 3D Interactive Animation. *CACM*, Vol. 36, No. 4, 1993, pp. 57-71.

16. Rouse W. B., Morris N. M. On looking into the black box: prospects and limits in the search for mental models. *Psychological Bulletin*, 100, 1986 pp. 349-363.

17. Stasko J. T. Animation in User Interfaces: Principles and Techniques. In Bass L., Dewan P. (Eds.). *User Interface Software*, John Wiley and Sons, Inc. NY, 1993.

Assessing the Effect of Non-Photorealistic Rendered Images in CAD

Jutta Schumann
Free University of Berlin
Dept. of Computer Science
Takustraße 9
D-14195 Berlin
phone: +49 (30) 838 75 132
schumann@inf.fu-berlin.de

Thomas Strothotte, Andreas Raab
University of Magdeburg
Dept. of Simulation and Graphics
Universitätsplatz 2
D-39106 Magdeburg
phone: +49 (391) 67 18 773
{tstr, raab}
@isg.cs.uni-magdeburg.de

Stefan Laser
University of Magdeburg
Dept. of Psychology
Virchowstraße 24
D-39104 Magdeburg
phone: +49 (391) 67 16 554
ls@isg.cs.uni-magdeburg.de

ABSTRACT

Recent work in computer graphics has resulted in new techniques for rendering so-called *non-photorealistic* images. While such features are now already appearing in commercially available software, little is known about the effect of non-photorealistic images on users and their usefulness in specific contexts.

In this paper we report on an empirical study with 54 architects who compared the output of a sketch-renderer for producing pencil-like drawings with standard output of CAD systems for architectural designs. The results show that the different kinds of renditions actually have a very different effect on viewers and that non-photorealistic images actually do deserve their place in the repertoire of CAD systems.

KEYWORDS: non-photorealistic rendering, architectural presentation, preliminary drafts, sketches, CAD.

INTRODUCTION

There has been a recent flurry of activity in the area of computer graphics away from the traditional photorealistic style of rendering. Rather than to mimic a camera taking a picture of a real scene, several new pieces of work have focused on producing images which look hand-made. Examples of this trend are a renderer which produces images which look like they were done using ink and pens [9][16], pencils [12] and paintbrushes on canvas [10]. Commercial rendering software like IRIS Inventor (Alias®) and KATY (5D Solutions®) are also beginning to offer such rendering possibilities.

CHI 96 Vancouver, BC Canada
© 1996 ACM 0-89791-777-4/96/04..$3.50

At first one may surmise that such features are merely marketing gimmicks to improve the sales of rendering software. In this paper we put this hypothesis to test and study the usefulness of such non-photorealistic rendered images. To do so, we work with a highly interactive sketch-renderer which was designed to produce pencil-like drawings of architectural designs prepared with CAD software. We report on a study with 54 architects who analysed several renditions of the same scene and reported on their impressions.

PHOTOREALISTIC AND NON-PHOTOREALISTIC IMAGES: A USER'S PERSPECTIVE

Techniques

It is no longer possible to define precisely what is meant when the term "computer graphics" is used in the literature. Most images which reach the eyes of viewers today were processed by computer somewhere along the line, be it by a scanner, a drawing program or a renderer.

Drawing programs and renderers lie on opposite ends of the spectrum with respect to user interaction. The former offer users almost complete freedom to draw an image given certain primitives; even the manipulation of individual pixels is possible. Renderers, on the other hand, read in a geometric model and generally produce an image whose appearance can hardly be modified, except by post-processing [13].

The style of rendering which practically all research has focused on in the last 15 years has been photorealism [3]. Hence users wishing to produce such images have some of the same freedom as a normal camera offers: the camera position and the lighting can be adjusted and in some cases also depth-blurring. Advanced features are often implemented, such as special environmental conditions like fog [2] or unusual perspective transformations [8].

This restriction to photorealism is convenient as its goal is well-defined, which is simply to convince viewers that the image is in fact a photo [3, plate III.19]. It is easily possible to assess the success or failure of a renderer to reach this goal (at least at a superficial level). Furthermore, photorealism poses no new problems with respect to usability, since the output is (at least in principle) the same as with a camera.

Non-photorealistic rendering software does not define the kind of output as precisely as when photorealism is the goal. Non-photorealistic images vary greatly in style and quality in the same way as human artists renditions vary. Such renderers provide interesting challenges from an algorithmic as well as from an artistic point of view. Lansdown and Schofield [7] recently surveyed the developments in this area.

The introduction of non-photorealism makes it much more difficult to define goals for what the software should actually be able to achieve and how it should be used. In the present context, it is important to note that such software also places a greater emphasis on the user, because he or she must interact with the renderer to fine-tune the image. This includes selecting the overall style of rendering as well as modifying individual features of the image. Hence aspects of human-computer interaction with rendering software are becoming important.

Interaction with a Sketch-Renderer

To illustrate how users interact with renderers which produce non-photorealistic images, we shall describe one such system. It is *the sketch-renderer*, a system developed by the authors [12] for producing images which resemble hand-made drawings with pencil on paper. It is the tool which was used to produce one of the images assessed later on in this paper.

The input to the sketch-renderer is a three-dimensional model in the DXF-format which is commonly used in CAD-software. The sketch-renderer first produces a wire-frame image as is normally produced in CAD. In order to give the user full control over the style of a presentation, the sketch-renderer strictly separates the geometric model from the stylistic information which can be assigned to single objects. This enables the sketch-renderer to read in models which were perhaps intended for another renderer, while keeping separate the stylistic information of which only the sketch-renderer makes use. The user can fine-tune the following parameters with the "point and click" method using the interactive sketch editor:

- *line styles* with width, edge quality, contour, waviness, colour saturation, saturation progression, length of segments, variation of segments from baseline, and connection of segments, and
- *hatching styles* with density of lines, line pattern, angle of lines, segmentation of hatching lines, and deviation from regular hatching.

These parameters can be combined with each other, e.g. the lines used for cross-hatching may be different from those used for contours. Hatching can be used to represent textures and shadows; the latter are calculated depending on a light source. Changes can be seen immediately on the screen and can be saved to so-called configuration file. An impression of how users can work with the sketch-renderer is given in Figure 1.

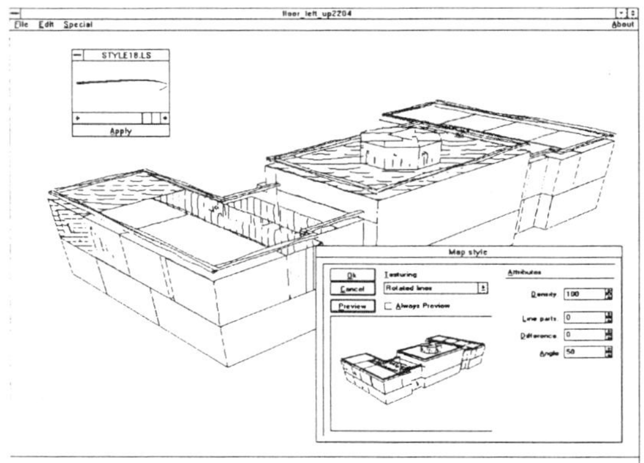

Figure 1: *The interactive sketch-renderer has an easy to use point-and-click interface.*

Open Problems

Graphics which are produced with current CAD programs do not reach the expressiveness of hand-made drawings. With the sketch-renderer, by contrast, an architect can produce more individual views of an object being planned; these seem to be appropriate especially in earlier stages of design. In order to verify this, we carried out a survey among potential users of the system. This is described in the following section.

AN EMPIRICAL STUDY[1]

Goals

The goal of our study is to compare the usability of computer-generated images with respect to communicative goals during development of design concepts. We use three computer-generated images: an exact CAD plot, a shaded image[2] and a sketch generated by our sketch renderer. The first of these is the "normal" output of CAD software; the second is often available in CAD software

[1] The study was conducted in German; the results of the verbal answers have been translated into English for the purposes of this paper, although we risk missing small nuances in some of the descriptions. All details of the experiments, including statistical analyses, may be found in [11].

[2] We use the term "shaded" rather than "photo-realistic" because *real* realistic images are used rather seldomly in architecture.

(though not used as much in practice), while the third is still at an experimental stage.

We are investigating three aspects of presentations:

1. use of different media in the different phases of the design process,
2. judgement of the impression which images make on viewers, and
3. how viewers are stimulated to express changes to the design.

Hypotheses

We are interested in the situation in which an architect would use the images. Since an architect's goal is in general to attract attention to the image, we hypothesize that

H1 For presentations of early drafts of architectural designs, sketches are the preferred over CAD plots and shaded images.

Furthermore, we hypothesize that there is a marked difference in the way the three images affect their viewers. To structure our hypothesis, we refer to the classification scheme of Peeck (see Willows and Houghton [15]), who divides the possible effects of an image into three groups:

- a *cognitive* group, pertaining to aspects like the understandability, clarity or spatiality of the image,
- an *affective* group, to assess emotional aspects, like how interesting or imaginative an image appears, and
- a *motivational* group, measuring to what extent users are encouraged to participate in the design process.

We hypothesize that

H2 Sketches perform better in the communication of affective and motivational aspects, while exact plots and shaded images perform better in cognitive aspects.

Finally, we expect the exact plot to arouse more interest in the actual design of the object being visualized, which leads us to the hypothesis that

H3 Sketches stimulate viewers more than shaded images to discuss and actively participate in design development

The psychological context of these hypotheses is taken up in the discussion section later on in the paper.

Method

Subjects. A questionnaire was given to approximate 150 architects and architectural students in several cities in Germany. Of these, 54 (36%) returned it, having answered the questions. Of those returning the questionnaire, 67% replied that they regularly use CAD.

Design. Subjects where shown three different images, each portraying the same object (see Figures 2 to 4) which was designed by students of architecture as a term project. The CAD plot (ordinary wire-frame image with hidden-line removal) was produced with AutoCAD™, the image with constant shading was generated by the RenderMan™ renderer, while the sketch was produced with the sketch-renderer described above. Note that all three images were produced from the same geometric model in the DXF-format.

After being shown the three images, subjects were asked to answer various questions. First, they

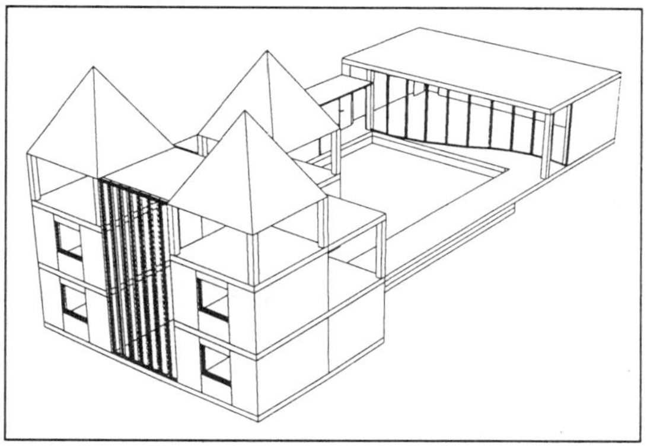

Figure 2: *The CAD plot*

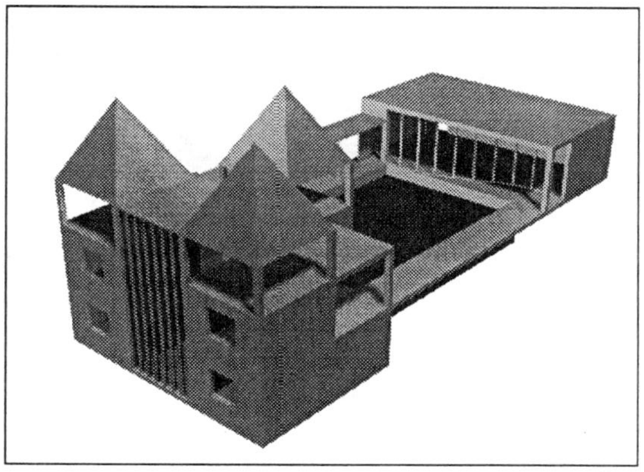

Figure 3: *The shaded image*

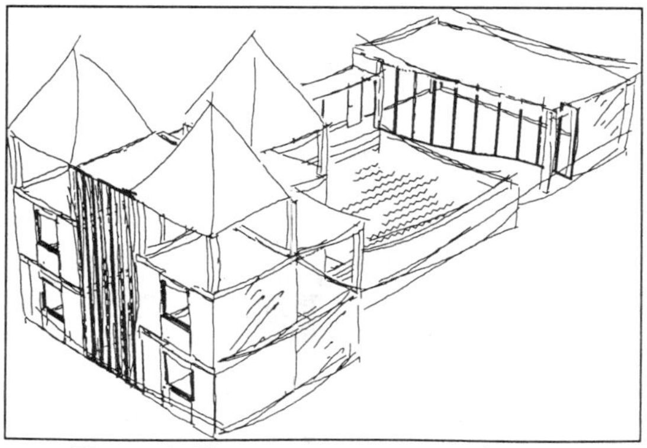

Figure 4: *The computer-generated sketch*

were asked to say which image(s) they would want to use to show a first draft to a client and which image they would use for a final presentation. They were also asked to provide a verbal explanation of their choice.

Next, subjects were asked about a number of (possible) effects of the images, classified according to Peeck's scheme mentioned above. These were to be rated on a scale of 5 ("strongly disagree") to 1 ("strongly agree"). Subjects were also asked to give an additional verbal judgement about the images, which is not described here but is valuable help for further implementations.

To test the third hypothesis, subjects were asked to say how they would make changes to the design being visualized. They were given four options to choose from:

(a) using a verbal description,
(b) by gesturing or by pointing relative to the image.
(c) by drawing on another sheet of paper, or
(d) by drawing directly onto the image.

RESULTS

Use of Images during the Design Process

Of those subjects using CAD, 53% chose the sketch as a suitable way to present a first draft to a client. This is significantly more than those suggesting the shaded image (22%), as well as the exact plot, which was chosen by 33% of subjects.

Subjects preferring the sketch generally argued that it best shows the preliminary character of the draft and does not focus on details which are, at this stage, not yet decided upon. Many of those who chose the shaded image commented that they appreciated the ability to present the spatial concept of the design.

By contrast, only 8% chose the sketch to present a final result to a client, which is significantly less than those choosing the exact plot (50%) and the shaded image (42%) ($p < 0.05$). Subjects who chose the exact plot or the shaded image often argued that the selection committee "want to see exact renditions", while those few who choose the sketch commented on its originality and the desire to stand out against competitors. Figure 5 summarizes the results.

Impression Made by the Images

Subjects had to assess the impression of the three images in more detail. The results in Figure 6 show that sketches were found significantly more interesting, lively, imaginative, creative, individual and less artificial than both the other media (affective group). Furthermore, they were found to stimulate significantly more to discussions and active changes, in which shaded images performed worst.

In sharp contrast to these affective criteria, the CAD plot performed significantly better in the cognitive group, being more comprehensible, recognizable and clear than both the other media. The shaded image was found to support spatial concepts better, but differences were not significant.

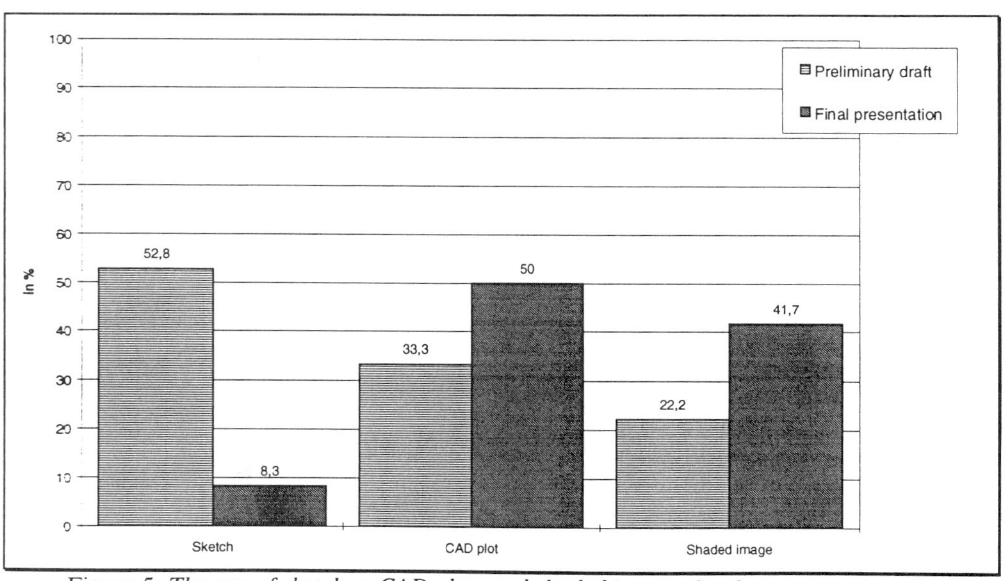

Figure 5: *The use of sketches, CAD plots and shaded images for the presentation of a first draft versus the presentation in a final presentation.*

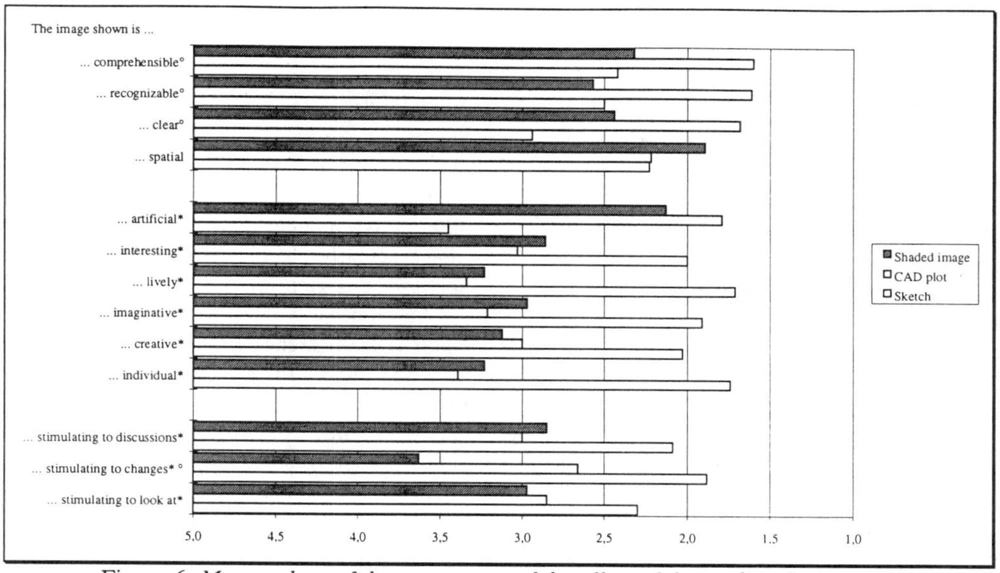

Figure 6: *Mean values of the assessment of the effect of the media (CAD users).*

*The left-most value on the scale (5.0) means complete disagreement, the rightmost value means complete agreement with statements made on the y-achsis. * denotes the items in which sketches differ significantly (p<0.05) from CAD plots and the shaded images. ° denotes the items in which CAD plots differ significantly (p<0.05) from sketches and shaded images.*

Expressing Changes in the Design

While the observations so far were concerned with assessing which impression architectural presentations make on viewers, it is an important goal of the communication between architects and their clients to explain ideas mutually and to develop them further. Therefore, an important criterion in the assessment of the effectiveness of a presentation medium is its ability to provoke active participation of the partners within a discussion.

The results in Figure 7 illustrate that in both media, the methods (a), (b) and (c) were used nearly equally often (the differences are not significant). However, drawing directly into the image was chosen significantly more often ($p < 0.05$) in sketches than in shaded images (69% vs. 33%).

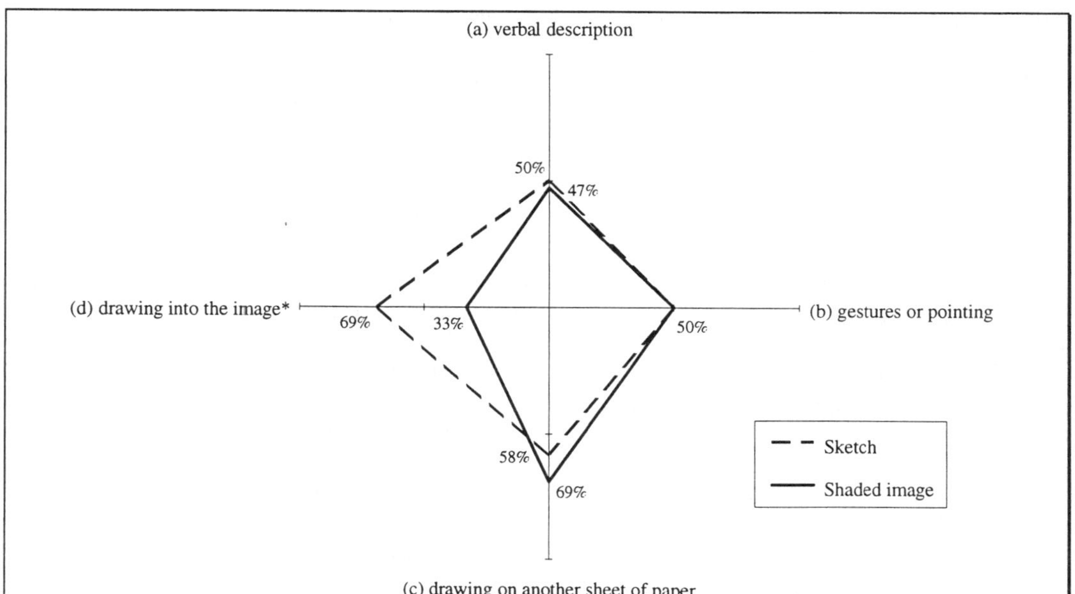

Figure 7: *How subjects would realize changes in a sketch vs. in a shaded image (CAD users). * means a significant (p<0.05) difference between the sketch and the shaded image.*

DISCUSSION

All three of our hypotheses could be proven by the experiments carried out. To explain the results, we shall now look at them from a theoretic point of view. We would expect the cognitive effort required by viewers to be greater for sketches than for the other two kinds of images tested. This is because sketches are more irregular in their form, which means that they transport more information to their viewers. This, in turn, increases the cognitive effort required to understand them (see Klix [6]).

Indeed, Weidenmann [13] speaks of *normalization demands* being placed on a viewer in order to decipher an image. By the above reasoning, these are higher for sketches than CAD plots or shaded images. Applying the ideas of Berlyne's "collative variables" [1], normalization demands lead to curiosity, which in turn is linked to interest and creativity, resulting in a high level of motivation [6].

Going back now to our hypothesis H2, we can explain the less favourable score of the sketch in the cognitive group with the difficulty in deciphering the irregular forms; the resultant ambiguities, however, are then responsible for the better scores in the affective and in the motivational groups.

This reasoning also explains the results of H1. In a first draft, architects reported they want to arouse interest in their designs, which by the reasoning above is higher with sketches. For a final draft, a good score in the cognitive group is more important, hence the shaded images and CAD plots are preferred.

To explain H3, we need to go one step further in the theoretic background. Gombrich [5] speaks of the process of *projection* of our experience and expectations onto the phenomena seen. This requires firstly empty or vague places in a picture which can act as a "projection screen", and secondly hints to direct the viewer as to how these gaps can be filled. By this reasoning, sketches provide more projection space than shaded images (because in these practically the whole area of the image is filled, and hence cannot act as a projection space quite as well). Sketches also provide more projection space than CAD plots, because there is no room for interpretation as to where and how lines (i.e., edges in the object visualized) meet. More projection space thus can explain the greater willingness of viewers of sketches to enter into a discussion about the design.

These explanations are only rudimentary analyses of the results; more would go beyond the scope of this paper (see [11] for more details).

CONCLUDING REMARKS

In this paper we have shown that indeed non-photorealistic images are able to affect viewers of images in a different way than photorealistic images are. Care must be taken not to overgeneralize the results by making specific claims about other kinds of images than the ones evaluated in this paper. However, the present study suggest that sketches in the context of CAD indeed deserve their place in rendering software and can be used in an effective manner by architects. Fine-tuning an image actually changes the way the viewer thinks about the design itself.

An intuitively pleasing result of our study is the significant difference in the way the cognitive and affective factors differ. Affective (i.e., emotional) factors are supported significantly more by sketches, while cognitive factors (like comprehensibility of the image) are significantly better with CAD plots or shaded images.

The results clearly indicate that using sketches encourages discourse about a design. Hence if an architect wishes to enter into such a discussion, a sketch is the medium of choice; if the design is no longer to be altered, CAD plots or shaded images are preferable. This conclusion is in tune with the observations of Yin Yin [17], who contends that sketches are more readily accepted as being incomplete representations than more polished forms of visualization.

We expect the ability to produce non-photorealistic images to alter significantly the way users work with CAD. No longer can users divorce themselves from the way their image looks in the final output; the user must take responsibility for the appearance and also its effect on the viewer. The new freedom which users have will also allow them to make mistakes, both in the equilibrium of the image as well as in the intended effect on the viewer. New concepts will have to be developed to help guide users in their work to fine-tune images for their final presentation.

From the technical point of view, the sketch-renderer must be extended to improve the output for large, complex architectural models. In particular, algorithms and interaction techniques must be found which will enable less detail to be visualized in an image than is actually encoded in the underlying model. This will be of particular importance when using such renditions as to show a first draft of a design to a client.

The bottom line is that the new features of non-photorealism in renderers are definitely worthwhile, as they offer users a new degree of freedom which can be used to affect the viewers of the images. However, users will need to learn more about when to use which image along the lines we have shown in this paper.

ACKNOWLEDGEMENTS

The authors wish to thank all those who helped prepare and carry out the survey, among them E.

Kernchen and H. Jesse of the Technical University of Berlin.

REFERENCES

1. D. E. Berlyne (1969), *Conflict, Arousal and Curiosity*, McGraw-Hill, New York.

2. R. Brugger (1993), *3D Computer Animimation with a Description of Autodesk 3D Studio* (in German), Addison-Wesley, Reading, MA

3. J.D. Foley, A. van Dam, S.K. Feiner, J.F. Hughes (1990), *Computer Graphics - Principles and Practice*, Second Edition, Addison-Wesley, Reading, MA.

4. G. Goldschmidt (1994), "On visual thinking: the vis kids of architecture", *Design Studies, 15* (2), Elsevier Science Ltd., Oxford, pp. 158-174.

5. E.H. Gombrich (1986), *Art and Illusion*, Belser Verlag, Zürich.

6. F. Klix (1992), *Die Natur des Verstandes*, Hogrefe, Göttingen.

7. J. Lansdown, S. Schofield (1995), "Expressive Rendering: A Review of Nonphotorealistic Techniques", *Computer Graphics & Applications*, May, pp. 29-37.

8. H. Löffelmann, E. Gröller (1995), "Ray Tracing with Extended Cameras", Technical Report TR-186-2-95-06, Technical University of Vienna.

9. M. Salisbury, S. Anderson, R. Barzel, D. Salesin (1994), "Interactive Pen-and-Ink Illustration", Siggraph '94, *Computer Graphics 28* (4), pp. 101-108.

10. S. Schofield (1994), *Non-photorealistic Rendering: A critical examination and proposed system*, PhD Thesis (unpublished), Middlesex University, UK.

11. J. Schumann (1995), *Effektivität von Computergraphiken in vorläufigen Präsentationen*, Technical Report B 95-12, Department of Computer Science, Free University of Berlin.

12. Th. Strothotte, B. Preim, A.Raab, J. Schumann, D. Forsey (1994), "How to render frames and influence people", *Computer Graphics Forum 13* (3), pp. 455-466.

13. W.D. van Bakergem, G. Obata (1991), "Free Hand Plotting: Is it Life or is it Digital?", *CAAD-Futures '91*, Verlag Schmitt/Vieweg, pp. 567-582.

14. B. Weidenmann (1988), *Psychische Prozesse beim Verstehen von Bildern*, Verlag Hans Huber, Bern-Stuttgart-Toronto.

15. D.M. Willows, H.A. Houghton (Eds.) (1987) *The Psychology of Illustration*, Springer-Verlag, Berlin-Heidelberg-New York.

16. G. Winkenbach, D.H. Salesin (1994), "Computer-Generated Pen-and-Ink Illustration", Siggraph '94, *Computer Graphics 28* (4), pp. 91-100.

17. W. Yin Yin (1992), "Rough and Ready Prototypes: Lessons from Graphics Design", *CHI '92 Short Paper Submission*.

Gratuitous Graphics? Putting Preferences in Perspective

Ellen Levy *†, **Jeff Zacks** *†, **Barbara Tversky***, and **Diane Schiano**†
Stanford University*
Department of Psychology,
Stanford, CA 94305-2130
and
Interval Research†
1801 Page Mill Road
Palo Alto, CA 94304
Tel: (415) 424-0722; E-mail: levy@psych.stanford.edu

ABSTRACT
Rapid growth in 3-D rendering technologies has deluged us with glitzy graphical representations. In what contexts do people find 3-D graphs of 2-D data both attractive and useful?

We examine students' preferences for graphical display formats under several use scenarios. Line graphs were preferred more for conveying trends than details, and more for promoting memorability than for immediate use; bar graphs showed the opposite pattern. 3-D graphs were preferred more for depicting details than trends, more for memorability than immediate use, and more for showing others than oneself. The reverse held for 2-D graphs.

KEYWORDS
Visualization, Spatial Representation, 3-D Graphics, User Interface Design.

INTRODUCTION

Graphical displays of quantitative information are becoming increasingly common in advertising and news reporting, as well as in the more traditional areas of business and science. As graphics technologies have become more sophisticated, graphical displays have grown more varied and more baroque. Until recently, 3-dimensional (3-D) displays were used primarily to render 3-D data sets in such specialized domains as CAD/CAM and geometric modeling. The ability to add depth cues to graphs of 2-dimensional (2-D) data is now commonplace in general-purpose analysis and visualization packages, and the demand for "sexy" but possibly gratuitous 3-D graphics is increasing.

Do glitzy graphics do more than attract the eye? How can quantitative information best be rendered on 2-D surfaces such as paper or computer screens to facilitate easy and accurate comprehension and memory? In this paper we report the results of three studies of people's preferences for graphical displays in which 2-dimensional data sets are rendered as dots, lines, or bars with or without 3-D depth cues. In these studies we focus on the cases in which 2-dimensional data had to be displayed, and a choice had to be made about the general type of display to use, as well as the preferred dimensionality of the graphical elements. Given the ease with which any of tens or hundreds of different graph types can be generated using even the most basic of available graphics packages, the question is one with which journalists, scientists, designers, and statisticians are confronted daily.

To be understood, graphics must first be accurately perceived. Cleveland and colleagues [3-5] have characterized the ability of the human perceptual system to extract information from graphs when presented in various geometric forms, such as angles, lengths, areas, and volumes. This low-level analysis has yielded "hierarchies" in which basic elements are ranked in terms of comprehension scores. For graphs of a dimensionality equal that of the data, accurately perceiving and understanding all of the properties of the display is critical to extracting the information. However, for 3-D displays in which the depth does not represent any additional quantitative information, the viewer must deal with redundant and extraneous cues.

One obvious place to turn for advice on selecting graphs is the graphic design community. The message from designers is straightforward: simple and clear is better, extra ink is bad, and extraneous information detracts from the impact of the graphic [11]. In one example, Tufte starts with a complex figure with extra 3-D shading and, in accordance with the goal of maximizing the ratio of data to ink in a graphic, strips out the elements generating the illusion of depth. The argument is that if the information being displayed is inherently 2-dimensional, the graphic should be 2-dimensional as well. According to Tufte, rendering uninformative depth is a bad idea in principle because it can lead to misperception of the information of interest, and it can hide the real content from the viewer.

These admonitions are largely based on the cumulative experience of talented professionals, and for the most part make sense. For empirical support we can turn to the literatures on visual perception and visual illusions. Early in this century, Gestalt psychologists repeatedly demonstrated that interactions among elements in a visual display can result in a perception very different from the simple physical description of the components of the display. In addition, there are countless examples of displays in which the perception of a given stimulus varies significantly, depending on its relationship to other, contextual elements in the visual field [6]). For example, Jordan & Schiano [7] found that the perceived length of a single test line can be greatly affected by the presence of one additional context line in the visual display; moreover, the size and direction of the resulting distortion depended systematically upon the relative proximity and size of the context line to the test line. In his how-to book on graphical design, Kosslyn points out that the ultimate goal of the designer is to have control over the perceived properties of a graph — not merely the physical properties of the page or screen rendering [8]. Given the sort of data described above, it could easily follow that rendering false depth cues in graphical displays of quantitative information amounts to placing extraneous information on the page at the risk of introducing perceptual distortions.

However, in the context of 3-D displays, the conclusions are not necessarily clear. Such displays may be difficult to perceive when there is ambiguity in the 2-D representation of a 3-D object, as in reversible figures such as the Necker cube or Escher drawings. What remains to be seen is whether 3-D objects are detrimental to accuracy and speed of judgments from graphics. Also, what parameters of 3-D rendering can be manipulated to minimize its harm? Finally, are there any benefits to depth cues, and what parameters maximize them?

The little research that does bear directly on the comparison of 2-D vs. 3-D displays of 2-dimensional data has focused primarily on the extent to which information is accurately perceived in graphs of different dimensionality. Results from both perceptual match and magnitude estimation studies have been interpreted as evidence that added dimensionality has little or no effect on accuracy [2, 10]. However, there are several alternative interpretations of these findings, some of which will be taken up in the Discussion.

Taken all together, the message would seem to be telling us to "keep it simple, stupid." However, this is not the way the world is. For one thing, the world we perceive is rich, complex, and even ambiguous. For another, a glance at the morning paper should convince anyone that the graphics arms race is on. The ratio of data to ink in many publications is going down fast. Information providers are increasingly producing graphics with colors, pictures, and all sorts of extraneous 3-D structure. Graph users as well as graph producers seem to have preferences and opinions about the effectiveness and appropriateness of these graphs.

Existing research on graphical displays suggests that the effectiveness of graphical formats varies with context and intended use, but little if any research exists that demonstrates the extent to which people have sound *intuitions* about which graph types are best. One exception is Carswell et al.'s study [2] in which students made judgments about imaginary universities. They were provided information about two different universities in the form of several graphic displays. The impressions that the students formed about each university were directly influenced by whether the information had been presented in 2-D or 3-D graphs. In three studies, we examine people's preferences for different types of graphics, depending on the use to which the graphic is to be put.

EXPERIMENT 1

This first study was designed to be a broad exploration of subjects' preferences for different graph types. Subjects were presented with 6 scenarios, and asked to choose a graph type from an array of 9 graphs. The scenarios and graph types were chosen to capture the varied situations in which graphs are used and the range of options commonly available [see Figure 1 for sample graphs used in questionnaire].

METHODS

Subjects

The subjects were 161 Stanford University undergraduates enrolled in an introductory Psychology course.

Questionnaire

Subjects were given a booklet with several questionnaires, including the one described below, which they were instructed to take home and complete over the course of two days. Estimated time to complete the entire packet was roughly 1-2 hours, with the page for this study taking no more than a few minutes.

A one-page questionnaire was used to probe subjects' attitudes about a set of graph formats: the top half of the questionnaire contained 9 panels of graphs illustrated below. The graph panels were arranged to form a 3 x 3 matrix, with each graph labeled with a letter from A to I. The bottom half of the page presented subjects with 6 scenarios to consider.

Data sets

The hypothetical data set displayed in each of the graphs was comprised of nine data points. The data set contained

6 trend reversals, where a trend reversal is defined as the change in slope of the graph (positive to negative or vice versa).

Graphs
Nine types of graphs were created in the software program Excel [1]: (1) a scatterplot, (2) a simple bar graph, (3) a 3-dimensional volume bar graph, displayed from the perspective of a viewer looking up from below the x-axis plane, (4) a 3-dimensional volume bar graph, displayed from the perspective of a viewer looking down from above the x-axis plane, (5) an area line graph, (6) a simple line graph, (7) a 3-dimensional volume line graph, displayed from the perspective of a viewer looking down from above the x-axis plane, (8) a 3-dimensional surface line graph, with the same perspective as the 3-dimensional volume line graph, and (9) a 3-dimensional volume pie graph. [see Figure 1]

The collection of graphs offered subjects very different options, with choices between certain pairs of graphs reflecting subtle variations along one dimension. For example, graphs 3 and 4 only varied in the perspective shown to the viewer — both were 3-dimensional volume bar graphs. Along the same lines, graphs 7 and 8 differ in that the former renders a volume by filling in the area underneath the curve, while the latter representation depicts a floating surface, even though both can rightly be called "3-dimensional graphs."

Scenarios
Subjects were asked to "imagine yourself as a research scientist working at a high-tech firm. You have been given the chance to present the findings from you work to the Board of Directors of the company. Your research assistant has been assigned the job of preparing the slides that you will need. Given each of the scenarios listed below, decide which graphs (give your first and second choice) you think would be the best given the circumstances." The 6 scenarios were: [note - *italicized labels did not appear on the actual questionnaires*]

1) [*patterns*] In preparation for your talk, you are trying to get a better feel for your data, and want to see a graph that will help you visualize the patterns and important aspects of your findings.
2) [*gist*] You have only a few minutes to get your points across to the board. In fact, you really don't want the board members to worry too much about details, but rather to focus on the "gist" of what you are saying.
3) [*details*] You've just been warned that the board is going to ask you very detailed questions about your work, and that you might have to get down to the "knitty gritty" [sic] of what your work shows.
4) [*trends*] From past experience, you know that your main objective should be to present information to the board in such a way that they can pick out the trends and extrapolate from your findings.
5) [*contrast*] You want to convey the fact that the most exciting part of your work is reflected in certain data points (such as the minimum and maximum values). You will be contrasting different data points to get this across.
6) [*memory*] You know that just after your presentation, your colleague will be presenting contradictory findings. You want the board to be able to remember your results, and compare them to what they hear in the next talk.

RESULTS

We report only subjects' first choices as their second choices do not substantially change the picture.

The pattern of preferences for the 9 graph types for each of the 6 scenarios is given as Table 1. Our subjects' choices were clearly not due to random variation ($\chi^2 = 304.959$, $p < .0001$). Due to the exploratory design of this study, the data do not lend themselves to a rigorous statistical analysis. Nevertheless, some conclusions do seem warranted. The area bar graph and the simple line graph, two familiar types, were the most popular overall. Of the two 3-D volume bar graphs, subjects greatly preferred the view from above to the view from below (94 to 19). Of the two 3-D line graphs, they chose the 3-D volume more often than the 3-D surface (90 to 41). For Scenario 1, which emphasized understanding the data for one's self, subjects liked a bar area graph best. (This type is arguably one of the most familiar.) For getting a point across quickly (Scenario 2) or picking out general trends (Scenario 4), subjects preferred a simple line graph.

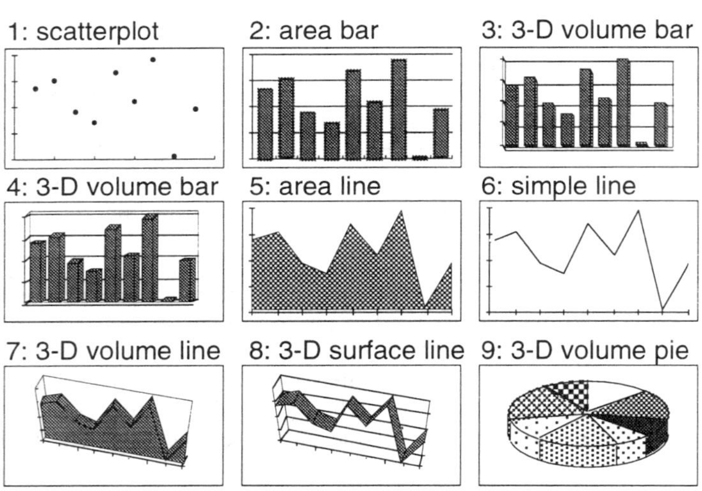

Figure 1: Graphs from Questionnaire 1.

1: Patterns	5	**48**	1	15	21	8	36	3	24
2: Gist	2	34	2	6	28	**47**	9	2	30
3: Details	32	20	6	**33**	12	20	10	5	23
4: Trends	3	20	4	7	33	**58**	15	10	10
5: Contrast	35	21	3	13	33	**39**	5	9	3
6: Memory	1	28	3	20	**31**	22	15	12	28
Total	78	171	19	94	158	194	90	41	118

Table 1: Data from Experiment 1. Table shows number of subjects choosing each graph as their first choice, for each question. Numbers in bold indicate the most popular graph for each scenarios.

EXPERIMENT 2

In this experiment, we sought to refine our initial findings by more carefully manipulating the graph types, scenarios and data sets employed. In the literature, the use of the term "3-D graph" has been applied to many different types of graphs. Here we distinguish between graphs that add depth to create the impression of a surface suspended in space and those that add depth to create the impression of an object with volume. The instructions for Experiment 1 suggested a very particular situation (the "board room"); here we created generic scenarios that avoided referencing specific situations and focused on more general circumstances.

METHODS

Subjects

The subjects were 110 Stanford University undergraduates enrolled in an introductory Psychology course.

Questionnaire

Subjects filled out a 1-page questionnaire, of the same format and distributed in the same manner as in Experiment 1.

Data sets

Two versions of the questionnaire were prepared, differing only in the nature of the data depicted in the graphs themselves. Each data set consisted of nine data points. In one version, the *general trend* (GT) data set, the graphs of the data formed a slightly right-skewed curve. In the second version, the data points were selected to create a *multiple reversal* (MR) data set. Applying the definition of a trend reversal as the change in slope of the graph (positive to negative or vice versa), the GT data set contained 1 trend reversal, while the MR data set involved 6 trend reversals. Data set (GT or MR) was a between-subject variable.

Graphs

Nine types of graphs were created. The graphs are shown in Figure 2, and included: (1) a scatterplot, (2) a simple line graph, (3) an area line graph, (4) a 3-dimensional volume line graph, (5) a 3-dimensional surface line graph, (6) a simple bar graph, (7) an area bar graph, (8) a 3-dimensional volume bar graph, and (9) a 3-dimensional surface bar graph, in which only the tops of 3-dimensional bars were used to indicate quantity on the y-axis.

With the exception of the scatterplot, the graphs were divided into two broad categories—*line graphs* that connected the data points(2,3,4,5), and *bar graphs* that plotted each data point independently with a vertical element of some sort (6,7,8,9). Within each category, an example of a simple graph, an area graph, a volume graph and a surface graph was created. While the simple graphs (2 & 6) and area graphs (3 & 7) are familiar formats that do not need much explanation, the distinctions between the 3-dimensional graph types are important and not as readily apparent.

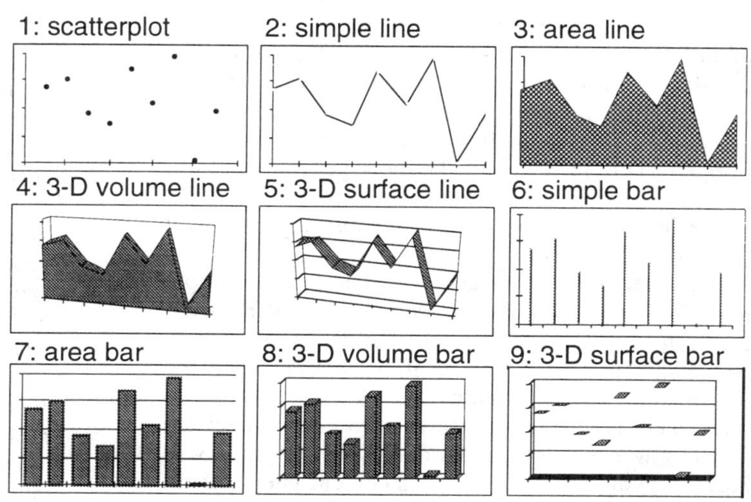

Figure 2: Graphs from Questionnaire 2 (multiple reversal data set)

1: Details	13	18	11	10	11	4	**21**	16	5
2: Trends	3	**36**	34	7	12	1	9	7	0
3: Self	6	**38**	5	8	1	2	31	18	0
4: Other	2	16	10	12	9	1	23	**36**	0
5: Now	6	14	19	6	6	4	**31**	22	1
6: Memory	2	7	**23**	22	14	1	17	21	2
Total	32	129	102	65	53	13	132	120	8

Table 2: Data from Experiment 2. Table shows number of subjects choosing each graph as their first choice, for each question, and combines results from both the GT & MR dataset versions . Numbers in bold indicate the most popular graph for each scenarios.

All graphs were created using standard graphing commands in Microsoft Excel [1], except for graphs 6 & 9, which were rendered in a drawing program.

Scenarios

The 6 scenarios listed below were designed to set up contrasts on three dimensions: *self* vs. *other* (scenarios 1 & 2), *details* vs. *trends* (scenarios 3 & 4), and *now* vs. *later* (scenarios 5 & 6).

1) [*self*] You've just finished collecting all this information. You want to see it graphically displayed so that you can understand what is going on. This is just for your own use; you won't be showing the graph to others.
2) [*other*] You need to represent your data graphically for a group of people. Conveying what is going on to them is critical. You want them to understand your findings as fully as possible.
3) [*details*] You want to make a graph that will show the detailed relationships in the data. It is important that the specifics of how each data point relates to the others be evident in the figure. The details are critical.
4) [*trends*] You need to quickly show general trends in the data. One should be able to just glance at the figure and understand what is going on. The important thing here is the "gist."
5) [*now*] You need to present your data to help people make an immediate decision. It makes no difference if they remember this next week--the decision needs to be made correctly today. The graph should convey the information right here and now.
6) [*memory*] Your data will be used to make a decision in a few weeks. Someone looking at your graph will need to be able to remember it's content later without referring back to it. You should make the figure as memorable as possible.

RESULTS

As in Experiment 1, we analyzed only subjects' first choices. As in the first study, our subjects' judgments were non-random. (For the multiple-reversal data set, $\chi^2 = 106.787$, $p < .0001$; for the general trend data set, $\chi^2 = 104.272$, $p < .0001$.) In general, their pattern of choices was quite similar for the multiple-reversal and general trend data sets ($r = 0.74$). Some obvious and non-surprising patterns jump out of the data (see Table 2). Our subjects clearly chose different graphs for different situations. Overall, they liked the familiar area bar and simple line graphs best (chosen 132 and 129 times out of 654, respectively). They rarely chose the simple bar (13 times) or 3-D surface bar graphs (9 times).

The more structured design of this survey also permits a more detailed analysis. We can look at preferences for graphs of different dimensionality by collapsing over data set and collapsing the line and bar graphs. When we do so, a consistent pattern emerges. For all of the 3 pairs of questions, subjects' preferences for simple, area, 3-D volume, and 3-D surface graphs changed systematically. Simple and area graphs were liked for some sets of circumstances, and 3-D volume and surface graphs for others (see Figure 3a). Subjects liked simple and area graphs better for their own use than for presenting to others; the opposite pattern held for 3-D volume and 3-D surface plots. They chose the 3-D graph types more often when the data had to be remembered, and simple and area graph types more often when the figure was for immediate use. Finally, they liked the two types of 3-D graphs better for showing detailed relationships than for showing the "gist", while the opposite pattern held for the simple and area graphs.

If we collapse over data set and collapse over dimensionality, another pattern emerges. Our subjects chose line and bar graphs for different uses. They chose line graphs more often when the data had to be remembered than when the graph was for immediate use; the opposite pattern held for bar graphs. Our subjects liked line graphs better for general trends than for details. Bar graphs, on the other hand, were chosen more for details than for trends (see Figure 3b).

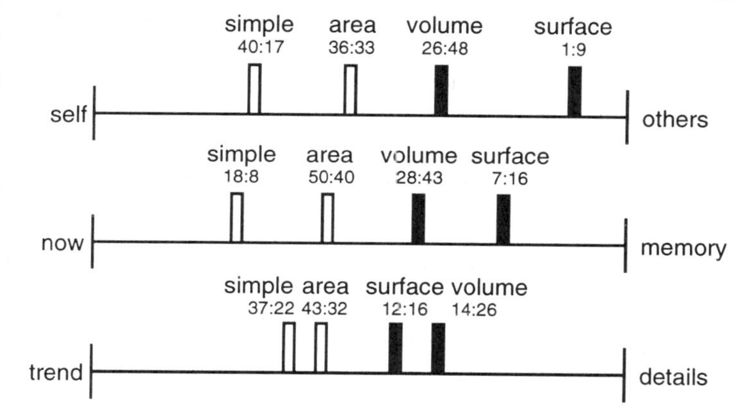

Figure 3a: Graph type choices for simple, area, volume, and surface graphs. Bar positions represent the relative frequency with which a graph type was chosen for two contrasting scenarios. Numbers below the graph type labels give the actual frequency. For example, simple graphs were chosen 40 times for the "self" scenario and 17 times for the "others" scenario.

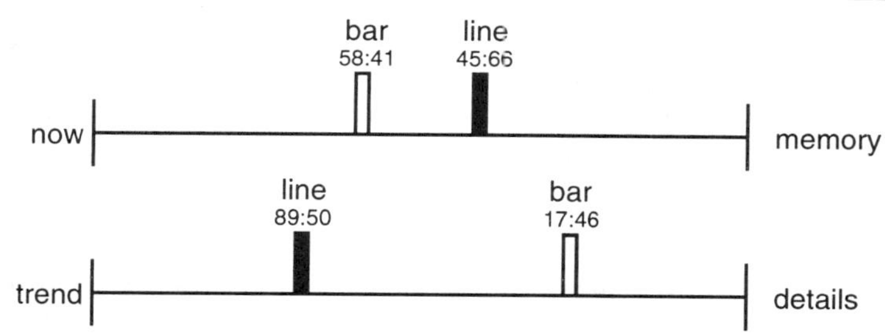

Figure 3b: Graph type choices for line and bar graphs. Bar positions represent the relative frequency with which a graph type was chosen for two contrasting scenarios. Numbers below the graph type labels give the actual frequency. For example, bar graphs were chosen 58 times for the "now" scenario and 41 times for the "memory" scenario.

Both of the patterns described above were robust; each holds for both the multiple reversal data set and the general trend data set results individually, as well as for the combined data.

EXPERIMENT 3

In this final experiment, we focused on the central question of preferences for "2-D vs 3-D" graphics by creating a two-alternative, forced-choice questionnaire. The format and procedures were identical to those described in Experiments 1 & 2, except for the number of graph panels presented.

METHODS

Subjects

The subjects were 157 Stanford University undergraduates enrolled in an introductory Psychology course.

Questionnaire

Subjects filled out a 1-page questionnaire, similar in format and distributed in the same manner as in the previous experiments. Four versions of the questionnaire were created by crossing type of graph (line vs. bar) and order of presentation (2-D area graph first vs. 3-D volume graph first).

Data sets

All versions of the questionnaire depicted the multiple reversal data set used in Experiment 2.

Graphs

Each questionnaire displayed only two graphs: an area graph and a volume graph. The graphs were either line graphs or bar graphs.

Scenarios

Subjects were shown the six scenarios used in Experiment 2, and were given the same instructions—to pick the graph most appropriate for each situation described.

RESULTS

A clear pattern of preferences that reinforce the findings from Experiments 1 & 2 emerged (see Figure 4). Not only can comparisons be made between preferences within each graph dimensionality (i.e., 2-D graphs were preferred more often for presenting to one's self than when presenting to others), but relative preferences for employing 2-D or 3-D graphs can also be assessed. For most situations, subjects preferred the 2-D area graph. Two exceptions are when graphs were to be used for presenting data to others, in which case there was no significant difference in preference for the two graph types ($p < 0.31$), and when the graph needed to be memorable, in which case the 3-D volume graph was significantly preferred ($p < 0.01$).

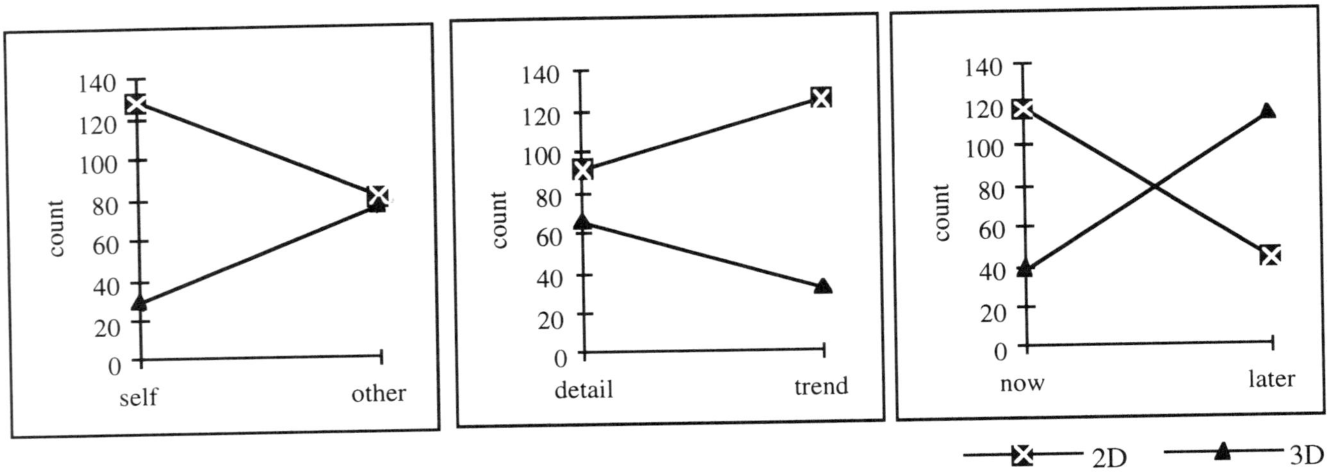

Figure 4: Graph type choices for area (2-D) and volume (3-D) graphs in Experiment 3. Graphs show the number of subjects selecting each of the two graph options, broken down by implied use scenario.

When assessing the pattern of results for each of the three continuum—self vs. other, detail vs. trend, and now vs. later—significant interactions exist between the dimensionality of the graph and the proposed use scenario ($\chi^2 = 62.59$, $\chi^2 = 59.07$, and $\chi^2 = 71.86$ respectively).

GENERAL DISCUSSION

The key findings of the three surveys can be described as follows. First, subjects were not leery of choosing graphs with 3-D shading. Second, they found different graph types appropriate for different rhetorical purposes. They systematically chose line graphs for different circumstances from bar graphs, and chose 3-D graphs for different situations from 2-D graphs. In particular, they chose 3-D graphs over 2-D graphs when the situation demanded memory, and equally often when it involved communication to others. In addition, the use of 3-D graphs was deemed more appropriate for certain scenarios than other scenarios: for examining details rather than trends in data, for making a memorable rather than an immediate impression, and when using a graph to communicate to others over situations in which the graph is for one's self. Finally, subjects preferred graphs that strongly suggested a 3-D volume to those that depicted a surface floating in space.

Why this robust pattern of preferences for these 3-D graphs? Our subjects consistently selected 3-D graphs for various scenarios, and rejected them for others. Moreover, out in the real world scientists and business-people are voting with their feet (and their trackballs and mice) for 3-D graphs. This may be just the tip of the iceberg, considering the general proliferation of 3-D interfaces and computing environments being developed.

We propose two possible explanations for these preferences. The more parsimonious of the two is a simple discriminability or salience account. In Experiments 2 & 3, subjects chose the 3-D volume (and surface) graphs more often when the scenario demanded memory or showing data to others. Under these conditions people may feel that extra graphical flourishes will make the figure stand out, making the graph both more memorable and more impressive to others.

A second explanation derives from the ecological and evolutionary situatedness of our visual systems. We have evolved to deal with a world of 3-D objects and 3-D scenes. Figures that more strongly suggest a spatially realistic environment may better engage our visual systems, and may be more easily coded in terms of schemas we have for visual scenes. This kind of facilitation could be helpful for communicating a pattern to others or keeping it distinct in memory. This hypothesis might also explain why people like 3-D volume graphs more than 3-D surface graphs: the former more closely resemble solid objects such as the ones we deal with in the real world. While this view is not directly addressed in the work we report here, it serves as an interesting and plausible explanation. Our subjects did seem to have had a sense that graphs with depth were more appropriate for communicating and remembering, and they found realistic volumes preferable to unlikely floating surfaces. Could it be that their intuitions were in line with their actual abilities?

This possibility has some support in the small literature directly comparing 2-D and 3-D graphs of quantitative information. Two recent studies [2, 10] failed to find a difference in accuracy of estimates from 2-D and 3-D graphs. However, one of these studies [2] failed to distinguish between 3-D surface and 3-D volume graphs; the other [10] averaged data over several heterogeneous 3-D graph types. In light of the great differences we found in peoples' preferences for these types of graphs, it seemed worthwhile to attempt a more direct comparison. In a recent series of studies in our laboratory [9], we compared analogous versions of 2-D area and 3-D volume bar graphs. Under these conditions, we found a reliable and suggestive effect of dimensionality: adding depth cues impaired accuracy in both a magnitude estimation and a perceptual match task. However, this performance difference was small. Moreover, it vanished when subjects had to make their judgments from memory (perceptual match task exercising a very short-term form of working memory).

At this point we can conclude with some certainty that people prefer graphs of quantitative information enhanced by 3-D shading for some situations. More pronounced and important is the fact that these preferences show a systematic structure. For our subjects, adding 3-D shading to 2-D displays amounted to more than simply adding more ink to the page, or pixels on the computer screen. The challenge for designers and consumers of graphics is to learn about and take advantage of these preferences for features inherent in graphic displays. For behavioral scientists, it is to discover the extent to which these preferences have a basis in the human perceptual system.

ACKNOWLEDGMENTS

The first and second authors are supported by National Science Foundation Fellowships. In addition, this research has been supported by Interval Research Corporation.

REFERENCES

1. Excel (1992). Microsoft: Redmond,WA.

2. Carswell, C.M., Frankenberger, S., and Bernhard, D. (1991). Graphing in depth: Perspectives on the use of three-dimensional graphs to represent lower-dimensional data, *Behaviour & Information Technology*, 10(6), 459-474.

3. Cleveland, W.S. (1985). The Elements of Graphing Data, Wadsworth Advance Books and Software, Monterey, CA.

4. Cleveland, W.S. and McGill, R. (1984). Graphical perception: Theory, experimentation, and application to the development of graphical methods, *Journal of the American Statistical Association*, 79, 531-553.

5. Cleveland, W.S. and McGill, R. (1985). Graphical perception and graphical methods for analyzing scientific data, *Science*, 229, 828-833.

6. Coren, S. and Girgus, J.S. (1978). Seeing is Deceiving: The Psychology of Visual Illusions, Lawrence Erlbaum Associates, Hillsdale, NJ.

7. Jordan, K. and Schiano, D.J. (1986). Serial processing and the parallel-lines illusion: Length contrast through relative spatial separation of contours, *Perception & Psychophysics*, 40(6), 384-390.

8. Kosslyn, S.M. (1994). Elements of Graph Design, W.H. Freeman and Company, New York, NY.

9. Levy, E., Schiano, D.J., Zacks, J., and Tversky, B. (1995). Representing information in graphs, *Paper presented at the meeting of the Psychonomics Society*, Los Angeles, CA.

10. Spence, I. (1990). Visual psychophysics of simple graphical elements, *Journal of Experimental Psychology: Human Perception and Performance*. 16, 683-692.

11. Tufte, E.R. (1990). The Visual Display of Quantitative Information, Graphics Press, Chesire, CT.

Beating the Limitations of Camera-Monitor Mediated Telepresence with Extra Eyes

Kimiya Yamaashi[1] Jeremy R. Cooperstock[2,4] Tracy Narine[2] William Buxton[2,3]

[1] Hitachi Research Laboratory
Hitachi Ltd.
7-1-1 Omika-cho Hitachi-shi
Ibaraki-ken 319-12 Japan
+81 294 52 5111
yamaashi@hrl.hitachi.co.jp

[2] Telepresence Project
University of Toronto
10 King's College Road
Toronto ON M5S 3G4 Canada
+1 416 978 0703
{jer, tracyn}@dgp.toronto.edu

[3] Alias|Wavefront
110 Richmond Street East
Toronto ON M5C 1P1
Canada
+1 416 362 8558
bbuxton@aw.sgi.com

ABSTRACT

In physical presence, you are most aware of your immediate surroundings, such as what is at your feet or who is beside you, and less aware of objects further away. In telepresence, almost the opposite is true. Due to the nature of the medium, you are most aware of what is in front, often at a distance, as dictated by the limited view of the camera. Even where remote camera control is possible, the range of exploration is limited and the logistics of control are typically awkward and slow. All of this adds up to a pronounced loss of awareness of the periphery in telepresence.

The research described here attempts to compensate for these problems through two mechanisms. First, we provide telepresence users with two separate views, one wide-angle and the other, a controllable, detailed view. To simplify navigation, the two views are seamlessly linked together, so that selecting a region of one will have an effect in the other. Second, we utilize sensor information from the remote location to provide the user with notification of relevant events that may require attention. Together, these tools significantly enhance users' awareness of their telepresence surroundings.

Keywords

Telepresence, teleconferencing, CSCW, multimedia

INTRODUCTION

Normal human vision can be conceived as consisting of two highly mobile cones of view. One is the focused foveal cone, one degree wide, while the second is the peripheral cone, or global field of view, spanning approximately 170 degrees [1]. Excellent spatial resolution is provided by the first, while the second, lower resolution view, provides us with stimulus that acts to redirect our attention.

Camera-monitor mediated vision, in contrast, suffers in resolution and due to the size of the display, uses limited azimuth of the visual field. Watching television, for instance, typically involves the foveal cone only. The narrow channel of information, both in the sense of bandwidth and field of view, imposes limitations on the ability to explore, follow conversations, check reactions, and generally sense significant actions in a remote space, such as people passing by or entering. In such situations, users must choose between a global and a focused view. With the former, resolution is sacrificed to permit a wide field of view and easy change of gaze direction. If only the focused view is provided, users obtain details but no peripheral awareness. This is typical of most videoconference settings [5] [11].

One approach to support both the foveal and peripheral cones is with multiple views. The problems with this approach are well understood. The Multiple Target Video (MTV) system of Gaver et. al. [12] first proposed the use of multiple cameras as a means of providing more flexible access to remote working environments. Users were offered sequential access to several different views of a remote space. However, as the authors noted, a static configuration of cameras will never be suitable for all tasks. Furthermore, switching between views introduces confusing spatial discontinuities. A further study (MTV II) by Heath et. al. [15] attempted to address this latter issue by providing several monitors, so that every camera view was simultaneously available. While this new configuration was more flexible, the inability of static cameras to provide complete access to a remote space still remained a problem. Furthermore, the various views were independent of one another, and the relationship between them was not made explicit. Consequently, spatial discontinuities persisted.

Another approach involved the Virtual Window concept [10], which uses the video image of a person's head to navigate a motorized camera in a remote location. Our user experience with this technique [7] revealed a significant improvement to the user's sense of engagement in

[4] Author is a Ph.D. student with the Department of Electrical and Computer Engineering, University of Toronto.

meetings. Unfortunately, when the camera was focused on a small area, the loss of global context often made the user unaware of important activity taking place out of view.

To compensate for the limitations on vision imposed by camera-monitor mediated telepresence, the work discussed here offers to:

1. Provide both a global (peripheral) and a detail (focused) view, simultaneously. We note that this approach has already been used extensively in the Ontario Telepresence Project [2] [3] [17] by combining the two views through a picture-in-picture device. The same approach with multiple views was also proposed by Kuzuoka et. al. [16]. However, as will be discussed later, providing a link between the two views is not only critical for usability, but also supports the goal of multiple views while avoiding the pitfalls of spatial discontinuities inherent in the MTV studies [12] [15].
2. Provide a navigation mechanism using these views, allowing users to redirect their view in both direction and scale, through a simple user interface.

However, even with these two goals satisfied, the user is still sensorally deprived to the extent that it may inhibit social interaction. Therefore, our third goal is as follows:

3. Provide a sensory surrogate or prosthesis to compensate for the limited scope of visual information.

SUPPORTING FOVEAL AND PERIPHERAL CONES

It has been suggested by several vision researchers that a brain mechanism exists to drive foveating saccades[1] of the eye in response to stimulus in the periphery region [14] [19]. In the discussion of their model of saccadic eye movement, Tsotsos et al. comment that these saccades play an important role in the exploration of the visual world [18]. Supporting evidence for this comes from neurophysiology. A region known as PO, which receives a representation of the periphery of the visual field, has been identified in the brains of primates [4]. Deprived of this information, individuals suffering from tunnel vision, or a loss of vision outside the fovea, exhibit severe problems navigating through their physical surroundings, even when these surroundings are familiar to them [13]. With this in mind, it becomes readily apparent that camera-monitor mediated telepresence is bound to suffer unless peripheral vision can be supported concurrently with a detailed, foveal view.

Overlaid Multiple Views

As an initial attempt to provide this support, we developed a prototype system, consisting of a large and small display, as shown in Figure 1. The large screen display provides the user with a wide angle view of the remote space while the small display provides a high resolution view of the area of interest. With the camera orientations fixed and the proper geometric positioning of the two displays, spatial discontinuities are minimized. The sensation of increased peripheral awareness obtained by this system is very powerful.

We note that this prototype requires two high-resolution displays, one of them quite large, in order to achieve a significant effect. As this may be prohibitively expensive for most videoconference users, we would like to unify the two views into a single display. Unfortunately, even with a large screen display, the limited resolution would make the quality of the foveal region unacceptable. Another approach is required.

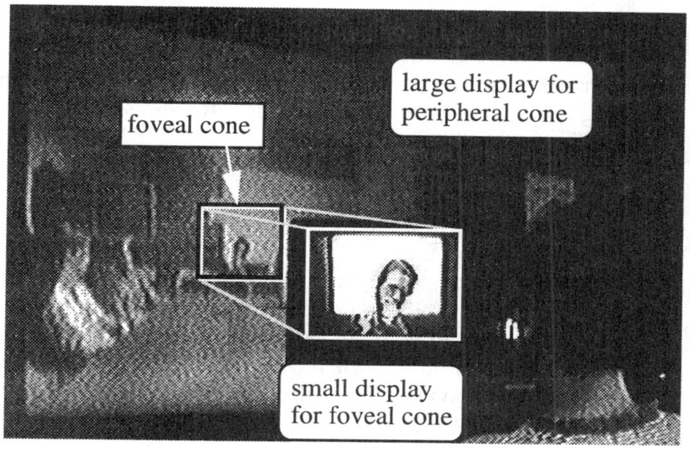

Figure 1. This prototype system uses a large screen display for the peripheral view and a small screen for the detail view.

Disjointed Multiple Views

Another approach to supporting both the foveal and peripheral views is to display the two separately on the same screen. Since the views are disjointed, each can have sufficient size and resolution, even with the limitations of current technology. Our implementation of this system is shown in Figure 2. The top portion of the display provides a foveal or detail view, obtained from a user-controlled motorized camera, while the lower portion provides the peripheral or global view from a fixed, wide-angle camera.

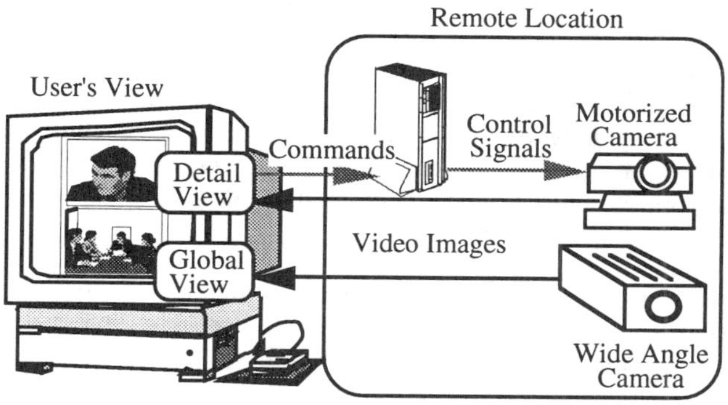

Figure 2. Architecture of the Extra Eyes system.

[1] Foveating saccades are rapid eye movements intended to direct the fovea to a desired orientation.

Since the views are independent of each another, there is no consistent geometric relationship between the two. This can result in an inability to locate the position of the detailed region within the peripheral view, once more bringing us back to the problem of spatial discontinuities. Navigation under these conditions is typically difficult and slow. This is especially severe when the scene being viewed is relatively homogeneous (e.g. through tele-education, a large class of students). Normal human vision does not suffer from this problem because the direction of the fovea explicitly dictates the peripheral view.

Linking Multiple Views

To address the lack of a geometric relationship between the two views, we indicate the detailed region within the global view by means of a yellow bounding box (detail frame), as shown in Figure 3. The enclosed region corresponds exactly to what is displayed in the detail view. As the detail view changes, the bounding box on the global view adjusts accordingly.

Because the two views are logically linked, users can select a desired region by sweeping out a bounding box or simply *point-and-click* on the global view. In the former case, the detail view is defined by the size of the bounding box, while in the latter, the detail view is centered at the selected position and displayed at the maximum zoom. These interaction techniques with the global view permit a far more efficient navigation mechanism than the effectively *blind* [2] view selection offered by both the original MTV system [12] and the Virtual Window system [10].

In addition to control via the global view, the detail view can be manipulated directly through the scroll bars, which provide tilt and pan control of the motorized camera. It is also possible to adjust the zoom factor of the detail view by pressing the left or right mouse button, or obtain a wide view by selecting the *wide* button.

To provide a linkage between the global and detail views, we require a mapping between the coordinate systems of each, dependent on the properties of the different cameras. We first define a global coordinate system, which covers the entire area visible to both cameras. Next, we define models for each camera, which consist of a view model, and in the case of the motorized camera, a transformation function. The models describe the relationship between pixel coordinates of each camera and the global coordinate system. In the case of our fixed wide-angle camera, this is simply a one-to-one mapping. The transformation function for the motorized camera maps pixel coordinates to the appropriate motor signals. The models and relationships are described in Figure 4.

When a user selects an area of the global view, the pixel coordinates of this region are first translated into global coordinates through the wide angle view model, and then into pixel coordinates of the detail view. The detail pixel coordinates are then mapped into motor signals via the transformation function. Finally, the motor signals are sent to the detail camera. At the same time, the updated location and dimensions of the bounding box are computed, and displayed on the global view. Similarly, when a user specifies an area of the detail view directly, the pixel coordinates of this region are transformed into motor signals for the camera, and to global coordinates describing the new bounding box (see Video Figure in the CHI 96 Video Program).

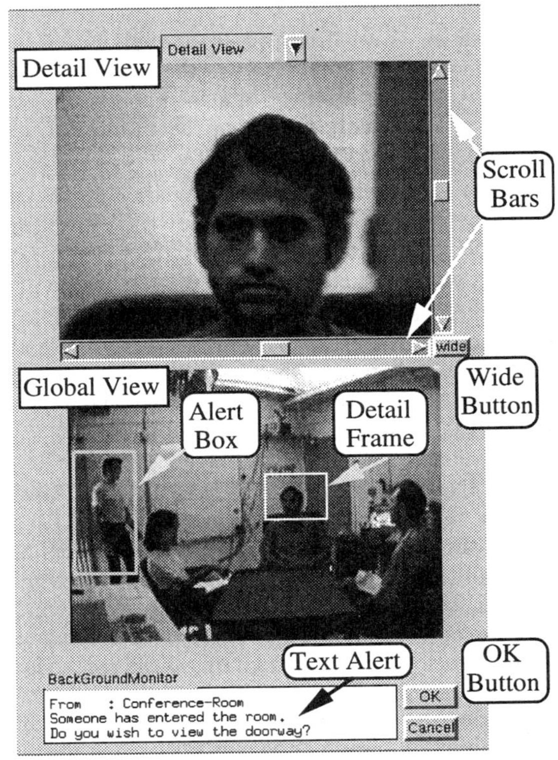

Figure 3. Screen layout of Extra Eyes.

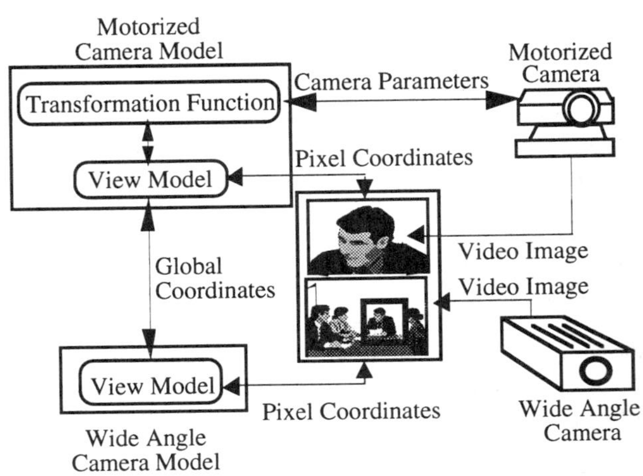

Figure 4. Camera models and their relationships.

[2] We use the term, *blind*, because no visual information apart from that appearing in the single view is available.

SENSORY SURROGATE

Sensory surrogate for environmental awareness

There exists no substitute for physical presence that offers the fidelity of rapidly directable stereo vision and spatially sensitive binaural audio, as manifested by the human senses. To help bridge the gap between physical presence and telepresence in this regard, our Extra Eyes system provides users with a *sensory surrogate* to increase their awareness of the remote environment. The surrogate monitors background information obtained by sensors and reports on relevant events through the use of sound, text, and graphics, or a combination of the three. In this manner, background processing by the computer is used to improve the user's foreground awareness.

Sensors in the room [6] monitor the status of presentation technology such as the VCR, document camera, and digital whiteboard, as well as the entry of new individuals as depicted in Figure 5. When an event occurs, it triggers an *alert-action sequence*. The alert corresponds to the screen message displayed (e.g. "Someone has entered the room. Do you wish to view the doorway?"), as well as the appearance of a blue bounding box (*alert box*) in the corresponding region of the global view, as shown in Figure 3. If the user acknowledges the alert by pushing the *OK* button or selecting the *alert box,* then an appropriate action is executed by the system (e.g. control the motorized camera to display the doorway). Another possible alert message is "The VCR is now playing. Do you wish to view the tape?" with the associated action of switching the user's view to the VCR output (see Video Figure in the CHI 96 Video Program).

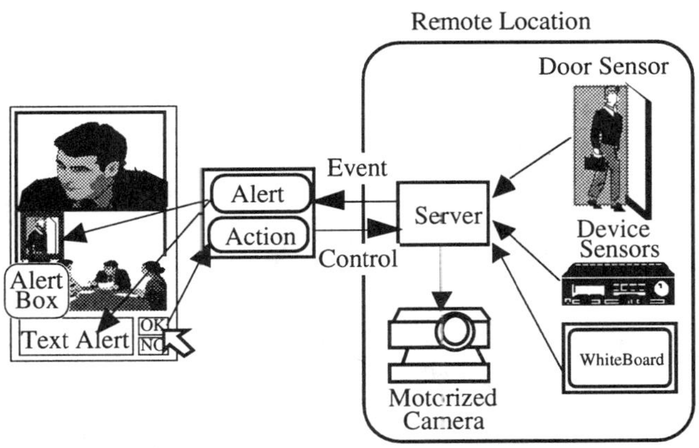

Figure 5. The sensory surrogate in operation.

Sensory surrogate for social awareness

We have also applied the sensory surrogate concept to increasing social awareness among individuals sharing the media space of the Ontario Telepresence Project [17]. The Postcards system (see Figure 6), based on Rank Xerox EuroPARC's Portholes [8], captures snapshots from each user's office at set intervals and distributes these to members of the media space. A sensory surrogate in the Postcards system compares every two consecutive frames from each office to determine if there is activity there. This is done by counting the number of pixels that have changed by more than a certain threshold amount between the two frames. Although the algorithm is susceptible to false detection of activity due to camera perturbations, it has worked reasonably well in our environment. Stored knowledge of activity allows Postcards to determine whether individuals are in or out, or have recently entered or vacated their offices.

Users can take advantage of this background monitoring feature by asking the system to *sense* activity and notify them when any number of individuals are simultaneously present in their offices. This permits informal group meetings to be established with a minimum of effort, freeing the user from the mundane task of repeatedly checking to see who is available.

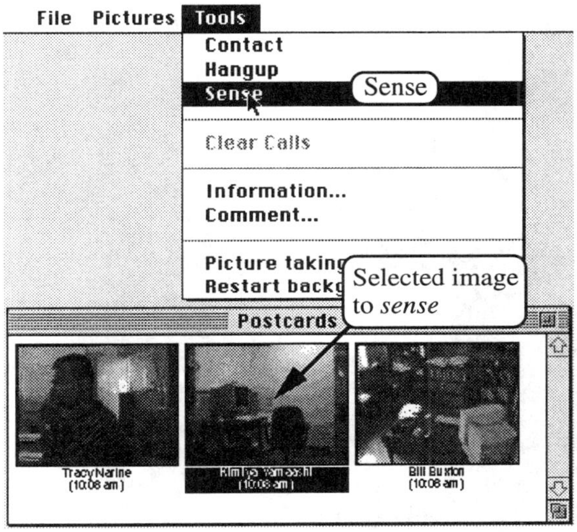

Figure 6. Screen layout of Postcards. Images from each room are captured periodically.

EVALUATION

User Study

We evaluated the performance of Extra Eyes through the following user study. Three television monitors were arranged in a remote location, as shown in Figure 7. Letters of the alphabet were displayed on a randomly chosen monitor, one at a time. The user's task was to use the Extra Eyes system to identify these letters as they appeared, as quickly as possible, while minimizing the number of errors. Each letter would remain on the monitor until the user had identified it, by typing its corresponding key. Once the letter was identified, it would be replaced by another letter on a different monitor. The font size was sufficiently small so that a zoom factor near the maximum was required for legibility. We tested each of our seven subjects on the following conditions, the order being randomly varied, with 20 repetitions per condition:

1. **No Global:** Only the detail view is visible. This situation is equivalent to typical telepresence systems.
2. **No Global + Text:** Same as 1. In addition, a text alert indicates the display on which the current letter appears.
3. **Unlinked:** Both the global and detail views are simultaneously visible, but the two views are not linked (i.e. neither view has effect on the other). This is equivalent to the MTV system.
4. **Linked:** Both the global and detail views are simultaneously visible and linked.
5. **Linked + Text:** Same as 4. In addition, a text alert indicates the display on which the current letter appears.
6. **Linked + Action:** Same as 5. In addition, an *alert box* appears, and the user can invoke the action corresponding to the alert by pushing the *OK* button or by clicking anywhere within the *alert box*. The action causes the camera to point directly to the new letter with maximum zoom factor.

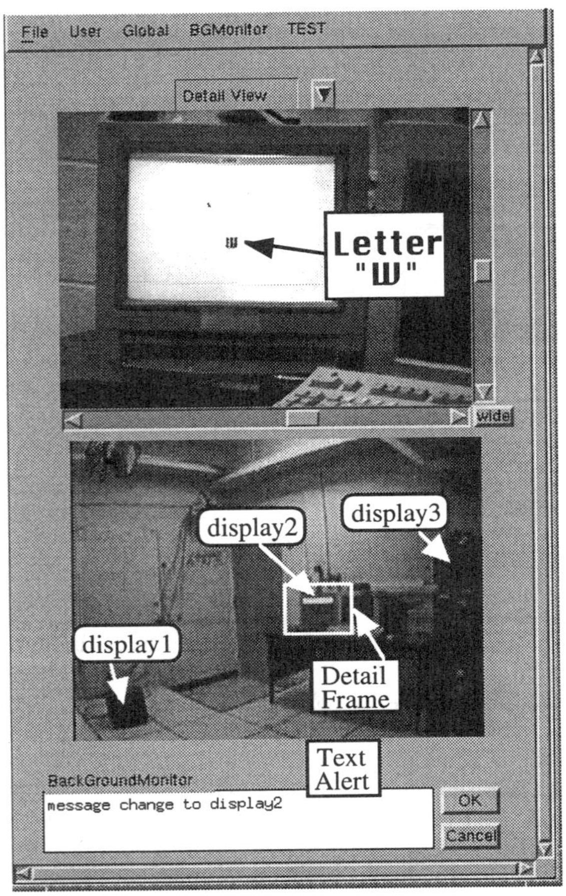

Figure 7. Configuration of user study.

Discussion and results of user study

For the first three conditions, users exhibited two strategies to identify the various letters. When no information beyond that of the detail view was available, users consistently zoomed out to obtain a wide angle view, then panned and tilted the camera to center the letter, before zooming in again. This *zoom-out* strategy, represented by the solid line in the space-scale diagram [9] of Figure 8a, requires over three camera operations, on average, to identify each letter. When an alert message was added, indicating the display on which the new letter appears, users tended to change their strategy. Knowing the approximate location of the desired monitor from past experience gathered during the study, users often tried to find this monitor by repeatedly panning and tilting the camera, as shown by the solid line in Figure 8b. This strategy is quite similar to searching for an object in a familiar room, while in the dark. Because users cannot accurately select a desired position with the *pan-tilt* strategy, this method often requires more operations than the *zoom-out* strategy. The same *pan-tilt* strategy was used when the global view was provided, but not linked to the detail view. For the remaining three conditions, users were able to identify the letters with only a single camera operation.

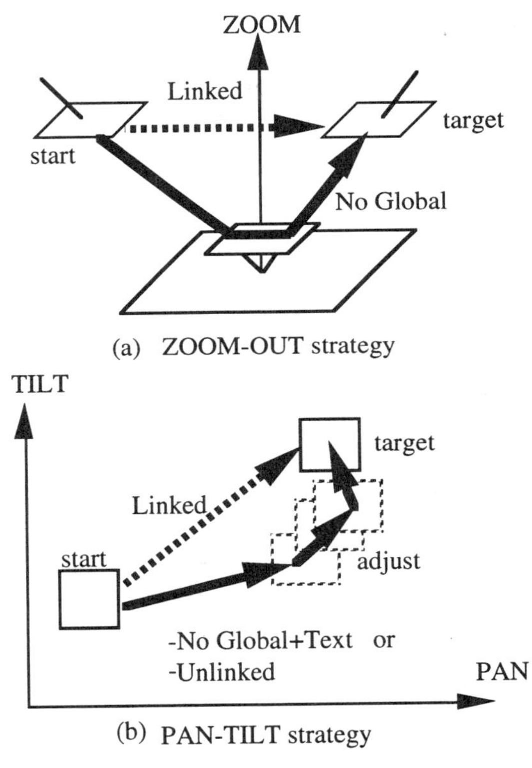

Figure 8. Space-scale diagram of camera movement. The solid arrows indicate the users' strategy typically adopted without linkage available, while the dashed arrows indicate the strategy taken when the global and detail views were linked.

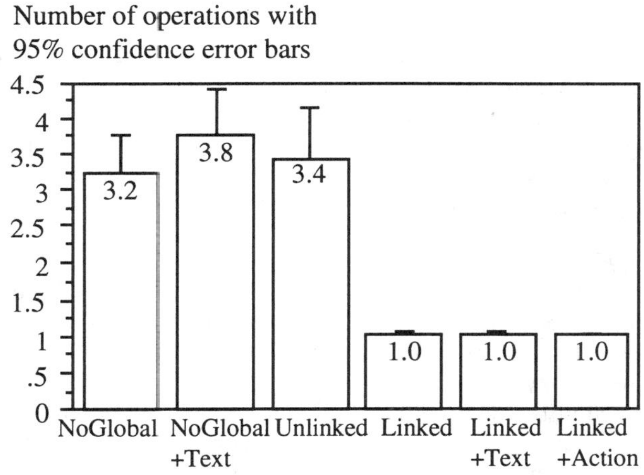

Figure 9. Means of number of operations in each experimental condition.

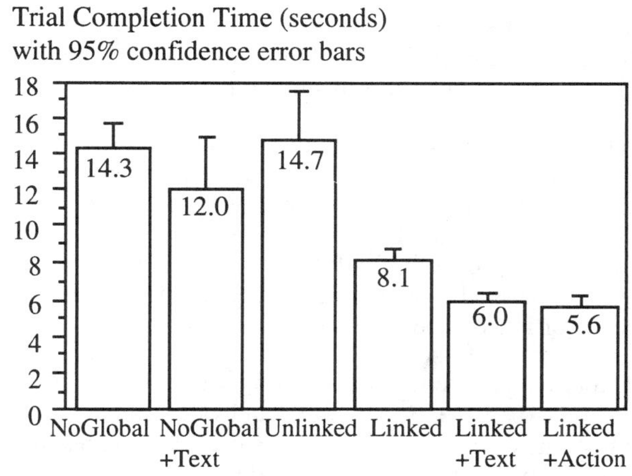

Figure 10. Means of completion time in each experimental condition.

Figure 9 and Figure 10 present the results of our user study, indicating the average number of camera operations users required to identify each letter, as well as the average completion time with 95% confidence error bars, with each of the six experimental conditions.

Analysis of variance (ANOVA) showed that both number of operations and trial completion times were significantly affected by the experimental conditions. For number of operations, $F(5, 30)=55.2$, $p<0.001$. For completion time, $F(5, 30)=40.1$, $p<0.001$.

As measured by number of operations (Table A1 in the Appendix), Fisher's protected LSD posthoc analyses showed that all linked conditions were significantly different from the Unlinked and NoGlobal conditions ($p<0.05$). However, there is no significant difference among linked conditions. The difference between Unlinked and NoGlobal, as well as Unlinked and NoGlobal+Text is also insignificant.

As measured by completion times (Table A2 in the Appendix), Fisher's protected LSD posthoc analyses showed that all conditions were significantly different from each other ($p<0.05$), except Linked+Action vs. Linked+Text condition ($p=0.64$) and NoGlobal vs. Unlinked ($p=0.66$).

Based on these results, we can draw the following conclusions.

Conclusion 1: Linkage between views is very important
When the two views were linked, navigation in the remote environment via selection in the global view was effortless. Any desired (visible) target could be selected directly with a single camera operation, as indicated by the dashed lines of Figures 8a and 8b (see also Figure 9). In this case, the previous indirect strategies of *zoom-out* and *pan-tilt*, which require almost twice as much time as direct selection, were never used. Users expressed their opinion that the direct selection mechanism was more natural than the indirect methods. Indeed, all linked conditions were significantly better than the unlinked one in terms of both number of operations and trial completion time.

Further user feedback was also highly informative. Some commented that the *detail frame* was useful as an indication of direction of camera motion. Furthermore, when the two views were not linked, users had to remain conscious of their current position in order to reach the desired view. This was a result of spatial discontinuities [12]. Linkage between the two views reduced the effect of these discontinuities, because a user action on one view has a direct effect on the other.

Conclusion 2: Sensory information is useful
The time improvement from linked views to linked views with a text alert ($p<0.05$, see Table A2) indicates the added value of sensory information. As most users explained, the alert allowed them to reduce the size of the visual search area. Users also appreciated the audio feedback of a *beep*, provided simultaneously with an alert message, indicating that a new letter was about to appear.

We note that sensory information may have compensated for the low update rate (approximately 1-2 frames/s in our present implementation) of the global view. In many instances, the indication of various alerts preceded the appearance of a new letter on the global view by one second or more. This enabled users to begin their navigation toward the desired monitor before the letter was actually visible.

Although the differences in time and number of operations between Linked+Text and Linked+Action were not statistically significant, users indicated that the graphic alerts were more useful than text messages. The graphic alerts completely specify the relevant visual regions, as opposed to text alerts, which require the user to read and then perform a search. Many users simply did not read the text alerts, preferring instead to watch only the graphics display.

FURTHER ISSUES

Having described Extra Eyes and our preliminary evaluation of this system, we now turn to some other issues.

The global view provided by our present system can not capture a view of the entire room. Other designers may prefer to use multiple cameras, or a very wide angle lens, possibly a fisheye, for this task. In the former case, some form of image processing will be required to combine the images, while in the latter, unwarping to compensate for image distortion will be necessary.

Detractors may argue that transmitting video for the global view is too expensive. Either more bandwidth is required, or the frame rate of the detail view will suffer. We suggest that since the global view is only required to provide a sense of peripheral awareness, both its frame rate and resolution can be relatively low. In fact, we reduced our global view to a quarter size (160 x 120 pixels), and found that users were still very aware of activities occurring in the periphery. If the global view is transmitted at this size, along with a full-frame detail view, both at the same rate, then the decrease in frame rate of the detail view would be less than 7%, assuming constant bandwidth consumption. We strongly believe that the benefit of peripheral awareness justifies this minor expense.

FUTURE WORK

While the sense of peripheral awareness offered by a fixed global view is a helpful navigation tool, it does not accurately replicate the mechanics of human vision, in which the periphery is dictated by the orientation of the fovea. A future version of Extra Eyes should remedy this shortcoming, either by attaching the global camera to the motorized detail camera, or by using another motorized camera for the global view, synchronized with the detail camera.

This improvement is presently being applied to our initial large-screen prototype, discussed earlier. To maximize effectiveness, we are locating the smaller display near the center of the large screen. This way, the foveal and peripheral cones will maintain the correct geometric relationship at all times. We are presently combining such a system with the Virtual Window head-tracking mechanism, and look forward to reporting on its results in the near future.

An alternative route to pursue may be to make use of image processing techniques, such as those of Warp California's Virtual TV (VTV) system, to selectively unwarp any portion of the image from a fisheye lens. As higher resolution and lower cost frame grabbers become available, this technology will offer many advantages over motor-driven cameras.

CONCLUSIONS

We have crossed the complexity barrier of current camera-monitor mediated telepresence applications. To beat the limitations imposed by this barrier, we propose a new design to support views of the foveal and peripheral cones simultaneously. To minimize the effects of spatial discontinuities, we also provide a seamless linkage between the two views. Furthermore, a sensory surrogate is needed to increase the remote user's sense of awareness. Acting together, as they do in the Extra Eyes system, these techniques serve dramatically to provide users with increased accessibility to remote locations.

ACKNOWLEDGMENTS

The authors would like to thank William Hunt and Shumin Zhai of the University of Toronto, Abigail Sellen of Rank Xerox EuroPARC and Masayuki Tani of Hitachi Research Laboratory, for their invaluable suggestions and contributions to this paper. We would also like to thank John Tsotsos of the University of Toronto for helping us sift through the relevant literature on biological vision.

This research has been undertaken as part of the Ontario Telepresence Project. Support has come from the Government of Ontario, the Information Technology Research Center of Ontario, the Telecommunications Research Institute of Ontario, the Natural Science and Engineering Research Council of Canada, Hitachi Ltd., Bell Canada, Xerox PARC, British Telecom, Alias|Wavefront, Hewlett Packard, Sun Microsystems, the Arnott Design Group and Adcom Electronics. This support is gratefully acknowledged.

REFERENCES

1. Barlow, H.B. and Mollon, J.D., The Senses, *Cambridge Texts in the Physiological Sciences,* 1982, Cambridge University Texts.

2. Buxton, W., Integrating the Periphery and Content: A New Model of Telematics, in *Proc. GI'95* (Quebec PQ, May 1995), Canadian Human-Computer Communications Society, 239-246.

3. Buxton, W., Telepresence: Integrating Shared Task and Person Spaces, in *Proc. GI'92* (Vancouver BC, May 1992), Canadian Human-Computer Communications Society, 123-129.

4. Colby, C.L., Gattass, R., Olson, C.R. and Gross, C.G., Topographical Organization of Cortical Afferents to Extrastriate Visual Area PO in the Macaque: A Dual Tracer Study, *Journal of Comparative Neurology, Vol. 269*, 1988, 392-413.

5. Cool, C., Fish, R.S., Kraut, R.E. and Lowery, C.M., Interactive Design of Video Communication Systems, in *Proc. CSCW'92* (Toronto ON, Oct. 1992), ACM Press, 25-32.

6. Cooperstock, J.R., Tanikoshi, K., Beirne,G., Narine, T. and Buxton, W., Evolution of a Reactive Environment, in *Proc. CHI'95* (Denver CO, May 1995), ACM Press, 170-177.

7. Cooperstock, J.R., Tanikoshi, K. and Buxton, W., Turning Your Video Monitor into a Virtual Window,

Proc. of IEEE PACRIM, Visualization and Signal Processing (Victoria BC, May 1995).

8. Dourish, P. and Bly, S., Portholes: Supporting Awareness in a Distributed Work Group, in *Proc. CHI'92* (Monterey CA, May 1992), ACM Press, 541-547.

9. Furnas, G. and Bederson, B., Space-Scale Diagrams: Understanding Multiscale Interfaces, in *Proc. CHI'95* (Denver CO, May 1995), ACM Press, 234-241.

10. Gaver, W., Smets, G. and Overbeeke, K., A Virtual Window on Media Space, in *Proc. CHI'95* (Denver CO, May 1995), ACM Press, 257-264.

11. Gaver, W., Realizing A Video Environment: EuroPARC's RAVE System, in *Proc. CHI'92* (Monterey CA, May 1992), ACM Press, 27-35.

12. Gaver, W., Sellen, A., Heath, C. and Luff, P., One is not Enough: Multiple Views in a Media Space, in *Proc. INTERCHI'93* (Amsterdam Netherlands, April 1993), ACM Press, 335-341.

13. Grusser, O. and Landis, T., Visual Agnosias and Other Disturbances of Visual Perception and Cognition, *Visual and Visual Dysfunction, Volume 12*, CRC Press.

14. Hallett, P., Primary and Secondary Saccades to Goals Defined by Instructions, *Vision Research 18*, 1978, 1279-1296.

15. Heath, C., Luff, P. and Sellen, A., Reconsidering the Virtual Workplace: Flexible Support for Collaborative Activity, to appear in *Proc. ECSCW '95* (Stockholm Sweden, September 1995)

16. Kuzuoka, H., Kosuge, T. and Tanaka, M., GestureCam: A Video Commutation System for Sympathetic Remote Collaboration, in *Proc. CSCW'94* (Chapel Hill NC, Oct. 1994), ACM Press, 35-43.

17. Riesenbach, R., The Ontario Telepresence Project, in *Conference Companion CHI'94* (Boston MA, April 1994), ACM Press, 173-174.

18. Tsotsos, J. K., Culhane, S. M., Wai, W., Y., K., Lai, Y., Davis, N., and Nuflo, F., Modeling Visual Attention via Selective Tuning. *To appear in Journal of Artificial Intelligence.*

19. Whittaker, S. and Cummings, R., Foveating Saccades, *Vision Research 30 (9)*, 1990, 1363-1366.

APPENDIX

Table A1. Posthoc analysis of six experimental conditions: number of operations.

	Vs.	Diff.	Crit. diff.	P-Value	
Linked +Action	Linked+Text	.008	.528	.9757	
	Linked	.008	.528	.9758	
	NoGlobal+Text	2.753	.528	.0001	S
	NoGlobal	2.226	.528	.0001	S
	Unlinked	2.416	.528	.0001	S
Linked +Text	Linked	4.2E-5	.528	.9999	
	NoGlobal+Text	2.746	.528	.0001	S
	NoGlobal	2.218	.528	.0001	S
	Unlinked	2.408	.528	.0001	S
Linked	NoGlobal+Text	2.746	.528	.0001	S
	NoGlobal	2.218	.528	.0001	S
	Unlinked	2.409	.528	.0001	S
NoGlobal +Text	NoGlobal	.528	.528	.0500	S
	Unlinked	.337	.528	.2022	
NoGlobal	Unlinked	.191	.528	.4660	

S = Significantly different at the level:0.05.

Table A2. Posthoc analysis of six experimental conditions: time (seconds).

	Vs.	Diff.	Crit. diff.	P-Value	
Linked +Action	Linked+Text	.440	1.872	.6350	
	Linked	2.554	1.872	.0092	S
	NoGlobal+Text	6.423	1.872	.0001	S
	NoGlobal	8.762	1.872	.0001	S
	Unlinked	9.172	1.872	.0001	S
Linked +Text	Linked	2.115	1.872	.0282	S
	NoGlobal+Text	5.983	1.872	.0001	S
	NoGlobal	8.323	1.872	.0001	S
	Unlinked	8.732	1.872	.0001	S
Linked	NoGlobal+Text	3.868	1.872	.0002	S
	NoGlobal	6.208	1.872	.0001	S
	Unlinked	6.617	1.872	.0001	S
NoGlobal +Text	NoGlobal	2.340	1.872	.0160	S
	Unlinked	2.749	1.872	.0054	S
NoGlobal	Unlinked	.409	1.872	.6585	

S = Significantly different at the level:0.05.

Talk and Embodiment in Collaborative Virtual Environments

John Bowers
Department of Psychology
Manchester University, U.K.
+44-161-275-2599
bowers@hera.psy.man.ac.uk

James Pycock
Department of Psychology
Manchester University, U.K.
+44-161-275-2682
pycockj@hera.psy.man.ac.uk

Jon O'Brien
Department of Sociology
Lancaster University, U.K.
+44-1524-594186
soajeo@cent1.lancs.ac.uk

ABSTRACT
This paper presents some qualitative, interpretative analyses of social interaction in an internationally distributed, real-time, multi-party meeting held within a collaborative virtual environment (CVE). The analyses reveal some systematic problems with turn taking and participation in such environments. We also examine how the simple polygonal shapes by means of which users were represented and embodied in the environment are deployed in social interaction. Strikingly, some familiar coordinations of body movement are observed even though such embodiments are very minimal shapes. The paper concludes with some suggestions for technical development, derived from the empirical analyses, which might enhance interactivity in virtual worlds for collaboration and cooperative work.

Keywords
Conversation analysis, interaction analysis, body movement, embodiment, virtual reality, CSCW.

INTRODUCTION
Collaborative Virtual Environments (CVEs), where multiple individuals interact with each other in a computational environment rendered by Virtual Reality (VR) technology, are of emerging interest from a number of perspectives. Several writers have claimed [e.g. 2] that such environments may support collaboration and interactivity (especially geographically distributed collaboration) in ways which go beyond what is possible using more familiar meeting room or teleconferencing technologies. The development of CVEs has also drawn interest as a complementary alternative to video and 'mediaspace' [5, 12] research. CVEs may provide a shared spatial environment where (in principle) people can employ communicative resources which are unavailable to them in other technical systems. For example, participants can have a degree of control over what they view in a CVE which is not generally possible with mediaspaces supported by a fixed camera and monitor system, and our ordinary means for coordinating turn-taking in social interaction can be deployed rather than some technical means such as 'floor control' policies as is commonly the case in traditional conferencing systems. Furthermore, if users in a CVE are all embodied in it so that their location and orientation can be represented, then a degree of mutual awareness of each other's activity may arise or be readily supported [1, 2].

This paper attempts to subject such claims to preliminary examination by giving a characterisation of what CVEs are like as environments for cooperative work and social interaction and seeing how ordinary conversational mechanisms are exploited or transformed in such environments. To these ends we employ empirical techniques derived from Conversation Analysis or CA [e.g. 14], which to our knowledge has not been attempted before in studying CVEs or other VR technologies, though CA has had some influence in HCI and CSCW in enabling detailed studies of interaction in the workplace [10], the impacts of new computer based technologies on 'talk at work' [8] as well as in motivating technical design choices [3] and assisting in the analysis of the design process itself [4]. Accordingly, we seek to add to this literature while extending it to the study of a novel setting (a work-related meeting being conducted in VR).

Finally, we are concerned to show how methods of interaction analysis might contribute to the evaluation and hence future requirements of CVEs. User-oriented evaluative studies of VR systems are still overwhelmingly dominated by investigations of such matters as motion sickness [13] and the characterisation of phenomena in terms of individual perceptual psychology [15]. We wish to study CVEs so as to extend the base in reference to which VR systems should be evaluated and developed. Through characterising the nature of social interaction in a CVE at least in a preliminary fashion, we hope to make a start on the task of exploring the worth of distributed VR technologies for the support of cooperative work and social interaction.

THE VIRTUAL MEETING
We have been working closely with CVE developers for some time in a number of research projects. As their CVE technologies have become more robust, our collaborators have begun to use their own systems as environments for the support of distributed research meetings. We have been present as participant-observers at a number of these meetings and have begun to accumulate a corpus of videos and other materials for analysis. At the time of its occurrence, probably the most significant of these meetings took place on 28th March 1995 as a working meeting of COMIC, a European ESPRIT project devoted to basic

research on CSCW. The significance of this meeting was that it involved real-time interaction in a number of virtual worlds between nine participants who were distributed across five sites and three countries (Germany, Sweden and the UK). According to many of the participants, this degree of international participation was a 'world first' and has been reported as such in a number of technical press articles.

The MASSIVE system [9] that was used for the virtual meeting supports multi-user interaction between distributed sites allowing participants to communicate over graphical, textual and audio media. The graphical interface provides a navigable 3D view of the shared virtual world and of other participants represented as simple graphical embodiments. For the current meeting the 3D view was presented on screen rather than immersively. The audio interface allows real-time conversation. The text interface provides a 2D plan view of a world and allows the exchange of text messages. MASSIVE employs client-server information distribution. The hardware used was exclusively Silicon Graphics for the interface clients with a Sun Sparc 10/51 at Nottingham University in the UK running server software.

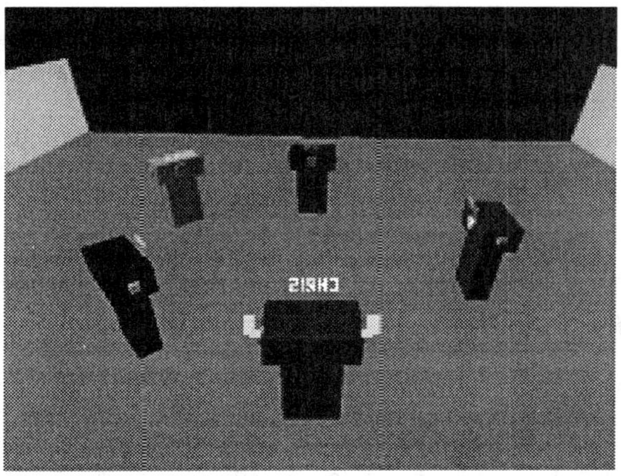

Figure 1. Blockies in a virtual meeting.

The user-embodiments or 'blockies' are made of simple 3D box-polygons with one square 'eye' on one vertical surface and the user's name 'suspended' above the top surface. As well as identity, this design affords a rudimentary sense of 'face', 'front' and 'back' which according to Goffman [6] are features of the human body of basic significance to social interaction enabling us to distinguish between, for example, talking to someone's face from talking behind their backs. Furthermore, the 3D view that a user has can relate to the blockie's face. Although different views are possible, the default is that one 'sees out of' the blockie's eye. This view, or one where one looks over the blockie's shoulders, are the ones typically employed by users. In this way, what other participants can see and where they are looking is often available from an inspection of their bodily orientation and, accordingly, a sense of mutual awareness can be sustained and transformed by aligning the blockies or moving them around. For example, 'full face encounters' [6] can be brought about by two participants aligning their blockies to face each other. Indeed, it has been precisely a consideration of what was the minimal geometrical object necessary to sustain basic interactional relations between participants which has informed the design of the blockies [1]. Insisting that the embodiments should be geometrically simple (yet still have interactional potential) is necessary because of the extreme computational complexity of distributed VR systems based on current technology.

The blockies also support minimal gesturing. They have 'ears' which can be 'flapped' in different ways (left one raised, right raised etc.). They can recline (or 'sleep'). This can be used, for example, to denote that the participant the blockie corresponds to has currently left their local machine and is not available for interaction. Gestures are controlled through simple key sequences and the blockie is moved by clicking the mouse on the 3D view or by using the arrow keys. Finally, the blockies have a 'mouth' which opens when a user's speech exceeds a certain amplitude threshold.

The overall business of the virtual meeting is well described by the following quote from the minutes which one of the participants distributed afterwards: "The time spent in the conferencing software, approximately an hour and a half, can be split up into three distinct periods. To begin with there was a fifteen minute mingling session where people arrived for the meeting and chatted socially ... This time was also spent making sure everybody could communicate with everybody else. At a quarter past two SB called the meeting to order and everybody trooped off to the designated meeting room where a pre-prepared agenda was awaiting on a noticeboard and ... introductions were carried out. CG then gave a tutorial on how to use MASSIVE ... [The items on the agenda were then discussed.] The formal meeting finished at about two fifty five, and after that much more informal communication took place." While some of the clients needed to be restarted from time to time, the server software and network connections were reliable throughout.

INTERACTION ANALYSIS

In this section, we report our analyses of the talk exchanged between participants in the virtual meeting. Specifically, we focus on two issues: the nature of turn taking in virtual environments and how the embodiments are used. Our interest is in the *interactional qualities* of CVEs, what these environments are like as arenas for social interaction as revealed in the moment-by-moment texture of talk and activity. Accordingly, our analyses work from transcript data which we analyse qualitatively and interpretatively.

Before we turn to some examples from our data, it is necessary to clarify the transcript conventions we have adopted. We employ an adapted version of the conventions devised by Jefferson and presented in a number of sources [e.g. 14]. Pauses and silences are notated by their length in seconds shown within round brackets: (1.2). Talk which receives more emphasis than the surrounding speech is underlined: someone else's turn. Parts of the transcript where we are unsure of what is said, but are able to guess, are notated with round brackets: thanks lennart (how) very eloquent. Where we are unable to guess the round brackets are empty. Prolonged sounds are indicated by inserting colons, and concatenated speech, where the words are quickly run together, is notated by hyphens placed between the words: an::d this wonderful VR system-MASSIVE-that-we're-using is wot i writ. An audible in-breath is notated .hhh and hhh. denotes an audible out-breath. Overlapping speech is notated by means of square brackets positioned to indicate where the overlaps occur. Speech which is distorted by, say, some malfunctioning of the audio link is placed within curly brackets: i'm john {b}owers from manchester {uni}versity. Our comments within the transcript are enclosed within angled brackets: <laughter>. We shall discuss our conventions for transcribing the movements of the blockies later.

Taking Turns at Talk

Turn taking is a basic and obvious feature of the organization of talk. Some aspects of how turn taking is managed by participants in ordinary conversation are analysed by Sacks, Schegloff and Jefferson [14] who propose what they call a 'simplest systematics' by means of which participants manage the exchange of speakers from turn to turn. In the analysis of turn taking, a basic distinction can be made between (i) turns which select who is next to speak by, for example, addressing a question (ahh lennart can you hear us?) or request (go on dave) to a specific, perhaps explicitly named, participant and (ii) turns which do not contain next-selecting components:

```
AB:     <mouth click> .hhh (2.2) <mouth click> .hhh-woahruh
        i'll go next (.) then if no one else is speaking.
        (0.6) uh i'm adrian bullock also from the
        university of nottingham.
```

In AB's turn here, it is AB who selects himself to speak, indeed he does so quite explicitly noting that 'self-selection' is exactly what he is doing (i'll go next). AB's turn itself contains no components which project who is next to speak after him. He introduces himself and then stops. At such moments, it is open for the other participants to either select themselves as next-to-speak or, for that matter, for AB to continue speaking prolonging his current turn.

Next Selected by Self

Our preliminary observations suggested to us that turn taking was often problematic in the virtual meeting. The transcript was marked by many long silences as participants seemed to wait for each other to say things. However, a closer inspection reveals that these silences are most prevalent when speakers have to select themselves as next-to-speak in the absence of any prior turn with next-selecting components. This is not to say that all such turn transitions break down. Rather it is to claim that the disfluencies in speech exchange are notably concentrated at transitions where speakers have to self-select. The following examples (from the early stages of the meeting where SB has invited participants to introduce themselves) reveal problems in speaker switches of this sort.

Example 1

```
SB:     someone else's turn. (1.2) thanks lennart (how)
        very eloquent. (1.2) maybe (eloquent.)
(12.0)
CG:     i'll 'ave a go then.
(1.2)
SB:     yeah please do.
(1.4)
CG:     i'm chris greenhalgh (0.4) also at nottingham (0.8)
        an::d this wonderful VR system-MASSIVE-that-we're-
        using is wot i writ.
```

Example 2

```
SB:     <laughter> how much does it cost?
CG:     oo to you nothing. bargain at double the price.
(1.0)
SB:     excellent.
(3.0)
AB:     <mouth click> .hhh (2.2) <mouth click> .hhh-woahruh
        i'll go next (.) then if no one else is speaking.
        (0.6) uh i'm adrian bullock also from the
        university of nottingham.
```

Example 3

```
SB:     anyone else?
(1.2)
AC:     {uh uh hello s-s-} can you hear me?
        [ (.)  ]=anyone? [ (.) ]=err
SB:     [ yeah=]         [ yea=]
AC:     it's andy at lancaster.
```

Example 4

```
(1.2)
( ):    (.hhh)
(4.0)
SB:     anyone else?
(2.8)
JB:     huhlow::. i'm john {b}owers from manchester
        {uni}versity currently v{i}sit{in}g sics. (0.8) i'm
        interes{ted in} lots-of stuff (0.4) {and i'm a
        c}apricorn.
SB:     <laughter>
```

In Examples 1, 3 and 4, SB does not explicitly name who is next to introduce themselves. Rather he invites contributions by means of anyone else? (Examples 3 and 4) or someone else's turn (Example 1), leaving it up to whoever is next to speak to select themselves. Such components are followed by quite lengthy silences. Indeed, in Example 1, after just over a second's silence, SB engages in some 'side talk' thanking LF in an ironically humorous fashion for his prior self-introduction. Another twelve seconds of silence follows before CG starts talking. In Example 2, SB and CG exchange some humorous remarks before SB utters excellent which can be heard as closing his exchange with CG. The three second pause that follows is then broken by AB selecting himself. In all of these examples, speakers only self-select after quite lengthy silences and with much preparatory activity (e.g. mouth clicks, in-breaths, protracted sounds, stammerings and so forth) or, as in Example 1, a minimal turn from CG (i'll 'ave a go then) which requires confirmation from SB (yeah please do) before CG continues.

This preparatory activity is often quite exaggerated as in Example 2 where a mouth click and an audible in-breath are heard from AB and then, after a pause of just over two seconds, there follows a second mouth click, another audible in-breath running into a vocalization transcribed as woahruh before AB explicitly self-selects. The interactional significance of such preparatory activity is worth noting. Audible in-breaths and the rest do not explicitly or fully claim a turn at talk in and of themselves. They could be interrupted by another participant immediately launching into a turn without such activity. Accordingly, such preparatory activity displays a participant's *readiness* to contribute as next-to-speak, without disqualifying others. Indeed, in Example 2, even *after* he self-selects, AB pauses very briefly (notated by (.)) after i'll go next and for about six tenths of a second after then if no one else is speaking. These are further junctures where another participant could have self-selected and claimed the floor to introduce themselves ahead of AB. These features of the examples suggest that self-selected turns are managed with considerable care by speakers - a matter borne out by the fact that AB in Example 2 is explicitly attentive to the possibility that others may speak ahead of him. The exaggeration of preparatory components in the virtual meeting is, we suggest, a means for managing turn taking at moments which can be problematic where, for example, in the absence of explicit next-selection, a number of speakers could start to speak simultaneously. Indeed, Examples 5 and 6 suggest that simultaneous self-selected turns are problematic for the smooth conduct of the virtual meeting and that the presence of audio distortion makes them especially hard to manage.

Example 5

```
(3.0)
SB:     [ (   '
JB:     [ (       )(fahlén)
(3.7)
LF:     okay. errm. (2.5) we have err (.) umm (.) a rather
        a serious echo here.
```

Example 6

```
(1.8)
LF:     {i think we ermm} (0.5)
KJ:     [ {(let's put) that upon} the agenda ] (1.0)
LF:     [ {(                             )} ] {uh }
KJ:     [ (       ) ]
LF:     [ {(        ] ) some kind of uh distortion (.) uhhhm
        (0.5) originating at K T H. you should probably
        lower yer input levels a bit.}
(1.0)
KJ:     okay i'll try.
```

In Example 5, after a three second silence, SB and JB start speaking together. JB's speech continues after SB's but neither of their turns are taken up by any other participant, rather the talk dies away into a silence of nearly four seconds before LF complains about the audio quality. In Example 6, KJ and LF talk together and then after LF utters `uh` while KJ falls silent, they both restart together again with LF's complaints about the audio again heard after KJ's talk finishes. In cases like these, the overlaps leave unfinished interactional business with one or both overlapping turns failing to be taken up by others in subsequent talk. The overlaps in Examples 5 and 6 are hard to transcribe for the precise reason that the voices tend to mask each other and this is exacerbated by the poor audio quality LF complains about. Not only do they mask each other so as to make transcription difficult, they interfere so as to make it hard for participants themselves to hear the talk and tease apart overlapping contributions. We suggest that it is because of the problems involved in the management of overlaps of turns that self-selected turns often manifest the preparatory activity we have noted.

Note again the presence of various artifacts (e.g. distortion) in JB's talk in Example 4. In the next example, this is particularly intense. SB does not hear DE's `eh:::m:. (0.5) yuh` as preparatory to a turn at all!

Example 7

```
(2.0)
SB:     okay-is there any shy: person who hasn't spoken
        yet?
(3.0)
DE:     {eh:::m:.} (1.5) {yuh}
SB:     i think that's everyone.=
DE:     ={ouh}=
LF:     =steve-d'yuh-think-i think you could probably
        [ err (0.9) ] raise your levels a bit?
DE:     [ {hallo::?} ]
SB:     who me? maybe.=
DE:     ={huhlo?}
AB:     <mouth click> yeah go on dave.
DE:     (2.5) {right. um. [ (.)  ] (first)ly can you hear
        me:?}=
LF:                       [ (   ) ]
        =you're much quieter [ (   )
AB:                          [ just about.
(2.8)
SB:     hi the[re.
AB:           [{ } breaking up (.) but you can just about
        make it out.
(0.8)
( ):    um.
(2.0)
DE:     {{(okay)}} (1.6) {{{(hiya (.) steve)(    [
        [
                [              )}}}
JB:                                              [<laughter>
SB:     [ ah ha. um.
AB:             [nah.
AB:     nah-that's unintelligible.
```

This example suggests the problems in coordinating speaker switches when at least one participant has a considerably degraded signal may be profound. It also further underlines the point we have been making about difficulties with self-selection and that these may be intensified when one's signal is poor. Indeed, very few of DE's turns at talk are brought off in Example 7 without some overlap or interruption from the other participants.

Interestingly, DE's first attempt to claim a self-selected turn at talk in this example manifests very similar preparatory features to those we have already seen in Examples 1 to 4. It is unsuccessful presumably because SB does not hear them as having this significance or as being any different from the artifacts, pops and crackles and other background noises that can be heard on the audio channel. DE having the poorest audio connection is doubly disadvantaged: first in that his speech is easily masked by others in overlap, secondly in that his routine attempts to anticipate the problems of overlap (e.g. protracting an `ehm` or uttering a preparatory `yup`) are not heard as such!

It is important to emphasise that the difficulties with turn taking we have noted cannot simply be reduced to problems with audio quality. We observe substantial silences in examples where there are no (Examples 1 and 2) or few (Examples 3 and 4) audio problems. Indeed the audio connections within the site accommodating SB, CG and AB were of good quality throughout the meeting, yet these provide some of the most notable silences in our transcripts. Hence we argue that the problems of self-selection are exacerbated by but not solely attributable to poor audio quality.

The lengthy silences before speaker-switches, we suggest, reflect problems due to managing self-selection with minimal embodiments which have restricted gestural abilities. In this regard, it is of interest that DE does not attempt to compensate for interactional difficulties by any form of virtual gesture or change of body orientation at any moment in Example 7. The embodiments are very rarely used concurrently to aid speakers in designing their own turns or in eliciting turns from others at such moments (in contrast to the use of gesture and body movement in ordinary co-present conversation, see [7, 11], or, for that matter, as reported in the videoconferencing literature, see [16]). This is a point we shall return to.

Next Selected by Prior Speaker

In contrast to the problems we have noted at moments where speakers have to self-select to claim a turn at talk, turn transitions are much smoother where the identity of the next person to speak is clear either because they have been explicitly named or due to some other contextual feature. In Example 8, AB gives JB instruction as to how to use the mouse button after he has been struggling to pass through a gateway to another virtual world. Similarly, in Example 9 KJ and SB discuss two different modes for 'focus' a technical feature of the MASSIVE system. Finally, in Example 10 SB notices the presence of LF and starts a discussion about the organization of a conference panel.

Example 8

AB: (you can use your right mouse button for lateral) translations john.
JB: i can do what?
AB: use your right mouse button (.) in the middle of the screen just to move you side ways.
<JB moves sideways>
AB: wrong way.
SB: oh he's gone. <through the gateway>

Example 9

(KJ): ( )
SB: (did you) change focus?
(0.5)
KJ: so what is the difference between narrow and directed
SB: directed is a sort of cone (.) in front of you erm i can't remember the angle it goes out to. narrow is like a really thin tube
(0.5)
KJ: ok
(0.5)
SB: you can try this thing out in the audio gallery and (you'll) probably notice the effect fairly well
KJ: alright

Example 10

SB: oh there you are. ok so w-what happened about this panel thing what's the (scam)?
LF: umm nothing much but erm we're still missing erm erm: the erm er spatial awareness versus (( )) versus media spaces kind of panel ya?
SB: arham are we liable t-to do one of these?
LF: ya <conversation between SB and LF continues for nearly a minute with many turns readily exchanged>

In all these examples, the speech exchange between participants is fluent and not marked by the hesitations, overlaps and other perturbations noted before. In each of them, though, who is next to speak is clear either as a result of explicit naming or the identification of 'you' even if several other parties are present. When speaker switches can be governed in this way, fluent conversations can occur between two parties in the virtual environment. (It should be noted that these examples involve fluent exchanges between people at distant sites: SB and AB are in Nottingham, the others in Stockholm. This suggest that the problems we have documented are interactional and not just due solely to technical reasons like network delays which were rarely notable in the meeting.)

Interpreting Silences and Absences

We have suggested that there are differences between turn transitions where the prior speaker has selected who is next to speak (these are carried off relatively fluently) and those where speakers have to self-select (these are the sites of the main breakdowns of fluency in the transcript). As noted by Sacks et al. [14], these different transition types give rise to differences in the significance of silences in talk. When the prior speaker has selected who is next-to-speak, any silence after next-selection is *attributable.* That is, it is 'owned by' the person who has been designated as next to speak. It is *their* silence and their next speech action is *noticeably absent.* Depending on the circumstances, a continued silence after next has been explicitly selected may licence inferences about the person who is remaining silent. For example, in a law court, persistent silence under cross examination may lead to suspicions of guilt or other culpability. On the other hand, when the prior speaker has not selected who is next-to-speak, such attributions are not standardly available and the silence is not uniquely 'owned'.

When conversations are technically mediated, technical failure can be inferred as a source of attributable silence. Indeed, in the data we have, technical failure (rather than some socially significant attribution like evasiveness or rudeness) is *invariably* first considered as accounting for an attributable silence. In Example 11, SB first asks a question about whether another meeting is intended. AB replies to this saying that a future meeting should use the DIVE system. SB continues by asking a question which is hearably directed at two of the current meeting's members who are also developers of DIVE. However, this receives no reply and after a one second silence, SB explicitly names (and aligns his embodiment in the virtual world so as to face) the two the question is addressed to. Again, a long silence follows and AB checks on LF's ability to hear. Another long silence: whereupon SB notices and brings to the attention of others that KJ has typed a message in the text window saying he cannot hear anything. The point of this example is that when next-to-speak has been explicitly selected and no reply is heard, this is interpreted here as arising from an inability to hear due to an audio failure.

Example 11

SB: are we going to have another one of these?
AB: we ought to have one with dive.
SB: yer (0.5) what's-what's the status of that stuff? (1.0) he says looking at lennart and kai.
(5.0)
AB: ah:: lennart can you hear us?
(5.0)
SB: (hi) if you look at the text window (.) kai says he's not hearing anything

Example 12

AB: can you hear me kai? (2.5) hello?
CG: he may be a corpse now. he's disappeared off my text (as far as)

Similarly, in Example 12 AB's repeated failure to elicit a reply from KJ is accounted for by CG. Amongst the VR research groups involved in this meeting 'corpse' is used to refer to an embodiment which lingers in the virtual world even though the local system which manages interaction with it (in this case the interface client running on KJ's machine) may have crashed or become disconnected. In both examples, noticeably absent 'seconds' in an 'adjacency pair' [14] like question-answer are first interpreted as indexing *technical problems and not accountable social behaviour* (e.g. rudeness etc) on the part of whoever has been selected to speak. In contrast, the silences in Examples 1 to 4 where SB did not select who was next to speak, are not uniquely attributable and hence, if anyone does happen to have audio connection or other technical problems, they will pass unnoticed and possibly for some time to follow. To put this point another way, silence can be hard to interpret and technical problems can be difficult to identify, even those originating from one's own local environment. A local failure can pass unnoticed for some time simply because an appropriate moment for the problem to be identified does not occur in the interaction. We shall return to the design implications of this in discussion at the end of this paper.

Embodiment, Talk and Movement

How are the embodiments used by participants in the virtual meeting and how are their movements coordinated with concurrent talk? A first observation is that participants do move the embodiments around to get a better view of those they wish to interact with or attend to. The provision of an audio channel does not *require* them to do so in order to speak to each other, but that we have examples of people navigating the embodiments in this way suggests that, in a simple sense, interactants are seeking to become 'face engaged' [6] when exchanging talk. Accordingly, the embodiments do seem to have a social *interactional* role and not merely a role in determining the view an individual has of the virtual world. Note how SB and LF establish contact in Example 13 before starting a lengthy exchange.

Example 13

```
SB:      (    ) lennart
LF:      yar (steve)
SB:      oh what happened about um the the panel for ecscw?
(LF):    (    )
SB:      c-could you turn (the) mic up a bit?
LF:      (    )
SB:      (    ) where has he gone lennart?
(2.0)
LF:      ar where's steve?
SB:      hi i'm i'm here behind kai i think
LF:      ye
(4.0)
<LF and SB move around the environment and finally turn to
face each other>
SB:      oh there you are. <continues as Example 10>
```

Do we have evidence from the recordings of the virtual meeting of any more subtle uses of virtual body movements to accompany ongoing interaction? To examine this, we first consider whether body movements exist in the virtual world as an accompaniment to one's own talk and then look at whether participants are able to coordinate their movements with those of others and their talk.

We remarked above that participants seem to rarely use virtual body movements to aid the design of their own turns, even when constructing turns by means of talk alone is problematic (as in Example 7). Indeed, it is rather rare in the virtual meetings we have studied for people to complement their own turns at talk with any concurrent movement of their embodiment. This may not strike one as surprising as talking down a potentially troublesome audio channel may be difficult enough without having to engage in simultaneous mouse movements to get one's embodiment to move! However, it presents a stark contrast with ordinary talk where a whole array of body and facial movements, gazings and changes in overall deportment can accompany and aid the design of turns at talk [7, 11]. Example 14 transcribes the body movement from Example 1. Here, CG raises and lowers the ears on his embodiment. These gestures span his breaking of the long silence we have already noted and aid the construction of his self-selected turn. This is however the only example we have yet found of gesture being used to aid the design of a speaker's concurrent turn. (It also introduces our transcript conventions for showing movement. The beginning and end of the movement are shown underneath the concurrent talk and described in italics on a line after that.)

Example 14

```
<The virtual body movements in Example 1>
         ( 12.0 )
CG:           ¶-
CG:      raises both ears

CG:      i'll 'ave a go then.
CG:      ------¶
CG:      and lowers them
```

While we have few examples of participants designing their own turns with the aid of some movement from the virtual embodiment, mutually coordinated movements between participants and movements coordinated with the speech of others are more commonly found in our data. Consider Example 15 which transcribes the body movements of a number of participants while LF is introducing himself to the meeting. We transcribe on the spot turnings about with ∞----∞ the length and the position of the symbol corresponding to the analogous position in the talk above it. We transcribe translation movements (xyz-displacements) with ^-----^. A verbal description of each movement is given just below each movement-transcription. A period (.) at the beginning of a line is used to match up lines of transcribed movement where no body movement occurred with the corresponding line of talk.

It is notoriously difficult to adequately and clearly transcribe body movement [8, 11] but we hope our conventions will become clear as we now explicate this example. Early in the example, AC turns towards AB just while LF utters `fahlén`. He then stays facing AB for the rest of LF's turn. A 0.6 second pause follows, at the very start of which AC begins to turn back towards SB, continuing this movement over a brief `uh hum` from SB and stopping the movement when LF begins to hesitate (`er:`) in his next turn. For his part, reciprocally, AB turns towards AC, again beginning the movement at a hesitancy in LF's turn (the initial `uhm:`). Immediately once AC has finished turning back towards SB and started to move away from the group, AB also turns back towards SB, starting this movement during LF's `er:`. AB makes a further movement towards SB while (again) LF is hesitating and pausing with `er:m (1.2)`. SB then makes a movement towards LF which starts during a 0.6 second pause in LF's talk. Following the start of SB's movement, LF continues talking with `and um:: i've been involved in these things for a long time`. When LF begins to utter `for a long time`, SB reciprocates AB's slightly earlier turn towards SB, before finally returning towards LF, initiating this movement again during a one second pause in LF's talk.

Example 15

```
<SB is facing the others who are looking towards him. After
some side-talk with LF, SB invites LF to introduce himself>
LF:      (1.6) um: (2.0) i'm um (.) lennart fahlén from the
         swedish institute of computer science
AC:                                              ∞----∞

AC:      turns to face AB
```

```
            ( 0.6 )
AC:         ∞------
AC:         turns to face SB
SB:         uh hum=
AC:         -------
AC:         continues turning
LF:                =uhm: (1.0) and er: in my spare time i try:
            to manage this (     ) virtual reality group in
            here-at er:m (1.2) sics as it's called (0.6) and
            um:: i've been involved in these things for a long
            time (1.0) so i'm starting to (         ) (1.0)
            that's very apparent i think
AC:         ---------------------∞ ^----------------------
            ---------------------------------------------
            ------------^ ∞------∞
            .
            .
            .
AC:         finishes turning to face SB then backs away from
            the rest of the group then turns towards AB
AB:                 ∞---------∞       ∞---------------------
            ---------∞
                       ∞--∞
            .
            .
            .
AB:         turns towards AC then returns to face SB then turns
            further towards the rest of the group
SB:         .
            .
                                                      ^-----
            -^                                       ∞--------
            ------------∞                             ∞---
            -------------------∞
SB:         moves towards LF then turns towards AB and then
            turns back towards LF
```

We suggest that this example on close examination compellingly shows *exchanges* of movement between first AC and AB and then AB and SB during LF's introduction of himself. To the extent that the blockies can exchange glances at each other, this is what they are doing here (even though for a blockie a 'glance' involves a whole body movement!). Thus, participants do seem to be able to use the blockies to enter into coordinated movements with one another. The blockies have an *interactional* significance and are not merely navigation devices. What is more these virtual body movements seem to be very precisely coordinated with LF's ongoing talk. It is in the pauses and hesitations in LF's talk that we see the majority of the movements initiated. Thus, strikingly, participants seem to be able to coordinate movements with each other while interleaving this with the talk of a 'third party'. It is also noticeable that SB's approach to LF initiated during a 0.6 second pause provokes LF to further add to his turn of self-introduction. In all these respects, we are witnessing residual though noticeable phenomena reminiscent of the coordination of action in ordinarily embodied conversation. In short, even if only to a limited extent, participants do seem to be able use the blockies in ways derivative from their ordinary interactional competencies.

DISCUSSION

We owe it to Heath et al. [12] to have drawn our attention to the following quote from a 1972 lecture of Harvey Sacks: "The technical apparatus [Sacks had in mind the telephone] is, then, being made at home with the rest of our world. And that's a thing that's routinely being done, and it's the source for the failures of technocratic dreams that if only we introduced some fantastic new communication machine the world will be transformed. What happens is that the object is made at home in the world that has whatever organisation it already has". We feel that our analyses of talk in virtual environments clearly exemplify Sacks' intuition that the new and technologically unfamiliar is often made to be 'at home' with our familiar world. If ever there were technocratic dreams, they have been thoroughly invested in VR! But what we see is the ordinary apparatus of conversation and the social interactional coordination of body movements being moulded and adapted to what the virtual environment affords so that participants can carry on as best they can with their business at hand.

Thus, we see systematic ways in which participants try to resolve or anticipate turn-taking problems, the elementary coordination of body movements between participants, the coordination of movements with ongoing speech, the utilisation of the bodies to engage others and initiate talk, amongst other phenomena. While, of course, we have concentrated on data from just one virtual meeting and it must be acknowledged that more meetings and more examples are required to develop yet more convincing generalisations, it is fascinating that what we have noted so far in the virtual world is in some way familiar.

Though familiar, this is not to say that improvements should not be made to systems such as MASSIVE to enhance their abilities to support multi-party collaborative activity in a virtual environment. Our interaction analytic techniques have been able to highlight problems, some of which may be amenable to technical solution or assistance. Let us discuss three classes of possibilities.

(1) We noted that it is possible for many technical failures to pass unnoticed for some time, simply because those moments which make them clear (a sufferer of technical failures being selected as next-to-speak, yet not responding) may not have arisen in the conduct of the meeting. This suggests to us that CVEs should support *local troubleshooting* because it may be very hard to bring to the attention of *others* that one is experiencing a local failure. This has implications for the overall distributed architecture that a system might exploit. An architecture must be not only robust in the face of local failure but it must also support graceful distributed recovery from local failures. A local failure must be remediable *at that site* and not require initiation from a remote site where participants may be unaware of the failure. Additionally, it should be possible to bring about such recovery by means within the expertise of any participant. These are actually quite demanding requirements and we believe they follow from our observations of how the structure of technically-mediated social interaction may lead to problems identifying ongoing failures in distributed systems such as MASSIVE.

(2) The overall design of virtual worlds should be considered in terms of how they afford social interaction and not just in terms, say, of their navigability, capability for presenting masses of information, or their thrilling aesthetics. The kinds of objects that we insert into a virtual world should be selected and designed with social interaction in mind. For example, a meeting table may be a simple device for people to gather around while affording them means for coordinating their talk, views of each other and mutual bodily orientation. Indeed, such a device may have aided our participants in solving some (not all) of

their turn-taking problems by suggesting a 'round the table' sequence for talk. Quite simple devices (e.g. a table as polygon on the base plane) may often be the most important from a social interactional standpoint yet their inclusion in the virtual world is easy to forget. Although the MASSIVE system can support a variety of 'meeting furniture', only a noticeboard was included on this occasion.

(3) While the blockies do afford various *social* interactional phenomena (and are not *merely* navigational aids or simple interface devices), it is worth reminding ourselves of the subtlety of interaction and participation which is much more readily possible with a real human body. The hands, the arms, the head, the neck, the torso permit a number of different orientations with respect to each other as well as with respect to co-interactants' bodies. In this way, we can glance without moving our heads, or turn our heads without moving the rest of our bodies.

Importantly, the coordinated flexibility of our eyes and heads enable us to look around without turning our backs on anyone. This, together with all the other kinds of embodied distinctions which are available for investing with interactional significance, is not available to the blockies. The only way for a blockie to 'glance' is by changing its whole bodily orientation. Accordingly, the blockies are considerably constrained in *just how* they can display their attentiveness to others and also in *just how* they can gesture or engage in whole body movements to aid the design of their own turns or to partake in a finely co-ordinated stream of talk. What perhaps is remarkable is that the minimal embodiments offer any interactional affordances at all. Nevertheless, introducing articulations (in the physical sense!) to the embodiments does seem to be worthwhile: e.g. so that a 'looking-around' can be distinguished from a 'turning-away'. Current VR systems essentially treat action in a virtual world as a matter of navigation or object manipulation. However, in CVEs where participants are interacting with one another, perhaps one should consider the direct support of actions of a 'higher-order' than mere movement, actions of *social interactional* significance (like approaches, turnings, glances and maybe some under collaborative control like 'form a circle' and so forth). In future work, we wish to study whether such higher-order actions can be sensibly added to the repertoire of interaction techniques available to the blockies and participants who 'inhabit' them. In this way, we may also be able to help users employ gestures to aid the concurrent construction of their turns - something which is currently problematic.

Of course, adding any further complexity to the blockies has to be reckoned with in the light of technical issues such as computational and network-transmission performance. We feel, though, that a viable and systematic research strategy for developing useful CVEs is to incrementally add further sophistication to very simple embodiments *as and when* analysis reveals that it is called for in the support of social interaction. Interestingly, this goes against the grain of many VR research trajectories which are devoted towards photorealistic body renderings and whole body movement detection. But, unless the social interactional significance of the body is understood, such developments may be not only unduly computationally expensive (especially when one considers distributed collaborative VR systems) but also lacking in social scientific motivation.

ACKNOWLEDGEMENTS

This research was supported by COMIC (Esprit BRA 6225) and VirtuOsi (DTI/EPSRC Initiative in CSCW).

REFERENCES

1. Benford, S., Bowers, J., Fahlén, L., Greenhalgh, C. & Snowdon, D. User Embodiment in Collaborative Virtual Environments, in *Proc. CHI'95*, ACM Press, 1995.
2. Benford, S., Bowers, J., Fahlén, L., Mariani, J. & Rodden, T. Supporting Co-operative Work in Virtual Environments. *The Computer Journal*, 37, 8 (1994), 653-668.
3. Bowers, J. & Churcher, J. Local and global structuring of computer mediated communication. In *Proc. CSCW '88*. ACM Press, 1988.
4. Bowers, J. & Pycock, J. Talking through design. In *Proc. CHI'94*, ACM Press, 1994.
5. Gaver, W. The Affordances of Media Spaces for Collaboration, in *Proc. CSCW'92*, ACM Press, 1992.
6. Goffman, E. *Forms of Talk.* Blackwell, Oxford, 1981.
7. Goodwin, C. *Conversational Organization.* Academic Press, New York, 1981.
8. Greatbatch, D., Luff, P., Heath, C. & Campion, P. Interpersonal communication and human computer interaction, *Interacting with Computers*, 5 (1993), 193-216.
9. Greenhalgh, C. and Benford, S. MASSIVE: A Virtual Reality System for Tele-conferencing, to appear in *ACM Transactions on Computer Human Interfaces.*
10. Heath, C. & Luff, P. Collaboration and control. *CSCW*, 1 (1992), 69-94.
11. Heath, C. *Speech and body movement in medical interaction.* CUP, Cambridge, 1985.
12. Heath, C., Luff, P. & Sellen, A. Reconsidering the virtual workplace, in *Proc. ECSCW'95*, Kluwer, 1995.
13. Presence. Special Issue on Simulator Sickness, *Presence*, 1.3 (1992).
14. Sacks, H., Schegloff, E. & Jefferson, G. A simplest systematics for the organization of turn-taking in conversation. *Language*, 50 (1974), 696-735.
15. Slater, M. & Usoh, M. Representations Systems, Perceptual Position and Presence in Immersive Virtual Environments. *Presence*, 2.3 (1994), 221-234.
16. Tang, J. & Issacs, E. Why do users like video? *CSCW*, 1 (1993), 163-196.

Emacspeak –A Speech Interface

T. V. Raman
Cambridge Research Lab
Digital Equipment Corp.
Bldg 650, One Kendall Square
Cambridge MA 02139
E-mail: ⟨raman@crl.dec.com⟩
Voice-mail: 1 (617) 692-7637
Fax: 1 (617) 692-6650

Abstract

Screen-readers —computer software that enables a visually impaired user to read the contents of a visual display— have been available for more than a decade. Screen-readers are separate from the user application. Consequently, they have little or no contextual information about the contents of the display. The author has used traditional screen-reading applications for the last five years. The design of the speech-enabling approach described here has been implemented in Emacspeak to overcome many of the shortcomings he has encountered with traditional screen-readers.

The approach used by Emacspeak is very different from that of traditional screen-readers. Screen-readers allow the user to listen to the contents appearing in different parts of the display; but the user is entirely responsible for building a mental model of the visual display in order to interpret what an application is trying to convey. Emacspeak, on the other hand, does not speak the screen. Instead, applications provide both visual and speech feedback, and the speech feedback is designed to be sufficient by itself.

This approach reduces cognitive load on the user and is relevant to providing general spoken access to information. Producing spoken output from *within* the application, rather than speaking the visually displayed information, vastly improves the quality of the spoken feedback. Thus, an application can *display* its results in a visually pleasing manner; the *speech-enabling* component renders the *same* in an aurally pleasing way.

Keywords: Speech Interface, Direct Access, Spoken Feedback, Audio Formatting, Speech as a first-class I/O medium.

Introduction

A screen-reader is a computer application designed to provide spoken feedback to a visually impaired user. Screen-readers have been available since the mid-80's. During the 80's, such applications relied on the character representation of the contents of the screen to produce the spoken feedback. The advent of bitmap displays led to a complete breakdown of this approach, since the contents of the screen were now light and dark pixels. A significant amount of research and development has been carried out to overcome this problem and provide speech-access to the Graphical User Interface (GUI).

The best and perhaps the most complete speech access system to the GUI is Screenreader/2 (ScreenReader For OS/2) developed by Dr. Jim Thatcher at the IBM Watson Research Center [Tha94]. This package provides robust spoken access to applications under the OS2 Presentation Manager and Windows 3.1. Commercial packages for Microsoft Windows 3.1 provide varying levels of spoken access to the GUI. The Mercator project [ME92, WKES94, MW94, Myn94] has focused on providing spoken access to the X-Windows system.

A common feature of traditional DOS-based screen-readers and speech access packages to the GUI is their attempt to convey the contents of the visual display via speech. In fact, a significant amount of the development effort required to design speech-access packages to the GUI has concentrated on building up robust *off-screen models* —a data structure that represents the contents of the GUI's visual display. Construction of such an off-screen model helps screen-readers regain the ground they lost due to the advent of graphical displays. However, the nature of spoken feedback provided does not change.

Shortcomings Of Reading The Screen

Screen-readers have helped open up the world of computing to visually impaired users[1]. However, the spoken interface they provide leaves a lot to be desired.

The primary shortcoming with such interfaces is their

[1] The author has used these for the last five years.

inability to convey the structure present in visually displayed information. Since the screen-reading application has only the contents of the visual display to examine, it conveys little or no contextual information about what is being displayed. Put another way:

> A Screen-reader speaks *what* is on the screen without conveying *why* it is there.

As a consequence, accessing applications that display highly structured output in a visually pleasing manner with screen-readers is cumbersome.

Here is a simple example to illustrate the above statement. A typical calendar display is made up of a table showing the days of the week. This information is visually laid out to allow the eye to quickly *see* what day a particular date of the month falls on. Thus, given the display shown in Fig. 1, it is easy to answer the question "What day is it today?". When this same *display* is

Jan 1995

S	M	T	W	Th	F	Sa
1	2	3	4	5	6	7
8	9	10	11	12	13	14
15	16	17	18	19	20	21
22	23	24	25	26	27	28
29	30	31				

Figure 1: A Typical Calendar Application

accessed with a screen-reader, the user *hears* the entire contents of the table Figure 1 on page spoken aloud. This results in the following set of meaningless utterances:

> pipe pipe 1 pipe 2 pipe 3 pipe 4 pipe 5 pipe 6 pipe 7 pipe pipe ... pipe pipe 29 pipe 30 pipe 31 pipe pipe pipe pipe pipe pipe

Alternatively, the characters under the application cursor can be spoken. In the case of Fig. 1, the listener would hear the system say "one". To answer the question "What day is it today?" the user has to first build a mental representation of the visual display, and then navigate around the screen, examining the contents that appear in the same screen column as the **1** in order to infer the fact that the date is Sunday, January 1, 1995.

Screen-readers for both character-cell and graphical displays suffer from this shortcoming. This is a consequence of trying to *read* the screen instead of providing true spoken feedback. The rest of this paper describes Emacspeak, an interface that treats speech as a first-class output medium. Screen-readers speak the screen contents after the application has displayed its results; Emacspeak integrates spoken feedback into the application itself. This tight integration between the spoken output and the user application enables Emacspeak to provide rich, context-sensitive spoken feedback. As a case in point, when using the calendar application, the user hears the current date as Sunday, January 1, 1995. For related work in integrating speech as a first-class I/O medium into general user applications, see [YLM95].

We conclude this introduction by pointing out that visual layout plays an important role in cuing the reader to information structure. Such visual cues reduce cognitive load by allowing the perceptual system to perceive the inherent structure present in the information, thereby freeing the cognitive system to process the information. Spoken feedback produced from the visual layout proves difficult to understand because many of the structural cues are lost; to make things worse, other structural cues turn into *noise* (the "pipe pipe ..." above is a case in point). This results in the listener having to spend a large number of cognitive cycles in trying to parse the spoken utterance, making understanding the information considerably harder. Speaking the information in an aurally pleasing manner alleviates this burden, leading to better aural comprehension.

A Different Approach

We tightly integrate spoken output with the user application. Such tight integration allows the functions providing spoken feedback direct access to the application context. Thus, in the case of the calendar example shown in Fig. 1, the speech feedback routines can access the runtime environment of the calendar application to find out that the current date is Sunday, January 1, 1995 instead of trying to guess this from the visual presentation of the calendar.

Thus, using speech as a first-class output medium provides *direct access* to the information displayed by an application —traditional screen-readers provide what can at best be described as *indirect* access.

Motivation

Every computer application (big or small) can be characterized as having the following structure:

- Accept user input
- Compute on the data
- Display results of the computation

Human computer interaction focuses on the first and third of these stages. Traditional WIMP interfaces[2] have assumed a purely visual interaction; applications designed for such interfaces naturally optimize their displays to this mode of interaction.

However, visual layout is not optimal for spoken interaction as evinced by the calendar application (See Section). By having the user interface (UI) components

[2] Windows, Icons, Mouse, and Pointer

of the application communicate directly with the speech subsystem, Emacspeak produces more *usable* output. Contrast this with the screen-reading paradigm, where spoken output is produced by a program that is *unaware of* and *separate from* the user application.

Implementation

We have motivated the design of Emacspeak with the help of the calendar example. However, Emacspeak is much more than a simple talking calendar; it extends all of GNU Emacs to provide full spoken feedback. The author uses Emacspeak on his Alpha AXP[3] workstation running Digital UNIX and on his laptop running Linux. Emacspeak has been made available on the Internet[4] and is currently being used by an increasing number of Digital's customers.

This paper will not go into implementation details —our purpose is to highlight the novel interface provided by Emacspeak. For the sake of completeness, here is a brief sketch of how the system is implemented.

Emacspeak consists of a core speech module that provides basic speech services to the rest of the system, e.g., functions that speak characters, words and lines. The *advice* facility of Emacs Lisp is used to integrate the speech feedback provided by these functions into Emacs. This facility allows us to specify program fragments that are to be run either before, after, or around any function. Since the user interface level of GNU Emacs is implemented entirely in Emacs Lisp, the functions making up this interface can be *advised* to speak. The primary advantage of this approach is that we have been able to speech-enable all of GNU Emacs —a large system— without modifying a single line of source code from the original Emacs distribution.

We conclude this sketch with an example. Function **next-line** implements movement of the editing cursor to the next line in GNU Emacs. Emacspeak provides the following *advice* to this function:

```
(defadvice next-line (after emacspeak )
  "Speak the line you moved to."
  (when (interactive-p)
    (emacspeak-speak-line )))
```

This advice specifies that if function **next-line** is called *interactively* (As the result of the user pressing a key.) then function **emacspeak-speak-line** should be called **after next-line** has done its work.

The next section Section gives examples of the spoken interaction provided by Emacspeak when performing several day-to-day computing tasks. All of the facilities described are implemented using the model described above.

Examples Of Common Computing Tasks

This section describes the user interface provided by Emacspeak when performing common-place computing tasks like editing and proof-reading, surfing the WWW, reading and replying to electronic mail and Usenet news. This paper description suffers from the natural shortcoming of elucidating in print what is essentially aural. Here are some features of the spoken feedback that are common to the different interaction scenarios:

- Speech output is always interruptible. Actions causing new information to be spoken first interrupt any ongoing output.
- Emacspeak provides a *voice-lock* facility that permits association of syntactic units of text with different voices. This is a powerful method of conveying structure succinctly and was first described in [Ram94]. Audio Formatting is used to aurally set apart different syntactic units, for example, highlight regions of text.
- Emacspeak uses auditory icons [SMG90, BGB88, Gav93, BGP93, JSBG86] —short snippets of sounds (under 0.25–0.5 seconds to cue common events such as *selecting*, *opening* and *closing* an object. Used consistently throughout the interface, these cues speed up user interaction —an experienced user can often continue to the next task when an aural cue[5] is heard without waiting for the spoken confirmation.

Editing Documents

Emacspeak speaks each character as it is typed. Pressing the space-bar causes the previous word to be spoken. Cursoring through a file speaks each line; speech is interrupted if the cursor is moved while a line is being spoken. This allows the user to efficiently browse files. All of the standard Emacs navigation commands, e.g., move to the next paragraph, skip this S-expression, give appropriate auditory feedback.

Emacs' knowledge of the syntax of what is being edited is used to advantage in enabling sophisticated navigation. For instance, the user can move across *statements* when browsing program source code. When navigating through a file of C code, the user gets relevant spoken feedback that conveys the structure of the program. Different syntactic units are spoken in different voices to increase the band-width of aural communication. In addition, the user can have the *semantics* of a line of source code spoken upon request. Thus, when the

[3] For the first time in five years, I can sit in front of a workstation, rather than in front of a DOS PC functioning as a terminal! UNIX is a trademark of Unix Systems Laboratories.
The following are trademarks of Digital Equipment Corporation: Alpha AXP, DEC, DECstation, DECtalk.

[4] *URL http://www.research.digital.com/CRL*

[5] Emacspeak will still produce the spoken confirmation, but continuing to the next task will interrupt this speech.

editing cursor is on the closing brace that ends a function block, Emacspeak says "brace that closes function" and then speaks the opening line of that function. This provides the listener the same kind of feedback that users of traditional visual interfaces have come to expect.

Spell Checking

Emacspeak provides a fluent aural interface to **ispell**, a powerful interactive spell checker. Here is a brief description of the visual interface provided by the spell checker for those unfamiliar with this system.

Typically, a file opened with Emacs can be spell-checked by invoking **ispell**. Errors are visually highlighted, with a separate window showing a list of possible corrections. The user can type a number to pick a choice from the list of corrections; alternatively, a replacement can be directly typed in.

Using this interface with a traditional screen-reader is painful to say the least[6]. A user of a screen-reader needs to query the position of the cursor to find out the erroneous word, then locate the window of corrections on the screen before continuing.

With Emacspeak, the fact that the list of possible corrections appears in a separate window is completely hidden from the listener. When running the spell checker, Emacspeak speaks the line containing the erroneous text with the incorrect word *aurally* highlighted. Next, the list of possible corrections is spoken; the user can pick a choice at any time. Based on the user action, the spell checker inserts the appropriate correction and continues to the next error.

A similar approach is used to provide aural feedback to the common editing task of interactively replacing a string by another. Emacspeak speaks the line containing the instance of the text being replaced, with the instance that will be replaced *aurally* highlighted. This allows the listener to respond correctly when there are multiple occurrences of the text being replaced within a line. Thus, the task of replacing the first occurrence of **foo** with **bar** while leaving the second instance of **foo** intact in the example

> Change this food, but do not touch this fool.

is trivial; the same task using a screen-reader is much harder.

Electronic Mail

Emacspeak provides a fluent spoken interface to electronic mail. Instead of having to listen to verbose utterances consisting of email headers, the listener hears a succinct summary of the form " *sender name* on *subject*.". Emacspeak also infers the dialogue structure present in electronic mail messages based on standard conventions used to cite the contents of previous messages in a conversation thread. When such dialogue structure is detected, the different parts of the dialogue are spoken using different voice characteristics. Hitting any key while a part of the dialogue is being spoken results in the system skipping to the next portion of the dialogue.

[6] Believe me, I've done it!

Usenet News

Emacspeak provides a fluent spoken extension to GNUS, the GNU Emacs news-reader. The interface permits the user to browse news using the four arrow keys.

We present the user with a simple metaphor of opening and closing objects. The up and down arrows navigate through objects at the current level; the right arrow opens the current object, while the left arrow closes it.

To begin with, the user opens up Usenet news. The up and down arrows navigate through the list of newsgroups, providing a succinct verbal description of the current group and the number of articles that are unread. Opening a group with the right arrow results in the up and down arrow keys moving through the list of unread articles; again, the article is succinctly summarized using utterances of the form "*Sender* on *topic*, 33 lines.". Opening an article by pressing right arrow speaks it; the listener can move to the next article merely by pressing the down arrow, which will interrupt the reading of the current article, and summarize the next article. The auditory icons described earlier are especially useful when browsing news; the aural cues for opening, closing and selecting objects allow the listener to quickly move to the next task in the interface.

All of the features described in the section on reading email are available when reading news; Emacspeak presents the dialogue structure present in news articles using the voice-lock feature described above.

Surfing The WWW

The WWW presents two interesting challenges to a spoken interface.

- Presence of hypertext links.
- Presence of interactive elements, e.g., fill-out forms consisting of UI elements such as input fields, check boxes and radio buttons.

Emacspeak provides a spoken extension to W3, the excellent Emacs-based WWW browser developed and maintained by William Perry.

Browsing A WWW Page. The listener can browse a WWW page just like any other document. Hyperlinks are spoken in a different voice. The listener can interrupt speech at any time and activate the link that was most recently spoken. The listener can also move the application focus between the various links on a page; jumping to a link results in the anchor text being spoken along with an auditory cue indicating a large movement. Activating a link plays the auditory icon for *opening* an object, retrieves the document, and finally announces the title of the newly opened WWW document.

Interactive WWW Documents. The W3 browser parses a WWW document before displaying it. Emacspeak relies on this internal representation to provide the spoken rendering, rather than examining the visually displayed document. This fits well with the overall design of Emacspeak; it also enables Emacspeak to produce spoken feedback that would be impossible to generate by merely examining the screen.

A typical interaction with a form element consists of:

- Moving system focus to the element.
- Changing the state of the form element, e.g., pressing a button or entering a value.
- Obtaining confirmation from the system about the recently performed action.

We illustrate this with examples of what happens when the user interacts with different form elements that are found on WWW documents.

Text Field
- Emacspeak summarizes the element under the focus with an utterance of the form "text field *field name* set to *value.*". The name of the text field and its value if any are retrieved from the internal representation.
- Pressing enter results in the spoken prompt "Enter value for *field name.*".
- After the value has been input, Emacspeak confirms this with the announcement "text field *field name* set to *value.*".

Check Box
- Emacspeak summarizes the check box with an utterance of the form "Check-box *name* is *checked.*", assuming the box has been previously checked.
- Pressing enter produces a button click.
- Emacspeak says "unchecked check box *name.*".

Radio Button The interaction parallels that described above for check boxes. The utterance uses the phrase "is pressed" to distinguish radio buttons from check boxes.

Navigating The File System

Emacs' **dired** mode, which is used to navigate the file system and perform operations such as moving, copying and deleting files, is extended to provide succinct aural feedback. When navigating through the file listing, the user hears the name of the current file or directory spoken; different *file types* e.g., directories, executables and symbolic links are distinguished by speaking their names in different voices. Opening a file plays the auditory icon for opening an object, and then speaks the name of the file just opened. Marking a file for later processing, deleting a file etc. all produce auditory icons. The auditory icons in this context are very useful because typically, performing an action such as deleting a file when using **dired** affects the current object and moves the focus. Visually, the file marked for deletion is set apart and the focus is moved. Combining the sound of a file being deleted with the speaking of the current object introduces the same level of parallelism in the aural interaction.

When navigating the *dired* buffer for the directory containing this paper, a screen-reader would speak a typical line shown below

> -rw-r–r– 1 raman users 11905 Aug 17 16:04 examples.tex

as " dash rw dash r dash dash r dash dash 1 raman users 11905 Aug 17 16:04 examples.tex", an utterance that is hard to parse and comprehend. In contrast, Emacspeak merely speaks the filename; the listener can repeatedly press the *tab* key to hear the various fields of the file listing. Below, we list the utterances produced by each repeated press of the *tab* key.

Permissions rw r r
Links 1
Owner raman
Group users
Size 11905
Last Modified Aug 17 16:04
Filename examples.tex

Figure 2: Tabbing through a file listing.

Notice that Emacspeak infers the meaning of each field in the file listing. Pressing the *tab* key while a field is being described interrupts speech immediately and moves to the next field.

Conclusion

We conclude with a summary of what we have learnt from the work on Emacspeak. Firstly, the design of Emacspeak as a speech interface as opposed to a system that reads the screen is radically different from what has been attempted in the past. The current implementation has achieved a remarkable level of success in providing fluent speech access to day-to-day computing tasks.

The convoluted interfaces provided by screen-readers proved moderately effective in the case of visually impaired users —there was no other choice and consequently, users had the motivation to learn and use these interfaces. However, general users who wish to use speech as an extra modality to enhance their interaction with the computer are unlikely to put up with such interfaces. The *direct* access provided by the speech-enabling approach is likely to produce more acceptable output and make deploying speech interfaces easier.

Finally, our implementation of Emacspeak has provided the first true speech access interface to UNIX workstations. To date, the only available solution for visually impaired users has been to access these using PC's running screen-readers as a talking terminal. Our work provides a viable alternative to accessing the power of UNIX and the wealth of communication and development tools that are commonplace in this environment.

Acknowledgements

We would like to thank the authors of the various Emacs subsystems such as the WWW browser, email and news readers. Without their work, Emacspeak would have remained a speech interface to a text editor; in itself not a very useful artifact. Special thanks go to Hans Chalupsky, author of the *advice* package, without which the implementation of Emacspeak would have been difficult, if not impossible. I would also like to thank Win Treese for drawing my attention to the power of the *advice* facility and Dave Wecker[7] for goading me into writing Emacspeak.

REFERENCES

[BGB88] W. Buxton, W. Gaver, and S. Bly. The use of nonspeech audio at the interface. *Tutorial Notes, CHI '88.*, 1988.

[BGP93] Meera M. Blattner, Ephraim P. Glinert, and Albert L. Papp. *Sonic Enhancements for 2-D Graphic Displays, and Auditory Displays.* To be published by Addison-Wesley in the Santa Fe Institute Series. IEEE, 1993.

[Gav93] William Gaver. Synthesizing auditory icons. *Proceedings of INTERCHI 1993*, pages 228–235, April 1993.

[JSBG86] K. I. Joy, D. A. Sumikawa, M. M. Blattner, and R. M. Greenberg. Guidelines for the syntactic design of audio cues in computer interfaces. *Nineteenth Annual Hawaii International Conference on System Sciences*, 1986.

[ME92] Elizabeth D. Mynatt and W. Keith Edwards. Mapping GUIs to auditory interfaces. *Proceedings ACM UIST92*, pages 61–70, 1992.

[MW94] E.D. Mynatt and G. Weber. Nonvisual presentation of graphical user interfaces: Contrasting two approaches. *Proceedings of the 1994 ACM Conference on Human Factors in Computing Systems (CHI'94)*, April 1994.

[Myn94] E.D. Mynatt. *Auditory Presentation of Graphical User Interfaces.* Santa Fe. Addison-Wesley: Reading MA.., 1994.

[Ram94] T. V. Raman. *Audio System for Technical Readings.* PhD thesis, Cornell University, May 1994. URL *http://www.research.digital.com/CRL* /personal/raman/raman.html.

[SMG90] D. A. Sumikawa, Blattner M. M., and R. M. Greenberg. Earcons and icons: Their structure and common design principles. *Visual Programming Environments*, 1990.

[Tha94] James Thatcher. Screen reader/2: Access to os/2 and the graphical user interface. *Proc. of The First Annual ACM Conference on Assistive Technologies (ASSETS '94)*, pages 39–47, Nov 1994.

[WKES94] E. D. Mynatt W. K. Edwards and K. Stockton. Providing access to graphical user interfaces - not graphical screens. *Proc. Of The First Annual ACM Conference on Assistive Technologies (ASSETS '94)*, pages 47–54, Nov 1994.

[YLM95] Nicole Yankelovich, Gina Anne Levow, and Matt Marx. Designing speechacts: Issues in speech user interfaces. In *Proceedings of CHI95, Human Factors In Computing Systems*, pages 369–376. Sun Micro Systems, May 1995.

[7] He got tired of listening to my complaints about how inadequate screen-readers were.

Audio Enhanced 3D Interfaces for Visually Impaired Users

Stephen W. Mereu, Rick Kazman
Department of Computer Science
University of Waterloo
Waterloo, ON, Canada, N2L 3G1
+1 519 888 4567 x4870
rnkazman@cgl.uwaterloo.ca

ABSTRACT

Three dimensional computer applications such as CAD packages are often difficult to use because of inadequate depth feedback to the user. It has, however, been shown that audio feedback can help improve a user's sense of depth perception. This paper describes an experiment which evaluates the use of three different audio environments in a 3D task undertakeh by visually impaired users. The three audio environments map tonal, musical, and orchestral sounds to an (x, y, z) position in a 3D environment. In each environment the user's task is to locate a target in three dimensions as accurately and quickly as possible. This experiment has three important results: that audio feedback improves performance in 3D applications for all users; that visually impaired users can use 3D applications with the accuracy of sighted users; and that visually impaired users can attain greater target accuracy than sighted users in a sound-only environment.

Keywords

User Interface, Auditory Interface, Disability Access, 3D Interface

INTRODUCTION

Audio feedback has proven itself to be an effective addition to human-computer interfaces in numerous studies. Many computer applications use sounds to present information to the user that would otherwise be difficult to convey through other means. Audio is also useful when the user's attention needs to be focussed away from a visual display. For example, Gaver, Smith and O'Shea demonstrated the utility of audio feedback with their Arkola cola factory simulator. In this experiment users "listened to" processes that were not visible in their view of the factory [4]. The bottle capper machine, for instance, normally made a rhythmic sound. When something went wrong with the capper, the rhythm changed thus alerting the user.

Along with monitoring background events, complex foreground events can also be aided using audio feedback. Di Giano and Baecker, for example, added sound to a programming environment [1]. By attaching a different sound to each routine or block of code, semantic errors, like infinite loops, were easily detected. Jackson and Francioni also used sound in a programming environment, but they focused on conveying the state of executing parallel programs to the user [6]. Although audio can help users monitor processes and events, it can also be used to listen to raw data. Hayward demonstrated this by attaching sounds to seismic signals [5]. By doing so, significant seismic events were then quickly determined by listening to changes in the data. The possibilities for listening to data are virtually endless. Known applications range from listening to the stock market, company annual sales, computer load, or even bodily functions like a heart beat and respiratory rate [3].

One use of audio feedback that has proven to have significant ramifications is improving the access of visually impaired users to computers. This is an increasingly important area of study as user interfaces are becoming more graphical and less text-based and thus hindering the visually impaired user (who previously managed reasonably well in text-based environments by using speech synthesis to "read" the contents of the screen). Some work has already been performed in the area of improving access to graphical environments for visually disabled users. Mansur, Blattner and Joy's Sound-Graphs showed how a sound could be mapped to (x, y) data so that visually impaired users could perceive the relationship between x and y. They did this by scanning along the x axis and adjusting the pitch of the sound according to the y value [7].

When given a choice between a text based application and a windows based one, visually impaired users prefer the text based product since it is easier for them to use. Edwards sought to help visually impaired users in using a windowing system [2]. He succeeded by attaching an identifying tone to each window including the edge of the screen. As the user moved the cursor around the screen, each entered window would play its identifying tone. The user would then know which window was the active window.

Sound can help visually impaired users function in a windowing interface—a 2D graphical environment. Can it also help them in a 3D environment: a CAD package, or a vir-

CHI 96 Vancouver, BC Canada
© 1996 ACM 0-89791-777-4/96/04..$3.50

tual environment? Such environments are difficult for normally sighted users, principally because they try to convey depth information in a 2D environment, typically through the use of orthogonal views. Sound has proven to be effective in improving the performance of users of such 3D environments [8].

If sound can be similarly used for visually impaired users, it would break down a substantial barrier, thus allowing visually impaired users access to 3D applications. The research of this paper seeks to answer this question, and gives reason to believe that this barrier can be surmounted.

PREVIOUS WORK

Before studying the effects of sound in a 3D computer interface with visually impaired users, we studied its effect with sighted users. This initial study served four purposes: a) to determine if sound could be used as an effective *depth cue* to improve depth perception in 3D interfaces, b) to compare the differences between various types of sound cues, c) to note how user performance changes when all visual aids are removed thus forcing users to rely solely on sound cues, d) to study the effect that learning has on user performance while using a sound based computer environment. [8]

The first three questions were studied using twenty sighted subjects. Subjects were presented with a randomly rotated "blobby" object that had a target dot randomly placed on its surface. Figure 1 shows an example blobby object. The user's task was to move the cursor to the target—shown as a white spot on the object's surface in Figure 1—in 3D space. Cursor movement was controlled using a standard mouse for the x and y directions and the up/down arrow keys for the z dimension. When the cursor was at the desired location, the user depressed the space bar signalling that the task was complete. Subject performance was measured by automatically recording both their target accuracy (distance from the target) and task time.

Subjects were tested on four types of environments: one that gave no audio feedback, a tonal environment that provided audio feedback by altering a simple sine wave tone, a musical environment that altered a piece of music being played for the user, and an orchestral environment that used an orchestral arrangement to play music.

During a task trial with each of the audio environments, the subject would continually "hear" the cursor's location. Upon depressing the left mouse button, however, the user would hear only the sound of the target location. By pressing and releasing the mouse button consecutively an audible comparison is made so that the subject can determine the similarity between the two sounds, and hence the relationship between the cursor and the target.

The tonal sound environment attached a simple sine wave tone to each location. As the cursor moved in 3D, the sound would change in three of its *sound dimensions*, such as pitch or volume. Pretest experiments found that the best mapping of spatial dimensions to sound dimensions was x (left/right) to balance (left/right), y (up/down) to pitch (high/low) and z (far/close) to volume (quiet/loud) [8].

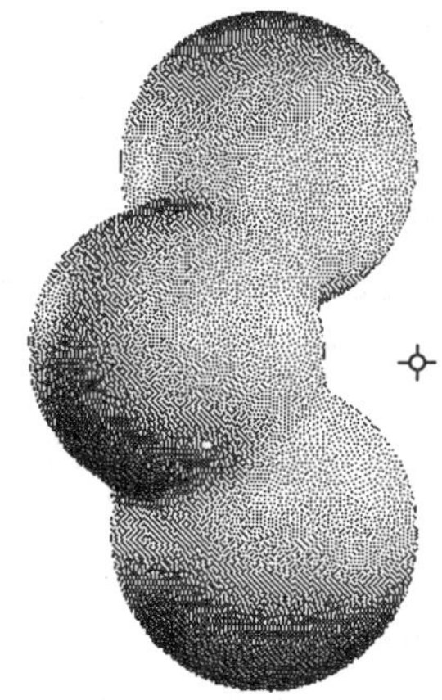

Figure 1: "Blobby" Object with Target Location
The "blobby" object's irregular shape and lack of hard edges minimize the visual depth cues provided to the user. Both the object's orientation and the location of the white target are randomly chosen per trial to reduce learning effects. Users moved the crosshair cursor in 3-space to locate the target dot.

In the musical environment a very similar approach was taken, but instead of modifying a simple tone, a randomly selected musical piece was played. This piece was modified according to the cursor's location. As with the tonal environment, pretests were carried out which determined the best sound dimension mappings. These were, as with the tonal environment, x to balance, y to pitch and z to volume.

The orchestral environment extended the idea of playing music by arranging a set of instruments into a standard configuration and using this to locate a sound in 2D. The initial motivation for this mapping was the observation that tonal and musical sounds are good for giving users relative position information but, excepting those rare users with perfect pitch, they are inadequate for giving absolute position information. An orchestra, on the other hand, is a fixed configuration and so, after a small amount of training, when a user hears a trumpet play, they know what location this represents. Absolute position information was thought to be valuable for visually impaired users.

In the orchestral environment the x-z horizontal plane was partitioned into eight instrument sections as shown in Figure 2. Each section was assigned a different instrument. Instruments were selected based on pretest results that determined the eight most identifiable instruments from the 128 available in the MIDI patch set.

Using this environment, the music played corresponding to a given cursor location would be dominated by the instrument in the cursor's orchestra section. For example, if the cursor was located in the 1/8th of the x-z plane that was occupied by the violin section, the violins would play the melody the loudest while the other sections would play a background part. Thus the orchestra metaphor provided the x and z components of the cursor's 3D location. The third spatial component, y, was mapped to oscillation. This mapping was selected based on pretest results.

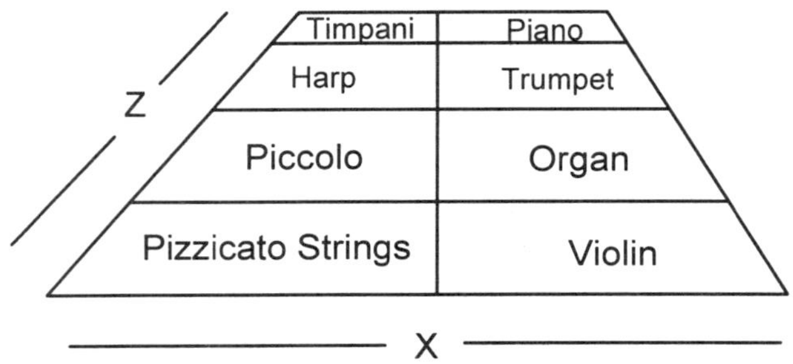

Figure 2: Orchestra Arrangement
The orchestral environment uses an orchestra consisting of eight instrument sections laid out on the x-z horizontal plane.

User performance in these three audio environments, plus a visual-only environment, was then studied.

RESULTS OF THE INITIAL STUDY

Twenty paid normally sighted subjects performed 25 trials on each of the four environments. All subjects performed the experiments in a quiet room using a Pentium[1] PC running Windows 3.1[2] equipped with a Gravis Ultrasound[3] card, a pair of headphones and the experiment application software. Subjects were instructed on each sound environment before beginning and were told that both speed and accuracy were equally important.

The order of exposure to the four environments was randomized. The set of trials for each environment was divided into 5 *learning* trails, 15 *visual* trials and 5 *"blind"* trials. After they had completed the learning and visual trials, the subjects performed what were termed the "blind" trials. These were exactly like the normal visual trials except the screen was blanked and the subjects had to rely entirely on audio feedback. In addition to the recorded measures of target error and task time, four subjective ratings were also measured per sound environment: subjective performance, preference, usability, and marketability.

Results showed that all three audible sound environments (tonal, musical, and orchestral) reduced target errors over the no sound environment by 78.9%, 61.1% and 32.4% respectively. Task time, however, suffered and increased over the no sound environment by 123.4%, 178.4% and 215.1% respectively.

The no visual "blind" tasks caused an increase in target error over the visual cases in only one of the three audio environment: orchestral sound. Normally sighted users were thus able to accurately locate the target in a "blind" environment relying only on tonal or musical feedback. This suggested the possibility of using the sound environments in a sound-only application when a sighted user needed to focus elsewhere, or in an application for visually impaired users.

Overall, subjects performed the best, in terms of speed and accuracy, using the tonal environment. However, they found tonal sound to be annoying and preferred to use the musical environment. Subject differences such as gender, area of study, musical ability and previous graphics experience made no significant difference to the results. The order that the environments were tested also caused no significant difference.

The results of this experiment prompted a second question: how would the results change when subjects were exposed to the sound environments over an extended period? Another experiment was therefore run with seven paid subjects. Subjects performed the same experiment on a Monday, Wednesday, and Friday of a single week. Results showed that target error remain the same as before, but task time was reduced significantly over the three days. Given that target error decreased but task time increased over the no sound environment in the initial study, this result is encouraging. It shows that, with a small amount of practice, the additional time required to attend to the audio cues can be mitigated.

AN EXPERIMENT WITH VISUALLY IMPAIRED USERS

The three sound environments (tonal, musical, and orchestral) proved to be effective position cues and, more importantly, depth cues, for normally sighted users. As a result we thought it likely that visually impaired users could also benefit from these audio environments. In a subsequent study eight paid visually impaired subjects (3 low vision and 5 blind) were used to test this hypothesis. The results of this study are the main topic of this paper.

The experimental design was similar to the previous study described above, having 25 trials per sound environment (tonal, musical, and orchestral) this time using 10 as learning and 15 as experiment trials. Since the no sound environment is a visual only environment, it was not tested with blind subjects and was used only as a learning tool for the low-vision subjects.

Results: Visually Impaired Subjects

The three sound environments were compared using one-way ANOVA tests with repeated measures on the sound environment. A significant difference in target error was found across the sound environments with $F(2,14)=87.12$, $p=0.0001$.

Figure 3 shows the difference in these target errors. The error level in the tonal environment was approximately

1.Pentium is a registered trademark of Intel.
2.Windows is a registered trademark of Microsoft Corp.
3.Gravis Ultrasound is a registered trademark of Advanced Gravis Computer Technology Ltd.

half that of the musical environment and almost a fifth of the orchestral environment.

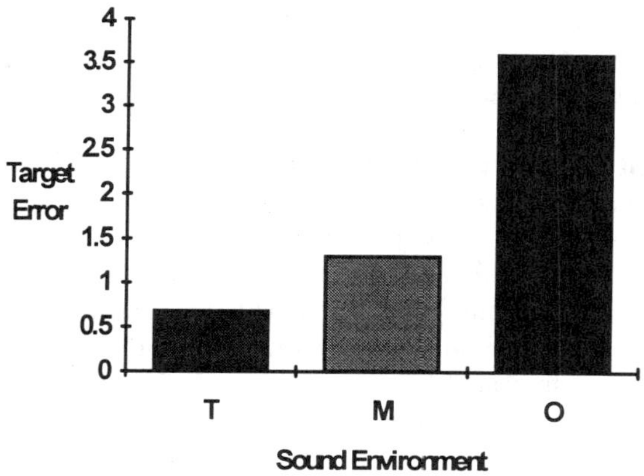

Figure 3: Sound Environment vs. Target Error
The above graph shows that errors were the least when subjects were using the tonal sound environment.

No significant difference was found in the task time across the three sound environments, as shown in Figure 4, with F(2,14)=0.75, p=0.4924.

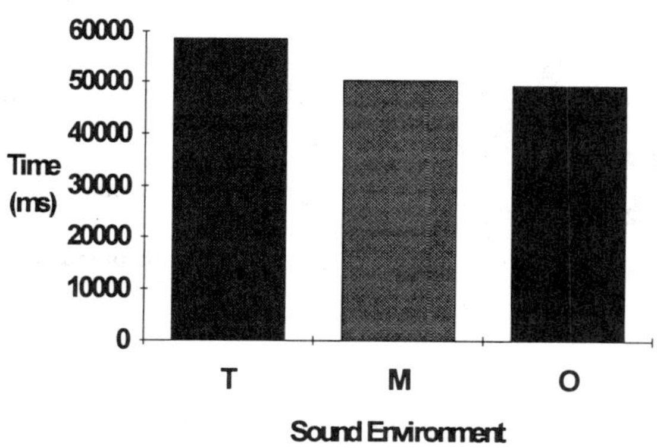

Figure 4: Sound Environment vs. Time
The time required to reach the target were approximately the same for each sound environment and showed no significant difference.

The visually impaired users rated the tonal sound environment higher than both the musical and orchestral environments with respect to subjective performance, preference, usability, and marketability, as shown in Figure 5. These differences, however, did not reach the 0.05 level of significance, likely due to the small number of subjects.

Sighted vs. Visually Impaired Subjects

Since the normally sighted subjects had already been tested on the three sound interfaces, it was of interest to see if there was any significant differences between their performance and preferences and the performance and preferences of the visually impaired subjects. As mentioned previously, the normally sighted subjects were tested on the sound environments both with and without visual cues, representing a *combined audio and visual* application and a *sound-only* application respectively. Both of these tests were compared to the responses of the visually impaired subjects.

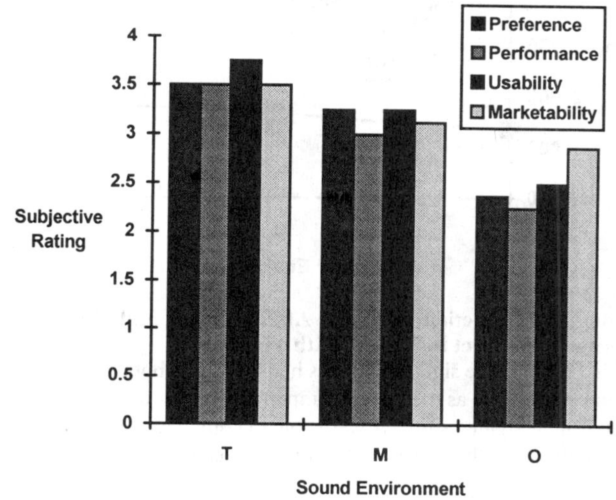

Figure 5: Sound Environment vs. Subjective Ratings
In this figure larger subjective results are better. The tonal sound environment was rated as the best sound environment over the musical and orchestral sound environments on all four of the subjective measures by visually impaired users.

Sighted Subjects with Audio and Visual Cues

The target error and task times of the sighted and visually impaired subjects showed a significant interaction with the sound environment. Figures 6 and 7 show the interactions of target error and task time respectively. It is not surprising to see that the sighted subjects had better accuracy and time throughout since they had the use of both audio and visual cues.

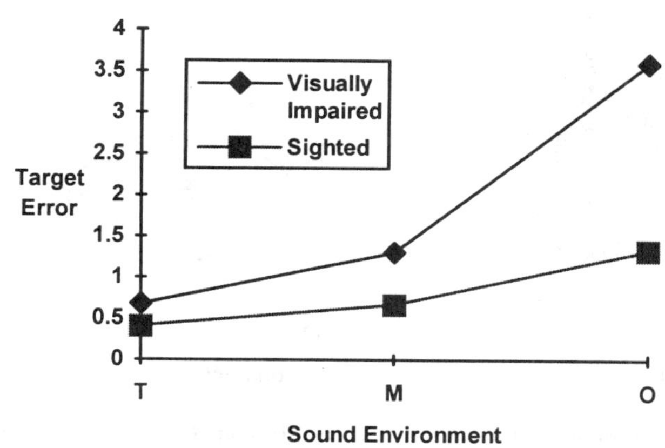

Figure 6: Interaction of Visual Ability and Sound Environment with Respect to Target Error
This graph shows the interaction of the subject's visual ability and the sound environment. Sighted users had the use of both audio and visual cues, whereas visually impaired users had only audio cues.

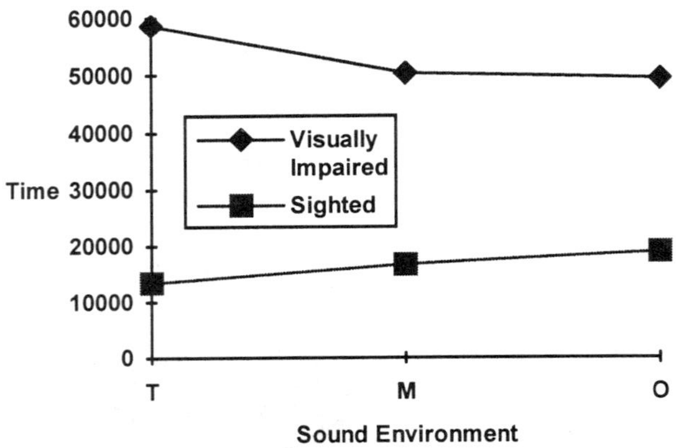

Figure 7: Interaction of Visual Ability and Sound Environment with Respect to Time—With Visuals
As in Figure 6, the sighted subjects had the use of both audio and visual cues where as the visually impaired subjects used only the audio cues. Sighted subjects were able to complete the task significantly faster than visually impaired subjects.

What is interesting is that although the visually impaired subjects took, on average, 4.3 times as long using the tonal environment, their accuracy (0.68) was comparable to the sighted user with the musical environment (0.67). This means that the tonal sound environment by itself is giving the visually impaired users as much information as the combination of visual and tonal cues gives a normally sighted user. It is not surprising that the times for visually impaired users were longer: the normally sighted users located the (x, y) position of the cursor very quickly, by simply placing the crosshair over the white target spot, and spent most of their time using the sound cues to locate the proper depth (z).

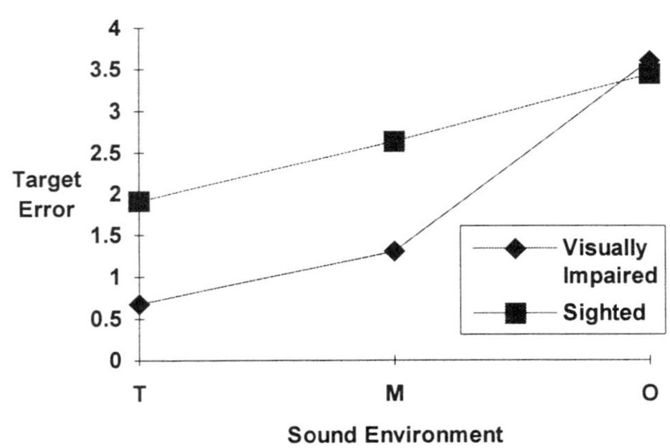

Figure 8: Interaction of Visual Ability and Sound Environment with Respect to Target Error
This graph is the same as Figure 6 except the sighted subjects could not use visual cues. Both the sighted and visually impaired subjects received only audio cues. The visually impaired subjects had target errors significantly *less* than the sighted subjects in both the tonal and musical environments.

The visually impaired users also performed as well with the musical environment (1.30) as the sighted user did with the orchestral environment (1.33). Least Significant Difference (LSD) T tests were performed on each sound environment comparing the responses of the two visual abilities and showed a significant difference in all cases at α=0.05

Sighted Subjects with Sound-only

When the sighted subjects had only audio feedback as did the visually impaired subjects, their performance degraded as seen in Figures 8 and 9. Target error for sighted subjects in the tonal and musical environments were now significantly *worse* than the visually impaired subjects' when compared using an LSD test at α=0.05. The orchestral sound environment's target error level showed no significant difference between the two visual abilities.

In addition to more target errors, the sighted users also took longer with this sound-only scenario than when they had both visual and audio cues. LSD tests at α=0.05 showed no significant difference between the time responses of the two visual abilities per sound environment.

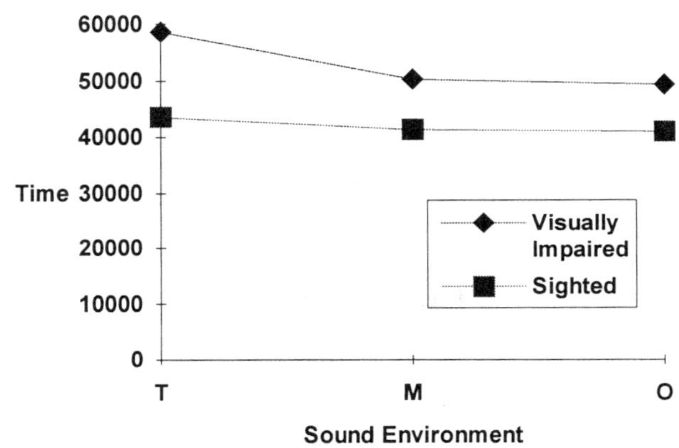

Figure 9: Interaction of Visual Ability and Sound Environment With Respect to Time—No Visuals
When sighted users were without visual aids their task times were significantly higher than in Figure 7. Compared to visually impaired users' task times, no significant difference was found.

Subjective Differences

The subjective measures (performance, preference, usability, and marketability) were all compared using ANOVA tests to note any differences between the sighted and visually impaired subjects. For subjective performance, usability, and marketability no significant interaction with the three sound environments was detected with $F(2,52)=0.48$, $p=0.62$; $F(2,52)=0.74$, $p=0.70$; $F(2,52)=0.48$, $p=0.62$ respectively. There was also no significant difference in the three subjective rating due to visual ability with $F(1,26)=1.05$, $p=0.32$; $F(1,26)=0.40$, $p=0.53$; and $F(1,26)=3.04$, $p=0.09$ respectively.

Subjective preference, however, did show a significant interaction ($F(2,52)=3.54$, $p=0.04$). Figure 10 shows this interaction with visually impaired subjects preferring the tonal environment and the sighted subjects preferring the musically-based environments.

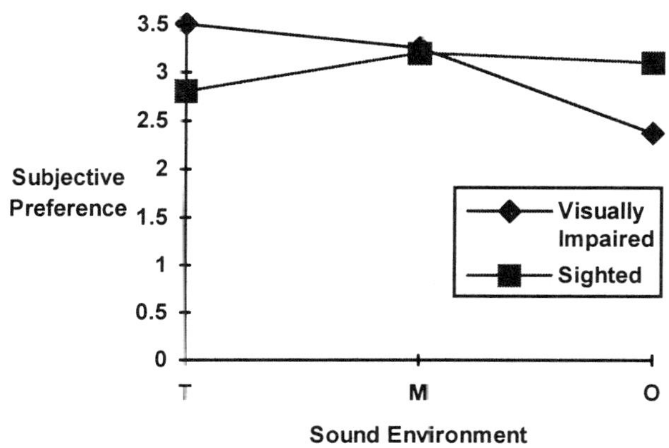

Figure 10: Interaction of Visual Ability and Sound Environment With Respect to Subjective Preference
This graph shows the differences in sound environment preference between subjects from the two visual groups. Visually impaired subjects preferred the tonal environment whereas the sighted users preferred the more musically-based environments.

DISCUSSION

These results have shown that visually impaired users can use the sound environments to perceive depth and position in a 3D application. Although the time for them to locate a position is significantly longer than a sighted user with a display, their accuracy was often very good. This is an important result; it means that a blind user using a tonal sound can perform 3D tasks with the accuracy of a sighted user. This opens a world of possibilities to the visually impaired user.

Comparing both visual ability groups with the sound-only environments showed that visually impaired subjects have a more developed sense of hearing. Sighted users rely on their sight, whereas visually impaired users rely on their sense of hearing. It isn't surprising therefore to find that they out-performed sighted users in this area.

Subjectively, sighted users preferred musical environments whereas visually impaired users preferred the tonal environment. It is thought that this result is due to the way both groups use the sound. Sighted users rely on their vision the most to complete the task. The sound provided is simply an additional cue which sighted users rely on only for depth information. Turning this cue into a musical piece makes it more pleasant for sighted users. Visually impaired users, however, rely only on the sound. The sound that is therefore the most accurate and least distracting is the sound cue of choice. The tonal sound environment was simple and provided visually impaired users enough information to be very accurate.

When designing these experiments, we expected the orchestral environment to perform better than it did, because it is tailorable (a user could play their favorite piece), and because it addresses a shortcoming of audio environments: the fact that positions are always relative, unless the user has perfect memory for pitch, volume, and balance. We attribute its poor showing to two factors: limited resolution and unfamiliarity. We discuss these two points next.

The orchestral environment had severely limited resolution. Owing to limitations in the audio hardware we could only construct an orchestra consisting of 8 distinct sections arranged in a 4x2 grid. This means that precise positioning had to be determined by the relative volumes of adjacent orchestral sections—a subtle distinction. This lack of resolution certainly contributed to the orchestral environment's poor target error performance.

In addition, the orchestral environment—the arrangement of a set of instruments on a 2D plane—was less familiar to our users than the more conceptually simple tonal or musical environments. In order to determine the effects of familiarity on performance and preference in the three sound environments, we performed a longitudinal study on normally sighted users [8]. This study tested the three environments over three days—a Monday, Wednesday, and Friday of a single week. The longitudinal study showed that performance on all environments (including the orchestral environment) improved over the three days, but the orchestral environment remained the worst performer. However, by the end of the third day it was preferred over the other two environments.

Persistent audio feedback, even when it provides valuable information, is often annoying to users. An environment which minimizes this annoyance is an environment which will actually be used. This appears to be the most important contribution of the orchestral environment for the moment.

In conclusion, sound can help both sighted and visual impaired users in 3D applications. The best sound environment depends on the user's visual ability: sighted users prefer music, visually impaired users prefer tonal. The usefulness of the orchestral environment remains to be shown.

Finally, we have seen that sound-only applications are also possible for both the sighted and visually impaired user, with the visually impaired user being more proficient. This raises the possibility of sighted users operating 3D interfaces in situations where their attention needs to be focussed elsewhere, and opens the world of 3D interfaces to blind users.

ACKNOWLEDGMENTS

Funding for this research was provided by the Natural Sciences and Engineering Research Council of Canada, the University of Waterloo/Institute for Computer Research, and Intel Corporation. We would also like to thank Kirk Reiser of the University of Western Ontario's Blind Lab facility for helping with the experiments.

REFERENCES

1. Di Giano, C.J. & Baecker R.M. Program Auralization: Sound Enhancements to the Programming Environment, in *Proc. Graphics Interface '92* (Vancouver BC, May 1992), CIPS, 44-52.

2. Edwards A.N. The Design of Auditory Interfaces for Visually Disabled Users, in *Proc. CHI'88*, (Washington D.C., May 1988), ACM Press, 83-88.

3. Fitch, W.T. & Kramer, G. Sonifying the Body Electric: Superiority of an Auditory over a Visual Display in a Complex, Multivariate System, in G. Kramer (ed.) *Auditory Display*, Addison-Wesley, Reading MA, 1994, 307-326.

4. Gaver, W.W, Smith, R.B, & O'Shea, T. Effective Sounds in Complex Systems: The Arkola Simulation. in *Proc. CHI'91*, (New Orleans LA, May 1991), ACM Press, 85-90.

5. Hayward, C. Listening to the Earth Sing, in G. Kramer (ed.) *Auditory Display*, Addison-Wesley, Reading MA, 1994, 369-416.

6. Jackson, J.A. & Francioni J.M. Synchronization of Visual and Aural Parallel Program Performance Data, in G. Kramer (ed.) *Auditory Display*, Addison-Wesley, Reading MA, 1994, 291-306.

7. Mansur, D.L, Blattner M.M, Joy, K.I. Sound-Graphs: A Numerical Data Analysis Method for The Blind, in *Proc. 18th Annual Hawaii International Conference on System Sciences*, (Honolulu HI, January 1985), 198-203.

8. Mereu S.W. Improving Depth Perception in 3D Interfaces with Sound, Technical Report No. CS95-35, University of Waterloo, 1995.

Dual Device User Interface Design: PDAs and Interactive Television

Scott Robertson, Cathleen Wharton, Catherine Ashworth, Marita Franzke

Applied Research, Collaborative Systems Group
U S WEST Advanced Technologies
4001 Discovery Dr.
Boulder, CO 80303 USA
+1 303 541 7028
scottrob@advtech.uswest.com, cwharton@advtech.uswest.com,
ashworth@clipr.colorado.edu, mfranzk@advtech.uswest.com

ABSTRACT

Computing environments which involve many interacting devices are a challenge for system and user interface designers. A prototype of a multiple-device application consisting of a personal digital assistant (PDA) that operates in conjunction with interactive television (ITV) was developed from user requirements for a real estate information service. The application is used both as a stand-alone service and in conjunction with a television. Users interact exclusively with the PDA. The television responds to PDA output and is used for the presentation of visual images and videos. In this paper the application is described and user interface design issues that arise in the context of multiple device systems are discussed.

Keywords: Personal digital assistants (PDA), interactive television (ITV), ubiquitous computing, mobile computing, multiple devices.

DESIGNING FOR MULTIPLE DEVICES

Future computing environments are likely to involve a combination of specialized personal devices that interact with each other. This will form a new class of systems in which multiple coordinated computing devices are used in various configurations at different times and places to achieve a task. Such systems, often referred as "ubiquitous computing" [4,8], support greater mobility and take advantage of the strengths of different specialized devices that are available at a particular time or place. Multiple device systems, and the concept of "ubiquitous computing," offer many new design challenges to the field of human-computer interaction.

The concept of multiple interacting devices is not new; however, in most cases the interaction is one-way and takes the form of a controlling device paired with a controlled device. Some examples include a television remote control in which input to the controller device causes the controlled device to change channels, modify volume, etc.; an electronic phone directory and dialer which emits tones that control the behavior of a telephone switch; or a stereo component system in which several independent, interacting devices send information to each other. Interestingly, Brown, Buxton, & Murtagh [2] observe that a multiple-device metaphor is used in a wide variety of computing applications which are not really multiple devices, e.g. the "Control Panel" for adjusting an application's or device's parameters.

In all of these cases, the particular devices that can interact are predetermined and the range of possible interactions is limited. We are interested in the design issues that arise when considering multiple computing devices, each of which is capable of carrying out a broad range of interactive applications, which might be combined in many different ways.

Our group has recently developed a prototype of real estate information service that uses a personal digital assistant (PDA) and a television that is part of an interactive television (ITV) services network. A PDA is a hand-held, mobile computing device that has built-in infrared and serial communications capabilities and which is designed to interact with other devices. PDAs are already used as remote controllers for televisions, however the power of PDAs will be most evident when they go beyond the role of a controlling device and are used as a companion computing device. A likely use for PDAs in the future is to interact with cable television services and networked computer systems as a companion device.

The primary goal of the PDA-ITV project was to investigate the design and use of this example of a multiple-device system. We hoped to support mobile users with the PDA, take advantage of the high-quality display capabilities of a television, and utilize the resources of a broadband information network. In this paper we describe the prototype and highlight several of the design challenges that arose.

Design Challenges

HCI researchers have emphasized the importance of understanding how the design space for user interfaces is influenced by characteristics of input and output devices [3,6] and how these characteristics interact with task characteristics [5]. Multiple coordinated computing systems are a new class of systems that complicates the understanding of both users' tasks and input and output characteristics of the system.

Design constraints are more fluid in a multiple-device system for several reasons. First, there are several devices which differ in their input and output characteristics, and differing combinations of devices have novel input-output characteristics. Second, the user may accomplish different parts of a task using different devices, and task characteristics can change depending on the particular device combination that is available. Third, input and output are confounded, with the output to one device (e.g. a touchscreen) becoming the input to another (e.g. a television).

We identified several general questions that arise in the context of designing for multiple-device systems. These include:

- How can a multiple device application be designed so that it is useful both as an ensemble and in individual parts?
- How can several information technologies be used in combination to support users' task goals?
- On which device(s) should each output be located, since devices differ in their display capabilities?
- On which device(s) should each input control be located, since devices differ in their input capabilities?
- When should input on one device control output on the other, and how is this "distributed control" accomplished?
- How can several information technologies be coordinated over space and time to avoid confusing users?

THE PDA-ITV APPLICATION

The domain of real estate information is information-rich, requires considerable database browsing, involves comparison of multiple selection criteria, and benefits greatly from multimedia presentation formats. It is a domain which traditionally requires the intervention of a human agent to mediate search and help in decision making. It also requires home buyers to be present in the new location and to spend considerable time traveling to homes and neighborhoods for a first-time look. A service that reduces any of these requirements would be highly valuable.

The prototype real estate information system was developed using data from interviews and participatory design sessions with potential users. The requirements gathering, design sessions, and development activities were all influenced by the fact that our system utilized more than one device.

The application architecture is illustrated in Figure 1. A user interacts with a PDA using the touchscreen. A PDA communicates with an ITV service through a television settop box. Communication between the PDA and the settop box uses wireless infrared technology. The settop box communicates with a server through a cable system. Communication is bi-directional between the device pairs. This enables complex user-system interactions. For example, a user can perform an action on the PDA which is received by the settop box, which then downloads data from the server, which can then be displayed on the television and/or transmitted back to the PDA.

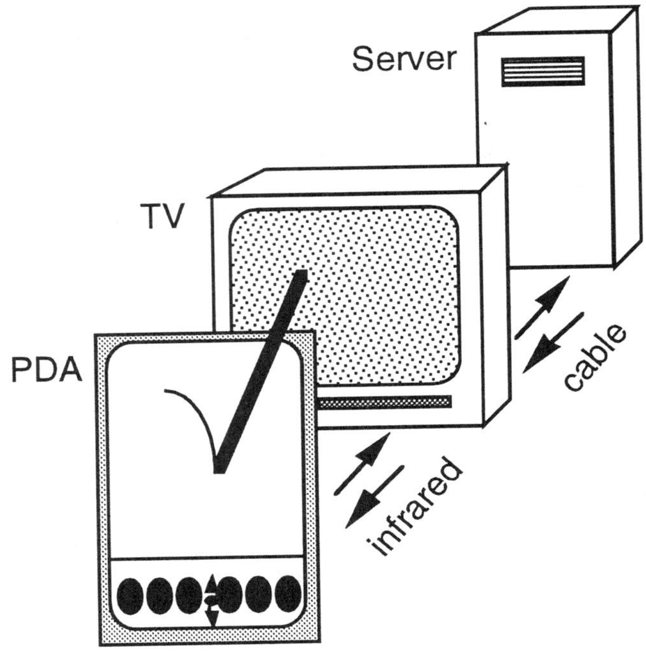

Figure 1. The user interacts with a hand-held PDA using a stylus to tap or write on a touchscreen. The PDA and a server interact with a television using a settop box with infrared and cable I/O.

We refer to this situation as a *dual*-device system since there are only two devices "visible" to the user: the PDA and the television. Here we discuss only the behavior of the PDA and television.

USER REQUIREMENTS

To inform our design of the PDA-ITV system, we conducted two user studies: a task analysis and a participatory design study.

Task Analysis

Four people who had bought a house within the last 5 years were asked to select three to five houses in an assigned price range from a traditional paper real estate catalogue with photos and text. Participants supplied verbal protocols as they searched for suitable homes. After identifying a set of homes, participants summarized their strategy and discussed what they did and did not like about doing the selection task with the paper catalogue. Finally, they described their

Task Structure	Search for a set of homes	Serial access to homes	Individual home browsing
PDA Screens		House Selection Screen	House Information Screen

Table 1. The task structure derived from user studies, and PDA screens developed for two of the tasks.

vision of a "magic catalogue" that would do the task in the manner that they wanted it done.

We identified a task structure composed of three phases: searching for candidate homes, serially accessing homes for inspection, and opportunistically exploring the information available about a particular home (top row of Table 1). Although the phases must occur in this order, an earlier phase can always be returned to directly from a later phase. We assumed that our overall design task was to support this task structure.

Participatory Design

Four new people who had bought a house within the last five years participated in a cooperative design exercise. With the help of a facilitator, the participants designed a paper version of an information system for browsing and selecting real estate using a PDA and a television.

Participants began by giving a general description of how they wanted the system to look and behave. Next they specified the design by creating a house shopping scenario. Participants created representations of their input controls and output displays on two pads of paper, one representing the television screen and the other the PDA. Successive pages showed changes in appearance.

All participants placed input controls on the PDA. They all utilized the touchscreen capabilities and created maps, icons, buttons, and other controls for the PDA. Even when menus were displayed on the television screen, a companion representation was used on the PDA for selection.

The participants clearly expected the information on the television to be coordinated with the information on the PDA. If a selection on the PDA resulted in the display of information about a particular house on the television, for example, the PDA touchscreen would also be updated. This is quite different from a traditional remote control which clearly does not change its characteristics in response to what it is controlling. We adopted several of the participants' ideas for coordinating the PDA and television in the prototype.

PROTOTYPE DESCRIPTION

A prototype was developed using Newton® MessagePads for the PDAs and a Macintosh® to simulate the interactive video service. The system fully supports the user scenarios described here, although it does not currently utilize an extensive real estate database.

Our design of the prototype interface had three aims: 1) to support users' task goals 2) to exploit users' major design ideas, and 3) to explore the design constraints of interacting devices. Participants suggested using the touch screen to display informative graphics such as a map or floor plan. Direct manipulation on the graphic displayed on the touch screen was used to control the television display. From this suggestion, we derived two of our design themes: 1) coordinated graphic displays on the PDA touch screen and television screen, and 2) direct manipulation on a PDA touch screen.

We decided that it was appropriate to have a separate PDA screen for each phase of the task analysis. The prototype supports the house selection and house information browsing components of the task analysis (Table 1 and Figure 2). We have not yet implemented the initial search phase. Consistent with the users' practice of moving between phases, navigation buttons allow users to go back to any previous screen.

During the house inspection phase, users wanted a variety of types of information in several categories. They also wanted to control the display of information from the PDA. We supported this by creating buttons for six types of house information on the House Inspection PDA screen. The buttons can be selected in any order to browse the information.

In the following sections, the House Selection screen and House Inspection screen are described in detail.

House Selection

The result of initial search is a set of candidate homes displayed on the *House Selection Screen* of the PDA and on the television (left portion of Figure 2). The homes are presented in the form of a map on the PDA and a mosaic of pictures on the television. The map includes the major roads for the area and the locations of the homes. Note that this combination display is useful for the "catalogue shopping" phase when a home buyer wants to see what the homes look like. Without the television, the PDA is still useful as a map which can be used to drive to different house locations.

From the *House Selection Screen*, the user may return to the earlier search phase by pressing the "Search" button at the bottom of the screen. If the user wishes to see details about a house, he or she taps on the appropriate house on the PDA map.

House Information Browsing

When a user selects a house on the *House Selection Screen*, the PDA displays a *House Information Screen* with a text description of the house, and the television (if present) displays a large view of the home (right portion of Figure 2). A low-resolution view of the house can also be

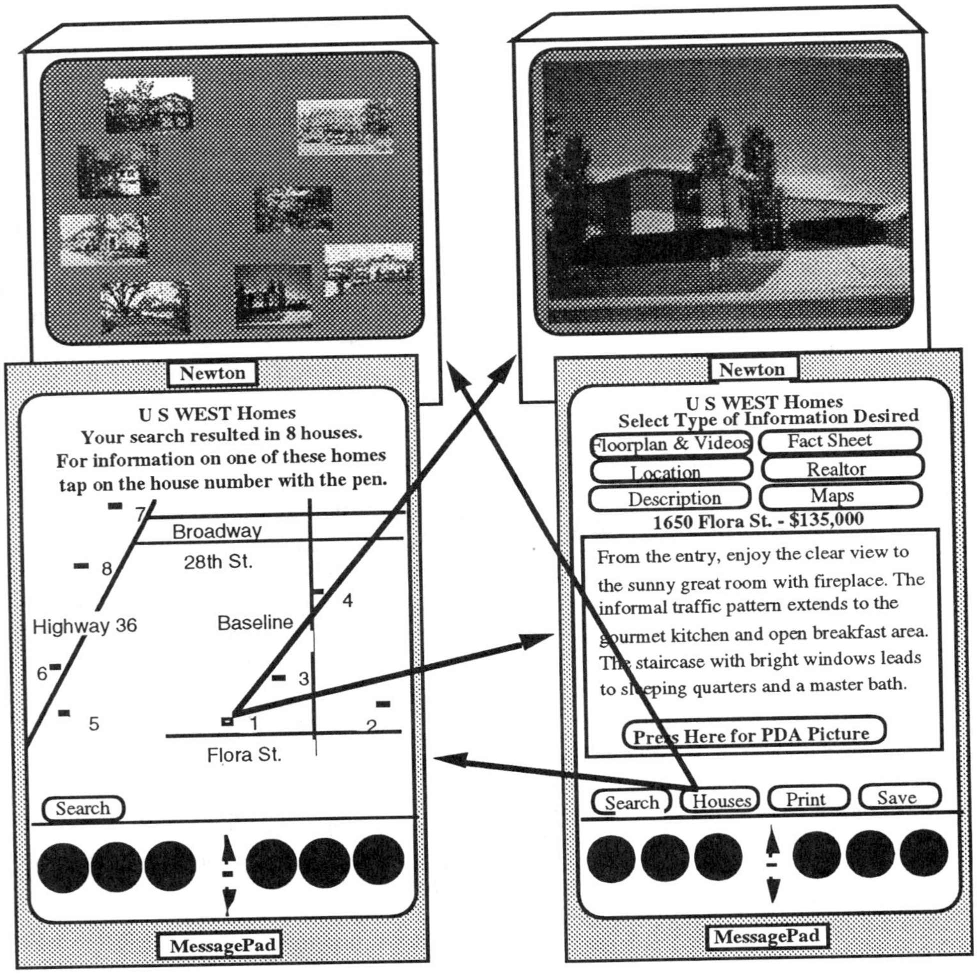

Figure 2. On the left is the PDA *House Selection Screen* (foreground) and accompanying mosaic of house pictures on the television (background). Touching a house on the PDA results in display of the PDA *House Information Screen* (right foreground) and accompanying picture of the house on the television (right background). Pressing "Houses" on the PDA returns the user to House Browsing. (Note that all figures in this paper represent actual prototype screens. Photographs of the prototype screens did not show sufficient detail.)

presented on the PDA screen. The PDA image, which appears as an overlay of the text, is useful if a television is not available. A "Houses" button will return the user to the House Selection state. The "Search" button remains available to initiate a new search. "Print"" and "Save" buttons are available at the bottom of the screen to create more permanent records of the information about the house being inspected.

The *House Information Screen* contains six house information buttons at the top and an information box in the center. The six information buttons provide access to various categories of information about the selected house. This information appears in the information box and may have accompanying information on the television screen.

Location
When a user presses the "Location" button, plain text describing the location is displayed in the information window. A picture of the street is shown on the television, if available. A "Play" button on the PDA allows users to see a "walking tour" of the street.

Description
When the "Description" button is pressed, plain text describing the home is displayed in the information window. This description corresponds to the "advertising" description that typically appears in printed catalogues or newspapers. A front view of the home is shown on the television. This is the initial state of the system when a user leaves the house selection screen (see Figure 2).

Fact Sheet
When a user presses the "Fact Sheet" button, plain text with technical details about the home is displayed in the information window. This text contains specifics like number of bedrooms, square footage, date of construction, type of heating, etc. that would appear on a typical detailed

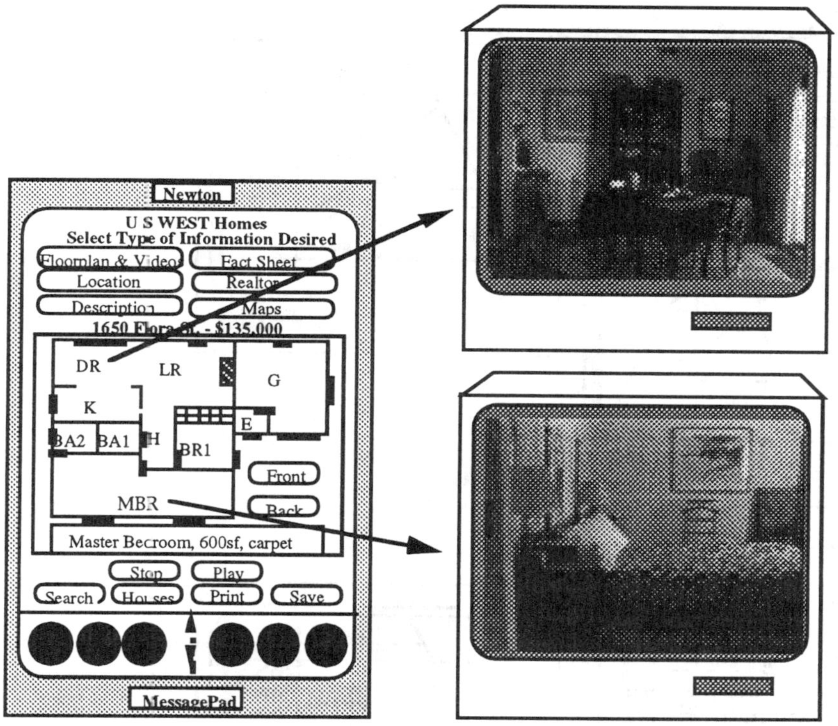

Figure 3. Pressing the "Floorplan and Videos" button results in display of a floorplan on the PDA. Touching a room causes a text description of the room to appear on the PDA and a picture of the room to appear on the television. Pressing the "Play" button shows a room walkthrough on the television.

fact sheet from a commercial listing service. A picture of the home is shown on the television.

Realtor
When a user presses the “Realtor” button, plain text giving background information about the realtor is displayed in the information window. The Realtor's picture appears on the television. A "Play" button on the PDA results in the display of a video of the realtor describing him/herself and the house. A button on the PDA can be pressed to show a low-resolution picture of the realtor on the PDA in case a television is not available.

Floorplan & Videos
When a user presses the “Floorplans & Videos” button, a floorplan of the currently selected house appears in the information window (Figure 3). When a room is touched with the stylus, information about the room (e.g. square footage, flooring type) appears in a text window on the PDA. In addition, if the user is using a television, touching a room causes the display of an image of the room on the television screen. “Play” and “Stop” video control buttons appear on the PDA screen when a floor plan is being studied. When the “Play” button is pressed, a video showing the entire room is presented on the television. Thus, the user can use the PDA to control a video walkthrough of the house. “Back” and “Front” buttons are also shown on the PDA, and pressing one of these yields either a front or back view of the home on the television.

If a television is not available, the floorplan presentation on the PDA is still useful as a stand-alone application. Users could navigate through a house and learn details about each room by taking the PDA with them on a real walkthrough, for example.

Maps
When a user presses the “Maps” button, several map icons are displayed in the information window of the PDA (Figure 4). The buttons are labeled with different types of maps, for example “RTD” (the local bus system), “Schools,” “Civic,” etc. The television shows a detailed map of the region. When a user presses one of the map types on the PDA, the PDA information screen shows a very general schematic of the appropriate map with important locations identified. The more detailed map on the television shows a highlight of the selected map component. For example, when "Civic" is selected, a map of main roads is shown on the PDA with locations like the Library and Police Station indicated. These landmarks are also highlighted on the television's detailed map.

When an item like a landmark or bus stop is touched on the PDA, an address appears on the PDA and a narration, if available, appears on the television. The user re-touches the "Maps" button to see another map.

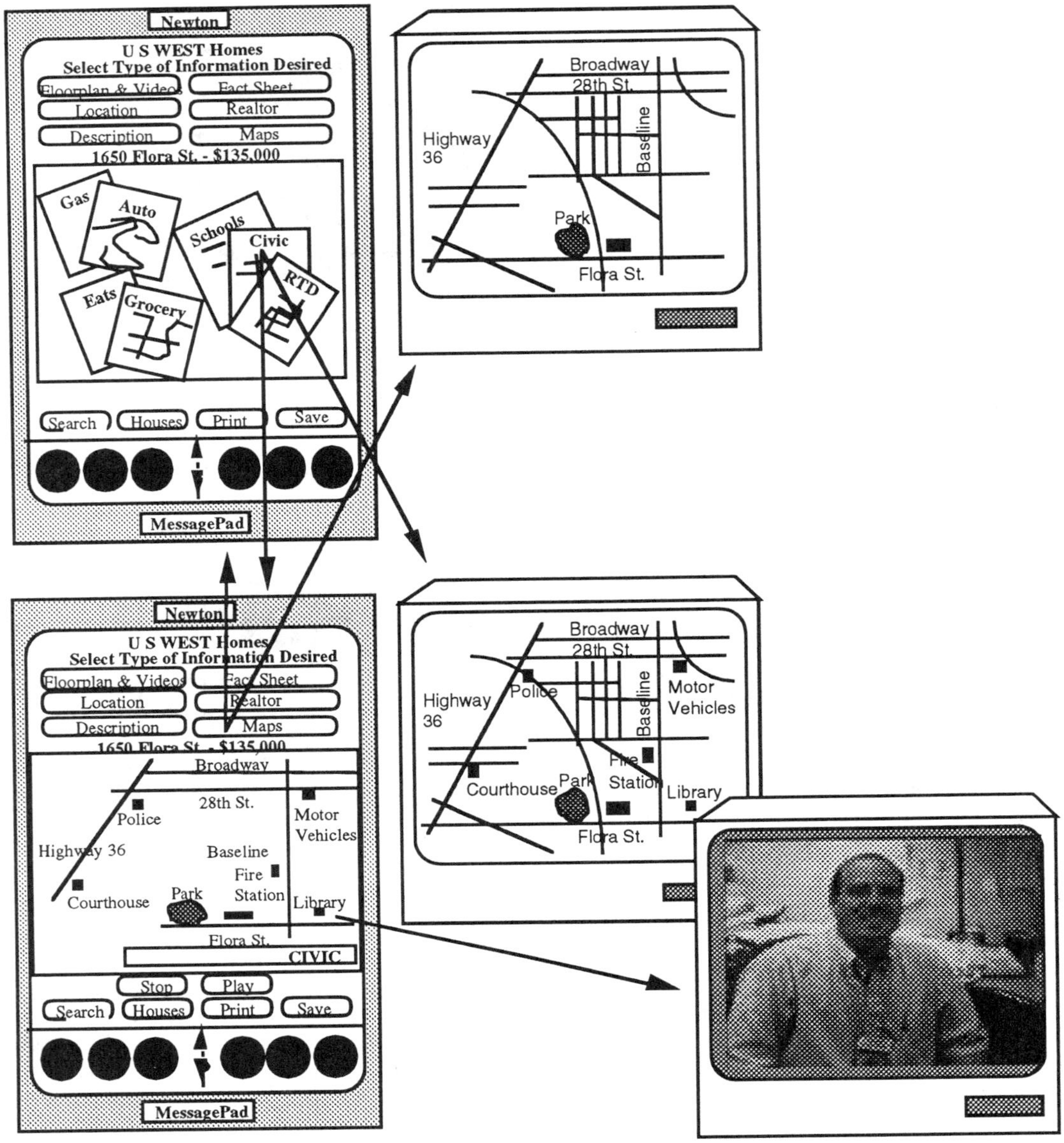

Figure 4. Pressing the "Maps" button results in a set of map icons on the PDA and a detailed regional map on the television (top PDA-TV pair). Tapping a map causes a schematic map of the area with locations of the chosen type to appear on the PDA and, in more detail, on the television (bottom PDA-TV pair). Tapping a location on the PDA causes a narrative to play on the television (bottom right) and an address to appear in a pop-up on the PDA (not shown).

Without a television, the maps can be used to navigate to different locations or simply learn about the neighborhood. With the television, the user gains a visual feel for the neighborhood and can gather considerable information about each of the establishments.

EXAMPLE TASK WALKTHROUGH

The following scenario describes how a prospective home buyer might use the PDA-ITV system. First, the buyer would use the PDA to access a home information service on their television. The buyer could be located anywhere with respect to their final destination (in fact, this service would be most useful to buyers who were far from their ultimate destination). The buyer would use the PDA to send search information (such as price range and location) to the information provider who, in turn, would download data about a set of candidate houses to the PDA. The candidate houses would appear on the PDA in the *House Selection Screen* and on the television as shown in the left portion of Figure 2.

The buyer could glance at the houses on the television and decide whether to begin a new search (if all of the houses looked like the wrong style, for example) or inspect some in detail. If a new search was desired, then the "Search" button at the bottom of the PDA screen is available.

The user may next wish to look at the details for a small number of candidate houses. By touching a house with the stylus, the user is taken directly to a description of the house on the *House Information Screen* and is shown a close up of the house on the television (right portion of Figure 2). By moving back and forth between these screens, the buyer simulates browsing the advertising section of a newspaper or real estate booklet.

Once a few candidates have been selected for serious consideration, the buyer might next begin examining the maps (Figure 4) to see where the candidate houses are located. Houses far from neighborhood schools or in undesirable locations could be rejected. After narrowing the search to a very few houses, the buyer might take video walkthroughs of each one (Figure 3). Finally, the buyer would use the "Realtor" button to get contact information about the realtor.

On a visit to the location, the buyer and realtor could take the PDA with them and use the "Maps" screen to navigate to the locations of candidate houses. Once at a house, the "Floorplan" screen would be used to find a house's rooms.

This scenario shows that a prospective buyer could learn a considerable amount about a home and a neighborhood before visiting the new location. The buyer could come to the realtor with several pre-selections. The scenario also shows the use of the system both in a dual-device situation and as a mobile, stand-alone PDA application (using data downloaded through the cable television system). In addition to the advantages of current online real estate systems and interactive home finding services [1,9], the PDA-ITV system enables mobility, multi-user information sharing, greater presentation control, and the ability to use the service in the multiple contexts of house selection.

DESIGN GUIDELINES

From on our experience in prototyping the PDA-ITV real estate information service, we developed several design guidelines for use in multiple-device situations. The guidelines result from an interaction of the constraints provided by devices, tasks, types of information, and user goals. Since they are "guidelines," and not rules, they will not always apply; however, they can guide designers in reasoning about multiple-device systems. The guidelines address many of the questions posed at the beginning of the paper.

- ***Distribute information across the appropriate devices.***

Information devices differ in their strengths. For example, a television is appropriate for pictures, videos, and audio output. PDAs are appropriate for display of text and some graphics such as simple maps or icons. An important part of our user requirements gathering was to capture information on which devices users might want to use for different information. We then placed graphical and schematic information on the PDA and detailed images and videos on the television (cf. [2]).

- ***Combine devices so that the ensemble provides more than each independent device.***

Value is added if applications on two (or more) devices are cooperative and complementary to each other. For example, a map on a PDA and pictures of houses on a television are useful in themselves. However, if the map on the PDA can be used to navigate through house pictures, then the combined application is more useful than either stand-alone application.

- ***Information content strongly determines display format, which should be mapped to the appropriate device(s).***

An analysis of materials currently used in real estate sales showed several types of information. The most basic information about real estate is textual, consisting of descriptions of houses' features and realtors' contact data. Pictures are very important and are typically the next step beyond text in house advertisements. Real estate offices also provide house pictures. Videos are also sometimes available. Later in the buying process, maps become important. Thus the nature of the information strongly biased where we wanted to place it. High resolution image information went on the television while textual and schematic information went on the PDA. In the case of the maps, an interactive schematic map with main streets only was displayed on the PDA, while a more detailed map or neighborhood scene was displayed on the television.

- ***User tasks influence which device is appropriate for particular types of information.***

Users need different types of information for different tasks. For example, we discovered that real estate buyers wish to perform an initial search without much effort. They are happy to view pictures and read descriptions in one location, at home or in a realtor's office for example. Thus we could provide information relevant to this activity on the television. Map and neighborhood information, on the other hand, is desired once buyers begin traveling to homes. Thus, this information must be represented on the mobile PDA.

- ***Device coordination is critical. Be sure that the information on different devices is coordinated, consistent, and up to date.***

All devices should be dealing with the same task, and a device should never be left in an old state. For example, a user may view a house on the television screen but then begin to read the description for a new house on the PDA. If a picture of the old house remains on the television there is potential for confusion.

- ***Combine the coordinated information guideline with the appropriate device guideline.***

Information about the same thing can be presented in more than one way. For example, information about a room can be conveyed in a picture, a text description, and a floorplan graphic. It is often desirable to display different types of information simultaneously on the same devices. Multiple representations allow systems to take advantage of the ability of users to manipulate one type of representation and see changes in another. For example, navigation through a house video is controlled on a schematic floorplan displayed on a PDA.

DISCUSSION

The PDA-ITV real estate prototype provides a multimedia information retrieval and browsing application that operates both as a stand-alone device and in conjunction with television images and videos. The design of this system was derived by combining user requirements analyses, participatory design outcomes, and guidelines for multiple device systems.

All control components and text information were placed on the hand-held device. Enough information was included on the PDA to enable users to perform some aspects of all the subtasks. Information on the television enhanced the ability of users to do the tasks, but it was not required.

PDA-augmented systems could support many different kinds of activities. For example, it is easy to imagine that a user might want to contact a realtor through the PDA (a communications application), use the PDA to calculate mortgage payments or apply for a loan analysis (financial services applications), or get instructions for how to get to an address from a current location (a transportation application that might even use global positioning data). In fact, future computing applications will involve a plethora of specialized devices.

While our initial prototype focused on the home buyer as a primary user, several other potential users would be involved in the use and support of a real system. A house seller might be interested in listing their home and need to arrange for the appropriate data to be gathered (e.g. video) and published. Real estate agents would become involved both using the system on behalf of their buyers and arranging for sellers to publish their house information. Information providers would become involved in the storage, maintenance, and delivery of the material.

Multiple-device applications complicate the problem of matching the capabilities of devices to users' tasks [5,7]. They also greatly complicate any attempt to produce a taxonomy of devices [3,6] since their usage patterns change through time and vary depending on their combination (e.g. is exploring a floorplan on a stand-alone PDA different from using the same PDA application to control a video walkthrough?). There are many new challenges and issues for user interface designers when they begin to think about multiple device environments. Our goal in this paper was to begin exploring some of these issues in the context of a dual-device system and to identify some principles for multiple-device user interface design.

ACKNOWLEDGMENTS

Newton and Macintosh are trademarks of Apple Computer, Inc. registered in the U.S.A. and other countries.

The authors would like to acknowledge the contributions of our colleagues: Mike King, Monica Marics, Michael Muller, Carrie Rudman, Patricia Somers, Lynn Streeter, and Scott Wolff; and a visiting colleague: Scott Hudson.

REFERENCES

1. Ahlberg, C., Williamson, C., & Shneiderman, B. Dynamic queries for information exploration: An implementation and evaluation. *Proceedings of CHI '92 Conference on Human Factors in Computing Systems.* ACM, New York, (1992), 619-626.

2. Brown, E., Buxton, W., & Murtagh, K. Windows on tablets as a means of achieving virtual input devices. *Proceedings of INTERACT-90: Third IFIP Conference on Human-Computer Interaction,* (1990), Amsterdam: Elsevier Science Publishers, 675-681.

3. Card, S., Mackinlay, J., & Robertson, G. A morphological analysis of the design space of input devices. *ACM Transactions on Information Systems, 9,* (1991), 99-122.

4. Fitzmaurice, G. Situated information spaces and spatially aware palmtop computers. *Communications of the ACM, 36,* 7, (July 1993), 39-49.

5. Jacob, R., Sibert, L., McFarlane, D., & Mullen M. Integrality and separability of input devices. *ACM Transactions on Computer-Human Interaction, 1,* (1994), 3-26.

6. Mackinlay, J., Card, S., & Robertson, G. A semantic analysis of the design space of input devices. *Human-Computer Interaction, 5,* (1990), 145-190.

7. Sears, A., & Shneiderman, B. High precision touchscreens: Design strategies and comparisons with a mouse. *International Journal of Man-Machine Studies, 34,* (1991), 593-613.

8. Weiser, M. Some computer science issues in ubiquitous computing. *Communications of the ACM, 36,* 7, (July 1993), 75-85.

9. Williamson, C, & Schneiderman, B. The Dynamic HomeFinder: Evaluating dynamic queries in a real-estate information exploration system. *Proceedings of SIGIR Conference*, ACM, (1992), 339-346.

Pen Computing for Air Traffic Control

Stéphane Chatty
Centre d'Études de la Navigation Aérienne
7 avenue Édouard Belin
31055 TOULOUSE CEDEX
France
chatty@cena.dgac.fr

Patrick Lecoanet
Centre d'Études de la Navigation Aérienne
Orly Sud 205
94542 ORLY AÉROGARES
France
lecoanet@cena.dgac.fr

ABSTRACT
Modernizing workstations for air traffic controllers is a challenge: designers must increase efficiency without affecting safety in any way. Air traffic control is a time-intensive and safety-critical activity, and thus interaction efficiency and low error rates are crucial. Classical interaction techniques have been used in prototype workstations, but the resulting efficiency is not always satisfactory. This leads designers to consider more advanced interaction techniques. This paper reports on the design and a preliminary evaluation of the first prototype of project IMAGINE, which represents the second generation of graphical interfaces for air traffic control. This prototype, GRIGRI, uses a high resolution touch screen and provides mark based input through the screen. The use of gestures, as well as the use of multi-modal techniques, make interaction faster, and closer to the controllers' habits.

Keywords
Air traffic control, gesture recognition, mark-based input, pen computing, touch-screen, direct manipulation, prototyping

INTRODUCTION

Air traffic control (ATC) is a fascinating application domain for human-computer interaction research, but it is also very challenging to interface designers. They face many difficulties, especially since safety requirements are essential. First, there are the requirements for the interface itself: low error rates are necessary for obvious reasons and interaction efficiency is required to avoid fatigue and to improve safety during periods of time-intensive work. Second, air traffic controllers and their management are understandably cautious about changing tools that affect hundreds of lives, and tend to resist new technologies. Other reasons include the need for finely tuned transition plans (the job must be done, even when the system is being changed), the cost of learning new procedures, and the cost of developing high quality hardware and software for a narrow market. Finally, even access to end users is sometimes a problem. In France, for instance, the number of air traffic controllers is often considered too low to allow for secondary tasks such as designing future systems. The consequence is that rather old technologies and designs are still used in air traffic control centers. Direct manipulation graphical user interfaces have been commonly available for ten years. But the air traffic control rooms of most advanced countries are still equipped with systems designed in the 60s and 70s, that are more and more expensive to maintain.

However, the need for new interfaces for air traffic control is getting more and more perceptible. Air traffic has been growing rapidly for the past ten years, and does not appear to be stabilizing. The increased workload has so far been balanced by a growth of the number of controllers (sometimes), and by growing individual workloads (most often). If the traffic keeps growing, more computerized systems and more efficient tools will be necessary. Despite the difficulties mentioned earlier, most air traffic control agencies embarked on projects based on graphical interfaces. The past ten years have been spent applying technologies and techniques from other application domains, identifying the specifics of ATC, and developing solutions when necessary.

France has such a plan, which is reaching its final development stage, and is aimed at replacing the current air traffic control workstations within the next few years. This plan, called PHIDIAS, makes heavy use of classical interaction techniques, and most of its original features are to be found in its hardware or low-level software components. PHIDIAS provides a standard WIMP (windows, icon, mouse, pointer) interface on two screens, one of which is very large. A lot of work has been spent on identifying and solving the software issues raised by such a large screen, and especially the management of many graphical objects moving independently. If those technical issues have now been solved, a number of design choices made in PHIDIAS can still be improved, if only because hardware, interaction techniques, and our knowledge of ATC have improved over time. This article describes the design of GRIGRI[1], the first prototype in project IMAGINE, which is a step toward the future generation of interfaces for air traffic control. GRIGRI implements design choices very remote from current designs, and finds its inspiration in pen computing. Contrasting with the notepads that made pen computing popular a few years ago, GRIGRI does not use handwriting recognition, but only the recognition of simple gestures, drawn with a pen or a fingertip. Those gestures (marks) are performed directly on the surface of the screen, thanks to a high resolution touch-screen. GRIGRI also uses direct manipulation for some functions and makes use of sam-

[1] *grigri* is a colloquial French word for *scribble*

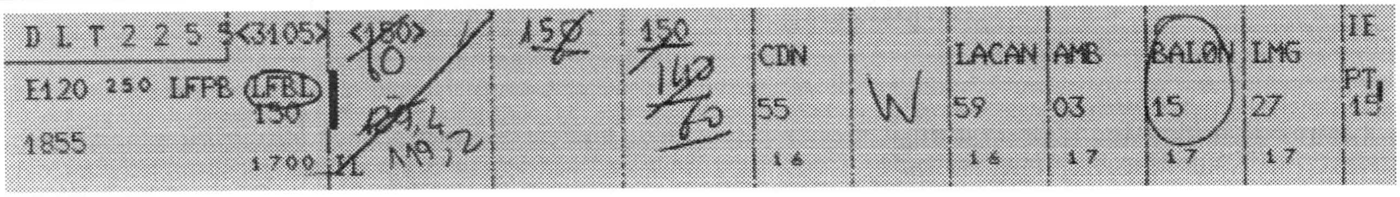

Figure 1: An annotated flight strip

pled sounds to improve the confidence of users and to make some interaction modes more explicit. Finally, the layout of GRIGRI was designed to encourage two-handed interaction.

This article is organized as follows. The first section is devoted to a description of the ATC task and the current environment of controllers. The second section identifies several drawbacks in the use of classical user interface techniques. The third section describes related work on gesture recognition and pen based computing. The following sections describe the design choices implemented in GRIGRI. The last section reports on preliminary evaluations of the system.

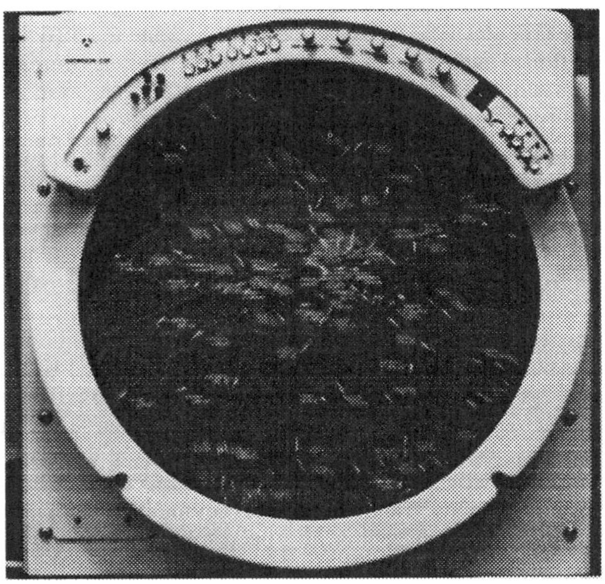

Figure 2: The current radar screen

THE AIR TRAFFIC CONTROL TASK

Air traffic control is a domain that encompasses a number of different tasks. We will focus here on the basic task of en-route air traffic controllers. These controllers mainly guide and monitor aircraft that follow airways, at a reasonable distance from airports. Airspace is usually divided in a number of sectors, each of which is managed by a team of two or three air traffic controllers. The most popular task is performed by so-called radar controllers, who monitor aircraft through radar screens and give vocal orders to pilots through radio links.

Today's radar screens are usually circular and monochrome. They provide a top view of airspace, and represent each aircraft with an icon showing its current position, smaller icons showing a few of its past positions, a line representing its speed, and a label containing its call-sign, speed, and altitude (see figure 2). This display enables radar controllers to identify problems, solve them in real time, and monitor the implementation of the solution. In this process, they also benefit from data about flight plans, that are printed on semi-rigid paper strips, called flight strips (see figure 1).

The flight strips are printed by the computing systems a few minutes before the estimated entry of an aircraft in the sector. The planning controller, who assists the radar controller by planning his work and managing the communications with other sectors, grabs the strips as soon as they are printed. Each strip is then inserted in the set of current strips, and the planning controller signals possible problems through voice, gestures, or layout conventions. The strips, which feature the call-signs of aircraft, the altitude requested by their pilots, and the planned route, are then used by the radar controller, mainly as a reminder. Strips are gathered in groups according to the current situation, and annotated with the orders given to pilots, as shown on figure 1. Most annotations are codified and documented in manuals. Finally, when an aircraft leaves for another sector, the corresponding strip is thrown away, as a sign that the radar controller may forget it.

LIMITS OF TRADITIONAL INTERACTION

When the plan for modernizing the French ATC workstations was launched in 1986, one of the goals, as in other countries, was to take advantage of new technologies in order to alleviate the workload of air traffic controllers. This goal had immediate consequences, such as the use of color screens to code information useful to radar controllers. It also had indirect but major consequences. A number of ATC experts placed hopes on intelligent tools that would help radar controllers solve problems. But such tools need data that are not available to the ATC system in its current state. For instance, the system does not know which controller is in charge of a given aircraft, because transfers are performed through procedures based on voice. Consequently, the idea of helping controllers quickly turned into the need for making them provide more data to the system. This is why they were interested in turning paper strips into a graphical interface: the information previously contained in annotations would then be known to the system.

These goals, as well as the set of available techniques, have had a strong influence on the design that was chosen for the new workstations. The screen gained even more importance and its size became critical. In addition to the radar image which covers a 50 cm wide round screen in the current system, the screen also has to display the new "electronic strips", as well as the potential intelligent tools. Air traffic controllers, afraid of missing important information that would be hidden, are generally opposed to overlapping windows. It was thus decided to use screens as large as possible, namely 50 cm wide square screens, featuring 2048x2048 pixels, developed by Sony for the US FAA. But those screens are so large that users must be seated far from them if they want to see the whole contents. This immediately excluded any possibility of direct interaction on the screen, and led designers to using a mouse and classical interaction techniques: menus, buttons, double clicks, etc. Studies were then focused on information coding (colors, icons, etc) and on the software techniques needed to efficiently display and move many objects on a large screen.

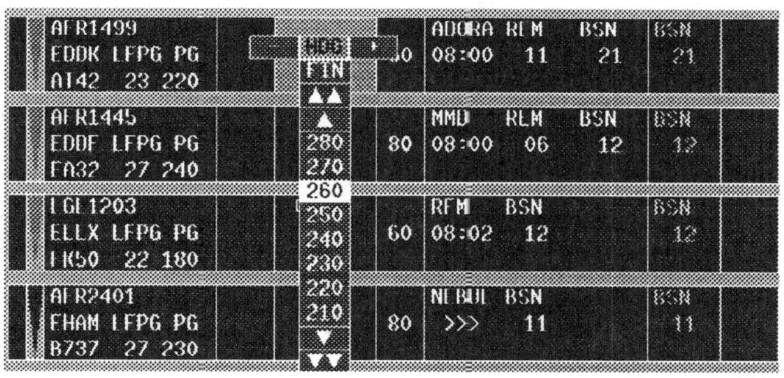

Figure 3: Manipulating a flight strip through menus.

On this screen, the main interactive areas are the fields of flight strips and aircraft labels on the radar image. Users may manipulate them to store a new heading or altitude or select an aircraft and display its route. All these manipulations require the designation of an aircraft or a strip, and the input of a command and its other parameters. Several commands are possible for nearly every active field (label, field of a label, part of a strip). Among the classical interaction techniques, menus seemed to be the most appropriate. But in order to minimize the number of items without having to use cascading menus, it was decided to associate a different menu with every field. For instance, figure 3 shows the menu associated to the "heading" field of a strip.

The system that we just described is still being developed. However, several design choices have been criticized by future users. For instance, the manipulations on electronic strips are considered slow and painful. It has been observed that with today's system, a controller writes an annotation on a strip every 17 seconds [6]. With such usage frequencies, manipulation times and the degree of attention needed are very important. But manipulating menus is relatively slow, and users have to pay attention to what they are doing. Even worse, before selecting an item in a menu, a controller has to click in a zone which is sometimes very small. This increases manipulation times according to Fitt's law. In the case of flight strips, the decrease in performance is noticeable, compared to manual manipulations that are often performed in parallel with other tasks, without paying much attention. With no simple solution to such problems, a number of users ask for the status quo, and want to keep paper strips until the time when alternative tools will make them really obsolete.

Even if electronic strips are discarded, manipulation times will still be an issue for radar images, and for every tool provided by the ATC system. This leads us to exploring possible solutions to that issue, by exploring new interaction techniques. Gesture recognition and mark-based input through a digitizing tablet or a touch screen look like a promising direction. Other techniques are also explored, among which are speech recognition and computer vision. But gesture recognition seemed mature enough to be proposed to air traffic controllers for a medium-term implementation.

RELATED WORK

Gesture recognition deals with the movements performed with one's hand, or any part of the body, with or without an instrument (pen, glove, etc). The input parameters are the successive positions of the tip of the pen, those of fingertips, or the successive angles of articulations, for instance. The devices used are pointing devices (mouse, digitizing tablet, touch-screen), digital gloves and position locators, or video cameras. Some of the techniques developed for 2D gestures performed with a pen can be transposed to more complex situations like 3D gestures performed with a glove [1]. Among those techniques, the most popular is Rubine's algorithm [12], which incrementally computes geometrical features of gestures, and uses statistical methods.

2D gestures, or marks, have been used in several ways in graphical interfaces. In addition to obvious applications to text input, gestures can be used to issue commands to the system. Kurtenbach has studied the issues raised by mark-based input, on the user's as well as on the system's side [9, 8]. Pie menus [3], although apparently close to traditional menus, are close to mark-based input, in that they use the orientation of gestures performed by the user. T-Cube even chains pie menus, thus associating each command to a broken line [13]. In T-Cube, menus are only displayed if the user hesitates while issuing a command. Unistrokes [7] fit between handwriting recognition and mark-based input. It models each letter with a simplified letter composed of only one stroke, in the same way as shorthand.

Pen computers, or notepads, which use the techniques mentioned above, have been popular at the beginning of the decade [10]. One of the first widely available environments was GO Corp's PenPoint. Apple's Newton uses handwriting recognition and mark-based input, combined with high quality feedback. But handwriting recognition accuracy often determines how such systems are accepted by users [5], and it is still difficult to achieve a very high accuracy, especially in countries where cursive writing is dominant, like France. Graffiti, a commercial variation of Unistrokes by Palm Computing, improves the accuracy and thus the usability of such systems at the cost of learning a simplified alphabet.

Finally, it is interesting to note that French air traffic controllers have been familiar with touch-screens for decades. The Digitatron, introduced in the 60s, is a touch sensitive alphanumeric screen with a low resolution. It gives access to a videotext system, used for infrequent operations such as checking which military zones are activated or modifying a flight plan.

A FIRST PROTOTYPE

As mentioned earlier, the management of flight strips is a good candidate for mark-based input. The annotations written on paper strips are made of numbers, and of simple and codified marks. Moreover, annotations are frequent, and the expected gain in time provides a good motivation. This led us to build a demonstrator in order to check whether gesture recognition was useful in this context. The proposed interface was based on the proposed format for electronic flight strips, itself very close to real flight strips. The recognized marks, made with a pen on a digitizing tablet, were of two types. First, it was possible to sort, group and shift strips, just as it is done with paper strips. Then, the usual annotations performed on paper strips were mimicked: highlighting of values by underlining them, modification of values by striking them off and writing the new ones, input of direct routes by drawing arrows between beacon names.

This prototype of flight strip management was soon enriched with a simplified radar image manipulated with gestures, so as to check how well the technique could be applied to interfaces where the use of gestures was not as obvious as for flight strips. This radar image was built with no button or menu, and every command was performed through gestures. There were gestures for zooming and panning, and for several operations on aircraft and beacons.

The results of this pilot study were very encouraging, as well as full of lessons. The lessons were related to the handling of errors, the acceptance of the system by users, and the type of applications that could easily take advantage of gesture recognition.

Errors

Error rates were a major concern, because high error rates would have meant that the technology could not be applied to air traffic control in its current state: errors make interaction slow and painful when they are noticed, and are dangerous when unnoticed. Although we did not carry serious evaluations at that stage of the project, the results were comforting. Our worst concern was interpretation errors: one gesture recognized as another gesture. But such errors were rare. More frequent were interpretation failures: gestures that could not be related to any gesture class. Those failures were especially numerous during the first contacts with the system. The absence of adequate feedback could induce users into errors and decrease their confidence in the system.

Acceptance

During this pilot study, the way the prototype was accepted by users was important: previous experience showed that full studies are useless if air traffic controllers are not confident about the system's potential usefulness. Comfortingly, the acceptance of the prototype by the first air traffic controllers who tried it was good. They found most gestures natural and fast enough, even when they had no equivalent in the current ATC system. The gestures proposed to interact with the radar image were especially well accepted, mainly because of the low precision that is required to perform operations. However, the physical setup, composed of a digitizing tablet and a normal workstation screen, was frustrating to users. They would have preferred a more direct interaction with the contents of the screen.

Potential applications

The use of gestures to interact with the radar image and the contents of flight strips was appreciated. However, the interface proposed for manipulating the strips themselves was the cause of problems. Users, who took pleasure in being able to use their pen again to annotate strips, were disappointed to be unable to move them with their bare fingers. Moving strips with a pen was far less natural. Moreover, the gestures for moving strips often caused confusion with gestures for annotating them. For instance, downward moves were interpreted as downward arrows when made close to a number representing a flight level. Consequently, we decided to discard that interaction technique.

We used the lessons learned with this first prototype when developing the prototype described in the rest of this article. First, we investigated the set of available hardware allowing direct interaction on the screen, either by projecting images on a digitizing tablet (like Rank Xerox EuroPARC's Digital Desk [14]), or by using touch-screens. Second, finding no simple solution for moving flight strips around, we decided to concentrate on radar images, leaving flight strip management for future research. Finally, we paid more attention to feedback during interaction.

Figure 4: The physical setup of GRIGRI

THE PROTOTYPE GRIGRI

Using our first results, we developed a second version of the system, devoted to more systematic evaluations with air traffic controllers. This version, described below, offers a more complete interface and set of functions than the first prototype, so as to allow more realistic tests.

The physical setup of our prototype uses a touch-screen. It includes a color screen built in the surface of a desk with an angle of approximately 30 degrees (see figure 4). The screen is covered with a high resolution touch sensitive layer, that can be used with a pen or a fingertip. It is used to display a radar image and a bar of controls, as shown on figure 5. Depending on their type, commands are issued through the bar of controls, through gestures on the radar image, or through longer direct manipulation interactions.

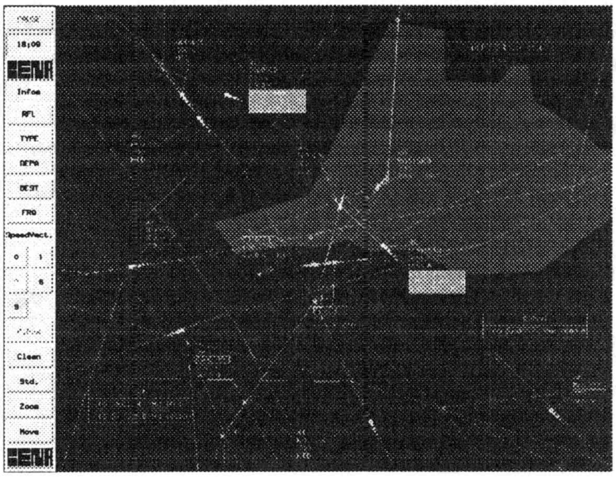

Figure 5: The screen of GRIGRI

Contents of the screen

For the reasons explained earlier, GRIGRI only features a radar image, and no flight strips. Our purpose is that evaluations yield results about mark-based input only, without introducing perturbations due to design choices in strip management. For similar reasons, the proposed radar image is not much different from radar images offered by PHIDIAS and its earlier prototypes. Controllers are familiar with their design, and we did not want to add novelties that would have changed their perception of the system. The radar image is thus composed of a plain background on which appear airways and restricted zones, represented by lines and polygons of a different color. Aircraft nearly have the same representation as on today's radar screen: icons for the current and past positions, a segment for speed. Labels are similar to those of PHIDIAS: they contain several text fields displaying the call sign of the aircraft, its speed, its flight level, etc. The label can be further enriched on demand, by displaying data from the flight plan of the aircraft: destination airport, route, etc. Users can also obtain graphical representations of routes on the display. Finally, the bar of controls on the side of the screen provides a number of global commands.

Global commands

Most commands offered by air traffic control interfaces are related to a given aircraft. Only a few commands are global to the radar image, and make it possible to change parameters of the display: filters to display only certain categories of flights, zoom factor, panning, length of speed vectors (expressed in minutes of flight), etc. Though we plan to return to real hardware buttons and knobs for a number of those parameters, we offered the corresponding controls in the form of software buttons, grouped in a bar on the side of the screen. The size of those buttons is large enough to allow fast manipulations with fingertips, without having to use a pen. We laid them on the side of the screen in order to study whether users would be tempted to use their non-dominant hand for pressing them. With this design, we hoped to observe a specialization of hands, the non-dominant one dealing with secondary tasks, and the dominant one being dedicated to fine manipulations on aircraft representations.

Mark-based commands

Most commands concerning a given aircraft are simple operations, for which one needs to specify the aircraft, the operation to be performed, and one or two additional parameters (field to be highlighted or modified, type of warning, etc.). When those parameters can have many values, special interactions will be necessary. But in other cases, the number of possibilities is low enough to code each combination of operation and parameters by a mark. For instance, controllers highlight the flight level or the heading of an aircraft to register the fact that the valued was confirmed to the pilot. This highlighting operation can be designed in two ways. It is possible to go for a unique, generic command, by assigning a specific behaviour to every field representing a value. It is the choice made in PHIDIAS: users click on the field they want to highlight, thus making a menu appear, and choose the appropriate item in the menu.

With mark-based input, another choice can be made: do not specialize fields, but have several marks for the same operation, and have each mark code for a field. For instance, instead of having a mark for the command "modify a field", that can be applied to any field, let us have a mark for "modify speed", a mark for "modify flight level", and so on, with the meaning of a mark being independent from the location where it is issued. This design choice yields a growth of the number of commands that must be learnt (about 15 different marks). But it dramatically lowers the constraints imposed on users, because gestures can be started anywhere on the label, and their sizes may vary much more. This choice allows us to expect a better efficiency in interaction, at the expense of some training, which is acceptable for professional users such as air traffic controllers.

However, even if we were confident that specific gestures were a good solution, we also implemented generic commands as an alternative way of performing operations. Those generic commands (modify, highlight) are interpreted according to the field on which they are performed. Doing this, we allowed users to choose the interaction style they preferred, thus getting some hints about whether our reasoning was right. The set of all possible gestures is shown in figure 6.

To recognize gestures, GRIGRI uses Rubine's classifying algorithm. This algorithm can classify gestures composed of a single stroke, and involves an individual training period. For each class of gestures, each user provides about fifteen examples, using a tool described later in this article. During this training, the geometrical features of each gesture are extracted, and are used to produce a dozen features that are significant of the class. Later, when using the system, the same features are extracted from every gesture drawn, and compared to those of the defined classes. The classifying

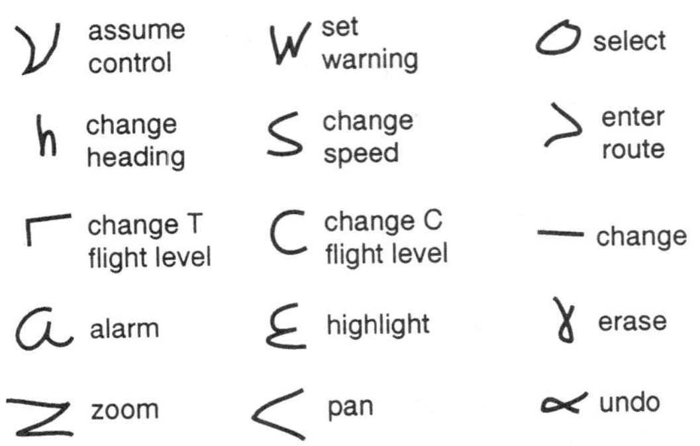

Figure 6: The set of gestures recognized.

algorithm identifies the class whose features are closest, or yields a recognition failure if the confidence ratio is too low. Classification is very fast (a few milliseconds), and response times are not perceptible by users. Having noticed that recognition failures had to be quickly and clearly signaled to users, we had to devise appropriate feedback. Considering that the visual channel was already very busy, we added sound capacities to GRIGRI. Two sampled sounds are used: one signals recognition failures, and the other signals gestures that are correct but meaningless at the place where they are performed. However, we did not use sound for successful operations yielding an immediate visual feedback, so as to restrict the use of sound to situations where it is necessary.

Long interactions

Some commands of GRIGRI involve the input of numerical or geometrical data, and cannot be implemented as a simple gesture or a button click. In the current version of GRIGRI, there are four of those "long interactions": heading input, warning input, flight level or speed input, and zooming. Heading and alarm input are triggered by a gesture on the label of an aircraft. Then begins an input sequence using classical techniques of direct manipulation: rubber band for headings, and palette for alarms. Input of flight levels and zoom are more complex.

To enter a flight level, one needs to specify an aircraft, the operation itself, and the new value. These data are entered as follows: Like other operations, the command begins with a gesture on the label of the appropriate aircraft. Then GRIGRI opens a window that allows the user to enter the new flight level. In many regions of airspace, only a few values are acceptable (330, 350, 370, 390, for instance), and PHIDIAS proposes to enter the new value through a menu, allowing itself to propose a default value. However, a number of air traffic controllers have to deal with many more possible flight levels, which makes this solution less acceptable. What we implemented in GRIGRI is the recognition of hand written numbers, in order to compare the efficiency of the two techniques. The input window has its own gesture classifier, independent from the one which is used in the radar image. It recognizes the ten digits (drawn with a single stroke) as well as gestures for correction and validation. The input window is fairly large, so as to let users write at their preferred size.

In order to avoid masking a large portion of the radar image for tool long, this window is semi-transparent, after Xerox's see-through tools [2] (see figure 7).

Changing the zoom factor involves a more classical type of interaction. The user first needs to go into zoom mode; this is done with a gesture, or by pressing a button in the bar of controls on the side of the screen. Then, the image is stretched or condensed by moving the pen outward or inward; the system goes back to normal mode when the user lifts the pen again. The two ways of starting the operation have been implemented because we hoped to identify whether users preferred to use a button or a gesture. We also hoped to induce users into using forms of two-handed interaction: the bar of controls is located on the side of the non-dominant hand, while the pen is usually held in the dominant hand. This is a situation where using two hands may be useful: the non-dominant hand rests on the border of the screen and presses buttons on demand, while the other hand stays where the attention of the user is focused, and keeps holding the pen. Even though it is impossible to perform parallel actions with current touch-screens (which might be a problem, as described in [4]), we wanted to assess whether a purely sequential operation was possible.

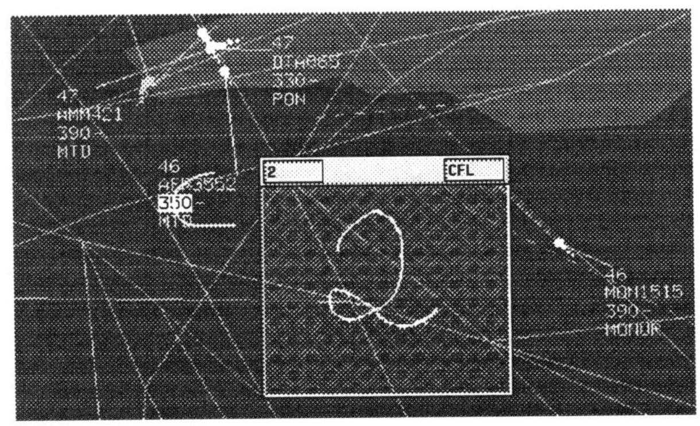

Figure 7: Entering a flight level

Finally, conscious that long interactions place the system in modes that should be made explicit to the user, we decided to use sounds. When the user starts a long interaction, or when the action is terminated, the system produces a fairly long sound of the kind which is usually associated to transitions, teleportations in science fiction movies, for instance. Though we have not yet planned to test the usefulness of such sounds, we believe they have a significant role in the perception users have of the results of their actions. However, air traffic controllers are still very cautious about sound, and this will need to be studied more closely.

Training

The algorithm we use for gesture recognition has a learning phase. Training has to be done for each user, even when the gesture set is fixed, which is the case for GRIGRI. This is partly because the dynamics of a gesture may vary, even if the result looks the same, and partly because complex gestures, such as digits, vary a lot. Although we could have used gesture editors that were already available, we decided to develop a new one, specific to our system, for several reasons. First, we wanted to make sure that the size and shape of gestures would not change between the learning phase and the evaluation phase, and we thought that the context, and especially the size of aircraft and labels, had a role. We also knew that the learning phase would be the first exposure of our users to GRIGRI, and we wanted to use it as a training period for them as well. Finally, we had noticed during the earlier experiments that gestures would vary when drawn near the edges of screen. Taking this into account, our training system makes users draw gestures in different locations of the screen, thus feeding the algorithm with all variations of gestures.

IMPLEMENTATION

GRIGRI was implemented on a Sun SPARCstation, with a software and hardware environment adapted to our needs. Only the screen of the workstation is accessible to users: the mouse was removed, and the keyboard is used by observers during tests. The screen is the standard screen of Sun workstations, attached to a custom made table. The input device is a resistive layer held between the screen and its frame, with a resolution of about 200 dots per inch.

Our system uses the X Input extension to the X Window System distributed by MIT, which had to be modified to suit our needs. With these extensions installed, the touch-screen replaces the mouse for every purpose. Gesture recognition is based on Rubine's algorithm, in its C version. The software layers that feed positions to it had to be modified to account for the slight unevenness of the screen that caused the pen to bounce. Rebounds were interpreted as the end of a mark and the start of a new one, which led to many interpretation failures. We introduced a time-based filter that removes most of those parasitic events.

GRIGRI was built using a hybrid prototyping environment developed at CENA. This environment is based on a public domain Scheme interpreter: time-intensive functions are programmed in C and exported as primitives of our environment, while most of the system is programmed in Scheme. This approach, similar to that of Tcl [11], combines the efficiency of C with the flexibility of an interpreted language, and proved very useful for prototyping. In GRIGRI, the most important primitives used are the gesture recognition algorithm and a graphical widget dedicated to animated interactive images.

EVALUATION

One of the main motivations in developing GRIGRI was to perform systematic evaluations with professional air traffic controllers in a semi-realistic environment. Those experiments, which are currently under way, have several phases. The first phase of tests relied on CENA staff as users. While not using the time of air traffic controllers, which is an expensive resource for us, those tests allowed us to identify and eliminate several design mistakes. They also helped us to design a training scheme for our new users. This first phase was sufficient to discover the drawbacks of our hardware setup. The worst problem was that the screen was too high above the working surface, thus provoking arm strain. This strain is aggravated by the fact that users cannot rest their wrists on the surface of the screen while interacting with the system, because that would confuse the touch-screen. Another problem is the thickness of the touch sensitive layer, which introduces parallax errors, that were identified as the cause of many out of context gestures: the user wants to highlight a field, but draws the corresponding mark on the background of the screen. Identifying this problem allowed us to adapt the measures that were taken during the next evaluations, and eventually led us to implementing a partial software correction. These defects did not prevent our first users from quickly getting used to the system. But this fast familiarization with the system also had a severe drawback: users immediately understood how the system worked, and soon wanted to use it like real pen and paper. This led them to increase their manipulation speed too much, and to produce many interpretation failures and errors, which was disappointing to us. We now prevent them from this disappointment by explaining the limits of the system at the first contact, before the first manipulation.

The second phase of the project, which is currently being carried out, is done with volunteer air traffic controllers. It is a first evaluation of how the system is accepted by controllers, as well as a means of getting data on how well the system works and how it is used. The obtained data will then be interpreted and used to improve the system, if it is considered promising. Other goals will then be set for the next evaluation phase, so as to understand better and better how this technology can be used in air traffic control systems. GRIGRI is evaluated by having it used in semi-realistic conditions by a radar controller. Simulated traffic is fed to the system and displayed on the radar image, while The controller is linked to pseudo-pilots through a simulated radio link. Measurements begin after one hour of simulation. What is observed is the way the radar controller interacts with the workstation. Some data is obtained by observing users and conducting interviews after every simulation. But the most objective data is obtained through the system itself, which is instrumented to output it. Among those data are the number of times every command is used, the frequencies of several types of errors, manipulation times, and even the trace of every gesture. Some errors which are difficult to detect automatically (errors on digits, for instance) are registered by an observer through the keyboard of the workstation.

This second phase involved 12 volunteer air traffic controllers. The data obtained during this phase is currently being interpreted, and only rough data are available. The first results, however, are very encouraging. The perception of the system by users is generally good, and they consider it as a potential alternative to classical interaction techniques, if it can be made reliable. The figures are encouraging as well. Out of a total number of 5200 marks drawn by the 12 users, we observed about 5% of gestures out of context, 5% of interpretation failures, and 1.3% of interpretation errors. Of course, these numbers will have to be interpreted, and the nature of interpretation errors and their impact will be studied carefully. But they prove that mark-based input is an option that can be considered further in the context of air traffic control. We already have indications that these figures can be improved easily. For the first six users, for instance, parallax errors accounted for half of the marks drawn out of context. Those parallax errors have then been partially corrected by applying a geometrical transformation to the coordinates provided by the touch-screen. They would even probably disappear with a more appropriate device, using overhead projection for instance. Similarly, half of interpretation failures have been identified as caused by technical problems that we should be able to solve (rebounds still poorly handled, or insufficiently sampled gestures). After devising and applying solutions, we will still have to determine whether the resulting error rates are satisfactory, or if they can be further improved by other means. However, even with the current 90% accuracy, our users accepted the system well, probably because of the low cost of mistakes: redoing a mark is fast enough.

Although we have gathered a lot of data that will help us to improve the system (for instance by taking into account the probability of each command according to the context), our experiment will not allow us to evaluate all the design choices made in GRIGRI. For example, we will have to determine whether users discarded generic gestures (such as the straight line associated to "modify") because they forgot about their existence, as they put it, or because of other reasons. Similarly, there were too few zoom actions (two) to gather any evidence about two-handed interaction. Finally, we now need to measure manipulation times with PHIDIAS in order to be able to compare them with the ones we obtained with GRIGRI.

Whereas some expected results are missing, we also made unexpected observations, that will have an influence on future research. For instance, we discovered that controllers liked the fact that two of them were able to share a screen, talk over it, and interact with it one after another without having to exchange mice. This opens new perspectives in the management of the collaboration between a radar controller and a planning controller. Such properties of the system will be studied in future phases of experimentation. Doing this, we hope to progress in our understanding of mark-based input while proposing a system that will be more and more usable.

CONCLUSION

We have described in this article the reasons why we considered mark-based input as an interaction technique for air traffic control. We have explained the choices made while designing an experimental workstation based on that technology, and we have described the most significant technical issues encountered. Finally, we have given first evaluation results that make us confident regarding the possible applications of pen computing to air traffic control. Nevertheless, as we explained in the introduction of this article, there are many obstacles when designing interactive systems for a domain such as air traffic control. The techniques that we are studying have only been through the first of those obstacles. Then, if they prove worthwhile, they will have to be integrated in a full size workstation. They will also have to be tested with air traffic controllers under stress; the fatigue induced by their use will have to be measured; their impact on the collaboration between a radar controller and a planning controller will have to be studied. A number of social issues will also probably appear. It takes all that to apply new technologies to our environment where efficiency and safety are so important.

ACKNOWLEDGMENTS

The first version of GRIGRI was developed by Gwenael Bothorel, using previous work by Thomas Baudel (LRI, Orsay). The current version was built with Jean-Luc Dubocq and Frédéric Lepied. Christophe Mertz supervises the evaluations that are being carried. Thomas Baudel and Wendy Mackay provided helpful comments and helped with English grammar.

REFERENCES

1. T. Baudel and M. Beaudouin-Lafon. Charade: remote control of objects using free-hand gestures. *Communications of the ACM*, pages 28–35, July 1993.

2. E. Bier, M. Stone, K. Fishkin, W. Buxton, and T. Baudel. A taxonomy of see-through tools. In *Proceedings of the ACM CHI*, pages 358–364. Addison-Wesley, 1994.

3. J. Callahan, D. Hopkins, M. Weiser, and B. Shneiderman. An empirical comparison of pie vs linear menus. In *Proceedings of the ACM CHI*, pages 95–100, 1988.

4. S. Chatty. Extending a graphical toolkit for two-handed interaction. In *Proceedings of the ACM UIST*, pages 195–204. Addison-Wesley, Nov. 1994.

5. C. Frankish. Recognition accuracy and user acceptance of pen interfaces. In *Proceedings of the ACM CHI*, pages 503–510. Addison-Wesley, 1995.

6. C. Garoff-Mercier and M. Chollet. Analyse de l'activité des contrôleurs du trafic aérien : utilisation des vecteurs d'information et des communications. Technical Report R90-07, Centre d'Études de la Navigation Aérienne, 1990.

7. D. Goldberg and C. Richardson. Touch-typing with a stylus. In *Proceedings of the ACM CHI*, pages 80–87, 1993.

8. G. Kurtenbach and T. Baudel. Hypermarks: issuing commands by drawing marks in Hypercard. In *CHI'92 Posters and Short Talks*, page 64, 1992.

9. G. Kurtenbach and W. Buxton. Issues in combining marking and direct manipulation techniques. In *Proceedings of the ACM UIST*, pages 137–144, 1991.

10. A. Meyer. Pen computing. A technology overview and a vision. *SIGCHI Bulletin*, 27(3):46–90, 1980.

11. J. K. Ousterhout. *Tcl and the Tk toolkit*. Addison-Wesley, 1994.

12. D. H. Rubine. *The automatic recognition of gestures*. PhD thesis, Carnegie Mellon University, 1991.

13. D. Venolia and F. Neiberg. T-Cube: a fast, self-disclosing pen-based alphabet. In *Proceedings of the ACM CHI*, pages 265–270, 1994.

14. P. Wellner. Interacting with paper on the Digital Desk. *Communications of the ACM*, 36(7), July 1993.

Multimodal Interfaces for Dynamic Interactive Maps*

Sharon Oviatt

Department of Computer Science and Engineering
Center for Human-Computer Communication
Oregon Graduate Institute of Science & Technology
P.O. Box 91000, Portland, Oregon 97291
(503) 690-1342; oviatt@cse.ogi.edu

ABSTRACT

Dynamic interactive maps with transparent but powerful human interface capabilities are beginning to emerge for a variety of geographical information systems, including ones situated on portables for travelers, students, business and service people, and others working in field settings. In the present research, interfaces supporting spoken, pen-based, and multimodal input were analyze for their potential effectiveness in interacting with this new generation of map systems. Input modality (speech, writing, multimodal) and map display format (highly versus minimally structured) were varied in a within-subject factorial design as people completed realistic tasks with a simulated map system. The results identified a constellation of performance difficulties associated with speech-only map interactions, including elevated performance errors, spontaneous disfluencies, and lengthier task completion time— problems that declined substantially when people could interact multimodally with the map. These performance advantages also mirrored a strong user preference to interact multimodally. The error-proneness and unacceptability of speech-only input to maps was attributed in large part to people's difficulty generating spoken descriptions of spatial location. Analyses also indicated that map display format can be used to minimize performance errors and disfluencies, and map interfaces that guide users' speech toward brevity can nearly eliminate disfluencies. Implications of this research are discussed for the design of high-performance multimodal interfaces for future map systems.

KEYWORDS: multimodal interface design, dynamic interactive maps, spoken, pen-based, and multimodal input, predictive modeling, robust processing

INTRODUCTION

Current research is progressing toward the creation of dynamically interactive on-line maps with transparent but powerful human interface capabilities. Improvement in speech and pen recognition are developing in parallel with visual display and database access capabilities to yield more broadly functional maps, with an increasingly diverse set of potential applications [1]. Map systems emphasize interfaces designed to permit users to browse, navigate, and grasp information from visual displays representing large amounts of data, and to retrieve and filter information in a tailored manner suiting a particular user and task. Finally, users can engage in rudimentary "information-seeking dialogues" with online maps, although further research will be needed to achieve the naturalness, flexibility, and expressive power one might desire.

With respect to formulation of dialogue exchanges, state-of-the-art map systems support human input using direct manipulation, speech-only input, or keyboard and speech combined with touch or mouse pointing. For example, map interaction based on direct manipulation permits the user to formulate "dynamic queries" by adjusting individual sliders for pre-selected types of information, such as Dynamic HomeFinder's ability to specify a desired real estate minimum and maximum price range by moving a slider to the desired multiple of some number [14]. This approach provides a nonlinguistic form of question-answer interaction, rather than an extended interactive dialogue. Compared with linguistic modes of interaction (e.g., speech, pen, keyboard), direct manipulation queries are relatively inflexible in their coverage, and are unable to support spontaneous description. For example, a language-based map system permits users to automatically locate out-of-view entities through simple description of landmarks and streets (e.g., "Where are the for-sale homes farthest from Yuba fault?").

Other systems such as Voyager and GeoSpace focus on spoken input as a means of conducting an information-seeking dialogue with a map [5, 15], for purposes like navigational assistance, tourist information, or information about local municipalities and their services. This class of systems emphasizes extended spoken dialogue, and in some cases provides multimodal output via text, graphics, and synthetic speech. However, human input relies exclusively on a single modality, rather than combining speech with a means of selectively pointing at the map display. On the other hand, map systems

CHI 96 Vancouver, BC Canada
© 1996 ACM 0-89791-777-4/96/04..$3.50

*This research was supported in part by Grant No. IRI-9213472 from the National Science Foundation and, as well as grants, contracts, and equipment donations from Apple Computer, ATR International, AT&T, ETRI, Intel, Scriptel, Sun Microsystems, and USWest.

such as Cubricon and Miltalk, a variant of Shoptalk, include multimodal input as well as output, with the user able to speak or use keyboard input combined with mouse pointing [4, 6]. These latter systems integrate direct manipulation and language input, yielding a potentially complementary spoken and manual input blend [4]. However, for functions like pointing on dense maps, or tracing fine-grained roadway networks, both mouse pointing and touch are relatively imprecise. They also are insufficiently versatile for creating the full array of gestures, symbols, and graphic drawings that are needed in different map applications.

In contrast, interfaces for combined spoken and pen-based input may be particularly effective for interacting with dynamic map systems, although multimodal interfaces that recognize two or more naturally-integrated input streams are still by and large in the planning stages. Although research relevant to the design of multimodal systems that incorporate speech and pen input is beginning to emerge [11, 12], the problem of how to optimize such interfaces for map displays has received little attention. In verbal and quantitative domains, interface design parameters clearly have a major impact on improving system robustness — for example, by guiding human input to coincide more closely with system processing capabilities. Empirical work within these domains indicates that basic interface design can be used to reduce difficult sources of linguistic variability in human speech and writing by a factor of 2- to 8-fold [8, 11]. More specifically, both input modality and presentation format have a documented influence on users' overall wordiness, utterance length, lexical variability, disfluencies, bigram perplexity, syntactic ambiguity (i.e., number of parses generated), and semantic integration. For instance, a highly structured form-based interface can successfully filter out difficult-to-process lexical content such as conjunctions, prepositions, and nonstandard abbreviations, can substantially lower perplexity and syntactic ambiguity scores, and can filter out 70% of the spontaneous disfluencies otherwise observed when the same person accomplishes the same task using an unconstrained interface [11, 8].

Apart from being difficult for recognition systems to process, spontaneous disfluencies present a particularly interesting source of linguistic variability because of their relation to sentential planning demands. During human-computer interaction in verbal and quantitative domains, it has been confirmed that disfluencies are elevated when an interface format is unconstrained, such that the user must take more initiative to self-structure the content and order of information presented to the system [8]. It also has been demonstrated that increased utterance length is a powerful predictor of spoken disfluencies during human-computer interaction, with a linear predictive model best summarizing this relation [8]. However, further research is needed on the source of planning load in complex visual domains, so that interfaces can be developed that effectively manage disfluencies and other difficult sources of input variability.

As a class of emerging systems, dynamic interactive maps have received little empirical guidance with respect to interface design. One aim of the present research was to explore interface issues relevant to the design of map-based systems, including assessment of human performance in terms of efficiency, accuracy, cognitive load, and preferential use. Another aim was to investigate performance in map tasks representing a range of different functions involved in seeking and filtering information from a map database, creation and editing of new map content, and control of the map display.

In this study, human performance was examined during spoken and pen-based input to dynamically interactive maps. Data were collected while people spoke, wrote, or combined speech and writing as they completed realistic tasks with a simulated map-based system. Communication modality (speech, writing, multimodal) and map display format (highly versus minimally structured) were varied in a within-subject factorial design. Consistent with previous research, it was predicted that people would prefer to interact multimodally rather than unimodally [12]. From a performance standpoint, the issue of whether unimodal or multimodal interactions would yield greater advantages in the map domain also was explored. It was hypothesized that users' preference for multimodal map interaction might be congruent with performance advantages in this modality — including faster completion time and fewer performance errors than during unimodal interaction. Cognitive load associated with the need to articulate spatial location descriptions was explored as a possible source of performance difficulty during speech-only interaction with maps.

In comparison with previously explored verbal and quantitative domains, the base-rate of disfluencies was predicted to be higher during interaction with map displays, in part due to a need to articulate abstract visual-spatial information pertaining to location, size, and shape. If elevated, this higher disfluency rate would represent a special difficulty requiring interface management in map domains. Based on previous research, it also was hypothesized that a highly-structured map display that effectively reduces users' need to self-structure their input would reduce both spoken disfluencies and performance errors. Finally, the rate of disfluencies was examined in sentences of varying length, to assess whether longer utterances in the map domain have an elevated rate of disfluencies per 100 words compared with briefer ones. Implications of this research are discussed for the design of future high-performance dynamic maps.

METHOD

This section summarizes a simulation experiment that was designed to examine people's highly interactive exchanges with a dynamic map system.

Subjects, Tasks, and Procedure

Eighteen subjects participated in this research as paid volunteers. A "Service Transaction System" was simulated that could assist users with map-based tasks. For example, during a real estate selection task, participants were asked to select an appropriate home for a client. They were provided with a thumbnail sketch of the client's needs, such as acceptable price range. Using a city map, they filtered available homes until locating one meeting their constraints. A person might circle a lakeside house icon with their pen and say "I don't want a house in a flood zone." In response, the system would display waterways and flood zones, and would filter out the house icon if it was located poorly. During a map update task, people added and modified information on a map representing a high-growth area. For example, they indicated new municipal buildings, parks, and road closures. During these tasks, people could manipulate the map display itself (e.g., zooming, scrolling, automatic location of entities), and they could retrieve and manipulate information relevant to the map-based application. Figure 1 illustrates a user's spoken request to automatically locate the hospital. Figure 2 shows a distance calculation during real estate selection, which the user performs by circling two entities and connecting a line between them while asking, "How far from here to here?"

During the study, subjects received a general orientation to the Service Transaction System, and on how to enter information on the LCD tablet when writing, speaking, and combining both modalities. When writing, they were free to use cursive handwriting or printing, gestures, symbols, graphics, pointing, or other marks. They were told to write information with the electronic stylus directly onto the color map displayed on their LCD tablet. When speaking, subjects were instructed to tap and hold the stylus on the map as they spoke. During free choice, people were completely free to use either modality in any way they wished. In all cases, they were encouraged to speak and write naturally, to work at their own pace, and simply to focus on completing their task.

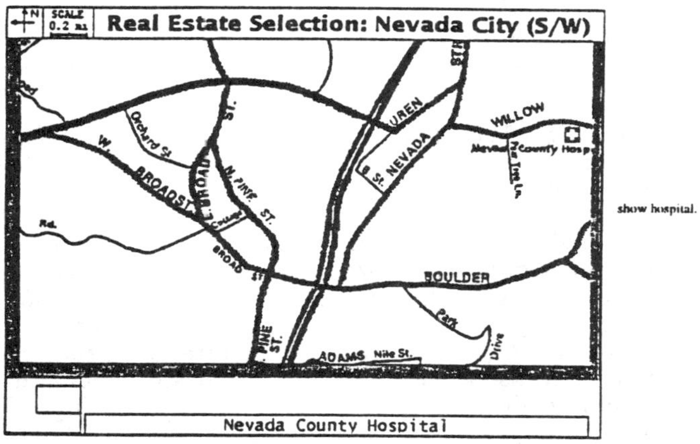

Figure 1: Minimally structured map display format during real estate selection

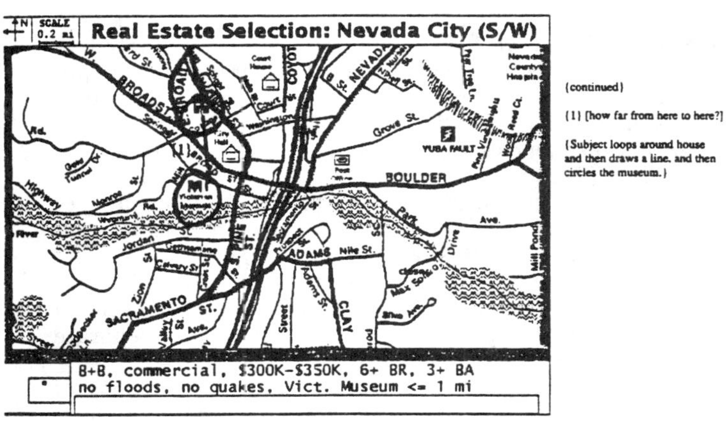

Figure 2: Highly structured map display format during real estate selection

People also were instructed on completing tasks using two different presentation formats. In one format illustrated in Figure 2, a detailed reference map displayed the full network of roadways, buildings, overlay information, and labels that are conventionally found on hard-copy reference maps. This format presented the most graphically and linguistically structured map. The second format, illustrated in Figure 1, displayed only a streamlined network of roads leading to available real estate, and only buildings and overlay information to which the user actually referred. Essentially, the default structure in this format was a less structured "minimalist" version of the reference map, with about one-third of the roadway and overlay information as the more structured display. However, people were free to add more information to this map format as they worked.

Other than specifying the available input modality and map format, an effort was made not to influence the manner in which people expressed themselves. People's input was received by an informed assistant, who performed the role of interpreting and responding as a fully functional system would. Essentially, the assistant tracked the subject's written or spoken input, and clicked on predefined fields at a Sun SPARCstation to send altered map displays and confirmations back to the subject. After the session, a post-experimental interview was conducted and subjects were debriefed.

Semi-Automatic Simulation Technique. In developing this simulation, an emphasis was placed on providing automated support for streamlining the simulation to the extent needed to create facile, subject-paced interactions with clear feedback, and to have comparable specifications for the different input modalities. In the present simulation environment, response delays averaged less than 1 second between subject input and system feedback. The simulation was designed to be sufficiently automated so that the assistant could concentrate attention on monitoring the accuracy of incoming information, and on maintaining sufficient vigilance to ensure prompt responding. Technical details of the general simulation method have been provided elsewhere [10]. However, the specific method used in this study was adapted extensively to handle the dynamic display and manipulation of maps, overlays, and photographs.

Research Design and Data Capture. The research design was a completely crossed factorial with repeated measures, with the following main factors: 1) communication modality – speech-only, pen-only, multimodal pen/voice, and 2) presentation format – highly structured map, minimally structured map. All 18 subjects completed two subtasks within each of these six conditions, with the order of conditions counterbalanced across subjects. In total, data were available from 216 tasks for analysis purposes. All human-computer interactions were videotaped. Hardcopy transcripts also were created, with the subject's handwritten input on the map captured automatically in context, and spoken input transcribed onto the printouts.

Transcript Coding. Coding was conducted for the following measures:

Total Words and Mean Length of Utterance (MLU)– The total number of spoken and written words, as well as the average number of words per utterance, was tabulated for each condition and subject.

Disfluencies and Self-Corrections– Spontaneously occurring disfluencies and self-corrections were totaled for each subject and condition. The total number of disfluencies per condition then was converted to a rate per 100 words, and average disfluency rates were summarized as a function of condition and utterance length. Disfluencies of the following types were coded: (1) Content self-corrections– e.g., "west of, no, *east* of Seven Hills School," (2) False starts– e.g., "I want to be...have the hospital within 1.5 miles," (3) Verbatim repetitions– e.g., "Victor...Victorian museum," (4) Spoken filled pauses– e.g., "uh," "um," (5) Written self-corrected spellings and abbreviations– e.g., "sroll...scroll;" "BA...bath." Details of disfluency definitions and classification have been provided elsewhere [8].

Spatial Location Descriptions– The total number of sentences containing a spatial location description were tabulated, as was the mean length of these utterances. Expressions scored as spatial location descriptions were those specifying an object's placement in relation to other objects, landmarks, or roads on the map. Typical location descriptions included simple locative prepositions (e.g., "Close Willow Road between the post office and May Lake"), approximate location descriptions (e.g., "Move the overpass a little farther to the right"), the relative orientation and/or distance between objects (e.g., "The apple orchard is 0.2 miles east of Sugarloaf Mountain Park"). To evaluate whether sentential content involving location descriptions is more prone to disfluency than other content, all sentences containing spatial location descriptions were scored for the rate of spoken disfluencies within constituent clauses representing the location description versus the rest of the sentence.

Task Completion Time– The number of seconds required to complete each subtask was totaled for each condition and subject.

Task-critical Content Errors– The total number of task-critical content errors was tabulated for each condition and subject. An example of such an error would be requesting a home with the wrong number of bedrooms for a client, or placing a new building at the wrong intersection.

Self-reported and Observed Preferences– During post-experimental interviews, people's self-reported preference was assessed for communicating in either combined pen/voice, unimodal speech, or unimodal writing. In addition, preference to complete tasks using the more structured reference map versus minimalist map was assessed. When subjects were free to use any input mode in the multimodal conditions, their observed preference to interact multimodally versus unimodally also was tabulated.

Reliability. All dependent measures reported in this paper had reliabilities of 0.80 or above, and 90% of the measures had reliabilities above 0.86.

RESULTS

Mean Length of Utterance. In these map-based interactions, utterances ranged from 1 to 32 words. Average utterance length during multimodal input was confirmed to be significantly briefer than that observed during speech-only input (i.e., 4.79 versus 6.22 words respectively), both in the structured map format, paired t (17) = 3.62, $p < .001$, one-tailed, and in the minimal map format, paired t (17) = 5.53, $p < .001$, one-tailed.

Disfluencies and Self-Corrections. The data yielded a corpus totaling over 12,000 words, including approximately 250 disfluencies for analysis. Since it was predicted that the disfluency rate would be more elevated in a complex visual domain than in verbal or quantitative domains reported previously [8], the average total disfluency rate was compared for verbal and map-based simulations. It was confirmed that the disfluency rate was significantly more elevated in the map domain than the verbal one, t (34) = 3.39, $p < .001$, one-tailed.

Table 1 summarizes the average spoken disfluency rates for six types of human-computer interaction, comparing human-computer map-based disfluencies with other kinds of spoken interaction reported previously [7, 8]. These disfluency rates all are lower than those reported for human-human spoken interactions which, for example, have been estimated at 5.50 disfluencies per 100 words for two-person face-to-face interaction involving verbal content [8] and 7.34 for two-person interaction involving map-based tasks [2].

	Structured	Unconstrained
Map Domain	1.70	2.14
Verbal Domain	0.78	1.74
Numeric Domain	0.87	1.87

Table 1: Spoken disfluency rate per 100 words for human-computer interaction involving different formats and content domains

As predicted, disfluencies in the multimodal conditions were significantly lower than those in the speech-only conditions, with average rates of 1.25 and 1.95, respectively, paired t (17) = 2.36, $p < .02$, one-tailed. With respect to format, the average rate of all spoken and written disfluencies also was significantly elevated in the minimally structured map compared to the highly structured one, with an average of 2.26 versus 1.68 disfluencies per 100 words, respectively, paired t (15) = 1.76, $p < .05$, one-tailed. This format effect also is illustrated in Table 1.

Since previous simulation studies in the verbal and numeric domains have demonstrated a strong relation between spoken utterance length and the likelihood of a disfluency, disfluency rates in the map domain were examined further for specific utterances graduated in length. Analyses indicated that the average rate of spoken disfluencies increased significantly with utterance length for lengths 2-21, r = +.89. When the rate of spoken disfluencies was compared for short (1-6 words), medium (7-12 words), and long utterances (13-21 words), it increased from 0.95, to 1.64, to 5.06 disfluencies per 100 words, respectively. Statistical comparisons confirmed that these rates represent a marginal increase between short and medium sentences, t = 1.73 (df = 10), $p < .06$ (one-tailed), and a significant increase between medium and long ones, t = 4.00 (df = 5.2, separate variances), $p < .005$ (one-tailed).

A regression analysis indicated that the strength of predictive association between utterance length and spoken disfluency rate was $\rho^2_{XY} = .79$ (N = 17). That is, 79% of the variance in the rate of spoken disfluencies was predictable simply by knowing an utterance's specific length. The following linear model, illustrated in the scatterplot in Figure 3, summarizes this relation: $Y_{ij} = \mu Y + \beta_{Y*X}(X_j - \mu X) + e_{ij}$, with a Y-axis constant coefficient of -0.84, and an X-axis beta coefficient of +0.35 representing utterance length. These data indicate that the demands associated with planning and generating longer constructions while interacting with a map lead to a substantial increase in the rate of disfluent speech, which generalizes a similar finding obtained in the verbal and numeric domains [8].

Since utterance length is strongly related with disfluency rates, and since the average utterance length varies between domains and input modalities, the present data

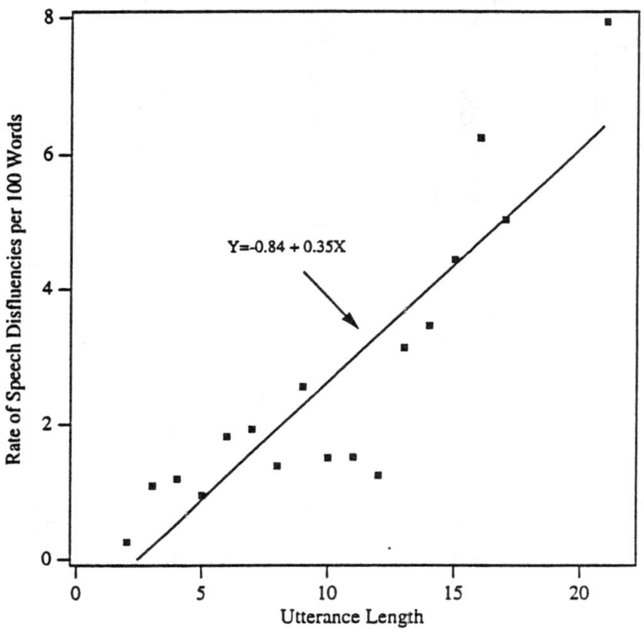

Figure 3: Linear regression model summarizing increasing rate of spoken disfluencies per 100 words as a function of utterance length during map interactions

were examined further to evaluate whether differences in utterance length alone could potentially account for the observed difference in disfluencies between: (1) verbal and map-based domains, or (2) speech-only and multimodal input conditions. To make this assessment, a comparison of disfluency rates was conducted for utterances matched on length. With utterance length controlled in this manner, the average spoken disfluency rate in the verbal versus map domains was 1.64 versus 1.70, with no significant difference as a function of domain content alone, paired t (10) < 1. Likewise, a comparison of disfluency rates in speech-only versus multimodal conditions, after matching samples on length, revealed averages of 1.86 and 1.99, respectively, paired t (16) < 1.

Spatial Location Descriptions. In light of the fact that utterance length may correlate with and simply be mediating other unique linguistic characteristics of speech to maps, spatial location descriptions were analyzed in terms of their relation to MLU and disfluencies. An average of 17.2 utterances per subject in the speech-only conditions contained adverbial locative descriptions, which was reduced significantly to 6.7 for the same subjects in the multimodal conditions, paired $t(17) = 10.04$, $p < .001$, one-tailed. Sentences containing location descriptions also were relatively lengthy, and they were significantly lengthier when spoken than when delivered multimodally (i.e., averaging 9.85 and 8.96 MLU, respectively), paired t test, $t(15) = 1.89$, $p < .04$, one-tailed. In contrast, the average MLU was just 6.22 for all spoken sentences, and 4.79 for all multimodal sentences in the map domain. Finally, sentences containing spatial location descriptions had an elevated rate of spoken disfluencies. Further analysis revealed that sentential constituents containing a location description averaged 2.51 spoken disfluencies per 100 words, which was significantly higher than 1.68 in the baseline constituent of the *same* sentences uttered by the *same* speaker, Wilcoxon Signed Ranks test, $z = 1.66$ ($N = 16$), $p < .05$, one-tailed. These findings confirm that longer and more disfluent utterances resulted when a spatial location description was produced while speaking to the map. Furthermore, the spatial location constituent of an utterance was significantly more disfluent than the baseline constituent of the same utterance.

Task Completion Time. Task completion times were significantly faster during multimodal map interactions (249 secs) than during either speech (278 secs) or writing (410 secs), paired t (17) $= 1.92$, $p < .04$ (one-tailed) and paired t (17) $= 8.19$, $p < .001$ (one-tailed), respectively. Figure 4 illustrates that this relative speed advantage of multimodal over speech-only input is unique to the visual/spatial map domain, and was not found in verbal or numeric domains.

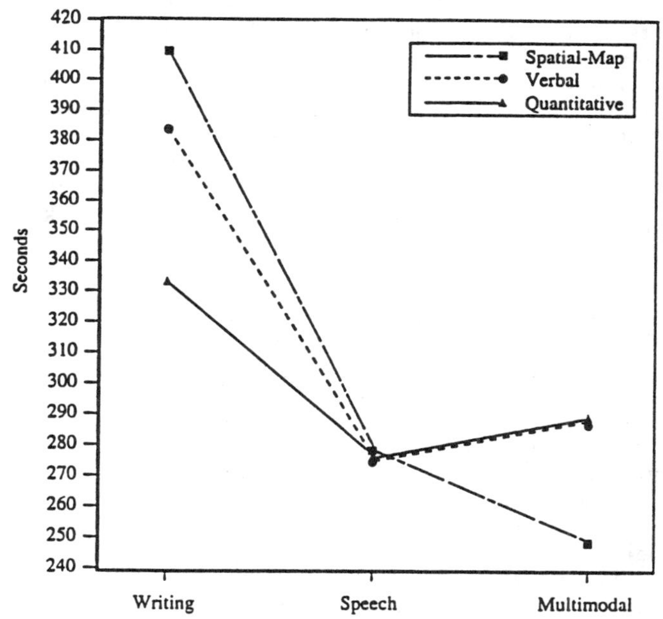

Figure 4: Task completion time as a function of input modality and content domain.

Task-critical Content Errors. Users averaged 0.54 content errors per task set overall, with the rate of errors during combined speech and writing just 0.39 per task set, compared with 0.67 for writing and 0.61 for speech. Wilcoxon signed ranks analysis confirmed that task-critical content errors were elevated significantly during speech-only interaction compared with multimodal input, $T+ = 83$ ($N = 14$), $p < .03$, one-tailed. However, analyses revealed neither a significant difference in content errors between speech-only and writing-only

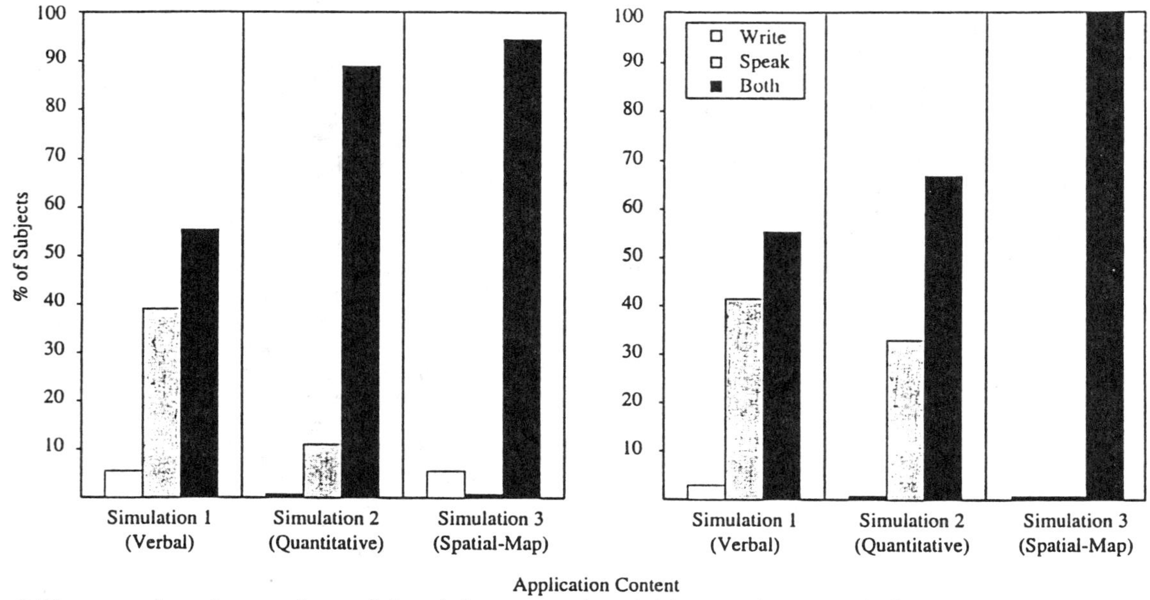

Figure 5: Self-reported preference for multimodal versus unimodal interaction in verbal, quantitative, and map-based simulations (left panel), and users' observed multimodal versus unimodal interaction during free choice (right panel)

interactions, nor between writing-only and multimodal interactions.

An analysis of the predominant type of content errors revealed that approximately 48% involved locating objects incorrectly in relation to landmarks or streets on the map. One common source of these location errors involved reversals of orientation (e.g., "The handicaped center is east, no, *west* of Deer Creek School"). Another common source accounting for 18% of all errors involved incorrectly specifying inclusion/exclusion relations with respect to a distance between two objects (e.g., "I'd like a house within a mile of the airport...I mean, at least a mile *away from* any airports.")

Self-reported and Observed Preferences. Results indicated that 94.5% of subjects preferred interacting with the map multimodally, 5.5% preferred exclusively written input, but none of the participants preferred unimodal spoken input. Figure 5 (left panel) illustrates this strong preference for multimodal versus unimodal interaction within the map-based domain, in comparison with recently reported preferences to interact multimodally in verbal and quantitative domains [12]. Figure 5 (right panel) illustrates that users also were observed to select multimodal over unimodal input 100% of the time in the map domain when they had free choice. Both self-reported and observed preference to use multimodal input were most pronounced in the complex visual domain, compared with others reported previously. With respect to display format, 83.5% of participants preferred interacting with the more structured map, whereas 11% reported no preference, and 5.5% preferred the minimally structured display format.

DISCUSSION

Within a visual-spatial domain such as maps, clear performance advantages exist for supporting human-computer interaction multimodally. In comparison with speech-only input to a map, combined use of pen and voice actually was faster, less error-prone, and input involved less complex linguistic expressions to be recognized and parsed. In fact, for the *same* user completing the *same* task, 36% of all content errors and 50% of spoken disfluencies could be eliminated simply by permitting people to interact multimodally, input involved shorter constructions with fewer complex spatial descriptions, and task completion time sped up 10%. Furthermore, this constellation of performance advantages was matched by a strong user preference to interact multimodally with maps.

In large part, the error-prone, slow, disfluent, and generally unacceptable nature of speech-only input to maps can be traced directly to people's difficulty articulating spatially-oriented descriptions. The following example illustrates one subject's difficulty articulating a location description: "Add an open space on the north lake to b- include the north lake part of the road and north." In contrast, the same task was achieved multimodally simply by circling an area and saying, "Open space." Analysis of task-critical performance errors revealed that approximately 48% of all content errors involved locating objects incorrectly in relation to landmarks or streets on the map. Of these, the largest subclass of location errors was reversals of orientation (e.g., "Close the road west, um, *east* of American Hill Park"). Another common subclass involved misspecification of containment or exclusion relations pertaining to a distance between two points (e.g., "Show me houses within a mile, I mean at *least a mile away* from highway 49").

A systematic analysis of all map utterances containing location descriptions revealed that the *same* person accomplishing the *same* task generated 157% more such sentences when speaking than when mixing modes, and that these spoken constructions averaged longer than their multimodal counterparts. During multimodal interactions, people selectively used the pen to point or create graphics in a way that effectively specified location, shape, and area— eliminating the need to articulate complex location descriptions. Further analysis of utterances containing location descriptions, in which baseline versus location constituents were compared, clarified that spoken disfluencies were concentrated 50% more heavily in location-descriptive constituents. That is, for utterances matched on both speaker and length, a significantly higher loading of spoken disfluencies was evident on sentential constituents describing location. Essentially, the need to speak spatial information can be viewed as a primary source of planning demand in map-based domains, and one that directly contributes to increased disfluent speech in this domain.

Spoken disfluencies during map interaction also were confirmed to be strikingly sensitive to utterance length. Of all the variance in spoken disfluencies in the present data, 79% was predictable simply by knowing an utterance's specific length. A linear model was provided, $Y = -0.84 + 0.35X$, to summarize the predicted rate of spoken disfluencies (Y) as a function of utterance length (X). This finding replicates and generalizes the linear predictive model between utterance length and spoken disfluencies reported previously by Oviatt and colleagues [11, 8], which was based on human-computer interaction involving verbal and quantitative content. In previous research, the best fitting linear model was a similar $Y = -0.32 + 0.26X$, which accounted for 77% of the variance in observed spoken disfluencies. In a recent analysis of disfluencies in the Air Travel Information System (ATIS) domain that involved a different data collection procedure, Shriberg [13] replicated this finding that a linear model provides the best fit between disfluencies and utterance length during human-computer interaction. Both the present research on map displays and Shriberg's research on ATIS data confirm that knowledge of utterance length is a powerful and robust predictor of spoken disfluencies during human-computer interaction — one with broad application to qualitatively different task domains and styles of query interaction. Although the increased planning demands of generating progressively longer utterances is an excellent predictor of disfluencies, nonetheless in the map domain utterance length *per se* is not necessarily the direct *cause* or the only factor driving heightened disfluencies, as indicated by the results on spatial location descriptions.

From a pragmatic viewpoint, interface techniques capable of guiding people's spoken input to avoid lengthy constructions (i.e., 13 words or more) could potentially reduce spoken disfluencies by a substantial 74%. Since lengthier utterances to the map frequently contained descriptions of spatial location, and since multimodal interaction typically circumvented location descriptions through pen-based pointing or marking, the most effective way to elicit brief input during map-based tasks appears to be selecting a multimodal interface design. Whether other complex visual-spatial domains involving graphic, photographic, or moving audio-visual images would benefit from similar performance advantages if implemented multimodally remains to be investigated.

With respect to relative efficiency, time required to complete map-based tasks actually was *shorter* during multimodal than speech-only input, primarily because location and shape can be designated more precisely, rapidly, and with less effort and error using the pen. Specifically, task completion time was 10% faster during combined pen/voice input, even though it included 13% writing. Perhaps the greatest speed advantage of multimodal input accrued from pen-based pointing and graphic marks to designate a point, line, or area on the map display, which then avoided the need to speak complex location descriptions. Multimodal input speed also can be attributed to the relative speed of forming many frequently occurring map-based pen gestures (e.g., —> to request scrolling), symbols (e.g., $), and abbreviations (e.g., "BA" for bathroom), especially when compared with speech input needed to achieve the same goal (e.g., drawing a circle to zoom on a house, versus saying "Show me the house at the southwest corner of Nevada and Broad Streets"). Although speech typically is reported to be two- to three-fold faster than writing or typing during human-human communication tasks [3, 9], in these map tasks speaking was only 32% faster than pen input. This constriction of the usual speed advantage of spoken over written input clearly occurred because of the frequent use of gestures, abbreviations, symbols, and digits in the map domain, rather than handwriting of full lexical expresssions as in formal text. Given the speed and other performance advantages of multimodal input revealed by this research, applications involving complex visual-spatial displays such as GIS systems appear to constitute an ideal domain for the development of early multimodal systems.

The degree of structure provided by a map's visual display also influenced spoken disfluencies and content errors substantially. The minimally structured map, which required speakers to self-structure and plan to a greater degree, precipitated a 43% higher rate of disfluencies and 31% higher rate of content errors than the highly structured display. Since this presentation format difference occurred in samples matched for length, it clearly exerted an influence on disfluencies independent of utterance length. These results on map format replicate and generalize the previous finding that degree of interface structure in verbal or quantitative tasks, defined as a form-based graphic versus unconstrained scratchpad, influences users' language and disfluency levels [8]. The majority of users, or 84%, also reported a preference for the more structured map display, which they said facilitated rapid orientation, provided better guidance, and required less effort to self-structure. Perhaps surprisingly, users did not appear to view flexible self-structuring of the map as an advantage, but rather as "more burden on you." Future research is needed to investigate methods of permitting users to flexibly self-structure interfaces without simultaneously driving up their cognitive load and difficult-to-process sources of variability in their language — since these goals currently appear to trade off, and therefore present a dilemna for interface designers. Research also should address what impact other dimensions of interface display may have on the processability of human language input.

The vast majority of users, or approximately 95%, reported preferring to interact with the map multimodally, another 5% were satisfied with pen-only map interaction, but *no users* reported a preference to speak to the map. This strong preference for multimodal map interaction was replicated in data indicating that 100% of users' interacted multimodally when observed during free choice. Although in verbal and quantitative domains, people also preferred multimodal over unimodal interaction, this preference clearly was most pronounced when manipulating complex visual-spatial displays. Self reports revealed that people preferred to use speech and writing for different and often complementary functions. For example, in most instances requiring specification of a location, users had a strong preference to interject pen use, thereby avoiding spoken location descriptions.

From a methodological point of view, there now is cumulative evidence from this study and previous research that disfluencies present a sensitive index of cognitive load during human-computer interaction [8]. That is, the spoken disfluency rate per 100 words provides a window on inferential and sentential planning demands within the normal working range, below the threshold for verbalizing stress or any specific difficulties with a task. As such, disfluency rates may present a valuable tool for evaluating the adequacy of future spoken language or multimodal interfaces in supporting human performance. Since multimodal interfaces are relatively complex, empirical assessment may be particularly valuable for proactively guiding their design. Without such guidance, multimodal/multimedia systems with too many input and output options, or that are poorly integrated, run a special risk of fragmenting user behavior and driving up cognitive load to unacceptable levels. This in turn risks increasing human performance errors and difficult sources of linguistic variability in human input, which can be expected to have a direct bearing on degradation of system robustness.

Among other things, the goals of designing multimodal rather than unimodal systems typically include enhanced ease of use, transparency, flexibility, and efficiency, as well as usability for more challenging applications, under more adverse conditions, and by a broader spectrum of the population. However, actually achieving these advantages will depend on basic empirical research on a variety of fundamental issues, as well as the construction of theoretical models that predict the performance advantages of spoken, manual, and combined input modes for different types of tasks. One implication of this research is that multimodal systems evidently can permit sufficient flexibility for users to avoid many errors, and to optimize speed through selection of a particular input mode or integrated use of modes at appropriate points during an interaction. In some tasks permitting multimodal input, it also appears that users are able to effectively self-manage their own cognitive load. The present research has elucidated one class of application domains likely to benefit from multimodal system design— that of complex visual displays involving maps. It also has provided information about specific performance advantages than can be anticipated for multimodal versus unimodal map-based systems.

References

[1] *1995 GIS World Sourcebook*. GIS World, Inc., Fort Collins, Colorado, 1995.

[2] J. Carletta, R. Caley, and S. Isard. A collection of self-repairs from the map task corpus. Tech. Rep. 47, Human Communication Research Centre, Edinburgh Univ., Scotland, 1993.

[3] A. Chapanis, R. N. Parrish, R. B. Ochsman, and G. D. Weeks. Studies in interactive communication: II. The effects of four communication modes on the linguistic performance of teams during cooperative problem solving. *Human Factors*, 1977, 19(2):101–125.

[4] P. R. Cohen, M. Dalrymple, D. B. Moran, F. C. N. Pereira, J. W. Sullivan, R. A. Gargan, J. L. Schlossberg, and S. W. Tyler. Synergistic use of direct manipulation and natural language. In *CHI'89 Conf. Proc.*, New York, 1989, ACM, Addison Wesley, 227–234.

[5] I. Lokuge and S. Ishizaki. Geospace: An interactive visualization system for exploring complex information spaces. In *CHI '95 Conf. Proc.*, New York, 1995, ACM:SIGCHI, 409–414.

[6] J. G. Neal and S. C. Shapiro. Intelligent multimedia interface technology. In J. W. Sullivan and S. W. Tyler (eds.), *Intelligent User Interfaces*, , ACM: Addison Wesley, New York, 1991, chap. 3, 45–68.

[7] S. L. Oviatt. Predicting spoken disfluencies during human-computer interaction. In K. Shirai (ed.), *Proc. of the International Symposium on Spoken Dialogue: New Directions in Human-Machine Communication*, Tokyo, Japan, Nov. 1993, 53-56.

[8] S. L. Oviatt. Predicting spoken disfluencies during human-computer interaction. *Computer Speech and Language*, 1995, 9:19–35.

[9] S. L. Oviatt and P. R. Cohen. Discourse structure and performance efficiency in interactive and noninteractive spoken modalities. *Computer Speech and Language*, 1991, 5(4):297–326.

[10] S. L. Oviatt, P. R. Cohen, M. W. Fong, and M. P. Frank. A rapid semi-automatic simulation technique for investigating interactive speech and handwriting. In J. Ohala (ed.), *Proc. of the ICSLP*, Univ. of Alberta, 1992, vol. 2, 1351–1354.

[11] S. L. Oviatt, P. R. Cohen, and M. Q. Wang. Toward interface design for human language technology: Modality and structure as determinants of linguistic complexity. *Speech Communication*, 1994, 15(3-4), 283-300.

[12] S. L. Oviatt and E. Olsen. Integration themes in multimodal human-computer interaction. In *Proc. of the ICSLP*, Acoust. Soc. of Japan, Yokohama, 1994, 551–554.

[13] E. Shriberg. *Preliminaries to a Theory of Speech Disfluencies*. PhD thesis, Univ. of California, Berkeley, 1994.

[14] C. Williamson and B. Schneiderman. The dynamic homefinder: Evaluating dynamic queries in a real estate information exploration system. In *SIGIR Conf. Proc.*, ACM, 1992, 339–346.

[15] V. Zue, J. Glass, D. Goddeau, D. Goodine, H. Leung, M. McCandless, M. Phillips, J. Polfroni, Seneff. S., and D. Whitney. Recent progress on the MIT voyager spoken language system. In *Proc. of the ICSLP*, Acoust. Soc. of Japan, Kobe, 1990, 1317–1320.

Using the Web Instead of a Window System

James Rice, Adam Farquhar, Philippe Piernot, and Thomas Gruber
Knowledge Systems Laboratory
Gates Building 2A, M/C 9020
Stanford, CA, 94305
+1 415 723 3444 http://www-ksl.stanford.edu/
{rice, axf, piernot, gruber}@ksl.stanford.edu

ABSTRACT

We show how to deliver a sophisticated, yet intuitive, interactive application over the web using off-the-shelf web browsers as the interaction medium. This attracts a large user community, improves the rate of user acceptance, and avoids many of the pitfalls of software distribution.

Web delivery imposes a novel set of constraints on user interface design. We outline the tradeoffs in this design space, motivate the choices necessary to deliver an application, and detail the lessons learned in the process.

These issues are crucial because the growing popularity of the web guarantees that software delivery over the web will become ever more wide-spread.

This application is publicly available at:
`http://www-ksl-svc.stanford.edu:5915/`

Keywords

Internet application, remote user interface, active document, CSCW, World Wide Web, Hypertext, HTML, HTTP, Java.

INTRODUCTION

The recent explosion in the popularity of the world-wide web and its associated hypertext markup language (HTML) and hypertext transfer protocol (HTTP) presents an exciting new opportunity to provide widely distributed access to sophisticated software applications [10]. The design of HTTP and HTML, however, place a number of novel and often severe constraints on the design of interfaces that use them. This paper outlines our approach to providing a rich user interface to a sophisticated application over the web, specifies our design objectives, the constraints imposed by HTML and HTTP, and the trade-offs that we made in order to meet these objectives whilst satisfying these constraints. We further document the evolution of the design and implementation of our application, and some of the lessons learned.

Space constraints prevent us from discussing a number of important issues, such as user preferences, the impact of Java, and ways in which HTML could easily be changed to support this sort of application better. These issues are discussed in the HTML version of this paper in these proceedings.

CHI 96 Vancouver, BC Canada

The Application

Our application [1] is a system for browsing, creating, and editing *Ontologies*. An ontology is a formal specification that defines the representational vocabulary in some domain of discourse [3]. While our ontologies are used for knowledge sharing and agent interoperability [2], they share many properties in common with class libraries, object-oriented specifications, object-oriented simulation components, database schema definitions, and knowledge-bases. We expect that many of our design decisions will apply to systems for browsing and editing these types of objects.

For example, we might define an ontology of units and dimensions. Such an ontology would provide us with a definition of what it means to be a unit of measure, or dimension, would provide all of the relations and axioms that interrelate units and dimensions, and would hook these concepts into more primitive concepts. Having defined this ontology, we would be able to reuse this work in any application that deals with the measurement of physical quantities.

Clearly, some ontologies are going to be largely static definitions of well understood and invariant domains, but an ontology of, say, therapeutic drugs would need to be updated almost every day. Such an ontology has to be the product of a concensus between practitioners in the field. Writing and editing such an ontology is, by its nature a distributed activity – hence our tool must support distributed, collaborative editing.

Ontology construction is, by nature, a distributed, collaborative activity [4]. In the medical domain, for example, no single person has the expertise necessary to construct an ontology for therapeutic drugs. It is essential for experts to collaborate on construction. Furthermore, it is essential for prospective users of an ontology to examine, evaluate, and critique it. These users will be geographically distributed across a variety of organizations (e.g., hospitals, insurers, government agencies).

Our application is unusual among web services because it allows users to create and edit objects, rather than simply retrieve them by following hypertext links or by making simple database queries.

The implemented application provides a full, distributed, collaborative editing environment with over a hundred user commands, context sensitive help, context sensitive user feedback and bug-report collection, multi-level undo/redo, multi-user sessions, and so on. It has been publicly available since February 1995 and (as of 1/96) supports about 900 users, about 150 of whom we would classify as "serious," who average over 2000 requests per day. Feedback from users and data collected online support the claim that it is possible to deploy richly interactive applications over the web. Based on our experience in developing the ontology editor, we offer an approach to developing and delivering web-based applications that instantiates this claim.

Providing Access to Applications Over the Web

We came to the web approach out of frustration with conventional approaches to software development and distribution. The costs of ensuring that software was portable over multiple hardware and software platforms together with the cost of distributing software releases, patches, and upgrades were simply too high for a small research institution. Indeed, these costs often dominated our efforts to develop and test new functionality. Providing a system to support distributed collaborative work would only make the situation worse.

The web appeared to be a reasonable alternative. We had previously developed experience in providing automatically generated HTML documents to describe ontologies and other structured objects [6]. People found that using their native hypertext browsing systems to examine these documents was both valuable and appealing.

The ontology editor is a good candidate for this approach because (1) it requires distributed access from heterogeneous environments; and (2) think-time dominates computation time. This makes it possible to provide a useful shared computational resource for a community of users from a centralized server without the hardware costs being too onerous.

PROBLEM ANALYSIS AND DESIGN

In this section we begin to describe how we addressed the problem of delivering our network-based application, and how we designed it.

Objectives

Our goal was to create a general environment to facilitate the development and sharing of ontologies. Such an environment must assist the user in the basic development tasks of browsing, creating, maintaining, sharing, and using ontologies. We also realized that many of our users want to develop ontologies through a consensus process; therefore, we needed to provides tools to help people collaborate during development.

From the outset, we wanted to make our potential user community as large as possible. The target community is diverse and includes academics, industrial researchers, and government employees. Once we had established our web-based system, our user community grew from a handful to hundreds in the space of a few months.

This was an additional incentive to use the web. Furthermore, distributed access eliminates the need for our users to have high-end hardware systems or expensive licenses for the proprietary software systems that we used to develop our application more efficiently. A centralized server model also means that we can make changes and upgrades to the server at a single site (or small number of controlled sites); the new, improved software is instantly accessible to all users. In short, we decided that it would be cheaper to provide free computational resources to our entire user community than to develop shrink-wrap software and distribute it to them.

Our challenge was to design a user interface that operates under the constraints of the web, remains intuitive and natural to users, and provides full access to the application.

Support for Naïve Users

In order to achieve our goal of broad impact, we worked to make our application intuitive and usable to anyone familiar with web browsers (e.g., Netscape Navigator or Mosaic) so that. a new user could pick up and productively use our application without any formal training or preparation. We explicitly addressed this by the following means:

HTML used for documentation: Our application has no manual at all *per se*. All documentation is provided on-line using the same browser that the user already employs to operate the application.

Guided tour: One important aspect of the documentation is a guided tour, which takes the new user through a credible editing scenario, motivating the different features of the system.

In-context, automatically-generated help: Unlike applications such as Microsoft Word 6.0, in which documentation is available only in an idiosyncratic hypertext browser, our application uses a standard hypertext browser for its full interface. This means that help and documentation are seamlessly integrated with the rest of the system. Indeed, the help facility builds help pages in real-time so as to give the most focused and helpful response in the user's context. A novel feature of the help facility is that the commands available to the user are echoed as widgets on the help page (figure 1 right). If the user clicks on the widget in the help page which has accompanying explanatory text and links to worked examples, then the command associated with that widget is activated just as if it were invoked on the page from which the user made the help request.

Familiar interface: There was no existing interface metaphor for ontology editing. We selected a document metaphor so that the application could be smoothly integrated into the HTML world. This allows users who are familiar with hypertext documents and browsers to make an easy transition into our interactive application.

Support for Power Users

Although we were keen to expand our user community as much as possible, we were aware that experienced ontology developers would not want to be held back by an interface that was optimized for naïve users. It is very important to us to support power users. The vast majority of meaningful ontologies are developed by such users, even if these ontologies are then used by the less experienced as building blocks. The issue of power user support was eventually resolved by providing a powerful user preference facility. This allows the experienced user to tailor the look and feel as well as the set of commands exposed at any given time.

User Support

In order to be responsive to our users, we wanted to provide an obvious mechanism that they could use to make

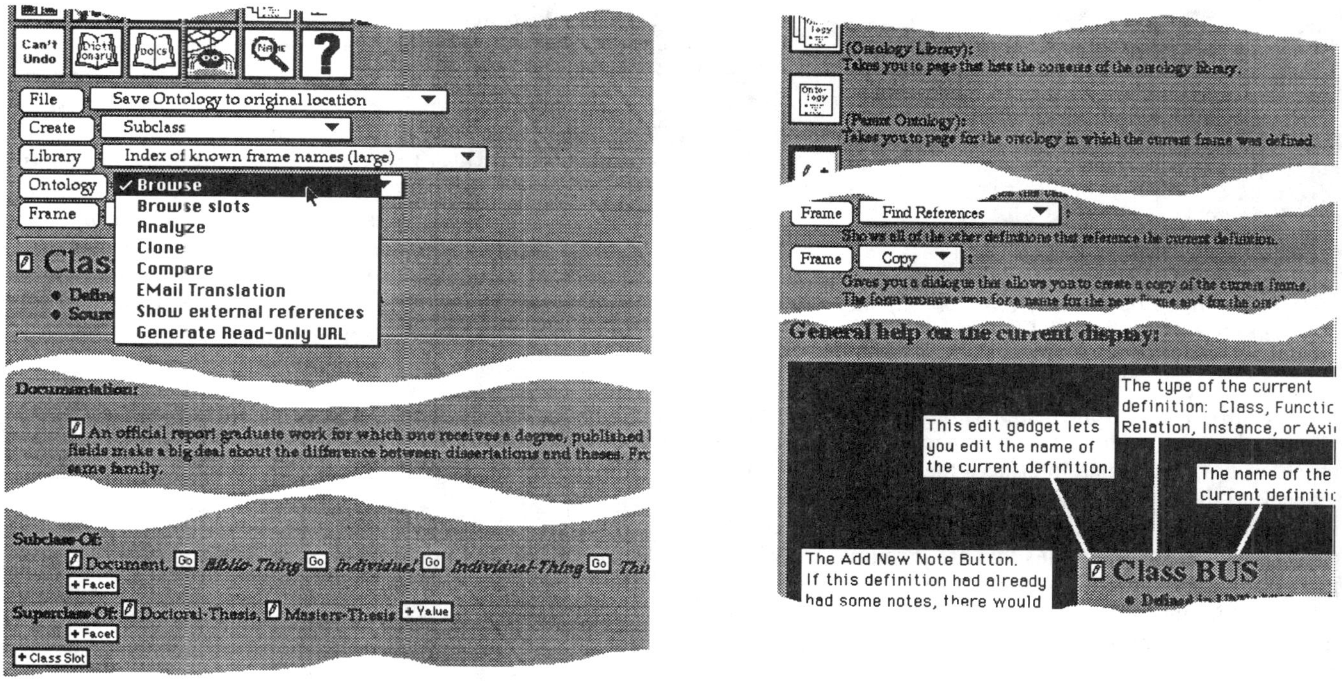

suggestions and report bugs. We resolved this by providing feedback buttons on *every page* for both comments, questions and bug reports. The application captures the user's context automatically so as to make the user's bug report as useful to the developers as possible.

Trustworthiness

Because we were intending to provide a multi-user shared resource, it was essential for the user community to find our application both reliable and trustworthy. Otherwise, they would not use it to develop confidential or proprietary ontologies. To this end, our application supports a user and group model similar to that provided by operating systems and password protection to ensure privacy and security. Ontologies are protected by maintaining multiple versions that the user can revert if necessary. At a finer granularity, a multi-level Undo/Redo feature allows the user to repair any mistakes. A sophisticated compare facility, which compares semantic units rather than text, allows the user to see exactly what has changed; an analysis facility tells the user what ought to be changed.

Overcome Previous Difficulties

Our previous software delivery attempts had been plagued by long release cycles, installation difficulties, and problems with patch distribution. Users had to acquire expensive proprietary software and high-end hardware to run the system. This was very unpopular, and substantially reduced the impact of our work by excluding PC and Mac users from the user community. We needed an approach that would overcome all of these problems.

There are a number of possible ways to deliver applications to a user community. In the past, we had always built our software to be as portable as possible, testing it on a number of platforms and with a number of different compilers from different vendors. This approach was necessary because our user community always wanted us to ship source code to them so that they could modify and experiment with our software. The cost of testing and ensuring cross-platform portability proved to be very high. Users would often employ versions of operating systems, platforms or compilers that we had no access to. One way to address this problem would have been to offer only shrink-wrap software releases to our users. This was not a tenable option because of the diversity of platforms in our user community. We simply could not build a "PC-only", or "SUN/OS-only" application. Our new approach of keeping control of the software, and shipping a *network service* seemed the best way for us to overcome the difficulties of shipping software, while being able to impact a wide user community.

Figure 1. *The final design (left) used a row of icons (top) for important or frequently used operations, and pop-up menus preceeded by submit buttons (e.g.,* "File" *top left) as labels Selecting the '?' help command (left) takes the user to a page explaining all applicable commands, and with a labeled explanation of the page (right) . The command widgets on the help page are real. Selecting one of these widgets will execute the command in the context of the page that the user was on. Tears in the figure elide material extraneous to this discussion.*

Constraints Imposed by HTML and HTTP

There are only two ways for the browser to transmit information to the server (i.e., the application). Selecting an *anchor* transmits a request to follow a hypertext link. Pressing a *submit* button transmits the widget state. It is not possible for the server to determine anything about intermediate activities that a user might perform such as typing text into an input field, toggling radio buttons or check boxes, selecting items from menus, moving the mouse, and so on.

The only way for the server to transmit information to a browser is in response to a submit or select action initiated by the user.

Figure 2. In early designs, radio buttons were used to select an argument (left). Selecting an operation from a pop-up menu and clicking on a submit button (top left) snipped suitable edit widgets into the flow of the page at the selected location (right).

Multiple Browsers
A growing number of web browsers from a variety of institutions and vendors make non-standard extensions to the published protocols. These browsers provide different levels of support for features in the protocols. Fortunately, the protocol provides a means for browsers to identify themselves (although they do not describe their capabilities in a meaningful way), which allows servers such as ours to be sensitive to some of the distinctions between them.

Consequently, it is currently impossible to implement many features of sophisticated user interfaces over the web. In particular, tightly coupled interfaces that provide immediate feedback to the users are not possible. For instance, given an initial menu selection, it is not possible for the application to gray out options that are incompatible with it. Furthermore, there can be no direct manipulation of objects such as one might find in a graphical class browser. Finally, it is not possible for the application to preempt the browser's activity or provide any asynchronous communication. For example, it is not possible to notify the user asynchronously about the results of a background task or remind the user to save work.

Bandwidth is a key constraint. Each user action (submit or select) causes an entire new page to be transmitted back to the browser over the network. There is no method for the application to cause an incremental update of a portion of the display. Even on high-bandwidth local area networks, transmitting and rendering large pages is time consuming; for distant browsers it becomes the dominant cost.

The application has very little control over appearance. HTML explicitly cedes rendering decisions to browsers. This has many advantages for browsing hypertext documents, but it proves awkward for interface design. There is little control over the location of displayed objects on the finally rendered page. In particular, if a page is too large to fit on a single screen, there is no way of controlling how and to where the browser will scroll the page. This *registration* problem can be very difficult to work around and frustrating for users (see the section on the breakdown of the Edit-in-place metaphor below).

The widget set available through HTML's forms capability is extremely restricted. It includes only pop-up menus, single/multiple selection scrolling lists, submit buttons, checkboxes, radio buttons, mapped images, and text type-in widgets (see figures 1 and 2). There is no way to combine either submit button or anchor behavior with a pop-up menu to provide the sort of command selection model that is present in so many user interfaces (e.g., the Macintosh menu bar). There is no way to associate a "right button" menu with items, nor is there a no way to provide constraints on selection elements (e.g., toggling "show text files" causes a scrolling list of files to filter out non-text files). There is also no way to include iconic elements in menus or scrollable lists.

Time-Travel in the Interface
A unique feature of web browsers is that they cache previously seen pages and allow the user to revisit these cached pages without notifying the server. In interactive applications delivered on the web, these "previously seen pages" can represent earlier states in a dialog with the user. As a consequence, the browser allows the user to travel back in time to an earlier interaction state and attempt to execute the commands as they were presented then. Since the state of the data on the server may have changed as a result of the user's interactions with the server, incoherent transactions can result. There are two alternative ways for applications to handle this. Applications must either support time-travel, or they must always reflect the most recent state. For example, suppose that a user engages in a dialog to delete an object and then backs up to a page on which the object is still present. If the user selects the deleted object as represented on that page, the application should either undo the deletion or report an error in a graceful way.

Choices and Design Principles
The underlying principle of our design was to minimize the cognitive load on the user imposed by the interface [5]. As we worked within the constraints of HTML and HTTP to meet our objectives, we used this principle to guide our design decisions. The steps we took included: minimizing the number of intermediate states in complex command execution, minimizing the number of distinct types of pages, the number of distinct widgets, working to achieve consistent appearance across browsers, but working within the widgets provided by the native window systems. In this section we discuss these issues in more detail.

Minimize Intermediate Pages and Number of Clicks
The restrictions on the widget set force complex interactions to be broken down into a sequence of simple ones punctuated by submit actions and the transmission of intermediate pages. To simplify the execution of complex commands, we chose (1) to minimize the number of actions that the user must perform, and (2) to minimize the number of pages presented during the course of the interaction. It is important to minimize these because of the cognitive effort required to parse and understand a new page, because displaying a new page makes it change registration (see the section on the Evolution of Design below), and because transmitting and rendering a page may take several seconds.

Edit-In-Place Metaphor
In order to minimize the number of different-looking pages to which the user would be exposed, we decided that the editing environment should look as much like the browsing environment as possible. This is natural in our application, because even when a user is creating new objects, most of a user's work is browsing. We preserve the browsing environment's look and feel by inserting edit widgets into the flow of the HTML page (see figures 2 and 3) in a manner similar to the `protoTextExpando` widget in the Newton user interface [8].

Pages Represent Objects
A page was to be a representation of a specific object. This meant that commands on the menu bar would implicitly apply to the underlying objects which may be nested (e.g., an attribute of a class in an ontology.) Commands applicable to all of these may appear on the menu bar.

Five Types of Interface Widgets
We decided that in the normal course of events the user should be exposed to the minimal number of distinct widgets. The final design includes only five types of widgets (see the section on the Early Implementation below).

Consistency Across Browsers
We wanted our user interface to work in the same way across all platforms and browsers. This would minimize training and documentation problems. We explicitly chose to limit use of undocumented or non-portable extensions provided by different browsers. One significant exception to this decision is HTML tables, which provide a much better way to present tabulated information than is otherwise possible. We use HTML tables when communicating with a Netscape browser [9] and use `PRE`formatted text for other browsers. Currently, Netscape is the only vendor that fully supports tables.

We explicitly decided to support multiple browsers. Some user interfaces on the web are almost unusable without using Netscape. We did not want to limit our user community in this way, and so preserved a consistent look and feel across platforms and browsers.

Native Window System's Submit Buttons
Many developers choose to exercise artistic control over the look and feel of their web pages by using custom bitmapped graphics instead of the native look and feel that the web browsers provide. Consequently, their web pages look more uniform across platforms, but users must learn to recognize buttons anew for each of these idiosyncratic applications. Furthermore, when this mapped graphic approach is used, the browser is not able to provide feedback to the user about which regions of the bitmap will result in commands being executed.

In contrast, we chose to use the native window system's submit buttons for our interface. Our application was going to be complex enough without the user having to relearn what a button is supposed to look like.

The constraint of supporting naïve users meant that we could not allow any user interface tricks such as having extremely stylized icons that cause differing behavior depending on where on the icon the user clicks. While such approaches allow very terse and dense displays that efficiently take advantage of the available screen real-estate and bandwidth, they would be difficult for members of our target community to understand and learn.

EVOLUTION OF DESIGN

As we saw above, the design for our user interface was influenced both by a number of hard constraints imposed by our need to deliver our application over the web, and a number of design choices that reflected our beliefs about the usage patterns of our system and our prospective user community. In this section we describe the evolution of our design and our software, and show how we changed our user interface as we learned more about the application and received user feedback. One of the significant advantages of our implementation approach – a central server and standard browsers, coupled with a dynamic, rapid-prototyping implementation infrastructure – was that we could rapidly receive user feedback and introduce changes in response, often within a few minutes or hours. This meant that as soon as the server was established, our design progressed very rapidly. In this section we describe several of the significant events in this evolutionary process.

Early Design and Mockup

We were fortunate to start this project with a preexisting substrate. Earlier work had enhanced Ontolingua [3], our ontology development tool so that ontologies could be compiled into static hyperwebs. These hyperwebs displayed the concepts in the ontology with one concept per page. Our first step, therefore was to take pages of hypertext generated by this compilation process and manually edit them so as to mock up the editing interface. This process of developing mockups lasted about two weeks and went through multiple iterations, experimenting with different ways to handle the perceived problems of having a simple user interface that was nevertheless powerful. Early designs experimented with putting edit widgets next to each of the potentially modifiable objects in the page being displayed. Selecting one of these edit widgets would take you to a different mockup page with, for example, a text widget allowing the user to edit the selected value.

We tried several different approaches to provide the functionality of a right button command menu, which is not supported by HTML. For example, in one mockup, there was a radio button in front of each editable object, and at the top of the page was a pop-up menu of operations to be applied to the object selected with the radio button (figure 2). A "Do It" submit button caused the execution of the selected operation. This method requires three different widget selections which involved mouse travel from the selected object back to the top of the page and often required the user to scroll the viewport. This would have been burdensome on our users.

We addressed this problem by using a single intermediate page for edit operations, and by limiting the expressiveness of the user interface – we do not allow the user to execute all conceivably legal operations at any given point. We eventually settled on a design in which a small edit widget would be placed next to any editable object. Selecting this widget would take the user to a page just like the current page, only with suitable edit widgets replacing the value that

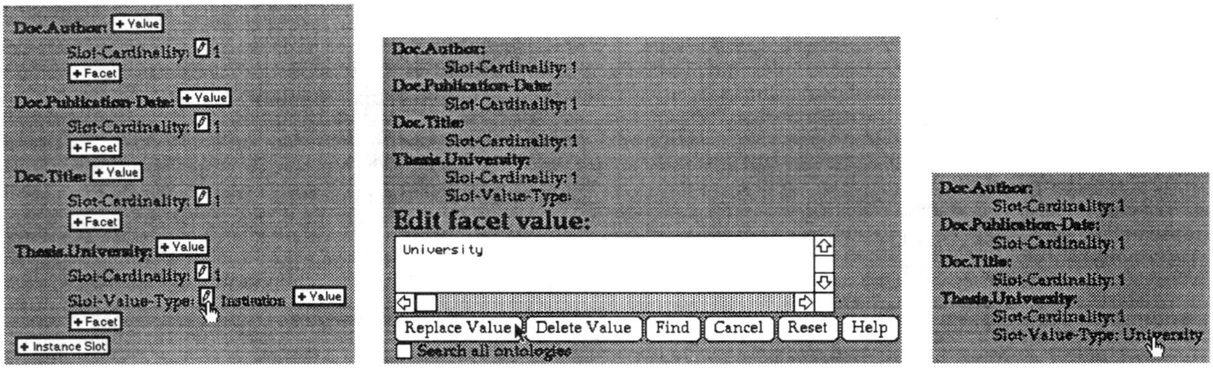

was selected, and allowing the user to select between a number of possible edit options.

In our application, it is necessary to be able both to create new objects (e.g., classes) and also to add objects to existing objects (e.g., add a property or value to a given object). Finding a good way to represent this proved tricky, and we experimented with several methods. For example, we tried using a "dummy" entry for values, so that for every list of values there would be an extra one at the beginning (or end) in italics that was a place holder for a new value to be added. This was found to be confusing, and was soon dropped in favor of the design described in the next section.

Early Implementation

Moving on from our mockups, our initial implementation of the editing environment attempted to implement the design that we had mocked up as closely as possible, but we rapidly ran into difficulties. For example, in the mockups, quite by chance, we had selected an object which had only one value for each of the attributes being displayed. This encouraged us to position a single edit widget in front of the set of attribute values in order to elicit and/or modify all of the values simultaneously in one text widget. We soon discovered that the more general case of there being several attribute values was very common and the single text widget approach was confusing to our users. Problems with eliciting multiple values in a single text widget were compounded by our desire to edit values in context, which made us want to minimize the size of the text widget. Values were sometimes scrolled out of the user's viewport, which resulted in erroneous editing operations and much confusion. Early user feedback quickly caused us to change our design in favor of eliciting or editing only one attribute value at a time. This had the side-effect of increasing screen clutter by putting individual edit widgets in front of every editable value (figure 3 left).

The next problem that arose was that users were confused by the methods for creating and adding objects and values. They often added values that were illegal or non-existent objects. The number of possible legal values for attributes in the system is typically too large to enumerate explicitly. Because of this, we developed a sophisticated, context-dependent completion facility, which space prevents us from describing here.

After a few iterations we ended up with a design which we have broadly kept since this early stage (see figure 3). In this design, we distinguish between five different types of widget: (1) the simple hyperlink, which always takes the user to a page showing the selected object. (2) edit widgets, represented by pencil icons that allow the user to edit an existing value and addition widgets, which are represented by icons such as +Value. Only one type of object can be added at each location; the type is indicated by the icon. (3) a submit button and pop-up menu combination for commands. (4) text widget and submit button combinations for value elicitation, and (5) tool bar icons presenting important, general commands.

***Figure 3**. The final version uses edit widgets in front of all editable objects, and "+" widgets wherever an addition is possible (left). In this example, we show editing the Slot-Value-Type facet value of* `Thesis.University` *from* `Institution` *to* `University`. *Selecting an edit pencil inserts the necessary widgets to elicit or modify the value in context (middle). The user has entered* `University` *instead of* `Institution`. *The user can remove screen clutter by inhibiting all edit widgets (right).*

Although we went to considerable effort to make the user interface clear and intuitive, it was still novel in many ways. To familiarize new users with the meaning of the various icons and edit widgets they might see, we introduced a "Welcome" page which displays the icon images together with a brief explanation. Users can suppress this page once they are familiar with its contents.

By this point, we were able to edit values and create new objects in our system, but we were unable to save our changes. Our user interface mockups had focused exclusively on the different ways to edit objects in the system – they completely neglected the sorts of operations that are typically found on the "File" menu of a normal user interface. This presented us with a problem. We already had a row of buttons at the top of the page that would provoke the creation of new objects. When we added the options that were necessary for typical file menu operations we found that we had a glut of buttons. The number of buttons would only increase as the system became more sophisticated.

At this point, we had to make a significant compromise. Again, because HTML does not support pop-up submit buttons, we were unable to implement the obvious and familiar behavior of a menu bar. The only "correct" model for command menus in HTML is the exhaustive enumeration of the commands as submit buttons. This was untenable because of the number of commands we needed to support (typically around 40 per page). As an alternative, we partitioned the commands into broad classes and put the commands on menus. In front of each menu we placed the name of the menu as a submit button (see figure 1, top left). This meant that the user had to select an option from the menu and then click on the submit button to execute the selected operation. This is non-standard, but we found that our users got used to it fairly quickly, probably because we went to significant effort to make sure that the system would always put the most likely choice as the default option on the menu. Thus, a single pointer operation often suffices.

Because we could not predict whether our users would find the factoring of commands onto menus with submit buttons described above reasonable, we introduced a user preferences mechanism that allowed the user to control, amongst other things, the look and feel of these menu commands. In practice, most users ended up accepting our default setting for the command menu's look and feel. The desire for menu flexibility was the impetus for us to introduce a user preferences facility, but this feature has become ever more important in our system. This is particularly the case because users connect to our application from all around the world from sites with widely differing quality of network connectivity. This has meant that it is very important to support options that let the user trade prettiness or verbosity for bandwidth.

The issue of how much power to give to the user came up with the introduction of this command menu model. Our system is non-modal in the sense that it is always theoretically legal to jump to (say) a class creation dialog from the middle of a different object creation dialog. By default, we choose to hide this fact from users in order to simplify the appearance of the user interface. However, power users resent such restrictions, and so we have had to add extra preferences to allow our power users full access to all applicable commands, irrespective of their current context.

Problems of Scale

By the time the system had reached this level of sophistication, we had made our application available to the public, and around one hundred users had tried it out. We quickly found that users were unable to visualize large ontologies with hundreds or thousands of concepts. This is a problem analogous to browsing a flat file system with hundreds or thousands of files. We considered using a graphical rendering of the hierarchy [7], but this had several problems: transmitting large images is too slow; it is not possible to position the image so that a particular object is visible; the browser cannot tell which portions of the image are links, and the browser may not be able to display graphical data. We chose to provide a hierarchical browsing mechanism with the same sort of triangular open/close widgets that are found in the Macintosh file system. The system uses a heuristic method to compute the appropriate initial set of objects to display in the "open" state (figure 4).

We found that however hard we might try, our application always produced pages that were multiple screens in height. Consequently, we replicated the menu bar at the bottom of the page so that the user could scroll to the nearest end of

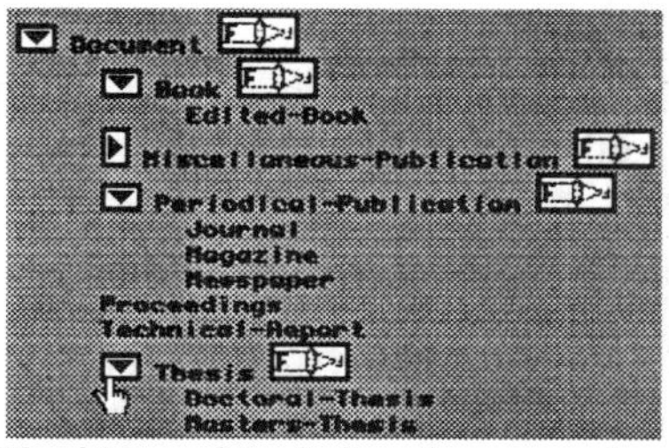

Figure 4. The hierarchical class browser shows large graphs of objects in a compact form. Triangular widgets open and close subgraphs. "Focus" widgets move the selected object to the root of the displayed tree.

the document in order to select one of these more global commands.

User feedback has caused us to spend more effort on displaying large ontologies. We have recently addressed this by factoring pages showing large ontologies automatically. We have also introduced a method of focusing the hierarchical browsing tool onto subgraphs of the class lattice, and for using this same hierarchical browsing technique to look at attributes as well as classes and instances.

Breakdown of the Edit-in-place Model

Our early design criteria had called for trying to preserve the illusion that there were only a few different types of pages: one for ontologies, one for the library, and one for frame objects. Edit widgets would be inserted in-place to preserve the look and feel of these pages (see figure 3). When it came to object creation, we did not, of course, have an object to display. When the user selected a creation operation, we presented the user with a fake page representing an object of the type being created, with a text widget into which the user could enter the new object's name. This preserved a uniform look and feel for all of our pages. We rapidly discovered that this approach confused our users. Their cognitive model of object creation was sufficiently different from normal editing and browsing operations that being presented with a fake page for the object to be created was confusing. The users clearly liked to think of the creation pages as being (pseudo) modal dialogs, and didn't want to view the creation page as an ersatz, incomplete object.

Another problem with the edit-in-place model of interaction is that HTML and HTTP give no effective control over viewport positioning. This means that when the user selects an edit operation, we have no choice but to refresh the whole page (unlike a more tightly-coupled user interface in which the system might push existing text aside in order to make room for the edit widgets). Although it is possible to tell the browser where to scroll to on the new page, this is very coarse-grained control. Browsers differ significantly in their scrolling behavior, and this typically results in a loss of registration of the user's viewport.

In practice we suspect that it might be better not to use this edit-in-place model, but rather to use simple pages that give the illusion of modal dialogs. This is an open design question and needs further investigation. Registration of the display is only reliable when the whole HTML page is less than one screen in height. Because browsers cannot inform the server of the browser's window size or exact viewport position within a document, this problem cannot be solved in general. Furthermore, our application typically generates HTML pages more than one screen high.

Observations on User Interaction

We have conducted one informal email survey of our users and have collected over 1500 in-context comments and bug reports. Together with informal observation of local users, we have observed several surprising characteristics of system usage.

Reluctance to Click

We have noticed that users are reluctant to experiment freely within the application. This becomes an issue when users are unable to understand an icon or command. They do not try it to see what it will do. This surprised us. We had expected that users would experiment freely because the network connection isolates them from most problems. There are several possible explanations for their behavior: They may be avoiding wasting their time. Some browsers are difficult to interrupt if an address is not well formed, a server refuses to respond or responds slowly, or if a large document is transmitted. They may be trying to protect their work. Many web-based applications are brittle and crash unexpectedly. Few applications provide as many safeguards as ours does against irrecoverable damage. They may also be trying to protect the work of other users by following only understood paths. It would be interesting to find out why users are so reluctant to experiment, since this could have significant impact on the design of networked application user interfaces if this behavior proved to be widespread.

Logging Out

We have observed that our users have a powerful desire to be able to log out of our system. Because a user's connection with our application lasts only as long as each individual request from the browser – typically only a second or two – and because the user could walk away, leaving the browser at any time – we have had to engineer the system so that logging out is not necessary. The system has a set of timeouts and defaults that allow it to recover quiescent resources. However, we have noticed that users feel a need to log out, even when they are told explicitly that it is not necessary. We have therefore provided a command to give the user the illusion of logging out.

CONCLUSIONS

We have shown how we were able to deliver a sophisticated, yet intuitive, interactive application as a network service. An off-the-shelf web browser provides the user's interaction medium. Leveraging standard browsers attracts a large user community, improves the rate of user acceptance, avoids software installation and distribution problems, and dramatically reduces turnaround time for software development.

The key contribution of this paper is to describe the constraints imposed on user interface design by this interaction medium, outline the tradeoffs in this design space, and motivate the choices we made in order to deliver our application over the web. We further outlined the lessons we learned and the design changes we made as the interface evolved in response to user feedback.

These issues are crucial because the growing popularity of the web ensures that this form of software delivery will become ever more wide-spread.

This application is available on the web at:
`http://www-ksl-svc.stanford.edu:5915/`

ACKNOWLEDGMENTS

The authors gratefully acknowledge the support of the following funding agencies: NASA Ames Research Center under contract NCC2-537, ARPA and NASA/ARC under contract NAG2-581 (ARPA order 8607), and CommerceNet under contract CN-1094 (TRP #F33615-94-4413). Numerous people in our user community were both influential and helpful in the development of this application, particularly Wanda Pratt, Rupert Brauch, and Richard Fikes.

REFERENCES

1 Farquhar, A, Fikes, R, Pratt, W, and Rice, J. *Collaborative Ontology Construction for Information Integration*. Technical Report KSL-95-63, Stanford University, Knowledge Systems Laboratory. 1995

2 Fikes, R., Cutkosky, M., Gruber, T., & van Baalen, J. *Knowledge Sharing Technology Project Overview*. Technical Report KSL 91-71, Stanford University, Knowledge Systems Laboratory. 1991

3 Gruber, T. R. A Translation Approach to Portable Ontology Specifications. *Knowledge Acquisition*, **5**(2), 199-220. 1993

4 Grudin, J. Groupware and Cooperative Work: Problems and Prospects, in *The Art of Human-Computer Interface Design*. Laurel, B., Ed. Addison-Wesley Publishing Company, Inc., Reading, Massachusetts, 1990, pp. 171-185.

5 Gygi, K. Recognizing the Symptoms of Hypertext... and What to do About it, in Laurel, B., ed., The Art of Human-Computer Interface Design. Addison-Wesley Publishing Company, Inc., Reading, Massachusetts, 1990, pp. 279-287.

6 Knowledge Sharing Technology Project. `http://www-ksl.stanford.edu/kst/kst-overview.html`

7 Lamping, J, Rao, R, Pirolli, P: A Focus+Context Technique Based on Hyperbolic Geometry for Visualizing Large Hierarchies. In *CHI'95 Human Factors in Computing Systems*. 1995. New York: ACM Press.

8 Newton Programmers Guide. Apple Computer Inc. Cupertino CA. 1993

9 Netscape Navigator Handbook, Netscape Communications Corporation, Mountain View, California. Also available on the world wide web at: `http://home.netscape.com/eng/mozilla/1.1/handbook/`

10 World Wide Web Consortium. `http://www.w3.org/`

The WebBook and the Web Forager: An Information Workspace for the World-Wide Web

Stuart K. Card, George G. Robertson, and William York
Xerox Palo Alto Research Center
3333 Coyote Hill Road
Palo Alto, California 94304
E-mail: {card | robertson | york}@parc.xerox.com

ABSTRACT
The World-Wide Web has achieved global connectivity stimulating the transition of computers from knowledge processors to knowledge sources. But the Web and its client software are seriously deficient for supporting users' interactive use of this information. This paper presents two related designs with which to evolve the Web and its clients. The first is the WebBook, a 3D interactive book of HTML pages. The WebBook allows rapid interaction with objects at a higher level of aggregation than pages. The second is the Web Forager, an application that embeds the WebBook and other objects in a hierarchical 3D workspace. Both designs are intended as exercises to play off against analytical studies of information workspaces.

Keywords
3D graphics, user interfaces, information access, World-Wide Web, information workspace, workspace.

INTRODUCTION

Whereas personal computers used to be viewed as knowledge processors—word processors or spreadsheet calculators, for instance, they are now becoming viewed as knowledge sources—portals to vast stores of information on-line or on CD-ROMs [1]. This is true because much work has become knowledge work and because the infrastructure for distributed knowledge access has been developing. The most dramatic development of this infrastructure has been the growth of the World Wide Web in the last couple of years. Uniform access protocols have enabled a person with a personal computer and a communications link access by button-click to millions of pages around the world.

Despite the exhilaration felt by many users at this achievement of wide-scale connectivity, there are problems that call for evolution of the medium: Pages are often hard to find, users get lost and have difficulty relocating previously-found pages, they have difficulty organizing things once found, difficulty doing knowledge processing on the found thing, and interacting with the Web is notoriously too slow to incorporate it gracefully into human activity. In this paper, we suggest a way of viewing the Web and its problems, then propose two related innovations, the WebBook and the Web Forager, to mitigate these problems.

INFORMATION FORAGING ON THE WEB

In an information-rich world, the limiting quantity for users isn't so much the information in the world as the user's own limited time. Just as animals forage for food and try to optimize their food rate of gain, users often seek strategies to optimize their information gain per unit time and in fact, we can make the analogy literal by thinking of the Web in terms of Information Foraging Theory [1], an analogue of foraging models from ecological biology [2].

In terms of this theory, the user stalks certain types of information. In a particular environment, this sort of information is encountered at a certain rate of λ relevant pages/hour, say. The Web is an evolving information ecology in which on the one hand users are trying to evolve methods to increase the encounter rates of relevant information and on the other hand information sources are trying to evolve their attractiveness to users. These result in a clumpy structure of patches of high λ. Three mechanisms in particular have evolved on the server side: First, indexes, such as Lycos [3] attempt to visit and form an inverted index of every page by following all the links. The user can formulate a keyword query and obtain a patch of possible links to forage. Creation of such a patch is a form of information enrichment.

A second sort of information enrichment is a table of contents lists such as Yahoo [4]. These systems provide typically a tree of categories with links of Web pages at their leaves. Again, this technique provides enriched patches for foraging. A third sort of enrichment are the home pages provided by many users, which collect together lists of related links. Again, these often provide patches with higher encounter rates. All three responses represent evolutionary adaptation (Lycos and Yahoo are successful enough that they have now been converted to businesses) and emergent self-organizing structure on the Web. Yet these innovations do not address the basic cost-structure problem of users using Web information as part of some activity.

THE COST STRUCTURE OF INFORMATION WORKSPACES

The Web maintains a uniform cost structure. The time per interaction is fast, compared to the time to, say, go to the library, but it is slow compared to interaction rates, say the time to interact with pieces of paper on a desk. Empirically, users tend to interact repeatedly with small clusters of information, a property known as locality of reference [5, 6]. As a result, information workspaces, that is, environments that are cost-tuned for doing information-based work, tend to exhibit a certain cost-structure of information: a small amount of information is organized to be available at very low cost, larger amounts are available at moderate costs, large amounts at high cost. By so doing, they capitalize on locality of reference and the activity is speeded considerably. A routine example would be a typical (ideal) office where a small amount of information is kept available on the desk; moderate amounts of information, moderately available in nearby files; and large amounts, slowly available are kept in a library down the hall. Users constantly rearrange their environments to *tune* the relative costs of the information, so as to make them efficient. And if they don't, they suffer accordingly. An important activity they do in such environments is to use them for *sensemaking* [7], that is, the restructuring, recoding, and analysis of information for purposes of insight.

But the Web does not exhibit the characteristics of a good information workspace. Users do not have the ability to create adequately tuned environments nor is sensemaking supported. The major effort to allow users to organize their workspaces has been the development of variants of the "hotlist" notion. Fig. 1 show a typical example from Netscape 1.1N. User actions are provided for adding or deleting an element to a hot list, arranging an element under a heading, changing it's position in the list, or searching for it. Because of the interface, these mechanisms are very slow to use and do not work well with more than a couple dozen entries. Even when the entry is found, the user must still wait for the slow access times before the page appears.

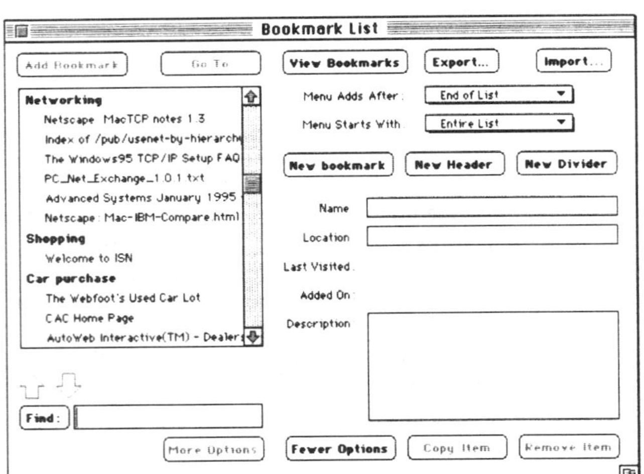

Fig. 1. Hotlist browser from Netscape.

Hence the space is not tunable to a reasonably cost-structured workspace. Multiple windows can be spawned for access to multiple pages, but these then slow the user down because they overlap. Finally, sensemaking is impeded. In the conventional Web browsers, users are always *at* a particular page. But the way a user works with information is to have multiple pages simultaneously available that can be juxtaposed, rapidly accessed, and structured, such as by grouping or other layout.

In order to make the use of the Web better able to support information work (or for that matter, entertainment), we propose in this paper two basic moves:

(1) A move from the single Web page as the unit of interaction to a higher, aggregate entity.

We call this entity a WebBook™, and it allows the user to group together related Web pages (an elementary form of sensemaking) and to manipulate these pages as a unit.

(2) A move from a work environment containing a single element to a workspace in which the page is contained with multiple other entities, including WebBooks.

We call this environment the Web Forager™. This information workspace allows for the intensive, rapid interaction among pages and allows for the assembly on the user side of hierarchical cost-structures of information necessary for the task tuning of the workspace.

Each of these has been implemented on a Silicon Graphics Iris computer using the Information Visualizer system [8]. Efforts are underway to reimplement them on a PC and to continue advancing the design.

THE WEBBOOK

Current Web servers and browsers focus attention at the link and page levels. These levels are too low to represent gracefully some higher-level structures, resulting in many more entities in the Web space than are necessary and

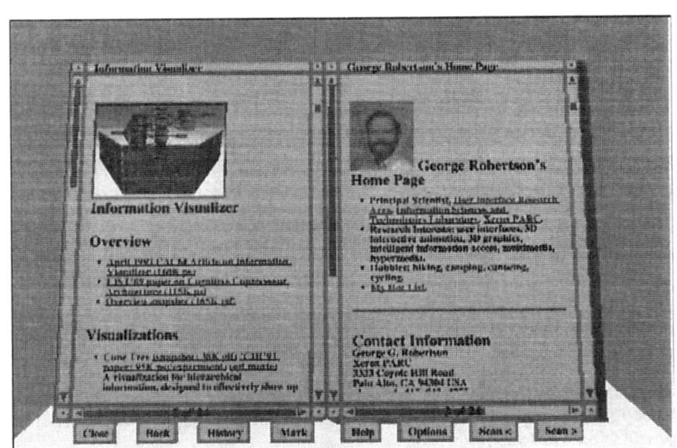

Fig. 2: Example of a WebBook (See Color Plate 2).

hence to orientation and sensemaking problems. We know from analysis of the web that there are structures that the user could take advantage of if the user were aware of their existence. For example, a typical home page on the web has a collection of related pages that can be reached with relative URLs (Uniform Resource Locators). It is very typical for the creator of such pages to use relative URLs instead of absolute URLs, so that the collection of pages can be physically moved easily. But current web browsers pay no attention to the distinction between relative and absolute URLs, and the user simply sees one page at a time, with no difference between a page "in the collection" and one outside the collection. Our proposal is to create a Web entity at a higher level of abstraction, a WebBook. A natural candidate structure to represent this abstraction is the book metaphor, which has been used by us [9] as well as others [10-18] previously.

Fig. 2 shows a picture of a WebBook. Given a collection of web pages, it preloads those pages and displays them as a collection using an augmented simulation of a physical book. 3D graphics and interactive animation are used to give the user a clear indication of the relationship between the pages of the book. Each page of the WebBook is a page from the web. Links are color coded so the user can easily tell the difference between a reference to another page in the book (red links) and a reference outside the book (blue links). Picking a red link will animate the flipping of pages to the desired page. Picking a blue link will close the current WebBook and look for the page elsewhere. If the page is in another WebBook stored on a bookshelf, that WebBook is opened to the desired page. If the page is in none of the WebBooks, then the Web Forager is used to display the individual page in the user's information workspace.

There are a number of features in the WebBook that make it intuitive to use. The user has several ways to flip through the pages of the book, all animated so the user can continue to see the text and images on pages while they turn. The simplest method is to click on a page (away from any link on that page); this will flip to the next or previous page

Fig. 3. Example of ruffling pages in a WebBook (See Color Plate 3)

depending on whether user clicked on the right or left page. The user can also click on the right or left edge of the book. The relative distance along that edge indicates how far to flip. The user can also scan the book with forward and backward scan controls (two of the buttons on the bottom of the book). The scan rate and pause time at each page is a user preference. When the user clicks on a page during a scan, the scan stops. Finally, the user can ruffle through the pages (Fig. 3) by clicking and holding the mouse button down. The ability to rapidly riffle through a set of pages has previously been a method of rapid scanning for information that could only be done with physical books.

In addition, the user can leave a bookmark on any page. When the book is closed, a bookmark is automatically left for the last page that was viewed. Also, there is a "Back" and "History" mechanism that follows the same convention as NetScape's versions of those commands. The WebBook can be stored on a bookshelf using a simple gesture. When it is removed from the bookshelf (by clicking on it), it reopens to the last page that was being viewed.

Each page in the WebBook has three scrollbars. Two of these are the familiar vertical and horizontal scrolling controls (left and bottom scrollbars). The third (on the right) is for scaling the font size, since the trade-off of font-size vs. amount of page viewed differs for individual pages. As the scale scrollbar is moved, images remain the same size but the text changes size and is refilled continuously. A menu command allows the user to apply a new font scale to all pages of the WebBook. The corners of each page of the WebBook are resize tabs, which the user can use to change the size of the book.

Books are compact but (except for bookmarks) sequential. Therefore we allow the user to explode the book out (in animation) so that all the pages are available simultaneously. The Document Lens [19] can then be used to inspect portions of interest. Fig. 4 shows the WebBook Document Lens view. The user is then able to pan and zoom over the entire set of pages, while retaining a focus plus context display of the book. When returning to the book view, the user sees an animation of the pages imploding into a book.

WebBook Applications

The WebBook can be used to view any collection of web pages. The principle difference is the method used to generate the URLs. The method used to collect URLs leads to a number of applications.

Relative-URL Books. One interesting choice of pages is based on recursively finding all relative URLs starting from a given page. These pages are intrinsically related because their creator wanted to be able to move them as a group. We have found this heuristic often produces coherent and interesting books.

Home-Page Books. Probably the simplest choice of pages is those pages referred to directly from a given page. Users throughout the net have strongly expressed their desire to make sense of the net by collecting sets of related URLs. The WebBook goes the next step and allows the collection of pages to be rapidly consulted without waiting for network delay speeds.

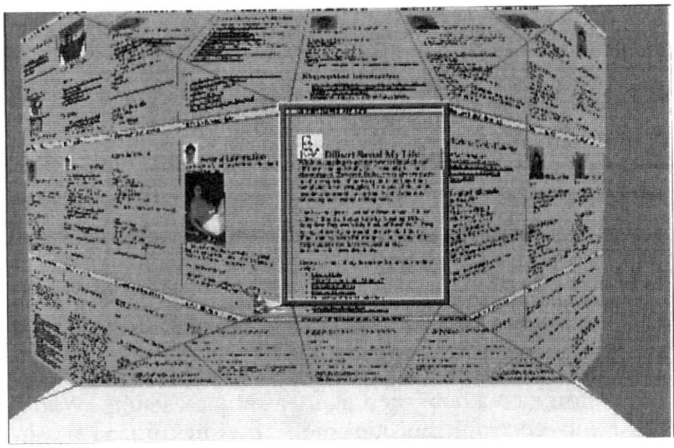

Fig. 4. WebBook viewed with a Document Lens. (See Color Plate 4)

Topic Books. A variant is to make sets of books on interesting topics. For example, in our area houses for sale are published on the Web, usually one page per house and usually organized off the home pages of the real-estate brokers. But we have rearranged these ads into houses from a given city. It is then possible rapidly to look back an forth in order to make house comparisons.

Hot List Books. Another variant is hotlist pages. Our system can read any user's Netscape hotlist and automatically fashion it into a set of WebBooks. Although exactly the same URLs are involved, the transformation is dramatic because all the information on all the pages is readily available.

Search Reports. Since WebBooks can be created dynamically, they can be used to display the results of a content based search, either keyword based or relevance feedback (looking for pages similar to a given page). Later results from the search can still be retrieving pages while the user is examining the first pages of the book.

Book Books. A final example comes from observing how some people take multi-page documents and put them on the web. One way to do this is with a series of pages, with next and previous links between pages. When viewing one of these pages with a traditional web browser, there is no indication of how the pages are related. But, such a structure can be easily discovered, and a WebBook constructed from those pages, resulting in a collection of obviously related pages.

Related Work: The Book Metaphor

The book metaphor has been used in both 2D and 3D applications by a number of people for some time. What is new about the WebBook is the integration of an animated 3D book, used to show collections of web pages, with an information workspace manager (the Web Forager) and the application to Web problems.

A book metaphor was chosen after careful examination of a large number of web pages and page collections, and for several reasons: Informally, information on the Web tends to have non-homogeneous character, with closely related weblets situated in more loosely structured environments. An important subset of these have 'next' and 'previous' links, and thus are thus close operational analogues to books. Furthermore, books as an invention make very efficient use of display space. Starting with a book metaphor, it is easy to escape the serial nature of the physical form by having alternate forms into which the book is transformed, such as the Document Lens in this paper. A book metaphor makes it easy to put actual books on the Internet, something not so at present. We use the book metaphor not primarily because it is familiar, but because of the operational match to a corpus of interest and the efficient display characterization. As a bargain, its familiarity allows us to exploit irresistible affordances for low training costs.

Early experiments with giving users access to books, like Brown's Intermedia [10] system in 1985, had limited 3D graphics capabilities. Instead of a simulation of a physical book, Intermedia used 2D layouts of the pages, showing relationships between pages with the layout and with lines drawn between pages. In 1987, Card and Henderson reported the use of a 2D book simulation called "Catalogues" as part of the Rooms system [9], although page turning was not animated. The Xerox TabWorks system [16] was directly inspired by Catalogues. Also in 1987, the BellCore SuperBook Document Browser [13], was designed to transform existing electronic documents into hypertext documents with indexing and a fisheye table of contents, although SuperBook did not use a simulation of a physical book.

Use of a 2D physical book simulation, including page turning, was done in 1987 by Benest [17] for hypertext documents. Similar systems were reported by Miyazawa in 1990 [11] and Ichimura in 1993 [18]. Recently, PenPoint [14] and General Magic [15] have offered commercial products that use a book metaphor with bookshelves. These are actually 2D animations painted on a background that give the impression of a 3D environment. In 1993, Silicon Graphics introduced the SGI Demo Book [12] as a way of distributing collections of applications, documents, and games. Demo Book is a 3D book that simulates page flipping with animation. The pages hold a collection of icons, 4 rows by 5 columns on each page. The page flipping appears to have flexible pages (broken on the columns). The WebBook page flip currently uses rigid pages, but is displaying text and images instead of rows and columns of icons. Demo Book also has the notion of a bookshelf, although the book always opens to the first page rather than the last page viewed.

Fig. 5: The Web Forager. (See Color Plate 1)

In 1995, Brown described an experimental web browser, called DeckScape [20], that used a metaphor of decks of cards. Although not a book metaphor, it was an alternative way to solve the problem.

All these systems exploit the human perceptual and cognitive systems by using familiar objects, images and affordances. The page turning of a book conveys information about the relationship of pages, the direction you are moving in the book, the size of the book, and the contents of the book. The WebBook takes advantage of advances in graphics and processor power to get much closer to a realistic simulation of a book. At the same time, it goes beyond what is possible with a physical book.

THE WEB FORAGER

The WebBook provides a representation of a more aggregate Web entity above the page and allows rapid local interaction with it. The Web Forager allows interaction with multiples of such entities and allows for the necessary tradeoffs among fast access, number of entities, and screen space. The Web Forager is a proposal for a task-tunable information workspace [21] (see Fig. 5).

An individual Web page or a WebBook is presented in a 3D document space (see[22], [23]). Users can click on links in the usual way causing the new linked-to page to fly into the space. The HTML image on the new page develops at the slow Internet speeds (often 15~30 sec). Web pages entered into the space are stored locally and thence forward are available at user interface speeds (around 1~0.1 sec), permitting high interaction rates. These pages can also be grabbed and placed into WebBooks.

Our primary interest in this style of workspace is in exploring the potential for rapid interaction with large numbers of pages. We have previously explored the use of animation, scaling, and 3D-based distortions for building a workspace [21] as a way of handling large numbers of objects. Ark Interface, Inc. [24] produced a pseudo-3D workspace in which functions were associated with parts of a picture of a design studio. Staples [23] did a design mockup study for a 3D user interface. Her goal was to enrich the graphic vocabulary of the workspace by applying perspective, light, and transparency. Ballay [22] with co-workers at the MAYA Design Group implemented a 3D design for an office system. Their design is artistically striking and claimed to be able to handle hundreds of documents. We have sought to break new ground relative to their design on several fronts. First, we tried to increase the speed with which objects can be moved around the space by using gestures. Second, we focused on the Web. Third, the WebBook provides a higher-level object. Fourth, we have experimented with observer movement in the space. And Fifth, we have used a structured model for the generation of the design.

Hierarchical Workspace
The Web Forager workspace (see Fig. 5) is arranged hierarchically (in terms of interaction rates) into three main levels: (1) a Focus Place (the large book or page) showing a page, a book, or an open book at full size for direct interaction between user and content; (2) an Immediate Memory space (the air and the desk), where pages or books can be placed when they are in use, but not the immediate focus (like pages on a desk). A Tertiary Place (the bookcase) where many pages and books can be stored.

The Immediate Storage place has several tiers. Documents are arranged at several distinct z-distances in the 3D space. The user can move these documents back in space (the farther back, the smaller they become and the more documents that fit). Objects in the Immediate Storage place can be moved around in X and Y and moved forward and backward (that is, in Z) using a simple gesture language. A separate Intermediate Storage area is represented by objects on the desk. When the user moves around in the space, the desk, and hence objects on the desk, moves.

The Tertiary Storage area is the bookcase. In normal view, the bookcase is seen at an angle to reduce screen pixels consumed, while at the same time displaying enough information that recently-used books can be recognized. If the user touches one of the books or pages in the bookcase, it will fly up to the focus area (an object occupying that area will automatically fly back to an Immediate Storage position). But if the user wants to examine better the books before making a choice, then touching the bookcase will cause the user, desk and all, to fly to the bookcase (Fig. 6). Touching a book will then cause the user to fly back to the home position and the book to fly to the focus position.

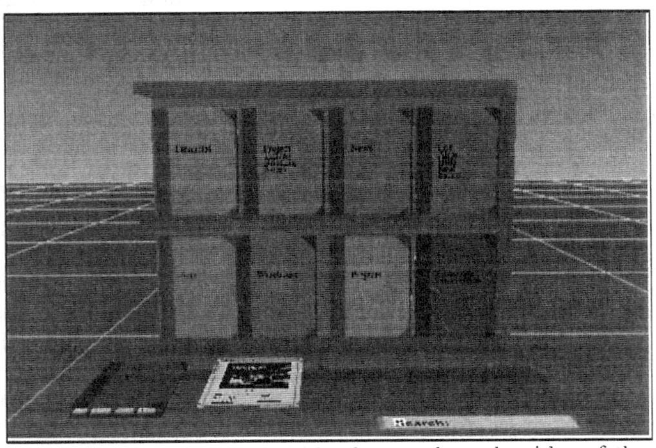

Fig. 6: User has flown to the bookcase where the titles of the books can be easily read. (See Color Plate 5)

The purpose of the workspace is to allow a number of objects to be displayed together (mitigating the limitations of the small screen space) in order to support information-intensive activities. The workspace sets up explicitly the capacity for speed/access-time tradeoff to allow tuning for such activities. The design aims to provide very rapid access to a small number of pages, smoothly integrated with the slower access to a large number. The Immediate

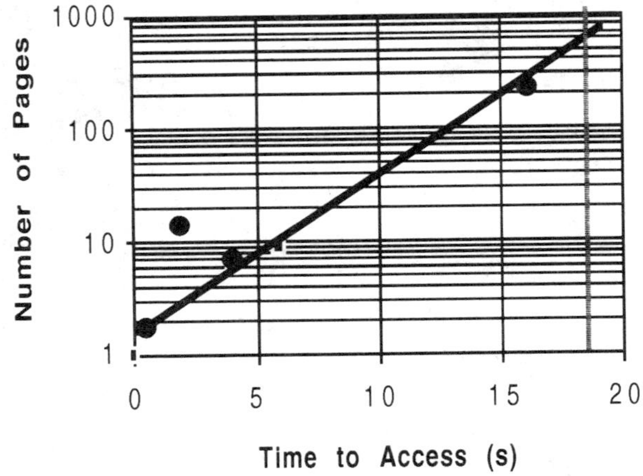

Fig. 7. Preliminary computation of Cost of Knowledge Characteristic Function for Web Forager.

Storage workspace can hold about 30 documents without occlusion, and over a hundred if occlusions are allowed (not counting book contents). Pages for ongoing activities migrate into the rapid access and manipulation region. In this way, repeated reference due to locality of reference statistics can result in faster interaction.

Cost of Knowledge Characteristic Function
In previous work [25], we have attempted to measure the access properties of a workspace by computing the Cost of Knowledge Characteristic Function, that is, a plot of how many objects can be accessed as a function of the time cost of accessing them. We surmise that a balanced workspace will exhibit an exponential relationship, most conveniently displayed as a straight line in semi-log coordinates. As a tool to use in refining our design, we have computed a preliminary version of this function. The computation assumes that there is a page in the Focus Position (hence the maximal occlusion), that the desk is full, and that one row of pages from each of the discrete Z-distances in the space shows (remember, the design of the space has been carefully set up to permit this).

The results are shown in Fig. 7. They are roughly in the expected relation, except that the images on the desk permit the fast part of the space to receive extra loading. An illustrative comparison with a conventional Web browser is shown as a gray line assuming a constant 18 sec per page retrieval. We hope to use this and related techniques to further refine the space in future research.

SUMMARY
The Web Forager workspace is intended to create patches from the Web where a high density of relevant pages can be combined with rapid access. In addition to multiple pages occurring simultaneously, the space contains groups of pages in the form of WebBooks, which can allow the user to express an elementary form of sensemaking by grouping and ordering. High density patches found around the net,

whether created explicitly by searchers or discovered through Web analysis methods can be put into a form where they can be rapidly interacted with. Through the invention of such techniques and analytical methods to help us understand them, it is hoped that the connectivity of the Web, which has been so successful, can be evolved into yet more useful forms.

REFERENCES

1. Pirolli, P. and S. Card, *Information Foraging in Information Access Environments,* in *CHI '95, ACM Conference on Human Factors in Software*. 1995, ACM: New York. p. 51–58.

2. Stephens, DEW. and J. R. Krebs, Foraging theory. 1986, Princeton: Princeton University Press.

3. Mauldin, M.L. and J.R.R. Leavitt. *Web-agent related research at the CMT*. in *SIGNIDR*. 1994. McLean, Virginia:

4. Filo, D. and J. Yang, *Yahoo (Yet Another Hierarchical Officious Oracle)*. 1994, Yahoo! Corp: Stanford, California.

5. D. A. Henderson, J. and S.K. Card, *Rooms: The use of multiple virtual workspaces to reduce space contention in a window-based graphical user interfaces.* ACM Transactions on Graphics, 1986. **5**(3 (July)): p. 211–241.

6. Card, S.K., M. Pavel, and J.E. Farrell, *Window-based computer dialogues.,* in *Human-Computer Interaction—INTERACT '84,* B. Shackel, Editor. 1984, Elsevier Science Publishers, B. V. (North-Holland): Amsterdam. p. 51–56.

7. Russell, D.M., *et al., The cost structure of sensemaking,* in *ACM/IFIPS InterCHI '3 Conference on Human Factors in Software*. 1993, ACM: New York. p. 269–276.

8. Robertson, G.G., S.K. Card, and J.D. Mackinlay, *Information visualization using 3D interactive animation.* Communications of the ACM, 1993. **36**(4 (April)): p. 57–71.

9. Card, S.K. and D.A. Henderson, *Catalogues: A Metaphor for Computer Application Delivery,* in *Human-Computer Interaction -- INTERACT'87*. 1987, Elsevier Science Publishers (North Holland): p. 959–963.

10. Yankelovich, N., N. Meyrowitz, and A. van Dam, *Reading and Writing the Electronic Book.* IEEE Computer, 1985. **18**(10 (October)): p. 15–30.

11. Miyazawa, M., *et al., An Electronic Book: APTBook,* in *Human-Computer Interaction -- INTERACT'90*. 1990, Elsevier Science Publishers (North Holland): Amsterdam. p. 513–519.

12. Silicon Graphics, *Demo Book*. 1993, Silicon Graphics: Mountain View, California.

13. Remde, J.R., L.M. Gomez, and T.K. Landauer, *Superbook: An Automatic Tool for Information Exploration,* in *ACM Hypertext '87 Proceedings*. 1987, p. 175–188.

14. Carr, R. and D. Shafer, *The Power of PenPoint*. 1992, New York: Addison-Wesley.

15. Sony Corporation, *Magic Link User's Guide, PIC-1000*. 1994, Tokyo: Sony Corporation. 203 pp.

16. Moll-Carrillo, H.J., *et al., Articulating a Metaphor Through User-Centered Design,* in *CHI '95, ACM Conference on Human Factors in Software*. 1995, ACM Press: New York. p. 566–572.

17. Benest, I.D., G. Morgan, and M.D. Smithurst, *A Humanized Interface to an Electronic Library,* in *Human-Computer Interaction -- INTERACT'87*. 1987, Elsevier Science Publishers (North Holland): Amsterdam. p. 905–910.

18. Ichimura, S. and Y., *Another Dimension to Hypermedia Access,* in *Hypertext '93*. 1993, ACM: New York. p. 63–72.

19. Robertson, G.G. and J.D. Mackinlay, *The Document Lens*. UST '93, ACM Conference on User Interface Software and Technology, 1993. : p. 101–108.

20. Brown, M.. and R. C. A. Shiner, *A New Paradigm for Browsing the Web,* in *CHI '95, ACM Conference on Human Factors in Software, Conference Companion*. 1995, ACM Press: New York. p. 320–321.

21. Card, S.K., J.D. Mackinlay, and G.G. Robertson. *The Information Visualizer: An information workspace*, in *CHI '91, ACM Conference on Human Factors in Computing Systems*. 1991.

22. Ballay, J.M. *Designing Workscape: An interdisciplinary experience*. in *ACM CHI '94, Human Factors in Computing Systems*. 1994. Boston: ACM.

23. Staples, L. *Representation in virtual space: Visual convention in the graphical user interface*. in *INTERCHI '93*. 1993. ACM.

24. Ark Interface Workspace *User's Guide*. 1990, Seattle, Washington: Ark Interface, Inc. 54.

25. Card, S.K., P. Pirolli, and J.D. Mackinlay, *The cost of knowledge characteristic function: Display evaluation for direct-walk dynamic information visualizations,* in *CHI '94, ACM Conference on Human Factors in Software*. 1994, ACM: New York. p. 238–244.

Silk from a Sow's Ear: Extracting Usable Structures from the Web

*Peter Pirolli, James Pitkow, Ramana Rao**

Xerox Palo Alto Research Center
3333 Coyote Hill Road
Palo Alto, CA 94304, USA
E-mail: {pirolli, rao}@parc.xerox.com, pitkow@cc.gatech.edu

**authors are ordered alphabetically*

ABSTRACT

In its current implementation, the World-Wide Web lacks much of the explicit structure and strong typing found in many closed hypertext systems. While this property probably relates to the explosive acceptance of the Web, it further complicates the already difficult problem of identifying usable structures and aggregates in large hypertext collections. These reduced structures, or localities, form the basis for simplifying visualizations of and navigation through complex hypertext systems. Much of the previous research into identifying aggregates utilize graph theoretic algorithms based upon structural topology, i.e., the linkages between items. Other research has focused on content analysis to form document collections. This paper presents our exploration into techniques that utilize both the topology and textual similarity between items as well as usage data collected by servers and page meta-information lke title and size. Linear equations and spreading activation models are employed to arrange Web pages based upon functional categories, node types, and relevancy.

Keywords

Information Visualization, World Wide Web, Hypertext.

INTRODUCTION

The apparent ease with which users can click from page to page on the World-Wide Web (WWW) belies the real difficulty of understanding the what and where of available information. The primary approaches widely provided for finding information are search systems like Lycos and Harvest and human-organized directory browsers like Yahoo and Internet Yellow Pages [18]. Though these approaches are quite powerful, they don't exhaust the potential space of approaches.

We suggest that the ecological approach of Information Foraging Theory [12] motivates the use of techniques for automatic categorization and a particular kind of associative retrieval of WWW pages involving *spreading activation* [4]. Categorization techniques are used to identify and rank particular kinds of WWW pages, such as "organization home pages" or "index pages." Associative retrieval techniques identify and rank pages predicted to be related and relevant to currently viewed pages. Both techniques work on the basis of a variety of features of WWW pages, including the text content, usage patterns, inter-page hypertext link topology, and meta-document data such as file size and file name. In combination, these techniques may be used in support of novel information visualization techniques, such as the WebBook [6], to form and present larger aggregates of related WWW pages. We will argue that these techniques can be used to optimize user information-seeking and sensemaking.

INFORMATION FORAGING ON THE WWW

In an information-rich world, the limiting resource is the time and attention of users. We are developing Information Foraging Theory [12] as an attempt to understand how people adaptively allocate their time and attention in the pursuit and consumption of valuable information. Foraging theory in anthropology [16] and biology [17] attempts to explain how humans and animals optimize their gain of food energy from flux of the physical and organic environment. Similarly, Information Foraging Theory attempts to explain how human *informavores* optimize their information gain from the flux of the cultural and technological environment. We can think of the WWW as an information environment in which information-seeking users will want optimized foraging technologies. We will argue that categorization and associative retrieval techniques improve the optimality of WWW interactions.

Categorizing to Optimize Foraging Decisions

We assume a scenario in which a user forages for relevant, valuable information at some *web locality*, meaning some collection of related WWW pages. Perhaps the pages are related because they are at some particular physical site or WWW server, or perhaps related because they have been collected by a particular community or organization. The optimal selection of WWW pages from the web locality to satisfy a user's information needs is a kind of *optimal information diet* problem discussed in Pirolli and Card [12]. The overall rate of gaining useful information will be improved by eliminating irrelevant or low-value categories of information from consideration. Simply put, to the

CHI 96 Vancouver, BC Canada

extent that one can rapidly distinguish junk categories from interesting or relevant ones, a person can allocate their time more usefully.

Imagine that a user coming upon a web locality is analogous to a predator such as a lion coming upon an open plain with a teeming array of potential prey species: The optimality of the diet or pursuit sequence chosen by the predator (or user) will depend on their ability to rapidly categorize the prey types (WWW page types), assess their prevalences on the plain (web locality), assess their profitabilities (amount of return over cost of pursuit), and decide which categories to pursue and which to ignore. The optimization can be further improved to the extent that the category members can be ranked, so that good examples of a good category could be pursued first. Figure 1 provides a graphical illustration of the improvements provided by categorization and ranking (see Pirolli and Card [12] for detailed technical discussion).

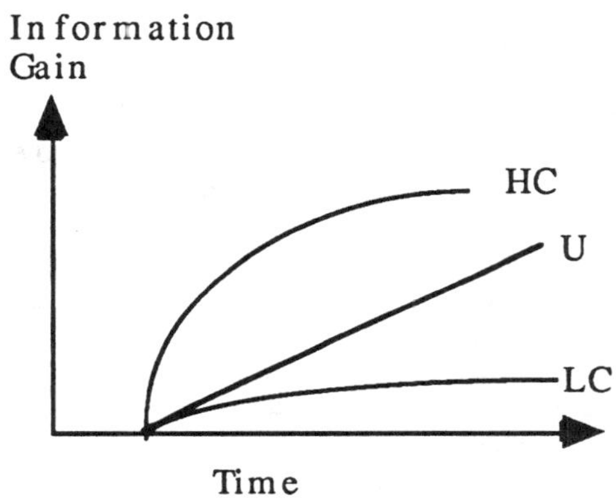

Figure 1. Uninformed search through an uncategorized web locality produces a linear information gain function as in U. Categorizing and ranking WWW pages allows an information forager to rapidly identify high value, ranked, categories (HC) and low value categories (LC) and concentrate on exploiting the HC gain curve.

Spreading Activation to Predict Needed Information

Anderson and Milson [1, 3] have recently argued that human memory has adapted through evolution to optimize the retrieval of needed information (memories) based on the current context of attention. Generally, one could say that their analysis relies on three general sorts of information to compute the *need probabilities* of all stored memories, given a current focus of attention: (1) past usage patterns, (2) degree of shared content, and (3) inter-memory associative link structures. More recently, Anderson [2] has proposed that spreading activation mechanisms can be used to implement and approximate such computations.

The WWW can be viewed as an external memory and a user-forager would be aided by retrieval mechanisms that predicted and returned the most likely needed WWW pages, given that the user is attending to some given page(s). We will use a kind of spreading activation mechanism [4] to predict the needed, relevant information, computed using past usage patterns, degree of shared content, and WWW hyperlink structure.

Monitoring the Evolution of Web Ecologies

The WWW itself is an evolving ecology of information-bearing items, each of which is competing for human attention. One can think of the knowledge content of the WWW as a collection of *memes* [9], or cultural knowledge units, analogous to genes, that are transmitted and replicated. People who manage WWW sites (e.g., Webmasters) may want to assess general properties of the information evolving at their sites, as well as general properties about which users are attending to which kinds of information. We will illustrate how categorization and associative retrieval techniques provide a means for monitoring the interaction of users and WWW pages in the information habitat of a WWW site.

RELATION TO WEB VISUALIZATION

Most current WWW browsers provide very little support for helping people gain an overall assessment of the structure and content of large collections of WWW pages. Information Visualization could be used to provide an interactive overview of web localities that facilitates navigation and general assessment. Visualizations have been developed that provide new interactive mechanisms for making sense of information sets with thousands of objects [15]. The general approach is to map properties and relations of large collections of objects onto visual, interactive structures. Such visualizations provide value to the extent that the mapped properties help users navigate around the space and remember locations or support the unit tasks of the user's work.

Visualizations can be applied to the Web by treating the pages of the Web as objects with properties. Mukerjea [11] has applied a number of visualizations to the Web. Each of these provides an overview of a Web locality in terms of some simple property of the pages. For example, a Cone Tree shows connectivity structure between pages and a Perspective Wall shows time-indexed accesses of the pages. Thus, these visualizations are based on one or a few characteristics of the pages.

As argued above, our approach to extracting structure from the Web using categorization and spreading activation, can be used to form higher level abstractions that reduce the complexity and increase the richness of an overview. We have developed methods for annotating pages with their functional types and relevancy/importance assessments as well as aggregating the Web into collections which can be treated as collections. These collections could be visualized as WebBooks in the WebForager [6].

OVERVIEW OF THE APPROACH

Many kinds of information can be used to classify or organize collections of WWW pages including the textual content, the connectivity (hyperlink) structure, and various characteristics of the pages including file-system attributes and access statistics, as well as usage statistics. Most of this information can be straight-forwardly gathered for fixed collections of pages, particularly with privileged access to the server's storage system. Over time, the Web infrastructure can be adapted to provide this information directly through standard protocols.

We have gathered information for several Web localities, but in this paper, we focus on the pages served by the Xerox WWW server. Our goal was to analyze this data and to design algorithms for various extractors which would annotate and aggregate WWW pages at this Web locality. In particular, we have designed methods for classifying nodes into a number of functional categories, and spreading activation based on selecting one or more source nodes (WWW pages) and dimensions of interest, and aggregating nodes into higher level collections.

Categorization techniques typically attempt to assign individual elements (e.g., WWW pages) into categories based on the features they exhibit. Based on category membership, we may quickly predict the functionality of an element. For instance, in the everyday world, identifying something as a "chair" enables the quick prediction that an object can be sat on. Our techniques rely on particular features we can extract about WWW pages at a Web locality.

One may conceive of a Web locality as a complex abstract space in which WWW pages of different functional categories or types are arranged. These functional categories might be defined by a user's specific set of interests, or the categories might be extracted from the collection itself through inductive technologies [13]. An example category might be *organizational home page*. Typical members of the category would describe an organization and have links to many other Web pages, providing relevant information about the organization, its divisions or departments, summaries of its purpose, and so on.

We specified a set of functional categories for this study that correspond to the various roles that Web pages typically play. Each functional category was defined in a manner that has a graded membership, with some pages being more typical of a category than others, and Web pages may belong to many categories. Specifically, we defined the following types of Web pages for our study:

- *head*: Typically a related set of pages will have one page that would best serve as the first one to visit. Head pages have two subclasses:
  - *organizational home page*: These are pages that represent the entry point for organizations and institutions, usually found as the default home page for servers, e.g., http://www.org/
  - *personal home page*: Usually, individuals have only one page within an organization that they place personal information and other tidbits on.
- *index*: These are pages that server to navigate users to a number of other pages that may or may not be related. Typical pages in this category have the words "Index" or "Table of Contents" or "toc" as part of their URL.
- *source index*: These pages are entry points and indices into a related information space. Thus they are also head nodes.
- *reference*: A page that is used to repeatedly explain a concept or contains actual references. References also have a special subclass:
  - *destination*: In graph theory these are best thought of as "sinks", pages that do not point elsewhere but that a number of other pages point to. Examples include pages of expanded acronyms, copyright notices, and bibliographic references.
- *content*: These are pages whose purpose is not to facilitate navigation, but to deliver information.

We will use spreading activation mechanisms to predict the relevance of Web pages at a locality to WWW pages that are in the a current focus of attention of the user. The degree of relevance of Web pages to one another can be conceived as similarities, or strength of associations, among Web pages located in an abstract space. These strength-of-association relations can be represented formally using a composite of several graph structures. Each graph structure contains nodes representing Web pages, and directed arcs among nodes are labeled with values representing strength of association among pages. One type of graph structure represents the hypertext link topology of a Web locality by using arcs labeled with unit strengths to connect one graph node to another when there exists a hypertext link between the corresponding Web pages. This is perhaps the most common intuition that people hold when thinking about a locality. A second type of graph structure represents the inter-page text content similarity by labeling arcs connecting nodes with the computed text similarities between corresponding Web pages. This is a common way of conceptualizing documents in search-based information retrieval. A third type of graph structure represents the flow of users through the locality by labeling the arcs between two nodes with the number of users that go from one page to another. This essentially reflects the mutual desirability of information among Web pages based on observed usage patterns. Predicted relevance of WWW pages can be based on one or all of the similarity structures represented by these graphs of hypertext links, text overlap, or usage patterns.

In summary, given this conception of a Web locality, we use three component processes to identify and extract Web structure. First is the categorization of Web pages into types and the users' selection of pages according to their degree of category membership in different types. Second is the spread of activation from the identified sources through some combination of the link connectivity, text similarity, and usage spaces. Third is the selection and aggregation of Web pages based on their pattern of relevancy as measured by activation.

DATA SOURCES AND COLLATION

The data used for subsequent analyses was derived from two sources: a traversal of the Xerox's external Web site, whose Uniform Resource Locator (URL) is http://www.xerox.com, and the logs of requested items maintained by the Xerox Web server. For this analysis, we choose the access logs from March through May of 1995, in which 1.4 million items were requested. Four basic kinds of data were extracted:

- *Topology* , which is the hyperlink structure among WWW pages at a Web locality.
- *Page meta-information*, which includes various features of the pages, such as file size and URL.
- *Usage frequency* and *usage paths*, which indicate how many times a WWW pages has been accessed and how many times a traversal was made from one WWW page to another.
- *Text similarity* among all text WWW pages at a Web locality

These data were used to construct two types of representation, used in the categorization and spreading activation computations respectively:

- Feature-vector representations of each WWW page that represent values of each page on each dimension.
- Graph representations (in matrix form) of the strength of association of WWW pages to one another.

Topology

The site's topology was ascertained via "the walker", an autonomous agent that, given a starting point, performs an exhaustive breadth-first traversal of pages within the locality. The walker used the Hypertext Transfer Protocol (HTTP) to request and retrieve items, parsing the returned object to extract hyperlinks. Only links that pointed to objects within the site were added to a list of items to explore. Thus, the walker produced a graph representation of hyperlink structure of the Web locality. The walker may not have reached all nodes that are accessible via a particular server -- only those nodes that were reachable from the starting point were included. This analysis produces an adjacency matrix for the particular locality that we call the *topology matrix.*

Page Meta-Information

For each node visited in a site at least the following meta-information properties was collected: name, file size, and the time the node was last modified. These and other page characteristics can be collected by the walker from the HTTP reply header or the HTML document header. In addition, another process, called "the ripper", was used to extract characteristics directly from the Web server's file system. The meta-information for each page was collected into *meta-document vectors.*

Usage Statistics and Paths, and Entry Points

Most servers have the ability to record transactional information about requested items. This information usually consists of at least the time and the name of the URL being requested as well as the machine name making the request. The latter field may represent only one user making requests from their local machine or it could represent a number of users whose requests are being issued through one machine, as is the case with firewalls and proxies. This makes differentiating the paths traversed by individual users from these access logs non-trivial, since numerous requests from proxied and firewalled domains can occur simultaneously. That is, if 200 users from behind an America Online proxy are simultaneously navigating the pages within a site, how does one determine which users took which paths? This problem is further complicated by local caches maintained by each browser and intentional reloading of pages by the user.

The algorithm we implemented to determine user's paths, a.k.a. "the whittler", utilized the Web locality's topology along with several heuristics. The topology was consulted to determine legitimate traversals while the heuristics were used to disambiguate user paths when multiple users from the same machine name were suspected. The latter scenario relies upon a least recently used bin packing strategy and session length time-outs as determined empirically from end-user navigation patterns [7]. Essentially, new paths were created for a machine name when the time between the

Table 1. Node type definitions and results.

Node Type	Size	Number Inlinks	Number Outlinks	Depth of Children	Similarity to Children	Freq.	Entry Point	Precision
Index	- (outlinks/size)		+					0.67
Source Index	- (outlinks/size)		+				+	0.53
Reference	+	-	-	-				0.64
Destination Reference	+	-	-	-			-	0.53
Head			+	+	+		+	0.70
Org. Home Page		+	+		+		+	0.30
Personal Home Page	> 1 k & < 3 k					-	-	0.51
Content	+	-	-					0.99

last request and the current request was greater than the session boundary limit, i.e., the session timed out. New paths were also created when the requested page was not connected to the last page in the currently maintained path. These tests were performed on all paths being maintained for that machine name, with the ordering of tests being the paths least recently extended. This produced a set of paths requested by each machine and the times for each request. From this, a vector that contained each node's frequency of requests and a matrix containing the number of traversals from one page to another were computed using software that identified the frequency of k-substrings for any n-string [14]. These are referred to hereafter as the *frequency vectors* and the *path matrix* respectively.

Additionally, the difference between the total number of requests for a page and the sum of the paths to the page was computed. Intuitively this generates a set of *entry point* candidates. These are the WWW pages at a Web locality that seem to be the starting points for many users. Entry points are defined as the set of pages that are pointed to by sources outside the locality, e.g., an organization's home page, a popular news article, etc. Table 2 shows the results of this analysis. The Xerox Home page and the 1995 Xerox Fact Book are the top pages identified are among the pages most visited by users, as might be expected of people seeking information about Xerox. Also among the top WWW pages are Xerox PARC's Digital Library Home Page, PARC's Map Viewer, the Bookwise Home Page, all of which have received substantial outside press or awards that would draw the attention of users. Entry points might provide useful insight to Web designers based on actual use, which may differ from their intended use on a Web locality. Entry points also may be used in providing a set of nodes from which to spread activation.

Inter-document Text Similarity

Techniques from information retrieval [19] can be applied to calculate a *text similarity matrix* which represents the inter-document text similarities among WWW pages. In particular, for each WWW page, we tokenized and indexed the text using the TDB full-text retrieval engine [8]. Like many schemes, each document is represented by a vector,

Table 2. The most popular starting points

% Visits Outside	Number Visits	Pages
99.96	2662	/95FactBook/Title.html
96.18	12377	/PARC/docs/mapviewer-legend-world.html
99.58	16004	/Products/XIS/BookWise.html
99.99	19130	/PARC/dlbx/library.html
94.29	24107	/ (the default Xerox Home Page)

where each component of the vector represents a word. Entries in the vector for a document indicate the presence or frequency of a word in the document. For each pair of pages, we computed the dot product of the these vectors, which produces a similarity measure, which was entered into the text similarity matrix for the Web locality.

WEB CATEGORIZATION

Previous hypertext research extols the value added of strongly typed node and link systems, yet most of the information available on the Web is poorly typed. Even so, a quick tour of WWW pages across Web localities reveals that certain classes of documents do indeed exist. This next section presents an approach to categorization and discussion of the results obtained from categorization of the Xerox Web locality.

Web Page Feature Vectors

In order to perform categorizations we represented each WWW page at the Xerox Web locality by a vector of features constructed from the above topology, meta-information, usage statistics and paths, and text similarities. These WWW page vectors were collected into a matrix. Specifically, a new matrix was created with each row representing a WWW page, and the columns representing the page's:

- *size*, in bytes, of the item
- *inlinks*, the number of hyperlinks that point to the item from the Xerox Web space
- *outlinks*, the number of hyperlinks the item contains that point to other items in the Xerox Web space
- *frequency*, the number of times the item was requested in the sample period
- *sources*, number of times the item was identified as the start of a path traversal
- *csim*, the textual similarity of the item to it's children based upon previous TDB calculation
- *cdepth*, the average depth of the item's children as measured by the number of '/' in the URL.

A logarithmic transform and a z-score normalization was applied to the size, inlinks, outlinks, frequency, and sources values. Two additional matrices were derived from the original dataset, one with zero size items removed and the other with only item whose sizes were between 1000 and 3000 bytes.

Given the above properties and shapes of the distributions, linear separable categories were assumed. This enabled categories to be identified by solving a set of linear equations of the form:

$$c_i = w_1 v_1 + w_2 v_2 + ... + w_n v_n \quad (1)$$

for all nodes i in Xerox Web space, where the v_j are the measured features of each Web page, and the w_j are weights. In what follows, these weights were set *a priori* by us to be either -1, 0, or +1. Future works may investigate classification algorithms for optimizing the setting of these weights, for instance, by using Linear Discriminant Analysis, or more sophisticated machine learning techniques.

Table 1 shows the weights used to order Web pages for each of the categories. For example, we hypothesized that Content Nodes would have few inlinks and few outlinks, but have relatively larger file sizes. The equation used to determine this category of nodes has a positive weight, +1 on the size feature, and negative weight, -1, on the inlink and outlink features. For Head Nodes, being the first pages of a collection of documents with like content, we expected such pages to have high text similarity between itself and its children, would have a high average depth of its children, and that it would be more likely to be an entry point based upon actual user navigation patterns.

Evaluation

Once the set of WWW pages for each category were identified, the top 25 members with the highest scores on Linear Equation 1 were extracted, and the first page of the corresponding Web pages printed for off-line evaluation. Each printed page was read and then rated by the three authors as either "belonging to" or "not belonging to" the category it had been associated with. Precision scores were computed for each retrieved set of 25 WWW pages, where precision was the proportion of pages rated as "belonging to" the category. Table 1 shows the average precision (geometric mean) for each node category.

As one would expect due the large number of content nodes in a Web locality, the precision at which content nodes can be identified was quite high (precision = .99). Equally encouraging was the identification of Head and Index Nodes (precisions of .70 and .67 respectively). Table 3 shows the list of top five Head Nodes. Not surprisingly, the lowest precision in Table 1 was associated with the correct identification of Organizational Home Pages, of which there are only about ten such pages at the Xerox Web locality.

Table 3. The top 5 head nodes.

Titles of Page
Digital Tradition Keywords
RXRC Cambridge Technical Report Series
Ken Fishkin's Public Home Page
Why are Black Boxes so Hard to Reuse?
Xerox Corporation 1994 Form 10-K

SPREADING ACTIVATION

Spreading activation can be characterized as a process that identifies knowledge predicted to be relevant to some focus of attention. The particular version we use is a leaky capacitor model developed in the ACT* theory [4] and studied parametrically by Huberman and Hogg [10].

Suppose a user is interested in a set of one or more Web pages and wants to find related pages to form a small Web aggregate, such as a WebBook [6]. We assume that the identification of such "interesting seed sets" of Web pages could also be automatically determined based on functional category using methods described above.

Networks for Spreading Activation

As outlined above, we used three kind of graphs, or networks, to represent strength of associations among WWW pages: (1) the hypertext link *topology* of a Web locality, (2) inter-page *text similarity*, and (3) the *usage paths*, or flow of users through the locality. each of these networks or graphs is represented by matrices in our spreading activation algorithm. That is, each row corresponds to a network node representing a page, and similarly each column corresponds to a network node representing a page. If we index the 1, 2, ...,N pages, there would be $i = 1, 2, ..N$ columns and $j = 1, 2, ..N$ rows for each matrix representing a graph network.

Each entry in the ith column and j^{th} row of a matrix represents the strength of connection between page i and page j (or similarly, the amount of potential activation flow or capacity). The meaning of these entries varies depending on the type of network through which activation is being spread:

- in topology networks, an entry of 0 in column i, row j, indicates no hypertext link between page i and page j, whereas an entry of 1 indicates a hypertext link.
- in text similarity networks, an entry of a real number, $s \geq 0$, in column i, row j indicates the inter-document similarity of page i to page j.
- in usage path networks an entry of an integer strength, $s \geq 0$, in column i row j, indicates the number of users that traversed from page i to page j

Conceptually, activation is pumped into one or more of the graph networks at nodes representing a starting set of Web pages and it flows through the arcs of the graph structure, with amount of flow modulated by arc strengths (which can also be thought of as arc flow capacities). The asymptotic pattern of activation over nodes will define the degree of predicted relevance of Web pages to the source pages. By selecting the topmost active nodes or those above some set criterion value, we may extract and rank WWW pages based on their predicted relevance.

Activation Algorithm

An activation network can be represented as a graph defined by matrix $\mathbf{R}$, where each off-diagonal element $\mathbf{R}_{i,j}$ contains the strength of association between nodes i and j, and the diagonal contains zeros. The strengths determine how much activation flows from node to node. The set of source nodes of activation being pumped into the network is represented by a vector $\mathbf{C}$, where $\mathbf{C}_i$ represents the activation pumped in by node i. The dynamics of activation can be modeled over discrete steps $t = 1, 2, ...N$, with activation at step t represented by a vector $\mathbf{A}(t)$, with element $\mathbf{A}(t, i)$ representing the activation at node i at step t. The time evolution of the flow of activation is determined by

$$\mathbf{A}(t) = \mathbf{C} + \mathbf{M}\,\mathbf{A}(t-1), \tag{2}$$

where **M** is a matrix that determines the flow and decay of activation among nodes. It is specified by

$$\mathbf{M} = (1 - \gamma)\,\mathbf{I} + \alpha\,\mathbf{R}, \quad (3)$$

where $\gamma < 1$ is a parameter determining the relaxation of node activity back to zero when it receives no additional activation input, and α is a parameter denoting the amount of activation spread from a node to its neighbors. **I** is the identity matrix.

Huberman and Hogg showed that the characteristic dynamical behavior of spreading activation depends on the relation among γ, α, and the mean number of arcs per node, μ. In the general case, there is a phase transition when $\alpha = \gamma$. When α/γ is small, the total activation in the net rapidly rises to an asymptotic pattern and is localized in the network. When $\alpha > \gamma$, there is another phase transition at $\mu = 1$. With $\alpha > \gamma$, when the network contains sparsely connected nodes with $\mu < 1$, the total activation rises indefinitely but the pattern remains localized. Our usage path graph structures are such sparse networks. With $\alpha > \gamma$, with richly connected nodes with $\mu > 1$, the total activation rises indefinitely and all parts of the network affect all others, so that inputs of activation at any node tend to create the same pattern of activation. Our text similarity graphs are richly connected graphs. Given this characterization of the phase space of spreading activation regimes, we chose parameters such that $\alpha/\gamma << 1$ to identify Web structure aggregates.

Example 1: Predicting the Interests of Home Page Visitors

To illustrate, consider the situation in which we identify the most frequently visited organization home page using our categorization information, and wish to construct a Web aggregate that contains the pages most visited from that page. The most popular organization page can be identified as we did in Table 1 and the corresponding component of **C** given a positive value, and the remaining elements set to zero. Setting the association matrix **R** to be the usage path matrix, we then iterate Equation 2 for N time steps (in our simulations we used $N = 10$). Selecting the 25 most active pages constructs the collection described in Table 4. We could have used an activation threshold rather than a fixed set size to circumscribe a Web aggregate.

In Table 4, it is evident that a user who is focused on the Xerox home page is predicted to then shift their attention (by traversing web links) to WWW pages describe mainly xerox products, businesses, and financial reports. From this, we might infer that users interested in the Xerox home page are also interested in what Xerox sells or how they are doing financially.

Example 2: Assessing the Typical Web Author at a Locality

Consider another situation in which we are interested in the Web pages having the highest text similarity to the most typical person page in a Web locality. In other words, we might be interested in understanding something about what a typical person publishing in a Web locality says about themselves. In this case, the most typical person page is identified as in Table 1, the corresponding **C** element set to positive activation input (zeros elsewhere), and **R** is set to the text similarity matrix. Iteration of this spread of activation for $N = 10$ time steps selects the collection described in Table 4. By reading the group project overviews, the home pages of related people, personal interest pages, and formal and informal groups to which the person belongs, we should get some sense of what people are like in the organization.

Combining Activation Nets

Because of the simple properties of our activation networks, it is easy to combine the spread of activation though any weighted combination of activation pumped from different sources and through different kinds of arc-- that is, simultaneously through the topology, usage, and text similarity connections. Consequently, the Web

Table 4. Examples of Web pages selected using spreading activation.

Activation Source	Network	Most Active Web Pages Found (No. found)
Xerox Home Page	Usage paths	Xerox product descriptions (10) Financial reports (6) Business Division home pages (5) General info (2) Search form (1)
Highest rated member of *Personal Home Page* category	Text similarity	Group project overviews (5) Other people hotlists (4) Company info (4) Personal interests (4) Other similar people (3) Informal groups (1) Workshop attendee list (1) Wildlife award report (1) Someone else's talk (1)

locality can be lit up from different directions and using different colors of predicted relevancy. For instance one might be interested in the identifying the pages most similar in content to the pages most popularly traversed.

PURE LINK TOPOLOGY-BASED APPROACHES

Botafoga et al [5] have reported on purely graph-theoretic techniques for splitting a hypertext into aggregates. These techniques are based on identifying articulation points in the undirected graph and removing them to create a set of subgraphs. A node is an articulation point if removing it and its edges would disconnect the graph. Botafoga et al describe two algorithms which repeat this procedure iteratively. These algorithms removes indices (nodes with relatively high number of out-links) and references (nodes with relatively lots of in-links) on each iteration in order to prevent these functional nodes from overconnecting the graph. However, in our case, many of the nodes identified were in fact table-of-contents-like nodes which are very important elements of a web group.

Applying their first algorithm to the graph structure of the Xerox Web produces 10 web groups with at least 10 nodes. In addition, we tried an algorithm which iteratively removes articulation points until all groups are below 25 nodes in size or contain no articulation points. We didn't remove indices or references during iteration. This leads to 9 clusters (again of at least 10 nodes. The two algorithm produced 8 web groups in common, though often not including the same nodes. In addition, the simplified algorithm produced one extra web group, while the 2 extras web groups produced by the Botafoga algorithm were caused by splitting a web group and by including a spurious web group.

These algorithms were quite effective at pulling out highly-connected book structures. For example, one 13 node book was a TOC with 12 nodes for sections which pointed back and forth. However such structures are highly-authored sections of the web and cluster together in a number of ways. For example, there was a high correlation between the URLs of the nodes within these web groups. Most of the nodes typically shared a prefix of two or three pathname parts, though web groups that were less book-like tended to also bring in a few nodes from other locations on the server. More systematic comparison of pure topology-based methods and those based on one or more of the sources outlined here is an open area for further work.

SUMMARY

Higher level abstractions over hypertext can be used to improve navigation and assimilation of hypertext spaces. Previous work on structure extraction has typically used topological or textual relationships to drive analysis. In this paper, we have integrated these data sources as well as new sources including usage statistics and page meta-information to develop new techniques for node typing, group extraction, and relevancy determination. These methods can provide leverage in designing more usable overviews and visualizations of Web spaces.

REFERENCES

1. Anderson, J.R., *The adaptive character of thought*. Lawrence Erlbaum Associates, Hillsdale, NJ, 1990.
2. Anderson, J.R., *Rules of the mind*. Lawrence Erlbaum Associates, Hillsdale, NJ, 1993.
3. Anderson, J.R. and R. Milson, Human memory: An adaptive perspective. *Psychological Review, 96* (1989). 703-719.
4. Anderson, J.R. and P.L. Pirolli, Spread of activation. *Journal of Experimental Psychology: Learning, Memory, and Cognition, 10* (1984). 791-798.
5. Botafogo, R.A. and B. Schneiderman. Indentifying aggregates in hypertext structures. in *Third ACM Conference on Hypertext*. (1991, San Antonio, TX). ACM. pp. 63-74.
6. Card, S.K., G.G. Robertson, and W.M. York. The WebBook and the Web Forager: An Information Workspace for the World-Wide Web. in *Conference on Human Factors in Computing Systems, CHI-95*. (1996, ACM. pp.
7. Catledge, L. and J. Pitkow, Characterizing browsing strategies in the World-Wide Web. *Computer Networks and ISDN Systems, 27* (1995). .
8. Cutting, D.R., J.O. Pedersen, and P.-K. Halvorsen. An Object-Oriented Architecture for Text Retrieval. in *RIAO '91 Intelligent Text and Image Handling*. (1991, Barcelona, Spain). pp. 285-298.
9. Dawkins, R., *The selfish gene*. Oxford University Press, Oxford, 1976.
10. Huberman, B.A. and T. Hogg, Phase transitions in artificial intelligence systems. *Artificial Intelligences, 33* (1987). 155-171.
11. Mukherjea,S., J.D.Foley, and S.Hudson. Visualizing complex hypermedia networks through multiple hierarchical views. in *Human Factors in Computing Systems CHI-95*.(1995, Denver, CO). ACM. pp. 331-337.
12. Pirolli, P. and S. Card. Information foraging in information access environments. in *Conference on Human Factors in Computing Systems, CHI-95*. (1995, Association for Computing Machinery. pp.
13. Pirolli, P., P. Schank, M. Hearst, and C. Diehl. Scatter/Gather browsing communicates the topic structure of a very large text collection. in *Conference on Human Factors in Computing Systems, CHI-96*. (1996, Association for Computing Machinery. pp.
14. Pitkow, J. and C. Jehow. Results from the Third WWW Survey. in *4th Annual International WWW Conference*. (1995, pp.
15. Robertson, G.G., S.K. Card, and J.D. Mackinlay, Information visualization using 3D interactive animation. *Communications of the ACM, 36* (1993). 57-71.
16. Smith,E.A.and B.Winterhalder,ed.*Evolutionary ecology and human behavior*. de Gruyter, New York, 1992.
17. Stephens, D.W. and J.R. Krebs, *Foraging theory*. Princeton University Press, Princeton, NJ, 1986.
18. Taubes, G., Indexing the internet. *Science, 8* (1995). 1354-1356.
19. vanRijsbergen, C.J., *Information retrieval*. Butterworth & Co., Boston, MA, 1979.

A Palmtop Display for Dextrous Manipulation with Haptic Sensation

Haruo NOMA Tsutomu MIYASATO Fumio KISHINO
ATR Communication Systems Research Laboratories
Seika-cho, Kyoto, 619-02, Japan
Tel : +81-774-95-1211
<noma,miyasato,kishino>@atr-sw.atr.co.jp

ABSTRACT

Palmtop displays have been extensively studied, but most of them simply refocus information in the real or virtual world. The palmtop display for dextrous manipulation (PDDM) proposed in this paper allows the users to manipulate a remote object as if they were holding it in their hands. The PDDM system has a small LCD, a 3D mouse and a mechanical linkage (force display). When the user locks onto an object in the center of the palmtop display, s/he can manipulate the object through motion input on the palmtop display with haptic sensation. In this paper, the features of the PDDM with haptic sensation are described, then four operating methods and the haptic representation methods for a trial model are proposed and evaluated. (see Video Figure in the CHI 96 Video Program)

Keywords

Palmtop display, Haptic sensation, Force display, Virtual reality, Teleconference, User interface

INTRODUCTION

A virtual world generated by VR is expected to accommodate applications in many fields, such as remote control, CAD and art. In general, such applications allow users to arrange both virtual and real objects in the virtual world by a number of methods. We will suppose that the basic operation is a sequence of the following three unit phases.

- Observe objects in the VR space from a suitable viewpoint.
- Control and transform the objects that are focused on.
- Confirm the results of the sequence.

These unit phases make up a basic motion, and a complex operation is considered to be an assemblage of basic motions. In many VR related studies, specialized interface devices are designed and applied based on a certain goal. However, not many VR interfaces are good at balancing both observing (output) and controlling (input) methods. If one side should prevail, the sequence of the unit phase becomes unstable and the user could encounter problems in use.

In this study, a new manipulating device using a palmtop display is proposed as one solution to this balancing problem. It is called the Palmtop Display for Dextrous Manipulation (PDDM) shown in Figure 1 and was designed especially for fine manipulating tasks in our virtual space teleconferencing system (VSTC) [7]. The most important design concept of the PDDM is an interface device which combines an input method and an output method. This device allows the user to be unaware of mode shifts, which interrupt the phase flow in manipulation.

In the next section, we explain the features of the PDDM and clarify its layout in other I/O devices. A trial PDDM system was designed, and four manipulating methods were tested. Additionally a haptic representation method was tested to evaluate our design. In the last section, the remaining problems and prospects of the PDDM are discussed.

PALMTOP DISPLAY FOR DEXTROUS MANIPULATION

The VSTC has been designed to generate a virtual conference room with a high realistic sensation. The trial VSTC has a large fixed screen, a glove-like device and a magnetic 3D position tracker. Generally, such a system provides a direct manipulating interface for the participants and they can handle virtual objects roughly without learning. It is, however, difficult to manipulate objects exactly with such devices. One of the main reasons for this is the excessive degrees of freedom (DOF) in the manipulation. When we wish to draw a straight line on a peace of paper, we use a straight scale to restrict the DOF of the hand to 1. At this point, two solutions can be proposed: one is to give a virtual constraint to the dynamical motion objects in the virtual space [5], and the other is to give a physical limitation to the user's motion using a mechanical

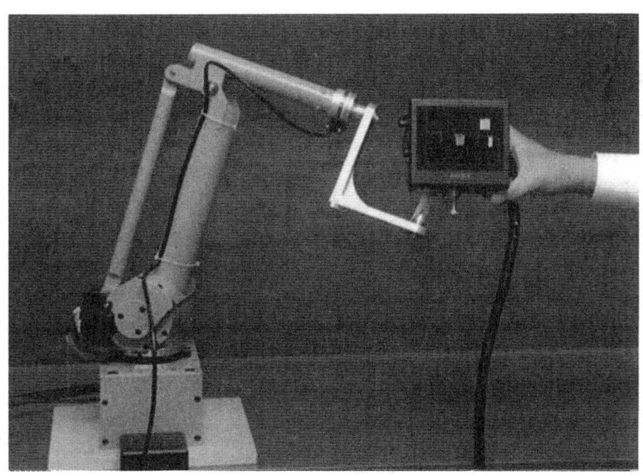

Figure 1 The Palmtop Display for Dextrous Manipulation

linkage [3][8]. A mechanical linkage that provides a reaction force for the user is called a force display.

In this paper, a kind of force display is introduced. In addition using reaction force to restrict the user's motion, the force display can render the features of objects, such as their weight, hardness, texture and so on. Almost everyone who has tried our trial VSTC has complained about the lack of haptic sensation, so it is assumed that these factors are important for generating a realistic manipulating environment. However, using a force display with a large fixed screen requires us to solve the following problems.

- The force display must generate a reaction force within the entire area of the virtual space on the display. This will make the force display quite large.
- The mechanical linkage connected to the user's hand are located between the user and the screen. This will cause a depth conflict and reduces the immersive sensation of the virtual world [12].

Considering these problems, we proposed a palmtop display as a motion input device. The PDDM consists of a palmtop display, a position and orientation sensor and a force display, and can act as a visual display and as a motion input device with haptic sensation in one unit.

The features of the PDDM will be explained using the ideal system in the VSTC shown in figure 2. The right side is a real space where the PDDM user is, and the left side is a virtual world where other participants and objects are displayed on the large screen. When the PDDM user wishes to modify the lidless box out of hand, the user copies it into the special space (local studio) in front of him/she. The camera metaphor could be introduced for this motion using the palmtop display. The local studio is the working area for the PDDM user and only s/he can modify objects in this space. A change in the copy is immediately reflected in the original. Here, s/he can observe the object from any viewpoint with the palmtop display (observing phase). Deciding the best viewpoint for the modification, s/he focuses on the part of the object that s/he intends to modify in any way (handling phase). Here, the motion of the palmtop display is directly related to the motion of the object. It will allow the user to feel as if s/he is grasping the object directly in front of him/herself. Moreover, the force display system applies a reaction force to the user through the palmtop display in the handling phase. After the user finishes modifying the object, s/he releases it and return to the palmtop display mode to confirm the result (confirming phase).

As the sequence of these operational phases is shifted with a grasping motion, the user does not need to pay much attention to the shifting operation. In the trial model mentioned later, this is realized by locating the object in the center of the display and pushing and holding a button behind the palmtop display. We can also propose a touch panel on the display as a more immersive method.

The problems with the force display in large-screen VR can thus be solved, as follows:

- The PDDM does not need a large space to handle objects. This is the biggest advantage of the force display
- Since the mechanical linkages are located behind the palmtop display, They never hide the image on the palmtop display. The depth sensation on the palmtop display is always kept.

Additionally, the following features are expected:

- Since the input device and the output device are combined into one unit, the whole device is quite small.
- As long as an object is displayed on the PDDM, the user can directly move and rotate it with his/her hand.
- The user does not have to wear any equipment.

In the following sections, additional features of the PDDM are described with comparison to other interface devices.

A LAYOUT OF THE PDDM IN INTERFACE DEVICES

As mentioned above, the PDDM is an interface device that has two faces: information output and operation input. We

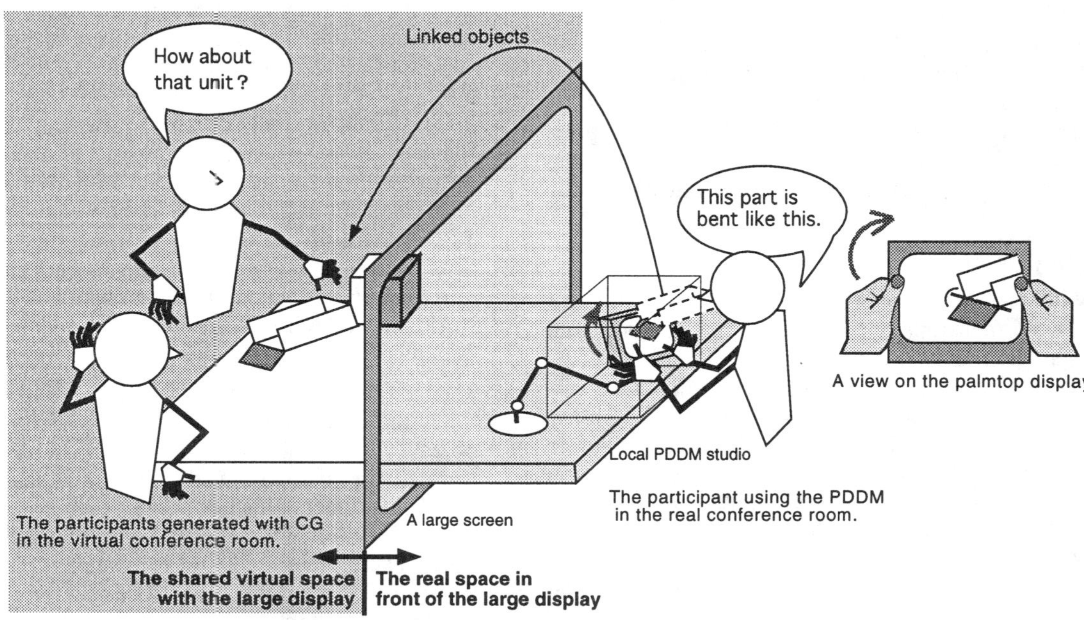

Figure 2 Conception of the PDDM system

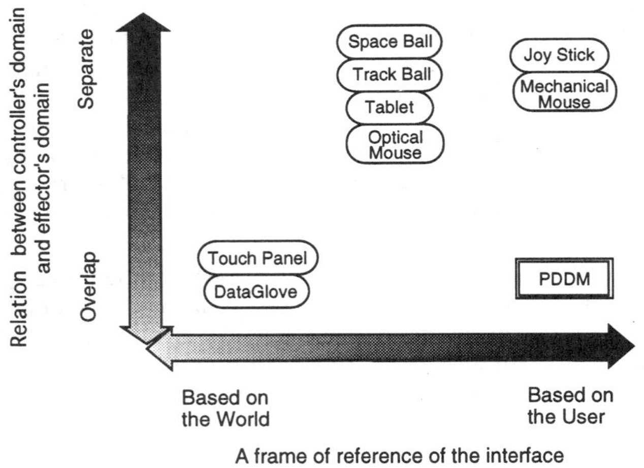

Figure 3 Taxonomy of the input device

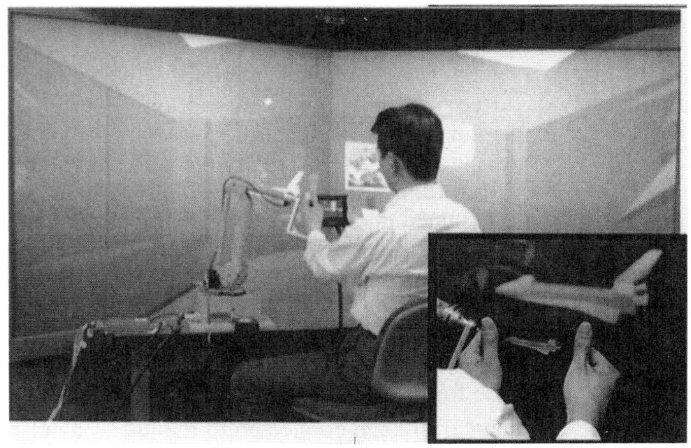

Figure 4 The PDDM with the VSTC

clarify the position of the PDDM in comparison with usual interface devices.

As an output device for visual information

A typical visual output device for VR systems makes virtual world images using a virtual camera that follows the user's motion. Through such animation, the user gets an intuitive sensation.

The PDDM employs a palmtop display for visual information. Palmtop displays [1,4,6,11] usually have a smaller display than other VR devices, such as fish tanks [2,9], large screens [7] and HMDs. Studies related to the palmtop display reported that the immersive sensation does not always depend on the screen size. This is because the palmtop display gives a higher degree of freedom than other devices, and the viewing point can be easily and intuitively changed to any place and direction the user wishes. The user can observe all of the directions with a palmtop type interface immediately.

As a related work, the Chameleon [4] is well known. The Chameleon allows a user to search information in virtual space interactively. In this case, the motion of the palmtop display is mapped to control the region where the user focuses upon in the database. The biggest difference between the PDDM and similar others is that the motion of the PDDM is applied not only to change the focused point, but also to manipulate remote objects as if they are in front of the user with kinesthetic feedback.

As an input device for motion

Next, we will propose a taxonomy for input devices. Figure 3 shows the two dimensions of the taxonomy. The horizontal dimension is "the frame of reference of the interface". This means what frame is referred for evaluating the input motion. The options are "user based" and "world based". The other dimension is "the relation between the controller's domain and the effector's domain." This means the spatial relation between the domain in which the user inputs motion and the domain in which the effector is controlled, and there are either tied to "overlap" or "separate". Almost all input interfaces can be classified into two groups: "based on the world and overlap" or "based on the user and separate".

Based on the world and overlap

This group contains a glove-like device and a touch panel. The user's motion is always evaluated according to the frame of reference fixed on the virtual world with them. The effector appears in the same domain where motions are input. For example, when the glove-like device user wants to move an object in the north direction, the user has to stretch his/her hand to the object and grasp it. Then, s/he has to move the hand in the north direction. Such a style is called direct manipulation and offers intuitive operation. Even a novice user can manipulate objects well without much practice. Conversely, the user's motion and the effector's motion must be directly engaged, so the operation strongly depends on the user's position in the virtual world. For instance, the user can't manipulate an object that is located out of his/her reach. When s/he wants to do so, s/he has to move beside the object.

Based on the user and separate

This group contains mechanical mouse, joystick and so on. The user's motion is evaluated according to the frame of reference based on the user with them. The domain where the motion is input is separate from the domain where the effector moves. An icon representing the user in the virtual world is an essential part of this category. As the input motion is mapped to the icon's motion with some transferring functions, it is difficult for a novice user to use this well. The transfer function, however, doesn't depend on the spacial relation between the user and the world. Usually, such devices can manipulate almost all objects in the virtual world within only a compact domain. Optical mouse, track ball, tablet and SpaceBall™ are very close to this category, but their frames of reference for evaluating input motion is semi-fixed in the world. These devices are located in the middle of the horizontal dimension.

The PDDM in this taxonomy

Since the user can fundamentally focus on and manipulate objects without an icon in the display, the PDDM is located vertically in "overlap". On the other hand, the user can directly handle an object in his/her frame of reference at the handling phase. This means that the PDDM is located in "based on the user". Therefore, the PDDM is located as a device "based on the user and overlap", and it is expected that the user can manipulate a remote object as if s/he is holding it in the frame based on him/her.

THE TRIAL MODEL

Configuration of the trial PDDM

The goal is to obtain an intuitive interface for manipulation in the VSTC. The PDDM is proposed as one solution. Evaluating this concept, we built a trial PDDM with an Ultra Sonic Motor (USM) force display [13]. (Figure 4)

The palmtop display of the PDDM is a 4-inch LCD (resolution 220x480 dots, weight 350 gf) and has two push-button on the back. The user holds both sides of the display and presses the buttons with the left fingertips. Here, only one push-button is used to shift between the observing and the handling phase. A magnetic position sensor is installed on the side of the display. This sensor provides the orientation and position of the palmtop display.

The display is connected to a 6 DOF USM force display that we have developed. 3 of these are actuated with USM and generate a force in any direction at the display. The others are an unactuated 3-axis universal joint at the end of the arm. Thus, the system can't restrict rotating torque. Each arm's length is 30 cm, and the workable volume is a half sphere with a radius of 60 cm. In this configuration, the force display can generate a maximum 5 N reacting and sustaining force in the volume.

A USM works with frictional force, which completely differs from an electric magnetic motor (EMM). It can generate a high sustaining and rotating torque in one component and the output can be controlled from a full sustaining torque to a full rotating torque continuously with our proposed method [13]. The rotating torque per unit weight of our USM is almost twofold that of a typical EMM. In addition, a USM can output maximum torque at lower speed (1.3 Nm at 60 rpm in ours), so it does not need reduction gears, which reduce back driveability. Furthermore, since a USM makes no magnetic noise at all, it does not affect the results from the magnetic position sensor introduced in many VR systems.

An electrical touch sensor is installed on the back of the palmtop display. When the user holding the display, all joints can be freely rotated. When the user releases it, the system detects it and immediately locks all joints. It is an important feature that the PDDM keeps the same position as that where the user released it. The system does not support this now, but the weight and the inertia of both the display and the mechanical linkage can be reduced to a level sufficiently small with dynamic impedance control. It is expected that fatigue in the user's arm through extended use can also be reduced.

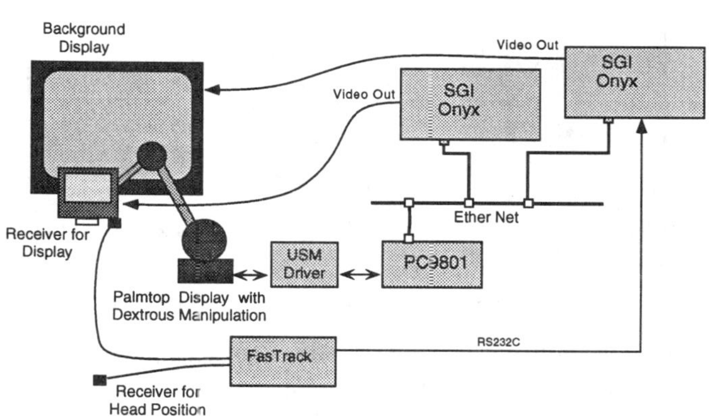

Figure 5 Configuration of the trial system

Figure 4 shows the configuration with the VSTC. Both the PDDM and the large screen display the same virtual world. Figure 5 is a diagram of the system. The SGI™ workstations contain a master server process, a drawing process and communication processes. A PC is used to control the force display and communicate with the server process through the ethernet. The drawing process can update an image in real time.

MANIPULATING METHOD

As the PDDM's operation in the observing phase is very similar to the use of a video camera with an LCD, even a novice user can use it well. On the other hand, the usage of the PDDM in the handling phase is highly unique. As shown in figure 6, the motion input on the display is reflected on the grabbed objects and the virtual camera in many way. The camera takes the image of the virtual space for the palmtop display. Four combinations can be offered for the handling phase: the view on the display is fixed on the background, fixed on the object, or two halfway between them. The features and acronyms of each method are described below and in figure 6-b,c,d,e . Table summarizes them.

Fixed View in Background (FVB)

In the FVB mode, the motion of the PDDM is directly reflected on the grabbed object as if the user is grasping it. The virtual camera is fixed when s/he grasps it. This means that the background image is fixed on the display. When the user releases the object, the direction of the PDDM contradicts the gazing vector of the virtual camera, and the user loses it from his/her view.

Semi Fixed View in an Object (SFVO)

In the SFVO mode, the motion of the PDDM is directly reflected on the grabbed object as with the FVB. When the object is grasped, not the rotated motion, but only the translated motion of the PDDM is reflected on the virtual camera. Then the grabbed object is fixed in the center of the display and its appearance is changed as the PDDM is rotated. When the object is released, the user loses it from his/her view.

Camera Centered Magic Hand (CCMH)

A magic hand is a toy for children and looks like an extended manipulator with only a link. In the CCMH mode, a metaphor of the magic hand is introduced. When a user grasps an object, a geometrical relation between the PDDM and the object is fixed as if it is being held with the magic hand attached behind the PDDM. When the PDDM is rotated, the object is rotated in the center of the PDDM. As the gazing vector of the virtual camera always follows the motion of the PDDM, the object is fixed in the center of the display and never changes its appearance. Additionally, the user never loses the object from his/her view.

Object Centered Magic Hand (OCMH)

The OCMH mode is similar to the CCMH mode, but the virtual camera is rotated in the center of the grasped object as the PDDM is rotated. Here, the motion of the PDDM is reflected on the motion of the object in the same way as the first two. Then the object is fixed in the center of the display and never changes its appearance. When a user releases the object, s/he loses it from view for a while.

When the same operation is applied to an object with these methods, the results of its motion are the same in the FVO, SFVO and OCMH methods. In the following section, an experiment to compare these methods is presented.

Experiment

The main purpose of the experiment was to clarify how these methods affect the performance and to find a standard method for future models.

The subjects were requested to put a cube in the marker on the left side corner as correctly and fast as possible. The distance between the target and the initial position of the cubes was 50 cm, but they appeared in different orientation.

Every subject tried each method 16 times in a training phase, at first. In the test phase, they tried each method 8 times. In each trial, the position and the orientation of the cube and how many times they grasped and released the cubes were recorded in every 3 sec. and in the end of trial. The completion of each trial was reported by each subject.

The subjects for this experiment were six volunteers from our staff. They are all computer engineers. The number of total trials was 6 (subjects) x 4 (methods) x 8 (trials) = 192 times. They were asked to fill in an interview sheet about the usability after all trials.

Results and Discussion

To limit the range of the force display, a large operation consisted of repetitive smaller operations in the same way as operation with a mouse. In this case, the number of grasps and releases means the number of these unit operations. The task completion time divided by this number means the passing time per unit operation. Using an analysis of the variance of test phase data, it was found that all subjects could do the unit operation within almost the same time for every method. Therefore, it was expected that they became sufficiently skillful in all methods within the test phase.

Figure 7 presents the four manipulating methods versus mean task completion time in the test phase. Some subjects spent

Method	The motion of an object	The motion of the camera	contradiction of the view
FVB	reflected directly	Fixed	contradict
SFVO	reflected directly	translation	contradict
CCMH	Magic Hand	centered on the camera	consistent
OCMH	reflected directly (Magic Hand)	centered on the object	contradict

Table 1 Four proposed methods in the handling phase

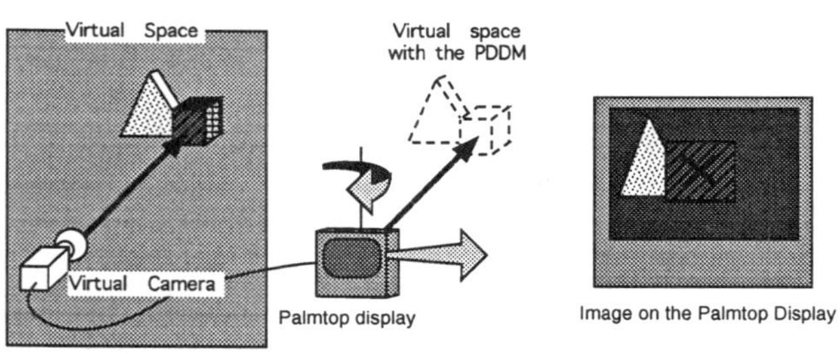

(a) Initial situation

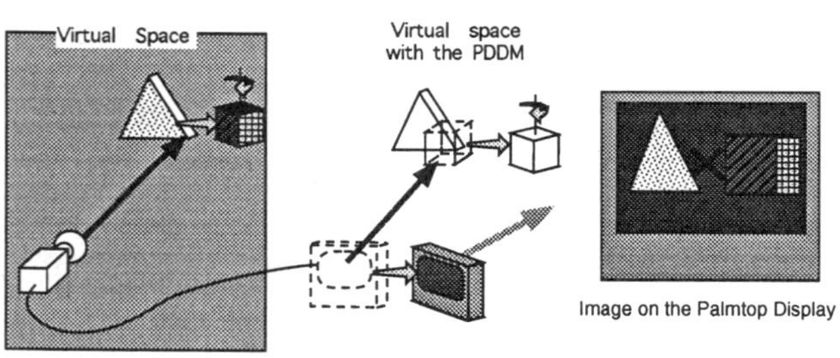

(b) Fixed View in Background: FVB

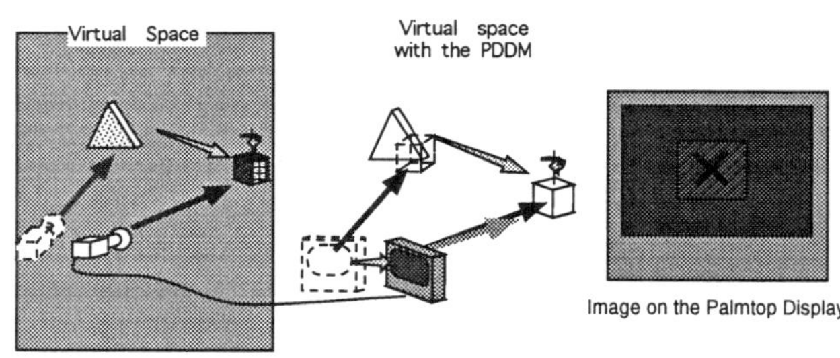

(d) Camera Centered Magic Hand: CCMH

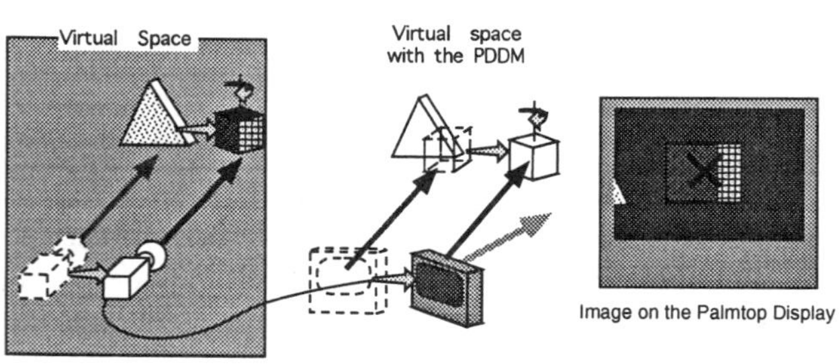

(c) Semi-Fixed View in the Object: SFVO

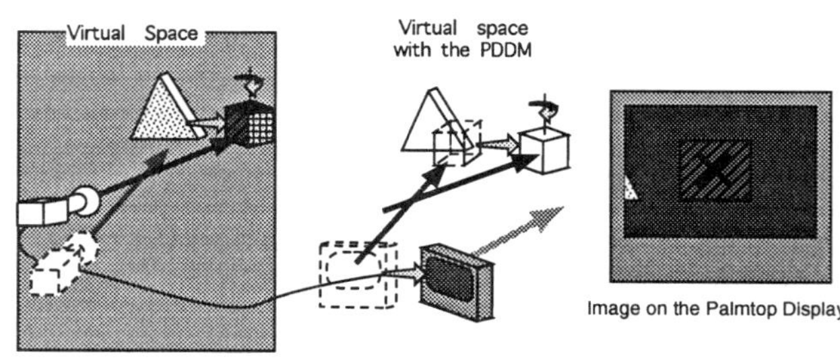

(e) Object Centered Magic Hand: OCMH

Figure 6 Four methods of manipulation : (a) shows an initial layout of the virtual world and an image on the palmtop display. (b)-(e) show results of the virtual world after same operations are applied and image on the palmtop display. In this case, a cube is manipulated and a palmtop display is shifted to right and rotated clockwise. Each image is taken by the virtual camera that is moved as a motion of the palmtop display.

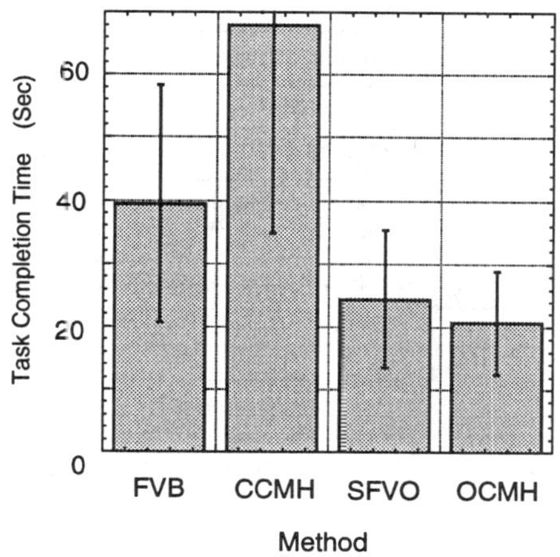

Figure 7 Mean completion time of four methods

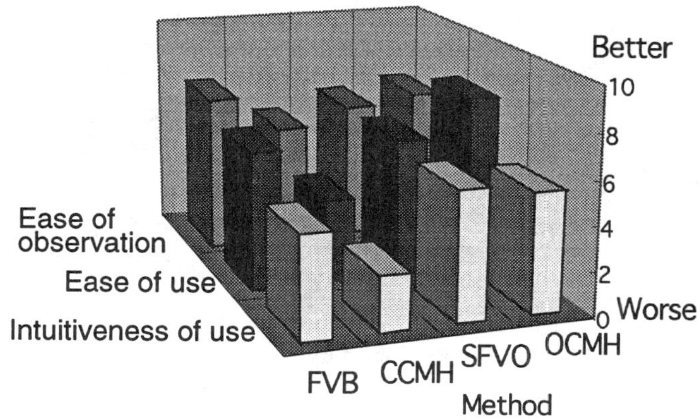

Figure 8 Subjective rating of the each method

too much time to place the cubes accurately. So each trial was terminated when the positional error between the cube and target was reduced to the level the accuracy defined from the results from each subject. The error bar shows the standard error of the results. This shows that all subjects needed much time in the CCMH method. On the other hand, the OCMH and the SFVO require shorter time than the others, and there is no significant difference between them (P(t>1.31)=0.19).

The subjective ratings from the interview sheets are shown in Figure 8. In the interview sheet, each subject was asked to decide scores from 0 to 10 for three questions: "ease of observing the result"," ease of use to manipulate" and "intuitiveness of use."

The CCMH method introduced the metaphor of the magic hand and is equal to a manipulator with a monitoring camera at the end effector. As it is difficult to realize other methods in the real world, we assumed that the CCMH method could provide the most intuitive interface. However, the CCMH's score in the interview was worst also. It is supposed that this is because input motion to the display is magnified and then reflected on the object. This means that the user can move an object from one point to another easier then with the others, but it is difficult to control the orientation of the object with the CCMH method. In this task, the subjects were asked to arrange both the position and orientation of the cubes, so it is guessed the CCMH method is not suit to such type task.

As for the other methods, the OCMH and SFVO methods got slightly better scores than the other methods. Especially in the OCMH method, some subjects reported that they felt as if they manipulated not the object but the background and they gave the OCMH method a full score for the question of "ease of use." This means that they used the PDDM according to the frame of reference based on the world in the observing phase, but that they could handle not the object but the world in the frame based on the user in the handling phase. This suggests that they were not aware of the shift in the frame of reference during in the repetitive operation. Since the methods are designed to afford the same result when the user applies the same operation, we believed that a difference in the motion of the virtual camera might cause such a result. In future research concerning the PDDM, we should clarify the relation among the frame of the world, the PDDM, the virtual camera, and the user operating with the PDDM.

HAPTIC REPRESENTATION WITH THE PDDM

In this section, the implementation of haptic feedback with the PDDM and an evaluation are described. As the gratest advantage of the PDDM, it provides reaction force in a VR space. A primitive operation for manipulating objects is to catch and place it next to another one, so we used a virtual flat wall at the beginning. As a most object consists of many pieces of small planes (polygons), this method can also be extended to such more complex objects.

Simulation of dynamics of the virtual wall

Figure 9 shows a diagram of a collision between a wall and a handled object. P(t) represents the position of the nearest vertex of the object to the wall and 't' is the cycle of the simulation. When a part of the object collides with the wall, the system generates a reaction force using a simulation of a virtual spring and a virtual damper. In the trial PDDM, the depth, 'Depth(t)', and the velocity, 'Vwall(t)', of the nearest vertex are used to determine the feedback mode.

Figure 10 shows a block diagram of the haptic simulation. The force display can generate passive force and active force for the user, and the passive force is larger than the active force. The system switches these modes according to the situation.

In the case of the first impact, as the normal velocity is sufficiently higher than the threshold (LIMIT_V), the impact of the collision is reduced by passive feedback, with the USMs acting as a brake. In another case, i.e., rubbing the surface of the wall, as the normal velocity is smaller than the threshold, the spring has lager effect than the damper in the dynamic simulation, and the active force mode operates. Controlling the coefficients of the spring and the damper, ks and Kd, the property of the wall can be changed from soft to semi-hard.

Experiment

Evaluating the proposed method for haptic representations with the PDDM, a "catch and placing" task was conducted.

The top view of the experimental setup is illustrated in Figure 11. The setup indicates a cube that the subject manipulates, a floor board and a wall. Each subject was asked to catch the cube and place it against the wall. The manipulating method of the PDDM is the OCMH. When the subject places the grabbed cube onto the wall, s/he gets the reaction force in the

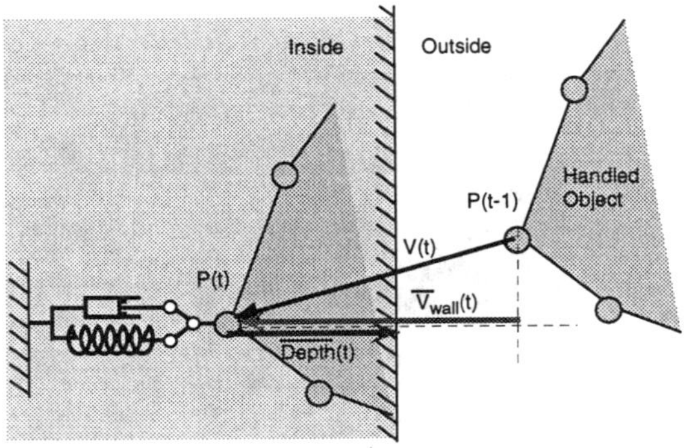

Figure 9 Simulation of dynamic of a wall

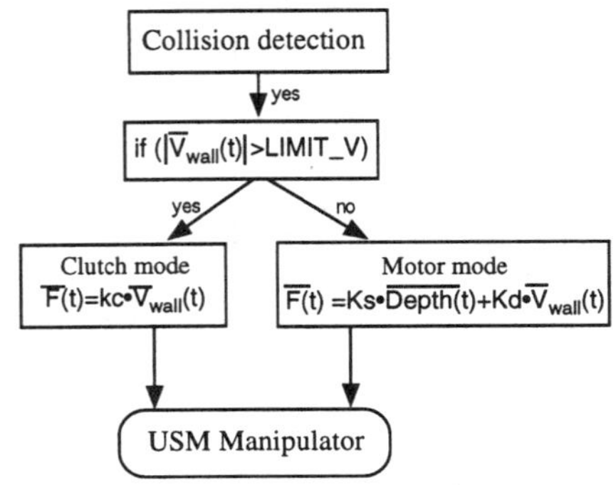

Figure 10 Block diagram of the simulation of a virtual wall

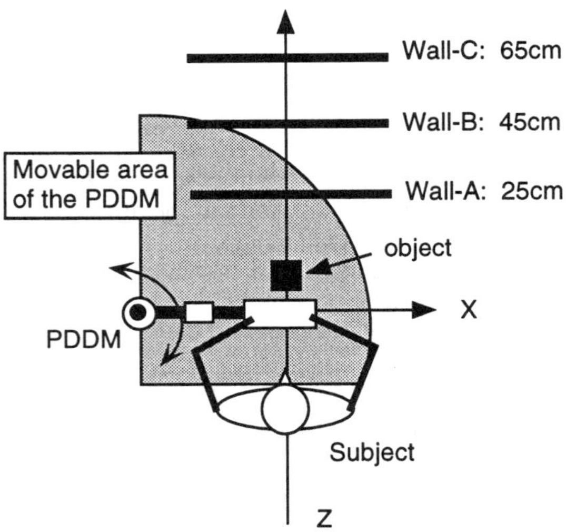

Figure 11 Experimental setup: Catch and place

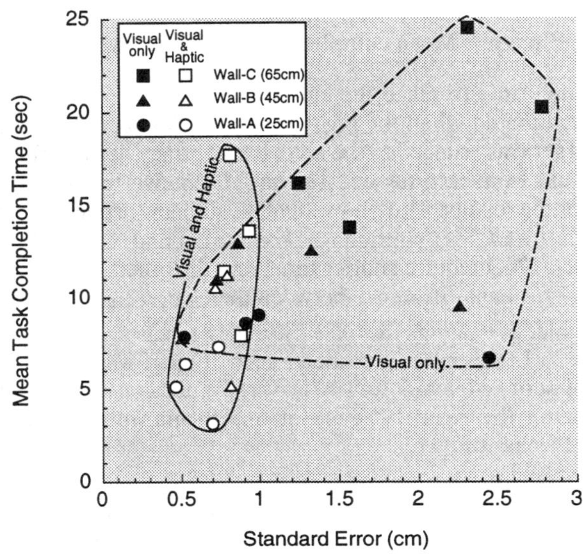

Figure 12 Results of the task

method stated above.

The initial position of each cube was constant (z=10cm,) and the position of the wall was selected randomly from three conditions:(Z=25, 45 and 65 cm.) The subjects sat down 50 cm away from the initial position of the cube. It is difficult for the traditional glove-like device user to manipulate the cube around to the farthest wall without changing the standing point in some way.

Each subject was asked to catch the cube and place it as fast and accurately as s/he could. To evaluate the effect of the haptic feedback, we held the two mode: "with visual feedback" and "with haptic and visual feedback". The subjects were four volunteers from ATR. They had all experienced the PDDM before. The total number of trials was 4 (subjects) x 3 (wall positions) x 2 (modes) x 10 (trials) = 240 times.

Results and Discussion

All subjects could put the cubes next to the wall. Here figure 12 shows the standard error of the cubes' position versus the mean task completion time for each condition (10 trials.)

The markers' character means the three positions of the wall and the feedback modes. Closed curves point up the modes. Generally, it is expected that both the standard error and the mean task completion time will correspond to the distance between the subject and the wall. However, from the curves' shape, it is found that the standard error with haptic and visual feedback is independent of the distance, and even in the farthest wall it is as small as in the nearest . Besides this, the mean task completion times with haptic feedback are shorter than those with visual feedback. It is supposed that the excessive time in the visual feedback mode was spent on final adjustments.

Additionally, it is worth noting that the darkened area in figure 11 shows the movable area of the PDDM, and walls B and C were located outside of this area. When the subject moved the PDDM near the edge of the movable area, they released the cube temporarily, then moved the PDDM to the center of the movable area and repeated the motion. This motion is the same as the repetitive motion mode with a mouse on a pad that is smaller than the display. This indicates that the subject can manipulate an object that is out of the movable area as well as an object that is in his/her hands. This is because the motion of the cube depends on the motion of the palmtop display.

As a suitable application for these PDDM's advantages, a large-scale simulation, such as an urban planning simulator, can be proposed. Using the PDDM, a reaction force against

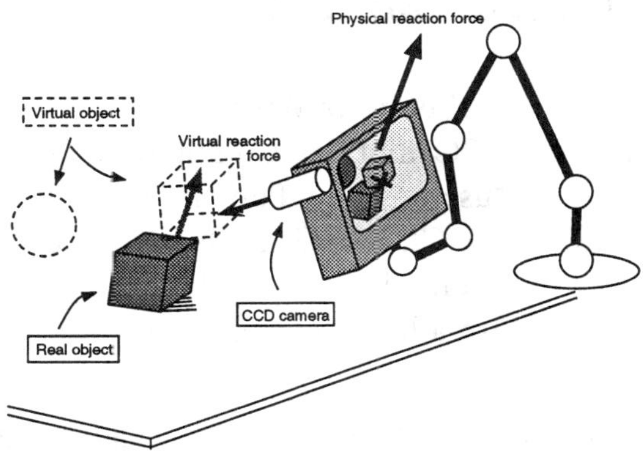

Figure 13 The PDDM system in an augmented reality

ground would assist an operator to arrange buildings straightly. The operator could manipulate the targets without having to move near them.

FUTURE WORKS

We employed 6 DOF force display, but 3 of these were unactuated, as stated above. We can construct a fully actuated 6 DOF force display using three of our arms. However, such a mechanism would become complicated and the movable area would be limited. As another solution, we are planning to employ a dynamic constraint method [5] to aid the lack of DOF.

As one future work for the PDDM, we have designed ,but have not yet achieved, a PDDM system in an augmented reality [10]. As shown in figure 13, a small CCD camera is mounted on the PDDM. The image on the PDDM is a superimposed one of a real scene captured with the camera. S/he can observe virtual and real objects on the PDDM. When the user manipulates a virtual object with the PDDM and it collides with another real/virtual object, the user will be able to feel the reaction force with the PDDM.

The system premeasures the shape of real objects. By measuring their position in any ways, i.e., a visual sensor or magnetic position sensor, the simulation process can treat real or virtual objects using the same method as we have now. The z-buffer method can be applied to effectively make such a superimposed image [14]. We expect the such a system could be applied to the engineering CAD.

CONCLUSION

We believe that the concept of the PDDM is new and unique and it offers possible applications in a wide variety of fields. In this paper, we proposed a PDDM for manipulating objects in the VSTC. First, we presented a conceptual design and then clarified its features in comparison with other devices. Offering the advantages of both a palmtop display and a direct manipulating device, the PDDM allows a user to handle a remote object as if it is within his/her own hands. Using a trial model, we conducted two experiments. In the first, we confined ourselves to four operational methods with the PDDM, and found that each of them had advantages and that the relation of the frame of the reference should be further clarified in the PDDM in future. In the second, we evaluated the combination of haptic and visual feedback. The results showed that the PDDM with haptic feedback offer grate positing accuracy in a catch and place task.

Acknowledgments

The authors wish to thank Dr. N. Terashima, President of ATR CSRL, and Dr. K. Habara, Executive Vice President of ATR International (Chairman of the Board of ATR CSRL), for their thoughtful advice and encouragement in this research. Authors also wish to thank Mr. Akaba, who took part in implementing the system.

Reference

1. Amselem, D., "A Window on Shared Virtual Environments", *Presence*, Vol. 4, No. 2. : pp.130-145. 1995
2. Arthur, K. W., Booth, K. S., and Ware, C., "Evaluating 3D Task Performance for Fish Tank Virtual Worlds", *ACM Transaction on Information System*, Vol. 11, No. 3 : pp.239-265. 1993
3. Brooks, F. P., Ough-Young, M., and J. Batter, J., "Project GROPE-Haptic Display for Scientific Visualization", *ACM Computer Graphics*, Vol. 24, No. 4 : pp.177-185. 1990
4. Fitzmaurice, G. W., Zhai, S., and Chignell, M.H., "Virtual Reality Palmtop Computers", *ACM Transactions on Information Systems,* Vol. 11, No. 3 : pp.197-218, 1993
5. Kitamura, Y., Miyasato, T., and Kishino, F. "A Sophisticated Manipulation Aid in a Virtual Environment Based on the Dynamic Constraints among Object Faces", *proc. of IEEE International Conference on Systems*, Man and Cybernetics. Vancouver, Canada: 1995.
6. Kuzuoka, H., Kosuge, T., and Tanaka, M. "GestureCam: A Video Communication System for Sympathetic Remote Collaboration" , *proc. of CSCW'94.* : pp.35-43. 1994.
7. Noma, H., et al., "Multi-Point Virtual Space Teleconferencing System", *IEICE Trans. on Com.*, Vol. E78-B, No.7 : pp.970-979. 1995.
8. Noma, H. and Iwata, H. "Presentation of multiple dimensional data by 6DOF force display", *proc. of IEEE/RSJ Intelligent Robots and Systems*, Yokohama, Japan: pp.1495-1500. 1993.
9. McKenna, M. "Interactive Viewpoint Control and Three Dimensional Operation" , *proc. of ACM Symposium on Interactive 3D Graphics*. pp.53-56. 1992.
10. Milgram, P. and Kishino, F., "A Taxonomy of Mixed Reality Visual Displays", *IEICE Trans. INF. & SYST.*, Vol. E77-D, No.12 : pp.1321-1329. 1994
11. Rekimoto, J. "Augmented Interaction: Interacting with the real world through a computer", *proc. of HCI'95.*, Yokohama, Japan : pp.225-264. 1995.
12. Shimojo, S. and Nakayama, K."Real World Occlusion Constraints and Binocular Rivalry", Vision Res. , Vol. 30, No. 1, pp.69-80. 1990
13. Takemura, H., and Kishino, F. "Cooperative Work Environment Using Visual Workspace", *proc. of CSCW '92* : pp.226-232. 1992.
14. Wloka, M. M. and Anderson, B.G. "Resolving Occlusion in Augmented Reality", *proc. of ACM 1995 Symposium on Interactive 3D Graphics.*, Monterey CA USA: pp.5-12. 1995.

BrightBoard: A Video-Augmented Environment

Quentin Stafford-Fraser †*
† Rank Xerox Research Centre (EuroPARC)
Ravenscroft House, 61 Regent Street
Cambridge CB2 1AB, United Kingdom
Tel: +44 1223 341521
E-mail: fraser@europarc.xerox.com

Peter Robinson *
* University of Cambridge Computer Laboratory
New Museums Site, Pembroke Street
Cambridge CB2 3QG, United Kingdom
Tel: +44 1223 334637
E-mail: pr@cl.cam.ac.uk

ABSTRACT

The goal of 'Computer Augmented Environments' is to bring computational power to everyday objects with which users are already familiar, so that the user interface to this computational power becomes almost invisible. Video is a very important tool in creating Augmented Environments and recent camera-manufacturing techniques make it an economically viable proposition in the general marketplace. BrightBoard is an example system which uses a video camera and audio feedback to enhance the facilities of an ordinary whiteboard, allowing a user to control a computer through simple marks made on the board. We describe its operation in some detail, and discuss how it tackles some of the problems common to these 'Video-Augmented Environments'.

KEYWORDS

Augmented reality, image processing, machine vision, pattern recognition, ubiquitous computing

INTRODUCTION

Video cameras can now be produced, with controlling circuitry, on a single chip. Digital output reduces the need for expensive frame-capture cards, and it is reasonable to assume that simple cameras, being devoid of moving parts, will soon be a cheaper accessory for personal computers than keyboards, microphones, and mice. The possibilities for video-conferencing and other human-human interactions are obvious, but how might the ready availability of video sources enrich the way we interact with the machines themselves?

Augmented Environments

In the office environment the computer has traditionally been thought of as a tool, in the same way that a typewriter or Rolodex is a tool. It is something employed by a user to accomplish a particular task. It is a very flexible tool, and can fulfil the roles of typewriter, Rolodex and calculator simultaneously, but the activity is generally initiated by a 'user', a term which succinctly describes the relationship.

CHI 96 Vancouver, BC Canada

We might hope that the computer of the future would be more like an assistant than like a typewriter, that it would perform mundane tasks *on your behalf* when it sees they are necessary rather than always operating directly *under your control*. The more a secretary knows about your way of life, your preferred modes of work, how cluttered your desk is and when you are in a meeting, the more useful he or she can be to you. The same applies to a computer, but the average PC has no knowledge of the world outside its box and has to be spoon-fed with information through its limited range of input devices.

This is part of the philosophy behind *Computer-Augmented Environments*; the desire to bring the computer 'out of its box' and give it more awareness of the world around, so that it *augments* and *enhances* daily life rather than attempting to replace it. Can we, for example, make the computer understand what we do in our offices rather than putting an impoverished 'office metaphor' on the machine's screen? Can we centre computational power around everyday objects with which users are already so familiar that they don't think of them as a human-computer interface? During work on the DigitalDesk [10,16], for example, we experimented with ways of enabling the computer to recognise an ordinary pencil eraser, and using that as the means of deleting parts of an electronic image projected onto the desk. The motivation was simple: people already know how to use erasers, and will continue to use them for hand-drawn pictures. By augmenting the eraser's capabilities we simply expand its scope of use. We neither detract from its abilities to erase pencil, nor require the user to learn a new tool.

ACHIEVING AUGMENTED ENVIRONMENTS

There is an inherent difficulty in the goals of Computer-Augmented Environments (CAEs). For computers to have much understanding of the world around, they must be equipped with sensors to monitor it. These may be directly connected to the computer, or they may relay information to it via some communication medium. The more sensors, the more complete will be the picture a computer can create of its surroundings and the activities of its users. However, the more sensors we embed in the environment, along with the associated cables, batteries and power supplies, the more investment is needed to bring about our goal and the more intrusive the technology becomes, so frustrating the aim of an 'invisible' user interface.

The solution is to give the computer a small number of senses which have a broad scope of application and which operate remotely, i.e. without direct contact with the objects being sensed. The obvious candidates are vision and hearing, through the use of video cameras and microphones. Similarly, if the computer is to communicate with humans, then the analogous output systems are audio feedback and perhaps some projection facilities. Not only do cameras and microphones have a broad range of application, they can often be applied to more than one task at the same time. A single camera might monitor a whole room, and detect when the room is occupied, when a meeting is in progress, and when an overhead projector is being used, as well as recording the meeting.

This paper describes the use of video in the creation of a Computer-Augmented Environment called *BrightBoard*, which uses a video camera and audio feedback to augment the facilities of an ordinary whiteboard. Until fairly recently the deployment of such systems in the average workplace would be limited by the cost both of cameras and of the computing power required to process video signals. However, manufacturing developments are making video cameras an economically viable alternative to more conventional sensors, and the typical office workstation is now fast enough for the simple image processing required for many of these 'Video-Augmented Environments' (VAEs).

BRIGHTBOARD: THE WHITEBOARD AS A USER INTERFACE

From prehistoric cave paintings to modern graffiti, mankind has conveyed information by writing on walls. They provide a working surface at a convenient angle for humans to use, with space for expansive self-expression, and they form a natural focus for a presentation or group discussion. The blackboard, the more recent whiteboard, and to some degree the overhead projector, are an extension of this basic theme, with the added facility of being able to erase easily any information which is no longer needed. Whiteboards have become very popular tools in environments ranging from the kindergarten to the company boardroom.

BrightBoard aims to capitalise on this natural means of expression by making use of the whiteboard as a user interface. It is not the first system to explore the whiteboard's potential. Projects such as Tivoli [11] have tried to capitalise on this natural means of expression, and have created note-taking, shared drawing and even remote conferencing systems by emulating and enhancing a whiteboard using a computer. There have been many variations on the whiteboard theme as well. VideoWhiteboard [15] used a translucent drawing screen on which the silhouette of the other party could be seen. Clearboard [8] was a similar system which used the metaphor of a glass whiteboard where the parties in a two-way video conference were on opposite sides of the glass, allowing both face-to-face discussion and shared use of a drawing space. Typically, these systems use a large-screen display and electronic pens whose position in the plane of the screen can be sensed and which may have pressure-sensitive tips to control the flow of 'ink', thus giving a more realistic feel to the whiteboard metaphor. The Xerox Liveboard [4] is an example of a complete, self-contained, commercially available unit built on this basis; it has a workstation, Tivoli software, display and pens in one ready-to-install package. The software allows several users (potentially at different locations) to draw on a shared multi-page whiteboard where each page may be larger than the screen and scrollable. The software is controlled by a combination of gestures, buttons and pop-up menus. A more recent commercial offering is *SoftBoard*. This is a special whiteboard which uses pens and erasers similar to conventional which have a reflective sleeve allowing their position to be detected by an infra-red laser scanning device fitted to the board. The movements of the pens and erasers are relayed by the board to a computer, which can then construct an electronic version of the image on the board.

Figure 1: BrightBoard in use

Such systems, while useful, have their failings. Their price is typically quoted in thousands of dollars, they are often delivered by a forklift truck, and are generally installed in board-rooms whose primary users have neither the time nor the inclination to master the software. They also fail to achieve the ease of use of a conventional whiteboard, even for those experienced with them. To quote one user, "The computer never quite gets out of the way".

Examples of whiteboard use observed by the author, which tend not to translate well into the electronic domain, include the following:

- A 'y' was written on the board, but looked rather like a 'g'. The writer used a finger to erase part of the letter before continuing; a process which barely interrupted the flow of the writing.
- During the design of a user interface, screen components such as buttons and scrollbars were drawn on Post-It notes or on pieces of paper affixed to the board with magnets. They could then be added, removed or repositioned easily within the sketches on the board.
- The whiteboard eraser had been temporarily mislaid, and a paper towel was used instead.

A computer-based "whiteboard metaphor" always breaks down somewhere because the computer's view of the board differs from the user's.

WHAT IS BRIGHTBOARD?

BrightBoard *is* a whiteboard. Anyone who can use an ordinary whiteboard can use it. In addition, it provides some of the functionality of electronic documents - the images on the board can be saved, printed, faxed and emailed simply by walking up to the board and making particular marks. (See examples in Figure 2, and the Video Figure in the CHI 96 Video Program).

BrightBoard can also operate as a more general input device for any computer-controlled system. An example of its use might be as follows:

> Eric is leading a meeting in a room equipped with a BrightBoard camera. He arrives early to discover that the room is a little chilly, so he writes the temperature he requires on the whiteboard, [T21], and the air-conditioning reacts appropriately. When the participants arrive, he makes a mark on the board to start the video-recording of the meeting, [V], and then uses the board as normal. During the meeting the participants request a copy of a diagram on the board, so Eric marks that area of the board and prints off six copies [P6]. As the meeting draws to a close, Eric scribbles a quick note requesting coffee for six, marks out the area as before, and mails it to his secretary [M]. Finally, he switches off the video-recorder and the air-conditioning by erasing his original marks.

All this control has been achieved without Eric leaving the focal point of the meeting – the whiteboard – and without direct interaction with any machines or controls. It is easy to configure:

- the marks that BrightBoard will recognise, by capturing and labelling samples. ("This mark is an 'S'.").
- the relationships between different marks required to constitute a command. ("A *save* command is an 'S' inside a box.").
- the action to be taken when a particular command is specified. ("When you see a *save* command, execute this shell script.")

Corner marks can be used to delimit an area of the board, and commands can then be made to act only on this area. Inexperienced users may find it useful to have a summary of the available commands posted beside the whiteboard.

BrightBoard uses a video camera pointed at a standard whiteboard (Figure 1), thus eliminating the need for expensive installations and electronic pens. It uses audio or other feedback, and so has no need of a large display. The program, once configured, puts minimal load on the workstation, and requires no manual intervention. The computer can therefore be shut away in a cupboard, or put in a separate room – particularly useful for meeting rooms where the hum of fans and the flicker of screens can be a distraction.

HOW DOES BRIGHTBOARD WORK?

BrightBoard consists of several programs, but the main one has a structure common to many VAE applications. It centres around a loop containing the following steps:

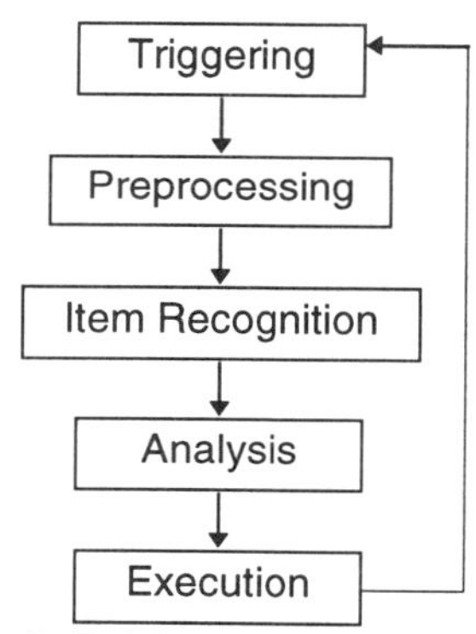

Figure 3: BrightBoard's main loop

1. Triggering – Wait until a suitable image can be captured, and then do so.
2. Preprocessing of the image. (Thresholding, in the case of BrightBoard)
3. Item Recognition. (Finding & Recognising marks)
4. Analysis of the items found looking for particular situations.

A 'Print' command *Selecting an area of the board* *A 'Fax to Peter' command*

Figure 2: Some sample BrightBoard commands

5. Execution of some action(s) based on the situations found.

In practice, these stages may not be strictly sequential. The triggering might be accomplished by dedicated hardware inside the camera, for example. In BrightBoard the execution of external commands is done as a separate background process.

We shall look at each of these stages in turn.

Triggering

There are two considerations here:

- Whiteboards suffer badly from obstruction – the interesting things are generally happening when somebody is obscuring the camera's view. We must detect when people are in the image and wait until they have moved out of the way. Humans have a very useful characteristic in that they tend to keep moving, and in many VAEs this can be sufficient to separate them from an inanimate background.
- One of the aims of BrightBoard is that it should be practical to have it running all the time. To start it up whenever a user wished to write on the board would largely defeat the object of the exercise, but, on the other hand, it would not be acceptable for an infrequently used facility to consume too many resources on the user's workstation.

Both problems can be solved by the use of a 'triggering' module. BrightBoard normally operates in a semi-dormant 'standby' mode. Every half-second or so, the triggering module captures a low-resolution image and examines a 40x30 grid of pixels, comparing each with the equivalent pixel in the previous image. It calculates the percentage P of these pixels which have changed by more than a certain threshold. This puts very little load on a typical workstation. The threshold for each pixel is based on the statistics of the noise seen at that pixel position in ten calibration frames captured at startup time. This allows the system to compensate for regions of the image which are inherently noisier due to lower light levels, reflections of flickering screens, etc. In addition, these thresholds are adjusted slowly over time, to cope with changes in lighting during the day.

The triggering module can wait either for movement, or for stability. By concatenating these two modes we say, in effect: "Ignore an unchanging whiteboard. Wait until you see movement in front of it, and when this movement has finished, then proceed with your analysis". A full-resolution image can then be captured, to be used in the following stages.

Thresholding

If we are to analyse the writing on the board, we must now distinguish it from the background of the board itself. A simple global threshold will not suffice, for two reasons:

a) The high proportion of white to black pixels means that analysis of the histogram does not generally reveal clear maxima and minima - the 'black peak' tends to get lost amid the noise of the 'white'.[1]

b) the level of illumination on the board often varies dramatically from one side to the other.

There are many sophisticated methods available which attempt to solve the former by examining only pixels near the black/white boundaries, thus giving a better balance of black and white pixels [5], and the latter by dividing the board into tiles, finding local thresholds suitable for the centre of each tile, and then extrapolating suitable values for points between these centres [3].

Unfortunately, these methods are rather too slow for an interactive system, so we use an adaptive thresholding algorithm developed by Wellner for the DigitalDesk [16]. This involves scanning the rows of pixels one at a time, alternating the direction of travel, and maintaining a running average of the pixel values. Any pixel significantly darker than the running average at that point is treated as black, while the others are taken to be white. This simple algorithm works remarkably well in cases where the image is known to have small areas of dark on a light background, such as we find in the typical printed page and on a whiteboard, and it only involves a single examination of each pixel.

Item recognition

There are two distinct operations here; first we find the marks on the image of the board, then we attempt to recognise them.

Finding

Each black 'blob' in the thresholded image is found and analysed. We are not interested in blobs consisting of only a few pixels. With the camera zoom setting chosen to include a reasonable amount of a whiteboard, the symbols we wish to recognise will generally contain between a hundred and a thousand pixels. We need not, therefore, examine every pixel in the image, but can look at every third or fourth pixel in each direction with fair confidence that we will still strike any areas of interest. This has the added benefit of 'missing' much of the noise in the image which appears as blobs of one or two pixels.

Once a black pixel is found, a flood-fill algorithm is used to find all the black pixels directly connected to that one. As the fill proceeds, statistics about the pixels in the blob are gathered which will be used later in the recognition process; for example, the bounding box of the blob, the distribution of the pixels in each axis, the number of pixels which have white above them and the number with white to the right of them. For the sake of speed, an 'upper limit' on the number of pixels is passed to the filling routine. Beyond this limit the blob is unlikely to be anything we wish to recognise, so the flood fill continues, marking the pixels as 'seen', but the statistics are not gathered. When the fill completes, if the number

[1] For simplicity we refer to the marks as being 'black' on a 'white' background. In fact, any coloured pens may be used, though the thresholding is easier with the darker colours.

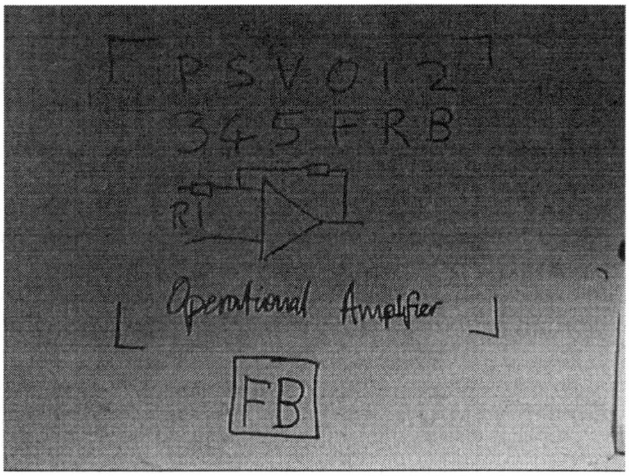

Figure 4: A sample image captured...

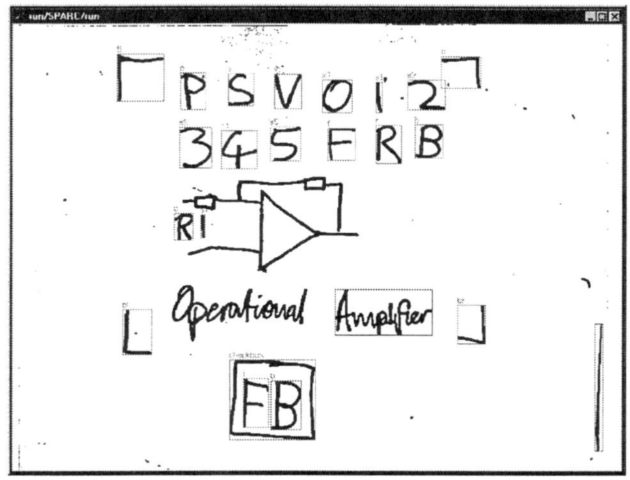

Figure 5: ...and processed by BrightBoard

of pixels is less than this upper limit but more than a specified lower limit, the blob's statistics are added to a list of items for further analysis.

Recognising

In the current system, no further processing of the image is carried out. The problem of off-line handwriting recognition is the subject of a large and active research field, and for a good overview the reader is referred to A.W.Senior [13]. Many things could be done by analysing the topology of each blob, for example, but this would involve a significant amount of pixel processing, which we have so far managed to avoid. In addition, topological analysis can cause problems with such a potentially noisy image. After the thresholding, the majority of white pixels have been ignored and each black one will have been examined maybe twice or three times. Yet, for the limited range of symbols we wish to recognise, the statistics gathered are sufficient. From these we can calculate a *feature vector* - a set of real numbers representing various characteristics of the blob, which can be thought of as coordinates positioning the blob in an n-dimensional space. At the time of writing, 12 dimensions are in use, and the values calculated are chosen to be reasonably independent of the scale of the blob or the thickness of the pen used. For example, one value is the ratio of the number of black pixels with white above them to the number of black pixels with white to the right of them. This gives a rough measure of the ratio of horizontal to vertical lines in the symbol. Another set of characteristics are based on moments about the centroid of the blob. Moments have been found to be very useful in this type of pattern recognition [2,7], and a hardware implementation is possible allowing substantial speed improvements [6].

The recognition is done by comparing the feature vector of each blob found to those of prototype copies of the symbols we wish to match. These are all calculated off-line in advance from a training set of board images. The simplest recogniser might just find the closest prototype in the n-dimensional space to the candidate blob, and identify the blob as being of the same type. This has several limitations, however:

- The scales of the dimensions are not in any way related, and a distance of 0.1 in one dimension may be far more significant than a distance of 1.0 in another. We therefore use the *Mahalanobis distance* instead of the *Euclidean distance*, which simply means that each dimension is scaled by dividing it by the standard deviation of the values found in this dimension amongst the prototypes.
- The second limitation is the absence of a rejection condition. We assume that all blobs can be recognised, which is most unlikely. Using the Mahalanobis distance, however, it makes more sense to reject blobs which are more than a certain distance from even the closest prototype. If this distance is more than $\sqrt{n}D$, where n is the number of dimensions, it means that the candidate blob is on average more than D standard deviations from the prototype in each dimension. By adjusting the value of D the selectiveness of our recogniser can be controlled.
- The third is that, in many of the dimensions, the groups formed by different symbols may overlap to a considerable degree. The capital letters *B* and *R*, for example, are similar in many ways, and it is quite possible that the statistics calculated for a candidate *R* may place it closest to a prototype *B* (see Figure 6). To help avoid this, we use a *k-nearest-neighbours* algorithm which states that X can be classified as being a symbol Y if at least a certain number of its *k* nearest prototypes are symbol Y. For BrightBoard, we classify X as being an *R* if at least 3 of its 5 nearest neighbours are *R*s. The cost of finding the *k* nearest neighbours is approximately proportional to the number of prototypes examined, if *k* is small.

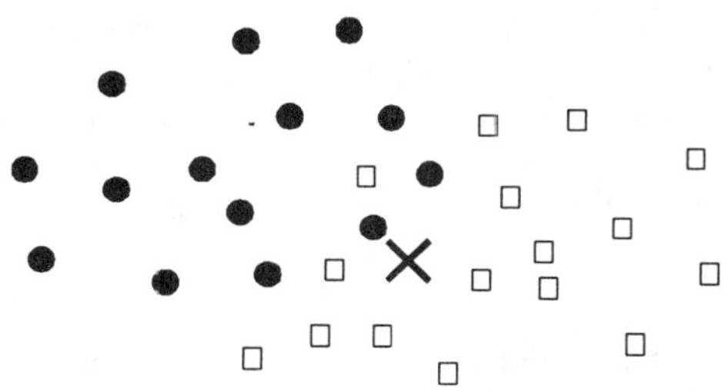

Figure 6: If circles are B prototypes and squares are R prototypes, what is X?

- Lastly, the values used for some dimensions are less reliable than others at distinguishing between symbols. We therefore have a set of dimension weightings which are adjusted by hand on a trial and error basis. All distances in a given dimension are multiplied by the appropriate weighting before being used. A number of methods for selecting weights automatically are described in [2].

Several methods are available to improve the partitioning of the *n*-space. The Karhunen-Loève transform can be used to choose alternative axes which highlight the distribution of the prototypes. Simard et al describe an alternative distance metric which is invariant to small transformations of the input image [14].

Neural Alternatives

This recognition phase is an obvious candidate for neural network-based solutions, and these are being investigated. The use of a neural net could mean improved reliability and constant recognition time, at the expense of less predictability and more time-consuming analysis of the training set. At present the training data consists of about 20 copies of each of the 17 symbols we recognise, and this is really far too small for neural net training. To combat this we are experimenting with the use of 'fake' training data, created by applying to the captured images the sort of variations that might be found in normal handwriting: small amounts of shear and rotation, and variations in scale and aspect ratio. This is less time-consuming than the capture of new training data, and early experiments show an encouraging improvement in both neural- and non-neural-based recognition rates.

The limitations of a very crude recogniser can be overcome to a substantial degree by the choice of command patterns. In practice we find that the current recogniser is capable of distinguishing well between the symbols in its known alphabet, (we measured recognition rates of 93-96%) but it has a tendency to be over-generous, and recognise as valid symbols some things which are not. The chances of these 'false' symbols occurring in such relationships as to constitute a valid command are, however, very small.

Analysing

We now have a system which waits for an opportune moment, captures an image of the board, and finds and recognises the symbols in the image. The next problem is how to describe the commands we wish to have executed in terms of these symbols. We do not wish to hard-code such descriptions into the program, so we need a grammar with which to specify the combination of symbols which constitute, say, a 'print' command.

Fortunately, there are languages available which specialise in the description and analysis of relationships: those designed for Logic Programming, of which Prolog is the most common. If the information from the recogniser is passed to a Prolog engine as a set of facts, we can then write Prolog rules to analyse the contents of the board. For each blob found, BrightBoard assigns a unique number *x* and adds a rule to a Prolog database an assertion of the form:

```
bounds( itemx, w, e, n, s )
```

which specifies that blob *x* has a bounding box delimited by the north-west corner (*w*, *n*) and the south-east corner (*e* , *s*). Simple rules can then be written to determine, for example, whether blob A is inside blob B, or to the right of it, or of a similar size, from these entries. In addition, if the blob has been recognised, a second assertion will be made, of the form:

```
issym( itemx, y )
```

which indicates that item *x* has been recognised as being symbol *y*. A 'Print' command might then be defined as follows:

```
doprint :-
    issym(X, p),
    issym(Y, checkbox),
    inside(X, Y),
    /+ (inside(Z, Y), Z \= X)
```

This can be roughly translated as "there is a print command if we can find blobs X and Y such that X is a 'P' and Y is a 'checkbox' and X is inside Y, and nothing else is inside Y [2]".

Both current and previous states can be passed to Prolog, so that the rules can also specify that printing should only occur if either X or Y or both were not present in the previous analysis. This prevents a command from being accidentally repeated.

On a SPARCstation 2, BrightBoard took 4.5 seconds to capture, threshold, display, analyse and recognise the 'Fax to Bob' command in the 740 x 570 image shown in Figure 4, from the time at which movement was no longer detected. There is much room for optimisation; speed was not a primary issue during BrightBoard's initial development.

Executing

The final stage is to take action based on the analysis. A 'command file' relates Prolog predicates such as 'doprint' to UNIX commands that will actually do the printing. Each line in this file has the form:

[2] The final part is more accurately transcribed as: 'The goal "Z is inside Y and Z is not equal to X" cannot be satisfied'

```
<predicate> <filetype> <command>
```

where <predicate> is, for example, 'doprint', <command> is any valid UNIX shell command, and <filetype> is either 'none' or the name of an image format[3]. If it is not 'none' then a temporary file of the specified format is created and its filename can be passed to the UNIX command by using '%s' in the command file. A print command might then be:

```
doprint   pgm   pgmtops %s | lpr
```

though more complicated actions would generally be implemented by a specially written script or another program. The commands currently employed also provide audio feedback to the user through the use of pre-recorded or synthesised speech. The user is informed not only when a print command has been seen, but also when the printing has been completed.

One predicate is given special treatment in the current version of BrightBoard. It is named 'inc_area' and checks for the presence of symbols which mark the bounds of the area to be included in the image file. This allows small areas of the board to be printed, saved, sent as messages etc.

The next version of BrightBoard (currently under development) uses an extended protocol for the interaction between Prolog and the UNIX commands. The number of parameters of the predicate may be specified in the command file, and, if greater than zero, the values of the variables returned by the evaluation are passed to the UNIX command as environment variables. The UNIX command is executed once for each match found in a given image, with a special variable set on the last match. This allows the function of 'inc_area' and similar predicates to be implemented by external programs, giving rise to much greater flexibility. As an example, a print command can consist of a *P* followed by a digit, where the digit represents the number of copies to be printed. The `doprint` predicate can then have a parameter in which it returns the digit found, and this information is passed to the executed command.

Until now, all use of BrightBoard has been by the author and two colleagues for a substantial number of demonstrations, but under fairly controlled lab conditions. The system has almost reached the stage where user testing is possible in a real office environment, and this is the obvious next step in its development.

FUTURE POSSIBILITIES

There are a few aspects of BrightBoard which are worth highlighting, especially in the context of possible future developments.

The first is that there is minimal configuration required to set it up. All that is needed is a camera with a fairly unobstructed and 'straight-on' view of the board, zoomed to a reasonable scale. It would be straightforward, therefore, to make a portable version of BrightBoard. A briefcase containing a laptop computer and a camera with a small tripod could be carried into any meeting room, the camera pointed at a board and the program started, and the whiteboard in the meeting room is immediately endowed with faxing, printing, and recording capabilities.

Secondly, the system is not limited to whiteboards – any white surface will suffice. Thus noticeboards, refrigerator doors, flipcharts, notebooks and papers on a desk can all be used as a simple user interface. The current version of BrightBoard has been switched from monitoring a whiteboard to providing a 'desktop photocopying' device without even stopping and restarting the program. A camera clipped to a bookshelf above the desk and plugged into a PC (which will often be on the desk anyway) enables any document on the desk to be copied, saved, faxed without the user moving from the desk or touching a machine. If the user does not wish to write on the documents themselves, then Post-it notes or cardboard cut-outs with the appropriate symbols drawn on them can be used. Parts of the paper documents can be selected using the area delimiting symbols, and pasted into electronic documents. Resolution is a slight problem here, as a typical frame-grabber capturing half a page will only provide about 100 dots-per-inch; the same resolution as a poor-quality fax. It does, however, capture a grey-scale image, and the anti-aliasing effects make the resolution appear much higher than would be the case with a purely black & white image. In situations where a binary image is definitely needed, the greyscale information can be used to enhance the resolution artificially. We have found the appearance of thresholded images to be greatly improved by inserting extra pixels between the original grey pixels and giving them values based on linear interpolation between the neighbouring originals. A double-resolution image is formed which is then passed to the thresholding module. Since this increases the time required for thresholding by a factor of four, the process is only used in the output of images, and not in BrightBoard's internal processing.

A richer interaction model would be possible by monitoring the position and gestures of a user's hands. The system, before acting on a command, for example, could request confirmation from the user which might be given with a 'thumbs-up' gesture. Conventional hand-tracking systems have generally required the user to wear special gloves and position-sensing devices [1], but systems have been built using video alone. Jakub Segen describes a system which allows the user to control a mouse-style pointer on the screen, or to 'fly' through a Virtual Reality-like environment, using hand movements and gestures watched by a camera [12]. Myron Krueger's *VideoPlace* combines projected graphics with the silhouette of the user to create an artistic medium which responds to full-body gestures [9]. Such a system would be easier to include in a portable BrightBoard, as described above, than one involving extra hardware.

[3] The formats 'pgm' (portable greymap) and 'pbm' (portable bitmap) are currently supported.

An interesting challenge would be the creation of a friendlier user interface to the Prolog rules. One of the aims of BrightBoard is that it should be accepted in a normal office environment, but the inhabitants of such an environment will not generally be Prolog programmers. A programming language allows us great flexibilty, however, which can be difficult to duplicate in other ways. Consider the following specification:

> 'A *P* in a box, possibly followed by another symbol representing a digit which is also inside the box, constitutes a print command, where the number of copies is given by the digit, or is one if no digit exists. There must be no other symbol inside the box.'

It is difficult to imagine an easy way of representing this graphically. Indeed, even the concept represented by the words 'followed by' must be explicitly defined. A textual front-end to the Prolog could possibly be created which would more closely resemble natural language, or a programming language with which users were more likely to be familiar. This is only an issue if the users are expected to customise the set of commands provided by BrightBoard.

CONCLUSIONS

The dramatic reduction in cost of video cameras and of the computing power needed to process their output opens up a wide variety of opportunities for novel human-computer interaction methods, especially by augmenting the capabilities of everyday objects and environments. This can be less intrusive than more conventional methods of interaction because of the large amount of data that can be gathered from a camera with only a small amount of wiring, and because the camera is a remote sensor and so does not in any way interfere with the user's normal use of the augmented objects.

BrightBoard is an example of this genre which illustrates some of the problems that will be issues to many video-augmented environments and shows what can be accomplished by combining relatively unsophisticated image processing and pattern recognition techniques with logic-based analysis of their results.

ACKNOWLEDGMENTS

This work has been sponsored by Rank Xerox Research Centre, Cambridge, England (better known as 'EuroPARC'). We are grateful for their support and to Dr Pierre Wellner, Mik Lamming, Mike Flynn and Dr Richard Bentley for advice and assistance.

All product names are acknowledged as the trademarks of their respective owners.

REFERENCES

1. Baudel, T. and Beaudouin-Lafon, M. "Charade: Remote Control of Objects using Free-Hand Gestures", *Comm. ACM,* Vol. 36 Number 7, July 1993, pp 28-37.
2. Cash, G.L. and Hatamian, M., "Optical Character Recognition by the Method of Moments", *Computer Vision, Graphics, and Image Processing,* Vol. 39, pp. 291-310 (1987)
3. Castleman, K., *Digital Image Processing,* Prentice-Hall Signal Processing Series, 1979. The tile-based thresholding algorithm was developed originally by R.J.Hall.
4. Elrod, S., Bruce,R., Gold, R., Goldberg, D., Halasz, F., Janssen, W., Lee, D., McCall, K., Pedersen, E., Pier, K., Tang, J., and Welch, B., "Liveboard: A Large Interactive Display Supporting Group Meetings, Presentations and Remote Collaboration", *Proceedings of CHI,* ACM, 1992, pp. 599-602.
5. Gonzalez, R.C., and Woods, R.E., *Digital Image Processing*, Addison-Wesley 1992
6. Hatamian, M., "A Real-Time Two-Dimensional Moment Generating Algorithm and Its Single Chip Implementation", *IEEE Trans. on Acoustics, Speech, and Signal Processing,* Vol ASSP-34, No. 3, June 1986, pp. 546-553
7. Hu, Ming-Kuei, "Visual Pattern Recognition by Moment Invariants", *IRE Trans. on Information Theory,* Vol. IT-8, 1962, pp. 179-187.
8. Ishii, H., Kobayashi, M., and Grudin, J., "Integration of Inter-Personal Space and Shared Workspace: ClearBoard Design and Experiments", *Proceedings of CHI,* ACM, 1992, pp. 33-42.
9. Krueger, M.W., *Artificial Reality II,* Addison Wesley, 1991
10. Newman, W. and Wellner, P., "A Desk Supporting Computer-based Interaction with Paper Documents", *Proceedings of CHI,* ACM, May 1992, pp. 587-592.
11. Pedersen, E., McCall, K., Moran, T.P. and Halasz, F.G., "Tivoli: An Electronic Whiteboard for Informal Workgroup Meetings", *Proceedings of INTERCHI,* ACM, 1993, pp. 391-398.
12. Segen, J., "Controlling Computers with Gloveless Gestures", *Proceedings of Virtual Reality Systems'93 conference*, NYC, March 15, 1993.
13. Senior, A.W, "Off-line Handwriting Recognition: A Review and Experiments". University of Cambridge Engineering Department technical report CUED/F-INFENG/TR105, December 1992. Available by FTP.
14. Simard, P.Y, Le Cun, Y., Denker, J.S, "Memory-Based Character Recognition Using a Transformation Invariant Metric" in *Proc. 12th IAPR International Conference on Pattern Recognition,* Jerusalem, 1994, Vol. II pp. 262-267.
15. Tang, J.C., and Minneman, S.L., "VideoWhiteboard: Video Shadows to Support Remote Collaboration", *Proceedings of CHI,* ACM, 1991, pp. 315-322.
16. Wellner, P., *Interacting with Paper on the DigitalDesk.* University of Cambridge Computer Laboratory Ph.D. Thesis, October 1993. Computer Lab Technical Report 330

Wayfinding Strategies and Behaviors in Large Virtual Worlds

Rudolph P. Darken
Naval Research Laboratory
Washington, D.C. 20375
+1-202-767-2236
darken@enews.nrl.navy.mil

John L. Sibert
The George Washington University
Washington, D.C. 20052
+1-202-994-4953
sibert@seas.gwu.edu

ABSTRACT

People have severe problems wayfinding in large virtual worlds. However, current implementations of virtual worlds provide little support for effective wayfinding. We assert that knowledge about human wayfinding in the physical world can be applied to construct aids for wayfinding in virtual worlds. An experiment was conducted to determine whether people use physical world wayfinding strategies in large virtual worlds. The study measures subject performance on a complex searching task in a number of virtual worlds with differing environmental cues. The results show that subjects in the treatment without any additional cues were often disoriented and had extreme difficulty completing the task. In general, subjects' wayfinding strategies and behaviors were strongly influenced by the environmental cues in ways suggested by the underlying design principles.

Keywords

Virtual worlds, wayfinding, navigation, environmental design, spatial orientation, cognitive maps

INTRODUCTION

Problems associated with wayfinding have been encountered in every large virtual world. These problems may manifest themselves in a number of ways. Virtual world navigators may wander aimlessly when attempting to find a place for the first time. They may then have difficulty relocating places recently visited. They are often unable to grasp the overall topological structure of the space. Any time an environment encompasses more space than can be viewed from a single vantage point, these problems will occur. Compounding the problem is the fact that many virtual worlds are rarely, if ever, revisited offering the navigator no opportunity to develop a usable cognitive map of the environment.

As important as these issues are to human performance in virtual environments and the eventual acceptance of virtual environment solutions to real problems, currently, only ad hoc remedies and case studies are available for guidance.

The overall objective of our research program is to develop design principles which can be incorporated into a methodology for the design of wayfinding augmentations to virtual worlds and which will facilitate expert-like navigation performance in novice users. This paper presents an analysis of searching behaviors observed in an experiment applying real-world wayfinding and environmental design principles to the design of virtual worlds. Our intent is to show that these same principles will produce skilled wayfinding behavior* in virtual worlds.

CHI 96 Vancouver, BC Canada
ACM 0-89791-777-4/96/04

BACKGROUND

The principles we are investigating are based on spatial knowledge theory and environmental design methodology. Our intent is not to find new principles which are unique to virtual worlds but rather to determine how much of what is already known about wayfinding in the physical world is independent of the type of space and therefore can be applied to abstract computer-generated environments.

Spatial Knowledge

Wayfinding tasks in general require that the navigator be able to conceptualize the space as a whole. This type of configurational or topological knowledge is defined by Thorndyke [10] as *survey knowledge*. Object locations and inter-object distances are encoded in terms of a geocentric, fixed, frame of reference. This is significantly different from *procedural knowledge* which is defined as the sequence of actions required to follow a particular route. The route may make use of *landmark knowledge* which is static information about the visual details of a specific location.

Survey knowledge is map-like in nature. Accordingly, it can be acquired directly from map use. However, survey knowledge acquired from a map tends to be orientation-specific. In contrast, prolonged exposure to navigating an environment directly is more likely to result in survey knowledge which is orientation-independent.

The relative inflexibility of spatial knowledge acquired only from maps led Levine [6] to study the effect of this phenomenon on map design. He found that in order to facilitate efficient map use, the map must be congruent with the environment it represents. This is illustrated in the *forward-up equivalence* principle which states that the upward direction on a map (assuming it is perpendicular to the floor) must always show what is in front of the viewer.

Survey knowledge is hierarchical in nature [9]. Rather than encode the absolute positions and directions to every place encountered, fewer large, general, logically selected places (e.g. Washington, D.C.) are encoded with subnetworks of smaller, more specific places (e.g. The White House) being defined within each.

Environmental Design

Based on the role of spatial knowledge in wayfinding tasks, environmental designers have concerned themselves with developing a design methodology focussed on environmen-

*.We define skilled wayfinding behavior to be purposeful, oriented movement during navigation.

tal organization and map use. Lynch [7] suggests that urban elements such as paths, landmarks, and districts be used to divide the environment into smaller, clearly connected, more manageable pieces. These pieces can then be directly encoded into a hierarchy of spatial knowledge. Lynch also notes the importance of frequent directional cues to orientation maintenance.

Passini [8] expands on these ideas applying them to architectural design. A space should have a basic organizational principle underlying it. For example, Manhattan's streets are organized in a grid. We use this information directly to structure spatial knowledge. Most importantly, a space must have in it a number of "places" which are easily discernible to any wayfinder. A "place" is most simply defined as a distinct, recognizable location or region of a larger space often associated with a landmark. Passini also notes that if a map is to be used, it should show the organizational principle of the space as well as the design elements described by Lynch. The observer's position must always be shown and Levine's forward-up principle must be adhered to.

APPROACH

Previously, we implemented a number of navigation aids and tested their effect on subjects' ability to perform wayfinding tasks in virtual worlds [4]. Although the earlier study addressed the fundamental issues of wayfinding, it did not culminate in a set of generalizable conclusions. Rather, it presented a number of alternative cues and tools which were shown to improve subjects' performance. In this paper we set out to capture subjects' behavior in an objective form from which we could readily infer the search strategies used in accomplishing wayfinding tasks.

Wayfinding Tasks

We classify wayfinding tasks into three primary categories:

1. *Naive search*: Any searching task in which the navigator has no a priori knowledge of the whereabouts of the target in question. A naive search implies that an exhaustive search must be performed.
2. *Primed search*: Any searching task in which the navigator knows the location of the target. The search is non-exhaustive.
3. *Exploration*: Any wayfinding task in which there is no target.

The classifications of wayfinding tasks are mutually exclusive. However, they are often compounded into sequences. In cases where the navigator has general knowledge of the target's position without enough precision to find it directly, a primed search is performed to the target's general proximity followed by a naive search within that area. The opposite ordering of tasks is equally common.

Although purely naive searches are rare in the real world, in virtual worlds, spatial naivete is common in first-time explorers of a space; even the world builder. A scientist visualizing data sets may have no preconceived idea as to the shape or organization of the data. Therefore, wayfinding aids must support both exhaustive and non-exhaustive searches and must facilitate survey knowledge acquisition.

An optimal exhaustive search requires that the navigator traverse the entire space once (in the worst case). To facilitate this, there must be a method of organizing the space to eliminate multiple passes or skipping entire areas. A primed search, on the other hand, requires only that the navigator know a path to the target. If movement is unrestricted (as it often is in virtual worlds), the navigator need only know the direction and distance to the target. Minimal survey knowledge is required relating the navigator's present position to the target's position. Lastly, exploration is the basic task of spatial comprehension. Its objective is to develop survey knowledge. Maps can be used and, similarly to naive searches, the space should be explicitly organized.

These requirements lead to the conclusion that survey knowledge is the key to successful wayfinding in any environment. Based on the literature previously introduced, we present the following set of design principles for wayfinding augmentations to virtual worlds.

Design Principles

Organizational principles are intended to provide the necessary structure by which an observer can mentally organize the environment into a spatial hierarchy capable of supporting wayfinding tasks. The basic principles are:

1. Divide the large-scale world into distinct small parts, preserving a sense of "place."
2. Organize the small parts under a simple organizational principle.
3. Provide frequent directional cues.

Although map use is not an appropriate tool for every situation, the ability to quickly extract spatial knowledge directly from a map often makes it a powerful navigation aid. Ideally, this knowledge should be flexible, as if the observer had obtained it from direct experience. Therefore, map design principles are intended to present spatial information in such a way as to produce a flexible, orientation-independent representation of the environment. The basic principles are:

1. Show all organizational elements (paths, landmarks, districts, etc.) and the organizational principle.
2. Always show the observer's position.
3. Orient the map with respect to the observer such that the forward-up equivalence principle is accommodated.

Note that the two latter principles are difficult to apply in the real-world when the observer is moving. In the virtual world they can be applied equally easily to a stationary or moving observer.

METHOD

The performance of each subject was observed and measured on wayfinding tasks in several virtual world treatments. Some treatments adhere to a subset of the wayfinding principles; others do not. (See Video Figure in the CHI 96 Video Program) The four treatments in the experiment are:

- **Control Treatment**: No wayfinding assistance provided
- **Grid Treatment**: Adherence to organizational principles
- **Map Treatment**: Adherence to map principles
- **Map/Grid Treatment**: Adherence to both organizational and map principles

In order to capture the subjects' behavior we asked each subject to sketch a map [5, 7] showing the location of land forms and targets after each treatment. We asked subjects to think aloud and recorded each treatment with video and audio tape. Finally, we sampled (once per second) the path of each subject through each treatment and superimposed it on a map of the environment (See below, Figure 4). In addition to visual comparison to the actual environment, we analyzed the sketch maps using a metric incorporating target distances and directions and land mass shapes developed for this particular purpose [3]. We analyzed the audio and video tape using a verbal protocol analysis [1] and captured observed behavior in the same notation used in CMN-GOMS [2]*.

Design

All subjects were tested on all treatments. Five male and five female subjects participated in the study. The availability of subjects is limited due to both the location of the laboratory and the total time required to complete all trials (approximately three hours for each subject). All subjects had a technical background and were between the ages of 20 and 45.

Stimuli and Apparatus

There were five environments built for this experiment, each of which was equivalent in extent to approximately 12,000 square kilometers in real-world dimensions. The worlds were constructed by hand using a geometric modeling tool. Each world contains large areas of open sea and several land masses. The land masses are colored by elevation and the ocean surface is textured. The land masses were shaped and scaled to be distinct from one another. The targets (ships) were manually placed in the worlds, each with a random orientation. They were also numbered in order to aid identification.

The viewpoint was restricted to movement above the terrain but below a maximum altitude of 400 meters. This is necessary to allow some vertical movement without allowing the subject to gain enough altitude to be able to look down on the entire environment from a "bird's eye view." Movement was constrained horizontally so that when an edge was encountered, there would be no distinguishable features by which to navigate. Contact with the virtual edge resulted in an audible "click" cue combined with immediate clamping of the viewpoint's movement at the point of contact.

The radial grid used in the grid treatment was constructed from a red center post and four different colored posts in each cardinal direction. The outer posts each have a "flag" which points inward toward the red inner post. There are three concentric rings marking range. The red, yellow, and white rings are placed at 10000m, 20000m, and 40000m radius respectively. The outer posts are placed on the white ring. Black radial lines are placed every 45 degrees and extend beyond the white ring.

The map used in the map treatment was identical to the actual environment except that the blue sea texture was replaced by a grey background for contrast with the environment. A red sphere was moved along the map surface to identify the viewpoint position during navigation. The map is presented flat and in the same orientation as the environment itself in conformance to the map principles. The map was placed relative to the viewpoint during movement such that it was visible at all times. The intent was for subjects to feel that the map was in front of their chest.

*.Although we used GOMS notation, this is not a traditional GOMS analysis since it was used only for capturing differences in search methods.

The map/grid treatment was implemented by placing the grid over the map and the world simultaneously. In the examples in Figure 1, the viewpoint in each case is near the home target facing the center of the world. The target is identified as target zero with a white numbered cube directly above it. The red center post is shown in both the grid and map/grid treatments.

This experiment is intended to study the validity of the design principles and spatial behaviors associated with environmental information rather than the effectiveness of these specific environmental cues. Although we have chosen representative cues for each treatment that adhere to the design principles, there are certainly many other ways to provide the same information.

The treatments were implemented on a Silicon Graphics Onyx™ Reality Engine 2™ workstation. The only peripheral device used was a Fakespace Inc. BOOM3C™ display and tracker. The BOOM3C is a full color, high resolution (1280x1024 pixels) CRT-based display mounted on a counter-balanced mechanical arm. The display is held to the eyes with one hand which controls a single button and a thumb-operated joystick. The position and orientation of the head are tracked through the mechanical arm. Motion is controlled via an acceleration metaphor by which the subject accelerates forward in the virtual world by pushing up on the joystick and backward by pulling down. Velocity is bounded by a maximum speed of approximately Mach 3 (993m/s or 2223mph). Movement is *always* in the direction of view. The subject may stop at any time by pushing the button on the hand controller.

Procedure

The order of treatment presentation and the environments to be used with each were predetermined at random. However, all subjects were given the control treatment on a separate environment as a training session. This was done to introduce the apparatus and the experimental procedure in such a way as to limit the order effect on the data.

The wayfinding task performed for all treatments required the subject to execute five naive searches followed by one primed search. The subject starts at the home target and proceeds to search the environment for each of the five ships which have been numbered and shown to the subject in the instructions. No a priori information is given as to their whereabouts. Once the last target has been located, the subject is required to return to the home target. Subjects were given as much time as needed to complete the task. However, the trial could be discontinued at the subject's request. This was allowed only in cases when either the subject felt unable to make any progress toward task completion after an extended period of time (always at least 15 minutes) or the subject became unable to continue for physical reasons.†

During task execution, subjects were asked to "think aloud" [1] as a method of knowledge elicitation specifically aimed at understanding search strategies. Following each trial, subjects were required to draw a map of the environment in as much detail as possible. Subjects were free to sketch the environment at will starting from a blank piece of paper.

†.There were two cases of motion sickness.

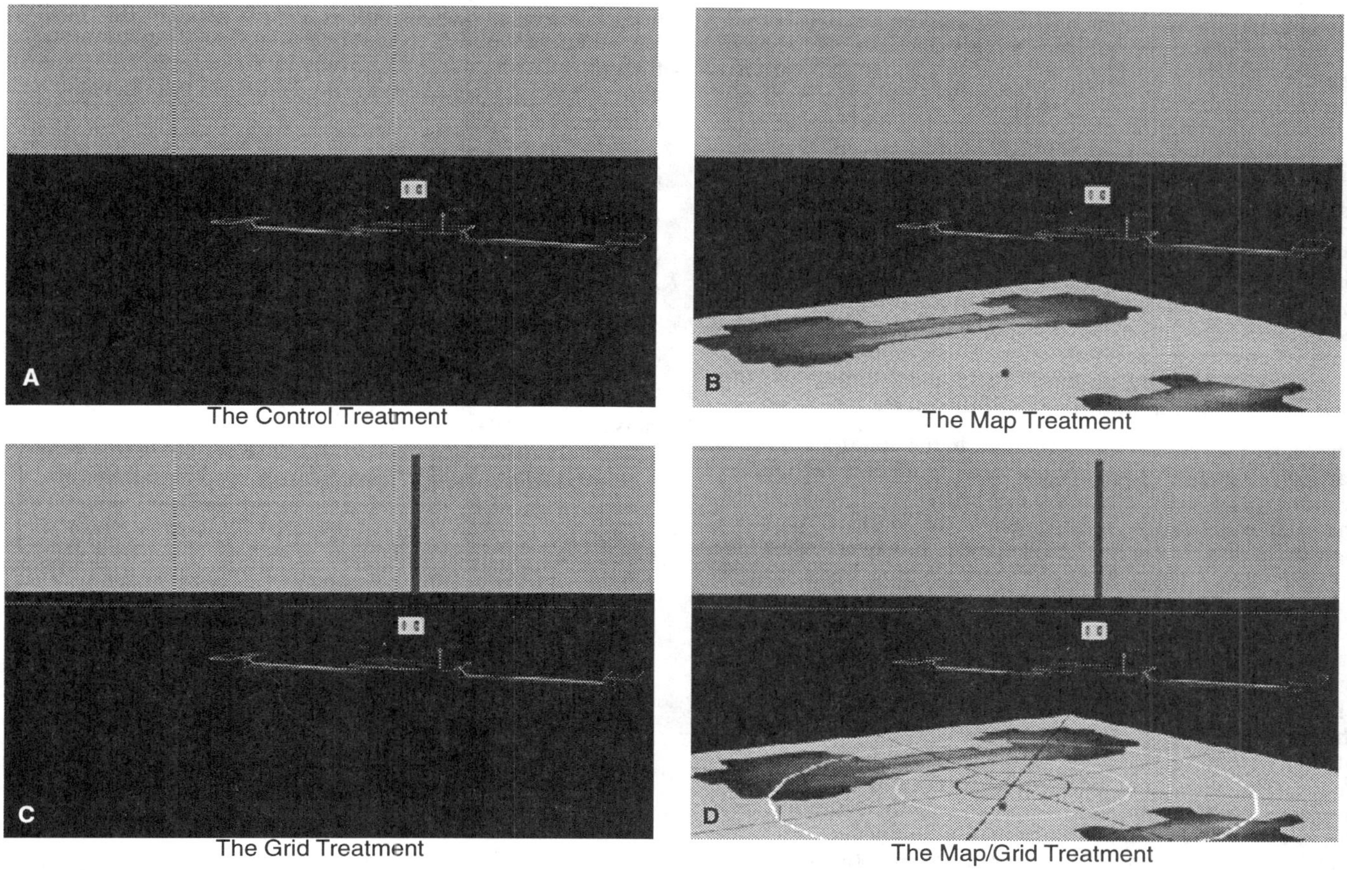

Figure 1: The four treatments as seen from identical locations in a sample environment.

RESULTS AND DISCUSSION

Our primary objective in this paper is to present the fundamental differences in spatial behavior associated with each experimental condition. Consequently, this section will be qualitative in nature. Quantitative results will be reviewed in the next section.

For the purpose of this study, the wayfinding tasks have been broken into their primary components (See Figure 2). Subjects must first ground themselves in the virtual world by acquiring their orientation and position. Then, they begin to undertake the explicit tasks of the five naive searches followed by one primed search. If at any time they lose their orientation or position, they must reacquire it before proceeding. Also, during task execution, actions may be taken which are specifically meant to help the subject maintain orientation and position and consequently, to develop a better cognitive representation. Finally, as targets and objects of interest are located in the world, they are explicitly placed into memory so that they may be recalled later for the map drawing exercise.

This linear description does not completely show the flow of execution. During a single task sequence, subjects may choose more than one method to achieve a goal. For example, when using a word processor, there are typically at least two ways to change the style of the selected text; either via the pull-down menu or using accelerator keys. Either method is acceptable but the subject will never execute both in a single task sequence. In the type of tasks described here, there are also several acceptable methods available to

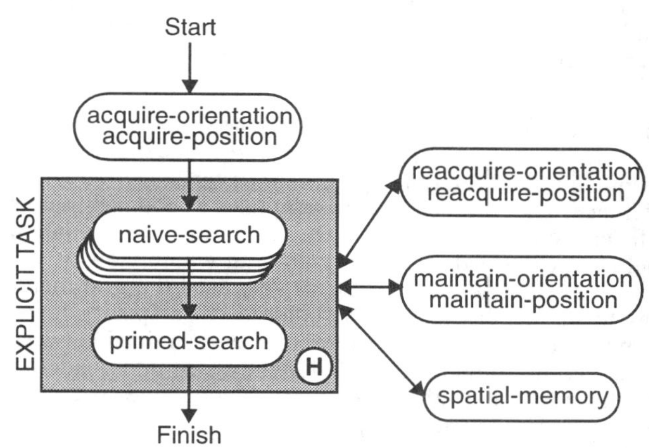

Figure 2: High-level schematic diagram of task execution. The H designates a history mechanism by which any arc traversed out of the gray, explicit task nodes returns to the node of departure.

complete any task, but it *is* feasible to choose more than one method for any given instance. This type of reinforcing or repetitive behavior is the rule rather than the exception in this analysis. Many subjects used several strategies during any one trial as they discovered better alternatives or found their current approach ineffective. Most commonly, subjects selected a method based on intuition restricted by the cues and information currently perceived or available.

The overall goal of the task is to execute an efficient, organized search locating all five targets and afterwards, the home target. The subject must also accumulate survey knowledge in order to draw an accurate map of the environment after completion of the task. Our interest here lies in the notable differences in behavior and in search strategies based on the differences in navigation aids provided (or not provided as the case may be).

Orientation and Position

Grounding the egocentric perspective within the cognitive map, which implies maintaining correct orientation, is an essential component of navigation. Without this grounding, survey knowledge cannot develop. This grounding information must be initially acquired, maintained throughout the task, and reacquired immediately if disorientation occurs.

The lack of suitable orientation cues in the control treatment caused subjects to use relatively weak grounding techniques which proved to be error prone. Most subjects tried to use the orientation of the home target or the initial view direction as a default "north." This failed, however, when the subject moved away from the start position because adequate reference information was no longer available if and when disorientation occurred. Some subjects tried to use targets and land features as reference points, and attempted to infer distance and direction by moving between them. However, this method was not very successful because of the large distances between targets. One subject even created an external reference by grounding one foot in physical space. The viewpoint was easily reoriented based on the subject's body posture. However, this method was not useful in extracting positional information. Subjects most often used a dead reckoning* technique with the home target as a reference point to determine position. This was a difficult task considering the lack of alternative reference points throughout the environment. However, it was often the only viable alternative. During navigation, subjects would frequently retrace their recent path or move between targets to estimate distances between them.

These same techniques were also observed in the grid treatment. However, the grid markings were frequently used as the predominant reference points for distance and direction inference. The four outer posts were used as compass points with any one arbitrarily chosen as "north." Reorientation could be performed by simply returning within view of any outer post. Alternatively, subjects also used the grid markings to divide the space. The colored rings specify range from the center post. Subjects were evenly divided between those who used the posts to divide the space into quadrants and those who used the radial lines to divide the space into wedge-shaped octants. Subjects also used the grid to maintain orientation and position by determining which bounded area they were currently in. These methods were more effective because the grid represented an absolute frame of reference.

The map provides a geocentric perspective to the environment. Consequently, many of the difficulties in acquiring and maintaining orientation and position are eliminated. The map shows the shape of the space and allows for the effective use of geographical landmarks† and world edges as reference points. The orientation of the map itself indicates the viewpoint orientation with respect to the world. Viewpoint position is available at a glance. The addition of the grid superimposed on the map in the map/grid treatment allows methods from both the map and grid treatments to be used together.

*.Dead reckoning is a technique by which future positions are determined based on movement at a constant velocity and direction from a known starting location.

Spatial Memory

This implicit subtask involves the structure of the cognitive map employed by the subject to encode spatial knowledge. Subjects would often pause after locating a target to decide how to remember its location for the map drawing exercise. This is also shown clearly by the subjects' paths (See Figure 4). Based on analysis of the paths and observed behaviors we defined structures (See Figure 3) which appear to have been used to represent spatial information. The chosen representation was most often closely related to the type of naive search used (See Table 1).

Spatial Memory	Naive Search	Primed Search
Graph	Local Search	Retrace Steps
Square Grid	Lawnmower	Manhattan
Anchor	Coastline	Direct Landmark
Radial Grid	Area Paths	Approximate Direct

Table 1: Spatial memory representations and their associated search methods

The amorphous nature of the control treatment allowed subjects to apply any structure to the environment. The targets could be connected in the form of a *graph* with the targets as nodes and the paths between them as edges. A *square grid* structure could also be applied dividing the space into smaller regions. Most commonly, targets were represented as *anchored* relative to the land masses.

In the grid treatment, the graph and anchoring methods are still utilized. However, the square grid method does not coincide with the shape of the radial grid and is consequently replaced by a *radial grid* structure.

The map does not impose any structure on the environment beyond that of the control treatment. Accordingly, the same conceptual structures were used in the map treatment as in the control treatment. In the map/grid treatment, however, subjects were not observed to use the graph method; presumably because the grid markings and geocentric perspective provided enough reference points to make this method inferior to others.

Naive Searching

An effective naive search requires that the subject conduct an organized, exhaustive traversal of the space. In the control treatment, since the space itself was not organized, subjects had extreme difficulty in organizing their search. The most common methods involved searching the area *local* to targets or to land masses by following *coastlines*. The local search method was most often used in concert with the graph structure while the coastline method was used with the anchor structure. The coastline method is improved by

†.These include unusual landforms such as a bay or peninsula.

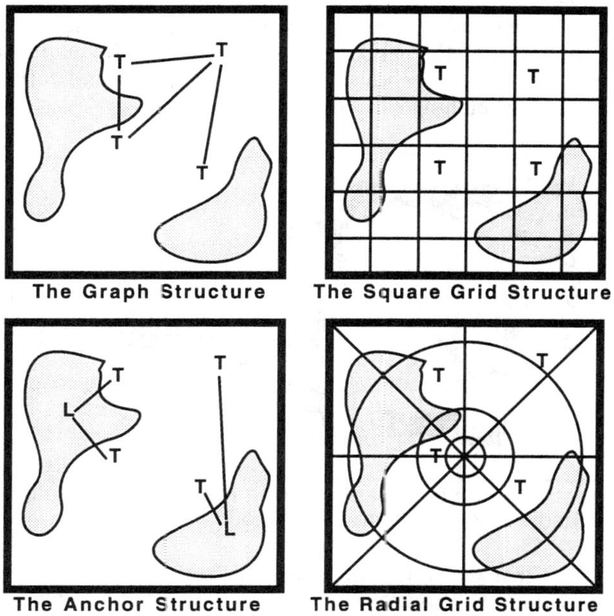

Figure 3: Cognitive representations for spatial memory

encircling the land multiple times, each time extending further out into open space. The subject using an external orientation method was able to conduct a very different type of search because of his superior ability to maintain orientation. He located a corner of the world by repeatedly bumping the edges, and then proceeded to cover the space in long strips moving across the length of the world (not unlike the path of a *lawnmower*; See Figure 4A)

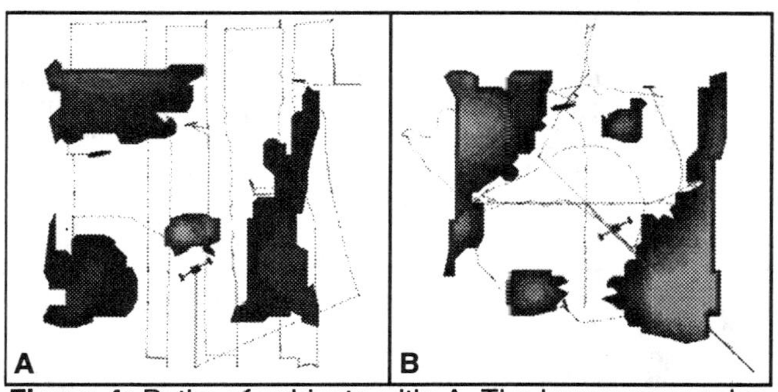

Figure 4: Paths of subjects with: A. The lawnmower naive search method. B. The radial grid used as paths.

When the grid was provided, it added two primary methods to those of the control treatment. The grid markings can be used as *paths*. The path trail line in Figure 4B clearly shows both the radial lines and the range rings which were used to guide the search. This was seen as a more comfortable alternative to searching open spaces. Also, the world could be divided into *areas* bounded by the grid lines, each to be searched sequentially.

The map allowed the search techniques of the control treatment to be executed more effectively and with optimizations. *Heuristic* searches were often used to initially visit places which subjects guessed would hide a target such as an inlet or bay. They can be used with any of the spatial memory representations. Also, the lawnmower method was optimized to eliminate searching over land. The addition of the grid to the map enabled combinations of methods. For example, heuristics were used to improve area searches.

Primed Searching

The ability to perform an efficient primed search is dependent on the level of useful spatial knowledge obtained during navigation. In the control treatment, many subjects had been disoriented for most of the trial and therefore conducted another naive search to locate the home target. Subjects who were able to connect targets in a chain-like fashion *retraced steps* back to familiar ground. If a grid structure was used to organize the space, a path was followed along the *Manhattan* distance* to the home target. Most often, subjects unsuccessfully attempted to infer a *direct* path.

The grid markings were used in one of two ways. If a post or line crossing was within view of the home target, that location was used as an *approximate* target from which the primed search could be completed easily. The alternative was to place the home target in the world relative to the grid and search for it directly.

When the map is used, the home target is placed relative to some predetermined geographical *landmark*. To relocate the target, the subject moves back to the general area and conducts a local search until successful. If the grid is added to the map, the grid markings are usually preferred over geographical landmarks for reference points.

In all treatments, dead reckoning was used extensively as a way to structure movement during a search (naive or primed). It was used frequently in the control and grid treatments but only intermittently in the map and map/grid treatments when not navigating from the map directly.

SEARCH EFFECTIVENESS

In addition to categorizing searching strategies and behavior, we evaluated search effectiveness across treatments. A Friedman two-way within-subject ANOVA was used to analyze the results. This is a nonparametric test of interval data suitable for experiments with small subject sample sizes.

A measure of total time to complete each trial (adjusted for incomplete attempts) showed significant effects across treatments (Friedman test statistic=15.96, $p \leq .001$)† indicating that subjects in the control treatment tended to execute ineffective searches and were unable to structure the space. This is further illustrated in the distance travelled during each treatment which also showed a significant effect (Friedman test statistic=17.4, $p \leq .001$). As seen in Figure 5, subjects repeatedly traversed the same space in the control treatment. Distances and times for the grid treatment were lower than the control treatment but higher than the map and map/grid treatments. Although the grid supplies enough information to structure a search, a significant amount of effort and reinforcing actions must be executed to maintain orientation.

A ratio of the percentage of space searched to total time is a coarse indicator of search effectiveness. This ratio was shown to be significant across treatments (Friedman test statistic=13.8, $p \leq .005$). In general, subjects were not able to coordinate an effective search in the control treatment due

*.A Manhattan distance measures movement constrained to horizontal and vertical directions.

†.For all quantitative results presented, no significant effect was found for gender or treatment order.

to disorientation. The grid significantly increased performance and ability to extract spatial information but the map and map/grid treatments supported the most effective searches.

A metric was developed to objectively evaluate the map sketches (See [3] for details) in terms of directional accuracy, relative distance estimation, and land form (shape, placement, and relative scale of the land masses). There were significant effects for directional accuracy across treatments (Friedman test statistic=14.52, p≤.005) as well as land form (Friedman test statistic=18.84, p≤.0001). However, distance estimation did not show a significant effect (Friedman test statistic=6.93, p>.05). Error in directional accuracy (range from 3%-60%) was significantly higher than error in distance estimation (range from 1%-10%). The ability of most subjects to efficiently dead reckon regardless of treatment is dependent on their ability to determine distance and speed. Therefore, it is not surprising that subjects were much more adept at estimating distance than direction in light of the prevalence of dead reckoning across treatments. Furthermore, disorientation often caused subjects to draw incomplete map sketches of the control treatment because they were unable to do more than randomly place targets on the map which were located while they were disoriented.

The disorientation most commonly associated with the control treatment is evident in a number of ways. A typical diagram of the route followed during an average control treatment shows significant confusion and a general inability to organize the space (See Figure 5). In this example, a

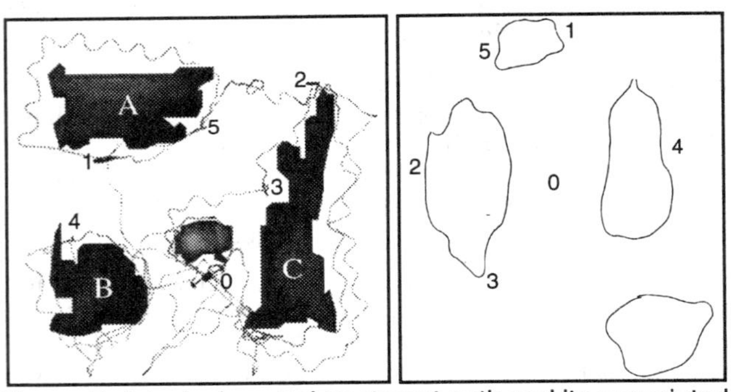

Figure 5: A typical control treatment path and its associated map drawing. Targets have been numbered on both figures.

coastline following method was used. The weaving motion during navigation is a behavior associated with widening the field of view. The subject looks back and forth while moving to compensate for the narrow view of the display. The path shows that this subject traversed each land mass multiple times with a single thread joining A to the others. There is no point in this environment from which A can be seen simultaneously with B or C. Consequently, most of the search was confined to familiar areas near the home target (labelled #0). This subject drew a map which shows a basic inability to extract spatial information from the space. The map is roughly a horizontal reflection of the actual environment.

The presence of the radial grid was shown to significantly improve directional accuracy. Map sketches of both the grid and map/grid treatments were more accurate in target placement than the control and map treatments. This is shown in Figure 6. This subject used an area search method in the grid treatment. The map shows that although the subject placed the targets very accurately, the land mass structure is incorrect. Due to the geocentric view provided, the map and map/grid treatments showed the most accurate land forms on the map sketching exercise.

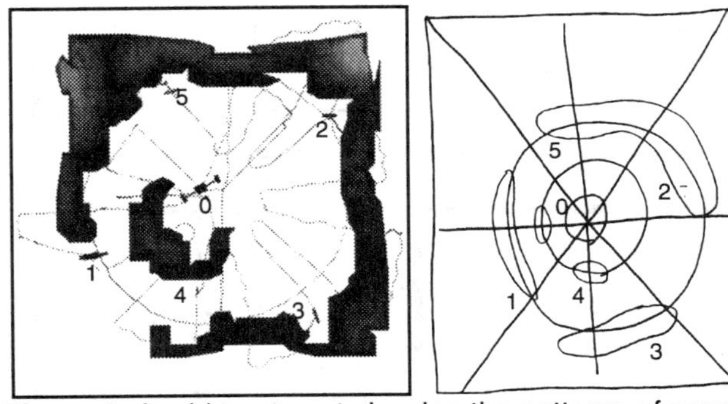

Figure 6: A grid treatment showing the patterns of search confined to sequential areas of the grid.

The fact that we were able to discern reasonable cognitive representations (Figure 3), even in the control treatment indicates that structure was imposed on the environments whether or not it was supported by the environment itself. This structure is a necessary precondition to execution of a searching task. Those subjects who did not conceptually organize the environment were unable to conduct an efficient search and in many cases, did not successfully complete the task.

Thorndyke [10] describes survey knowledge in part as configurational knowledge, often acquired via a map, allowing short-cuts and the ability to infer new paths. The optimizations to the control treatment search methods observed in the map treatment illustrate this point exactly. The path shown in Figure 7 is cut short around target 5 rather than cross a land mass of known shape. This path can be compared to Figure 4A which shows the same search technique used in the control treatment. The subject is unsure of the shape and size of the land masses and therefore does not deviate from the pattern.

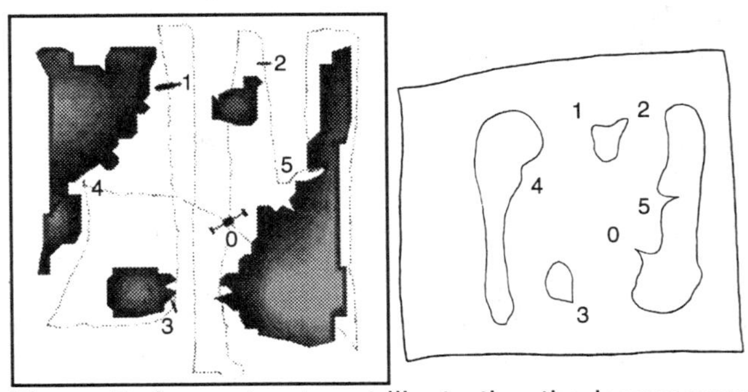

Figure 7: A map treatment illustrating the lawnmower method of search.

Behavior observed during all four treatments indicates that organizational structure and restriction of movement are an essential part of navigation. Subjects were uncomfortable with completely free and unrestricted movement in sparsely populated space because it led to disorientation much of the time. When the grid was added, this discomfort subsided as subjects found structure to guide and direct their search and consequently, avoid disorientation. The importance of paths as described by Lynch [7] indicates that in virtual and physical spaces alike, navigators need structured movement for effective navigation and spatial knowledge acquisition. This should not be interpreted as a recommendation of rigid movement restriction in virtual worlds. A lack of freedom in movement and choice inhibits exploration. Rather, we advocate the augmentation of large virtual worlds with directional cues and a simple, well-defined structure that facilitates subjects' construction of their own paths.

The frequent use of dead reckoning across treatments was not an anticipated behavior. Effective use of this technique requires three necessary components:

- the current position
- the direction of movement, and
- the velocity of movement.

The effectiveness of the technique is much improved if there are reference points within view of the path of travel which can be used as "checkpoints" marking progress along the way. This was only the case when the grid was present. Form the relative success of dead reckoning in the non-grid treatments we conclude that the frame rate (≥15 frames/second) and visual cues (specifically the sea texture) provided enough feedback to maintain a consistent estimation of velocity. The technique is further encouraged by the method of movement since the subject must always look in the direction of movement.

CONCLUSIONS

The methods employed in each subtask were profoundly affected by the stimuli presented. The lack of directional cues and spatial organization in the control treatment led to ineffective search strategies and frequent disorientation. The radial grid provided enough information to successfully execute a search but required reinforcing actions to maintain orientation. The map provides a simultaneous geocentric perspective augmenting the egocentric perspective and fostering the use of geographical landmarks and optimizations to search methods. General conclusions drawn from this work include:

1. When not given an adequate source of directional cues, disorientation will inhibit both wayfinding performance and spatial knowledge acquisition.
2. A large world with no explicit structure is difficult, if not impossible, to search exhaustively. This was shown by repeated reacquisition behavior in the control treatment.
3. A conceptual coordinate system is often imposed on the world to act as a divider. This is a side-effect of not being able to divide the world explicitly. A structure must be imposed on the world if an organized exhaustive search is to be attempted.
4. Our observations support the notion that path following is a natural spatial behavior. Subjects frequently used features such as coastlines or grid lines as if they were paths.
5. A map allows for optimizations to be made to search strategies. This is because it can be considered a supplement to survey knowledge.
6. Dead reckoning was observed to be an intuitive and natural part of navigation; all subjects exhibited this behavior even though frequently unaware of it. The ability to infer position from a past location and constant velocity over time, while sometimes complex in reality, appears to be more easily understood and implemented in virtual spaces.

We are encouraged that the observations reported in this paper support the application of environmental design principles to virtual world design. We expect to broaden our investigation in the future to include environments with vastly different spatial characteristics. As environments become more complex and abstract, we will need to determine whether or not a human's conception of an abstract space is analogous to that of a physical space. Early indications are that this is the case, but a definitive statement at this time requires us to speculate as to the nature of virtual environment representations of the future.

ACKNOWLEDGEMENTS

This research was conducted through support by the Virtual Environment Laboratory of the Tactical Electronic Warfare Division of the Naval Research Laboratory in Washington, D.C. The authors would like to thank Manuel Pérez and Dan McFarlane for their assistance as well as our experimental subjects at NRL for their time and effort.

REFERENCES

1. Byrne, R., *Protocol Analysis in Problem Solving*, in *Thinking and Reasoning: Psychological Approaches*, J.B.T. Evans, Editor. 1983, Routledge & Kegan Paul: London. p. 227-249.
2. Card, S.K., T.P. Moran, and A. Newell, *The Psychology of Human-Computer Interaction*. 1983, Hillsdale, N.J.: Lawrence Erlbaum Associates.
3. Darken, R.P., *Wayfinding in Large-Scale Virtual Worlds*, Doctoral dissertation, 1996, The George Washington University, Washington, D.C.
4. Darken, R.P. and J.L. Sibert, *A Toolset for Navigation in Virtual Environments*. User Interface Software and Technology, 1993: p. 157-165.
5. Howard, J.H. and S.M. Kerst, *Memory and Perception of Cartographic Information for Familiar and Unfamiliar Environments*. Human Factors, 1981. **23**(4): p. 495-504.
6. Levine, M., I. Marchon, and G. Hanley, *The Placement and Misplacement of You-Are-Here Maps*. Environment and Behavior, 1984. **16**(2): p. 139-157.
7. Lynch, K., *The Image of the City*. 1960, Cambridge: MIT Press. 194.
8. Passini, R., *Wayfinding in Architecture*. 1984, New York: Van Nostrand Reinhold Company Inc.
9. Stevens, A. and P. Coupe, *Distortions in Judged Spatial Relations*. Cognitive Psychology, 1978. **10**: p. 422-437.
10. Thorndyke, P.W. and S.E. Goldin, *Spatial Learning and Reasoning Skill*, in *Spatial Orientation: Theory, Research, and Application*, H.L. Pick and L.P. Acredolo, Editors. 1983, Plenum Press: New York. p. 195-217.

An Empirical Evaluation of Design Rationale Documents

Laurent Karsenty
ARAMIIHS
31 rue des Cosmonautes, Z.I. du Palays
F-31077 Toulouse, FRANCE
+33 62 24 75 55
karsenty@jazz.matra-espace.fr

ABSTRACT
While several studies propose methods and notations for "capturing" design rationale (DR), there is to date little data available on how useful this information is when a designer needs to reuse a previous design. This paper presents the results of an empirical evaluation of DR documents, carried out with six experienced professional designers who were asked to understand and to assess a past design. These designers were provided with documents that described the solution and documents describing the DR. These DR documents were constructed using the QOC method. To determine the usefulness of DR documents, we attempt to answer the three following questions: (1) Do designers confronted with an unknown design need to know the design rationales? (2) How designers use design rationale documents? (3) Do we succeed in capturing the rationales looked for by designers? The results provided by this study lead us to conclude that DR should be useful, at least for some designers who use it as a support to their reasoning, but not sufficient. Indeed, this study exhibits some limitations of the traditional approaches for recording DR. We discuss these limitations and some solutions needed to go beyond them.

Keywords
Design Rationale, Design methodology, Reuse

1. INTRODUCTION

Recent studies have used methods, notations and tools for recording, representing and accessing design rationale [5, 2]. It is argued that design rationale (DR) is necessary for reusing past designs, coordinating people involved in a long project [6], promoting critical reflection during design [7], facilitating maintenance and the use of the artifact [3]. A commonly advocated framework for recording and representing design rationale is argument structure (e.g., gIBIS [6], DRL [11], QOC [12], DRCS [10]). This framework proposes to represent DR with a semi-structured approach, implying different nodes: *questions* or *issues*, *options* related to these issues, *arguments* or *criteria* involved in the assessment of these options, and *justifications*.

CHI 96 Vancouver, BC Canada

While this framework is claimed to be appropriate for the capture and subsequent use of DR, there is little empirical data on how useful DR documents constructed using this framework really are (but see [13] for a review related to this issue). By DR documents, we mean paper documents or electronic documents containing a semi-formal description of the DR. This paper presents a first experiment aimed at evaluating the usefulness of such documents.

The first requirement of this evaluation was to record the DR of a design project. This has been possible with the collaboration of a French aerospace company, Aerospatiale. We recorded the DR of a real industrial project conducted in a design office of this company. This design office specialises in mechanical engineering design. The goal of the design project was to evolve one of their products to meet new requirements (redesign). We examined the first phase of this project, which lasted for nine months. This study received the project manager's support, because he was convinced that a DR document could be a helpful information tool for those in charge of the next phases of the project.

To record the DR of this project, we used the QOC formalism [12]. Two reasons explain this choice: (1) to carry out a first experiment in an industrial setting, we needed a fairly simple method; IBIS (see [6]) and QOC meet this requirement; (2) one of the main differences between IBIS and QOC is that it is necessary to make *design criteria* explicit with QOC, while they may remain hidden in the *arguments* defending the *positions* with IBIS. The ability to be directly informed about the design criteria was judged by the project manager to be an indispensable requirement. Indeed, this makes it possible to immediately know the project objectives, and thus, to better assess the solution.

The record of the DR was ensured by two scribes, a company documentation specialist and the author. This was a condition required by the design office chief, who did not believe that the designers would take the time to document the DR themselves. Both scribes played a purely passive role in the design process. The DR record was based on the analysis of 4 audiotaped design meetings, bringing together mechanical engineers and technicians. Each design meeting lasted two hours.

The DR document was structured by reporting the new facts discussed at each new design meeting. After each formalization of a meeting using QOC, we asked the project team to review the new version of the DR document. The final document contains 31 questions, 46 document. The final document contains 31 questions, 46 options, 25 criteria, and 12 justifications of the option assessments.

This document was paper-based. Indeed, the company where the study was carried out preferred to first test the DR capturing method without any computer support, before investing in such a tool. One consequence of this choice is that the evaluation performed and presented in this paper does not cope with some aspects affecting the usefulness of DR documents. In particular, we do not evaluate how easy the access to the DR is, because this feature is completely dependant on the provided means for access.

Because the document was paper-based, we tried to respect the following rules intended to make it easier to read : (i) one problem per page; (ii) a recall of the origin of each question with a title at the top of each page, (iii) a graphic symbol for each type of node (questions were encircled, chosen options in a square frame, etc.), (iv) each node numbered to provide annexes with complete lists of each type of node (list of questions, list of criteria, etc.), with the number of each node and its wording.

In order to explore how useful DR documents are, three questions were addressed: (1) Do designers confronted with an unknown design need to know the design rationales? Depending on this answer, we will be able to say at least if DR documents should be useful; (2) Do designers use design rationale documents? Indeed, no matter what the designers' need for DR is, if they do not use DR documents, this would highlight serious limitations of our approach; (3) Do we succeed in capturing the rationales looked for by designers? Here too, if designers need DR, but if they do not find the facts that they are looking for in the DR documents, we will need to revise our approach. This paper presents the results of different analyses related to these three issues. We will finally conclude by recalling the lessons learned by this study.

The experiment presented in this paper was carried out in the field of mechanical engineering design. However, we believe that the lessons learned by this study should be valuable for other fields of design, because our conclusions are more concerned with the approach for capturing DR than with the application domain.

2. METHOD

In order to evaluate the usefulness of DR documents (for convenience, we will use "DR" to refer to "DR document"), we asked six experienced, professional designers (three engineers and three technicians), all external to the project that we examined, to understand and to assess the solution proposed by the project team. These tasks were chosen because they are considered by the designers themselves as the most important when they need to work on the results of a previous study.

During an evaluation meeting, a designer was provided with two kinds of information: (i) information describing the solution, and consisting mostly of blueprints; (ii) information describing the reasons for design decisions, and reported in a paper-document.

Designers were free to use blueprints and DR as they chose: this means that we did not force them to use the DR. This was necessary because we were interested in knowing how they would spontaneously use it. In addition, the documentation specialist and I were present to help find the information looked for by designers, or to answer their questions. Actually, our initial intention was to let the designers finding themselves their answers in the DR. However, because some of them systematically asked questions to us, we decided to give the appropriate answers, and thus, not to jam the natural process. One consequence of this decision is that we will not be able to draw conclusions about the usability of DR documents (but see [13], which reports some empirical data on usability of DR).

Each evaluation meeting proceeded as follows: we described the tasks assigned to the designer, and presented the documents available. Because the DR was a new type of document, we described its properties and how it should be interpreted. Then the designer began his/her tasks, without time constraints. At the end, we asked a few questions on his/her opinions concerning the usefulness of the DR. These evaluation meetings lasted about one hour each, and were all taped.

3. DO DESIGNERS CONFRONTED WITH AN UNKNOWN DESIGN NEED TO KNOW THE DESIGN RATIONALE?

In order to measure the importance of knowing the design rationales, we examine the *questions* raised by the designers confronted with a design solution during the evaluation meetings.

One hundred and thirty eight questions were extracted from the 6 evaluation meetings. These questions were coded according to the following categories:

1. *Blueprints questions*: they aim at clarifying the objects represented (e.g., pointing at a blueprint "what is this element?"); this category also includes requests for other blueprints.
2. *Structure questions:* they concern the material used, the forms and the size of the objects composing the whole artifact, and the properties of the interfaces between these objects (e.g., "how is the plate that carries the equipment fixed?")
3. *Behavior questions:* they focus on the way the artifact carries out its functions (e.g., "What are the moves allowed by this arm?")
4. *Design rationale questions:* they ask about the initial motivations of the project, the reasons for the design decisions, the different possible choices and the comparison between these different choices (e.g., "Why 6 fuel tanks, and not just 4 bigger ones?").
5. *History questions*: typically, they include questions about what has changed between the previous design and the new one, mostly concentrating on the structural aspect of the artifact ("Did you change the way the plate is fixed?")
6. *Document questions*: they aim at clarifying the terms used in the DR documents, and to better understand

the way these documents were constructed (e.g., "How did you decide to link one criteria to one option?").

Figure 1 gives the percentages of occurrence that we found for each category of questions.

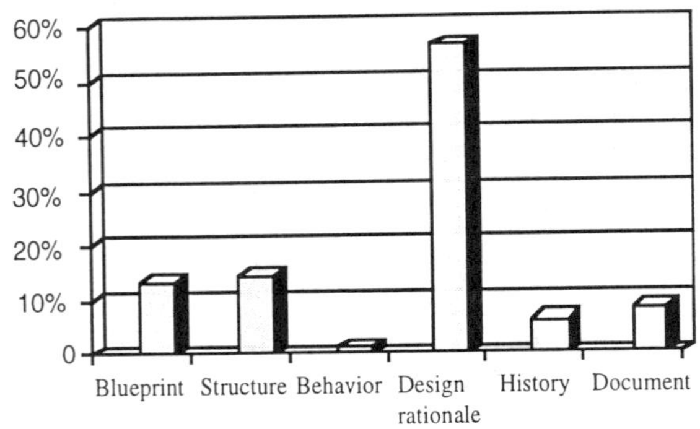

Figure 1. *Percentage of questions during evaluation meetings*

This diagram shows that *DR questions are by far the most frequent*. In addition, this result remains true whatever the designers' competence is (63% of DR questions for engineers; 49% for technicians).

Discussion

These results clearly establish that designers need to know the design rationale to understand and assess an unknown design.

However, one must note that these results contradict Herbsled and Kuwana's observations [8]: their analysis of questions in design meetings stated that design rationale questions (referred to as *why* questions) were rare. They then proposed different possible explanations of this result, among which: "the rationale behind decisions is simply relatively unimportant" (p.13). If this is true, how can we explain the high frequency of DR questions in our study ?

The discrepancy between our respective results might be due to the fact that *question asking is a situated, context-dependent activity*. In other words, questions observed in a specific situation, namely design meetings, cannot be considered as representative of questions asked in another situation, namely reuse situations. And indeed, there are two major differences between both situations:

1. Some previous studies [9] highlight the fact that explanations are most of the time given *spontaneously* in design dialogues, and not in response to a question. More precisely, in analyzing database design dialogues, it was found that 83% of the explanations were volunteered when one member of the group wanted to submit a proposal or to address a critic. As a consequence, one observes few explicit why questions in such design dialogues.

2. Furthermore, because participants in a project accumulate knowledge on this project (the requirements, constraints, problems with different alternatives. etc.). they are able to infer, in some cases, why such a proposal or such a criticism is relevant, without asking the corresponding why question.

Both aspects are present in the design meetings studied by Herbsleb and Kuwana, and missing from our evaluation meetings, where designers had to work with a previous design without having the historical knowledge of the project. Our conclusion is that knowing the design rationale is important, especially when the project team works on someone else's design.

This conclusion would appear as a strong argument for claiming the usefulness of DR documents if at least two conditions were satisfied: the first condition would be that designers want to use DR documents; the second condition would be that DR documents constructed with the QOC method contain the information looked for by designers. We test these conditions in the two following sections.

4. DO DESIGNERS USE DESIGN RATIONALE DOCUMENTS?

The evaluation meetings have allowed us to identify two very distinctive ways of using the DR: an opportunistic use and an extensive use.

The opportunistic use of DR

The first way of using the DR is to look at it only when no other means allow a designer to answer his her question. Among these other means are: the inference of the reasons for the decisions, and the verbal asking.

Indeed, very often when a designer raises a DR question. he/she first looks more precisely at the blueprints. In doing so, he/she tries to gain more information on the structural and functional aspects of the artifact. The new information found in this way (they also might ask a question) helps to infer the reasons for the design decisions. The following extract gives an example of how a better understanding of the artifact helps to discover the design rationale ("D" stands for designer, "DS" for documentation specialist, "* *" for personal comments):

D: (talking to himself) *So, what lead to the choice of these tanks?* (Now, he turns towards us) *What is the principle of these tanks? Is the pressurization external or internal?*

DS: *Internal.*

D: *Ok, so one may assume that the cost was a criteria of choice in this case* (*in fact, internal pressurization is cheaper than external pressurization*).

This extract highlights the fact that an improved understanding of the structure or of the behavior of the artifact makes it possible in numerous cases to answer DR questions. However, this is not always possible. The designer may then try to find the information looked for in the DR. This is what we call an opportunistic use of a document.

This kind of use could have been expected if we had related the use of DR with the use of manuals, guidelines, written instructions, etc. Indeed, several user studies (e.g., [4]) reported that users usually prefer to act before reading any documentation. This is what seems to happen with our designers.

No other study could have prepared us to observe the opposite way of using the DR, which we call an extensive use.

The extensive use of DR

All three engineers, and two of them more significantly, began to analyze the blueprints, then looked for information in the DR, and based their understanding of the design on an extensive reading of the DR. By extensive reading, we mean the attempt to understand each issue reported inside the document, one after the other. However, we also noted that these designers rarely used the DR alone: regularly, they went back to the blueprints. In doing so, they expressed not only the need for visualizing the chosen option referred to in the DR, but also their desire to make their own judgement. The following extract illustrates this sequence of behaviors:

D: (reading a DR question) "*How can we reduce the vibrations at the DAAV level?"...first option "Design with DIAS"...ok, but it does not satisfy the weight criteria Right. "New design of the high level without DIAS"* (*this is the second option*) *... ok ...could we look at the blueprints now* (turning towards the blueprints) *...Ah ok, so here, the bottom of the ferrule comes under the DAAV, doesn't it ?* (*this structural item explains how it is possible to reduce vibrations and weight at the same time by comparison with the previous design*).

DS : *Yes, that's it.*

In contrast to the opportunistic use, an extensive reading of the DR then mainly implies the following behavioral pattern: from DR to blueprints, or in other words, from design reasoning to the solution.

Note that for designers who extensively read the DR, a paper format of the DR might be more appropriate than a computerized format.

Discussion: An explanation of why designers use the DR differently

We asked one engineer why he seemed to prefer reading the DR over a deeper analysis of the blueprints. He commented: "With the blueprints, I can only notice that the new design is different from the previous one. But to understand why and to assess the results of the project, I need to know the problems raised by the previous design. This document (the DR) provides such information." This comment suggests that some designers will use the DR not just as a punctual provider of information, but more significantly as a support for their reasoning. However this comment does not account for those designers who do not express the need to extensively read the DR, except if we consider that those designers have some *contextualization capacities* that others do not. By contextualization capacities, we mean the cognitive ability to create a context of information that will help in understanding and assessing a design. In fact, this is what we observed: the three designers who developed an opportunistic use of the DR found out by themselves (i.e., without reading the DR) numerous problems raised by the previous design once they knew the specific requirements for the new design; they evoked many alternatives, which helped them to make some comparisons with the presented design; and they constructed their own explanations of the choices made by deducing some possible criteria used by the project team. Probably because they were more experienced, and certainly because they were used to working on initial phases of projects where it is usual to search for and to balance many alternatives, they were able to provide by themselves a context sufficient to interpret the design rationales.

However, it is also important to stress the fact that the reasons found by these more experienced designers were not always right, even if they were satisfied by them[1]. This reveals that designers do not look for the *real reasons* for design decisions: finding out *some good reasons* seems sufficient. This also explains the fact that some designers rarely consult the DR, even if they are interested in the design rationales.

All these considerations lead us to revise our initial assumptions about DR documents: it is not because such documents (whether paper or electronic) are available that they will be consulted, even if they contain information needed by designers!

Our approach to circumvent this difficulty, at least partially, consists in including some facts which make up the design rationale such as comments on the blueprints (or any representation of the solution). Such an approach assumes that the documentation specialist will be able to select the important facts from the sets of facts composing the DR. It also assumes that designers will use an interface that offers them the possibility of hiding or showing the DR comments.

[1] Note that the incorrect inference of the DR may lead designers to wrong conclusions. For instance, the observed designers sometimes came to the conclusion that other alternatives were better, while this was not the case. This is actually one of the main problems that has motivated our study: when designers have to reuse a previous design, and do not have access to the corresponding DR, they often figure out one alternative which seems preferable; they then elaborate on this alternative, sometimes for one or two months before discovering that it presents a major drawback. At the same time, they understand the rationale of the previous design, and sometimes come back to it!

5. DO WE SUCCEED IN CAPTURING THE RATIONALES LOOKED FOR BY DESIGNERS?

In order to evaluate the usefulness of DR documents, it is necessary to compare the designers' questions with the content of these documents. Indeed, it will be possible to claim that DR is useful only if designers' questions can be answered by such documents.

To address this issue, we accounted for the DR questions expressed by the designers that were answered by the DR. We considered that a designer's DR question was answered by the DR either if the designer found an answer in it, or if we provided him/her with a verbal answer which existed in the document. Seventy six DR questions were identified in this way.

We found that *41%* of the designers' DR questions (31 out of 76) were answered by the DR. In addition, we noticed that this result did not significantly vary according to the designers' competence (43% for the technicians, 38% for the engineers).

These results alone are difficult to judge: for some, they may be viewed as a good result, because nothing existed before! For others, they may be considered as insufficient. To better assess these results, an analysis of the causes explaining why some DR questions were not answered by the DR was performed.

Analyzing the discrepancy between DR questions and the DR captured

Four categories of causes were identified, each one including different types of causes (see table 1):

Types of cause	Frequency of occurrence
1. Causes related to the analysts:	*14*
- Known justifications not reported	10
- Known issues not reported	2
- Known criteria not reported	2
2. Causes related to the QOC method:	*1*
- Lack of weighted assessments	1
3. Causes related to the readers:	*19*
- Misconceptions	12
- Inappropriate questions (Need for formal proofs)	7
4. Causes related to the project team:	*11*
- Issue not handled	2
- Criteria not taken into account	2
- Option not considered	4
- Lack of global assessment	3

Table 1. *The causes and their frequencies explaining the discrepancy between designers' DR questions and the content of the DR document*

1. *Causes related to the DR analysts*: 14 designers' questions were not answered because the analysts had not reported some facts, even though these facts were discussed during the design meetings recorded. Looking at these facts more closely, we found that some of them were not reported because the analysts had simply forgotten to report them. Others were not reported because the analysts might decide, not always consciously, that given information was not important, because given the current state of design elaboration, it was not essential. For instance, during the project, the designers had decided to elaborate one alternative among three, simply because they wanted to quickly test one idea, and not because this alternative was judged better than the other ones; however, at the end of the first phase of the project, only this alternative was elaborated, and during the evaluation meetings, the designers were provided only with the blueprints of this solution. Some of them asked why. We knew the answer, but it was not reported in the DR. In short, for different reasons related to the analyst, some known facts may not be included in the DR document. This observation may induce two opposite reactions: one may want to reduce this number, for instance by asking the analyst to be more "rigorous", or by introducing more controls in the DR elaboration. We believe that such an approach will be inadequate. Indeed, one has to note that, because it was the first time that we tried to capture the DR, we were as "rigorous" as

possible. Introducing more controls does not seem to be the solution either: we did ask the project team to review the DR document after each new meeting; this team was also motivated by the fact that it was the first time that such an experiment was attempted within the company. However, these review meetings also were not sufficient to ensure the completeness of our document.

Considering these arguments, another reaction is possible: we need to introduce an *iterative approach* to DR capture. We believe that a DR document must be conceived as something unfinished at the end of a project. This document should be improved with the questions raised by its subsequent use. This improvement process should be centralized at the level of the DR analyst: he/she should receive the designers' questions, then answer them, and at the same time decide if some facts need to be added to the existing documents or not. If a computer tool is introduced to access the design rationale, this means that we must provide the user with the possibility of asking questions and receiving answers through the system (electronic mail for instance).

2. *Causes related to the QOC method*: the only problem noticed with QOC concerned its relative inability to represent weighted evaluation (X is better than Y according to criteria Z). Actually, it is possible with the use of link-thickness, but readers often fail to correctly interpret it. As a consequence, it was not possible to answer questions like "According to criteria Z, is X or Y better?" Some authors (e.g., [11]) claim that this kind of information is necessary, and include it as a requirement for DR capture support tools. However, because this problem was noticed only once in our study, we did not decide to modify our original notation.

3. *Causes related to the readers*: this category contains the highest number of questions unanswered (19 out of 45 in all). It includes two different types of cause:

- *readers' misconceptions*: most of the time, a DR question based on a misconception has no DR answer. For instance, a question such as "Why did they change the whole structure?" has no answer if only some parts of the whole structure were changed. The most frequent misconceptions encountered in our data were due either to a misundertanding of the artifact structure (4/12), a misunderstanding of the artifact functions (3/12), an incomplete or incorrect knowledge of the previous design (2/12), or facts learned during the meeting that were forgotten (2/12). It is important to note that misconceptions represent one factor that contributes to making wrong decisions in design, especially when a designer has to choose between different alternatives. These misconceptions were often not due to a lack of information, but to an incomplete analysis of the blueprints provided. We then believe that these misconceptions will always exist, because it is difficult to change the way people work in their daily settings. If we accept this statement, we must look for mechanisms of detection and correction of these misconceptions. One possible approach that we choose to explore further consists in taking advantage of the internal network of the company. We have said that designers should be able to ask questions directly to the DR analyst. The analyst will then be able to correct some designers' misconceptions.

- the problem of *inappropriate questions* is specific to our study. Because the design presented was only the result of the first phase of the project, several formal proofs (calculations) were not yet available. The designers may ask for these formal proofs if they are not convinced by the justifications provided in the DR. These questions are inappropriate, given the current state of design development. However, they are not inappropriate with respect to the designer's needs. As a consequence, we have learned from this observation that we will need to include in the DR the formal proofs that will be established later. These formal proofs will be represented as justifications of evaluations.

4. *Causes related to the project team*: this last category of causes is one of the most interesting, because it highlights that some claims concerning the benefits gained with a DR documentation rely on a false assumption (which we shared at the beginning of this study). It is common to think that a design *has* a rationale. This is what makes the idea of "capture" possible. Some authors (e.g., [12]) also promote the idea that the *design space* (i.e., the space of possibilities) can be analyzed by designers. All of these ideas have some limitations, because the space of possibilities is not fixed in time. Not only this space, which depends on the designers' background and experience, changes according to the designers involved in a project, but it also evolves with time (because technologies change, experience is growing, industrial strategies are different, etc.). This is what explains why some questions were not answered by the DR: some designers asked questions about issues, options or criteria not taken into account during the design. For instance, "why did they choose option X (reported in the DR) and not option Y (not handled during the project)?" It is then obvious that such questions have no answer in the DR, but it is also important to consider that it will never be possible to avoid such questions. Moreover, we can anticipate that the frequency of occurrence of this class of questions (currently 8/45) will increase, as the time goes by and designers' culture changes. We then speculate that long-term reuse of DR should be more problematic that short-term reuse.

In considering this problem, Terveen *et al.* [14] promoted the idea of a "living design memory". This approach consists of the creation of a design knowledge base and a design assistant program aimed at giving advice to the designer. The designer can accept or refuse the advice. The refused advice is discussed during a design review. These discussions may produce further knowledge which will be incorporated into the design knowledge base. This living approach to the design memory, while interesting, presents two limitations: firstly, Terveen *et al.*'s paper reports that many users still have problems with the current system; secondly, this approach radically changes the way designers are currently working. Designers at the design office where our study was conducted have rejected this approach for this reason.

Another possible approach exists, which acknowledges the intrinsic limitations of any memory system and develops a social approach to design memory [1]. According to this approach, the emphasis must be on dialogue in work settings, because it is there that people collectively (re)interpret past experience and control others' interpretations. Putting this approach into practice means giving the opportunity to designers to collaborate more easily and more often. CSCW applications may be a technical solution to this problem. However, they will not be sufficient. New work organizations must also be defined. We are currently attempting to put these ideas into practice at Aerospatiale.

6. CONCLUSION

The goal of this study was to evaluate how useful DR documents are. The analyses presented here are not sufficient to give a complete answer to this question, in particular because we did not investigate the potential difficulties for accessing pieces of information composing the DR. However, given that (1) more than half of the designers' questions concern DR, and (2) some designers extensively use the DR document as a support for understanding and assessing a previous design, (3) less than half of the designers' DR questions were answered with the QOC-based document, our first conclusion is that DR documents *should be useful*, at least for the designers who want to extensively read it, but *not sufficient*.

This study highlights that traditional approaches for capturing DR exhibit some limitations. Possible adaptations of these approaches are then necessary. In this paper, we have considered (1) the integration of the DR with the information currently processed by designers (in our case, this means integrating DR with blueprints), (2) the introduction of an iterative approach to the DR capture, going beyond the design period, and (3) the need to promote collaboration between designers.

ACKNOWLEDGMENTS

The author acknowledges support from Aerospatiale and the Ergonomics Laboratory of the CNAM (Paris) for funding this research. Thanks also to the design office team at Aerospatiale, Les Mureaux. This work was carried on while the author worked at EURISCO. Thanks to the EURISCO team, and more particularly to Martin Hollender, Helen Wilson, Guy Boy, and Markus Durstewitz, for their comments on the first drafts of this paper.

REFERENCES

1. Bannon L.J. and Kuutti K. *Shifting Perspectives on Organizational Memory: From Storage to Active Remembering.* IEEE Hawaii Inteernational Conference on System Sciences (HICSS'96), January 1996.

2. Boose, J.H., Bradshaw, J., and Shema D.B. Knowledge-based Design Rationale Capture: Automating Engineering Trade Studies. In: Green M. (Ed.) *Knowledge Aided Design*, NY: Academic Press, 1992.

3. Boy, G. Supportability-based design rationale. In *Proceedings of the 6th IFAC Symposium on Analysis, Design and Evaluation of Man-Machine Systems*, 1995.

4. Carroll, J.M. *The Nurberg Funnel: Designing minimalist instruction for practical computer skill.* Cambridge, MA: MIT Press, 1990.

5. Carroll J.M. and Moran T.P. (Eds.) *Human-Computer Interaction, Special Issue on Design Rationale*, 6(3&4), 1991.

6. Conklin, J.E. and Begeman, M.L. gIBIS: A Hypertext Tool for Exploratory Policy Discussion, *ACM Transactions on Office Information Systems*, 6,303-331, 1988.

7. Fischer, G., McCall, R. and Morch A.I. Design environments for constructive and argumentative design. In *CHI'89*, 1989.

8. Herbsleb, J.D., and Kuwana, E. Preserving Knowledge in Design Projects: What Designers Need to Know. *INTERCHI'93*, 1993.

9. Karsenty, L., and Brézillon, P. Cooperative problem solving and explanation. *Expert Systems with Application,* 8(4), 445-462, 1995.

10. Klein, M. Capturing Design Rationale in Concurrent Engineering Teams. *IEEE Computer*, 26(1), 39-47, 1993.

11. Lee J. and Lai K. What's in Design Rationale?. *Human-Computer Interaction*, 6(3&4), 251-280, 1991.

12. MacLean, A., Young, R.M., Bellotti, V. and Moran T.P., Questions, options and criteria: Elements of design space analysis, *Human-Computer Interaction*, 6(3&4), 201-250, 1991.

13. Shum S. & Hammond N., Argumentation-based design rationale: what use at what cost? *International Journal of Human-Computer Studies*, 40, 603-652, 1994.

14. Terveen, L.G., Selfridge, P.G. and Long, M.D. From "Folklore" to "Living Design Memory". In *INTERCHI'93*, 1993.

Systematic Design of Spoken Prompts

Brian Hansen, David G. Novick, Stephen Sutton
Center for Spoken Language Understanding
Oregon Graduate Institute of Science & Technology
20000 N.W. Walker Road
Beaverton, OR, 97006
brianh@jib.cse.ogi.edu, novick@cse.ogi.edu, sutton@cse.ogi.edu
(503) 690-1121

ABSTRACT

Designers of system prompts for interactive spoken-language systems typically seek 1) to constrain users so that they say things that the system can understand accurately and 2) to produce "natural" interaction that maximizes users' satisfaction. Unfortunately, these goals are often at odds.

We present a set of heuristics for choosing appropriate prompt styles and show that a set of dimensions can be formulated from these heuristics. A point (or region) in the space formed by these dimensions is a "style" for prompts. We develop and apply metrics for empirically testing different prompt styles. Finally, we describe a toolkit that automatically generates prompts in a variety of styles for spoken-language dialogues.

Keywords

Interaction design, auditory I/O, dialog analysis, design techniques, evaluation, toolkits

INTRODUCTION

Between the attainable practicality of command-based speech recognition and the elusive attraction of "natural" spoken-language interaction lies the growing use of spoken dialogue systems (SDSs). This middle ground includes applications such as the AT&T long-distance billing system, the OGI automated spoken questionnaire for the U.S. Census [6], and systems performing the ATIS travel information task [15]. These systems engage in relatively simple task-based dialogues, often expecting users' utterances to consist of a single word or a short phrase; they are analogous in complexity to graphical user interfaces (GUIs). Like GUIs, SDSs generally do not generate their output at run time; they instead use pre-specified phrases or templates as prompts. Development of these prompts is usually taken to be more art than science; to create the system's prompts, designers most often rely on expert intuition and tacit experience. But beyond intuition and experience we propose systematic methods for characterizing and generating spoken-dialogue prompts. In this paper, we present these methods and show their usefulness for developing effective SDSs. Although we concentrate on SDS development, these methods have a natural extension to the speech component of multimedia systems.

CHI 96 Vancouver, BC Canada
© 1996 ACM 0-89791-777-4/96/04..$3.50

For effective interaction, SDSs must rely on directive prompts [7] to increase user compliance with system requirements. The best intuitively-designed prompts serve two functions though: they not only constrain the user's response so that speech recognizers—all too fallible—stand a better chance of success, but also provide a feeling of "natural" dialogue for the user so that the overall interaction is not aversive. These two functions provide a basis for a more systematic approach to generation of prompts. From our own experiences in designing SDSs, we have developed a set of heuristics for designing system output. From these heuristics, we have further developed a framework for analyzing and designing prompts in terms of dimensions, features and styles.

Our interest in identifying dimensions of dialogue variation grew out of our need to translate a written questionnaire for the US Census (the 1990 Census Short Form) into a configuration usable with a SDS. The first problem we encountered was a proliferation of possible ways of structuring and phrasing census questions. For each written question, there seemed a nearly infinite variety of ways of expressing its underlying meaning to users. We needed a way to choose only a few representatives from the profusion of conceivable treatments; we could not test the effectiveness of every variation and needed to converge quickly on solutions better suited to SDS technology. Unfortunately we did not know, *a priori*, which solutions would be best. To ensure adequate performance of the speech recognition component of a SDS, while avoiding confusing or alienating users, we needed to find a way to characterize the "space" of ways to formulate questions, and to predict the results obtained by using prompts in different points of that space.

We derive a space of possible system prompts by first producing and analyzing heuristics offering different treatments, or *styles*, for handling various aspects of spoken interaction. These styles suggest several ways to present automated human-computer dialogues, with an emphasis on the ways of phrasing system prompts. By abstracting across the heuristics, we have identified a set of *features* associated with each style, and a set of *dimensions* covering and containing the feature set. A point in the space described by the dimensions is a "style" for prompts.

In this paper, we present a framework of heuristics, dimensions and styles for spoken dialogue prompts. We define the notion of a SDS's overall stylistic consistency. We outline metrics for empirically testing different prompt styles in terms of their effects on constraint of user speech and on user satisfaction, and briefly present results of our use of this approach. Finally, we describe a SDS toolkit we are developing that incorporates some of this framework in the automated generation of system prompts.

THE PROBLEM

Current speech recognition algorithms match the features of a speech signal with models of the features of known phonemes via a statistical process. One effect of this statistical matching is that recognition is probabilistic. In a GUI, only the set of relevant user actions are defined at any given moment. This is equivalent to imposing a vocabulary of legal actions. It is generally not possible to enforce the same rigid constraints in a spoken interface. Unfortunately, the need for a high-degree of recognition accuracy in speaker-independent speech recognition imposes the requirement that the words to be recognized come from a relatively small set of candidates. The overall effectiveness [8] of a SDS, then, is dependent upon the ability of dialogue designers to produce prompts that constrain users' possible responses. One of the subtleties of dialogue design lies in giving users a feeling of naturalness and freedom of response although underlying constraints exist.

In an ideal SDS, the naturalness and accuracy criteria would both be satisfied. Users would be free from artificial constraints on their use of vocabulary, grammar, or the interactional fluidity that characterize routine task-based human-human telephone speech. Unfortunately, this ideal is unrealistic given current technology [5,12,13]. Indeed, given the limitations inherent in current speech recognition technology and the need for near-perfect recognition accuracy, dialogue designers must often make compromises between accuracy and naturalness. While these criteria may sometimes agree on the best way to present system prompts, most often a tension exists between them.

We have used different versions of dialogues to refine our understanding of this tension. Consider, for example, a dialogue in which the system sought to elicit certain information from the user by asking only yes/no questions. Such an approach would likely be very accurate from a speech recognition standpoint, yet fairly unnatural and inappropriate for many situations. Determining a user's age by means of yes/no questions, for example, would most certainly be a laborious and unacceptable approach, unpleasant for the user and time-consuming for both user and system.

Finally, where limits of speech recognition technology force dialogue designers to adopt solutions that are not maximally pleasing or natural, it is essential that they have a clear understanding of the implications of the compromises they make. Only then are they in a position to take advantage of improvements in the accuracy and robustness of that technology as they become available.

HEURISTICS, DIMENSIONS AND STYLES

To advance the production of voice-response questionnaires from an *ad hoc*, mostly intuitive "craft" into more of an engineering discipline, we have developed a method using a set of heuristics for transforming [16] a written version of a questionnaire into a script (or protocol) for use with speech-recognition systems. From these heuristics, we then developed a systematic approach to the design of spoken prompts; this approach is based on defining a space of possible system prompts that can be described by a set of task-independent descriptive dimensions. We identify a set of fourteen dimensions of system prompts, and define a point in the space they form as a "style" for prompts.

Heuristics for Designing Dialogues

In designing prompts for the census task, we quickly saw that for each question there was a myriad of ways of expressing its underlying intent. To converge on a practical number of dialogue designs to test, we needed a principled way of deciding which, out of thousands of wording variations, we should use. One limiting factor for this particular project derived from the nature of the census task itself: we needed the spoken questionnaire to be as true to the original written form as possible in order to avoid distorting census results. This concern led us to examine ways of transforming the original written questionnaire into a form suitable for use with a SDS. One result of our investigation was a set of heuristics for translating from written to spoken media.

Associated with each heuristic are 1) a *pattern*, or a set of pre-conditions, specifying where the heuristic may be used; 2) a set of *styles* into which a question (or other aspect of the interaction) can be transformed; and 3) a discussion of the trade-offs between the styles. The discussions of the trade-offs constitute informal hypotheses about the effects of the different styles on the accuracy of speech recognition, the naturalness of the interaction, and the interaction's length. As an example, consider a heuristic applicable to multiple-choice questions (described below). This heuristic applies when transforming, from written to spoken form, questions involving a choice among three to six options. We have informally specified five different styles of structuring and phrasing such questions, and have analyzed their implications on speech recognition accuracy as well as their expected effect on the naturalness and length of the interaction.

The styles associated with each heuristic are representative samples, depicting not every way of phrasing or presenting prompts but rather a reasonable breadth of approaches. Although many of the heuristics are associated with the forms that questions may take, some are applicable to the interaction as a whole or to a particular aspect of interaction, such as ways of accomplishing turn-taking. Multiple heuristics may apply to a single prompt and, in the case of heuristics describing the re-structuring of complex questions, may be cascaded; one heuristic may partially break down the question while another may finish the translation.

We developed these heuristics in order to provide a principled starting point for an iterative dialogue design prototyping effort, but their value is not limited to this particular usage. In general, the prompt heuristics have several important uses, including:

- developing designs for a set of initial dialogues,
- categorizing existing dialogues,
- testing hypotheses about the effectiveness and naturalness of different styles, and
- implementation via rapid prototyping toolkits.

In our efforts, these heuristics have been useful for reducing the expected user vocabulary, reducing the effects of user intonation, mitigating the reduced level of system's understanding and interactive abilities, and compensating for the loss of visual access to the written form (including the ability to scan ahead) [3]. Perhaps the greatest benefit of this framework is that it encourages an empirical approach to dialogue design. By making and testing predictions about the effects of various styles, we can reject inappropriate dialogue styles and reduce the dialogue designer's reliance on intuition and hand-crafting.

The following sections describe individual heuristics we devised in the course of the census project. In many cases the styles associated with a heuristic are presented as hypothetical interactions between the system ("S") and a user ("U").

Questions Containing Presuppositions

Figure 1 depicts two different styles for dealing with questions containing presuppositions. Style 1.1 ignores the possibility of a question eliciting an unexpected response due to an invalid presupposition on the systems's part.

Style 1.1: S: What is your home phone number (including area code)?
U: I don't have a phone.

Style 1.2: S: Do you have a home phone number?
U: Yes.
S: What is your home phone number (including area code)?
U: <telephone number>

Figure 1: Questions containing presuppositions

Alternately, style 1.2, employs a "guard question" that reduces the difficulty of interpreting a response where the precondition does not hold. It also increases the length of the interaction, though it may be relevant for only a fraction of the cases encountered. In those cases, guard questions may reduce the chance of communication breakdown. In the context of a large number of yes/no questions, however, style 1.2 could become tedious for users.

Questions Eliciting Compound Answers

Figure 2 shows different styles of structuring questions to elicit compound, or multi-part, answers. Style 2.1 offers the fewest constraints as to how the user may answer and, if successful, is the quickest and most efficient. The lack of expressed constraints on the form of the expected reply may not be too damaging where a standard way of specifying the information is already well-established in the minds of most users. Style 2.2 breaks the question down into an explanatory sentence and several prompts, a pattern that style 2.3 takes one step further. The extreme of this approach would be to ask for each digit of the number separately, clearly an arduous task especially considering the costs of turn-taking. It is, however, likely to be the style having the highest recognition accuracy.

Style 2.1: S: What is your home phone number
U: 503...um... 690...

Style 2.2: S: We need to know your home phone number.
S: What is the area code?
U: 503
S: and the number?
U: <tel number>

Style 2.3: S: We need to know your home phone number.
S: What is the area code?
U: 503
S: and the exchange?
U: 226
S: and...

Style 2.4: S: We need to know your home phone number.
S: Please state the area code <pause> 3-digit exchange, and 4-digit...
U: 503 226 2...

Style 2.5: S: We need to know your home phone number. Please state your number, area code first.
U: 503
S: Mmm-hmm
U: 690
S: Yes.
U: 1121
S: 1121. Ok.

Figure 2: Questions eliciting compound answers

Style 2.4, like style 2.3, specifies each component the user is expected to provide, sharing with style 2.3 the danger of confusing people unfamiliar with the notion of a telephone "exchange" or, more generally, the names of the individual components. Style 2.4 encourages the user, however, to supply all components within a single turn at speech. The need to forestall extended repair sub-dialogues may require that the system offer acceptances [4] of users' utterances after the components of multi-part answers are received. Style 2.5 depicts such a case in which the system provides feedback in the form of acknowledgments and echoing [2,10].

Questions Involving Choice Between Two Options

The heuristic depicted in Figure 3 describes the different ways of asking questions where only two responses are expected (for example "Are you male or female?"). Style 3.1 invites uncooperative users to answer "Yes" or "No", especially if minimal or non-intuitive intonation is used in presenting the question. This may require a clarifying repair sub-dialogue perhaps employing a style-3.2 type interaction.

Style 3.2 increases the number of interactions required in the average case, subsequently increasing the survey time overall. Further, if the two options are truly mutually exclusive, users, recognizing the overall intent of the series of questions, and volunteer the answer to the underlying question (e.g., U: "No, I'm a B."), or worse (U: "If I said I wasn't female, then what else could I be but male?"). In both cases the variety and complexity of expressions that must be recognized are greatly increased.

Style 3.1: S: A or B?
U: B

Style 3.2: S: A?
U: No.
S: B?
U: Yes.

Style 3.3: S: A?
U: No.
S: Then B, correct?
U: Yes/No.

Figure 3: Questions involving choice between two options

Questions Involving Choice Among Three to Six Options
Figure 4 depicts a heuristic for multiple choice questions having more than two but still only a few alternatives. We judge that among the different treatments, style 4.1 is somewhat less natural than styles 4.2 and 4.3. This is especially true for questions having stereotypical answers (E.g. "What's your marital status?" "Single"). It is slightly less natural than Style 4.2, because a human operator can compensate for the user's not mentioning an option name directly and can either interpret a response as indicating a category, or can move toward a Style 4.3 interaction if necessary. While style 4.1 may be expected to elicit more constrained responses, it may suggest that the user cannot be trusted to recognize the choices, an indication that may appear to be insulting or condescending if obvious choices are spelled out.

Style 4.1: S: <ask question, give options>
U: <option-name>

Style 4.2: S: <ask question without giving options>
U: <option-name>

Style 4.3: <transform question into series of sub-questions (a decision tree) having yes/no answers>

Style 4.4: <for each option, ask if it is the case>

Style 4.5: Similar to style 3, except when number of options is reduced to 2-3, ask for the option-name

Figure 4: Questions involving choice among three to six options

Style 4.2 constrains the response the least (e.g., S: "What is your current marital status?") and would therefore be presumed to elicit answers having greater variability (U: "I've been living with X for..."), again tending to reduce recognition accuracy.

Style 4.4 takes the longest to achieve but does employ only yes/no questions, as does style 4.3. Both invite the user to anticipate the line of reasoning implied by the sequence and to volunteer the response that the sequence of questions suggests, increasing variability and reducing recognition accuracy.

Style 4.5 may be a good compromise between styles 4.1 and 4.3, allowing recognition of only a few keywords at any one time, without the rigidity of a strict binary tree style.

Questions Involving Choice Among More Than Six Options
The analysis here is similar to that for styles presented in the previous section except that with more choices the problems become more severe. Use of style 4.1 for more than six options may put a severe strain on the user's short-term memory, while style 4.2 may leave the user even more adrift as to what exactly constitutes a proper answer. The decision tree of style 4.3 becomes deeper, though not so quickly as the option-checking sequence of style 4.4, which becomes clearly unnatural as the number of options increases.

Style 5.1: <reduce problem to fewer options and include "other", then use more choice-constrained heuristics, in the case of "other", either store what the user says for later interpretation, or ask the same question with the next group of options>

Style 5.2: S: <ask question, give explanation of n-at-a-time style, loop through the options n at a time>
U: <option name, or special phrases for user initiated repair>

Figure 5: Questions involving choice among more than six options

Figure 5 shows two more styles that may be useful in cases where there are a large number of options. Style 5.1 is quite similar to style 4.5, with 5.1's "other" serving to help control the flow of the dialogue. In style 5.1 and 5.2, recognition of the word "other" must already be in place. Using style 5.1, the overall gains in automation may be reduced by requiring human interpretation.

Encouraging Brief Answers
Figure 6 shows three different styles for eliciting brief, concise answers.Of these, style 6.1 is quick and formal, though not particularly "friendly," and is likely to evoke a

Style 6.1: Give "telegraphic" questions. For example,
S: Date of birth?

Style 6.2: Explicitly state what information is wanted, and what form it should take as a parenthetical to the question. for example,
S: "We now ask about your date of birth. Please say the month, the day and then the year or your birth."

Style 6.3: Phrase question "naturally" and hope user provides a short, appropriate response. For example,
S: "What is your date of birth?"

Figure 6: Encouraging brief answers

reasonably focussed response. Style 6.2 takes longer but is likely to elicit fewer open-ended responses. It is also likely to be frustrating for expert users. Style 6.3 is most natural in presentation but does little to constrain the response. Style 6.3 might require increasing the coverage of grammar to accommodate more verbose or non-standard responses, thereby decreasing recognition accuracy

Other Heuristics
In this section we briefly describe some additional heuristics that serve to illustrate the breadth and utility of this approach. In particular, we sketch the expected trade-offs of using:

- different techniques for turn-taking
- more or less explanatory text in prompts,
- human versus computer voice,
- different personas (such as a spokesperson or, in the case of the census, a particular census taker),
- faster or slower rate of speech, and
- stronger or weaker confirmation requirements after giving user information.

It is difficult, using current speech recognition methods, to accurately gauge when a user has finished his or her turn at speech. Moreover, it is difficult to provide timely feedback to the user as to whose turn it is. We have identified at least three possible implementations of turn-taking. If the system employs "natural" intonation patterns to signal end-of-turn, it may encourage users to encode information in intonation, possibly causing misunderstanding. If it relies only on illocutionary expectations, the dialogue may be vulnerable to communication breakdowns following turn confusion. If it uses beeps or other tone patterns to indicate turn completion, it may require some explanation to the user, increasing the number of utterances made by the system.

For questions that require prior explanations, there are two general styles: 1) provide as short an explanation as possible, or 2) provide longer explanations. Longer or more frequent explanatory text describing the intent of the question or the form of the expected answer tends to increase the output time and the output vocabulary. Increasing the output vocabulary may serve to entrain users into believing the system is able to recognize a large vocabulary, leading them to use out-of-vocabulary keywords or complex grammatical constructs.

In the case of the system's voice (either recorded human or computer synthesized), we expect to find that users react negatively to the use of synthesized speech. Not only is such technology not "natural," but often difficult for human hearers to understand. We expect, however, that users provide more concise answers when prompted by a synthesized voice. In the course of developing the census system, this heuristic was tested [11] with mixed results.

Related to system voice is the choice of the persona within which the system interacts [9]. Although we make no clear prediction as to the effects of varying the persona on speech recognition accuracy, the choice of persona may affect users' acceptance of the system. Different personas in our case included the government, a census taker, or a spokesperson. In the census project, the system persona was an anonymous census enumerator.

An area not explicitly tested in the census project was to vary the rate of speech of the system voice. On one hand, we predict that faster speech may be more compelling but entrains users to use faster speech in response, possibly degrading speech recognition accuracy. A slower rate of speech, on the other hand, may increase user frustration and lead to users interrupting (or "barging in on") the system voice, again degrading recognition accuracy.

Finally, as the census project was concerned primarily with asking questions, we did not develop extensive heuristics addressing how best to convey information to, or answer questions of, the users. Where the objective is primarily to convey information to the user, the quickest style for presenting information would be simply to present it and go on to the next stage of the dialogue. If it were critical that the information be understood, the system might ask for confirmation and go on if confirmed. Alternately, if the system detected silence or sounds indicating that the user was uncertain or did not understand, it could present the information again or inquire as to possible sources of misunderstandings.

Dimensions of Prompts
Although the heuristics described above were useful in the initial stages of our project, they still did not capture what we term the dimensions of spoken prompts. By examining the ways in which styles varied within a single heuristic, we were able to identify different "features" that characterized the various styles. By examining features used in different heuristics, we distinguished which features were in opposition. These mutually exclusive features formed points within a single dimension.

The dimensions may be thought of as naming a way of varying a system prompt. The dimension *PreExplanation*, for example, denotes the degree to which the intent behind the prompt is described to the user before the question is actually given. Although in this case, as in many of the other dimensions, a whole continuum could be imagined, we often limited our analysis to polar opposites (e.g. *+PreExplanation* and *-PreExplanation*). In other cases, such as *Decomposition*, ordering the points within the dimension was less clear.

By revisiting the various styles for each of the heuristics, we identified a set of dimensions characterizing the phrasing of system prompts. These dimensions include the following ten:

- *PreExplanation*. Should preparatory text be included before posing the question(s)?
- *Terse*. Should the question be posed as tersely as possible?
- *ListOptions*. Should we list the set of words from which we expect an answer?
- *CompoundQuestion*. Should we break the question down into its component parts or leave it as one question?

- *Polite.* Should the question be phrased politely [9]?
- *Decomposition.* Should we break down the selection from a list of options into a decision tree, a partial decision tree, a decision list, or not at all?
- *AllowOther.* Should we formulate the question so as to allow the user to specify "other" as an option?
- *Indirection.* Should we ask the question indirectly (for example "Could you spell that?) or should we require that questions be posed directly, perhaps as commands (for example, "Please spell that.")?
- *GiveOptionName.* Should we mention the "name", or topic, of the information desired (for example "Are you married or single" does not mention "marital status")?
- *GuardQuestion.* Should we ask initial questions to rule out incorrect presuppositions?

In addition, we also identified a number of dimensions characterizing the interaction as a whole, including:

- *Voice* (human or synthesized),
- *Intonation* (minimal or natural),
- *Persona*, and
- *Turn-taking cues.*

In total, these dimensions define a fourteen-dimensional space of system prompts.

Dialogue Styles

Having defined the dimensions of spoken prompts in terms of the features of styles, we can now define more formally the concept of a style as being a collection of points within a number of dimensions. Since each style within a heuristic uses only a few of the identified dimensions, a style can be described as a *region* in the space of possible ways of expressing prompts. Figure 8 shows different styles (described in terms of features) for eliciting the user's marital status. Again, not all dimensions are explored equally. Instead, we examine those regions in the space of system prompts that best suit the needs of our dialogue evaluation effort.

One of the advantages of using styles defined in terms of features is that it allows us to characterize the *overall* style of the interaction rather than limiting our analysis to identifying the style of a single prompt. We thus define overall stylistic consistency of a SDS as the property of a dialogue in which the styles associated with each prompt do not conflict.

EVALUATING DIALOGUE STYLES

In our development of the census dialogue model, we went through several iterations of dialogue design, using up to four competing designs in a test of which worked best. In order to converge quickly on reasonable solutions, we started by identifying criteria that the various dialogue models should meet. In particular, we considered potential dialogues that were (a) closest to original form, (b) most constrained, (c) most "natural", (d) clearest to the hearer, (e) tersest, (f) most polite, (g) most open-ended, and (h) most recognizable. By identifying the features that best

Style 1: (+Terse, -PreExplanation, -ListOptions)
S: Marital status?

Style 2: (+Terse, -PreExplanation, +ListOptions)
S: Marital status? Now married, widowed, divorced, separated, or never married?

Style 3: (-Terse, -PreExplanation, +ListOptions)
S: What is your marital status, now married, widowed, divorced, separated, or never married?

Style 4: (+PartialDecisionTree, -Terse, +GiveOptions, -PreExplanation)
S: Are you now married (yes or no)?
if no, then
S: Have you ever been married (yes or no)?
if yes, then
S: Were you widowed, divorced or separated (please say one)?

Style 5: (+PreExplanation, +ListOptions, -Terse, +GiveOption)
S: The next question will determine your marital status. The categories are: now married, widowed, divorced, separated, and never married. What is your marital status?

Figure 7: Examples of styles for marital status question

met each criterion, we were able to characterize the region in the space of dialogue prompts best suiting our needs.

The iterative approach required us to produce a method for assessing the merit of each design as a basis for further refinement. We addressed this problem from two perspectives: accuracy of recognition and naturalness of interaction. To evaluate our dialogue designs we used an objective measure of the conciseness of users' responses in combination with a subjective measure of naturalness as reflected in users' feedback to evaluation questions. Together these metrics supplied grounds for making a wide range of dialogue design decisions, including evaluating candidate styles. In addition, these evaluation metrics provided a means to test the predictions made by our heuristics. These predictions effectively narrowed the search space of subsequent prompt refinements.

We now briefly present a behavioral coding scheme, a subjective evaluation metric, and some results from using our approach to dialogue development for the census system.

Behavioral Coding Scheme

The need to refine our system prompts so as to elicit only the most concise and recognizable user responses led us to develop a behavioral coding scheme (BCS) as an evaluation metric [11]. The BCS is used to characterize a user's utterance into one of eleven classes. Each class has an associated code which is used to label users' responses during transcription. Table 1 provides a summary of the behavioral coding scheme showing the eleven response classes, a brief description of each, and an example system prompt and user response.

The BCS can characterize a set of utterances; the distribution of BCS codes associated with responses to a given question in different treatments, or regions of the space of dialogue prompts, can be used as a basis for evaluation. For example, suppose we have three candidate prompt styles and wish to select the one that is the most constraining. First, we collect data for the three prompt styles, then label these data according to the BCS. Comparing the frequency of class "Adequate Answer 1" for the three styles shows which style elicited the most constrained responses.

Subjective Evaluation Questions

Given the potential trade-off between recognition accuracy and naturalness of interaction, reliance on the BCS as our sole criterion when designing prompts might lead us to dialogues that were very effective from the standpoint of eliciting highly recognizable responses but rather awkward or frustrating for users. We balance the behavioral coding evaluation of prompt styles with feedback from users. We solicited this feedback through evaluation questions presented at the end of the questionnaire providing users the opportunity to express their likes and dislikes regarding any aspect of the dialogue, including question topics, the wording of prompts, and the manner in which the prompts were presented.

Results of Evaluations

We used the behavioral coding scheme (and its predecessor versions), task completion rates, and responses to evaluation questions in three formal rounds of dialogue development in the Census project. The first round (based on roughly 100 callers) involved comparisons of the strongest differences among three overall styles. Our evaluation enabled us to pursue only those designs that elicited constrained answers and were generally acceptable to users.

Subsequent rounds focused on increasingly smaller differences among dialogue styles and thus required greater numbers of respondents. By round three (involving nearly 4000 callers) the differences between proposed dialogue designs were quite small and concise (AA1) responses were elicited over 90 percent of the time for all census questions.

DEPLOYMENT OF STYLES IN CSLURP TOOLKIT

The styles developed in the census project are proving useful in a broad range of applications. As part of on-going research in SDSs we have incorporated the notion of dialogue style into a toolkit [1] for creating spoken-language applications. This toolkit provides state-of-the-art speaker- and vocabulary-independent spoken-language recognition technology allowing developers to design, test and deploy spoken language interfaces rapidly for useful (real world) applications. The toolkit greatly simplifies the process of specifying a SDS by use of the Center for Spoken Language Understanding's rapid prototyper (CSLUrp), a graphically-based SDS authoring environment. CSLUrp currently provides a small set of style templates which a developer may use to generate a prompt. A corresponding template is displayed and slots in the template are filled with current vocabulary items.

If, for example, a dialogue designer were given the task of developing an automated pizza-ordering system, and needed to generate a prompt to elicit the size of pizza the user wanted, they would first specify the vocabulary to be recognized (small, medium, or large). He or she would then specify the style to be used in expressing the question (Polite1, Polite2, or Terse). CSLUrp would then generate a

Response Class	Description	System prompt	User response
Adequate Answer 1	Answer is concise and responsive.	Have you ever been married?	Yes
Adequate Answer 2	Answer is usable but not concise.	Have you ever been married?	No I haven't
Adequate Answer 3	Answer is responsive but not usable.	Have you ever been married?	Unfortunately
Inadequate Answer 1	Answer does not appear to be responsive.	What is your sex, female or male?	Neither
Inadequate Answer 2	User says nothing at all.	What is your sex, female or male?	<silence>
Qualified Answer	User expresses uncertainty in an otherwise adequate answer.	What year were you born?	Nineteen fifty five I think
Request for Clarification	User requests clarification as to the meaning of a concept or survey question.	Are you black, white or other?	What do you mean?
Interruption	User interrupts the speaking of the question.	What year were you born?	*teen fifty five
Don't Know	User responds "I don't know" or equivalent.	Are you black, white or other?	I'm not sure
Refusal	User refuses to answer.	What year were you born?	I'm not telling you
Other	User behavior not captured by the above codes	What year were you born?	Thirt... <noise>

Table 1: Summary of behavioral coding scheme

prompt incorporating both the vocabulary words and the style specification. Table 2 shows the prompts generated in this case. After the prompt has been generated, the designer is free to modify the text to better serve the situation. Although its implementation of our framework is incomplete, the repertoire of styles provided by CSLUrp has been used in the development of a variety of SDSs, including e-mail browsers, ordering and other form-filling systems, and even games.

Style	Generated prompt
Polite1	Please choose one of the following options: small, medium or large.
Polite2	Please say: small, medium or large.
Terse	Small, medium or large?

Table 2: CSLUrp generated prompts

CONCLUSION

In this paper we have presented a set of heuristics describing different styles of transforming a written questionnaire into a form usable with a SDS. We have identified a set of features that characterize these styles and a set of dimensions that cover and contain the feature set. Taken together, the fourteen dimensions we have presented define a space of system prompts. We refine the notion of "style" as being a set of features characterizing a prompt. Alternately, we define a prompt style as being a region in a space of prompts.

In order to evaluate the degree to which different prompt styles constrain users' responses while maintaining a sense of natural interaction, we have devised a behavioral coding scheme. Additionally, we have sketched our initial efforts at incorporating prompt styles in a rapid-prototyping toolkit.

Scope for further integrating dimensions into the dialogue design process, especially during prompt specification and dialogue critiquing, offer promising areas for further research. It is our hope that others will find this framework helpful, and we invite dialogue designers to develop their own heuristics, features, dimensions, and styles.

ACKNOWLDEGMENTS

This research was funded by the U.S. Bureau of the Census, U S WEST, the Office of Naval Research, the National Science Foundation, ARPA and the OGI CSLU.

REFERENCES

1. Colton, D., Cole, R., Novick, D., & Sutton, S. A laboratory course for designing and testing spoken dialogue systems, Proceedings of ICASSP-96, Atlanta, GA, May, 1996 (in press).
2. Clark, H. & Brennan, S. Grounding in communication, *Shared Cognition: Thinking as Social Practice*, APA Books (1991).
3. Clark, H. & Marshall, C. Definite reference and mutual knowledge, *Elements of Discourse Understanding*, Cambridge University Press, 1981, 10-63.
4. Clark, H. & Shaefer, E. Contributing to Discourse, *Cognitive Science*, **13** (1989), 259-294.
5. Cole, R., Hirschman, L., et al. *Workshop on Spoken Language Understanding, 1992*, Technical Report CSE92-014, Department of Computer Science and Engineering, Oregon Graduate Institute, 1992.
6. Cole, R., Novick, D.G., Burnett, D., Hansen, B., Sutton, S. & Fanty, M. Towards automatic collection of the U.S. Census, *Proceedings of the 1994 International Conference on Acoustics, Speech and Signal Processing* (1994), I:93-96.
7. Kamm, C. User interfaces for voice applications, *Voice Communications between Humans and Machines*, National Academy Press, 1994, 422-442.
8. Marshall, C., & Novick, D. G. Conversational effectiveness in multimedia communications, *Information, Technology & People*, **8** (1) (1995), 54-79.
9. Nass, C. Steuer, J. & Tauber, E.R. Computers are social actors, *Proceedings of Computer Human Interaction* (1994), 72-78.
10. Novick, D. & Hansen, B. Mutuality strategies for reference in task-oriented dialogue, *Twente Workshop on Language Technology, Corpus-Based Approaches to Dialogue Modeling* (TWLT 9), Enschede, The Netherlands (June, 1995), 83-93.
11. Novick, D.G., Sutton, S., Vermeulen, P. & Fanty, M. *Rapid design and deployment of spoken dialogue systems*, Technical Report CSLU95-008, Department of Computer Science and Engineering, Oregon Graduate Institute, 1995.
12. Rudnicky, A., Hauptmann, A. & Lee, K. Survey of current speech technology, *Communications of the ACM* (March 1994), **37**(3), 52-57.
13. Schmandt, C. *Voice communication with computers*, Van Nostrand Reinhold, 1994.
14. Sutton, S., Hansen, B., Lander, T., Novick, D.G. & Cole, R. *Evaluating the effectiveness of dialogue for an automated spoken questionnaire*, Technical Report CSE95-12, Department of Computer Science and Engineering, Oregon Graduate Institute, 1995.
15. Ward, W. The CMU Air Travel Information Service: Understanding spontaneous speech, *Proceedings of the DARPA Speech and Natural Language Workshop* (1990), 127-129.
16. Yankelovich, Levow, G & Marx, M. Designing SpeechActs: Issues in speech user interfaces, *Proceedings of Computer Human Interaction* (1995), 369-376.

MailCall: Message Presentation and Navigation in a Nonvisual Environment

Matthew Marx* and Chris Schmandt
groucho@media.mit.edu, geek@media.mit.edu
Speech Research Group, MIT Media Laboratory
E15-252, 20 Ames St., Cambridge, MA 02139

ABSTRACT
MailCall is a telephone-based messaging system using speech recognition and synthesis. Its nonvisual interaction approaches the usability of visual systems through a combination of intelligent message categorization, efficient presentation, and random-access navigation. MailCall offers improved feedback, error-correction, and online help by considering the conversational context of the current session. Studies suggest that its nonvisual approach to handling messages is especially effective when the user has a large number of messages.

KEYWORDS: Auditory I/O, interaction design, mobile computing, speech recognition, speech interface design.

INTRODUCTION

The telephone is as an ideal remote access tool for those who need to keep abreast of incoming messages. Unlike laptop computers and PDAs, which can be unwieldy or difficult to connect to the network, the telephone is ubiquitous and necessarily networked. Smaller size and better networking capabilities will make PDAs increasingly attractive, especially because of their graphical user interfaces, but they will never be ideal in situations where the user's hands or eyes are busy, such as driving. Speech-driven messaging systems, however, will continue to be indispensable in such situations, which compose much of the mobile user's activity. Thus nonvisual systems are important both because of their current practicality over the telephone as well as the fundamental suitability of audio-only interaction to hands/eyes busy situations.

The nonvisual modality, however, introduces obstacles for the user interface designer. The slow, serial, and transient nature of speech makes finding important messages not only frustrating but also expensive if calling long-distance or from a cellular phone. Furthermore, a system that gives repetitive or superfluous feedback can feel mechanical and unfriendly.

* Currently affiliated with Applied Language Technologies: Cambridge Massachusetts, 617.225.0012.

CHI 96 Vancouver, BC Canada
© 1996 ACM 0-89791-777-4/96/04..$3.50

An effective nonvisual messaging system must support rapid access by giving an overview of the information space and supporting random access to individual messages. Feedback must be accordingly efficient and appropriate. Since, as will be discussed, these interactional demands exceed the capabilities of touch-tone input, speech recognition must be incorporated. Thus the system must wrestle with additional issues regarding helping users learn the command set as well as handling recognition errors.

This paper describes the design of MailCall, a telephone-based messaging system that supports in a nonvisual environment the flexible message access available in visual messaging systems. MailCall categorizes incoming messages by importance, summarizes categories, and allows random access. It also strives to meet user expectations of conversational interaction by customizing feedback according to conversational context, tracking recognition errors, and offering online help.

RELATED WORK

Phoneshell [6] offers telephone-based access via touch-tones to incoming messages as well as rolodex, calendar, news, weather, and traffic. Since many users receive dozens of messages a day, Phoneshell supports rule-based filtering to group messages into categories such as "important" and "mass mailings." The user is principally restricted to sequential navigation, however—either reading the next message or the previous one, and many find it tedious to process a long list of messages.

Chatter [4] used speech recognition to allow the user to retrieve email messages, send voice messages, look up information in a personal rolodex, place outgoing calls, and ask the location of other Chatter users. Messages were presented in order of relevance based on the user's past usage. Chatter used a sophisticated discourse model to track the conversation, although it did not handle recognition errors.

SpeechActs [9] combines the conversational style of Chatter with the broad functionality of Phoneshell, offering a speech interface to mail, calendar, stock quotes, and weather forecasts. SpeechActs improves upon sequential navigation by allowing the user to access messages by number (e.g., "read message 17"). Recognition errors are addressed by SpeechActs, which explicitly verifies requests that are irreversible (e.g., "delete message") and offers progressively more detailed assistance when the system fails to understand the user.

The Wildfire electronic assistant is a commercial system that screens and routes incoming calls, schedules reminders, and retrieves voice mail (but not email). Wildfire allows the user to sort messages, but navigation is chiefly sequential.

Phoneshell, Chatter, SpeechActs, and Wildfire all provide remote access to messages, but none of them offers interaction comparable to what users enjoy with a GUI mail reader. Phoneshell and Chatter prioritize messages but neither summarize them nor allow random access. SpeechActs scans message headers and allows the user to pick out a message by number, but remembering the number of a message adds to the user's cognitive load. Wildfire allows the user to ask if there are messages from people in the rolodex but does not summarize incoming messages and allow users to pick from them at random. To improve upon previous work, MailCall must support methods of finding important messages quickly without imposing excessive cognitive demands on the user.

MAILCALL

MailCall is a telephone-based messaging system that employs speech recognition for input and speech synthesis for output. It was developed on a Sun Sparcstation 20 under both SunOS 4.1.3 and Solaris, using the DAGGER speech recognizer from Texas Instruments and DECtalk for text-to-speech synthesis. Call control is facilitated by XTL, ISDN software from Sun Microsystems. The following paragraphs give a high-level summary of MailCall's behavior and capabilities; see [5] for a complete description of MailCall's functionality, recognition vocabulary, and software architecture.

Unified voice/text message retrieval. MailCall retrieves and categorizes incoming email and voice mail messages. The user can ask the sender, subject, arrival time, or recipients of any message. Audio attachments are processed and played as sound files, and email notification sent by the voice mail system acts as a pointer to the original voice message. Messaging is "unified" in that there is no differentiation by media; email and voice mail from the same person are grouped together.

Sending messages. The user can send a voice message in reply to any message, or to anyone in the rolodex. If the recipient is a local voice mail subscriber, it will be placed in the appropriate mailbox; if not, then it is encoded—available formats include MIME, NextMail, Sun, and uuencode—and sent as electronic mail. (Speech recognition is not yet accurate enough to transcribe without editing, so dictating replies to be sent as text is not supported.)

Voice Dialing. Instead of sending a voice message, the user may elect to place a call. If the person's phone number is available in the rolodex, MailCall uses it—and if there is both a home and work number, MailCall prompts the user to choose one or the other. If the phone number cannot be found, the user is prompted to enter it.

Usage Scenarios

MailCall is especially useful when the user has a long list of incoming messages or when time is short. In the first example, Pat is in a hurry trying to meet a deadline, waiting for Lynn to send a critical piece of information. MailCall enables Pat to check for it quickly.

MailCall: You have seven personal messages.
Pat: Is there anything from Lynn Smith?
MailCall: Sorry, no messages from Lynn Smith.
Pat: How about Renee Foster?
MailCall: Nothing from Renee Foster, either.
Pat: Good-bye.

In a second example, Pat calls up after a marathon afternoon meeting to find over 100 new messages. MailCall enables Pat to hear the most important ones first.

MailCall: Welcome to MailCall. Who's there?
Pat: It's Pat Peterson again.
MailCall: Pat Peterson, correct?
Pat: Correct.
MailCall: Hello, Pat. Please say your six-digit password.
Pat: 5-6-5-5-1-9.
MailCall: Hold on while I get your messages...Just a second...Okay! You have 16 timely messages, 33 personal ones, and 150 others.
Pat: Is there anything from Lynn Smith?
MailCall: Personal messages from Lynn Smith. Message 25 from Lynn Smith about "here's the information you requested."
Pat: When did that arrive?
MailCall: It arrived about three hours ago.
Pat: Send a reply.
MailCall: Record your message for Lynn Smith. Pause for several seconds when finished.
Pat: *Lynn, thanks for finally sending the info, but it was a bit too late. Let's try to coordinate a little better next time.*
MailCall: Got it. Review the message, send it, or cancel?
Pat: Send it.
MailCall: Did you say "send it"?
Pat: Yes.
MailCall: Sending your message. Please wait....... What now?
Pat: Go to my timely messages.
MailCall: Timely messages. I can read the summary, or you can start with the first one.
Pat: Read me the summary.
MailCall: You have a bunch from Chris Barry, a few from Mark Matthews, one each from Deb Cohen and Dominique Farnsworth, and many others.
Pat: Read me the ones from Mark Matthews.
MailCall: Messages from Mark Matthews. Message 5 from Mark Matthews about "can we meet?"
Pat: Let me hear it.
MailCall: (playing voice message) *Hey Pat, I've got a*

great new pyramid scheme I'd like to get you involved in. We'll make millions!

Pat: Delete it.
MailCall: Did you say to delete the message?
Pat: That's correct.
MailCall: Deleting message 5.
Pat: Go to my other messages.
MailCall: Other messages. Read the summary, or read the first header?
Pat: Read me the summary.
MailCall: You have an incredible number from Mail Delivery Subsystem, a few from Fran Tess, several from Joyce Ball, one from listserv@mit.edu, and several others.
Pat: Read the one from listserv at MIT dot e d u.
MailCall: Message 121 from listserv@mit.edu about "your request for privacywatch." You have been added to the privacywatch mailing list.
Pat: That's all for now.
MailCall: Did you say to hang up?
Pat: Yep.
MailCall: Pat, thanks for calling. Good-bye!

As the above examples demonstrate, MailCall enables the user to find important messages quickly. Its *organization* of incoming messages into categories makes it feasible to provide efficient *presentation*, which in turn affords effective *navigation* of the information space. Further, its attention to conversational context helps establish its credibility as a cooperative conversant. The next two sections describe MailCall's approach to nonvisual information management and its strategies for crafting conversation.

DESIGN CHALLENGE: NONVISUAL NAVIGATION

Retrieving messages over the phone is more cumbersome than with a GUI-based mail reader. With a visual interface, the user can immediately see what messages are available and access the desired one directly via point and click. In a nonvisual environment, however, a system must list the messages serially, and since speech is slow, care must be taken not to overburden the user with long lists of choices. Indeed, a recent empirical study of speech vs. GUI-based message retrieval [8] revealed that a major problem with the otherwise well-received speech interface was finding important messages. The following three sections describe how MailCall supports effective nonvisual messaging through a combination of intelligent filtering, efficient presentation, and random access navigation.

Information organization

A first step towards effective message management in a nonvisual environment is prioritizing and categorizing messages. Like other mail readers, MailCall filters incoming messages based on a user profile that contains a set of rules for assigning messages to various categories or deleting them entirely. Although rule-based filtering is powerful, writing rules to keep up with dynamic user interests can require significant user effort. We considered memory-based reasoning (as adopted by Chatter) to lighten the burden on the user, but decided against it since the associated learning curve can be too slow to capture quickly changing interests.

Our approach to finding important messages exploits the wealth of information that can be present in a desktop environment. The user's calendar, for instance, keeps track of timely appointments, and a record of email the user has sent suggests people from whom the user might be awaiting replies. MailCall exploits these information sources through a background process, CLUES, that scans various databases and automatically generates filtering rules. (For details on the mechanics of CLUES see [5]). The rules generated by CLUES are available to other applications, as well; both Phoneshell [6] and an HTML-based visual mail reader described in [5] utilize CLUES' filtering rules to categorize messages.

The rules generated by CLUES are integrated into an existing filtering system; thus the user can benefit from both static rules in the filtering profile and dynamic ones generated automatically by CLUES. Below are described several information sources and how CLUES uses them to prioritize messages. The elements that match entries in the information sources are printed in bold.

CALENDAR	
Monday	Tuesday
10am Motorola visit	visiting Sun all day
5pm leave for airport	fax: 415-555-5555
ROLODEX CARD 32 OF 89	
Name: Kim Silverstone	
Address: 25 Harshwood Way, Palo Alto CA 94306	
Phone: (415) 555-5555	
Email: ksilvers@eng.sun.com	
OUTGOING EMAIL	
To: geek@media.mit.edu *Subject: latest draft of paper*	
To: chi96@sigchi.acm.org *Subject: deadline extension?*	
OUTGOING PHONE CALLS	
dialed 215-555-5555 (Charles Hemphill)	
dialed 8-5956 (unknown)	

Figure 1: Various information sources available in the user's computing environment, including calendar, rolodex, and records of outgoing email and phone calls.

Calendar. Assuming an "interest window" of approximately two weeks ahead of the current date and a few days back, CLUES extracts salient items from calendar entries. Thus the following message is marked even though it was not addressed directly to the user.

From lad@media.mit.edu
To: demo-staff@media.mit.edu
Subject: visitors from **Motorola** delayed until 3:30

Email replies. CLUES scans the user's record of outgoing messages to see who might be sending a reply and what they might be replying about. For instance, CLUES would automatically mark the following message.

From **chi96@sigchi.acm.org**
Subject: Re: **deadline extension?**

Returned phone calls. Similarly, CLUES can detect when someone returns a call by correlating the user's record of outgoing phone calls—created when the user dials using MailCall, Phoneshell [6], or a desktop dialing utility—with the Caller ID number of voice mail. Our voice mail system sends the user email with the Caller ID of the incoming message. Thus, CLUES would mark the following:

From Operator <root@media.mit.edu>
Subject: Voice message from **8-5956**

Medium-independent filtering. Often, someone does not reply using the same medium; one may call in response to an email message or vice versa. After finding the email address of the person the user has called by cross-referencing the phone number in the rolodex, CLUES can mark an email reply to an outgoing phone call. In this example, CLUES marks the email message from Charles Hemphill since the user recently tried to call him.

From **hemphill@csc.ti.com** (Charles Hemphill)
Subject: I just got your voice mail; here's what I think

Geographic filtering. Business travelers often leave behind a phone number where they can be reached. CLUES correlates a phone number found in the calendar with the user's rolodex to produce a list of people who live in that area. (CLUES also keeps a small table of co-located area codes such as 408 and 415.) A message from any of those people is then marked under the assumption that the user might be trying to coordinate with them while in town. Hence, messages from those the user is visiting suddenly become important, as when the calendar has a fax number in an area code near where Kim Silverstone lives:

From **ksilvers@eng.sun.com**
Subject: Let's do lunch while you're in town!

Domain-based filtering. CLUES also extracts the domain names from the email addresses for the people the user has recently sent messages, presuming that messages from people at the same site may too be relevant. Since CLUES identified Kim Silverstone as someone whom the user might want to visit on Tuesday's trip, messages from anyone at the same domain are marked.

From smith@**eng.sun.com**
Subject: Kim Silverstone told me you're in town...

Isolating the important part of a domain name is nontrivial. Some people may receive email at one sub-domain (groucho@media-lab.media.mit.edu) but send from another (groucho@timpanogos.media.mit.edu). Some corporations are geographically distributed; *eng.sun.com* is in California, but *east.sun.com* is in Massachusetts. Others like *aol.com* are non-location specific, so they are useless for geographic filtering. CLUES prunes domain names as appropriate.

MailCall's categorization breaks up a long list of messages into several smaller lists, one of those being the messages marked by CLUES. Once the messages have been sorted into various categories, the user can jump from category to category in nonlinear fashion, saying "go to my personal messages" or "go back to my important messages."

Nonvisual presentation

Categorization of messages helps to segment the information space, but when there are many messages within a single category, the user again is faced with the challenge of finding important messages in a long list. Creating more and more categories merely shifts the burden from navigating among messages to navigating among categories, so the user must have a method of navigating within a large category—or, more generally, of finding one's way through a long list of messages. Efficiently summarizing the information space is the second step toward effective nonvisual messaging.

With a GUI-based mail reader, the user is treated to a visual summary of messages and may point and click on items of interest. This works because a list of the message headers quickly summarizes the set and affords rapid selection of individual messages but is difficult to achieve aurally, due to the slow, non-persistent nature of speech. Whereas the eyes can scan a list of several dozen messages in a matter of seconds, the ear may take several minutes to listen to the same list read aloud. Further, one must rely on short-term memory to recall the spoken items whereas the screen serves as a persistent reminder of one's choices.

Since speech is slow, summaries must be streamlined, avoiding extraneous information or repetition. The approach adopted by SpeechActs is to read the headers one by one, which was necessary to list the number of each message:

SpeechActs: Your next six messages are from MIT.
User: Scan the headers.
SpeechActs: Message 1 from Gina-Anne Levow about "final draft changes." Message 2 from Chris Schmandt about "visit Friday." Message 3 from Chris Schmandt about "visit Friday—correction." Message 4 from Matt Marx about "videotape."........(etc.)........Message 10 from Matt Marx about "final draft changes." Message 7 from Matt Marx about "hello."

MailCall's summary is more concise, though at the expense of some detail.

MailCall: Personal messages. Read the summary, or read the first header?
User: Read me the summary.
MailCall: You have several from Matt Marx, a couple from Chris Schmandt, and one from Gina-Anne Levow.

Although the latter summary does not list the subject of each message, it is more quickly conveyed and easier to remember. By grouping messages from the same sender, it avoids mentioning each message individually, instead providing a summary of what is available.

In addition, MailCall attempts not to overburden the user with information. When reading the list, for instance, it does not say the exact number of messages but rather a *fuzzy quantification* of the number: e.g., "several from Matt Marx" instead of "six from Matt Marx." And if there are messages from many different people in the same category, MailCall will mention only the first four or five and add "...among others."

Nonvisual navigation

The fact that MailCall summarizes the contents of a category implies that the user is able to pick from them at random. Random access refers to the act of nonlinear information access—i.e., something other than the neighboring items in a list. The chart below delineates four general types of random access.

	location-based	content-based
relative	"skip ahead five messages"	"read the next one about 'meeting'"
absolute	"read me message thirty-five"	"read the message from John Linn"

Figure 2: Four types of random access.

By *location-based* random access we mean that the user is picking out a certain item by virtue of its position or placement in a list. Location-based random access may either be *absolute* (e.g., "Read message 10."), when the user has a specific message in mind, or *relative*, when one moves by a certain offset (e.g., "skip ahead five messages.") (It may be noted that sequential navigation is a form of *relative location-based* navigation where the increment is one.) SpeechActs supports both absolute and relative location-based random access, and suggests their use by reading the number of each message while scanning the headers in a message category. Location-based random access imposes an additional cognitive burden on the user, who must remember the numbering of a certain message in order to access it. Indeed, participants in the SpeechActs usability study were often observed jotting down the numbering of messages, though doing so would be most difficult in situations where speech is maximally beneficial, such as while driving.

With *content-based random access*, the user may reference an item by one of its inherent attributes: sender, subject, date, etc. For instance, the user may say "read me the message from John Linn" without having to recall the numbering scheme. As with location-based navigation, both relative and absolute modes exist. *Relative content-based* access associated with following "threads," multiple messages on the same subject. Phoneshell, for instance, allows the user to drop into "scan mode," which reads the next message on the current topic or from the current sender; this is feasible with touch-tones since the user need not specify the desired topic explicitly but signify that the current topic is to be followed. *Absolute content-based navigation* is the contribution of MailCall, allowing the user to pick the interesting message(s) from a summary.

> MailCall: You have several messages from Lisa Stifelman, a few from Mike Phillips, and one each from Jill Kliger and Steve Lee.
> User: Read me the ones from Mike Phillips.

It is practical to support absolute content-based navigation with recent advances in speech recognition. Traditionally, a speech recognizer loads a precompiled vocabulary that cannot be modified at runtime. This makes it impractical for the speech recognizer to know about new messages that arrive constantly. (One can imagine recompiling the grammar whenever a new message arrives, but this is both computationally intensive and susceptible to race conditions, as when the user calls while the grammar is being recompiled to reflect new messages.) Recently, however, a dynamic vocabulary updating feature of the DAGGER speech recognizer [3] supports runtime vocabulary modification. When the user enters a category, MailCall adds the names of the senders in that category to the recognizer's vocabulary. Thus the user may ask for a message from those senders listed in a summary. One may also ask if there are messages from anyone in the rolodex, or from someone whom one has recently sent a message or called (as determined by CLUES).

Absolute content-based random access combined with intelligent categorization and category summarization brings MailCall closer in line with the experience one expects from a graphical mail reader, although a GUI mail reader on a large display has the potential to communicate more information more quickly about the available messages. It satisfies some criteria for an effective nonvisual navigational scheme [8]: users do not have to learn many additional commands, short-term memory is not overburdened, and the structure of the mailbox is not complicated excessively.

DESIGN CHALLENGE: CRAFTING CONVERSATION

MailCall uses speech recognition because it is not practical to support absolute content-based navigation with touch tones. Expressing the command "read the message from Mark Matthews," for instance, would require a command for "read the message from..." and then a mechanism for spelling the desired name, which is especially difficult when dealing with email addresses. (MailCall does support touch-tone equivalents for sequential navigation and other simple functions; see [5].) The use of speech for both input and output, however, raises user expectations of the interaction since it implicitly resembles a human conversation. These heightened expectations can be damning, however, since speech recognizers are far less adept than humans. Knowing what to say is a stumbling block for beginners, yet taking the time to explain one's options can be tiresome for "power users." Further, speech recognition errors slow down the interaction, requiring the system to perform constant "grounding" [1] between the system and user to insure that they share a common perception of what is transpiring. This section describes strategies for avoiding conversational breakdown.

Communicating capabilities with help

People have very different expectations for "conversational" systems: some speak as if chatting with a good friend, expecting the machine to perform human-level language understanding. Experience [9], however, demonstrates that many people do not ascribe much competence to a spoken language application and instead expect to be led step-by-step as with a menu-driven IVR system. In both cases, it is essential to guide users to speak requests that the system understands. Given the range of expectations, a major responsibility of the speech interface designer is to communicate system capabilities to the user.

Like SpeechActs, MailCall avoids explicitly listing options in the form of a menu, instead opting for a conversational style, which is both more familiar and also faster for experts who have learned the system's vocabulary. Still, novice users need to know what their options are. The SpeechActs strategy involved giving each user a printed card with a list of sample commands. In the usability study, this proved successful, as most users spoke only the commands listed on the card. For MailCall, our goal is an "out-of-box" experience, meaning that we want users to be able to learn the system without reading manuals or carrying instruction pamphlets. MailCall users are informed at the beginning of a session that they can ask "what can I say now?" or press the '0' telephone key for assistance.

The first step in providing help is *reestablishing context*—reminding users where they are and how they got there, usually by revisiting the last action taken by the system and explaining what the system thought the user said. Next, a list of *currently available options* is given with an explanation of each command. Finally, the user is reminded of the *global reset* command ("start over from the beginning") so that the user can begin the session anew instead of hanging up in disgust.

Handling recognition errors

Like other speech systems [1, 7, 9], MailCall invests significant effort in detecting and correcting speech recognition errors. It handles rejection errors by apologizing and giving *progressive assistance* [9] and verifies potential substitution errors, allowing the user to correct them quickly (e.g., "No, I said *read* the message.").

Its contribution to error-handling is ErrorLock, a general "interface algorithm" for handling recognition errors. (See [5] for a complete description and a diagram.) Instead of dealing with errors on a case-by-case basis, each incoming utterance is passed through ErrorLock for evaluation and confirmation. Aside from insuring uniform error-handling among varied input, it also keeps track of past recognition errors and deals more intelligently with consecutive errors. If, for instance, the recognizer consistently picks a hypothesis but its confidence is just under the cutoff threshold, ErrorLock temporarily relaxes the threshold and asks if that is what the user meant. Error-tracking also helps to keep MailCall from sounding oblivious to context. In the following example, MailCall makes the same mistake twice but reflects that knowledge in its feedback.

> MailCall: Welcome to MailCall. Who's this?
> User: Matt Marx.
> MailCall: Nat Parker, correct?
> User: No, Matt Marx.
> MailCall: I thought I heard "Nat Parker" again, but you just said that. Is that right?

If the speech recognizer were able to return more than one hypothesis (an N-best list), ErrorLock would be able to discard the hypothesis that was already rejected and try the next-most-likely one. Besides facilitating better interaction, ErrorLock is a convenience for the developer. Centralizing error-handling removes the need to copy error-handling code all over the application, and since ErrorLock is domain-independent, it can be reused for other applications, changing prompts as necessary.

ErrorLock is, not, however, a complete discourse model like that of Chatter [4]. And although its verification of potential misrecognitions is invaluable when the speech recognizer is having difficulty, its constant verification can become annoying when the speech recognizer is performing well. An adaptive model of feedback such as described in [1] may help MailCall appear less rote in deciding when to ask for feedback.

Contextually customized feedback

Grice's cooperative principle of conversation [2] as applied to spoken language systems might read as follows: "give as little feedback as possible, but no less." Giving too much is a vice, but failing to give enough is the greater sin if the user becomes confused for lack of explanation. Both the user's competence and the conversational context of the current session are factors in deciding how to give feedback.

Varying the length of feedback. Like other speech systems [6, 7], MailCall offers various levels of feedback, with longer prompts for novices than experts. MailCall goes a step further, however, adapting its feedback based on the conversational context through the use of *ellipsis*. Ellipsis refers to the omission of words or phrases that have already been established earlier in the conversation, with the assumption that the intended meaning can be reconstructed from a shorter prompt and the existing context. In the following example, the user is asked twice whether to review, send, or cancel a message. Items omitted by ellipsis appear in strikeout text.

> User: Send a message to Jordan Slott.
> MailCall: Record your message for Jordan Slott. Pause for several seconds when finished.
> User: *records a voice message*
> MailCall: Got it. Review the message, send it, or cancel?

User: Send.
MailCall: Sending your message. Please wait.
User: Send a message to Steve Lee.
MailCall: Record your message for Steve Lee. ~~Pause for several seconds when finished.~~
User: *records a voice message*
MailCall: Got it. Review ~~the message~~, send ~~it~~, or cancel?
User: Send.
MailCall: Sending your message. Please wait.

As the above example demonstrates, MailCall uses ellipsis on individual words, phrases, and even sentences. Ellipsis helps to streamline the interaction and may help users to perceive the interface as non-repetitive.

Varying the speed of feedback. Like other speech systems [6, 7], MailCall allows the user to set a default speech output rate or change it during a session. It also recognizes that certain items are more familiar than others, having been established earlier in the conversation. Prompts, for instance, become familiar with use. Items that are new to the conversation, however, may be harder to understand. Thus MailCall temporarily slows down its speech when presenting the sender or subject of a message. It does so in the following example, with the words spoken more slowly rendered in expanded text.

User: Start with the first message.
MailCall: Message 1 is from S t u a r t A d a m s about a response to "n e x t w e e k ."

Temporarily slowing down for new information can allow the user to set a higher default speaking rate, speeding the presentation of prompts. Ellipsis and automatic speed adaptation help to reduce the repetitiveness of repeated prompts while helping to insure that new, unfamiliar information can be comprehended. This is especially important when using synthetic speech, which is necessary when delivering dynamic data such as email messages.

USER STUDY

To evaluate the effectiveness of MailCall, a user study was conducted. The goal was not only to determine how usable the system was for a novice, but also how useful it would prove long-term as a tool for mobile messaging.

Method

Since our goal was not only to evaluate ease of learning but likelihood of continued use, we conducted a five-week study involving four Media Lab affiliates with varying experience using speech recognition. In order to gauge the learning curve, minimal instruction was given except upon request. Sessions were neither recorded nor monitored due to privacy concerns surrounding personal messages, so the results described below are based chiefly on user reports. The experiences of the two system designers using MailCall over a period of three months were also considered.

Results

Feedback from beginning users centered mainly on the process of learning the system, though as users became more familiar with the system, they also commented on the utility of MailCall's nonvisual presentation. Seasoned users offered more comments on navigation as well as the limits of MailCall in various acoustic contexts.

Bootstrapping. As described above, our approach was to provide a conversational interface supported by a help system. All users experienced difficulty with recognition errors, but those who used the help facility found they could sustain a conversation in many cases. A participant familiar with other speech systems found the combination of error-handling and help especially useful:

> I have never heard such a robust system before. I like all the help it gives. I said something and it didn't understand, so it gave suggestions on what to say.

Other participants were less enthusiastic, though nearly all reported that their MailCall sessions became more successful with experience.

Recognition robustness. MailCall has a very large vocabulary, pushing the limits of the speech recognizer. Two factors were identified in the success of the system: vocabulary size and acoustic context. Since the user can ask if there are messages from anyone in the rolodex, send them messages, or call them at any time, MailCall's vocabulary size varies directly with the number of people in the user's rolodex. An experienced user with well over 100 names in his rolodex found recognition to be unreliable when talking over a noisy cellular connection.

Specifying Names. A difficulty common to all users was getting MailCall to understand names, both in asking for messages from certain people and simply identifying one's self. Unlike Chatter, which used first names only, MailCall requires the user to say full names. Everyone responded to the prompt "Welcome to MailCall. Who's this?" with "It's Matt!" or something similar. Furthermore, users were disappointed when they had to refer to someone the same way that MailCall did; instead of saying "read the one from groucho at M I T dot E D U," they wanted to say "read the one from groucho" which, given the conversational context, is all that is required to uniquely specify that person.

Navigation. Users cited absolute content-based navigation as a highlight of MailCall. One beginning user said "I like being able to check if there are messages from people in my rolodex." And one of the system designers, a diehard Phoneshell user, admits that he uses MailCall instead of Phoneshell when facing an unusually large number of messages because he can ask for a summary of a category and then pick the ones he wants to hear first.

For sequential navigation, however, speech was in fact a *dis*advantage. The time necessary to say "next" and then wait for the recognizer to respond can be greater than just pushing a touch-tone, especially when the recognizer may misunderstand. Indeed, several used touch-tone equivalents for "next" and "previous." And since some participants in the study received few messages, they were content to step through them one by one. MailCall's touch-tone equivalents address this preference.

These results suggest that MailCall is most useful to people with high message traffic, whereas those with a low volume of messages may be content to simply step through the list with touch-tones, avoiding recognition errors.

Implications for redesign

The results of our user study suggested several areas where MailCall could improve, particularly for novice users. Some changes have already been made, though others will require more significant redesign of the system.

More explanation for beginners. Supporting conversational prompts with help appears to be a useful method of communicating system capabilities to novices. Our experience with four novice users, however, suggests that our prompts and help were not explicit enough. As an iterative design step, we lengthened several prompts, especially those at the beginning of the session, and lengthened the help messages. A fifth user who joined late in the study after these changes had been made was able to log on, navigate, and send messages on his very first try without major difficulties. This suggests that prompts for beginners should err on the side of lengthy exposition.

More flexible specification of names. Specifying names continues to be an elusive problem. MailCall should allow the user to refer to someone using as few items as necessary to uniquely specify them. Doing so would involve two additions to MailCall: first, a "nickname generator," which creates a list of acceptable alternatives for a given name; second, an interface algorithm for disambiguating names with multiple referents as in [9].

Moded vs. Modeless interaction. If MailCall is to be usable in weak acoustic contexts (like the cellular phone) for people with a large rolodex, its interaction may need to become more modal. We intentionally designed MailCall to be modeless so that users would not have to switch back and forth among applications, but as the number of people in the rolodex grows, it may become necessary to define a separate "rolodex" segment of the application to constrain the recognition task. Wildfire has segmented their recognition of names (necessitated by other constraints), though the resulting interaction is less conversational.

CONCLUSIONS

Nonvisual messaging systems can approach their visual counterparts in usability and usefulness if users can quickly access the messages they want. Through a combination of intelligent organization, efficient presentation, and random-access navigation, MailCall offers interaction similar to that of a visual messaging system. Consideration of context helps to meet user expectations of error-handling and feedback, though beginning users may require more assistance than was anticipated. Results suggest, however, that a large-vocabulary conversational system like MailCall can be both usable and useful for mobile messaging.

ACKNOWLEDGMENTS

Jordan Slott implemented the ISDN software, and several research associates of the MIT Media Lab Speech Group have contributed to infrastructure. Raja Rajasekharan and Charles Hemphill made it possible for us to use DAGGER. Nicole Yankelovich reviewed a draft of this paper. This work was supported by Sun Microsystems and Motorola.

REFERENCES

[1] S. Brennan and E. Hulteen. "Interaction and feedback in a spoken language system: a theoretical framework." *Knowledge-Based Systems*, April/June 1995, pp. 143-151.

[2] H. Grice. "Logic and Conversation," *Syntax and Semantics: Speech Acts*, Cole & Morgan, editors, Volume 3, Academic Press, 1975.

[3] C. Hemphill & P. Thrift. "Surfing the Web by Voice." *In Proceedings of ACM Multimedia '95*, San Francisco, CA, Nov. 5–9, 1995.

[4] E. Ly. "Chatter: A Conversational Telephone Agent" MIT Master's Thesis, Program in Media Arts and Sciences, 1993.

[5] M. Marx. "Toward Effective Conversational Messaging." MIT Master's Thesis, Program in Media Arts and Sciences, 1995.

[6] C. Schmandt. "Phoneshell: the Telephone as Computer Terminal" *Proceedings of ACM Multimedia Conference*, August 1993.

[7] L. Stifelman, B. Arons, C. Schmandt, and E. Hulteen. "VoiceNotes: A Speech Interface for a Hand-Held Voice Notetaker, *ACM INTERCHI '93 Conference Proceedings*, Amsterdam, The Netherlands, April 24–29, 1993.

[8] C. Wolf, L. Koved, and E. Kunzinger, (1995) Ubiquitous Mail: Speech and Graphical User Interfaces to an Integrated Voice/E-Mail Mailbox, Interact '95, 247-252.

[9] N. Yankelovich, G. Levow, and M. Marx. "Designing SpeechActs: Issues in Speech Interfaces." *Proceedings of CHI '95*, Denver, CO, May 8–11, 1995.

NewsComm: A Hand-Held Interface for Interactive Access to Structured Audio

Deb K. Roy and Chris Schmandt

Speech Research Group
MIT Media Lab
20 Ames Street, Cambridge, MA 02139
dkroy@media.mit.edu and geek@media.mit.edu

ABSTRACT
The NewsComm system delivers personalized news and other program material as audio to mobile users through a hand-held playback device. This paper focuses on the iterative design and user testing of the hand-held interface. The interface was first designed and tested in a software-only environment and then ported to a custom hardware platform. The hand-held device enables navigation through audio recordings based on structural information which is extracted from the audio using digital signal processing techniques. The interface design addresses the problems of designing a hand-held and primarily non-visual interface for accessing large amounts of structured audio recordings.

KEYWORDS
Audio interfaces, hand-held computers, structured audio.

INTRODUCTION
This paper describes the design of the interface for a hand-held device called NewsComm (Figure 1) which provides mobile access to dynamic databases of large audio recordings. The motivation for this work is to deliver personalized news and other program material to mobile listeners as audio. The device is hand-held and incorporates a primarily non-visual interface which can be used while performing other tasks such as walking or exercising, and by visually impaired users.

In a typical user scenario, one or more audio servers would be established which receive audio programs from various sources, process them, and then store them on disk. The user intermittently connects the hand-held to one of the servers through a high-bandwidth connection such as a television cable or an ISDN line. The server then selects a subset of the available recordings and down-loads them into the local memory of the hand-held (the server selects recordings based on the user's preferences and listening history). The user then disconnects the hand-held from the server and listens off-line.

The interface contains two sets of controls. The first set allows the user to select recordings and to indicate which recordings were interesting (the server uses this information to determine which recordings are likely to be of interest in the future). In certain cases where the server does not have sufficient confidence to down-load an entire recording to the hand-held, an automatic summary of the recording is generated and down-loaded instead. If the user indicates interest in the summary, the entire recording is down-loaded the next time the user connects to the server.

The second set of controls are used to navigate within recordings. The term "navigate" refers to the control of the play position within a recording. For example, the navigation control of a conventional tape deck usually includes a fast-forward and rewind button. In NewsComm the navigation controls use structural information about the audio to make searching and browsing more efficient.

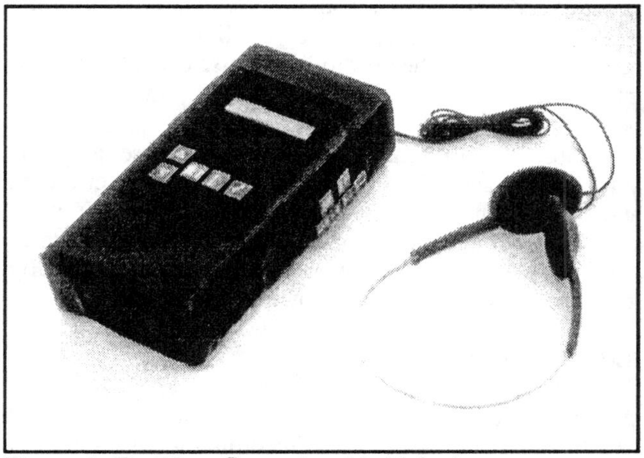

Figure 1: The NewsComm hand-held device.

This paper focuses on three aspects of the design of the hand-held interface:

- What are the design criteria for a primarily non-visual interface for use in mobile situations?

- How can we make an interface which uses multiple structural descriptions of varying accuracy to assist in navigating an audio recording?

- What is the optimal balance between automatic and manual navigation when accessing large structured audio recordings?

MOTIVATIONS

One motivation for this work is to overcome the shallow and repetitive coverage of conventional broadcast media due to its need to reach large audiences. NewsComm creates a mechanism for one-to-one connections between individuals and information providers resulting in an increase in both the depth and breadth of information which the listener can access.

A second motivation for creating NewsComm is to provide filtering mechanisms which help the user find information of interest. The need for filtering is steadily increasing since there is a rapidly growing number of information providers producing, distributing, and archiving audio programs in digital form. One example of this is the Internet Multicasting Service which multicasts (a method of sending real-time audio and video to one or more destinations on the Internet) and archives the audio proceedings of the U.S. House and Senate, producing over 20 hours of digital audio daily [5]. A second example is the Forum project at Sun Microsystems which provides lectures in audio over the Internet [10]. Additionally, as large existing information providers such as network news agencies begin providing on-line services, the amount of digital audio available will increase dramatically.

NewsComm filters information at two levels. At the first level, it relies on usage history and user preferences to select recordings to down-load from the audio server to the hand-held. At the second level of filtering, interactive navigation enables the user to listen to selected portions of interest from the down-loaded recordings.

We chose to build an audio device because audio is attractive for accessing information while the user's eyes and hands are busy. NewsComm is aimed at mobile users who are performing some other simultaneous task such as walking, exercising, or the morning commute. Visually impaired individuals are also potential users.

RELATED WORK

SpeechSkimmer is a hand-held interface for interactively skimming speech recordings [1]. The interface enables the user to listen to a single speech recording at four levels of skimming. At the lowest level the entire recording is heard. At the second level pauses are shortened. At the third level, only short segments (highlights) of the recording following long pauses are played. Level four plays highlights selected using pitch analysis. NewsComm is similar to SpeechSkimmer as it also provides a hand-held navigation interface for skimming and searching audio recordings. NewsComm is different from SpeechSkimmer in two major ways, other than in its physical redesign. First, it uses a new framework for combining structural descriptions allowing one interface to make use of varying degrees of structural description. In contrast, the number of controls and resulting complexity of SpeechSkimmer grows with greater structural description. Second, NewsComm provides support for accessing and managing multiple recordings.

VoiceNotes is an interface for a hand-held portable audio note taking device which can be used to capture and organize short spoken notes [9]. NewsComm is also a hand-held device but uses only buttons to navigate audio recordings. The main difference between the two devices is the genre of audio they are designed to operate with. VoiceNotes is designed for short recordings made by the user which are later reviewed; NewsComm is designed for longer structured audio programs which are produced by information providers.

Whittaker et. al. have developed a system called Filochat which integrates handwriting and recorded audio in a portable system [11]. The system records audio and time-synchronized written notes. Audio can later be accessed by selecting a written note which automatically moves the play position to the audio which was recorded at the time the note was written. Similar to Filochat, NewsComm relies on annotated audio to find useful entry points into a long recording. However Filochat uses written annotations to index audio, while NewsComm relies on automatic audio processing. Also, Filochat is intended for retrieving previously heard material whereas NewsComm is designed for listening to previously unheard recordings.

Hindus et. al. designed a set of applications for capturing and structuring audio from two-person telephone calls, and a screen based interface for displaying and retrieving the contents of the conversations [4]. The conversations are annotated by using a simple audio detector to separate speakers talking over a telephone line. NewsComm is similar to this work since it also structures audio by annotating speaker changes. In contrast to Hindus's system, NewsComm uses a more sophisticated signal processing algorithm to locate speaker changes which will work on a much broader range of audio recordings. NewsComm is also a primarily non-visual interface, and designed to navigate longer recordings.

Kimber et. al. have built a system which automatically divides a multi-speaker recording into speaker segments and displays the information in a graphical browsing tool [6]. NewsComm also uses automatic speaker segmentation to index recordings. However, in contrast to Kimber's Hidden Markov Model based segmentation system, NewsComm uses a neural network approach [7]. Also, similar to Hindus's system, Kimber's system is designed to review meetings and conversations rather than listen to new material, and uses a screen based interface rather than a hand-held non-visual one.

THE NEWSCOMM SYSTEM

Figure 2 gives an architectural overview of the NewsComm system. The audio server (top part of Figure 2) collects and processes audio from various sources including radio broadcasts, books and journals on tape, and internet audio multicasts. Typical content might include newscasts, talk shows, books on tape, and lectures. The hand-held down-loads recordings from the audio server through intermittent high-bandwidth connections.

The audio processor module in the server automatically finds two classes of features in each audio recording: pauses in speech, and speaker changes (points in the recording where the person talking switches). The locations of these features constitute a structural description of the recording. The audio and associated structural description are collectively referred to as structured audio. All audio in the server is structured by the audio processor and then stored in the audio library, a large network-mounted hard disk drive.

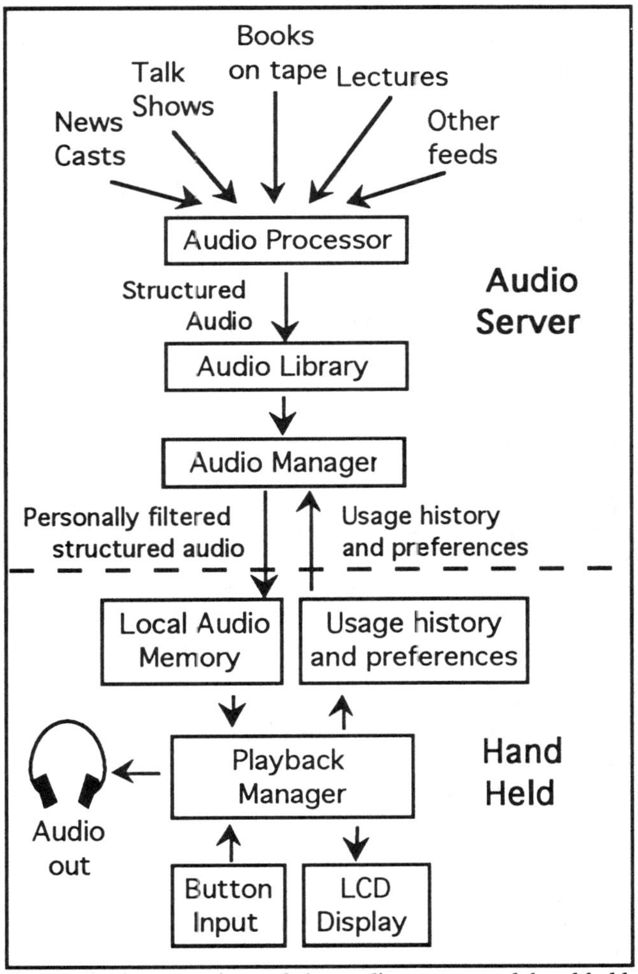

Figure 2: An overview of the audio server and hand-held playback device.

Users can down-load structured audio from the server by connecting their hand-held to the audio manager. The audio manager decides which recordings to down-load based on a preference file which the user has previously specified, and also based on the recent usage history uploaded from the hand-held. The preferences file specifies interest rankings for each available source of audio. The server uses these rankings to determine which recordings to down-load to meet the user's interests. The preference file is currently created by editing a text file manually. The usage history is generated as a result of interaction with the hand-held interface and is discussed in the section on the design of the interface.

Once the down-load is complete, the user disconnects and interactively accesses the recordings using the navigation interface of the hand-held. The playback manager in the hand-held uses the structural description of the audio to enable efficient navigation of the recordings. It does this by ensuring that when the user jumps forward or backward in a recording, the jump "lands" in a meaningful place. The structural description of each recording contains the location of all suitable jump destinations within the recording. The interface enables the user to efficiently skim and search audio, and to listen selectively to portions of interest.

STRUCTURED AUDIO

Audio is difficult to browse and access randomly due to its serial nature. To facilitate efficient navigation it is useful to annotate significant features of a long audio recording which can serve as "entry points" or "jump locations" within the recording. Ideally these annotations would point to semantically meaningful events such as a change of speaker, change of topic, or start of a new sentence. Arons found that simple techniques using pause and pitch analysis can be used to locate features which are often semantically significant [1]. We adopt this approach in the NewsComm system which uses pause and voice analysis to locate long pauses and changes in speaker [7].

The locations and lengths of all pauses in a recording constitute a structural description of a recording. The locations of all speaker changes constitute a second description of the same recording. In general there may be any number such descriptions derived from various automatic and manual annotation methods.

We have developed a general framework for combining any number of such descriptions. The framework provides a standard programming interface to the underlying description(s) so that interface design can be isolated from the class and number of structural descriptions available.

We now define a set of terms which are used in the remainder of this paper. A **jump location** is a location in the recording selected using the structural representation framework. A **jump** is made when the play position is moved to the next or previous jump location (relative to the current play position). A **highlight** is a short segment of audio following a jump location. **Skimming** is a mode of playback in which only the highlights of the recording are played in sequence; the portions of the recording between highlights are skipped. The **jump range** is the maximum distance a jump can move the play position from its current position. The **jump granularity** is a qualitative measure of the spacing between jumps in a recording. Short jumps result in fine granularity; long jumps result in coarse granularity.

The framework performs a weighted sum of available descriptions and then selects jump locations at any desired granularity based on the jump range [8]. For example, in the current system the weight of each pause is proportional to its length reflecting our assumption that long pauses precede interesting events in an audio stream. Speaker changes are assigned the highest possible weight to assure that they are always selected as jump locations (assuming the jump granularity is fine enough to hit every speaker change in the recording).

INTERFACE DESIGN

This section describes the design of the NewsComm interface.

Design Objectives

The following objectives were set for the hand-held interface design:

(1) Enable natural and efficient audio navigation

(2) Be small enough to be held and controlled with one hand

(3) Require little or no visual attention to operate, especially for common operations such as jumping within a recording

(4) Facilitate selecting recordings and communicating simple requests to the server.

Usability Testing

For each iteration of the interface design four subjects were asked to perform the following four steps:

- Visually inspect the interface and describe what the subject believes each element of the interface will do if activated.
- Explore the interface without instruction from the investigator. The purpose was to determine if the interface design is intuitive for users who have no information about how to use it.
- Perform a search task. The subject was asked to find a specific news story within a recording of a 20 minute newscast using the interface.
- Describe features of the interface which were found easy to use or useful and features which were found difficult to use or of no use, and additional features the subject would like to have added to the interface.

Notes were taken at each step of this process and used to redesign the interface. The goal of the user studies was to expose flaws in the design and determine the set of features users find useful for skimming and searching audio recordings.

Implementation Strategy

We took the approach of separating function from the form of the interface. The first three iterations of the interface are implemented in software-only using Tcl/Tk on a Sun workstation. These three interfaces rely on screen based display of controls and status information, and use a mouse for input. Our intent was to focus on the appropriate controls and functionality of the interface. In the fourth iteration the design was transferred to a custom made hardware device. This two-stage design implementation strategy facilitated rapid prototyping in the initial phases and reduced hardware development time.

Summary of the Design Process

We designed and implemented four iterations of the interface. The first (software-only) design represents our initial hypothesis for an interface which meets design objective (1). Usability testing exposed several poor design decisions and highlighted missing and unused functions. These tests led to the second iteration which additionally addresses design objectives (2) and (3). Further usability tests of this second design led to the third and final software design which also addresses design objective (4), the ability to access and manage multiple recordings. The fourth design is implemented in hardware and focuses on the selection and placement of buttons and a liquid crystal display (LCD), and the overall shape and feel of the device.

The first and fourth designs are comparable in complexity, however the functionality and usability improved considerably. User studies indicate that users easily understand and use the final interface whereas the initial interfaces are virtually unusable. As developers we exhibited a tendency to expose increasing control to the underlying indexing abilities of the system but usability studies consistently showed that a simple interface retaining only basic indexing control was preferred.

Description of Each Design

We now give descriptions of each iteration of the interface design. For clarity, the names of all controls (buttons and sliders) are written in upper case.

Iteration 1

Figure 3 shows a screen capture of the interface which was designed to navigate a single audio recording. The interface consists of three main areas, the audio display at the top, a row of control buttons in the center, and two slider controls at the bottom.

The window at the top displays the structural descriptions of the audio, current play position and jump range setting, and a "trace" of the play position. The structural description of the recording is displayed by vertical bars indicating the locations of speaker changes and pauses. The length of the bar is proportional to the duration of the pause, and speaker changes are indicated in red. The display resembles Degen et. al.'s audio display [3], although in contrast to that system, the feature markings in this display are generated automatically by the pause and voice analysis software. A black diamond tracks the play position in real-time. A trace of the areas where the diamond has traversed is recorded using a black bar which serves as a visual reminder of which parts of the recording have been played. A square bracket centered on the diamond shows the current jump range.

Five buttons are arranged in a row in the center of the window. Three of the buttons provide conventional rewind, stop and play operation. A fourth button jumps backwards to the previous jump location, and the fifth button puts the system into skim mode. Finally, two sliders enable the user to set the jump-range and playback speed.

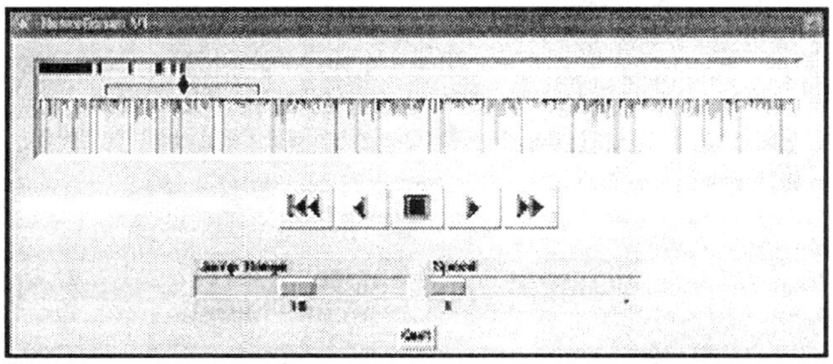

Figure 3: Iteration 1 of the interface includes (from top to bottom) a display of the structural description, five navigation buttons, and two parameter control sliders.

Usability tests were made on a 20 minute BBC news recording. During initial visual inspection the subjects correctly guessed the functions of the conventional stop, play and rewind buttons, but failed to guess the function of the jump-back and skim buttons.

To our surprise, after trying the interface on the sample audio, none of the subjects learned the function of the skim mode. The two main reasons for the confusion were (1) there was no way to know that a new mode was being activated, and (2) the pause separated highlights are semantically unconnected and difficult to follow (some subjects thought the system was malfunctioning). When given a simple search task, the subjects used a combination of REWIND, JUMP-BACK, and PLAY to locate specific parts of the recording. The SKIM function was not used.

Subjects were asked what they would like change in the interface. They all asked for direct manipulation of the play position by clicking and dragging the diamond icon to a different position.

Iteration 2

Figure 4 shows the redesign of the interface based on the usability studies on Iteration 1, and additional constraints of design objectives (2) and (3). Major changes include:

- The audio display window was replaced with a single line text display which shows the duration of the recording and the current play position. We found these to be the two most important pieces of information in the previous display. We limited the display to one text line so that it can be implemented using a small LCD in the final hand-held hardware. The text display also indicates the current mode of operation (stop, play, or skim) to help reduce the confusion over the skim mode in the first design.

- An auditory icon of sped-up speech was added to all jump functions. The duration of the icon is logarithmically proportional to the length of the corresponding jump. Whenever the user jumps, or when automatically jumping between highlights in the skim mode, the icon is played to indicate movement of the play position.

- A new slider was added to control the length of highlights (which was fixed in the first iteration), and a new button was added to jump-forward.

- The button layout was re-organized with modal buttons in one row, and navigation buttons in a second.

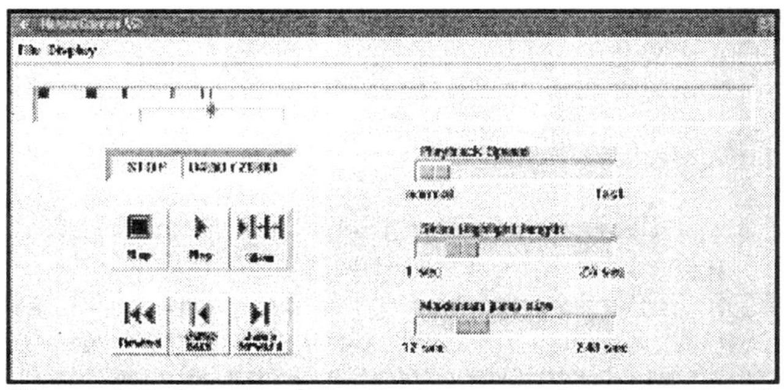

Figure 4: In Iteration 2 the display was reduced to a small text display (above the navigation buttons). The functionality, icons, and layout of the navigation buttons were redesigned; a new slider for controlling highlight length was added.

Icons and labels were also redesigned to reduce confusion (based on observations from Iteration 1 tests). For example, in the first design the PLAY icon is a triangle pointing right, and the JUMP-BACK a triangle pointing left. This opposite-symmetric choice led to confusion (users guessed pressing the JUMP-BACK would play the audio backwards). The JUMP-BACK icon in Iteration 2 was redesigned to differentiate it from the play operation.

Another four subjects tested this new design. There was a clear improvement in the usability of the buttons.

Subjects quickly understood the distinction between modal and navigational control, although the function of the skim mode was less obvious. Subjects easily understood the purpose of the single line display.

The auditory icon for jumping was found useful and intuitive. One subject commented that the jump-back sound should be different from the jump forward sound.

The skim mode continued to cause confusion and was not used in the sample search tasks. It became clear that adding controls (such as the highlight length slider) only made the skimming function more difficult to use.

Iteration 3
Figure 5 shows the next interface design.

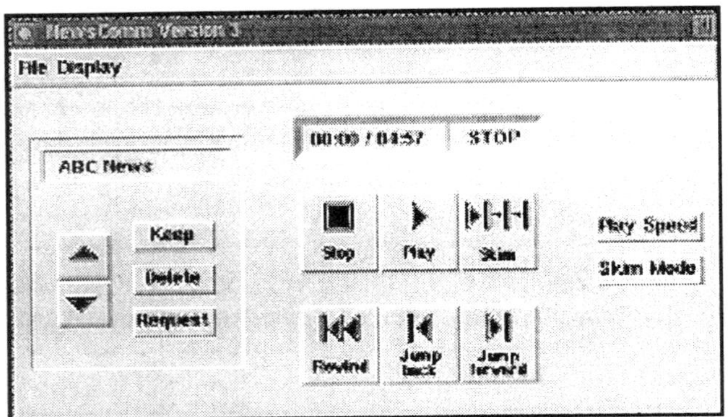

Figure 5: In Iteration 3 sliders were replaced with two buttons which cycle through preset (discrete) settings of the three control parameters. A new set of controls and display were added (on the left) to select and manage multiple audio recordings.

Two major changes were made in the third and final software-only design:

- The sliders were replaced with two buttons labeled PLAY-SPEED and SKIM-MODE. Pressing PLAY-SPEED cycles the play speed through three settings (1.0, 1.4, and 1.8 times faster than normal speed). SKIM-MODE cycles through three combinations of settings of the highlight-length and jump-range. The three skim mode settings correspond to skimming with fine, medium, and course granularity.

- A new set of buttons and line of display was added to support multiple recordings (fulfilling design objective 4). The display shows the name of the current recording. Up and down arrow buttons (on the left) enable the user to move through a list of available recordings. The interface also announces the name of the new recording using prerecorded audio.

The KEEP and DELETE buttons let the user mark recordings to be retained or discarded at the next connection with the server. The REQUEST button is used to request full versions of recordings when only a summary of the recording has been down-loaded. These three buttons could not be tested in usability studies for Iteration 3 since the audio server had not been implemented at that time, but subsequent tests of the buttons in the hardware prototype were successful.

Summaries were introduced in this version. A summary of a recording is a concatenation of only the highlights of the original recording, with 200ms 200Hz tones separating each highlight. This is similar to the summaries generated by Chen et. al. based on pitch analysis [2]. The summary is generated by the audio server and is usually sufficient for the listener to decide whether he or she wants to download the entire recording during the next connection to the server.

Tests of Version 4 suggested that the skim mode was still unclear, and users continued to feel a need for more direct navigational control.

In all of the first three designs, the search engine used to find jump locations computes the locations relative to the current play position. We found that this caused confusion since jumping back twice from slightly different originating locations will not necessarily land the play position in the same place. The result is that the jumping function seems to have inconsistent behavior.

Iteration 4
Iteration 4 of the interface was implemented in hardware as shown in Figures 1 and 6. Three main changes were made to the interface:

- The skim mode was eliminated

- Two pairs of direct navigation buttons were added which enable coarse and fine granularity jumps

- Jump locations were precomputed and fixed rather than dynamically computed on the fly

The function of the recording selection and management controls were not changed but all of the icons were redesigned.

The granularity of jumps tied to the COARSE-JUMP buttons depend on the type of audio being played and is set manually in the audio server. For example, a granularity of approximately 30 second jumps using a 60 second jump range was found appropriate for navigating newscasts. The FINE-JUMP buttons are tied to jumps roughly 5 seconds apart and usually correspond to grammatical sentence breaks. For two person interview shows we found a jump range of 120 seconds to be appropriate for the coarse granularity jumps (we used the same fine-jump granularity for news shows and interviews).

Although the skim mode was removed, a similar function can be achieved by holding down any of the jump buttons; doing so plays 0.5 second segments of the recording and then jumps automatically to the next jump location. This is similar to the scan operation of a CD player and is understood easily by users.

Tests of this interface have indicated that the four button interactive navigation is preferred to an automatic skim mode since the system never initiates a jump automatically (which causes a feeling of lack of control). The two levels of granularity seem sufficient for navigation; there seems to be no need for more elaborate control over the jump algorithm afforded by the earlier more complex interfaces.

The fixed jump locations were a major improvement to the usability of the device. The locations serve as landmarks within the recording which can be revisited as points of reference.

DISCUSSION

In this section we highlight some of the lessons learned from the design process.

We have presented the design of a simple interface for navigating audio recordings. Usability tests were essential in guiding the design process. An important lesson learned from these tests was that although the authors had a tendency to design powerful but complex interfaces, in most cases users preferred a less powerful, simpler interface. For example, early versions of the interface include a skimming mode which plays selected highlights of a recording. Additional controls enable the user to adjust parameters of the skimming mode. Although users generally agreed that the skimming mode is useful, they consistently preferred a simpler interface with no second modality; the users could achieve the same affect of skimming by manually pressing a jump forward button after hearing each highlight. Although this method of skimming requires more input from the user, it reduces the confusion of having a hidden mode, and eliminates the feeling of an interface which "takes over" the navigation task.

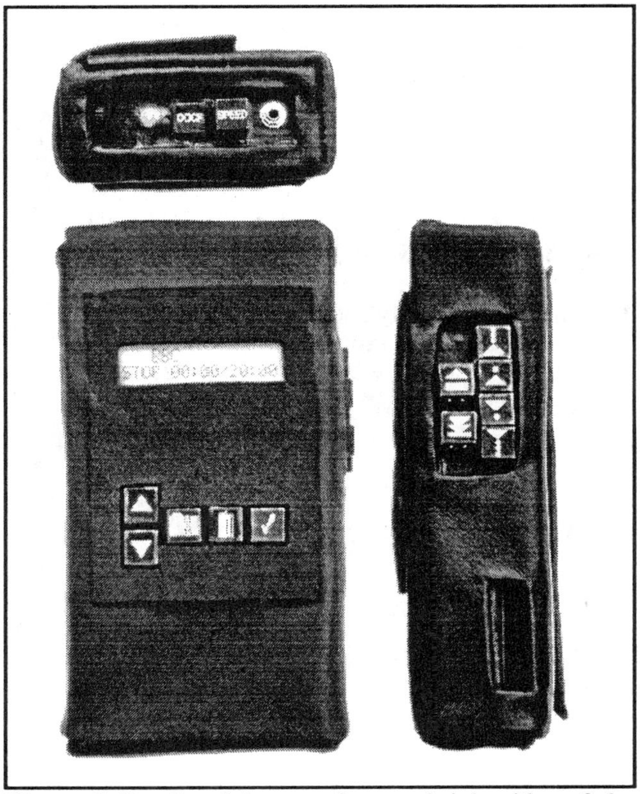

Figure 6: Details of the top, front and right sides of the final hand-held which incorporates Iteration 4 of the interface design. The front panel houses the recording selection and management controls and a 2x16 character LCD screen, and the right side houses the navigation controls. The case is made of soft leather and measures 7.5"(h) x 3.75"(w) x 2.0"(d).

In the final design the two levels of jumping provided an ideal balance of direct control and intelligent jumping. The coarse grain jumps usually move the play position to a meaningful new entry point in the audio and the variable duration fast-forward sound provides a cue of how far the position moved. However, due to the limited accuracy of the speaker indexing algorithm, the coarse jump locations are sometimes chosen in poor locations. The fine grain jump controls provide a highly interactive and reliable second level of control which is easily used to correct errors in the coarse jump selection. We found that users naturally combined the two levels of jumps.

The framework for combining annotations was successfully used to combine the output of the speaker indexing algorithm and pause detection. The framework was used to provide jump locations for four different interface designs which demonstrates the separation of interface design from the underlying representation of the media. The highly interactive nature of the interface overcomes inaccuracies in the annotations; users can compensate for poor jump selection by using finer granularity direct control.

The two-stage interface implementation strategy was found to be an excellent approach and we would recommend it to any similar hardware interface design. Software implementation allows the designer to explore options which would be to costly to consider in a hardware-only design strategy.

FUTURE WORK

We are currently porting the hand-held to a standard PC laptop platform so that any laptop equipped with a large hard drive and sound card can run the NewsComm system. This will enable better long-term usability testing.

Time scale modification can be added to the hand-held device as an additional method of speeding up access to recordings.

The annotation framework can combine any number of structural descriptions. In the current system only two types of annotations have been demonstrated (speaker changes and pauses). Other possible additional annotations include pitch based locations, topic changes (located by modeling the output of a speech recognizer run on the audio), key word spotting, and human editing.

The current implementation of NewsComm supports only simple notions of user history and preferences. In the future, the user history may include tracking which portions of a recording are skipped and which portions are heard and user preferences could include topics and keywords which are of interest.

Although primarily non-visual, NewsComm uses an LCD to display the name and length of recording, and the current play position. We are exploring audio-only solutions to each of these display components based on a combination of additional sound cues and interactive query controls.

ACKNOWLEDGMENTS
We received help and useful comments from Jeff Herman, Sandra Bunch, Nicola Shaw, Josh Bers, Sara Elo, Nicolas Saint-Arnaud, Walter Bender, Bob Donnelly, John Makhoul, Jack Driscoll, Sumit Basu, Vadim Gerasimov, Lisa Stifelman, and Yin Yin Wong. Lena Davis assisted with editing.

This work was supported by the MIT News in the Future Consortium.

REFERENCES

1. Arons, B. Speech Skimmer: Interactively Skimming Recorded Speech. Ph.D. thesis, MIT Media Lab, 1994.

2. Chen, F., M. Withgott, "The Use of Emphasis to Automatically Summarize a Spoken Discourse". *Proc. Int. Conf. Acoustics, Speech and Signal Processing*. Vol. 1, pp. 229-232, 1992.

3. Degen, L., R. Mander, G. Salomon, "Working with Audio: Integrating Personal Tape Recorders and Desktop Computers". *Proc. of CHI '92*, pp. 413-418, ACM, 1992.

4. Hindus, D., C. Schmandt, C. Horner, "Capturing, Structuring, and Representing Ubiquitous Audio." *ACM Trans. on Information Systems*, Vol. 11, No. 4, pp. 376-400, 1993.

5. Internet Multicasting Service, URL: http://town.hall.org/.

6. Kimber, D., L. Wilcox,, F. Chen,, T. Moran, "Speaker Segmentation for Browsing Recorded Audio". *Proc. of CHI '95*, pp. 212-213, ACM, 1995.

7. Roy, D. "Speaker Indexing Using Neural Network Clustering of Vowel Spectra", upcoming issue of *International Journal of Speech Technology*, 1995.

8. Roy, D. NewsComm: A Hand-Held Device for Interactive Access to Structured Audio. Masters thesis, MIT Media Laboratory, 1995.

9. Stifelman, L., B. Arons, C. Schmandt, "VoiceNotes: A Speech Interface for a hand-held voice notetaker". *Proc. of CHI '93*, pp. 179-186, ACM, 1993.

10. Isaacs, E., T. Morris, T. K. Rodriguez, "A Forum for Supporting Interactive Presentations to Distributed Audiences". *Proc. of CSCWI '94*, pp. 405-416, ACM, 1994.

11. Whittaker, S., P. Hyland, M. Wiley, "Filochat: Handwritten Notes Provide Access to Recorded Conversations". *Proc. of CHI '94*, pp. 271-279, ACM, 1994.

The Thin Glass Line: Designing Interfaces to Algorithms

Michael Eisenberg
Department of Computer Science and Institute of Cognitive Science
Campus Box 430
University of Colorado, Boulder CO USA 80309-0430
duck@cs.colorado.edu; (303-) 492-8091

ABSTRACT

Modern application software often includes operations that are performed by complex mathematical algorithms. These algorithms—far from being the "black boxes" typically portrayed in computer science courses— may instead be viewed as interactive processes, each presenting its own particular "interface" to the user. This paper, then, offers a number of *interface guidelines for mathematical algorithms*—principles whose purpose is to suggest ways in which users may employ algorithms with greater control and expressiveness. As a source of examples, we illustrate the guidelines through a particular complex mathematical problem—that of generating a "folding net" for a three-dimensional solid.

Keywords

Algorithms, human-computer interaction, polyhedra, folding nets.

INTRODUCTION

Implicit in almost every university catalog is a taxonomy of knowledge—the world is divided into discrete subjects such as physics, history, and (in most universities) computer science. These subjects themselves are likewise divided into subdisciplines, as reflected by the individual courses. Delving further, and exploring the offerings within computer science departments, one will usually find both an algorithms course and a human-computer interaction course. It is overwhelmingly likely that these two courses will be taught by different faculty, employ different teaching assistants, share no readings, and make use of little of the same language or technical background. Within computer science, algorithm design and human-computer interaction are about as different as subdisciplines can be.

CHI 96 Vancouver, BC Canada
© 1996 ACM 0-89791-777-4/96/04..$3.50

But in practice, mathematical algorithms do, after all, present something of an interface to their users—even if that interface is as simple as a request for parameters. And increasingly, as computer applications become more powerful and complex, they employ algorithms whose behavior is more varied, more unpredictable to the user. A paint program may, for instance, include something like a "select region" function whose behavior is defined as "selecting all nearby pixels whose current color, when compared with the color of the selected pixel, is within some distance in an abstract color-space." A mathematical algebra program may automatically regroup terms in polynomials, following some algorithm whose behavior it is left to the user to induce (and whose results may often leave the user perplexed). "Intelligent" help systems may construct models of users' backgrounds or intentions through algorithms whose details, or even outlines, remain mysterious.

This paper presents a number of broad design guidelines, or principles, for creating interfaces to mathematical algorithms—in effect, for bridging the "thin glass line" of the computer screen that separates the worlds of algorithm and interface design. The governing assumption in seeking these guidelines is that we would like to provide the user with flexible means both for controlling and understanding the algorithm in question. If we assume, in contrast, that users are incapable of understanding even the outlines of the algorithm—for instance, that our hypothetical paint program user would be unable to understand the notion of testing the distance of two colors in an abstract color space—then the issue is resolved before we begin, and we can at best present the user with a choice of typical parameters to our algorithm. In this argument, we assume that users will exhibit a high level of interest in and (potential) understanding of the algorithms that they employ in a professional context, and we seek means of providing users with effective and expressive control over those algorithms.

By way of presenting the suggested guidelines, this paper will use an illustrative algorithm for solving (if partially) an interesting and complex mathematical problem—namely, the problem of generating a two-dimensional "folding net" for a three-dimensional solid. The following section briefly describes this problem and its history, and shows a general algorithm for solving it in certain instances. In the third section we extend this basic algorithm with a variety of suggested improvements; these improvements are motivated by (and, in succession, illustrate) the principles for creating "algorithm interfaces". The fourth section draws out the links between the principles as they appear in the context of this particular sample problem, and the same principles applied to other similarly complex mathematical algorithms that crop up within software applications; this section also describes the relation between this effort and other work, especially in the area of algorithm animation. The fifth section concludes with some directions for future research.

THE FOLDING NET PROBLEM

Consider the polyhedral solid shown in Figure 1a, and imagine that our goal is to create a paper model of this solid. One means of doing so would be first to find a two-dimensional "net" of the solid, as in Figure 1b, which we could print on paper; then we would cut around the outlines of this net, and fold along the edges to form the desired polyhedron. The notion of producing a folding net for a solid is credited (along with the term "net" for the pattern itself) to the 16th-century artist Albrecht Dürer, who devised the first such nets for the five Platonic (or regular) solids, among others. [12] (The solid shown in Figure 1 is, in fact, one of these regular solids—the dodecahedron.)

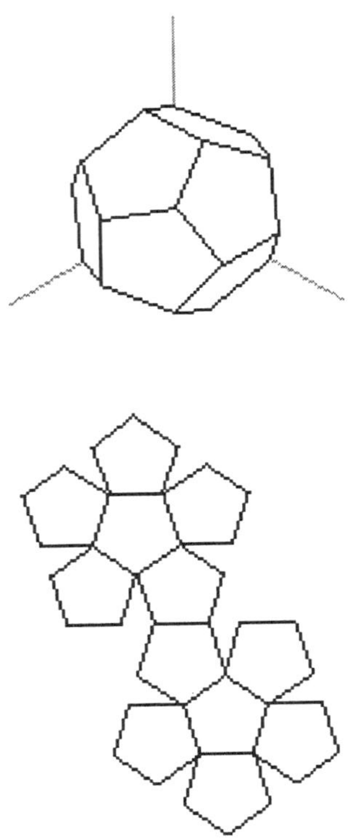

Figure 1a (top). A regular dodecahedron.
Figure 1b (bottom). A "folding net" for the solid.

In utilitarian terms, the generation of folding nets for solid is potentially important: one could imagine uses for nets in (say) packaging, architectural modelling, or three-dimensional illustration. In purely mathematical terms, the problem of generating a folding net for a solid is complex, for a variety of reasons. First, it is unclear how we might determine whether a given solid even has a viable folding net (i.e., one in which the solid has been cut and "unfolded" along some of its edges to form a connected set of two-dimensional polygons, and in which the polygons don't overlap so that the net can be printed on a single sheet of paper). The net in Figure 1b is viable—none of the pentagons overlap, the solid has been sliced along its edges, and the entire two-dimensional shape folds back into a dodecahedron; but in fact there are some nonconvex solids for which no such net exists. The question of whether every convex polyhedron has some folding net (allowing "cuts" of any kind) is an open problem in computational geometry [4]; and to my knowledge, no one has demonstrated a "bad" convex polyhedron for which a viable folding net (allowing only cuts along edges) cannot be produced.

In short, then, we do not know, when given a polyhedron, whether a net can be found (though for convex polyhedra, we might at least be hopeful of obtaining one). There is also a flip side to this issue: a particular solid may admit of several (or perhaps many) nets. Figure 2, for example, shows two other distinct nets (besides that in Figure 1b) for the dodecahedron. The problem of finding a folding net for a solid is thus difficult in two opposing senses: we are not sure if there is any solution, and—having found some solution—we cannot be sure that we have found (for our purposes) the best possible solution.

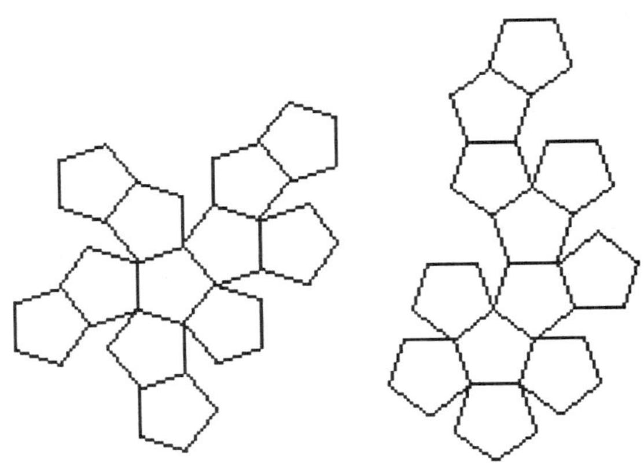

Figure 2. Two additional nets for the dodecahedron.

Algorithms for dealing with problems of this "uncertain" kind generally fall under the heading of heuristic or approximate search. (NP-complete problems, such as the famous "travelling salesman" problem, are typically approached this way as well [3]). We look to find some realistic solution with an eye not toward guaranteeing the best solution, but to "satisficing" (in Simon's [16] term):

essentially, getting a livable solution without spending inordinate amounts of time and effort trying to obtain a slightly better solution.

Here, then, is the broad outline of an algorithm that can often manage to solve the folding net problem (though it is by no means guaranteed to do so). This algorithm will be our starting point for the explorations of the following section.

Algorithm 1
For unfolding a polyhedron P-3D with faces {F-3D} to produce a planar net N with faces {F-2D}:

(1) Begin by choosing a face F from {F-3D}. On the 2D plane, place a polygon f congruent to F. This single polygon now constitutes the net in progress.

{2} If there are no more unaccounted-for faces in {F-3D}—that is, if there are no more faces whose equivalents have not been placed in the net N—then we are done. Return the net N.

{3} Otherwise, choose a face f within the net corresponding to a face F in {F-3D}, and see if F shares an edge with an unaccounted-for face F' in {F-3D}. Place a 2D face congruent to F' in the net so that it shares an edge with the appropriate net polygon congruent to F, along the corresponding shared edge. Check whether the newly-placed net polygon overlaps any other polygon currently in the net. If there is no overlap, go back to step {2}.

{4} If there is an overlap, look to see whether F shares an edge with some other unaccounted-for face F". If so, go back to step {3} (using F" in the role of the face F'). If not, go back to step {3}, attempting an alternative choice for the face f. If there are no remaining choices for the face f in step {3}—i.e., if we have unsuccessfully tried every available face in the net as the face from which to "expand" the net—then announce failure.

Figure 3 illustrates several successive "snapshots" of this algorithm at work in the case of the regular octahedron. Here, the algorithm begins by placing one of the triangular faces of the octahedron on the 2D plane; it then "grows" the net incrementally by finding polygons in the net that border unaccounted-for faces on the solid, and adding those faces to the two-dimensional net. The final result, once all eight faces are accounted for, is shown at the end of the second row in Figure 3.

PRINCIPLES OF "ALGORITHM INTERFACE DESIGN": THE FOLDING NET PROBLEM REVISITED

Algorithm 1, as presented in the previous section, is a workable (though far from ideal) solution to the problem of generating folding nets. One could certainly imagine incorporating this algorithm into a larger application—indeed, something like this algorithm is included in a polyhedral-modelling system developed in our laboratory, "HyperGami" [8], in which the user designs three-dimensional solids on the screen and is then able to create decorated folding nets for those solids.

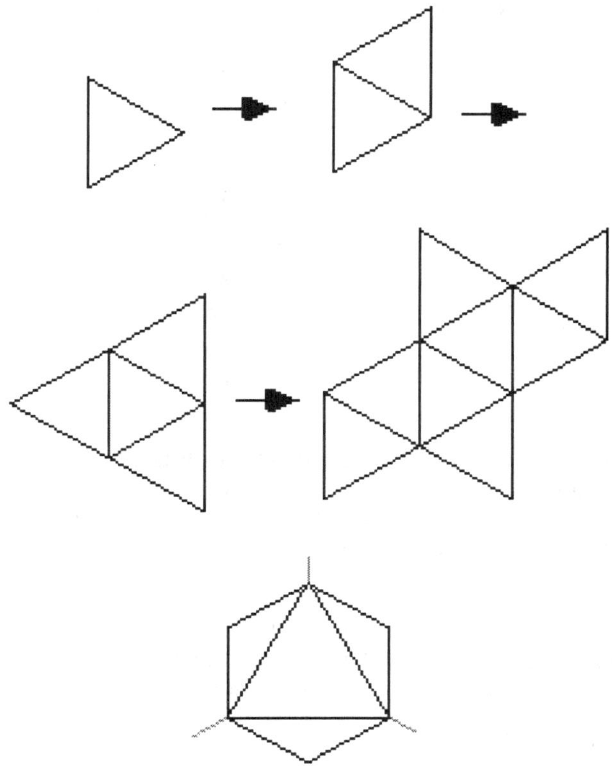

Figure 3a (top two rows). Successive "snapshots" in the generation of a net for a regular octahedron.
Figure 3b (bottom). The octahedron.

In principle, then, we could simply present the user with a button or menu choice of the form "Generate Net for Current Solid"; when the user selects this choice, Algorithm 1 will be run. Such a plan is problematic, however, for two reasons:

(a) Algorithm 1, as written, simply makes one single attempt to generate a net. That attempt may fail; whereas, if the algorithm were to be re-run under slightly different conditions (e.g., choosing a different starting face F in step 1), the algorithm may succeed. Thus, if the algorithm fails, the user should not be left utterly without options until she is satisfied that no solution (or at least no easily obtained solution) exists.

(b) Even if the algorithm succeeds, it may find a net that the user would prefer to avoid. Consider, for instance, the problem of generating a net for an octagonal pyramid, as shown in Figure 4a (this is a loose approximation to a cone). Running Algorithm 1 on this solid may well produce the net shown in Figure 4b. While this is a perfectly reasonable folding net from the mathematical standpoint, it is a poor choice from the human standpoint: the process of actually cutting and folding the net in Figure 4b would require folding eight separate triangles toward a single point, and gluing the edges of those triangles together (an extremely tedious and error-prone chore).

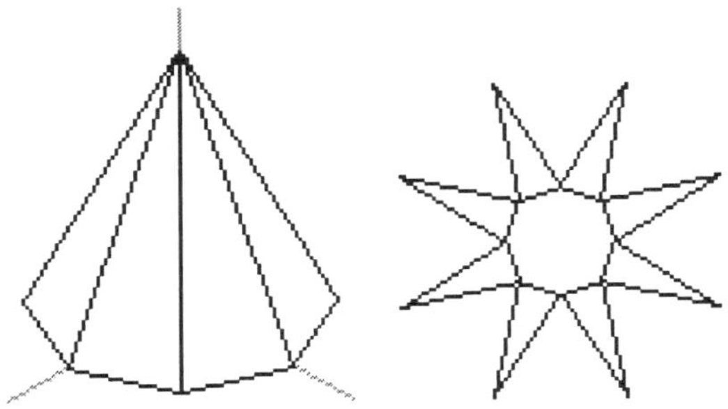

Figure 4a (left). A pyramid whose base is a regular octagon.
Figure 4b (right). A technically correct, but manually problematic, net for the pyramid.

It is worth taking a moment to reflect on the issues described in (b) above. Over and over, what at first blush appears to be a purely mathematical problem—finding a net, arranging terms of a polynomial, presenting steps in a proof, finding a path for a robot through a maze of obstacles—turns out to include highly contextualized, difficult-to-formalize aspects. We wish to express a polynomial, *calling attention* to the higher-order terms in one particular variable; we wish to present steps in a proof so that coherent *patterns of reasoning* are visible (i.e., the steps should not be placed in a technically valid but incoherent order); we want a path for the robot that not only achieves the goal but does so while providing the visual appearance of *purposeful behavior*; or, in our present case, we wish to find a folding net that does not presume inordinate manual skill.

In any event, the issues raised in (a) and (b) suggest that we would like to provide the user with some sense of how our algorithm ran in some particular case—i.e., where it may have gone astray; and moreover, we would like to provide the user with means for rerunning the algorithm with alternative choices of running parameters. This can be summarized in the first two design principles for algorithm interaction:

Principle 1.
When creating an interface to some algorithm, allow for a version that permits the user to observe the algorithm's effects as it runs.

Principle 2.
Create means that allow the user to learn and understand the effect of altering constant parameters within the algorithm, and to perform those alterations.

Realizing Principle 1 in the case of the present algorithm is relatively straightforward—if we do not interpret the principle too strictly. We can simply allow the algorithm to run in normal fashion, placing its various choices of net polygons on the plane as it obtains them (as opposed to simply working in silence and either announcing "failure" or producing a fully-blown net at the end of the process). Thus, the algorithm would produce, as it runs, a sequence of visible nets like those shown in Figure 3 earlier.

Conceivably, Principle 1 could be employed more creatively than this. We might, for instance, need to allow the user to slow down or "tune" the running speed of the algorithm so as to observe its effects; running the algorithm at its maximal speed may prove counterproductive if it hinders understanding. We might also augment the algorithm with a variety of visual cues to indicate the path taken; in our present case, for instance, the most-recently-placed polygon in the net could be shown in red. Going a bit further, we might present the user with both a three-dimensional rendering of the solid being unfolded, and a two-dimensional rendering of the net-in-progress; and the most-recently-placed net polygon could be shown in the same color as its corresponding three-dimensional face.

An extreme version of this idea might entail elaborating the algorithm with more and more visual information, all with the intent of illustrating the operation of the algorithm. Where possible, such additional information should appear unobtrusive within the working context of the algorithm—that is, the visual information should not render the overall application a purely pedagogical exercise. (We will return to this issue in a later section.)

Principle 2 appears rather straightforward at first—presumably, the user should be able to specify important parameters to any complex algorithm. Thus, in the present case, the user should be able to select (for instance) the 3-dimensional polyhedral face from which the net-generation process will begin in Step 1 of the algorithm.

There are subtle problems encountered, however, in trying to interpret Principle 2 more creatively. A "parameter" to an algorithm such as Algorithm 1 above may not be quite as straightforward as a number or polygon. Consider, for instance, the third step: it involves choosing a "frontier" polygon in the net, and finding an edge of that polygon corresponding to a 3d (solid) edge bordering a still-unaccounted-for face. The choice rules for both these operations may themselves be parameters to the algorithm: for instance, we might wish to specify that the algorithm will always choose the most recently-placed polygon in the net as the "frontier" from which to attempt expanding the net (in effect, performing a depth-first search). Specifying a choice rule—as opposed to a simple value such as a number—as input to an algorithm touches upon the often controversial notion of end-user programming [5, 7, 13, 14]: conceivably, the user should be given something like a programming language with which to express "choice rules" in complex algorithms. A less contentious position in this situation would be that the user should have, at the very least, a set of discrete "typical" choice rules from which to select, or (somewhat more powerful) an algorithm-specific "grammar"—perhaps less extensive than a complete programming language—with which to express notions such as choice rules.

Considering the notion of a "choice rule" as an algorithm parameter leads to yet another principle, regarding when such a choice rule is most effectively considered by the user. The standard assumption for algorithm design is that parameters are dictated as initial fixed inputs to the algorithm, which is then run to completion. But in the case of a procedure such as Algorithm 1, we may have a better sense of what parameters to choose once the algorithm has actually begun operation: for instance, we may have a more informed notion of what would constitute a good choice rule at the moment that the choice rule needs to be employed. Moreover, we might well want this type of repeatedly-employed parameter to be dictated dynamically, more than once in the course of the running algorithm (as opposed to being dictated in static and irrevocable fashion at the outset).

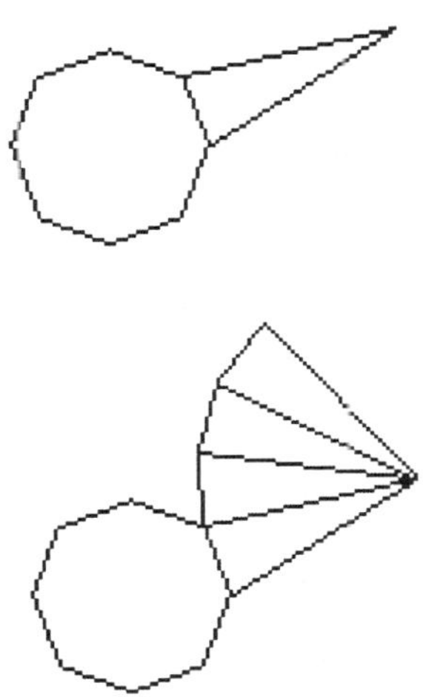

Figure 5a. The net-in-progress for the pyramid of Figure 4a, after just two steps.
Figure 5b. The net after several more steps, using a rule in which each new polygon is attached to the most recently-placed available polygon.

To take a specific example: suppose, once more, that we are generating a net for an octagonal pyramid. The algorithm might begin by placing the solid's base octagon as the first face in the two-dimensional net, and then a neighboring triangle corresponding to one of the "side" faces of the pyramid. (See Figure 5a for illustration.) The algorithm might then—and only then—pause for the user's input as to choice rule for next polygon in the net to expand. In this case, the user might select as choice rule "most recently-placed net polygon", so that the algorithm attempts to attach the next net polygon to an edge of the triangle (as opposed to an edge of the octagon). The net produced after several more such steps is shown in Figure 5b. At this juncture, the user might interrupt the algorithm once more to re-define the choice rule, indicating that (e.g.) future new polygons should be joined (if possible) to those polygons with few vertices that were placed earlier. The algorithm would then continue by placing its next triangle on the bottom edge of the earliest-placed triangle (the one in Figure 5a).

The rationale behind a scenario of this kind is based upon the notion of "reflection-in-action" described by Schoen [15] and eloquently advocated in the realm of user interfaces by Fischer and his colleagues [10]. These writers present a portrait of design activity in which decisions are often made not in the manner of *a priori* specifications, but rather in a more dynamic fashion, as the need for the decision arises. Such notions can be applied to interaction with algorithms just as they can with the sorts of design domains considered by Schoen. (This extension of an "improvisatory" style of work to computational media also resonates strongly with the ideas expressed by Dourish [6] in designing systems that present dynamic "accounts", or self-generated representations, of system behavior.) In any event, we can summarize by stating our third principle of algorithm interaction:

Principle 3.
There should be means for permitting users to specify parameters to the algorithm at the time they are employed; and for those parameters that are employed repeatedly, there should be means of treating those parameters as "fluid" by altering them in mid-process.

This principle leads, in turn, to a fourth which implements the notion of at least a single level "undo": if we have chosen a particular fluid parameter and run into trouble as a result, we should be able to return to the state of the algorithm at the moment of the last (apparently flawed) decision—a form of user-directed "backtracking."

Principle 4.
For those parameter choices that have been dynamically specified midway, there should be means for storing the state of the algorithm at the time of the most recent specification and returning to that state in order to revisit the user's previous decision.

To return to the (somewhat artificially simple) example of the octagonal-base pyramid: suppose that after two polygons in the net have been placed (as in Figure 5a), we specify that the rule for choosing the next polygon to expand will be to select the least-recently-placed polygon. After a second triangle has been placed (in Figure 6a), we realize that our choice is going to produce a problematic net, so we should be able to interrupt the algorithm and return it to the state in which we made the previous decision. From this point, we choose an alternative next-polygon rule and resume the algorithm, generating (after a second triangle has been placed) the net shown in Figure 6b.

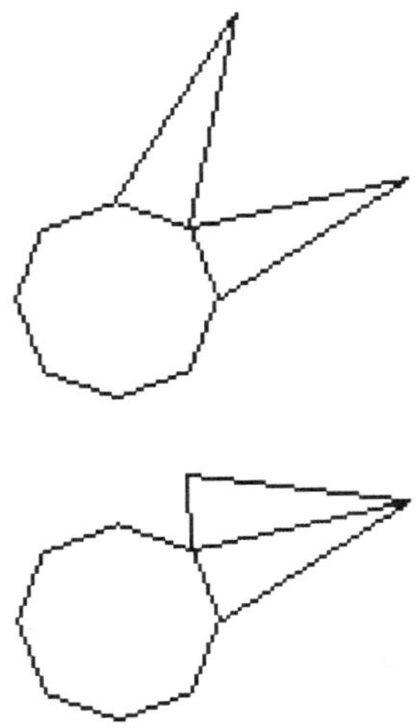

Figure 6a (top). The net for the pyramid in Figure 4a, after three polygons have been placed.
Figure 6b (bottom). A more promising start for the net.

"Undo" facilities of the type suggested by Principle 4 are a staple of user interface design courses, but in practice they typically apply to discrete actions taken via direct manipulation by the user, not to parameter choices for running algorithms.

Finally, even when a complex algorithm has run to successful completion, users (being only human, after all) may still be dissatisfied. For instance, even if our algorithm has produced a successful folding net, we may still sense a possibility for improvement after the fact. In this instance, an algorithm should provide means for *post hoc* "adjustment" of its solution to a particular problem.

Consider, as an example, the folding net shown in Figure 7a. In this case, the user has produced a perfectly reasonable net for a truncated prism—but she would still like to tinker. She could now be presented with a "post-algorithm" operation allowing her both to select an "end polygon" in the net (a polygon with only one net-connected edge) and to observe which other edges in the net could be attached to that same polygon. Using this operation she should now be able to repeatedly shift end polygons to other available positions, as illustrated for one such shift in Figure 7b.

Our fifth principle for interacting with algorithms, then, is:

Principle 5.
Algorithms should not run to an irretrievable conclusion, but should wherever possible be accompanied by "post-algorithmic" operations that allow the user to modify (if only slightly, in accordance with "legal" moves) the solution produced by the algorithm.

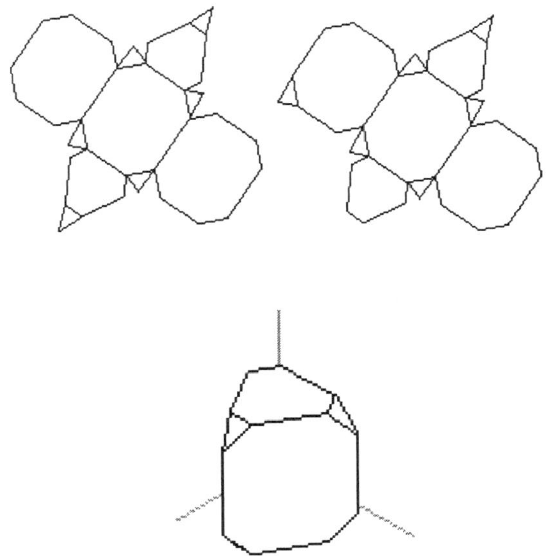

Figure 7a (top left). A folding net for a truncated prism.
Figure 7b (top right). An alternative net, differing in the position of one triangle.
Figure 7c (bottom). A view of the solid itself.

THE "ALGORITHM INTERFACE PRINCIPLES" IN OTHER CONTEXTS

To this point, the principles described in the previous section have all been illustrated through one (conceivably artificial) problem—that of generating a folding net for a solid. To suggest the ways in which such principles might be employed in other contexts, this section presents an extended scenario in which "conventional" application behavior might be profitably perturbed to accommodate the principles.

Suppose, then, that the user of a hypothetical paint program selects a starting point on some picture; his intent is that this will be the point from which he would like to select a region of contiguous pixels within the picture, all within a given "RGB color distance" d of the starting point. Instead of selecting this color distance via some abstract symbol (such as "high/medium/low distance"), or through some unexplained numeric value, the algorithm presents the user with a representation of the RGB "color cube" (cf. the representation in [11]) and allows him to select the desired parameter by drawing a sphere of radius *d* around the color of the starting point. (Principle 2: the algorithm presents its parameters in a manner faithful to their use and meaning within the process itself.) Once invoked, the algorithm, rather than simply presenting a final boundary to this region "by magic", instead may be slowed down to portray the way in which the boundary of the region is incrementally obtained. (Principle 1: the algorithm slows down to indicate its mode of operation to the user.)

Over time, the user becomes sufficiently familiar with this algorithm that he is able to use a more advanced version in which, as the region around the starting point is incrementally searched (at moderate to slow speed, so that the search process is visible), the color distance used as the effective search "filter" may be altered: that is, rather than merely produce a region whose RGB-distance from the starting pixel is less than *d* throughout, the user may "tune" or vary the parameter *d* as he observes the region grow on the screen. (Principle 3: a parameter used repeatedly in the course of the running algorithm may be made "fluid" in practice.) The overall region thus generated may reflect multiple choices of the distance *d*: e.g., the region might use a "loose" distance filter over some portions of the boundary, a "strict" color filter over other portions. In employing this more complex version of the "region selection" routine, the user is also able to "back up" the search process to the point where the last change in the parameter *d* was made (Principle 4.) Overall, the boundaries of the regions generated in this "tunable" search process may be much more complex than those generated in a simpler, "fixed-parameter" version.

Finally, once a region has been generated, the user is able to revisit the region boundary (perhaps "zooming in" on those portions), selectively moving small portions of the boundary outward or inward. (Principle 5: Once the algorithm is run, its results may be modified by related "post-algorithmic" operations.)

It may be argued at this juncture that the principles articulated for "algorithm interaction" are hardly anything new: after all, when selecting an operation within some application, we would *always* wish to choose a parameter for that operation in an informative way (Principle 2), to see the operation itself performed in instructive fashion (Principle 1), to have the option to undo some recent set of decisions (Principle 4), and so forth. This is true: but in practice, applications tend to treat the invocation of algorithms as atomic actions, employing algorithms in the "black box" fashion more typical of presentations in computer science courses. Algorithms tend to be written to run at maximum speed rather than with maximum transparency, and as a consequence, users are left with (at best) a very coarse-grained picture of how many popular operations are actually performed: region fills, spline creation, digital image warping, text justification all remain mysterious. Of course, for many users the "black box" assumption is perfectly reasonable—the majority of us may not be especially interested in how the standard "fill" operation is actually performed in most paint programs, and may be satisfied to employ a black-box version of the algorithm to run at maximal speed. But the option either of understanding or interacting with such an algorithm is rarely offered. The purpose of presenting these principles as means of interacting with algorithms is merely to suggest that in many cases, algorithms may themselves be thought of as the subjects of interface construction.

It should also be mentioned that there are definite commonalities of interest between the principles suggested here and many of the techniques used for algorithm animation [1, 2, 17]. Most efforts at algorithm animation, however, focus on presenting algorithms strictly for pedagogical purposes: i.e., the user's presumed intent (at least in the short term) is to understand but not actually employ the algorithm. Moreover, algorithm animations typically present processes at a level somewhat abstracted from use within applications: we may see an animation of a depth-first search routine, but not the use of that routine in the course of generating (say) a folding net for a solid. The argument of this paper, in contrast, is to weave at least some of the ideas associated with algorithm animation into the actual working contexts of applications themselves.

ALGORITHM INTERFACES: SOME DIRECTIONS FOR RESEARCH

The previous section concluded with a distinction drawn between the "practical" context suggested for the principles described here, and the "pedagogical" context assumed for most algorithm animation efforts. Merely because the interface principles suggested here are intended for integration within working algorithms, however, does not imply that they have no pedagogical value. In fact, it may well be that users who learn about (say) depth-first search in the course of ongoing, and personally meaningful, professional work will have more motivation to experiment with the algorithm than those who learn of the algorithm in the rather abstract setting of a computer science course (even if that course is augmented by beautifully prepared animations). Again, this echoes the sentiments of Fischer [9], who argues for effective learning in the context of ongoing work (the basis for what he has dubbed "learning on demand").

It would be of particular interest, then, to incorporate (some of) these principles within selected complex algorithms in professional applications, and to study the pedagogical effectiveness of the principles in that context. Such an effort might, if the results are encouraging, lead professional application designers to incorporate more "transparent" algorithms into their systems. While this might appear to be a utopian wish in an era when algorithms are treated as proprietary information, designing applications with transparent algorithms might actually prove of financial benefit if it lends greater expressiveness (and hence satisfaction) to an application's user community. And placing transparent algorithms within applications might serve the purpose of enlisting the culture of professional application design, easily and unobtrusively, in the larger task of computer science education.

Moreover—returning to the academic theme with which we began—thinking of algorithms as interactive (rather than purely and majestically deterministic) processes might lend an interesting twist to the study of algorithms themselves. Currently, it is rare to see algorithms analyzed in any terms other than those of computational requirements in space or time. Nonetheless, an algorithm which, in practice, lends itself to expressive interaction might be far superior than one that runs faster but offers no avenues for creativity to its users. As suggested earlier, it would appear that especially difficult problems—including, one might guess, many NP-complete problems—are good candidates for the design of interactive algorithms. Rather than run a non-interactive algorithm for (say) a variant of the "travelling salesman" problem, one might enlist the occasional aid of the user—particularly if (as so often happens), the user is aware of relevant context-specific information for this particular instance of the problem. Pursuing this direction might lead us to analyze the performance of algorithms as augmented by human interaction: we might find, in practice, that an algorithm rich in its interactive capabilities actually outperforms (in the quality of its solutions) a more time-efficient "black box" algorithm. This type of study might lead us in turn to analyze algorithms, on occasion, in terms of the interactions that they afford, rather than the resources that they require. And eventually—perhaps—our university courses in human-computer interaction and algorithm design might actually share the occasional reading.

ACKNOWLEDGMENTS

This work owes much to the influence of Hal Abelson and Gerald Jay Sussman. The HyperGami program—the source of the "folding net problem"—was developed with the collaboration of Ann Nishioka and the assistance of Zach Nies and Jay Smith. I would also like to thank Gerhard Fischer and the members of the Center for LifeLong Learning and Design at the University of Colorado for wonderful conversations. The author is supported in part by NSF grants RED-9253425 and IRI-9210324, and by a Young Investigator award IRI-9258684.

REFERENCES

1. Brown, M. Exploring Algorithms Using Balsa-II. *IEEE Computer*, May 1988, pp. 14-36.

2. Brown, M. H. and Sedgewick, R. Techniques for Algorithm Animation. *IEEE Software*, Jan. 1985, pp. 28-39.

3. Cormen, T.; Leiserson, C.; and Rivest, R. *Introduction to Algorithms*. McGraw-Hill, New York, 1990.

4. Croft, H.; Falconer, K.; and Guy, R. *Unsolved Problems in Geometry*. Springer-Verlag, New York, 1991.

5. Cypher, A., ed. *Watch What I Do*. MIT Press, Cambridge MA, 1993

6. Dourish, P. Accounting for System Behavior: Representation, Reflection, and Resourceful Action. *Proc. of Third Decennial Aarhus Conference*, Aarhus Denmark, Aug. 1995, pp. 147-156.

7. Eisenberg, M. Programmable Applications: Interpreter Meets Interface. *SIGCHI Bulletin*, 27:2, 1995, pp. 68-83.

8. Eisenberg, M. and Nishioka, A. Creating Polyhedral Models by Computer. To appear in *Journal of Computers in Mathematics and Science Teaching*, 1996.

9. Fischer, G. Supporting Learning on Demand with Design Environments. In *Proceedings of the International Conference on the Learning Sciences*, Charlottesville, VA, 1991, pp. 165-172.

10. Fischer, G., Lemke, A.C., Mastaglio, T. and Morch, A. The Role of Critiquing in Cooperative Problem Solving. *ACM Transactions on Information Systems*, Vol. 9, No. 2, 1991, pp. 123-151.

11. Foley, J; Van Dam, A.; Feiner, S.; and Hughes, J. *Computer Graphics: Principles and Practice*. Addison-Wesley, Reading, MA, 1990.

12. Malkevitch, J. Milestones in the history of polyhedra. In M. Senechal and G. Fleck (eds.), *Shaping Space: A Polyhedral Approach*, Birkhäuser, Boston, 1988, pp. 80-92.

13. Myers, B.; Smith, D. C.; and Horn, B. Report of the "End-User Programming" Working Group. In B. Myers (ed.), *Languages for Developing User Interfaces*. Jones and Bartlett, Boston, 1992, pp. 343-366.

14. Nardi, B. *A Small Matter of Programming*. MIT Press, Cambridge, MA 1993.

15. Schoen, D. A. *The Reflective Practitioner: How Professionals Think in Action*. Basic Books, New York, 1983.

16. Simon, H. *The Sciences of the Artificial*. MIT Press, Cambridge, MA, 1981.

17. Stasko, J. and Patterson, C. Understanding and Characterizing Software Visualization Systems. *1992 IEEE Workshop on Visual Languages*, Seattle, Sept. 1992, pp. 3-10.

Learning Theory in Practice:

Case Studies of Learner-Centered Design

Elliot Soloway, Shari L. Jackson, Jonathan Klein, Chris Quintana, James Reed, Jeff Spitulnik, Steven J. Stratford, Scott Studer, Jim Eng, Nancy Scala

University of Michigan
1101 Beal Ave.
Ann Arbor, MI 48109, USA
+1 313 763 6988
soloway@umich.edu

ABSTRACT
The design of software for learners must be guided by educational theory. We present a framework for learner-centered design (LCD) that is theoretically motivated by sociocultural and constructivist theories of learning. LCD guides the design of software in order to support the unique needs of learners: growth, diversity, and motivation. To address these needs, we incorporate scaffolding into the context, tasks, tools, and interface of software learning environments. We demonstrate the application of our methodology by presenting two case studies of LCD in practice.

Keywords Learner-Centered Design, Educational Applications, Science Applications, Socioculturalism, Constructivism, Case Study, Scaffolding.

INTRODUCTION: MOTIVATION AND GOALS

The push for educational reform in the U.S. is strong. Currently, the dominant educational paradigm is "didactic instruction," where learning is viewed as an *information transmission process*: teachers have the information, students don't, and teachers' lectures serve to move information into the heads of students. In contrast, national and state education reform movements are advocating for students to be actively engaged in learning, *constructing understanding and meaning*, not receiving it. Project 2061, a national science curriculum developed by the American Association for the Advancement of Science [1] calls for students to engage in long-term, authentic investigations.

Computing and communications technologies can play a key role in supporting students and teachers as they engage in such authentic tasks as question-generating, model-building, report-publishing. However, constructing software that truly addresses the needs of learners is a challenge: while learners are also users, and thus the principles of user-centered design apply, learners additionally have a set of unique needs that must be addressed in software:

- **Growth**. At the core of education is the growth of the learner; promoting the development of expertise must be the primary goal of educational software. Rather than just support "doing" tasks, software designed for learners must support "learning while doing."
- **Diversity**. Developmental differences, cultural differences, and gender differences play a major role in the suitability of materials for learners. To be usable by all learners, a range of software tools that address these differences must be available.
- **Motivation**. In contrast to software developed for professionals, the student's initial interest and continuing engagement cannot be taken for granted.

To address these unique needs of learners, we are developing learner-centered design (LCD) guidelines [24] to augment the user-centered design (UCD) framework [15]. Our current focus is on K-16 learners; however, given Senge's [22] compelling arguments that an organization must be a *learning* organization in order to be productive, LCD should also have validity for the workplace.

The central claim of LCD is that software can embody learning supports—*scaffolding*—that can address the learner's growth, diversity, and motivation. Scaffolding is an educational term that refers to providing support to learners while they engage in activities that are normally out of their reach [28, 30]. For example, n undertaking an authentic science inquiry, e.g., what is the quality of water in the stream behind my school, the tasks are more complex and diverse than those in traditional, follow-the-steps, lab-style experiments. Software-realized scaffolding can reduce the complexity of these tasks, for example, by relating discrete subtasks to their current mental representations.

From edutainment to context-sensitive help systems, the need to support learners is well recognized. That said, there are precious few resounding successes (e.g., [6, 16]). Given the formidable educational problems that face our society and the almost-availability of consumer-priced, high-performance computing and communications technologies, the opportunity to actually make-a-difference in education is truly at hand.

In LCD we (see also [12, 14, 20]) are attempting to explore the design implications of learning theories -- constructivism and socioculturism -- that have heretofore received less attention than, say, behaviorism (upon which computer-assisted instruction (CAI) is built) and information processing psychology (upon which intelligent tutoring systems are built). While the work reported here is clearly only now maturing, our intent is to focus attention on a fertile, promising direction for research and development.

In this paper, then, we:

- **Articulate the Theoretical Rationale and Design Implications.** The scaffolding design guidelines of LCD build directly on constructivist & sociocultural theories of learning.
- **Illustrate LCD via Case Studies.** Two examples of how LCD has informed the design of educational software are presented.
- **Summarize the Key Issues in LCD.**

THEORETICAL RATIONALE & IMPLICATIONS

Two resonating theoretical frameworks underlie both the education reform movement (e.g., [3, 4, 7] as well as our evolving the LCD framework:

- *In constructivism* (e.g., [14, 16, 17, 28]) the central notion is that understanding and learning are active, constructive, generative processes such as assimilation, augmentation, and self-reorganization. For example, a teacher's words do not simply become directly engraved in a student's mind, after passing through the ear, but rather, those words are acted upon and interpreted by the student.
- *In socioculturism*, the central notion is that learning is enculturation, the process by which learners become collaborative meaning-makers among a group defined by common practices, language, use of tools, values, beliefs, and so on [5, 14, 21, 29]. The goal is to enable practices and meaning making that are appropriate in the professional culture of the domain under study. For example, scientists understand science as those ideas are embodied in their everyday practices. Contrast this way of knowing with traditional science classrooms where, *from the students' perspective,* concepts come from textbooks and lectures, and lab experiments are tightly-controlled exercises that fit into the requisite 50 minute period.

These two theoretical perspectives are consistent with each other; they just emphasize different themes: the former speaks to the individual's cognition, while the latter speaks to the contributions of the surroundings to that cognition.

From socio-constructivism, then, guidelines for the design of learning environments and the supporting scaffolding can be developed (e.g., [9, 11, 20]). In particular, in LCD, *we are attempting to provide guidelines for the construction of scaffolding strategies, to address the three unique needs of learners* (growth, diversity and motivation) *for each of the four components in a learning environment:*

- **Context**: What is the environment in which the software will be embedded? How will it be used, and by whom?
- **Tasks**: What are the tasks the software will support?
- **Tools**: What tools will perform these tasks?
- **Interface**: What is the interface to those tools?

Examples of LCD scaffolding guidelines are given in the following case studies.

LCD: TWO CASE STUDIES

Model-It and NoRIS are learner-centered software tools which we have designed for two different contexts:

- Model-It: High school, project-based science classroom: We are working with science teachers at Community High School in Ann Arbor to develop a new high school science curriculum in which computing technologies are routinely used, and in which the subject matter of earth science, chemistry, and biology is combined and taught in the context of meaningful, long term projects. *Model-It,* software for building and testing computational models, is one of the tools we are developing for use in this environment.
- NoRIS: University nuclear engineering classroom: The University of Michigan Nuclear Engineering department encourages the use of computational science in the upper-level undergraduate curriculum. *NoRIS* is a problem-solving environment we have developed for use in these classrooms.

While on the surface these two contexts are different, at their core they both require the same sorts of scaffolding; the only real difference is one of emphasis. In the high-school context, motivation is a big issue, while it is less so in the undergraduate context. However, in the undergraduate context, structuring the complex tasks that make up a computational science-style argument is the real challenge.

In our discussion of each example, we first present the software design, and how it incorporates scaffolding to address learner's needs regarding software context, tasks, tools, and interface. Then, we present examples from the user testing data which illustrate the impact of specific software features designed to provide scaffolding.

Case Study One: Model-It

Model-It is designed to support learners in building and testing models of dynamic systems. Scientists build models to test theories and to develop a better understanding of complex systems [13]. Similarly, we want to support students in the building of models, as sociocultural learning theory says that learners should be involved in professional practices. Constructivist learning theory predicts that by constructing external representations of scientific phenomena, learners are building an internal, mental model of the phenomena. We believe that by building models, students will support, refine, and develop their understanding of a scientific system by constructing models to represent their understanding of the phenomenon and its complex interrelationships.

The modeling tools that have typically been designed for students fall into two categories: pre-defined simulations, and modeling environments. Pre-defined simulations, such as Maxis' SimEarth and Wings for Learning's Explorer, are not constructivist; although user-friendly and informative within their pre-programmed domains, they do not provide access to underlying functions and representations which drive the simulation, nor the ability to add or change functionality. On the other hand, modeling environments, such as High Performance System's Stella or Knowledge Revolution's Working Model, allow unlimited flexibility in building models. However, they are difficult to learn because they don't support the novice's knowledge representation of the domain; for these tools, building complex models requires mastery of a complex authoring language [26]. Thus, current modeling tools inadequately address the needs of learners.

Design and LCD Scaffolding

Context: Model-It, with its emphasis on *building and testing models*, is designed to be used in an authentic, project-based science curriculum, grounded in constructivist and sociocultural educational paradigms. The 9th and 10th grade students in our pilot studies have been engaged in a long-term project investigating the question "How safe is our water?" Specifically, they are studying a tributary of the Huron River which flows near the school, collecting a variety of data to determine the quality of the water. Since this water eventually ends up in their drinking fountains, the question is motivating and personally meaningful to the students.

Using Model-It, the students constructed models of the stream ecosystem,[1] and were assigned open-ended projects in which they were asked to build models to represent their choice of particular stream phenomena, e.g., land use practices: the impact of man-made structures such a golf course or parking lot on stream quality. Creating models is motivating to students because the students are engaged and challenged to create an original artifact. Furthermore, as students have more input into the choice and control of their environments, their motivation for pursuing cognitively challenging problems increases [2]. Allowing students to decide how to plan, design, and work on their models can engage them in the learning process.

Tasks: Model-It scaffolds the complexity of the modeling task by providing a set of *pre-defined high-level objects* (e.g. stream, bugs, golf course). These physical objects match the learner's knowledge representation of the domain, in contrast to an expert's knowledge representation which might consist of domain-independent primitives of inputs, outputs, functions and states.

Students select from this set of objects, define factors of the objects, and relationships between the factors. Model-It redefines the task of defining relationships by supporting a *qualitative representation of relationships*, rather than requiring formal mathematical expressions. This scaffolding is important for learners because their knowledge structures don't initially include a quantitative command of the concepts involved.

Tools: Learners need tools appropriate for their learning styles and levels of expertise; therefore Model-It provides tools for *both qualitative and quantitative definition* of relationships. Initially, relationships can be defined qualitatively by selecting descriptors in a sentence, e.g., "As stream phosphate increases, stream quality decreases by less and less" (Figure 1). As students' knowledge representations of the domain become more expert-like, they have the option of defining the relationship more quantitatively, e.g., by entering data points into a table (Figure 2). Model-It also supports a similar qualitative definition of rate relationships which define how one factor sets the rate of change of another factor over time.

To support different learning styles, and to facilitate the learner's shift to more abstract mental representations, these tools provide both *textual and graphical representations of relationships*. Given a qualitative definition, the software translates the text into a quantitative visual representation; e.g. "decreases by less and less" is interpreted as shown by the graph in Figure 1.

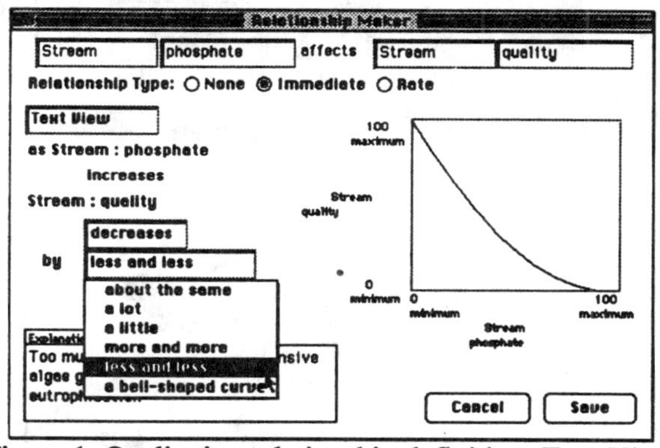

Figure 1: Qualitative relationship definition: Text View

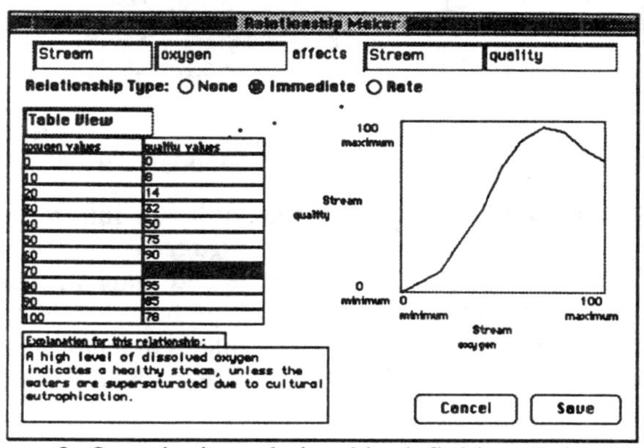

Figure 2: Quantitative relationship definition: Table View

Interface: Learners often need extra motivation to sustain interest in a task, and the interactivity and engaging personal graphics of Model-It can help provide that motivation. To make the task more concrete and authentic, objects are represented with *actual digitized photographs* and

[1]Model-It can be used to build a wide range of process flow models; for our preliminary classroom study we chose the domain of stream ecosystems. In our description of the program, we use examples from this domain.

user-defined graphics. Students can create their own objects and paste in their own pictures. In Figure 3, the background graphic is a photograph of the actual stream the students studied. According to sociocultural perspectives of learning, this personalized representation creates a context through which the activity has meaning.

The Factor Map (Figure 4) provides an *interactive overview of the model.* It helps students structure the task by providing a means of visualizing the network of factors and relationships, rearranging the nodes in a meaningful way, and making changes (e.g., drawing an arrow to create a new relationship).

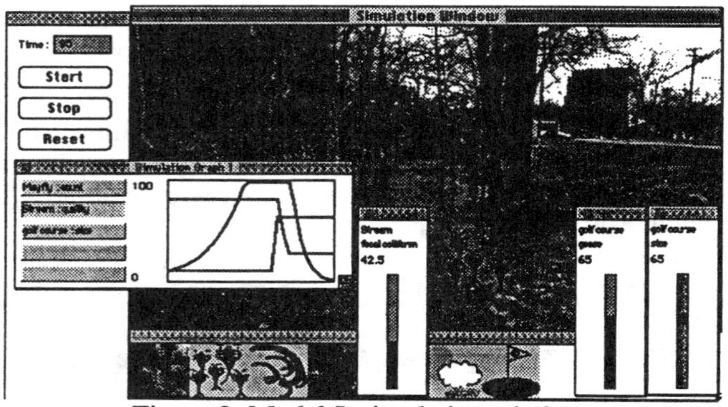

Figure 3: Model-It simulation window

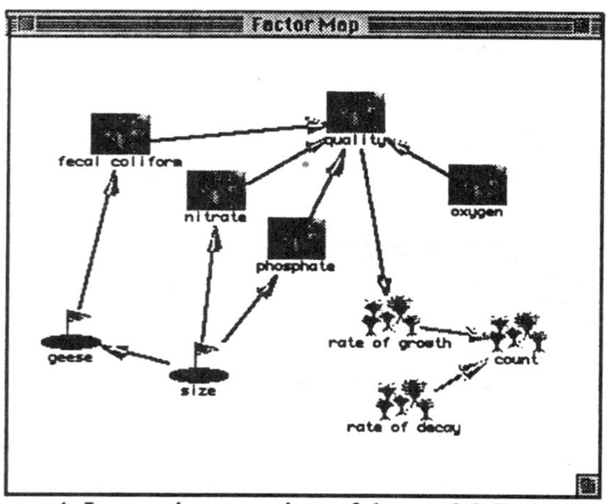

Figure 4: Interactive overview of the model: Factor Map

The highly interactive, direct manipulation interface of Model-It can help provide *sustained engagement* in the task [15, 23]. During a simulation, meters and graphs provide *immediate feedback* of factor values as they change over time (Figure 4). Students can make changes in factor values even while the model is running, and immediately see the impact.

From a constructivist perspective, interactively working and reworking the representation enables the student to continue constructing their knowledge representations [17]. By integrating the building and testing components of modeling, Model-It supports an iterative process of model construction.

Finally, to encourage students to reflect, and therefore extend their knowledge and their metacognitive skills, the interface encourages articulation by providing *explanation fields* (e.g., Figure 2) where students can enter explanations for the objects, factors and relationships they create.

Results

Versions of Model-It have been used in several classroom studies with 9th and 10th grade students. In each, students have worked in groups of two with the program, over a period of one or two weeks. Each study culminated in the assignment of an open-ended modeling task, where students were asked to create their own models to represent some chosen ecological phenomenon. In [12], we present a detailed analysis of the data. The following discussion focuses on a representative pair of students, Paul and Jim, two 9th graders from our first classroom study, and how Model-It scaffolded them in creating a complex model in just one 45-minute period.

Context: The open-ended modeling task assigned to the students gave them the flexibility to branch off and explore different topics, and to express their own understanding. For example, to demonstrate land use impacts, Paul and Jim chose to put the golf course object into their model, and show how factors of the golf course might affect the stream and the organisms living in it:

J: Let's use that one.
P: The golf course?
J: Yeah, we haven't used that one yet.
P: How the golf course affects what, though?
J: How the golf course affects, um, bacteria.
P: Too hard.
J: It's easy. Because the golf course, a lot of geese are on the golf course, and the geese feces go in the water.
P: Oh, and it affects fecal coliform
J: Which in turn affects the bacteria, and the fecal coliform grows on bacteria.
P: Okay, where do you want the golf course?
J: Right there.

This opportunity to build their own models was extremely motivating for Paul and Jim; they displayed excitement and enthusiasm for the project throughout the class period. Once they had completed their initial goal of representing the golf course impact, they branched out on their own to create more relationships, from the stream quality to the mayfly population. They expressed pride in their model, and called the teacher over to show it off to her. This reaction was typical of the entire class; as one student said in post-interviews, "It makes you think more about a real-life situation, where's there's no real answer—*you* set it up and everything."

Tasks: Students were comfortable expressing themselves qualitatively, and using the qualitative definition of relationships, they were able to build complex relationships very quickly:

P: As geese increases fecal coliform increases at about the same. And then if we want, it won't take long to put in nitrates.
J: Okay.
P: We can add that in.
J: Cause that's part of fertilizer...
P: Cause that's part of fertilizer, yeah. So we go to stream...okay...to nitrates N I T nitrates.
J: Lesser and lesser.

Paul and Jim created four accurate, interrelated relationships in four minutes, and in the next four minutes, tested and verified their model, and found another relationship to add (they realized that the size of the golf course should affect the number of geese on it). Figure 4, above, shows the factor map of their final model. In class discussion, they proudly described how their model worked:

P: The size of the golf course affected the geese, the number of geese...
J: The more land there is the more geese... And the more geese the more fecal coliform.
P: The golf course size affected nitrates and phosphates...because the bigger golf course has more fertilizer and fertilizer has nitrates and phosphates in it.
Teacher: Do you have any [relationships] going to quality?
P: Well I'm getting there, okay? This is complicated! Okay, fecal coliform goes to quality, phosphate goes to quality, nitrate goes to quality... And then the quality went to rate of growth.
Teacher: Why?
P: Because the better quality...
J: There is the more mayflies can grow. And then the growth went to count and the decay went to the count.

Tools: Providing a variety of modeling and visualization tools proved very useful for learning, as students could choose the tool which made the most sense to them. For example, we provide both qualitative and quantitative means of defining relationships to support students at different levels of expertise. While Paul and Jim exclusively used the qualitative "text view" tool, another classmate preferred the precision afforded by the quantitative "table view." Often, students transitioned from one to the other during our longer studies, switching to the "table view" when they realized a need to make their models more accurate.

Interface: Meters and graphs provided visualization of simulations as they ran, and were used for model testing and verification. For instance, during their testing, Paul and Jim used the meters to try different values of golf course size, and realized that it should affect the number of geese on the golf course, so they went back to put that relationship in: "So, golf course size affects golf course geese. Yeah, we can do it. As golf course size increases, geese increases by about the same."

Summary

Our Model-It testing showed that the software design scaffolded the learners' growth, diversity, and motivation. Within the context of this project-based classroom, working on an authentic problem, students were able to build and test computational models, a task which is usually inaccessible to learners in high school science classrooms. Students used modeling tools provided by the software in ways reflective of their learning styles; their engagement with the modeling task was evident in their interaction with the interface as they built and tested their models.

Case Study Two: NoRIS

NoRIS is designed to provide an environment that will enable students to use professional computational science tools to carry out a scientific investigation. More and more researchers are turning to computational science when they investigate problems because increased computing power allows them to model physical phenomena, giving more explanatory power to their arguments. Therefore, it is important for students to use authentic tools as they learn to conduct investigations and construct scientific arguments [8]. However, learning to use computational science tools and techniques is a complex process that poses difficulties to the learner.

• First, there are many different individual computational tools available to scientists, but few tools that provide comprehensive support for the entire investigative process. For example, visualization packages are very powerful, but very specific for a certain subtask of an investigation. Others, such as Mathematica, Maple, etc., are attempting to integrate more functionality within a single package, but the packages are still complex and do not support all investigative tasks [25], nor do they provide support for learners.

• Second, computational science results in artifacts of different media types, but there is no support for the construction of the scientific argument, or for the management of the artifacts necessary to support the investigatory process [10]. For example, in a given situation, a student may need to refer to a source code file, data file, and graph, all of which may reside in different directories. The responsibility for organization and access of these artifacts is with the student.

• Finally, students are confronted with a variety of different interfaces and tools, which adds an additional level of complexity to the investigation.

In order to address these shortcomings and provide computer-based support to help students learn the investigative process, we have developed NoRIS (Notebook-based Research and Investigative process Support system).

Design and LCD Scaffolding

Context: NoRIS provides a platform that *enables students to use computational science* so that they can carry out a scientific investigation. NoRIS is being used in a senior-level nuclear engineering class where students investigate numerical methods. NoRIS assumes more of a sociocultural perspective: by giving these students an environment that reduces many of the complexities inherent in computational science, NoRIS aims to support students as they begin learning the tools and practices of the professional researcher.

Tasks: Students with little expertise can be hindered by having to remember the variety of disjointed, lower-level tasks that make up an investigation. NoRIS therefore restructures an investigation in terms of *high-level tasks*:

- Notekeeping: Students continually record important observations, data, etc. throughout an investigation.
- Building cases: A case encompasses the major tasks that use computational tools, such as writing numerical-method programs, visualizing data, etc.

By providing support and structure for these high-level tasks, NoRIS allows the student to begin constructing an understanding of the investigative activities that researchers perform.

As well as restructuring the investigative process, NoRIS also reduces complexity by handling the student's managerial tasks, such as *artifact management.* Artifact management is important because throughout an investigation, the student may have to re-use, modify, or refer to artifacts such as notes, source code, data files, etc. However, it becomes tedious and distracting for a student to coherently organize their artifacts. By supporting artifact management, the student can focus more on their investigation less on mundane, bookkeeping tasks.

Tools: In order to provide an environment that students can use for scientific inquiry, NoRIS provides the variety of tools needed by beginning students to complete their tasks. As we have seen, there are many computer tools that can be used in a scientific investigation: *computational tools* (such as compilers and algebraic/mathematical software), *visualization tools*, etc. NoRIS provides this functionality by integrating existing software packages.

However, for tasks such as artifact management, there are no existing tools that the student can use. NoRIS is designed as a *computer notebook*, a metaphor that corresponds to the student's current mental representations—they know what it is and how to use it. The notebook metaphor provides an organizational structure to help students manage the different artifacts that they have created during the argument. For example, NoRIS includes the Notebook Summary window (Figure 5) that summarizes the different numerical-method programs that have been written by the student.

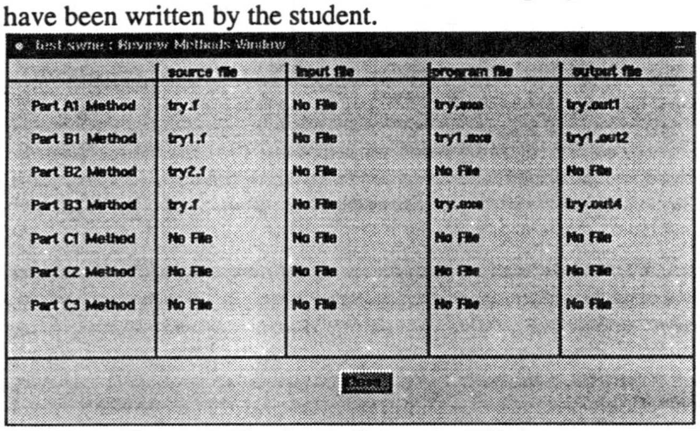

Figure 5: Notebook Summary Window

Interface: One of the complexities of computational science is having to learn different computer tools and interfaces. Students may have access to the necessary functionality, but if they do not have an accessible interface to that functionality, they will not use the tools. Therefore, NoRIS has a *simple, consistent interface* to all of the different tools, by providing button and menu-based access to each tool. This corresponds to the constructivist principle that complexity is reduced by offering similar processes that match current mental structures for a range of tasks. Examples include:

- The Workspace Tool (Figure 6) provides button and menu-based access to the tools needed by the student to build and analyze numerical method cases.

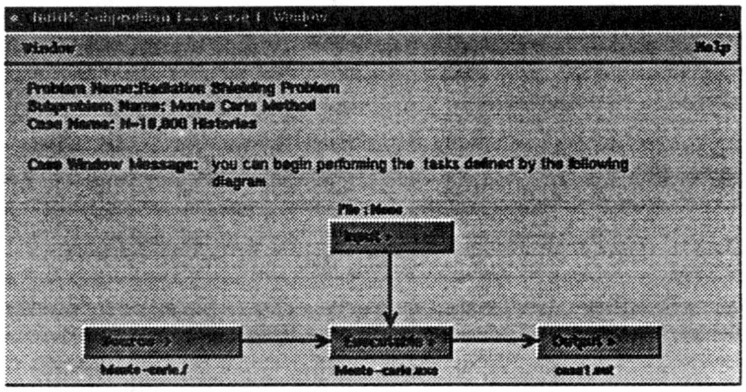

Figure 6: The Workspace Tool

- The Multiplot Tool (Figure 7) allows the researcher to easily plot data files in the same graph window for analysis. The student can simply "check off" all of the files that they want to plot and then press the Plot button.

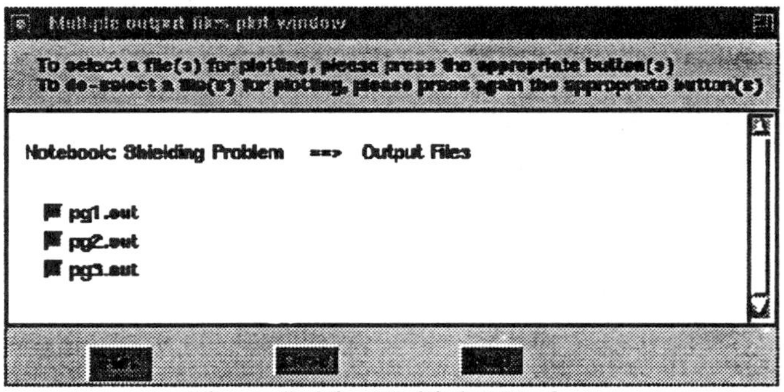

Figure 7: The Multiplot Tool

Once students can access the necessary functionality, they need further support to help them identify and complete their investigative tasks. To further sustain the students as they proceed through their investigation, NoRIS provides visual cues in the interface so that the students can see the different steps in the process, and the different types of information that they must record. Examples include:

- The Workspace Tool (Figure 6) contains a *task diagram* (a constructivist concept) of the process used to construct a case for the numerical method that they are investigating. Each button represents a different stage in the case-building process. Pressing a button presents the user with a menu identifying their options for that particular stage.

- Notepad windows (Figure 8) contain *button palettes* that identify to the student the different types of information that they should be thinking about and recording throughout the investigation, such as problem objectives, descriptions of the numerical methods they are investigating, etc. This structure encourages students to reflect and keep important notes throughout their investigation.

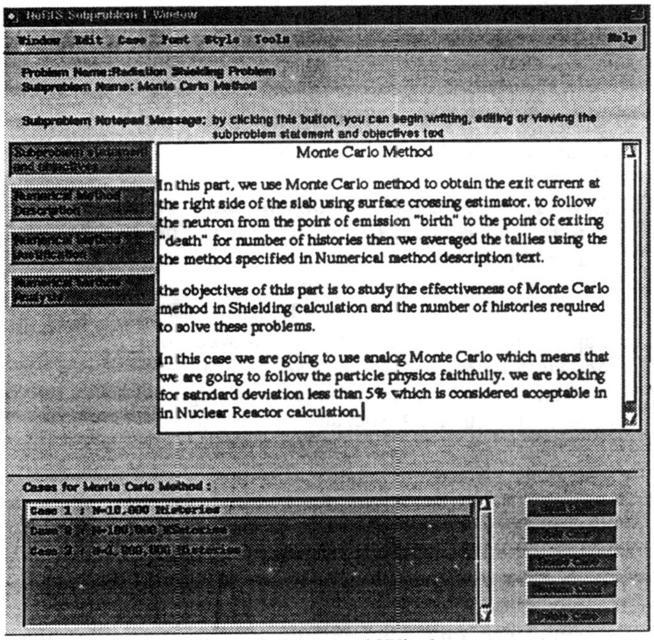

Figure 8: Notepad Window

Results

NoRIS was initially tested in three two-week trials with two nuclear engineering students in each trial. For each trial, the students were given a problem to work on using NoRIS. More recently, NoRIS was used in a nuclear engineering class by five senior-level undergraduate students who worked on week-long, project-based assignments to analyze numerical methods in particle-distribution problems.

Context: Using NoRIS, students were able to complete their particle-distribution assignments, verifying that NoRIS facilitates their investigatory process. We saw that NoRIS gave students an environment that made computational science accessible and investigations manageable.

Tasks: The task decomposition defined in NoRIS helped reduce the complexity of an investigation, and students quickly caught on to the tasks decomposition. They saw that their investigation involved setting up different cases for their different numerical methods and keeping notes on those cases. We soon observed students trying out new experiments by simply setting up new cases, even though their problem did not necessarily indicate that they needed to do so.

We also saw that it was useful for NoRIS to handle some of the student's tasks, such as artifact management. One student noted the advantages of this:

> "I am usually disorganized and after a while, I spend a lot of time organizing things—setting up directories, putting codes and things in the right places. NoRIS takes care of this—this really helps because it lets me concentrate on the problem.."

We also saw that automatic artifact management helped students manage the complexity of re-using and modifying existing artifacts to build new cases. Since it was easy for students to find and re-use old artifacts, students could build new cases from old cases quickly; this encouraged students to experiment with numerical methods by continually modifying a base case for the different experiments.

Tools: Students liked the fact that they had all of the necessary tools available to them in one application. Since students are not experts in using computational science, they may not know what tools to use in given situations:

> "[NoRIS] really provides an integrated package that beginning students can really use...having all of the needed information 'at my fingertips' is an advantage so that I do not have to bounce around different programs...this is good for students who are inexperienced with [computers]"

By having all of the functionality available to them in one application, the students did not have to be moving from application to application, which can be a problem for students who have little expertise with computational science.

Interface: Students liked using the interface because it was easy to invoke their different tools. The fact that they could use menus and buttons to access many of their tools made it easy for the student to quickly get started with their investigation.

Students also appreciated the different visual cues provided by the interface. For example, one student commented on the notepad button palette that identifies important pieces of information that should be recorded:

> "[The button palette] helps lay out the thought process I should be following when I start working on my problem...Seeing [the buttons] makes me pause and think about the problem rather than just jumping in and starting to write programs, which is what I might normally do."

The visual cues of the interface therefore structure the task and articulate their thoughts.

Summary

Our user testing has shown that students are able to use NoRIS to complete authentic scientific investigations, and that they find the structure provided by the program helpful. Furthermore, by providing an accessible interface to the array of computational tools used by professional researchers, NoRIS supports learners in their enculturation into professional practices.

CONCLUDING REMARKS

Model-It and NoRIS are two components of the ScienceWare suite of tools, a "computational workbench" that we are developing to scaffold learners engaged in the full range of scientific investigatory activities. As we apply our LCD strategies to the design of the ScienceWare tools, and study the use of these tools in classroom settings, our goal is to develop a fully-articulated LCD framework in which the needs of learners are specifically addressed by theoretically-motivated scaffolding for each element of the learning environment.

In putting forth the notion of UCD, Norman, Draper, and their book contributors [15] sought to focus attention on the needs of users at a time when there was growing interest in developing usable and productive interfaces and interaction paradigms. Similarly, in putting forth the notion of LCD, our intent is to focus discussion on work that is expressly intended for learners at a time when, as *Business Week* [2] declared, there is a "revolution" going on in educational software. UCD has proven itself to be a useful notion; time will tell whether LCD is similarly so.

ACKNOWLEDGMENTS

This research has been supported by the NSF (RED 9353481 and IRI 9117084), and the Univ. of Michigan.

REFERENCES

1. American Association for the Advancement of Science (1992) *Science for all Americans: A Project 2061 Report on Literary Goals in Science, Mathematics, and Technology,* AAAS Technical Report, Washington, D.C.
2. Armstrong, L., Yang, D.J., & Cuneo, A., (1994) The Learning Revolution, *Business Week,* No. 3360, Feb. 28, 80-88
3. Blumenfeld, P. C., Soloway, E., Marx, R. W., Krajcik, J. S., Guzdial, M., & Palinscar, A. (1991) Motivating Project-Based Learning: Sustaining the Doing, Supporting the Learning. *Educational Psychologist, 26*(3 & 4)
4. Brown, A., & Campione, J. (1990) Communities of learning, or A context by any other name. *Contributions to Human Development, 21*, 108-125.
5. Brown, J. S., Collins, A., & Duguid, P. (1989) Situated Cognition and the Culture of Learning. *Educational Researcher*, Jan - Feb, 32 - 42.
6. Carroll, J. M., & Carrithers, C. (1984) Training Wheels in a User Interface, *CACM*, Vol. 27, No.8, August, 800-806
7. Collins, A., Brown, J. S., & Newman, J. (1989) Cognitive Apprenticeship: Teaching the craft of reading, writing, and mathematics. In L. B. Resnick (Eds.), *Cognition and instruction: Issues and agendas* Hillsdale, NJ: Lawrence Erlbaum Associates.
8. Cunningham, S., Brown, J. R., McGrath, M. (1990) Visualization in Science and Engineering Education, *Visualization in Scientific Computing*, IEEE Computer Society Press, 48-57.
9. Fischer, G., Nakakoji, K., Ostwald, J., Stahl, G., & Sumner, T., (1993) Embedding Computer-Based Critics in the Contexts of Design, *Human Factos in Computing Systems, INTERCHI '93 Conference Proceedings,* Amsterdam, 157-164.
10. Gallopoulos, E., Houstis, E., Rice, J. R. (1994) Computer as Thinker/Doer: Problem-Solving Environments for Computational Science, IEEE Computational Science & Engineering, Vol. 1, No. 2, Summer 1994, 11-23.
11. Guzdial, M. (1993) Emile: Software-Realized Scaffolding for Science Learners Programming in Mixed Media. Unpublished Ph.D. dissertation, University of Michigan.
12. Jackson, S. L., Stratford, S. J., Krajcik, J. S., & Soloway, E. (1995) Learner-Centered Software Design to Support Students Building Models, *Interactive Learning Environments*, to appear.
13. Kreutzer, W. (1986) *Systems Simulation: Programming Styles and Languages,* Addison-Wesley, Wokingham, England.
14. Lave, J. (1993) *Understanding practice: perspectives on activity and context.* Cambridge; New York: Cambridge University Press.
15. Norman, D., Draper, S. (1986) *User Centered System Design,* L. Erlbaum & Assoc., Hillsdale, NJ.
16. Papert, S. (1993) *The Children's Machine: Rethinking School in the Age of the Computer*, Basic Books, NY
17. Perkins, A. (1986) *Knowledge as Design.* Hillsdale, NJ: Lawrence Erlbaum Associates.
18. Piaget, J. (1954) *The construction of reality in the child.* New York: Basic Books.
19. Resnick, L. B., & Glaser, R. (1976) Problem solving and intelligence. In L. B. Resnick (Eds.), *The nature of intelligence*. Hillsdale, NJ: Erlbaum.
20. Resnick, M. (1992) *Beyond the Centralized Mindset: Explorations in Massively-Parallel Microworlds*, Unpublished Ph.D. dissertation. Massachusetts Institute of Technology.
21. Rogoff, B. (1990) *Apprenticeship in thinking: Cognitive development in social context.* New York: Oxford University Press.
22. Senge, P. (1990) *The Fifth Discipline: The Art and Practice of The Learning Organization,* Doubleday, New York, NY
23. Shneiderman, B. (1983) Direct Manipulation: A Step Beyond Programming Languages, *IEEE Computer.* Vol. 16, No. 8, August, 57-69
24. Soloway, E., Guzdial, M., & Hay, K. E. (1994) Learner-Centered Design: The Challenge for HCI in the 21st Century, *Interactions*, Vol. 1, No. 2, April, 36-48
25. Springmeyer, R. R., Blattner, M. M., & Marx, N. L. (1992) A Characterization of the Scientific Data Analysis Process, *Proceedings of IEEE Visualization '92*, 235-242.
26. Tinker, R. F. (1990) Teaching Theory Building: Modeling: Instructional Materials and Software for Theory Building, NSF Final Report, TERC.
27. vonGlaserfeld, E. (1989) Cognition, construction of knowledge, and teaching. *Synthese,* 80, 121-140.
28. Vygotsky (1978) *Mind in Society.* Cambridge, MA: Cambridge University Press.
29. Wertsch, J. (Ed.) (1985) *Culture, communication and cognition: Vygotskian perspectives.* Cambridge, MA: Cambridge University Press.
30. Wood, D., Bruner, J. S., & Ross, G. (1975) The role of tutoring in problem-solving. *Journal of Child Psychology and Psychiatry*, 17, 89-100.

Assessing Dynamics in Computer-Based Instruction

John F. Pane
Computer Science Department
Carnegie Mellon University
Pittsburgh, PA 15213 USA
+1 412 268 1449
pane+chi96@cs.cmu.edu

Albert T. Corbett
HCI Institute
Carnegie Mellon University
Pittsburgh, PA 15213 USA
+1 412 268 8808
corbett@cmu.edu

Bonnie E. John
Computer Science Department,
Psychology, and HCI Institute
Carnegie Mellon University
Pittsburgh, PA 15213 USA
+1 412 268 7182
bej+@cs.cmu.edu

ABSTRACT
We present an evaluation of a multimedia educational software system that includes text, graphics, animations, and simulations. When compared with an informationally equivalent control environment that used text and carefully selected still images, we found little evidence that the dynamic presentations enhanced student understanding of the declarative information in this lesson. Furthermore, students cannot be relied on to take full advantage of exploratory opportunities in computer-based instruction. These results prescribe further investigation of whether and how computer-based multimedia can be used effectively in education and training.

Keywords
animation, simulation, multimedia, computer-based learning.

INTRODUCTION
Multimedia educational environments are rapidly growing in popularity. Journals and international conferences devoted to educational multimedia have sprung up, multimedia encyclopedias are a popular throw-in with personal computer hardware, and as computing costs decline multimedia learning environments are destined to make substantial inroads into schools at all levels. It is plausibly assumed that the interactive nature of multimedia environments along with video and audio presentations will engage the students' interest and intellect, particularly contemporary students who have grown up with television and video games. However, relatively little is known about the conditions under which multimedia presentations are effective.

In this paper we examine the impact of computer-based movies and simulations on students' understanding of time-varying biological processes. A variety of studies have examined the use of such animations in computer-based education. A range of results has been obtained, but many studies report a positive impact of animations on learning and student motivation. In most, but not all, of these studies, the computer-based animation condition is compared to a control condition in which students either do nothing, just read text or just examine still graphics. While these outcomes are of practical importance in education, they do not directly bear on the genuine value-added of dynamic computer-based presentations on learning unless a principled effort is made to develop an informationally equivalent control condition. In this paper we focus on the process of developing an informationally equivalent control condition in assessing the value added by dynamic presentations.

THE ACSE ENVIRONMENT
This study employs the Advanced Computing for Science Education (ACSE) environment [12]. The ACSE environment focuses on the understanding of complex time-varying processes. It is designed to afford students the opportunity to actively design and execute experimental investigations of the mechanisms underlying these dynamic processes and to be a living document of the student's investigation and growing understanding.

The ACSE software provides a multimedia document containing text, still graphics, movies, and simulations. The system provides the student with tools for navigating through the lesson, viewing the movies, and manipulating and running the simulations. Movies include any dynamic presentations that are the same each time they are viewed, e.g., animations, videos, and time-lapse photography. Simulations include any graphics, tables or other output generated under programmatic control of the student. Simulation outcomes are subject to changes the student makes, as well as probabilistic variations, and thus may be different each time they are viewed.

In this study we are interested in the impact of both movies and simulations on students' understanding of declarative facts about time-varying biological processes. As described in the next section, a major thrust of this study was to

CHI 96 Vancouver, BC Canada

design a formative evaluation that would reveal the real value added by dynamic presentations. Much of the effort went into developing an informationally equivalent control condition that relied exclusively on static images and text.

Other research has investigated the effectiveness of movies and simulations for declarative knowledge acquisition, with mixed results. Studies investigating the use of movies to teach mathematics and dental hygiene have found positive effects [1, 4]. In addition, studies using simulations in biology and economics found positive effects [3, 6]. But these results are balanced by similar studies in content areas such as physics and computer science where no significant improvements are found [5, 13, 14, 15]. Overall, none of the above studies took a disciplined approach to information equivalence between the experimental and control conditions.

Some studies are notable for the care with which they constructed equivalent comparison conditions. One study found an advantage of movies for long-term recall of episodic story structure, although not for immediate recall [2]. Here the comparison condition was a text-only condition that controlled for episodic story structure rather than information equivalence. Other studies have found value-added for movies in acquiring procedural knowledge, where movies improved immediate recall, but not long term recall, of how to use a direct-manipulation computer interface [8, 9, 10]. It is questionable whether procedural results are applicable to the acquisition of declarative knowledge in any case, but again, these studies employed a text-only comparison condition.

We don't doubt that visual images can convey information that is difficult to capture in text. In contrast, this study examines the relative impact of dynamic visual presentations on the acquisition of declarative knowledge. We compare the impact of two informationally equivalent environments, one that combines text, still graphics and dynamic presentations, with a second that uses only text and still graphics.

FORMATIVE EVALUATION DESIGN

Development and evaluation of educational software depends on a close collaboration between software developers and instructors. The ACSE project is a collaboration among the following Carnegie Mellon departments: Computer Science, Human Computer Interaction Institute, Biological Sciences, and Center for Light Microscope Imaging and Biotechnology. The target domain is an upper level undergraduate course in developmental biology and the course instructor identified two topics involving dynamic processes that he viewed as difficult to teach.

The first lesson is titled *Sea Urchin Gastrulation* and examines a process common to many organisms in early development in which cells adopt specialized roles and migrate to appropriate locations in the embryo. The second lesson is titled *The Early Development of Drosophila Melanogaster* and examines the way that gradients of molecules produced by the mother and stored within the fertilized egg can result in differences among embryonic cells and the generation of patterns in the organism. Each lesson is about 50 pages long, although these pages correspond to the size of the content window on a 13-inch computer screen, and thus have less information than a typical textbook page. The lessons contain multiple high-resolution light microscope images and movies, as well as multiple simulations.

Review questions are incorporated in each lesson and serve as the dependent measure of student learning. Three classes of review questions are distinguished, based on the form in which relevant information is presented in the ACSE condition. The review questions tapped information that was presented primarily in the form of (1) text and static graphics, (2) movies, or (3) simulations. In the control condition all of the questions were based on information that was presented in form of text and static graphics.

Control Condition

The most challenging issue in evaluating multimedia learning environments is the construction of an appropriate comparison condition. The goal in this condition is to convey the information presented in the movies and simulations as well as possible with still images and text. In our ACSE evaluation, we adopted the model of a conventional biology textbook for the comparison condition. We developed a *textbook* variation of the ACSE environment in order to reduce the possible confounding effects of comparing the computer with a paper-based control condition. We used the following guidelines in constructing the contents of the control condition.

Select Key Frames

One great challenge in setting up the textbook comparison condition was selecting the appropriate still images. The lesson designer was interviewed to determine the replacement elements for the control condition. For each movie and simulation element, we asked him to reflect on the pedagogical goal of the element by asking questions like: What is the student expected to learn from this lesson element? What are the important events in this time-varying process? Which still images best represent these important events? What captions are required? How would a textbook best describe this material? Videotapes of these sessions were inspected to create the following strategy: choose frames representing the initial and final conditions, and intermediate frames that represent important incidents. However, in the event that there is a series of simulations with identical initial conditions, it is not necessary to repeat the frame representing the initial condition each time.

Choose Illustrative Simulation Runs

In the ACSE lesson, when students encounter a simulation, they are directed to run it without modification. Then they are instructed to make a specific modification to the simulation and to run it again. After these directed runs, they are encouraged to make further modifications to explore the behavior of the system. In deriving the control

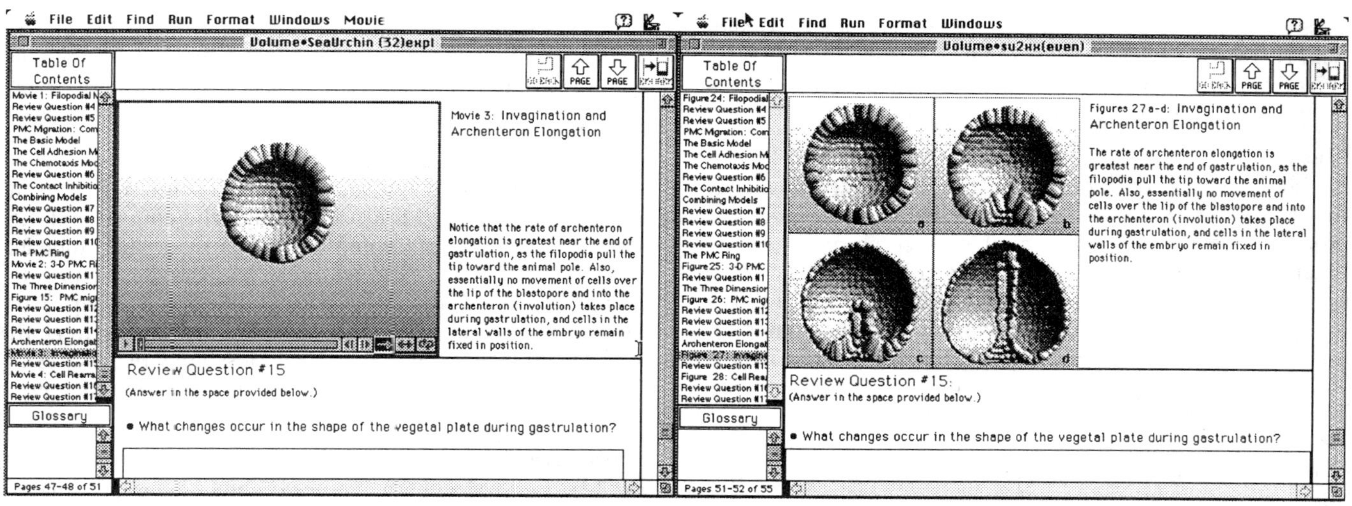

Figure 1: (a) ACSE lesson containing a movie. (b) Equivalent lesson with text and graphics.

lesson, each of the specified simulation runs is represented by still images. It is essential that these actually illustrate the necessary dynamics, so that the review question is answerable in the control condition.

Locality and Economy of Space

Biology textbooks typically have space limitations and a survey of representative books revealed that they seldom devote more than two still pictures to a particular topic. Furthermore, it is desirable to maintain locality of information. We limited the number of still pictures that replace each movie and simulation to a maximum of four, occupying a maximum of two lesson pages. The average number of still pictures representing each movie or simulation was two.

Preserve Visual Quality

Since visual quality may affect the information a student can get from an image, we prohibit any reduction in the number of pixels per image (spatial resolution) or number of bits/pixel (pixel resolution) between the images used in the movies or simulations and their still-graphic counterparts.

Replace Program Code with Text

ACSE shows small pieces of the Pascal simulation programs to the student. In some instances, this Pascal code is displayed in a natural language form, but in other cases the syntax of the programming language shows through. In the control lesson, simulation code is always translated into natural language or simple mathematical formulas.

Explanatory Text

In deriving the control elements for movies and simulations, it is often necessary to supplement the selected still images with explanatory text that describes some behavior that is observable in the movie or simulation, or to fill in the gaps between the chosen stills. This text was provided in both the ACSE and the control lessons.

Figure 1 displays the two versions of one page of the developmental biology lesson about sea urchin gastrulation. Figure 1(a) displays an animation of a stage of development in the sea urchin embryo. The student clicks the play button to watch the process unfold. Figure 1(b) displays the equivalant still images. Students can scroll through the lesson pages with the scroll bar, or page up and down with the buttons located in the upper right corner of the window. The Table of Contents allows students to directly access major sections in the text.

HYPOTHESIS ON MEDIA EFFECTIVENESS

Our interviews of the instructor on curriculum goals and a careful inspection of the review questions led us to formulate a hypothesis concerning the effective deployment of educational multimedia. We informally observed two distinct instructional goals: some review questions tended to focus on understanding processes, while other review questions tended to focus on end products. An example of the former is, "Describe the appearance and motile behavior of these cell processes," while an example of the latter is, "At the end of active migration, what is the arrangement of [cells] in the embryo?" Our tentative hypothesis is that dynamic presentations are more effective to portray processes, while still images are sufficient to portray end products.

THE EXPERIMENT

Participants

Thirty four Carnegie Mellon students (13 male, 21 female) taking an upper level developmental biology class participated in the study. Performance in the lab session constituted 10% of their course grade.

This set of students was divided into two groups of seventeen through a matching process. Students were rank ordered on the basis of prior test performance in the course, with QPA used to break ties. Within successive pairs in this list, one student was randomly assigned to group A and the other to group B. The two groups were well matched on class performance (68.0 vs. 68.0), QPA (3.08 vs. 3.14) and sex (10 vs. 11 females). All except one student (group A) had completed or placed out of at least one university-level computer programming course.

Materials

All students worked through the two ACSE lessons. The first lesson, entitled *Sea Urchin Gastrulation*, examines a process in early development that is common to many organisms, where cells adopt certain roles and migrate to appropriate locations in the embryo in order to fulfill those roles. It is 51 pages long, and in addition to text contains 15 images and figures, 4 movies, 18 fragments of simulation code drawn from 6 simulations, and 17 review questions. The second lesson, entitled *The Early Development of Drosophila Melanogaster,* examines the way that gradients of molecules produced by the mother and stored within the unfertilized egg can result in differences among embryonic cells and the generation of patterns in the organism. It is 55 pages long, and in addition to the text contains 23 images and figures, 3 movies, 10 fragments of simulation code drawn from 7 simulations, and 10 review questions.

During the time span between the first and second lessons, a table of contents feature was added to the software to assist the student in navigating and tracking progress through the lesson. This new feature was present for lesson 2 for both the ACSE and control conditions. In addition, in order to foster greater use of the simulations in lesson 2, we focused most of the review questions on the processes portrayed in the simulations, and introduced explicit recommendations to run the simulations along with suggested manipulations to perform between runs.

Each review question was sorted into one of three categories, by determining the lesson element that was most relevant to answering the question: text or still graphics; movies; or simulations. The 17 review questions in the first lesson fall into the following categories. Seven questions focused on the initial material in the lesson that contained no movies or simulations. These questions serve as a control to ensure the equivalence of the two student groups. Five questions focused on the movies and five focused on the simulations. In the second lesson nine review questions focused on the simulations while the tenth question focused on a movie. The movie and simulation questions were further classified depending on whether they focused on dynamic processes or end results. A biology graduate student performed this classification, which is shown in Table 1.

	Lesson 1	Lesson 2
Movie	4P / 1E	0P / 1E
Simulation	4P / 1E	3P / 6E

Table 1: Classification of review questions into *process* or *end result*. (P=process; E=end result).

After finishing work on each lesson, participants were given a short paper questionnaire. It asked about prior computer experience and satisfaction with the lesson, as well as opinions about the best and worst aspects of the system and suggestions for improvements.

Design

The study was conducted during two evening lab sessions at appropriate points in the course curriculum. The first lesson was presented midway through the course, and the second lesson was presented in the last week. All students worked through the first lesson in the first session, with group A in the dynamic ACSE condition and group B in the static control condition. In the second session, all students worked through the second lesson, with group B in the dynamic ACSE condition and group A in the static control condition.

Procedure

Each session was held in a large computer laboratory that is partitioned into two sections. All of the ACSE participants were assigned to one half of the lab; and all of the control participants were assigned to the other. Participants received a one-page instruction sheet about the features of the ACSE environment. A proctor directed them to a computer which had the appropriate lesson opened to page one and recorded the starting time. Participants worked on identically configured Macintosh IIsi computers with 9 MB of memory and 13-inch 8-bit color monitors.

Students had no *a priori* knowledge that there were two different lesson formats. Students were permitted to work as long as they wished, were informed that their answers to the review questions would be graded, and that each lesson was worth 5% of their course grade. There was the additional motivation that the material might appear on an exam. The lessons were not made available to the students for study outside the laboratory session.

Feature usage and user inputs were timestamped and automatically logged by the software. When participants indicated that they were finished, the time was recorded by the proctor, and they were given the questionnaire.

Due to scheduling conflicts, there were six students who attended a makeup session for the first lesson (four ACSE; two control) and two students who attended a makeup session for the second lesson (one ACSE; one control). The procedure used during these makeup sessions was identical to the main session. The only known confounding factor is the possibility that these participants discussed the lessons with their peers before attending the makeup session. Three students who participated in the first session did not participate in the second session (second session group assignments: one ACSE, two control).

The answers to review questions were scored by an independent grader, a biology graduate student, who was blind to condition. The grader was not familiar with the details of this study. In a debriefing session after the experiment concluded, she reported nothing that would have biased the grading.

QUANTITATIVE PERFORMANCE RESULTS

Pretest Measures as Performance Predictors

We found no significant correlation between the pretest measures (QPA, Prior Exams) and performance overall or performance on any of the categories of questions.

Time on Task

On the first lesson, the ACSE group took 146 min (sd=36) to finish, while the control group took 101 min (sd=23). This difference was significant [t(32)=4.4, p<.001]. On the second lesson, the ACSE group took 130 min (sd=32) to finish, while the control group took 100 min (sd=35). This difference was significant [t(28)=2.5, p<.05].

Performance on Review Questions

We measured the students' scores on the four categories of questions based on (a) identical static text and still images at the beginning of lesson 1, (b) lesson 1 movies, (c) lesson 1 simulations and (d) lesson 2 simulations.[1] Recall that the movie and simulation questions in lesson 1 focus overwhelmingly on dynamic processes while the simulation questions in lesson 2 focus mostly on end-products. The results are shown in Table 2. The numbers represent the average score on questions in the categories listed, expressed as a percentage of the possible points in that category. A significant difference between groups was found only on the lesson 1 simulation questions. There the ACSE group scored about 10% higher than the control group [t(32)=2.153, p<.05].

	Lesson 1			Lesson 2
	Static (7)	Movie (5)	Simulation (5)	Simulation (9)
ACSE	72 (sd=10)	70 (sd=12)	78 (sd=10)	64 (sd=12)
Control	71 (sd=10)	72 (sd=14)	71 (sd=9)	68 (sd=17)

Table 2: Performance on review questions in percent correct by question type (# of questions in parenthesis).

The lesson 1 simulation questions focused heavily on dynamic processes rather than end products. To determine if this distinction accounts for the significant effect in Table 2, we combined the simulation questions for lessons 1 and 2, and performed a pairwise t-test comparing the process-oriented questions and product-oriented questions. This test was non-significant.

STUDENT ATTITUDES

There were no significant differences between the ACSE condition and control condition on any of the survey questions, although the responses were generally favorable. Further information about the survey responses can be found in [11].

[1] On Lesson 2, one participant visited only 34 of the 55 lesson pages, ran only three of the seven simulations, and answered only two of the ten review questions. On the questionnaire, this participant reported that "I didn't have time to do it because of other work (tests)." This participant was removed from the analysis of lesson 2.

FORMATIVE USABILITY EVALUATION

We collected both direct feedback from the students with the questionnaire, and software logs containing records of usage patterns and problems. These provide insight into the usability of the ACSE environment which we can use to improve future versions of the system.

Lesson 1

Students made far less use of the movies and simulations than we anticipated. Students ran each movie an average of 1.4 times and ran each simulation an average of 1.3 times.

Three types of student comments stood out after the session. First, students praised the high quality of the graphics. Second, they complained that the system ran slowly, particularly the simulations. Third, they complained that there was no table of contents to assist them in finding relevant information when answering the review questions.

Lesson 2

As described above, we introduced two changes for lesson 2. First, a table of contents was provided to make it easier for the student to navigate through the environment. Secondly, we focused the review questions on the simulations and added explicit recommendations to run the simulations along with suggested manipulations to perform between runs. These relatively small changes in the environment had a small positive impact on usage of the ACSE features. While the average number of movie runs remained essentially unchanged at 1.3, the average number of runs per simulation increased to 2.0. Software logs show that the table of contents was heavily used and three students reported that this feature was the best thing about their experience with lesson 2.

GENERAL DISCUSSION OF PERFORMANCE

We draw several important conclusions from this evaluation of the dynamic presentations in a computer-based environment. First, dynamic presentations are not a panacea for instructional difficulties. With well-defined instructional goals, appropriate learning data, and an informationally equivalent control environment with text and carefully selected still images, we found little evidence that dynamic presentations enhance student understanding. Moreover, student attitudes concerning the dynamic and static conditions did not vary significantly.

Second, even motivated students cannot be relied on to take full advantage of exploratory opportunities. The upper level biology class was largely populated by biology majors at a selective university. This group of students reflects about the highest general motivation level that can be realistically expected in a K-12 or university environment. Nevertheless, we were disappointed that students made relatively little use of the potential to explore the experimental manipulations afforded by the simulations. Students ran an average of 1.3 simulations in the first lesson. When two specific simulations were recommended in the second lesson, students averaged exactly 2.0 simulation runs. This suggests that substantially more guidance must be built into such experimentation environments.

Comprehension Differences

Despite these general caveats, dynamic presentations did enhance student comprehension in lesson 1 simulation questions and this is a moderately large, 0.7 standard deviation effect. Further analyses indicated that this effect did not depend on process-oriented questions, contrary to our hypothesis.

However, the lesson 1 simulation questions did have a unique property. This was the one situation where students in the dynamic condition could receive more visual information than was present in the control condition. Each time students ran the sea urchin simulations in lesson 1, they observed a different probabilistically varying development sequence (in addition to the set of static images that were presented in both the dynamic and static environments). This was not true of the movies, which always display exactly the same dynamic sequence, or the lesson 2 simulations which did not have probabilistic behavior. In short, the lesson 1 simulation condition presented more visual information than the corresponding control condition. This suggests that dynamic presentations will be useful when information concerning process variability can be gleaned from multiple runs – more runs than can be reasonably portrayed in a set of still images.

It should be emphasized that these conclusions are limited to dynamic presentation of declarative knowledge. We have no reason to expect that they generalize to the acquisition of procedural knowledge.

The magnitude of the performance improvement should be considered in the context of the small amount of time allotted to each lesson. We do not believe the minimal effect obtained in this study generalizes to a situation in which students are actively engaged in experimentation and modifying simulation parameters. The challenge is to engage students in this activity; it does not come readily even to students who are well prepared and relatively motivated. The tools themselves are complex as are the reasoning patterns they support. Students received no instruction on the features and effective use of the system. Instead, students jumped right into using the system with difficult topics that normally arise near the end of the course. It may be necessary to scaffold effective feature usage with more modest topics introduced right from the beginning of the course. In addition, the teacher may need to demonstrate the features of the system through routine use in the classroom lectures before students will adopt and benefit from advanced capabilities [7].

It may also be the case that even the control lesson in this study was superior to the other teaching materials that are available to the instructor. It is derived from a carefully constructed lesson that covers exactly the topics desired, in exactly the order that this particular instructor would choose to present them. It uses still graphics that were generated by a simulation which would otherwise not have been available were it not for the ACSE environment. This is analogous to writing a custom textbook for the course and instructor. This spin off of the careful formative evaluation is of educational significance, although it does not bear directly on human computer interaction issues.

Time Differences

In both lessons, the control lesson is approximately the same length as the ACSE lesson. However, the process used to derive the control ensures that it has no more total information than the ACSE lesson. This, in combination with the fact that each ACSE simulation takes several minutes to run and can be run an unlimited number of times, suggests that the ACSE group will take more time to work through the material. This is confirmed by our observations of total time.

While much of the additional time used by the ACSE group is spent in running simulations, we found no significant correlation between the number of simulations run by the student and their performance on those review questions that were directly related to those simulations.

Analysis of the first 20 pages of lesson 1, which are the same between groups, supports the expectation that any time or performance difference between groups is due to the experimental manipulation that appears later in the lesson. Participants might have spent more time on a lesson if they were enjoying the experience or felt that it was a productive use of their time. Alternatively, participants might have felt some obligation to complete the lesson, and thus would have been less satisfied if it was not enjoyable or seemed an unproductive use of time. Since student satisfaction measures do not show significant correlations to time spent, neither of these speculations can be confirmed.

USABILITY RESULTS AND DISCUSSION

Navigation

As discussed earlier, the table of contents feature proved essential in allowing students to effectively navigate through the environment and in shaping their overall evaluation of the environment.

However, not every page of the lesson has a table of contents entry, so some other method of scrolling must be used to reach those pages. One student exclusively used the table of contents for navigation, thus skipping pages of the lesson that do not appear there. This happened even though (a) this student had used the other scrolling mechanisms on lesson 1, (b) there is a page number indicator visible at all times, and (c) the text had several cross references to these pages. This student's behavior surprised us and suggested that page numbers next to the table of contents entries might alleviate this problem.

Management of Information

There were six comments (one ACSE, five control) about difficulty in remembering material from page to page. The logs showed that when students are answering the review questions, they often scroll back through the material multiple times in the midst of typing their answers. This problem may be relieved when previously-planned features of ACSE – a glossary, bookmarks and live cross-reference links – are completed. One subject suggested that the system provide a scratchpad that the user can use to record notes and simulation results.

Modifying Simulations

In ACSE, we experimented with using natural language syntax for presenting simulation code. One example is a transformation of Pascal procedure calls, where:

```
Regulator(bicoid,1000,activates,hunchback,50);
```

becomes:

Regulator: when the concentration of **bicoid** is greater than **1000** units, it **activates** the expression of **hunchback** with an efficiency of **50%**.

This special formatting posed some problems for students when they attempted to edit the statement, because the underlying Pascal syntax appears at that time and changes must be entered using that syntax. The natural language syntax reappears when editing is completed. The logs show that this transition between representations was a problem for many students: they encountered syntax errors and sometimes inadvertently destroyed the annotations that provide the natural language syntax. We conclude that while this implementation was easiest for the development of the ACSE software, we must change the editor so students can work exclusively in the natural language syntax.

We also observed students having difficulty with the Pascal syntax in other cases: a) real numbers must have a digit before the decimal place, so values like **.8** are not accepted; and b) commas are not permitted in large numbers, so **32,000** must be entered as **32000**. These problems highlight the limitations of using a programming language in the context of natural language. Buttons and sliders, which were previously-planned but not yet implemented features of the software design, can be used to provide a direct-manipulation interface to numeric parameters. The system could also have been improved to selectively allow deviation from the Pascal standard, to permit incorrect but unambiguous syntax to be interpreted in the expected way.

Workstation Requirements

The predominant positive comment from both groups concerned image quality (22 comments from the ACSE group, and 20 from the control group). Of these, 10 of the ACSE comments specifically mentioned movies and simulations. The lessons make extensive use of large, high resolution color graphics. It would be inappropriate to attempt to use these lessons on systems that do not support color graphics or that have miniature screens. The memory and processing demands of these high-quality graphics were at the upper limit of the capabilities of the systems that were used in this study.

The most common negative comment regarded speed, and this was biased heavily toward users of the ACSE lesson. Forty ACSE comments and 7 control comments indicated that the system was too slow. In addition, on lesson 2, three students who has been in the ACSE condition for lesson 1 commented that the best thing about lesson 2 (when they were in the control group) is that it was faster than lesson 1. This can be explained by the processing requirements of the simulations, which are present only in the ACSE condition. In many cases the simulations took several minutes to run on the participants' computers. This indicates that the system was underpowered for this task. Clearly it would be unwise to attempt to use these fully featured lessons on less powerful machines. However, despite this performance, students seemed to like using the simulations, as nine students who had been in the ACSE group for lesson 1 complained about missing the interactivity when placed into the control group for lesson 2.

CONCLUSIONS

While the usability problems listed above may have had a negative impact on student performance, this evaluation suggests that designers of educational software should exercise caution in their use of multimedia in computer-based instruction. The mixed results of the comprehension and time measures dictate that we look carefully at the underlying pedagogy of science education. Merely using animation and simulation capabilities of modern computers does not guarantee improvement in students' learning. Well designed static graphics and text may be just as effective, and much cheaper to produce and use, than animations and simulations.

We need to find ways to measure investigative thinking more objectively, so that we can test multimedia learning environments in many educational situations. Perhaps movies and simulations are more motivating, so students will spontaneously spend more time with them even outside a structured laboratory setting, and thereby learn more. Perhaps longer-term usage of the ACSE environment for homework assignments or routine use of ACSE in classroom lectures would magnify the performance benefits. Or, these dynamic media may be more effective with student populations different than the high achievement group examined in this study. In short, much more research needs to be done to understand the requirements in lesson content and presentation media to realize the educational potential of computer-based learning environments. The method used in this study to carefully construct an informationally equivalent control condition can serve as a guide to this research.

ACKNOWLEDGMENTS

This research was supported by National Science Foundation Grant Number MDR-9150211. Bonnie John's participation is supported by the Advanced Research

Projects Agency, DoD, and monitored by the Office of Naval Research under contract N00014-93-1-0934. Al Corbett's participation is supported by the Office of Naval Research Grant Number N00014-91-J-1597. The views and conclusions contained in this document are those of the authors and should not be interpreted as representing the official policies, either expressed or implied, of NSF, ARPA, ONR, or the U.S. Government. The authors acknowledge Laurie Damianos, Chuck Ettensohn, Kirsten Guss, Ken Koedinger, Glenn Meter, Phil Miller, and Scott Vorthmann for their contributions to the ACSE project and this evaluation.

REFERENCES

1. Baek, Y. K. and Layne, B. H. Color, Graphics, and Animation in a Computer-Assisted Learning Tutorial Lesson. *Journal of Computer-Based Instruction, 15,* 4 (Autumn 1988), 131-135.

2. Baggett, P. Structurally Equivalent Stories in Movie and Text and the Effect of the Medium on Recall. *Journal of Verbal Learning and Verbal Behavior, 18* (1979), 333-356.

3. Grimes, P. W. and Willey, T. E. The Effectiveness of Microcomputer Simulations in the Principles of Economics Course. *Computers & Education, 14,* 1 (1990), 81-86.

4. Lautar-Lemay, C. Comparison of Computer-Assisted-Learning With Traditional Lecture and Reading Assignment. In *Proceedings of the International Conference on Computer Assisted Learning in Post-Secondary Education.* (Calgary, Canada, May 1987), 293-294.

5. Lawrence, A. W., Badre, A. N., and Stasko, J. T. Empirically Evaluating the Use of Animations to Teach Algorithms. Georgia Institute of Technology, Technical Report GIT-GVU-94-07, (Atlanta, 1994).

6. Lazarowitz, R. and Huppert, J. Science Process Skills of 10th-Grade Biology Students in a Computer-Assisted Learning Setting. *Journal of Research on Computing in Education, 25,* 3 (Spring 1993), 366-382.

7. Miller, P., Pane, J., Meter, G., and Vorthmann, S. Evolution of Novice Programming Environments: The Structure Editors of Carnegie Mellon University. *Interactive Learning Environments, 4,* 2 (1994), 140-158.

8. Palmiter, S. and Elkerton, J. An Evaluation of Animated Demonstrations for Learning Computer-based Tasks. In *Proceedings of the ACM CHI'91 Conference on Human Factors in Computing Systems.* (New Orleans, April 1991), 257-263.

9. Palmiter, S. and Elkerton, J. Animated Demonstrations for Learning Procedural Computer-Based Tasks. *Human-Computer Interaction, 8* (1993), 193-216.

10. Palmiter, S., Elkerton, J., and Baggett, P. Animated Demonstrations vs Written Instructions for Learning Procedural Tasks: a Preliminary Investigation. *International Journal of Man-Machine Studies, 34,* 5 (1991), 687-701.

11. Pane, J. F. Assessment of the ACSE Science Learning Environment and the Impact of Movies and Simulations. Carnegie Mellon University, School of Computer Science Technical Report CMU-CS-94-162, (Pittsburgh, PA, June 1994).

12. Pane, J. F. and Miller, P. L. The ACSE Multimedia Science Learning Environment. In *Proceedings of the 1993 International Conference on Computers in Education,* T.-W. Chan, Ed. (Taipei, Taiwan, December 1993), 168-173.

13. Rieber, L. P. The Effects of Computer Animated Elaboration Strategies and Practice on Factual and Application Learning in an Elementary Science Lesson. *Journal of Educational Computing Research, 5,* 4 (1989), 431-444.

14. Rieber, L. P., Boyce, M. J., and Assad, C. The Effects of Computer Animation on Adult Learning and Retrieval Tasks. *Journal of Computer-Based Instruction, 17,* 2 (Spring 1990), 46-52.

15. Stasko, J., Badre, A., and Lewis, C. Do Algorithm Animations Assist Learning? An Empirical Study and Analysis. In *Proceedings of ACM INTERCHI'93 Conference on Human Factors in Computing Systems.* (Amsterdam, April 1993), 61-66.

A Case For Interaction: A Study of Interactive Information Retrieval Behavior and Effectiveness

Jürgen Koenemann
Center for Cognitive Science
Rutgers University
Psychology Bldg.
Frelinghuysen Rd.
Piscataway, NJ 08855 USA
+1 908 445 6122
koeneman@ruccs.rutgers.edu

Nicholas J. Belkin
School of Communication,
Information, and Library Studies
Rutgers University
4 Huntington Street
New Brunswick, NJ 08901-1071 USA
+1 908 932 8585
nick@belkin.rutgers.edu

ABSTRACT

This study investigates the use and effectiveness of an advanced information retrieval (IR) system (INQUERY). 64 novice IR system users were studied in their use of a baseline version of INQUERY compared with one of three experimental versions, each offering a different level of interaction with a relevance feedback facility for automatic query reformulation. Results, in an information filtering task, indicate that: these subjects, after minimal training, were able to use the baseline system reasonably effectively; availability and use of relevance feedback increased retrieval effectiveness; and increased opportunity for user interaction with and control of relevance feedback made the interactions more efficient and usable while maintaining or increasing effectiveness.

Keywords:

information retrieval, user interfaces, evaluation, empirical studies, relevance feedback

INTRODUCTION

We are experiencing in our work and home environments a dramatic explosion of information sources that become available to an exponentially growing number of users. This has resulted in a shift in the profiles of users of online information systems: more users with no or minimal training in information retrieval (IR) have gained access to tools that were once the almost exclusive domain of librarians who served as intermediaries between end-users with their particular information needs and the information retrieval tools.

This situation has stimulated increasing interest in computerized tools that support end-users in their information seeking tasks. One important such situation is the information filtering (or *routing*) task, in which streams of information (such as email messages, newswire articles, or net news postings) are automatically filtered by a program based on specifications that are directly or indirectly obtained from the user. How these specifications should be obtained and used, and in particular, whether such programs should be autonomous or interactive are unresolved and controversial issues, which are explicitly addressed in the study reported here. This paper describes an experiment investigating the information seeking behavior of 64 novice searchers who used one of four versions of an advanced IR system to formulate routing queries for two given search topics. Each version offered a different level of interaction with a query formulation support mechanism called *relevance feedback*.

The paper is organized as follows: we first present the rationale for using an interactive, best-match, ranked-output, unstructured input, full-text IR system (INQUERY), and we discuss relevance feedback as a support tool for query reformulation. We then detail the design of the four different interfaces employed in our study, and describe the experiment which we conducted. The major portion of the paper focuses on a comparative description of the information retrieval behavior and effectiveness we observed in the use of these systems. We conclude with some general recommendations for the design of effective interfaces for information retrieval suggested by our results.

SUPPORTING END USERS

Users in all types of IR systems face the central difficulty of effective, interactive (re)formulation of queries which represent their information problems. Professional searchers using commercial IR systems have developed a variety of techniques and heuristics for addressing this difficulty in the context of Boolean query languages for exact-match, set-based retrieval from databases of indexed citations and abstracts of documents. Conversely, the difficulties faced by end-users with no training or experience in the use of these systems have been well documented. From experimental studies it has been known for some time that best-match, ranked-

CHI 96 Vancouver, BC Canada
© 1996 ACM 0-89791-777-4/96/04..$3.50

output retrieval techniques are in general superior in non-interactive settings to exact-match systems, such as commercial Boolean IR systems, in terms of recall and precision performance measures [2].

In response to such results, our study used the INQUERY retrieval engine developed at the University of Massachusetts [3]. The underlying mechanism of INQUERY is a Bayesian probabilistic inference network which provides rules for the computation of probabilistic belief values for each document in the collection. These belief values are based on the terms that are shared by the query and the *full text* of the document, and on the operators used to combine these terms. The system returns a *ranked* list of documents with documents that *best match* a given query being ranked at the top.

Research has shown that end-users with little or no training in query formulation have severe difficulties in making use of available operators and in mapping their intent to the appropriate logical query structure; it seems that systems which allow queries to be put in unstructured form allow easier query formulation than those which require Boolean structure, and are, at least for end-users, more effective [5, 13]. We therefore restricted queries to simple lists of terms. The only (implicit) operator allowed was the concatenation of terms to form multi-term phrases such as "automobile recall".

One particularly interesting and promising tool to support (or even replace) query reformulation in the context of these systems is *relevance feedback*. Relevance feedback modifies an existing query based on available relevance judgements for previously retrieved documents. For example, the system may add key terms from documents that the user has indicated as being relevant to the list of query terms, or the system may assign higher weights to terms in a user query that also appear in documents that have been marked "relevant" by the user. The goal of relevance feedback is to retrieve and rank highly those documents that are similar to the document(s) the user found to be relevant.

It is quite clear that automatic relevance feedback significantly improves retrieval performance in *fully automated* retrieval systems without user interaction, and with many relevance judgments[11]. Our concern is with determining how a relevance feedback component impacts the information seeking behavior and effectiveness of *novice* searchers in an *interactive* environment, and therefore with relatively few relevance judgments.

There have been many studies of user interaction with traditional boolean systems (e.g. [8]) and some studies that have focused on novel interaction techniques (e.g. [1, 10]). A few observational studies are concerned with relevance feedback [4, 6] but we are not aware of studies that have looked at relevance feedback in an experimental setting except for our own work in the context of the interactive track of TREC-3 [9].

A central question for the design of interactive systems in general is the amount of knowledge a user is required or expected to have about the functioning of the system and the level of control a user can exert. We share the "task-centered" view that interfaces for the occasional user should hide as much as possible of the inner workings of a system and should instead present users with a view that focuses on the user's task. However, the question arises of *how much* knowledge and control a user should have in order to best interact with components such as relevance feedback that are central to the user task, here the formulation of an information need. At one extreme, the existence of such a tool can be completely hidden from the user: the set of "relevant" documents could be determined by some algorithm that takes as input a user's behavior such as the viewing, saving, or printing of documents. The other extreme would be a system that provides the user with complete control over the feedback mechanism: a user could provide lists of "good" documents to the mechanism, manipulate the query modifications (changed weights and added terms) suggested by the relevance feedback component, and even adjust internal parameters such as belief thresholds. Between these two extremes there is a large space of possible designs; the goal of this study was to explore this space through the design of four interfaces described in the next section.

THE SYSTEMS

We designed and implemented (Tcl/Tk) a **baseline** interface to the INQUERY (V.2.1) retrieval engine, RU-INQUERY, (Figure 1) that allowed users to enter queries and to view the results. Users entered one-by-one single or compound terms (phrases) into the term entry window. An entered term was checked against the database and was either rejected if it did not appear in the collection or added in its stemmed form to the query term list. Words that appeared on a stop word list were ignored. Subjects submitted a query for retrieval by hitting the `Run Query` button. The total number of retrieved documents and the titles of the top five (5) ranked retrieved documents were displayed. Users could scroll through the entire list of titles and look at the full text of any document by double-clicking on its title. A check box next to each title allowed keeping track of documents between iterations. A single-step undo mechanism allowed users to return to the previously run query. The system blocked most inappropriate user activities in order to prevent error episodes. Subjects could view the results of a query, and then reformulate the query by manually adding or deleting terms.

Performance in this baseline system was compared with one of three experimental versions, each offering (in addition to the baseline facilities) a different level of interaction with a relevance feedback facility for automatic query reformulation.

In the **opaque** interface relevance feedback was treated as a black-box, a "magical" tool that hid the functionality of the relevance feedback component from the user. Searchers were simply told that marking documents as relevant would cause the system to retrieve additional documents that were similar to the ones marked as relevant and/or that similar documents would be ranked higher. Thus, users only needed to acquire

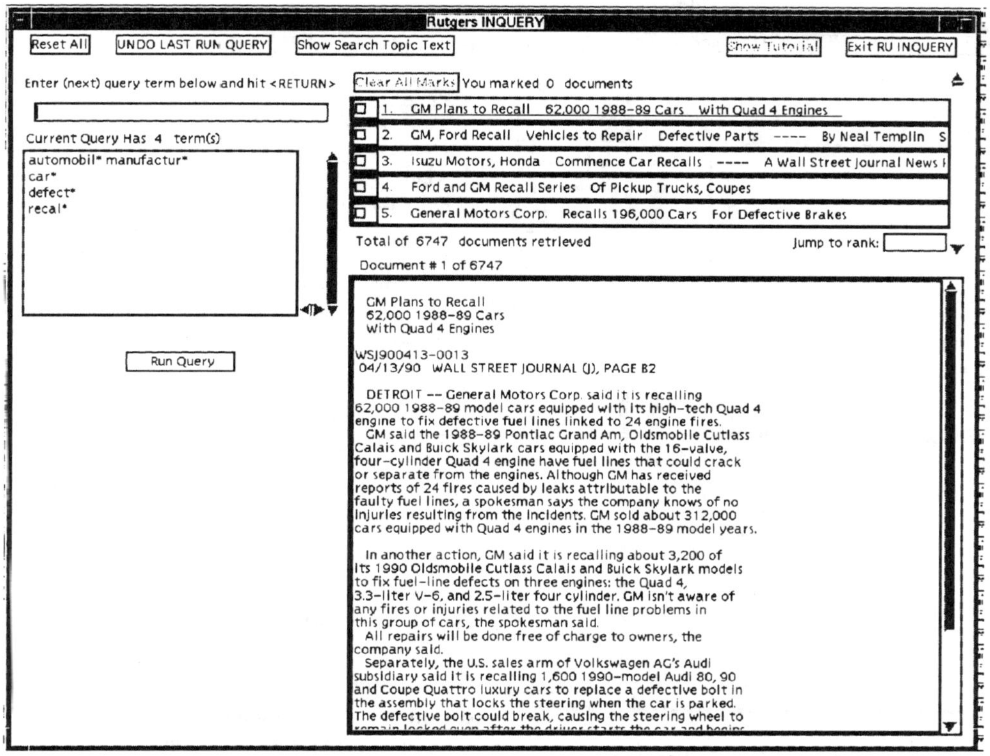

Figure 1: The RU-INQUERY Interface: Base Version Without Relevance Feedback

minimal knowledge about the feedback tool and could focus on the evaluation of documents rather than on the resulting reformulation of queries. Users marked a document "relevant" by clicking on the check box next to its title. Relevance feedback took effect the next time a query was run.

The **transparent** relevance feedback interface had the same functionality as the opaque version with the following addition: after a relevance feedback query had been executed searchers were shown the list of terms that had been added to the user-entered terms by the relevance feedback component. This additional information could be used to develop a more accurate model of the tool. Feedback terms could also be used as a source for future queries.

The **penetrable** relevance feedback interface (Figure 2) took the transparent version one step further: in addition to providing information about the functioning of the relevance feedback mechanism it provided the ability to manipulate the output of the relevance feedback component *prior* to query evaluation. The execution of the query was interrupted and the user was presented with the list of terms suggested by the feedback component. Users had the opportunity to add none, some, or all of the suggested terms prior to the continuation of the query evaluation. For example, the user might select only terms that appear to be central to the search topic.

THE EXPERIMENT

Given the research results and considerations discussed above, our experiment was designed to investigate the following questions:

- Can best-match, ranked-output, full-text retrieval systems combined with an operator-free query language be used in an effective way by end-users with little training?
- Is relevance feedback effective? That is, do users using one of the three systems with relevance feedback perform better on the routing task compared to subjects who use the baseline system without relevance feedback?
- Is user knowledge about the output of the relevance feedback system helpful? If so, users in the transparent and penetrable conditions should perform better than subjects using the opaque relevance feedback system.
- Is user control over the operation of the relevance feedback system helpful? If so, users in the penetrable condition should perform better than subjects using the transparent feedback system and better than users using the opaque system.
- How do different levels of interaction impact the information seeking behavior of users such as the number of queries developed and the way these queries are formed?

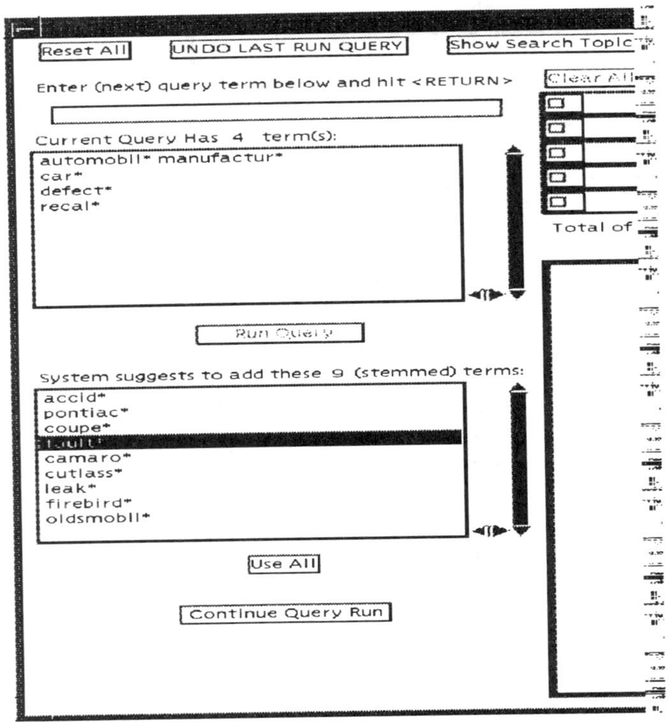

Figure 2: **Penetrable Relevance Feedback Version** (View of Feedback Component)

Subjects

64 Rutgers University Undergraduates (43 females, 21 males) with (self-reported) native-like English competence participated in the study. None of the subjects had any formal training in library and information science. Their IR searching experience was limited to the occasional use of a computerized library card catalog. In addition, a few isolated instances of Psych-Lit searches and WorldWideWeb browsing were reported.

Materials

The system and interfaces used are described in the previous section. The INQUERY system and the RU-INQUERY interfaces were installed on a SPARC 2 workstation and users interacted with it via a networked SUN 3/50 with monochrome monitor, standard keyboard, and mouse.

Recently, in the context of the ARPA-sponsored TIPSTER project and the ARPA/NIST TREC studies [7], a test collection of reasonably realistic information problems, together with a large database (ca. 3GB) of the full texts of a wide variety of documents, and relevance judgments on up to 2000 documents per information problem has become available. For our experiment, we used a subset of the TREC test collection, consisting of 74,520 articles from the Wall Street Journal between 1990 and 1992.

Two search topics (162 - *Automobile Recalls* and 165 - *Tobacco Advertising and the Young*) were selected from the set of TREC search topics. Each topic consisted of a title, a short description, and narrative that spelled out what would constitute a relevant article (figure 3).

Topic: Tobacco company advertising and the young
Description: A document will provide information on what is a widely held opinion that the tobacco industry aims its advertising at the young.
Narrative: A relevant document must report on tobacco company advertising and its relation to young people. A relevant document can address either side of the question: (1) Do tobacco companies consciously target the young, or (2) As the tobacco industry argues, is this an erroneous public perception. The "young" may be identified as youth, children, adolescents, teenagers, high school students, and college students.

Figure 3: Search Topic Definition For Topic 165

Each of the unique 2000 retrieved documents was rated by the first author as being relevant or not relevant to the topic on hand. These ratings were compared to TREC relevance judgments made by the originators of the topic descriptions that were available for a subset of about 560 of the 2000 retrieved documents. The inter-rater agreement between the experimenter and the TREC evaluators was almost perfect (98%) for topic 162 and very good for topic 165 (94%); cases of disagreement were resolved by careful reexamination of the documents. These judgements served as the basis for the performance evaluation.

The task for this study was a query construction task, i.e. subjects had to develop a final routing query for a given information problem, or *topic*, that could be run repeatedly against changing document collections. Specifically, we asked subjects to devise a single final query that retrieved at least 30 documents from the current collection, of which as many documents as possible in the top 30 were relevant to the provided topic. A focus on the top 30 articles mirrors realistic retrieval situations in which users are only interested in a small number of documents. We focused on retrieval for the current collection because a previous study [9] had shown that even experienced searchers did not reason about the effect of changing collection content and collection characteristics on query effectiveness. The task of developing a final query is different from a standard adhoc retrieval task in which users focus on finding relevant documents throughout the interaction and across multiple queries and where the end result is a set of documents, not a single final query. Our routing task is typical of a situation where a user wants to develop a profile for the filtering of information and uses an existing current collection to develop and test this profile.

A short (30-40 minutes long) interactive tutorial was integrated into the interface. It guided subjects through a sequence of exercises using the baseline system without relevance feedback in the form of a sample search. Three additional, very short online tutorials were developed that taught the use of the respective relevance feedback interface.

Experimental Design and Procedure

Subjects performed two (2) searches: all subjects used the baseline system without relevance feedback for their first search, followed by a second search on a different topic using either one of the three relevance feedback systems or continuing the use of the baseline system (control group). The order of topics was counterbalanced between searches, leading to eight (8) different conditions based on the topic order employed (2) and the type of system used during the second search (4). Subjects were assigned to one of the eight conditions in a block-randomized fashion.

After giving their informed consent and filling out the online questionnaire subjects worked through the online tutorial at their own pace. After subjects ended the tutorial or after the allotted time of 45 minutes had expired they were given twenty minutes to formulate a routing query for their first topic. At the twenty minute mark subjects were told that time was up and that they should wrap up the current action. After a short break subjects worked for up to ten minutes either through one of the three relevance feedback tutorials (experimental groups) or returned to a review of the original baseline tutorial (control group). Next, subjects were again given twenty minutes to formulate a routing query for the second topic, using the system and interface they just had learned about. A short interview concluded the experiment. Users were asked to comment on their overall experience and to state which interface they liked better.

All interactions with the system were automatically recorded by the system, creating a timed log of user and system actions. Subjects were instructed to think aloud during their two searches and the utterances were video-taped along with the current screen image. Independent of actual performance, subjects were told that they did well.

RESULTS AND DISCUSSION

Information Retrieval Evaluation

Although IR has a long history and extensive experience of evaluation (see, e.g. [12]), evaluation of interactive IR systems is still in its infancy. The two standard measures of retrieval effectiveness are **precision**, the number of relevant retrieved documents over the total number of retrieved documents, and **recall**, the ratio of relevant retrieved documents to the total number of (known) relevant documents. For the purposes of this paper we use *precision at 30 retrieved documents*, the cut-off level determined by the task that we set for our searchers in the experiment.

We used the non-parametric Kruskal-Wallis and Mann-Whitney U tests with corrections for tied ranks to analyze precision results since the normality and homogeneity assumptions for an ANOVA were violated. We report medians (M), the interquartile range (IQR), means ($\overline{X}$), and standard deviations (s) for descriptive purposes.

Training

Searchers trained on the baseline system on average about 26 minutes; the fastest subject finished the tutorial in 9.5 minutes whereas one subject had to be stopped after 45 minutes. There were no differences in training time between conditions. There was no correlation between training times and performance on the first search topic ($r = .08, p > .5$).

Note that we designed the training to ensure (for experimental purposes) that all subjects were comfortable with the baseline system and had used all its features. Thus, the training times we observed do not reflect the minimum time that would be required to make use of the system in a walk-up situation. Indeed, a few subjects "jumped the gun" and issued quite successful queries prior to studying the tutorial.

Baseline: Search Task 1

There were no differences in mean search-times for the first search by topic or experimental condition. All subjects used up (most of) the allotted time (17-21 minutes).

Three quarters of all subjects retrieved at least 8 relevant documents and half the subjects located over 12 relevant documents in the top 30 with the baseline system ($M = .40$, $IQR = .27 - .67$, $\overline{X} = .45$, $s = .24$). The lowest precision was 0, i.e. no relevant documents were ranked in the top 30 (but appeared in lower ranks); the best final queries had a precision of .87. Topic 162 on "Automobile Recall" had 2.5 times as many relevant documents in the collection compared to topic 165 on "Tobacco Advertising And the Young" (83 versus 33). As a result, finding relevant documents and ranking them high was significantly more difficult for the latter: the median precision for topic 162 was $M = .67$ ($IQR = .28 - .78$, $\overline{X} = .56$, $s = .28$) as compared to a median precision of $M = .33$ ($IQR = .27 - .42$, $\overline{X} = .34$, $s = .09$) for topic 165 (Kruskal-Wallis $H' = 10.17$, $df = 1, p \leq .01$). The average and median performance on the first search did not differ for the four experimental groups that searched for topic 165 in their baseline search. Among the groups that were given topic 162 first, only the group that would later use the opaque relevance feedback version performed on a level that was borderline significantly lower than the other groups.

Relevance Feedback Training

After completion of the first search subjects were trained on the feedback mechanism or reviewed the baseline tutorial (control). Subjects completed the second part of the tutorial on average within 8 minutes. Subjects in the control group finished their review on average in 6.5 minutes; the opaque feedback group who had only to learn about the marking of documents for relevance feedback but not about interaction with the output of the relevance feedback mechanism finished equally fast ($\overline{X} = 6.5$ minutes). Subjects in the transparent and penetrable condition used the allotted 10 minutes to finish the tutorial.

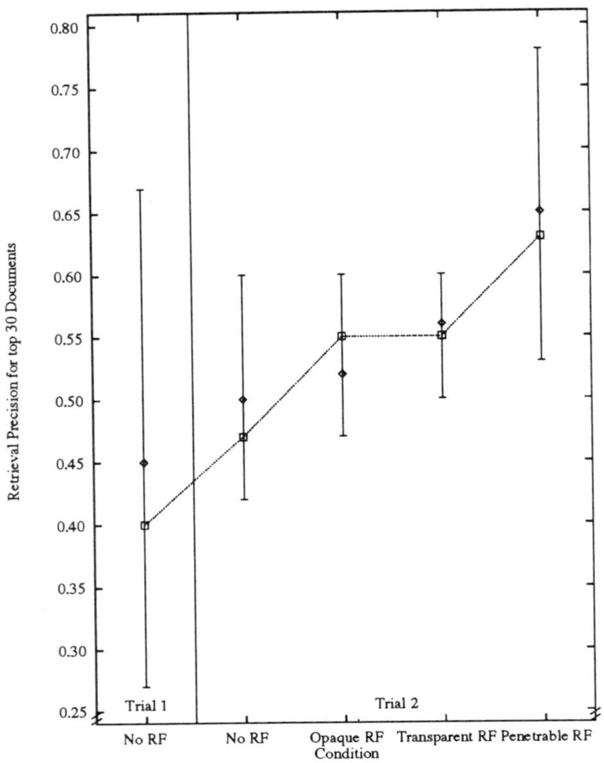

Figure 4: **Retrieval Precision at 30 Documents for Final Queries.** Given are median precision (□), mean (◇), and the interquartile range for search task 1 (No RF, n=64) and for each of the four conditions used for search task 2 (n=16).

Second Search Task - Effectiveness

At the top 30 cutoff level we found (see Figure 4) that overall retrieval performance differed significantly between conditions (Kruskal-Wallis test, $H' = 8.27, df = 3, p < .05$). Subjects who used relevance feedback had 17% to 34% better performance than subjects who continued in the control condition. Subjects in the penetrable feedback condition performed as a group 15% better than subjects in the opaque and transparent feedback conditions. Pairwise comparisons were, however, not significant except for the difference between the penetrable and baseline conditions (Mann-Whitney $U' = 72, p < .05$) due to large within-group variations and the relatively small sample size. The same general pattern held when data were analyzed separately for both topics. Again, topic 165 proved to be more difficult compared to topic 162, but the difference was less pronounced compared to the baseline search ($M_{165} = .50$ vs. $M_{162} = .63$, Mann-Whitney $U' = 212, p < .05$).

This overall performance is quite impressive, considering that our users had no search experience. The median performance exceeded the performance of INQUERY in fully automated mode (.23 for topic 162 and .40 for topic 165 on this collection), INQUERY being one of the best performing systems in the TREC context.

We can compare the performance on the two topics by considering R-precision, the proportion of relevant retrieved documents at the number of relevant documents in the collection, i.e. precision at the point where 100% recall would be possible. Topic 162 had 83 relevant documents compared to only 33 relevant documents for topic 165. The median R-precision for all subjects searching on topic 162 was .39 as compared to .48 for all subjects working on topic 165. Thus, subjects who searched on topic 165 were able to retrieve a larger proportion of those relevant documents known to be in the collection

Although the task specified 30 documents as the cutoff level, it is instructive to note the performance at other cutoffs as well. At 100 retrieved documents the relative performances mirror the results from the top 30 cutoff: the control group did worst ($M = .22$), the penetrable group did almost 50% better ($M = .32$), and the groups in the opaque and transparent condition fell in between ($M = .27$ and $M = .26$, respectively). If one only considers the top 5 and top 10 ranked documents, an even more dramatic (and significant) difference in favor of relevance feedback materializes: typically 5 out of 5 and 9 out of the top 10 documents were relevant for subjects in the feedback conditions whereas subjects in the control group managed to manually design final queries that had 3 out of the top 5 and 7 out of the top 10 being relevant.

A potential limitation of our study is the use of relevance feedback as a simple query expansion tool without a re-weighting of user terms. It remains an open issue whether or not the more massive query expansion through automatic, opaque relevance feedback may do better under particular term re-weighting schemes and how search tasks and collection characteristics impact performance of the various interfaces.

Second Search Task – Behavior

Search times for the second search did not differ significantly for either topics or conditions: 80% of the subjects used up the allotted time of 20 minutes, 19% searched for 16-19 min., and one subject stopped after 11 minutes, having found a very good query.

Interactive query formulation is an iterative process of query design and entry, query execution, and query evaluation. The number of iterations for each condition is depicted in figure 5. There were significant differences in the number of iterations (Kruskal Wallis $H' = 8.52, p < .05$). The control group ($M = 7, \overline{X} = 8.2$) and opaque feedback group ($M = 7, \overline{X} = 7.7$) went through roughly the same number of iterations, whereas subjects in the transparent condition performed an extra iteration ($M = 8, \overline{X} = 8.8$). The penetrable feedback group needed less iterations ($M = 6, \overline{X} = 5.8$) to develop equally good or better queries. Interaction was clearly beneficial: initial queries had much lower precision (Topic 162: $M_1 = .06$ vs. $M = .63$, Topic 165: $M_1 = .33$ vs. M=.50) and on average precision increased with the first few iterations.

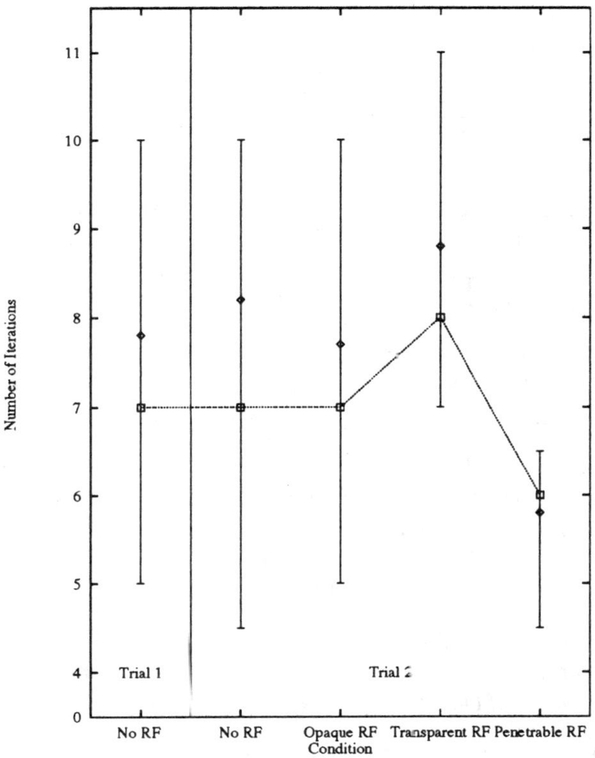

Figure 5: **Number of Iterations** (Number of Unique Queries Developed, Run, and Evaluated); both topics combined. Given are median number of iterations (□), the mean (◇), and the interquartile range for search task 1 (No RF, n=64) and for each of the four search task 2 conditions (n=16).

The four different interfaces shaped how subjects constructed their final queries over the course of the interaction. Table 1 provides a summary of the analysis of final queries and their constituent terms. The rightmost column lists the total number of query terms for each of the four conditions and for the two search topics separately and combined. Users in the baseline condition without relevance feedback entered on average 6.4 terms (s = 4.2), 1.8 of which were compound terms of 2 or 3 words each. The use of relevance feedback led to a dramatic increase in query length. In the opaque condition, the final query comprised on average 35.5 terms (s = 17.92). This was not a result of users entering more terms ($\overline{X} = 7.3, s = 9.36$), but a result of the automatic query expansion through relevance feedback which added on average 28.2 terms (s = 15.38). This expansion was caused by searchers having marked on average 12.6 documents as being relevant when running the final query. The average query length for queries by subjects in the transparent condition is even larger: final queries had on average 41.2 terms, 30.3 of which were automatically added by the feedback component based on an average of 13.6 documents being marked as relevant. User queries had on average about 11 terms; only 3.8 of these terms were entered by the user, almost twice that many

Mean Number & Sources of Query Terms					
Relevance Feedback Condition	User Controlled: User Typed	Copy from RF	Σ	Added by RF SYS	Σ
Topic 162:					
None	6.9	n/a	6.9	n/a	6.9
Opaque	10.9	n/a	10.9	35.9	46.8
Transparent	3.3	9.1	12.4	42.8	55.1
Penetrable	6.3	24.4	30.6	n/a	30.6
Topic 165:					
None	6.0	n/a	6.0	n/a	6.0
Opaque	3.8	n/a	3.8	20.5	24.3
Transparent	4.3	5.3	9.5	17.8	27.3
Penetrable	3.3	9.5	12.8	n/a	12.8
162&165:					
None	6.4	n/a	6.4	n/a	6.4
Opaque	7.3	n/a	7.3	28.2	35.5
Transparent	3.8	7.2	10.9	30.3	41.2
Penetrable	4.8	16.9	21.7	n/a	21.7

Table 1: Number and Sources of Query Terms in Final Queries for Second Search, Both Topics. Given are the mean number of query terms for each of three possible sources: user entry, copied by user from relevance feedback output, and automatic query expansion through relevance feedback.

($\overline{X}$ = 7.2) were terms the user had copied from the display of automatically added terms or through relevance feedback expansion during prior iterations.

Finally, the average length of final queries by subjects in the penetrable feedback condition was 21.7 (s = 29.4). This number is lower compared to the other feedback conditions because on average final queries contained only 16.9 terms (s = 27.3) suggested by the feedback component. Subjects in the penetrable condition marked a comparable number of documents as being relevant but were quite selective in using suggested feedback terms: throughout the search they used only 349 of a total of 1259 suggested terms. Furthermore, five (5) instances in which users copied all suggested terms in one step accounted for 233 of these terms. An initial content analysis of copied terms suggests that users primarily copied those terms which had a clear and central semantic relation to the search topic. At the same time, subjects entered fewer terms ($\overline{X} = 4.8, s = 3.94$) manually. Indeed, subjects commented that they preferred the "lazy" approach of term selection over term generation.

Given that relevance feedback depends on the marking of relevant documents and that topic 165 was much harder than topic 162, it is not surprising that there were significant differences in query length between the two topics ($F(1, 56) = 16.3, p < .001$). However, table 1 shows that the pattern described above also holds for each topic in isolation.

CONCLUSIONS

Subjects used our system and interface quite effectively and very few usability problems surfaced. Users had little problem formulating their queries and the observed retrieval effectiveness of final queries supports the view that interactive best-match, ranked-output, unstructured input, full-text retrieval systems are suitable tools for end users with limited search experience. Users clearly benefited from the opportunity to revise queries in an iterative process.

Overall, relevance feedback appears to be a beneficial mechanism. All users declared their preference for the relevance feedback mechanism over the baseline system in a post-search interview. Relevance Feedback did improve median performance by 10% (or more) at 30 retrieved documents. Even larger gains were observed if one only considers the top 10 or top 20 documents retrieved, a situation quite common in many application domains. However, substantial subject and topic variation precluded statistical significant findings at the chosen level of $p \leq .05$.

Subjects that interacted with the penetrable version of relevance feedback did best in our study overall and significantly better than users of the baseline system without relevance feedback.

Perceived performance, trust in the system, and subjective usability are important issues, in particular for such sensitive domains as the filtering of one's personal email or news. Subjects really "liked" the penetrable version that allowed them to manipulate the list of suggested terms. Indeed, subjects in the opaque condition and in another study currently in progress routinely expressed their desire to "see and control" what the feedback component did to their queries. People commented that using the feedback component as a suggestion device made them "lazy": the task of generating terms was replaced by the easier task of term selection. Furthermore, users in the penetrable condition needed fewer iterations to achieve results comparable to, or better than the other, less interactive, feedback conditions.

Although a number of issues need to be further addressed, these results suggest that interfaces for IR systems for end users should be designed to support interactive collaboration in query formulation and reformulation between the users and the "intelligent" programs which support them.

ACKNOWLEDGMENTS

This work is supported by NIST Cooperative Agreement 70NANB5H0050. Thanks to the Rutgers University Center for Cognitive Science (RuCCS) for providing equipment loans and infrastructure support and to Jamie Callan, Bruce Croft, and Steve Harding of the Center for Intelligent Information Retrieval at the University of Massachusetts at Amherst for their unstinting support of our use of INQUERY.

REFERENCES

1 Ahlberg, C., and Shneiderman, B. Visual information seeking: Tight coupling of dynamic query filters with starfield displays. In *Proc. CHI'94*. ACM Press, New York, 1994, pp. 313–317.

2 Belkin, N. J., and Croft, W. B. Retrieval techniques. In *ARIST*, M. E. Williams, Ed. Elsevier, 1987, ch. 4, pp. 109–145.

3 Callan, J. P., Croft, W. B., and Harding, S. M. The inquery retrieval system. In *DEXA 3: Proceedings of the Third International Conference on Database and Expert Systems Applications* (Berlin, 1992), Springer Verlag, pp. 83–87.

4 Efthimiadis, E. *Interactive Query expansion and Relevance Feedback for document Retrieval Systems.* PhD thesis, City University, London, UK, 1992.

5 Frei, H., and Qiu, Y. Effectiveness of weighted searching in an operational IR environment. In *Information Retrieval 93: von der Modellierung zur Anwendung; Proc. der 1. Tagung Information Retrieval '93* (Konstanz, 1993), Universitätsverlag Konstanz, pp. 41–54.

6 Hancock-Beaulieu, M., and Walker, S. An evaluation of automatic query expansion in an online library catalogue. *Journal of Documentation 48*, 4 (1992), 406–421.

7 Harman, D. Overview of the second text retrieval conference. *IPM 31*, 3 (1995), 271–289.

8 Hewett, T., and Scott, S. The use of thinking-out-loud and protocol analysis in development of a process model of interactive database searching. In *Proceedings of INTERACT'87* (Amsterdam, 1987), Elsevier, pp. 51–56.

9 Koenemann, J., Quatrain, R., Cool, C., and Belkin, N. J. New tools and old habits: The interactive searching behavior of expert online searchers using inquery. In *TREC-3. Proceedings of the Third Text REtrieval Conference* (Washington, D.C., 1995), D. Harman, Ed., Government Printing Office, pp. 144–177.

10 Landauer, T., Egan, D., Remde, J., Lesk, M., Lochbaum, C., and Ketchum, D. Enhancing the usability of text through computer delivery. In *Hypertext: A psychological perspective*, C. McKnight, A. Dillon, and J. Richardson, Eds. Ellis Horwood, New York:, 1993, pp. 72–136.

11 Salton, G., and Buckley, C. Improving retrieval performance by relevance feedback. *JASIS 41*, 4 (1990), 288–297.

12 Sparck Jones, K. *Information Retrieval Experiment*. Butterworths, London, 1981.

13 Turtle, H. Natural language vs. boolean query evaluation: A comparison of retrieval performance. In *SIGIR'94. Proc. of the Seventeenth Annual ACM SIGIR Conference on Research and Development in Information Retrieval* (London, 1994), Springer Verlag, pp. 212–220.

Scatter/Gather Browsing Communicates the Topic Structure of a Very Large Text Collection

Peter Pirolli, Patricia Schank, Marti Hearst, Christine Diehl

Xerox Palo Alto Research Center
3333 Coyote Hill Road
Palo Alto, CA 94304, USA
pirolli@parc.xerox.com, schank@unix.sri.com,
hearst@parc.xerox.com, cdiehl@violet.berkeley.edu

ABSTRACT
Scatter/Gather is a cluster-based browsing technique for large text collections. Users are presented with automatically computed summaries of the contents of clusters of similar documents and provided with a method for navigating through these summaries at different levels of granularity. The aim of the technique is to communicate information about the topic structure of very large collections. We tested the effectiveness of Scatter/Gather as a simple pure document retrieval tool, and studied its effects on the incidental learning of topic structure. When compared to interactions involving simple keyword-based search, the results suggest that Scatter/Gather induces a more coherent conceptual image of a text collection, a richer vocabulary for constructing search queries, and communicates the distribution of relevant documents over clusters of documents in the collection.

Keywords
Information retrieval; Scatter/Gather; Clustering; Browsing.

INTRODUCTION
When faced with ill-defined problems requiring information access, we often want to explore the resources available to us before exploiting them. This exploration may be partly aimed at refining our understanding of the potential space of content that is available, and partly aimed at formulating a concrete course of action for getting specific documents. Interfaces that support the *browsing* of a collection, as opposed to *searching* a collection, are aimed at satisfying this need to learn more about a collection before taking action.

Scatter/Gather is a document browsing technique aimed at supporting such exploratory learning [3, 4]. The emphasis in this browsing technique is to present users with an automatically computed overview of the contents of a document collection, and to provide a method for navigating through this summary at different levels of granularity. The central primitive operation in Scatter/Gather involves document clustering based on pairwise document similarity. The technique aims to place similar documents into the same cluster. Recursively clustering a collection produces a *cluster hierarchy.*

For each cluster, at each level of this hierarchy, the user is presented with summary information about the cluster that presumably communicates something about the kinds of documents it contains. The user may then select (*gather*) those clusters that seem interesting or relevant. This subset of clusters can then be reclustered (*scattered*) to reveal more fine-grained clusters of documents. With each successive iteration of scattering and gathering clusters, the clusters become smaller and more detailed, eventually bottoming out at the level of individual documents.

In this paper we present experimental evidence to support the view that Scatter/Gather interaction induces the development of a better understanding of the contents of large text collections, refines users' formulations of search queries, and is a feasible information retrieval technique in its own right when compared to standard search techniques.

METHODOLOGICAL ISSUES
Much of the discussion on the evaluation of textual information access systems has focused on how to improve the traditional measures of *precision* and *recall* (e.g., [6, 11]). Precision is the proportion of relevant documents retrieved among a set of retrieved documents, whereas recall is the proportion of relevant documents in the original collection that were retrieved. Some researchers argue the need to move away from strict measures of overall precision and recall toward other measures of search success or to what is termed user-centric evaluation [5]. However, most of the analyses that offer alternatives to precision and recall measures focus on how well the user's information need is satisfied (and in some cases on the progression of familiarity with the system under study), rather than what is learned incidentally about the collection itself. Pirolli and Card [8] suggest evaluating information access search strategies using a theoretical model based on optimal foraging theory from biology. Foraging often involves a

CHI 96 Vancouver, BC Canada
© 1996 ACM 0-89791-777-4/96/04..$3.50

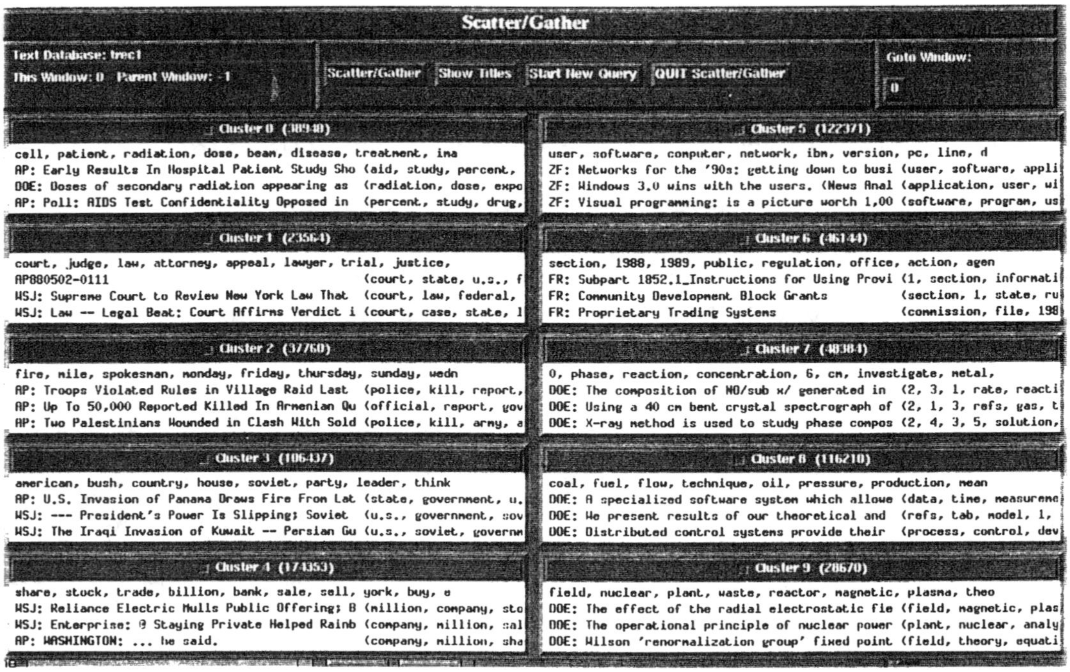

Figure 1. The Scatter/Gather interface presents a user with clusters of like documents.

phase of exploration to gain knowledge about the distribution and cost structure of access to resources and this knowledge determines later patterns of foraging [1].

Although there are some subtle issues involved in the assessment of precision and recall measures (such as deciding on how to evaluate documents as being "relevant"), even more difficulties arise when trying to assess whether a browsing system is communicating knowledge to a user about the structure of a document collection. As will become clear, this was a major challenge to our research. We have had to develop multiple methodologies and analyses in order to converge on an assessment of the mental models that people get from interacting with Scatter/Gather.

DOCUMENT CLUSTERING IN SCATTER/GATHER

Clustering techniques have been used in the past as an enhancement to keyword-search retrieval algorithms [3, 4]. The novelty of the Scatter/Gather approach is its use of clustering as the basis of an interactive method that supports the browsing of a summary of the structure and content of a text collection–a summary intended to be like a table of contents. This raises two essential requirements [4]. First, the clustering method has to be fast enough to support real user interaction. Second, there must be a method of cluster summarization that enables a user to make sense of the text collection content and to navigate its structure.

Clustering depends on some measure of inter-document similarity. A common approach [10], with a number of variants, is to represent documents as vectors of equal length, where each component of a vector is associated with one of the unique content words in the document collection. In some schemes, the component may contain a value indicating the presence of a word in the document (i.e., a binary coding). In other schemes, a vector component may indicate the frequency or some normalized frequency of a word in the document. The similarity of two documents can then be computed by a *cosine measure*, which is the cosine of the angle between two vectors, which is sometimes also known as a *normalized correlation.*

Single-linkage *hierarchical clustering* is a commonly used method outside of information access. For instance, we use it below in our data analysis. It is, however, too slow for even moderately large document collections. Beginning with individual documents, single-linkage hierarchical clustering iteratively agglomerates the most similar pair of clusters built so far into a new cluster. The global consideration of all pairwise similarities at each stage of clustering leads to running times of $\Omega(n^2)$ in the number, n, of documents.

Speedier algorithms [4] were developed for Scatter/Gather based on a nonagglomerative *partitional clustering* scheme. The essence of this approach is to flatly partition a collection into k subsets, and recursively partition the subsets as needed to induce a hierarchical structure. At each partitioning, k document seeds are selected and remaining documents are clustered with the most similar seed. At each stage the procedure may be run further to iteratively improve the selection of seeds and improve the clustering. The developed schemes have running times of $O(kn)$.

Linear $O(kn)$ run-times are still too slow for very large collections. Constant-time interaction costs for Scatter/Gather navigation through a cluster hierarchy are achieved by precomputing a cluster hierarchy to be used in Scatter/Gather interaction [3]. The off-line precomputation uses the linear-time algorithms and summarizes document clusters by *meta-documents* containing profiles of topical words and the most typical titles.

These topical words and typical titles are also used to present users a summary of the documents in a cluster. Topical words are those that occur most frequently in a cluster, and typical titles are those with the highest similarity to a centroid of the cluster. Together, the topical words and typical titles form a *cluster digest*. The cluster digest scheme combined with the constant-time interaction cost satisfy the two requirements desired for a cluster-based browsing method.

A SCATTER/GATHER INTERFACE

Figure 1 presents a typical view of the Scatter/Gather interface. There are ten clusters, with each cluster represented by a separate area in Figure 1. For each cluster, the user is presented with the topical words that occur in the text contents of documents in a cluster, as well as the titles of the three most typical documents. The user may *gather* some subset of those clusters, by pointing and selecting buttons above each cluster, and then ask the system to *scatter* that subcollection into another 10 subclusters, by selecting a Scatter/Gather button at the top of the display in Figure 1.

Users could also select one or more clusters and then select the Show Titles button at the top of Figure 1, which would then display all of the document titles in the selected clusters, in a separate Show Titles Window. The user can scan the displayed list of titles, seeking those that appear relevant to the task at hand. Relevant documents can be selected by pointing, and then saved to file by cut and paste techniques.

OVERVIEW OF THE EXPERIMENT

Although Scatter/Gather has not been developed as a stand-alone information access technique [4], we felt that a stern trial of its efficacy would be to test it as a stand-alone search tool and determine how it fared in support of (a) finding relevant documents and (b) incidental learning about the text collection. We compared Scatter/Gather to a word-based search interface we called SimSearch. This interface allowed users to enter an arbitrary collection of words based on a topic query and it retrieved a fixed small set of documents most similar to the query, as determined by a similarity in a vector space model [2].

METHOD

Participants

Sixteen adults participated in this study. Three of the participants were Xerox PARC employees, one was a PARC employee family member, and the remaining 12 participants were graduate students from Stanford University. PARC employees volunteered their time for the study; the remaining subjects were paid $10/hour for their participation.

Materials and Procedure

Participants were asked to read the instructions for the experiment and then use one of the interfaces to find articles relevant to given topics in a large and complex collection of text documents. There were four phases to the experiment: (1) finding articles relevant to a topic using Scatter/Gather or Similarity Search, (2) writing search queries and drawing a diagram representing the topic structure of the collection, (3) a replication of Phase 1, and (4) a replication of Phase 2. Phases 1 and 3 were aimed at providing participants with exposure to one of the information access techniques, and Phases 2 and 4 were aimed at assessing the impact of that exposure on query formulation and the users' conception of the text collection.

The experiment used the 2.2 gigabyte TIPSTER text collection created for the TREC conference [7]. Twelve topics were drawn from the first 100 topics used in the TREC conference. These twelve were chosen based on a level of difficulty measured by the mean number of relevant documents in the Tipster collection as identified by information retrieval experts associated with TREC [7]. The four topics with the fewest (expert-identified) relevant documents (M = 46) were placed in the "hard" group, the four topics with the most relevant documents (M = 865) were placed in the "easy" group, and the four topics about the median number of relevant documents were placed in the "medium" group (M = 303).

Participants spent between two and five hours total on study activities, with two phases a day over the course of two days. Four blocks of topics were constructed for presentation over the four phases of tasks. Each topic-block contained one easy topic, one medium topic, and one hard topic, in that order. The order of blocks across phases was counterbalanced over sets of four participants, within groups, according to a randomized Latin square.

Participants were randomly assigned to one of three study conditions: Scatter/Gather Speeded (SGS, N = 4), Scatter/Gather with Relevance Ratings (SGR, N = 4), and SimSearch (SS, N = 8). Phases 1 and 3 varied by condition, and Phases 2 and 4 were identical across conditions. In the SGS condition, subjects were given one hour to find articles in each of Phases 1 and 3. In the SGR condition, subjects were not given a time limit, and were asked to complete additional classification and relevance activities: Given worksheets, they were asked to indicate how they would classify each presented cluster (i.e., using words or short phrases), and to estimate what percentage of texts in a cluster seemed relevant to the topic. In the SS condition, subjects used SimSearch rather than Scatter/Gather to find their relevant articles in phases one and three. Note that SGR and SGS conditions were combined for some analyses into one group (SG; see below).

RESULTS

Our first set of analyses will concentrate on comparisons of Scatter/Gather versus SimSearch, with respect to their effectiveness as information retrieval tools. Subsequent analyses will focus on comparisons with respect to enhancement of users' understandings of the text collection.

Finding Relevant Articles (Phases 1 and 3)

Table 1 presents summary data for the mean time spent per query, the mean number of documents selected (saved) for retrieval, mean number of those that were relevant (according to TREC identification), and the mean *precision* of the retrieved documents (No. relevant ÷ No. saved). For each type of data in Table 1, (i.e., each row) we conducted an analysis of variance (ANOVA) for the two Groups (SG, SS) × Query Difficulty (Easy, Medium, Hard) × Phase (1, 3) factorial design.

Interface Effects

Examining Table 1, it is apparent that participants who used the Scatter/Gather interface to answer queries took substantially longer than those using SimSearch, and the SG vs SS group difference in Table 1 was significant, $F(1, 14) = 34.07$, $MSE = 297.79$, $p < .001$. The SGR participants took about twice as long as the SGS participants to answer queries. This is attributable to the ancillary rating task performed by the SGR participants. Still, SGS participants took about twice as long as SS participants, so that, even when instructed to use the Scatter/Gather interface as quickly as possible to answer queries, Scatter/Gather users were substantially outhustled by SimSearch users.

Although there was not a significant difference in the total number of documents saved by SG ($M = 12.26$) versus SS ($M = 16.44$) participants [$F(1, 14) = .24$, $MSE = 2355.77$], there was a difference in number of relevant documents saved, $F(1, 14) = 5.44$, $MSE = 108.55$, $p = .04$, with SS participants ($M = 10.40$) outgaining SG participants ($M = 5.44$). This is reflected in the differences in precision scores in Table 1.

The SG group showed substantially more variation in number of documents saved ($SD = 65.21$; $SD = 17.94$ with largest outlier removed) than the SS group ($SD = 11.27$). Furthermore, 27% of SG queries (13 of the 48), resulted in no documents saved, whereas all the SS participants saved at least one document on each query. These results suggest that the chance of finding relevant documents is a bit more "hit and miss" for participants using a pure SG system.

Query Effects

Both the total number of documents saved and the number of relevant documents saved decreased significantly with increases in Query Difficulty: (a) Easy No. saved $M = 34.91$ and No. relevant $M = 15.06$, (b) Medium No. saved $M = 15.72$ and No. relevant $M = 5.81$, and (c) Hard No. saved $M = 6.00$ and No. relevant $M = 2.88$ [for No. saved, $F(2, 28) = 3.99$, $MSE = 1737.52$, $p = .03$; for No. relevant $F(2, 28) = 10.04$, $MSE = 128.98$, $p = .001$]. Query Difficulty had a significant, although complex main effect on task time, $F(2, 28) = 3.73$, $MSE = 75.71$, $p < .05$, with participants spending more time on Easy ($M = 23.42$ mins) and Hard ($M = 20.15$ mins) queries than on Medium queries ($M = 17.50$ mins). This main effect did not interact with the type of interface used, $F(1, 14) = 1.56$. Perhaps participants monitored the rates at which they encountered relevant documents and this rate did not exhibit substantial depression before the 30 min cutoff for Easy and Hard queries, but did so for the Medium queries. That is, the rate of encounter with relevant documents should be highest for Easy queries, less for Medium, and less still for Hard queries, but the point at which there is a noticeable drop-off in this rate (indicating a near-depletion of relevant documents) may occur earliest for the Medium queries. Clearly the users' judgments about when to give up is complex and requires further investigation.

Table 1. Per-query averages for SimSearch (SS) and Scatter/Gather (SG) groups (SGS = Speeded, SGR = Rating conditions).

	SS	SG		
		SGS	SGR	Both
Time (min)	10.10	22.10	39.18	30.64
No. Saved	16.44	7.71	17.09	12.26
No. Relevant	10.40	2.45	8.42	5.44
Precision	.63	.32	.49	.44

Practice Effects

Although there were trends indicating that participants increased the number of documents saved as they gained more experience (Phase 1 $M = 11.92$; Phase 3 $M = 25.83$) and increased the number of relevant documents saved with increased practice (Phase 1 $M = 6.81$; Phase 3 $M = 9.02$), neither increase was significant, nor did the trends show a significant interaction with the type of interface used. There was also no main effect of practice on time per query (Phase 1 $M = 19.78$; Phase 3 $M = 20.94$). It could be that our participants found both SimSearch and Scatter/Gather to be rather easy to learn during the warm-up exercises and therefore showed relatively little additional learning during the experimental phases.

Summary

As a stand-alone information retrieval tool, Scatter/Gather is not as effective as a common word-based search technique. As we noted, however, this is a stern test of the technique, since it has really been aimed at communicating the topic structure of a collection. In the following sections we examine the incidental learning about topic structure that Scatter/Gather induced in the SG participants.

Communicating the Distribution of Relevant Texts

We expect the Scatter/Gather browser to provide users who are working on a query with a sense of the distribution of relevant documents across clusters. The SGR participants were asked to rate the precision of each cluster encountered (No. relevant documents ÷ No. documents). Ideally, one would like to match these ratings against the actual precisions to assess how well Scatter/Gather communicates the location of relevant documents, but it is currently infeasible to carry out this computation.

As an approximation, however, we were able to formulate the expected distribution of relevant documents across clusters and to compare this against the observed distribution of ratings. The distribution of relevant documents across clusters was examined for each of 29 queries used in TREC. Sets of the 200 most similar documents were retrieved using the SimSearch technique and then these retrieved sets were clustered using the Scatter/Gather clustering algorithm into five partitions. The clustering, however, proceeded wihout any information about the nature of the query used to select the initial 200 documents. Clusters larger than a criterion size were clustered again, and this process recursed. For each query, the clusters were ranked $i = 1, 2, ..., 5$ by the number of relevant documents u_i assigned to cluster i from the U relevant documents contained in the original set that was clustered. Among regressions of linear, exponential, and power functions, the best fit was obtained by an exponential distribution of relevant documents across clusters,

$$u_i = .47Ue^{-.57(i-1)}, \qquad (1)$$

with $R^2 = .92$.

Using Equation 1, we estimated the distribution of relevant documents (those identified by TREC experts) across the 10 topmost clusters and compared this against the mean precision estimates given by SGR participants, and these data are presented in Figure 2. (For the sake of clarity, Figure 2 omits estimates of zero precision by our participants.) This makes the assumption the rank ordering of people's ratings mirror the rank ordering of No. relevant documents in clusters.

The linear relationships apparent in the log-log coordinates of Figure 2 suggest that the Scatter/Gather users perceive a distribution of relevant documents across clusters that has a power law relation to the expected distribution of relevant documents. Such relations are common in many domains where people must assess the strength of evidence to judge the probability of events [9]. Users apparently show the same biases in estimating how many relevant documents are in a collection as they do in estimations of events in other domains, such as sports or health risks.

It seems, then, that three conclusions can be drawn about how well Scatter/Gather communicates the location of relevant documents among the clusters presented to users: (1) even though the clustering algorithm obtains no information about users' queries, most of the documents relevant to a typical (TREC) query will tend to be grouped into few clusters, (2) users judge most of the relevant documents to be grouped into few clusters, and (3) the users' judgments appear to have a well-defined power-law relationship to the actual distribution of relevant documents.

Communicating Effective Query Terminology

We might also expect that exploring a text collection with the Scatter/Gather interface improves the ability of users to formulate better key-word search queries. We examined this expectation through an analysis of the search queries formulated by participants in our study. Both SG and SS subjects were given the task to generate search words for given query topics after having used their systems. Table 2 shows the mean number of keywords participants used in their keyword queries, and the mean number of new keywords in their query (i.e., keywords that didn't appear in the topic description). SG participants used significantly more new terms not given in the topic description than SS participants, $t(15) = 2.01$, $p < .05$, and this was more apparent early in Phase 2, $t(15) = 1.84$, $p < .05$. In Phase 2, SG subjects also generated significantly more terms than SS subjects, $t(15) = 1.79$, $p < .05$, although SS subjects marginally increased the number of terms they used from Phase 2 to Phase 4. These results support the hypothesis that Scatter/Gather users are learning about the effective topic language from which to generate their search queries.

Communicating a Conceptual Model of Topic Structure

In Phases 2 and 4 we had asked all participants to draw tree diagrams representing the topic structure of the text collection. Descriptive statistics for subjects' drawn diagrams are given in Table 3. SGR participants' diagrams had the most nodes and links, significantly more than SGS [$t(7) = 2.78$, $p < .05$], but not significantly more than SS [$t(11) = 1.45$, $p > .10$]. For all three groups, the number of nodes did not significantly differ from number of links. SGR diagrams were significantly more deep than SGS diagrams [$t(7) = 2.82$, $p < .05$), but not significantly deeper than SS diagrams. SGR diagrams were significantly broader than both SGS and SS diagrams [$t(7) = 2.22$ and $t(11) = 4.77$, respectively, both p's $< .05$]. Although SGS diagrams were not significantly broader than SS diagrams

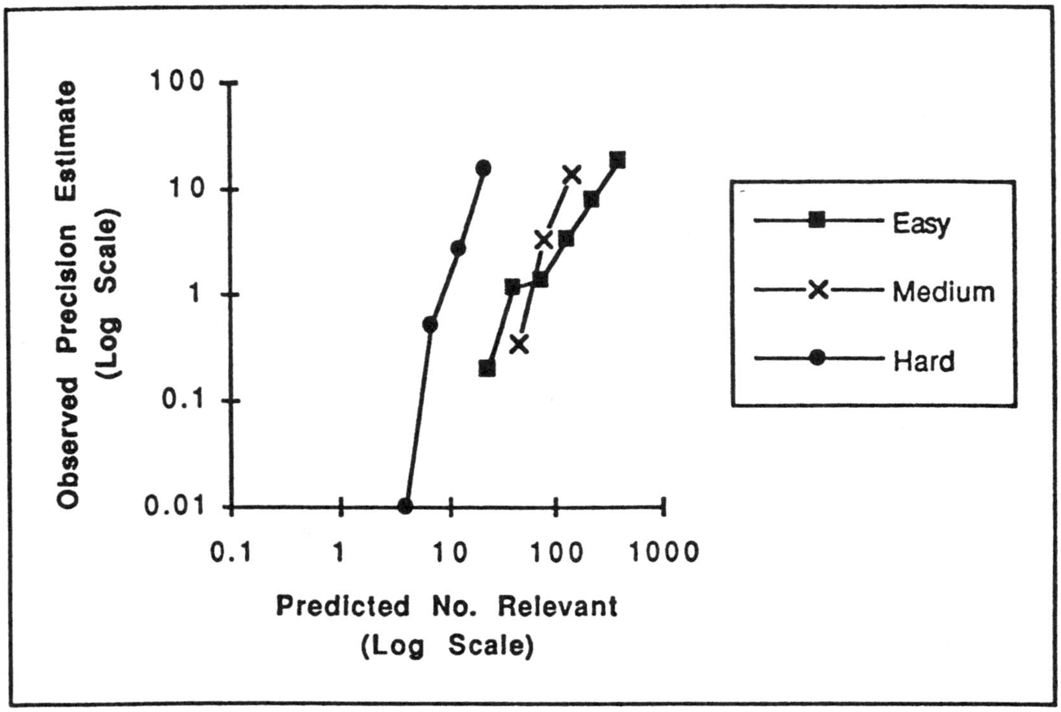

Figure 2. The match of the perceived precision (No. relevant + No. total documents) of clusters to the predicted distribution of relevant documents for different degrees of Query Difficulty.

overall, both SGS and SGR diagrams were significantly broader than SS diagrams at the highest level [$t(11) = 2.81$, $p < .01$, and $t(11)=4.71$, $p<.001$, respectively]. That is, the SG subjects used a greater number of primary (or organizing) topics in their diagrams (see Table 3).

Table 2. Search terms used, Phases 2 and 4.

Group	Number of Terms Used	Number of New Terms
SS	5.77	0.73
Phase 2	4.75	0.54
Phase 4	6.79	0.91
SG	6.44	1.84[a]
Phase 2	6.67[a]	2.04[a]
Phase 4	6.21	1.63

[a]significantly greater than other group, same condition, $p < .05$

If it is the browsing interaction with Scatter/Gather that induces the topic structure in users, then we should expect the richness of the diagrams drawn by SG participants to increase with increased browsing. Figure 3 shows that, indeed, the breadth of SG diagrams was highly correlated with the number of Scatter/Gather cluster windows (windows such as Figure 1) that participants saw during a block of queries. The number of cluster windows was not correlated at all, however, with the depth of the diagrams or the number of nodes or links.

Regarding content, there seemed to be more diversity in topics listed in SGR diagrams, e.g., in addition to terms used in the given query topics. The SS group listed items more related to their specific query topics, as well as more general nodes like "news," "AP," "WSJ," etc. Finally, the SGS diagrams seem to have a few new topics not given in the queries (e.g., "medicine," "science"), but not as many as the SGR group. Two judges rated the topics appearing in the diagrams on a three-point "specific-general" scale to determine the diversity of topics contained in the diagrams (a rating of one was assigned to a topic judged to be very specific, e.g., "corrupt government officials", and a rating of three was assigned to a very general topic, e.g., "law"). There was an 82% inter-rater agreement overall and 85% agreement on the most general topics (i.e, those having a rating of three). Forty diagram topics (20% of the distinct topics used) were rated as most general by both judges, and the groups were compared on the proportion of "general" topics their diagrams contained. Overall, the SG subjects used a significantly greater percentage of general topics than the SS subjects (52% and 31% respectively; $t(15)=2.56$, $p < .05$). The SGS and SGR subjects did not differ significantly in the proportion of general topics they included in their diagrams (54% and 49% respectively). There were no significant between- or within-group differences in the number of general topics for diagrams drawn in Phase 2 versus Phase 4.

Table 3. Diagram analyses, Phases 2 and 4.

Group	Mean #Nodes	Mean #Links	Mean Depth	Mean Breadth	Breadth to Depth Ratio	Mean #Primary Topics
SS	12.5	11.8	2.8	3.9	1.4	3.1
SGS	7.5	7.3	1.9	4.4	2.3	4.9[b]
SGR	15.1[a]	14.4[a]	3.0[a]	6.0[ab]	2.0	6.6[ab]

[a]significantly greater than SGS group, $p < .05$
[b]significantly greater than SS group, $p < .05$

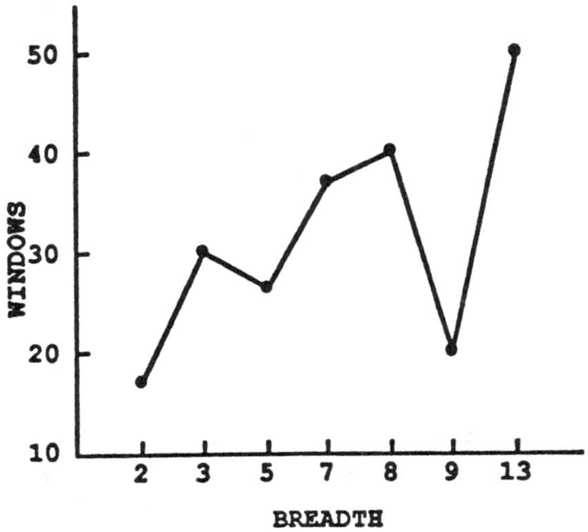

Figure 3. Relation of No. Scatter/Gather windows seen to the breadth of a subject's topic structure diagram.

A multi-dimensional scaling analysis was used to assess the similarity of participants' diagrams based on the number of shared topics. Such an analysis attempts to arrange entities in a space such that the distances between the entities in that space correspond (as much as possible) to some measured differences (or similarities) between all pairs of entities. We wanted to look at the output of such an analysis to see which users (the entities in our analysis) seemed to cluster together in terms of their conception of the topics contained in the text collection. That is, multi-dimensional analysis was used to lay out a kind of semantic space for users conceptions of topics in the collection.

The similarity matrix we used for this analysis indicated the proportion of shared topics between any two diagrams (number of topics in common divided by the number of topic nodes in the larger diagram). One SS participant did not use topics and was not included in the analysis. On average, SGS and SGR participants' diagrams were more similar to each other than they were to SS participants' diagrams (sharing 10% versus 5% of topics, respectively). SS participants' diagrams were no more similar to each other than they were to SG participants' diagrams (sharing only 5% of topics). The SGS diagrams were the most similar of the three groups, sharing an average of 14% of their topics. Figure 4 shows a three-dimensional multi-dimensional scaling solution for these diagram topic similarity data. The circles represent SG participants and the boxes represent SS participants. In addition, a minimal spanning tree has been laid over the points in Figure 4 to highlight clusterings. Overall, it appears that SG participants are more central and closer to one another in Figure 4 than SS participants. As a measure of incoherence, we computed the root mean squared (*RMS*) distances among points in the Figure 4. This incoherence measure was lower for the SGS (*RMS* = 1.08) and SGR (*RMS* = 1.22) participants than for the SS participants (*RMS* = 1.68). The people using Scatter/Gather seemed to be closer to one another in terms of their conception of the topics contained in the collection

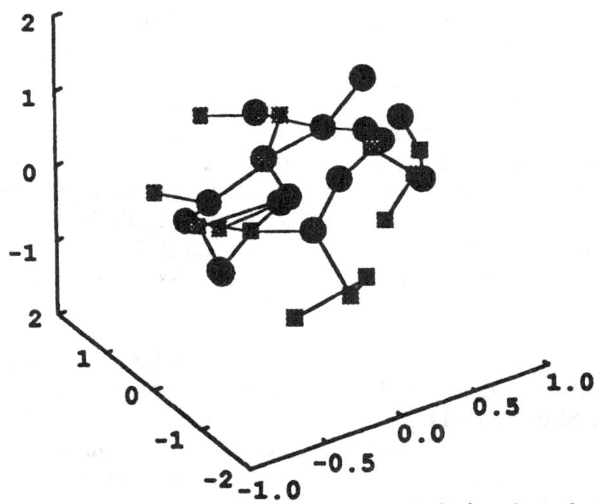

Figure 4. Multi-dimensional scaling solution based on diagram content similarity for the Scatter/Gather (circles) and SimSearch (boxes) participants.

Figure 5 shows a hierarchical clustering based on the similarity data for the diagrams from Phase 4. This is another way of seeing how individual people cluster together in terms of their conception of the topics in the collection. This tree representation clearly shows the strong similarity grouping of the SGS and SGR diagrams. Overall then, it appears that the Scatter/Gather interface is inducing a more coherent view of the text collection than SimSearch.

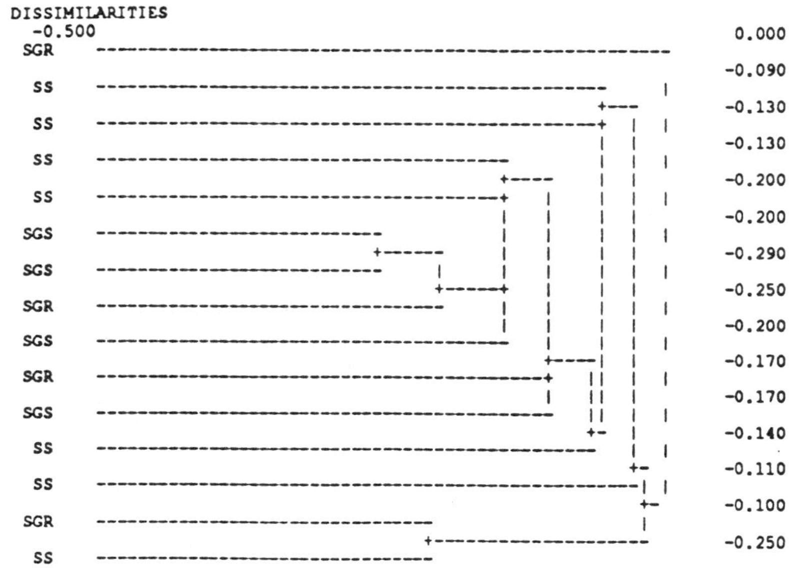

Figure 5. Hierarchical clustering of diagram topic similarity data from Phase 4 (single linkage method, nearest neighbor). SG diagrams (SGS and SGR) appear to be the most similar grouping.

GENERAL DISCUSSION

The results indicate that Scatter/Gather communicates several kinds of information about the topic structure of a large text collection. It is, by itself, not a superior information retrieval tool when the goal is to locate specific documents. Scatter/Gather may be useful in support of the kind of exploratory sensemaking activities that occur when users encounter large unknown text collections, and it should be coupled with other kinds of retrieval techniques, such as SimSearch, that can be enhanced by the knowledge that users gain through preliminary Scatter/Gather browsing. We are currently in the process of testing such a multi-functional browsing/search engine.

In conducting this research, we also faced numerous methodological problems. It is easy to collect measures based on counts of documents retrieved, but not so easy to assess the knowledge about a collection that is communicated by a browsing technique. We developed several convergent assessment measures in this regard, though clearly a great deal of refinement remains to be done.

ACKNOWLEDGMENTS

We thank Jan Pedersen for discussions and advice throughout this study, and Stuart Card for similar interactions during the initial experimental design.

REFERENCES

1. Bell, W.J., Searching behavior: The behavioral ecology of finding resources. Chapman and Hall, New York, 1991.
2. Buckley, C., J. Allan, and G. Salton. Automatic routing and ad-hoc retrieval using SMART. in Second Text Retrieval Conference TREC-2. (1994), National Institute of Standards and Technology.
3. Cutting, D.R., D.R. Karger, and J.O. Pedersen. Constant interaction-time Scatter/Gather browsing of very large document collections. in SIGIR '93. (1993).
4. Cutting, D.R., D.R. Karger, J.O. Pedersen, and J.W. Tukey. Scatter/gather: A cluster-based approach to browsing large document collections. in SIGIR '92. (1992), pp. 318-329.
5. Froehlich, T.J., Relevance reconsidered -- Towards an agenda for the 21st century. Journal of the American Society for Information Science, 45 (1994). 124-134.
6. Harman, D., Evaluation issues in information retrieval. Jorunal of the American Society for Information Science, 28 (1992). 439-440.
7. Harman, D. Overview of the first text retrieval conference. in 16th Annuam International ACM/SIGIR Conference. (1993), Pittsburgh, PA. ACM. pp. 36-38.
8. Pirolli, P. and S. Card. Information foraging in information access environments. in Conference on Human Factors in Computing Systems, CHI-95. (1995, Association for Computing Machinery.
9. Tversky, A. and C.R. Fox, Weighing risk and uncertainty. Psychological Review, 102 (1995). 269-283.
10. vanRijsbergen, C.J., Information retrieval. Butterworth & Co., Boston, MA, 1979.
11. Wildemuth, B.M. and R.D. Bliek, Measures of searcher performance: A psychometric evaluation. Information Processing and Management, 29 (1993). 533-550.

LifeLines: Visualizing Personal Histories

Catherine Plaisant, Brett Milash*, Anne Rose, Seth Widoff, Ben Shneiderman*^
Human-Computer Interaction Laboratory
*Computer Science Dept., ^Institute for Systems Research
University of Maryland
A.V. Williams Bldg. College Park MD 20742
http://www.cs.umd.edu/projects/hcil
(301) 405-2768 - email: plaisant@cs.umd.edu

ABSTRACT
LifeLines provide a general visualization environment for personal histories that can be applied to medical and court records, professional histories and other types of biographical data. A one screen overview shows multiple facets of the records. Aspects, for example medical conditions or legal cases, are displayed as individual time lines, while icons indicate discrete events, such as physician consultations or legal reviews. Line color and thickness illustrate relationships or significance, rescaling tools and filters allow users to focus on part of the information. LifeLines reduce the chances of missing information, facilitate spotting anomalies and trends, streamline access to details, while remaining tailorable and easily transferable between applications. The paper describes the use of LifeLines for youth records of the Maryland Department of Juvenile Justice and also for medical records. User's feedback was collected using a Visual Basic prototype for the youth record.

Keywords
Visualization, history, timeline, personal record, justice, medical record, screen design, overview, screen management.

INTRODUCTION
Records of personal histories are needed in a variety of applications. Members of the medical and legal professions examine a record to garner information that will allow them to make an informed decision regarding their patient or case. Decision making critically depends on gleaning the complete story, spotting trends, noting critical incidents or cause-effect relationships and reviewing previous actions. Professional histories, in the form of résumés, help employers relate a prospect's skills and experiences to employment and education. Financial and retirement plans associate past and upcoming events to culminate in an expected result. In child and family social services, complex problems may require review of multiple related personal histories.

In most applications delays in gathering the information to elaborate a meaningful overview of the record can have deleterious effects. In a medical situation, a patient's treatment may be delayed while charts and lab results are assembled. In a social work situation, assistance to a youth in detention may be delayed for weeks while school and court records are brought together.

CHI 96 Vancouver, BC Canada
© 1996 ACM 0-89791-777-4/96/04..$3.50

Once gathered in a single record, the information is often in the form of a puzzle and the reader has to browse the data in order to form the big picture of the record. The reader must pour through lengthy and diverse pages. Missing or overlooking a piece of the puzzle can have dramatic effects.

While more attention is now put on developing standards for gathering and exchanging personal records (especially in the medical field), we found that virtually no effort had been made to design appropriate visualization and navigation techniques to present and explore personal history records.

An intuitive approach to visualizing histories is to use graphical time scales. The flexible and natural ordering of the time scale in months, weeks, days and even minutes, gives the design an efficient and facile interpretation and the ability to divulge detail. The consistent linear time scale allows comparisons and relations between the quantities displayed. Most importantly, large data sets can be displayed along the time line to help relate a story [15].

We propose LifeLines as a general technique for visualizing summaries of personal histories. On a one screen overview multiple facets of the records are displayed. Aspects with varying status, such as medical conditions or legal cases, are displayed as horizontal lines, while icons indicate discrete events, such as physician consultations or legal reviews. Line color and thickness illustrate relationships or the significance of events. LifeLines always begin with a one screen overview of the record, and rescaling tools or filters allow users to focus on part of the record and see more details, providing a general visualization environment. Techniques to deal with complex records and issues of a standard personal record format are discussed.

This general visualization environment is not computationally demanding, requires only high level data descriptions, and can handle a variety of records. Those characteristics make LifeLines a practical example of a personal record format that could be rapidly exchanged or synchronized between multiple services.

THE CHALLENGE OF PERSONAL HISTORIES
In order to be a general tool LifeLines have to be able to present different facets of a person's life (medical, financial, education, work, hobbies, legal, etc.). A particular application might use LifeLines for only a subset of those facets. Each facet includes different stories or aspects. For example the medical facet of a person's history might include a 5 years story about their back pain. A famous artist's biography might include facets on painting, writing and

influential personalities, its painting facet would then have different aspects such as style and themes. Each story or aspect includes events (e.g. an operation, a police arrest) and periods (e.g. two weeks of acute pain, the blue and pink period in Picasso's biography).

LifeLines present the personal history in a single screen, facets are shown as regions of the screens distinguished by alternating background colors, stories or aspects are lines, periods correspond to changes of size or color along the line, while discrete events are marked by icons.

Our work on the visualization of personal history started with a project with the Maryland Department of Juvenile Justice (DJJ), a Visual Basic prototype was developed to illustrate the principle of LifeLines (Figure 2 and 3), collect user feedback on the youth record design and explore the applicability of the LifeLines to other domains. Screen mockups have been prepared (Figure 4 and Color Plate 2) to discuss refined designs and particularly the use of LifeLines for medical records. .A video is also available in the CHI 96 Video [10].

RELATED WORK

Tufte [15] describes timelines as a frequent and powerful form of graphic design and presents many examples. An experiment in home automation showed that timelines could be quickly understood and used for data entry when scheduling devices in the home [10]. Novel techniques have been proposed to present calendars and timed information [9] and to analyze and search time scales [5] [14]. A design using timelines for medical records was proposed by Powsner and Tufte [13] who developed a graphical summary using a table of individual plots of test results and treatment data. In project management the Gantt chart [8] and PERT chart display the duration and type of tasks in a project. Many attributes of the tasks are stored but only synchronization and dependencies of tasks themselves are shown on the diagram. Software such as Microsoft Project uses these charts but the overviews do not provide the richness needed for personal histories, which are not carefully planned series of tasks but a mosaic of information that still need to be related to each other.

When navigating large spaces overviews have been found helpful [12] [2]. In the medical domain studies have shown the benefits of record summary. The Summary Time-Oriented Record, a pure text flowchart, was found to be helpful in an arthritis clinic [16]. Another text summary record uses scaled values to indicate the severity of a symptom and also notes the duration of the symptoms, allowing the timing of clinical events to become apparent [17]. Intensive care summary visualization software includes notions of filtering, severity scaling, and details on demand [4].

JUVENILE JUSTICE YOUTH RECORD

About 600 employees of the Maryland Department of Juvenile Justice are using an information system to process over 50,000 cases of delinquent youth behavior per year. In general a 'case' is opened when a complaint is filed against the youth (usually after a police intervention.) The success of a DJJ case worker's decisions relies greatly on knowledge of the youth's current status and previous case history. With the current system cryptic codes are used to access screens packed with lists of cases, placements or reviews, and to browse complex forms (Figure 1) while searching for detail information in dozens of screens. Important notes and decisions are often difficult to find in the deeply nested structure and more importantly it is very difficult to get an overview of the whole record. While attending a standard training session for the system we were told that the "trick is that you have to find the magic case", i.e. you have to be lucky and follow the right path to a case where a lot of information is available. The data entry is done over months or years, by clerical staff, field workers or detention facilities staff, geographically dispersed and with limited communication. Newly added or updated data may not be noticed, data entry errors are common and often remain unseen in the text screens. Delays are difficult to notice when browsing tables of dates.

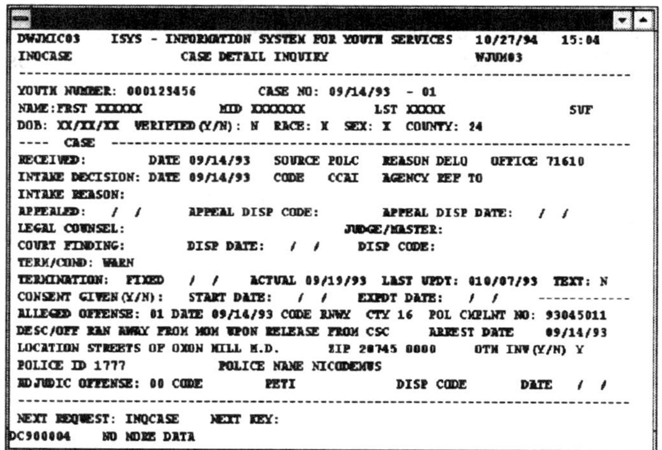

```
DWJMIC03     ISYS - INFORMATION SYSTEM FOR YOUTH SERVICES   10/27/94   15:04
INQCASE                 CASE DETAIL INQUIRY                  WJUM03
------------------------------------------------------------------------------
YOUTH NUMBER: 000123456        CASE NO: 09/14/93  - 01
NAME:FRST XXXXXX          MID XXXXXXX         LST XXXXX                SUF
DOB: XX/XX/XX  VERIFIED(Y/N): N  RACE: X  SEX: X  COUNTY: 24
----  CASE  --------------------------------------------------------------
RECEIVED:          DATE 09/14/93   SOURCE POLC   REASON DELO   OFFICE 71610
INTAKE DECISION: DATE 09/14/93   CODE    CCAI   AGENCY REF TO
INTAKE REASON:
APPEALED:   / /       APPEAL DISP CODE:          APPEAL DISP DATE:    / /
LEGAL COUNSEL:                               JUDGE/MASTER:
COURT FINDING:        DISP DATE:   / /      DISP CODE:
TERM/COND: WARN
TERMINATION:  FIXED    / /    ACTUAL 09/19/93  LAST UPDT: 010/07/93  TEXT: N
CONSENT GIVEN(Y/N):   START DATE:   / /     EXPDT DATE:   / /     -----------
ALLEGED OFFENSE: 01 DATE 09/14/93 CODE RNWY  CTY 16  POL CMPLNT NO: 93045011
DESC/OFF RAN AWAY FROM MOM UPON RELEASE FROM CSC     ARREST DATE    09/14/93
LOCATION STREETS OF OXON HILL M.D.       ZIP 20745 0000     OTH INV(Y/N) Y
POLICE ID 1777               POLICE NAME NICODEMUS
ADJUDIC OFFENSE: 00 CODE         PETI               DISP CODE        DATE   / /
------------------------------------------------------------------------------
NEXT REQUEST: INQCASE    NEXT KEY:
DC900004     NO MORE DATA
```

Figure 1: Sample screen from the existing DJJ system .

In response the LifeLines were designed to 1) present a youth record visual overview on a single screen, 2) provide direct access to all detail information from the overview with one or two clicks of the mouse, 3) promote critical information or alerts to the overview level.

Description of the interface

In this LifeLines design the facets of the youth records were chosen to be the cases, placements, case worker assignments and reviews (Color Plate 1 and Figure 2). Each facet is distinguished from the next by a switch of background color. The dates of the timeline legend shows that the youth Bart Simpson has been involved with DJJ for about a year. Thin vertical lines across the whole timeline mark each new year, giving a sense of scale to the diagram (e.g. compare Figure 2 and Figure 3). The first facet of the record shows the cases. There are 4 lines indicating four cases in Bart's record. Bart was first referred to DJJ for "breaking and entering" (B&E code). The case was handled informally and then closed after 3 months. He was referred again for the same offense, also handled informally and then for a more serious auto theft. That time the case was handled formally (i.e. went to court, i.e. to the States Attorney's Office - SAO) and Bart was adjudged delinquent DLNQ (i.e. was found guilty). The case was closed several months later. The right end of the timelines area shows today's status: we can see that there is only one case currently open, an attempted murder case for which a decision has not been made yet. Below the cases the placement facet shows that Bart is currently at Waxter (a detention center), in relation to the attempted murder case. We can see that last year Bart went to a drug abuse program for a while and later was placed at Cheltenham (a residential treatment center) when he was found guilty in the auto theft case. The assignment lines show who has been assigned to Bart over time. The currently assigned worker is Brown. The last facet in this record is the set of reviews. Reviews are discrete events where the youth's needs or progress are assessed. A click on Smith's name gives the worker's contact information. A click on a review icon brings the text of the review report on an overlapping window. Similarly details about cases or placement are obtained by clicking on the lines or labels.

Interrelationships between periods or events on the lines can be highlighted. For example one cannot tell by looking at the timelines if the drug abuse program was recorded as part of the auto theft case or the breaking and entering case, but clicking on the drug abuse program placement highlights the related case (i.e. in this instance the B&E case) and the social worker assigned to that case (Color Plate 1).

Line thickness and color are used to indicate the severity of the offense and the depth of penetration in the system (Color Plate 1). For example underage drinking would be a very thin line, but the alleged auto theft offense is a medium thickness line, which in the example of Color Plate 1 and Figure 2 is getting darker as the case progresses to court and darker again when Bart is found guilty (delinquent). On the other hand the recent case of alleged murder appears as a thick line but remains of light color because the case has not progressed yet. Severity levels are set following a policy.

At the top of the screen, next to the name, age and picture of the youth, a set of buttons gives access to the general contact information, aliases used, education, work and medical status screens but critical keywords from those screens always appear on the overview screen (e. g. suicide risk). Color coding could also be used for those buttons to suggest how recently the information was updated. A pale button can indicate 'out of date' data, a bright button recently modified information.

THE BENEFITS OF LIFELINES

LifeLines can:

1 - Reduce the chances of missing information. Because the data entry is performed over a long period of time by different people the LifeLines overview assists users in reviewing a disparate record. Yet unseen, or recently added and updated information can be revealed by highlighting.

2 - Facilitate the spotting of anomalies and trends. Intervals are easier to estimate on a timeline than in a table of dates. Repetitions of series of events result in visible patterns.

3 - Streamline the access to details. LifeLines act as large menus from which large numbers of detail screens can be accessed in a single step (about 35 from the record of Figure 2, and 100 in Figure 3)

4 - Remain simple and tailorable to various applications. The long term success of any record format depends on its sharability among collaborating services. LifeLines only uses high level data that can act as reference pointers to other services records.

DEALING WITH COMPLEX RECORDS

Keeping the overview

LifeLines begin with an overview of the entire record. Seeing this overview gives users a better sense of the type and volume of information available. Unfortunately, many youth records include so many cases that one page is not enough. Other applications such as medical records or biographies might require 50 or 100 lines. Screen size limits the number of lines which can be displayed, and the number of events and periods which can be identified on a line. Scroll bars are the common answer to pixel shortage but scrollbars are inadequate - if not harmful - when presenting overviews as users often forget to browse the complete image, or worse

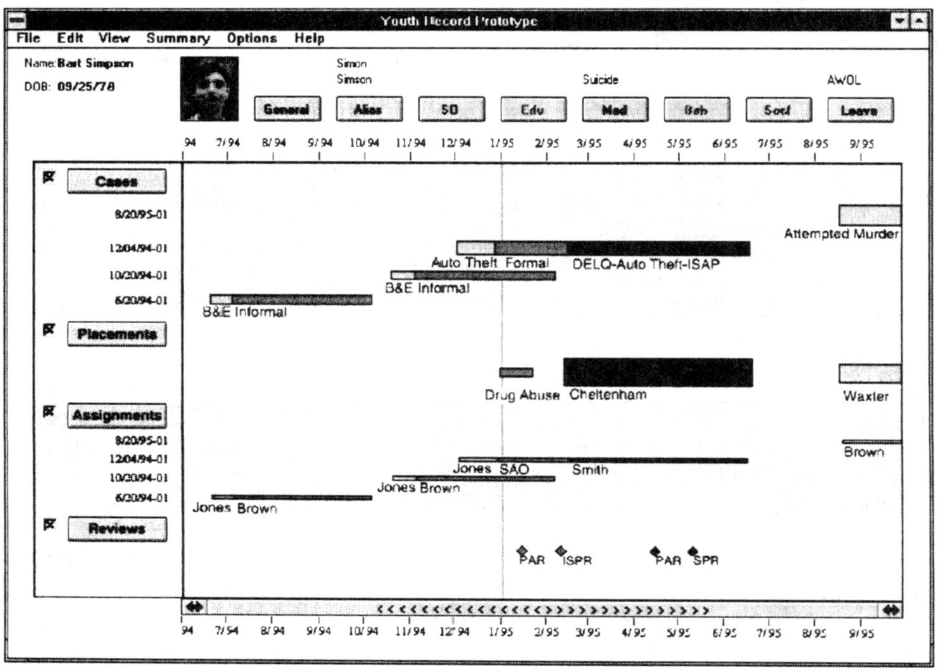

Figure 2:
A simple hypothetical youth record showing four cases, 3 placements, workers' assignments and review markers.

are even unaware that part of the image is hidden. To guarantee complete coverage of the overview, detail must be sacrificed for completeness in the first viewing of LifeLines. This raises two issues for the designer: how to represent all the information at the overview level , and how to reveal the next level of detail. Those problems are general to the design of image browsers for monitoring and decision making [12], and we propose a series of techniques tailored to LifeLines.

Silhouette and shadow

When all the lines and labels cannot be shown in the first screen the lines are brought closer to each other and the labels disappear (Figure 3a and 3b). It remains possible to see on this silhouette the number and importance of the cases, the type of placement and the number and date of reviews. Each line, period or event can still be selected individually. A background sensitive cursor can display the label of the underlying object (Figure 3a) and selecting a line or icon can display the labels of all associated events (i.e. the corresponding case, placements, assignments and reviews (Figure 3b)).

The natural next step for unusually large records is to remove all blank space and thickness coding, clumping all lines together to show a mere colored shadow of the record (which could then show hundreds of lines in one screen). Once the overview has been appreciated, semantic zooming can be used [18] as users expand desired facets to show thickness and labels again, zoom to a particular time period, or focus on a given case. Scrollable, resizable windows should only become necessary when the overview has been examined. Then filters can be offered to search, sort or hide items of a given type.

Facet hierarchy

LifeLines are organized by facets of the record. A complex record may require a hierarchy of facets containing the headings of the facets, stories and aspects. Displayed in the classic outline format (Color Plate 2), facets can be expanded and contracted to show increasing or decreasing levels of detail. Through direct manipulation, the user may rearrange the headings within any level of the tree. Sorting specified levels of the tree by importance, name, date or other factors becomes useful.

Rescaling

When the sheer density of periods and events on a time line requires intervals so small that they challenge the granularity of the time line a sub-time-line icon (or a special line style) can signify a section of the time line where the data density is too large. Details of that time period can be revealed progressively by rescaling (zooming in) or by opening a sub-time-line into a detail window. The term rescaling is preferred to zooming since only the horizontal dimension is modified. We were surprised by the diversity of design solutions to perform the time rescaling. Figure 2 shows a flexible-interval scroll bar, which is adjustable at both ends to represent the width of the desired interval of time, it offers adequate control, but requires the manipulation of a widget that is not altogether familiar. The screen mockup of Color Plate 2 shows compressed and stretched clock tools allowing the user to alternately compress or stretch the time scale centered on the last selected item. Another design is to separate the horizontal scroll bar from the selection of the time interval (e.g. week, month or year, which can be chosen in a menu or with a different slider). This is advantageous for reviewing specific fixed periods but requires users to focus their attention on the time period selection, rather than the data displayed. The 3D animation technique of the perspective wall [9] which folds the display in 3 panels could also be used but the facet hierarchy legend becomes an intrusion into the continuous scrolling. Lastly, the time scrollbar can be designed to allow multiple foci by dividing it into independent scrolling regions.

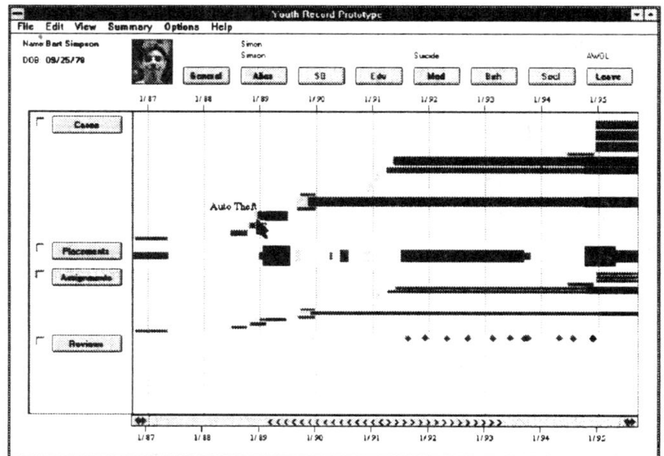

Figure 3a: Silhouette of a more complex record. Placing the cursor on a line displays the corresponding label.

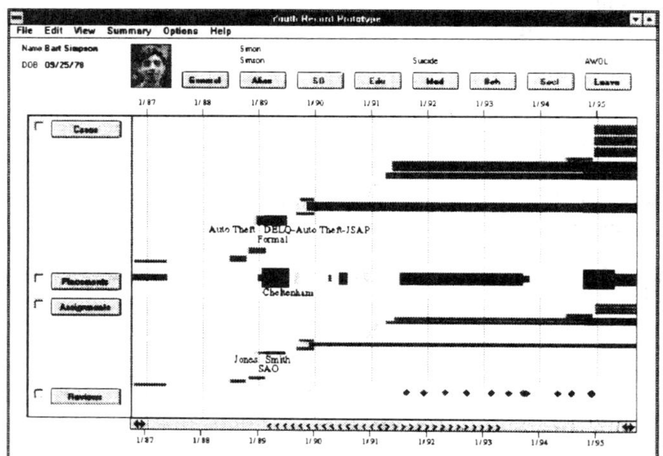

Figure 3b: Silhouette of a more complex record. Selecting a line or icon displays all the labels for the corresponding case and associated events.

Layout issues

Optimized layout algorithms have not been explored in our project but the abbreviation and layout of the labels and compact layout of the lines is definitively a critical part of dealing with large records. We are not satisfied with the current prototype as too much space is left unused yielding a low "data-ink ratio" [15].

USER'S FEEDBACK FROM DESIGN REVIEW

The Visual Basic prototype was demonstrated to about 60 users during an all-day review. Small groups of 4 to 5 users were given a 20 minute demonstration of the LifeLines prototype. They were able to use the interface to explore a few record overviews that we had prepared based on real records. They were asked to comment on perceived advantages and problems, and to consider what additional data would be useful to display in the overview. Users were a representative group of social workers, supervisors and a few administrators of varying age, gender and computer experience recruited from field offices, detention facilities, program services and administrative services.

Most users were very enthusiastic about the interface. A few others appreciated the interface but expressed concerns about the possible bias associated with the color and thickness coding. Showing the offense severity brought to the surface underlying issues such as the data "quality" (possibility of errors or cases of uncertainty). The paradox might be that error prone data buried in a hard to navigate system seems less offensive than when the same data is made visible. The use of color and thickness coding is very powerful, and should be used carefully to avoid misleading overviews.

Positive comments were related to:

- the importance of the overview. Even if all the information is case based, the overview presents a youth record in one screen with more information than the current list of cases' screen .
- the ease of access to details. For example seeing the existence of the reviews and being able to read them by a single click - as opposed to a series of codes and screens- was highly appreciated.

Data entry errors were found in the records we used, which would have been difficult to locate in the multiple screens of the current text record. The long tables of dates used in the current system are difficult to review, while the timelines make more visible the fact that a case was left open by mistake, that reviews are overdue or that the court is taking too long to make a decision.

Many recommendations were made:

- the ability to show future events, e.g. to show the end of a placement or probation, a scheduled court hearing or review deadline.
- the need to be able to see exact dates, which can be done with a status bar or special cursor which could be moved from event to event to show dates and ordering of events.
- the marking of informal groups of related cases or events, e.g. stealing car radios from 10 cars can result in 10 individual cases that would be marked and seen as a group.
- the integration with data entry techniques.

Alternative layouts were proposed; additional data to be displayed was discussed. This suggests that control panels are necessary to let users or technical support staff modify the mapping of the data onto the LifeLines.

LIFELINES FOR MEDICAL RECORDS

Because our youth record Visual Basic prototype reads a simple format as input it was easy for us to explore other data sets such as our own personal resumes and sample medical records, which lead to new designs and layouts shown in the medical record screen mockups of Figure 4 and Color Plate 2.

An appropriate use of LifeLines

A patient's medical record is an important source of information for the physician. Medical records can be extremely complex, with data intervals ranging from seconds to decades. Clinical data lend themselves to a multimedia presentations, with sounds, such as patient interviews; images, such as X ray images or MRIs; quantitative data, e.g. lab test results or vital signs; and qualitative data, such as visual observations.

Certain characteristics make medical records specially suited for the LifeLines format:

- Clinical data can divide into scalable quantities and related free text [3]. For example, a quantitative blood pressure measurement may be classified as normal, elevated, or reduced, and may be linked to doctor's notes about a change in diet and exercise.
- Clinical data categorize neatly into sections on history, specimens, labs, reports, previous encounters and actions taken [17].
- Medical records use scaled values for simplicity of interpretation [13].
- Symptoms, treatments and assessments can easily by related graphically on the timeline where the temporal relation of clinical events becomes apparent.
- Events scheduled for the future can be viewed along with past events and current status.
- Medical records benefit from a concise summary. When summaries were introduced to cardiac, pulmonary and renal clinics, in the second year hospital stays were shorter by an average of one week. [13]

Scenario

In the sample medical record (Figure 4), we see that the patient is diabetic from medical alerts section at the top of the page and from the line in the manifestation facet. For treatment, he has regular, bimonthly consultations with an endocrinologist and administers insulin to control the symptoms. Early in May, this patient sprained his knee and visited an internist, his primary care physician, for suggestions. Dr. Wood referred him to an orthopedist, Dr. Jones, whom he visited for an opinion on his knee. The patient, however, desired a second opinion and visited Dr. Hansen who suggested arthroscopic surgery and prescribed acetaminophen to relieve the pain. Shortly after, the patient entered University Hospital where Dr. Hansen operated on the damaged ligament. Having received surgical treatment, the knee proceeded to heal and the severity of the tear, implied by the thickness of the line, decreased and the dosage of acetaminophen also decreased.

After leaving the hospital, the patient began physical therapy sessions with Dr. Carter. As the ligament continued to heal, sessions became farther apart, with two more scheduled appointments past the current date marked by the dashed red line in this example. Future events occur to the right of the current date line and appear gray. Meanwhile, the patient developed ear pain and returned to his internist. The internist saw in the medical alerts that the patient is allergic to penicillin and prescribed the antibiotic doxycycline for the diagnosed ear infection. The ear infection quickly healed and the patient finished off all of the antibiotic.

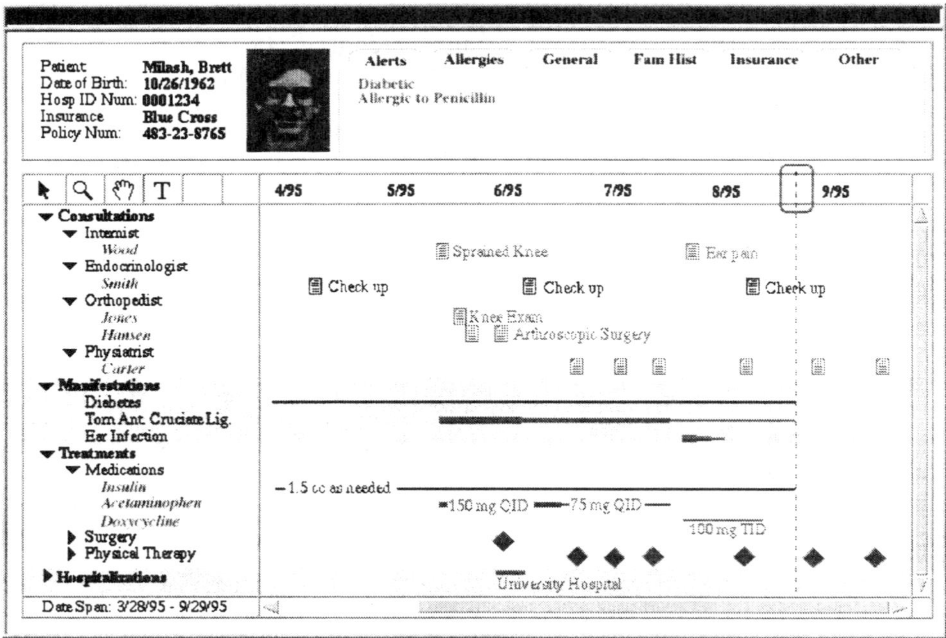

Figure 4 :
A medical record overview.
On the right of the dashed vertical line are shown the scheduled appointments (as seen around the end of August).

Encoding information

Labels for the consultation events in Figure 4 denote the chief complaints of the patient. They may, however, contain other information, such as the resulting diagnosis, or a suggested course of action, for example, a referral to a specialist. Other icons may be more indicative of the nature of the consultations: A clipboard or writing hand may represent a purely observational consultation, a flask means that lab results are available, an ambulance suggests an emergency situation and a syringe indicates that medications were administered (Color Plate 2).

Showing relationships

Quantities sharing a critical quality are grouped into similar facets but it may be important to view relationships between items outside of facet boundaries. Through the simple and consistent use of colors, groups can be identified. For example, color can be used to signify lines and events related to a diagnosis listed in the manifestations heading. In the example printed in Figure 4 all information related to the sprained knee was green and all information related to ear pain was magenta. This is a very telling scheme. However, it may be crucial to locate every consultation, illness and treatment related to Dr. Wood. Color Plate 2 shows how each physician can be assigned a color to mark his or her consultations, letters, prescriptions etc. The list of doctors serves as the color legend for the diagram.

OVERVIEW AND DETAILS - ELASTIC WINDOWS

Assuming that a large screen is available multiple windows can be used to see detailed reports while keeping the overview (Color Plate 2). By dragging an event icon to the region, space is allocated for a formatted report of all information associated with the icon. As more icons are placed on the region, the region divides into independently scrolling segments, with the new report placed in relation to the other reports with respect to where it was dropped on the screen [7].

When large records have been expanded in scrollable facets windows and multiple detail windows, new methods are needed to manipulate them beside the traditional vertical scroll bar assigned to each region, 1) the pump tool, available from the tool bar in the upper left corner of the time line region (Color Plate 2) is used to expand or contract the region from both ends, shrinking the adjacent regions [1], 2) the hook tool expands or contracts the region from one end and shrinks the adjacent region [1]. The master vertical scroll bar on the right hand side of the LifeLines allows the user to navigate across all the top-level facets.

TOWARD A PERSONAL HISTORY RECORD FORMAT

In order to develop a standard for the display of personal histories certain concessions are necessary to maximize the chances of their use. The use of pointers to other data sources offers an alternative to the unsuccessful attempts at all-inclusive, redundant records. The knowledge of the existence and type of an event is in some cases all that matters, and in all cases better that not having any record of the event at all because the information is in an incompatible format. Because of its simplicity and tailorability the overview of the LifeLines could act as a referencing tool to a complete physical record, with immediate access only to high level data. As more detail is needed, a system using LifeLines can establish a network connection with the appropriate system if possible or use contact instructions stored in the LifeLines to avoid an irking ϶data not found message.

LifeLines offer an effective visualization tool, but reality often thwarts complete and immaculate record keeping. Imprecise data should be acknowledged with adequate coding (e.g. an approximate date of birth should appear differently than a verified one). Confidentiality needs to be secured at least at the same degree as a paper record. The record owned by an individual would include a medical facet which can be copied when visiting a new doctor's office, providing basic summary data and pointers to other physician's records. But the patient would not authorize the doctors' office to copy bank account summaries or pointers to school records. Similarly social services could be authorized by the person or by the court to synchronize their records with court systems or school systems and speed up their required data gathering.

LIMITATIONS

For the designers, agreeing on an appropriate data encoding scheme is difficult. Icons, color and thickness codes have to be carefully designed to avoid biases. For the developers appropriate labeling of the timelines remains hard to optimize and smooth rescaling depends on efficient display algorithms, [6] [17].

Only the visualization aspect of the record has been discussed here and none of the data entry issues. Even if in many applications tedious data entry remains separated from the decision making task, it is clear that a complete implementation of the LifeLines will need some data entry mechanism to append or correct existing records. Our previous experience shows that constructing time lines by direct manipulation was an adequate solution in scheduling home automation devices [11].

CONCLUSION

Personal histories contain information that plays an important role in decision making. LifeLines are proposed as a simple and tailorable technique to represent a variety of personal history records. They provide a complete visualization environment offering overview, zooming, filtering and details on demand. Color coding, filtering and dynamic highlighting unveil relationships between events that may otherwise be difficult to see in paper records. Finally, techniques have been described to handle large records and to facilitate the associated window management, making LifeLines a useful starting point toward a standard personal history format.

ACKNOWLEDGMENT

This work was supported in part by the Maryland Department of Juvenile Justice and by the NSF grant NSF EEC 94-02384. We want to acknowledge Chris Cassatt from DJJ for his participation in this work, and Teresa Cronnell for her help with graphic design.

REFERENCES

1. Asahi T., Turo, D., Shneiderman, B. Using treemaps to visualize the analytic hierarchy process, to appear in *Information Systems Research*, (1996).

2. Beard, D., Walker II, J., Navigational techniques to improve the display of large two-dimensional spaces. *Behaviour and Information Technology 9* , 6 (1990), 451-466.

3. Boens, J., Borst, F., Scherrer, J., Organizing the clinical data in the medical record. *MD Computing* ; 9 (1992) 149-155.

4. Factor, M., Gelernter, D.H., Kolb, C.E., Miller, P.L., Sittig, D.F. Real-time dasta fusion in the intensive care unit. *IEEE Computer*, 24 (1991) 45-54.

5. Hibino, S., Rundensteiner, E. A., A visual query language for identifying temporal trends in video data, *Proceedings of the 1995 International Workshop on Multi-Media Database Management Systems.*, pp 74-81.

6. Jog, N., Shneiderman, B. Starfield information visualization with interactive smooth zooming. *Proc. of IFIP 2.6 Visual Databases Systems.* (Lausanne, Switzerland, March 27-29, 1995) 1-10.

7. Kandogan, E. , Shneiderman, B., Elastic windows: improved spacial layout and rapid multiple windows operations. Technical report CS-TR-3522, University of Maryland, (1995).

8. Lientz, B.P., Rea, K.P. *Project Management for the 21st Century.* Academic Press, San Diego, California, 1995.

9. Mackinlay, J.D., Robertson, G.G., Card, S.K. The Perspective Wall: detail and context smoothly integrated. In *Proceedings of SIGCHI '91* , (1991) 173-179, ACM, New York.

10. Milash, B., Plaisant, C., Rose. A., LifeLines: Visualizing Personal Histories, in CHI 96 Video Program, ACM, New York, (1996).

11. Plaisant, C., Shneiderman, B. Scheduling home control devices: design issues and usability evaluation of four touchscreen interfaces. *Int. J. Man-Machine Studies*, 36 (1992), 375-393.

12. Plaisant, C., Carr, D., Shneiderman, B., Image Browsers: Taxonomy, Guidelines, and Informal Specifications, *IEEE Software* , 12:2 (1995), 21-32.

13. Powsner, S.M., Tufte, E.R., Graphical summary of patient status. *The Lancet*, 344:8919 (August 6, 1994), 386-389.

14. Sanderson, P., Scott, J., Johnston, T., Mainzer, J., Watanabe, L., James, J., MacSHAPA and the enterprise of exploring sequential data analysis (ESDA), *Int. J Man-Machine Studies*, 41 (1992), 633-681.

15. Tufte, E.R., *The Visual Display of Quantitative Information.* Graphics Press, Cheshire, Connecticut, 1983.

16. Whiting-O'Keefe, Q.E., Simbork, D.W., Epstein, W.V., Warger, A. A Computerized summary medical record system can provide more information than the standard medical record. *JAMA*, 254:9 (1985), 1185-1192.

17. Wyatt J.C., Clinical data systems, Part 1: data and medical records. *The Lancet*, 344 (December 3, 1994), 1543-1547.

18. Bederson, B.B., Hollan, James D., Pad++: A Zooming Graphical Interface for Exploring Alternate Interface Physics, *Proceedings of UIST '94*, (Marina del Rey, California, November 2-4, 1994), 17-26, ACM, New York.

Remote Evaluation: The Network as an Extension of the Usability Laboratory

H. Rex Hartson, José C. Castillo, and John Kelso
Department of Computer Science
Jonathan Kamler
Department of Forestry
Virginia Tech
Blacksburg, VA 24061
Tel: +1-540-231-4857
Email: hartson@vt.edu

Wayne C. Neale
Eastman Kodak Company
901 Elmgrove Road
Rochester, NY 14653-5800
Tel: +1-716-726-0953
Email: neale@pixel.kodak.com

ABSTRACT

Traditional user interface evaluation usually is conducted in a laboratory where users are observed directly by evaluators. However, the remote and distributed location of users on the network precludes the opportunity for direct observation in usability testing. Further, the network itself and the remote work setting have become intrinsic parts of usage patterns, difficult to reproduce in a laboratory setting, and developers often have limited access to representative users for usability testing in the laboratory. In all of these cases, the cost of transporting users or developers to remote locations can be prohibitive.

These barriers have led us to consider methods for remote usability evaluation wherein the evaluator, performing observation and analysis, is separated in space and/or time from the user. The network itself serves as a bridge to take interface evaluation to a broad range of networked users, in their natural work settings.

Several types of remote evaluation are defined and described in terms of their advantages and disadvantages to usability testing. The initial results of two case studies show potential for remote evaluation. Remote evaluation using video teleconferencing uses the network as a mechanism to transport video data in real time, so that the observer can evaluate user interfaces in remote locations as they are being used. Semi-instrumented remote evaluation is based on critical incident gathering by the user within the normal work context. Additionally, both methods can take advantage of automating data collection through questionnaires and instrumented applications.

Keywords

Remote evaluation, formative evaluation, usability testing, usability method, usability engineering, semi-instrumented, empirical, critical incident, video conferencing

INTRODUCTION

A large share of traditional user interface evaluation is conducted in the laboratory where users are observed directly by evaluators. However, the remote and distributed location of users—often on the network, now a major environment for distribution and usage of software applications, such as CSCW—precludes the opportunity for direct observation in usability testing. Further, the network itself and the remote work setting have become intrinsic parts of usage patterns. Additionally, developers often have limited access to representative users for usability testing in the laboratory and the users' work context is difficult or impossible to reproduce in a laboratory setting. In all of these cases, the cost of transporting users or developers to remote locations can be prohibitive.

These barriers to usability evaluation have led us to extend the concept of formative evaluation beyond the usability laboratory to methods for remote usability evaluation, typically employing the network itself as a bridge to take interface evaluation to a broad range of network users, in their natural work settings.

In the following sections we briefly survey several kinds of remote evaluation as distinguished by the methods used and data collected. In brief case studies, we then explore two approaches specific to our own work, concluding with a glimpse at possible future directions for this work.

TYPES OF REMOTE EVALUATION

A brief listing of some possible approaches to remote evaluation is useful to understand the range of possibilities and to avoid comparison of unlike methods. We define *remote evaluation* to be usability evaluation wherein the evaluator, performing observation and analysis, is separated in space and/or time from the user. Much of our discussion could apply to other kinds of usability evaluation, but we limit our focus to empirical formative usability evaluation (i.e., evaluation used for improving user interaction designs, especially early in the system life cycle). No claim is made for the completeness of this list of types.

Local Evaluation

Local evaluation is included here as a benchmark method for comparison with remote evaluation methods. In local evaluation the user and evaluator are usually in the same or adjacent rooms at the same time. This somewhat formal evaluation is usually conducted within a usability laboratory using controlled tasks and often driven by quantitative usability specifications [8]. Data collected are both quantitative (e.g., task performance time and error count) and qualitative (e.g., verbal protocol), and both objective (e.g., observed user performance metrics) and subjective (e.g., user preference questionnaire scores). Sessions are usually videotaped for backup and review. Typically, the quantitative data are used to determine if and when usability specifications are met so that iteration can halt. Qualitative data serve to identify usability problems, their causes within the interface design, and potential redesign solutions [4].

Portable Evaluation

Some remote evaluation situations call for a portable usability evaluation unit, by means of which the laboratory (often special portable usability testing equipment) is taken to the users in their normal work environments. While this is an area of growing interest, it is outside the scope of this paper.

Local Evaluation at Remote Site

A number of commercial services are now available to developers lacking their own local evaluation expertise or facilities. Clients use the network to communicate design documents, software samples, and/or prototypes to the remote evaluators, but the network is not used to connect to remote users. The evaluation is local to the evaluators and remote from the developers, with results being returned via the network. This kind of "contracted out" evaluation is a useful service for development groups without their own evaluation facilities. However, the quality of these services can vary, the methods can be ad hoc (e.g., intuitive inspection without use of guidelines), and the process is not always suitable for the specific needs of a development group.

Remote Laboratory Testing

Formal laboratory-based usability evaluation, offered by consulting groups, provides usability testing with representative users and tasks. Results include quantitative user performance measures, user opinions and satisfaction ratings, recommendations for application improvement, and sometimes even a copy of the evaluation session videotapes for review by the development team.

Remote Inspection

Some developers send their designs to remote contractors who perform local evaluation using ad hoc, intuitive interface inspection, drawing on design guidelines, user profiles, and software standards. Without empirical observation of users and a more formal process, results can vary depending on the knowledge and skills of the evaluators. As an example, this kind of evaluation is done by Vertical Research, Inc. [6] for Microsoft Windows™-based products. In a variation of remote inspection called collaborative inspection, evaluators work remotely with developers to inspect interface design, documents, and code.

Remote Questionnaire/Survey

A software application can be augmented to display a user questionnaire to gather subjective user preference data about the application and its interface. The appearance of the questionnaire, requesting feedback related to usability, is triggered by an event (including task completion) during usage. Responses are batched and sent to the developers. As an example, the User Partnering (UP) Module™ from UP Technology [1] uses event-driven triggers to "awaken" dialogues that ask users questions about their usage.

Approaches based on remote questionnaires have the advantage that they capture remote user reactions while they are fresh, but they are limited to subjective data based on questions pre-written by developers or evaluators. Thus, many of the qualitative data normally acquired in laboratory testing, i.e., the data directly useful in identifying specific usability problems, are lost.

Remote-Control Evaluation

The remote-control method of remote evaluation employs control of a local computer from another computer at a remote site. The user is separated from the evaluator in space and possibly in time. The two computers can be connected through the Internet or a direct dial-up telephone line with commercially available software (e.g., Timbuktu™, PC Anywhere™). Using this method places the evaluator's computer in the usability lab where a video camera or scan converter captures the users' actions. The remote users remain in their work environment. Audio capture is made via the computer or telephone. If audio capture is via telephone, the evaluator and user remain connected in time. Alternatively, equipment in the usability lab could be configured to automatically activate data-capture tools based on usage of a particular application. This flexibility is important when collecting data remotely from many different time zones. This type of asynchronous remote evaluation also gives the evaluator the flexibility to do the evaluation all at once and at a time that is convenient.

Video Conferencing as an Extension of the Usability Laboratory

Local usability evaluation, where the user and evaluator are in adjacent rooms, requires a video/audio cable (or wireless communication) between the rooms. Users located more remotely can be connected to evaluators using the network and video conferencing software, as an extension of the video/audio cable between user and evaluator. This kind of remote evaluation, using video teleconferencing over the network as a mechanism to transport video data in real time, perhaps comes the closest to the effect of local evaluation. Currently, the primary obstacle to this approach is the limited bandwidth of the network, occasioning communication delays and low video frame rates.

Instrumented Remote Evaluation

An application and its interface can be instrumented with embedded metering code to collect and return a journal or log of data occurring as a natural result of usage in the users' normal working environment. The data represent various user actions made during task performance, often as detailed as keystrokes and mouse movements. The logs or journals are later analyzed using pattern recognition techniques [7] to deduce where usability problems have occurred. This approach has the advantage of not interfering at all with work activities of the user and, in theory, can provide automated usability evaluation for certain kinds of usability problems. However, for formative evaluation it can be difficult to infer many types of usability problems effectively. This method has been used successfully for summative evaluation, marketing trials, and beta testing.

Semi-Instrumented Remote Evaluation

Semi-instrumented remote evaluation uses selective data collection triggered directly by users performing tasks in their normal work context. Users are trained to identify usage events having significant negative or positive effects on their task performance or satisfaction. In particular, a negative effect is usually an indicator of a usability problem. Information about these events is transmitted to developers along with context information about system, task, and interface history and state. Developers use these data, approximating the qualitative data normally taken in the usability laboratory, to determine the usability problems.

The semi-instrumented approach has potential for cost-effectiveness, since the user and the system gather the data and evaluators look only at data that relate to usability problems. However, reliance on users with only minimal training to identify critical incidents during their performance of on-the-job tasks, makes it a technique with as yet unproved effectiveness.

CASE STUDY: TELECONFERENCING AS AN EXTENSION OF THE USABILITY LAB

Goal of Study

The goal of evaluating teleconferencing as a vehicle for remote evaluation is to examine the degree to which the quality and quantity of data collection are affected by this new approach. In addition to evaluating teleconferencing, specifically desktop video conferencing, as a usability tool, automation of data collection and use of the Internet as part of the evaluation process was evaluated in terms of its fit, effectiveness, and efficiency. Several phases of evaluation were used in the case study, each with a corresponding type of network support (Figure 1). A scan converter was used in the remote usability lab, and digital video captured from the computer monitor was sent back to the evaluator via the Internet. In this way, desktop video conferencing extends the usability lab to the users' work environment rather than physically bringing the user to the usability lab.

Set-up/Design

This case study compared a typical usability lab evaluation to a remote usability evaluation using desktop video conferencing. The Kodak server on the World Wide Web (WWW) was used as the application interface under evaluation. Four participants using the Kodak WWW server were observed in a typical usability lab with the scan converted view of the computer monitor (lab condition). In this lab condition, the evaluator was located in the control room of the usability lab receiving the scan converted view of the monitor and an audio connection.

Four other participants' monitors were observed through desktop video conferencing software from a remote location (remote condition). Pilot tests were performed between Kodak (Rochester, NY) and Virginia Tech (Blacksburg, VA) to test the feasibility of the remote condition. In the remote condition for the main part of the study the evaluator was located in a remote office within Kodak. The screen output was captured by a scan converter and a video digitization board. The digital video was sent via the Internet to the remote evaluator by the desktop video conferencing software. Fifteen frames per second was the average video frame rate. A telephone connection was used to transmit each user's voice in this condition.

The participants in the lab condition were given printed paper questionnaires while the participants in the remote condition were given on-line questionnaires. The content of the questions were identical. The on-line questionnaire, however, was designed to format and export the quantitative data in specific file formats (e.g., Microsoft Excel™, StatView™, Superanova™) for statistical

Evaluation Process	Network/Automation Support
Defining protocol and method of data collection (distributed contributors)	Network and CSCW tools (email, WWW, groupware)
Document sharing (questionnaires, protocol, data, report, etc.)	Network and CSCW tools (email, WWW, groupware), desktop video conferencing
Subject profile questionnaire	Digital questionnaire
Training, instructions, set-up	Network, digital questionnaire, desktop video conferencing
Direct observation	Desktop video conferencing
Post-test questionnaires	Digital questionnaire
Debriefing	Desktop video conferencing
Distribution of results/final report	Network and CSCW tools (email, WWW, groupware), desktop video conferencing

Figure 1. Evaluation process and matching network and/or automated data collection support

analysis. The qualitative data of the questionnaire (i.e., open ended questions) were entered into text fields and saved as word processor files. The questionnaire was sent to the remote machine via the Internet, and the exported files were sent back to the remote evaluator.

Procedure

Eight subjects participated in this study. All were daily computer users with no experience using the WWW browsers. The eight participants were randomly assigned to the study treatments (lab and remote). Participants were given approximately five minutes of introduction and ten minutes of training using a popular WWW browser. Training was conducted on a server other than the one used in the study. Participants were given five benchmark tasks to complete. The tasks consisted of locating various pieces of information and requesting technical support via a form. The evaluator noted usability problems in both conditions by typing them into a text file. Time and navigation errors were logged through instrumenting the application, thereby affording the evaluator time to focus on observation. Both conditions were videotaped as a back-up. The same evaluator was used with all eight users to eliminate variation across evaluators.

Results

The total number of usability problems in both conditions was listed by the evaluator (Lab condition = 12; Remote condition = 14). The questionnaires (paper and on-line) contained nine semantic rating scale questions. The results of the questionnaires were compared between the two conditions, lab (paper) and remote (on-line). The results of a standard t-test were not reported because the small number of subjects did not support the assumption of a normal distribution. The Kolmogorov-Smirnov non-parametric test was applied to each question with no significant differences between the two groups on all nine questions (p values > 0.2170 for all nine questions). Additionally, both versions of the questionnaire had three open-ended usability questions. We compared the total number of paper vs. on-line responses, and based on the Kolmogorov-Smirnov test, we found no significant differences between the lab and remote conditions, χ^2 = 0.50, $p > 0.999$.

Conclusions

Remote evaluation using desktop video conferencing appears to be feasible given recent technical advances in computer processing speed and digital video applications. Typical in-lab video observation can be extended to virtually anywhere in the world without a significant detriment in the quality and quantity of usability problem list generation. An evaluation can be conducted anywhere a computer is connected to the Internet and a phone line. This gives the evaluator the opportunity to test a broad sample of users on an international scope in their own work context. This approach may help solve the "homogeneous subject pool" problem developed at many universities and companies by running the same subjects repeatedly. Instead of on-site visitation, traveling can now be virtual, saving thousands of dollars. Furthermore, using digital questionnaires improved efficiency gains in data collection and analysis. Many variables can affect the quality of digital video (e.g., software algorithms, camera, LAN and Internet bandwidth, network traffic, sample rate, processor speed, display size and video board).

There were times when it was difficult in the remote condition to interpret what the user was doing on the screen. Most of the time the users' verbal comments, in addition to the video window, were sufficient to identify the problem. Mimicking the users' actions with the same application at the evaluator's computer also helped resolve the users' actions that were difficult to see in the desktop video conferencing software window.

CASE STUDY: SEMI-INSTRUMENTED CRITICAL INCIDENT GATHERING

Ideal Comparison with Laboratory-Based Formative Evaluation

As in the fully instrumented case, semi-instrumented evaluation occurs while users are working on their own real tasks in their own work environment. Usage patterns will include naturally occurring interruptions and other influences from the work setting and the network environment. In contrast to the fully instrumented case, however, the semi-instrumented approach employs users to identify *critical incidents* (CIs)—occurrences during system usage that reflect usability problems, missing functionality, and other ways in which the system fails to meet user needs.

Success of the semi-instrumented method of remote usability evaluation depends on the ability of typical users effectively to recognize CIs. This issue was explored in the case study and will be the object of further studies. The current laboratory-based formative usability evaluation practice of having CI identification done by a trained HCI evaluator might lead to skepticism about casting the user in that role. However, critical incidents in human factors experiments, before the CI technique was adapted for HCI [2], were originally identified by the *subject* during his or her own task performance [3]. Thus, we expect our users with minimal training to be able recognize CIs, an expectation supported by our initial case study. Our users cannot be expected to be generally trained in HCI, but they can be given minimal training for the specific task of spotting CIs.

The goal of semi-instrumented remote evaluation is to gather qualitative data (e.g., CIs and verbal protocol), rather than quantitative data (e.g., timing or error rates). We consider qualitative data to be the most useful for identifying and fixing usability problems.

For comparison, Figure 2 depicts one view of the "traditional" laboratory-based formative evaluation process. While directly observing user task performance, evaluators

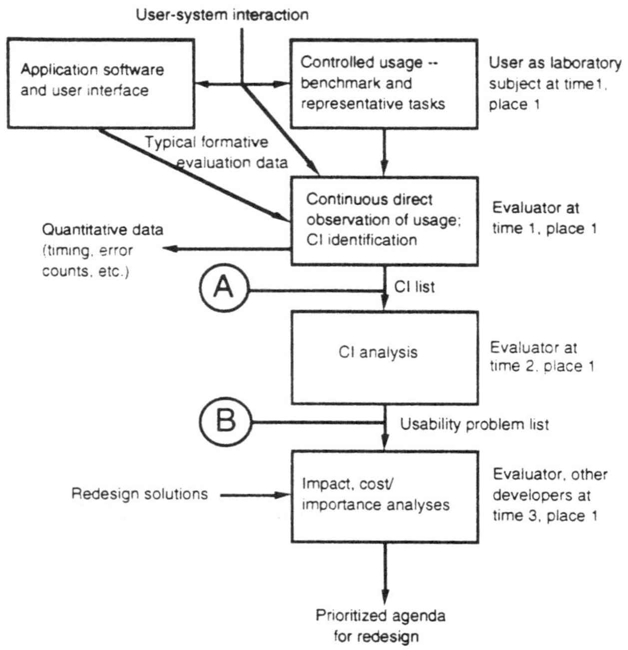

Figure 2. One view of local formative evaluation

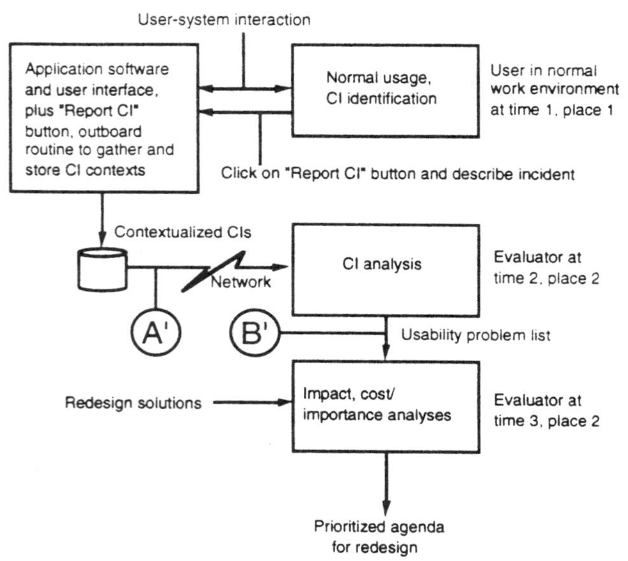

Figure 3. Semi-instrumented remote evaluation

produce a list of CIs (at point A) that are later analyzed by evaluators into a usability problem list (at point B).

In semi-instrumented remote evaluation, as shown in Figure 3, users themselves identify CIs during the normal course of on-the-job task performance.

Whenever usage difficulty is encountered, the user clicks on a "Report CI" button, a single added object consistently appearing on all screens of the application. The click activates the instrumentation routine (software outside the application) causing the system to store the incident indicator and data about its context (e.g., system, interface, task state information, and video clips or screen image sequences with audio), to be sent later to developers. This package of data, the CI and its context taken together, is called a *contextualized critical incident* (CCI). Thus, the semi-instrumented evaluation process is a user-triggered CI-reporting mechanism that produces sets of CCIs (at point A'), sent asynchronously via the network to remote evaluators to be later analyzed into a usability problem list (at point B').

Raison d'être of the Semi-Instrumented Approach

In the absence of a direct observer, the user is the only one who has knowledge of CIs as they occur. This knowledge is essential to identifying design problems that impact usability. The identification of CIs is arguably the single most important information associated with task performance in a usability-oriented context. This knowledge is also perishable. This information is lost in the fully instrumented approach, because it is not captured immediately as it arises during usage. Much of the fully instrumented method consists of applying complex pattern recognition to regain a small portion of this lost information from the usage patterns. Processing journal files of user and system actions in search of usability problems can be like looking for a needle in a haystack. However, if users can deliver the "needles" directly, we can avoid the haystack.

The major working hypothesis of semi-instrumented remote evaluation is that it will provide approximately the same quantity and quality of qualitative data that can be obtained from formative laboratory-based usability evaluation.

Goals of the Case Study

Our eventual goal is to compare the effectiveness in producing usability problem lists of two formative evaluation approaches: semi-instrumented remote and normal usability lab-based evaluation. Of the following three steps for approaching this goal, the first is reported in this paper:

1. initial case study to explore relevant issues and to find intuitive indications of the validity of our working hypotheses;
2. controlled laboratory-based experiments validating the hypotheses; and
3. fields studies conducted in real work environments, accounting for work context factors (noise, interruptions, multi-thread task performance, etc.).

The primary goal of the first step, the case study, was to judge feasibility of the process. As a bottom-line, we wanted to see whether this new method could provide approximately the same quantity and quality of qualitative data that can be obtained from laboratory-based formative evaluation. Specifically, we wished to see if the list of usability problems at B' in Figure 3 is a good approximation to the list at B in Figure 2. Finally, we wanted to appraise the likelihood of achieving all these goals in a way that is cost-effective for both developer (e.g., minimal resources for data collection and analysis) and user (e.g., minimal interference with work).

Questions Addressed by the Case Study

The case study used two kinds of subjects—user subjects and expert subjects. User subjects were not trained in usability methods, but were given minimal training to recognize CIs in their own usage—five minutes of lecture and a 10-minute demonstration. Expert subjects were interface developers, who are trained in usability methods and who normally perform evaluations in the usability lab.

For the case study the goals stated in the previous section translate into two research questions related to the hypotheses of the semi-instrumented remote approach:

Question 1: Can user subjects identify CIs approximately as well as the expert subjects?

Question 2: Can expert subjects transform contextualized CIs from user subjects into a usability problem list approximately as well as they can produce a usability problem list in the normal lab-based approach?

Steps of the Case Study

1. Three user subjects not knowledgeable in usability methods were trained to identify CIs in task performance.
2. Sessions of user subjects performing tasks and simultaneously identifying CIs were videotaped. The test application was a program for viewing and manipulating images from a digital still camera.
3. A panel of three expert subjects viewed the tapes to detect any CIs missed by the user subjects.
4. The tape sets were edited into sets of CCI packages.
5. Two expert subjects (different ones) were asked to convert the CCI sets into usability problem lists.

The results of Step 3 provided answers to Question 1 and results of Step 5 gave answers to Question 2.

Using Videotapes as Input to Expert Subjects

Normal lab-based evaluation employs expert evaluators recording their own lists of CIs while observing user subjects in the same or an adjacent room. For evaluation experts, viewing tapes of users is nearly equivalent to observing users in real-time via video monitors in an adjacent room.

In this case study, however, we wished to make direct comparisons of exactly the same CIs, between expert subjects in the "normal" case and user subjects in the remote case. This meant the experts had to view tapes of user subjects made in the remote evaluation case. Thus, the experts also saw the users identifying their own CIs. This aspect of user subject behavior could not be ignored by the expert subjects and could not be edited from the tapes without gaps or "glitches" in the tape, thus revealing the presence of CIs. We could have masked this effect somewhat by introducing additional "decoy" glitches, but we felt that line of reasoning would divert us from the goal at hand. Thus, we settled on using the expert subjects to judge user subject performance in CI identification. We felt this produced results essentially equivalent to a direct comparison, especially for the most important case of CIs not found by the user subjects. In future controlled experiments we plan to compare user and expert subject performance directly, without tapes, but this will require large numbers of subjects and CIs in order to establish statistical significance.

Two tapes were made simultaneously during each task performance. One video camera was used to record users in the normal way, including audio of user comments. The second tape captured screen activity via a scan converter connected to the computer monitor. The experimenters set up the hardware and software, and the subjects were in a controlled setting in a laboratory, with no interruptions.

To address Question 1, the panel of expert subjects viewed these unedited tapes on a pair of monitors, watching user subjects identifying their own CIs as they performed tasks, especially looking for CIs the user subjects failed to identify.

Anything considered by a user subject to be a CI was deemed so, by definition. Thus, we did not look for any "false positive" identifications.

Incidentally, we found that IDEAL [5], a tool designed to support laboratory-based formative user interface evaluation, was also useful in supporting evaluation methods research. IDEAL provided controls for marking, viewing, editing, and synchronizing the videotapes. IDEAL also supported marking tapes where CIs begin and end, allowing rapid wind/rewind to view and analyze a given CI. CIs could also be annotated in IDEAL by any of the case study participants.

Reporting CIs

The instrumentation was easily simulated. First, to simulate clicking of the software "Report CI" button, user subjects pushed the space bar on the keyboard, which caused a sound that could be heard in the audio portion of the tape.

As a substitute for entering text in a dialogue box (for example) to describe a CI, subject users gave a verbal description that was captured on an audio track of the videotape. Verbal descriptions (which use a non-visual output channel) did not interfere, to the extent that typing would, with task performance during capture and observation during evaluation.

The CI Contexts

The videotapes, including verbal comments by user subjects, provided a complete history of user activity. To address Question 2, the context of each CI was "packaged" by editing a short clip from the tapes.

By informal experimentation we determined to use a 60 second video clip centered around the CI identification. This interval provided economical coverage for most of the data in this study. However, the tradeoff between bandwidth requirements to transmit clips on the network and richness of context will be the subject of a future study.

Question 2 was approximated by the following question: How easily can expert subjects turn CCI sets into usability problem lists? Expert subjects reviewed the CCIs found by user subjects and tried to transform each CCI into one or more specific usability problems, while the experimenters judged how well they did this. In the future, it would be possible to use multiple expert subjects for each user subject and/or to use different expert subjects to judge these results.

Results, Discussion, Lessons Learned

Although this case study was informal and no quantitative data were recorded, it did yield considerable understanding of problems and solutions regarding semi-instrumented remote evaluation and did lend insight useful in directing future studies.

Users liked the idea of having a sounding mechanism for reporting the CIs, which we discovered in pilot testing needed to be distinguishable from all other system sounds. We used a "gong" sound, activated by pressing the space bar, which the users liked because it was a bit like "gonging" out the designer for bad parts of the interface. Users indicated a preference for using the same sound to report both positive and negative CIs, and in the end we found that users rarely, if ever, identify positive critical incidents, anyway. Also, user subjects usually reserved gong ringing for cases where task performance was blocked and usually did not ring the gong for situations where they could perform the task but it was awkward or confusing. For example, most users had minor trouble rotating an image, but they all eventually figured it out and none signaled a CI associated with this part of the task. The experts did see this trouble with rotation as a CI, one of the few examples of the ones they recognized but users did not. There was also one case of a CI spotted by an experimenter and missed by both user and expert subjects.

To summarize the results for Question 1, there were very few CIs missed by the users but found by the experts, and the problems missed were ones of less importance.

The tape of the scan-converted screen provided the most valuable data for the experts and the experimenter. The camera on the user was occasionally useful for revealing when the user was struggling or frustrated (e.g., pounding on the gong key).

The principal problem exposed by the study was the need to prompt users continually for the verbal protocol that is so essential in the tape clips for establishing task context to the CIs. Even though users were asked up-front to give a running verbal commentary, they generally did not speak much without prompting. This problem is exacerbated in the case of remote evaluation, since the experimenter will not be present and the user must be self-actuated in this regard. Verbal protocol was essential for the experts to establish for each CI what the task was, what the user was trying to do, and why the user was having trouble.

A second major area where insight was gained involved the question of how to "package" CCIs in the most cost-effective way with respect to network transmission cost (e.g., bandwidth) and usefulness to the developers. The study indicates the need to examine the use of screen capture only. For remote evaluation, CCI packages are sent over the network from users to developers. Existing digital screen capture programs can overlay audio and text (e.g., for task descriptions) on the screen image, requiring less storage and bandwidth to transmit than continuous video.

One problem with "automatically" packaging CCIs is that different kinds of CIs need different intervals. For example, it is not surprising that we found more pre-gong time is needed to establish clear context for goal-related problems than for action-level problems.

With regard to Question 2, when task information was not given (experts not told what user was trying to do), expert subjects had difficulty guessing what was happening and did not do well in identifying the usability problems associated with the CI. When CI clips were augmented with verbal protocol about intended task and context of where the user was in the task when the CI occurred, the expert subjects were generally able to identify the associated usability problems and design flaws that led to them.

Conclusions

Semi-instrumented remote evaluation appears to be a feasible technique meriting further development. The method has potential to exploit the value of real work context, allowing usability testing over a broad range of users and tasks. It requires very little embedded code for instrumentation. Data collection cost is very low (almost zero) to developers, because users gather the data. Data analysis costs are lowered (cf. laboratory-based methods) because users perform "time filtering" of the raw task performance data, singling out CIs from usage activities not useful in finding usability problems.

FUTURE DIRECTIONS

We found these case studies valuable, both for what we learned and for the insight they provided for directing future research. For example, we will address the effect of video quality on usability list generation. Evaluators will need to determine values for variables such as sufficient frame rates and processing power. We will examine various levels of screen detail and their effect on the ability to discern useful information about usability problems.

We will also investigate the number of camera views that are necessary for quality observation. A sufficient base of research is needed to guide development of tools that would control and streamline remote data collection. The result of such work would reduce the cycle time for designing interfaces in the overall development process. This work is being continued at Virginia Tech and at Kodak.

Future studies will also focus on how much context to include in a CCI package for the semi-instrumented approach. Typically, users ring the gong some time after the beginning of a CI. The context of a CI continues to develop some time after the gong, as well. Thus, a CI and its context typically span both sides of the gong. We plan empirical studies to determine the best pre-gong and post-gong time intervals for CCI clips.

The design and evaluation of specific user training for identifying CIs is an important focus of our work. Cost-effective on-demand availability of this training to potentially large numbers of users requires a self-paced module. The subject matter is appropriate for multi-media with at least video and sound, delivered on the network (e.g., through the World-Wide Web).

Further, a clear need for a remote method for user prompting emerged as a lesson learned from the studies. As a result of this study we intend to investigate social, psychological, and organizational issues in prompting users at a distance to maintain verbalization. We expect to explore voice and/or dialogue boxes for conveying a request for information about the task and the problem, either when the CI button is pushed (e.g., in the semi-instrumented case) or if the user is inactive for too long.

An additional area of study will focus on the necessity for the user to pause and identify the CI, and the effect that this task interruption might have on usability of the application itself. We also plan to catalog which types of applications work best with remote evaluation, and possibly identify predictor characteristics for new applications. We also hope to qualify which of the two methods we studied are best suited for collecting data from a given type of application.

The Montgomery County, Virginia, school system will serve as a near-term testbed for remote evaluation methods. We, in the Department of Computer Science at Virginia Tech, are working with the public schools to design, implement, and evaluate a software architecture, software tools, and courseware to construct a virtual physics laboratory to support broadly collaborative, highly interactive physical science education for middle school and high school students. The virtual laboratories will be accessed via the Internet and the Blacksburg Electronic Village, a densely interconnected community in Southwestern Virginia. Remote evaluation will be a necessity for this project.

In the longer term, we expect to be working with the U.S Forestry Service and the Bureau of Land Management, who are using an expert system for landscape architecture as part of a very large scale geographical information system. We look forward to the possibility of using remote evaluation methods with literally hundreds of remote users across the country.

REFERENCES

1. Abelow, D. Automating Feedback on Software Product Use. *CASE Trends* (December 1993), 15-17.
2. del Galdo, E. M., Williges, R. C., Williges, B. H., and Wixon, D. R. An Evaluation of Critical Incidents for Software Documentation Design. In *Proceedings of Thirtieth Annual Human Factors Society Conference* Human Factors Society, Anaheim, CA, 1986, 19-23.
3. Fitts, P. M., and Jones, R. E. "Psychological aspects of instrument display." *Selected Papers on Human Factors in the Design and Use of Control Systems. 1: Analysis of 270 "Pilot Error" Experiences in Reading and Interpreting Aircraft Instruments.* Sinaiko ed., Dover Publications, Inc., New York, 1947.
4. Hix, D., and Hartson, H. R. *Developing User Interfaces: Ensuring Usability Through Product and Process.* John Wiley & Sons, Inc., New York, 1993.
5. Hix, D., and Hartson, H. R. IDEAL: An Environment for User-Centered Development of User Interfaces. In Proceedings of *EWHCI'94: Fourth East-West International Conference on Human-Computer Interaction* (St. Petersburg, Russia, August 2-6), 1994, 195-211.
6. Nolan, P. R. Welcome to Vertical Research. Vertical Research, Inc., P.O. Box 1214, Brookline, MA 02146, USA. (1995). http://www.nolan.com/~pnolan/vertical.html.
7. Siochi, A. C., and Ehrich, R. W. Computer Analysis of User Interfaces Based on Repetition in Transcripts of User Sessions. *ACM TOIS. 9*, 4 (October 1991), 309-335.
8. Whiteside, J., Bennett, J., and Holtzblatt, K. "Usability Engineering: Our Experience and Evolution." Chapter 36 in Handbook of Human-*Computer Interaction.* Helander ed., Elsevier North-Holland, Amsterdam, 1988, 791-817.

Usability Problem Identification Using Both Low- and High-Fidelity Prototypes

Robert A. Virzi, Jeffrey L. Sokolov, Demetrios Karis

GTE Laboratories Incorporated
40 Sylvan Road
Waltham, MA 02254 USA
{rvirzi, jsokolov, dkaris}@gte.com

ABSTRACT

In two experiments, each using a different product (either a CD-ROM based electronic book or an interactive voice response system), we compared the usability problems uncovered using low- and high-fidelity prototypes. One group of subjects performed a series of tasks using a paper-based low-fidelity prototype, while another performed the same tasks using either a high-fidelity prototype or the actual product. In both experiments, substantially the same sets of usability problems were found in the low- and high-fidelity conditions. Moreover, there was a significant correlation between the proportion of subjects detecting particular problems in the low- and high-fidelity groups. In other words, individual problems were detected by a similar proportion of subjects in both the low- and high-fidelity conditions. We conclude that the use of low-fidelity prototypes can be effective throughout the product development cycle, not just during the initial stages of design.

Keywords

Method, usability testing, low-fidelity prototyping

INTRODUCTION

The use of low-fidelity prototyping techniques has blossomed over the last five years, with researchers claiming low-fidelity prototypes: (1) are an efficient way to search the design space [7]; (2) are predictive of preferences in the actual product [9]; (3) enhance user participation in the design process [4]; (4) enable visualization of possible design solutions [3]; and (5) provoke innovation [10]. While there have been dissenting voices to the acceptance of prototyping in general [6], current practice seems to demand some level of prototyping activity during the design process. As a profession, it is incumbent upon us to define ways to use this tool effectively, while at the same time understanding its limitations.

CHI 96 Vancouver, BC Canada

In this paper, we address a critical question that appears to remain open: *In the later stages of user-interface design, are low-fidelity prototypes as effective as high-fidelity prototypes in identifying usability problems?* We cast the question this way because we think it is apparent that low-fidelity prototypes are useful in the early stages of design, before the details of the user interface are well known. One might also argue that even in later design phases, when it would be possible to build a high-fidelity working simulation of the product, low-fidelity techniques could be as effective in identifying usability problems. If this were true, then the choice of using low- or high-fidelity techniques would be based on considerations other than efficacy (e.g., cost). Alternatively, one could argue that low-fidelity prototypes can never be as effective as high-fidelity prototypes late in the design process. That is, one should build as high fidelity a prototype as possible, striving for realism as design activities progress. There are two forms this argument might take. First, one might suppose that there are particular aspects of a design that cannot be adequately simulated in a low-fidelity prototype. Thus, in using a low-fidelity prototype a usability specialist would risk missing an entire class of usability problems. A second argument against low-fidelity prototypes is that, due to their very nature, they are less effective in detecting problems; that is, they are a blunt instrument when compared to a high-fidelity prototype. Thus, use of a low-fidelity prototype would mean risking sensitivity in detecting problems. That is, any given subject would detect a smaller percentage of the total problems using a low-fidelity prototype compared to a high-fidelity prototype. An investigator could compensate for this, however, merely by increasing the number of subjects when using a low-fidelity prototype.

Two recent studies are relevant to the current question. Nielsen [5] compared the effectiveness of two types of prototypes in a heuristic evaluation, a low-fidelity paper mockup and a higher fidelity (but not high fidelity) computer mockup. Nielsen claimed that evaluators using the computer mockup were more likely to find the major problems than evaluators using the paper mockup, but the study is difficult to evaluate because he provides very few procedural details. Some of the differences between mockups could have arisen from evaluator variability, and the most important result, the difference between conditions in finding major problems, was based on a measure of problem severity that was not validated.

Wiklund et al. [9] examined the relationship between the aesthetic refinement of a prototype and perceived usability. They created four versions of an electronic dictionary that varied in how realistically they represented what the actual product looked like. Subjects rated the prototypes on a variety of scales including ease of use and ease of learning, both before and after using the prototypes. These ratings were not affected by level of realism. They also had these subjects use the actual device, and provide the same ratings. This manipulation pointed out one of the pitfalls of low-fidelity prototyping. Because they did not accurately represent the slow response times for some aspects of the actual device's performance, estimates of usability for all the prototypes were greater than that of the actual device. Wiklund et al. argue that prototype fidelity does not affect how sensitive the test is, that is, low-fidelity tools are not blunt, but it does affect the kinds of problems one can detect.

Prototype fidelity is a continuum, not a dichotomy, and a prototype can vary from the final product along several orthogonal dimensions, including breadth of features, degree of functionality, similarity of interaction, and aesthetic refinement. Breadth of features refers to the number of features the prototype supports. Each of these features can then vary in its degree of functionality, or the extent to which the details of its operation are complete. Similarity of interaction refers to how one communicates with the product (whether by pressing buttons, clicking a mouse, touching a screen, speaking, etc.), and aesthetic refinement refers to aspects of the product that do not directly influence its functionality, such as choice of colors and graphic design. Although prototype fidelity is difficult to define precisely, a prototype that compromises on one or more of these four dimensions in a way that is obvious to the user is a low-fidelity prototype.

Low fidelity prototypes may have fairly complete breadth of features and degree of functionality and so may be similar to the final product on these dimensions, but users do not typically interact with low-fidelity prototypes in the same manner as the final product, and they do not typically look and feel the same with respect to the last dimension, aesthetic refinement.

Although illuminating, the studies reviewed above have not addressed our particular issue. We wanted to know if low-fidelity prototypes are as effective as high fidelity prototypes in detecting problems under the following conditions: (1) at the later stages of the product design process (i.e., when enough is known about the application to build a high-fidelity prototype); (2) when the study is under the supervision of usability specialists; (3) when the think-aloud protocol is used [1]; and (4) when the primary measure of effectiveness is the number of usability problems uncovered in a user interface.

We present the results of two separate experiments designed to examine this question. In both experiments, we ran two usability studies, one using a low-fidelity paper prototype, and one using a high-fidelity prototype. In experiment 1, we used an encyclopedia in electronic book form. Experiment 2 is essentially a replication of experiment 1 using a different product, an Interactive Voice Response (IVR) system for a new telecommunications service. We chose these two applications because of the differences in the products and in the low-fidelity prototyping techniques we could use. The low-fidelity version of the electronic book was created using paper and index cards, while the IVR system was simulated by a person reading the prompts aloud from written specifications.

EXPERIMENT 1 METHOD

Description of Application and Prototypes

We used a portable electronic-book player running an abridged encyclopedia. The player and the encyclopedia were tested as a complete system. The device itself is capable of displaying text and limited graphics on a flip-up, backlit LCD screen approximately 2.5" x 2.5". The overall device is 6" x 4" x 2". The device includes a limited QWERTY keyboard and some dedicated function keys. The software running on the device, a highly abridged encyclopedia, allows users to search the database and retrieve articles using any of 5 different search functions. Most articles are purely text; however, a small subset of articles have associated pictures. All graphics and text appear as black lines on a white screen. The actual electronic-book served as our high-fidelity prototype.

For the low-fidelity version of the electronic book, we created a simulation of the screens and keyboard on paper. The text and pictures used for the prototype were based on the screens from the actual product. They were prepared using a computer drawing program (Claris MacDraw Pro™), and printed on index cards. As users interacted with the paper prototype, by pressing the buttons on the paper rendition of the keyboard, they called out the keys they were pressing. The experimenter then simulated the action of the actual device by changing the display on the prototype (i.e., by removing the current card and substituting the card for the next screen). Even actions as simple as moving a highlighter from one item to the next were simulated by changing index cards. Over 100 cards were prepared that could represent not only the correct sequence of actions to complete the tasks, but also the most frequent mistakes, based on pilot testing.

Subjects

Twenty college-age subjects were recruited from local universities and paid a small fee for their participation in the study.

Procedures

Three tasks were devised that exercised the functionality of the electronic book (find the birth date of Increase Mather, a Puritan clergyman; find a list of different types of governments; find a picture of a map of Afghanistan then determine the literacy rate for that country in the early 1980s). Half the subjects (10) performed these tasks using the actual electronic book while the other half performed the tasks using the paper prototype. All subjects were instructed to think-aloud while interacting with the system. The entire session was videotaped, and these videotapes were later used for analysis. Sessions lasted from 30 to 45 minutes.

After all testing was completed the tapes were coded. We filled out a separate incident sheet for each usability problem encountered by a subject. We declared a usability problem had occurred when: (1) the user verbally indicated that something was unclear or confusing, even if they did not make an error; (2) the user's utterances indicated a misconception regarding what was happening or what function a particular button may have had; or (3) the user's actions indicated an incorrect path or course of action, even if the user was not conscious of the problem. The number of times that a problem was identified by a given subject was also indicated on the sheets.

When all the problem sheets had been prepared, we created a single list of problems by sorting the sheets into groups of behaviors that underlay the same usability problem (problem sheets from both conditions were combined). For example, even though subjects exhibited different sorts of behaviors that indicated they did not know how to use the search facility, we grouped all tokens of this problem into a single problem type. We did this for both the high- and low-fidelity subjects at the same time. It is important to note that we were blind to the condition under which each problem sheet was generated during the sorting process. After completion of the sorting task, we generated two matrices of subjects by problem type, one for each condition of the study (low- versus high-fidelity).

EXPERIMENT 1 RESULTS

A total of 38 distinct usability problems were identified over both the low- and high-fidelity conditions (e.g., item selection was difficult; there were no instructions on how to use the search facility; function keys were not always available; their placement was inconsistent; and their labels were not descriptive). The proportion of the 10 subjects in the two conditions who identified each problem was calculated. Thus, for each problem we had a measure of how likely it was to be detected using the two prototypes. These measures form the basis of our analyses.

The first question we tried to answer was, do the techniques differ in their overall sensitivity in detecting problems? If one of the techniques was more sensitive, we would expect that the proportion of subjects finding problems using that technique would be systematically higher. In the high-fidelity group, each subject found, on average, 38% of the problems, while in the low fidelity group each subject found 34% of the problems. We tested the difference between the groups using a two-tailed paired t-test, with problems forming the unit of analysis. The two conditions did not differ significantly in their overall sensitivity ($t(37) = 1.08$, $p = .29$). The most prevalent problem, which involved a key labeled "YES" instead of an "ENTER" key, was found by 80% of the subjects (70% in the high-fidelity group, 90% in the low-fidelity group). The three least prevalent problems were found by only one subject each. Only one person in the high-fidelity condition complained about not having a "backspace" key to fix typos by deleting single characters. A single subject in the low-fidelity condition had difficulty determining from screen feedback whether the page-down command had worked as intended. The last idiosyncratic problem was also found by a low-fidelity subject who had trouble determining the boundaries of the screen in the prototype.

Figure 1 plots the average proportion of the total set of usability problems one would expect to uncover as a function of the number of subjects run in the evaluation. This is calculated using the formula described in [8],

$$1 - (1 - p)^n$$

where p is the mean probability of problem identification and n is the number of subjects in the evaluation. Separate plots are presented for the two groups. The closeness of the two curves reflects the similarity in detection ability using the two prototypes.

We realize that it is impossible to prove the null hypothesis that the two techniques are equally sensitive. We present an additional analysis here in which we ask whether or not the two kinds of prototypes were finding the same sorts of problems. It is possible for the two techniques to have approximately the same mean sensitivity, while tapping into different pools of problems. If this were true, then we would expect to find a poor correlation between the conditions. On the other hand, if the two techniques tend to uncover the same problems at comparable levels of detectability, we would expect a high correlation. Figure 2 presents a scatter plot of the data, where the proportion of low-fidelity subjects finding a problem appears on the X-axis, and the proportion of high-fidelity subjects finding the same problem appears on the Y-axis. Dots represent single problems and co-occurring points are mapped to spiked icons, where the number of points in a symbol corresponds to the number of overlapping points (e.g., a bar is two coincident points, etc.).

The ability to detect problems using the two techniques is highly correlated, $r = .58$, $p < .01$. This indicates that the two prototypes were indeed tapping into the same problems with roughly the same degree of sensitivity to most problems. Problems that were found by a high proportion of subjects in the low-fidelity condition were also found by a high proportion of subjects in the high-fidelity condition, and vice versa. Of the 38 total problems, 34 were found by subjects in the high-fidelity group, and 32 were found by subjects in the low fidelity-group.

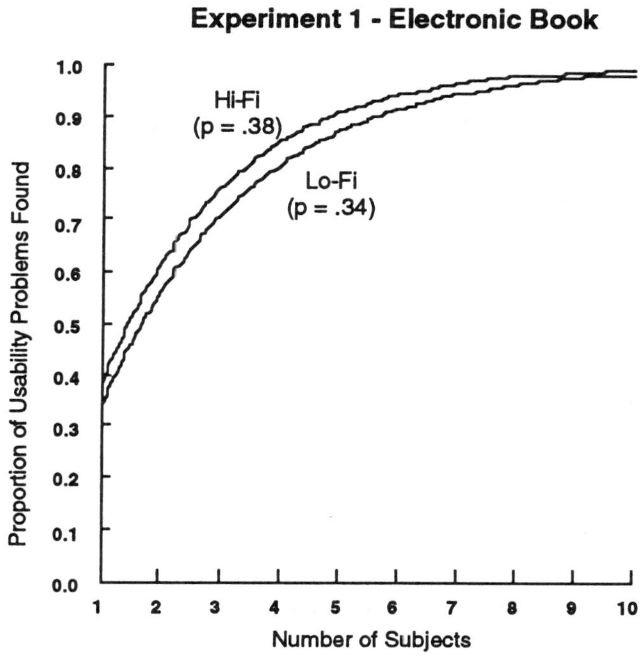

Figure 1. The proportion of usability problems one would expect to detect for a given number of subjects in the evaluation is shown for both low- and high-fidelity conditions in Experiment 1.

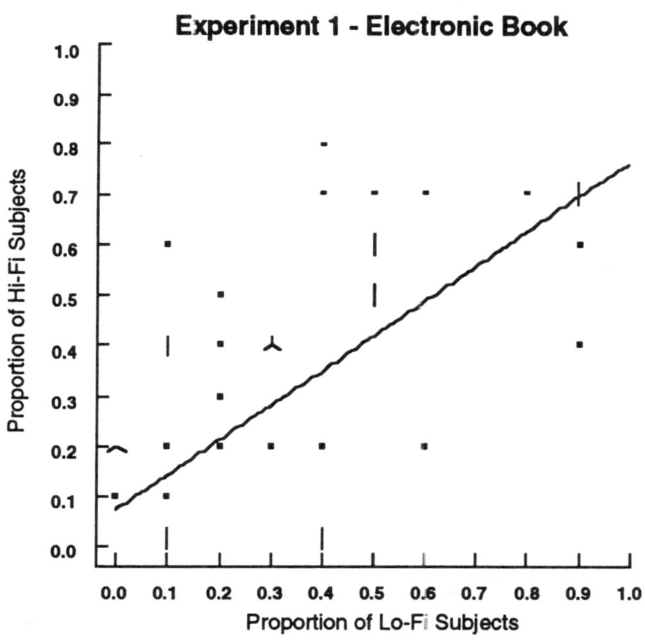

Figure 2. The proportion of subjects identifying individual problem types in the two conditions of Experiment 1 are plotted. The regression line shown corresponds to the equation: $y = .075 + .690(x)$, $r = .576$.

EXPERIMENT 2 METHOD

Description of Application and Prototypes

In experiment 2, we used an Interactive Voice Response (IVR) system for a new telecommunication service. The high-fidelity prototype was built using TFLX™, a Magnum Software product for the Apple Macintosh™ computer. Users interacted with the system by calling the computer from a touch-tone phone. In response to their keypresses, the computer played back recorded digital speech via the telephone network. The application allowed callers to setup and maintain a fairly complicated telephony service that included caller identification, call screening, and automatic callback functions.

For the low-fidelity version of the IVR system, we enacted the system with one of the authors playing the part of the computer. Subjects sat in a room with the experimenter and indicated what they would do by pressing buttons on a telephone (which was not attached to the network). The experimenter read out loud what the computer would say based on the subject's input.

Subjects

Twenty college-age subjects were recruited from local universities and paid a small fee for their participation in the study.

Procedures

A series of tasks were devised that exercised the functionality of the IVR system (e.g., create a caller acceptance list; define call routing options). Ten subjects performed these tasks using the high-fidelity prototype while the other half performed the tasks using the low-fidelity prototype. All subjects were instructed to think-aloud while interacting with the system. The entire session was videotaped, and these videotapes were used for later analysis. In this experiment, the low fidelity prototype matched the high-fidelity prototype in terms of completeness; any action possible in the final system could be taken by subjects using either the low- or high-fidelity prototypes.

After user testing was completed, the tapes were coded and problem sheets were sorted as in Experiment 1, producing a subject by problem matrix for each condition.

EXPERIMENT 2 RESULTS

A total of 21 distinct usability problems were identified over both the low- and high-fidelity conditions (e.g., difficulty finding the setting for blocked calls; confusing terminology; misleading prompt order on a menu; and inconsistent key mappings). The proportion of the 10 subjects in the two conditions who identified each problem was calculated, as in experiment 1.

A t-test on these data replicated the finding from experiment 1: The two techniques did not differ significantly in their overall ability to detect usability problems ($t(20) = .870$, $p = .39$). In the high-fidelity group, each subject found, on average, 40% of the problems, while in the low-fidelity group subjects found 46% of the problems. Figure 3 shows these results graphically.

Figure 4 presents a scatter plot of the data for experiment 2. As in experiment 1, the ability to detect problems using the two techniques is correlated, $r = .49$, $p < .05$. This indicates that the two prototypes were indeed tapping into the same problems with roughly the same degree of sensitivity to most problems. Of the 21 total problems, 19 were found by subjects in the high-fidelity group, and 20 were found by subjects in the low-fidelity group. Two problems appear to be outliers in that they were identified by almost all the subjects in the high-fidelity condition but relatively few of the subjects in the low-fidelity condition (see Figure 4). The two problems were related in that they were both caused by the failure of the high-fidelity prototype to automatically save users' changes upon returning to the main menu from a sub-menu. The low-fidelity prototype handled this function slightly differently, thus subjects were not as likely to detect the problem.

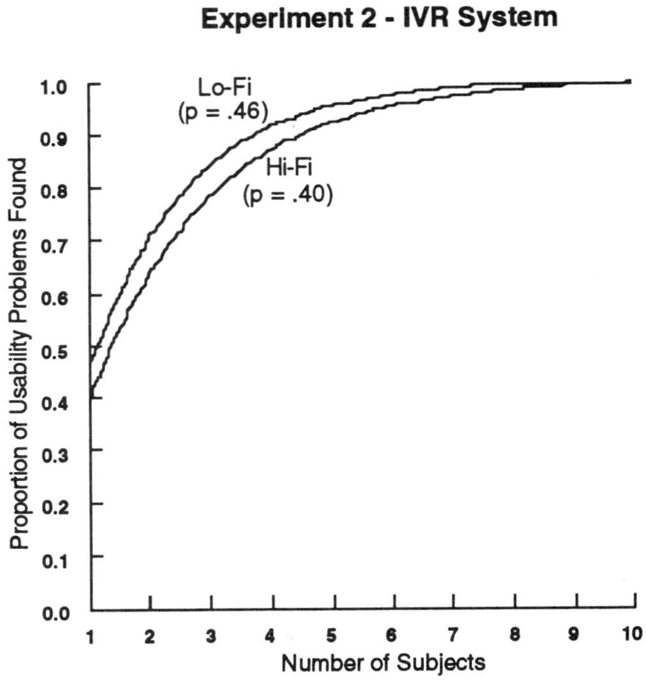

Figure 3. The proportion of usability problems one would expect to detect for a given number of subjects in the evaluation is shown for both low- and high-fidelity conditions in Experiment 2.

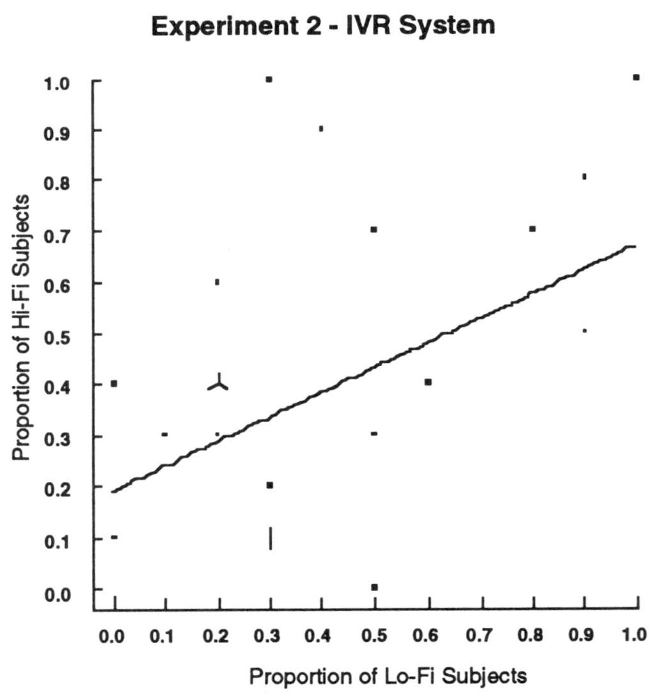

Figure 4. The proportion of subjects identifying individual problem types in the two conditions of Experiment 2 are plotted. The regression line shown corresponds to the equation: $y = .181 + .480(x)$, $r = .487$.

DISCUSSION

Are Low-Fidelity Prototypes a Blunt Tool?

The first question we attempted to answer was, *Are low-fidelity prototypes a blunt tool?* The results of both experiments were highly consistent, and indicated that low-fidelity prototypes are as effective as high-fidelity prototypes at detecting usability problems. Thus low-fidelity prototyping is not a blunt tool, or at least it is as sharp as high-fidelity prototyping in detecting usability problems. We employed a usability technique involving a think-aloud protocol, and we are not claiming that our results would apply equally well to other usability techniques. The types of low-fidelity prototypes used here require extensive manipulation by the experimenter as well as frequent interaction between experimenter and subject. The think-aloud technique also requires interaction, as the experimenter sometimes needs to ask questions to understand the problems a subject is experiencing, and this technique is a nice complement to the use of low-fidelity prototypes.

While we acknowledge that one cannot prove the null hypothesis (that there is no difference between prototyping techniques), we would hasten to point out the practical importance of the finding. Both studies showed that substantially the same sets of problems were found in the low- and high-fidelity groups. Thus a user-interface designer would have essentially the same amount of information regardless of the technique employed. Note that low fidelity does not imply a lack of functionality. In the IVR system the functionality of the prototypes in both conditions were almost identical, and complete. For the low-fidelity version of the electronic book, just enough functionality was provided to allow the user to perform the tasks. The electronic book itself was obviously fully functional.

Although the products in the two experiments were quite different, and used different low-fidelity prototyping techniques, the results were essentially the same. How generalizable are these results? Surely they would not apply, we have heard colleagues say, to direct manipulation interfaces, virtual reality or other immersive systems, or to systems that are extremely response-time sensitive [2]. We are not so sure. The exact bounds of our results must await additional research with a variety of products. In a third experiment (not reported here), we tested a complex, CD-ROM, multimedia Macintosh™ product that had a graphical user interface. Our preliminary analysis finds very few differences in the usability problems discovered using a paper-based low-fidelity prototype versus the actual product.

Do Low-Fidelity Prototypes Find Different Problems?

Our second question was, *Do low-fidelity prototypes tend to find different problems than high-fidelity prototypes?* The question appears to be answered with a qualified, *No.* Both techniques uncovered the same usability problems for the most part, and at about the same level of sensitivity, as witnessed by the high positive correlations in the two studies between the proportion of low- and high-fidelity subjects finding particular problems. That is, when a problem was found by a high proportion of subjects in the high-fidelity group, it also tended to be found by a high proportion in the low-fidelity group. However, some problems that were found in the high-fidelity condition were not found in the low-fidelity condition, and vice versa. This is true for both studies. There are many reasons why this result might obtain, but inspection of the actual problems did not lead to any obvious conclusions. We believe, that except as noted earlier, this is probably a result of normal variability, given the small number of subjects, rather than a function of differences between the two prototypes, but we currently have no evidence to substantiate this belief.

Would there have been differences between the two conditions if we had considered problem severity? It is very difficult to come up with adequate techniques for defining and labeling problem severity, and we did not attempt to do so in these experiments. However, based on an "eye-ball" examination of the problems uncovered, we could see no striking differences as a function of our rough estimates of problem severity. Both groups found many severe problems, as well as many we would categorize as minor. Where there were large differences between the two conditions, it was difficult to attribute this to aspects of the prototypes. For example, in experiment 1, problem 32 involved using the graphic search capability: an instruction screen was presented showing three screen locations where a cursor could be located to navigate through graphics screens or select the associated article. Not only was this difficult to understand as presented, but this information had to be remembered, because when the graphics appeared all instructions disappeared. This resulted in a variety of related problems that we categorized together. In the low-fidelity group, 90% of the subjects experienced these problems, while only 40% experienced them in the high-fidelity group. We just don't know whether there is some reason for this difference related to how the subjects performed the task in the two groups, or whether this is random variability. It was clear after watching only one or two subjects struggle with this problem that it was quite serious. Problems that were found by only one or two subjects did not appear to be as serious, but we have no real data to support this claim.

It is also important to remember that practically all problems were identified within each condition (i.e., across subjects). In experiment 1, the high- and low- fidelity groups uncovered 34 and 32 of the 38 problems, respectively, while in experiment 2, the numbers were 19 and 20 out of 21.

In both experiments we set up and performed the usability evaluation as realistically as possible, and chose what we considered a representative set of tasks that exercised all the main functions of the product. In fact, the IVR system in experiment 2 was part of a new telecommunication service that GTE planned to offer, and the high-fidelity prototype was built to support our user-interface design effort. It was built from specifications we prepared, and used for usability testing essentially identical to that reported here. That is, the same tasks, instructions, and procedures used in usability tests for the commercial product were used in the usability tests reported here. The high-fidelity prototype provided full functionality and was quite complex; it contained over 5,000 TFLX™ "icons," seven databases, over 500 sound files, and took over two months to develop. As we note below, this prototype served several purposes. However, with respect to usability testing, had we performed an experiment like the one reported here a year earlier, *we would not have spent the time and effort to build a high-fidelity prototype, and would have conducted all usability testing with the low-fidelity prototyping techniques reported here.* In fact, this is how we currently design IVR systems in practice.

In experiment 1, the commercial electronic-book product served as the high-fidelity prototype. This is actually a conservative approach because a high-fidelity prototype, by definition, can equal, but never surpass, the fidelity of the actual product. Using the actual product instead of a high-fidelity prototype would tend to increase, not decrease, the differences between our groups if the high-fidelity prototype failed to incorporate some of the features or attributes of the real product.

The Need for High-Fidelity Prototypes

Although we found substantially the same set of usability problems in both the low and high-fidelity groups, we are not arguing that there is no place in the development cycle for high-fidelity prototypes. There are several circumstances in which high-fidelity prototypes are useful. First, there will probably be a set of usability problems for which any particular low fidelity prototype will be inadequate. For example, in experiment 1 there were no tasks requiring the user to physically manipulate the electronic book, which would be required when opening it to insert a diskette. It would not have been possible to complete this task given the two dimensional paper and cardboard low-fidelity prototype. We should note, however, that a low fidelity prototype that allowed physical manipulation could have been constructed. Low-fidelity prototypes will always be limited, by definition, on some dimensions; however, given a particular set of tasks, it is almost always possible to construct a low fidelity prototype that can support their execution. In a low-fidelity prototype of an IVR system, as in our second experiment, it is not possible to check for possible problems with the concatenation of prompts, or their intelligibility (especially, for example, if synthetic speech were to be used) because the experimenter reads the prompts from the specification. However, even with a high-fidelity prototype of an IVR system, it is not typically possible to check concatenation or intelligibility unless special care was taken to build the prototype to match the commercial product (e.g., by breaking up and concatenating messages in the same way, or using the same text-to-speech synthesizer).

Even though we are focusing here on the prototype itself, it may be helpful to step back and consider what is happening from a broader perspective. The task in a usability evaluation is to identify problems. When this is done in the laboratory, even when using a high-fidelity prototype, we are simulating not only the product, but also the tasks, the environment, the data used by the product, and so on. Thus even a high-fidelity prototype can lead to a noisy approximation of the actual way in which people will use a product. The focus of this paper is the artifact (the prototype), but it is also important to focus attention on these other aspects of testing as well.

Another general class of problems that may be identified differentially in low- and high-fidelity prototypes involve performance measures such as the time to complete certain operations. In many cases, of course, it takes longer for an experimenter to manipulate a low-fidelity prototype in response to a user's action than for a computer running a high-fidelity prototype to respond. We are currently quantifying the magnitude of these differences in another experiment that measures time to complete tasks and other performance measures, including the number of tasks completed and the number of steps required per task.

Once we leave the realm of usability, there are a variety of areas in which increasing the fidelity of certain aspects of the prototype will prove much more useful. In selecting the fonts, images, and colors to use in a graphical user interface, for example, a prototype that can provide displays nearly identical to the actual product will be far superior to a paper simulation.

In our development work, we have found three broad areas, apart from usability testing, where high-fidelity prototypes are valuable. First, prototypes are effective in communication with marketing departments, and here the high face validity of high-fidelity prototypes can be critical. Both positive and negative information about a product can be communicated effectively, either via videotapes of usability sessions or via direct interaction by marketing personnel. Marketing can also use the prototype as part of early demonstrations to their clients. The second area involves communication with developers. A prototype, as an adjunct to a user-interface specification, can be very effective in conveying a sense of system behavior, and in helping the development team to read and understand a detailed specification. A corollary to this is that the process of building a high-fidelity prototype always helps to identify weaknesses and omissions in a user-interface specification. The third area involves communication with people writing documentation or preparing training materials. Since technical writers often need to start their work long before a working version of the product is available, having access to a prototype can be valuable in helping to develop an understanding of exactly how the product works, as well as providing easy access to details such as specific prompt wording or screen designs.

Implications for Practitioners

We interpret these results to mean that a designer or usability tester need not consider sensitivity when selecting a method for representing an interface in a test, provided comparable functionality is maintained. We would condition this recommendation to the case where the designer is seeking to identify problems and is willing to use the think-aloud protocol. Given these conditions and the limited number of subjects typically used in an evaluation, the designer is likely to uncover about as many problems at any one level of fidelity as another. Moreover, using a carefully constructed low-fidelity prototype, the designer should be uncovering the same types of problems as if a high-fidelity prototype were used.

ACKNOWLEDGMENTS

We would like to thank Devorah Klein for her assistance in conducting these studies. This work has also benefited from comments and discussions with department members, notably David Fay and Greg Cermak. Finally, we would like to thank Larry Wood, Alan Asper, Frank Reiff, Joe Dumas, Jonas Lowgren, and other members of the U-TEST mailing list for comments on a draft of this paper, as well as the CHI '96 reviewers.

REFERENCES

1. Lewis, C. Using the "thinking- aloud" method in cognitive interface design. IBM Technical Report RC

9265 (#40713), 2/17/82.

2. Lowgren, J. Personal communication, September, 1995.

3. Moggridge, B. Design by story-telling. Applied Ergonomics, 24(1), (1993) pp. 15 - 18.

4. Muller, M. PICTIVE - An exploration in participatory design. In Proc. of the Conference on Human Factors in Computing Systems. ACM:New York, (1991) pp. 225 - 231.

5. Nielsen, J. Paper versus Computer Implementations as Mockup Scenarios for Heuristic Evaluation. In Proceedings of IFIP INTERACT'90: Human-Computer Interaction, (1990) pp. 315 - 320.

6. Thimbleby, H. Failure in the technical user-interface design process. Computers and Graphics, 9, (1985), pp. 187 - 193.

7. Virzi, R. What can you learn from a low-fidelity prototype? In Proc. of the Human Factors Society 33rd Annual Meeting, HFES: Santa Monica, CA (1989), pp. 224 - 228.

8. Virzi. R. Refining the test phase of usability evaluation: How many subjects is enough? Human Factors, 34(4), (1992), pp. 457 - 468.

9. Wiklund, M., Thurrott, C., and Dumas, J. Does the fidelity of software prototypes affect the perception of usability? In Proc. of the Human Factors Society 36th Annual Meeting, HFES: Santa Monica, CA, (1992), 399 - 403.

10. Wulff, W., Evensen, S., and Rheinfrank, J. Animating interfaces. In CSCW '90 Proc., ACM: New York, (1990), pp. 241 - 254.

Toward Automatic Generation of Novice User Test Scripts

David J. Kasik and Harry G. George
Boeing Commercial Airplane Group
P.O. Box 3707, Mail Stop 6H-WT
Seattle WA 98124 USA
+1 206 234 0575
kasik@ata.ca.boeing.com

ABSTRACT

Graphical user interfaces (GUI's) make applications easier to learn and use. At the same time, they make application design, construction, and especially test more difficult because user-directed dialogs increase the number of potential execution paths. This paper considers a subset of GUI-based application testing: how to exercise an application like a novice user. We discuss different solutions and a specific implementation that uses genetic algorithms to automatically generate user events in an unpredictable yet controlled manner to produce novice-like test scripts.

Keywords

Automated test generation, dialog model specification, genetic algorithms, software engineering test process.

INTRODUCTION

The role of the user interface has become increasingly important to the success of computer applications. Graphical interfaces make complex applications visually attractive and accessible to a wide range of users.

Users can exercise an interactive application in many different ways. In reactive, GUI-based applications, even more options are available because multiple widgets and paths can be active concurrently. This causes problems as an application is tested for failures, especially when the it is made available to a large user community. Unsophisticated and novice users often exercise applications in ways that the designer, the developer, and the tester did not anticipate.

Tools and techniques to improve testing for program failures (e.g., capture/playback tools) are becoming more widely available.

As the tools have been deployed, the prime beneficiaries have been experts. An expert user or tester usually follows a predictable path through an application to accomplish a familiar task. A developer knows where to probe to find the 'weak points' in an application.

As a result, applications contain state transitions that work well for predicted usage patterns but become unstable when given to novice users. Novices follow unexpected paths and do things 'no one would ever do.' Such program failures are hard to generate, reproduce, diagnose, and predict. Current methods (e.g., recruiting naive users, beta testing) are manual, costly, and usually occur after development is finished.

This paper presents a technique to move novice-like testing earlier in the overall system test process. We use genetic algorithms as a repeatable technique for generating user events that drive conventional automated test tools. Reprogramming the genetic algorithm reward system can mimic different forms of novice user behavior. Our prototype implementation works at run-time and is independent of application design and development tools.

MOTIVATION

Testing is the subject of an entire branch of computer science [1, 13]. The test process is shown in Figure 1.

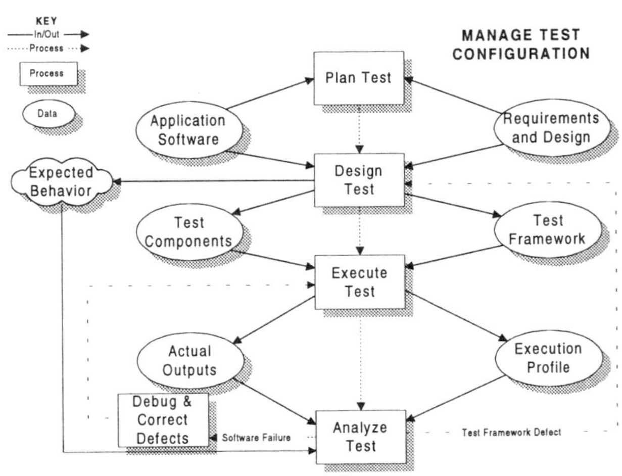

Figure 1. Test Process Framework

This paper deals with one aspect of the overall test process: how to automate generation of test scripts that exhibit novice user characteristics as part of **Design Test**. Novice-like testing is often the target of beta programs and can involve many people (e.g., Microsoft's 400,000 beta copies of Windows95). When this type of novice testing is done, it is designed to find program failures rather than to determine usability characteristics.

GUI-based applications present special problems in test design. Older interactive applications often embedded command hierarchies directly in the structure of the program. The user then followed the command tree while navigating from one function to another. The test designer could assume that certain logical conditions held because the user could not deviate from the program-controlled sequence.

Multiple dialog sequences are available concurrently in a GUI-based application. The application becomes reactive and paths more unpredictable. Therefore, a test designer must consciously assure that the program maintains logical relationships through the state changes needed to control:

- Interleaved function execution.
- Exit from a partially completed function.
- User or program generated asynchronous events.
- User or program generated error conditions.

The size and complexity of both the application program and the test set grow dramatically when concurrent dialog is involved. Industry statistics [12] indicate that many GUI-based applications devote half of the code to managing the user interface. As discussed in the next section, there are a number of different techniques for improving the user interface design/build process. Testing is still required even with improvements in the early stages of the system engineering process.

The general problem of test automation for GUI-based applications has received some attention. The principal effort has been in the area of automated record/playback tools [16]. Such tools accept input at two levels:

1. Raw keystroke capture saves individual user keyboard and mouse events.
2. Logical widget names provide higher level specifications that are screen position insensitive.

The tools generally offer a language that can be used to program test scripts. Some form of bitmap compare is included to help a tester compare results of a test run with a known-good result.

Test automation tools work well when given to an expert and poorly when given to a novice because:

- An expert knows how an application should respond to a particular input, and a novice does not have such knowledge. In other words, an expert knows what an application can or cannot do as a task is being performed and a companion script written.
- A large set of test scripts is needed to faithfully represent how a novice might exercise an application. Generating such scripts by hand is tedious and needs to be re-done for each new version.

Novice Testing

Testing can be conducted on a number of different levels to discover application failures and to measure and verify acceptable performance. The most common characterization of testing describes phases where:

- *Unit test* attempts to find failures in a logical unit in isolation from others.
- *Functional test* attempts to find failures as logical units are connected together to perform specific functions.
- *System test* attempts to find failures as the whole application is used and to verify that the application meets requirements.

Different people are assigned responsibilities for testing. Developers isolate specific application functions and interfaces during unit and functional test. These tests require extensive knowledge and analysis of code internals. System test is more task oriented. In addition to finding failures, system test determines if an application can be used to accomplish tasks. The testing is done in a black box manner and must be driven from the user interface. Experts perform most system testing, and novices are occasionally recruited to find application weak spots.

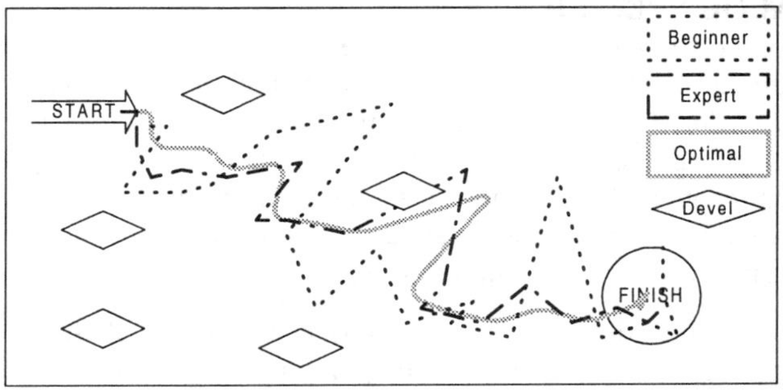

Figure 2. Different Paths through an Application

As shown in Figure 2, there are three paths that can be taken to perform a task during system test:

- The optimal path lets a user perform the task in the shortest time or fewest steps.
- The expert comes close to exercising an application in a semantically optimal manner. Experts know enough about program state to be able to work efficiently and define a reusable test script. Work has been done in the area of task analysis, cognitive simulation, and interface complexity with Goals, Operators, Methods (GOMS) models [10] to clearly define how an expert might use a complex application.
- The novice wanders in a reasonable but unpredictable manner. The novice gradually builds a more accurate

mental model of the application. The better mental model results in paths closer to the optimal.

Novices do not work at random: they learn the application by performing a task. Random testing does have a role in exploring the outer limits of an application but is not our primary focus.

Novice testing is often ignored. At worst, some applications have been released in anticipation that users will find errors and accept fixes in the next version. Beta programs find some failures caused by novice, but beta users are often quite literate in an application domain. Some companies recruit large numbers of naive users to test true novice behavior prior to beta release.

All three approaches to novice testing are costly. Not only do they occur late in the cycle, but a novice's actions are also hard to replicate. Novices wander through convoluted paths that only rigorous keystroke recording can capture. Large numbers of novice keystroke files become difficult to manage and upgrade to the next version.

We chose to automate generation of novice test scripts to address these problems. Automation requires a script environment to record and playback sessions and a method to generate user events in a novice-like manner for those scripts. Our approach assumes the existence of an automated record/playback tool. The automation effort focused on user event generation.

DIALOG SPECIFICATION ALTERNATIVES

In order to generate meaningful events for a script, we require a clear, accurate specification of both the user interface dialog [14] and the program state information. The state information controls the legality of specific dialog components and the names of the legal commands during a session. Without access to state, the generator could produce many meaningless input events.

This section contains a brief review and analysis of three techniques designers and developers use to specify user interface dialog and control its state.

GUI Toolkits and Source Code

The most commonly used form of dialog and state specification is the application program itself. The UI designer and implementer often use a GUI toolkit to specify graphical layout and input gathering mechanics.

A GUI toolkit does not manage state information. Therefore, both logical relationships and concurrency must be managed in programmer maintained code. Application code grows more complex as the number of relationships increases. In addition, the way in which a programmer manages logical relationships and concurrency is different from but interleaved with the algorithmic code that performs a requested function.

Because the code is an integral part of the specification and state information cannot be derived from static code analysis, any automated test generation scheme needs to be able to obtain current user interface and state information from the application code itself.

User Interface Management Systems

The second alternative is a user interface management system (UIMS). UIMSs have been formally pursued since the early 1980's [4, 9]. The UIMS ideal is to operate the same application across a wide variety of interface styles (e.g., GUI, command line, form, script file) with little or no change to the dialog or application.

This is possible because a UIMS contains a dialog specification language that contains state information. The language is translated into an informal model that is interpreted to control program execution. Because they contain state information, UIMS specifications are inherently more complete than GUI widget hierarchies and more suitable for use in generating test scripts.

However, few applications are specified with a UIMS. Applying any automated test generation technique to a manually developed application requires reverse engineering to derive the UIMS model. This is a daunting task: a working program often contains 'features' and loopholes that are difficult to capture in a more abstract UIMS model.

Process Modeling

The third specification alternative for dialog is formal process modeling. Formal models are commonly used in time and state sensitive areas (e.g., real time software, business process modeling, temporal protocol logic).

In contrast to the informal models in UIMSs, formal models can be validated prior to execution. Theorem proving techniques can be used to determine correctness for text-based formal specifications [5]. Graphical formal models like Petri nets can be analyzed mathematically [17] or via discrete event simulation [7].

Formal models have been used as direct input to the test process, especially for safety critical applications. Two examples are path models built from source code to generate test data values [6] and finite state models to reduce the number of required tests [2]. Little has been done to automate the generation of the scripts themselves.

Petri nets have been used as a type of process model applied to dialog [15, 19]. Palanque and Bastide have documented reasonably complex interfaces based on Petri nets. The nets proved to be an effective specification technique. However, they were manually verified and translated into an executable application. Manual translation of a formal model to an executing program can contain errors and deviations from the specification.

Summary

Both user interface management systems and formal process models contain the information necessary to generate test scripts automatically from the specification itself. But neither technique is used widely. As a result, we would have needed to build a reverse engineering tool to recreate either a UIMS or formal model specification from an existing program. This approach would make the automated test generator itself difficult to use and error prone. Formal models also suffer from a lack of tools to translate the abstract specification into an executable form.

Therefore, we chose to work with the application itself as the dialog specification. Moreover, we chose to use the executing application rather than the source code. Source code analysis techniques cannot deduce program and dialog state changes that occur during execution. The state changes allow each new step in the script send syntactically correct input to an active part of the application.

PROTOTYPE IMPLEMENTATION

Given that an executing program specifies the application user interface dialog, we needed to develop methods to:

1. Simulate user inputs. Genetic algorithms proved to be a good method to control the generation of random numbers used to simulate input events.
2. Capture the current state of the user interface during application execution. Our implementation approach requires no added processing logic in the application.
3. Tie the genetic algorithm generated input values to the user interface during execution in an application independent manner.
4. Allow the tester to generate and save novice-like scripts.

The prototype uses standard tools and techniques wherever possible. The prototype is application independent and needs no special application dialog design or code structure.

Simulated User Inputs

Commercial test tools provide a mechanism to drive a GUI-based application from captured keystrokes. Automation requires a method to generate keystrokes.

Analyzing user behavior led to the conclusion that emulating novice user behavior requires a way to 'remember' success. Both novices and experts use an application to perform tasks. Novices explore to learn the semantics of individual functions and how to combine sequences of functions into meaningful work. Experts have already discovered successful paths through an application and rely on past experience to accomplish new tasks.

Random number generators alone are inadequate because they do not rely on past history to govern future choices. Genetic algorithms do rely on past history. Success has been reported in applying genetic algorithms to hardware test sequence generation [18]. Therefore, we chose to use genetic algorithms to simulate novice user events.

Genetic Algorithms

Genetic algorithms [11] can be programmed to simulate a pseudo-natural selection process. In its simplest form, a genetic algorithm manipulates a table (or pool) of random numbers. Each row in the table represents a different gene. The individual components of a gene are called alleles and contain a numeric genetic 'code.' The interpretation of the allele values varies according to application.

Allele values start as random numbers that define an initial 'genetic code'. The genetic algorithm lets genes that contain 'better' alleles survive to compete against new genes in subsequent generations.

During a run through multiple generations to determine the best genes, the gene pool contains the same number of genes that have the same number of alleles. The number of genes in the pool and the number of alleles in a gene can vary from run to run.

A basic genetic algorithm:

- Initializes the alleles with valid random numbers.
- Repeats the following until its goal is reached:
  - Generates a score for each gene in the pool by trying the allele values.
  - Rewards the genes that produce the best results by replicating them and allowing them to live to a new generation. A defined fraction of genes with the highest scores live and the remainder are thrown away.
  - Completes the pool in the next generation with new genes created by crossover of previous allele values.
  - Mutates some of the genes in the new generation. Mutation can occur in either surviving or new genes.

Gene crossover styles, mutation rates, and death rates can be programmed and varied. These techniques are useful in determining how many genes survive into a new generation, how existing allele values are swapped among genes, and how new random allele values are inserted into surviving or new genes. Each generation is guaranteed to produce a set of genes that survive. Allowing a genetic algorithm user to vary survival techniques lets the user tune the algorithm to a particular problem.

Genetic algorithms are not an effective way to explore all possible paths in a dialog sequence. Instead, a genetic algorithm uses previous sets of random numbers as the basis for new ones. This means that the method used to compute the 'best results' becomes the key factor in any application that uses genetic algorithms. As applied to user interface event generation, 'best results' meant designing an algorithm that represents how novice users learn to use an application.

Run-time User Interface Capture

At run-time, different GUIs require different implementations to capture the current state of the user interface as the Application Under Test executes. Our prototype, whose architecture is shown in Figure 3, works with applications built with Motif 1.2 and X11R5. All software components are written as objects in Modula-3 [3].

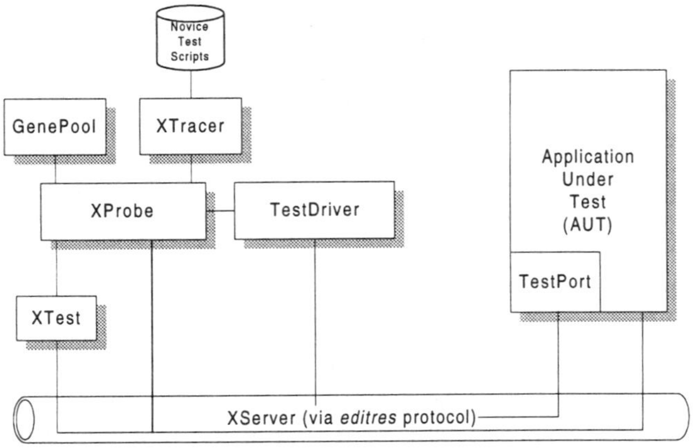

Figure 3. Run-time Architecture

The test script generator (XTest) can be applied to different Applications Under Test (AUT). During execution,

- TestPort and TestDriver establish the connection between the AUT and Xtest processes.
- XProbe selects events and sends them to the AUT.
- GenePool uses the genetic algorithms to tune XProbe's selections and events.
- XTracer generates the genetically engineered test script at the end of a session.

XProbe, TestDriver, and TestPort use standard Motif and X communications with a protocol based on the *editres* protocol. This approach proved superior to other UNIX techniques for sharing information across process spaces like shared memory, rpc servers, pipes, and shared files.

Xtest controls the AUT through the standard XSendEvent mechanism. While this technique works, XSendEvent operates strictly at the keystroke level. Therefore, XTracer generates test scripts at the keystroke level. A reasonable extension is to implement a reverse protocol to pass widget-level information to the application under test and to generate a more readable test script based on widget names.

The *editres* protocol asks the AUT to put some of its process-specific information into a form for use by TestDriver. The prototype requires only one slight modification to the AUT source code. Two procedure calls must be inserted to establish the TestPort callback and to provide the ID of its top level window. These calls are executed only once during AUT initialization, and all other processing happens transparently. A preferable approach would require no source code change.

Integrating Genetic Algorithms and UI Capture

The prototype interprets the alleles in each gene to dynamically generate events that are legal for the AUT. At run-time, TestDriver observes and controls the AUT as shown in Figure 4.

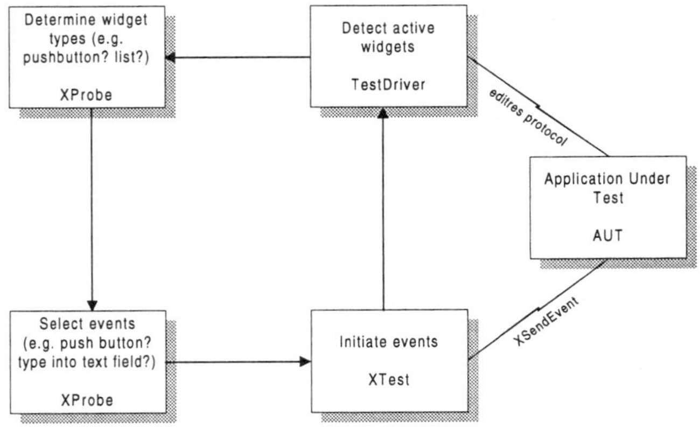

Figure 4. Observe and Control Loop

Prior to execution, the tester defines the number of alleles in each gene and the total number of genes in the pool. The following steps are executed for each gene in the gene pool in XProbe:

- Restart the AUT, set the active_allele_index to 1, and total_score for this gene to 0.
- Loop until the active_allele_index is greater than the number of alleles in the gene:
  - Read the current AUT widget tree.
  - Use the active_allele_index in the current gene as the start point to search for an active widget in current AUT widget tree. The search technique we implemented randomly chooses one of the active widgets in the current tree to minimize repetition of the same dialog sequence.
  - Depending on the active widget type, use the next *n* allele values to simulate user input events with XTest. XSendEvent send each events to AUT as it moves to its next state.
  - Increment active_allele_index by *n*.
  - Increment the total_score for this gene by the amount computed using the technique described in the next section.
- Save the total_score for the current gene.

Each gene in the pool restarts the application to insure an identical initial state. From then on, each gene can start at a different spot because allele values are used to randomly select an active widget. Finally, even though the number of alleles is the same for all genes, the number of input events varies from gene to gene because a different number of input events is needed for each dialog state.

After all the genes in the pool are tried, the genetic algorithm in GenePool (refer back to Figure 3) lets the winning genes survive, generates new genes, and mutates the pool before proceeding to the next generation. The script that corresponds to the top scoring gene in the last generation is output via XTracer.

Reward System

A realistic reward system lets the genes that generated the 'best' novice-like behavior survive by assigning a weighted score to user events. For example, one score can be given to a set of alleles that picks a list widget, a second to a set that types in specific characters, and a third to a set that provides input to a widget on the same window as the previous widget. Adjusting the weights allows the reward system to represent different types of novice user behavior.

We based our prototype reward system on the observation that a novice user often learns how to use an application via controlled exploration. A novice starts one function in a dialog sequence and experiments with a number of different parameters. In this way, the novice uses localized parameter settings to understand the overall effect of a single function. This is only one of the possible characterizations of novice user behavior.

To implement this reward system, we set the weight for all user events to zero except one. A gene receives a positive score each time its allele value(s) generate input for a widget (e.g., entering data into a text field, choosing an item from a list, selecting a radio button) that has the same window name as the last active window name. No additional score is generated to differentiate among the possible types of widgets on the window. The net result is that the longer a gene stays on the same window, the higher its score and better its odds of survival.

Tester's Interface

To simulate novice behavior, a tester:

- May begin with an expert generated test script.
- Inserts one or more *DEVIATE* commands into the script. *DEVIATE* departs from the existing script via the genetic algorithm and tries to return to the script.
- Tunes the genetic algorithm parameters to build up a set of scripts that represent novice behavior.

Because the prototype works outside an automated test tool, we defined a simplified script language to specify the expert test. A postprocessor generates scripts for commercial test tools. The resulting scripts can then be included as part of a complete test suite. The tester can use realistic, previously created scripts that contain novice behavior to initiate new simulations.

This interface strategy lets the tester control when deviations occur because a *DEVIATE* command can be inserted at arbitrary script locations. The script can then continue in either of the two modes shown in Figure 5. Pullback mode rewards genes for returning to the original script, while meander mode allows the activity to wander indefinitely. Even though pullback mode returns to the expert script, it will generally not generate the same results because additional functions are exercised.

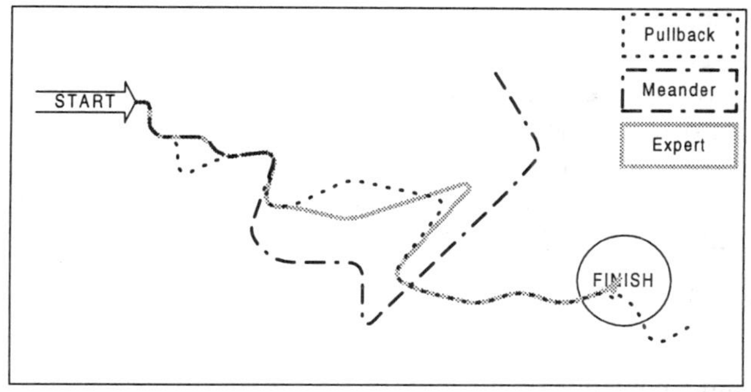

Figure 5. Deviation Modes

The following script demonstrates pullback mode. It opens and loads a data file and deviates to see that an application can still enter data for an x,y graphing program after novice-like activity:

```
(# expert script, in the form of a list of
   window, widget pairs with pullback #)
("SGE: On Version Dialog" "Cancel")
("Style Guide Example - <New File>" "file")
("Root" "open")
("SGE: Open Dialog" "sb_text" "solardat")
("SGE: Open Dialog" "OK")
Deviate
("Root" "dataTable")
("SGE: Table Dialog" "text" 4 "30")
("SGE: Table Dialog" "text" 5 "40")
("SGE: Table Dialog" "OK")
```

The implementation of meander mode is simple: execute the expert script and turn control over to the genetic algorithm when the *DEVIATE* command is encountered. The reward system then identifies genes that stay on the same window.

Pullback mode relies on the ability to look ahead to the next command in the expert script when processing a *DEVIATE* command. To implement pullback mode,

- The script processor acquires the window name (next_window) and the widget name (next_widget) of the next command. As the gene generates new events, each allele provides input to a named window (allele_window) and widget (allele_widget).
- The reward system scores are based on the following comparisons:
  1. allele_window <> next_window and allele_widget <> next_widget. This is a miss; the gene gets no points.
  2. allele_window <> next_window and allele_widget = next_widget. The gene gets 10 points because getting to a widget with the same name has some value, but we give preference to a gene that generates input for next_window.
  3. allele_window = next_window and allele_widget <> next_widget. This continues the philosophy of rewarding genes that stay on the same window. The gene gets 50 points for getting to the window of the next command. The score accumulates rapidly if the gene stays on the same window.

4. allele_window = next_window and allele_widget = next_widget. This means that the gene has reconnected with the next command. So when the genetic algorithm processor encounters the same window name and the same widget name, interpreting the gene is stopped. The gene is given an artificially high score to make it highly probable that it will survive.

RESULTS ANALYSIS

This section analyzes specific aspects of the prototype:

- Implementation architecture.
- Reward system.
- Impact on test process.

Implementation Architecture

The multi-process implementation architecture proved to be flexible, adaptable, and application independent. The widget tree was correctly captured during execution and keystrokes successfully sent to different AUTs without changing TestDriver. The applications we instrumented were small but did support concurrent dialog sequences. Isolating GenePool let us change the reward system without affecting the basic observe and control loop.

Reward System

We quickly discovered that implementation of the reward system was the most sensitive part of the genetic algorithm. The reward system governs which genes survive to generate a novice-like test script that a tester can keep.

We first tried our reward system to see if the genes could learn to simulate novice-like behavior in a standalone manner. The test script was a single *DEVIATE* command. We varied the genetic algorithm parameters to let the algorithm itself generate novice-like events. At best, the resulting scripts seemed more chimpanzee-like than novice-like. Getting a script to accomplish anything meaningful was unlikely. This occurred because we could not provide any application semantic knowledge based on GUI widgets alone. A higher level specification (as found in a UIMS or process modeler) is needed to insure that a particular run can even open a file.

We then used meander mode and inserted a *DEVIATE* command at the end of an existing expert script. In this way, we were able to open files and do other activities before turning control over to the genetic algorithm. The results were better but could be attributed more to starting with something already done than to the genetic algorithm.

Pullback mode produced the best results. This occurred because pullback mode forces the script back to a state in which the script performs some meaningful activity. We were able to insert more than one *DEVIATE* command in a script to insure that the application could continue to operate through multiple encounters with unpredictable user events.

We have been able to evaluate the 'novice-ness' of the resulting scripts only on an informal basis. We asked other group members to observe a set of automatically generated scripts and collected their feedback. The scripts used with pullback mode were judged to be the best representation of their understanding of novice user behavior.

Impact on Test Process

Our experiments demonstrate the ability to use a small number of inputs to generate a large number of test scripts in an hour. The tester decides how many scripts should be saved as 'winners' that represent novice behavior.

Using automated script generation decreases the total number of scripts that need to be saved and modified as application versions change. Only the parameters that govern genetic algorithm execution are saved. Therefore, new novice scripts can be regenerated for a new user interface and application. The regeneration process does not guarantee identical scripts because the application dialog state changes when the user interface changes.

REMAINING ISSUES

Our implementation resulted in a framework that can be used to simulate novice user behavior and solve some real problems. It provides a basis that demonstrates the potential of automated script generation and can be used for additional projects area to improve:

Test script configuration management. Our approach can be used to generate a large number of novice test scripts quickly. Measures must be developed to determine when enough novice testing has occurred.

Test results evaluation and comparison. The results of each novice test script must be evaluated to insure that the system has worked properly. At a minimum, the novice tests can be used to insure that the application does not break. The applications we tested with the prototype did not fail, which increased our confidence in them. We used manual observation to determine that the applications continued to work properly.

More work is required to develop effective ways for determining that a script produces the proper results. A simple comparison of the results produced by a companion script is inadequate even in pullback mode. The deviation may have deleted or edited data in a way that makes direct results comparison impossible.

Emulation and evaluation of more types of novice user behavior. Additional genetic scoring algorithms and reward systems will expand the repertoire of characterizations of novice user behavior beyond our learning-by-experimentation style.

Care must be taken to formally evaluate the results of any automated techniques to insure their value and validity. The context for such comparisons is well documented (for a good example, see [8]). Usability testing facilities offer a solid technology foundation for conducting real versus automated novice evaluations.

Integration with automated test tools. Given the current implementation of the novice test script generator, the use of genetic algorithms could be incorporated as a new command in any existing widget-based test tool.

Higher level user interface specifications. In the long term, higher level dialog models than a GUI widget tree should be used to generate both application user interface code and test scripts. Automatic UI code generation will decrease user interface state management errors (although application code errors will still occur). Such specifications should be analyzable for usability for experts or novices. Testing will still be needed across multiple user skill levels to determine if program failures occur whether the application is driven by real or simulated events.

CONCLUSION

Using automated test script generation to simulate novice users can be used to help identify application failures earlier than beta test or production. Such failures are costly to fix and frustrating to users, especially novices.

Our technique works best as a companion to automated test tools and expert test scripts. Expert users still must generate complex scripts that exercise an application thoroughly. Genetic algorithms provide a controllable method of emulating novice input events to test an application in an unexpected, but not purely random, way. Including automated novice testing early in the development process should improve overall application quality.

Acknowledgments

Rob Jasper and Dan Murphy of the Boeing Commercial Airplane Group provided insight into the issues involved with testing and genetic algorithms. Keith Butler of Boeing Information and Support Services helped mold early drafts. The SIGCHI referees provided excellent comments as part of their reviews.

REFERENCES

1. Beizer, B. *Software System Testing and Quality Assurance*, Van Nostrand, 1984.
2. Bernhard, P.J. A Reduced Test Suite for Protocol Conformance Testing. *ACM Transactions on Software Engineering and Methodology 3*, 3 (Jul 1994), 201-220.
3. Harbison, S.P. *Modula-3*, Prentice-Hall, 1992.
4. Hartson, H.R. and Hix, D. Human Computer Interface Development: Concepts and Systems. *ACM Computing Surveys 21*, 1 (Mar. 1989), 5-92.
5. Hoare, C.A.R. *Communicating Sequential Processes*, Prentice-Hall International, 1985.
6. Jasper, R., Brennan, M., Williamson, K., Currier, W., and Zimmerman, D. Test Data Generation and Feasible Path Analysis. *International Symposium on Software Testing and Analysis* (Seattle, Aug. 1994).
7. Jensen, K. Coloured Petri Nets: A High Level Language for System Design and Analysis. Advances in Petri Nets 1990 (G. Rozenberg editor), *Lecture Notes in Computer Science 483*, Springer-Verlag, pp. 342-416.
8. Karat, C-M., Campbell, R., and Fiegel, T. Comparison of Empirical Testing and Walkthrough Methods in User Interface Evaluation. *Proc. CHI'92 Human Factors in Computing Systems* (May 1992), ACM Press, 397-404.
9. Kasik, D.J. A User Interface Management System. *Computer Graphics (Proc. SIGGRAPH 82)*, July 1982, ACM Press, pp. 99-106.
10. Kieras, D.E. Towards a Practical GOMS Model Methodology for User Interface Design. *Handbook of Human-Computer Interaction* (M. Helander editor), Elsevier Science, 1988, pp. 135-157.
11. Michalewicz, Z. *Genetic Algorithms + Data Structures = Evolution Programs*, Springer-Verlag, 1992.
12. Myers, B.A. and Rosson, M.B. Survey on User Interface Programming. *Proc. CHI'92 Human Factors in Computing Systems* (May 1992), ACM Press, 195-202.
13. Myers, G.J. *The Art of Software Testing*, Van Nostrand, 1978.
14. Olsen, D.R. *User Interface Management Systems: Models and Algorithms*, Morgan Kaufmann, 1992.
15. Palanque, P., Bastide, R., Dourte, L., and Sibertin-Blanc, C. Design of User-Driven Interfaces Using Petri Nets and Objects. *Proc. Advanced Information Systems Engineering: 5th International Conference, CAiSE 93*, Springer-Verlag, pp. 569-585.
16. Parker, T. Automated Software Testing. *Unix Review*, January 1995, pp. 49-56.
17. Peterson, J.L. *Petri Net Theory and the Modeling of Systems*, Prentice-Hall, 1981.
18. Rudnick, E., Patel, J., Greenstein, G., and Niewmann, T. Sequential Circuit Generation in a Genetic Algorithm Framework. *Proc. 31st Design Automation Conference* (Jun 1994), 698-704.
19. vanBiljon, W.R. Extending Petri Nets for Specifying Man-machine Dialogues. *International Journal Man-Machine Studies 28*, 1988, 437-455.

Pavlov: Programming By *Stimulus-Response* Demonstration

David Wolber
Department of Computer Science, University of San Francisco
2130 Fulton St., San Francisco, CA., 94117-1080
(415) 666-6451
wolber@usfca.edu

ABSTRACT
Pavlov is a Programming By Demonstration (PBD) system that allows animated interfaces to be created without programming. Using a drawing editor and a clock, designers specify the behavior of a target interface by demonstrating stimuli (end-user actions or time) and the (time-stamped) graphical transformations that should be executed in response. This stimulus-response model allows interaction and animation to be defined in a uniform manner, and it allows for the demonstration of *interactive animation*, i.e., game-like behaviors in which the end-user (player) controls the speed and direction of object movement.

KEYWORDS
End User Programming, UIMS, Programming By Demonstration, Programming By Example, Animation

INTRODUCTION
A visitor to our planet might deduce that most computer users have the necessary skills to quickly and easily graphical user interfaces (GUIs). First, computer users know what they want: any user of today's popular applications is now quite capable of delivering a detailed (and passionate!) discussion on the strengths and flaws of computer interfaces. Second, most computer users have the mechanical skills required to demonstrate the appearance and behavior of an interface: anyone that has used a drawing editor knows how to draw objects with a computer, click on them, and transform them.

But today's development tools have yet to fully tap the potential of the computer user. Though interface builders like Visual Basic have significantly decreased the time and expertise necessary to build *standard* interfaces, the development of more graphical, animated interfaces is still mostly performed by skilled programmers. This time-consuming and costly development is particularly unfortunate given the exploding demand for computer games, interactive entertainment, and animation in even "standard" interfaces, and the recognized importance of more end-user participation in designing interfaces. There has been some progress: an entire book has been published describing research systems that allow interfaces to be created or extended by demonstration rather than programming [2] ; commercially, tools like Macromedia's *Director* allow non-programmers to develop animation and some interaction.

CHI 96 Vancouver, BC Canada
© 1996 ACM 0-89791-777-4/96/04..$3.50

But none of these systems cohesively combine interactive techniques for specifying end-user interaction, graphical transformation, and timing, the three primary ingredients of an animated interface. *Director* is powerful for specifying transformation and timing, but designing simple interaction requires some programming, and more complex interaction requires an expert. The Programming By Demonstration (PBD) systems in [2] present powerful techniques for specifying transformation and some interaction, but do not provide the timing mechanisms necessary for animation.

This paper presents Pavlov, a GUI development system based on the *stimulus-response* model. Stimulus-response provides a cohesive model for demonstrating interaction, transformation, and timing. The model seeks to minimize the cognitive dissonance between concept and design by allowing designers to demonstrate the behavior of an interface exactly as they think of it: "When I do A, B occurs", or "two seconds after the start of the program, this animation begins." Beginning with a blank *target interface*, tabula rasa if you will, the designer uses a drawing tool to draw the interface, then uses the same tool and a clock to demonstrate stimulus-response pairs. In essence, the designer teaches the system in a way that is intuitive to humans:

> The basic physiological function of the cerebral hemisphere throughout the subsequent individual life consists in a constant addition of numberless signaling conditioned stimuli to the limited number of in-born unconditional stimuli, in other words, in constantly supplementing the unconditioned reflexes by conditioned ones.
>
> Ivan Petrovich Pavlov

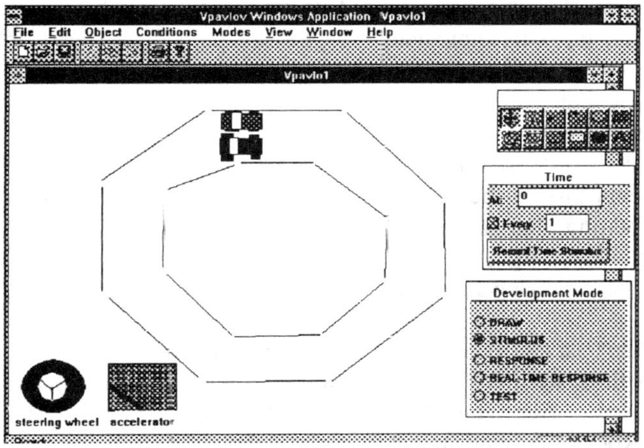

Figure 1. Pavlov Development of a Driving Simulator

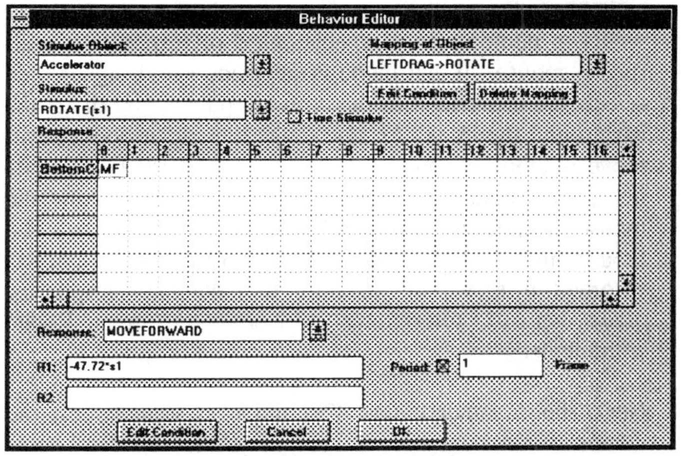

Figure 2. The Pavlov Editor

This stimulus-response model was first used in the author's DEMO system [13] to demonstrate *non-animated* interface behaviors. The model has been extended in Pavlov so that an interface can be taught about time, periodic activity, and the inherent *direction* of some objects. These extensions allow animation as well as interaction to be designed *within the stimulus-response framework*. It is this intersection between animation and interaction, not animation per se, that distinguishes Pavlov from other PBD systems. Because of it, designers can demonstrate most behaviors that combine interaction and animation, including game-like behaviors in which the end-user (player) controls the speed and direction of object movement.

A DRIVING SIMULATOR EXAMPLE

In the driving simulator, the top car begins moving when the program begins, follows a pre-defined path around the track, then stops near its starting point. The bottom car begins moving only when the driver rotates the "accelerator". Its speed and direction is controlled by the driver (the end-user) manipulating the accelerator and the steering wheel.

Figure 1 shows the Pavlov environment during development of the driving simulator (also see the Video Figure in the CHI 96 Video Program). The basic tools are the drawing editor in the top-right corner, the clock (middle-right), and the Development Mode Palette (lower-right). The designer uses the development modes to inform the system as to whether s/he is just drawing the interface (Draw mode), demonstrating an end-user or time stimulus (Stimulus mode), demonstrating how the system should respond to a stimulus (Response or Real-Time Response mode), or testing an interface (Test mode). The designer uses the clock to demonstrate when an operation should be executed (using the top *At:* box), or if an operation should be executed periodically (the middle *Every:* box). The lower button on the clock, labeled *Record Time Stimulus*, allows the designer to specify that the following responses should be triggered by time.

Another important part of the environment is the editor, shown in Figure 2. This editor displays a textual description of the interface being designed. It serves to provide feedback to a designer as demonstrations are performed, and it allows the designer to modify the behaviors "learned" by the system when necessary. Details of this editor are provided later in the paper.

The first task in creating the Drawing Simulator is to draw the two cars, the road, the accelerator, and the steering wheel. To do so, the designer selects Draw mode from the Development Mode Palette, and makes use of the graphic primitives and grouping mechanisms available in the drawing palette. He also provides names to the drawn objects for later reference.

Next, the designer begins specifying the behavior of the interface. Because s/he wants the two objects shaped like cars to move as cars do, s/he selects each, chooses Object | Set Direction from the menu and enters an angle that defines the *direction attribute* of the particular car. In the simulator, both cars initially face straight ahead on the x-axis, so the designer sets the angle to 0. A vector emanating from its center appears on each car to signify that the car will only move forward and backward in relation to its direction, and must be rotated to change direction. The vector does not appear during execution of the target interface.

The designer is now ready to demonstrate the stimulus-response behavior of the top car. In this case, the stimulus is time: at time 0 (the beginning of execution) the car should begin moving. To demonstrate, the designer selects Stimulus mode, sets the clock *At:* box to 0, and clicks on the Record Time Stimulus button. The system reports that a *time stimulus* has been recorded, and automatically switches to Response mode. For this behavior, the designer wants to demonstrate a special kind of response, a real-time response, so that mode is selected. The designer then selects the move icon in the drawing palette and drags the car around the track. As s/he drags the car, it doesn't ever move diagonally, but instead moves forward towards its nose, and rotates its base (turns) in order to follow the mouse around the track. After the designer releases the mouse button, s/he sees from the editor that the system has recorded a series of discrete, time-stamped responses, made up of alternating MoveForward and Rotate commands.

Next, the designer enters Test mode to visually test the demonstrated behavior. Immediately, the top car begins moving and follows the path that was demonstrated. The designer knows s/he could edit the recorded responses in the editor to modify the path, but for now s/he is satisfied with the behavior of the top car.

The designer then turns his attention to the bottom car. The bottom car's behavior is not triggered by time, but by an end-user action. Thus, instead of demonstrating a time stimulus, the designer plays the role of the end-user and demonstrates an action. After entering Stimulus mode, s/he selects the Rotate icon in the drawing palette, presses the left-mouse button on the rectangle denoting the accelerator, and rotates it clockwise some amount, say -0.36 radians. The system reports that a stimulus was recorded and automatically switches the development mode to Response. The system also records an implicit stimulus-response descriptor mapping the physical action used to the higher-level operation:

(1) On Accelerator.LeftDrag --> Accelerator.Rotate

At this point, the designer needs to demonstrate that the rotation of the accelerator should cause a response of accelerating the movement of the bottom car. First, s/he enters 1 in the *Every:* box of the clock. S/he knows that this will cause the upcoming demonstrated response to be executed periodically every time frame in the target interface. Next, s/he moves the car some amount, say 17 units. Because the car is a "directed" object, the car's movement is restricted: it can only be moved on the vector defined by its direction arrow (note that in Real-Time Response mode this vector is allowed to change). This restriction is as the designer desired: in response to the rotation of the accelerator, s/he wants the car to *move forward*, not change direction. The system reports the recorded stimulus-response descriptor containing a proportional constant (-47.22 = 17/-.36)

(2) On Accelerator.Rotate(s1)-->
BottomCar.MoveForward(-47.22*s1) At 0 Every 1

Next, the designer enters Test mode to check his work. The top car immediately begins its path. The designer, playing the role of the end-user, rotates the accelerator. The bottom car begins moving, and continues to move even after the designer releases the mouse from the accelerator. As the car leaves the right side of the screen, it reappears on the left. The designer again experiments with rotating the accelerator and notices that rotating it clockwise speeds up the car, while rotating it counter-clockwise slows it down.

The designer is nearly satisfied but thinks the accelerator is a little sensitive. He enters the editor (see Figure 2) and selects "Accelerator" as the stimulus object. The stimulus "Rotate(s1)" appears in the box labeled stimulus, and a single response appears in the first cell of the score row labeled BottomCar. The response box below the score contains the response "MoveForward". Its parameter, as in descriptor (2) above, is -47.22*s1. The period box contains "1". To reduce how much the car speeds up in response to the rotate, the designer changes the proportional factor from -47 to -30.0. (alternatively, the period could have been increased). When s/he re-enters Test mode, s/he is satisfied to see that the accelerator is indeed less sensitive.

The next task is to specify the behavior of the steering wheel so the end-user can control the direction of the bottom car. The designer enters Stimulus mode and rotates the steering wheel. Then, in Response mode, s/he sets the *Every:* box in the clock to 1, and rotates the bottom car. The following descriptor is recorded:

(3) On Wheel.Rotate(s1)-->
BottomCar.Rotate(0.25*s1) At 0 Every 1

To test this new behavior, the designer once again enters Test mode. The top car immediately begins its path. The designer rotates the accelerator to get the bottom car moving, then releases the accelerator and rotates the steering wheel to control its direction. He is pleased to note that s/he was correct to set the *Every:* box before demonstrating the rotation of the bottom car: just like a real one, the car continues to turn if the steering wheel remains rotated from its original setting.

The designer continues to test the interface, and soon realizes that if s/he rotates the accelerator counter-clockwise past its origin, the car begins moving backward. To alleviate this problem, s/he uses the editor to delete the previously recorded accelerator behavior, and then re-demonstrates it. First, in Draw mode, s/he sets the top-left point of the accelerator on the left edge of the enclosing rectangle and chooses *Conditions | Generate* from the menu. Then s/he demonstrates the stimulus of rotating the accelerator. A dialog appears listing a set of graphical conditions relating the stimulus object to other objects in the interface. The designer selects the condition "Accelerator.Within(EnclosingRectangle)", and the system records a modified version of the originally recorded stimulus-response descriptor (1).

(4) On Accelerator.LeftDrag --> Accelerator.Rotate
When Accelerator.Within(EnclosingRectangle)

The designer proceeds to demonstrate the response of moving the car forward, as s/he did in the first iteration. Afterwards, s/he re-enters Test mode, and is satisfied to see that s/he (playing the role of the end-user) is restricted from rotating the accelerator outside its enclosing rectangle. Since the top-left point of the accelerator begins on the left edge of the enclosing rectangle, there is no way to rotate it counter-clockwise past its origin, so the car cannot move backward.

THE STIMULUS-RESPONSE MODEL

The driving simulator example illustrates many features of the stimulus-response model, including the extensions that allow interactive animation to be defined. This section describes the model in more general terms in order to 1) explain the inferences made by the system in the example, and 2) bridge the gap between the specific and the general, i.e., persuade the reader that Pavlov is useful for designing all kinds of interfaces, not just driving simulators.

An interface is viewed as a stimulus-response machine. Stimuli are either physical actions (e.g., drag the mouse while pressing the left-button), higher level operations, or time. The interface responds to stimuli by executing a set of time-stamped operations. Operations either create, transform, or delete objects. The set of operations includes the primitives found in most drawing editors and one additional primitive, *move forward*. This additional primitive allows an object to be moved while constrained to the vector defined by its direction attribute. Together, the operations offer the base functionality necessary to demonstrate nearly all animated interface behaviors.

The Semantics of Stimulus-Response

The challenge of a stimulus-response development system is to provide clear syntax and semantics for how the designer uses the set of physical actions and operations to demonstrate the behavior of the target interface. The "syntax" of Pavlov is straight forward: the designer changes development modes to inform the system whether his intent is to draw, demonstrate a stimulus or response, or test the interface.

Providing clear semantics is a more challenging problem: the goal is for the system to always record a stimulus-response descriptor that perfectly matches the intent of the designer's demonstration (this is the primary challenge of all PBD systems). Pavlov uses an *explanation-based learning* approach: from a single demonstration of a stimulus-response pair, the system uses domain knowledge and the information provided by the demonstration to record as reasonable a stimulus-response descriptor as possible. If necessary, the designer can then use Pavlov's powerful editing facilities to modify the descriptor.

This simplistic strategy differs from other systems that allow a designer to refine behavior descriptions through multiple demonstrations. Such an *empirical-based learning* approach allows more complex behavior to be specified, but complicates the semantics of the system.

The Semantics of a Stimulus Demonstration

In Stimulus mode, the designer demonstrates the operations the end-user can perform in the target interface. When the designer performs an operation in this mode, Pavlov records 1) a stimulus-response pair mapping the physical action used to the operation that was executed, and 2) the first part of a second stimulus-response pair that will eventually map the operation to one or more operations demonstrated as the response.

Mapping the physical action to the operation is important because the drawing palette used during development to demonstrate operations does not appear when the target interface is executed (Test mode). In Test mode, the end-user can only use the operations that the designer has explicitly demonstrated as stimuli, and can only access those operations using the physical action (mouse button, auxiliary key) used in the demonstration. For example, in the driving simulator the end-user can only rotate the accelerator by dragging the mouse with the left-mouse button down, because that is how it was demonstrated. The designer cannot manipulate the car directly in any manner, because no such stimulus was demonstrated. This positive example method of specifying the functionality of the system is in contrast to the scheme of [9] in which the designer "freezes" the objects that cannot be manipulated.

The second recording made from a Stimulus demonstration records the high-level operation demonstrated as a stimulus (e.g., Accelerator.Rotate). It is the execution of this high-level stimulus that will trigger the execution of the responses demonstrated in Response mode.

The only complication to the semantics of a stimulus demonstration is that a designer may demonstrate a stimulus on a *representative* object. At run-time, the same stimulus applied to any member of the set represented will trigger the demonstrated response. Dynamically allocated objects, which can be specified by creating an object in stimulus or response mode (see [13]), are by default marked as representative objects. Pavlov also allows the designer to designate behavior groups, and marks each element as representative of the group (a similar approach is used in [12]).

The Semantics of a Response Demonstration

When the designer demonstrates an operation R on object O in response mode, the system connects a response of the form "O.R $(r_1,r_2,...)$ when C" to the previously demonstrated stimulus, where each r_i is a function of zero or more stimulus parameters, and C is an optional context for when R should be executed.

The simplest semantic rule is to execute the demonstrated response each time the demonstrated stimulus occurs in the target interface. However, such a simple rule would preclude the designer from demonstrating the context for when an operation should be executed; semantics such as "execute R is response to stimulus S only when the environment is in state s" could not be demonstrated.

By setting a toggle, the Pavlov designer explicitly states if context should be taken into account. If it is, the designer configures the interface into the desired context (or the negation of the desired context) prior to a response demonstration. After the demonstration, the system runs a set of tests to identify graphical conditions describing the state of the interface. The designer is allowed to select one or more of these conditions and combine them with logical operators to define the context for when a response should be executed.

In the driving simulator, a context was defined on the description mapping the physical stimulus "Accelerator.LeftDrag" and the response "Accelerator.Rotate". A context could also be demonstrated so that the bottom car doesn't run into the top one: the designer demonstrates the stimulus of rotating the accelerator, tells the system to identify context, then demonstrates a response of moving the bottom car so that it intersects the top car. When the system identifies BottomCar.Intersects(TopCar) amongst other conditions, the designer selects it and negates it, and the following behavior is recorded:

```
(5) On Accelerator.Rotate(s1)->
      BottomCar.MoveForward(47.22*s1)  At 0 Every 1
        When  Not (BottomCar.Intersects(TopCar))
```

In general, there are many true conditions concerning the state of the interface. To reduce the number of conditions listed for the designer, the system only identifies those conditions relating the response object and all other objects in the interface. Because the stimulus object has also been signified as important, relationships found concerning it and the response object are shown at the top of the list of found conditions. When necessary, the designer can use the editor to specify a condition not identified by the system.

A second complication to the response semantics is similar to that discussed in the stimulus section: if the demonstrated response object is representative of a set, the response is applied to the entire set during execution (or a subset, as defined by a context conditional [13]).

A third complication to the response semantics concerns determining the response parameters. The simplest solution is, of course, to execute R during execution with the same parameters as in the demonstration. This is the best solution when the corresponding stimulus has no parameters (e.g., the stimulus is a button click and the response is a move(x=5,y=7)). However, for stimuli that do have parameters, it is often the case that the reaction is proportional, i.e., the response parameter(s) are proportional to the parameters of the stimulus. For instance, the car in the Driving Simulator is rotated an amount proportional to the amount the steering wheel is rotated. Thus, when such a stimulus-response is demonstrated, Pavlov infers proportional constants $C_i = r_i/s_i$ that relate each of the stimulus and response parameters. When the stimulus $S(s_1,s_2,...)$ occurs during execution, the response $R(s_1{*}C_1,\ s_2{*}\ C_2)$ is executed.

The formula for R illustrates that the system infers the first parameter of the stimulus to be related to the first parameter of the response, the second to the second, and so on. The basis of this inference is that most interface operations either have a single parameter or they have two parameters denoting x and y coordinates, so in practice the corresponding stimulus and response are often related. As with conditionals, the editor can be used to modify the response formulas recorded.

EXTENSIONS FOR ANIMATION

Systems for demonstrating animation have existed for over twenty-five years [1]. Pavlov's contribution is the integration of animation demonstration with the stimulus-response model for defining interaction.

An animation path can be demonstrated with a real-time response demonstration, with a series of time-stamped response demonstrations (the editor can be used for in-betweening), or with a periodic response. Like any other response, an animation path can be triggered by any kind of end-user or time stimulus.

When a designer demonstrates the transformation of an object in real-time response mode, the system records a series of time-stamped operations. Because operations are recorded instead of picture frames (as in *Director*), the recorded path is not constrained to a particular starting point or object. Thus, reuse is facilitated. The mechanism is also slightly more general than in systems such as *Director* because any operation, not just move, can be demonstrated in real-time.

A Notion of Direction

An important contribution of Pavlov is that a designer can demonstrate animation in which the end-user not only initiates movement, but accelerates it and changes its direction. Though such behavior is the primary activity in many game-like applications, there has been little research in this area, and commercial systems such as *Director* require extensive programming to develop this part of an application.

From struggling with how to allow game-like behavior to be demonstrated, the following observations were made: In many games, one input control (e.g., steering wheel) is used to control direction, and a different control (accelerator) to control speed. Also, many objects do not move in an arbitrary manner, but are restricted to moving forward and backward, and must rotate their base to turn. From these observations it became clear that the standard Move(x,y) operation in Pavlov's drawing editor is not sufficient for the demonstration of movement because it specifies both a distance and an absolute direction.

To solve the problem, a notion of direction was added to the stimulus-response model. Designers can set a *current direction* attribute for an object that is displayed during development. The direction attribute makes it possible for the designer to demonstrate a *MoveForward(d)* operation. This operation causes an object to move forward (or backward, if d<0) in the direction it is facing. Thus, it is much better suited for the demonstration of acceleration than Move(x,y).

Periodic Responses

The notion of a periodic response is also useful in demonstrating acceleration. In the driving simulator, when the end-user rotates the accelerator, the car should begin moving and *continue to move*, even after the end-user releases the mouse. In Pavlov, the designer explicitly specifies continuous movement by setting the *Every:* box on the clock before the demonstration of a forward movement. In essence, when a "MoveForward (d) Every t" is demonstrated, the system infers that the object should move forward at a speed of d/t.

The following run-time rule follows from these semantics: the execution of successive periodic MoveForward operations on the same object results not in two alternating and possibly opposite actions, but in a single action combining the magnitudes of the operations. For example, in the driving simulator, when the car is already moving at 4 units/frame and the end-user rotates the accelerator again, say back towards the origin, it causes a response of MoveForward (-1) units/frame. This second operation is combined with the existing one so that the car slows down to 4-1=3 units/frame, instead of alternating between moving forward 4 units, and backward 1 unit.

The system only uses these semantics for periodic MoveForward operations. For other operations, successive periodic responses will execute in tandem. Thus, using two periodic, regular Move demonstrations, the designer can demonstrate that an object move back and forth, such as in an *animated move icon.*

An alternative method of demonstrating acceleration has also been added to the Pavlov environment. After demonstrating a stimulus that should cause the acceleration, the designer enters *real-time* response mode and moves an object forward at the desired speed. Generally, a real-time response is used to demonstrate a fixed animation path as a response to a simple button-click or time. When a real-time Move Forward is demonstrated as a response to a transformational stimulus (one with parameters), the system does not record a series of discrete time-stamped operations as usual, but instead records a single periodic operation. The distance parameter is computed by dividing the total distance of the demonstrated movement by the time of the movement (d/t), and the period is set to 1 (ms).

The advantage of this scheme is that the designer truly demonstrates the speed of the movement; the disadvantage is it complicates the semantics of the system. A more thorough analysis will be provided after more feedback is gathered from users.

THE PAVLOV EDITOR

An important aspect of a PBD system is how a designer edits the behaviors inferred by the system. Pavlov's editor borrows from *Director* by providing a time-line view of activity (a score). However, because interaction is emphasized, Pavlov provides multiple timelines: one for the events that occur without an end-user stimulus, and one for the events triggered by each end-user stimulus that was demonstrated. This method of organizing events by stimulus significantly eases the editing task compared to the single score editors found in most animation systems.

Pavlov's editor, shown in Figure 2, can be viewed simultaneously with the main development window. In order to view the operations that occur in response to a particular stimulus, the designer selects an object and a particular stimulus in the top-left list boxes. To view the operations that occur without an end-user stimulus, the designer selects the "Time Stimulus" check box to the right of the stimulus list.

The objects that respond to the listed stimulus are shown in the rows of the score. The designer can select a particular response in a cell, and the inferred response parameters appear in the edit boxes labeled R1 and R2. Any expression consisting of constants, stimuli parameters, and system-supplied object attribute functions may be entered as a response parameter. In essence, editing behavior formulas is very similar to entering a formula in a spreadsheet.

IMPLEMENTATION

At the beginning of execution (Test mode), the time stimulated operations defined in the target interface are placed in the *execution list* with their respective time stamps. For each end-user stimulus that occurs, the *sr processor* traverses the selected object's stimulus-response list to find the response operations associated with the stimulus. These responses are copied into the execution list with a time-stamp of $t + t_r$, where t is the time the stimulus occurred (the current time), and t_r is the recorded time-stamp of the response (which is relative to the stimulus). When the system is not processing end-user stimuli in this manner, the execution list is traversed and all operations whose time-stamp is less than the current time are executed. A non-periodic operation is removed from the execution list immediately after execution; a periodic operation is left in the list, with its time-stamp incremented by the size of its periodic interval. In either case, the executed operation is sent as a stimulus to the sr processor, so a chaining of events can occur.

Though the scheme does not guarantee that operations will be executed before or on their time-stamp, in practice it provides visually acceptable performance even for interfaces with lots of interaction and concurrent animation (Pavlov runs on a 486 PC).

RELATED RESEARCH

Rehearsal World [5] and *Peridot* [7] were early PBD systems that inspired the stimulus-response framework. The first systems to allow direct graphical demonstration of a full range of stimuli and responses were *DEMO* [13] and *Marquise* [8]. *DEMO* introduced the stimulus-response model and a technique for demonstrating dynamically created objects, while *Marquise* focused on the demonstration of graphical editors, including those with palettes and modes.

DEMO II [3] and [4] are stimulus-response systems that allow the designer to perform multiple demonstrations of the same behavior to refine the system's inferences. [4] uses multiple examples to make sophisticated inferences concerning response parameters-- inferred formulas may depend on attributes of arbitrary objects as well as stimulus parameter values. *DEMO II* uses multiple examples to refine inferences concerning the context for when a response should be executed.

Pavlov is the first *stimulus-response* system to focus on animation, though there are a few PBD systems not based on stimulus-response that allow some animation to be demonstrated: *KidSim* [12] and *Agent Sheets* [10] use graphical rewrite rules to allow designers to demonstrate the context for when an operation should be executed. The systems are powerful for creating non-interactive simulations, but the rewrite-rule method of defining context is not integrated with a method of specifying end-user stimuli, so interactive simulations cannot be designed without coding; *Dance* [11] allows the demonstration of animation for the purpose of program visualization. *Chimera* [6] and *LEMMING* [9] allow interface behavior to be specified with multiple demonstrations of *constraints*, but do not cover time-based animation or acceleration.

Director is representative of the commercial animation systems that provide facilities for both animation and interaction design. These systems allow animation to be designed quickly and easily using a combination of frame-by-frame animation, in-betweening, and real-time recording. These systems also allow sound and video to be linked into presentations, and provide a range of features for creating special effects such as *slow-in/slow-out*, *motion blur*, and *squash and stretch*.

Though powerful for defining animation, these systems do not provide a PBD method of defining interaction. The systems all allow button-click triggered animation to be defined in a relatively simple manner. However, more complex stimulus-response behaviors, such as the steering-wheel and accelerator controlled animation in the driving simulator, require expert-level programming.

A second difficulty in defining interaction with animation systems is that they are based on a single-score editor: all the animation sequences of an application are shown on a single time-line. Though such a score is sufficient for non-interactive animation (which was its original purpose), it is too unstructured for applications with interactive as well as time-stimulated animation. Like the programs written before the advent of structured programming (sub-procedures), the designer is forced to program control, i.e., where one animation ends and another begins, using *goto* statements. For complex applications with lots of movement and interaction, the result is a *spaghetti score*.

The multiple score scheme in the Pavlov editor alleviates this problem, and allows the designer to edit the different interactive behaviors and animation sequences separately.

LIMITATIONS

The major practical limitation of Pavlov is that interfaces created with it cannot be connected to application code. In the next version, designers will be able to make this connection by 1) demonstrating a function call as a stimulus or response, and 2) calling an application function within a response or conditional formula. Pavlov's single demonstration scheme might also be considered a limitation: more behaviors could be inferred if a multiple demonstration inference engine, such as [4], was integrated. Before doing so, however, we want to study whether the additional inferred operations justify the additional complexity that would be added to the environment. A third limitation is that *acceleration* can be demonstrated for an object that has no pre-defined path, but cannot be demonstrated for an object that must stay on a *fixed path.* In this regard, we are exploring both the use of parametric functions to model some animation paths, and the use of "conductor" objects with special properties [10].

SUMMARY

Pavlov contributes a cohesive model for demonstrating animation and interaction, and innovative techniques for demonstrating interfaces in which the end-user controls both the speed and direction of animation paths. Using these techniques, interfaces like the driving simulator can be created in less than fifteen minutes.

Development is by no means restricted to driving simulators or similar applications. A number of other interfaces have also been developed, including a wide variety of games, a diagram editor with animated icons, and an educational solar system program. We attribute the general usefulness of Pavlov to the generality of the stimulus-response model, and its powerful multiple-score-based editing facility.

Besides increasing the range of PBD, the stimulus-response model provides a very intuitive method for defining interfaces. A usability test was performed with a number of non-technical designers. Subjects were given a manual describing the stimulus-response model, and then were asked to design two interfaces equal in complexity to the driving simulator. Seven of ten were able to create the interfaces within an hour; the three others completed the tasks after asking a few questions (specific questions concerning how to complete the tasks were not allowed). We were extremely encouraged by the results, as well as the enthusiasm the subjects expressed for exploring once the formal tests were completed (though we could get none to salivate!).

REFERENCES

1. Baecker, R., Picture-Driven Animation, *Proceedings of the Spring Joint Computer Conf.*, AFIPS Press, 1969, pp. 273-288.
2. Cypher, A., ed., *Watch What I Do: Programming By Demonstration*, MIT Press, Cambridge, Mass., 1993.
3. Fisher, G., Busse, D.,and Wolber, D.,"Adding Rule Based Reasoning to a Demonstrational Interface Builder,*Proceedings of UIST'92*,Nov. 1992, pp.89-97.
4. Frank, M. and Foley, J., "A Pure Reasoning Engine for Programming By Demonstration", *Proceedings of UIST '94*, Nov. 1994, pp. 95-102.
5. Gould, L. and Finzer, W., "Programming By Rehearsal", *Byte,* v. 9, no. 6., 1984.
6. Kurlander, D. and Feiner, S., "Inferring Constraints from Multiple Snapshots", *ACM Transcations on Graphics*, May, 1991.
7. Myers, B., *Creating User Interfaces By Demonstration*, Academic Press, San Diego, 1988.
8. Myers, B., McDaniel,R.,Kosbie, D.,"Marquise: Creating Complete User Interfaces By Demonstration, *Proceedings of INTERCHI '93*, Amsterdam, April,1993, pp.293-300.
9. Olsen, D., Ahlstrom, B., Kohlert, D., ,"Building Geometry- based Widgets by Example", *Proceedings of CHI '95*, May, 1995, pp.35-42.
10. Repenning, A., "Agent Sheets: A Medium for Creating Domain-Oriented Visual Languages", *Computer*, V.28, 1995, pp. 17-25.
11. Stasko, J., "Using Direct Manipulation To Build Algorithm Animations By Demonstration", *Proceedings of CHI '91*, 1991, pp. 307-314.
12. Smith, D.C., Cypher A., "KidSim: End-User Programming of Simulations", *Proceedings of CHI '95*,May 1995, pp.27-34.
13. Wolber, D., and Fisher, Gene, "A Demonstrational Technique for Developing Interfaces with Dynamically Created Objects." *Proc. of UIST '91*, 1991, pp. 221-230.

Reusable Hierarchical Command Objects

Brad A. Myers
Human Computer Interaction Institute
School of Computer Science
Carnegie Mellon University
Pittsburgh, PA 15213
bam@cs.cmu.edu
http://www.cs.cmu.edu/~bam

David S. Kosbie
Microsoft Corporation
One Microsoft Way
Redmond, WA 98052
dkosbie@microsoft.com

ABSTRACT

The Amulet user interface development environment uses hierarchical command objects to support the creation of highly-interactive graphical user interfaces. When input arrives or a widget is operated by the user, instead of invoking a call-back procedure as in most other toolkits, Amulet allocates a command object and calls its DO method. Unlike previous uses of command objects, Amulet organizes the commands into a hierarchy, so that low-level operations like dragging or selection invoke low-level commands, which in turn might invoke widget-level commands, which invoke high-level, application-specific commands, and so on. The top-level commands correspond to semantic actions of the program. The result is better modularization because different levels of the user interface are independent, and better code reuse because the lower-level commands, and even many high-level commands such as cut, copy, paste, text edit, and change-color, can be reused from the library. Furthermore, the commands in Amulet support a new form of Undo, where the user can select any previous operation and selectively undo it, repeat it on the same objects, or repeat it on new objects. In addition, operations like scrolling and selections can be undone or repeated, which can be very useful. Thus, the command objects in Amulet make it easier for developers by providing more reusable components, while at the same time providing new capabilities for users.

KEYWORDS: Amulet, User Interface Development Environment, Toolkits, Command Objects, Undo, Redo.

INTRODUCTION

One of the primary and oldest software engineering principles is to use a "layered architecture," where each layer "is a useful subset of the system" [9]. It would seem that user interface software would naturally decompose into these layers. For example, deleting a file in the finder might decompose into a delete operation, a drag-icon operation, and a low-level object-follows-mouse operation.

Unfortunately, today's toolkits and user interface environments do not support layered software design well, especially for the handling of the users' inputs. Typically, the window manager sends the hardware-level mouse and keyboard events, which the application code directly handles. When using widgets like buttons and menus, the programmer does not have to deal with the low-level events, but programmers still find that the "call-back procedures" invoked by the widgets often become an unstructured and unlayered maze of code. Furthermore, the widgets' implementations are not layered: they directly handle the hardware events. Other toolkits have tried to increase the modularity and reuse by providing a *single* layer. For example, Garnet [6] provides Interactors to handle low-level input, Gina [1] and MacApp [12] provide a single "command" layer, Chiron-1 [10] has the "Artist" layer, and the Macintosh provides the "Apple Events" layer. In all of these systems, the result is that programmers find it difficult to modularize their implementation, because the code must be "factored" into exactly two layers. Since most of the behavior is implemented in application-specific code, there is less reuse of code.

To address these problems, Amulet provides *hierarchical command objects*, where each application-level operation is typically implemented using a number of layers of command objects. This is based on the PhD research on "hierarchical events" by the second author [3, 4, 5]. Instead of invoking a call-back procedure, all interaction techniques and widgets allocate a command object and call its DO method. The DO method will take some action, store any data needed for UNDO, and then invoke the DO method of a higher-level command. For example, when the user selects a menu item to delete a graphical object, the mouse events are first passed to a general-purpose "Choice-Interactor" object [6] which can handle any kind of selection. The DO method in the command object associated with that Interactor calls the command object associated with the menu, which knows how to update the feedback to show which menu item is selected. This command object in turn calls the higher-level Cut command, which removes the object from the window and stores it in the invisible clipboard, as well as in the command object to support undo. Another use for hierarchical commands supports modal dialog boxes. The widgets of a dialog box typically should *not* cause any effect until the OK button is selected. Amulet groups all the commands from the dialog boxes as children of the dialog box's high-level command.

The hierarchical nature of Amulet's commands promotes reuse, since the various layers of Amulet provide libraries of commands that can be used by applications, usually *without change*. For example, the basic low-level text field editing, mouse-based selection, and mouse-based moving and growing of objects are supported by built-in commands. These command objects also support undoing of the operations. Higher-level commands, such as cut, copy, paste, delete, object creation, object property changing (such as changing a color or line-style), are also supplied. Unlike some systems like MacApp, commands in Amulet are used for all application-specific behaviors, including directly manipulating objects. These custom behaviors can often be achieved by simply linking a new command as the parent of an existing command, and then the system will perform (and undo) both. The custom command does not have to repeat any of the code in the lower-level commands.

In addition to increasing the modularity and reuse of code, Amulet's command objects also support a powerful undo mechanism. One of the most difficult tasks when programming an interactive application is providing *undo* for every operation. Thus, while most commercial applications provide Undo, very few research ones do. Because supporting user interface researchers is an important goal of Amulet, the undo mechanism is easy-to-use, flexible and entirely replaceable. So far, we have developed three different undo mechanisms. One is a Macintosh-like single undo, and another supports conventional multiple undo, where the user can undo all operations in sequence. The third form is an innovative *selective undo* mechanism that allows the user to select any previous operation and undo it, as in Gina [1]. Unlike Gina, Amulet also allows the user to *repeat* any previous operation, and to repeat previous operation on a different set of objects. This allows the user to express with a single command, "change the color of *these* objects to be the same as the color that I set *that* object to."

This new undo mechanism also allows the user to easily undo or repeat supporting operations like selections and scrolling. It is common that setting up a complex selection will take a number of steps. The user might accidently clear the selection with a single click in the wrong place. In other systems, the user then needs to start over, but in Amulet, the user can simply undo the last incorrect selection action. Undoing and repeating scrolling is useful when the user wants to repeatedly switch among two or more specific locations in a document. By combining this feature with Amulet's general-purpose facility that allows any command to be marked and executed with a single keystroke, the user can easily set up "bookmarks" in any application, and even in scrollable file lists.

Another innovation in Amulet's undo mechanism is that when a command operates on multiple objects, users can undo the command on a *subset* of the objects. For example, if the user selects a number of objects and then deletes them with a single command, the command can be expanded in the undo dialog box and the user can specifically undo the delete of a single object and leave the rest deleted.

The hierarchical command objects in Amulet also support a number of other important aspects of UI development:

- **Enabling:** A standard field of the command objects controls enabling and disabling of commands (and whether the associated widget is grayed out).
- **Help:** Another field supplies a short help string that can be used for the "help line" in Microsoft Windows or for the "balloon help" on the Macintosh. There is also a pointer that can be used when longer help is needed, which will typically bring up the help dialog box.
- **External Control:** The command objects also allow a program to control another program as if it was the user (a program can easily "push the buttons" of another without requiring any changes in the target application). Since the command objects have a simple, fixed protocol, a program simply sets the `VALUE` slot of the desired command object, and calls its `DO` method.
- **Macros and Programming by Demonstration:** In the future, command objects will be used to create a flexible macro facility (by having the recorder save the commands and call the `DO` methods) [5]. Since this will be supported at the system level, applications will not have to invent their own independent macro mechanisms.
- **Analyzing User Interfaces:** We expect the command objects to be useful for transcribing and analyzing the user's actions, since the hierarchical decomposition of the commands seems to map closely to users' task decomposition.

RELATED WORK

The Amulet system draws much inspiration from the Garnet system [7]. In particular, the low-level input event handling in Amulet uses Interactor objects based on the design from Garnet [6]. However, Garnet did not support any form of command objects, undo, or hierarchical layers for behaviors.

Using command objects to support undo was introduced in MacApp [12] and has been used in many systems including InterViews [11] and Gina [1]. All of these use a similar single-level command architecture. Katie introduced the idea of hierarchical events and explored some implementation issues [3, 4, 5]. Katie also proposed mechanisms for using hierarchical events for scripting and undo. Amulet is the first system to fully explore hierarchical command objects as a way to support large-scale applications, modularity, reuse, and undo.

There is a long history of research into various new undo mechanisms, and Amulet is specifically designed to allow new mechanisms to be explored. Berlage [1] has a good survey of previous undo mechanisms. The selective undo mechanism described here is closest to the Gina mechanism [1], but adds the ability to repeat previous commands, even on new objects. Furthermore, Gina did not support undoing parts of commands or undoing selections and scrolling.

COMMAND OBJECTS

A command object is defined for each operation in the system. Many command objects are built into the system, and others are created by application programmers. For example, there are built-in command objects for dragging graphical objects, changing objects' colors, and copying objects. Typically, each menu item and widget has an associated command object. Because command objects can be hierarchical, composite objects like menus and menubars can have a separate command object for each item (e.g., a separate command for cut, copy and paste). Alternatively, there might be a single command for an entire menu where the VALUE of the command is determined by the menu choice. For example, in a menu for picking a font, the change-font command can be attached to the menu itself and each menu item can simply be a font value.

Command objects can be attached to widgets either by writing code or by using an interactive tool like an Interface Builder, which might display a menu of built-in and programmer-defined commands. The command object associated with a widget can even be computed by a *constraint*, which is a function that recomputes the value whenever needed. This makes it easy to support ''menubar sharing'' where the global menubar items change based on which window or sub-window is active.

Slots of Command Objects

Instance variables of Amulet objects, called *slots*, can be dynamically added and removed from any object. Slots that are not set locally are inherited from prototypes. Methods are implemented as function pointers stored in slots. Command objects in Amulet have a number of default slots and methods. The LABEL slot of a command object holds a string or object that will typically be displayed in the widget. For example, menus, buttons and text input fields use the value of the LABEL slot as their label. Because Amulet allows slots to contain any type of value, the LABEL slot can contain a graphical object instead of a string. This allows any picture to be a widget's label, not just bitmaps or strings as in most other toolkits. Keeping the label with the command object rather than with the widget ensures that the same operation consistently uses the same name. Instead of a regular value, the LABEL slot can contain a *constraint* that calculates the value. This is very useful when the label should change. For example, implementing a cycle button that alternates between "turn grid ON" and "turn grid OFF" is trivial.

The ACTIVE slot of a command object controls whether the associated widget, Interactor, or menu item should be enabled or not (grayed out). Typically, the ACTIVE slot contains a constraint. For example, the Cut command object's ACTIVE slot contains a constraint that returns false when no objects are selected. The VISIBLE slot of a command object can be used to control widgets, dialog boxes and windows that appear and disappear. If the VISIBLE slot is true, the associated graphical object is visible, and if false, then it is invisible. Using the VISIBLE slot of the attached command object to control pop-up dialogs provides a nice, uniform interface.

Command objects can also contain HELP and SHORT_HELP slots to support the help-line and full help text for the command. The help string in a command can be computed by a constraint. This makes it easy, for example, to change the string from telling what the command does to telling why it is not available based on whether the ACTIVE slot is true or false.

Since Amulet allows a program to dynamically add slots to objects and since a slot can hold any type of data, command objects typically store their current and previous states as slot values. Four standard slots are defined, but custom command objects can add other slots as necessary. The standard slots are the VALUE slot for the current value, the OLD_VALUE slot for the previous value, the OBJECT_MODIFIED slot for the object or list of objects modified by this command, and the OLD_OWNER slot for the widget or Interactor that invoked the command. By using these standard slots for holding the data of the command, the standard undo mechanisms can provide default ways of checking and displaying the commands, as described below. These slots also form the interface between lower-level and higher-level command objects in the hierarchy. For example, the low-level Interactor which moves objects is used in the scroll bar widget to let the user drag the indicator. When the user drags the indicator, the DO method in the command in the Interactor sets its VALUE to the current position. The scroll bar command's DO method then uses this value to compute the appropriate percent value, which is then set into its own VALUE slot.

Methods in Command Objects

Amulet calls the command's DO method when the command should be invoked. The various kinds of undo mechanisms require additional methods in each command, as described below. The standard single and multiple undo require two methods (for undo and undo-the-undo), and the selective undo mechanism requires six methods. In some situations, even for custom commands, it may not be necessary to use a DO method at all. Instead, constraints can be used. For example, the default change-property command stores the current value of the property in the VALUE slot of the command, and often a constraint can be put into objects to get the current value of this slot. Then, the DO method can be NULL (empty), and the UNDO method will be the default, which simply swaps the values in the VALUE and OLD_VALUE slots of the command. For commands like cut or delete-file, however, both DO and the various UNDO methods are needed.

Command Object Hierarchies

Command objects in Amulet use *four* different hierarchies (see Figures 1 and 2). All Amulet objects, including commands, are in a prototype-instance hierarchy. This is used to control the inheritance of default values for slots and methods, and corresponds to the class hierarchy in C++. In Figure 1, the command in item 1 is an instance of the Cut command, and inherits a number of methods and slots from it. Other methods and slots might have local, application-specific values. The Cut command, in turn, is an instance of the root Command object.

Most objects in Amulet also participate in a part-owner hierarchy. This corresponds to the grouping mechanism in other toolkits. Graphical objects are typically part of

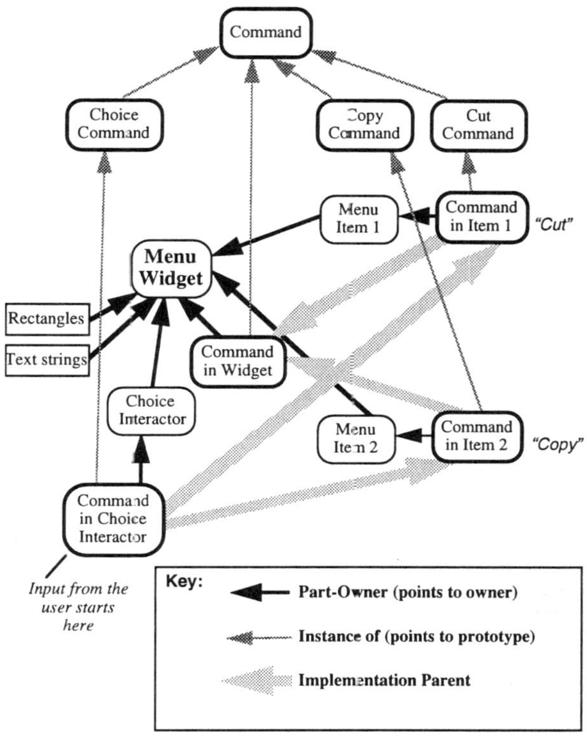

Figure 1:
Three of the hierarchies that command objects use.

groups, which are part of a window, which are part of the screen. Non-graphical objects can also be added as parts. This supports *structural inheritance* because all parts of an object are copied when an object is copied. In Figure 1, the menu widget contains various rectangle and string graphical objects as parts, as well as a Choice-Interactor object, the command object for the widget, and the command objects for the various menu items. When a copy or instance is made of the menu object, Amulet also copies all of these parts. Programs can safely store local values into the command objects since a unique command object will be allocated for each menu and menu item.

The other two hierarchies are specific to command objects, and are not used by other kinds of Amulet objects. The first one supports lower-level commands executing the higher-level commands. For example, in a menu, the low-level command associated with a Choice-Interactor deals with the interim feedback that shows which menu item the mouse is over. When the user releases the mouse over a menu item, the Choice-Interactor's command turns off the interim feedback, and then calls the DO method of the appropriate command associated with that item. If desired, the menu's command object would be invoked next. We call this the ''implementation hierarchy,'' since all the commands work together to implement the operation.

The implementation hierarchy is quite different from the prototype-instance inheritance hierarchy, since in the prototype-instance hierarchy, an instance's DO method *replaces* the parent's DO method. In the implementation hierarchy, however, the child's DO method is run in addition to the parent's DO method (specifically, the child's runs *before* the parent's).

Amulet uses the IMPLEMENTATION_PARENT as follows: when an input event arrives, Amulet finds the Interactor object to handle it. Then, that Interactor's command object's DO method is invoked, followed by its IMPLEMENTATION_PARENT command's DO method. In pseudo-code:

```
cmd = current_interactor.COMMAND;
do {
     cmd.DO_Method();
     undo_handler.Register_Command(cmd);
     cmd = cmd.IMPLEMENTATION_PARENT;
     }
 while (cmd.Valid());
```

Of course, the standard widgets set the IMPLEMENTATION_PARENT slots of internal commands automatically, so the programmer is only responsible for higher-level parts of this hierarchy. For custom widgets and behaviors on application-specific objects, programmers will typically use the lower-level commands from the library and attach their own higher-level commands as the IMPLEMENTATION_PARENTs.

Originally, we thought that the part-owner hierarchy would serve as the implementation hierarchy as well, since in most cases commands in parts would call the commands in the owners. For instance, the command in the Move-Interactor in a scroll bar calls the command in the scroll bar, and the scroll bar is the Move-Interactor's owner. However, there are a number of situations where the part-owner hierarchy does not match the required implementation hierarchy. For example, a single Choice-Interactor is attached to an entire menu widget, whereas there may be command objects associated with each individual menu item (see Figure 1). In this case, the Choice-Interactor's command object *dynamically* computes its implementation hierarchy parent based on where the user points. Another example is the selection handles widget, that allows graphical objects to be selected, moved, and grown, and displays the standard square handles around the objects selected. Since this single widget performs multiple actions, it contains a number of Interactors as parts (each with its own low-level commands), and the widget also contains multiple high-level semantic commands such as ''become selected'' and ''move.'' The part-owner hierarchy is insufficient to match these up.

Our original design for the implementation hierarchy required that programmers call the correct methods as part of their DO and UNDO code, but the programmers using Amulet found it difficult to know what code was supposed to be called when. Therefore, the current design uses a *declarative* approach where the IMPLEMENTATION_PARENT slot in each command object is set with the parent object. Now, the application's DO and UNDO methods can contain arbitrary code, or even be empty. This seems to be much more intuitive.

By contrast, the programming model introduced in Katie [4] provides for the automatic determination of parent information in events by using a nondeterministic parsing scheme operating on a declarative specification of events accepted by each event handler.

The final hierarchy used by command objects is for situations where multiple widgets are used to construct a single operation, such as with dialog boxes. So far, every command has been either a top-level command (i.e., like ''Cut'') that will show up in the undo menu, or else the IMPLEMENTATION_CHILD of a top-level command.[1] We found that these two options were not sufficient for every case, since all commands on the implementation hierarchy are executed at the same time. In particular, dialog boxes are often used to execute a single command, but the dialog box itself is composed of many widgets each of which has its own command. In Figure 2, the Change-Font command should *not* be executed when the font-size widget's commands are executed, but only when the OK or Apply buttons of the dialog box are hit. Thus, the Change-Font command cannot be the IMPLEMENTATION_PARENT of the font-size widget. However, we still would like the font-size command to be associated with the Change-Font command for later undoing or transcription. Therefore, commands can have their DEFERRED_EXECUTION_PARENT slot[2] set with the top level command that will eventually be executed. Unlike the IMPLEMENTATION_PARENT command, the DEFERRED_EXECUTION_PARENT command is *not* executed when the child's is. Tools that help programmers build dialog boxes in Amulet, like Interface Builders, will set the DEFERRED_EXECUTION_PARENT slots appropriately, so we do not expect that most programmers will directly need to deal with this hierarchy.

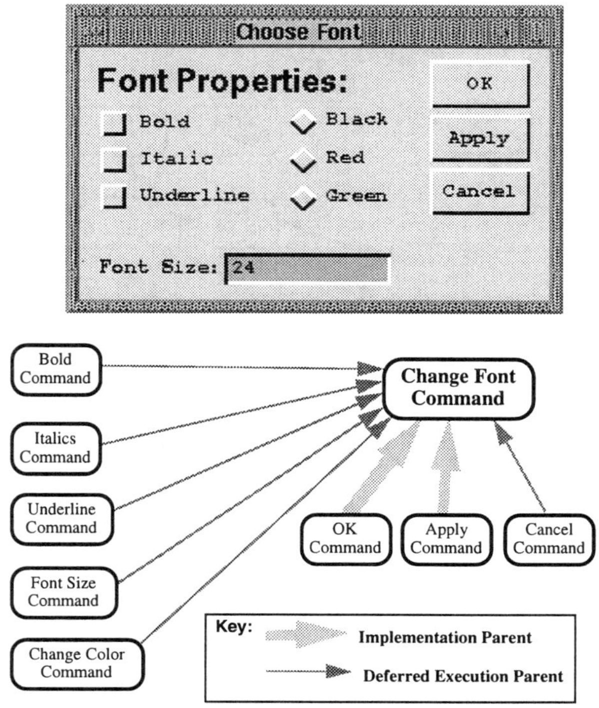

Figure 2:
The Change-Font command is the IMPLEMENTATION_PARENT of the OK and APPLY commands so it will be executed automatically when they are executed, but it is the DEFERRED_EXECUTION_PARENT of the other commands so it will *not* be executed when they are executed, but so the commands will still be linked to the Change Font command.

UNDO AND REPEAT MECHANISMS

User Interface

The command objects themselves have no user interface, since they are used as an execution framework. The general undo mechanism supports a variety of user interfaces, and any Amulet application can supply a custom user interface to the undo mechanisms. This section presents the default user interface for the three undo mechanisms, which we have used to verify that the various options can be presented in an understandable way.

At the top of the Edit pull-down menu in applications is the usual ''Undo'' option, which undoes the last command. In the Macintosh-like single undo mechanism, this menu item changes to ''Redo'' after an undo has been performed, which will undo the undo. The usual keyboard accelerator keys can be used for the menu items.

In the multi-level undo mechanism, there are two undo menu items: ''Undo'' which undoes the last operation that has not been undone, and ''Redo'' which undoes the previous Undo. The ''Undo'' option is always available unless the user has undone all the operations back to the initial state. The ''Redo'' option is only available if the previous operation was an Undo, since this undo model does not support trees of commands, just a linear list.

With the selective undo mechanism, there are three undo menu items in the Edit menu: ''Undo,'' ''Redo'' or ''Repeat,'' and ''Selective Undo/Redo/Repeat...''. ''Undo'' and ''Redo'' operate the same as for the multi-level undo mechanism. ''Repeat'' is a quick way to selectively repeat the previous command. ''Repeat'' shares the same menu item as ''Redo'' to save space, as in Microsoft Word version 6. The final option brings up the dialog box for selective undo shown in Figure 3.

The undo dialog box lists all the commands, and has buttons for the various undo and repeat actions. The dialog box is not modal, and if it is left visible, the user can see each new command added to the top of the list. The commands are described by their type, the name or a picture of the object modified (if any), and the value of the command (such as the resulting color for a change-color command). If the names of the object is not sufficiently meaningful, the object associated with a command can be made to flash. The user can easily undo or repeat the command to see if it is the desired operation. If the selected command cannot be undone or repeated, the appropriate action buttons are grayed out. This would typically happen if the objects the command affects are no longer valid, for example if the objects have been deleted.

[1]The IMPLEMENTATION_CHILDREN of a command C are all the commands whose IMPLEMENTATION_PARENT is C.

[2]Better suggestions for the name would be appreciated!

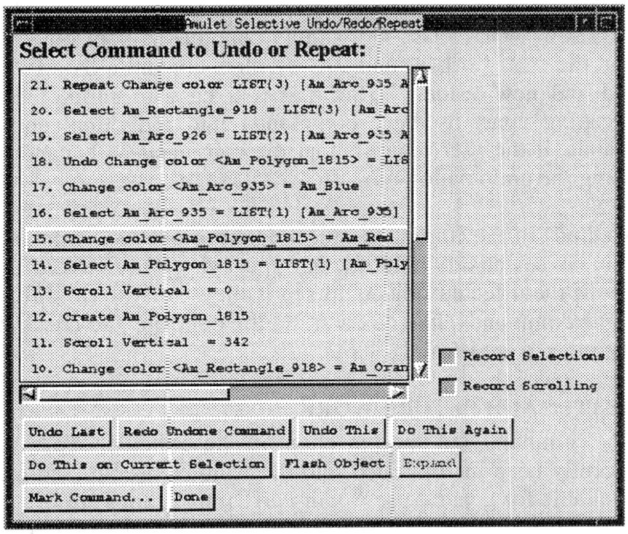

Figure 3:
The dialog box currently used for selective undo, redo and repeat. Command 11 has been marked with the F9 accelerator key.

The meaning of selectively undoing a command has been adopted from Gina [1]: the affected values of the objects are returned to the state just before the command was executed. If a command turns an object from blue to yellow, selectively undoing the command will make it blue, no matter what its current color is. Similarly, selectively repeating the command will turn the object yellow again. Selectively repeating a command on new objects will do the same operation to the new objects. In this case, the new objects would turn yellow. The selective operations also generate a new command object which is put at the top of the command list, and this new command can then be undone using the normal mechanisms. The name of the new command is prefixed with "Undo" or "Repeat," as shown by commands 18 and 21 in Figure 3.

Selective repeating of some commands might mean different things. For example, we decided that repeating a "move" command should put the object in the same place as the original move. However, it might alternatively mean to move by the same *relative* distance. User testing will be required to see which meaning is more often desired, or if users would prefer to have a choice of both options.

The check boxes at the right of the dialog box in Figure 3 control whether scrolling and selections should be queued for undoing. If so, they are added to the command list like regular commands.

The `Expand` button in the dialog box expands an operation that affects multiple objects into a set of commands, so they can individually be undone or repeated The selected command can be *marked* and given a user-defined name and keyboard accelerator that will selectively perform the command again on the same object or the currently-selected objects. This can be used, for example, to create "bookmarks" for scrolling to specific places in a document, or to create a command to set any object to a particular custom color. Another use would be to mark the final command which selects a set of objects so that various operations can be applied to them without having to laboriously re-select them or place them into a group. Eventually, marking will be augmented by a full macro facility.

Implementation of Undo

Amulet is designed to be flexible to support user interface researchers. In particular, the undo mechanism is completely replaceable. An undo-handler object is attached to each window, and Amulet calls a standard method in it to process each command executed. Programmers can use one of the three undo-handlers supplied in the library, or they can write their own. Amulet simply requires that each undo-handler support the method `REGISTER_COMMAND` which takes a command object, and saves it for later undoing.

The undo-handler's `REGISTER_COMMAND` method checks to see if a command has an `IMPLEMENTATION_PARENT` or `DEFERRED_EXECUTION_PARENT`, and if not, then it makes a copy of the command and all of its children. If a command does have an `IMPLEMENTATION_PARENT` or `DEFERRED_EXECUTION_PARENT`, the parent command will eventually be executed, and it will then be queued for undo along with its parent, so there is no need for the undo-handler to queue it.

When a single command is undone or repeated, all of its `IMPLEMENTATION_CHILDREN` commands have to be undone or repeated also, since they all participated in the operation of the command. Consider a widget to change an object's color in a graphics editor. When the user clicks on it, the `DO` method of the command in the widget changes the widget to show the current color, and the `DO` method of the application's Change-Color command (which is the `IMPLEMENTATION_PARENT` of the widget's command) changes the color of the selected objects. If this command is undone, then *both* the widget and the selected objects should return to their previous states. Therefore, the `UNDO` method in the command object in the widget *and* the `UNDO` method in the application command should be executed. This clearly shows the advantages of the hierarchical commands, since in other toolkits, the undo method for the application has to know which widget it was part of and how to reset the widget. In Amulet, however, the application command can be exclusively concerned with updating the application's data structures, and the child command for the widget will update the widget.

It is important that the `UNDO` methods be executed in the *same* order as the `DO` methods (from child to parent) since often the higher-level commands compute their values from the values of lower-level commands. For example, since the widget's command's `DO` and `UNDO` methods will always be executed first, the methods in the application's Change-Color command do not need to store an old value since they can simply access the current value of the widget's command object.

We have found that the `DEFERRED_EXECUTION_CHILDREN` of a command do *not* need to be undone when a command is undone. For example, undoing the font setting command should usually not reset the various widgets in the font dialog box. If necessary, an undo method is free to call the undo methods of its DEFERRED_EXECUTION_CHILDREN, and some future undo mechanisms might even allow the DEFERRED_EXECUTION_CHILDREN commands to be individually undone by the user.

Some commands are not undoable (like Save File) but should still be queued on the undo list to show that they were executed. Other commands are not normally queued on the undo list at all (like scrolling and selection). Commands that are not undoable but should still be queued can simply leave their UNDO_METHOD as empty (NULL). The undo-handlers grey-out commands without an undo method. Commands that are not normally queued for undo are so marked, but they still have UNDO_METHODs, so the user can dynamically decide whether they should be queued for undo, for example by using the check boxes in Figure 3.

When an command object can no longer be repeated or undone, it is destroyed. The single undo mechanism destroys the old command object whenever a new command is executed. The multiple command mechanism currently supports unlimited undo, so command objects are only destroyed if they are undone, and then a new command is executed, since at that point, redo is no longer available.

Implementation of Selective Undo and Repeat

Implementing selective undo and repeat is not much harder than implementing regular undo. All the required information is already stored in the command object. The major new complication is that for selective undo or repeat, the affected object's *current* values must be loaded into the command object, in case the selective undo command itself is undone. To facilitate this, the undo mechanism first makes a copy of the command object to be undone or repeated before calling the selective undo or repeat method. Therefore, the methods are free to reload the OLD_VALUE slot from the current object without affecting the original command. For example, the method that implements all the undo and repeat operations for property changing commands looks like (in pseudo-code):

```
//undo is true when undoing and false when repeating.
//on_new is true when applying this to the new object new_obj.
void property_repeat_undo(Am_Object cmd,
         bool undo, bool on_new,
         Am_Object new_obj) {
 if (on_new) {
   cmd.OBJECT_MODIFIED = new_obj;
   object = new_obj;
   }
 else object = cmd.OBJECT_MODIFIED;
 cur_value = object.property_slot;
 if (undo) new_value = cmd.OLD_VALUE;
 else new_value = cmd.VALUE; //repeat
 object.property_slot = new_value; //Set it
 //now swap old and new values in command
 cmd.VALUE = new_value;
 cmd.OLD_VALUE = cur_value;
}
```

If the command affects a *set* of objects, then the OBJECT_MODIFIED slot simply contains a list of objects, and the OLD_VALUE and VALUE slots contain a list of the old and new values. This makes it easy to support the breaking apart of these commands into individual commands, if the user requests that the command be expanded using the undo dialog box.

Methods in the command object determine if the command can be selectively undone or repeated. These typically check the affected objects to see if they are still valid (but some commands, like deletion, do the opposite and check if the objects are invalid).

STATUS AND FUTURE WORK

The command and undo mechanisms described above have recently been incorporated into the Amulet system, and are available for general use.[3] Our early impressions are that it is not difficult to construct applications using the hierarchical command architecture, supporting selective undo is only slightly harder than regular undo, and both are facilitated by the hierarchical commands. In the future, we hope to gather some data about end user's feelings about the selective undo mechanisms: Is the meaning of selective undo and repeat clear? Can users pick the correct command from the dialog box? Is undoing and repeating of selections and scrolling useful and easy enough to do?

Currently, the undo mechanism only allows the user to select the top-level command for undoing and repeating, and this automatically undoes or repeats all the children commands. It would be interesting to explore whether it is useful for users to be able to undo only the children commands, for example, to re-enter a dialog box or other multi-step action and finish it differently. Given the ease of creating new undo mechanisms in Amulet, it becomes attractive to explore many other forms of Undo. For example, what if the previously undone operations were not flushed when new operations were entered, but instead the system supported multiple paths of execution with the possibilities of skipping around? Then the command history might become a complex tree. Combined with the bookmark facility, this might allow "what if" explorations, where the user can try different sequences of actions, and then use the one that works best (even if it wasn't the last one tried).

A number of researchers have explored undo in the context of multi-user applications, and the selective undo model described here seems ideal for this. The interface could easily allow commands like "Undo *my* last action" versus "Undo *the* last action" by simply marking each command with a user ID.

Another important direction for future work is to support scripting and programming by demonstration [8] using the

---

[3]The complete Amulet system is available for free by anonymous FTP, including the command and undo model described here. See http://www.cs.cmu.edu/~amulet or contact the first author for more information.

command objects so users can aggregate several actions into a single new command. Scripts can be record the command objects at any level: at the low level input events (left button down at (45,30), move to (54,31), ...), at the intermediate command level (move file_object_461 to (54,31)), or at a higher semantic command level (move_file "commands_paper" from folder "submitted" to folder "CHI96"). Different uses of scripts may require recording at any of these levels and having the semantic level will make scripting more useful than previous systems [5]. It will be interesting to explore how to let the user choose which level is desired. Having scripting at the toolkit level, instead of using a different scripting mechanism for every application, will allow users to transfer their knowledge and to create more elaborate programs that use multiple applications.

Transcripts of the multi-level commands may be useful for analysis. The time spent scrolling, selecting, using help, aborting commands, and undoing, can be clearly differentiated from productive work, and it might be possible to write programs to filter the transcript to look for problem areas. Also, it appears that the command hierarchy matches the NGOMSL method decomposition [2] so model-based evaluation of Amulet interfaces may be possible even before testing with any subjects.

Another direction for future work is to extend the selective undo mechanism to text editing. The main problem for selectively undoing and repeating will be *where* in the document a command refers, given that the text may have been substantially edited since the command was first executed.

CONCLUSIONS

The hierarchical command objects in Amulet make it easier to build interactive applications, because low-level commands can be reused from the library without change, and application-specific properties can be easily expressed with constraints and methods in high-level commands. At the same time, the command objects enable a very flexible Undo mechanism that supports selective undoing and repeating of previous actions, and new undo mechanisms can be easily added. We are very excited about the potential of Amulet's command objects as a foundation for future research and for general user interface development.

ACKNOWLEDGEMENTS

For help with this paper, we would like to thank Alan Ferrency, Rich McDaniel, Brad Vander Zanden, John Pane, and Bernita Myers. The Amulet system is being developed by Brad Myers, Rich McDaniel, Alan Ferrency, Andy Mickish, and Alex Klimovitski.

This research was partially sponsored by NCCOSC under Contract No. N66001-94-C-6037, Arpa Order No. B326, and partially by NSF under grant number IRI-9319969. The views and conclusions contained in this document are those of the authors and should not be interpreted as representing the official policies, either expressed or implied, of the U.S. Government.

REFERENCES

1. Thomas Berlage. "A Selective Undo Mechanism for Graphical User Interfaces Based on Command Objects". *ACM Transactions on Computer Human Interaction 1* (Sept. 1994), 269-294.

2. Michael D. Byrne, Scott D. Wood, Piyawadee Sukaviriya, James D. Foley and David E. Kieras. Automating Interface Evaluation. Human Factors in Computing Systems, Proceedings SIGCHI'94, Boston, MA, April, 1994, pp. 232-237.

3. David S. Kosbie and Brad A. Myers. A System-Wide Macro Facility Based on Aggregate Events: A Proposal. In Allen Cypher, Ed., *Watch What I Do: Programming by Demonstration*, MIT Press, Cambridge, MA, 1993, pp. 433-444.

4. David Kosbie. *Hierarchical Event Histories in Graphical User Interfaces*. Ph.D. Th., Computer Science Department, Carnegie Mellon University, 1996. In progress.

5. David S. Kosbie and Brad A. Myers. Extending Programming By Demonstration With Hierarchical Event Histories. In Brad Blumenthal, Juri Gornostaev and Claus Unger, Ed., *Human-Computer Interaction: 4th International Conference EWHCI'94, Lecture Notes in Computer Science, Vol. 876,*, Springer-Verlag, Berlin, 1994, pp. 128-139.

6. Brad A. Myers. "A New Model for Handling Input". *ACM Transactions on Information Systems 8*, 3 (July 1990), 289-320.

7. Brad A. Myers, Dario A. Giuse, Roger B. Dannenberg, Brad Vander Zanden, David S. Kosbie, Edward Pervin, Andrew Mickish, and Philippe Marchal. "Garnet: Comprehensive Support for Graphical, Highly-Interactive User Interfaces". *IEEE Computer 23*, 11 (Nov. 1990), 71-85.

8. Brad A. Myers. "Demonstrational Interfaces: A Step Beyond Direct Manipulation". *IEEE Computer 25*, 8 (August 1992), 61-73.

9. David L. Parnas. "Designing Software for Ease of Extension and Constraction". *IEEE Transactions on Software Engineering SE-5*, 2 (March 1979), 128-138.

10. R. Taylor, K. Nies, G. Bolcer, C. MacFarlane, and K. Anderson. "Chiron-1: A Software Architecture for User Interface Development, Maintenance, and Run-Time Support". *ACM Transactions on Computer Human Interaction 2* (June 1995), 105-144.

11. John M. Vlissides and Mark A. Linton. "Unidraw: A Framework for Building Domain-Specific Graphical Editors". *ACM Transactions on Information Systems 8*, 3 (July 1990), 204-236.

12. David Wilson. *Programming with MacApp*. Addison-Wesley Publishing Company, Reading, MA, 1990.

The Zephyr Help Instance: Promoting Ongoing Activity in a CSCW System

Mark S. Ackerman
Leysia Palen
Department of Information and Computer Science
University of California, Irvine
Irvine, CA 92717
ackerman, palen@ics.uci.edu
http://www.ics.uci.edu/CORPS/ackerman.html

ABSTRACT

If Computer-Supported Cooperative Work (CSCW) systems are to be successful over time, it will be necessary to promote ongoing and continuing activity, not just initial adoption. In this paper, we consider what technical and social affordances are required to encourage the continued use of a CSCW system.

To explore these issues, we examine a chat-like system, the Zephyr Help Instance, which is used extensively at MIT. The Help Instance facilitates users asking questions of one another, and is an example of a distributed help and problem-solving system. We provide an overview of the system's use as well as those mechanisms, both technical and social, that facilitate continuing its use over time.

KEYWORDS: computer-supported cooperative work, CSCW, help, computer-mediated communications, CMC, norms, organizational interfaces, social maintenance, electronic social spaces.

INTRODUCTION

> Worlds are socially constructed and socially maintained. Their continuing reality... depends on specific social processes, namely those processes that ongoingly reconstruct and maintain the particular worlds in question. (Berger [2], p. 45)

If Computer-Supported Cooperative Work (CSCW) systems are to be successful, it will be necessary to promote ongoing, continuing activity. Even once a CSCW system gets past the critical mass problem, users must continue to find it not only useful, but usable. Only some CSCW systems will provide the social and technical affordances necessary to promote the social maintenance required for continued use.

We examine this issue through the study of a particular system, the Zephyr Help Instance, at MIT. The Zephyr Help Instance is a chat-like system that allows users to ask questions and other users to answer. The Zephyr Help Instance serves as an interesting field study site for several reasons:

- Zephyr is a successful CSCW system in production use.

At CSCW'94, a call was made to find "real" CSCW systems in wide-scale use. The Zephyr Help Instance has been in heavy use for 7 years (at over 30,000 messages per semester). In its organizational setting, this computer-mediated communication (CMC) system is not monitored or maintained by any authority; its existence is sustained and organized solely by its users. Because its use is discretionary, it serves as an excellent opportunity to study how users might organize their electronic social space.

- Zephyr ameliorates an important help problem by providing a mechanism for distributed help and problem-solving. It does this by allowing users to help one another.

Relatively little is known about how people can best assist one another in a computationally distributed environment. With the Zephyr Help Instance, users help one another in a cooperative environment to continue their work tasks. There have been many times, some highlighted below, where no single person could answer the question posed, but a group of people could. Of course, this type of help would be of little value if the system were not an ongoing source of answers.

- Zephyr has a simple user interface, making it easier to determine the interaction of system affordances and social maintenance.

Zephyr is a bit of a paradox. The standard interface is rudimentary, consisting of either a text-based, tty interface or a simple X-based interface. Yet, the system *is* used extensively for technical problem-solving, as well as other types of work and social communication. The simplicity of the user interface allows us to more easily see the social affordances. It is our contention that the system allows participants to invoke a rich set of social behaviors and adaptations. Not only do these interactions allow them to problem-solve, it also allows them to maintain and organize their electronic social space. This usability capability is partially dependent on the user interface, as normally construed, and partially on the organizational or external interface [14].

CHI 96 Vancouver, BC Canada
© 1996 ACM 0-89791-777-4/96/04..$3.50

Therefore, this system provides an interesting and important study. Simply put, the Zephyr Help Instance highlights some critical CSCW requirements -- requirements that have enabled it to be a success within its environment of use *over time*.

We begin the paper with a brief examination of the CSCW literature concerning continued use over time. Following this, we describe Zephyr in general and the Help Instance in particular. With a firm base in the use of the system, we then analyze why the Zephyr Help Instance has continued to be used.

CSCW SYSTEMS AND ONGOING ACTIVITY

Numerous CSCW and information technology studies have examined the adoption of group and organizational systems (e.g., [9]). The social impacts of computational systems have also been heavily studied (e.g., [16]).

Determining the conditions of success and continuation has been much less clear. One strand of research argues that within many organizations, where use may be mandated, continued use is dependent primarily on either coercion or user satisfaction. The studies assume that with high user satisfaction, systems will be effectively used. Many user involvement and participatory design studies fall within this research stream.

Another line of argument assumes that fit to the social situation provides for system success (or failure) over the long run. In her study of Lotus Notes, Orlikowski [15] claimed that the system assumptions cannot be contrary to the reward schemes and mental maps of the organization or of key groups. Bowers [3] came to similar conclusions in his study of a British government office. Both Orlikowski and Bowers acknowledge the necessity of organizational fit, but also paint a considerably more complex picture that requires a consideration of individuals' goals, shared understandings, and system affordances. Unfortunately, both studied implementations that were failures at the time of study, swaying their conclusions.

While there are few field-based studies of continuing use of computational systems, to our knowledge, there are no studies examining how CMC-based help systems maintain themselves over time. Help has been extensively studied: There is a plethora of studies of technical systems (e.g., [4]), help information design (e.g., [13]), and face-to-face interactions between users and expert consultants (e.g., [1]). Nonetheless, while CMCs have considerable potential for providing access to distributed colleagues for help and problem solving, there is mostly anecdotal evidence for this capability. Sproull and Kiesler do report on a number of CMC uses, including the norms of use, in [17]. Similarly, Finholt reported on the use of distribution lists and their archives in [7]. Outside of these studies, little attention has been paid to how groups using CMCs (particularly for help) organize themselves to maintain their social spaces.

ZEPHYR MESSAGE SYSTEM AT MIT

The Zephyr system is a synchronous chat facility supported on MIT/Project Athena workstations [6]. In Athena, users can use any public-access workstation in any location. Zephyr provides a synchronous method of both communicating and finding other people in a geographically and computationally distributed environment.

Zephyr messages can be sent to a channel, called an "instance", to which multiple people are subscribed. Messages can also be sent to individuals or groups of individuals. (We are omitting description of some advanced features from our discussion here.) Sending a message to an instance is the equivalent of participating in a chat channel; the message is sent to all the people who are subscribing to the instance at that time.

Methods and data

The analysis presented here was largely based on a qualitative examination of the publicly-available message log for one semester, Autumn, 1993. The log consists of 30,052 messages, providing data for 93 days of the 105-day semester. There are gaps of 9 days and of 4 days because of failures in the logging mechanism. There are also some days with only partial data, although it is often difficult to determine when Zephyr was inactive, the logging application was broken, or the Athena system was down.

In addition to our analysis of the message log, the first author has been a participant-observer on the system for approximately three years (and a casual participant for much longer). We have also interviewed the people that started the Help Instance, and interviewed a small number of heavy and light users. We conducted 19 interviews in total. We have used this additional data to corroborate and inform our analysis.

The analysis followed qualitative techniques standardly used to examine small-scale interactions (as in [12]). We were careful to triangulate among our data.

Users

Help Instance users are entirely MIT affiliates, mostly undergraduates, since they are the typical Athena user. This does provide a different type of user population than in many organizations. For example, undergraduates have more time and more willingness to engage new technologies. Additionally, MIT has a distinct technical culture. On the other hand, MIT undergraduates have a wide diversity of technical competence and interest. In general, we believe that the Zephyr users are typical of many technical users, but we will discuss the impact of MIT as an organizational culture below.

In Autumn, 1993, there were 540 users. Usage followed the familiar exponential curve of CMCs [10]. It is important to note that there were a number of user groups. Based on our analyses of the message log, it is clear that there was a core group of "regulars" on the Help Instance (approximately 8% of users). Some people lived on the system. One user had nearly 2400 messages on the Help Instance alone. There was also an intermediate group of intermittent users (the middle of the exponential curve), who participated over the extent of the quarter but at a lower level. Some appeared to stay subscribed to the Help Instance but participated at a lower level; others may have subscribed when they wanted to ask a question or had the time to answer. There were a large number of users (39%) who sent four or fewer messages. Our interview data suggest that the tire-kickers (the tail of the curve) subscribed only when they wanted to ask a question.

Although we have interview and observation evidence that person-to-person exchanges are more common than broadcasting to public instances, we are emphasizing one particular chat channel, the Help Instance, in this paper. It should be noted that the Help Instance is only one channel on the system. Still, the Help Instance was enormously popular and useful.

Zephyr in use

The following sections show how Zephyr is used. Before discussing the technical and social mechanisms by which the Help Instance continues over time as a social space, we need to ground that discussion by describing what occurs on the system.

In the following two message exchange, the user named `azir` asks a question, and `clee` answers it. (All names and other identifiers have been changed in any data presented here. Additionally, we have modified the headers and messages slightly for readability and because of page constraints.)

```
Time: 18:57:10 Date: Fri Oct 29 1993
From: @times(@b(@i( Course II ))) <azir>
after i change a list to a group, how long
before i can use it?

Time: 18:57:52 Date: Fri Oct 29 1993
From: starlight on a moonless night <clee>
you can use it immediately
```

The rapidity and burstiness of interaction are impossible to duplicate in print, but long lulls are punctuated with frantic bursts of activity. That these messages are only 42 seconds apart is normal. This pacing gives the system a flavor very different from net news or e-mail.

The pace of query and response is an extremely important feature of the system. Messages fly by. If they are not answered within a few minutes, it is likely that they never will be. In general, users ignore any older messages; the system is effectively memoryless.

Several additional things about the messages should be noted. First, the example messages above are unusually short, but the available editors as well as the rapidity of the exchanges tend to keep messages below 10 lines long. All of the lines arrive together. Second, the user must keep track of the conversational threads to know how a message fits into potentially many simultaneous exchanges.

Third, there is some identifying information in addition to the message itself. The timestamp, originating machine, and user id are provided by the system and guaranteed to be correct. The signature on the From line, however, is set by the user. These signatures, or "zsigs", are extremely interesting in their own right. Unfortunately, the zsigs have been shortened here because of space constraints. Finally, the messages are simple in format and flexible in structure. As can be noted from the first From line, there are markup codes for fonts, font styles, and color. (The formatting appears as only markup commands on the tty interface.) There are no other embellishments to the messages.

As mentioned, the user interface for Zephyr is rudimentary. Incoming messages pop up on the user's X screen or scroll by in a tty window; outgoing messages are written with a line-oriented editor. More sophisticated interfaces exist, but are seldom used.

Distributed use of the Help Instance

Many exchanges are like the one presented above -- a single question followed by a single answer. However, one of the advantages of distributed problem solving is that a community of people is involved and many people can attend to each question. Some of the most interesting interactions on the Help Instance capitalize on its distributed nature; these interactions occur when an answer could not be readily provided, and it takes several people multiple iterations to arrive at a solution. Below is an exchange where one person adds to the answer of another:

```
Time: 20:48:09 Date: Fri Oct 29 1993
From: @i[@(blue)Faded] <chatter>
Thanks for helping me before, but now I have
another problem.
I'm trying to use ftp.
I've gotten into another schools files, but
how do you open them

Time: 20:48:38 Date: Fri Oct 29 1993
From: The Ranger <ranger>
get filename

Time: 20:49:25 Date: Fri Oct 29 1993
From: @tt{@i{The next zsig lies.}} <phopkins>
that copies the file into your current directory
"man ftp" at an athena prompt for more info

Time: 20:49:57 Date: Fri Oct 29 1993
From: @i[@color (blue)Faded] <chatter>
Thanks again!
```

In this situation, `chatter` has asked a question about getting files from another site. `ranger` answers succinctly but his answer "corrects" the naively formed question by `chatter`. `ranger`'s answer tells `chatter` how to retrieve files, but not to open them as `chatter` asks, because that cannot be done with ftp. After the time for a conversational turn for `chatter` has elapsed, `phopkins` decides to add more information that elaborates on `ranger`'s answer and provides more help for a novice's use of ftp. Finally, `chatter` thanks everyone for the help.

The CMC nature of the Help Instance also allows corrections and modifications where necessary. In the following exchange, `rpt` corrects the initial response.

```
Time: 06:27:32 Date: Thu Oct 14 93
From: Health is merely the slowest possible
rate at which one can die. <elf>
Who wrote "Hallelujah!"? Or is the author
unknown?

Time: 06:28:27 Date: Thu Oct 14 93
From: band-aid <johnson>
If you're speaking of the Halleljuah chorus,
it is from Hayden's Messiah.

Time: 06:28:36 Date: Thu Oct 14 93
From: Robert Talbott <rpt>
Handel, not Hayden
```

In addition to multi-party answers, the chat-like nature of the Help Instance allows a user to ask for additional help if he doesn't understand the answer:

```
Time: 15:44:28 Date: Fri Oct 29 1993
From: Snoozin' <felly>
Why is a load average made up of three
numbers? What do the numbers mean?

Time: 15:45:24 Date: Fri Oct 29 1993
From: Redhead at the wheel <kat>
I think they are short, medium, and long-
term numbers, but I'm not sure. I think they
mean nothing, but I'm not sure

Time: 15:46:05 Date: Fri Oct 29 1993
From: Mythical man-month at work <dan>
1 5 15

Time: 15:46:35 Date: Fri Oct 29 1993
From: Snoozin' <felly>
Huh?

Time: 15:47:07 Date: Fri Oct 29 1993
From: Synthetic syntax spoken <descartes>
Load averaged over the last 1, 5, and 15
minutes, respectively
```

In this example, user `felly` posted a question; `kat` gave a partial response. Another user `dan` gave a different partial response, perhaps in an effort to disambiguate `kat`'s. Yet another user, `huey`, gave the final correct answer which disambiguated the previous partial responses. While `kat` made the initial effort to help `felly`, both `dan` and `huey` joined the conversation in an attempt to make the answer as precise and helpful as possible. This example is one kind of collaborative interaction that illustrates the distributed problem-solving that takes place on the Help Instance. More complex problem-solving also takes place, with extensive iteration and negotiation among users to understand and define the problem.

Finally, many questions get posted that never receive an answer, while others receive responses from many people at once. While this appears to be a failure of the system, it is expected by users. Realizing that one might not get an answer is actually very important to the sustained functioning of the system. Additionally, some questions get a single response referring to a place where a "stock" answer or other information resources can be found.

To summarize, the Zephyr Help Instance provides a mechanism by which users can answer one another's questions. They do this in a distributed environment, and many people can listen and participate in the exchanges. Because participation is always discretionary, users can answer, modify answers, or correct mistakes as they wish. Furthermore, many users can simultaneously participate to solve complex problems. The pace of the system provides immediate feedback and response.

The system capabilities must be augmented by social mechanisms for the system to actually work. For example, the synchroneity of Zephyr promotes use when urgency matters, but a human consultant is not available. However, there must also be enough people on the system to hear the request. The next section examines the social conditions of use.

WHY ZEPHYR CONTINUES TO WORK

Technically, Zephyr and its Help Instance are relatively simple. What makes the Help Instance interesting is not its technical capabilities, but that it works so successfully. Its viability is partially dependent on its technical affordances for social use and partially on the social mechanisms in place for maintaining the sociality. We will discuss those social mechanisms in the following sections.

A shared understanding of the purpose

The Help Instance was begun purposefully as a forum for user questions. It was begun in 1988 by a small group of technically expert undergraduates who were willing to answer questions, and it has maintained the same basic format since.

The Help Instance is now a well-known and well-defined place to ask questions and provide answers within the MIT community. The regularity of activity reinforces that same activity [8]. On the Help Instance, asking questions and finding answers reinforces the actors' providing questions and answers in the same location. Indeed, the actors would be disconcerted if they came to the Help Instance, and it did not contain questions and answers.

Social policing removes wildly deviant behavior on the Help Instance. This is made possible by a system affordance. Because Zephyr has a number of channels—and even more can be created dynamically by any user—it is easy to take an exchange off the Help Instance and continue to exchange Zephyr messages elsewhere. In fact, the Help.d Instance provides an established forum for discussing opinions, analyzing previous help responses, or flaming. Users often tell people to take a dialog to the discussion channel:

```
Time: 14:32:17 Date: Fri Nov 19 1993
From: Mike <mavedon>
I can go faster not having to take my hands
off the keybd to operate a mouse. also, mousing
bothers my wrist more than typing..

Time: 14:33:15 Date: Fri Nov 19 1993
From: Andrew Topper <andrew>
then use xrn, and stop flaming.
the nature of this sort of thing is that there
*cannot* be One Perfect Interface For Everyone.
```

```
Time: 14:32:37 Date: Fri Nov 19 1993
From: Mike <mavedon>
(and this should really go to help.d)
```

They also reinforce that users should stick to the proper content for a channel:

```
Time: 21:20:24 Date: Fri Oct 29 1993
From: I'd explain it, but there's a
lot of math. <susan>
please, stick to the appropriate instance,
chang, we're on help.d
```

Like all the norms discussed here, the playing out of this norm is dependent on the situational context and on the players involved [18]. Flames and opinions do exist; users complain about print quotas, compilers, and their workloads. Still, the content of the Help Instance is remarkably consistent. There is a "common-enough" understanding of the space's purpose.

Roles of asker and answerer

The Help Instance, as a sociality, must reinforce the desire of people to ask questions and for people to answer. While there are many potential questioners, users will not come to the Help Instance unless they can expect their questions to be answered in a manner that is not psychologically or socially problematic. Likewise, potential answerers must find it socially or psychologically beneficial to expend the time and effort to answer questions.

If the system use is to be stable, the creation of potential benefits and the removal of potential liabilities for both questioners and answerers must be institutionalized through some norms and roles. In this, we follow Strauss that these roles will not be extensively and consciously elaborated, and they are partially dependent on the specifics of the participants [18].

For the Help Instance participants, there appear to be two active roles, that of asker and that of answerer. The role of asker is more elaborated in that there is a recognition that users progress from "frosh" (freshman) to more expert users, and this progression should be accounted for in potential answers.

These two roles are heavily intertwined with the attribute of "cluefulness", where people range along a continuum of "clueless" (e.g., freshmen and other naive questioners) to "clueful" or "clued" (e.g., those who answer well). This attribute of "cluefulness" is deeply rooted in the MIT culture, but is often found in technical organizations. It is most often associated with a level of technical expertise and understanding, but it also connotes an internalization of specific institutional and professional norms such as deference to expert authority. We will remark on those aspects "cluefulness" that are important to Zephyr use in our discussion below.

Socially, these two roles -- asker and answerer -- reinforce each other. Indeed, it is important to remember that participants move fluidly between the two. Because of the link to "cluefulness", the roles are also socially reinforced by and are socially reinforcing with the organizational culture of MIT. This process of reinforcement is key to the system's success. However, system affordances make the reinforcements visible and possible.

In the following two sections, we discuss these roles, their norms, and the resulting reinforcements. We will then be able to discuss the system affordances that enable these social mechanisms.

Reducing burden: the role of asker

The information seeker creates a tension within the Help Instance. The purpose of the Help Instance is to provide answers; however, this will be continued only if any burden on the answerers is minimal. Since reciprocality (i.e., the returning an item of similar value) cannot always be met, this need often gets expressed through demands that the asker take the proper actions to seek out the answer through other means:

```
Time: 16:47:40 Date: Thu Oct  7 1993
From: Brian Burke <brian>
Can someone help me find the E-mail
address of a friend of mine at another
college?

Time: 16:48:10 Date: Thu Oct  7 1993
From: May I help you? <erikson>
You might add consult and look in
/mit/consult/doc/college-email-* first.

Time: 16:48:28 Date: Thu Oct  7 1993
From: in complete contrast <mayabe>
if it's at cornell, maybe.
otherwise, read the stock answers.
there's also a FAQ in news.answers
about finding addresses for colleges.
```

Knowing to first search the system and external sources of information is part of being "clueful", and therefore part of what distinguishes people capable of answering from those who are "clueless". In the following message, `bsutton`, one of the more prolific providers of information, admonishes one of his colleagues who did not first search the Unix help pages:

```
Time: 14:35:55 Date: Wed Nov 10 1993
From: That is not my beautiful house. <bsutton>
*you* I expect to read the manpage when you're
 dealing with something you don't know.
```

This requirement to exhaust other information sources before coming to the Help Instance is not always invoked. It is not invoked for "regulars" of the system, perhaps because they have been presumed to have searched or because they will reciprocally provide other information.

Even when this norm is invoked, it is most often invoked gently. The following exchange provides an example. A freshman, `diamond`, wants to know how to use uuencode, a program that produces ascii output from binary data. This program is a fairly common application, and on-line help exists in several forms. Two users, `arno` and `chang`, tell him to consult external sources. `shasha` tells him, unusually, to "rtfm", or to read the manuals. Shortly afterwards, however, `chang` also gives him the answer. In this manner, diamond gets his answer but is also provided with a sharp reminder to check other sources first. He is not told to go away, but neither is his behavior completely tolerated:

```
Time: 02:12:50 Date: Fri Nov 12 1993
From: @color(red)Intuition refund <diamond>
anyone knows how to use uuencode
and then send it thru mail (which one)?

Time: 02:13:29 Date: Fri Nov 12 1993
From: Sh! I'm hunting foah a rabbit! <arno>
There is a stock answer on that, I think.
Look under MAIL.

Time: 02:13:51 Date: Fri Nov 12 1993
From: <chang>
man uuencode

Time: 02:14:08 Date: Fri Nov 12 1993
From: @bold(Well!  morning to you, too.) <shasha>
to summarize the answers, rtfm :-)

Time: 02:16:52 Date: Fri Nov 12 1993
From: <chang>
uuencode <filename | mhmail ......

Time: 02:17:12 Date: Fri Nov 12 1993
From: @color(red)Intuition refund <diamond>
thanks
```

Another part of being "clueful" is knowing how to phrase a question satisfactorily. This is something that users have to learn, since Zephyr messages are relatively short. In an exchange too long to reproduce here, a freshman regarded publicly as a "clueless frosh" has been told to seek out one of the experts for a face-to-face tutorial. He asks whether it is really necessary, given the lateness of the hour. cmkao comes back with:

```
Time: 02:02:01 Date: Sat Nov  6 1993
From: Familiar Assonance <cmkao>
Yes, but stop asking
us questions that we're getting frustrated
with in that case :-)
```

The freshman asks why this is a problem repeatedly. Finally, bsutton informs him:

```
Time: 02:03:27 Date: Sat Nov  6 1993
From: Psycho killer, anyone? <bsutton>
because, bluntly, you don't know enough
to ask meaningfull questions or
to realize why we can't give you answers
when you ignore our questions to you
or even to understand that you don't know
some things and can't ignore some things.
```

Of course, the role of the information seeker requires the complementary role of information provider. We next turn to this role.

The role of provider

Concurrently with the need to reduce potential burden on the answerers, the askers need to know that they can ask their questions without psychological or social cost. To effectively continue the Help Instance as a sociality, then, the answerers must not belittle or berate the askers. While being clueful provides the understanding necessary to provide answers, it does not necessarily result in suitable exchanges. Users must also learn how to answer appropriately for the social space.

The responses are expected to be nuanced according to the asker's capabilities and to be polite. In the following example, taken from a longer exchange, hasan has asked how to change permissions on a subdirectory so that other users can access it. This is an arcane task in the Athena environment because of its complex access control. The entire exchange takes 41 minutes (interwoven with several others) and has 9 participants. At one point, sirius tries to be helpful and provides some elementary information. hasan gets indignant at the assumption, and sirius tells him that he was trying to be a helpful information provider. The [...] indicates that several extraneous messages were omitted between hasan's message and sirius's response.

```
Time: 10:49:17 Date: Mon Oct 18 1993
From: he said, she said. <sirius>
by the way, hasan,  ~ means your home
directory, which, in your case, is
/mit/hasan

Time: 10:50:18 Date: Mon Oct 18 1993
From: Hasan <hasan>
Bloody hell, I did know that. Humph.

[...]
Time: 10:53:31 Date: Mon Oct 18 1993
From: Moonlight reflects the rain. <sirius>
hasan -- sorry if some of the things
I'm telling you are things you
already know ... but it's difficult to
judge how much someone knows, and lots
of people will not ask about confusing
jargon even if it is meaningless t
to them.
```

Sharp or acerbic answers often bring a response from other answerers. After one answerer was curt with a naive questioner, he was taken to task not to be sharp:

```
Time: 16:15:02 Date: Sat Dec 11 1993
From: Paul Su <pauls>
Switch to help.d?

"Which word didn't you understand?" is one of my
pet peeves. The true answer is typically "It is
not a particular word, but how the word is
related to the concepts under discussion". But
almost always the person on the receiving end of
this doesn't have the tolerance to formulate such
a formal answer.
```

We should note that the Help Instance is "polite enough." There are no doubt users who find the tone dismissive, difficult, or problematic. Nonetheless, we have noted a usual tone of politeness in the Zephyr exchanges. Askers often send an extra message of thanks, and the answerers seldom are dismissive.

The visibility of expertise

The two roles of asker and answerer get played out in a very publicly visible environment. Zephyr's user interface requires messages to be highly public and visible, which adds to the system's social reinforcement. The visibility affords for public acceptance of an answerer's expertise, requires self-control over incorrect answers, as well as provides an easy path by which people can be recruited for the role of answerer.

Answering questions *correctly* is extremely self-reinforcing in the MIT culture. With the culture's anchor in technical expertise (as is "cluefulness"), one can gain the admiration of colleagues for showing proficiency. Said one interviewee, "I answer partially to be helpful, and I answer partially to show off." One's performance on the Help Instance is public -- and visible to anyone subscribing. If one is capable of correct answers, then the Help Instance is a good forum for garnering the attention most prized by the organizational culture.

For undergraduates, who form the major population of Help Instance users, this visibility and public performance have extra force. As Davis found with his student nurses [5], students must articulate and rehearse their future professional roles to be successful within school and later in their careers. Successful students come to understand this need, and quickly begin to practice what Davis terms "role simulations" of "valued performances".

The public performance of one's Help Instance activity also diminishes the number of incorrect answers. Since "cluefulness" or technical expertise is enacted (i.e., agreed upon by both the participant and his audience), providing incorrect answers detracts from one's preferred persona. Information providers seldom answer when they are uncertain, and if they do (e.g., when directly asked) will mark uncertain answers appropriately.

The public performance, combined with the ease of response, also results in recruitment of new members. The Help Instance "regulars" provide a stable collectivity which a new recruit may gradually join. Seeing one's questions answered makes it more likely that one will ask questions. Opportunities to correct or elaborate on another's answers provide a forum for slowly increasing one's answering without discomfort. In a situation where no one is compelled to answer, the opportunity to correct or supplement another (politely and non-hostilely) is of high motivation. New members, then, are gradually recruited.

Background attending and lightweightness

While the roles and norms are elaborated to reduce psychological cost for users, participation might still be onerous or problematic without the ability to ignore the Help Instance while attending to one's work.

As mentioned, for people to ask questions, they must feel that they will find an answer. In order for the Help Instance to support collaborative problem solving for its users, it must be attended by many users with various areas of expertise. However, requiring that any given individual provide answers could be onerous, especially if that individual were a volunteer as in the case of the Help Instance. Furthermore, answering or even attending could interfere with one's work performance, thus reducing the likelihood of participation. Consequently, the system must allow many people to follow the progress of a topic and join in the activity voluntarily, as they see fit. Because the interactions are rapid, conversation topics change quickly, allowing users to phase in and out of attending without substantial loss. The amount of work and time required of users to help other users is dictated only by the helper him- or herself.

It appears to be socially permissible to not answer a question, even if questions from other people are being answered. We saw no evidence that this was problematic. If someone doesn't know the answer to question, it is rarely said; the question simply goes unanswered. These same guidelines enable others to not answer a question even if they might know the answer. For this reason, answering a question is seen as a voluntary gesture, and users asking questions should not expect help. In the following exchange, `loy` is told that he should be patient with not getting a response:

```
Time: 21:09:07 Date: Wed Oct  6 1993
From: Why are wrong numbers never busy? <loy>
anyone heard of a software company called
metrowerks?

Time: 21:14:18 Date: Wed Oct  6 1993
From: No hypothetical situations? <loy>
has anyone heard of a company called
metrowerks?
(if this is the second time this went here,
then I wasn't subbed before, out of practice,
sorry)

Time: 21:14:44 Date: Wed Oct  6 1993
From: Synthetic syntax spoken <descartes>
No one answered the first time; presumably no
one here has heard of it.
```

Background attending of a large silent audience also works as a check on the quality of answers given by individuals. As an earlier example showed, users will correct answers, and the large attendant audience serves as a safety net for people who ask questions. Accordingly, there may be less fear of asking questions or of misinforming others.

The system capability for this lightweight attending assists in sustaining the Help Instance. Interestingly, the technical features that afford lightweight attending include the limited display options. The teletype window option lets the Help Instance messages scroll by. The scrolling action allows the user to be conversationally current only on the messages that are still displayed on the screen, reducing the burden on the user to immerse him or herself in a longer-term context. When Zephyr messages are displayed using pop-up windows, each message has its own window. When someone chooses not to attend, the windows pile up on one another, with the most recent Zephyr message on top. Users can then attend to only the most recent message which appears on top. The system is largely memoryless. This lack of memory and the possibility of background attending provide for lightweight help; users need answer only as they wish.

CONCLUSIONS

The Zephyr Help Instance is a place where users can ask questions and get expert, but polite answers. It is also a place where users can answer questions and feel satisfaction and social approval.

To continue providing help, the Help Instance requires, like any sociality, a common-enough understanding of the space's purpose, a shared understanding of the key roles (i.e., questioners and answerers), some norms about acceptable and preferred behavior, and a positive adaptation to the organizational culture. In other words, in order to continue as a social place, there must be a negotiated order of some sort. The Zephyr Help Instance is a simple example of this, but one that is effective and successful.

These social mechanisms rely on several system features. Zephyr is simple technically. But, we have discussed the usefulness found in its capabilities for new instances (for policing of the topics), the system speed (for background attending), the public messages (for rewarding and recruiting answerers), as well as, paradoxically, the lack of memory and the poor display options (for background attending). Most importantly, the generality of messaging allows users to negotiate their status and roles on the system. Perhaps because the system is so simple, the users are able to effectively negotiate their roles and statuses through the system.

Some of the particular social mechanisms described here are specific to MIT or similar organizations. We would not expect to find "cluelessness" per se in many other organizations (although we might find similar labels for new and naive members). Thus, these system affordances do not necessarily enable the social mechanisms. Instead, we note that the users have made creative use of system affordances to organize and regulate their electronic social space. Users were able to seize upon the system features for their own social purposes. The system affordances became resources in the users' world [11], allowing the users to create and maintain a socially useful and usable system over time. Indeed, it is likely that other successful CSCW systems will have similar adaptations.

Acknowledgments
This work continues the Answer Garden project. This began when the first author was at Project Athena, and the authors are indebted to Wendy Mackay, Beth Anderson, and the many users and originators of the Help Instance. Wayne Lutters provided the usage statistics. Bob Halperin, Lisa Covi, Christine Halverson, David Redmiles, and Jonathan Grudin provided additional help with this paper.

The MIT Center for Coordination Science provided continued assistance for this study. This research was supported by grants from NASA (NRA-93-OSSA-09) and the UCI Committee on Research. The second author was supported through an NSF graduate fellowship.

References

1. Aaronson, A. and J. Carroll. Intelligent Help in a One-Shot Dialog: A Protocol Study. *Proceedings of CHI + GI '87*, 1987: 163-168.
2. Berger, P. *The Sacred Canopy*. Anchor, New York, 1967.
3. Bowers, J. The Work to Make a Network Work: Studying CSCW in Action. *Proceedings of CSCW'94*, 1994: 287-298.
4. Campagnoni, F. R. and K. Ehrlich. Information Retrieval Using a Hypertext-Based Help System. *Proceedings of SIGIR '89*, 1989: 212-220.
5. Davis, F. Professional Socialization as Subjective Experience. In Becker, H., B. Geer, D. Riesman and R. Weiss (ed). *Institutions and the Person: Papers Presented to Everett C. Hughes*. Aldine, Chicago, 1968.
6. DellaFera, C., M. Eichin, R. French, D. Jedlinsky, J. Kohl and W. Sommerfeld. The Zephyr Notification Service. *Proceedings of the Usenix Technical Conference*, 1988: 213-220.
7. Finholt, T. Outsiders on the Inside: Sharing Information through a Computer Archive. Carnegie Mellon University, Ph.D. thesis, 1993.
8. Garfinkel, H. *Studies in Ethnomethodology*. Prentice-Hall, Englewood Cliffs, NJ, 1967.
9. Grudin, J. and L. Palen. Groupware Success Factors: A Study of Meeting Scheduling. *Proceedings of European CSCW Conference*, 1995: forthcoming.
10. Hiltz, S. R. and M. Turoff. The Evolution of User Behavior in a Computerized Conferencing System. *Communications of the ACM*, 1981, 24(11): 739-762.
11. Hutchins, E. *Cognition in the Wild*. MIT Press, Cambridge, MA, 1995.
12. Hutchins, E. and L. Palen. Constructing Meaning from Space, Gesture and Talk. *Proceedings of NATO Workshop on Discourse, Tools and Reasoning*, 1993.
13. Kearsley, G. *Online Help Systems : Design and Implementation*. Ablex, Norwood, NJ, 1988.
14. Malone, T. W. Designing Organizational Interfaces. *Proceedings of CHI'85*, 1985: 66-71.
15. Orlikowski, W. Learning from Notes: Organizational Issues in Groupware Implementation. *Proceedings of CSCW'92*, 1992: 362-369.
16. Randall, D. and J. A. Hughes. Sociology, CSCW, and working with customers. In Thomas, P. J. (ed). *The Social and Interactional Dimensions of Human-Computer Interaction*. Cambridge University, New York, 1995.
17. Sproull, L. and S. Kiesler. *Connections*. MIT Press, Cambridge, MA, 1991.
18. Strauss, A. *Creating Sociological Awareness*. Transaction, New Brunswick, 1991.

Email overload: exploring personal information management of email

Steve Whittaker **Candace Sidner**
Lotus Development Corporation
One Rogers St
Cambridge MA. 02142, USA
+1 (617) 693 5003 +1 (617) 693 7737
Steve_Whittaker@crd.lotus.com Candy_Sidner@crd.lotus.com

ABSTRACT

Email is one of the most successful computer applications yet devised. Our empirical data show however, that although email was originally designed as a *communications* application, it is now being used for additional functions, that it was not designed for, such as *task management* and *personal archiving*. We call this *email overload*. We demonstrate that *email overload* creates problems for personal information management: users often have cluttered inboxes containing hundreds of messages, including outstanding tasks, partially read documents and conversational threads. Furthermore, user attempts to rationalise their inboxes by filing are often unsuccessful, with the consequence that important messages get overlooked, or "lost" in archives. We explain how *email overloading* arises and propose technical solutions to the problem.

Keywords

Email, information overload, personal information management, asynchronous communication, filing, task management, interpersonal communication, ethnography, empirical studies.

WHY STUDY EMAIL?

Email is one of the most successful computer applications yet devised. There are millions of email users world-wide who often spend significant proportions of their work time using email. Research suggests that email has contributed to the growth of distributed organisations, by allowing people in different geographical areas to communicate across time and space. It has also led to the emergence of on-line communities by supporting asynchronous communication [8]. Email has been the subject of many studies, including pioneering early work that focussed on the social and communicative aspects of email, comparing its usage with face-to-face communication [8]. Nevertheless, there is little systematic data on its usage and utility as a workplace technology. Furthermore, the success and popularity of email has led to high daily volumes of email being sent and received. Research has not yet addressed how people organise and manage large amounts of information. This study therefore presents a quantitative analysis of the mailboxes of 20 users, along with 34 hours of interviews to address these new questions.

Email applications were originally designed for *asynchronous communication*, but as our analysis will show, email has evolved to a point where it is now used for multiple purposes: document delivery and archiving; work task delegation; and task tracking. It is also used for storing personal names and addresses, for sending reminders, asking for assistance, scheduling appointments, and for handling technical support queries. We use the term *email overload* to describe the use of email for functions that it was not designed for. We discuss three main email functions: *task management, personal archiving* and *asynchronous communications*. The central question is how well a single tool can support all these functions. Subsidiary questions must also be asked in each category.

Task management requires users to ensure that information relating to current tasks is readily *available*. This both preserves *task context* and allows users to determine the progress of ongoing tasks. Task management also involves *reminding* oneself about when particular tasks or actions have to be executed [1,2,4,6]. How do people do this in email?

Personal archiving or *filing* addresses how people organise and categorise longer term information, so that it can later be retrieved. *Archives* are not of immediate relevance to current tasks, but are constructed for reference or anticipated future use. Research shows that users experience major problems in generating appropriate folder labels when *filing* longer term information for later retrieval, and in *reconstructing* these labels when they engage in later retrieval [1,2,4,6]. To what extent do these problems occur in email?

Asynchronous communication is concerned with interaction in a permanent medium across space and time. Research has characterised face-to-face workplace communications as consisting of repeated brief communications [3,10]. Such interactions are seldom one-shot, and workers often engage in multiple intermittent interactions in order to complete a task. Workers are also usually engaged in several independent, but concurrent ongoing conversations, with the requirements of tracking separate conversational threads and switching contexts between conversations [10]. Does email communication have these characteristics, and how are *asynchronous communications* conducted?

To provide preliminary answers to these questions, this study presents qualitative and quantitative information about the use of email for *task management, personal archiving* and *asynchronous communication*. We describe the problems people experience with each of these functions, and the strategies they invoke to address the problems. Finally we suggest potential technical solutions.

SYSTEM AND METHOD

We studied users of NotesMail, the email component of Lotus Notes. This client-server system has a GUI with a number of standard features, including the ability to compose, reply to, copy (*cc*), and blind copy (*bcc*) messages to other users. Incoming unread messages are delivered into the inbox (called "uncategorised" in Notes), where they appear in a different colour from messages the user has "opened" and read. Once "opened", they appear in the standard colour. The system provides users with the ability to file information: they do so by creating categories (equivalent to folders in other email systems), so that related messages can be stored and accessed together, by category label. There is no conversational threading of messages: although responses generated using the reply option appear with *re* in the subject line, the system does not allow the user to automatically view messages from a given thread together. It is, however, possible for users to view messages in terms of various other properties. One can view by sender, date, size, or category. The system also has a text search capability: email databases can be full text indexed, so that key word or Boolean queries are possible. There is no formal support, or policy for, archiving.

The 20 study participants were office workers representing four major job types: 4 high level managers, i.e. people who had other managers reporting to them; 5 first level managers; 9 professional workers with no management responsibility, and 2 administrative assistants. All participants were experienced users with between 2 and 15 years experience of email. They had all used NotesMail for more than one year. All participants were employees of Lotus Development Corporation, a software development firm. We chose our subjects because we wanted to investigate email use in multiple job types, with different responsibilities. Our participants were drawn from marketing, consultancy, software development, support and research groups. We chose the organisation both because of its pervasive use of email and ready access to subjects. Given these choices, we studied NotesMail because it was the most frequently used system in the Lotus organisation.

We collected quantitative data about the mailbox of 18 users: (a) total number, age, and size of messages in their mailbox; (b) number of messages in each archival folder, (c) conversational threads. Due to technical difficulties, we were unable to collect quantitative data for the final two users. Ideally we would have wished to collect longitudinal data over an extended time period, to look at changes in mailbox size and structure, but the logistics of repeated access to personal data prevented this. We were however, able to collect a "snapshot" of each mailbox at a given point, from which we drew important inferences, which we report below.

We also interviewed all 20 participants for 1-2 hours using semi-structured questions. We asked them to describe: (a) the volume of email they sent and received; (b) their prioritisation, reading and reply strategies; (c) their correspondence management, e.g. when they used *reply, cc* and *bcc* features and how they managed conversational threads; (d) their filing behaviours. We also discussed: (e) the main problems they were experiencing with email; and (f) their reactions to certain technical solutions addressing these problems. Interviews were carried out in people's offices and participants were encouraged to demonstrate their statements and strategies with reference to their actual systems.

We analysed our interviews by collecting user comments about each issue described above. We present representative quotes from participants about these, and where there was substantial disagreement or inconsistency between participants' opinions, then we present quotes representing alternative points of view.

EMAIL OVERLOAD: THE PROBLEM

Participants were generally highly positive about email as a communication tool. They stressed how it enabled them to collaborate with others across time and distance [8]. They also pointed out its advantages over other technologies such as the telephone, and even face-to-face interaction. Nevertheless certain individuals experienced major problems in reading and replying to email in a timely manner, with backlogs of unanswered email, and in finding information in email systems. The inability to effectively manage communication means lost information, and reduced responsiveness. These have clear negative outcomes for both individual and corporate productivity.

"Waiting to hear back from another ...employee can mean delays in accomplishing a particular task, which can ... have significant impact on our overall operations. Depending on the situation, it can either be critical or just frustrating."

"One of my pet-peeves is when someone does not get back to me, but I am one of the worst offenders. I get so many e-mails (average 30-40/day) and phone messages (15-20) that I cannot keep up and also do my real job..."

"given the sheer volume of stuff that passes through here. I mean I couldn't even give you a percentage of how much is missed. I mean -- not necessarily missed but certainly recorded but never followed up on"

"I dedicate somewhere between minimally two hours at the outlying range, up to ten hours on any given day trying to stay on top of email"

So why do these problems arise? A simple *one-touch* model of email might assume: incoming messages that are *informational,* i.e. those not requiring a response, are read, and then either deleted or filed, depending on their relevance. Incoming messages that form part of a *correspondence,* (i.e. requiring a response), are answered, and then either deleted or filed. According to the *one-touch* model, information can therefore be in two possible states: unread and filed. The user's inbox at any point should solely consist of a small number of unread incoming messages, and the rest of their mailbox consist of filed items.

Our quantitative data show the *one touch* model is patently incorrect. The mean number of inbox items is 2482, and the mean number of filed items (858) is small compared with the number of inbox items, so that the inbox constitutes on average 53% of people's mailfiles. It is implausible that users receive 2482 new items each day, so what is happening and why is the inbox so full? It turns out that there are two related reasons for this: (a) the inbox operates as a *task manager,* where people are *reminded* of current tasks, and where people can keep information relevant to those tasks *accessible*; (b) people find it hard to *file* information to remove it from their inbox, both because filing into folders is difficult and there may also be few benefits to creating folders.

EXPLAINING THE FULL INBOX: MANAGING WORKING INFORMATION

Our users received a large number of messages each day (mean 49). One reason for the large volume of incoming messages is that email is now the *source* of many different office tasks, serving as the place in which work is received and delegated.

"it's where things come into your life in a way. It's the place where ... people hand things off to you, it's the electronic office"

Email can be an important determinant of how people spend their working day, again suggesting that it is a place that users receive and hand off tasks:

"I check it before I leave the house just in case there's anything I didn't get the night before. I read it as soon as I get into the office. ..... It does change what I do throughout the day, like what – I may come in thinking I was going to do one thing, but get mail that sort of diverts me into doing something else..... If I haven't checked my mail it makes me uncomfortable. And there's invariably a piece of something I was supposed to do, that's time sensitive".

Both the volume of incoming mail and the fact that mail is being used for task management, leads to a breakdown in the *one-touch* model. While there is evidence that users try and process information at once, there are a number of reasons why immediate responses are sometimes not possible or not appropriate, so that incoming messages remain undischarged in the inbox.

One general reason relates to the amount of time users have currently available. If the message requires more than a certain amount of time or effort to process, then users delay dealing with it and proceed to other potentially more urgent or manageable messages in the inbox. There are also specific types of messages that are often not discharged immediately:

(a) *"To dos"* These are messages which require the user to execute some action. In some cases, the message may require the user to engage in further complex activities which might take days to achieve. The user does not usually suspend the process of reading email to discharge these activities. These "to dos" are commonly kept in the inbox as *reminders* of unfinished tasks.

(b) *"To reads"* Alternatively, messages might be long documents. Although these are often informational and do not require a reply, they still take time and effort to read, and users often delay reading them, so that the inbox may contain unread or partially read documents. The quantitative data support this. We found that on average 21% of the inbox (i.e. an average of 334 messages) were long, when a long message was defined as more than 10Kbytes (~5 screensfull).

(c) *Messages of indeterminate status* One issue with informational messages, is that users are often unsure of the significance of an incoming message when it first arrives. Rather than investing valuable time in reading it at once, they register its arrival, but delay dealing with it until some later point when they are more certain of its importance. What makes immediate decisions difficult, is that the value of a given message may depend on events that occur *after* the message has been received: a flurry of subsequent messages on the topic may reveal its importance, or else it may turn out to be a "dead-end" with no follow-up being necessary. Rather than delete it immediately, users often conservatively retain it just in case it turns out to be important. This user describes keeping such documents in her inbox:

"I've gotten messages, I haven't dealt with them, haven't known what to do about them. And starting this new position, ... I got a lot of mail messages, but I didn't have the knowledge to know what on earth they were about ... You know, people were talking about servers and infrastructure....I just realized some day I would understand it, and I saved a lot of that stuff, and actually had to make a presentation where it all came in handy – where I went, I've been sitting with this information all this time and I didn't know it..... so you're conservative about keeping stuff, and ...at some point in the future it may come in useful."

People also explained how retaining such unread messages was useful for unplanned contingencies, e.g. when they received surprise phone calls about them. They were able to read the documents in the course of the call, while pretending to have already read them.

"[email] is the best that's ever happened for covering your ass ... because while the guy's on the phone, he says, well, I sent that to you a week and a half ago, and you think, shit, I never saw that. But you say, 'really? Yeah, oh yeah, I remember reading that', as you're reading it."

(d) *Ongoing correspondence.* Finally the inbox is sometimes used for ongoing, but incomplete, threads of asynchronous conversations. The user may delay responding to a question from another person because a careful reply is necessary which takes more time than is currently available. Alternatively, users may be unable to reply immediately, because they currently do not have the answer, and they await further information from other people.

For more complex interactions involving multiple exchanges over an extended time period, users may also track and sometimes save, both their own and other people's contributions to the conversation. An issue may take several email exchanges to be resolved, or users may require the responses of multiple individuals in order to collate opinion, or reach consensus. A major problem with email correspondence is that there are no agreed conventions about whether to include the context or history of prior messages as the conversation proceeds. Often this context is important, because it is necessary for interpreting what each subsequent message means. One user describes this problem with one of his coworkers.

"X is unbelievable in that he never puts the context in which, of what he's replying to. He always comes up with these one line responses, and I have no idea what it is that he's talking about, you know, it's like, "Re: the Internet." ... And, in many cases, he's replying to something that somebody else sent, but I wasn't on the original distribution list, but he thinks that I'd be interested ...So I get this totally out-of-context great idea"

For multiple interchanges extending over periods of days or weeks, it is easy to forget who said what and to whom. For legal purposes, it can also be important on occasion to record exactly what was said by whom. For these reasons, for certain critical interactions, users sometimes save both the originating message, as well as subsequent interactions.

"the people that I consider some of the best problem-solvers in my organization are fanatical about the history. And you get the whole thing. Yeah, the audit trail of what happens. We do that, have to do that a lot in support...Because you could be dealing with an extended customer issue that bounced around ... especially the people that are right on the front lines, it's almost like second nature to them... It's not only everything that's being said... It's every person that has been involved"

This conversational record serves multiple functions: an archive of what has been discussed; a *reminder* to the user that the conversation is in progress; and a record of the status of the conversation, and whether one "owes" or is "owed" a response. The importance of conversational tracking, as well as the absence of conventions about whether others will include history, can mean that each exchange of a lengthy conversation will appear as a separate message in the inbox. Not only does this increase the number of messages in the inbox, it is often difficult to gather together the related threads of a conversation, because conversational exchanges are often interleaved with other unrelated information.

"That reply with the history of previous stuff.... when some people do that and some don't and the fact that it's all interspersed with all other kinds of crap in my e-mail, and then I just can't pick up an e-mail and find out what else it belongs with".

The quantitative data indicate the pervasiveness of inbox conversational threads. We examined the subject line of each message and counted the number of instances in which it contained "*re*", signalling it was a reply to an original message. By this metric[1], we found that inboxes contain a mean of 209 such messages, and that these constitute 12% of the total inbox messages.

To summarise, multiple types of items linger in users' inboxes: actions the user has yet to do; documents that are partially read or unread, and correspondence that is still in progress. What unifies these is that they are all *incomplete*, and the usual strategy is to leave them in the inbox to serve as *reminders* that some further action is required. They are not normally filed away, because filing would mean that they are no longer visible whenever new email is read or the inbox searched.

"the reason that I don't categorize things but leave them in here [the inbox] is that I realize .... there are a certain number of things that I keep in my mind, and I will go back for... And others, I do have to count on tripping over them. And as long as there is that mess that I know I have to do the multiple passes of reading over... I'm kind of depending on that serendipitous tripping over it again as a way to remind me"

The importance of this visual reminding function is evidenced by the fact that five users had experimented with a strategy of filing undischarged information in an "action", or "to do", folder. In all but one of these cases, this action folder was abandoned, because users had to *explicitly remember* to go to it, open it and view its contents, rather than being reminded of these unintentionally, by the mere fact of being in the inbox reading new email[2].

"I used to have an "unread" folder. Which was messages I'd opened up, but I had never finished reading. Like those big ones that ... I didn't get through right away. I didn't go back to it [the unread folder] often enough though".

The single person who *was* successfully using "to do" folders had reconfigured her mailbox UI, so as to be reminded about this folder. Her "to do" folder appeared immediately above the first new unread item in her inbox, so that she would automatically see the "to do" folder whenever she read new email.

A second reason for leaving information in the inbox concerns its *availability*. In the case of extended interactions, users often keep conversational history in the inbox, because they believe it to be more *accessible* there.

"you may not want to file it. Because it might be something you need to refer to. .... I don't want to file that yet, because it's active ... there are things that are happening as a result of that. It's easier for me to find it. So I want to keep in my "in" box, keep it current"

GETTING INFORMATION OUT OF THE INBOX: THE PROBLEM OF FILING

We have seen that incomplete tasks being "kept around" can lead the inbox to be full. A second complementary reason is that users find it difficult to move messages out of the inbox by filing them into folders containing collections of related messages. Why is this? Firstly generating and maintaining these folder collections requires considerable effort. Secondly, and more importantly, the resulting collections may be of little use in message retrieval.

Filing is a cognitively difficult task [2,4]. Successful filing is highly dependent on being able to imagine future retrieval requirements. It is hard to decide which existing folder is appropriate, or, if a new folder is needed, how to give it a memorable name.

"any piece of information longer than five lines has at least several axes along which you might want to look it up and it really depends how you're coming at it and what you're thinking about at the time. [Filing] isn't reliable."

Users also may not file messages because they are concerned about failure to remember where information has been filed. Failure can have severe consequences especially if the message requires action:

"I don't know where to put it. And.. by making a wrong decision, I could really forget about it..."

---

[1]This measures the number of messages that are part of extended conversations, rather than the total number of conversational threads. It *underestimates* the proliferation of threaded messages, because it does not detect the message that originated the thread. It also occasionally *overestimates:* people report taking the last message by another person and simply *replying*, to avoid having to regenerate another user's mailing address, and on rare occasions forgetting to modify the subject line when they do this.

[2]An exception occurs when users create a folder for an ongoing conversational thread, for which there is a large number of daily incoming messages. There seem to be two reasons for this: the first is the pressing need to remove the multiple interactions *"cluttering up"* the inbox, and the second is that the frequency of these messages means that the user will be *reminded* of the fact that the conversation is still in progress.

Another reason for not filing is that users want to postpone their judgement in order to determine the value of information. Users do not want to create archives containing information that later turn out to be useless or irrelevant. The strategy here is to wait and see the extent to which subsequent events indicate a message is valuable.

"I'm reluctant to archive junk. ... I know that the consequence of archiving junk is to make it that much harder to find the good stuff... in the archive...Especially if information seems like it eventually will be overcome by events, I'd be very loath to move it into a [folder]. I'd be more likely to kind of hold it in my "in" box"

Folders may also not be useful after they are constructed. One problem is that users may not be able to remember folder labels, especially after a time has elapsed: *"if it's sort of older stuff, the category names are not going to mean anything to me any more".* Users experienced special problems when they had large numbers of folders. They had to remember the definition of each when filing and to be careful not to introduce duplication by creating new folders that were synonymous with pre-existing ones. Duplication detracts from their use in retrieval.

In addition, folders can be *too small* to be useful. A major aim of filing is to reduce the huge number of undifferentiated inbox items into a relatively small set of folders each containing multiple related messages. Filing is clearly not successful if the number of messages in a given folder is small: if a folder contains only one or two items, then its existence has not significantly reduced the complexity of the inbox, nor gathered together significant amounts of related material. However our data show that filing often fails: on average 35% of users' folders contain only one or two items. Furthermore, not only do these tiny "failed folders" not significantly reduce the complexity of the inbox, the user has the dual overheads of (a) creating them in the first place, and (b) remembering multiple definitions every time there is a decision about filing an new inbox item.

The quantitative data reflect the problem of trying to remember multiple folder definitions. The larger the number of folders a user has, the more likely that person is to generate "failed folders" containing only one or two items ($r_{(16)} = 0.75$, $p < 0.001$). User statements bear this out:

"I wish I viewed creating a category as a lightweight activity. And for some reason I don't .... it seems like, you know the more of them I create, the harder it is to find any of them that are there".

Folders can also fail because they are *too big.* When there are too many messages in a folder, it becomes unwieldy. It is difficult to find the relevant message in a large folder, the relationships between different messages in the folder become tenuous, so that one benefit of keeping them together is much reduced.

"So what happened was the size of the chunks associated with the categories got large. So now one key stroke would get me to a hundred things. So I really was no better off (filing information)"

To conclude, we have seen that users experience difficulties in creating folders. In addition, the returns for this effort may not be great: folders can be too large, too small or they may be too numerous for people to remember their individual definitions. As a consequence, folders may be of little use either for retrieval or for viewing related messages together. There is also a third problem: filing information means that it is less available to *remind* users about that topic. Some users therefore to finesse this problem: instead of filing incoming information, they simply leave it all in their inbox and use full-text search to find individual messages. We now examine users' strategies with respect to the problems of organising the inbox, so that it can be an effective method for managing ongoing tasks and conversations.

STRATEGIES FOR HANDLING EMAIL OVERLOAD

Given the dual problems of managing ongoing conversations and tasks, combined with the issue of filing, we identify three different user strategies, based on two criteria: (a) whether or not users currently use folders; (b) whether they "clean up" their inbox on a daily basis. This yields 3 strategies: *no filers* (no use of folders); *frequent filers* (folder users who try and clean up their inbox daily); *spring cleaners* (folder users who clean up their inbox only periodically). The data associated with each are shown in Table 1.

No filers: made no current use of folders (mean 11.33), but relied on full-text search to find information. Their folders were historic remnants from when two of the *no-filers* still filed. As a consequence of not filing, their inboxes were huge (3093.5 items, making up 95% of all their email). Their inboxes were overloaded: they included a large numbers of conversational threads (mean, 288). More significantly, over half of their inbox was old information that arrived more than 3 months ago. Their strategy for reducing the size of the overloaded inbox was periodic purges in which they deleted large numbers of old items or copied them to a separate independent archive. Four of the six *no filers* were managers.

Frequent filers: made strenuous attempts to minimise the numbers of inbox messages. They made daily passes through their inbox filing or deleting its contents. Their inboxes were relatively small, containing only 43.4 items, which was a very small percentage (5%) of the total number of mailbox messages. In addition, the inbox consisted almost exclusively of new items (90% were less than a month old, and only 5% were older than 3 months), and it was almost devoid of conversational threads (mean 3.6). They made frequent use of folders, and were relatively successful in their use of these, with only 21% being "failed folders". The five frequent filers included both the administrative assistants, but only one manager.

Spring Cleaners: dealt with the overloaded nature of their inboxes by intermittent *clean-ups* - normally every 1-3 months. They made extensive use of folders, even though this was often unsuccessful, as evidenced by the fact that over half of their folders "failed". They also had large overloaded inboxes (mean, 1492.3), containing large numbers of conversational threads (mean, 258). Over 40% of their inbox messages were more than 3 months old. Four of the seven *spring cleaners* were managers.

Impact, Overhead And Choice Of Strategies

All quantitative results are summarised in Table 1. In the remainder of the section, this data will be used to explore the impact of strategy choice. We discuss the trade-offs between strategies, and look at *why* users choose different strategies by examining the relationship between (a) strategy choice; and (b) factors such as job function and incoming message volume.

Strategy	N	# Inbox items	Total # items	Inbox as % of total mailbox	Old inbox items (%inbox> 3month old)	New inbox items (%inbox< 1month old)	# Inbox conversation threads	# Folders	Failed folders (# folders with < 3 items)	Daily # messages received
No filers	6	3093.5	3271.1	95.25	51.58	11.78	287.5	11.33	4.5	58
Spring Cleaners	7	1492.29	2818.71	51.02	40.15	24.22	257.86	61.43	30.85	45.71
Frequent filers	5	43.4	1062.2	4.96	4.75	90.34	3.6	70.6	16.6	42

Table 1 - The three strategies for managing email

The three strategies differ in terms of their benefits and maintenance costs. A major advantage of the *frequent filing* strategy is that the inbox can function as a genuine "to do" list containing a small number of outstanding messages relating to key current tasks, rather than having these items interspersed with huge numbers of conversational threads or unfiled old messages. It is also noteworthy that the average number of items in a frequent filer's inbox (43) can fit in two screens, and frequent filers report that it is important for them to be able to see items in this way. They are able to capitalise on the fact that when they view incoming unread email, they should be reminded of the majority of their outstanding tasks, because these should be visible or immediately accessible in the inbox.

"I don't have any other system, that keeps track of an e-mail message that needs a response .... usually the next day, hopefully it's still sort of near the bottom of the [inbox], ... I will see it when I look at new mail messages, so it won't get scrolled off the screen".

"But I live in the inbox And that is kind of my to-do list. I'll keep things in there ... there's probably about twenty or thirty in there now of things that I want to keep like in my frontal lobes, that I have to deal with"

Frequent filers are effective in their use of folders, experiencing fewer "failed folders". This may be because of frequency with which they file enables them to remember the label definition and contents of each folder. However, despite the benefits of the clean "to do" list, opportunistic reminding, and the availability of current projects, there are major costs to this strategy. It requires significant maintenance: users have to make frequent passes through the inbox, filing and removing discharged items.

".. after I read the new day's mail... I go back to the whole "in" box, right back. And there's almost like a sifting that keeps happening, where the less pressing ones start ageing. And it gets to the point where I say, "I'm either not going to do something about this" .... And I just delete them".

It may be that frequent filing is only possible for lower volumes of incoming email, and for job specifications which do not require users to be away from their desk for long periods of time. Workers such as managers receiving higher volumes with less time to process email may not be in a position to exploit frequent filing.

The *no filing* strategy stands in direct contrast to *frequent filing*. Here users make few attempts to reduce the complexity of their inbox. When possible they answer messages as they receive them, but they seldom review the inbox for outstanding undischarged messages. The fact that their inbox is cluttered with threads, as well as partially read and unread messages, means that outstanding tasks are not easily visible and are quickly displaced and scroll out of sight. Opportunistic reminding and task tracking are therefore unlikely to occur[3]. Users of this strategy admit that the clutter in their inboxes results in important tasks sometimes being overlooked.

"When you're dodging all this other stuff it's hard to pull out what could potentially be pretty important... like anyone else who may have that volume.... after a couple of days you're not going five screens up anymore. You're just looking at your current screen or maybe one more. Who knows what you've missed. I was on vacation for two weeks. Who knows what ... passed through ... e-mail during that time.... I saw a lot of it but I ... let a lot go by. I find that the most aggravating thing is when the inbox starts to grow and I don't know what to do with it necessarily".

When high volume of incoming email is accompanied by large amounts of time away from their desks, this may reduce the likelihood of *no-filers* constructing elaborate filing systems or engaging in extensive periodic clean-ups. The following *no-filer* described why he had abandoned any attempt to manage his inbox.

"Because what I used to do was use [spring cleaning] as a way as organizing and reviewing and catching anything that was falling off the end of the earth. I've given up on it. ... where am I going to get that time? If I wake up at three AM, and I've got nothing else to do, that's when I'm going to do it".

The *spring cleaners* are intermediate to the two other strategies. As with *no-filers*, as their inbox gets large, its size and complexity makes it ineffective as a "to do" list. The fact that it is usually cluttered with threads and unread messages means it is poor for task management, so opportunistic reminding is unlikely to occur. Furthermore the inbox was perceived to be of little archival use.

"it might as well be deleted as buried in this pile of junk .... E-mail may have value, but I will never avail myself in its current form, in this mail file. And so, it might as well be gone as sitting there, because either way I don't have it. It's not at my disposal and not usable".

Spring Cleaners have very strong feelings about the disorder of their inboxes: they use terms like *"disgust"* to describe their reactions to their inbox and are motivated by *"seizures"* to clean up. However the fact that they do occasionally go through the inbox means that

[3]One reason for the lack of task tracking may derive from *no filers'* organisational status: since they are usually managers, they tend to delegate tasks. They expect their employees to carry out the task, and report when it is done.

outstanding unprocessed messages are detected and can be replied to, even if these are sometimes late.

"So what I started to do was, either weekly, ... then monthly, I would go back to my mail, partly to categorize it and actually truthfully to catch things that I had just dropped the ball on"

This group seems to be less successful at creating useful folders than frequent filers. One possibility is that spring cleaners create folders infrequently, so that they forget folder definitions. Hence they may create duplicates of already existing folders. In terms of maintenance this strategy stands between the others: it does not require the daily efforts of *frequent filing,* but occasional clean-ups are required. This strategy choice may be explained by the inputs and workload of *spring cleaners:* they receive fewer messages and are less likely to be managers than *non-filers*, giving them more time to devote to managing their email.

We then tested these observations statistically. Because of our small subject pool, we were forced to combine data from both *spring cleaners* and *no filers,* in order to make comparisons. The analysis shows that *frequent filers* differ from the other strategies in a number of respects: they have smaller mailboxes ($t_{(16)} = 2.35, p < 0.05$), and smaller inboxes ($t_{(16)} = 3.94$, $p < 0.005$). Frequent filer's inboxes contain fewer inbox threads ($t_{(16)} = 3.99, p < 0.005$), and also tend to consist of newer items ($t_{(16)} = 2.41$, $p < 0.05$). Furthermore, there is a suggestion that they are more successful filers, with fewer "failed folders" ($t_{(16)} = 2.06, p = 0.058$).

Finally we looked at the impact on strategy choice, of factors such as organisational role and incoming volume of messages. We found only partial statistical evidence for the effects of role and volume. Managers were more likely to receive greater volumes of email ($t_{(16)} = 3.06, p < 0.005$). We then looked at whether managers were less likely to be frequent filers, given their higher volume of received email and greater time spent in meetings. Although only one frequent filer was a manager, there was no strong evidence of a direct relationship between strategy and status (*chi squared* (1 df) = 2.49, $p > 0.05$).

REDESIGNING EMAIL TO FIT ITS FUNCTIONS

There are both design and theoretical implications to these results. Although email was originally designed for *asynchronous communication*, the application is actually being used for multiple functions. Email therefore needs to be redesigned to support *filing* and *task management* as well as *asynchronous communication.* Our analysis of different users' strategies shows that both *non-filers* and *spring cleaners* experience problems with both *filing* and *task management.* These problems lead to backlogs of unanswered messages and "lost" information in archives. Furthermore, the group who experienced fewest problems, namely *frequent filers,* may only be able to operate successfully because of strenuous efforts to trim their inboxes. It is therefore important that we address overload. As email volumes continue to increase, even those users who are currently *frequent filers* may end up spending much of their energy in reading and responding to messages, leaving them with little time to maintain their inboxes, and folders. As a result, they may be forced to behave more like *spring cleaners* or even *non-filers.*

We now discuss possible techniques to support the three functions. We have shown that the inbox is often used as a place for incomplete tasks, unfiled information and ongoing conversations. In all these cases, users preserve *working information* in the inbox both to keep it *available* and as a *reminder* that further actions are required. We have also seen, however, that opportunistic reminding is compromised when the number of inbox messages is too large, because messages scroll off the screen and remain unseen. A key technical requirement is therefore to *reduce inbox clutter* to allow visual reminding, but without compromising the *availability* of working information. We now present technical solutions for each email function addressing different ways of presenting and viewing the inbox to support both availability and reminding for working information.

Although email was originally designed for *asynchronous communication,* the current system has limitations in supporting this function. The key requirements for asynchronous communication are: (a) *threading* to support context regeneration and the management of conversational history, and (b) the ability to track the *status* of a conversation. Users want to avoid: scrolling back through large numbers of heterogeneous inbox messages to find all previous elements of a conversational thread; lost context when someone omits message history; forgetting who has the next turn in the conversational sequence.

How can we address these asynchronous communication problems? One solution to the problem of communication management automatically marks email messages from the same conversation using a common thread ID, allowing the user to collect related messages together, and trace back through conversations. The user would subsequently be able to *view by thread.* Viewing by thread allows a user to select any message, use that message to access all messages from that conversation, and hence view any message in its conversational context. This functionality is equivalent to having a single message containing the forwarded history of an entire conversation. Unlike a single message, viewing by conversation is not beset by the navigational problem of trying to follow a conversation that is many layers deep, where information may be buried within a single message. Viewing by thread provides several additional benefits. It helps determine *conversational status:* by looking at the last message in a thread, the user should be able see whether they "owe" or are "owed" a response. Furthermore, it should be possible to file an entire thread, but *leave a representative message from that thread in the inbox*. This serves the purpose of *reducing inbox clutter,* even when users choose to copy themselves on every response. As we have seen with *frequent filing,* a representative message in an uncluttered inbox can *remind* the user that a conversation is in progress. When the conversation is concluded, the entire thread can also be archived or deleted as the user wishes.

What about *filing?* Given users' uncertainty about the value of much incoming information, they often end up with large numbers of incoming informational messages in their inbox. These documents are in a "holding pattern", while users attempt to determine their relevance and importance. In addition, our data show that filing may not be crucial for retrieval, because it may ultimately be superceded by full-text search. Nevertheless, users may want to cluster and view semantically related messages together, for example while they learn about a new topic.

How might we support this temporary buffering of incoming information? Information retrieval techniques could be used to cluster semantically related documents automatically, and the presentation of these clustered documents might be analogous with *conversational threads*. Users might therefore reduce the clutter of their inboxes, by leaving one semantic category exemplar in their inbox as a reminder and filing the rest. As with *threads*, each incoming message could be viewed in the context of other (in this case *semantically*) related information. This may partly address the problem of *failed folders*, and it might also help users to decide the usefulness of an arriving message. Two provisos are necessary here. First incoming documents should not be "filed" before the user has seen them. User comments and their experience with email filters clearly indicated that "automatic filing" was not desirable: users wanted to *be made aware* of the arrival of incoming documents, otherwise they would be ignorant of their existence. Furthermore, users were concerned that automatic filing would mean they wouldn't know the folder in which a given message had been filed*. Second, this semantic classification needs to be *dynamic*, given that the status of a document can be changed by the arrival of subsequent ones.

Finally, when we consider *task management*, it is clear that conversational *threading* and *semantic clustering* should reduce the amount of inbox clutter by having each conversation or folder represented by one inbox message. The consequent reduction of the number of visible items in the inbox should help users to more easily see their outstanding tasks, and hence support *reminding* and *tracking*. Keeping important things "in view" could also be helped by having the inbox temporally sequenced and having threads and folders gradually "decay" by scrolling off the screen if they have not shown recent activity. Two further requirements seem to be crucial for task management. The first is the ability to *mark* particular inbox items as requiring action. This marker should be highly visible, and it should be possible to view only the "action items" in the absence of threads or folders. Note that this is different from creating an action *folder:* the action items are not filed away, but remain visible in the inbox, to serve their reminding function. The second requirement is the ability to *program reminders*. A critical problem occurs with "action items" that either can't be done immediately or don't need to be done at once. Here it would be useful to program these items so they would *re-appear* as an action item, as the deadline approaches.

Turning to outstanding research issues, we need to test the generality of these results. Although NotesMail is representative of current technology, we must see how the findings extend to both different email systems and a broader user population. It would be of particular interest to investigate systems lacking some of the features in NotesMail, e.g. text search, and also systems that have sophisticated filtering mechanisms, which NotesMail does not possess. To what extent do different features affect handling strategies? Our results about the effects of email volume and job specification on email processing strategies also need to be replicated with larger numbers of subjects.

Lastly, this work supports the findings of recent theoretical studies pointing to the interactive nature of cognition, and the fact that people use external environmental sources or artifacts to mediate cognition [7,9,10,11]. We saw that email folders function as an external archival memory store. More importantly, people frequently access the email inbox, which means that properly organised it can operate as a visual device for attention manipulation and reminding, as a way of extending working memory, and maintaining the context of ongoing activities in an interrupt-driven environment. The importance of visual reminding and need to manage working information are reinforced by recent research on the organisation of physical and electronic desktops [1,2,6]. Past work has focussed almost exclusively on long term storage [3]. Future theoretical work should address these new issues of attention and the management of ephemeral and working information.

ACKNOWLEDGEMENTS

Thanks to the users for participating, to Sal Mazzotta for writing the analysis macros, also to Marilyn Walker, John Patterson, Irene Grief, Sara Kiesler and the members of Egrpsem for comments.

REFERENCES

1. Barreau, D. and Nardi, B. Finding and retrieving information: file organization from the desktop. To appear in *SIGCHI Bulletin*.

2. Kidd, A. The marks are on the knowledge worker. In *Proceedings of CHI'94 Human Factors in Computing Systems*, 186-191, ACM Press, New York, 1994.

3. Kraut, R., Fish, R., Root, B., & Chalfonte, B. Informal communication in organizations. In R. Baecker (Ed.), *Groupware and Computer Supported Co-operative Work*, 287-314, Morgan Kaufman, 1992.

4. Lansdale, M. The psychology of personal information management. *Applied Ergonomics*, 19, 55-66, 1988.

5. Maes, P. Agents that reduce work and information overload. *In Communications of the ACM*, **37**, 31-40, 1994.

6. Malone, T. How do people organize their desktops? Implications for the design of Office Information Systems. *ACM Transactions on Office Information Systems*, **1**, 99-112, 1983.

7. Norman, D. The psychology of everyday things. Basic Books: New York, 1988.

8. Sproull, L., and Kiesler, S. *Connections*. MIT Press, Cambridge, Mass., 1991.

9. Walker, M. Limited attention and discourse structure. *Computational Linguistics*, in press.

10. Whittaker, S., Frohlich., & Daly-Jones, O. Informal workplace communication: what is it like and how might we support it? In *Proceedings of CHI'94 Human Factors in Computing Systems*, 130-137, ACM Press, New York, 1994.

11. Whittaker, S., & Schwarz, H. Back to the future: pen and paper technology supports complex group co-ordination. In *Proceedings of CHI'95 Human Factors in Computing Systems*, 495-502, 1995.

*The observation that users do not want "automatic filing" has important implications for work advocating automatic filtering techniques [5].

HomeNet: A Field Trial of Residential Internet Services

Robert Kraut 1-412-268-7694 | **William Scherlis** 1-412-268-8741 | **Tridas Mukhopadhyay** 1-412-268-2307 | **Jane Manning** 1-412-268-1551 | **Sara Kiesler** 1-412-268-2888

Human Computer Interaction Institute
Carnegie Mellon University
Pittsburgh, PA 15213, USA

robert.kraut@cmu.edu
scherlis@cs.cmu.edu
tridas@andrew.cmu.edu
jmanning@andrew.cmu.edu
kiesler+@andrew.cmu.edu

ABSTRACT
HomeNet is a field trial of residential Internet use with lowered barriers to use. We use multiple longitudinal data collection techniques, including server-side instrumentation. This paper is an initial description of how diverse families used the Internet in the first five months of the trial, and of variables that predicted this usage. The results have implications for design (e.g., provide more help for adults to get started), for marketing (e.g., lower income people have as much desire for on-line services as do upper income people), and for research (e.g., understand why teenagers' lead family computing).

Keywords
Human factors, communication applications, empirical studies, Internet, electronic mail, world wide web, social impact.

THE HOMENET PROJECT

> "I really want to move to Antarctica—I'd want my cat and Internet access and I'd be happy."
> —16 year old HomeNet participant, 1995.

In the 1980s, personal computers and networking transformed workplace communication [11]. As these social changes took place, few researchers and developers looked at networking in the home. And when they did look, they did so narrowly—seeing networking at home as an extension of networking in the office.

In the 1990s, computers are moving into the home at an enormous rate. In contrast to the 1980s, telecommuting and other workplace applications are not the only, or even the main, reasons for this change. By 1994, approximately 31% of US households had a computer [12], and in 1994, computers for the home represented 40% of PC sales. The potential for families, businesses, and community services is enormous. Yet we still lack an understanding of the changes taking place. In particular, we know very little about which electronic services are valuable to people across incomes in diverse communities. We also know little about how to make electronic services more valuable—whether through better design, better training, or a different array of services.

HomeNet is an empirical field trial of residential Internet use whose goal is to increase our knowledge about the use and impact of residential electronic services. It is a true, pretest-posttest field experiment. It uses a longitudinal panel design to study families over time. The project soon begins its second year. Our goal in this early report is to describe how average citizens (as represented in our study) use the Internet and to predict what leads them to use it.

Diverse HomeNet Families

Our current knowledge of electronic services in general and the Internet in particular is based upon the behavior of the predominately upper income, white male professionals who buy computers and have used these services in the past (e.g., [13]). Moreover, the income and education gap between users and non-users of on-line services has been increasing during the last ten years [1]. Our research presumes that as computers become cheaper and on-line services easier to use, future users of these services may well be unlike current users. Therefore we set out to investigate how a broader sample of people would use and value electronic services.

To accomplish this goal, the HomeNet project is based on a service model with low barriers to entry. We loaned families a computer, or if they preferred, sold it to them at half price. Each family also received a high speed modem, and an extra telephone line as well as full Internet accounts

CHI 96 Vancouver, BC Canada
© 1996 ACM 0-89791-777-4/96/04..$3.50

for each family member above age 8 who wanted one. We simplified Internet access. All computers included a turnkey system—for access to the entire Internet—to newsgroups, the World Wide Web, electronic mail, MUDs, and special HomeNet chat newsgroups. Our software configuration allowed family members to use Internet services without learning the details of any computer operating system. Their Internet services were individualized, for example, by providing each family with a Web homepage pointing to information sources tailored to their identified interests. They received approximately three hours of training. We also offered on-line support through a help newsgroup and email, and an evening telephone help desk staffed by college students.

We recruited an initial sample of 48 families (157 individuals) through the public high schools of four neighborhoods in Pittsburgh, PA, selected for their demographic diversity. In each school, we recruited students who worked on the school newspaper and their families, as well as at least one journalism teacher and teacher's family. The common bond of journalism gave students from different schools something to discuss as we put the project on-line.

The result of these procedures is that while the HomeNet sample is not representative of the US population, it is more demographically diverse than existing Internet demographics (see Table 1).

N	157
Race	24% minority
Gender	57% female
Generation	42% <18 years old
Family income	25% <$35,000

Table 1: HomeNet sample demographics

DATA COLLECTION

The HomeNet project uses five sources of data: (1) computer-generated usage records of email traffic, newsgroups read and posted to, Web sites and MUDs visited, and time on the Internet; (2) pre-trial, bi-monthly, and post-trial questionnaires; (3) an archive of HomeNet newsgroup messages; (4) a log of help requests, and (5) home interviews. The analyses reported in this paper rely mainly on the computer-generated usage data, in-depth interviews with 14 families, and the pretest questionnaire. All subjects signed detailed informed consent forms.

HOW DO FAMILIES USE THE NET?

It is hard to get started

Currently, even the easiest-to-use computers and applications pose significant barriers to peoples' use of on-line services. Potential Internet users vary widely in their computer skill, and many have little computer experience. Among the HomeNet participants, 21% reported never having used a computer before the trial started. In contrast, 17% used a home computer at least daily.

Getting started was a major problem for many of the families. Connecting to the Internet is far more difficult than getting telephone or TV service. It requires that people correctly navigate a complex sequence of steps, from obtaining and setting up a computer, to establishing telephone service, to learning application software, to defining and remembering a password. Even with help and our simplified procedure, HomeNet participants had trouble connecting to the Internet for a wide variety of reasons—bad telephone lines and busy signals, passwords forgotten, depressed shift-lock keys on keyboards, erased login scripts, buggy software, and so forth.

Many participants lacked the skills to diagnose problems, in part because they did not have clear models of how components of the overall system operated. Their problems were more likely to be solved quickly if other family members or friends were more sophisticated than they or if they felt comfortable revealing their ignorance to the strangers on a help desk. Although teens typically became the most skilled computer users in their families, they were sometimes reluctant to share their expertise with their parents. Some participants blamed themselves for problems that were due to software bugs or overtaxed servers. Others asked for help from the project staff—122 times over the first 6 weeks of the trial period. The frequency of requesting help declined as people got started (or gave up), and as participants became more skilled in navigating the Internet.

Internet Use Is Strong in the Aggregate, But Varies Widely and Declines With Time

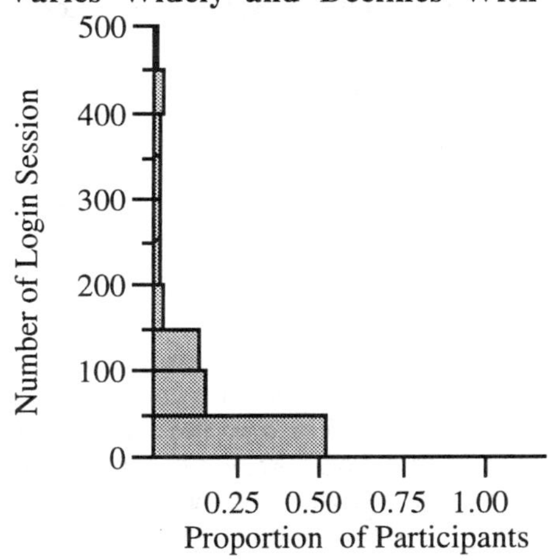

Figure 1. Distribution of logging into the Internet.

Of the 157 participants who received Internet accounts, 126 logged into the Internet (i.e., dialed in to the HomeNet server) from home at least once during the first 22 weeks of the trial. Participation differed enormously among them. Figure 1 shows the distribution of Internet sessions per person. While the modal number of logins was less than twice a week, some participants logged in multiple times per day and had accumulated almost 500 logins during the first 22 weeks of the trial. The first three columns in Table 2 show some descriptive statistics about participants'

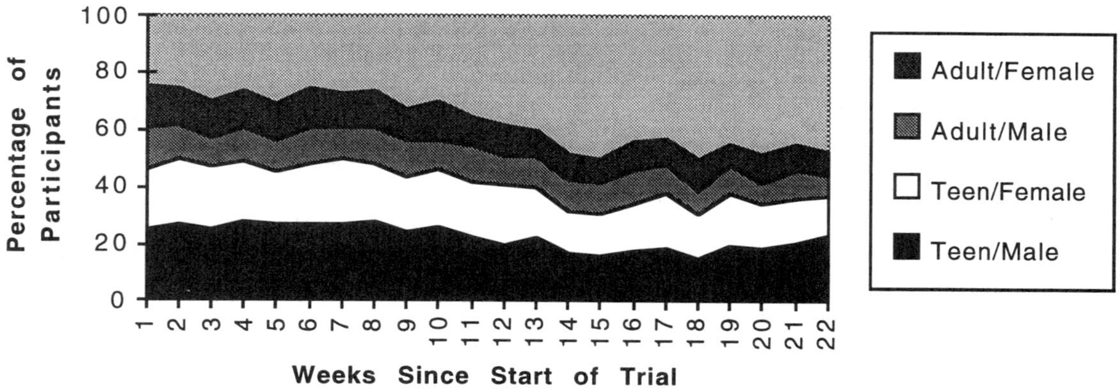

Figure 2. Percent of Participants Logging in Per Week

Note: Percentages have been normalized to a equal number of participants in each demographic group. If everyone in each group used the Internet weekly, then the graph would show four parallel bands, each representing 25% of the users.

use of different Internet services. The distribution of each of these measures is also highly skewed. For example, approximately 12% of those who logged in sent no electronic mail messages over the study period, but one user sent over 2500 messages.

Internet use was initially strong, but declined over time. During the first weeks of the trial approximately three-quarters of the participants logged in at least weekly (see Figure 2). Usage declined to about fifty percent by week 22. A noticeable dip occurred in week 14, when school let out for the summer, as travel, summer jobs, and outdoor activities cut into time on the computer.

Usage differed by generation and gender. For example, at the midpoint of the trial (week 11), 62% of the teenagers logged into the Internet compared to only about 45% of the adults. Among the teenagers, males were much heavier users than females; among adults, males were slightly higher user than females.

Net Use Is Interrelated

Most discussion of the Internet distinguishes communication services like electronic mail, from information services like the World Wide Web. The boundary, however, is blurry and growing blurrier as individuals learn to be their own broadcasters or post information to a newsgroup to response to a particular message.

We find that these conceptually distinct services are complementary. People who used communication services were also likely to use information services, and vice versa, and both kinds of use predicted the number of logins to the Internet and the number of hours spent engaged with it. Table 2 shows the descriptive statistics for various measures of Internet use and the correlations among them. Because usage was skewed, measures were converted to the log scale before the correlations were calculated. The average correlation is high (.70 for all participants shown in Table 1 and .52 for the 88 heaviest users). This result indicates that HomeNet participants who used any Internet service used most of them—electronic mail, newsgroups, and the World Wide Web. Follow-up time-series analyses will allow us to determine whether communication or information consumption is causally prior.

Teens Lead the Family

Our data also showed that usage within families was interrelated. In 41 of the 48 families, the heaviest user was one of the children. There was a significant correlation (r=.54, n=48, p < .01) between the usage of the heaviest user in the family and the average use by other family members. Heavy use by a child predicted both siblings' (r = .43) and parental use (r = .42). Because so few adults were heavy users, we cannot tell if their use also drove that of their spouses or children.

Participants Discover Communication

According to their pretrial questionnaires, participants didn't see computers as particularly useful for interpersonal communication. They thought computers were valuable for doing school work, for learning, and for performing household chores. Yet like people discovering the telephone at the turn of the century, chit-chat quickly became the dominant use of the Internet, and especially so for teenagers.

Overall, the median teenager sent almost six times as many electronic mail messages as the median adult. The generation difference, however, was greater for males than for females. Teenage males sent 25 times more messages than adult males, while teenage girls sent only six times more messages than adult males. Teenage boys sent almost twice as many messages as teenage girls. Almost all of the teenagers' messages went to other teens (94%), whereas the adults communicated approximately equally to teens and other adults.

	1st quartile	Median	3rd quartile	Logins	Connect hours	Email traffic	Newsgroup messages read
Logins	2	21	91	1.00			
Connect hours	.6	10.9	40.7	.95	1.00		
Email messages sent	0	6	39	.75	.78	1.00	
Newsgroup reads	0	2	36	.63	.66	.67	1.00
WWW hits	0	684	3604	.77	.85	.51	.48

Table 2: Descriptive statistics about measures of Internet use and correlations among them

Note. Descriptive statistics are in raw units. Measures were converted to a log scale for correlations.

Several of the teens discovered communication services that allowed them to exchange messages with friends and strangers in real time (Internet Relay Chat and various MUDs). One girl who had never dated started dating a boy she met over a chat service. Because of what seemed to be almost addictive behavior among some of the teenagers who used the real-time communication services, several parents imposed limits on their children's computer use.

Both Mass Market and Individualized Information Services Have Appeal

Directories and popular culture

Only a few newsgroups and World Wide Web sites were popular with most participants. The most frequently accessed services were directories and indexes, like Yahoo and Lycos, which provide taxonomies and search capabilities for people to find information. Directory and repository Web sites represented half of the top 10 Web sites, ordered by number of users accessing each site. Many participants accessed information about popular culture, including sports and entertainment, from newsgroups and Web sites. For example, men visited sites that provided information about the Pittsburgh Penguins, Pirates and Steelers, the local sports teams, and teens downloaded cartoons and songs from rock groups. One mother and her teenage-daughter regularly participated in a newsgroup to keep up with the soap operas they missed.

Sex

HomeNet participants also looked at sexually-oriented newsgroups, such as the alt.sex.* hierarchy and the Web sites published by Penthouse and Playboy. When newsgroups were ordered by the number of users who examined them one or more times over the first 5 months of the study, 13 of the top 30 newsgroups had sexual themes. But the sexually-oriented newsgroups do not hold their readers. When newsgroups were ordered by the number of "followers"— users who read them 3 or more times over the 5 months—then only 4 of the top 30 of this group were sexually oriented. Males were more likely to access these offerings than females and teens of both genders accessed them more frequently than adults, holding constant their overall use of the Internet. But less than 50% of the sample ever accessed a sexually-oriented newsgroup even once, and only 20% accessed a sexually-oriented newsgroup three or more times.

When asked about their children's access to pornography on the net, parents told us they trusted their children to avoid inappropriate content. Some said the sexually-oriented materials that they personally checked out were no worse that the materials easily available to their children in the corner drug store. It is unclear, however, how general are these attitudes, given our sample of urban parents.

Local services

Local information and communication services had special appeal to participants in the trial for two reasons. First, times for movies houses, buses schedules, and information on sports teams, social services and community development are all more useful when they are local. In one local newsgroup, teens from several area high schools shared information about which Department of Motor Vehicle testing station gave the easiest parallel parking tests. Local information services also provide people with satisfying social identities. People want to participate in and be part of groups, and geography provides one basis for group formation. Teenagers preferred communication forums that were limited to their own high schools. They complained when their communication areas were "invaded" (their term) by interlopers from other schools, and asked for controlled-access forums for their own groups.

Individualized services

Although services providing directory information and information about popular culture and the local environment appealed to many participants, the modal information service appealed to only one or two participants. The 126 participants who used the Internet accessed 1146 different newsgroups and more than 4000 different Web sites. Of the 1146 newsgroups visited, 328 were "followed"—accessed at least 3 or more times by at least one reader. When subset of newsgroups are ranked by number of followers, 78% were followed by just one user and only 10% were followed by 3 or more users. Similarly, 62% of followed Web sites were followed by only 1 reader and 23% were followed by 3 or more.

The information services that appealed to one or two people were extremely varied. Newgroups ranged from those associated with hobbies (e.g., needlepoint) to religion (e.g., Jewish culture) to professions (e.g., tax preparation).

Internet Use is Expressive
Our discussion of using the Internet to this point has focused on interpersonal communication as a way to build and maintain social relationships and on information services as a way to become informed or entertained. Participants also used their computers and the Internet as ways to express themselves. Six trial participants wrote their own World Wide Web home pages, one touting his high school and another showing off his creative writing. Besides this public expression, some participants personalized their home computers by creating new background patterns or substituting curses or musical phrases for the traditional warning sounds. Teenagers were most likely to engage in both types of expression. Many reported that mastering the techniques necessary to personalize their computers was satisfying in its own right. Most of the adults whom we interviewed considered mastering these techniques to be a waste of time and an obstacle to their use of the computer.

Communication networks have long been known as vehicles for people to express themselves, for example, by assuming different personas in newsgroups [4]. Among our sample, group communication was easier technically than personalization of the computer (although we found in our home visits that some participants had trouble locating desirable newsgroups and Web sites). Both adults and teens engaged in group communication, and many became consistent members of virtual groups. Teens who became relatively sophisticated computer users gave advice in the HomeNet help group to strangers in the trial who were having trouble. Several adults shared their professional expertise on newsgroups: an accountant his tax knowledge and a doctor his knowledge of arthritis. Others offered advice on their hobbies: one woman gave advice on raising exotic pets.

PREDICTORS OF INTERNET USE
We used linear regression analyses to identify the characteristics of HomeNet participants that predicted Internet usage differences. Because of the high correlations among usage measures, our dependent variable in this analysis is a composite, operationalized as the average of the standardized usage scores for sending and receiving electronic mail, reading and posting in newsgroups, and accessing World Wide Web sites (all in the log scale) across the first 5 months of the study. The predictor variables were measured on the pretrial questionnaires, before participants had Internet access.

These variables were grouped into four categories for purposes of analysis (Table 3). The category boundaries are arbitrary, but generally conform to the way home computing has been discussed in the literature, that is, as influenced primarily by economic and demographic factors, psychological or personality dispositions, computer skill and experience, and interest in various information sources (e.g., [12],[14]).

Below, we discuss each category of variables and the effects of each category singly. Then we construct an overall model, using all the significant variables from the previous analyses. This is an exploratory analysis, and does not use strong theory to test a deductive model. Also, it is a preliminary analysis examining only main effects on aggregate use. In later stages of this research we will investigate interactions, effects over time and differential predictions for communication and information services.

Demographics
Five demographic/economic variables are cited often in the literature on home computing: income, education, race, gender, and generation.

Income
Given the substantial investment required to purchase a computer, few families with low incomes have one [1]. By making computers and Internet access available to all participants in the trial, we are able to determine whether income has an effect on using the Internet once families have passed the hurdle of acquiring a computer. Household income was operationalized as the average of the household incomes reported by adults in a family.

Household education
Early adopters of home computing were well educated, professional people who often used computers to extend their work hours [14]. The task of purchasing the right hardware and software package, assembling the computer at home, and using the machine for useful purposes against the odds of breakdowns, was daunting. We made usability a strong goal in our trial, and asked whether enhanced usability might reduce the impact of education on usage. Household education was operationalized as the average of the highest grade completed by the adults in the family.

Race.
Home computers are less common in minority households than white ones, even controlling for income and education [1]. It has been argued that minority students do not have equal access to computing both at school and at home [10]. We tested if race difference in computing holds for home use of the Internet, once families have acquired a computer. Race was treated as a binary variable, coded as 1 for whites and 0 for others.

Gender
In schools, playrooms, and computer clusters, girls often do not seem as attracted to computers as boys do. A host of stereotypes including societal, educational and familial attitudes are said be working against women in computing [7]. We tested whether the gender gap often discussed in the literature affected Internet use at home. Gender was treated as a binary variable, coded as 1 for males and 0 for females.

Generation
A generation gap in adopting new technology seems as strong today as ever. Youngsters and young people typically adopt many new electronic home technologies (such as VCRs and Walkmen) well before adults. We expected the students in the sample to be heavier users of the Internet because they are curious, have time for exploration, and have had some formal training on computers. Generation was treated as a binary variable,

Predictor Variable	Demographic	Psychological	Computer	Media	Overall
Intercept	-.07 (.73)	.08 (.29)	.11 (.18)	.07 (.95)	-.05 (.75)
Income	-.03 (.89)				
Education	-.01 (.23)				
Race (white = 1, other = 0)	.52 (.00)				.46 (.01)
Gender (male = 1, female = 0)	.29 (.03)				.32 (.02)
Generation (adult = 1, child = 0)	-.86 (.00)				-.61 (.00)
Innovativeness		.23 (.00)			.13 (.05)
Sociability		.19 (.01)			.10 (.12)
Hassles		-.17 (.04)			-.11 (.13)
Time pressure		.03 (.71)			
Depression		.26 (.00)			.12 (.13)
Computer Skills			.29 (.01)		.18 (.01)
Computer Experience			-.26 (.00)		-.24 (.00)
Computer Value			.10 (.32)		
Applications' Value			-.11 (.19)		
Phone				.09 (.23)	
Newspaper				.05 (.51)	
Books				.18 (.02)	.03(.67)
Music				.14 (.07)	
TV				-.16 (.03)	-.14 (.03)
R Square	.33	.17	.14	.12	.45
N	132	131	121	129	129

Table 3. Predicting Internet Use.

Note. - Table entries are Beta coefficients for predicting Internet use. Except for the binary variable of race, gender, and generation, the independent variables have been standardized with a mean of 0 and a standard deviation of 1. *P*-values are in parentheses.

coded as 1 if a participant's age was 21 or greater and 0 otherwise.

The second column of Table 3 shows how the demographic variables were related to Internet usage in our sample. Neither income nor education predicted usage. This finding suggests strongly that once economic barriers are removed, people across socioeconomic lines will use the Internet. By contrast, race, gender, and, especially, generation were strong predictors of Internet usage in our sample: whites, males, and teens were more likely to use the Internet than minorities, females, and adults, respectively. These effects all speak to strong cultural or social forces on Internet usage. Of all the variables, the difference between children and adults was the strongest predictor in the category, and turned out to be the strongest predictor across all analyses.

Psychological dispositions

We chose five variables within the category of psychological dispositions.

Innovativeness

We measured people's willingness to experiment with new ideas and fashions. We adapted an innovativeness scale [8] used by marketing researchers to predict people's adoption of new products and services (e.g., "I like to experiment with new ways of doing things."; Cronbach's Alpha = .41).

Sociability

Since several of the most popular services on the Internet support interpersonal communication, we measured a person's tendency to socialize and have social skills, adapting a social extroversion scale [2] (e.g., "I like to mix socially with people."; Cronbach's Alpha = .74).

Hassles

Hassles are problems in daily life ranging from one's car breaking down to one's child getting sick at school. We speculated that those with a more harried lifestyle would be less likely to learn and use the Internet. This measure is the number of daily hassles each subject reported in the week prior to the pretrial survey [6].

Time pressure

People with too many responsibilities and little free time are unlikely to have the slack resources necessary to learn a new technology or to explore its value. We measured time pressure by adapting a scale measuring overload in organizations [3] (e.g., "I often feel under stress because I don't have enough time."; Cronbach's Alpha = .74).

Depression

The Internet could provide social support for those who lack it locally. We measured depression to investigate whether those measuring higher on this variable would be more likely to use the Internet to try to obtain support. It is possible, however, that the lack of energy and enthusiasm associated with depression would inhibit people from using the Internet. Our measure of depression was taken from [9]. (e.g., "I felt sad"; Cronbach's Alpha = .83)

The results of this analysis, shown in the third column of Table 3, are that innovative and sociable people used the Internet more, and those who listed many hassles used the Internet less. People under time pressure did not use the Internet less than people with more free time. (This result is the same when we used time diary data on hours spent at work or school.) Also, depressed people used the Internet more than those who were not depressed. Innovativeness and sociability are correlated with healthy psychological status whereas depression is not. These results suggest that the Internet appeals to people at both ends of the continuum of psychological status, perhaps for different reasons.

Computer experience and attitudes

The literature on individual differences in computing performance strongly suggests that technical abilities, experience, and attitudes will predict Internet usage.

Computer Skills
People with good computer skills should have an advantage in attempting to use the Internet, if only because they can deal with some of the technical problems that invariably arise. We developed a five-item scale to measure perceived computer skills. (e.g., "I am very skilled at using computers."; Cronbach's Alpha = .86).

Computer Experience
People with more years of experience also might have an advantage in using the Internet. Our computer experience measure is the number of years participants reported using computers.

Computer Value
People with more favorable attitudes about the usefulness of computers for work, communication, entertainment, education, and other functions, might use the Internet more. We developed a scale with twelve items to measure the perceived usefulness of home computers across several domains. (Cronbach's Alpha = .83)

Value of Computer Applications
This construct measured directly the perceived value of popular computer applications, such as word processing, spreadsheets and games as well as networked applications such as e-mail, newsgroups, and file downloading (Cronbach's Alpha = .76).

People with more skill used the Internet more, but surprisingly, people with greater experience with a computer used the Internet less, holding constant their skill. (See the fourth column of Table 3.) Possibly the Internet appealed to veteran computer users less than to novices because exploring computers was less of a novelty. Or, veterans' might have developed an instrumental view of computing, a view inconsistent with the communication, casual exchange of information, and fun that they saw in the Internet culture. The perceived usefulness of computers and applications was unrelated to participants' use of the Internet.

Use of other media

The Internet may serve as an alternative for other media such as books, telephones, newspapers and TV. Previous literature suggests both substitution and complementarity (e.g., [12]). However, this earlier research did not test whether, for example, TV watchers avoid computers or whether computers pull people away from their TVs. To test this hypothesis, we measured the times per week participants used a home telephone, read a newspaper, read a book, listened to music, and watched TV.

People who read books were more likely to use the Internet, whereas people who watched TV were less likely to use it. (See the fifth column in Table 3.) The text-based nature of most services on the Internet may appeal most to people who read for information and entertainment.

Overall Model

We constructed a combined model predicting Internet usage in our sample, by including variables from the previous analyses that significantly predicted use. The model explains 45% of the variance in participants' use of a range of Internet services. Generation is the strongest individual predictor; teenagers were much more likely to use the Internet than adults. Race is the second strongest predictor; whites use the Internet more than minorities. This race effect is strongest among the teens (analysis is not shown). Similarly, females used the Internet less than males, and again the effect is largest among the teens (not shown).

Entering the demographic variables into the model reduces the effects of all the psychological dispositions, although participants' innovativeness reliably predicts their Internet use. Among the computer variables, those with more computer skill used the Internet more, whereas those with more computer experience used it less. Finally, people who watch TV were less likely to use the Internet.

CONCLUSION

When ordinary people are given access to the Internet from home, half of them use it regularly after 5 months. Teenagers are central to Internet use at home, at least in the present sample. They often provided the motivation for their parents to invest in a computer, were often the heaviest users in the family, became sources of expertise within the household, and catalyzed Internet use by other family members. If these findings are generally true, then the family dynamics that characterize teenagers' interactions within families will influence the diffusion of home computing.

Though studies show that high-income, educated white males dominate the Internet, the HomeNet study shows that once financial barriers are lowered, lower income and less well educated people are as likely to become enthusiasts. Race and gender, however, remain associated with Internet usage, perhaps because the Internet's mainly white, male users has created a resource environment most attractive to men and whites. (One HomeNet women complained that there was so much football and so little about fashions on the Web.) The bias in Internet resources might change if more women and minorities sign on.

HomeNet participants communicated heavily and used a wide range of information services. Only a few of the information services were broadly popular. People gravitate towards services that address their idiosyncratic interests. Since most individuals will be interested in only a few of the thousands of services offered them, they need easy ways to personalize their information space so that it reflects their interests as the interests and their resources change over time.

This report on the HomeNet project is preliminary. Later reports will include a larger sample, and will focus on family interactions, on dynamic processes, on use over time of different electronic services, and on the impact of Internet use on individuals, groups, and families. Additional documents about HomeNet are at: `http://homenet.andrew.cmu.edu/Progress/`.

ACKNOWLEDGEMENTS

HomeNet is funded by grants from Apple Computer, Bell Atlantic, Bellcore, Intel, The Markle Foundation, The NPD Group, The US Postal Service, and US West. Farallon Computing and Netscape Communications contributed software.

REFERENCES

1. Anderson, R., Bikson, T, Law, S. & Mitchell. *Universal Access of E-Mail: Feasibility and Societal Implications*. MR-650-MF. Santa Monica, CA: Rand Corporation. 1995.
2. Bendig, A. W., The Pittsburgh Scales of Social Extroversion, Introversion and Emotionality, *The Journal of Psychology*, 53: 199-209, 1962.
3. Cammann, Cortlandt, Mark Fishman, Douglas Jenkins, Jr. and John R. Klesh. Assessing the attitudes and perceptions of organizational members. Pp. 71-138 in Stanley E. Seashore, Edward Lawler, Philip H. Mirvis, and Cortlandt Cammann (Eds.), *Assessing Organizational Change*. New York: John Wiley & Sons, 1983.
4. Finholt, T., and L. Sproull, Electronic Groups at Work. *Organization Science*, 1, 41-64, 1989.
5. Igbaria, M. and W. M. Wormley, Race Differences in Job Performance and Career Success, *Communications of the ACM*,, 38(3):82-92, March 1995.
6. Kanner, A. D., J. C. Coyne, C. Schaefer and R. S. Lazarus, Comparisons of Two Modes of Stress Measurement: Daily Hassles and Uplifts versus Major Life Events, *Journal of Behavioral Medicine*, 4: 1-39, 1981.
7. Klawe, M. and N. Levenson, Women in Computing: Where are We Now? *Communications of the ACM*, 38(1):29-44, January 1995.
8. Leavitt, C. and J. R. Walton, Innovativeness: Openness of Information Processing, in (Eds.) W. O. Bearden, R. G. Netemeyer and M. F. Mobley, *Handbook of Marketing Scales*, Newbury Park, CA: Sage Publications, 1993.
9. Radloff, L., The CES-D Scale: A Self-Report Depression Scale for Research in the General Population, *Applied Psychological Measurement*, 1: 385-401, 1977.
10. Rockman, S., In School or Out: Technology, Equity and the Future of our Kids, *Communications of the ACM*, 38(6):25-29, June 1995.
11. Sproull, L. & S. Kiesler, *Connections: New Ways of Working in the Networked Organization*. Cambridge, MA: MIT Press, 1991.
12. Times Mirror Center for the People and the Press. *The Role of Technology in American Life*. 1994
13. Venkatesh, A. and N. Vitalari, An Emerging Distributed Work Arrangement: An Investigation of Computer- Based Supplemental Work at Home, Management Science, 38(12):1687-1706, December 1992.
14. Vitalari, N. P., A. Venkatesh and K. Gronhaug, Computing in the Home: Shifts in the Time Allocation Patterns of Households, *Communications of the ACM*, 28(5):512-522, May 1985.

Physical Versus Virtual Pointing

Evan D. Graham
School of Kinesiology
Simon Fraser University
Burnaby, BC
Canada V5A 1S6
(604) 291-5794
evan_graham@sfu.ca

Christine L. MacKenzie
School of Kinesiology
Simon Fraser University
Burnaby, BC
Canada V5A 1S6
(604) 291-3004
christine_mackenzie@sfu.ca

ABSTRACT

An experiment was conducted to investigate differences in performance between virtual pointing, where a 2-D computer image representing the hand and targets was superimposed on the workspace, and physical pointing with vision of the hand and targets painted on the work surface. A detailed examination of movement kinematics revealed no differences in the initial phase of the movement, but that the final phase of homing in on smaller targets was more difficult in the virtual condition. These differences are summarised by a two-part model of movement time which also captures the effects of scaling distances to, and sizes of, targets. The implications of this model for design, analysis, and classification of pointing devices and positioning tasks are discussed.

Keywords

Analysis methods, Fitts' law, human performance modelling, input devices, pointing, virtual environments.

INTRODUCTION

Pointing to a location on a graphics display is an elemental gesture in many forms of human-computer interaction (HCI). Pointing movements have been studied in an attempt to understand perceptual-motor processes when we interact with real objects in the physical world. Our interest is in relating these theories and models from motor control to human performance in more abstract environments, where objects and actions represented on a graphics display are mediated by pointing devices. In particular, we wonder how limitations of current 2-D and 3–D virtual environments affect planning and control of natural movements like aiming, pointing, reaching, grasping, and manipulating objects; and how detailed analyses of movement kinematics can be used to reveal systematic effects of these constraints on human performance, in the HCI context.

Woodworth [12] first proposed that human pointing movements can been understood in terms of two movement phases: an initial planned impulse which covers most of the distance, followed by a second phase of deceleration to the target under current control. According to Fitts [3], total movement time involves a tradeoff between speed (distance covering) and accuracy (deceleration to the target). One version of Fitts' law states that on average, total movement time (MT) is a linear function of the index of difficulty (ID) of pointing to a target, where ID, in units of bits, is defined as $\log_2(2A/W)$, A being the distance to the target, and W the width of the target:

$$MT = a + b\ ID \tag{1}$$

This relation has been demonstrated in a number of studies of discrete and repetitive tapping and pointing with physical targets, using an tool such as a stylus [4] [2] [11], and also confirmed with computer systems and pointing devices ([1],[10], for a review see [8]) under a wide range of conditions.

In more recent studies of movement kinematics, Soechting [6], and Langolf et al. [9] examined velocity profiles along the path of a pointing movement, showing that the shape of the profiles was skewed for smaller, more difficult targets. MacKenzie et al. [7] showed how this effect was systematic for three-dimensional pointing movements, and suggested that a base trajectory representation of the velocity profile exists for a given size (W) of physical target, and is scaled according to the amplitude (A) of movement. They also proposed that for different combinations of A and W which give rise to the same ID, the shape and scaling effects cancel one another to give equal movement times as predicted by Fitts' law, even though the shape of the velocity profiles vary dramatically

CHI 96 Vancouver, BC Canada
© 1996 ACM 0-89791-777-4/96/04..$3.50

as A and W are scaled in proportion. In a previous study [5] where subjects used 3-D pointing movements to control a cursor on a 2-D computer display with varying control-display gain settings, we demonstrated these separable effects of A and W on the velocity profiles of both the hand and cursor. We found that:

a) the timing and magnitude of the initial velocity peak were a function of the distance to be covered by the hand, regardless of the scale of the display and target width; and

b) the proportion of time spent after the first deceleration peak was a function of the target width as an accuracy constraint for the hand, regardless of the size of its graphical representation or distance covered on the display.

In our study, however, we also observed unequal scaling of these amplitude and width effects. The overall size of the velocity profile was more sensitive to changes in amplitude than its change of shape for differing target widths. As a result, movement times were significantly longer to more distant targets with the same index of difficulty. We used a two-part model from Welford [11, p. 157] to summarise these results:

$$MT = a + b_1 \log_2 A - b_2 \log_2 W \quad (2)$$

In Welford's original formulation of the model, the units for b_1 and b_2 were bits per second. For linear regression on our data, we used this simplified form which distinguishes two ways of altering the index of difficulty for a pointing task: changing A or changing W. The first coefficient b_1, related to distance-covering, gives the sensitivity of MT to changes in A. The second coefficient b_2, related to deceleration to the target, gives the sensitivity to changes in W. In the case where b_1 and b_2 are approximately equal, Fitts' law would give a good account of the data. In our study of 3-D pointing to control a cursor on a 2-D display, we found that:

$$MT = 129 + 153 \log_2 A - 83 \log_2 W \quad (R^2 = .97) \quad (3)$$

with units of milliseconds and millimetres. We wondered if the large difference between coefficients might be due to a particular aspect of the setup used in the experiment which made the task more difficult than the corresponding task of pointing to a physical target with full vision of the hand. In our study, the subject made pointing movements with the hand on a table top in front and to the right of the body while viewing a display placed directly in front, tilted slightly away from vertical. We refer to this configuration as the "standard HCI setup", typically used with systems employing a mouse or tablet as a pointing device. We felt the main differences between our task and physical pointing were:

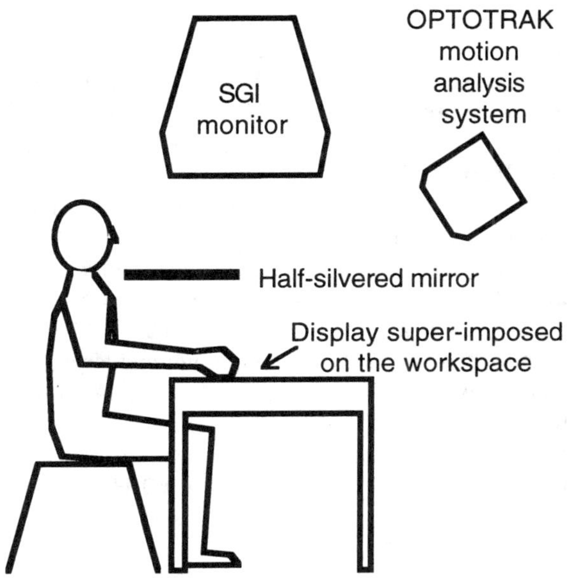

Figure 1. Layout of the experimental setup. Subjects made pointing movements while viewing either a graphics image of targets and a pointer superimposed on the workspace, or a physical pointer mounted on their index finger and targets painted on the table surface. Kinematic data for hand position was captured by an OPTOTRAK motion analysis system.

1) In the HCI configuration the display space is physically separate from working space for the hand. Movement planning requires learning a sensorimotor transformation to map the direction and extent of hand movements to corresponding cursor movements on the display.

2) The 2-D display presents no visual information about height of the hand above the table top, even though this dimension is important in control of the hand to achieve contact with the target location.

For the present study we eliminated the first difference (1 above) by superimposing a graphics image directly on the working space for the hand, and contrasted virtual (using a 2-D display) and physical (using full vision of the hand and physical targets) versions of the pointing task.

METHOD

Subjects

Six volunteers from the local community were paid to participate in the experiment. All had normal or corrected vision, had experience with computer pointing devices, and preferred to use the right hand in this context.

Apparatus

Subjects were comfortably seated in front of a table, viewing the work surface through a half-silvered mirror as shown in Figure 1. An OPTOTRAK motion analysis system recorded the three-dimensional position of infrared markers (IREDS) placed on the index finger, hand and arm, and stored the results in data files for further analysis. Coordinates from the OPTOTRAK were also used in real time by a Silicon Graphics Indigo Extreme workstation to update a 19" RGB monitor, double buffered at 60 frames per second. Sensing lag due to the OPTOTRAK was approximately 5 ms., and both the pointer and targets were represented as flat polygons on the display. As a result, the total system lag from hand (through OPTOTRAK, workstation, and display) to the eye was verified to be no greater than 25 ms, or 1 1/2 frames at 60 Hz. Subjects performed two versions of the pointing task:

1) Virtual pointing, where the half-silvered mirror was blocked so that only the graphics display image was visible. Targets were represented as white circles on a black background, while the two IRED markers on the index finger were used to superimpose an image of a red pencil-shaped "virtual finger" on the actual position of the subjects' finger over the work surface.

2) Physical pointing, where the graphics display was turned off and the mirror was unblocked, so that subjects could see through the mirror to the workspace below, illuminated by a task light. White circular targets were painted on a black background to correspond to the images generated by the graphics display for the virtual task. The subjects wore a fluorescent red pencil-shaped pointer, having the same dimensions as the virtual finger above, on their index finger.

Procedure

For each trial, a subject held the tip of the red pointer on a start mark. On instruction from the experimenter, the subject lifted the hand and quickly pointed to a spot on the table surface so that the tip of the red pointer ended anywhere inside the target circle. Movement speed was emphasised, with small corrections allowed if the target was missed. Four target sizes (W = 6, 12, 24, 48 mm) were combined with four movement distances (A = 37.5, 75, 150, 300 mm) for a total of sixteen A and W combinations.

Data for each subject were collected during a single session lasting about 1 1/2 hours. After a practice session with one of the display configurations, subjects performed twelve movements in each A and W combination, with a short break between each set of twelve trials while the target was changed. The order of presentation of A and W combinations was randomised, and the order of presentation of the virtual or physical task was counterbalanced across subjects.

Table 1. Summary of main effects for display.

Display	Virtual	Physical	
MT (ms)	610	538	**
PA (mm/s/s)	7688	8514	
TPA (ms)	100	97.8	
PV (mm/s/s)	721	751	
TPV (ms)	192	186	
%TAPD	56.1	53.7	

** $p < .01$

Data Analysis

Three-dimensional position data for each trial were rotated and translated to a convenient coordinate system where: the x-axis represents the principal direction of movement, away from the subject; the y-axis points to the left of the subject, and the z-axis points up. Data were then smoothed by a low-pass second order bidirectional Butterworth digital filter with a cutoff of 8 Hz. The three-dimensional trajectories of the fingertip were numerically differentiated to produce a velocity profile, and the resultant (speed of the movement along its path) further differentiated to produce an acceleration profile.

A series of computer programs were used on the resultant of the velocity profile to calculate movement time (MT), and the timing (TPV) and magnitude (PV) of the first velocity peak. Another program used the acceleration profile to calculate the timing (TPA) and magnitude (PA) of the initial acceleration peak, and also the per cent of movement time after the first deceleration peak (%TAPD). The variability of the end point was computed in both the principal direction of movement (VEx) and orthogonal to the principal direction of movement (VEy). VE measures were used to determine [8] the effective target widths (We), where We = 4.133 VE.

The within subject means of the last ten good trials in each A and W combination were analysed using ANOVA with repeated measures (BMDP 8V and 2V) on a subjects (6) by display (2) by movement amplitude (4) by target width (4) design. We also performed separate multiple regressions (BMDP 2R) on means for MT as a function of A, W, and We for the model of equation 2 for both virtual and physical pointing.

Table 2. Summary of main effects for movement amplitude.

A (mm)	37.5	75	150	300	
MT (ms)	420	510	613	753	***
PA (mm/s/s)	5148	6114	9187	11957	***
TPA (ms)	89.1	99.3	104	104	***
PV (mm/s/s)	324	471	837	1312	***
TPV (ms)	143	177	201	236	***
%TAPD	57.1	53.6	54.3	54.6	

*** p < .001

Table 3. Summary of main effects for target width.

W (mm)	3	6	12	24	
MT (ms)	657	607	536	496	***
PA (mm/s/s)	7487	8041	8672	8806	**
TPA (ms)	97.1	99.5	98.7	101	
PV (mm/s/s)	719	747	712	766	
TPV (ms)	190	190	190	187	
%TAPD	61.7	57.0	51.9	49.1	***

** p < .01, *** p < .001

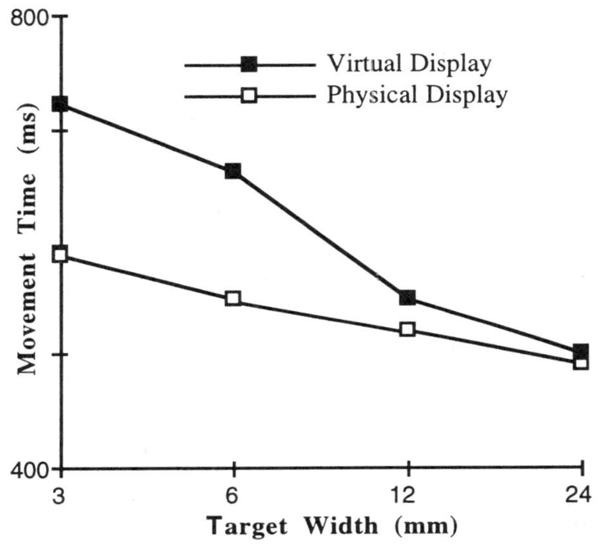

Figure 2. Mean movement times as a function of target width for virtual and physical displays, showing a display by target width interaction. Target width effects on MT are more pronounced for the virtual than the physical display.

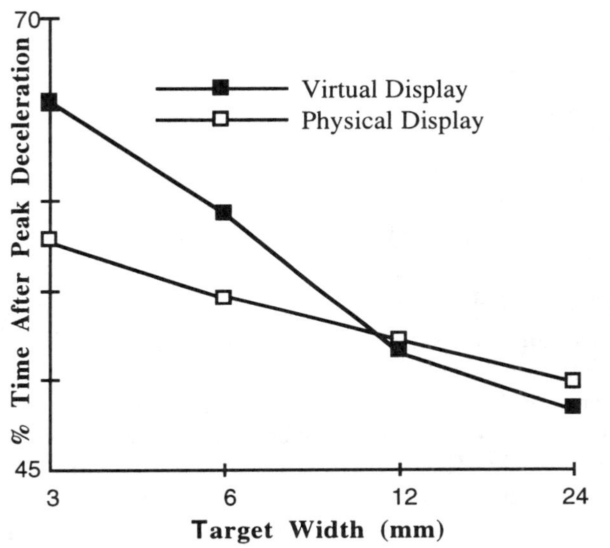

Figure 3. Mean proportion of time spent in deceleration to targets of different widths for virtual and physical display, showing a display by target width interaction. Target width effects on %TAPD are more pronounced for the virtual than the physical display.

RESULTS

Overall differences in 3-D kinematic measures for the hand due to the display are shown in Table 1. Movement times were about 80 ms slower ($F_{1,5}=25.35$, $p < .01$) with the virtual display than for physical pointing. Differences in MT were evident in a display by target width interaction ($F_{3,15} = 22.9$, $p < .01$). Shown in Figure 2, the increase in movement times as target size decreased was more evident for the virtual display compared to the physical display condition.

There were no significant differences between the physical and virtual display condition for the initial movement phase, up to the time of peak velocity. The slightly longer proportion of movement time (%TAPD) for the virtual display (56.1 versus 53.7 per cent) was not statistically significant, but revealed itself in a display by width interaction ($F_{3,15}=4.97$, $p < .02$) as shown in Figure 3. For smaller targets, the %TAPD increased more with the virtual display than with the physical display. In contrast, the %TAPD was similar across displays for the largest targets. This interaction parallels the interaction for MT, and demonstrates that the longer movement times for virtual compared to physical pointing are mainly due to extra time in deceleration to smaller targets when the virtual display was used.

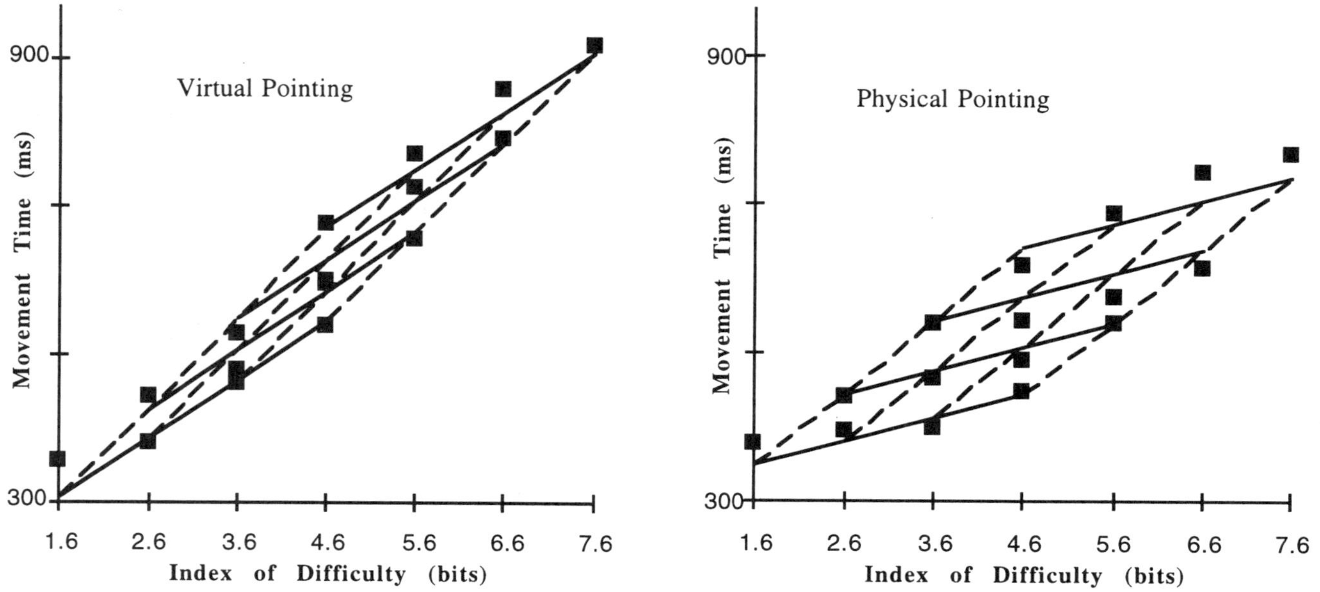

Figure 4. On the left, the two-part model of equation 4 is superimposed on actual data points for virtual pointing. Similarly on the right, the two-part model of equation 5 is superimposed on actual data points for physical pointing. Movement times (black squares) are plotted as a function of index of difficulty (ID). Dashed lines show predicted MT when target width is held constant, and ID is changed by varying A. Solid lines show predicted MT when amplitude is held constant, and ID is changed by varying W.

The main effects for movement amplitude are shown in Table 2. As predicted by Fitts' law, movement time increased for longer distances. Differences in the velocity profile due to movement amplitude are evident up to the time of the first velocity peak. In particular, the magnitudes of the initial acceleration and velocity peaks (PA and PV) increase with longer distances, and the timing of these peaks is also delayed for longer distances in a systematic fashion. All these effects were highly significant ($p < .001$). Although there were small differences in %TAPD for different movement amplitudes, this effect did not approach statistical significance.

Main effects for target width are shown in Table 3. As expected, movement time decreased for larger targets. Target size showed little effect on the first movement phase, although there was a slight increase in the magnitude of the first acceleration peak ($F_{3,15} = 5.59$, $p < .01$) for larger targets. The proportion of movement time spent in deceleration increased systematically from 49.1 to 61.7 per cent as target size decreased ($F_{3,15} = 22.14$, $p < .001$) from the large to small. We captured the effects of A and W on movement time using multiple linear regression to fit the model of equation 2 to means of MT for each A and W combination (units are millimetres and milliseconds). For virtual pointing:

$$MT = 22 + 123 \log_2 A - 79 \log_2 W \quad (R^2 = .99) \qquad (4)$$

and for physical pointing:

$$MT = -24 + 98 \log_2 A - 32 \log_2 W \quad (R^2 = .96) \qquad (5)$$

Note that in both conditions MT is more sensitive to changes in A (virtual 123 ms/bit, physical 98 ms/bit) than in W (virtual 79 ms/bit, physical 32 ms/bit), and this asymmetry is even more marked for the physical display than for virtual pointing. One explanation for this phenomenon is that subjects were not taking advantage of the relaxed accuracy constraint to improve their speed in reaching larger targets, so that effective target width was not varying as much as the actual width presented during trials. Since our analysis of variable error (VE) revealed the greatest deviations along the principal axis of movement (x), we used VEx to compute an effective target width (We) for each amplitude and width mean. Modelling MT with We rather than W revealed the same pattern of coefficients as equations 4 and 5 (units are mm and ms). For virtual pointing:

$$MT = 30 + 132 \log_2 A - 89 \log_2 We \quad (R^2 = .93) \qquad (6)$$

and for physical pointing:

$$MT = -28 + 101 \log_2 A - 41 \log_2 We \quad (R^2 = .95) \qquad (7)$$

This indicates two things: first, that the subjects were

taking advantage of larger targets to increase the movement speed, and second, that equations 4 and 5 effectively describe subjects' performance in the task.

To visualise the two-part model of equation 4, in Figure 4 on the left we have plotted actual and predicted movement times against ID for virtual pointing. Similarly, the model of equation 5 is depicted in Figure 4 on the right for physical pointing. As explained in the figure caption:

a) Movement times are plotted as black squares. Differences for various A and W combinations giving rise to the same ID are evident by the vertical spread of the data points.

b) The dashed lines represent predicted movement times when target width is held constant, and ID is changed by varying A.

c) The solid lines represent predicted movement times when amplitude is held constant, and ID is changed by varying W.

Looking at Figure 4, two features are evident. First, changing A (dashed lines) gives rise to a steeper slope than changing W (solid lines) for both display conditions. Second, the difference in slopes for A (dashed lines) and W (solid lines) is more marked for physical pointing than for virtual pointing.

DISCUSSION

Theory

The results suggest that movement planning is similar for both virtual and physical pointing in our experiment, evidenced by the lack of differences in kinematic features of the initial phase of the movement. The difference between the virtual and physical display is apparent only in the second movement phase, where visual control of deceleration to the smaller targets in the virtual task took more time than in the physical task. This interpretation is also supported by contrasting the models of equations 4 and 5: The coefficients (b_1) for the A term are of similar magnitude, but there is a marked difference in the coefficients for the W term (b_2), making MT much more sensitive to the increased accuracy constraint of a smaller target in virtual pointing.

A key feature of our virtual display is that it is flat — it presents no visual information to show the height of the finger above the table top, even though this dimension is used as part of the deceleration strategy to contact the table surface at the target location. This lack of the third dimension could account for the difficulty with visual control during final positioning in virtual pointing, and suggests further study using a more realistic 3-D virtual environment to clarify this issue.

To our surprise, we found that even with physical pointing changes in the size and shape of the velocity profile did not cancel when A and W were increased in proportion, as would be predicted by Fitts' Law. The spread of movement times for similar IDs in physical pointing was even greater than either virtual pointing, or our previous results using the standard HCI configuration. Thus, the fact that movement times increase as A and W are scaled up in size seems to be a feature of the pointing task per se, not a result of limitations in motor control processes associated with using a computer display.

Although the two-part model due to Welford (equation 2) is difficult to interpret in terms of an information-theoretic account of movement planning and control processes, it does capture the large and significant differences in movement time due to scaling. We suggest that the two-part models captured in equations 4 and 5 promise some utility from an engineering perspective. First, as a predictive model of performance, it takes into account the size or scale of hand movements appropriate for a particular interface. Second, as a diagnostic, it can serve to identify the type of constraint leading to speed-accuracy tradeoffs in a variety of positioning tasks.

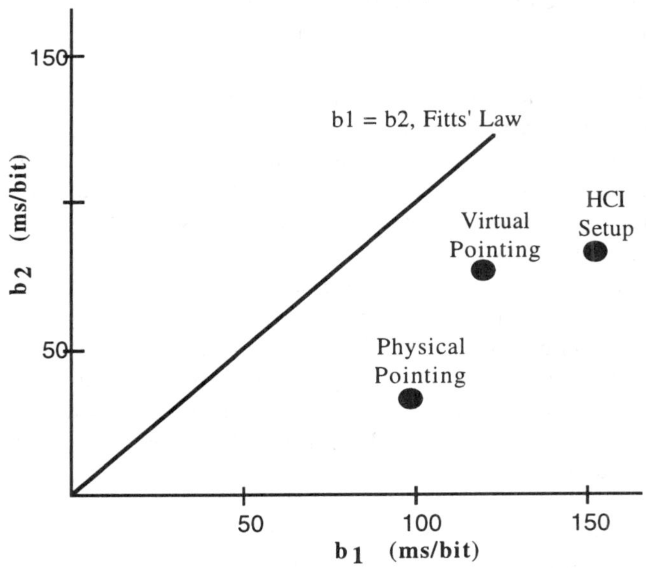

Figure 5. Parameter space for the model of equation 2, showing the data points for virtual and physical pointing, and also for pointing using the HCI setup in a previous study.

Application

In a graphical interface design, there is often some leeway in the choice of size both for a visual representation, and for the hand movements to operate an interface. For example, a set of buttons can be sized and spaced in various ways on the screen. There are obvious limitations on the lower limit of size, such as visual acuity and pointing device and display resolution, as well as on the upper limit, such as the footprint for working with a pointing device, but within these bounds the designer has to make an informed choice.

Figure 5 represents a parameter space for the coefficients of the two-part model of equation 2. In this figure we have plotted the data points for virtual and physical pointing from equations 4 and 5. In addition, we have added the point for our previous study [5], showing where equation 3, representing the standard HCI setup, falls in the parameter space. If the data from our studies were well characterised by Fitts' law, they would fall on the line $b_1 = b_2$. In our case, all points fall below this line by different amounts. In this region, below the Fitts' law line, movement time increases as the movement distance (and target width) for the hand are scaled up in size. Tasks associated with points in this region of the parameter space ($b_1 > b_2$) will be performed faster when hand movements are scaled to a smaller size - smaller is better. A glance at the points on the graph of Figure 5 tells us that our tasks will be performed faster if the movement distance and target size are reduced to the smallest practical value. In contrast, if we were to find a two-part model for a task which fell above the Fitts' law line ($b_1 < b_2$), this task would benefit from being scaled up - bigger is better.

The parameter space of Figure 5 may also be useful to classify pointing devices and display systems. Approximate values for the two-part model coefficients for a particular configuration can be readily identified by testing a small number of representative users with a large and small target, and a large and small movement amplitude, to form a total of four A and W combinations. We suggest that data points that fall higher on the graph (b_2 is large) indicate a task or device which involves more difficulty in final positioning on the target. A data point which falls more to the right (b_1 is large) indicates difficulty in planning and control of the distance covering phase of the movement with that system.

We plan to follow up these results in two ways. First, the study described here will be repeated using a 3-D stereographic display superimposed on the workspace, in order to see if the differences between the virtual and physical task we reported are due to lack of visual information about the height of the hand above the workspace in our 2-D virtual environment. Second, we are compiling data from some of our other studies, as well as revisiting data reported both in the HCI and motor control literature on discrete and repetitive pointing, in order to model and plot additional points in the parameter space shown in Figure 5. We hope to develop this approach into a useful technique for characterising and quantifying human performance for different combinations of positioning task and input device.

ACKNOWLEDGEMENTS

The authors thank Anita Trip for her assistance in data collection. This research was supported from research and strategic grants from the Natural Sciences and Engineering Research Council of Canada.

REFERENCES

1. Boritz, J., Booth, K.S., and Cowan, W.B. (1991). Fitts' law studies of directional mouse movement. In proc. of Graphics Interface '91. Toronto: Canadian Information Processing Society, 216-223.

2. Crossman, E.R.F.W., and Goodeve, P.J. (1983). Feedback and control of hand movement and Fitts' law. Quarterly Journal of Experimental Psychology, 35A, 251-278.

3. Fitts, P.M. (1954). The information capacity of the human motor system in controlling the amplitude of movement. J. Exp. Psych., 47(6), 381-391.

4. Fitts, P.M., and Peterson, J.P. (1964). Information capacity of discrete motor responses. J. Exp. Psych., 67(2), 103-112.

5. Graham, E.D. and MacKenzie, C.L. (1995). Pointing on a computer display. CHI '95 Conference Companion, Denver, Colorado, May, pp. 314-315.

6. Langolf, G.D., Chaffin, D.B., and Foulke, J.A. (1976). An investigation of Fitts' law using a wide range of movement amplitudes. J. of Motor Behaviour, 8, 113-128.

7. MacKenzie, C.L., Marteniuk, R.G., Dugas, C., Liske, D., and Eickmeier, B. (1987). Three-dimensional movement trajectories in Fitts' task: implications for control. Q. J. Exp. Psych., 39A, 629-647.

8. MacKenzie, S. (1992). Fitts' law as a research and design tool in human-computer interaction. Human-Computer Interaction, 7, 91-139..

9. Soechting, J.F. (1984). Effect of target size on spatial and temporal characteristics of a pointing movement in man. Experimental Brain Research, 54, 212-132.

10. Walker, N., Meyer, D.E., Smelcer, J.B. (1993). Spatial and temporal characteristics of rapid cursor-positioning movements with electromechanical mice in human-computer interaction. Human Factors, 35(3), 431-458.

11. Welford, A.T. (1968). Fundamentals of Skill. London: Methuen.

12. Woodworth, R. (1899). The accuracy of voluntary movement, Psych. Review Monograph Supplement, 3.

Differences in Movement Microstructure of the Mouse and the Finger-Controlled Isometric Joystick

Anant Kartik Mithal
Sunsoft Developer Products
2550 Garcia Ave MS MPK16-303
Mountain View CA 94043
anant.mithal@eng.sun.com

Sarah A. Douglas
Department of Computer Science
University of Oregon
Eugene, OR 97403-1202
douglas@cs.uoregon.edu

ABSTRACT
This paper describes a study comparing the movement characteristics of the mouse and the velocity-control isometric joystick. These characteristics are called the microstructure of movement. The comparison found random variations in the velocity of the isometric joystick that make it hard to control. The study shows that the microstructure of movement can explain differences in performance among devices.

KEYWORDS:
Fitts' law, pointing devices, mouse, isometric joystick, psychomotor models, movement microstructure, characteristics of movement, performance differences

INTRODUCTION

Since the early work by Card [2] extending Fitts' law [6] to pointing devices, extensive research has shown that it is a valuable tool for comparing pointing devices [9]. Fitts' law holds across a wide range of devices and conditions [1, 3, 5, 10]. While Fitts' law is unquestionably the best available tool to compare pointing device performance [9], it is not much help in understanding why such differences in performance exist.

For instance, a number of studies have shown that the mouse is substantially faster than the isometric joystick [2, 3, 5, 13]. For example, in an earlier study, we, reported that the isometric joystick was 70% slower than the mouse [4], but none of the studies explains the reason for the performance difference.

A possible explanation for this is that all these studies examine the gross characteristics of movement, such as target width, target distance and movement time, which are the variables in the Fitts' law equation. In doing so, they ignore the path the cursor follows in its movement towards the target, and so cannot describe the manner in which movement occurs.

For example, Figure 1 illustrates two hypothetical movements. It plots the velocity towards the target on the Y-axis, and distance from the start on the X-axis. From the plot, we can see the speed at which the cursor was moving at any point towards the target. Both trials have the same target distance and width, and take the same amount of time. From the point of view of a Fitts' law analysis, they are identical, but they have different movement microstructures. The first trial is made up of three submovements, all in the direction of the target. The second trial has two submovements, the first of which overshoots the target, and the second doubles back.

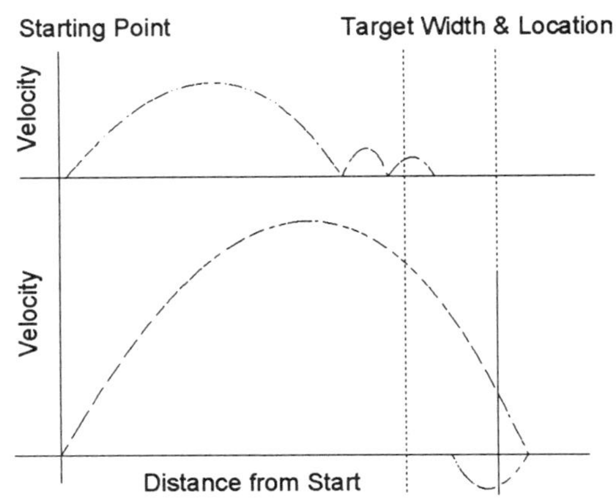

Figure 1: Two trials (not to scale) which are identical from the point of view of Fitts' law, but have different microstructures of movement.

In addition, to ignoring the structure of movement, the Fitts' law analysis is performed by averaging the movement times for a given target and width combination. What happens during a single movement of the cursor towards a target is ignored both by the type of data gathered and by the analysis technique used. As a result, current research on pointing devices has no way to explain why performance differences exist between pointing devices.

In building models that describe movement, psychomotor research examines the microstructure of movement. As the cursor moves towards the target, time and displacement data is gathered for each trial. Velocity is then derived and plotted as a function of time as shown in Figure 1. From this the pattern of submovements is studied.

This methodology can be used to study pointing devices as shown in this paper. We describe here the results obtained from comparing the movement microstructure of two devices, the mouse and the isometric joystick. Our analysis shows that there are random variations in the velocity of the cursor which are evident in the microstructure of the joystick but not the mouse. These variations would make fine control difficult with the isometric joystick. Thus differences in performance can be attributed directly to differences observed in their movement microstructures.

PREVIOUS RESEARCH

The mouse is the ubiquitous pointing device. Early work [2] showed that it was very fast and had few errors. Since then numerous studies have supported its superiority and only the touch tablet seems to have similar performance [10].

The isometric joystick is a device that does not move when force is applied to it, but is able to sense the applied force and translate that into a velocity of the cursor on the screen. It has attracted a great deal of research interest because its small size makes it ideal for notebook computers where space is at a premium making it popular in current PC-compatible notebook computers.

However, research dating back to the early Card study has consistently shown it to be slower and have more errors than the mouse. Epps [5] and Rutledge and Selker [13] similarly found poor performance with the joystick. Subjects in one study complained that the isometric joystick "was hard to control" [4]. Thus there is ample evidence that there is a substantial difference in performance between mice and isometric joysticks, but the literature does not explain why.

There are three major differences between the mouse and the isometric joystick that can account for differences in performance, the isometricity of the joystick, the order of control and finger vs. wrist control. Because the isometric joystick does not move when pressure is applied to it, the amount of kinesthetic feedback that the user gets is drastically reduced. [12]

The second major difference is that the joystick controls the velocity of the cursor on the screen [12]. The harder that a user pushes, the faster the cursor moves, like a car's accelerator. This is referred to as first order control, while the mouse's mapping of mouse displacement to cursor displacement is called zero order control. Jagacinski showed that for isotonic joysticks, displacement control is better for stationary targets, while velocity control is better for targets moving at constant velocity [7]. These results have not been tested for isometric joysticks, possibly because it is difficult if not impossible to construct a displacement control isometric joystick.

In addition, most isometric joysticks in use today are controlled by the tip of the index finger, while the mouse is controlled by the wrist. Langolf showed that the finger had a higher Fitts' law index of performance than the wrist, but again, he was studying isotonic movement. Any of these differences could cause the performance differences between the devices.

The characteristics of movement have been of interest to psychomotor researchers for a while, and were first used in the Langolf study [8]. The term microstructure of movement was coined by Jagacinski in his study of isotonic joysticks [7]. Figure 1 indicates what the microstructure might be. The upper figure shows a trial consisting of a rapid submovement that covers most of the distance to the target, followed by two smaller, relatively less accurate submovements. Jagacinski's data showed that a single movement towards a target is made up of a sequence of one or more submovements (rarely more than three), and the first submovement tends to be much larger and faster than the rest of the submovements.

Meyer et al. developed a model, the stochastic optimized submovement model based on the idea that a movement is made up of submovements, and optimizes the conflicting goals of rapid movement and low error rates [11]. The model predicts a close approximation to Fitts' law and also predicts that the first submovement is faster and more accurate than the rest of the submovements. This was verified for wrist movements, supporting Jagacinski's observations, and subsequent research has extended this model to movement with the mouse [15].

The present study gathered data on the microstructure of movement for mouse and isometric joystick to see if the observations about movement characteristics of the mouse were applicable to the isometric joystick, and to see whether differences in the movement microstructure could be used to explain differences in performance.

METHOD

This study was performed in two parts, a pilot study to test the equipment and software, and the main study. Data from both parts is presented here.

Subjects

For the main study there were 6 subjects, all from the University of Oregon, volunteers who were promised a home cooked Indian meal on completion of the study. Four subjects were from the Computer Science department, two were staff and two were graduate students. The remaining two were graduate students from the College of Business. There were two women among the subjects. All subjects were right handed and used the pointing devices with their preferred hand. Five of the subjects were expert mouse users prior to the study and used a mouse every day. Similarly, two subjects were expert with the kind of isometric joystick used in the experiment, using it every day in their work.

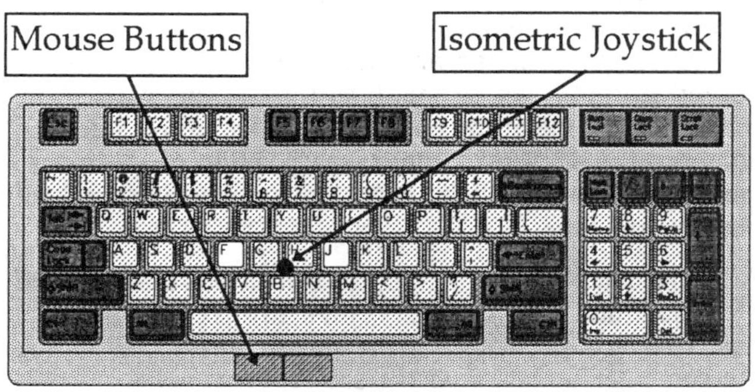

Figure 2. The IBM TrackPoint II keyboard.

Equipment

The mouse used was a Microsoft Mouse ver. 2.0", FCC ID C3KSMP1. It mapped displacement on the mousepad to displacement on the screen using the default non-linear display control function in the Windows NT 3.5 mouse driver. The isometric joystick used was an IBM TrackPoint II keyboard with embedded pointing device, shown in Figure 2. The keyboard has an isometric joystick embedded between the 'G', 'H' and 'B' keys. It protrudes 1 mm above the keycaps and thus does not interfere with typing. There are two buttons below the space bar that correspond to the two buttons on a mouse. Users control the cursor by pushing on the joystick. The joystick maps force into the velocity of the cursor on the screen. It picks up the magnitude and direction of the applied force and moves the cursor correspondingly. Its hardware uses a discontinuous non-linear display control function that is fed to the Windows NT mouse driver [13].

Both devices were connected to an MS-DOS compatible 90 Mhz Pentium running Windows NT 3.5. An MS-DOS computer has one connection for keyboard data. A pointing device can be connected either through a PS/2 mouse port, or through a serial port (Figure 3). The TrackPoint keyboard has two cables that come out of it, one going to the PS/2 keyboard port, and the other going to the PS/2 mouse port. In addition, there is a PS/2 mouse port on the keyboard that allows a user to attach a mouse to the keyboard for use in addition to the TrackPoint joystick. This configuration was used in the study, and is shown in Figure 3.

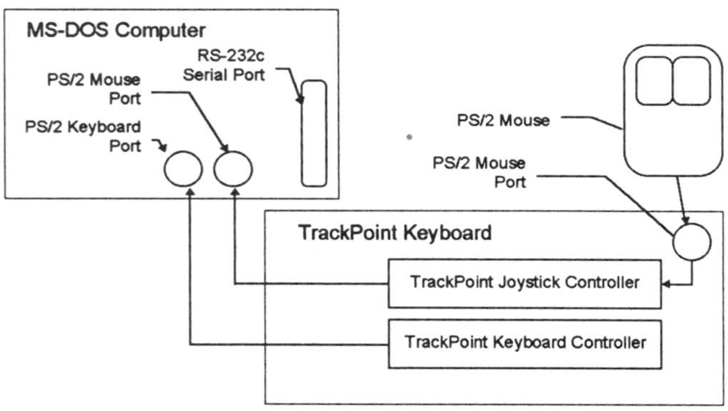

Figure 3. Connections for the TrackPoint keyboard.

Experimental Task

The experimental program presented subjects with the screen shown in Figure 4. A trial began when the subject clicked in the home square, and ended when the subject clicked in the target ribbon. The time at the start of the trial and the time at the end of the trial were recorded. In addition, the software sampled the position of the mouse cursor between the clicks every 16 ms, keeping track of position and time.

After the completion of a trial, the screen was blanked, and the data from the trial was written to disk and then the next trial was presented. If the subject missed the target, the computer beeped, and the subjects was made to complete the trial. The trial was marked as an error and written to the data file, and presented again to the subject at the end of the block.

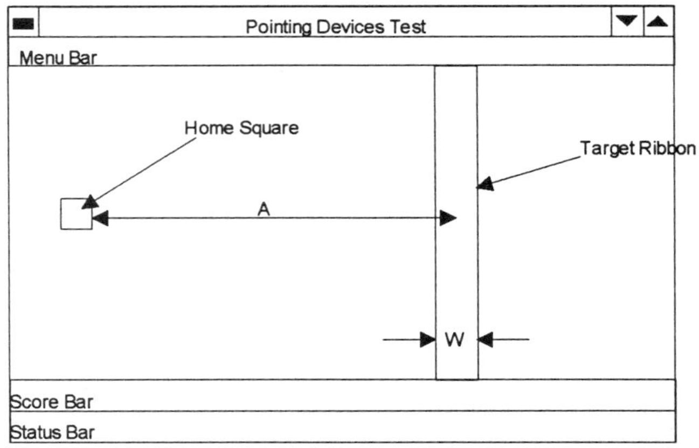

Figure 4. The experimental task

The cursor was re-centered on the home square prior to each trial, and the home square always appeared in the same location. The width and location of the target ribbon were varied as indicated in Table 1. These values generated the following six amplitude to width ratios (A/W): 48, 24, 12, 6, 3, 1.5.

Table 1. Values distance to target and width of target used.

Amplitude (A)		*Width (W)*	
Pixels	mm	Pixels	mm
768	232.5	16	4.84
384	116.3	32	9.69
192	58.1	64	19.38
96	29.1		

Experimental Design

Subjects completed the experiment in six sessions, three with each device. Three subjects did the three mouse sessions before the joystick sessions, and the other three reversed the order of the experiment. Subjects were randomly assigned to the orders. This was done to control for order effects.

One area of concern was that the subjects on the average had more experience with the mouse than the isometric joystick. In order to counteract this, subjects were given a large number of trials with each device, 600 randomly presented trials per session, or 1800 trials with each device. Earlier work indicates that after approximately 1200 trials, subjects do not have significant improvement in performance from one block of 120 trials to the next [2, 4]. Subjects were given 1800 trials so that the data from the last block of 120 trials would represent practiced performance.

RESULTS

The data from the experiment was analyzed in two ways, a gross level analysis, and a micro level analysis. The gross level analysis helped to validate the data and examined learning effects and did a Fitts' law analysis. In order to see the effect of learning, the data was grouped into blocks of 120 trials, 5 per session, and 15 per device. A pair-wise *t*-test between successive blocks showed that there was no significant learning ($p \leq 0.5$) after block 3 for the mouse and block 7 for the joystick. Thus we can assume that by the end of the experiment subjects were sufficiently practiced on both devices.

An analysis of the last block of 120 trials for all subjects showed that both devices followed Fitts' law, with an r^2 of .998 for the mouse, .991 for the joystick, and IP of 8.13 for the mouse, and 5.75 for the joystick.

Movement Microstructure for the Mouse

The second part of the analysis was of the movement microstructure for each device. Figure 5 represents a single trial from the pilot study, with the time in milliseconds on the x-axis, and distance from the start on the first y-axis. This curve is difficult to interpret, and is generally not used for analysis. Velocity is plotted on the second y-axis and provides more information. We can see how the velocity varied over the duration of the trial. There was almost no movement for 200 milliseconds, which corresponds well to the reaction time found in other studies [2]. There was then a large, rapid submovement, followed by a two smaller submovements. The first of these overshot the target (which was at 768 pixels), and the second was a corrective submovement that moved back to the target.

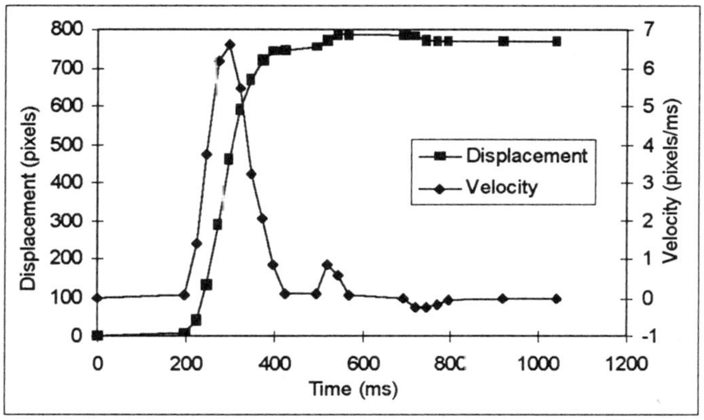

Figure 5. PS/2 mouse — trial from pilot study, A = 768 pixels.

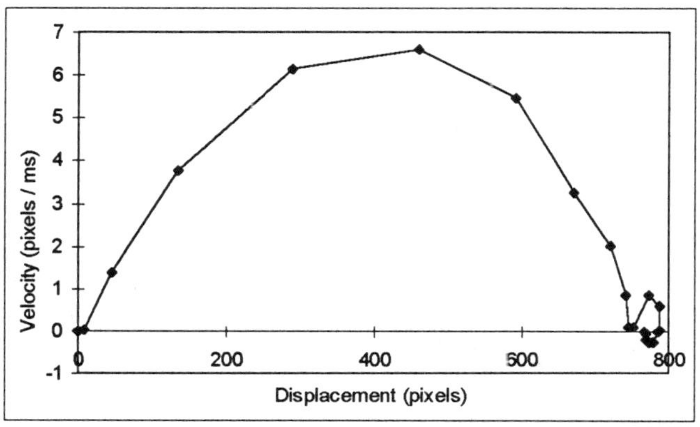

Figure 6. PS/2 mouse trial with velocity as a function of distance. A = 768 pixels.

A better way of looking at these data is shown in Figure 6, with displacement on the x-axis, and velocity on the y-axis. From this graph, we can see the speed of the cursor at any point along the path to the target. This graph shows that the movement is a sequence of three submovements. The first submovement covers most of the distance to the target and reaches a high peak velocity. The next two submovements are smaller, covering smaller proportions of the distance to the target. The second submovement overshot the target and the third submovement was a correction, bringing the cursor back to the target.

The plot in Figure 6 is a prototypical trial, that supports earlier findings that the first submovement tends to be larger and faster than the subsequent submovements. It is representative of the data obtained for a number of different types of mice in the pilot study, as well as in the data from the main study.

Mouse data from the main study was similar. Figure 7 and Figure 8 represent mouse movement data from the main experiment. They trials have been selected because they are representative of mouse trials from the main study.

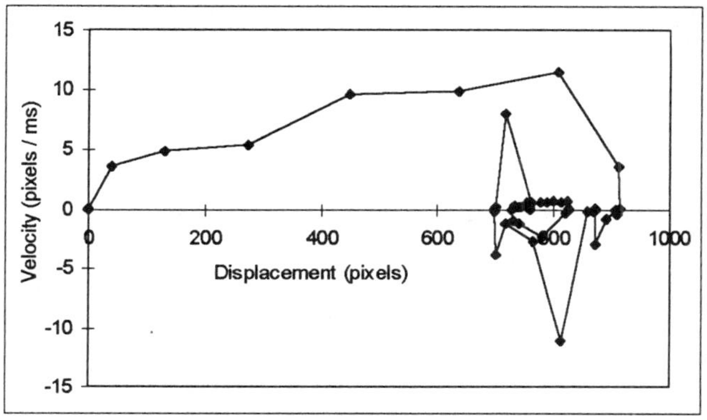

Figure 7. First mouse trial subject DD5 - raw data. A = 768 pixels

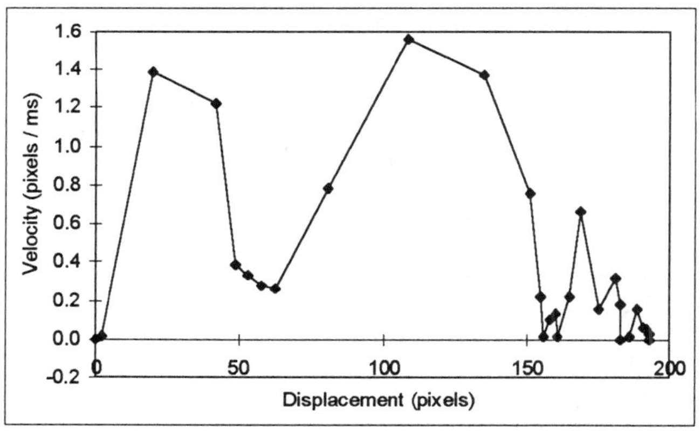

Figure 8. Middle mouse trial subject DD1 - raw data. A = 192 pixels

Figure 7 shows that the subject made a rapid primary submovement towards the target that overshot. The subject doubled back with the second submovement and overshot again. The third submovement also overshot, and the subject oscillated around the target till it was reached. This trial also has a large primary submovement, followed by smaller secondary submovements. Figure 8 deviates from the prototype in that there appear to be two large movements followed by smaller movements.

These figures show that in general, mouse movements have a large primary submovement, followed by smaller submovements, which is consistent with the data from earlier studies. This characteristic held throughout the experiment, from the early trials to the end of the study, and across all subjects. Note that each graph has been picked out of 3600 such graphs of mouse movement for each session. (Each of 6 subjects did 600 trials per session, and only one graph from each session has been shown.)

Movement Microstructure for the Isometric Joystick

Data for the isometric joystick was also obtained both pilot and main studies, and revealed an unexpected characteristic.

Figure 9 and Figure 10 show a joystick trial from the pilot study. The distance vs. time sub-plot in Figure 9 does not reveal anything out of the ordinary, but the velocity vs. time sub-plot shows a strange pattern of jitter in the velocity.

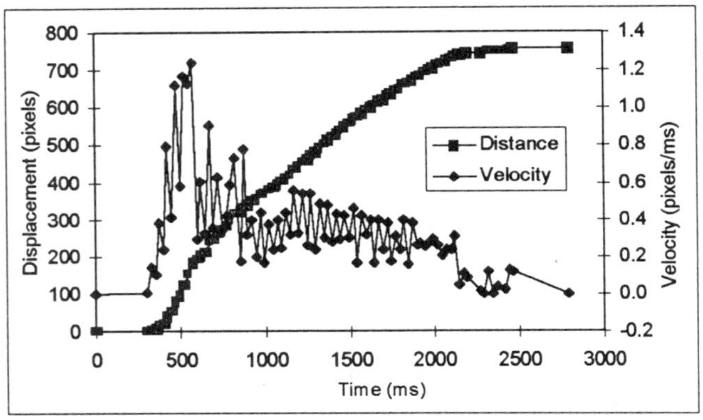

Figure 9. Isometric joystick - trial from preliminary tests. A = 768 pixels.

This jitter is more clearly evident when the velocity vs. distance plot (Figure 10) is examined. The jitter appeared in all the isometric joystick trials. This particular trial was one of the first attempted by the test subject, but persisted after 50 trials, and also occurred in trials by others.

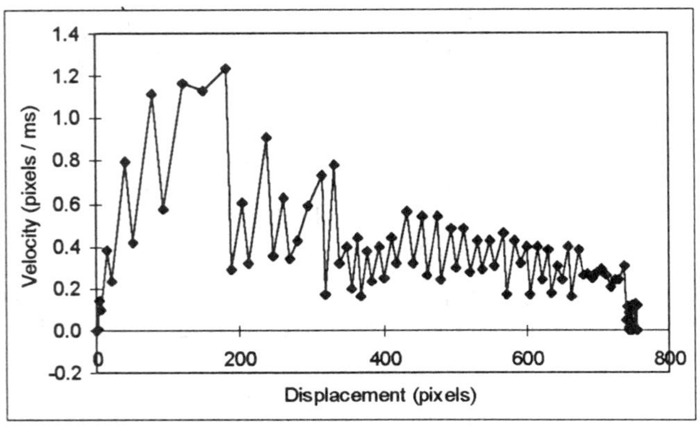

Figure 10. Isometric joystick preliminary tests. (Same trial as Figure 9.) A = 768 pixels.

There are a number of things that could account for this jitter. Among other things, it could be caused by an interaction between the joystick and the computer, it could be an artifact of the program gathering the data, it could be the subject, and it could be caused by the computer.

To eliminate the possibility that the error was caused by an interaction between the computer and the joystick, the TrackPoint keyboard was connected to another computer, with the same result, i.e., the jitter was still present.

Figure 3 showed the different ways in which pointing devices can be connected to MS-DOS computers. To eliminate the possibility that the jitter was due to the PS/2 connection used by the isometric joystick, tests were performed with four different pointing device configurations with the TrackPoint keyboard or a separate keyboard as appropriate. These configurations were the TrackPoint keyboard by itself, the PS/2 mouse by itself, the PS/2 mouse connected through the TrackPoint's PS/2 port, and an identical RS-232c serial mouse. In all cases, graphs for the mouse did not show jitter, with graphs similar to Figure 6, and jitter was present in the TrackPoint joystick.

To eliminate the possibility that there was a flaw in this particular joystick, the software was recompiled to run on a smaller screen (640x480, the standard size for notebook computers), and the test carried out on two IBM ThinkPads (which have built-in TrackPoints) and on an NEC Versa notebook (that has a similar isometric joystick, but is not called a TrackPoint), and the tremor was still present.

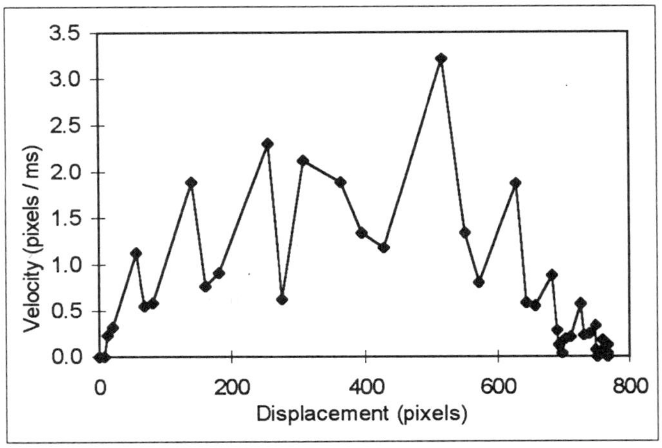

Figure 11. PortaPoint trial showing jitter. A = 768 pixels.

The last isometric device tested was a PortaPoint. It is a separate isometric joystick that uses the same electronics that are used in the Home Row 'J' mouse keyboard [4, 3]. The PortaPoint is mounted in a housing similar in shape to a mouse, and attaches to the computer through the PS/2 mouse port. Figure 11 is a trial from this device, showing jitter.

In all the tests conducted, none of the mouse configurations showed jitter, and all of the isometric joystick configurations showed jitter. If we go back to the base condition, the PS/2 mouse, by being connected to the TrackPoint's PS/2 connector, feeds data to the CPU through the same cable to the same software. Therefore there is something about the isometric joystick that causes the jitter.

After carefully considering all possible sources that could cause this jerkiness, the only explanation we found that fit all the available data was that the isometric joystick, which is force sensitive, was picking up physiological tremor in the finger. Tremor is a series of random variations in force that occur in the finger (and the rest of the human body), and the isometric joystick translates these changes into variations in cursor velocity. Tremor occurs during the application of force, during steady movement, and even at rest. It tends to increase with increased force [14].

The effect of tremor on the joystick's movement micro-structure was a totally unexpected phenomenon. When the main study was conducted, jitter continued to be evident in joystick trials throughout the experiment.

The graphs shown in Figure 12, Figure 13 and Figure 14 are representative samples of joystick trials from the main study. Figure 12 shows that the movement towards the target was made up of a sequence of movements that had rapidly changing velocity. Figure 13 shows a period in the beginning of the movement which might represent a primary submovement with rapid movement towards the target, relatively unaffected by tremor. The rest of the movement is quite badly obscured by tremor.

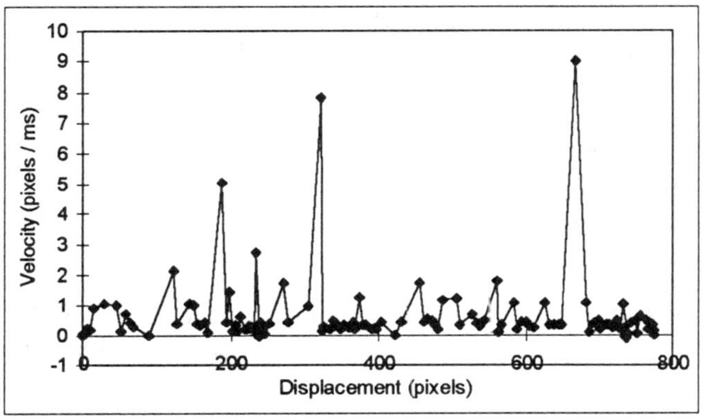

Figure 12. First joystick trial subject DD4 - raw data.

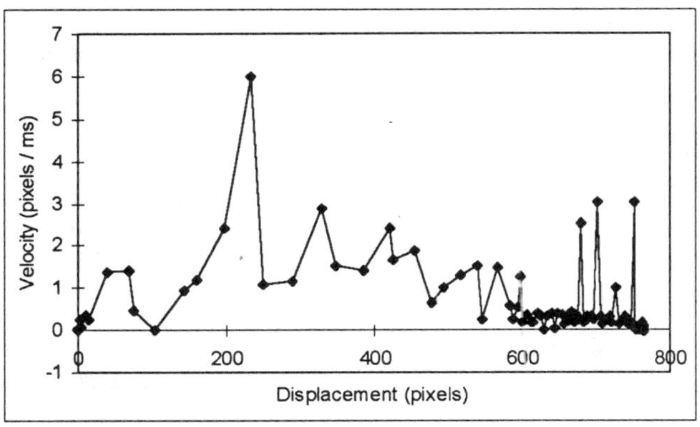

Figure 13. Middle joystick trial subject DD2 - raw data. A = 768 pixels.

Joystick trials were thus characterized by jerkiness that is visible only when the velocity of the trial is studied either over time or over movement distance. The jerkiness was evident in early trials in the pilot study and persisted throughout the duration of the main study.

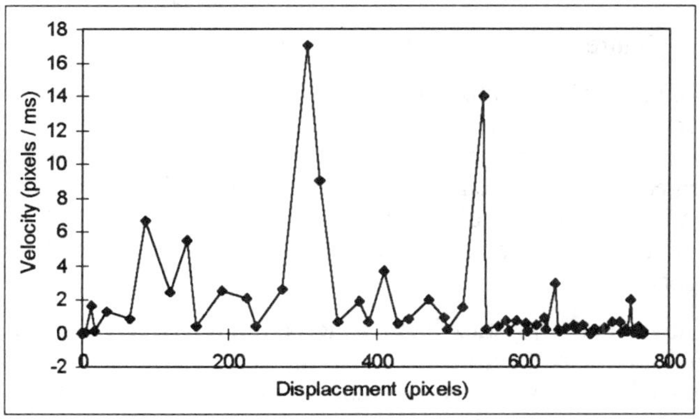

Figure 14. Last joystick trial subject DD1 - raw data.

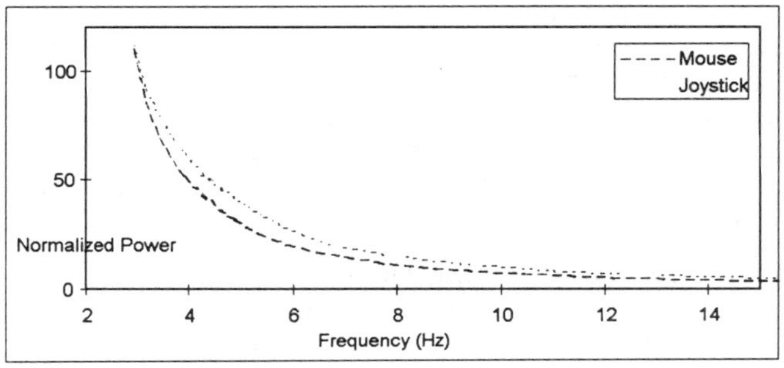

Figure 15. Comparison of spectrograms from mouse and isometric joystick for all trials from last block for all subjects.

The presence of the jitter in the isometric joystick trials suggests higher frequency components in joystick trials than mouse trials. This was verified through spectral analysis. Figure 15 presents the frequency data for the mouse for all subjects compared to the frequency data for the joystick all subjects. It clearly shows a that there is a greater percentage of the power for higher frequencies (between 3 and 10 Hz) for the joystick than for the mouse, which is consistent with higher frequencies in the jitter.

DISCUSSION

Tremor and the Isometric Joystick

The jerkiness in the velocity domain did not appear either in the analyses of mouse movement, nor in plots of cursor position vs. time for the joystick. But when the velocity of the joystick was plotted, either against time or against distance, the jitter leapt out. On reflection, this is not surprising.

Consider Figure 16 which shows a block diagram of an isometric joystick. The joystick is a force sensitive device that translates input force into changes in cursor velocity. Note that because the joystick is using the same hardware connections and software drivers as the mouse, it must send data to the OS in the same form as the mouse. The mouse sends the OS data about displacement, and so the isometric joystick performs an integration of velocity over time in order to send similar displacement information.

Figure 16. Block diagram of isometric joystick.

When there is tremor present in the finger, the tremor is perceived as changes in applied force. These in turn are mapped onto changes in velocity which of course get integrated into displacements and sent to the OS. As long as we look at plots of displacement, nothing is apparent. The moment we look at plots in the velocity domain, the tremor appears.

The isometric joystick happens to be unique in the manner in which it picks up tremor and the way in which it is affected by it. Consider for a moment the finger that controls the joystick. It is applying a lateral force on the joystick, and it is unsupported. It also does not move. Therefore there is little to damp the tremor. In other types of movement, tremor is damped by two things, inertial mass and friction. Because the finger does not move, inertial mass does not play a role and so does not damp tremor. Again, because nothing moves, friction does not play a role. In fact, the only damping factor that we have been able to uncover is the friction that exists between adjacent muscle fibers in the finger [14].

Tremor also occurs during mouse movement, but it does not have the same effect for two reasons. First, the mouse operates in the displacement domain, and is not sensitive to changes in applied force in the manner that the joystick is. It responds only to changes in displacement. The mouse is therefore not directly affected by tremor. Second, when a mouse is moving across a mousepad, any tremor is damped by the friction of the mouse and the hand on the mousepad, as well as by the mass of the hand, wrist and mouse (and perhaps the forearm). Due to these reasons, tremor does not appear in plots of mouse movement. So the physical construction of the joystick makes it susceptible to tremor in a manner that devices such as the mouse are not.

The effect of tremor on other pointing devices is still an open question. Two devices that use relatively unsupported limbs are the trackball and the touch tablet. The trackball is typically controlled by a single thumb or single finger, while touch tablets are controlled either by a finger, or by a stylus. While inertial mass and friction still play a role in these devices, the lack of support for the controlling limb suggests that a similar study needs to be performed on these devices to determine how they are affected by tremor.

The joystick also accentuates tremor. This tremor is picked up by the joystick and passed on to the joystick's hardware controller. The joystick's controller employs an 'accelerated' design, i.e. it employs a non-linear translation between input force and output displacement. This transfer function accentuates the effect that changes in input have on the output. So the changes caused by tremor are exaggerated in the displacement data that is sent to the software driver. The software driver is in turn accelerated, and accentuates changes in displacement into larger changes in the position of the cursor. The net result is that the velocity of the cursor varies widely as it moves across the screen. Thus the design of the joystick makes it unique in the way that it amplifies tremor.

The effect of tremor might be reduced by introducing digital signal processing routines into the joystick's hardware or in its software drivers. These routines could filter out the tremor. Making the joystick slightly deformable might introduce enough inertia into the system to damp the tremor. Additionally, a support for the finger might also reduce tremor.

To summarize, studying the movement microstructure for the joystick revealed that tremor causes involuntary changes in cursor velocity. Taking a closer look at the characteristics of the joystick and its connections to the computer showed that the isometric joystick is unique in the way that it is affected by tremor and the way in which it accentuates the effects of tremor.

CONCLUSIONS AND FURTHER RESEARCH

The study leads to a number of conclusions: about the effect of tremor on controlling pointing devices, about the value of the microstructure level analysis, and about the importance of examining the variable being controlled.

Tremor Makes Isometric Devices Difficult to Control

During an earlier study with a finger-controlled isometric joystick [4], subjects were interviewed to get qualitative feedback from them about their experience. A surprisingly large number of them said that they had a lot of trouble getting the joystick to stop in small targets (the smallest target was 8 pixels across).

The reason for this is now easy to understand. Tremor causes involuntary changes in the velocity at which the cursor moves. This makes it difficult for users to achieve fine control over the cursor making it difficult to stop the cursor at a desired point on the screen and explains why isometric joysticks are hard to control.

The Need to Examine the Variable Being Controlled

A simple lesson from this study is that when a pointing device is being studied, we need to examine its effect on the variable it controls. The isometric joystick controls the velocity of the cursor (even though it integrates the velocity over time and sends the computer displacement information). The effect of tremor was visible only when velocity was plotted against time or displacement.

Taking this argument to the next stage, the implication is that we should look at graphs of the appropriate variable. For example, if we control acceleration, we should look at graphs of acceleration.

Future Research

This study opened avenues of additional research, some of which has been completed and is outside the scope of this paper. A more extensive Fourier analysis has been completed, which revealed patterns of individual differences and learning. One of our originals goal was to model movement with the isometric joystick, but we were confounded by the problems that we were unable to differentiate voluntary from involuntary submovements in the case of the isometric joystick. We believe that studying muscle activations and neuron firings will help in this area. While our goal was understanding movement with the isometric joystick, our study has suggested ways in which it can be improved. These improvements have to be incorporated and tested.

The Microstructure Level Analysis as a Research Tool

The microstructure level analysis was extremely effective in providing information about what happened during joystick trials. The next step in the development of research on pointing devices should be to study movement microstructure in the manner that a Fitts' law analysis is routinely done. The manner in which this study uncovered tremor in the isometric devices strongly supports this suggestion.

Fitts' law, which is the tool most often used in understanding pointing devices, is excellent for comparing devices, but does not help explain why some devices perform better than others. The study of the microstructure of movement of a device helps explain device performance.

We need inventories of knowledge of the microstructure of movement with different devices just like we have a corpus of knowledge about gross movement and the applicability of Fitts' law.

Research on pointing devices will feed off research on the human psychomotor system, and is likely provide an impetus for new discoveries about how humans move. In this effort, Fitts' law must be augmented by microstructure level analysis as the primary research and design tool for pointing devices [9]. This work is the first step in that direction.

REFERENCES

1. Boritz, J., Booth, K.S. and Cowan, W.B. Fitts' Law Studies of Directional Mouse Movement. in *Graphics Interface '91*. 1991. Toronto, Ontario, Canada: Canadian Man-Computer Communications Society p. 216-233.
2. Card, S.K., English, W.K., and Burr, B.J. Evaluation of Mouse, Rate-Controlled Isometric Joystick, Step Keys, and Text Keys for Text Selection on a CRT. *Ergonomics*, 1978. 21(8): p. 601-613.
3. Douglas, S.A. and Mithal, A.K. The Effect of Reducing Homing Time on the Speed of a Finger-Controlled Isometric Pointing Device. *Proc. CHI '94*. 1994. Boston: ACM p. 411-416.
4. Douglas, S.A. and Mithal, A.K. *Human Performance Evaluation of a Finger-Controlled Pointing Device*. 1993, TR 93-11, Dept. of Computer Science, University of Oregon, Eugene, OR 97403-1202.
5. Epps, B.W., Comparison of Six Cursor Control Devices Based on Fitts' Law Models. *Proc. of the Annual Meeting of the Human Factors Society*, 1986: p. 327-331.
6. Fitts, P.M., The Information Capacity of the Human Motor System in Controlling the Amplitude of Movement. *Journal of Experimental Psychology*, 1954. 47(6): p. 381-391.
7. Jagacinski, R.J., Repperger, D.W., Moran, M.S., Ward, S.L., and Glass, B., Fitts' Law and the Microstructure of Rapid Discrete Movements. *Journal of Experimental Psychology: Human Perception and Performance*, 1980. *6*(2): p. 309-320..
8. Langolf, G.D., Chaffin, D.B., and Foulke, J.A. An investigation of Fitts' Law using a wide range of movement amplitudes. *Journal of Motor Behavior*, 1976. *8*(2): p. 113-128.
9. MacKenzie, I.S., Fitts' Law as a Research and Design Tool in Human-Computer Interaction. *Human-Computer Interaction*, 1992. 7(1): p. 91-139.
10. MacKenzie, I.S., Sellen, A. and Buxton, W. A Comparison of Input Devices in Elemental Pointing and Dragging Tasks. in Human Factors in Computing Systems: *Proc. CHI '91*. 1991. New Orleans: ACM p. 161-166.
11. Meyer, D.E., Smith, K.J.E., Kornblum, S., Abrams, R.A., and Wright, C.E., Speed-Accuracy Tradeoffs in Aimed Movements: Toward a Theory of Rapid Voluntary Action. in *Attention and Performance XIII*. M. Jeanerod, Ed. 1990, Erlbaum: Hillsdale, NJ. p. 173-226.
12. Mithal, A.K., *Using Psychomotor Models of Movement in the Analysis and Design of Computer Pointing Devices*. Doctoral Dissertation, Computer and Information Science. 1995, University of Oregon: Eugene. p. 176.
13. Rutledge, J.D. and T. Selker. Force-to-Motion Functions for Pointing. in Human-Computer Interaction - *INTERACT '90*. 1990. Amsterdam: North-Holland p. 701 706.
14. Stein, R.B. and R.G. Lee, Tremor and Clonus, in *Handbook of Physiology: The Nervous System II*. 1989. p. 325-342.
15. Walker, N., Meyer, D.E., and Smelcer, J.B. Spatial and Temporal Characteristics of Rapid Cursor Positioning Movements with Electromechanical Mice in Human Computer Interaction. *Human Factors*, 1993. *35*(3): p. 431-458.

The Influence of Muscle Groups on Performance of Multiple Degree-of-Freedom Input

Shumin Zhai[1,2] **Paul Milgram**[1] **William Buxton**[2]

[1]Department of Industrial Engineering and [2]Department of Computer Science
University of Toronto, Toronto, Ontario, Canada, MS4 1A4
+1-416-978-1976 +1-416-978-3662 +1-416-978-1961
zhai@dgp.toronto.edu milgram@ie.toronto.edu buxton@dgp.toronto.edu

ABSTRACT
The literature has long suggested that the design of computer input devices should make use of the fine, smaller muscle groups and joints in the fingers, since they are richly represented in the human motor and sensory cortex and they have higher information processing bandwidth than other body parts. This hypothesis, however, has not been conclusively verified with empirical research. The present work studied such a hypothesis in the context of designing 6 degree-of-freedom (DOF) input devices. The work attempts to address both a practical need - designing efficient 6 DOF input devices - and the theoretical issue of muscle group differences in input control. Two alternative 6 DOF input devices, one including and the other excluding the fingers from the 6 DOF manipulation, were designed and tested in a 3D object docking experiment. Users' task completion times were significantly shorter with the device that utilised the fingers. The results of this study strongly suggest that the shape and size of future input device designs should constitute affordances that invite finger participation in input control.

Keywords
Input devices, 3-D interface, 6 DOF input, motor control, muscle group differences, hand, fingers, arm, homunculus model.

INTRODUCTION
This paper studies the effects of using different muscle groups in 6 degree-of-freedom (DOF) manipulation. In particular, it investigates human performance differences in 6 DOF input control with and without the involvement of the small muscle groups and joints in the user's fingers.

Increasingly, the user interfaces that we are designing and using involve higher degrees of freedom than were found in first generation GUIs. This places a higher load on the operators of such systems. Consequently, it is all the more important that the motor and cognitive resources of the operator be used to their greatest effect. Many studies have already been conducted which address issues in multiple DOF input (e.g. [11], [12], [14], [25], [26] and [27]).

The study reported in this paper adds to this literature. It investigates how human performance in 6 DOF tasks varies according to the muscle groups employed. The implications of this research are very practical. If performance for a given task is higher when a particular muscle group is employed, then future input devices can be tailored accordingly, with affordances [8] that encourage the use of that group.

The present study was inspired by Card, Mackinlay and Robertson's "morphological analysis" of the design space of input devices, which suggested "a promising direction for developing a device to beat the mouse by using the bandwidth of the fingers" [2]. This prediction was based upon the well-established "homunculus model" from neurophysiology (Figure 1) and some motor bandwidth studies using Fitts' law tasks. However, empirical HCI studies that support such a prediction have not been conclusive. One candidate device which affords finger based manipulation and could therefore conceivably "beat" the mouse is a pen shaped 2 DOF input device such as the stylus studied by MacKenzie, Sellen and Buxton [19]. In their comparison of a stylus with a mouse, however, the results were inconclusive: the stylus outperformed the mouse in dragging but not in pointing tasks. Furthermore, in the context of conventional GUIs, even if the stylus were shown to result in higher performance, the issue may well be moot. This is because the time to acquire the device (i.e. the time for moving between the keyboard and pointing device, which is much longer with the stylus) may dominate the overall performance. We feel that such "side effects" and the collective user experience with the mouse as the "standard" 2 DOF computer input device may make the replacement of the mouse with a finger operated device a futile pursuit.

In the present study, for several reasons, we have chosen to focus on 6 DOF tasks. First of all, there is not yet an accepted standard 6 DOF input device. Secondly, few would disagree that 6 DOF input tasks are much more demanding than 2 DOF input tasks. Consequently, if one particular design factor results in a slight advantage in a 2 DOF input task, that same subtle advantage may manifest itself to a much larger extent in 6 DOF input tasks.

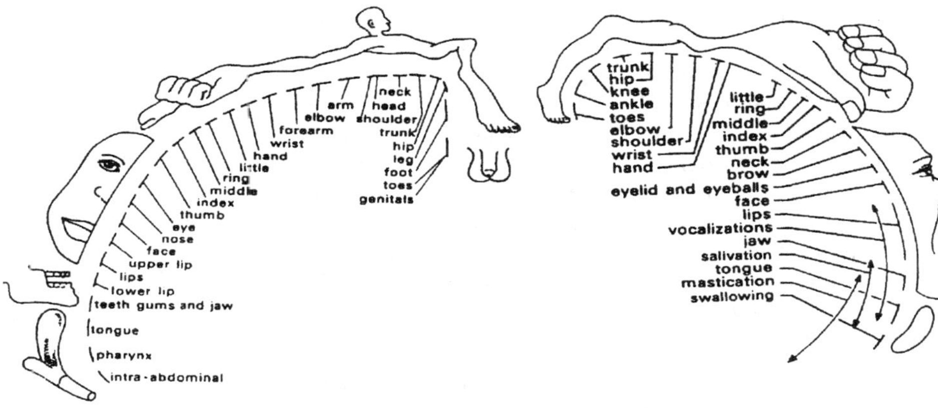

Figure 1 Homunculus model of somatosensory (left) and motor (right) cortex (Adapted from [23], G. H . Sage, Introduction to Motor Behavior, ©1977 Addison-Wesley Publishing Company Inc. Reprinted by permission of Addison-Wesley Publishing Company, Inc.)

THE LITERATURE

As mentioned earlier, neurophysiological studies have shown that various parts of the human body are anatomically reflected in the brain disproportionately relative to their physical size and mass, as illustrated by the homunculus model (Figure 1). Of particular interest to the present study is the fact that representations of the fingers and the hands in both the somatosensory cortex and the motor cortex are much richer than those of the wrists, elbows and shoulders. We may therefore expect performance enhancement if fine muscle groups (i.e. fingers) are allowed to take part in handling an input device. On the other hand, one should note that the relationship between the size of cortical area and dexterity has not been definitively proven in the field of neuroscience.

One of the first studies on the effects of different body parts in manual control was done by Gibbs [6]. In a one dimensional target acquisition task, Gibbs studied task performance of three different body parts: the thumb (activated by the carpometacarpal joint), the hand (activated by the wrist), and the forearm (activated by the elbow), in both position and rate control systems with various control gains and time delays. The performance ranking in Gibbs' study was, in decreasing order: hand, forearm, thumb.

Hammerton and Tickner later replicated Gibbs' study in a 2 DOF target acquisition task [9]. Although Gibbs and Hammerton *et al* subsequently argued about their experimental methodology [7][10], the two studies in fact arrived at very similar conclusions, that performance with the hand (wrist movement) was superior to that of the thumb and the forearm. This advantage was greater for more difficult tasks, such as those with long time delays [9]. Note that both studies found that the wrist was more effective than the thumb. Neither Gibbs nor Hammerton and Ticker included fingers in their studies, however.

The motor performance of different limbs has also been investigated in various Fitts' law studies. Fitts' law established the simple linear relationship: MT = a + b ID in repetitive tapping tasks, where MT is the movement time, ID = $\log_2(2A/W)$ is the Index of Difficulty, A is the movement amplitude and W is the width of the target area [4]. The slope parameter b, in units of seconds/bit, is the inverse of the motor system information processing rate. Fitts' law studies have typically found this rate (1/b) to be in the vicinity of 10 bits/second when the arm is involved in the movement.

Fitts speculated that other limbs, such as fingers, may show different processing rates [4]. Subsequent studies in fact supported this hypothesis. Langolf, Chaffin, and Foulke investigated the Fitts' law relationship using amplitudes of A = 0.25 cm, A = 1.27 cm and A > 5.08 cm [16]. For the first two amplitudes, the experiment was carried out using a microscope. For the large amplitude (>5.08 cm), the experiment was carried with direct vision. Langolf and colleagues observed that for A = 0.25 cm subjects moved the stylus tip (a 1.1 mm peg) primarily with finger flexion and extension. For A = 1.27 cm, flexion and extension of both wrist and fingers occurred. For A > 5.08 cm, the forearm and upper arm were involved in the movements. On the basis of this method of allocating actuation to different muscle groups by controlling the range of movement, Langolf and colleagues concluded that the information processing rates (1/b) for the fingers, wrist, and arm were 38 bits/sec, 23 bits/sec and 10 bits/sec respectively (see Figure 6 in [16]). This study has been widely cited in the literature (e.g. [1]; [15]; [2]) as evidence that fingers are among the most dextrous organs. Card and colleagues recently reviewed Fitts' law studies with various body parts (finger, wrist, arm, neck) and pointed out the limitations of the widely used computer input device - the mouse [2].

In summary, both neurophysiological studies (the homunculus model) and Fitts' law studies suggest that use of the small muscle groups (fingers and thumbs) should result in better performance than the large muscle groups (arm and shoulder). However some studies in manual control, such as Gibbs' study [6] and Hammerton and Tickner's study [9], are not completely consistent with such a prediction.

Due to the theoretical motivation, most studies in the literature tend to compare performance of different muscle groups *against* each other. From a practical and ecological point of view, such a contrast is not necessary for the design of 6 DOF input devices. The human upper limb as a whole (from shoulder to finger tips) has evolved to be highly dextrous yet powerful. Every part of it has its purpose and function. What is needed in input device design is to make use of all parts of the associated limb, according to their respective advantages. The larger muscle groups that operate the wrist, elbow, and shoulder have more power and a larger range of movement. The smaller muscle groups that operate the fingers and thumb have more dexterity. When all the parts work in synergy, movement range and dexterity can both be maximised.

TWO ALTERNATIVE DESIGNS

The preceding discussion suggests that performance improvement in 6 DOF input does not necessarily lie simply in moving operations from the large muscle groups to the smaller ones, but rather in using the small muscle groups *in addition to* the large ones. Motivated by this hypothesis, we designed and implemented two alternative 6 DOF devices for this experiment: the Glove and the FingerBall. The two designs were based on a single common sensing technology, an Ascension Bird™, and both were free moving, isotonic devices operating in position control mode [27]. The critical difference between the two devices, therefore, lay in the involvement of fingers in the manipulation of the 6 degrees of freedom.

The Glove

The first design was an instrumented glove (Figure 2) that had been used in previous experiments [e.g. 28]. An Ascension Bird™ magnetic tracker was attached to the centre of the palm of the glove, the rotational centre of the hand. Also mounted on the palm of the glove was a button with a T-bar. The clutch could easily be pressed down by closing the fingers. The entire glove device weighs 70g.

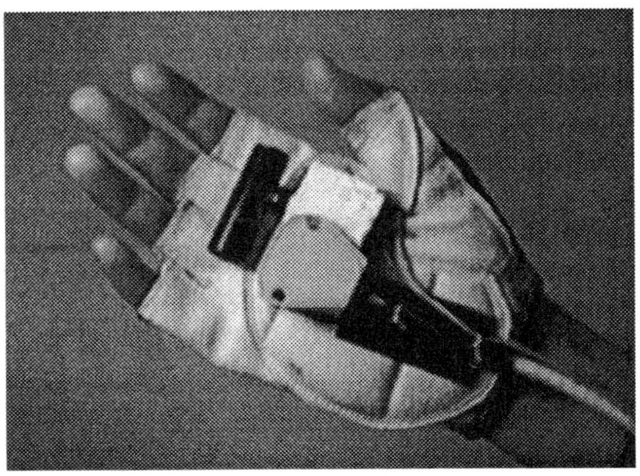

Figure 2 The 6 DOF glove

The Glove design resembles many of the common virtual reality input devices. When using the Glove, all translation and rotation operations are carried out by the user's shoulder, elbow and wrist, i.e., the gross joints and muscle groups in the human limb. Other than pressing the T-button, the smaller, finer joints and muscle groups on the fingers were not utilised for the 6 DOF manipulation.

The T-button was an essential component of the input glove. Since the Glove requires rotation to be made with the wrist, the elbow and the shoulder, its range of rotation is limited. Whenever a limit is reached, the user needs the clutch to disengage the manipulated object (by releasing the T-button under the fingers) and restore the hand to a more comfortable posture, and then recommence the manipulation (by re-closing the fingers). This is very similar to lifting a 2 DOF mouse and starting from a new position on the mouse pad. We refer to this process as "re-clutching".

The majority of existing designs of freely moving 6 DOF devices, such as the "Bat" [25], the "Cricket" [3] and the 3D mouse [17] are similar to the glove design in assigning wrist, elbow and shoulder muscle groups for manipulating the six degrees of freedom; however, none of these make use of the fingers.

The FingerBall

The second design is shown in Figure 3. This device has been dubbed the FingerBall, to reflect the ability to operate it with both arm and fingers.

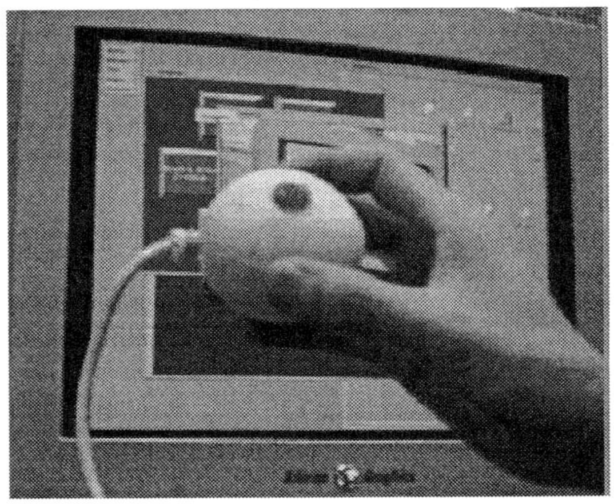

Figure 3 The FingerBall

The ball shape was chosen because a symmetrical ball shape can easily be grasped and manipulated by the fingers in all directions. The FingerBall is designed to be held and moved (rolled) by the fingers, wrist, elbow and shoulder, in postures that have been classified as "precision grasp", as opposed to "power grasp" [18]. Precision grasping, while holding objects with the finger tips, places emphasis on dexterity and sensitivity. In contrast, power grasping, while holding objects against the palm, puts emphasis on security and power. The FingerBall has been designed with a versatile shape that is compatible with a variety of virtual object shapes. This approach of choosing a versatile shape is an alternative to the approach of making "props" that are designed to resemble features of virtual objects being manipulated [11]. The FingerBall instead is similar to the concept of "bricks" [5], which are universal physical handles to various virtual objects.

To take maximum advantage of finger operations, two additional features would be desirable. One is to make the ball *tetherless*, so that the user can roll it freely between her fingers without interference. The second desirable feature is that the ball be made of an elastic, conductive material, so that the entire ball functions as a button that can be squeezed from any direction. Since enabling technology for wireless design is not easily available, the FingerBall currently uses the Ascension Bird™ tracker mounted in the centre of a sponge filled ball 6 cm in diameter. The entire FingerBall weighs 66g. The cord of the Bird is pointed away from the hand in the null position, so as to maximise the range of rotation without interference from the cord (Figure 3). Furthermore, since the FingerBall can be rotated up to 180 degrees in any direction, it did not require a clutch as in the glove design for the task used in the following experiment. It was therefore not necessary to implement a button for the FingerBall in the experiment.

The 3Ball™, manufactured by Polhemus [20], is a commercial product similar to the FingerBall design. The limitation of the 3Ball is its fixed button location. In order to access this button, users can not freely roll the ball between their fingers. Another spherical implementation of a 6 DOF tracker, the "Cue Ball," was demonstrated by Dan Venolia at the CHI'90 Interactive Experience.

EXPERIMENT

Experimental Set-up

Experimental Platform and Display
The experiment was conducted with a desktop stereoscopic virtual environment, MITS (Manipulation In Three Space). As illustrated in Figure 4, MITS consists of a SGI IRIS 4D/310 GTX graphics workstation, CrystalEyes™ stereoscopic glasses, several 6 DOF input devices and a software system developed by the first author.

Since the overall objective of this experiment was to evaluate 6 DOF input interfaces, the emphasis in designing the display was to provide the largest possible number of 3D spatial cues. This was to ensure that the task performance was driven predominantly by differences in input controller conditions rather than by difficulties in perceiving depth information. A 120 Hz sequential switching stereoscopic display was employed, which has been shown to be a necessary feature for this kind of experiment. To enhance the 3D effect, perspective projection and interposition cues were also implemented. The tetrahedra were drawn in wireframe so that all edges and corners of the objects could be perceived simultaneously. Subjects were asked to sit on a chair approximately 60 cm away from the computer screen for all experimental conditions (Figure 4).

Experimental Conditions
Two experimental conditions, the Glove and the FingerBall, were used in this experiment. A pilot study showed that the best performances for both conditions were achieved when the control display ratio (control gain) was 1 (both translation and rotation). In such cases, subjects can take the advantage of the direct, one-to-one correspondence between the input and the display.

Experimental Task
A 6 DOF docking task, illustrated in Figure 5, was used for this experiment. This represents a common elemental task that is involved in many higher level interactions. In the experiment, subjects were asked to move a 3D cursor as quickly as possible to align it with a 3D target. The cursor and the target were two tetrahedra of equal size (4.2 cm from the centre to each vertex). The edges and vertex markers (bars and spherical stars) of both tetrahedra were coloured so that there was only one correct match in orientation. The markers superimposed on each corner of the tetrahedra served multiple purposes. The stars on the target indicated the acceptable 3D error tolerance for each vertex (0.84 cm). The two types of markers (stars and bars) served also to differentiate the target from the cursor.

At the beginning of each experimental trial the cursor appeared in the centre of the 3D space while the target randomly appeared in one of five pre-set locations (14 cm, 11.5 cm, 12 cm, 7 cm, and 10 cm away from the centre of the cursor in five arbitrary directions) and orientations (110°, 98°, 106°, 140°, and 115°, mismatched with the cursor about five arbitrary axes). In contrast to the data

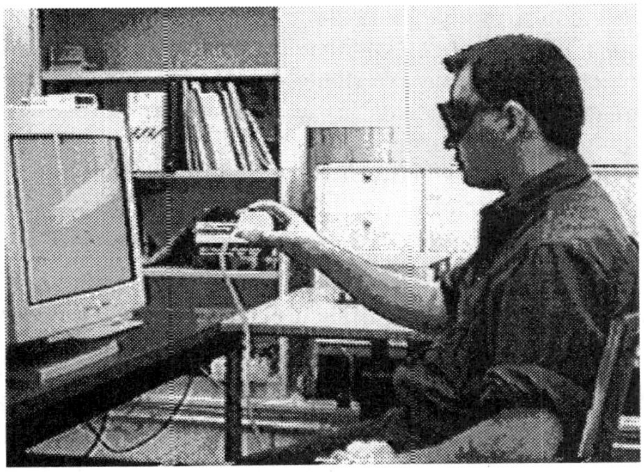

Figure 4 Experiment Set-up

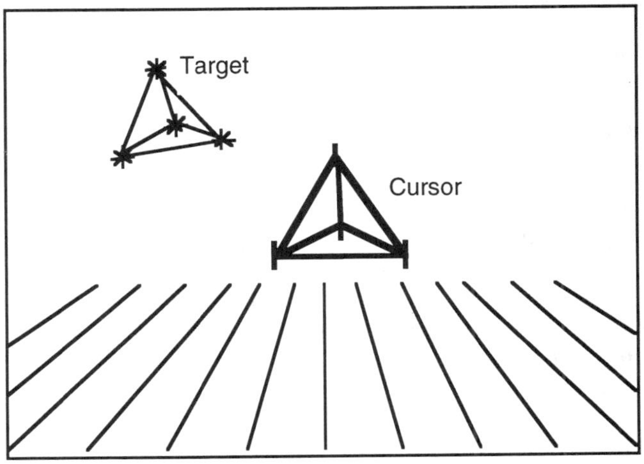

Figure 5 The Experimental Task

gathering trials, during practice sessions the target appeared in completely random locations and orientations.

During the trial, whenever a corner of the cursor entered into the tolerance volume surrounding the *corresponding* corner of the target, the star on that corner changed its colour as an indication of capture. Whenever all four corresponding corners stayed concurrently matched for 0.7 seconds, the trial was deemed completed. At the end of each trial, the trial completion time was printed on the screen. The beginning of each trial was signalled with a long auditory beep and the end of each trial was signalled with a short beep.

Experimental Design
A within-subjects design was used in this experiment, in consideration of efficiency. Each subject was tested with both of the two conditions, Glove and FingerBall, on the same day. According to the results of our previous research in [27-29], users' performance with 6 DOF isotonic position control inputs tended to stabilise after 20 minutes of practice. In this experiment, each condition was given about 25 minutes of exposure, which comprised a short demonstration, two warm-up trials, five tests and some practice trials between tests. Each test consisted of two identical blocks of trials. Each block had 5 trials with 5 distinctive initial target locations in random order. Test 1 started after a short demonstration and two warm-up trials. Test 2, Test 3, Test 4 and Test 5 started 5, 10, 15, and 20 minutes after the beginning of Test 1 respectively. Subjects were alternatively assigned to one of the two experiment orders: Glove first (GB) and FingerBall first (BG). After completing the first condition, each subject received a short break before proceeding to the second condition.

Subjects
Twelve paid volunteers who had no previous experience with 6 DOF input devices were recruited. Two of them failed to pass the screening test due to weak stereopsis (using a Baush and Lomb Orthorator). The remaining 10 participated in the complete experiment. Their ages ranged from 22 to 33, with a median of 29. Eight of the subjects were right handed and two were left handed. Subjects were asked to use their dominant hand with both input devices (FingerBall or Glove).

Experimental Results and Discussion

First Analysis of the Overall Results
In the following data analyses, statistical model residuals were analysed first and it was found that the residual distributions were skewed towards lower scores. This is typical when completion time is used as a performance measure. Data with such skewed distributions do not strictly meet the assumption of analysis of variance (ANOVA). We therefore applied a common correction technique, log transformation [13], to all time data in the following ANOVA significance tests. For ease of comprehension, however, all numbers and figures illustrating results are still presented according to the original, untransformed scale.

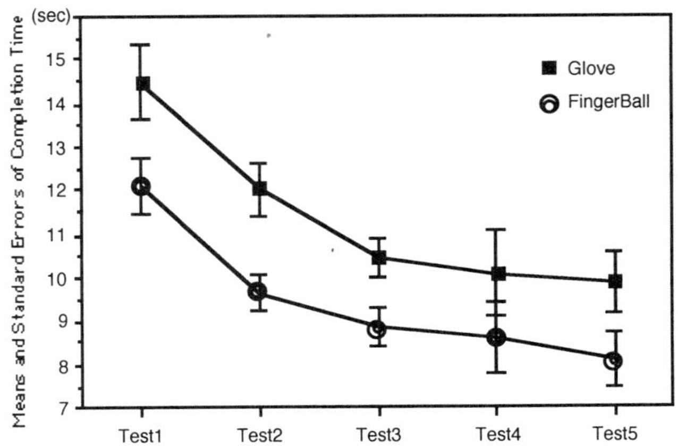

Figure 6 Task completion times with FingerBall and Glove (data from all 10 subjects)

Figure 6 shows the subjects' mean trial completion times for each of the five tests. On average, task completion times were clearly shorter for the FingerBall than for the glove in each of the five tests. Repeated measure variance analysis showed that overall performance scores for the two devices were significantly different: $F(1, 8) = 26.554$, $p < 0.005$.

With both modes, subjects significantly improved their performances over the course of the five experimental phases: $F(4, 32) = 34.04$, $p < 0.0001$. In addition, the performance differences between the two modes were independent of experimental phase, as indicated by the absence of a significant Device x Phase interaction: $F(4, 32) < 1$, $p > 0.5$. The performance differences between the two modes were also independent of initial target location / orientation: $F(4, 32) = 1.28$, $p = 0.3$.

Other significant factors included Block: $F(1,8) = 26.44$, $p < 0.001$. As stated earlier, each test consisted of two blocks of trials. Completion times in the second block were significantly shorter than for the first block, due to an obvious learning effect.

The presentation order of the two modes was not significant: $F(1,8) = 2.2$, $p = 0.17$, but the Order x Device interaction was significant: $F(1,8) = 22.587$, $p < 0.005$. This could imply the presence of an *asymmetrical skill transfer* as an artifact of the within-subjects design, a factor which is an often overlooked and which can result in misleading conclusions in such experimental research. As Poulton [21, 22] argued, with a within-subjects design, the actual skill transfer from one condition to another might not be symmetrical, even though subjects' exposures to the two conditions are ostensibly equalised.

In the present experiment, the Order x Device x Phase interaction is also significant ($F(4,32) = 8.7$, $p < 0.0001$) indicating that, if there was an asymmetrical transfer effect, it varied with experimental phase. It is thus very likely that asymmetrical transfer might have been a significant factor in the early experimental phases but not in the later phases. Two approaches were therefore taken, respectively described in the following two subsections, to test if asymmetrical skill transfer was likely to have been the only cause of the performance difference between the FingerBall and the Glove.

A Between-Subjects Analysis
In order to remove the possibility that the preceding results were due solely to asymmetrical skill transfer, an equivalent between subjects analysis was carried out using only the data for the first device used by each group of subjects, thereby eliminating any potential asymmetrical ordering effects. In other words, subjects were divided into two groups, where members of the FingerBall group were the subjects who were tested with the FingerBall first and the Glove later. Their data with the Glove were discarded for the between subject analysis. Similarly, the FingerBall data were discarded for the group who tested the Glove first. This approach was expected to be much less sensitive than the within subject analysis in the preceding section.

Figure 7 shows the results after discarding half of the data in this fashion. Results of a repeated measure variance analysis based on these between-subjects data were consistent with the early analysis, i.e., completion times with the FingerBall were significantly shorter than the glove: $F(1,8) = 3.6$, $p < 0.05$. Learning apparently did not reduce this difference, as the Phase x Device interaction was not significant: $F(4, 32) < 1$, $p > 0.5$.

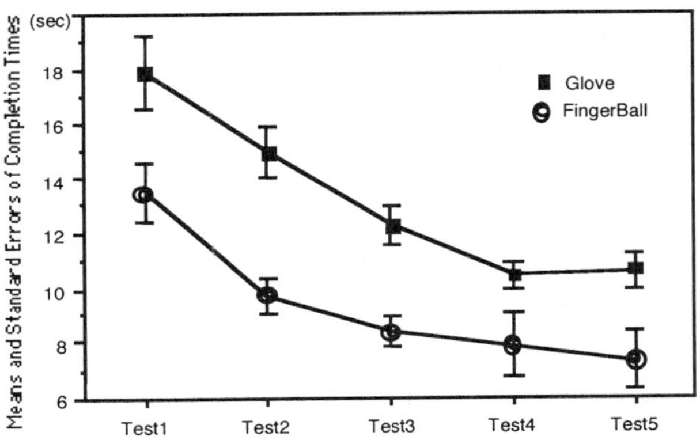

Figure 7 The FingerBall vs. the glove with 5 subjects in each group (between-subjects)

Performance Analysis of the Final Test
As an additional verification that asymmetrical skill transfer effect was indeed not the fundamental cause of the performance difference between the Glove and the FingerBall, we also analysed users' performance in the final test for each condition. As implied by the significant Order x Device x Phase interaction in the initial within-subjects analysis, it was very unlikely that asymmetrical skill transfer was still in effect in Test 5, after 4 tests and 20 minutes of practice with the second device. Indeed, a repeated measure within-subjects variance analysis on the data from Test 5 again confirmed the previous conclusions: completion time was significantly shorter with the FingerBall than with the Glove: $F(1, 8) = 15.8$, $p < 0.005$. Furthermore, neither Order of presentation nor Order x Device interaction was significant, implying that any possible skill transfer effect between conditions did not significantly affect performance in the final test.

On the basis of all three of the above analyses, we can therefore confidently conclude that the FingerBall significantly outperformed the Glove in the experiment.

The Effect of Clutching vs. Muscle Groups
From a practical point of view, the above analyses have concluded that the FingerBall is a more efficient device than the Glove. However, from a more theoretical point of view, the cause of the performance differences is still not clear. As described earlier, the FingerBall differs from the glove in two major aspects: the use of finger joints and the absence of a button (and the accompanying re-clutching processes). With the Glove, the re-clutching process takes time to complete. Subjects usually carried out 1 to 3 clutches / declutches in each trial. This could therefore have been the sole cause of the performance differences in the above analyses, while obfuscating any effects of using finger joints / muscle groups.

This issue had in fact been considered during the design stage of the experiment, however, and the re-clutching times (from the moment of disengaging to the moment of re-engaging) accumulated in each trial were measured and recorded during each trial. In the following analysis, the re-clutching times were subtracted from the trial completion times for the Glove condition. The resulting net score is labelled as "C-R time". For the FingerBall condition, for which no clutching was necessary, C-R time was identical to the original completion time itself. Figure 8 shows the mean completion time with the FingerBall, the mean completion time with the Glove, and the re-clutching time with the Glove, all from Test 5. The mean re-clutching time in Test 5 was 1.06 seconds, accounting for 10.7% of the mean completion time with the Glove (Figure 8).

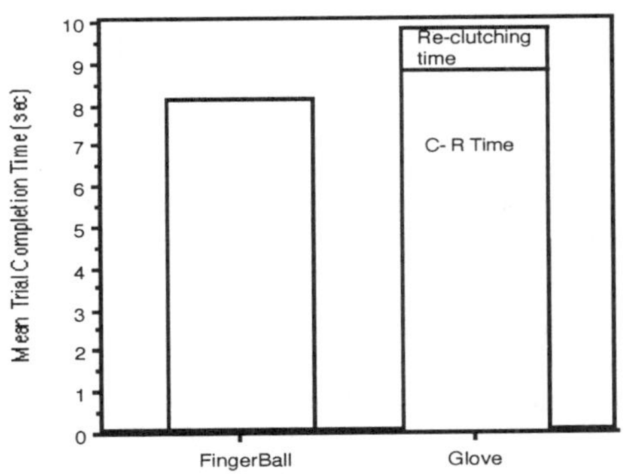

Figure 8 Mean completion time in Test 5

Note that the C-R time measure is biased against the FingerBall condition, for two reasons. First, with the FingerBall, the re-clutching process still exists effectively, although not explicitly. From time to time subjects had to move their fingers to different parts of the ball's surface to make further rotation. This effort (and associated time) was not taken into account by the adjusted C-R time measure, since no explicit re-clutching time could be measured. Second, during the re-clutching time with the Glove, subjects were not necessarily idle but probably were instead engaged in mentally making decisions about what to do next. Since it is known that mental rotation takes up a certain amount of time [24], this time may overlap with the re-clutching time in the Glove condition and is therefore reduced in the C-R time measure. Nevertheless, C-R time serves as a conservative measure to test if the use of fingers really was advantageous. If the FingerBall still outperformed the Glove, as measured by C-R time, the advantage of using fine joints must therefore exist. The converse may not be true, however.

Figure 9 shows the performance differences between the FingerBall and the Glove as measured by C-R time. As can be seen, the mean completion times with the FingerBall were still shorter than the mean C-R times with the Glove. Repeated measure variance analysis of C-R times collected in Test 5 (final phase of the experiment) showed that the difference between completion times with the FingerBall and the C-R times with the Glove was still significant: $F(1,8) = 5.324$, $p < 0.05$. Neither the order of presentation nor its interaction with the device was statistically significant, suggesting that this difference was not caused by asymmetrical skill transfer. This analysis therefore further supports the conclusion that the use of different muscle groups was indeed a major cause of the superior performance of the FingerBall as compared to the Glove.

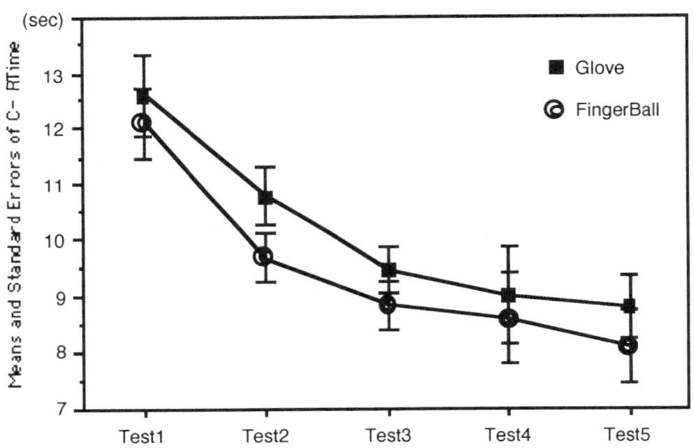

Figure 9 Comparison between the FingerBall and the Glove after discounting re-clutching time with the Glove

Subjective Evaluation

Upon completing the experimental trials, subjects subjectively rated each of the devices on a continuous scale ranging from -2 to +2 (-2: very low, -1: low, 0: OK, 1: high, 2: very high). On average, the FingerBall received higher ratings than the Glove (mean value: 0.78 vs. 0.60). Of the 10 subjects, however, only 6 rated the FingerBall higher than the Glove; the other 4 subjects rated the Glove higher than the FingerBall (Figure 10). This is an interesting contrast to the task performance measures. In the final test, all subjects, except subject A, had shorter task completion times with the FingerBall than with the Glove. It appeared, therefore, that subjective preferences were strongly affected by some salient features of the devices other than performance. Subjects were encouraged to jot down comments on features about which they felt strongly.

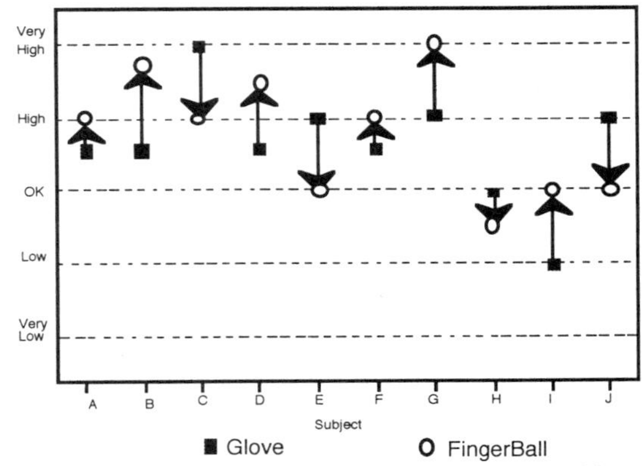

Figure 10 Subjective Ratings of FingerBall vs. Glove Upward arrows indicate that the FingerBall was preferred

Seven subjects felt that the cord with the FingerBall got in the way. Three subjects did not like the wrist rotations imposed by the Glove. Two subjects wrote that the FingerBall was less natural than the Glove. Surprisingly, one subject particularly liked the clutch function with the Glove. One subject reported fatigue with both devices. The fact that the Glove device is closer to what is typically encountered in "virtual reality" systems could also have been an influential factor in subjects' preferences.

CONCLUSIONS

On the basis of neurophysiological findings (the homunculus model) and Fitts' law studies, researchers have hypothesised that computer input devices that are manipulated by fingers (the small muscle groups) should have performance advantages over devices that are operated by the wrist and/or elbow and/or shoulder (the large muscle groups) [2]. It was believed that devices designed to conform to such a hypothesis would outperform the mouse - the standard 2 DOF computer input device. Follow- up studies that test such a hypothesis or apply it to new designs have not been reported in the literature, however. Designing efficient 6 DOF input devices thus presents a practical need, as well as a research opportunity to test the hypothesis of muscle group differences. Through an empirical study it was found that assignment of the muscle groups in manipulating an input device was indeed a very critical factor determining user performance. Our results show that in a 6 DOF docking task, trial completion times for an input device that included fingers during 6 DOF manipulation (the FingerBall) were significantly shorter than those of a device that excluded the fingers from the 6 DOF manipulation (the Glove). The results of our study strongly suggest that future designers of such input devices should design the affordances of input devices (i.e. shape and size) such that the fingers are included in their operation to whatever extent is feasible.

ACKNOWLEDGEMENTS

This paper is based on Chapter 4 of the first author's doctoral thesis [27]. We would like to thank George Fitzmaurice and other members of the ETC Lab and the IRG group at the University of Toronto for their comments, advice and assistance. Primary support for this work has come from the Information Technology Research Centre (ITRC) of Ontario, the Defence and Civil Institute of Environmental Medicine (DCIEM), and the Natural Sciences and Engineering Research Council of Canada (NSERC).

REFERENCES

1. Boff, K. R. and Lincoln, J. E. *Engineering Data Compendium - Human Perception and Performance.* Armstrong Aerospace Medical Research Laboratory, Wright-Patterson Air Force Base, Ohio, 1988.

2. Card, S. K., Mackinlay, J. D., and Robertson, G. G. A morphological analysis of the design space of input devices. *ACM Transactions on Information Systems, 9,* 2 (1991), 99-122.

3. Digital Image Design Inc. The Cricket, product information. New York, NY., 1993.

4. Fitts, P. M. The information capacity of the human motor system in controlling the amplitude of movement. *Journal of Experimental Psychology, 47,* (1954), 381-391.

5. Fitzmaurice, G. W., Ishii, H., and Buxton, W. Bricks: Laying the foundation for graspable user interfaces, in *Proc. of CHI'95: ACM Conference on Human Factors in Computing Systems* (Denver, Colorado, USA, 1995), pp. 442-449.

6. Gibbs, C. B. Controller design: Interactions of controlling limbs, time-lags and gains in positional and velocity systems. *Ergonomics, 5,* 2 (1962), 385-402.

7. Gibbs, C. B. Comments on 'An investigation into the comparative suitability of forearm, hand and thumb controls in acquisition tasks' by Hammerton and Tickner. *Ergonomics, 10,* 4 (1967), 431-432.

8. Gibson, J. J. *The ecological approach to visual perception.* Houghton Mifflin Company, Boston, 1979.

9. Hammerton, M. and Tickner, A. H. An investigation into the comparative suitability of forearm, hand and thumb controls in acquisition tasks. *Ergonomics, 9,* 2 (1966), 125-130.

10. Hammerton, M. and Tickner, A. H. Reply to Comments by C.B. Gibbs. *Ergonomics, 10,* 4 (1967), 433.

11. Hinckley, K., Pausch, R., Goble, J. C., and Kassell, N. F. Passive real-world interface props for neurosurgical visualization, in *Proc. of CHI'94: ACM conference on Human Factors in Computing Systems* (Boston, 1994), pp. 452-458.

12. Hinckley, K., Pausch, R., Goble, J. C., and Kassell, N. F. A survey of design issues in spatial input, in *Proc. of ACM Conference on User Interface Software and Technology* (1994), pp. 213-222.

13. Howell, D. C. *Statistical Methods for Psychology* (Third ed.). PWS-KENT Publishing Company, Boston, 1992.

14. Jacob, R. J. K., Sibert, L. E., McFarlane, D. C., and Mullen, M. P. Integrality and separability of input devices. *ACM Transactions on Computer-Human Interaction, 1,* 1 (1994), 3-26.

15. Keele, S. W. Motor Control, in K. R. Boff, L. Kaufman, & J. P. Thomas (Eds.), *Handbook of Perception and Human Performance.* (pp. 30.1-30.60). John Wiley & Sons, New York, 1986.

16. Langolf, G. D., Chaffin, D. B., and Foulke, J. A. An investigation of Fitts' law using a wide range of movement amplitudes. *Journal of Motor Behavior, 8,* 2 (1976), 113-128.

17. Logitech. 2D/6D Mouse technical reference manual. In Fremont, CA 94555: Logitech Inc., 1991.

18. MacKenzie, C. L. and Iberall, T. *The Grasping Hand.* North-Holand, Amsterdam, 1994.

19. MacKenzie, I. S., Sellen, A., and Buxton, W. A comparison of input devices in elemental pointing and dragging tasks, in *Proc. of CHI'91: ACM Conference on Human Factors in Computing Systems* (New Orleans, Lousiana, 1991), pp. 161-166.

20. Polhemus. 3Ball™, product information. Polhemus, Cochester, VT., 1993.

21. Poulton, E. C. Unwanted asymmetrical transfer effects with balanced experimental designs. *Psychological Bulletin, 66,* 1 (1966), 1-8.

22. Poulton, E. C. *Bias in Quantifying Judgements.* Lawrence Erlbaum Associates, Hove and London, 1989.

23. Sage, G. H. *Introduction to Motor Behavior, A Neuropsychological Approach* (2nd ed). Addison-Wesley Publishing Company, 1977.

24. Shepard, R. N. and Metzler, J. Mental rotation of three-dimensional objects. *Science, 171,* 3972 (1971), 701-703.

25. Ware, C. Using hand position for virtual object placement. *The Visual Computer, 6,* (1990), 245-253.

26. Ware, C. and Jessom, D. R. Using the bat: a six dimensional mouse for object placement. *IEEE Computer Graphics and Applications, 8,* 6 (1988), 155-160.

27. Zhai, S. Human Performance in Six Degree of Freedom Input Control. Ph.D. Thesis, University of Toronto,1995. (http://vered.rose.toronto.edu/people/shumin.html)

28. Zhai, S. and Milgram, P. Human performance evaluation of manipulation schemes in virtual environments, in *Proc. of VRAIS'93: the first IEEE Virtual Reality Annual International Symposium* (Seattle, USA, 1993), pp. 155-161.

29. Zhai, S. and Milgram, P. Input Techniques for HCI in 3D Environments, in *Proc. of Conference Companion of CHI'94: ACM conference on Human Factors in Computing Systems* (Boston, 1994), pp. 85-86.

A Collaborative Model of Feedback in Human-Computer Interaction

Manuel A. Pérez-Quiñones
Human-Computer Interaction Laboratory
Naval Research Laboratory, Code 5512
Washington, DC 20375-5337
perez@aic.nrl.navy.mil
+1-202-767-9003

John L. Sibert
Department of EE and CS
The George Washington University
Washington, DC 20052
sibert@seas.gwu.edu
+1-202-994-4953

ABSTRACT
Feedback plays an important role in human-computer interaction. It provides the user with evidence of closure, thus satisfying the communication expectations that users have when engaging in a dialogue. In this paper we present a model identifying five feedback states that must be communicated to the user to fulfill the communication expectations of a dialogue. The model is based on a linguistics theory of conversation, but is applied to a graphical user interface. An experiment is described in which we test users' expectations and their behavior when those expectations are not met. The model subsumes some of the temporal requirements for feedback previously reported in the human-computer interaction literature.

Keywords
Human-computer dialogues, feedback, conversational dialogues, states of understanding, collaborative view of conversations.

INTRODUCTION
Adequate feedback is a necessary component of both human-human and human-computer interaction. In human conversations, we use language, gestures, and body language to inform our conversational partners that we have heard and understood their communication. These communicative events fulfill a very important role in a conversation; they satisfy certain communication expectations of the dialogue participant. To understand these expectations imagine what happens when they are missing. In a conversation, if you do not hear a short uh hum or see a nod of the head, you might think that the other person did not understand and as a result you might interrupt the conversation while you question the listener's attentiveness; "hey, are you awake?"

This idea of communication expectations, also called "psychological closure" [16, 25], is a common human behavioral characteristic that also exists when we are interacting with a computer. For example, if the user types a command but receives no response from the user interface, the user might repeatedly press the return key to make sure that the system has "heard" (or received) the command. At times it is not even clear "who is waiting for whom" [17].

Many studies of feedback have been reported in the literature. Some deal with response times guidelines for feedback, others have addressed performance penalties caused by delayed responses [26], while others deal with the form feedback should take. What is lacking in all of these studies is a behavioral model that explains users' communication expectations and their behavior. In this paper we present such a model of feedback based on principles of conversation derived from linguistic theory and on graphical user interface design guidelines. We also describe an experiment in which we test some of the expectations proposed by the model.

CHI 96 Vancouver, BC Canada
ACM 0-89791-777-4/96/04

BACKGROUND
Feedback, in most of the human-computer interaction literature, refers to communication from the system to the user as a direct result of a user's action [24]. Most user interface design guidelines also stress the importance of this type of feedback, for example [1] recommends "keep the user informed" and use feedback to confirm "that the operation is being carried out, and (eventually) that it's finished." Gaines [10] states that the response to a user's action "should be sufficient to identify the type of activity taking place."

However, feedback also can be used to communicate the state of the system independently of the user's action [1]. The system, at times, can be busy processing incoming events like mail messages, or alarm notifications that the user has preset days in advance. In these cases, the system must let the user know its current state of processing so that the user does not feel frustrated or locked out of the dialogue.

Foley and van Dam [8] describe feedback in terms of interpersonal conversations, such as responses to questions or "signs of attentiveness." Both of these conversational devices are classified as forms of feedback.

What is common in all of these views of feedback is that it serves a behavioral purpose in interaction. This purpose represents the communication expectations that humans have from a conversational participant, even when this conversational participant is a computer system.

Collaborative View of Conversations

Our model is based on Clark, et. al [5-7] who view a conversation between two humans as a collaborative process. Previously, conversations were seen as turns taken by two participants, where the turns were related by a series of adjacency pair relations. The collaborative view extends this turn-taking model by looking at the cooperation between conversational partners to agree on common ground, sometimes without taking extra turns.

The collaborative model states that conversations are really negotiations over the contents of the conversation between two participants. One participant, the speaker, makes a presentation and the other participant, the listener, accepts it. A *contribution* to a conversation occurs only after the presentation is accepted. It is defined to be the pair of presentation and acceptance turns.

This theory of contributions to conversations has already been applied in the study of human-computer dialogues. Payne [19, 20] analyzed the interaction in MacDraw based on presentation/acceptance trees. Brennan and Hulteen have defined a model of adaptive speech feedback [3] based on the states of understanding principles. A similar model is used in Apple Computer's speech input system [15], PlainTalk. The different states of feedback are identified with icons, as shown below.

Figure 1. SOU in Apple's Casper

States of Understanding

States of understanding (SOU) are the states that a listener believes he or she is in, after receiving a presentation from the speaker [6]. SOU is one of many ways participants in conversations fulfill their goals in the collaborative process. The listener provides evidence of his or her SOU thus allowing the speaker to adapt according to the specific SOU.

The states are defined as follows. When speaker *A* issues an utterance, listener *B* believes he or she is in one of the following states:

State 0: *B* is not aware of the utterance
State 1: *B* is aware of the utterance, but did not hear it
State 2: *B* heard the utterance, but did not understand it
State 3: *B* fully understood the utterance

Evidence of understanding (i.e. identification of the state) must be provided by the listener, thus allowing the other participant to adapt accordingly. For example, if after presenting a question, the speaker receives evidence that the listener is in state 1, the speaker might repeat or rephrase the question to help the listener reach state 3. The two partners follow the principle of least collaborative effort [7]. This principle states that speaker and hearer will try to minimize the collaborative effort it takes to reach a level of understanding. If a SOU is not clearly communicated by the listener, the speaker will seek further evidence that the communication was received. This is a form of repair behavior guided by the SOU principles.

The SOU can be communicated without using a verbal utterance. For example, the use of a confused facial expression can be enough to indicate that the listener is in state 2. Also, several signals together can be used to signal a single state. A facial expression together with a hand gesture, for example, can be interpreted as a single indication of a state.

PROPOSED MODEL

Human behavior in a human-computer dialogue, when a communication expectation is not met, is similar to the repair behavior found in human-human dialogues. For example, consider the use of the performance meter on a workstation. Many workstation users keep one at the bottom of their screen to get an indication of the amount of work the CPU is currently performing. This information is used to identify whether the system is locked or just slow because it is overloaded. When users initiate an action but obtain no response within some expected amount of time, they face one of two situations: did the computer received my action or should I repeat it? The performance meter allows the user to determine if the system is busy, and thus may have received the action but is just slow in the response. If the system is not busy, the action was lost or ignored in which case the user must repeat the action if the results are desired. In this example, the user interface of the application in use did not meet the user's communication expectations and thus the user had to resort to an extra "device" (the performance meter) to find out extra information to match the communication expectations.

Based on the states of understanding principles and on graphical user interface design guidelines, such as [1], we have identified a number of feedback states needed in a human-computer dialogue to meet the human's communication expectations.

Our model contains five *simulated states of understanding* (SSOU): *ready*, *processing*, *reporting*, *busy-no-response*, and *busy-delayed-response*. Each state is intended to produce conversational behaviors on the part of the user similar to those produced by the SOU in human-human conversations. The model prescribes the type of feedback to be provided based on communication expectations but not the specific form in which it must be provided. The states are called *simulated* to emphasize the notion that this is not a model of understanding or of some other cognitive process. The model represents the communication expectations from a user's point of view. It does not address the communication expectations that the computer could or should have in a human-computer dialogue, see [17] for a discussion of this issue.

A user interface is a collection of concurrent dialogues between the user and the computing system[1]. For each one

1.In this context, system refers to the user interface component of the software system. The rest of the software system can be doing processing in the background asynchronously with what is happening at the user interface.

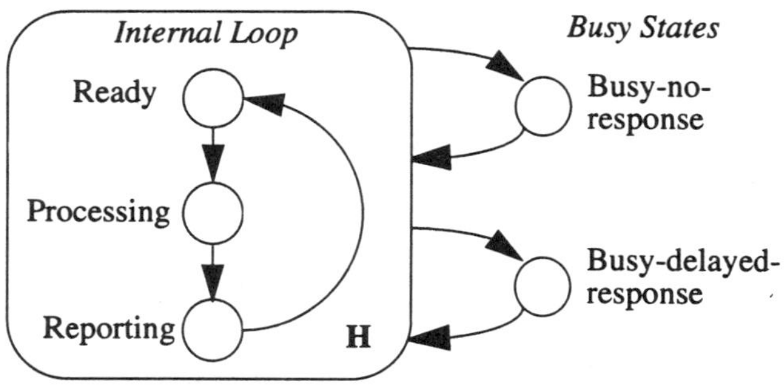

Figure 2. SSOU Feedback States

of these dialogues, the user interface *must provide* some form of evidence about the state of the dialogue. Each dialogue is *always* in one (and only one) of the states shown in Figure 2. In the performance meter example above, the application had possibly several dialogues with the user, and the performance meter had at least another one. In addition, the state of the dialogue can be indicated using more than one signal, as it is often done in human conversations. For example, a cursor change and a progress bar are used at the same time in some situations to indicate that a particular dialogue is processing a user request.

The *ready, processing*, and *reporting* states are known as the internal loop and represent feedback as responses to users' actions. The other two states are collectively known as the busy states and represent feedback as an indicator of system state. The notation used on Figure 2 is a modification of that presented in [12]. The internal loop has a history component. When a transition is made to one of the busy states, the internal loop "remembers" the state in which it was. When the transition is made back into the loop, it returns to the state "remembered." This is used as a short hand to avoid explicit portrayal of transitions from every node in the internal loop to both busy states and back.

Ready State

The system must provide evidence that it is in the *ready* state when it can receive and process user actions. When evidence of this state is presented, the user might initiate the next action and will expect to see some form of feedback indicating that the action has been received by the system. The behavioral role of this state is to inform the user that the system is ready to accept the next action.

Processing State

In the *processing* state, the system communicates to the user that an action was received in the *ready* state, and that something is being processed before providing the results of the action. Note that no results are displayed in this state, that is done in the *reporting* state. The behavioral role here is to inform the user that his or her action was received and it is being processed.

Sometimes, the *processing* state appears to be skipped if the results can be calculated so fast that there is no apparent delay in it. An example of this situation is dragging an object with the mouse. The object being dragged follows the mouse location continuously, giving the appearance of no time spent on the *processing* state.

On the other hand, the *processing* state sometimes requires a separate notification. For example, copying a very large number of files on the Macintosh Finder can produce feedback of processing and reporting. The system shows the *processing* state before it starts copying the files by displaying the message "Preparing to copy files..." This is a case where a separate *processing* feedback is used from the feedback used in the *reporting* state due to the length of time spent in the *processing* state.

Reporting State

In the *reporting* state, the system informs the user of the results of the action initiated in the *ready* state. Once this information is given to the user, the system is expected to go back to the *ready* state where it will be ready to accept the next user action. The behavioral role here is to inform the user of the results of a user action, thus providing closure to the action.

Busy States

Our model includes two busy states that are used to provide feedback about system state. The *busy-**no**-response* state is a state in which the system is "unaware" of any possible action the user might initiate. While in this state, all user initiated actions are ignored and lost. In the other busy state, *busy-**delayed**-response*, all user initiated actions are saved and processed later. This state has been called "type-ahead" in command line interfaces.

It is important that the busy states be signalled to the user to maintain a "sense of presence" [17] of the interface. It has been recommended that some form of "placebo" [9] is provided to ensure the user the system has not crashed. In our model we have subclassified the busy states into two separate states because of the different behavioral role each fulfills in the dialogue.

If the user is presented with evidence that the system is in the *busy-**no**-response* state, the user will opt to wait until the system returns to the *ready* state, since all actions are ignored by the system. This is the traditional busy state in most user interfaces. On the other hand, if the system is in *busy-**delayed**-response* and the user is aware of it, then the user might take advantage of the state and perform some actions even though no immediate response is provided. This has been seen in command line interfaces for years, but it also occurs in graphical interfaces.

In the *busy-**no**-response* state, the behavioral role is to communicate to the user that nothing can be done at this point. Any user actions will result in wasted effort on the user's part. In the *busy-**delayed**-response*, however, the behavioral role of the feedback is to inform the user that actions *will* be accepted but processed after a delay. In effect, it is as if the system was telling the user "I am listening, but will respond after a short delay... go ahead keep working." The analogue in human conversations is when a participant gives the other participant consent to continue talking even though no feedback will be provided. This might occur, for example, when their visual communication is interrupted and thus feedback cannot be provided using the usual mechanisms. In this case, feedback and responses might be provided only after a delay.

Unfortunately, in today's interfaces these two states normally are not signalled differently to the user. As a result, taking advantage of the "type-ahead" features is left as a "goodie" that only advanced users learn. For example, printing a document on the Macintosh using the default choices of the Print dialogue box can be done with just two keystrokes: command-P followed by the return key. Most of the time, the dialogue box will not be displayed in its entirety. This is a nice shortcut that uses a *busy-delayed-response* state, but only advanced users know about it.

Failure to represent adequately the *busy-delayed-response* state can cause undesirable side effects. Consider the case when the user interface indicates that it is in the *ready* state, but it is really in the *busy-delayed-response* state. If the user initiates the next action, the action is stored and processed after the delay. But if the context of the interface changes during the delay, the user's action might have unintended side effects. There are many examples of this in today's desktop applications. The Sun (OpenWindows) File Manager allows the user to delete files by dragging their iconic representation to a trash can. After a file has been deleted, there is a small delay in user event processing without an indication. The user sees the interface in a *ready* state and initiates the next action. During the short delay, all icons in the window are redrawn to fill the gap where the deleted file was located. This change in location of icons combined with the delay in processing causes the icon under the cursor when the event occurred to be a different one when the event is processed, resulting in the user grabbing the wrong icon.

The problem in this example is that the system indicates that it is in a *ready* state, when it really is in a *busy-delayed-response* state and the context changes before user actions are processed. The solution to this problem is simple. If a context change will occur, then the system should signal the state as *busy-no-response* and flush the event queue when coming back into the *ready* state.

Repair Behavior and Effort

In general, when a simulated state of understanding is not communicated effectively to the user, the user will enter a repair dialogue to find evidence of the correct state. The performance meter example is one example of this repair behavior. The user is not receiving enough feedback of whether the system is ready or not and thus decides to rely on the performance meter as a source of feedback. Looking at the performance meter is a repair dialogue resulting from the need for feedback when the system provides the wrong evidence, or no evidence at all.

A repair dialogue may or may not be disruptive to the user. The level of disruption of the current user's goals depends on the task at hand. What is true always, is that the user will have to spend more overall effort to accomplish his or her goals when the system is not cooperating.

Busy States

Another interesting behavioral aspect of this model is the separation of the *busy-no-response* state from the *busy-delayed-response* state. The current practice is to not signal the *busy-delayed-response* state.

When both busy states are signalled as a single state, the user will rarely take advantage of the *busy-delayed-response* state, since the information the system is providing indicates that the system is busy. Furthermore, at times the user will seek extra evidence to determine which state the system is in. That is, the user covers the collaborative gap left by the lack of appropriate feedback.

When *busy-delayed-response* has the same feedback as the *ready* state, the user will spend extra effort and possibly even obtain unwanted results because he or she will act at times when the system was not in the correct state.

If the system does provide accurate indication of the *busy-delayed-response* state, the user is more likely to take advantage of "type-ahead", or "drag-ahead" in the case of a graphical user interface. This will occur even if no feedback for the dragging action is provided during the delayed period. In this case, the user is attempting to reach the goal of the interaction without requiring the full feedback that could be provided by the system.

The busy states are a good example of where the user's repair behavior and extra effort will be spent overcoming "miscommunication" from the system. The user fills the conversational gap left by the system with extra effort exhibited in the form of repair behavior. The experiment described below studies the repair behavior and the extra effort caused by this behavior when users participate in a dialogue without good communication of the SSOU.

Related Work in the Context of Our Model

Our model incorporates many findings reported in the literature dealing with feedback and response times. The internal loop in the model includes the three states emphasized by proponents of direct manipulation interfaces [13, 14, 23]. User actions in the *ready* state require short and quick responses from the system in the form of the *reporting* state. Because most actions are short there is little need for feedback in the *processing* state.

Most response time studies [10, 11, 16, 17] are also related to this internal loop. Depending on the complexity of the action requested by the user, the time requirements for the response vary. If the user moves the mouse, he or she would expect the cursor on the screen to be moved accordingly. Such short actions, sometimes called "reflex" actions, require a response of less than 0.1 seconds [18]. In these cases, this is the timing constraint for a complete pass through the internal loop of the model. For more complex actions, for example actions that take more than 10 seconds, a progress bar should be displayed. This progress bar indicates the amount of work being done inside of either the *processing* or *reporting* state, as in the Macintosh file copying example.

A closely related model, Brennan and Hulteen's speech feedback model [3] differs from our model's structure only in that their model does not account for our *busy-delayed-response* state, possibly because it is not a common state in

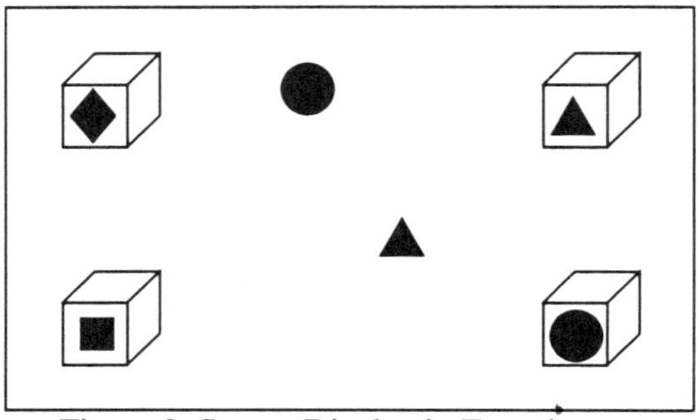

Figure 3. Screen Display in Experiment

a speech understanding system. The other states can be directly translated between the two models; some of their states are further decompositions of our states.

EXPERIMENT

We designed an experiment to explore the effect different forms of feedback have on users behavior in a direct manipulation task. Based on our model, we tried to answer three main questions: Do users engage in a repair behavior when the state of the system is not communicated correctly? Does this repair behavior amount to a significant extra effort on the user's part? And, how do users take advantage of the *busy-delayed-response* state?

Method

Thirty participants were recruited from NRL summer coop students, George Washington University computer science students and U.S. Naval Academy computer science students. All participants had comparable experience with graphical user interfaces (9 use MS-Windows, 19 use X-WIndows), and they all use the mouse on a daily basis (average 4.9 hours a day). All participants had high school degrees, 10 had completed undergraduate studies, 5 had graduate degrees.

The task to be performed by each participant involved the movement with the mouse of geometrical icons from their original location to a target location. The shapes used for the icons were circles, triangles, squares, and diamonds. The target locations were boxes with one of the shapes drawn on the front face of the box. In Figure 3, all four boxes are shown with two shapes, a circle and a triangle. Participants were asked to drag the shapes over to the corresponding box. When the object was dragged over a box, the box highlights, independent of whether it was a correct assignment or not. When the object was dropped on a box it disappeared, whether it was the right box or not.

The dependent measures used in the experiment were: number of interaction techniques (ITs), number of assignments, and number of incomplete actions. All of these measures were computed as totals and as measure per time unit (seconds). IT were all mouse-down actions, including clicks and drags. Assignments were subdivided into valid assignments and invalid assignments (assignment to the wrong box). Incomplete actions were ITs that did not result in an assignment. Time and distance moved were captured for possible future analysis but were not used in this experiment.

Procedure

The experiment consisted of three sessions of about five minutes and forty seconds each. In each session, the participant was presented with objects that appeared at a random location on the display. New objects appeared approximately every 3 seconds. The participants were instructed to assign the objects to their corresponding boxes as quickly and accurately as possible, with both criteria having equal importance.

Based on pilot data, the event rate was kept slow so that all participants would be able to complete the task. It was our desire to study the repair behavior exhibited by participants without causing frustration by making the task too difficult to complete. We were not concerned with performance effects in this study.

Three of the SSOU were used in the experiment (Table 1). In the *ready* state, all user actions were accepted and processed as soon as they occurred. In the *busy-no-response* state all user actions were ignored. In the *busy-delayed-response* all user actions were recorded but processed after a delay of approximately 2 seconds. User actions were played back after the delay, exactly as they had been performed.

State	User Action	System Response
Ready	Accepted	Yes, without a delay
Busy-No-Response	Ignored	None
Busy-delayed-response	Accepted	Yes, after 2 second delay

Table 1: SSOU in Experiment

Each session started in the *ready* state, then went to the *busy-delayed-response* state, back to *ready*, next *busy-no-response*, and then the whole cycle was repeated. Each phase was approximately 12 seconds long and participants were presented with approximately 4 objects per phase. There were a total of 29 phases, with the first one and the last one being *ready* phases, yielding a total of 7 *busy-delayed-response*, 7 *busy-no-response*, and 15 *ready* phases.

As an indication of feedback, we chose to use mouse cursor changes because this is a common use of mouse cursors in all the graphical user interfaces with which our subjects had familiarity. Treatments differed only in the type of feedback provided to indicate the state of processing. The user interface was always in one of the three states shown in Table 1. Indication of the state was given by changing the mouse cursor, as shown in Table 2. The watch in treatment B under the busy states was not reused in treatment C to avoid transfer effects in the recognition of the cursor.

Each participant was assigned randomly to one of three groups. Each group was presented with the three different treatments, counter-balanced according to a latin square design [4]. All participants received written instructions explaining the task to be performed. A three minute practice

Treat-ment	Ready	Busy-No-Response	Busy-Delayed-Response
A	Arrow	Arrow	Arrow
B	Arrow	Watch	Watch
C	Arrow	Stop Sign	Hour Glass

Table 2: Three Treatments in Experiment

session was given, during which participants saw only the *ready* state. All user and system actions were recorded for analysis. At the end of all three treatments, the participants were given a questionnaire to obtain demographic information (e.g. age, education, etc.).

To avoid biasing the participants towards a specific behavior, participants were not told of the busy states that were to occur in the three experimental conditions. They neither saw these states in the practice session nor did they know the different cursors associated with the different treatments.

RESULTS AND DISCUSSION

Performance in the task was not significantly different over any of the independent variables. This was expected, as explained earlier, because we maintained a relatively slow event rate. On the average, participants assigned 96.8% of the objects they were presented. The only significant performance-related result was the number of incorrectly assigned objects (objects assigned to the wrong box). The mean number of incorrect assignments for all participants was only 0.32 objects per session, yet there was an interaction effect between session and state of processing, $F(2, 139)= 3.89$, $p=0.0227$. In the ready states of the first session, participants incorrectly assigned more objects than in the ready states of the second session, $F(1)=8.08$, $p =0.0051$.

Repair Behavior

Our model suggests that if no information about state is provided to the user when the system is in *busy-delayed-response* or *busy-no-response*, then the user will perform extra actions to elicit the state of the system. These extra actions in our experiment are in the form of incomplete actions, clicks and drags that do not result in assignment of objects. Treatment A did not provide any feedback for the two busy states. As a result, treatment A should produce some form of repair behavior from the user.

Treatment ($F(2,224)=31.89$, $p=0.0001$) and state ($F(2,224)= 78.03$, $p=0.0001$) were significant for the number of incomplete actions per second (Figure 4), and the interaction effect between these two factors was also significant, $F(4, 224)=12.31$, $p=0.0001$. There were almost no incomplete actions in the ready phases for all three treatments (means were < 0.0001 for all three treatments). Treatment A produced more incomplete actions per second than treatment B

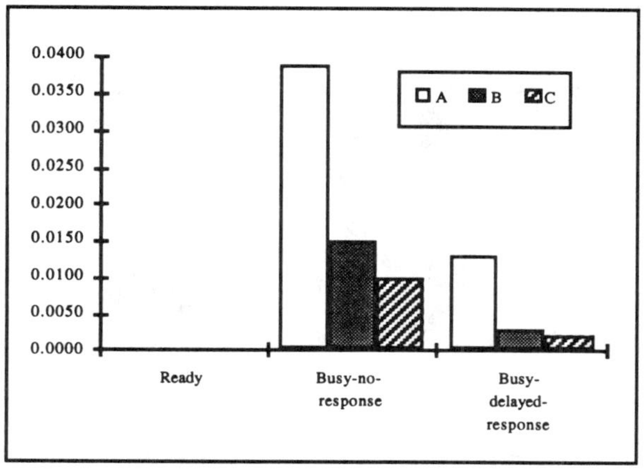

Figure 4. Incomplete Actions per Second

and C in the *busy-no-response* state, $F(1)=94.56$, $p=0.0001$. Treatment A also had significantly more incomplete actions per second in the *busy-delayed-response* state, $F(1)=15.64$, $p=0.0001$.

A very similar effect is found in total number of interaction techniques (IT) per seconds (Figure 5). This total includes incomplete actions and all the assignments[1] performed. Treatment ($F(2,224)=47.30$, $p=0.0001$) and state ($F(2,224)= 69.74$, $p=0.0001$) had significant effects on total IT, and there was an interaction effect between these two factors, $F(4, 224)=14.67$, $p=0.0001$. There was no significant difference among all treatments in the ready state. However, there was a significant difference in the *busy-delayed-response* state caused by treatment. Treatment A produced significantly more ITs than the other two treatments, $F(1)=34.37$, $p=0.0001$. Treatment B had fewer ITs than treatment C, but the difference was not significant[2].

These differences in incomplete actions and interaction techniques provide significant evidence that participants who are not given correct feedback of the state of the system engage in repair behavior. Treatment A produced the largest amount of repair behavior in the two busy states.

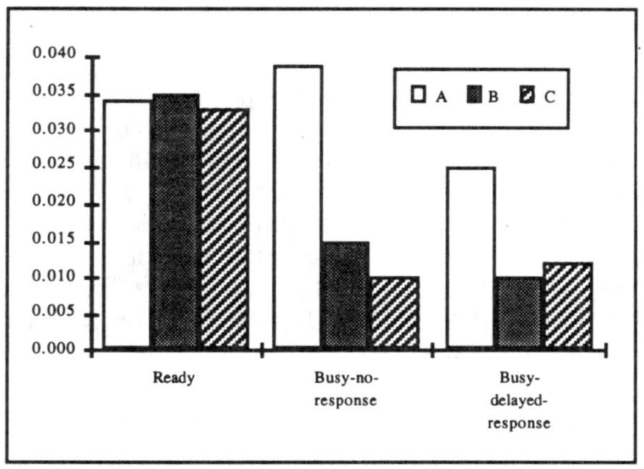

Figure 5. Interaction Techniques per Second

1. Assignments were not possible in the *busy-no-response* state.

2. The number of ITs in *busy-no-response* state is the same as the number of incomplete actions since no assignments were possible.

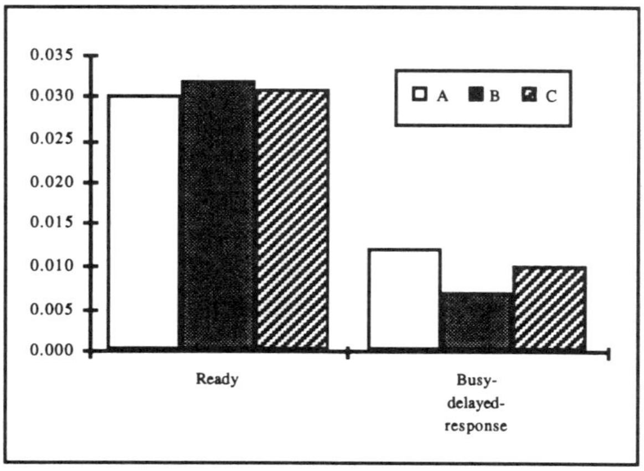

Figure 6. Total Assignments per Second

Participants in this group received no indication from the system that the state had changed. They not only had to figure out what was happening once they clicked for the first time in that state, but also had to continue clicking to determine when either busy state was over. Anyone who has ever faced a situation in which the computer does not respond to their actions understands this basic behavior.

Behavior in *busy-delayed-response*

We found evidence that users can take advantage of the *busy-delayed-response* state, once they understood that the system is responding after a delay. The participants had no a priori knowledge of the busy states or the meaning of the cursors. So in treatment A they had to figure out what was happening in the busy states without help from the system. Treatment B provided the same feedback, the wrist-watch, for both busy states. Treatment C provided differing feedback, but its meaning was not specified ahead of time. So, subjects in Treatment C also had to do some experimentation to understand the states.

State of processing had a significant effect $F(1,139)= 1256.22$, $p=0.0001$ on the number of assignments per seconds done (Figure 6). There were significantly more assignments per second in the *ready* state than in the *busy-delayed-response* state. We also found an interaction effect between state and treatment $F(2,139)=11.59$, $p=0.0001$. Treatment A had more assignments per second in the *busy-delayed-response* state than C, $F(1)=4.09$, $p=0.0450$, and B, $F(1)=22.63$, $p=0.0001$. Treatment B had significantly fewer assignments per seconds than treatment C, $F=7.475$, $p= 0.0071$. There was no significant difference due to treatment in the ready state. Session had a significant effect, $F=3.100$, $p=0.0482$; there were more assignments in the first session than in the other two, $F(1)=6.11$, $p=0.0146$. This represents a slight learning effect, but there was no interaction with any of the other variables.

Participants in all treatments were successful assigning objects in all states. Performance in the *busy-delayed-response* state was slower than in the *ready* state. Nevertheless users were able to perform assignments.

Surprisingly, participants in treatment A assigned the highest number of objects in the *busy-delayed-response* state. Perhaps this is merely an artifact of the smaller number of assignments for treatment A in the *ready* state. It is also possible that subjects in Treatment A had more trouble identifying the beginning of each new ready state and therefore did not make full use of it, hence making fewer overall assignments in the *ready* state.

Although the difference was not statistically significant, participants in treatment B did assign fewer objects during the *busy-delayed-response* state than those in treatment C. A possible explanation is that participants in treatment B assumed a more passive role in their *busy-delayed-response* state because they received the same feedback for both busy states. They could be interpreting both states as *busy-no-response*. Further data would be needed to fully explain this result.

CONCLUSIONS

We have taken a model of human conversation and reformulated some of the principles to cover human-computer interaction feedback. This is similar to the approach described in [2, 9, 17, 19]. Here, a theory of collaborative conversations served as the basis for the definition of states of feedback, with each representing different communication expectations users have when interacting with a computer.

The experiment showed that failure to properly identify a SSOU produces repair behavior by users, and that this repair behavior can be a significant amount of their effort. The study also shows that a different behavior is associated with each of the two busy states. It provides evidence that if a delayed state is identified, users do indeed take advantage of this "type-ahead" state.

The model presented, coupled with the feedback timings reported in the literature, gives the user interface designer the feedback requirements for the design of new interaction techniques and dialogues. More importantly, our model does so in a style-independent manner, so it is not specific to one platform or one style of interaction. As is common in our field, adherence to the principles of this model does not guarantee a good interface. But based on the empirical evidence and on our observations of commercial applications, violation of the principles embodied in the model does produce disruption on the human-computer dialogue as evidenced by the repair behavior. In this light, the model provides feedback design guidelines for interaction techniques and human-computer dialogues.

The model prescribes the feedback states for each dialogue in a human-computer interface. But, each user interface can have several human-computer dialogues, with each dialogue possibly having multiple cues communicating state information. The user integrates several cues into a single communicative event to identify the SSOU of the system. The model presented here does not address how this combination is done. It seems that some hierarchical combination of cues is done, but more work is needed to extend the model in that direction.

Finally, the goal of our research is to identify principles from human conversations that are desirable in human-computer dialogues [21, 22]. The feedback model presented here provides a behavioral description of direct manipulation interactions and their feedback requirements. This model is the lower level of a human-computer dialogue framework, currently under development, that studies dialogue at the feedback level and at the turn-taking level.

ACKNOWLEDGMENTS

We would like to thank Jim Ballas, Astrid Schmidt-Nielsen, and Greg Trafton for their many helpful comments about the design of this experiment. We also would like to thank the Computer Science Department at the U. S. Naval Academy and Rudy Darken at NRL, for allowing us to run most of the study at their facilities. The GWUHCI research group provided many helpful ideas in the design and the analysis of the data. This research was funded in part by the Economic Development Administration of the Government of Puerto Rico, and by NRL.

REFERENCES

1. Apple Computer Inc. *Human Interface Guidelines: The Apple Desktop Interface*. Addison-Wesley Publishing Company, Inc., Reading, Masachusetts, 1987.
2. Brennan, S.E., Conversation as Direct Manipulation: An iconoclastic view, in *The Art of Human-Computer Interface Design*, B. Laurel, Editor. 1990, Addison-Wesley Publishing Company, Inc.: Reading, Massachusetts.
3. Brennan, S.E. and Hulteen, E.A. Interaction and Feedback in a Spoken Language System, in *AAAI-93 Fall Symposium on Human-Computer Collaboration: Reconciling Theory, Synthesizing Practice*, (1993), AAAI Technical Report FS93-05.
4. Bruning, J.L. and Kintz, B.L. *Computational Handbook of Statistics*. Scott, Foresman and Company, Glenview, Illinois, 1987.
5. Clark, H.H. and Brennan, S.E., Grounding in Communication, in *Shared Cognition: Thinking as Social Practice*, J. Levine, L.B. Resnick, and S.D. Behrend, Editor. 1991, APA Books: Washington, D. C.
6. Clark, H.H. and Schaefer, E.F. Collaborating on contributions to conversations. *Language and Cognitive Processes, 2, 1* (1987), pp. 19-41.
7. Clark, H.H. and Wilkes-Gibbs, D. Referring as a collaborative process. *Cognition, 11,* (1986), pp. 1-39.
8. Foley, J.D. and Dam, A.v. *Fundamentals of Interactive Computer Graphics*. Addison-Wesley System Programming Series, ed. I.E. Board. Addison-Wesley Publishing Company, Reading, Massachusetts, 1982.
9. Foley, J.D. and Wallace, V.L. The Art of Natural Graphic Man-Machine Conversation. *Proceedings of the IEEE, 62, 4* (1974), pp. 462-471.
10. Gaines, B.R. The technology of interaction- dialogue programming rules. *IJMMS, 14,* (1981), pp. 133-150.
11. Gallaway, G.R. Response Times To User Activities in Interactive Man/Machine Computer Systems, in *Proceedings of the Human Factors Society-25th Annual Meeting*, (1981), pp. 754-758.
12. Harel, D. On Visual Formalisms. *CACM, 31, 5* (1988), pp. 514-530.
13. Hutchins, E.L., Hollan, J.D., and Norman, D.A., Direct Manipulation Interfaces, in *User Centered System Design: New Perspectives on Human-Computer Interaction*, D.A. Norman and S.W. Draper, Editor. 1986, Lawrence Erlbaum Associates: Hillsdale, NJ.
14. Jacob, R.J.K. Direct Manipulation, in *Proceedings of the IEEE International Conference on Systems, Man, and Cybernetics*, (Atlanta, GA, 1986), IEEE, pp. 384-388.
15. Lee, K.-F. The Conversational Computer: An Apple Perspective, in *Proceedings of Eurospeech*, (1993), pp. 1377-1384.
16. Miller, R.B. Response time in man-computer conversational transactions, in *Proceedings of Fall Joint Computer Conference*, (1968), pp. 267-277.
17. Nickerson, R.S. On Conversational Interaction with Computers, in *User Oriented Design of Interactive Graphics Systems: Proceedings of the ACM SIGGRAPH Workshop.*, (1976), ACM Press, pp. 681-683.
18. Nielsen, J. *Usability Engineering*. AP Professional, Cambridge, MA, 1993.
19. Payne, S.J. Looking HCI in the I, in *Human-Computer Interaction - INTERACT '90*, (1990), Elsevier Science Publishers B.V., pp. 185-191.
20. Payne, S.J. Display-based action at the user interface. *IJMMS, 35,* (1991), pp. 275-289.
21. Pérez, M.A. Conversational Dialogue in Graphical User Interfaces: Interaction Technique Feedback and Dialogue Structure, in *Proceedings Companion of the ACM CHI'95 Conference on Human Factors in Computing Systems*, (Denver, Colorado, 1995), Addison-Wesley, pp. 71-72.
22. Pérez, M.A. and Sibert, J.L. Focus on Graphical User Interfaces, in *Proceedings of the International Workshop on Intelligent User Interfaces*, (Orlando, Florida, 1993), ACM Press, pp. 255-257.
23. Shneiderman, B. The future of interactive systems and the emergence of direct manipulation. *BIT, 1,* (1982), pp. 237-256.
24. Shneiderman, B. *Designing the User Interface: Strategies for Effective Human-Computer Interaction.* Addison-Wesley Publishing Co., Reading, Masachusetts, 1987.
25. Simes, D.K. and Sirsky, P.A., Human Factors: An Exploration of the Psychology of Human-Computer Dialogues, in *Advances in Human-Computer Interaction*, H.R. Hartson, Editor. 1988, Ablex Publishing Corporation: Norwood, New Jersey.
26. Teal, S.L. and Rudnicky, A.I. A Performance Model of System Delay and User Strategy Selection, in *Proceedings of ACM CHI'92 Conference on Human Factors in Computing Systems*, (Monterey, California, 1992), Addison-Wesley, pp. 295-305.

A Comprehension-Based Model of Exploration

Muneo Kitajima
National Institute of
Bioscience and Human-Technology
1-1 Higashi Tsukuba Ibaraki 305, JAPAN
Tel: +81 (298) 54-6730
E-mail: kitajima@nibh.go.jp

Peter G. Polson
Institute of Cognitive Science
University of Colorado
Boulder, CO 80309-0345, USA
Tel: +1 (303) 492-5622
E-mail: ppolson@psych.colorado.edu

ABSTRACT

This paper describes a comprehension-based model of how experienced Macintosh users learn a new application by doing a task presented as a series of exercises. A comprehension mechanism transforms written instructions into goals that control an action planning process proposed by Kitajima and Polson [11]. The transformation process is based on a theory of solving word problems developed by Kintsch [8,9]. The comprehension and action planning processes define constraints on the wording of effective instructions. The combined model is evaluated using data from Franzke [3]. We discuss implications of these results for Minimalist Instructions [1] and Cognitive Walkthroughs [17].

Keywords

cognitive theory; display-based systems; exploration

INTRODUCTION

The goal of this article is to describe the LICAI[1] model, which extends the Kitajima and Polson [11] action planning model of skilled, display-based, human–computer interaction to account for learning by exploration. Learning by exploration involves discovering how to do a novel task by generalizing from past experience or by searching successfully for a correct action sequence. The LICAI model describes how experienced Macintosh users accomplish a task using a new application by doing a series of exercises. These users are familiar with the standard Macintosh interface conventions. They must combine their existing knowledge of the interface conventions with the task described in each exercise to generate the actions required by the new application to perform each task.

The LICAI model incorporates processes from Kintsch's [8,9] theory of text comprehension. The LICAI model uses comprehension strategies to transform written instructions into goals. In this paper, we propose three comprehension strategies in the form of schemata. Schemata are specialized knowledge structures whose slots are filled with crucial elements extracted from the instructions. The output of the comprehension processes are goals that control the action generation processes.

The LICAI model uses the action planning processes developed by Kitajima and Polson [11]. Their action planning model can simulate the behavior of skilled users interacting with a graphing application hosted on the Macintosh. The comprehension-based model of goal formation processes and the model of action planning processes are combined to describe the behavior of experienced Macintosh users learning a new application. The LICAI model defines constraints on the wording of effective instructions.

The LICAI model is evaluated using data from Franzke [3], who had experienced Macintosh users do a graphing task using one of three different graphing applications with which they had no prior experience. The graphing task was presented to users as a series of exercises. The instructions for each exercise contained no information about the action sequences required to complete each subtask. Franzke's [3] experimental task is similar to actual learning and use of an application. Users formulate tasks for themselves or are given written specification for a new task.

Franzke [3] found large variations in difficulty of subtasks both within and across different applications. We argue that Franzke's [3] participants had to comprehend the goal of each exercise and then infer, or try to discover by exploration the action sequence that would accomplish the goal. The goal formation processes attempted to build specialized goals required by Kitajima and Polson's action planning model [11] to generate correct actions for a subtask. These goal structures provided links between

[1] LICAI is acronym for the **LI**nked model of **C**omprehension-based **A**ction planning and **I**nstruction taking. When LICAI is pronounced like "Lee CHI (χ)," the pronunciation represents the two-kanji character Japanese word, 理解, which means comprehension.

users' understanding of a subtask and the low-level details of the interface to the new application, (e.g., menu labels).

Building these linking goal structures is a difficult and highly specialized comprehension task, analogous to processes required to successfully solve word problems studied by Kintsch [8,9]. The goal formation processes can fail. Users may not have all of the necessary comprehension strategies and/or knowledge about the task or about the application interface. Our theoretical analysis of Franzke's [3] results refines and extends her analyses, which were based on the model of learning by exploration [17] underlying the Cognitive Walkthrough [18,19].

Previous Research

The LICAI model characterizes skilled performance as involving comprehension processes that map an initial task description onto a specialized problem-solving representation. Greeno and Simon [4] showed that such mapping processes are a recurrent theme in the problem-solving literature. A good example is Hayes and Simon's [5] model of solving simple laboratory problems (e.g., tower of Hanoi and water jugs) described to participants in written instructions. Their model took as input the problem text and mapped it onto the representation required by the General Problem Solver [2] to solve the problem. Howes and Young [6] developed a SOAR model that analyzed interactions among the content of instructions given during learning by exploration, the details of the interface, and users' background knowledge.

Outline of the Paper

The next section describes the theoretical foundations and the action planning model of skilled, display-based human–computer interaction developed by Kitajima and Polson [11] and summarizes the results of a series of simulation experiments reported by Kitajima [10]. We then describe our comprehension-based model of goal formation that maps an initial description of a task onto the specific goals required by Kitajima and Polson's [11] action generation process. We evaluate the LICAI model using Franzke's [3] results. Finally, we summarize the implications of our results for practice. These results have importation implications for the design of interfaces and training materials that support learning by exploration [18] [1].

ACTION PLANNING MODEL OF DISPLAY-BASED HUMAN–COMPUTER INTERACTION

Kitajima and Polson's [11] model of action planning is synthetic in that it attempts to integrate the views of numerous researchers on the nature of display-based, human–computer interaction (e.g., [7]), theoretical ideas about the nature of display-based problem-solving (e.g., [13]), action planning [15], and task and device representations [16].

There are two core ideas underlying the action planning model. First, Kitajima and Polson [11] proposed that display-based HCI is analogous to *text comprehension*. In reading text, readers use large amounts of knowledge to comprehend the meaning of texts. In display-based HCI, users must comprehend the display and then select appropriate actions with the help of knowledge about the interface, the task to be performed, and so on. Second, the model is mapped onto Hutchins et al.'s [7] analysis of direct manipulation based on their action theory framework. This framework describes action planning as a goal driven process that evaluates the consequences of the last action and then generates the next action to be executed (see Figure 1).

Display-Based HCI and Text Comprehension

The action planning model implements a version of the action theory framework by extending Mannes and Kintsch's [15] theory of action planning, which is based on Kintsch's [8] construction–integration model of text comprehension. Kintsch proposed a model of comprehension that combines elements of symbolic and connectionist models of cognitive processes. Text comprehension is a cyclic process where readers process a sentence, or the major constituent of a longer sentence, during a single cycle; reading a text involves a sequence of such cycles. On each construction–integration cycle, the model takes as input a representation of the reader's goals, key elements of the text comprehended so far, and a propositional representation of the next sentence or major sentence fragment. Kintsch's model outputs a representation of this latest sentence or fragment consistent with the reader's goals and the context provided by the previous text.

The construction–integration cycle is a two-phase process. In the first phase, a network of propositions is created that contains possible alternative meanings of the current sentence or fragment. The *construction process* generates an associative network whose nodes are propositions representing the input text, the meanings of words in the input text retrieved from long-term memory, the current context, and the reader's goals. Construction is a bottom-up process that is not guided by context. Thus, at the end of the construction process, the model has multiple possible meanings for the input text.

The *integration process*, the second phase, selects an interpretation of the input sentence consistent with the current context and the reader's goals. The integration process is connectionist in nature and uses a spreading activation mechanism. The most highly activated nodes in the network represent the reader's interpretation.

Mannes and Kintsch [15] extended the construction–integration theory to action planning. Their task domain was human–computer interaction. Their action-planning model took as input a representation of users' or planners' goals, a propositional representation of the text containing the task description, and a very schematic representation of the task context. Their model generated the commands required to perform the task described in the text. Mannes and Kintsch argued that text comprehension and action planning can be conceived as similar tasks. Readers and planners must integrate their goals and information from other diverse sources to select one out of many alternative interpretations of a text or one out of many competing plans for action.

Kitajima and Polson's Model of Action Planning

Kitajima and Polson [11] developed an action planning model of display-based HCI based on Mannes and Kintsch's [15] construction–integration model of action planning, mapped onto the action cycle theory framework of Hutchins et al. [7]. The outline of the Kitajima and Polson model is shown in Figure 1.

Example Task

We will describe the action planning model by tracing its behavior during part of the task involving drawing a line graph for data contained in a table with columns labeled with variable names. The example plotting task is represented as follows:

Plotting-task: Plot numbers in the column labeled 'Observed' as a function of numbers in the column labeled 'Serial Position' (1)

Users first select a graph type from a pull-down menu, causing the dialog box in Figure 2 to appear. The column labels are displayed in two scrolling lists. Note that the label Serial Position appears in both X and Y axis scrolling lists. The dialog box partially occludes the table, but the column of numbers labeled Serial Position is visible in the background. To plot Observed as a function of Serial Position, users must click on and highlight Serial Position in the X-axis scrolling list and Observed in the Y-axis scrolling list. Finally, users point at the button New Plot and single-click it.

Goals

Kitajima and Polson's [11] action planning model assumes that skilled users have a schematic representation of the task in the form of a hierarchical structure involving two kinds of goals: task goals and device goals [16]. They assumed that each task goal is associated with one or more device goals. The device goals specify device states that must be achieved to satisfy an associated task goal. When the action planning model is provided with a new display, the model retrieves task and device goals. The task and device goals were:

Task goal: Perform "Put Serial Position on the X-axis" (2)

Device goal: Realize "Serial-Position-in-X-axis-scrolling-list is-highlighted" (3)

The Evaluation Stage

The action planning model is given a representation of a new display in the form of a large collection of screen objects; each screen object is described by several propositions. These descriptions include only limited information about the identity of each object and its appearance, including visual attributes (e.g., color, highlighting).

The model simulates Hutchins et al.'s [7] evaluation stage (shown in Figure 1) by elaborating the display representation with knowledge retrieved from long-term memory. The retrieval cues are the task and device goals and the propositions representing the current display. The probability that a cue retrieves a particular proposition representing a piece of knowledge in long-term memory is proportional to the strength of the link between them. The

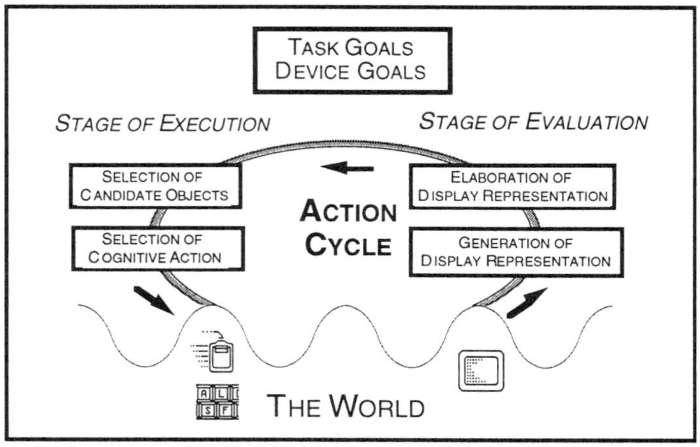

Figure 1. The action planning model of correct performance and errors in skilled, display-based HCI [11].

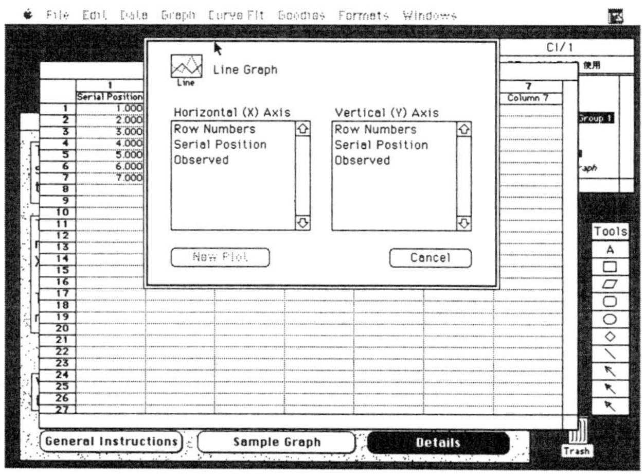

Figure 2. Example task.

propositions in long-term memory represent knowledge about the screen objects. For example, if Object23 is the scrolling list item labeled Serial Position, then the following knowledge items are stored in long-term memory about Object23: Object23 *has-label* Serial Position; Object23 *is-a-member-of* Line-Graph-Dialog-Box; Object23 *can-be-pointed-at;* Object23 *can-be-selected.* The elaboration process is stochastic and is taken from Kintsch [8]. Kitajima and Polson [11] discussed in detail the predictions and implications that follow from this stochastic elaboration process.

The Execution Stage

The execution stage of Hutchins et al.'s framework [7] is modeled by two construction–integration cycles. The first construction–integration cycle selects three screen objects as possible candidates for action. An important feature of the Kitajima and Polson's [11] action planning model is that the display representation is a detailed description of an actual large format display. Thus, the model's display representation can incorporate up to 100 screen objects. All screen objects are candidates for possible actions. During the initial construction phase, representations of all screen objects are combined with the goals and the elaborated display representation to construct the network. When the integration process converges, the model selects the three most highly activated screen objects as candidates for the next action.

This process is dominated by two factors. First, strong links from the goals to propositions in the network that share arguments with the goals, and second, the number of propositions necessary to link goals to candidate objects. As a result, the action planning model selects candidate objects closely related to the task and device goals. Device goals can directly specify a screen object, and thus can be directly linked to the screen object represented in the network. Task goals can be linked to screen objects through labels. Thus, the task goal shown in (2) is linked to the object representing the variable Serial Position in the X-axis scrolling list by the overlap of the labels that are part of the display representation.

The second construction–integration cycle selects an action to be performed on one of the three candidate objects. During the construction phase of this second cycle, the model generates a network with representations of all possible actions on each candidate object. Examples would include single-clicking and moving the screen object labeled Serial Position in the X-axis scrolling list. At the end of the second integration phase, the action planning model selects the most highly activated object–action pair as the next action to be executed. The process is dominated by the same two factors described above. However, the relevant interaction knowledge must be retrieved during the evaluation stage. For example, the action planning model must retrieve the fact that objects in the scrolling list can be selected.

Goal Specificity

Kitajima and Polson [11] assumed that they were modeling skilled users of the graphing package, and they gave the action planning model the very explicit goals required, examples of which are shown in (2) and (3). In a series of simulation experiments reported by Kitajima [10], we explored whether the model could successfully perform tasks with vague, incomplete, or even missing goals. Our initial conjecture was that users of a new application would have some understanding of the tasks they were going to perform, and they would be able to formulate more-or-less complete task goals. However, new users would not be able to formulate the precise device goals required, because they had never interacted with the application before.

The Kitajima [10] simulations focused on the two actions related to the task and device goals given in (2) and (3). The correct action sequence involved moving the mouse cursor to point at the label Serial Position in the X-axis scrolling list, followed by single-clicking on that object. The simulation experiments started with a display representation defined by Figure 2, and then the model attempted to perform the sequence of correct actions.

Kitajima [10] found that the action planning model can reliably generate the correct action sequence with no device goal. However, the task goal had to be stated exactly as given in (2). A perfectly reasonable task goal like "Plot Observed as a function of Serial Position" does not work. Kitajima [10] concluded from his simulations that the task goal had to be directly linked to the labels for the X-axis scrolling list and for the correct object in that scrolling list.

Furthermore, Kitajima [10] found an effect of number of competing screen objects. If the model was required to make the correct actions with a screen representation that included both the dialog box as well as the data table in the background with the distracting label Serial Position, these additional distracting objects prevented the action planning model from successfully generating the correct action sequence. However, limiting the focus of attention to the nine screen objects defined by the dialog box shown in Figure 2 enabled the specific task goal shown in (2) to generate the correct action sequence.

The action planning model always performed the correct actions given the device goal (3). The direct link between the device goal and the correct screen object caused the model to include the correct screen object in the list of the three candidate screen objects during the first phase of the execution stage. During the second phase, when selecting the correct action, information retrieved from long-term memory enabled the model to decide that the only possible action was to single-click on this object. The action planning model performed the task perfectly because the correct action was the only possible action.

A COMPREHENSION-BASED MODEL OF GOAL FORMATION

Kitajima's [10] results show that we can extend Kitajima and Polson's [11] original action planning model to account for people with a lot of background experience learning a novel application by describing how they formulate very specific task and device goals. Our goal-formation model assumes that this process is analogous to solving word-problems. The text comprehension processes take a semantic representation of the next task as input and combine this representation with highly specialized background knowledge to generate the required task goals. Device goals are acquired by interacting with the interface.

Problem Schemata for HCI

Task and interface specific problem schemata guide the transformation of the semantic representation of the original problem description and experiences of interacting with the program into a useful problem model (i.e., correct task and device goals). Problem schema is a notion proposed by Kintsch and Greeno [9] and further amplified by Kintsch [8]. A schema is a knowledge structure that takes a semantic representation of instructions as input and generates one or more specialized propositions defined by a predicate and slots with strong constraints on the admissible arguments.

The original problem statement "Plot Observed as a function of Serial Position" is transformed by two task specific problem schemata associated with the task Plot:

Put *variable-label*$_1$ on X-axis (4)
Put *variable-label*$_2$ on Y-axis (5)

In addition, specialized comprehension knowledge incorporated into the schema is required to fill the slots (i.e., "as a function of" means that the variable label before the phrase is put in the Y-axis slot, and the variable after the phrase is put in the X-axis slot). In the following section, we propose problem schemata that map instructions into task and device goals.

Schemata for Task Goal Formation

We assume two general schemata for task goal formation. The schemata construct propositions of the form (perform *action object*) which are used as task goals to generate associated actions.

TASK Schema

The TASK schema takes the original task instructions and transforms them into one or more propositions representing a task goal. This set of propositions is of the form, "perform *task-action* on *task-object* with *additional task-specification*," where both task-action and task-objects are constrained to be concepts for the task-domain. For example, transforming (4) generates the following instance of a TASK schema:

TASK schema	
task-action:	put
task-object:	Serial Position
task-specification:	on X-axis

The resulting task goal description is represented by two propositions: (perform put Serial_Position) and (location-of Serial_Position on_X-axis). Kitajima and Polson's [11] action planning processes then generates the sequence of actions that achieve this task goal.

The transformations performed by the TASK schema can be complex. The original task instructions can contain information irrelevant to the task goal, and thus the TASK schema must summarize the instructions to generate a task goal. The transformation shown in the above example is a simple paraphrase into a form that links directly to the labels of screen objects defined by the interface. The TASK schema can also generate necessary elaborations of terse instructions.

DO-IT Schema

In Franzke's [3] experiment, if participants were not making any progress on a subtask, they were given hints like "Click on Serial Position in the X-axis scrolling list." Observe that following such an instruction involves nontrivial inferences. 'Click on' must be mapped onto the action: Single-click with the mouse button after moving the mouse cursor to the required screen object. Serial Position must be mapped onto the screen object with the label Serial Position that is in the X-axis scrolling list.

The DO-IT schema maps instructions that describe a single legal action for the interface on a screen object with various attributes into a description of the form "perform *device-action* on *device-object* with *additional device-specification*." For example, the instruction, "Click on Serial Position in the X-axis scrolling list," is transformed into the following instance of the DO-IT schema:

DO-IT schema	
device-action:	single-click
device-object:	$; *variable undefined*
ID:	scrolling-list-item
attribute	
label:	Serial Position
location:	X-axis scrolling list

The resulting task goal is the following set of propositions: (perform single-click $), (isa $ scrolling-list-item), (has-label $ Serial_Position), (location-of $ X-axis_scrolling_list). Observe that this task goal specifies a single action. It's arguments link to the screen representation and action representation. The action planning processes can generate the specified step.

Schema for Device Goal Formation

It is unlikely that new users of an application would generate descriptions of a novel task that could be transformed by a schema into a device goal. Generating such descriptions requires detailed knowledge of the interface that can be only obtained by interacting with the particular application. For example, to be able to infer the device goal shown in (3) from the task description (1), users must know that a screen object labeled by the variable to be placed on the X-axis will be displayed as a scrolling list item and that this scrolling list item should be highlighted.

The DEVICE Schema transforms experiences interacting with the interface into device goals. The schema generates one or more propositions of the form "realize *device-object is-in-device-state* with *additional device-specification.*" The result is a device goal like (3). For example, the experience of successfully highlighting Serial Position in the X-axis scrolling list generates the following instance of the DEVICE schema:

DEVICE schema	
device-object:	Object23
ID:	list-item
attribute	
label:	Serial Position
location:	X-axis scrolling list
display-state:	highlighted
associated-task-goal:	perform "put Serial Position on X-axis"

Experienced users employ the current task goal and / or display as a cue to retrieve device goals from long-term memory.

EVALUATION OF THE LICAI MODEL

In this section, we evaluate the LICAI model using data from Franzke [3]. Experienced Macintosh users were given the task of creating a new graph with a novel graphing application, Cricket Graph I[2] or III[3], or one of two forms of the EXCEL 3.0[4] interface. The graphing task was divided

---

2 CA Cricket Graph, version 1.3.2, 1989.

3 CA Cricket Graph III, version 1.01, 1992.

4 MS EXCEL, version 3.0, 1990.

into two subtasks. The first was to create a default line graph by opening a document containing the data to be plotted, selecting the correct graph style (e.g., line graph) from a menu, and assigning the designated variables to the X- and Y-axis. The second subtask was to edit the default line graph. The edits were done in a specific order. The descriptions of the edits were very terse. Participants learned to do subtasks by exploration. If they had not made any progress toward the next correct action for more than 2 minutes on a particular step, they were given brief hints like "select line graph from the graph menu," or "double-click on legend text."

The goal formation processes of the LICAI model have been simulated using Franzke's [3] experimental paradigm [12]. The LICAI model only makes course grain predictions about the behavior of Franzke's participants. The instructions and the schemata assumed by the model may or may not enable participants to generate the correct task goal. If they generate the correct task goal, the action planning processes will generate the correct action sequence. However, the LICAI model does not describe the search behavior that occurs if the task goal construction process fails. We account for the initial success or failure of the goal formulation process. If instructions for a given exercise contain the necessary information, the comprehension processes will generate the goals that enable the action planning processes to generate the correct action sequence for the exercise. Thus, the LICAI model partitions the exercises given to Franzke's participants to tasks that can be done with little or no trial-and-error search and those that the model cannot perform because it can't generate the necessary task goal from the instructions. However, the model is able to generate a qualitative account of Franzke's results.

Label Following

Franzke [3] found strong support for the label following strategy [17,18] (see Figure 5 in Franzke [3]). Participants used overlap between task descriptions contained in instructions with labels on menus, buttons and other interface objects when learning by exploration. The degree of success of the label following strategy depended on the quality of the label and on the number of competing screen objects. Franzke [3] (Figure 7) obtained an interaction between number of objects (2 – 10) on the screen and quality of the label match (good, poor). There was no effects of number of objects for good labels and a large effect for poor labels. A unique, good label caused the user to attend to the correct screen object independent of the number of competing screen objects.

Label following is consistent with the LICAI model. If instructions contained a description of either an action or an object that matched a screen object label, those labels were preserved when the propositional representation of the instructions was mapped into a task goal. The links between the task goal and the correct screen object can mediate performance of the correct action if participants have the necessary knowledge about the screen object.

Direct Manipulation

Franzke [3] also found that participants had trouble on their first encounter with direct manipulation actions like double-click to gain access to an editing dialog box. Kitajima and Polson's [11] action planning model of skilled performance successfully performed such actions. The action planning model had propositions describing links among actions like double-clicking and tasks like edit for each object. Franzke's [3] participants did not have the knowledge that would enable them to infer that an object's attributes could be manipulated by double-clicking on it.

Use of DO-IT Schema

In navigating through the instructions or responding to hints, participants received instructions that described one or more legal actions on a screen object. No participant had any trouble following these instructions. Such instructions are mapped into specific task goals using the DO-IT schema. The resulting task goal is specific enough to enable the action planning process to select the correct object–action pair.

Use of TASK Schema

Participants were asked to "change the legend text to: Geneva, 9, bold." To accomplish this and related tasks in Cricket Graph I, participants had to first double-click on the appropriate text screen object, which opened a dialog box. This dialog box contained a copy of the title-text and three scrolling lists labeled font, size, and style.

Because all participants were experienced Word users, we can assume that they had the knowledge necessary to elaborate this cryptic instruction by assigning appropriate attributes to Geneva, 9, bold, and knowledge to transform them using the TASK schema into a series of subtask goals for font, size, and style. The following is the TASK schema instance for font:

TASK schema		
task-action:		change
task-object:		legend-text
task-specification		
	attribute:	font
	target:	Geneva

Observe that the task instructions do not give any support for finding access to the action double-click.

Franzke [3] found that almost all her participants had to be given a hint to double-click on legend-text. There was no evidence that they had any difficulty forming the correct task goal, change the legend-text. The screen object representing legend-text could easily be identified if participants had general knowledge about graphs. The task goal overlapped with the label for that screen object, so the action planning model would include the correct screen object as one of the three candidate screen objects for action. Participants did not know that the legend-text could be double-clicked, or that to edit the legend-text, it must be double-clicked. Thus, there was no link between the action specified by the task goal, change, and the action required by the device to complete this task, double-click. However, the action planning model will never generate the correct action without these links.

Once the dialog box was open, participants had no trouble completing the task. This result is consistent with the LICAI model's behavior. The model can perform each subtask specified by the instruction because the subtask goals link directly to a scrolling list title and to the relevant item in the scrolling list.

Use of DEVICE Schema

Franzke's [3] participants did the graphing task twice. Half did the task again after a 5-min. delay, and the remainder returned in one week. The LICAI model has no learning mechanisms, but participants probably would remember successful task and device goals generated by the various schemata. They would have some chance of remembering hints provided by the experimenter.

There were large practice effects. Mean task completion times dropped from about 15 min. for the first attempt on the task to about 7 min. on the second attempt. There was a small effect of delay of about 1.5 min. Most improvements resulting from practice were found on tasks where terms used in the instructions did not mach labels on the interface (see ref. [3], figures 5, 6, 7, and 8).

Consider the subtask of moving the legend. A significant number of participants had some difficulty with this task during the first session. When this difficulty occurred, the experimenter gave a hint, "Grab the legend which is to the right of the plot symbol, open circle, labeled as Observed." The hint would be comprehended by instantiating DO-IT schema, and the results of performing the hint would be encoded by the following instance of the DEVICE schema:

DEVICE schema	
device-object:	Object56
ID:	legend-text
attribute	
label:	Observed
display state:	grabbed
associated-task-goal:	perform "move legend"

Object56 represents the legend-text on the graph. Participants would also acquire knowledge that would enable them to correctly recognize new objects as a legend. During the second session, respondents were asked to do the same task 'move the legend,' but with different graph and data. The TASK schema would generate the identical task goal, which would serve as a retrieval cue for device goal. Participants would have acquired knowledge to recognize Object67 as legend and replace Object56 with Object67.

In summary, the large improvements in performance that Franzke [3] observed resulted from improvements on subtasks where the TASK or DO-IT schemata could not generate an effective task goal. One result of successfully performing the interaction is to gain information required by the DEVICE schema to generate the correct device goal. Participants were likely to retrieve these device goals on the second attempt at the task. Kitajima [10] showed that the action planning model always performed correctly when given the correct device goal.

CONCLUSION

We developed and evaluated the LICAI model of display-based human–computer interaction that has goal formation processes and action planning processes, both based on the construction–integration model. The goal formation processes transform initial task descriptions into the precise goals that enable the action planning processes to generate the correct actions. These processes are specialized comprehension strategies that employ task and interface specific schemata to construct goals. The action planning processes use representations strongly constrained by the superficial details of the interface (i.e., labels, menus, and buttons) and the interaction conventions of the host operating system. The goal formation processes must transform task descriptions into goals that link directly to the action planning representations. Most of the power and flexibility of this LICAI model is in the goal formation component.

Implication for Learning by Exploration

Our results have important implications for the development of training materials that support learning by exploration. Carroll [1] summarized an influential research program on the design and evaluation of training materials for application programs. This program led to the development of the Minimalist Instruction paradigm. The minimalist approach focuses on users' tasks rather than on describing a system function by function, minimizes the amount of written material, tries to foster learning by exploration rather than attempting to provide detailed step-by-step instructions, and supports error recognition and recovery.

The development of the Minimalist Instruction paradigm was stimulated by the then-surprising result that detailed and carefully designed training and reference materials for early versions of word-processors were unusable (e.g., [14]). This result is not surprising in light of research on word problems and the LICAI model. Mack et al.'s [14] participants did not have the necessary schemata or action planning knowledge, and attempts to include explicitly all necessary background information lead to long and confusing documentation for these new users.

Our LICAI model suggests that strong constraints on the content of instructional materials exist. Materials generated by minimalist design heuristics are constrained by the interface to an application and users' background knowledge. Although minimalist instructional materials are designed to support learning by exploration, the interface also must facilitate learning by exploration. Otherwise, instructional materials must provide a step-by-step description of how to perform every task. Carroll [1] and his collaborators have shown that most users are unwilling to read such detailed instructions, and users have a great deal of difficulty even if they try to use the step-by-step instructions.

Our LICAI model can be used to develop explicit design guidelines for content. The model's focus on task goals is consistent with the minimalist paradigm. The model makes very clear the kinds of constraints that must be understood in following Carroll's [1] design heuristic of minimizing the amount of written material. We showed that comprehending the very terse instructions used by Franzke [3] required specialized background knowledge about task and interface. "Change the legend text to: Geneva, 9, bold" cannot be understood by someone who has no experience with a modern word-processor. Effectively minimizing the amount of written material requires careful attention to the action and display knowledge and schemata assumed in the user population. A minimalist version of a complete manual for a modern word-processor would have to assume that users have the TASK and DO-IT schemata described in this paper.

The analysis presented in this article strongly reinforces the importance of the label following strategy. In addition, it shows that even when a correct task goal is generated by instantiating TASK and/or DO-IT schemata, a significant amount of background knowledge is needed to select correct actions. These results provide support for the Cognitive Walkthrough [19] methodology, which evaluates the effectiveness of the label following strategy and characterizes the background knowledge necessary to infer correct actions, serving as a design evaluation technique for application interfaces that support learning by exploration.

ACKNOWLEDGMENTS

The authors gratefully acknowledge research support from the National Science Foundation Grant IRI 91-16640. We thank Walter Kintsch and Clayton Lewis for ideas, direction, and comments on earlier versions of this paper.

REFERENCES

1. Carroll, J. M. The Nuremberg Funnel: Designing Minimalist Instruction for Practical Computer Skills. MIT Press, Cambridge, Mass., 1990.
2. Ernst, G.W., and Newell, A. *GPS: A Case Study in Generality and Problem Solving*. Academic Press, New York, 1969.
3. Franzke, M. Turning research into practice: characteristics of display-Based interaction. In *Proceedings of CHI '95*, 421–428. ACM, New York, 1995.
4. Greeno, J.G., and Simon, H.A. Problem solving and reasoning. In R.C. Atkinson, R. Herrnstein, G. Lindzey, and R.D. Luce, eds., *Steven's Handbook of Experimental Psychology*, 589–639. John Wiley and Sons, New York, 1988.
5. Hayes, J. R., and Simon, H.A. Understanding problem instructions. In L.W. Gregg, ed., *Knowledge and Cognition*. Erlbaum, Hillsdale, N.J., 1974.
6. Howes, A., and Young, R. Learning consistent, interactive, and meaningful task-action mappings: a computational model. *Cognitive Science* (in press).
7. Hutchins, E.L., Hollan, J.D., and Norman, D.A. Direct manipulation interfaces. In D.A. Norman, and S.W. Draper, eds., *User Centered System Design*, 87–124. Erlbaum, Hillsdale, N.J., 1986.
8. Kintsch, W. The role of knowledge in discourse comprehension: a construction-integration model. *Psychological Review*, **95**, 163–182, 1988.
9. Kintsch, W., and Greeno, J.G. Understanding and solving word arithmetic problems. *Psychological Review*, **92**, 109–129, 1985.
10. Kitajima, M. Model-based analysis of required knowledge for successful interaction with complex display. ICS Technical Report. Institute of Cognitive Science, University of Colorado, 1995.
11. Kitajima, M., and Polson, P.G. A comprehension-based model of correct performance and errors in skilled, display-based human–computer interaction. *International Journal of Human–Computer Systems*, **43**, 65–99, 1995.
12. Kitajima, M., and Polson, P.G. A comprehension-based model of exploration. ICS Technical Report. Institute of Cognitive Science, University of Colorado, 1995.
13. Larkin, J.H. Display-based problem solving. In D. Klahr and K. Kotovsky, eds., *Complex Information Processing: The Impact of Herbert A. Simon*. 319–342. Erlbaum, Hillsdale, N.J., 1989.
14. Mack, R.L., Lewis, C.H., and Carroll, J.M. Learning to use word processors: problems and prospects. *ACM Transactions on Office Information Systems*, **1**, 254–271, 1983.
15. Mannes, S.M., and Kintsch, W. Routine computing tasks: planning as understanding. *Cognitive Science*, **15**, 305–342, 1991.
16. Payne, S.J., Squibb, H.R., and Howes, A. The nature of device models: the yoked state hypothesis and some experiments with text editors. *Human–Computer Interaction*, **5**, 415–444, 1990.
17. Polson, P.G., and Lewis, C, Theory-based design for easily learned interfaces. *Human–Computer Interaction*, **5**, 191–220, 1990.
18. Polson, P.G., Lewis, C., Rieman, J., and Wharton, C. Cognitive Walkthroughs: a method for theory-based evaluation of user interfaces. *International Journal of Man-Machine Studies*, **36**, 741–773, 1992.
19. Wharton, C., Rieman, J., Lewis, C., and Polson, P. The cognitive walkthrough method: a practitioner's guide. In J. Nielsen and R. Mack, eds., *Usability Inspection Methods*. John Wiley, New York, 1994.

Exploring the Unrealized Potential of Computer-Aided Drafting

Suresh K. Bhavnani
Dept. of Architecture
Carnegie Mellon University
Pittsburgh PA 15213 USA
Tel: +1-412-363-8308
E-mail: suresh@andrew.cmu.edu

Bonnie E. John
Depts. of Computer Science and Psychology
HCI Institute
Carnegie Mellon University
Pittsburgh PA 15213 USA
Tel: +1-412-268-7182
E-mail: Bonnie.John@cs.cmu.edu

ABSTRACT

Despite huge investments by vendors and users, CAD productivity remains disappointing. Our analysis of real-world CAD usage shows that even after many years of experience, users tend to use suboptimal strategies to perform complex CAD tasks. Additionally, some of these strategies have a marked resemblance to manual drafting techniques. Although this phenomenon has been previously reported, this paper explores explanations for its causes and persistence. We argue that the strategic knowledge to use CAD effectively is neither defined nor explicitly taught. In the absence of a well-formed strategy, users often develop a synthetic mental model of CAD containing a mixture of manual and CAD methods. As these suboptimal strategies do not necessarily prevent users from producing clean, accurate drawings, the inefficiencies tend to remain unrecognized and users have little motivation to develop better strategies. To reverse this situation we recommend that the strategic knowledge to use CAD effectively should be made explicit and provided early in training. We use our analysis to begin the process of making this strategic knowledge explicit. We conclude by discussing the ramifications of this research in training as well as in the development of future computer aids for drawing and design.

Keywords

CAD, Task Decomposition, Learning.

INTRODUCTION

Productivity increases through the use of computers have been negligible or difficult to achieve in various application domains. The huge investments in the computer revolution, in general, have not paid off in terms of productivity growth [18], a phenomenon that is commonly referred to as the *productivity puzzle*. While phase one computers, designed to automate tasks requiring mathematical calculations have had impressive successes, phase two computers designed to augment human capabilities typically have shown disappointing results [11]. Productivity in firms using Computer-Aided Drafting (CAD) systems does not differ much from this general picture. Firms that have used their system for one year report productivity increases of only 5% and typically do not report the maximum productivity growth until they have worked with CAD for five years [17].

The few laboratory and field studies on CAD usage that are available present a dismal picture. Bietz et al. [3] found that mechanical engineering students who had passed a CAD course produce better and more complete drawings with less effort using paper and pencil than on a CAD system. Luczak et al. [13] studied 43 subjects using 11 CAD systems in 11 factories. They found that even when the subjects were highly trained, the high complexity of the commands (due to many input parameters, restrictions, and requirements) led to low performance, reduced creativity, frictions, and frustrations. Finally, Majchrzak [15] found no improvement in the performance of 25 engineers and 60 drafters using CAD systems in comparison to non-CAD users.

In order to understand the problems faced by CAD users, we observed and recorded professional architects using a CAD system in their natural environment [4]. We begin by analyzing an example of suboptimal CAD usage from those real-world data in addition to another example from a study by Lang et al. [12]. These examples will demonstrate that the efficient use of CAD is dependent on the use of strategies that take advantage of CAD capabilities. To understand why experienced users do not have this strategic knowledge, we explore three approaches. First, we review some of the training literature and demonstrate that this strategic knowledge is not defined or taught explicitly. Second, we suggest that in the absence of these strategies, users develop an approach that is a mixture of manual and CAD methods resulting in suboptimal strategies. Third, we attempt to understand why experienced users do not themselves realize and change their suboptimal strategies. This is done by analyzing the relationship between drawing strategies and the quality of drawing produced for manual drafting as well as for CAD. We conclude with an attempt to define explicitly some of the strategies that would improve the use of CAD systems and discuss the ramifications for training and design.

ANATOMY OF THE SUBOPTIMAL STRATEGY

We shall describe two examples where users demonstrate suboptimal strategies while performing CAD tasks.

CHI 96 Vancouver, BC Canada
© 1996 ACM 0-89791-777-4/96/04..$3.50

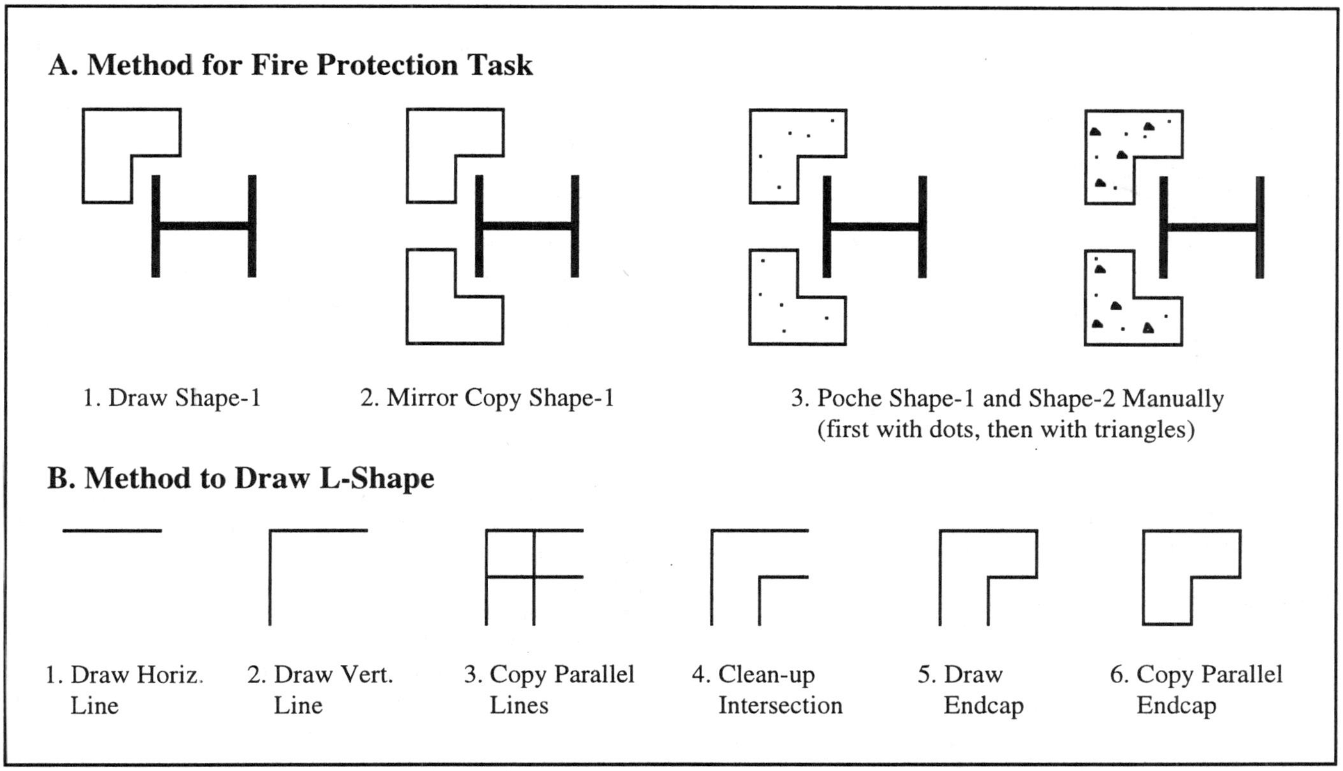

Figure1. Methods used by B1 to draw the fire protection.

Example 1
One of the users in our study (referred to as B1) modified a design file from a marked-up hard copy. His task was to draw fire protection enclosures around columns in a floor plan. The fire protections are polygons patterned with dots and triangles symbolizing concrete.

To construct the fire protection enclosures for the first column, B1 had to draw two identically patterned, L-shaped polygons. As shown in Figure 1a, he first drew the top shape (1), and then mirror-copied the shape to create the bottom shape (2). He then poched (patterned) each of the shapes (3). A more efficient way would have been to detail the first shape by drawing and patterning it, and then mirror-copying the patterned shape to create the second shape. This strategy would have saved him the extra operations for patterning Shape-2.

In addition to the above strategy to complete the entire task, B1 also used a suboptimal method to complete the subtask of drawing the L-shaped polygon. To draw a closed shape that could be patterned, he used the method shown in Figure 1b which was very similar to a manual drafting technique. First he drew the top horizontal line (1), and then the left-most vertical line (2). Next he used the COPY PARALLEL command to make copies of the two lines drawn, (3), and used the MODIFY TO INTERSECTION command to cleanup the intersection of the two lines (4). Finally, he drew one endcap of the shape (5) and used the COPY PARALLEL command to make a copy of the inner elbow of the shape to create the lower endcap of the shape (6).

The above method to draw a shape with lines had two repercussions. First, as the automatic PATTERN command is designed to pattern only closed shapes, he had to pattern each shape by copying individual dots and triangles from a nearby concrete shape. Second, when he decided to mirror-copy the shape, he had to temporarily group the individual line segments together using the FENCE command before he could mirror-copy the shape. In the version of the CAD system used in our study, this procedure included several actions requiring the user to select individual pixels. This difficult perceptual/motor task was quite error-prone. Instead, if he had used the command PLACE ORTHOGONAL BLOCK to create the shape as a closed polygon, he could have used the automatic PATTERN command as well as the regular MIRROR COPY. These would have avoided the errorful steps of precise line drawing, manually patterning, and creating a fence to achieve the grouping.

It is pertinent to note that B1 had no difficulty in interacting with the commands he used. He rapidly executed commands like MIRROR COPY and even more complex commands like MODIFY TO INTERSECTION with only minor motor slips. However, what B1 did not exhibit was a strategy to decompose the task so these very commands are used in a way to avoid unnecessary steps.

Example 2
Lang et al. [12] describes a similar suboptimal strategy used by an experienced CAD user. In their experiment, users were given the top and side view of a mechanical part drawn on paper. Their task was to construct three orthographic

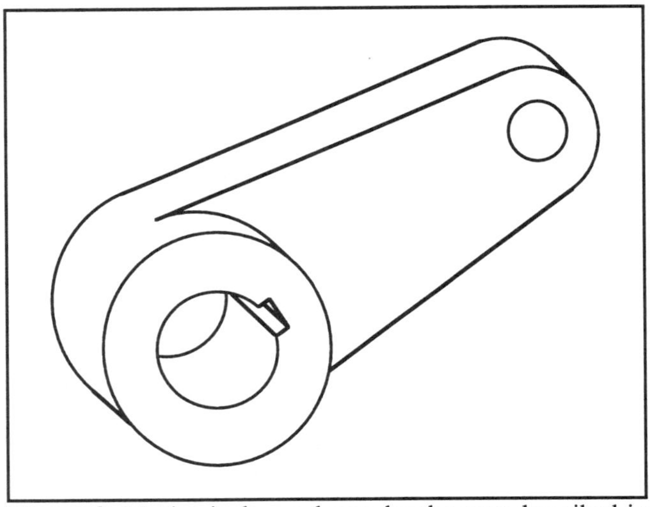

Figure 2. Mechanical part drawn by the user described in example 2 (reconstructed from Figure 2 in [12]).

views and one isometric view of the part shown in Figure 2. According to the authors, the following four steps are an efficient way to complete the task:

1. Draw the four circles representing the arcs and holes.
2. Draw lines connecting the outer arcs as well as the lines constituting part of the keyhole.
3. Clean up the drawing by trimming lines that are not accurate or those used for construction.
4. Group appropriate elements in the two dimensional drawing and project them into the third dimension.

However, an experienced user in the experiment (referred to here as L1), executed the task differently from the efficient way described by the authors. L1 skipped step 3 and projected the two dimensional drawing before cleaning it up. Therefore, he had to clean up the drawing in two places. Similar to B1 in the previous example, L1 had little trouble using the commands. However, because the task was not decomposed into the proper subgoals, the resulting command sequence caused him to execute more steps than needed.

Lack of an Efficient CAD Strategy

The above examples show the effects of not using efficient CAD strategies. In example 1, the step of copying a group of elements only after all the details are completed is an important strategy to take full advantage of the `MIRROR COPY` command. In example 2, the step of projecting a group of elements only after all the details are finished is once again an important strategy to take full advantage of the `PROJECT` command. Both examples demonstrate a strategy that requires the explicit sequence of first detailing all the parts, then aggregating those parts, followed by manipulating the aggregation. This strategy has no clear advantage in manual drafting as there is no way to produce elements automatically. However, this strategy is particularly useful in CAD as it can assist in reducing the number of steps to complete certain tasks.

Example 1 also demonstrates a suboptimal strategy that occurs at the lower level of drawing a shape. The example shows the effects of not using an efficient CAD strategy of using shapes to draw closed polygons. This "closed shape" strategy, of course, has no meaning for manual drafting. There is only one way to draw the shape - with individual lines.

Although both the above users had many years of experience using CAD, they used suboptimal strategies to complete their tasks. To understand why these users did not demonstrate the use of efficient strategies, we investigated the nature of CAD knowledge and instruction provided in CAD manuals and books.

SEARCHING FOR EFFICIENT CAD STRATEGIES

To understand more clearly the levels of knowledge that were known and not known to users, we constructed a task decomposition of example 1 expressed as a GOMS model [7]. Figure 3a shows a partial task decomposition of B1 drawing the fire protection shapes. When compared to the efficient way to accomplish the task (Figure 3b), we can see that B1 executed the `MIRROR COPY` too early, and therefore had to pattern both the shapes. Additionally, he drew the shape with single lines and patterned each shape manually by copying dots and triangles. Therefore he used 4 cursor inputs just to place dots in the first shape. Instead, as shown in Figure 3b, if he had used a closed shape combined with the automatic pattern command, he would have to select the shape only once to pattern it automatically. As this patterned shape can be mirror-copied, it would have saved him the extra step of patterning both shapes.

Therefore, while B1 was proficient in executing the commands in the lower part of the task decomposition, he did not demonstrate knowledge of an efficient strategy at the higher level. We therefore investigated whether the higher level strategic knowledge was contained in vendor provided manuals and other sources.

We found that the highly competitive CAD industry had spawned an explosion of features in CAD systems resulting in systems with upto 2000 commands and a corresponding increase of instruction material. Manuals provided by the market leaders AutoCAD and Intergraph, focus on providing users with volumes of information about the numerous features available. The MicroStation user's guide, for example, begins with *MicroStation Fundamentals* which contains numerous exercises centered around commands like `SAVE AS` and `DRAW LINE`. Although these descriptions are well presented, they are limited to the location of commands and the steps to use them. In addition to vendor supplied manuals, commercially available supplementary volumes reveal a similar pattern. They include only details of specific commands without any higher level strategies.

In a library search of CAD books for architects, we found only two books that went beyond the description of commands. One of the books [16] states, "It might be

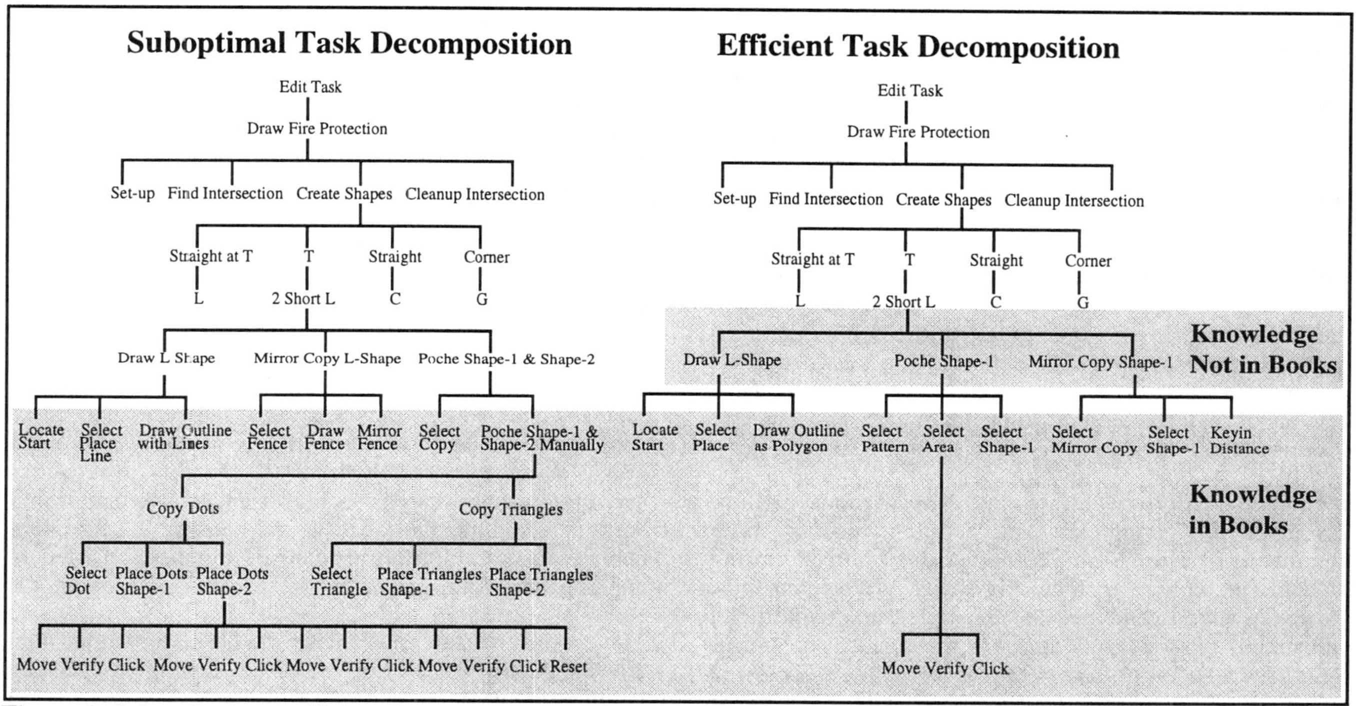

Figure 3. Suboptimal and efficient decompositions of the fire protection task. Only the subtasks of patterning (poche) a shape have been decomposed upto the keystroke level.

necessary to discard some traditional drafting concepts as you learn the sophistication of AutoCAD" (pg. v). The other book by Crosley [10], describes the importance of "thinking CAD". He states, "It's possible to use computer-aided drawing without really taking advantage of its capabilities. Even some experienced CAD users have simply transferred all their manual-drawing habits over to the computer." (pg. 6). Later he adds "Thus, the advantages of CAD are not free; they come at the expense of having to actually design the drawing" (pg. 11). While describing the COPY command he advises users to "never draw anything twice!" (pg. 41).

While such advice goes a long way in stressing the importance of using commands like COPY, he does not discuss explicit strategies to "design the drawing". Therefore, because commands like COPY are learned without a specific strategy, their power remains unrealized. In a book on computer graphics programming, Mitchell et al. [14] liken the efficient use of CAD systems to programming where "you must think carefully about the structure of the drawing in terms of repetition, conditionals, the hierarchy of parts, and the use of transformations." (pg. 515). However, because this knowledge has never been made explicit in any of the sources described, users are left to infer or develop it during use.

Therefore, it appears, that the manuals and books concentrate on providing knowledge at the lower levels of the task decompositions as shown in Figure 3a. This is also the knowledge that is fairly well understood by experienced users. However, the knowledge that is not demonstrated is higher up in the task decomposition which is exactly the knowledge that is absent in the manuals and books we reviewed.

While the experienced users were quite proficient in using complex CAD commands like MODIFY TO INTERSECTION that were not present in manual drafting, it was not clear why the high level strategies like drawing a shape with single lines had such a remarkable resemblance to manual drafting. We therefore reviewed research in the area of knowledge acquisition and conceptual change to see if we could find an explanation.

MENTAL MODELS AND CONCEPTUAL CHANGE

Research on mental models describe a convincing picture of the stages that people go through while undergoing conceptual change in various domains. Clement [9], for example, describes many adults who have a naive view of mechanics that has a striking resemblance to pre-Newtonian physics. The process of knowledge acquisition can be seen as the restructuring of these models that are based on naive or prior knowledge, to fit new information. Vosniaou et al. [19] describe this change in terms of synthetic models that have to go through weak restructuring to make them consistent with new information. Occasionally, however, when these synthetic models are faced with major anomalies, they have to undergo a radical restructuring before they can fit with the real world conceptual model.

The theory of mental models and conceptual change can be used to explain what appears to be occurring in the learning and use of CAD systems [Jackobson, M., personal communication]. Based on the way CAD systems are described and designed, users might begin by forming a mental model of the CAD system as merely an electronic drafting tool requiring little change in the way drawing tasks are performed. Introductory descriptions often have statements like "CAD is an expansion of the way you draw" [16] (pg. v), and go on by describing the use of the commands like `DRAW LINE`. The model of an electronic drafting tool is further reinforced by having concepts such as "drawings" and "layers" that are directly connected to the real world concepts of drawing sheets and overlay drafting (the use of overlapping tracing sheets). Following such introductions, the user is exposed to the details of using many different computer commands. The knowledge, as discussed earlier, is mainly about the location of these commands in deep hierarchical menus, and the procedure to execute them.

Inundated with tool knowledge but without explicit strategies to decompose tasks to make use of those commands, the users simply adjust their initial drafting model to incorporate the new knowledge of the commands. However, as described in the examples, this superficial adjustment causes problems. On the surface the use of `MIRROR COPY` and `PROJECT` appear to have been mastered as the users have no problem executing them. Because the underlying conceptual model is still an electronic drafting tool rather than a CAD system requiring different strategies, the overall use of these commands is suboptimal.

Although the above explanation appears plausible, it cannot explain why CAD users do not discover the strategies over time and make a deeper conceptual change to their mental models. These users, performing complex drawing tasks for many years, have many opportunities for serendipitous discoveries of efficient strategies. Research in the stages of skill acquisition in many domains show people who have successfully reached a stage of strategic learning. Strategic learning is described as "the improvement that comes about because people learn the optimal way to organize their problem solving for a particular domain" [1] (pg. 257). Why have the CAD users that we observed not reached this level of learning?

To understand why this change has not occurred, we contrasted the relationship between strategies and the quality of the product in manual as well as in CAD systems. We also explored the nature of the feedback loop for strategic knowledge in CAD systems.

THE RELATIONSHIP BETWEEN TECHNIQUE AND QUALITY

Manual drafting books have detailed descriptions of tools, techniques on how to use them, and simple rules to compose and perform a drawing task. Beakley et al., [2] (pg. 47), for example state that "When drawing, the lead should be pulled (not pushed) across the paper. To achieve this, tilt the lead holder in the direction of the hand movement when drawing a line. To reduce the frequency of sharpening standard size leads, slowly rotate the pencil as you draw a line". The book shows examples of 7 poorly drawn lines and their probable causes such as "pencil lifted too soon". In addition, techniques are provided to prevent lines from getting smudged and drawings getting dirty, for example, "... it is good practice always to begin work at the upper left corner of the sheet of drafting paper and to finish at the lower right corner of the sheet. Left-handed drafters may want to begin at the upper right corner of the sheet" (pg. 47). Still other techniques are provided to perform tasks requiring tool changes; "To avoid noticeably mismatched tangents, always draw circular segments first, then draw straight-line segments from the curved lines" [8] (pg. 19).

These procedures are designed explicitly to achieve drawing accuracy and quality. In most cases, if these procedures are not followed, it is very hard to produce a quality drawing; a wrong strategy invariably leads to a visibly low quality drawing. Because there is such a strong causal relationship between technique and quality, and because the flaws are publicly visible, drafters tend to be highly motivated to improve their technique.

This strong causal relationship between technique and drawing quality is absent in CAD. The drawing produced by B1 in example 1, is accurate and clean. This is easy to achieve as it requires only basic CAD knowledge to place accurate lines that meet at intersections. Therefore, there is no visible indication that the drawing was produced by a suboptimal strategy. As the flaws in the technique are not publicly visible, the users neither notice their suboptimal techniques, nor have motivation to change them.

In cases when drawings are shared and manipulated within a group working on the same project, a poorly constructed CAD drawing can cause irritations and problems to other users. For example, a user might expect to move a shape by grabbing a side and realize it was constructed by single lines. In cases like this the drawing strategy becomes public. However, if all the users in a group share a common mental model of the CAD system, the suboptimal strategy can remain undetected. This is exactly the situation at the office where example 1 occurred.

The nature of the feedback could also explain why CAD users never reach the level of strategic learning. In the study by Lang et al. [12], we find two examples of the value of feedback. When L1, in example 2, attempted to draw a line connecting two arcs, he drew only one arc before he started to draw the connecting line. As the line needed to be connected to the second arc, he did not have a precise location to end it. Having failed to complete the task of drawing the line, he abandoned the line to draw the second arc, after which he redrew the line connecting both the arcs. Therefore, the failure to complete the task provided him feedback to change his strategy. Furthermore, to test if he could perform the task more efficiently, L1 was asked to discuss his strategy with another user who had used the more efficient strategy, and then redo the task. In his second attempt, L1 completed the task with the efficient strategy using many fewer steps. This demonstrated that remediation can help even an experienced user to realize and execute a better strategy.

However, while feedback through failure can occur for some tasks, and remediation might occur through peer contact, in most real-world situations they do not occur. In CAD, using a high level suboptimal strategy typically does not preclude the user from completing the task as there are many brute force ways to complete the task. Additionally, as observed in our site visit, while users frequently discuss design issues, they rarely discuss drawing strategies or look over each other's shoulders during the drawing process. Therefore, as feedback through failure and remediation rarely occur, CAD users may never reach a level of strategic learning even after many years of experience.

AN APPROACH TO CHANGE THE CONCEPTUAL MODEL OF CAD

Understanding the structure and causes of a problem usually suggest solutions. First, we have seen that although strategic knowledge in manual drafting has been made explicit in books, there has been no such attempts for CAD. Second, while the products of CAD usage are public, the process of producing them is mostly private. We therefore have begun to explore ideas to address both these issues.

Making CAD Strategies Explicit

Whether the ultimate goal is to provide better training, feedback, or motivation, the first step is to make efficient CAD strategies explicit. An efficient CAD strategy is one that decomposes a task in a way that makes efficient use of the tools available. Additionally, these strategies should be sufficiently abstract so that, once learned, they can be used in a variety of contexts.

One way to identify efficient CAD strategies is to understand where CAD offers advantages over manual drafting. Figure 4 contrasts the task decomposition for manual drawing and CAD. The task is to draw three identical complex shapes consisting of lines and arcs. (We assume that the locations of these shapes have been determined through grids or construction lines). Due to the inaccuracy of the compass in manual drafting, the arc must be drawn first. However, to minimize tool changes, all the arcs must be drawn together (1). Next, the vertical lines can be drawn moving the set square from left to right to avoid smudging the lines (2). Finally, the horizontal lines are drawn for all the shapes (3). Therefore, the efficient task decomposition is determined by the nature of the manual tools.

In CAD, as shown in Figure 4b, the efficient way to decompose the same task is different. Because CAD provides aggregation and manipulation commands, it is better to first draw all the lines of the shape (1 & 2), group them (3), and then make two copies (4). This strategy is what we call the Detail-Aggregate-Manipulate (DAM) strategy. The suboptimal strategies in example 1 and 2 described earlier, occurred because the detailing stage of the DAM strategy was not completed before starting the aggregation stage. B1 mirror-copied the shape before patterning it, and L1 projected the two dimensional drawing before cleaning up the lines.

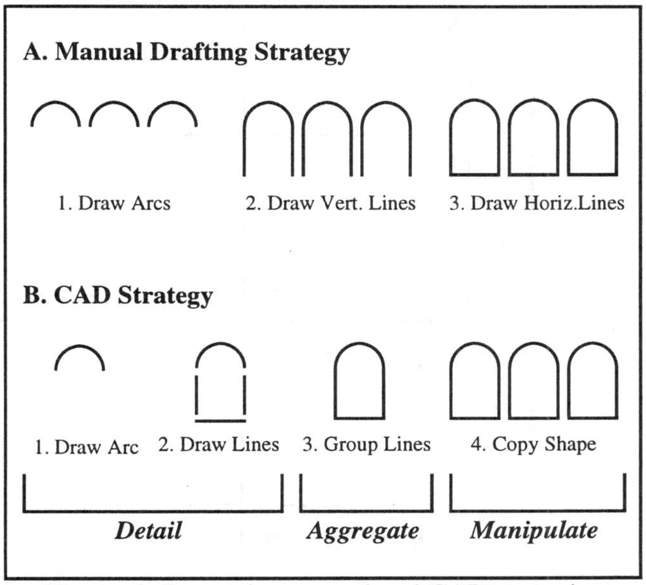

Figure 4. Comparing manual and CAD strategies

The contrast between the manual and CAD way to decompose the same task, as shown in Figure 4, suggests an important difference in the nature of assistance provide by the two media. While the manual drafting medium assists in the creation of geometry (lines, arcs etc.), it does not assist in exploiting the structure of a drawing (repetition, symmetry, projection, configuration). In contrast, the CAD medium, while supporting geometry creation, also provides assistance to exploit the structure of a drawing. However, this assistance can be beneficial only if a strategy such as DAM is used. The DAM strategy appears to be powerful as it has numerous applications, some of which are shown in Figure 5. Given the description of this strategy, one can begin to imagine other forms of suboptimal behavior. A user, for example, might detail the shape, ignore the aggregation stage, and proceed to copy the shape element by element.

CAD systems also provide powerful modification commands such as ADD VERTEX and PARTIAL DELETE. Such commands in combination with manipulation commands allow a user to exploit the occurrence of compositions that are similar in a drawing, a capability that is not supported in manual drafting. The CAD system can therefore assist the user to access and locate any part of a drawing (PAN, ZOOM, REFERENCE FILES), aggregate elements that are similar to the task at hand (FENCE, GRAPHIC GROUP, CELLS), manipulate the aggregation (MOVE, COPY, ROTATE) and modify them (SCALE, PARTIAL DELETE, ADD VERTEX) to create a similar but not identical result. This strategy can therefore be called Locate-Aggregate-Manipulate-Modify (LAMM) and can be applied in many different contexts.

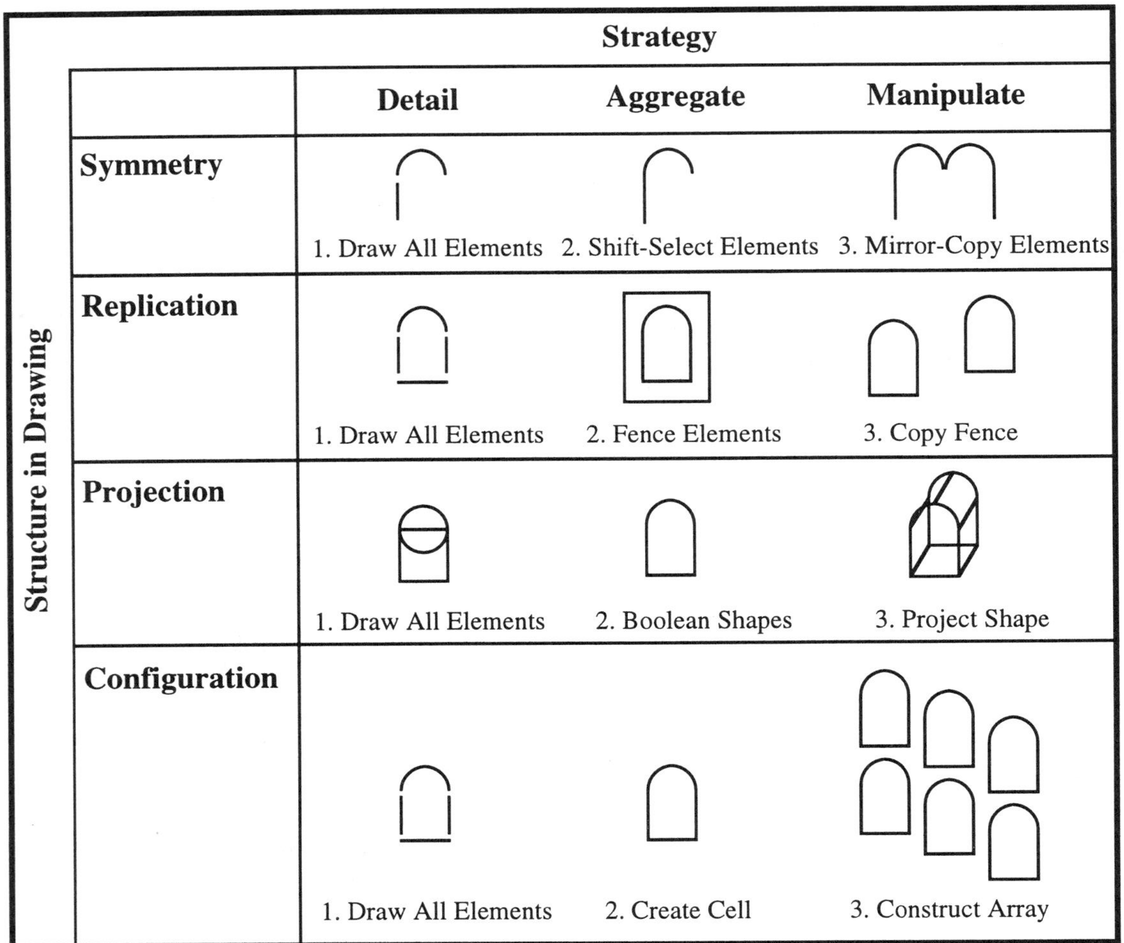

Figure 5. Applications of the DAM strategy. Each row represents a type of structure found in drawings, with a single instance of a command sequence to exploit that structure.

We suspect that there are efficient strategies at every level of CAD that need to be made explicit, from organizing a project to accurate cursor input. While strategies such as DAM and LAMM might appear obvious, the value of stating them explicitly cannot be ignored as even experienced users do not seem to be using them. However, it is yet an empirical question as to whether these strategies can be conveyed and learned by users through well-designed instructional aids. It appears that if these strategies and their applications are taught early during training, users can be encouraged to decompose drawings in terms of concepts like repetition and similarity. Such concepts are not new to designers who use them constantly in their designs. However, for reasons we have offered, many users may not be using the CAD medium to exploit the very concepts that they use in design. In addition, if CAD users are introduced early on how to decompose a drawing task ("thinking CAD"), they might be motivated to search for and learn the commands that allow for actions like aggregation and manipulation. In fact it might be possible to reorganize the commands in an interface based on task goals such as symmetry and similarity. This might encourage users to recognize and exploit the structure in a drawing.

Providing Feedback

Another approach that we are exploring is to provide computer based feedback to users when they use suboptimal strategies. We have prototyped a system called Active Assistant [4,5] that monitors various events while the system is being used, and provides unobtrusive assistance when appropriate. So, for example, the system might detect that a closed shape has been drawn with single enclosing elements and trigger the assistance. The assistance might replay the steps that a user executed to create the shape and present advantages of doing it another way. It is hoped that because the feedback is immediate and situated, the user will learn to look critically at their drawing process and motivate them to use better strategies. However, it remains to be seen if such a system would actually produce a change in the behavior of a user. Encouraging peer interaction and review might be equally powerful mechanisms.

CONCLUSION

We have attempted to explain why experienced CAD users not only use suboptimal strategies to complete drawing tasks, but also continue to do so even after many years of CAD usage. This, we believe, has three causes. First, the strategic knowledge to use a CAD system efficiently has never been made explicit, and therefore never taught. Second, as there are few mechanisms that provide feedback about suboptimal usage, users frequently may not be aware of their suboptimal usage. Third, as users can most often produce clean accurate drawings however suboptimal their strategies, there is little motivation to look critically at their drawing process.

In an attempt to reverse this situation, we showed two examples of how CAD strategies can be abstracted and explicitly stated. Such strategies could be used to design various forms of instruction as well as to redesign the interface. We also briefly described an approach to provide unobtrusive feedback to users if they performed tasks using suboptimal strategies.

One of the most common and favorite explanations for the low productivity in CAD systems is that the "D" in CAD does not stand for Design. Many claim that architects design, not just draw and therefore CAD systems as they stand today should be abandoned and approached differently. We believe this line of argument misses the point. Whatever the original acronym meant, CAD systems were designed to assist in drawing and not in design. While new paradigms for design assistance have to emerge and prove themselves, there are lessons to be learned from the CAD productivity problem.

The CAD productivity problem, as we have demonstrated, has to do with deeper mechanisms that can plague the proper use of any new technology or medium. If the CAD productivity phenomena is ignored or explained away by the nature of what CAD systems do, then we are doomed to repeat their mistakes. If, on the other hand, we understand that a new technology often requires reformulating old tasks, then we can spend more time in making that knowledge explicit and minimally disruptive. Bowen [6] studying the *productivity puzzle* states: "The large payoffs come not from increasing the efficiency with which people perform their old jobs, but from changing the way work is done". However, it appears, that the knowledge to make this change is often not as obvious to users as we might assume and while serendipitous discoveries by users are possible, it is not something we should depend upon.

ACKNOWLEDGMENTS

This research was supported in part by the U. S. Army Corps of Engineers Construction Engineering Research Laboratory (USA-CERL) Contract# DACA88-94-K-0006 and by the National Science Foundation, Award# IRI-9457628. The views and conclusions contained in this document are those of the authors and should not be interpreted as representing the official policies, either expressed or implied, of USA-CERL, NSF, or the U. S. Government. The authors acknowledge the contributions of O. Akin, U. Flemming, J. Garrett, D. Shaw; and Bentley Systems for the academic edition of MicroStation.

REFERENCES

1. Anderson, J.R. *Cognitive Psychology and its Implications.* W.H.Freeman and Company, New York, 1990.
2. Beakley, G.C., Autore, D.D., and Patterson, T.L. *Architectural Drawing and Design.* Macmillan Publishing Company, New York, 1984.
3. Bietz, W., Langner, T., Luczak, H., Muller, T. and Springer, J. Evaluation of a compact CAD-course in laboratory experiments, *International Journal of Human Computer Interaction*, (1990): 2, 2, 111-135.
4. Bhavnani, S.K., Flemming, U., Forsythe, D.E., Garrett, J.H., Shaw, D.S., and Tsai, A. CAD Usage in an Architectural Office: From Observations to Active Assistance. *Automation in Construction* (in press).
5. Bhavnani, S.K., Garrett, J.H., Flemming, U., and Shaw, D.S. Towards Active Assistance. *Bridging the Generations-Proceedings of the International Workshop on the Future Directions of Computer-Aided Engineering*, D. Rehak, (Ed.), (1994) 1183-1188. Carnegie Mellon University, Pittsburgh, PA.
6. Bowen W. The Puny Payoff from Office Computers. In T. Forester, (Ed.), *Computers in the Human Context,* Basil Blackwell, New York, 1989.
7. Card, S.K., Moran, T.P., and Newell, A. *The Psychology of Human-Computer Interaction.* Hillsdale, NJ: Lawrence Erlbaum Associates, 1983.
8. Ching, F. *Architectural Graphics.* Van Nostrand Reinhold Company, New York, 1975.
9. Clement, J. A Conceptual Model Discussed by Galileo and Used Intuitively by Physics Students. In Gentner D., and Stevens D (Eds.), *Mental Models.* Lawrence Erlbaum Associates, Publishers, Hillsdale, 1983.
10. Crosley, L.M. *The Architect's Guide to Computer-Aided Design.* John Wiley and Sons, New York, 1988.
11. Landauer, T. K. *The trouble with computers: Usefulness, usability, and productivity.* 1995 Cambridge, Mass: MIT Press.
12. Lang, G.T., Eberts, R. E., Gabel, M. G., and Barash, M.M. Extracting and Using Procedural Knowledge in a CAD Task. *IEEE Transactions on Engineering Management,* (1991) 38, 257-68.
13. Luczak, H., Beitz, W., Springer, J. and Langner, T. Frictions and frustrations in creative-informatory work with computer aided design-CAD-systems. *Proceedings of the Fourth International Conference on Human-Computer Interaction,* (1991), 175-9.
14. Mitchell, W.J., Liggett, R.S., and Kevan, T. *The Art of Computer Graphics Programming.* Van Nostrand Reinhold Company, New York, 1987.
15. Majchrzak, A. Effect of CAD on the jobs of drafters and engineers: a quantitative case study, *International Journal of Man-Machine Studies*, (1990): 32, 3, 245-62.
16. Obermeyer, T.L. *AutoCAD Architectural Lab Manual.* McGraw-Hill Book Company, 1987.
17. PSMJ. *CADD application and user survey* (Professional Services Management Journal, 1994).
18. Strassmann, P.A. *The Business Value of Computers.* The Information Economics Press New Canaan, CT, 1990.
19. Vosniadou, S., and Brewer, W.F. Mental Models of Earth: A Study of Conceptual Change in Childhood. *Cognitive Psychology,* (1992), 24, 535-538.

User Customization of a Word Processor

Stanley R. Page
Novell Incorporated
1555 N Technology Way
Orem, UT 84057 USA
+1 801 222 7016
stanp@novell.com

Todd J. Johnsgard
Novell Incorporated
1555 N Technology Way
Orem, UT 84057
+1 801 222 5112
tjohnsgard@novell.com

Uhl Albert
Intel Corporation
734 E Utah Valley Dr
American Fork, UT 84003
+1 801 763 2242
uhl_albert@ccm.ut.intel.com

C. Dennis Allen
Customer Satisfaction by Design
810 Skylake Dr
Woodland Hills, UT 84653
+1 801 423 1599
cdennisa@aol.com

ABSTRACT

The purpose of the study was to identify the customization changes users typically make to their word processor. Ninety-two percent of the participants customized their software in some way. Participants who used the software most heavily also did the most customization ($p < .05$). Most of the customization was done to facilitate the participants' work practices. The most common changes involved providing easier access to custom or often-used functionality. Button Bars seemed to provide an easy and effective means for participants to customize access to the functionality they wanted. Few participants customized the visual appearance of the interface.

Keywords

Adaptability, adaptable, customization, customize, tailor

INTRODUCTION

It is common for commercial software to allow user customization. Users are allowed to add ruler bars, change menus, add custom macros and applications to menus and button bars, and rearrange elements on the screen. The theory is that customization makes users more productive because they can tailor the software to their work practice. However, do users really make use of customization options? What kinds of customization do users want to do?

Do Users Customize?

Rosson [8] did extensive research on users of a text-editor. She found that programmers made extensive use of customization features (reassigning keys and writing macros) but secretaries did not. She also found that the amount of experience with the editor and text-editors in general was a good predictor of the amount of customization done.

Mackay [5] found that users did not take advantage of the customization features of software as often or successfully as they could, and she identified some of the triggers and barriers to customization. The three most commonly cited reasons for customizing software were that users: 1) noticed their own repeated patterns and wanted to customize to match those patterns, 2) wanted to fix or stop something that was annoying or slow, and 3) wanted to retrofit new versions of software to make them work as they did in the previous version. The most often mentioned barriers to customizing software were lack of time followed by how difficult the software was to customize.

Oppermann and Simm [7] studied the use of customization features in word-processing, spreadsheet, database, and drawing applications. About one-half of the users stated that they had tried some of the customization options. They made changes to preference settings (e.g. changed display measurements from inches to cm) and created styles. A few users recorded macros and made modifications to the menus when these options were available. They indicated that customization options made their work easier and saved time. However, many users said that they simply made changes out of curiosity or for fun.

Successful Customization

Customization is a key element of many types of applications. Trigg, Moran and Halasz [9] described the importance of customization in the design of an information structuring application called NoteCards. HyperCard [10] was one of the first commercial products designed to make it easy for users to create customized applications. Jones [1] found that customization was one of four major recurring themes among users of different styles of e-mail systems.

MacLean, Carter, Lövstrand, and Moran [6] were able to establish a successful "tailoring culture" within an organization. They first developed a software system that was easy to customize. Then, they "seeded" the novice users' systems with sample custom tools built by expert peers. They also provided ways to share customization files through e-mail. Providing simple tools and a support system of experts for helping with customization made it possible for the novice users to become proficient at customizing their software.

Others have found that customization can be successful when the proper formal and informal support is in place. Krogsæter, Oppermann, and Thomas [3] designed a successful automated system that analyzed user actions in a spreadsheet application and suggested ways of customizing the interface to make their work easier. Mackay [4] found that users spontaneously shared customization files within their organization. Gantt and Nardi [2] found that informal experts naturally emerged who helped co-workers customize their systems.

METHODS

The purpose of the current study was to identify the customization features used in a commercial word-processing application (WordPerfect 6.0a for Windows). This information will help software developers make informed decisions about how successful they have been in providing customization features, what aspects of the interface users want to customize, and how to provide an optimal set of functionalities by default.

Participants

Potential participants were drawn from the WordPerfect 6.0a for Windows software registration database. They were called and told that we were doing a study of general use of word processors and asked whether they were willing to participate. They were not told that software customization was the focus of the study.

A total of 101 participants from across the United States completed the study. Participants matched the distribution of users in our fourteen top market segments. For example, if the government industry accounted for 19% of our sales we collected 19% of our data from government sites.

Although we did not control for user characteristics we noticed several interesting demographics about our sample population:

- Computer experience of the participants ranged from "one year or less" to "ten years or more" with 57.4% having ten or more years of computer experience
- Experience with word processors went from "one year or less" to "ten years or more" with 40.6% of the participants having ten or more years experience.

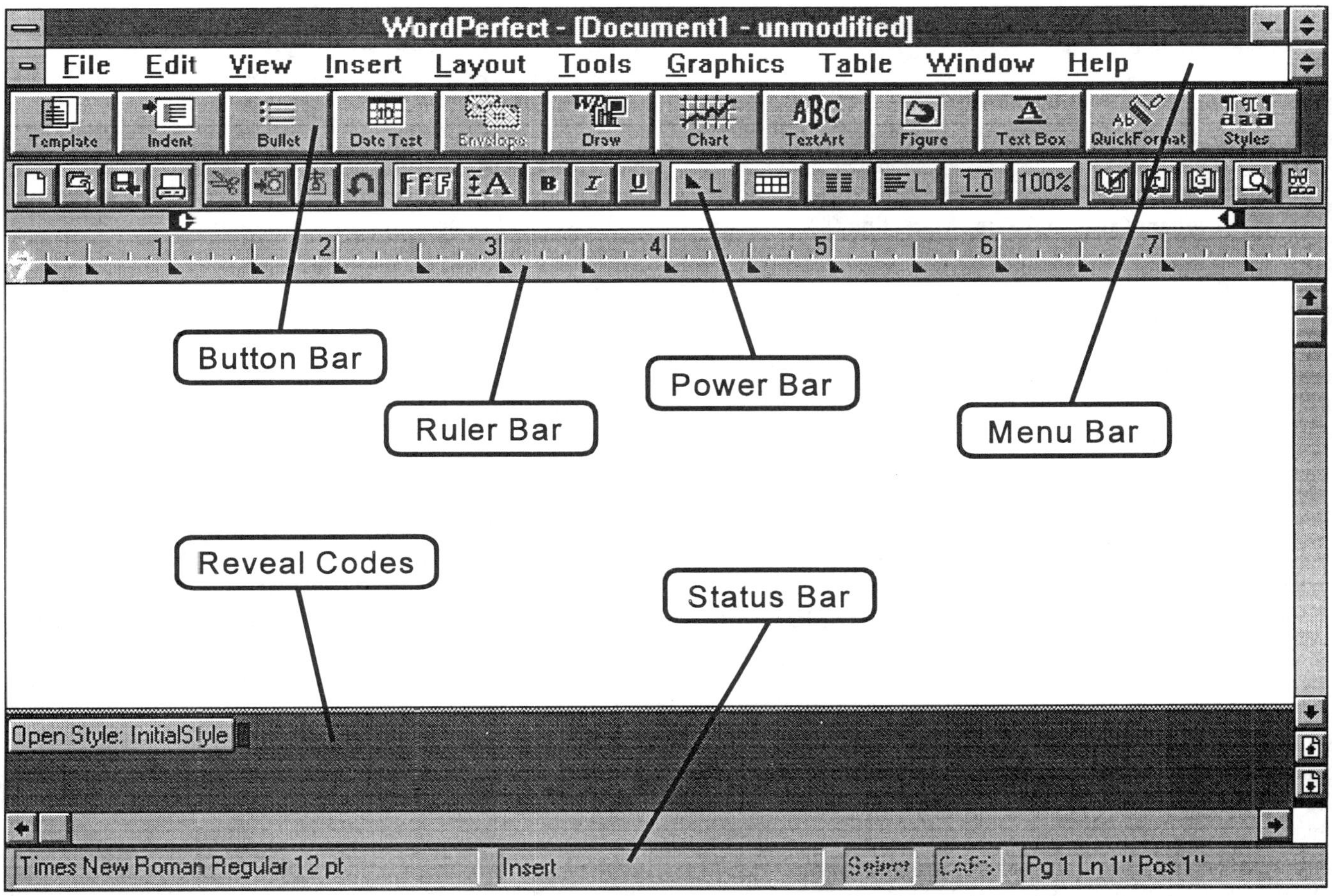

Figure 1. Application window with all interface tools showing. The Button Bar, Power Bar, and Status Bar were showing by default when users started the application. Reveal Codes and the Ruler Bar were hidden at startup.

Table 1. Purposes for Interface tools included in the study and descriptions of their customization options.

Interface Tool	Purpose	Customization Options
Menu Bar	Provides access to most of the features and functions in WordPerfect.	Contents and order.
Button Bar	Offers quick access to common features.	Position, contents, order, labels (text, icon, text and icon), font, font size, and whether or not displayed.
Power Bar	Offers a quick way of performing common tasks.	Contents, order, and whether or not displayed.
Ruler Bar	Displays margins, tab settings, and other formatting information.	Appearance and whether or not displayed.
Reveal Codes	Displays the codes that WordPerfect inserts for every formatting feature used in a document.	Whether or not displayed.
Status Bar	Displays document information, such as the type of font.	Contents, order, appearance, and font.

- The age of the participants varied from "under 25 years of age" to "over 65 years of age" with 50.5% falling between the ages of 40 and 54.
- The gender breakdown of the participants was 55.4% female and 44.6% male.

The job categories listed by the participants covered a broad spectrum and included: Administrative Assistant (13.9%), Secretary/Data Entry (18.8%), Manager (11.9%), Educator/Trainer (10.9%), Programmer/MIS (9.9%), Engineer (6.9%), Consultant (5%), and Sales/Marketing (4%).

Data Collected

One type of data we collected was how participants customized the interface elements of the software. Figure 1 shows the interface tools within the application window. Table 1 defines each of the interface tools and describes their customization options.

We also collected data about the amount of work participants did in the software along with their use of styles and macros for 28 days. A style is a collection of font attributes and other text formatting properties (such as justification) that can be reused and applied to several areas of text. Macros can record and play back a series of actions to perform repetitive tasks quickly.

A questionnaire was used to collect data about user characteristics. The questionnaire contained 31 questions in the following categories: experience levels, organizational characteristics, WordPerfect usage, documentation and training, interface preferences, personal characteristics, comfort with computers, system characteristics, and work characteristics.

Procedure

Participants performed the study on their own IBM-compatible computers running WordPerfect 6.0a for Windows. Participants received a diskette in the mail and ran a macro on the disk which presented them with the questionnaire. After 28 days the software customization and usage files were copied from their hard disk.

The disks were mailed back to us for analysis. There were three types of files on the disks: 1) questionnaire responses, 2) software and macro usage files, and 3) customization configuration files. We analyzed the responses from the questionnaire and were able to re-create each participant's WordPerfect configuration with the obtained customization files. Screen shots were generated based upon the configuration files and compared against the default configuration to assess the amount of customization performed.

FINDINGS

A surprising 92% of the participants in this study did some form of customization of the software. The maximum number of changes made by a participant was 54. The mean was 9.1. Eighty-six percent made changes to their general preferences settings (e.g., number of minutes between automatic file backups). Sixty-three percent made use of custom functionality in macros. Seventy-seven percent customized the software interface (primarily through the customizable Button Bar) to add or change access to their functionality.

Tests of effects were run to compare the level of customization to the user characteristics captured in the questionnaire. There was no significant correlation between the level of customization and user characteristics including computer experience, job title, education, age, gender, or learning method.

The only significant variable found was the relationship between the amount of customization and how much the software was used ($p < .05$). The more the software was used, the higher the level of customization.

We identified five categories of customization activities from the data collected: 1) customizing functionality, 2) customizing access to interface tools, 3) customizing access to functionality, 4) customizing visual appearance, and 5) setting general preferences. Findings in each of these categories are described below.

Customizing the Functionality

Because macros allow users to automate a series of steps they are a primary means for creating custom functionality. Sixty-three percent of the participants used macros. These macros included some that shipped with the application, macros that participants had created for themselves previously, or macros that others had created and shared with them. The use of macros suggests that participants want custom functionality that more directly supports their work.

The application contained a "macro recorder" that allowed participants to capture or record a series of actions (such as keystrokes and mouse clicks) and play them back at will. Sixteen percent of the participants created their own macros using the macro recorder during the 28 days of the study. The mean number of macros created was nine. One participant recorded 25 macros.

Styles was another feature that allowed users to create custom functionality. Styles in WordPerfect provide a way to format similar types of text, such as headings and lists. Thirty-three percent of the participants made use of the styles functionality.

Customizing Access to Interface Tools

Figure 1 shows the various interface tools that were available for display in the product. When participants started the application the Button Bar, Power Bar, and Status Bar were displayed by default. The Ruler Bar and Reveal Codes were hidden by default.

Table 2 lists the permanent changes that participants made to the display of the interface tools. Twenty-five percent of the participants changed their preference settings to always display the Ruler Bar. The Ruler Bar provides an easy way to visually check and make changes to document margins and tab settings.

Sixteen percent of the users removed the Button Bar. The Button Bar provided quick and easy access to functionality that was also available through the pull-down menus. Presumably these individuals preferred to have more room for the display of their document than easy access to those functions.

Table 2. Percentages of users making customization changes to the display of interface tools.

Display of Tools	Percent
Showed Ruler Bar	25%
Removed Button Bar	16%
Showed Reveal Codes	4%
Removed Power Bar	2%
Removed Status Bar	0%

As shown in Table 3, the button bar was positioned at the top of the application window by default and most users (78%) left it there. Over half of those who moved the bar moved it to the left side of the window. Only one person positioned the button bar as a floating palette (separate window that overlaps the application window).

Table 3. Percentages of users positioning the Button Bar at various window locations.

Position of Button Bar	Percent
Top of Window (Default)	78%
Left Side of Window	12%
Bottom of Window	5%
Right Side of Window	4%
Floating Palette	1%

Customizing Access to Functionality

The Button Bar was the most customizable of the available interface tools. It allows users to add buttons for virtually any feature of the product. Users can also add buttons for running macros or launching other applications. Buttons can be removed, spaces can be added to form groups of buttons, and the order of buttons can be changed. Seventy-seven percent of the users did something to customize their Button Bar. The Button Bar is an ideal customization tool because it is easy to customize and makes the desired functionality visible and accessible.

Table 4 shows the types of customizations made to the button bar. The high number of users who customized the Button Bar show that users want easy access to functions that are important to them. The fact that 44% of the users removed buttons that were on the bar by default suggests that better defaults could have been chosen by the designers.

Table 4. Percentage of users customizing options on the Button Bar.

Button Bar Customization	Percent
Added buttons for new features	55%
Removed buttons	44%
Re-arranged the buttons	39%
Added buttons for macros or applications	16%

The application allowed customization of the pull-down menus, but only 4% of the participants made any changes to them. Two percent added specific macros to their pull-down menus. That few participants made changes to the menus suggests that they are more concerned about surfacing desired functionality than reorganizing it.

Customizing Visual Appearance

Changes made to the appearance of buttons on the Button Bar are shown in Table 5. Most users (83%) did not change the appearance of the buttons from the default of text and icon. Some of those who changed the buttons to display text only did so in order to fit more buttons on the screen to provide quick access to more functions (Figure 2). It is interesting to note that many applications currently display an icon-only view of the buttons on their button bars, but only five percent of the participants in this study set their buttons that way. This data suggests that people prefer text only to icon only.

General Preferences

General preferences allowed participants to customize a number of elements of the software such as where documents are stored by default, the amount of time between automatic backup of files, and how graphics and other elements are displayed on the screen. Eighty-six percent of the participants made changes to their general preference settings. The most interesting changes were to the "Minutes Between Backups" and the "Zoom Percentage."

The program contains a feature that automatically saves backup copies of the file the participant is working on. The "Minutes Between Backups" setting controls how frequently these backups are made. The default setting on "Minutes Between Backups" was ten minutes. Thirty-seven percent of the participants changed this setting. Seventy-six percent of those making a change reduced the amount of time between backups (mode = 5 minutes). It appears that because of the importance of documents, participants want the security of frequent backups in case something goes wrong.

Table 5. Percentages of users customizing the visual appearance of buttons on the Button Bar.

Appearance of Buttons on Button Bar	Percent
Text and Icon (Default)	83%
Text Only	12%
Icon Only	5%
Made Text Larger on Buttons	6%
Made Text Smaller on Buttons	1%

The "Zoom Percentage" controls the size of the text on the screen without changing the size on the printed page. The default setting was "100%." Fifteen percent of the participants changed the zoom setting. Most of these participants set the zoom slightly larger (mean = 117%). One of the zoom setting options was "Margin Width" which set the zoom display to the largest possible setting while still displaying all the text between the side margins. Since most of the changed zoom percentage settings were not rounded numbers (i.e. 133,119, 107, etc.) it is probable that they were set with the "Margin Width" option. It appears that these participants wanted the text to be as large as possible on the screen without having to scroll horizontally to see their text.

CONCLUSIONS

We have shown that 92% of word processing users customize their software. We think this unexpectedly high number is due primarily to two things: 1) Work needs. Users who most heavily use their systems have the highest levels of customization. These users seem to customize to facilitate

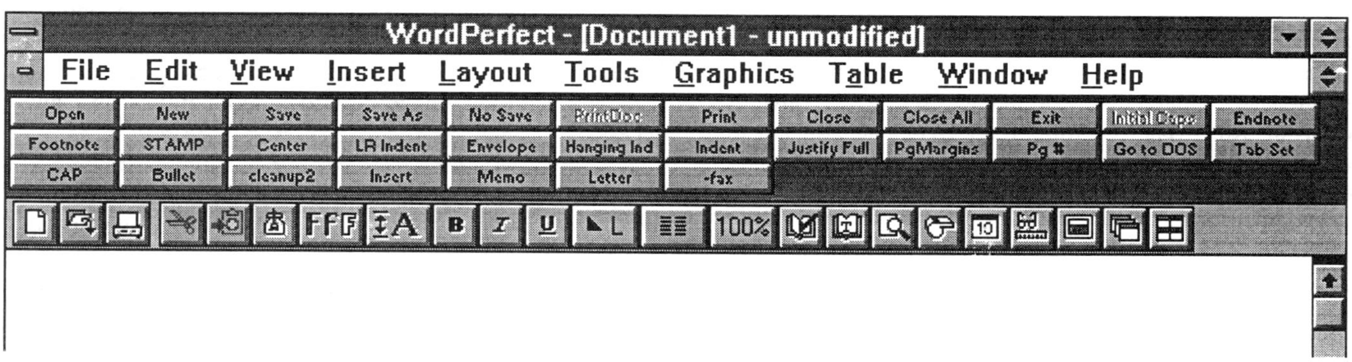

Figure 2. Button Bar with text-only buttons to allow room for multiple-rows of buttons.

their work. 2) Ease of customization. Customization features that were simple to adapt (like the Button Bar) tended to have higher incidences of tailoring.

In this study we identified five types of software customization: customizing functionality, access to interface tools, access to functionality, visual appearance, and general preferences. Here is an overview of their usage:

- The greatest proportion of participants customized the general preferences of the software, with 86% of the participants making some change.
- The second greatest proportion of participants made changes by adding software functionality, with 63% using macros and 16% recording macros.
- The third greatest proportion of participants made changes by giving more direct access to needed functionality. Fifty-five percent of the participants accomplished this by putting new buttons on the Button Bar. Sixteen percent put macros on their Button Bar.
- The fourth largest proportion of participants tailored their system by changing which interface tools were displayed, with 25% of participants displaying the Ruler Bar.
- The category of customization with the smallest proportion of participants making changes is visual appearance, with fewer than 15% of the participants making any type of change.

Mackay [5] states that her "data support the idea that users 'satisfice' rather than optimize." They do the minimum necessary to get by. We found that participants who used the software heavily also did a lot of customization. So, rather than being "too busy" to bother customizing, our data suggest that users with high levels of product use adapt the software to complete tasks more easily. That only 4% of the participants in this study modified the menu bar, suggests that users are making required functionality more visible rather than reorganizing it.

Recommendations

- Expect users to customize the software. Our pre-existing belief was that few users customize their software. The data from this study suggests that most users want to tailor the software to fit their needs.

- Make customization easy. To meet the needs of the many users who adapt their software, customization features need to be simple, easy, and fast to use.

- Make customization fit the work. Since tailoring is driven by need, customization features need to be designed to maintain users' work flow and rhythm. This requires that the customization features become an integral part of the system and its user interface; moving between task and customization activities needs to be as seamless as possible.

- Optimize default settings for casual users. Since infrequent or casual users do less tailoring of their software default settings must be optimized for these users.

Future Research

- In this study we concentrated on learning what users customize in their word processor. We would like to follow up this study with research aimed at learning more about why users customize their software and what we can do to facilitate customization.

- The Button Bar proved to be an effective tool for customization. Additional studies should be done to compare alternative methods and tools for customization to identify those that are most effective.

- Finally, studying the patterns of users' customization should help us move our adaptable systems to self adapting ones; systems that will accurately anticipate the customers' work and respond by providing the appropriate tools and services. To this end we need to continue to study when, why, and how users tailor software to accomplish their work.

ACKNOWLEDGMENTS

Nolan Larsen provided management support and encouragement on the project. Robert Bailey provided guidance on the survey and study design. Don Griffes did most of the programming of the tools to capture the data. Grant Johnson tested, refined, and integrated the data collection tools. Susan Zeller-Smith created the user documentation. Jennifer Pugmire helped with the survey and statistical analysis of the data. Chris Andrews and Karen Beus helped with the questionnaire and provided the market segmentation data used to select participants. Deirdre Calhoun edited the final version of the paper.

REFERENCES

1. Jones, S., Bock, G., and Brassard, A. Using electronic mail: Themes across three user interface paradigms. *ACM SIGCHI Bulletin* (1990) 21, 45-48.

2. Gantt, M. and Nardi, B.A. Gardeners and gurus: Patterns of cooperation among CAD users. In *Proceedings of CHI'92 Conference on Human Factors in Computing Systems* (Monterey, California, May 3-7, 1992), ACM SIGCHI, pp. 107-117.

3. Krogsæter, M., Oppermann, R., and Thomas, C.G. A user interface integrating adaptability and adaptivity. In Oppermann, R. (Editor), *Adaptive User Support: Ergonomic Design of Manually and Automatically Adaptable Software*, Hillsdale, NJ: Lawrence Erlbaum Associates, 1994, pp. 97-125.

4. Mackay, W.E. Patterns of sharing customizable software. In *Proceedings of the Conference on Computer-Supported Cooperative Work* (Los Angeles, California, October 7-10, 1990), ACM SIGCHI & SIGOIS, pp. 209-221.

5. Mackay, W.E. Triggers and barriers to customizing software. In *Proceedings of CHI'91 Conference on Human Factors in Computing Systems* (New Orleans, Louisiana, April 27-May 2, 1991), ACM SIGCHI, pp. 153-160.

6. MacLean, A., Carter, K., Lövstrand, L, and Moran, T. User-tailorability systems: Pressing the issues with buttons. In *Proceedings of CHI'90 Conference on Human Factors in Computing Systems* (Seattle, Washington, April 1-5, 1990), ACM SIGCHI, pp. 175-182.

7. Oppermann, R. and Simm, H. Adaptability: user-initiated individualization. In Oppermann, R. (Editor), *Adaptive User Support: Ergonomic Design of Manually and Automatically Adaptable Software*, Hillsdale, NJ: Lawrence Erlbaum Associates, 1994, pp. 14-64.

8. Rosson, M.B. The effects of experience on learning, using, and evaluating a text-editor. *Human Factors* (1984) 26, 463-475.

9. Trigg, R.H., Moran, T.P., and Halasz, F.G. Adaptability and tailorability in NoteCards. *Proceedings of IFIP INTERACT'87: Human-Computer Interaction* (1987), 723-728.

10. Williams, Gregg. HyperCard: HyperCard extends the Macintosh user interface and makes everybody a programmer. *Byte* (December 1987) 12, 109-117.

Multiagent Model of Dynamic Design

Visualization as an Emergent Behavior of Active Design Agents

Suguru Ishizaki[+]

Design Department · Carnegie Mellon University
MMC 110 · Pittsburgh · PA 15213
phone 412-268-6952 · email suguru+@cmu.edu

Abstract

This research has been motivated by the lack of models and languages in the visual design field that are able to address design solutions, which continuously adapt in response to the dynamic changes both in the information itself and in the goals or intentions of the information recipient. This paper postulates *a multiagent model of dynamic design*—a theoretical framework of design that provides a model with which the visual designer can think during the course of designing. The model employs a decentralized model of design as a premise, and borrows its conceptual model from the improvisational performance, such as dance and music, and bases its theoretical and technical framework on the field of multiagent systems. A design solution is considered an emergent behavior of a collection of active design agents, *or performers*, each of which is responsible for presenting a particular segment of information. The graphical behaviors of design agents are described by their dynamic activities—rather than by the traditional method of fixed attributes. The model is illustrated with two design projects, Dynamic News Display System and E-Mail Display, both of which were implemented using a multiagent design simulation system, **perForm**, along with an agent description language, **persona**.

Keywords: visual design, visualization, dynamic information, automatic design, multiagent systems

1. Introduction

1.1 Problems and Opportunities

Traditional visual design encapsulates information into fixed forms, such as print or film, so that the message can be distributed or stored. In the design of computer-based communication, design problems become more dynamic as the media become more interactive and include more temporal information. It is therefore important to create a design that continuously adapts in response to the dynamic changes of context, that is, information and the reader's intention. I argue that visual design as a field limits its own contributions to traditional methodologies, despite increasing efforts from within the field to improve the visual design of digital media. This lack of models and languages prevents designers from exploring those solutions that are unique to computer-based communication.

The problem on which I have focused in this research is identified by two unique characteristics of computer-based communication: dynamic change in context; and the capability of temporal presentation (Fig.1).

CHI 96 Vancouver, BC Canada
© 1996 ACM 0-89791-777-4/96/04..$3.50

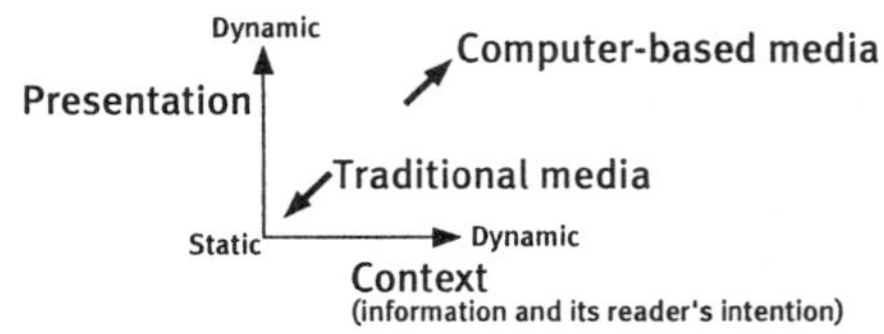

Fig.1. Two unique characteristics of computer-based communication raise new problems in design.

First, dynamic change in context (*i.e.,* information and the reader's intention) raises a new problem in the design of computer-based media. For example, on-line information systems, such as news databases and traffic information systems, are updated as information changes. The design in such a medium must reflect the dynamic changes in information over time. Interactive media provide readers with personalized access to information. The pace and order of reading and the amount and selection of information change over time based on the intention of the individual user. Consequently, in the design of computer-based media, a designer often finds it impossible to design for solving a particular problem, and instead must represent *a way of designing* in a form of a computer program that can generate design solutions at run-time.

But, what do I mean by a way of designing, or process of designing? What kind of *form* does this process take? In this paper, "a way of designing" is an explicit description of how individual design elements, unknown at the time of designing, change over time according to changes in the immediate context. A goal of this research has been to propose a conceptual model and a descriptive language that designers can use in the course of creating such dynamic design solutions.

The second characteristic of computer-based media is the capability of temporal presentation. It introduces new challenges and opportunities in design. Designers are no longer limited to fixed forms in order to communicate information. For example, a gradual color shift can be used to convey complex emotional quality; or a rapid repetitive movement can be used to indicate a quantity.

However, although traditional visual design has dealt with temporal presentation media, such as television and film, there have been only a few studies on temporal forms [4]. As a consequence, the visual design field lacks the rich models and languages that would allow designers to discuss visual forms presented over time. A classic example of such a model is a color space, *e.g.,* the Munsell model [6], which has provided designers with a conceptual model of color, along with a vocabulary set, allowing the use of rich color harmony as well as the analysis of complex interaction of

[+] *This work was done while the author was at the MIT Media Laboratory's Visible Language Workshop. (MIT Media Laboratory, E15-443, 20 Ames St. Cambridge, MA 02139)*

color. This research proposes such a model for the visual forms that change over time.

These characteristics have raised various questions that need to be answered: How can a designer conceptualize and describe a solution that can be interrupted by some immediate changes in information and in the reader's intention? How can a designer describe a design that contains an undetermined number of design elements constantly changing? How can a designer contemplate design problems as continuous problems, rather than a series of discrete problems?

I suggest that it is valuable to develop a model of design that would provide designers with a conceptual framework during the course of solving design problems, in order to extend the fixed nature of the traditional design-object so that it will include more continuous and responsive characteristics. The model is also intended to contribute to the development of computer systems that *represent* and *generate* continuous and responsive design solutions. In this paper, I shall call this framework *a multiagent model of dynamic design*, or **maDes**.

1.2 Background

There have been a number of researchers that proposed generative design systems (*e.g.*, [3][5][8][11]). However, most of their representation schemes do not consider the fluid nature of computer-based communication. Rather, those representations are modeled after traditional static design (*e.g.*, a layout, or a presentation) where a design solution is described as a collection of declarative statements that are intended to fix formal attributes. On the other hand, **maDes** is intended to encourage designers to perceive (1) a design problem in computer-based communication as a continuous stream, instead of a collection of discrete problems; and (2) a design solution as a fluid emergent entity generated by dynamic activities of design elements, instead of a set of design elements with fixed attributes.

maDes has been influenced by three distinct areas of studies. First is the cognitive models of design that suggest the multiplicity of knowledge involved in designing (*e.g.*, [10][12]). These theories have encouraged a distributed representation as a natural means for representing a generative design process. Second, in order to develop a distributed model, I have drawn an analogy from improvisational performance, such as dance and music [1][7]. The intrinsic nature of improvisation that addresses performers' responses to the spontaneous changes in context during a performance has provided an insight for a design solution that must respond to dynamic changes in its context. Finally, the research in multiagent systems—a branch of distributed AI—has provided a theoretical and technical foundation to this research [2]. In particular, **maDes** has adopted cooperative reactive (or situated) agents [9] as constituents of multiagent design systems.

2. A Scenario

Imagine that you are a designer. Think of a news display system that allows users to access a news database that is constantly updated. News stories arrive at the display system as they are issued, and a user can view them as they are published. The purpose, or more precisely, intention, of a user may also vary over time. For example, a user may want to read news articles according to locations; or a user may need to look at a particular category. Your task as a designer is to create a visual design solution for the display

Fig.2. A screenshot of Dynamic News Display, showing a scene while a user is reading a news story, after its headline is selected.

that reflects the dynamic changes in both reader's intention and the database. Since information is only available at run-time, you are not allowed to directly adjust attributes of potential design elements, such as typeface and color, unlike the newspaper design. Thus, you must design a way of designing, or design process, in order to dynamically solve this continuous design problem. In addition, since the display is capable of presenting temporal expressions (*e.g.*, animation), you are not limited to the traditional notion of static design solutions. Rather, you are free to use *temporal forms*. For example, you may use repetitive motion (*e.g.*, up and down) as a "label" for an important news story, as you would use a hue (*e.g.*, red) for the same purpose in the design of a news magazine.

I have just described that your task as a designer is to create a design solution that is responsive. And the solution is a way of designing that you have to describe. Now, how would you want to *describe* such a design solution?

maDes provides a designer with a unique framework for describing such a design solution. For example, Fig.2 is a scene from an experimental on-line news display designed based on the proposed model. Here, the design solution is an emergent expression created by the situated activities of design agents that are responsible for presenting headlines, news stories, placenames, a clock, a date text, and a map, each of which has its behavior specified by a designer. A headline agent left-aligns its text to its placename first when it is born; and when a new headline is issued at the same location it aligns the text to the new headline. Headline agents also change the translucency of its text based on its age. Placename agents change their text color when there is a headline associated with their location. When a news story is being read by a user, other design agents make their visual representations highly translucent so that they do not distract the user's reading. And so on... The solution here is created by a team of collaborating agents.

A designer's task when working with **maDes** is to anticipate potential changes in the context, and specify kinds of expressive forms for design agents to perform according to their immediate situations. An analogy to the designer's role here can be made with that of a director of an improvisational dance performance—selecting dancers with the desired expressive skill (body forms) and coaching their situated acting through a thorough rehearsal. In the course of creating a final dynamic solution, a designer would have to rehearse behaviors of agents iteratively by simulating real dynamic design situations.

3. A Multiagent Model of Dynamic Design

3.1. Overview

maDes models a design solution as a system consisting of a collection of smaller design systems. Each system, or *design agent*, is responsible for presenting a particular segment of information. A design agent is a system that can modify its expressive behavior as the context changes and can cooperate with other design agents. In traditional visual design, a design element is usually described by a set of fixed attributes; while in **maDes**, a design element is described by *a set of dynamic activities*.

The term *context* here is used from the perspective of an agent, and it is comprised of the information, the reader's intention, and the immediate presentation environment (*i.e.*, surrounding visual elements). Any of the three constituents is potentially dynamic.

3.2. Agent's ability

I have described that the design agent presents information according to a given context. But, how can a designer describe agents' activities? The proposed multiagent model of design adopts reactive agents as its constituents [9]. As described in Scenario, design agents are like performers in an improvisational performance, in that they perform reactively using their skills, without deliberately planning their actions. Performers seem to simply act on immediate situations, but it does not imply their performance is not intelligent. Rather, deliberation is considered embedded in their reactive pattern, or skill, through previous training. In dynamic design, the behavior of the design agent is described as a set of situation-action patterns. If a design agent is capable of communicating a particular segment of information at any given situation in such a manner that a designer desires, the agent's *ability* is said to satisfy the designer's intention.

Agent's ability is specified either for a particular agent, or for a class of agents. When it is specified for a class of agents, agents that belong to the same class share their ability. For example, there may be a set of design agents belonging to one class that are all responsible for presenting a headline in a dynamic electronic news system. In dynamic design, a designer often has to focus on behaviors for a class of design agents, rather than a particular design agent, since a particular information set is usually unknown at the time of designing. However, there is nothing to prevent the designers from creating a single unique agent. A clock agent in Dynamic News System is an example of such a unique agent.

In **maDes**, the ability of the agent is determined as well as described by the following characteristics:

Physical Realization

Physical realization is a perceivable representation of the agent. It is important to recognize that an agent is not bound to a particular type of expression. For example, an agent that is responsible for presenting a headline in Dynamic News Display may express itself using text or through voice. Since the agent is an active system, it chooses an appropriate realization according to a given context. Physical realization(s) for an agent is determined based on the available technology and a particular design problem at hand.

State and Sensor

State is a unit of what the agent "knows." State includes: physical properties (*e.g.*, color) that are determined by the agent's physical realization and changed by actions described next; information about other related agents, and information about user's intention; and changes in information for which the agent is responsible.

The design agent is assumed capable of sensing information from the external world (external to itself), which include: information to be presented (*e.g.*, news data), the reader's intention, and other agents' activities. A set of sensors is defined for an agent by a designer, and the value observed by a sensor is a special type of state.

Action

Action is the abstraction for the agent's basic ability—just as body-form is the abstraction for describing performer's skill in dance. There are three basic categories of actions that the agents can perform: formal, communicative, and external. Formal action is an expressive action that influences the agent's form, such as typography and color. For example, a flash shown in Fig.3, which can be used to attract a reader's attention, is a formal action. Communicative action is the act of sending a message to other agents, which is used when explicit coordination is necessary. An example of communicative action is a message sending action taken by a placename agent to inform its selection to the associated headline agents. Finally, external action is a type of action used to influence outside the multiagent system, such as an application program. For example, there can be a quit button agent that terminates the application program.

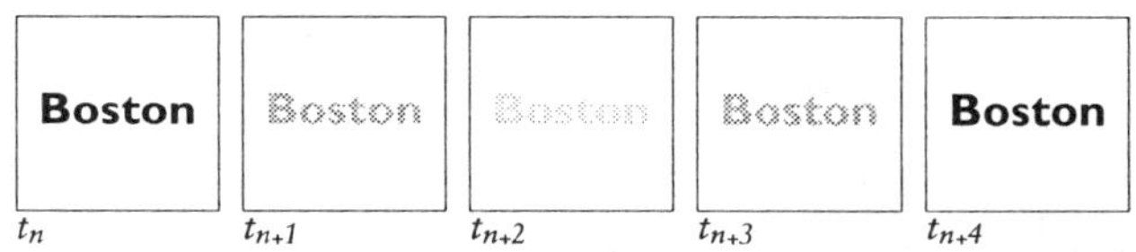

Fig.3. A simplified view of a flash action.

Each formal action—*or temporal form*—must be carefully described by a designer for a particular design problem. An action can be performed instantaneously (*e.g.*, change font), or it may take a certain duration (*e.g.*, gradually glow size). **maDes** provides an abstraction that allows structural and analytical descriptions of forms expressed over time.

Any meaningful formal expression can be considered an action. However, what is considered a meaningful action is determined by how a designer views a design problem and its solution. For example, consider the flash action shown in Fig.3. A designer may consider it as a meaningful action to attract a reader's attention. Alternatively, the first half of the same action (t_n~t_{n+2}), which changes the color of text from dark to bright, can be considered another action that serves a different purpose. *The abstraction of action provides a framework to structure design as a set of meaningful temporal forms.*

Strategy

Strategy is the abstraction over actions, which describes the agent's ability to achieve a particular goal. Strategy is like a performer's ability to express a certain theme in a musical improvisation. A player achieves a particular theme by selecting an appropriate action sequence at the right timing. A set of strategies determines the ability of a design agent.

To select an appropriate action as a response to its immediate situation, the agent must be able to recognize various *contexts* by which it is potentially situated. In other words, the designer of a dynamic design solution must identify possible situations for individual agents. A situation can depend on an agent's own state, another agent's state, information it's presenting, a reader's intention, or a combination of these. For example, the placename agent in the news display can recognize when a cursor is above its text, when its text is clicked, when there are headline agents associated with its place, and when some news story is being presented.

Situations are structured in a hierarchical manner. Suppose a user is interested in reading news articles based on locations (sit-1). Then, if a reader selects a placename with which a headline agent is associated, it generates a sub-situation for the headline: a reader is potentially interested in reading its story (sit-2). Notice that, sit-2 is situated within a larger situation sit-1. You can also find another substitution within sit-2 when a reader selects the headline agent: a reader is interested in reading its story (sit-3). In other words, when the agent is situated in one situation, it does not have to watch out for all the situations it can recognize; rather it only has to consider sub-situations that potentially happen within the immediate high level situation. Fig.4 presents a schematic diagram of situations that are hierarchically defined. *The abstraction of strategy and situation provides designers with a means of analyzing and structuring dynamic design problems in a systematic manner.*

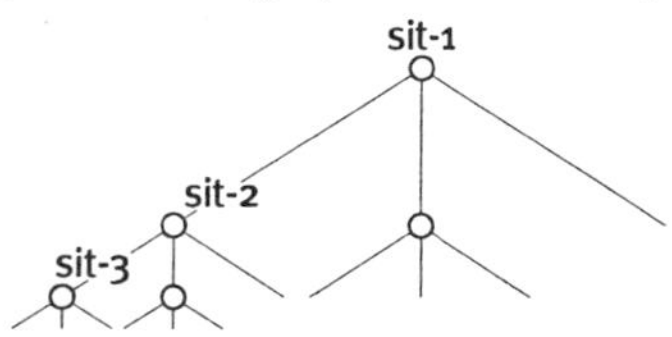

Fig.4. A schematic diagram of a situation hierarchy.

Given abilities to recognize necessary situations, a strategy is specified as a simple procedure and is composed of a set of actions and a set of reactive rules, based on the reactive agent model proposed by Singh [9]. The simplest strategy consists of a sequence of one or more design action. For example, a headline's strategy to attract a viewer's attention may consist of an action to gradually become red and increase its size. From a perspective of a headline agent, this strategy can be written as:

S-1 ***attract-viewer's-attention-strategy:***
perform ***flash-action***

More complex strategies provide the agent an ability to determine an appropriate action to perform according to its immediate context. An example of this type of strategy, for the headline agent, is to attract a viewer when the news item is important. This strategy is achieved by adding a conditional statement to *S-1*:

S-2 ***attract-viewer's-attention-strategy:***
If my news article is important to my reader
perform ***flash-action***
otherwise
do-nothing

A strategy can also consist of a set of other strategies. For instance, a simple strategy for a headline agent to use ***attract-viewer's-attention-strategy*** until it is deleted by a user can be defined as follows:

S-3 ***basic-strategy:***
while I am not deleted,
use ***attract-viewer's-attention-strategy***

Also, a strategy can consist of a sequence of multiple strategies.

Notice that these two strategies, ***basic-strategy*** and ***attract-viewer's-attention-strategy***, involve three situations as shown in Fig.5. First the top level situation is when the headline agent is not deleted. Then, there are two sub-situations: one when the agent's news article is important, another when it is not.

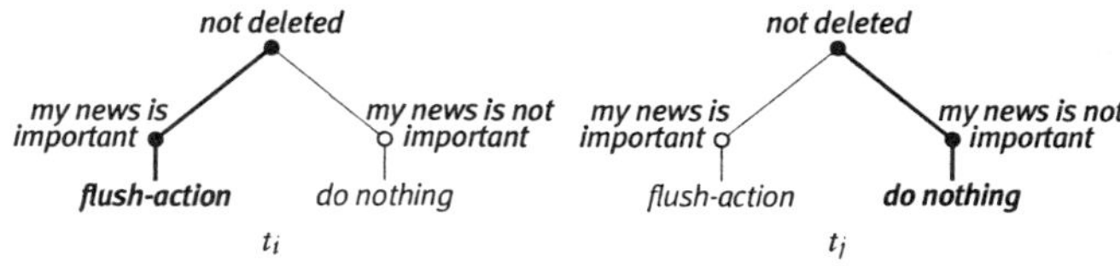

Fig.5. A schematic diagram of a situation hierarchy.

Strategy is a useful abstraction which a designer can use in the course of exploring design solutions, as well as in describing the final solution. *It provides designers with a framework for identifying changes in context, and for determining appropriate dynamic and responsive design solutions.*

3.3. External view

Fig.6 summarizes the agent's ability. The design agent acts on the immediate situation using a strategy that is designed to achieve its current goal. The information observed from the external world and messages sent from other agents are used by the strategy to determine appropriate actions to perform.

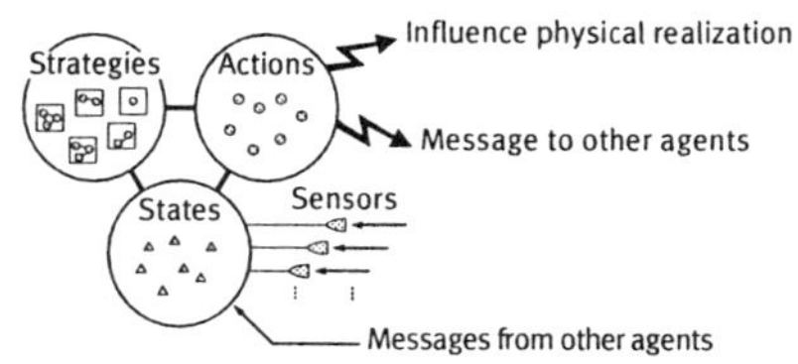

Fig.6. A summary of the agent's ability.

It may seem complex to understand how an agent behaves, with a given set of strategies and actions. One method that helps one understand an agent's behavior is to consider its history. Fig.7 shows a history of a headline agent. The agent repeated performing ***flash-action*** through t_i since its news story is important. Then, its situation changed at t_n, where the news story became no longer important. At t_n, the agent stopped performing ***flash-action*** and started perform ***do-nothing*** and kept doing nothing until now through t_j.

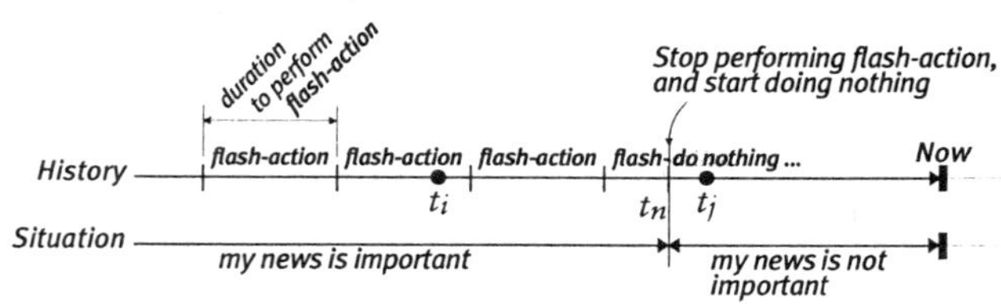

Fig.7. A historical view of a headline agent.

Also, an agent's future can be understood in terms of *histories*. Given a particular point in time, there are many possible histories. As time progresses, an agent possesses one history in its past. Fig.8 is a schematic diagram showing the concept of possible histories found in the future of an agent. The notion of history is an external description of the agent behavior, but it is not explicitly represented.

History is simply an analytical device that can be used to understand the agent's behaviors.

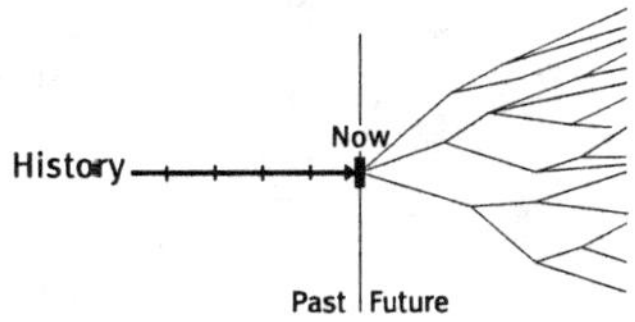

Fig.8. A schematic diagram of future histories of an agent.

3.4. Organization of Agents

maDes emphasizes a decentralized and lateral interaction among design agents, as opposed to a centralized and hierarchical one (Fig.9). Like dancers or players on a football team, who do not have strict hierarchical control, the design agents collaboratively act in order to achieve a global goal. However, an agent can become a local leader with some authority over other agents, like the lead dancer or the quarterback. The leaders can orchestrate other agents. For example, a headline agent in the dynamic news design can be a leader that oversees a story agent and a photograph agent.

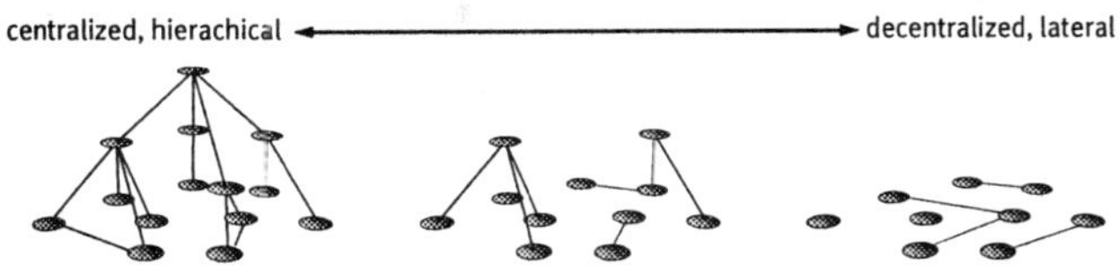

Fig.9. A range of organizational styles.

I have described that a design solution as a whole is an emergent behavior generated by both implicit and explicit collaborations among design agents. This emergent solution is considered a group strategy, and its communicative quality is considered the ability of a group. However, there is no explicit description about group strategies. Group strategy and group ability are like those of a football team, and composed of a collection of strategies used by individual agents.

3.5. Design Method

In addition to the theoretical framework, this research suggests a methodical process which a designer can follow through to solve a design problem. Fig.10 shows a schematic flow of a design process with **maDes**. This method fundamentally resembles a typical prescriptive design process paradigm—analysis, synthesis, and evaluation.

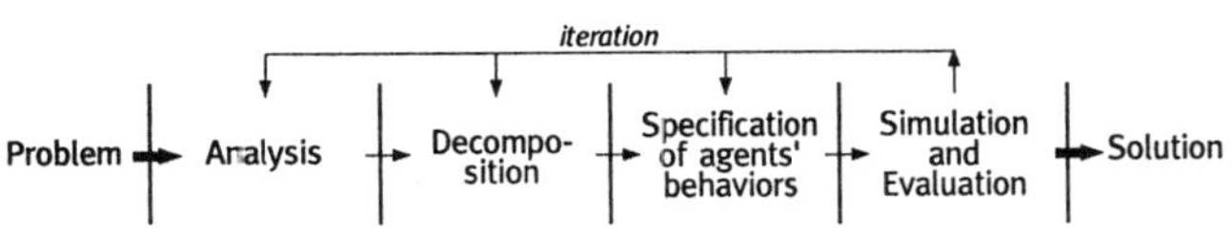

Figure 10. A design method that uses the multiagent model of dynamic design.

The first phase is the analysis of a design problem. The designer must understand the nature of information, the goal of communication, and types of intended readers. The second phase is the decomposition of the problem. A design problem is described as a set of design agents. In this phase, types of design agents, their roles and organizational style are determined. The third phase is the specification of the agents' behaviors. Here, a designer specifies the behaviors for individual classes of design agents using actions and strategies. Then the solution, or partial solution, created in the third phase is evaluated by simulating agents' behaviors in various contexts.

Although the design method is described in a linear fashion, the design is not completed by a simple four-stage process; rather it is an iteration of exploring and examining agents' behaviors and relations among them. The role of a designer is like that of a director in the performing arts, in that, the design process consists of a course of *dialogue* between a designer and the design agents. A designer must carefully determine the behaviors of agents in such a way that each agent can play its role according to the changes in the immediate context, and can contribute to an emergent design solution.

4. perForm: A Multiagent Design Simulation System

perForm is an experimental software program that was implemented based on **maDes** to examine its theoretical framework with concrete design examples. **perForm** provides an agent description language called **persona**, along with a multiagent design simulation engine, which simulates parallel activities of design agents. **persona** is implemented in LISP and provides a set of macros that are used to define agents' abilities, including actions, strategies, sensors, and messages. **perForm** uses a special 3D graphics library for the realization of the design agent, enabling the use of high quality typography to examine **maDes** with design solutions that are not too simplistic. The software is written using SGI's Performer graphics library on SGI's ONYX Workstation with the Reality Engine graphics.

The following sections illustrate how dynamic design can be created with **maDes**, using **perForm**. Because of the space limitation, the description of agents' behaviors are given in the style of stories, instead of strategies written in **persona**.

5. Case Study 1: Dynamic News Display

5.1. Overview

The design problem is to create a visual interface to an online news database, as introduced in Section 2. In this experimental project, I intended to create a visual interface that can continuously provide users with an overview of entire news articles issued within a certain time period (*e.g.*, past 12 hours). I also decided to present news articles based on their physical locations where they are issued.

5.2. Decomposition and Roles of Agents

The information is decomposed into the following agent types: Headline Agent, Story Agent, Map Agent, Placename Agent, Clock Agent, and Date Agent. Notice that a news article is represented by a headline agent and a story agent. The role of the Headline Agent is to quickly inform the content, as well as to present the age of its associated news article. The role of the Story Agent is simply to provide its message content. The reason to decompose a news article in two different agents (headline and story) is to create a visually less overwhelming interface. It is also conceivable to create a class of design agent that is responsible for presenting the entire news article. However, it was rather meaningful to represent a news story using two agents.

5.3. Solution

This particular example used a set of news articles categorized as top U.S. news from the Clarinet database on May 19, 1995. Fig.11.a shows the display just before 9 o'clock in the morning. There are three headlines at Los Angels, one at Kansas City, and one at Washington D.C. The place-

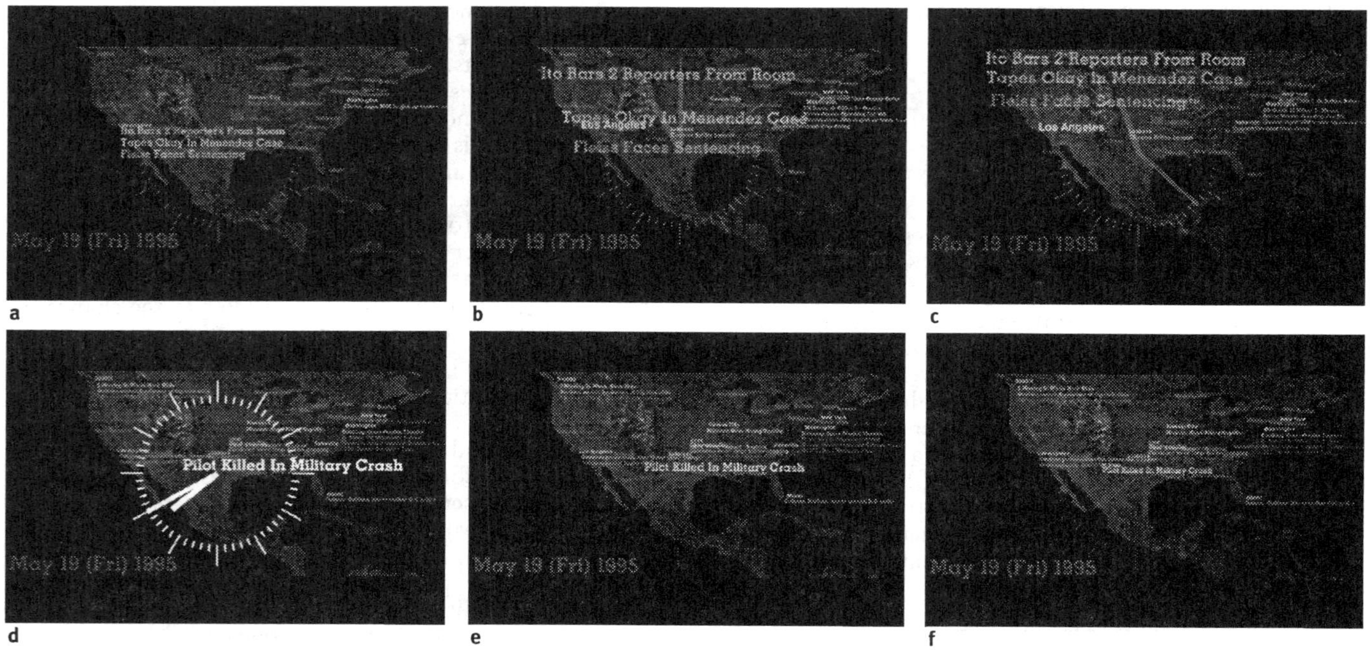

Fig.11. Interactive scenes from the Dynamic News Display. **a-c** show a sequence after Los Angles is selected. **d-f** show an introductory action of a headline agent.

name agents responsible for presenting these three placenames have recognized that there are news stories associated with them, and changed their color from light gray to bright orange. Also, notice that three headlines at Los Angeles have larger type size than the others. This scene is taken right after a reader moved a cursor over to the text "Los Angeles." First, the Los Angeles agent notices that a cursor is on top of it—a new situation; and then it informs headlines associated with it that it is being focused upon. Having been informed by the placename, those headline agents now "know" that their placename is being focused upon. According to my instruction for this situation, headline agents gradually grew their type size. It then kept that size while a cursor was on its associated placename, in order to make their text more readable.

When a headline agent is born, it first flashes its text close to a viewpoint (in *z-axis*) using white (Fig.11.d-f). Then, right after that, it gradually aligns the text to its placename. This introductory action is achieved by using a strategy with a flash action and a move action. After introducing its text, the Headline Agent uses a higher level strategy until the age of its news article reaches to the specified limit. This strategy provides the headline agent an ability to act based on how a user is interacting with its associated placename as well as with itself.

Each headline agent left-aligns its text to a headline that is issued next at the same place; or to its placename if it is the most recent one. The Headline Agent always tries to maintain this alignment using the *same* strategy. The Headline Agent also looks at the age of its new article and changes the translucency of its text proportional to its age. For example, the headline presented at Kansas City shows that its story is older than other news stories.

If a placename is selected, headline agents associated with that place use a different strategy to grow their text size, and to move to the top left position. Fig.11.b-c presents a sequence of scenes after Los Angels is selected. Three headline agents gradually move their text to the upper left part of the display. In this design, selecting a placename means to further examine articles at that place. Thereafter, if a user selects a headline by clicking its text, it informs its news story agent of its selection. This changes the situation for a story agent, which has been using a strategy to hide. Then, it uses another strategy to make its text visible (Fig.2). Notice that there have been other news stories arrived to other cities, while a user has been interacting with news articles at Los Angeles.

Behaviors of the other agents are relatively simple. The Clock Agent finds current time based on whether the system is used in quick review mode or real-time mode, and displays it in the form of a clock. It also changes color of its clock every hour based on a previously chosen set of 24 colors around a hue circle. The Date Agent keeps checking current date and displays it in the from of a text. The Map Agent just keeps displaying a map. In an earlier design The Map Agent changed the brightness of the map based on the time of a day; however, I decided not to use that strategy since color coding schemes of other agents were difficult to maintain.

Finally, notice that, in Fig.2, texts representing placenames and headlines, other than the selected headlines and its news story, are highly translucent. When the headline and the placename agents notice (using their sensors) a situation in which a news story is being presented , they use a strategy which tries not to visually distract the user's reading.

5.4. Summary

Imagine the design of a newspaper, for instance. The design of Dynamic News Display clearly has shown a different method in which designers can approach a problem, when compared to a traditional model. **maDes** was able to highlight the fluid nature of design problems and the potential of dynamic and responsive design solutions. **maDes** also provides a means to describe a rich and emergent solution out of relatively simple distributed agents.

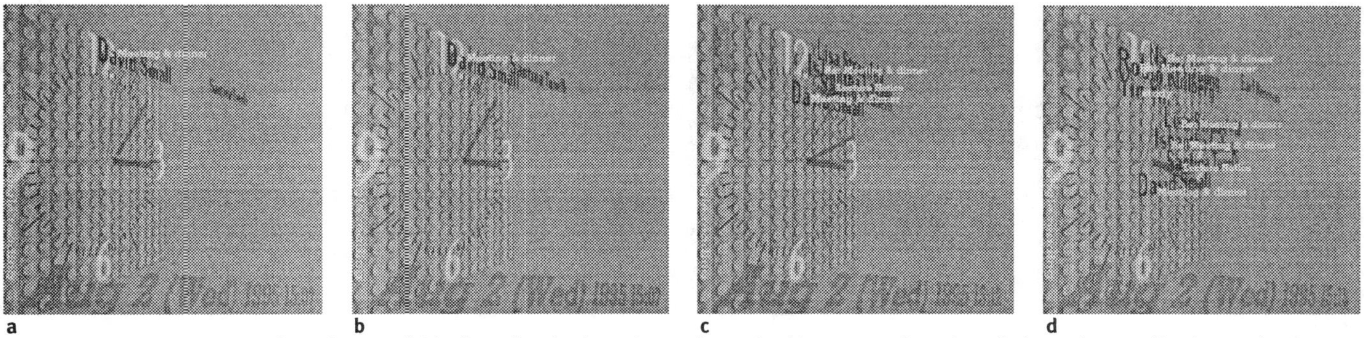

Fig.12. Interactive screens from the E-Mail Displlay, showing how the sender and subject agents introduce their text by coordinating each other.

6. Case Study 2: E-Mail Display

6.1. Overview

The design problem in the second case study is to create a visual interface to an e-mail system, E-Mail Display. The interface must represent: an arrival of a new message; reply-replied message relationships; whether or not a message is read by the user; and the number of mail messages. In addition, I intended to make the interface playful, avoiding conservative structured layout, using interesting temporal forms and vivid colors.

6.2. Decomposition and Roles of Agents

The information is decomposed into the following design agents: Sender Agent, Subject Agent, Message Agent, Clock Agent, Number-of-Messages-Agent (MumMsg agent), Reading-Mode-Switch-Agent (Switch agent), and Date Agent (Fig.12). Similar to a news article in the Dynamic News Display, a mail message is decomposed into three design agents: a sender, a subject, and a message. In addition to the obvious roles that are implied by these three agents, additional communicative roles are assigned to them. First, Sender Agent is responsible for representing whether or not its message is read, the temporal relationship to other messages, and reply-replied relationships. Sender Agent is also responsible for informing its message agent when it is selected by the user. Subject Agent must visually represent its relationship to its sender. The message agent must present its text when its sender is clicked. The roles of Clock Agent, Date Agent, and NumMsg Agent are those of which their names suggest. The role of Switch Agent is to indicate the current *reading mode* of the system, and to switch a reading mode between single and relational (discussed later) when it is clicked.

6.3. Solution

Similar to the Dynamic News Display, design agents are realized using a 3D space. However, unlike the News Display, the view point is rotated 45 degrees clockwise around the *y-axis*, creating a sense of perspective (Fig.12). The clock agent uses a LEGO-block pattern to create a playful atmosphere. Unlike other graphical elements, which use a single realization element such as text, the clock agent uses multiple parts: numbers, LEGO background, in addition to the clock itself. There is no need to decompose a clock into smaller design agents since it is a meaningful unit.

When a new email message arrives in the mail system, the sender agent presents its name text at the far right in the *x-axis* and at about the height of the clock in the *y-axis*; and then moves the text towards the clock. The sender agent randomly chooses the position for its text somewhere between the center and right edge of the clock (Fig.12.a-c). This random positioning in the *x-axis* is intended to make the names of senders easier to distinguish from adjacent ones, and to create a playful emergent form. As the sender agent approaches the clock, it uses squashing and stretching action, and stops. The design of this action is influenced by a technique used in traditional animation in order to provide a viewer a sense of life. After arriving at the clock, the sender agent adjusts the *y* position of its text at the top of the clock if it is responsible for the most recent message, and otherwise places it just below the next sender text (Fig.12.d).

As the sender agent finishes performing its introductory action, its associated subject agents introduce its text by gradually showing the text right next to the name of the sender, using its introductory strategy (Fig.13.a). Since the sender agent stops at a random location, its associated subject agent uses its sensor to adjust its final location.

The Sender Agent is sensitive to a reader's clicking, and if its text is clicked, it informs its associated message agent about the selection. After receiving a message from its associated sender agent, the Message Agent recognizes a new situation, and uses a different strategy to present its text in front of other graphical element facing towards the view point (Fig.13.b-c). The Message Agent keeps the text visible until a reader clicks the text. Simultaneously, the sender agent that is clicked faces its text to the view point, become translucent, and start "dancing" in the background. The subject agent associated with the message places its text just behind the message and rotates it 60 degrees counter clockwise in order to make it readable. While a message text is presented—a new situation—other sender agents make their text *defocused*, decreasing the contrast, and their associated subject agents make their text transparent, in order to make the message currently chosen easier to read.

Individual strategies, as well as group strategies, introduced by now are relatively short-sighted. In other words, although a group of agents presents a complex visual message with multiple contents, such as sender's name, message text, and subject, each of which uses its own strategies in *parallel*, each presentation remains relatively brief. What if there is more information than that can fit in a screen? What if a designer desires to present a chain of causal relationships in sequence? The next simple example will illustrate how a group of agents can collaborate to create a sequence of presentation.

Fig.13.d shows a scene after the agent whose sender name is "Ishantha Lokuge" is selected under the relational reading mode, and becomes *a leader*. Since Ishantha's message is a reply to the message sent by David Small, the leader agent (responsible for Ishantha's name) requests the agent responsible for David's name (*replied agent*) to start a pre-

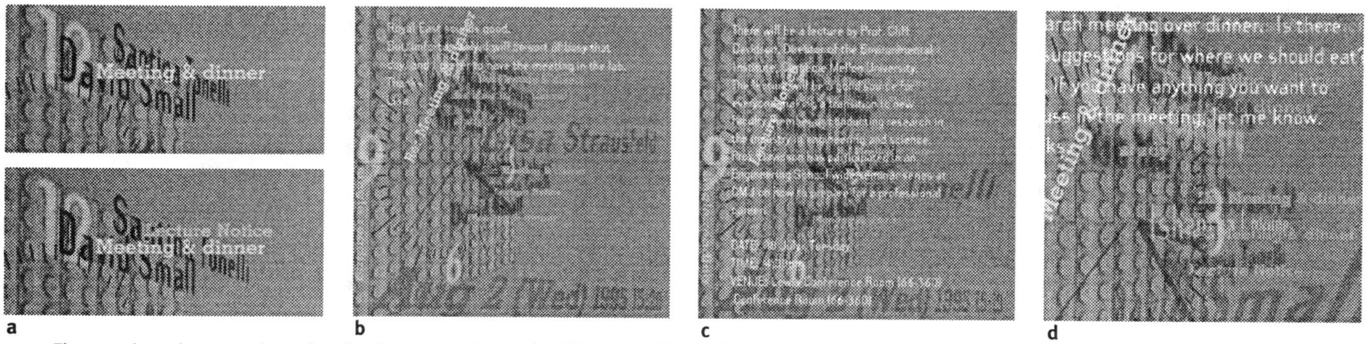

Fig.13. **a** is a close-up view showing how a sender and subject coordinate. **b-c** are scenes while a message is presented by a message agent. In **d**, a leader agent is waiting for a previous message to finish its presentation, by moving back and forth.

sentation. While David's message is being presented, the leader agent waits and visually indicates the fact that it is performing next, by shrinking and stretching in the *x-axis* (***waiting-action***). Then, after a user finishes reading David's message, the leader agent recognizes it and begins its own presentation. Simultaneously, the leader agent informs *reply agents* (sender agent whose messages are the reply to the message associated with its message) so that they can present their messages after its own presentation is over. This action changes the situation of the *reply agents*; and the closest *reply agent*, which is presenting next, starts performing ***waiting-action*** indicating its next presentation. Finally, when a user finishes reading the leader agent's message (Ishantha's), the leader agent stops its presentation and asks the closest reply agent to start its performance. The first reply agent informs the next reply agent when it is deselected. The remaining reply agents simply relay their presentation, one by one. Fig.14 shows a schematic diagram of this collaborative presentation.

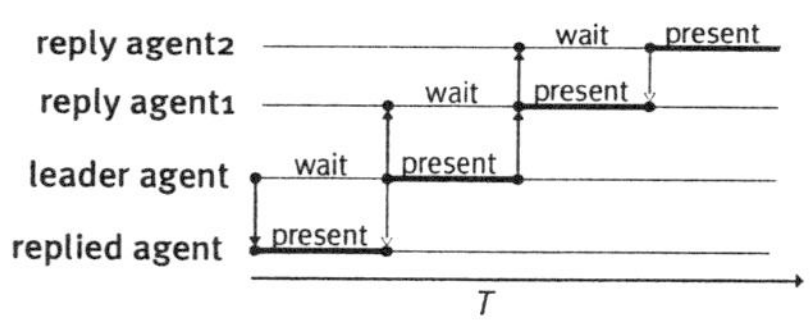

Fig.14. A historical view of the interaction among a group of agents. *(thick arrow=a message sending, thin arrow=sensing)*

6.4. Summary

The second study experimented with another type of collaboration orchestrated by a temporary leader agent. It has demonstrated that a collection of agents can generate a rather longer presentation sequence, as opposed to a short-sighted reactive design solution. I also tried to utilize temporal form as a more meaningful way to communicate messages. For example, the squash/stretch action for the sender agent is used to generate a sense of life; the dancing action for the sender agent is used as an "icon" expressing a sender's name for the message currently presented.

7. Conclusion

I have presented *a multiagent model of dynamic design*—a theoretical framework which provides designers with an approach towards creating design solutions that are responsive to dynamic changes in information and the user's intention. I have also emphasized the opportunity of utilizing *temporal forms* as a communicative means. Two case studies have demonstrated that the model is a plausible framework for highlighting the dynamic nature of computer-based communication, and for creating complex design solutions in a systematic manner with simpler descriptions of design agents.

Acknowledgement

I would like to thank the members of the Media Laboratory's Visible Language Workshop for their suggestions, and Munindar Singh for our conversation via email on his theory of multiagent systems.

This work was performed at the MIT Media Laboratory, and supported, in part, by ARPA, NYNEX, and Alenia Corporation.

References

1. Blom, L.A. and Chaplin, T.L. ***The Moment of Movement: Dance Improvisation.*** Univ. of Pittsburgh Press. 1988.
2. Bond, A.H. and Gasser, L. (eds.) ***Readings in Distributed Artificial Intelligence.*** Morgan Kaufmann. 1988.
3. Feiner, S.K. and McKeown K.R. **Automating the generation of coordinated multimedia explanations.** *IEEE Computer,* 24 10. 1991.
4. Hiebert, K. ***Graphic Design Processes: universal to unique.*** VanNostrand Reinhold. 1992.
5. Mackinlay, J.D. **Automating the design of graphical presentations of relational information.** *ACM Transactions on Graphics,* 5 2. 1986.
6. ***Munsell Book of Color: Defining, Explaining, and Illustrating the Fundamental Characteristics of Color,*** Munsell Color Company, Inc. 1929.
7. Pressing, J. **Cognitive processes in improvisation. In Cognitive Processes,** In the Perception of Art. W.R. Crozier and A.J.Chapman (eds.). Elsevier Science. 1987.
8. Roth, S.F. and Hefley,W.E. **Intelligent multimedia presentation systems: Research and principles,** In Intelligent Multimedia Interfaces, M.T. Maybury (ed.). MIT Press. 1993.
9. Singh, M.P. ***Multiagent Systems: A Theoretical Framework for Intentions, Know-How, and Communications.*** Springer Verlag. 1994.
10. Schön, D.A. and Wiggins, G. **Kinds of seeing and their functions in designing.** *Design Studies,* 13, No.2. 1992.
11. Weitzman, L. and Kent,W. **Automatic presentation of multimedia documents using relational grammars.** *Proceedings of ACM Multimedia* '94. 1994.
12. Whitefield, A. and Warren,C. **A blackboard framework for modeling designers' behavior.** *Design Studies,* Vol.10, No.3. 1989.

Helping Users Program Their Personal Agents

Loren G. Terveen
AT&T Bell Laboratories
600 Mountain Avenue
Murray Hill, NJ 07974
+1 908 582 2608
terveen@research.att.com

La Tondra Murray
North Carolina State University
Box 7906
Raleigh, North Carolina 27695
+1 919 515 7198
lamurra1@eos.ncsu.edu

ABSTRACT
Software agents are computer programs that act on behalf of users to perform routine, tedious, and time-consuming tasks. To be useful to an individual user, an agent must be *personalized* to his or her goals, habits, and preferences. We have created an end-user programming system that makes it easy for users to state rules for their agents to follow. The main advance over previous approaches is that the system automatically determines conflicts between rules and guides users in resolving the conflicts. Thus, user and system *collaborate* in developing and managing a set of rules that embody the user's preferences for handling a wide variety of situations.

Keywords
agents, end-user programming, intelligent systems

INTRODUCTION
Software agents are the focus of much interest in the popular press and are a hot research topic in human-computer interaction [3,5,7,8,9,10,12], artificial intelligence [16], and distributed computing [15]. HCI research on agents can be distinguished by its user-centered approach. The focus is on how agents can *empower users* to work more effectively in the vast, rich, ever-changing world of electronic communication and information.

One of the major promises of agents is *personal assistance* — each user can have an agent that serves his or her individual goals and preferences. This means that the agent must acquire appropriate knowledge about the user. This paper advocates an *end-user programming, human-computer collaboration* [13] approach to this problem. We have created a system called the Agent Manager that embodies the approach. Users state rules with a domain-specific graphical interface. The system analyzes rules for problems, computes methods of repairing the problems, and guides the user in selecting and applying repairs. Over time, user and system collaborate to evolve a set of rules that embody the user's goals and preferences.

We begin the paper by presenting a framework for agents that lets us identify the type of knowledge a personal agent requires. We then analyze existing approaches to agent personalization, showing when an end-user programming approach is appropriate and motivating the unique features of our system. We then describe the Agent Manager system, explain its representation and reasoning components, and illustrate how it helps users. We conclude by discussing the system development process, its current status, and our future plans.

A FRAMEWORK FOR PERSONAL AGENTS
The notion of an agent is notoriously vague. Although we do not expect to resolve this problem here, we will characterize the functionality we ascribe to agents. We do so to clarify the knowledge they need to perform their tasks, especially the user-specific knowledge required to be a *personal* agent.

The agent first needs knowledge of the task domains it is to operate in, such as messaging, electronic banking, or personal financial services. This knowledge is not specific to a particular user, so it can be supplied by the application developer. The fundamental ontology (or vocabulary) usually consists of objects, their attributes, and actions. In messaging, for example, objects include messages, folders, persons, and groups, and actions include moving a message to a folder, forwarding the message to another user, and replying to the sender. Some objects and actions are very general and thus useful in many domains, e.g., notification actions such as popping up a window on a computer screen, placing a call, and paging.

A personal agent needs knowledge about its owner's goals, habits, and preferences. Much of this type of knowledge can be expressed as rules of the form *when these conditions are true, take these actions*. Examples include:

- (messaging) When I get a message from my boss with the subject "urgent" after business hours, notify me by calling my home number.
- (banking) When the balance in my checking account falls below $500 and the balance in my savings account is above $2000, transfer $500 from savings to checking.
- (finances) When the price of XYZ stock falls below $30, buy 100 shares.

Another important function of an agent is to communicate on behalf of its owner. This includes notifying the owner when specified conditions occur, delivering messages to and responding to calls or messages from other users. To specify how a dialogue should be carried out, an appropriate set of abstractions is required. Ideally, the abstractions should be realizable on different devices, such as PCs and telephones. Our previous work [14] addresses these issues and complements the techniques for specifying rules that we discuss in this paper. Figure 1 summarizes our framework for personal agents.

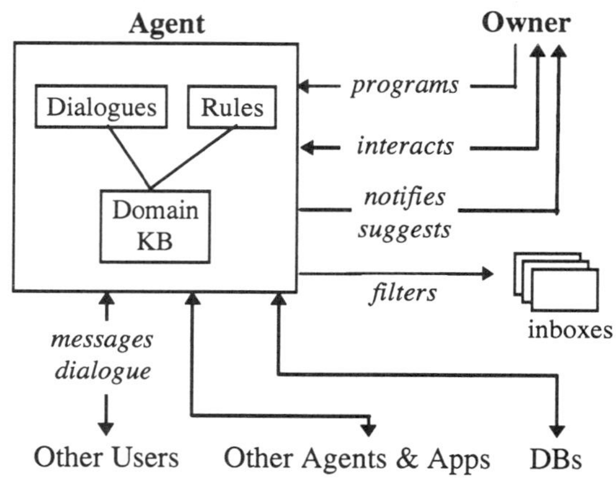

Figure 1: A Framework for Personal Agents

APPROACHES TO AGENT PERSONALIZATION

The research community has explored three major ways an agent may acquire the knowledge it needs: (1) end user programming, (2) learning, and (3) programming by demonstration.

End-User Programming (EUP)

The work of Malone and colleagues that began with the Information Lens and culminated with Oval [10] is the foundational research on end-user programming of rules. It popularized a basic method for expressing rules. The user first indicates the type of object the rule applies to, such as a message. The user then describes the conditions of the rule by filling out a form that contains a field for each attribute of the object; for messages, the attributes would include sender, subject, recipient, etc. Finally, the user specifies the actions of the rule by selecting from a list of all the actions that could apply to this type of object; a message can be moved, copied, forwarded, deleted, etc.

The most obvious advantage of this approach is that it is easy to implement. However, it has a number of disadvantages [8]: (1) users must recognize the opportunity to state a rule, (2) users must express the rule in the (textual or graphical) language of the system, and (3) users must maintain their rules over time, as their habits change.

Learning

Maes and colleagues [8,9] have explored a learning approach to acquiring agent rules, which they argue overcomes the problems with end-user programming. Rather than users being in charge of stating rules, the agent learns rules by watching user behavior and detecting patterns and regularities. The agent records a user's activity in terms of situation-action pairs. For example, a situation could be an email message and an action the way the user processed the message. The system predicts how a new situation should be handled by finding the most similar previously seen situation. After seeing enough examples, the system is able to make good predictions, which it uses to make suggestions to the user. The user also may instruct the agent to act on its own when its confidence in its predictions exceeds a specified threshold.

The basic learning model had its own shortcomings [8]: (1) the agent has a slow learning curve, so it cannot offer advice until it has seen quite a few examples, and (2) the agent cannot offer assistance in truly new situations, since it has not seen any examples of them. To remedy these shortcomings, the model has been extended to allow agents to collaborate with other agents. An agent can ask other agents for advice about how to handle a particular situation. This approach raises interesting issues of how agents interact with other agents, such as how an agent can learn to trust suggestions from some agents more than from others.

Programming by Demonstration (PBD)

In programming by demonstration (PBD) [4], a user "puts a system into 'record mode', then continues to operate the system in the ordinary way, and the system records the actions in an executable program" [12]. The prototypical PBD systems operate in domains that have a natural graphical representation. KidSim [5,12] is a good example. Kids create simulations in which characters move around in a two dimensional world. They create rules by using a graphical editor to depict changes of state; that is, they draw the configuration of the world before and after the rule has applied. The system generalizes from the concrete objects in the demonstration to create an abstract rule, e.g., replacing a particular character by any character of a certain type and replacing absolute locations by relative changes in location.

When kids want to write rules that mention properties not directly shown in the graphical simulation, such as the "hunger" rather than the location of a character, they use simple end-user programming tools. PBD thus combines elements of end-user programming (although users often work with concrete elements rather than abstract concepts) and learning (generalization from concrete examples to general rules).

When End-User Programming is Appropriate — and What Improvements It Needs

Despite the criticisms of EUP, all approaches retain it in at least some form. It is worth being explicit about the conditions under which it is appropriate:

- When users do have particular rules in mind, they should be able to express them. For example, I may want all messages from my boss put in a certain folder, and when I am on vacation, I may want a vacation message sent in response to all incoming messages. The second rule shows when learning is not appropriate. I want the rule to take effect immediately, so there is no time to collect examples. Further, the definition of the "situation" — i.e., the dates of the vacation — changes from one vacation to another, so there is no stable rule to learn.
- The rules the user is interested in may define the behavior of a "personal assistant", and the user may never engage in the behavior him or herself. Notifications are a good example: I may want to be paged when I get an email message from my boss with the subject "urgent", yet I certainly never have paged myself in the past. Therefore, this is another case where there will be no base of examples for a learning approach to work from.
- There is clear evidence that well-designed interfaces enable end-users to program. Bonnie Nardi made this case very eloquently in *A Small Matter of Programming* [11]. She identified domain-specificity as the key, giving many examples of domain-specific notations that people have mastered, from computer software such as spreadsheets to baseball scorecards. Nardi pointed out that spreadsheets are so successful because they allow users to express rich *domain* knowledge, while the spreadsheet framework encapsulates *programming* knowledge that would have to be made explicit in a conventional programming language. Most knowledge is local to a single cell. The spreadsheet automatically manages cell dependencies set up by formulas, a sophisticated control structure that no end-user could program. Commercial email filtering systems such as the MailBot (Daxtron Laboratories, Inc.) also offer an existence proof of the feasibility of end-user programming of rules.

Thus, we conclude that end-user programming still must play an important role in personalizing software agents. However, Nardi's studies of spreadsheets show one outstanding problem. Stating a single rule is fairly easy — it is roughly analogous to stating a formula in a spreadsheet cell. However, managing interactions between rules is much harder — it is more analogous to the control flow issues that a spreadsheet manages for users. The latter task takes the type of programming expertise that end-users do not have. Thus, our system, the Agent Manager, takes on this task. As a user creates rules, it analyzes the rules for problems, computes methods of repairing the problems, and guides the user in selecting and applying repairs.

THE AGENT MANAGER: COLLABORATIVE CONSTRUCTION OF AGENT RULES

The Agent Manager currently works in the domain of message processing. The primary user interface is a rule editor (Figure 2). Users specify rule conditions by restricting the values of the message type, sender, recipient, subject, and the date/time of arrival, thus defining the set of messages to which the rule applies. As users specify the conditions, the system continuously updates and displays the rule's context, i.e., its relationship to other rules and actions the rule will inherit from more general rules. Figure 2 shows a rule that applies to email messages from Julia Hirschberg whose subject field contains the word "important". Users select rule actions from a set that includes Move Message, Forward Message, Notify by Paging, Notify with Popup Alert, etc. The rule in Figure 2 contains a single action that moves messages to a folder named "julia". The system has determined that one rule named "Email" is more general, and that one action, *Copy Message "email archive"*, will be inherited to this rule.

A second editor lets the user specify two types of conditions about the arrival date/time of messages. First, users may specify messages that arrive in a particular interval, such as "between 4:00 p.m. on September 15, 1995 and 8:00 a.m. on September 20, 1995". Users also may specify intervals like "from November 1995 to March 1996", "before November 4, 1995", and "after 5:00 p.m. on September 15, 1995". Second, users can specify messages that arrive during a particular period, such as "during June, July, and August", "on Saturday or Sunday", "between 18:00 and 8:00", "on the first Monday of each month", and "on the last working day of the month". This is the most expressive editor for specifying date/time knowledge that we know of.

To understand how the Agent Manager assists users, we first must describe the representation and reasoning technology it uses.

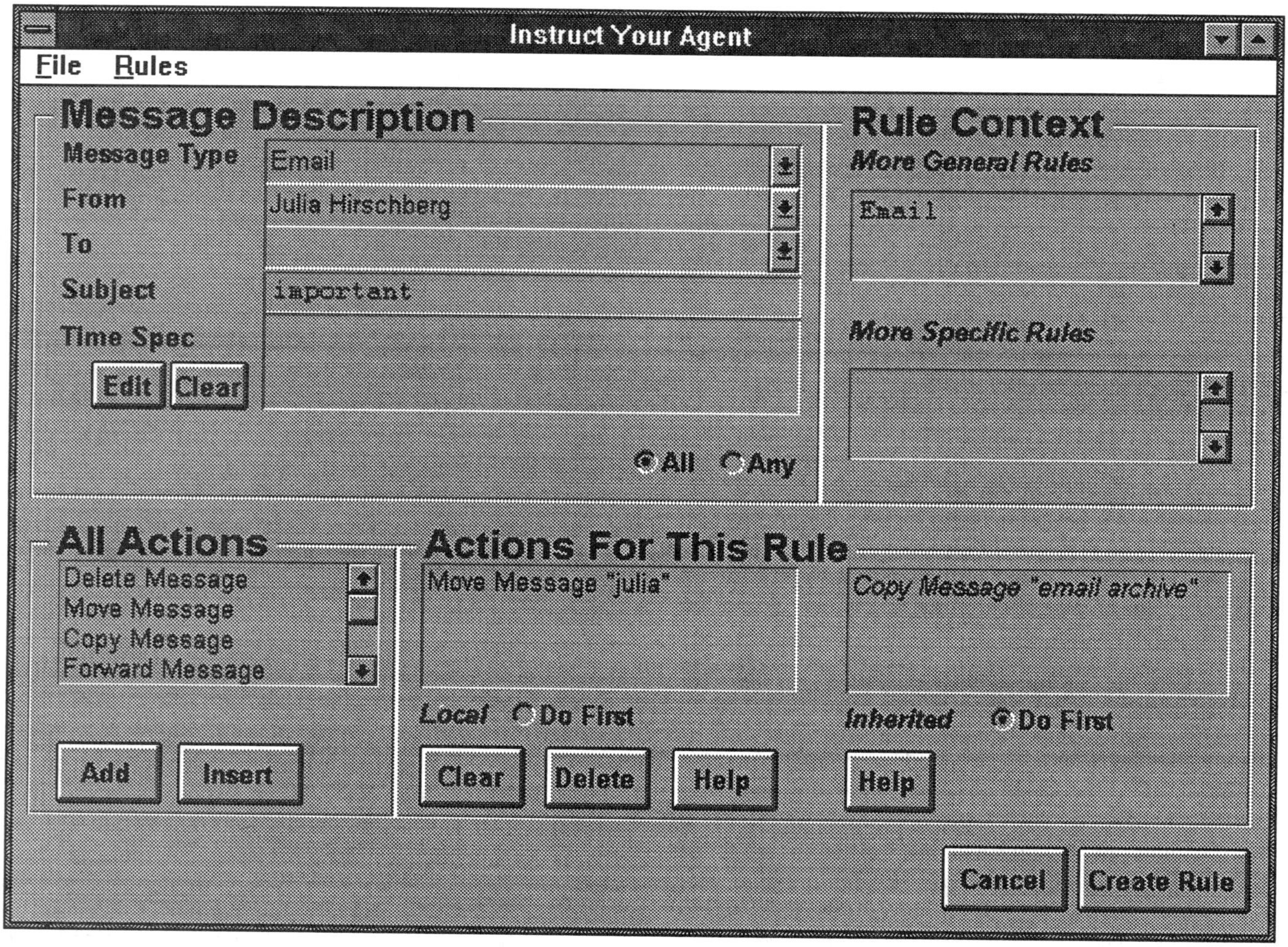

Figure 2: Rule Editor

Representation of Rules

Our representation of rules must enable these functions:

- determine whether an action may apply in a given context (e.g., to a specified set of messages, or after certain other actions),
- determine when one rule *subsumes* another — the set of objects to which the first rule applies is a superset of the set of objects to which the second rule applies, and
- determine when two rules intersect — the set of objects to which the first rule applies intersects the set of objects to which the second rule applies.

We represent rules using a version of CLASSIC [1,2] enhanced by Alex Borgida and Charles Isbell. CLASSIC is a *description logic*; as such, it permits users to create structured descriptions of sets of objects (known as *concepts*) and individual objects. As with any standard knowledge representation or object-oriented language, users may state hierarchical relationships between concepts; however, the main service CLASSIC provides is to determine subsumption relationships automatically by analyzing concept descriptions.

Determining subsumption relationships is one of our key requirements. By representing rule conditions as CLASSIC concepts, we get CLASSIC to maintain a rule hierarchy for us automatically. For example, the conditions of the rule being edited in Figure 2 would be represented as the following concept (call it C_0):

```
C0 – messageType = email and
     sender = Julia-Hirschberg and
     subject contains "important"
```

Examples of concepts that subsume C_0 include concepts formed from a subset of its conjuncts, such as `messageType = email` (the more general rule shown in Figure 2) or `sender = Julia-Hirschberg`. The object hierarchy is used, so `messageType = Message` also subsumes C_0. In addition, the semantics of substrings are used, so a concept like `subject contains "port"` also subsumes C_0.

CLASSIC also determines the intersection between two concepts. This is very useful because our experience has shown that users often state simple, general rules that categorize messages by a single attribute, such as

```
sender = Julia-Hirschberg, or
subject contains "important".
```

CLASSIC will determine that these rules do intersect. In this case, the intersection is simply the conjunction of the two concepts. However, in general, CLASSIC may have to combine parts of two concepts to determine the intersection. For example, consider the two descriptions of message arrival times "between 12:00 on November 8, 1995 and 12:00 on November 10, 1995" and "between 18:00 and 8:00". CLASSIC determines that the intersection is "18:00 to 23:59 on November 8, 1995, midnight to 8:00 and 18:00 to 23:59 on November 9, 1995, and midnight to 8:00 on November 10, 1995".

Like rule conditions, rule actions are represented as CLASSIC concepts. Actions are described in terms of a basic AI planning model [6]. Each action applies in a particular "state of the world", represented as a list of facts, and each action may change the state of the world. Thus, an action is defined in terms of its *preconditions* (facts which must be true for the action to be applied), *add list* (facts added by the action), and *delete list* (facts deleted by the action). For example, the action PickupCall is defined as:

```
preconditions: TelephoneCall
add: CallPickedUp
```

If an action A_1 occurs in a plan before an action A_2, and A_1 deletes a precondition of A_2, then A_1 defeats A_2.

AI planning research explores plan *synthesis* (creating a plan that transforms a specified initial sate to a specified final state) and *recognition* (inferring an agent's plan by observing his/her/its actions), both of which are very hard computational problems. In our case, the user constructs a plan — i.e., the actions of a rule — so the Agent Manager only has to check plan validity, a much simpler computational task.

Agent Manager Assistance

The Agent Manager's role is to watch for problems as users edit rules and help users to repair problems that it detects. Specifically, the Agent Manager detects when a rule's plan is not valid, i.e., some action does not apply. This can occur either as a user edits a rule or when the rule is added to the hierarchy (due to interactions with other rules). When the Agent Manager finds an invalid plan, it computes *repairs* — changes to the plan that will make it valid. It then presents an interactive explanation that explains the nature of the problem and guides the user in selecting a repair. We now describe the assistance process in more detail.

Verifying Plan Validity

The task of verifying plan validity centers around the notion of the *current state*. The conditions of a rule define the initial state (the class of messages to which the actions apply), and each action transforms the state by adding or deleting facts. For example, the initial state for the rule in Figure 2 is

```
InSpool and
messageType = email and
sender = Julia-Hirschberg and
subject contains "important"
```

`InSpool` is a special tag indicating that the message has not yet been disposed of, i.e., deleted or moved to a folder. All actions have at least one precondition — `InSpool` — which also is the one fact in the delete list of `Move Message`. Thus, adding a `Move Message` action results in the removal of `InSpool` from the current state. If any other actions are subsequently added to the rule, the system will find that they do not apply.

The system has to update the current state whenever an action is added, deleted, or inserted, or the conditions are changed. When an action is added to the end of the plan, all that has to be checked is that action's applicability. Changing the conditions redefines the initial state, so the validity of the whole plan must be rechecked. When an action is inserted into or deleted from the middle of the plan, the whole plan again is checked. (Although the checking could begin from the insertion/deletion point, this would require keeping around previous states and would result in more complex code. Since recomputing plan validity is efficient, we have chosen this route.) Figure 3 summarizes the task of verifying plan validity.

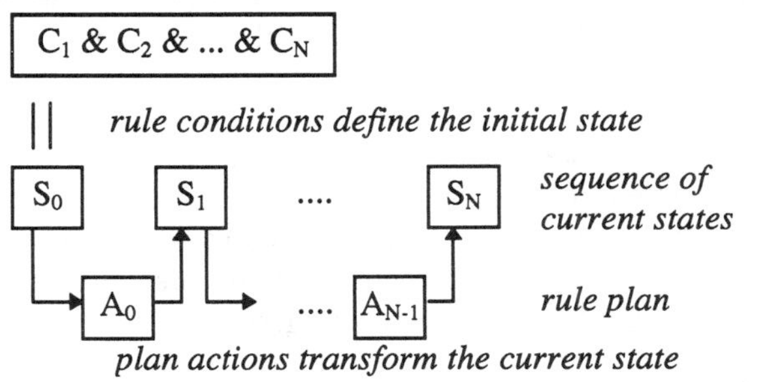

When an action A_i is added, the system first checks that it applies to state S_i, then computes state S_{i+1}.

Figure 3: Verifying Plan Validity Using the Current State

Computing Rule Interactions and Composing Plans

As a user edits a rule, the Agent Manager continuously recomputes its position in the rule hierarchy, thus determining the actions to inherit to the rule from more general rules. Either the locally defined or the inherited actions of a rule may be done first. If the user has not specified an order, the system will prefer the local-first ordering, but if this results in an invalid plan, it will try inherited-first. For example, in Figure 2, if the local `Move Message` action were ordered before the inherited `Copy Message` action, the plan would be invalid, so the system selected the inherited-first ordering.

When a rule is added to the hierarchy, the Agent Manager inherits its plan to all more specific rules. It also considers rules resulting from the intersection of the new rule and its sibling rules. These cases all result in new plans being composed, all of whose validity must be tested. Notice that users become aware of intersection rules only if their plans are invalid.

Categorizing Invalid Rules

When the Agent Manager detects that a rule has an invalid plan, it attempts to categorize the rule as one of a pre-defined set of invalid rule types. For example, the intersection of a rule that files messages by sender (e.g., "move messages from Tom to the folder Tom-Mail") and a rule that files messages by subject (e.g., "move messages with the subject "RDDI" to the folder RDDI-Project") constitutes a common type of problem. The benefit of categorizing problems is that multiple instances of a given category may occur as a user works, and the user may specify that all problems of a particular category should be repaired in the same way.

Computing Explanations and Repairs

When an action in a plan does not apply, the system computes an interactive dialogue that explains why the action does not apply and suggests repairs to the plan that will enable the action. The dialogue contains a component for each unsatisfied precondition of the action. The text is created by composing templates associated with actions, preconditions, and plan modification operators.

If a precondition was deleted by a previous action in the plan, the system looks for alternative actions whose add list is a superset of the defeating action and whose delete list does not contain the unsatisfied precondition. Consider the rule formed from the intersection of

```
messageType = email and
sender = Julia-Hirschberg
==> Move Message "julia", and

messageType = email and
subject contains "important"
==> Move Message "important".
```

The two `Move Message` actions conflict with each other, since each deletes `InSpool` from the current state, and `InSpool` is a precondition of all actions. Since `Copy Message` adds the same facts as `Move Message` (the message is filed), but does not delete `InSpool`, substituting it for one of the `Move Message` actions would result in a valid plan. The following explanation illustrates this type of repair:

> "Move Message" does not apply because
> the effect of a previous "Move Message" action was to move the message out of the mail spool —
> you can take care of this by replacing the previous "Move Message" action by "Copy Message"
> **Do It**[1]

If no action in the plan defeated an unsatisfied precondition, the system looks for actions that satisfy the precondition and do not defeat any other actions in the plan. Consider the rule

```
messageType = Message
==> Play Greeting "Greeting 1"
```

`Play Greeting` applies only to telephone calls, and only after a call has been picked up. Since the action `Pickup Call` results in the call being picked up, inserting it into the plan would repair the second problem. The following explanation illustrates this type of repair:

> "Play Greeting" does not apply because
> 1) the current message is not a Telephone Call —
> you can take care of this by selecting the Message Type Telephone Call
> **Do It**
>
> 2) the call has not yet been picked up —
> you can take care of this by inserting the action "Pickup Call" before "Play Greeting"
> **Do It**

To summarize, the algorithm for computing repairs is:

For each unsatisfied action A
  For each unsatisfied precondition P
    If ∃B in plan before A, and B deletes P
    Then Repairs = {B´ such that B´.add ⊇ B.add & P ∉ B´.delete}
    Else Repairs = {B´ such that P ∈ B´.add & B´ can apply before A & B´ does not defeat any later actions}

Repair Presentation and Interaction

The Agent Manager visually indicates rules with invalid plans and problematic actions in each plan. A user may access the repair dialogue associated with an action by clicking on the action. After the user selects a repair, the system applies the repair, checks the validity of the plan again to see whether the status of any other actions has

[1] When the user presses a **Do It** button, the system performs the specified repair.

changed, and updates the repair dialogue to show the new status of the plan.

After all the problems with a rule have been repaired, the system checks whether (1) the rule was a member of a problem category, and (2) other rules also belong to the same category. In such cases, the system asks whether the user wants the same repairs applied to all other rules in the category.

DISCUSSION

The Agent Manager has evolved through a series of stages, all developed on a PC. The current implementation uses Allegro Common Lisp for Windows and the enhanced version of CLASSIC developed by Alex Borgida and Charles Isbell. The Agent Manager is designed to be a general user programming tool for rule-based agents. However, it must be deployed with some particular agent. We are considering integrating it with Ishmail, an email filtering agent with a significant AT&T user community.

We are exploring several additional avenues of research. First, applying the Agent Manager to a domain other than messaging would verify its generality. Second, extending the Agent Manager to allow users to express dialogue knowledge would enable agents to communicate flexibly with both their owners and other users. Our experience in device-independent interaction design [14] is relevant here. Third, we are exploring an integration of our end-user programming, rule-based approach with machine learning techniques. One interesting issue is how to enable rules stated by users to be taken as "suggestions" by ML programs and how modifications generated by the ML programs may be re-expressed as rules. Finally, we will explore more sophisticated plan repair algorithms.

ACKNOWLEDGMENTS

We thank Alex Borgida and Charles Isbell for their extensions to CLASSIC. We also thank Julia Hirschberg, Henry Kautz, Mark Jones, Bob Klein, Bob Hall, Amir Mané, and Mark Tuomenoksa for many productive conversations about agents. Finally, we thank the anonymous CHI'96 reviewers for their excellent suggestions.

REFERENCES

1. Borgida, A., Brachman, R.J., McGuiness, D.L., and Resnick, L.A. CLASSIC: A Structural Data Model for Objects, in *Proc. SIGMOD'89* (1989).

2. Brachman, R.J., McGuinness, D.L., Patel-Schneider, P.F., Resnick, L.A., and Borgida, A. Living With Classic: When and How to Use a KL-ONE-Like Language, in *Formal Aspects of Semantic Networks*, J. Sowa, Ed., Morgan Kaufmann, Los Altos, CA, 1990.

3. Cypher, A. Eager: Programming Repetitive Tasks by Example, in *Proc. CHI'91* (New Orleans LA, April 1991), ACM Press, 33-39.

4. Cypher, A., Ed. *Watch What I Do: Programming by Demonstration.* MIT Press, Cambridge MA, 1993.

5. Cypher, A. and Smith, D.C. KidSim: End User Programming of Simulation. in *Proc. CHI'95* (Denver CO, May 1995), ACM Press, 27-34.

6. Fikes, R.E. and Nilsson, N.J. STRIPS: A New Approach to the Application of Theorem Proving to Problem Solving. *Artificial Intelligence 2, 3/4* (1971), 189-208.

7. Fischer, G., Nakakoji, K., Ostwald, J., Stahl, G., and Sumner, T. Embedding Computer-Based Critics in the Contexts of Design. in *Proc. INTERCHI'93* (Amsterdam, April 1995), ACM Press, 157-164.

8. Lashkari, Y., Metral, M., and Maes, P. Collaborative Interface Agents, in *Proc. AAAI'94*, (Seattle WA, July 1994), AAAI Press, 444-449.

9. Maes, P. Agents that Reduce Work and Information Overload. *CACM 37, 7* (July 1994), 30-40.

10. Malone, T.W., Lai, K.Y., and Fry, C. Experiments with Oval: A Radically Tailorable Tool for Cooperative Work. *ACM Transactions on Information Systems 13, 2* (April 1995), 177-205.

11. Nardi, B. *A Small Matter of Programming*. MIT Press, Cambridge MA, 1993.

12. Smith, D.C., Cypher, A., and Spohrer, J. KIDSIM: Programming Agents Without a Programming Language, *CACM 37, 7* (July 1994), 55-67.

13. Terveen, L.G. An Overview of Human-Computer Collaboration. *Knowledge-Based Systems 8,2/3* (April-June 1995), 67-31.

14. Terveen, L.G. and Tuomenoksa, M.L. DynaDesigner: A Tool for Rapid Creation of Device-Independent Interactive Services. in *Proc. Interact'95*, (Lillehammer NO, June 1995), Chapman & Hall, 386-389.

15. White, J.E., Telescript Technology: The Foundation for the Electronic Marketplace. General Magic White Paper, 1994.

16. Woodridge, M. and Jennings, N.R. Intelligent Agents: Theory and Practice. *Knowledge Engineering Review* (1995).

A Collaborative Approach to Developing Style Guides

Stephen Gale
AIT Limited
The Malthouse, 45 New Street,
Henley-on-Thames, RG9 2BP, UK.
+44-1491-416600
srg@ait.co.uk

ABSTRACT

A vital element in exploiting the benefits of Graphical User Interfaces (GUIs) is the use of an appropriate Style Guide. This paper outlines a collaborative approach to the development of Style Guides and highlights the associated benefits and pitfalls.

Keywords

Style Guides, Graphical User Interfaces, User Interface Design, Standards

INTRODUCTION

Over the past five years there have been a large number of technological developments which have impacted the availability of technology to business users. Colour displays, windowing systems, mice and icons offer application developers tremendous design freedom. This provides software developers with an opportunity to create truly innovative and creative designs. However, this increased design freedom also provides a greater number of opportunities to produce poor, ineffective designs.

Style Guides have become critical in exploiting the business benefits of GUIs. Although in the graphic design world, Style Guides are not new - many organisations have been using them for decades, but usually only for paper based materials - their application to computer software is still relatively immature.

Shortly after the introduction of the first GUIs the relevant manufacturers started producing Style Guides. The first to appear were developed by Apple for the Macintosh [1], but shortly afterwards both IBM and Microsoft developed Style Guides for Common User Access [2,3] and the Windows [4,5,6] platform respectively. While these guides have gained moderate acceptance, in practice they have not provided developers with sufficient detail; it is still possible to produce radically different user interfaces all of which comply with the relevant Style Guide.

CHI 96 Vancouver, BC Canada
© 1996 ACM 0-89791-777-4/96/04..$3.50

As a consequence, end user organisations have started to develop their own Style Guides which add detail and higher level guidance to the industry standard guides. For these organisations there are a number of motivating factors:

- They may have a large, and growing, number of GUI developments. In some cases, these organisations are trying to build an integrated environment where a number of applications are presented to the end user as a single coherent system. Consistent user interfaces are critical in these cases.
- A lack of consistency between applications is a very clear problem - you don't have to be a usability expert to be able to spot it!
- While the process of applying Human Computer Interaction (HCI) can be viewed as a change in perspective and possibly culture, a Style Guide is something tangible that can be funded and has clear definable outputs.
- The proliferation of different GUI platforms and development tools has increased the risk of inconsistent user interfaces dramatically.

With the advent of customer facing systems, (i.e. systems that are used in front of the customer) another requirement has started to emerge - to ensure consistent communication of a corporate image to customers. For many financial and retail organisations, where similar products are offered, it is important to differentiate not just by product, but also on image and service quality. This image can only be communicated effectively and systematically with customers if it is present throughout all product and corporate literature, whether computer or paper based. Hence the importance of a Style Guide.

STYLE GUIDES

What is a Style Guide?

The objectives of a Style Guide are to:

- Promote visual and functional consistency within and between different applications;
- Promote good design practice;
- Reinforce company branding or an organisation's public image.

Visual consistency ensures that applications appear the same in terms of colour, icons etc. whereas functional consistency ensures that the application operates in the same manner, e.g. the same metaphors are used for browsing data records.

It is well known in HCI literature that consistency is important:

- Once users have learnt how to use one application this knowledge will be applicable to other applications. This will minimise the amount of training required as well as encouraging users to use and explore different applications;
- Consistent applications will help staff to appear confident and competent in front of customers. This will improve the customer's perception of staff service. This is particularly important in customer facing situations;
- Consistency between the applications will allow the different project teams to share code, whether it is via custom controls or some other means. This will not only reduce the implementation time, but also produces less code which in the longer term will be easier and more cost effective to maintain. This is particularly important with GUIs where increasing amounts of code are associated with the user interface.

However, ensuring consistency does not ensure usability. Although an application may be highly consistent, it does not automatically follow that the application will be useful. Compliance with a low level Style Guide will ensure consistency. However, it will not ensure that the applications themselves perform the tasks required either by the end users or the business. Ensuring that the applications contain the appropriate functionality is usually the joint responsibility of the relevant business and IT departments. However, incorporating HCI principles which help ensure ease of use and minimise learning of the application should be an objective of a comprehensive Style Guide.

Consistency can be enforced by standardising on bad as well as good design and one of the necessities of a Style Guide is that it is built on good practice. As the body of knowledge of user interface design expands Style Guides will evolve.

Contents

While the exact content of a Style Guide may vary, the following format has been used successfully in a number of cases. The contents will depend on a number of factors:

- Internationalisation might not be an issue for some companies;
- The development methodology used;
- The type of systems and end users involved;
- The level of integration with existing guides.

TABLE OF CONTENTS

About this document
Who should use this Style Guide
When to use this Style Guide
How to use this Style Guide

DESIGN PRINCIPLES
What is usability
Why usability is important
Developing appropriate functionality
Strive for consistency
Aim for flexibility
Ensure visual clarity
Use colour effectively
Allow reversible actions
....

BUILDING APPLICATIONS
Navigation
Interaction Style
Feedback
Presentation of information
- When to use graphs
- When to use tables
Help
.....

APPLICATION COMPONENTS
Message boxes
Toolbars
Forms
Card Index
....

USER INTERFACE COMPONENTS
Buttons
Text boxes
Fields and Field labels
Scroll bars
Option buttons
.....

INTERNATIONALISATION
- Language Considerations
- GUI Considerations

COMPATIBILITY WITH OTHER STYLE GUIDES
- Microsoft
  - Windows 3.1 standards
  - Microsoft Office Compliance
  - Migrating to Windows 95
- IBM
  - Common User Access 91
  - Common User Access 93
- Motif

TERMINOLOGY
COMPLIANCE CHECK LIST
RESPONSE FORM
- Your comments
- How to ensure you get the latest release
- Where to get help

Benefits

As with many activities in user interface design the objectives are relatively straightforward, however, there are a wide variety of benefits.

From the end user perspective, the following benefits may be obtained from a Style Guide:

- Reduced errors - less frustration;
- Increased confidence in the system;
- Reduced training requirements;
- Increased morale;
- Improved use of system functionality;
- Improved productivity;
- Reduced resistance to the use of new technology.

However, other groups can also expect to benefit from the use of a Style Guide. From the IT developers' perspective, Style Guides may have the following benefits:

- Maintain control over look and feel;
- Control 3rd parties during the tendering and implementation phases;
- Reduce arbitrary design decisions and re-invention;
- Capitalise on learning/iteration;
- Enable production of re-usable software;
- Reduce development time.

From the Business perspective, there are a number of potential benefits:

- Produce usable systems enhancing customer service/satisfaction;
- Increase market awareness;
- Increase product awareness;
- Reduce training costs;
- Facilitate helpline support;
- Improve staff retention;
- Increase user acceptance of new systems.

When all these benefits are taken into account the case for developing a Style Guide can be very persuasive. However, many organisations have failed to reap the benefits. The remainder of this paper looks at why and presents an alternative approach.

REASONS WHY STYLE GUIDES FAIL

Obviously different Style Guides fail for different reasons. Many organisations have tried on more than one occasion to solve the "Style Guide problem". The following is a list of the more common reasons for failure:

- Often the documentation runs into hundreds of pages. The material becomes difficult to use and read. It is ironic that many of the existing Style Guides, aimed at producing usable systems, are themselves difficult to use.
- The guide attempts to be too prescriptive and tackle too many application domains or different types of end users. The result is that it is not appropriate for a number of target applications.
- The document is never updated - either because no one realises that it needs to be updated or because no one is sure about who should update it.
- Little consideration is given to how the Style Guide is introduced into the organisation - there is no supporting material and no one is there to encourage developers to use it. When there are problems there is no one around to listen and amend the guide (if necessary).
- Often the use of the Style Guide alone is perceived to solve the "usability problem". For example, many organisations seem to believe that once a Style Guide is in place no further action is required to ensure usability. The production of a Style Guide is seen as a substitute for iterative design and user testing.
- Another group, or person, is perceived to be responsible for the system's usability and the development team are no longer responsible for the usability of their own system.
- Developers and users are not involved in the content and development of the Style Guide.
- The guide does not address how it should be used in practice or how it should be integrated with development methods.

AN ALTERNATIVE APPROACH

In order to overcome these issues we have developed an alternative approach based on involving developers and end users throughout the production of the Style Guide. The approach involves 5 steps:

1. *Raising awareness amongst developers and end users*

   Often it is assumed that both the developers and end users understand the rationale for developing the Style Guide. This assumption is often not correct and leads to misunderstandings later in the process. Including management in this awareness raising process often pays dividends later on.

2. *Building consensus*
   One of the most successful approaches has been built on the use of a working party consisting of key developers and end users from each of the teams within the organisations. On a weekly basis over a period of 2 months specific topics (e.g. Keyboard Interaction, Navigation, Terminology) are presented to the working party for their review and input. This material is subsequently revised and forms a chapter in the Style Guide.

3. *Documenting the Style Guide*
   Only once a certain level of consensus has been reached, is the Style Guide documented. This approach ensures that the commitment and understanding of the developers is gained and the best of their ideas are documented.

4. *Providing training and support material*
   The way the document is introduced into the organisation is critical. The document should be supported by the use of training and support materials. The members of the working party who help develop the guide preferably provide the introductory presentations and the subsequent training.

5. *Establishing an environment which enables the guide to evolve*
   In many organisations evolution is perceived to be another word for "putting right previous mistakes". The Style Guide should be viewed as a repository for good ideas and this will constitute a body of knowledge which will grow over time. This is often the most difficult part of the approach to control, particularly because it is so dependant on an organisation's culture. The creation of this environment can be facilitated by using presentations, workshops, seminars, bulletin boards and roadshows.

As well as these five steps there are other aspects which are inherent in this approach.

Integrated with the development process
If a Style Guide is to be successful it must be designed to support the development methods being used. One of the most frequent problems with Style Guides is that they do not address the different ways in which they could be used. In fact, frequently the Style Guide is not aimed at supporting any kind of development process.

A critical part of the production of a Style Guide is understanding the development environment and culture of an organisation.

Getting it right in the first place
Style Guides are often used as a means of checking the conformance of a user interface once it has been implemented. While this is a valid use of a Style Guide it is not the most productive.

Our experience is that the Style Guide is best used from the outset of the project. With one organisation that we have worked with the Style Guide is taught to all new Visual Basic programmers. This organisation now has a number of developers that routinely use the Style Guide and would not consider developing a user interface without it.

Allowing evolution
The Style Guide must be based on good practice and as the organisation learns more about what is appropriate in their particular environment this knowledge need to be incorporated into the guide.

This evolution relies on setting the guide in the correct context and establishing a process that deals with requests for change impartially.

Communicate strong visual and functional style
The challenge here is to produce designs which are distinctive, but still conform with the industry standards. Maintaining a distinctive look and feel, while allowing the guide to evolve, presents a significant challenge. In addition, in many organisations their corporate image is constantly evolving.

Encompass relevant platforms and functionality
The scope of the Style Guide may have to be restricted as it is impossible to have a guide which will cover all systems - from back office to customer facing touchscreen systems.

Developed alongside a development team
Often Style Guides are developed in isolation from "real" projects. The result is a Style Guide that is impractical and frequently un-implementable in the chosen development environment. In addition, developers will often resist using the guide because they have not been involved in its production.

Our approach has been to develop the Style Guide alongside a development team and immerse ourselves in a real development project. From the development team's perspective, they receive HCI and graphic design input into their project. From the Style Guide team's perspective we know that the designs are practical and implementable. In our experience this is the quickest and most effective way of gaining commitment to the use of the guide.

This approach also has the added advantage that this is often the quickest way of ensuring an early success. Once developers realise that the Style Guide can improve their project, other projects are often very quick to follow suit.

Not just a document

Developers do not tend to read large documents. Ultimately we are attempting to change the way software is developed and if we want to achieve this it will be difficult to achieve via documentation alone. In our experience, other communication methods must be used. In the past we have produced:

- Interactive demonstrations to illustrate the look and feel. Some of these demonstrations have a mode which allow developers to browse the layout of the screen to pixel level;
- Checklists to ensure conformity;
- Reference tables for quick reference of critical data. These have been produced as "bumper stickers" which developers have attached to their monitors;
- Competitions to spot the deliberate mistakes in a user interface design. This was originally based on an idea by Molich and Nielsen [7], but later GUI versions were developed;
- Source code, custom controls and property tables which promote sharing user interface code.

Skills transfer

Often organisations find there is a shortfall in the skills required to develop these new GUI based applications. The most obvious skill is that of graphic design - once a niche skill restricted to those involved in paper based communication, but now particularly relevant in user interface design.

Our approach is to provide training, on an informal as well as a formal basis. However, our preferred approach is to work alongside a development team and develop the Style Guide with them. In our experience, this is the most effective and quickest way of developing a practical, usable Style Guide.

Ensuring ownership

This is one of the key factors and often one of the most difficult to achieve, particularly when the Style Guide has been put together by a third party. This collaborative approach to developing a Style Guide greatly helps to produce a feeling of ownership, however, a group or individual in the organisation must be identified as being responsible for the maintenance and updating of the guide. Such individuals often become the focal point for the guide and end up providing developers with ad hoc advice on generic user interface design issues.

DISCUSSION

For many organisations the production of a Style Guide is the first time they have come into contact with HCI specialists. Although there are a great many benefits to be gained there are also a number of pitfalls. If HCI as a function is going to gain the confidence and respect of the business and IT communities we must ensure that this initial contact is as fruitful as possible.

The issue of Style Guides raises some interesting issues for the HCI community:

- Rather than being concerned with document production, Style Guides are about changing culture and influencing developers. If one set out explicitly to change the way people work our first choice would not be to write a document. Style Guides are about winning hearts and minds.
- Style Guides also raise the issue of the difference between analysis and design and the difference in the skill sets required. The majority of HCI is based upon analysis and amongst many practitioners there seems to be a belief that design is just another form of analysis. However, the skills required to design something are very different (although complimentary) to being able to analyse something. For example, can an art critic paint?

  The answer to this particular issue lies in the combination of graphic design and HCI - neither party has the total answer - but both are holding different pieces of the same jigsaw puzzle.
- It is important that Style Guides are positioned properly in the development lifecycle. It is also important that their limitations are fully understood. On a number of occasions Style Guides have been seen to be the panacea to an organisation's usability problems. Whereas a clear definition of a systems requirements might have been more appropriate.
- A number of practitioners seem to perceive their role to be one of policing a Style Guide. While this is a valid role on certain occasions (and only then when accompanied with constructive criticism), a much more positive role would be for the practitioners to help get the design right from the outset. This again raises the issue of the difference between analysis and design.
- The Style Guide should be well presented and easy to use. It is ironic that many commercially available Style Guides are difficult to use - either because of poor structure or layout.
- The guide should be designed for the intended use - it should be easy to read, cross referenced and ideally available in softcopy.

If you are a developer or business user you might like to consider the following:

- Many of the benefits of a Style Guide are not directly related to the guide itself, but are the consequence of ensuring different implementation activities are co-ordinated. As a consequence of the production of Style Guides one organisation decided to set up a database of error messages (once they had been sorted out for one application the customer decided to share them across applications) and of custom controls (where different custom controls are used to perform very similar operations).
- Be aware of the pitfalls. The majority of them are related to the soft side of implementation and there are a number of ways avoiding them, e.g. making sure the key influencers are involved, making sure the views of the end users are taken into account.
- Make sure developers feel involved throughout the lifecycle. It is important that the developers feel that the Style Guide is theirs and it has not been imposed on them by senior management.
- Standards are often perceived as boring, out of date, old fashioned and slowing down development. If the Style Guide is perceived in this light then it is unlikely to succeed.
- Appropriate development methodologies for GUIs are still emerging. In many organisations different development teams are using different methods, in some cases it almost seems as if they are making it up as they go along on a per project basis. This makes it very difficult to integrate a Style Guide.
- Style Guides also have a role in end user involvement. Frequently, the difference in vocabulary between developers and users is so great that it can become a barrier to forming a successful partnership. Style Guides, because of their very graphical nature can help solve this problem.

CONCLUSION

The most effective Style Guides are not those that are imposed on developers by senior management, but those that have been developed with the developers themselves so that they perceive the Style Guide as being "theirs".

This paper outlines a collaborative approach to developing Style Guides. We have used the term collaborative because if the Style Guide is to be successful then it must be developed in conjunction with the software developers and end users. This approach has been used successfully with a number of different commercial organisations.

ACKNOWLEDGEMENTS

I would like to acknowledge the contributions of my colleagues at AIT, particularly Tracy Ashdown, Morgan Lynch, Jane Watts, Anil Patel and Garf Collins. Of our many clients, particular thanks to Daniel Jordan at the National Westminster Bank Plc and Lesley Hancock at Marks and Spencer Plc with whom we worked very successfully in applying and refining this approach.

REFERENCES

1. Apple Computers, Inc. *Macintosh Human Interface Guidelines.* Addison-Wesley, Reading, MA., 1992.
2. IBM Corporation, *Common User Access: Advanced Interface Design Guide.* IBM, 1989. (Part no. SC26-4582).
3. IBM Corporation, *Object-Oriented Interface Design: IBM Common User Access Guidelines.* QUE. 1992.
4. Microsoft Corporation, *The Windows Interface: An Application Design Guide.* Microsoft Press, Redmond, WA.,. 1992.
5. Microsoft Corporation, *Microsoft Windows 95 User Interface Design Guide: Preliminary Draft 5.00.* Microsoft Corp. October 1994
6. Microsoft Corporation, *The Windows Interface Guidelines for Software Design.* Microsoft Press, Redmond, WA., 1995.
7. Molich, R. and Nielsen, J. Improving a Human-Computer Dialogue. *Communications of the ACM*, 33(3), (March 1990), 338-348.

Integrating Human Factors in Customer Support Systems development using a multi-level organisational approach.

Anne Miller
Customer Support Platform Usability Team
Information Technology Group
Telstra, Australia
E-mail: amiller@vitgdts1.telecom.com.au

ABSTRACT

Integrating usability into software development projects involves working across multiple organisational levels. Aligning the Customer Support Platform Usability (CSPU) Teams objectives with those of the organisation allowed more effective integration of usability activities within project teams. Primarily, corporate alignment provided a legitimate mandate for the CSPU Team to develop standards and guidelines, and to require that usability activities be undertaken by project teams. However, at the project team level, integration was achieved by definition of roles, activities and processes according to the objectives, constraints and processes of project teams. Achieving common ground in project teams involved a willingness to work with, and to actively adapt to both organisational and project based needs.

Key words
human factors; usability; corporate mandate; Graphical User Interface; systems development life cycle; standards and guidelines; resourcing.

INTRODUCTION

The CSPU Team was formed within Telstra in August 1994 for the purpose of implementing usability in Customer Support Systems, (i.e. computer systems used by Telstra's customer facing staff). The Teams establishment and development bears a striking similarity to efforts described by Billingsley (1995), at Union Pacific Railroad. Like Billingsley (1995), formation of the CSPU Team:

- Involved forming a *new usabilty group,* (i.e. the CSPU Team), within Telstra,
- Was part of a *broader strategy* spearheaded by Dr. Gitte Lindgaard at the Telstra Research Laboratories, (TRL), to more effectively integrate human factors principles into product development projects,
- Depended on *preliminary planning* to align the CSPU Team's objectives with those of the organisation,
- Recruited and *utilised senior managers* to represent the aspirations of the CSPU Team at senior management levels,
- *Selected projects* that helped the CSPU Team develop methods and processes for effective involvement in project teams, and,
- Developed strategies that *promoted knowledge transfer and incentives* for project team involvement in usability activities.

However, unlike Billingsley's (1995), experience at Union Pacific Railroad, Telstra:

- Is a public service utility, (rather than a private enterprise), which had developed an organisational culture similar to that described by Lund (1994), at Ameritech, i.e. up until the late 1980's, Telstra was a monopoly; it was not market oriented; it was slow to introduce new products; and there was an expectation among employees that they would begin and end their working lives with Telstra,
- Has been subject to substantial organisational restructuring that, according to Moyal (1984), involved regionalising (or decentralising), centralised State and headquarter management in the mid 1970's,
- Already had a well-established Human Factors Research Group (HFRG), at TRL, which was having difficulty integrating human factors principles into product development across the organisation.

In this climate, successful integration of usability principles within project teams required substantial cultural change across multiple levels within Telstra.

This was recognised by Lindgaard (1995), as being "no mean feat".

Lindgaard (1995), states that, "if we want to ensure serious application of human factors principles in all telecommunications products, we are forced to bring about significant cultural change in design and development philosophy and approach in our organisation" (p. 362).

Effecting cultural change required:

- An understanding of present day problems as the result of past decision making, e.g. system incompatiblity and inconsistency were a consequence of regionalisation,
- An understanding of current organisational objectives, with the ability to define human factors potential in terms of global organisational goals. This meant moving from what Lindgaard (1995), describes as "putting out fires" at the end of project development to 'legislating' for human factors across entire projects at the level of Strategy and Direction departments, (this process is described in detail by Lindgaard, 1995), and,
- Integration of usability activities and personnel within projects by developing an understanding of, and a willingness to be involved with project teams on their terms.

ORGANISATIONAL CONTEXT

Historically within Telstra, 1970's regionalisation and organisational separation into relatively autonomous business units, had resulted in poor communication and a relative lack of organisational integration. This lead to fragmented and often isolated development of customer support applications. The net result was that applications were built using a variety of platforms that were not always consistent or compatible with one another, despite similar functionality.

By the late 1980's, senior management was addressing system inconsistency and incompatibility problems across the organisation. A key element in this process was Telstra's Information Technology Group (ITG), who in 1991, published the 'Overall Systems Architecture Strategy' (the 'Blue Book'). The 'Blue Book' set out a strategic framework for integrating technological operating systems around largely independent core business activities.

The second phase of the 'Overall Systems Architecture Strategy' was to link the separate technology bases. The most recent update of this strategy, the 'Overall Systems Architecture Phase 2 Update', 1994, defined the architectural framework for all computer systems within Telstra. Identification of opportunities for systems rationalisation through standardised convergence, and reuse was also a major objective.

In addition, Dr. Deborah Zinn, (a senior manager in ITG's Strategy and Direction department), outlined, within the Overall Systems Architecture, a sub-strategy for Customer Support Systems. Customer Support Systems are defined as, "applications that support the interface between the Customer and Telstra for all Customer Sales, Service and Support activities" (p. 10, Overall Systems Architecture Phase 2 Update, 1994).

Within this context, Dr. Gitte Lindgaard, (a manager at TRL), argued that usable interfaces were critical to effective customer support. As a consequence, usability was identified as one of five key principles driving development of all applications used by customer facing staff. Under this principle usability specialists would be employed to:

"implement standards for usability leading to ease-of-use and a common look and feel across all systems used by customer facing staff". (p.10, Overall Systems Architecture Phase 2 Update, 1994).

This single phrase was critical. It provided a corporate mandate for usability within Customer Support System development projects within Telstra. The next step was implementation of the mandate.

THE CUSTOMER SUPPORT PLATFORM USABILITY TEAM

Dr. Lindgaard and Dr. Zinn were highly instrumental in advocating for, and forming the CSPU Team, which was initially comprised of two human factors researchers from TRL and three members from the Hiser Consulting Group (HCG). The CSPU Team later recruited four new staff members over a twelve month period. These people, with other recruits will form the permanent CSPU Team, allowing TRL and HCG personnel to be gradually phased out. Other external consultants were recruited on a needs basis.

The professional composition of the CSPU Team was an important ingredient in a multi-level organisational approach. Experimental psychologists from TRL contributed a sound understanding of Telstra's corporate culture and a strong track record in human factors research. However, these people had very little experience applying human factors methods outside of the research environment. Conversely, the HCG was known to Dr. Zinn as having considerable expertise in designing Graphical User Interfaces (GUI's), while working closely with project teams in large public and private sector organisations. The HCG contributed highly experienced human factors specialists, and an ergonomist. Later recruits contributed skill in industrial and organisational psychology, industrial and interaction design, systems analysis, computer programming, and education.

This multi-disciplinary mix of expertise allowed high levels of flexibility and responsiveness at levels of:

- The organisation, as the CSPU Teams survival depended on appropriate strategy development which was communicated at senior and middle management levels,
- Project teams and work groups, in terms of understanding group processes and dynamics,
- Applied human factors expertise, which was utilised at the level of application users, and,
- Application design, in terms of ability to meet increasingly complex design problems with innovative solutions.

The CSPU Team's first goal was to demonstrate that usability could be integrated within existing project development teams.

Four strategically significant Customer Support development projects were targeted for usability intervention, involvement or activities. All projects were building applications for use by customer facing staff, and all involved the development of GUI's. One project was 'green-fields', (i.e. it had no precedent prior to conceptualisation), one was a project of high organisational significance that was near deployment, (organisational significance being defined according to the number of users affected, i.e. in excess of 2000 internal staff, and the estimated total budget of the project), and two projects in early stages of development.

One CSPU Team member was allocated to work on-site with each of the targeted project teams. Often, inexperienced CSPU Team members worked with more experienced staff, who acted as mentors. On-site Team members returned to a central location for a four hour meeting once per week to provide feedback about on-site involvement; to raise issues and to develop group strategies for solving a multiplicity of problems. Many methods and techniques used in the field, as well as screen design ideas, were developed in these sessions that often followed a workshop type format. These sessions were an important mechanism for knowledge sharing and transfer among CSPU Team members.

IMPLEMENTING SOFTWARE USABILITY IN PROJECT TEAMS

While allocating CSPU Team members to project teams was a relatively easy task, integrating usability activities within project development was another issue entirely. Project teams had not been required to include usability specialists in development teams; they did not understand the role of usability specialists and were concerned that inclusion would increase development time and expense.

Overcoming these obstacles involved a two pronged approach.

The first approach involved 'legislating' for the inclusion of usability expertise in project development. At Telstra projects pass through a project control process known as the Gating process. This is administered by ITG and ensures that all significant projects conform to the Overall Systems Architecture Strategy. The mechanism by which conformity is ensured is the allocation of funding, i.e. projects must complete key activities in order to receive funding for the next stage. By including usability tasks (e.g. user profiling; task analysis) as requirements for progression to the next gate, CSPU Team involvement became essential, as these tasks required specialist expertise.

The second approach was education. Required inclusion could not ensure that usability principles would actually be embraced by development teams. And further, mandatory requirements tended to cast the CSPU Team in the role of 'usability police'. As a result CSPU Team services were often requested too late, and recommendations involved substantial changes to work already completed. This fuelled the view that usability was too expensive and caused unnecessary delay.

To change this perception the CSPU Team organised presentations to project, as well as business unit managers. Presentations focussed on defining usability and its benefits in reduced training costs, enhanced user productivity and greater likelihood of user acceptance. The latter emerged as a key area of concern for project managers, since poor user acceptance often negatively affected the professional reputations of project team members, both from the point of view of negative user attitudes, and from the perspective of increased cost in post-deployment redesign work.

The CSPU Team also embarked on a policy of project team participation in almost every area of work. The Team strongly pushed for project team member involvement in usability activities. Project representatives were recruited as advisers, observers, as well as data collectors. This had the dual outcome of educating project members about usability activities, and by exposing these people to problems experienced by actual users, recommendations had a greater chance of being accepted as legitimate and justified.

In as much as project teams learnt about usability, CSPU Team members benefited from exposure to the day to day problems experienced by project teams. CSPU Team members knew that early involvement was critical to successfully integrating usability principles, but had only a broad understanding of development processes. The CSPU Team could not identify exactly what was required, when, and hence could not make accurate recommendations about specific usability activities or the timing of CSPU Team involvement.

Clearly the CSPU Team needed a better understanding of development processes. Drawing on Ernst & Young's Navigator System Series - Version 3.0®, (E&YNSS), documentation (a prevailing development method used at Telstra), and with the experience of HCG personnel, the CSPU Team explicitly defined usability activities in terms of phases of the systems development life cycle. This enabled the Team to:

- Identify existing processes, that could be used, modified or supplemented by usability input. For example, Design Facilitated Sessions, (an E&YNSS process in the Client/Server Development module), were augmented by natural workflow studies similar to those advocated by Holtzblatt and Jones (1993), and PICTIVE design sessions, (see Muller [1993]).
- Define not only the information or techniques required at various stages, but also the level of measurement required, i.e. population statistics at the project definition phase and sample statistics for the analysis phase. This facilitated better planning.
- Determine more accurately the cost to project teams of additional usability activities, e.g. design workshops were not identified as a requirement of the Gating process, but facilitated participatory design sessions were perceived as beneficial by project teams who had been finding their own methods inadequate.
- Identify the flow of information within the development process, i.e. the results of Contextual Inquiry, (Holtzblatt & Jones, 1993), or hierarchical task analysis, (Lindgaard, 1994), fed directly into natural workflow diagrams that were used in the design phase. This reduced unnecessary or redundant analyses.

Clearly defining the systems development life cycle also taught the CSPU Team the language of project teams. This allowed better communication of the Teams role and relevance.

An example of the effects of language differences, leading to poor communication, was the term 'task analysis'. Project managers, when asked whether they had completed a 'task analysis' as required by the Gating process, invariably replied that 'yes, they had'. When asked how this had been completed and by whom, CSPU Team members were told that business requirements had been documented by business analysts, and data flow requirements had been completed by systems analysts. This, according to Project managers, constituted a 'task analysis', but was clearly not a 'task analysis' as conducted by usability specialists. To avoid confusion the CSPU Team has since renamed its 'task analysis', to 'natural workflow analysis', which better describes and differentiates this process from other task related processes.

Systems development life cycle definition had a second outcome. The different groups comprising the CSPU Team, i.e. TRL and HCG, had very different approaches to applied research. TRL personnel preferred more experimentally 'correct' approaches, while HCG preferred a 'user centred' design approach. TRL expressed the need for accurately defined and well constructed studies that ensured accurate information and hence decision making. HCG emphasised the need for efficiency, project member acceptance of usability, and knowledge transfer.

At a more practical level, problems were being identified with some methods used in the field, particularly as the CSPU Team was encouraging project member participation. For example:

- Some methods e.g. a formal Task Analysis, took too long,
- Project team members and user representatives did not have the observation skills required to accurately time subtasks, or identify user errors,
- Use of video technology as a data collection tool drew an angry response from public sector trade unions and was abandoned,
- When working with customer facing staff, individual differences in the style of service provision and the general randomness of customer enquires and problems meant that environmental conditions could not be controlled as in the experimental setting, and it was argued that these situations should not be controlled, and,
- Opportunities to interact with customer facing staff as they worked were also extremely limited. It was

not uncommon to conduct studies using 4-6 participants.

Identifying stages within the systems development life cycle played a key role in resolving these issues. Process definition allowed the CSPU Team to determine:

- Stages where highly structured methods were appropriate, e.g. formal usability testing was used for assessing electronic prototypes prior to full development,
- Stages where information could be checked against results of previous studies or information seeking activities within the same project, if less rigorous methods or small samples were used, e.g. user profiling could be used to check the reliability of demographic information accessed from human resource departments,
- Stages where participatory approaches could be incorporated, e.g. PICTIVE sessions, (see Muller, 1993), were appropriate during design phases as participatory design workshops,
- Frequently and infrequently used methods, e.g. conceptual walkthrough's, (Lindgaard, 1994), were rarely used whereas heuristic evaluation, (Lindgaard, 1994), and Standards Compliance Assessments developed by the CSPU Team, where used frequently,
- Gaps in the CSPU Team's tools and techniques repository, e.g. specific user profile questionnaires.

By focussing on questions like 'what information do we need at this stage and why', the CSPU Team selected methods appropriate to this question and circumvented arguments about appropriate methods based purely on ideological or philosophical grounds.

Uncertainty about the utility of different levels of measurement, e.g. population versus sample measures, also emerged as an issue. In particular, project teams had been requesting information about the cost justification of software usability. As the CSPU Team had not conducted cost-benefit analysis studies previously, there was a need to establish usability benchmarks by which benefits could be quantified early in the development life cycle.

The question became 'What variables could reflect benefits of usable applications and how should these be measured?' Possible alternatives included staff turnover and attrition rates, and formal training time; this data being collected at the level of the various customer facing staff populations. Other indices included comparisons between mean or median common task completion times prior to application development and post application development; this data being collected at the level of samples.

More recently, the number of post-deployment change requests resulting from interface inadequacies, e.g. failure of customer facing staff to perceive critical information as a result of inappropriate screen placement, has also emerged as a possible indicator of benefit. It is expected that the number of post-deployment interface change requests would be much less for projects including usability expertise, than for projects with no or limited usability involvement. Fewer change requests would reduce post-deployment cost, given that interface redesign is said to be more expensive after deployment, than if inadequacies had been identified and resolved earlier, e.g. during prototyping.

Hence, defining the systems development life cycle allowed the CSPU Team to better understand the types of information; appropriate levels of measurement and the most efficient tools and techniques required at different phases. Using this approach also circumvented heated debate about the appropriateness of different types of methods and measures.

THE ROLE OF STANDARDS.

Prior to establishing the CSPU Team, the HFRG at TRL had published the Human Factors Kit, (HFK), as a set of standards and guidelines for the design and implementation of usable technology within Telstra. The HFK is discussed in detail by Burger (1995), and Lindgaard (1995). Suffice it to say here, that the HFK was a decisive and important instrument with a range of strategic benefits for usability i.e.:

- As a set of eight small booklets the HFK introduced and explained the importance of human factors principles in technological design, in language accessible to non-human factors professionals,
- It explained and illustrated by scenarios, common methods used in human factors research,
- It described and outlined when and how in broad terms, human factors could be included into a broad range of projects, not just in the development of GUI's,
- In electronic form it could be broadly accessed,
- It operationalised and made tangible often abstract concepts.

MAKING THE STANDARDS A REALITY WITHIN PROJECTS.

Despite its success the HFK had several problems:

- As a general document it was often difficult to apply in very specific circumstances,

- The kit tended to prescribe methods, but gave very limited advice regarding how these could be modified to suit different situations and constraints,
- Some of the methods described required considerable human factors skill,
- As a set of eight documents, the HFK tended to overwhelm. It was often difficult to navigate through if one wanted a solution to a specific problem, and,
- The kit was developed outside the processes by which project teams worked, hence some recommended activities were not appropriate to the realities of project development.

Also prior to formation of the CSPU Team, Telstra had commissioned, on the recommendation of Dr. Zinn, the HCG to develop a set of standards, (the Customer Support Systems Usability Standards and Guidelines), specific to software design for Customer Support Systems. These standards leveraged initial work done in the HFK, but were written specifically for use by projects teams designing either Graphical or Character Based User Interfaces for customer facing staff.

However, the introduction of standards has long been difficult. For those who write or advocate them, standards embody principles that move a technological device towards an abstracted ideal, for example, 'common look and feel'.

For those required to conform to them, standards can be perceived as a set of inflexible rules, a time consuming nuisance, and a limitation on the creative input of non-human factors interface designers. Initially the task for the CSPU Team was not so much to ensure that the standards were adhered to, (the policing role), as much as it was to evangelise and make concrete the 'common look and feel'. This involved addressing questions, such as:

- What will the application look like if standards are implemented?
- Can we demonstrate that the standards conforming interface is qualitatively and quantifiably better than the alternative?
- Can we show project teams that the development process is made easier; less time consuming; more successful in terms of user acceptance if the standards are conformed to?

The answer to these questions was 'yes', but only if there was a visual embodiment of the standards, that could be tested with users and demonstrated to project teams. This involved designing a standards compliant electronic prototype, the Corporate Graphical User Interface, (CGUI).

However, if the prototype was to be successful it needed to account for the same problems that project teams encountered. Most importantly, it needed to fit the needs of users.

Early in its life, the CSPU Team worked with a 'greenfields' project for customer facing staff dealing with Commercial (small business) and Consumer (residential) customers. Involvement in this project allowed CSPU Team members to lever off already completed analysis work, and to conduct participatory design sessions similar to those described by Holtzblatt and Jones (1993), and others, (see, Constantine & Lockwood, 1994). This involvement resulted in the first iteration of the 'common look and feel' interface, and allowed informed elaboration of the first version of the Customer Support Systems Usability Standards and Guidelines.

However, as the CSPU Team became involved with a broader range of projects, the 'one-fits-all-situations' prototype began to founder as a result of different user requirements. For example, applications designed for use by customer facing staff servicing large corporate customers required far more sophisticated design solutions compared to applications designed for use by customer facing staff servicing domestic consumers.

In resolving this problem, the CSPU Team observed that applications shared some commonalities irrespective of situational complexity. For example, function and 'hot' key allocation, colour schemes, application entry points, gross navigation techniques, the look and behaviour of application and document windows, and dialogue boxes could be standardised within a skeletal framework, irrespective of the complexity of customer requirements.

Variation arose in the behaviour of on-screen elements. For example, widgets allowing customer facing staff to order single services for a domestic consumer required design solutions quite different to solutions allowing single or multiple services to be ordered for organisations divided into regions and then into individual branch outlets.

More recently, the CGUI has taken the form of a basic or skeletal framework, into which a range of design options of varying complexity can be modified and inserted according to need.

An added advantage of this approach is ability to demonstrate various design possibilities. To illustrate, this writer recently had a delightful experience, (while facilitating a design workshop with users and developers), of meeting the challenge that "the current application works perfectly well, thankyou", with a demonstration of a range of more efficient alternatives. This demonstration immediately broadened participants' horizons of what was possible. It also generated a range of sometimes 'wild' additional alternatives, and a complete change of attitude from scepticism to creative involvement on the part of participants. Demonstration allowed participants to move beyond constraints of the familiar.

Standards compliance does not, however, ensure usable interfaces. To ensure that new design solutions are usable, all prototype applications, with CSPU Team involvement, are tested for usability as part of the development process.

Another outcome, in the evolving story of the CGUI are requests from project teams for reusable on-screen objects templates. This will increasingly involve the development of libraries of re-usable on screen elements and widgets; icon libraries; and libraries of standard language and terminology. These initiatives are expected to:

- Reduce development time by reducing the need to re-design on-screen elements and code with each new project, and by reducing the time spent debating a broad range of design alternatives, and,
- Increase user acceptance of the final product, as designs involve considerable input from and testing with users.

The next step in development of the standards and the CGUI is cost-benefit justification studies.

By shifting the emphasis on 'Standards - a set of rules' to 'Standards - a practical and creative tool' more applications are expected to converge to a standards compliant user interface.

RESOURCING USABILITY

With greater acceptance of usability within project teams, requests for CSPU Team involvement has increased.

As a small group (the CSPU Team is not anticipated to grow beyond 8-10 permanent members), resourcing has become a problem. The Team can not place members in every project. Education in the form of skills transfer provides a solution.

Recently CSPU Team members developed a series of workshops aimed as providing project teams with a 'do-it-yourself' capability. Two of the workshops target project managers and key decision makers. These workshops reinforce usability definitions, benefits and role in the development process. Four workshops, using a 'tell-show-do' format, introduce allocated or interested project members to usability skills, e.g. conducting design workshops; natural workflow analyses, etc.

The workshop series runs in tandem with a strategy borrowed from Mrazek and Rafeld (1992), for introducing non-CSPU Team usability representatives or ‘champions’ into project teams. These people are anticipated to carry out day to day usability tasks under CSPU Team supervision. The Team is also setting in place strategies for establishing a usability special interest group and a usability network for within project usability representatives.

CONCLUSION

In conclusion integrating usability across an organisation involves establishing 'common ground' between usability professionals and:

- Organisational objectives, through Strategy and Direction departments in this instance. Usability professionals cannot expect organisations to invest resources in usability, if it is not shown that usability is consistent with immediate and future organisational objectives. This also achieves a legitimised mandate which can be more effectively communicated within organisations.
- Project teams who own projects. The CSPU Team recognised that usability professionals are 'guests' in projects. To be invited and involved, the Team needed to communicate its objectives and role clearly. This involved defining roles in terms of project based processes. Second, usability concepts needed to be demonstrated in concrete but highly flexible terms. Abstract messages even when these were enshrined as standards were not sufficient. Third, CSPU Team members needed to be cognisant of project team objectives and constraints. There is little gained by introducing methods that are time consuming, not perceived as useful to projects or which duplicate existing knowledge or activities.

A prime reason for CSPU Team success has been its willingness to work with and adapt to the needs of the organisation as a whole.

ACKNOWLEDGMENTS

The author acknowledges the contribution of the Telstra Research Laboratories, specifically the Human Factors

Research Group and the Hiser Consulting Group to the activities undertaken by the CSPU Team. In particular the author acknowledges the support and advice offered by Helen Kieboom (HCG); Dr. John Craick (TRL) for some of the organisational context; Dr. Joe Havloujian (TRL), Daniel Szuc (CSPU Team) and Sheryl Lumb (Interactive Courseware Pty. Ltd.) for encouragement and assistance with editing; Dr Deborah Zinn, and Dr. Gitte Lindgaard for their energy and vision, without which this paper would not have been possible.

REFERENCES

1. Burger, K. (1995). Applying Usability Standards and Guidelines within a Multi-disciplinary Team. Conference Proceedings: Human Factors in Telecommunications, 15th International Symposium on Human Factors in Telecommunications. Melbourne.

2. Billingsley, P. (1995). Starting from scratch: Building a usability program at Union Pacific Railroad. Interactions, Oct '95.

3. Constantine, L. & Lockwood, L. (1994) Essential modelling for user interface design: essential use of cases and use context. OZCHI'94 Tutorials. Melbourne: Computer Human Special Interest Group of the Ergonomics Society of Australia.

4. Ernst & Young International. (1995). Ernst & Young Navigator Systems Series - Version 3.0: Client/Server Analysis using a 4GL/GUI. USA: Ernst & Young International, Ltd.

5. Holtzblatt, K & Jones, S. (1993). Contextual Inquiry: A participatory technique for system design. In Schuler, D & Namioka, A. (Eds), (1993). Participatory design, principles and practice. New Jersey: Lawrence Erlbaum Associates, Inc.

6. Lindgaard, G. (1994). Usability Testing and System Evaluation: A Guide for Designing Useful Computer Systems. London: Chapman & Hall.

7. Lindgaard, G. (1995). Cementing human factors into product design: Moving beyond policies. Conference Proceedings: Human Factors in Telecommunications, 15th International Symposium on Human Factors in Telecommunications. Melbourne.

8. Lund, A.M. (1994). The evolution of broad-band work in Ameritech's customer interface systems and human factors department. In M.E. Wiklund (Ed.), (1994) Usability in Practice: How companies develop user-friendly products. Cambridge, Massachusetts: AP Professional.

9. Moyal, A. (1984). Clear across Australia: a history of telecommunications. Melbourne: Thomas Nelson Australia

10. Mrazek, D & Rafeld, M. (1992). Integrating human factors on a large scale: Product usability champions. Proceedings CHI'92. p. 565-570.

11. Muller, M. (1993). PICTIVE: Democratizing the dynamics of the design session. In Schuler, D & Namioka, A. (Eds), (1993). Participatory design, principles and practice. New Jersey: Lawrence Erlbaum Associates, Inc.

12. Telstra. (1994). The Overall Systems Architecture: Phase 2 Update. Melbourne: Telstra Australia

Making A Difference - The Impact of Inspections

Paul Sawyer
Digital Equipment Corporation
LKG 2-2/Z7
550 King Street
Littleton, MA 01460-1289
(508) 486-7119
sawyer@tnpubs.enet.dec.com

Alicia Flanders
Digital Equipment Corporation
ZKO 2-3/R77
110 Spit Brook Rd,
Nashua, NH 03062-2642
(603) 881-1337
flanders@casdoc.enet.dec.com

Dennis Wixon
Digital Equipment Corporation
ZKO 2-3/R44
110 Spit Brook Rd,
Nashua, NH 03062-2642
(603) 881-2276
wixon@usable.enet.dec.com

ABSTRACT
In this methodology paper we define a metric we call *impact ratio*. We use this ratio to measure the effectiveness of inspections and other evaluative techniques in getting usability improvements into products. We inspected ten commercial software products and achieved an average impact ratio of 78%. We discuss factors affecting this ratio and its value in helping us to appraise usability engineering's impact on products.

Keywords
Formal inspections, heuristic evaluations, usability metrics, user testing, walkthroughs, impact ratio usability problems.

INTRODUCTION
Usability as a discipline, and usability organizations, face the challenge of measuring the effectiveness of the methods they use. The possibility of making such measurements varies with the type of work. For long-term consulting work, where usability consultants work as members of a development team from its inception, the relative contributions of usability professionals versus other contributors is difficult to distinguish. However, in the case of more tightly-focused, shorter-term methods, the ability to measure effectiveness is substantially higher because these projects offer the possibility of a before-intervention versus after-intervention comparison. One can assess an interface and collect such metrics as number of problems uncovered [6] or measure improvements in user performance [1, 16]. In addition, one can measure the relative effectiveness of one method over another [7, 8]. While these kinds of measures help usability professionals decide on the optimal method for their situation, they do not measure the effectiveness of any given method's ability to leverage product improvement.

Recent papers have begun discussing the need to measure the number of changes made to products as a result of a usability method [1, 5, 16]. We suggest that including the number of problems fixed is a more complete way of measuring the impact of usability activities.

The Usability Expertise Center offers both short-term and long-term consulting on usability issues within Digital Equipment Corporation. Our long-term work is often strategic in nature. This paper focuses on our activity as short-term consultants, called on by a development group to measure and improve the usability of a product by applying focused, well-defined tactical methods to achieve a quick result. In a tactical setting, the client needs specific suggestions that will solve specific problems. In other words, they need impact. Contributing to our need to measure our effectiveness is our own management who must be shown that we have a positive, measurable impact on the usability of the company's products. We must, therefore, measure the impact we have had on products to show that we accomplished something and to understand where we can be more effective [11].

In this paper we list a number of projects we have done, showing how many problems we found and how many of those problems were fixed by the development groups. We look at a few of these projects in detail by way of example to understand our relative impact and the factors contributing to it. Finally we describe conclusions about impact, which we have drawn based on all the projects we've listed. Although the projects we discuss here involved usability inspections, we believe the measurement of impact applies to any usability evaluation method.

FINDING THE PROBLEMS
One of our primary responsibilities as usability professionals is to find problems in user interfaces. A good deal of attention has been focused on efficient and effective

ways to find all of the problems that exist in a given interface. Nielsen has nicely summarized these methods [12].

In the Usability Expertise Center at Digital, we make frequent use of user testing and usability inspections. These methods often find different problems, so that the best coverage of a product results from using both methods [3, 8]. In practice we are usually constrained by development-group budget and preference to one or the other. To those clients who are short on time (and budget) and who value "expert opinion", we suggest an inspection. Inspections take less time. To those clients who have a little more time and budget or who do not value the opinions of experts, we suggest user testing. (However we find that we can often insert a little expert opinion into user testing.)

In the past we had been asked to do reviews of designs. We did these reviews, but there was no follow-up so we had no idea of how effective the review was. Since usability is a scarce resource, we decided to institute a structured process to assess our effectiveness and to winnow out any client groups who were asking for input that they did not plan to use. Specifically we decided to adopt a review format similar to that used in software code inspections. [18]

Here is our standard procedure for doing an inspection.

1. After talking with the client, we give them a written proposal that states which parts of the product we will inspect and which aspects of usability we will cover. Our coverage can include general usability principles, style-guide compliance, visual design principles, and online information (help and tutorials) principles.

2. We provide the client with a document describing the principles on which we base our inspection.

3. Our proposal states that we will provide a written report enumerating problems found and including for each problem the severity (with a specific scale), the specific principles violated, and a recommendation for ways to fix the problem.

4. The proposal further states that the client must make a written response that includes, for each problem: a statement of whether they will fix the problem immediately or in a later release or not at all; if not at all, why not; an estimate of the work required to fix the problem; and a statement of what fix they will use (our recommendation or their own alternative).

5. We have pairs of inspectors work as a team on each aspect of usability to be evaluated. (Although Nielsen discusses the advantages of multiple inspectors [13, 14, 15], he has evaluators work independently to ensure that one does not bias the other. This produces greater variability in the kinds of errors found.) Our experience is that having inspectors look at the interface together results in finding more problems and suggesting better solutions than if the inspectors work alone. However, having more inspectors is not necessarily better. We also find that two is the optimal number for interacting with each other and recording the findings efficiently. With more than two, the person taking notes becomes a bottleneck and the other inspectors become bored.

6. One person compiles a single report from all of the inspection comments from each pair of inspectors.

7. All inspectors review the final report and, if necessary, meet to resolve any gaps, contradictions, or disagreements.

8. We give this written report to the client team to read and act on, and if we are suggesting major design changes, we may walk through the suggested new design with the client team.

9. We use the feedback from the development group to evaluate our impact and to look for ways to improve our process.

HOW WE MEASURED IMPACT

As described above, we require the client to provide a written response. From that report we measure the number of problems that the client commits to fixing. We define a metric called *impact ratio* as the number of problems that the client commits to fix divided by the total number of problems that we found, expressed as a percentage:

$$\text{impact ratio} = \left(\frac{\text{problems committed to fix}}{\text{total problems found}}\right) * 100$$

FINDINGS

Table 1 summarizes our activity on ten projects. These inspections took place from August of 1994 to September of 1995 and represent all of the inspections that we delivered to clients during this time that used this framework. The table shows the result of these usability inspections ranked in descending order based on their impact ratios. The average number of usability problems found is 66 with a range of 26 to 111. The average number of committed fixes is 52 with a range of 24 to 84. The average Committed Impact Ratio is 78% with a range of 58% to 96%.

Table 1 – Commitment Ratios from 10 Inspections

Product	Issues Found	Committed Fixes	Committed Impact Ratio
A	26	24	92%
B	85	77	91%
C	78	63	81%
D	111	84	76%
E	33	24	73%
F	46	33	72%
G	89	63	71%
H	59	39	66%
I	52	30	58%
J	85	82	96%
Total	664	519	
Average	66	52	78%
Range	26-111	24-84	58% - 96%

A salient feature of the committed impact ratio is that it measures a commitment that we get from product development. One might wonder if this commitment is predictive of the actual number of fixes. For six usability inspections, we have had access to the version of the product produced after our inspection. This allowed us to see which usability issues development actually addressed.

When evaluating the number of usability issues fixed, it is important to keep in mind that product development is an ongoing process. Issues that are not addressed in one version of a product are sometimes deferred to another version. Therefore, a seemingly large divergence between the committed impact ratio and the completed-to-date impact ratio does not invalidate the committed impact ratio. The *completed-to-date* impact ratio is a measure of how far the development team has come towards addressing all of the problems identified.

For five out of the six inspections, the committed impact ratios are the same as the completed-to-date. The reasons for this reside in the pressures of the software development environment. In some cases, because of compressed schedules and the need to ship, developers implemented our recommendations before reporting back to us, so their reports reflected what they had actually done. This is an example of development's propensity to not commit to anything until they are sure they can do it.

For product G the response from development showed a *committed impact ratio* of 71%; however, when we were able to follow-up on the product, the actual number of recommendations implemented resulted in a *completed-to-date impact ratio* of only 37%. This ratio was partly due to the nature of the recommendations. For example, one recommendation was to implement mnemonics for every button in the interface. Developing a set of mnemonics for an interface requires some thought and planning, in addition to the actual coding. Other recommendations affected the entire interface. These included changing the action of scroll bars, providing progress indicators, making buttons, labels and placement consistent, allowing for maximizing and minimizing windows, and providing a task-oriented help system. Recommendations from our inspection represented only one set of pressures on the developers. Other pressures included the need to implement new features, fix bugs, and meet their deadlines for each release. The way that this development team balanced the demands was by staging their approach to implementing the usability recommendations over more than one version. and by placing a higher priority on software bugs than usability issues.

Gunn [5] reported that 14 inspections produced an average fix rate of 74% with a range of 50% to 95%. In addition, Muller [10] reported for one heuristic evaluation that 89 recommendations were made, 87% were committed to and 72% were actually implemented.

Our data as well as that of Gunn [5] demonstrate that formal inspections are a relatively effective method of getting usability problems fixed. These findings qualify Klemmer's [9] assertion that expert opinion is not as effective as data from usability studies in facilitating product improvement and suggest that, when embedded in an appropriate process, expert opinion can be quite effective.

WHAT AFFECTS IMPACT

There are a number of factors that affect the impact of a usability method. The following is a discussion of some of these factors, based on our experiences delivering inspections and our reflection on these experiences.

Written Report

Providing a written report has an obvious positive effect on our impact: The problem descriptions and specific solutions are available for all group members to read and reference, and the written word removes some (but not all) ambiguity about what we intend to say. The written report also has a less-obvious effect that has been reported earlier [18]: We avoid being used as an approval agency, wherein our recommendations may be ignored while "usability approval" is cited. In such situations, our impact would actually be negative: no changes would be made, and the incentive to make changes would be lessened.

Multiple Methods

Since inspections and user tests are known often to discover different problems [6], a way to improve impact is to do both kinds (or other kinds) of evaluations. It should be noted that inspections usually provide more systematic coverage of an interface than user testing.

Written Response

Requiring a client to respond in writing to our report changes the client's response. We ask our clients to include a work-time estimate for each problem fix as part of their response. Having invested the time to consider each problem, its fix, and the time required to implement it, development groups tend to actually do what they tell us they will do, though we have no authority to ask for commitments. This is the request form of speech acts [17] which provides for a clear specification of action, a responsible person, and a date to be completed.

In addition, requesting engineering to agree to respond to our report in writing often helps us to eliminate clients who are unlikely to implement our recommendations. That is, if they cannot agree to respond to our report, it follows that they probably will not have time to implement our recommendations either. Therefore the context in which we measure our impact actually helps us to identify optimal ways to apply our resources.

We find that requiring a written response from a development team is good practice for any usability technique. It is also one of the operational aspects of any kind of engineering. [16].

Easier Response Process

Client responses are important, but we know that they impose additional work on engineering. Therefore, we try to make the process easier. One way we do this is to set up a meeting where we go over the report with the client. We answer any questions they might have about the recommendations and they give us their response to each recommendation, which we record on the spot. Sometimes we provide our report document to clients so they can add their information to the report without having to reference each recommendation in a separate file. We are usually willing to adapt our process to achieve our desired result.

Specific Recommendations

Providing specific recommendations to fix specific problems has a tremendous positive effect: The development group need not spend time thinking of a solution, plus we gain a psychological advantage in offering constructive suggestions rather than just criticism. To the extent that we have the expertise, we include enough technical details in our recommendations so that the solution becomes "a mere matter of coding." Modern GUI toolkits are complicated, and many development groups do not have a GUI guru available, so we can often provide enough details to change a programmer's estimate from "Can't do that" or "That would take a month" to "I can have that done tomorrow".

Along that line, we sometimes offer two or more recommendations to solve a given problem, suggesting a better but more complex solution if there is time and talent available, and a less desirable but still acceptable solution that can be implemented more quickly. Some impact is definitely better than no impact.

Severity Level

We rate each problem found with a severity level of low, medium, or high according to that problem's effect on usability. This allows the development group to focus on the fixes that will have the most usability impact. We have found, however, that the severity of the issues that we report does not appear to have any effect on whether or not development will commit to addressing an issue. For the inspections shown in Table 1, the impact ratio for high, medium, and low usability issues is 72%, 71% and 72% respectively. This finding suggests the need to further examine the reporting of severity levels to learn if other factors (such as time, effort, and risk involved in addressing an issue) influence whether or not development will commit to addressing a usability issue.

We find that reporting severity makes our report more like engineering quality assurance reports and as a result adds more credibility to our process and findings. Therefore we will continue reporting severity levels.

We also encourage developers to go for some "cheap wins," problems that are easy to fix irrespective of severity. When a number of "cheap wins" are aggregated, the result can be a significant improvement in the perceived quality of the interface.

Client Participation

Having a member of the client development team sit in on an inspection or user test sometimes has a big impact. Karat has observed [7] that this is due to the "seeing is believing" phenomenon and the developer's involvement in and commitment to the usability evaluation process. We affirm this observation, noting that some developers and managers do not value expert opinion at all, so direct participation gives them assurance that the data we collect is credible. [4, 18]

Early Involvement

An obvious factor for impact is being able to work with a development group as early in the development cycle as possible, since it is well known that solving quality problems (whether software bugs or usability bugs) earlier is cheaper. We have less control over this factor, but we have found that we get a fair bit of repeat business from satisfied clients, and that our involvement with the next project for a client often happens earlier in the development cycle. Earlier involvement is, of course, advantageous to the client: inspections and user testing operate in a scrap and rework mode, so from a larger perspective they are less efficient than an approach which focuses on getting the design right earlier in the process. One might think of inspections as both a short-term aid to usability and a long-term investment in changing development processes.

FACTORS BEYOND OUR CONTROL

Some factors that affect impact are beyond our control. Although we believe that usability problems are real bugs and can often convince development groups of this, usability bugs most often are given lower priority in comparison to software bugs, for a good reason: if the product doesn't work, usability doesn't matter much. For products that have a high number of software bugs, impact from usability evaluations is likely to be low.

The following are reasons for not implementing a recommendation that we feel are beyond the control of usability practitioners:

- The development team did not have enough time or resources to implement the change. Shipping the product is the highest priority.
- Implementing the recommendation would have a negative impact on performance.
- The product was canceled.
- The problem existed only in prototype code and not in the actual product. When we compute the impact ratio for an inspection of a prototype, we base the impact ratio on the number of valid recommendations. That is, we subtract from the total number of problems identified any that were invalid because they described problems existing only in the prototype.

FACTORS AFFECTING SPECIFIC INSPECTIONS

A number of factors contributed to the high impact ratios of 92% and 91% for products A and B. Both of the products are part of a tightly integrated product set. The usability engineers who participated in the inspection enjoyed a long-term relationship with the development group and had earned the respect of the developers. The usability engineers worked on an ongoing basis with the developers, performing many kinds of usability processes and evaluations at various points in the development cycle. However, the inspections noted here were the first formal inspections performed in that product space. Previously a single usability engineer might review an interface and provide feedback to the developers. Formal inspections were a departure from the existing process because usability engineers worked as a team to review the interface and requested a written response from engineering. The novelty of the formal inspection process generated a lot of excitement and interest. Working as a team, the usability engineers were able to produce a comprehensive report in a relatively short time. The report categorized usability issues by screen and severity ratings. The development teams were pleased to be able to get usability feedback in time for current releases and the severity ratings helped them to focus on the most pressing issues.

Another factor contributing to the high success rate for the inspection of Product B (91% impact ratio) was that the development team was located in Valbonne, France and was appreciative of having the spotlight of attention from the "home office" focused on their product. Being in the spotlight might have also encouraged them to higher levels of cooperation.

On the other hand, a completely different set of factors contributed to the low impact ratio of Product H (66% impact ratio). The developer responsible for the first version was reassigned to another product. The new developer who was finally assigned lacked vital product knowledge and expertise to address the usability issues. In addition, the future of the product was uncertain because high-level strategy decisions were threatening to render it obsolete. Therefore development was unwilling to invest a lot of resources on the product unless its future was more certain. For future projects we will ask questions during our initial contact with clients to determine how stable a product is before we commit to performing an inspection on it. This will help us to avoid performing inspections on products to which development is not fully committed.

Here are some of the factors contributing to the 58% impact ratio of Product I. It is intended for internal use. The initial client request was for specific consultation on Motif style guide issues, but in looking at the interface with the client to understand the Motif issues, our consultant observed several usability problems that were not related to style-guide compliance. We suggested an inspection. The development manager acknowledged that the product had not had any involvement of a design professional, and that there were likely many problems that would not be observed until the product was actually deployed, so the manager was enthusiastic about an inspection. The inspection was done in our standard way (described earlier), and the client requested a consultation meeting to clarify some of the recommendations made.

When the client response came back, we discovered that our impact had been lower than usual. Analysis of the specific responses revealed several factors. Development time and resources were very limited, so most work was deferred to a later release. The developers had some strongly-held beliefs on how Motif applications are supposed to work, at least partly based on the *default* behavior of several Motif widgets. But the largest single factor was a strongly-held belief that users of the product must be domain experts (in an aspect of the company's business) and must undergo training before using the product. Although we demonstrated alternative designs that were not especially difficult to implement and that would remove the training requirement, the development team opted to assume the need for training (adding to the cost of use for every product user) in order to reduce their development cost (since they had already implemented the products). Only strong user criticism has a chance of changing their minds on this issue.

WAYS THAT WE CAN IMPROVE OUR IMPACT

Reflection on our processes has shown us that many factors affect our impact. This section describes some process improvements that resulted from analyzing the written responses from product development.

The following are reasons that clients gave us for not implementing our recommendations that we feel are within the control of usability practitioners:

- The recommendation is not in keeping with product goals. This reason was the most common reason that we encountered. It occurred in development responses from seven of the ten studies. It reveals the need for usability engineers to take more time to become familiar with the products they evaluate. They could do this by reviewing product brochures and product descriptions before beginning the inspection.

- The recommendation would make this component inconsistent with other components in the product family. If a product is one of a family of products, usability engineers could request access to the entire family, or at least major components. They could then reference other components to ensure that they do not make recommendations that compromise consistency in the product family.

- Product developers expressed strong (erroneous) opinion that the current implementation is satisfactory. Developers gave this as the reason for not implementing recommendations in half of the studies. The best way to counter this kind of complacency with the product is with usability testing rather than inspection methods. Expert opinion, one distinguishing characteristic of inspection methods, is only as effective as development's willingness to accept it. [2]

- The software platform or development tool seems to impose restrictions. This reason was present in the responses of five of the ten usability studies. Often the restriction is real. However, just as frequently, implementation requires a complex solution of which the developer is unaware. Usability engineers with technical expertise can influence a positive decision by describing a workable solution.

The impact ratio is a quantitative measure of how many of our recommendations the development team will implement. It provides us feedback on how we are doing. However, it is only a metric and not an end in itself. For example, we frequently make recommendations even when we are unsure whether a problem exists. We feel obligated to bring these kinds of ambiguous issues to the attention of the developers, even if there is a chance that they will not accept the recommendation and thus reduce our impact ratio. We do not limit our reports to items that we are sure development will address.

CONCLUSION

It is important for usability professionals to find usability problems quickly and effectively, but it is equally important to have an impact on the usability of products examined and to reflect on the effectiveness of usability practice. We have described here a simple way to measure the probable impact on product usability by (1) producing a written report, (2) requiring a response from the client, and (3) calculating the ratio of problems the client says will be fixed to the total number of problems found.

We have also described factors that we have found affect our impact: (1) providing severity levels for problems; (2) making recommendations that are both detailed and technically-specific; (3) requiring a client response; (4) getting involved as early as possible, (5) becoming familiar with the product and its design goals prior to the inspection, and (6) inspecting the product within the context of its product family.

Using these methods, we have satisfied our clients, improved the usability of our company's products, and measurably justified our existence to our management. In addition, we now have a database of results to which we can compare future evaluations to spot deviant cases and investigate them.

ACKNOWLEDGMENTS

We gratefully acknowledge the contributions to the usability methods described here of the other members of the Usability Expertise Center: Minette Beabes, George Casaday, Elizabeth Comstock, Nancy Clark, Debby Falck, Rick Frankosky, Tom Graefe, Trudi Leone, Mike Paciello, Anne Parshall, Sharon Smith, Linda Sue Trapasso.

REFERENCES

1. Bias, R.G. and Mayhew, D. J. *Cost Justifying Usability*, Academic Press, New York, 1994.

2. Brooks, P., Adding Value to Usability Testing. In *Usability Inspection Methods,* Nielsen, J and Mack, R.L., Eds. John Wiley & Sons, Inc., New York 1994, pp 255-271.

3. Desurvire, H.W. Faster, Cheaper!! Are usability inspection methods as effective as empirical testing? In *Usability Inspection Methods,* Neilsen, J. and Mack, R.L., Eds. John Wiley and Sons, New York, 1994, pp 173-202.

4. Dumas, J., and Redish, J.C., *A Practical Guide to Usability Testing*. Ablex, Norwood, NJ, 1993.

5. Gunn, C., An Example of Formal Usability Inspections in Practice at Hewlett-Packard Company. In *Human Factors in Computing Systems CHI'95 Conference Companion* (May 7-11, Denver, Colorado) ACM/SIGCHI, New York, 1995, pp 103-104.

6. Jeffries, R., Miller, J.R., Wharton, C., and Uyeda, K.M. User Interface Evaluation in the Real World: A Comparison of Four Techniques. In *Proceedings of CHI'91 Human Factors in Computing Systems* (April 27-May 2, 1991, New Orleans, Louisiana). ACM/SIGCHI, New York, 1991, pp 119-124.

7. Karat, C-M, A Comparison of User Interface Evaluation Methods. In *Usability Inspection Methods,* Nielsen, J and R.L. Mack, Eds. John Wiley & Sons, Inc., New York, 1994, pp 203-233.

8. Karat, C-M, Campbell, R, and Fiegel, Comparison of Empirical Testing and Walkthrough Methods in User Interface Evaluation. In *CHI '92 Conference Proceedings* (May 3-7, 1992, Monterey, California). ACM SIGCHI, New York, 1992, pp 397-404.

9. Klemmer, E.T., *Impact in Ergonomics: Harness the Power of Human Factors in your Business*. Ablex, Norwood, NJ: 1989, pp 45-87.

10. Muller, M. McClard, A., Bell, B., Dooley, S., Meiskey, L., Meskill, A., Sparks, R., and Tellam, D., Validating an Extension to Participatory Heuristic Evaluation: Quality of Work and Quality of Work Life. In *Human Factors In Computing Systems CHI'95 Conference Companion* (May 7-11, Denver, Colorado). ACM/SIGCHI, New York, 1995, pp 115-116.

11. Muller, M. , Wildman, D. and White, D. Taxonomy of PD Practices: A Brief Practitioners Guide. In *Communications of the ACM* , Vol. 36. No 4, (Oct. 1993) 26-28

12. Nielsen, J., Usability Inspection Methods. In *Human Factors in Computing Systems CHI'95 Conference Companion* (May 7-11, Denver, Colorado). ACM/SIGCHI, New York, 1995, pp 377-378.

13. Nielsen, J., and Landauer, T., (1993) A Mathematical Model of the Finding of Usability Problems. In *Human Factors in Computing Systems INTERCHI '93 Conference Proceedings* (April 24-29, 1993, Amsterdam, The Netherlands). ACM/SIGCHI New York, 1993, pp 206-213.

14. Nielsen, J., and Molich, R. (1990) Heuristic Evaluation of User Interfaces. In *Human Factors in Computing Systems, CHI '90 Conference Proceedings* (April 1-5, 1990, Seattle, Washington), ACM/ SIGCHI, New York, 1990, pp 249-256

15. Neilsen, J. and Phillips, V. Estimating the Relative Usability of Two Interfaces: Heuristic, Formal, and Empirical Methods Compared. In *INTERCHI'93 Conference Proceedings* (24-29 April, Amsterdam, The Netherlands). ACM/SIGCHI, New York, 1993, pp 214-221.

16. Whiteside, J. Bennett, J. and Holtzblatt, K. Usability Engineering: Our Experience and Evolution, in *Handbook of Human Computer Interaction*, North Holland, New York, 1988.

17. Winograd, T., and Flores, F. *Understanding Computers and Cognition.* Ablex Publishing Corporation, Norwood, NJ, 1986.

18. Wixon, D., Jones, S., Tse, L., and Casaday, G. Inspections and Design Reviews: Framework, History, and Reflection. In *Usability Inspection Methods,* J. Nielsen and R.L. Mack, Eds. John Wiley & Sons, Inc. New York, 1994, pp 77-103.

Using small screen space more efficiently

Tomonari Kamba[(1)], Shawn A. Elson[(2)], Terry Harpold[(2)]
Tim Stamper[(2)], Piyawadee "Noi" Sukaviriya[(1)]

(1) Graphics, Visualization, and Usability Center
College of Computing
Georgia Institute of Technology

(2) School of Literature, Communication, and Culture
Georgia Institute of Technology
Atlanta, GA 30332-0165

tomo@cc.gatech.edu, elson@cc.gatech.edu, terry.harpold@lcc.gatech.edu, tstamp@mindspring.com, noi@cc.gatech.edu

ABSTRACT

This paper describes techniques for maximizing the efficient use of small screen space by combining delayed response with semi-transparency of control objects ("widgets") and on-screen text. Most research on the limitations of small display screens has focused on methods for optimizing concurrent display of text and widgets at the same level of transparency (that is, both are equally opaque). Prior research which proposes that widgets may be made semi-transparent is promising, but it does not, we feel, adequately address problems associated with user interaction with text that is partially obscured by the widgets. In this paper, we will propose that a variable delay in the response of overlapping widgets and text improves the effectiveness of the semi-transparent widget/text model. Our conclusions are based on usability studies of a prototype of an online newspaper that combined transparency and delayed-response techniques.

Keywords

PDAs, icons, transparency, usability study

INTRODUCTION AND PROBLEM STATEMENT

The dramatic growth in recent years of the personal digital assistant (PDA) market demonstrates that users are willing to put up with small, hard-to-read, displays, limited storage and battery life, slow CPU speeds and cumbersome data transfer, in the hope of achieving truly portable access to electronic data. It is probably safe to predict that devices available only a few years from now will be dramatically improved. Future generations of PDAs will have higher-contrast, easier-to-read displays, they will have greater storage capacities, they will be much faster and run for longer periods of time between charges, and they will be more flexible in how they communicate with each other and with other computing devices. These probable changes in PDAs are, however, limited by two constraining factors: the dimensions of displayed text and of the screens on which the text is displayed are unlikely to change very much. Reductions in the size of displayed text will be limited by the ability of users to discern small type sizes on any display device, especially one of relatively low resolution. Our informal observations of PDAs based on the Apple Newton and General Magic's Magic Cap operating systems suggests that a practical threshold of legibility for most users lies somewhere between 9 and 12 points (72 points = 2.5 cm.) The small screen size of PDAs is not a technical limitation, but a key factor in their usefulness. Users clearly want devices that can be easily carried about and held in one hand. It is not difficult to imagine even smaller PDAs, worn on the wrist or carried on a keychain.

The small physical size of a PDA limits the maximum size of its screen, which can be no larger than the dimensions of the machine in which it is embedded. On the other hand, the need for displayed text to be legible defines another, more subtle boundary: if the size of text cannot be reduced below a threshold of legibility, then, as the screen shrinks in size, and less information may be shown on it, and the user will be required to increase the level of interaction with the device in order to get to desired information.

The design of user interfaces for PDAs must balance two opposing forces: the need to shrink the screen to a size that fits inside a very small box (we'll call this the "physical" limitation), and the need to keep the screen sufficiently large to show enough information that the device is actually useful (we'll call this the "functional" limitation.) This balance becomes particularly difficult in the case of navigational or functional controls, the widgets that must somehow be made available to the user to allow interaction with the information on-screen (switching between tasks, selecting information to be changed in some way, adding new information, etc.).

Most of the interface objects used in desktop computing environments – pull-down or popup menus, multiple windows, icons – consume a great deal of valuable screen space on the PDA screen. This accounts, we believe, for the efforts of the designers of the current crop of PDAs to minimize the size of these interface objects, or, in some cases, to eschew them altogether. It explains also the emphasis that many of these systems place on handwriting recognition technologies – the keyboard is perhaps the most cumbersome of control widgets. (The document-oriented, pen- and gesture-driven elements of the Newton interface are a good example of these approaches.)

Once again, however, the interface designer faces a version of the functional limitation: the user will expect not only to passively read content displayed on the device, but also to do something with it (to select it, modify it, or enter new content, etc.), and this means that he or she will need to interact with objects (widgets) that are different from the text, but equally available. These widgets must be large enough to be readily distinguished from the content and from each other, and to be practical targets for some kind of interaction (by means of a finger or pen, for example.) But if they are displayed all or most of the time, they will consume screen space that could otherwise be used to display content. Because the number of these widgets will depend on the functions supported by the active application, and not on the size of the screen, the portion of screen that must be surrendered to them will increase as the screen grows smaller, as illustrated in Figure 1.

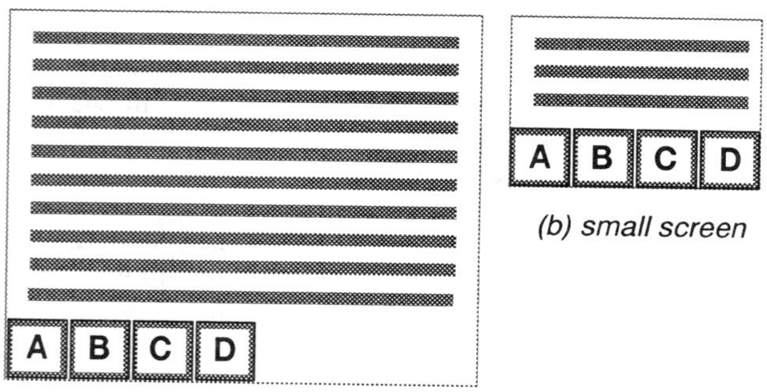

(b) small screen

(a) large screen

FIGURE 1. Surrendering screen space to widgets

The price paid for showing control widgets can be substantial – in the Magic Cap interface, for example, nearly 25% of the screen is used to display icons along the bottom and right edge of the screen.

Our research focused on techniques for reducing the screen space that must be surrendered to widgets, thereby maximizing the available space for display of content. In the next section, we will review general solutions to this problem suggested by the work of other researchers and designers working with interfaces of both handheld devices and desktop computers. Among these solutions, we will single out one approach that seems especially promising to us: the use of semi-transparent widgets, laid over text, so that both are present on the screen at the same time, but the text is able to fill nearly the entire screen. We will, however, point out a serious limitation with this solution, related to user interaction with the text. In the remaining sections of the paper, we will propose a variation of the semi-transparent widget/text model that improves its responsiveness to user interaction, and describe the results of a series of usability studies of a prototype that applies this improved model.

RELATED WORK

Showing Information Structure More Efficiently

One approach to the problem of maximizing the display of content is to improve the efficiency by which its underlying structure is represented on-screen. Several tools in Information Visualizer [4] take this approach. Cone Tree [13] and Hyperbolic Geometry [8] display in lucid forms complicated data hierarchies that might be otherwise invisible to the user, and Perspective Wall [10] does much the same for complex linear data structures. Cone Tree represents data hierarchies in 3D cone-shaped graphics. Hyperbolic Geometry displays a focused point within a data hierarchy in a large bounded space, and its context in a smaller bounded space. Perspective Wall displays relations between different nodes within the same document on two adjacent planes ("walls"), with semantic or structural differences between the nodes represented by the relative positions of the nodes on these walls. These methods for representing underlying data structure are arguably more precise and efficient than, for example, the very concrete "desktop" paradigm of Magic Cap (in which, for example, the Datebook application is accessed by tapping on a miniature appointment book), but they do not address the functional limitation of simultaneous display of widgets and content on a small screen.

Showing Information Content More Efficiently

A second approach to the problem directly addresses the presentation of the displayed content. Magic Lens [3] is a filtering tool that can change or modify the presentation strategy of objects on the screen over which it is laid. For example, a portion of a geographical map can change into a weather map or a population map when a special lens is applied to it. Starfield [6] displays a two-dimensional scatterplot of a multidimensional database, applying a dynamic filtering mechanism which continuously controls the density of information shown on the screen, and panning/zooming techniques to focus on the portion of the content displayed. Table Lens [11] represents large databases in table format. The user can zoom in on an arbitrary part of a table, and view it alongside a global view of the table.

Pad++ applies another kind of zooming/panning technique to displayed content [2]. The user can focus on and zoom into any part of the content, and smooth animation during the zoom insures that the semantic link between the zoomed information and its context are maintained. Galaxy of News [12] uses similar zooming techniques combined with dynamic restructuring of data hierarchies during the zooming/panning process.

We feel that these methods suggest several improvements on the simple, scrolling displays of long lists or blocks of text that are commonly encountered when using PDAs. However, they suffer from a critical limitation: filtering information content so that it may be displayed in smaller chunks that require less screen space does not obviate the need for widgets required to apply the filters, or to enable manipulation of the filtered content.

Showing Widgets More Efficiently

We were surprised to find little research that directly addresses the efficient display of the widgets themselves. We suspect that this may be because the physical/functional opposition outlined above is both obvious and intractable – designers know that widgets can only be so small before they cease to be useful, so they have concentrated their efforts on increasing the intelligence or functionality of the widgets, rather than how much screen space must be sacrificed because of them.

Gestural interfaces, like that used in Apple's Newton operating system, mark an important departure from the paradigm of on-screen control objects. Tying functionality to pen-based gestures frees up valuable screen space, because the user can directly interact with displayed content by simply drawing over it with the pen. This technique works well in many applications, but it also has limitations. First, the user must learn the gestures, and be able to reproduce them accurately. (The list of gestures on the inside of the screen covers of the Newton MessagePad 110 and 120 suggests that users are unlikely to be able to recall all the possible gestures without a mnemonic aid.) Second, not all functions supported by current PDAs can be mapped to intuitive gestures. There is a row of unchanging iconic buttons below the active screen space of the MessagePads. These buttons are used to switch between applications, and to undo previous tasks. By moving these buttons out of the active screen space, Apple has reclaimed area for displaying information, but in so doing has also underscored the difficulty of the problem illustrated in Figure 1.

Kurtenbach and Buxton's Marking Menus [7] offer an interesting variation on the gestural interface. In their system, when the user holds a pen to the screen for a predefined period of time, a pie-shaped menu is displayed below the pen, and the user can select an item in the menu by stroking toward it. Users who are familiar with the structure of the menu can select menu items without waiting for the pie to be displayed, by simply stroking in the direction of that slice of the pie. This approach appears to combine strengths of a gestural interface and a menu- or icon-driven interface, as it hides widgets until they are needed, and allows the content to fill the entire screen. For these reasons, Marking Menus may be a good solution for reclaiming space on small screens. It does not, however, permit simultaneous display of widgets and content. Because the pie menu is opaque, it will at least temporarily obscure underlying content.

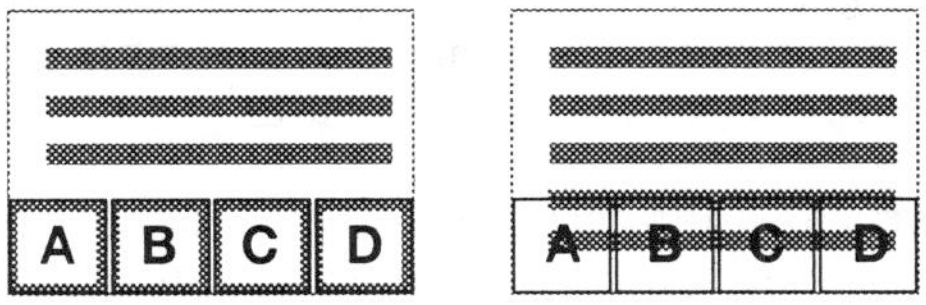

(a) *opaque widgets* (b) *semi-transparent widgets*

Figure 2. Selecting content beneath semi-transparent widgets

Semi-transparent Widgets And Their Limitations

An approach that begins to address this objection makes use of semi-transparent popup menus that do not completely obscure underlying content [5]. (Lieberman, et al. have used a similar semi-transparency method to show data context in a zooming interface [9].) Harrison, et al. proposed allowing users to define the level of menu transparency. They showed that the transparency levels selected by users will vary, depending on the tasks to be completed, and each user's level of expertise.

We believe that the use of control widgets of variable transparency is a promising method for maximizing usable screen space. If the transparency of widgets is adjusted so that the content with which they intersect on-screen is nonetheless legible, then it should be possible to display both the widgets and a full screen of content without sacrificing any screen space reserved for the latter. There is, however, a serious obstacle that must be overcome before this method will support user interaction with the content.

For the purposes of our argument, let us assume that the widget layer is on top of the content layer. If opaque widgets obscure otherwise selectable content, and no mechanism is provided for passing through the widget layer to the content, then the user will be able to interact with only those parts of the content which are not obscured. If, however, the widget layer is semi-transparent – that is, if the underlying content and the widgets are legible at the same time – then it is not immediately clear which of the two layers is selectable (for copying, editing, etc.), *even if there is no formal mechanism for selecting the bottom layer*. This is illustrated in Figure 2.

One solution to this problem is to turn off the selectability of underlying objects, even when they are visible. However, this is likely to confuse and frustrate users, who will reasonably expect that visible objects will sustain some degree of interaction, simply because they are visible. It is, moreover, fairly easy to build a scenario where this solution will effectively prevent underlying objects from ever being selected – if, for example, the upper layer cannot be moved, and the lower layer cannot be scrolled so as to move the partially-obscured content into a selectable region of the screen. The only course of action in this case would be a hardware toggle of some kind to force selectability – an awkward exception to the normal behavior of the interface and an unnecessary extra task for the user.

Instead, we propose a technique for determining the layer receiving user interaction that does not require an additional modifying step, as it based upon variations in the duration of the interaction. In this variation on the transparent widget/content model, the length of time during which the user engages with a region of the physical screen (wherein widgets and content overlap) would determine which virtual layer of the screen receives the interaction.

THE EXPERIMENT

Overview

To evaluate the merits of this technique in a practical example, we decided upon a prototype emulating a text-based online newspaper. PDAs are widely used to read text downloaded from digital news sources. These applications involve moderate quantities of relatively unstructured text, and usually support limited interactivity – simple navigation between stories, or between issues, searching for text strings, transferring information from a story to another application (for example, a scrapbook), and hypertext linking between stories or issues. The emulation of hypertext linking offered a focused example of object selection through layers – how, we wondered, would users attempting to select a passage of "hot" text (that is, a hypertext link) that was partially covered by a semi-transparent icon (or vice-versa) manage the transition between layers?

The prototype was implemented on a Macintosh in Allegiant SuperCard. Although the mouse-driven interface of the Macintosh differs from the pen-based interfaces of many PDAs, we believed that using a desktop computer for initial evaluation would nonetheless generate valuable data. Though we have emphasized in this paper the importance of the issue of screen size for PDAs, the balancing of window size with maximum content display in small windows is of value on desktop computers, where multiple windows may be open at any one time, and the user may wish to reduce the size of any given window to a practical minimum, while still being able to display as much content as possible. Interaction techniques developed for small screens would in this case apply equally well to larger screens displaying many small windows. Moreover, this initial run of the experiment was designed to test the merits of varying the responsiveness of semi-transparent objects (widgets and text), and those kinds of objects need not exist only on PDAs.

The overall design of the prototype strongly resembled that of AT&T's PersonaLink news reader for Magic Cap devices (see Figure 3). The active screen region in the prototype was 320 x 240 pixels. The top portion of most screens in the prototype contained labels identifying the current story and icons used to move between stories or to return to an index for that issue of the newspaper. The text of the story filled the center of the screen. Hypertext links in the story were underlined. Along the bottom of the screen were seven icons (shown left to right in Figure 3): Desk (to quit the newspaper and return to a hypothetical desktop), Search, Archive (to display previous issues of the newspaper), Append (to copy the current story to a Scrapbook), Scrapbook (to open a hypothetical Scrapbook application), and Trash. Along the right edge of the screen were icons for moving "up" or "down," to the next or previous page of the current story.

Most of the icons, and all of the hypertext links were only partially functional – when the user successfully highlighted a link or icon, a status message was briefly displayed in a floating palette on the screen. (This palette is not shown in Figure 3.)

Figure 3. Typical screens in the prototype

The layered icons and text at the bottom of the screen – comprising nearly 20% of the total screen space – were of variable translucency. As the icon layer was made more translucent, the text layer became more opaque, and vice-versa. After a small series of pilot tests, we decided to fix the translucency settings at 80% opacity for the text, and 20% for the icons, to insure good legibility of both icons and text. As we were principally interested in recording the test subjects' reactions to changes in the responsiveness of links and icons, we did not allow the subjects to change the transparency settings, nor did we run the test at other transparency levels.

Sixteen volunteer subjects were selected from among the faculty, graduate students and staff of the Graphics, Visualization and Usability Center, and the School of Literature, Communication and Culture of the Georgia Institute of Technology. Most of the subjects were expert users of the Macintosh or another mouse-driven graphical user interface. Most were familiar with hypertext concepts. Fewer than half had any experience with PDAs.

After a brief training session with the prototype to demonstrate the functions of the semi-transparent icons and the delayed response behavior of the software, each subject was asked to perform eight tasks:

1) From the story index (not shown in Figure 3), select a story title overlapping an icon. (Selecting a story title jumps the user to the first page of that story.)

2) From the story index, select a story title that does not overlap an icon, scroll two pages into the story, and select a link overlapping an icon.

3) From the story index, select a story title that does not overlap an icon, and select an icon that does not overlap with any linked text.

4) On the same page, select a link that does not overlap with any linked text.

5) From the story index, select a story title that does not overlap with an icon, scroll three pages into the story, and select a link overlapping an icon.

6) From the story index, select a story title that does not overlap with an icon, and select a link overlapping an icon. (The "Greenpeace" link shown in Figure 3.)

7) From the story index, select a story title that does not overlap with an icon, And select an icon that does not overlap with any linked text.

8) On the same page, select an icon that does not overlap with any linked text.

(The actual instructions given to subjects were more specific than those listed above.)

Each subject repeated the eight tasks six times: three times with the prototype configured to favor link selection (that is, to initially highlight the link when the mouse was clicked where a link and an icon overlapped, as if the link were on top of the icon), and three times with the prototype configured to favor icon selection. In both selection methods, if the mousebutton were held down for longer than a predefined period of time, the click would appear to pass through the object on top, highlighting the object under it. The association between response delays and layers was rigorously enforced: if selection of links was favored, the subject was required to hold down the mousebutton for the stipulated period of time before any icon would be selected, even if the icon did not overlap with any links.

We further divided the link-first and icon-first selection groups according to the response delay that determined the switching between layers. Each subject attempted all eight tasks for each method of selection with preset delays of 2/5 second and 4/5 second. In the third set of tasks for each selection method, the subjects were allowed to adjust the response delay, between a range of 1/5 of a second and a full second. The sequence in which the subjects performed the series of tasks was shuffled to compensate for learning effects.

	Task 1	Task 2	Task 3	Task 4	Task 5	Task 6	Task 7	Task 8	*Total*
Links-first, 2/5 sec	9	3	5	3	4	0	2	1	27
Links-first, 4/5 sec	11	2	9	1	7	1	3	1	35
Icons-first, 2/5 sec	7	16	8	0	5	8	6	0	50
Icons-first, 4/5 sec	2	11	6	0	7	3	1	0	30
Total	29	32	28	4	23	12	12	2	142

TABLE 1. Raw error counts

("Links-first 2/5 sec" = Links selected first, with a 2/5 second delay between icon and link layers)

	Task 1	Task 2	Task 3	Task 4	Task 5	Task 6	Task 7	Task 8	*Total*
Links-first, 2/5 sec	1.053	0.388	0.793	0.355	0.513	0.000	0.148	0.077	**3.327**
Links-first, 4/5 sec	1.323	0.424	0.833	0.250	0.641	0.077	0.234	0.125	**3.907**
Icons-first, 2/5 sec	0.731	1.469	0.794	0.000	0.504	1.089	0.609	0.000	**5.196**
Icons-first, 4/5 sec	0.361	1.354	0.800	0.000	0.664	0.302	0.167	0.000	**3.648**
Total	**3.468**	**3.635**	**3.220**	**0.605**	**2.322**	**1.468**	**1.158**	**0.202**	**16.078**

Table 2. Normalized error counts

("Links-first, 2/5 sec" = Links selected first, with a 2/5 second delay between icon and link layers)

At the conclusion of the experiment, each subject was given a brief questionnaire that reviewed the test, and included questions asking which of the selection methods was preferred (links first or icons first), and which switching delay (between 1/5 and 1 second) was preferred for each method.

The Results

As the subjects attempted the eight tasks, the prototype recorded every mouseclick, tabulating successful and unsuccessful hits on targets (links or icons). Gross errors (unsuccessful hits) for all subjects for the task series during which we controlled the delay times are summarized in Table 1.

The error counts shown in Table 2 have been normalized so that each subject's contribution to the total errors is (Standard deviations were calculated for each subject to insure that there were no outliers included in the data.) Figure 4 shows a simple line graph of the data in Table 2.

DISCUSSION

After analyzing the results of the experiment, we arrived at the following conclusions:

- Despite an overwhelming preference expressed for the links-first method of selection (15 of the 16 subjects), the overall error rate for the two methods of selection (links-first and icons-first) were very similar.
- The subjects' error rates decreased as they became more familiar with a method of interaction.

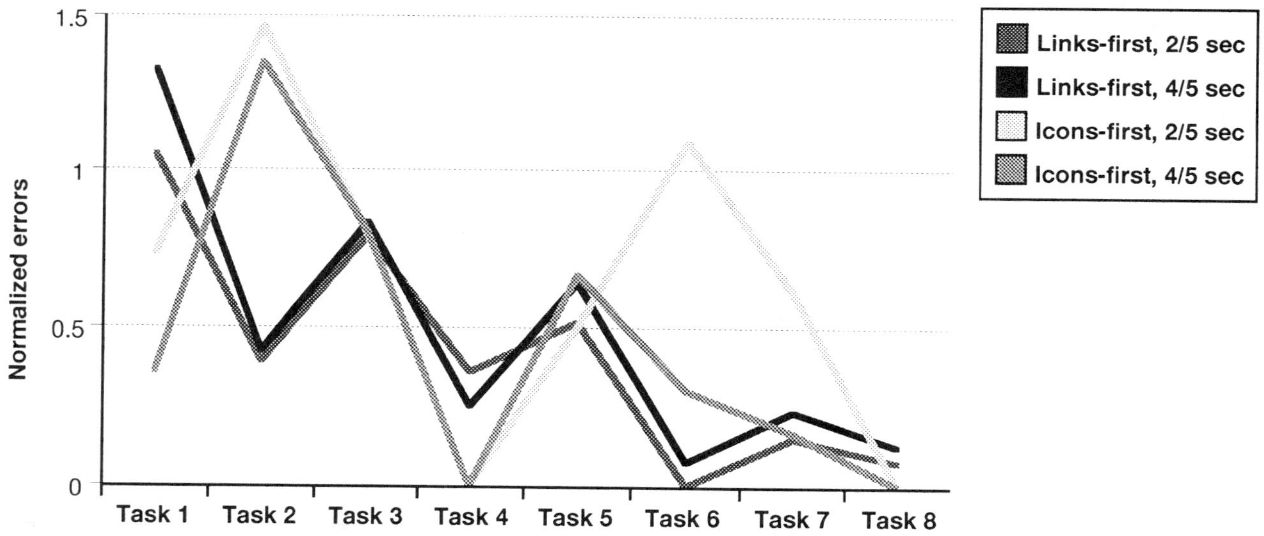

Figure 4. Line graph of data from Table 2

- Subjects had greater difficulty selecting links in icons-first mode, and vice versa. This accounts for the alternating peaks and troughs of Figure 4.
- In the questionnaire, we asked subjects how they would change the behavior of the delayed response. Many expressed the same desire: that all objects in one layer that did not overlap with objects in the other layer should be immediately responsive – in other words, that the subject should not have to wait for the mouseclick to pass through to the lower level if there is nothing on top of it in the upper level. This result surprised us, as we expected that a rigorous and consistent distinction between the layers would make it easier for subjects to conceptualize the two layers.
- The request for immediate responsiveness was given added weight by the subjects' answer to another question. When asked which delay time they preferred, most (12 of 16) responded that they preferred a delay time of 1/5 second – the minimum allowed by the prototype, regardless of which selection method they used. What the subjects appeared to be asking for was a way to simulate immediate responsiveness of non-intersecting objects, within the constraints of the prototype.
- The request was further supported by the difficulties that all subjects had with selection of non-obscured text while using the icons-first selection method. This may account for the high error rate in Task 6, when performed in icons-first, 2/5 second mode (see Figure 4). Users performing the same task in icons-first, 4/5 second mode had less trouble, possibly because they were by Task 6 accustomed to holding down the mousebutton for the extended duration required to select a text link.

DIRECTIONS FOR FUTURE WORK

This expressed preference for immediate responsiveness of non-intersecting objects merits additional research. How, for example, would this change to the delayed-response model affect complex text selection, such as the drag-select gesture supported by many PDAs? How would it affect selection of objects in PDA-based drawing applications? Would novices find this inconsistency in the method of object selection confusing? Would further experiments support the subjects' intuition that immediate responsiveness is a more efficient way to select non-intersecting objects, and might the data from those experiments reveal differences between the links-first and icons-first methods?

CONCLUSION

The very small screens of PDAs severely limit the space available for the display of both text and the widgets required to navigate within or modify that text. A promising method for maximizing the usable screen space of PDAs is to vary the transparency of overlapping objects on the screen, so that objects beneath other objects are still visible, and valuable screen space is not sacrificed in order to display both widgets and information at the same time. In this paper, we have proposed that a variable delay in the response of overlapping widget and text improves the effectiveness of the semi-transparent widget/text model. We assumed that varying the delay by which objects in different virtual layers of the screen responded to users' attempts to select those objects would make it possible for users to select partially-obscured objects without having to resort to a toggle to switch between layers.

Our experiment with a prototype for an online newspaper that uses this selection technique bears out this assumption, and raises additional questions. After an initial learning period, the test subjects were able to select underlying screen objects, regardless of whether those objects were text or icons. Subjects did, however, have greater difficulty successfully selecting objects of one kind when the other kind of object was on the top layer. Our results suggest that it may be easier for subjects to use a variant of the semi-transparency/delayed response model, in which the delay in responsiveness does not apply to objects in one layer which do not appear to intersect with objects in the other layer.

Nothing in our experiment calls into question the merits of techniques for maximizing usable screen space that rely on alternative views of information content. Indeed, it should be possible to combine this semi-transparency/delayed response model with content-based methods for reclaiming space on small screens.

ACKNOWLEDGEMENTS

We show great thanks to the News and Observers who allowed us to user their articles for our internal experimental newspaper.

REFERENCES

1. Ahlberg, C., Shneiderman, B., Visual Information Seeking: Tight Coupling of Dynamic Query Filters With Starfield Displays, CHI'94 Proceedings, pp. 313–17, 1994.

2. Benderson, B., Hollan, J., Pad++: A Zooming Graphical Interface for Exploring Alternate Interface Physics, UIST'94, pp. 17–26, 1994.

3. Bier, E., Stone, M., Pier, K., Buxton, W., DeRose, T., Toolglass and Magic Lenses: The See-through Interface. SIGGRAPH'93 Conference Proceedings, pp. 73–80, 1993.

4. Card, S., Robertson, G., Mackinlay, J., The Information Visualizer, an Information Workspace, CHI'91 Proceedings, pp. 181–88, 1991.

5. Harrison, B. L., Ishii, H., Vicente, K. J., Buxton, W., Transparent Layered User Interfaces: An Evaluation of a Display Design to Enhance Focused and Divided Attention, CHI'95 Proceedings, 1995.

6. Jog, N., Shneiderman, B., Interactive Smooth Zooming

in a Starfield Information Visualizer, University of Maryland Technical Reports, CS-TR-3286, 1994.

7. Kurtenbach, G., Buxton, W., User Learning and Performance with Marking Menus. CHI'94 Proceedings, pp. 258–64, 1994.

8. Lamping, J., Rao, R., Piroli, P., A Focus+Context Technique Based on Hyperbolic Geometry for Visualizing Large Hierarchies, CHI'95 Proceedings, 1995.

9. Lieberman H., Powers of Ten Thousand: Navigating in Large Information Spaces, UIST'94 Proceedings, pp. 15–16, 1994

10. Mackinlay, J., Robertson, G., Card, S., The Perspective Wall: Detail and Context Smoothly Integrated, CHI '91 Proceedings, pp. 173–79, 1991.

11. Rao, R., Card, S. K., The Table Lens: Merging Graphical and Symbolic Representations in an Interactive Focus+Context Visualization for Tabular Information, CHI'94 Proceedings, pp. 318-322, 1994.

12. Rennison, E., Galaxy of News, UIST'94 Proceedings, pp. 3–12, 1994.

13. Robertson, G. G., Mackinlay, J. D., The Document Lens, UIST'93 Proceedings, 1993.

An Experimental Evaluation of Transparent Menu Usage

Beverly L. Harrison

Dept. of Industrial Engineering
University of Toronto
Toronto, Ontario, Canada
M5S 3G9
beverly@dgp.utoronto.ca

and

Alias|Wavefront
110 Richmond Street East
Toronto, Ontario, Canada
M5C 1P1

Kim J. Vicente

Dept. of Industrial Engineering
University of Toronto
Toronto, Ontario, Canada
M5S 3G9
benfica@ie.utoronto.ca

ABSTRACT

This paper reports a systematic evaluation of transparent user interfaces. It reflects our progression from theoretically–based experiments in focused attention to more representative application–based experiments on selection response times and error rates. We outline how our previous research relates to both the design and the results reported here. For this study, we used a variably-transparent, text menu superimposed over different backgrounds: text pages, wire-frame images, and solid images. We compared "standard" text (Motif style, Helvetica, 14 point) and a proposed font enhancement technique ("Anti-Interference" outlining). More generally, this experimental evaluation provides information about the interaction between transparency and text legibility.

KEYWORDS: display design, evaluation, transparency, user interface design, interaction technology, toolglass

INTRODUCTION

This paper describes an empirical evaluation using variably-transparent, linear menus superimposed over different background content: text, wire-frame images, and solid images (Figure 1). The menu contains text items presented in either regular Motif-style fonts or our proposed "Anti-Interference" (AI) font. We evaluated the effect of varying transparency levels (from opaque menus to highly-transparent menus), the visual interference produced by different types of background content, and the performance of AI fonts. More generally, this will determine the interaction effect between transparency and text legibility.

The *technological problem* addressed by transparent interfaces is that of screen size constraints. Limited screen real estate combined with graphical interface design has resulted in systems with a proliferation of overlapping windows, menus, dialog boxes, and tool palettes. It is not

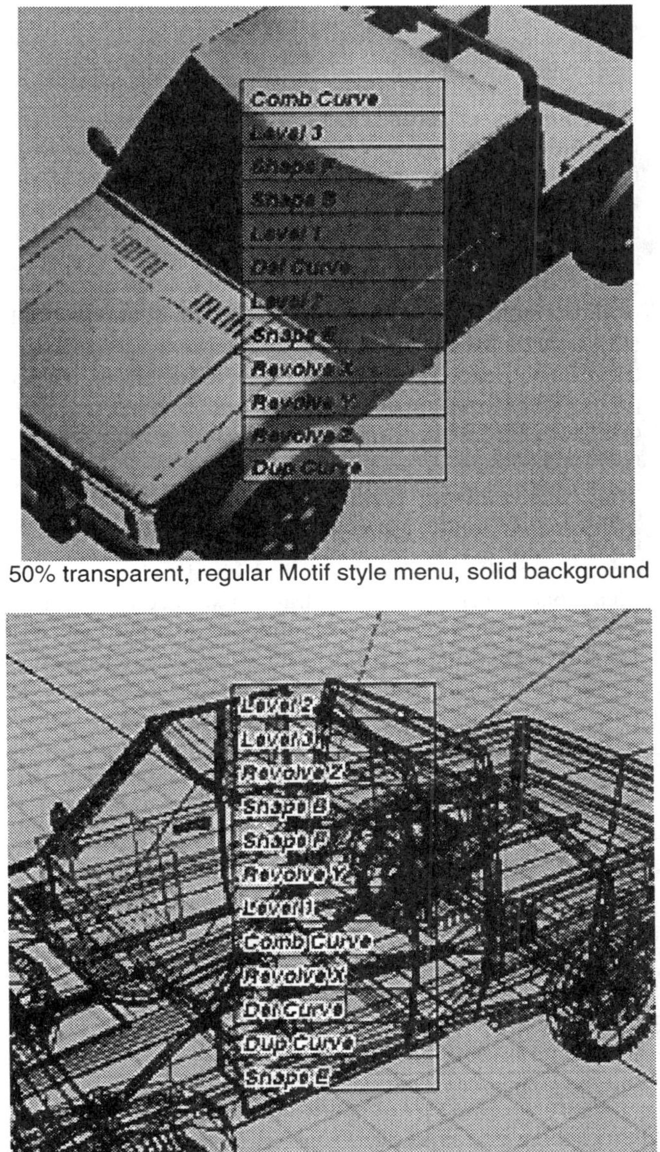

50% transparent, regular Motif style menu, solid background

100% transparent, AI font style menu, wire frame background

FIGURE 1. Experimental Sample Images. (Image resolution degraded due to scaling. Actual screen images were of much higher quality and resolution.)

feasible to "tile" computer workspaces; there are too many objects. Overlapping opaque objects obscure information we may need to see and therefore may also be undesirable. Transparent interfaces address these issues, but may also introduce new challenges for designers.

The associated *psychological problem* we are addressing is that of focused and divided attention. When there are multiple sources of information we must make choices about what to attend to and when. At times, we need to focus our attention exclusively on a single item without interference from other items. At other times, we may need to time share or divide our attention between two (or more) items of interest. In this case, we rapidly switch attention back and forth between the items (necessitating minimal "switching costs"). There is a trade-off between these attentional requirements.

Transparency is perhaps most useful in achieving better integration between task space and tool space, between multiple tools, or between multiple views. Many applications are designed with a large work space or data area which is the primary focus of attention, while the tools to manipulate the data appear in windows and palettes over top of the work area. These tools divert or block our attention from our work, which is often providing feedback about the actions we apply, for example, painting or drawing systems and the traditional UI tools to change paint brushes and colors. However, there are several examples of highly-advanced systems which exemplify more seamless task-tool integration through the application of transparent user interfaces. In Heads Up Display (HUD) design, aircraft instrumentation (a graphical computer interface) is superimposed on the external real world scene, using specially engineered windshields [12]. In the ClearBoard work [7], a large drawing surface is overlayed on a video image of the user's collaborative partner. The TeamWorkStation system [6], predecessor to ClearBoard, created semi-transparent computer work space windows superimposed with video image windows (e.g., a person, an object being discussed). The ToolGlass and MagicLens work [1, 2, 10] reflects a tight coupling between tool function, target object specification, and transparency. Other designs include such things as video overlays like those used in presenting sports scores in broadcast television.

Some designs combine transparency and 3-D projected views of the user interface. Several examples are: the work on "3-D silk (volume) cursors" [13], the work by Knowlton [8], which used graphical overlays projected down onto half-silvered mirrors over blank keyboard keys to dynamically re-label buttons and functions keys (e.g., for telephone operators), and the work by Schmandt [9], who built a system to allow users to manually manipulate and interact with objects in a 3-D computer space using a 3-D wand. Again a half-silvered mirror was used to project the computer space over the user's hand(s) and the input device. Disney has also developed a product called the "ImaginEasel" for animators and artists. ImaginEasel keeps the user's hand and input device in the workspace (using mirrors). In every case transparency provided a more seamless integration between the data or work and the UI tools.

The study described in this paper represents an "applied" experiment to evaluate transparency and text menu item selection, but it is intended to inform us about transparency and text legibility in general. Text labels are either selectable in themselves (e.g., as menu items, hypertext links) or they are important cues in differentiating and identifying graphical window items for subsequent selection (e.g., button labels, data entry fields). Also we wish to apply transparency to help systems and on-line documentation. Clearly the effect of transparency on overall text legibility is a critical consideration in these situations.

PROGRESSION OF RESEARCH

We conducted a series of experiments, reflecting the progression from tightly-controlled, theoretically based, empirical work [4] to studies which sacrifice some experimental control in order to increase the realism (and presumably applicability to everyday tasks) [5, and this paper]. In our previous research, we conducted a *theoretically motivated experiment* [4], which tested a hypothesized model of focused attention and interference. The stimuli for that experiment were specific to the Stroop Effect [12] and therefore were necessarily simplistic and non-representative of real applications, i.e., a text word is seen through a variably transparent colored rectangle.

Significant main effects were found for transparency level, word type, and color (all p<.001). Transparency increases resulted in performance improvements in word naming, since the word was more legible (Graph 1). There was a significant interaction between transparency and color F(12, 163)=6.17, p <.0001, suggesting that word legibility is affected not only by level of transparency (i.e., visibility) but also by the properties of the color used (i.e., saturation and luminance). Post-hoc analysis showed 3 significantly different groupings of transparency levels: 5%, 10%, 100%+50%+20%+0%. Most illegible trials occured at 5%; above 10%, subjects made virtually no errors.

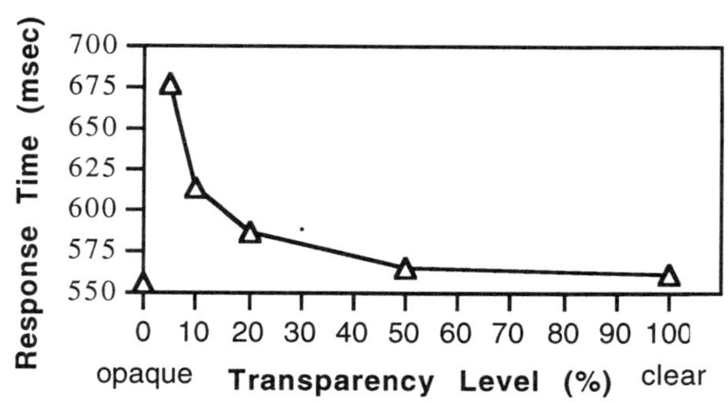

Graph 1. Mean Response Time Results from the Stroop Experiment - Word Naming (**Background**) Task. (Invert X axis to reflect foreground menu task relevant to ~~text~~ selection experiment.)

We subsequently changed the stimuli to more complex and realistic images. In the place of the Stroop color patch, we inserted either an iconic tool palette [5] or a linear text menu [this paper]. Both of these represent highly realistic foreground tasks in most user interface applications. We replaced verbal response times with mouse click selection times, also highly representative of realistic applications. Finally, we replaced our 78-point Helvetica word from the previous Stroop experiments with complex background images taken from product libraries. These images reflect a "snapshot" in time for several task domains we have targeted for later case study evaluation. While the images used as stimuli are not interactive, they do reasonably reflect a static moment in time for our choice of tasks. As in the Stroop experiment series, we ran both foreground focused attention tasks and background focused attention tasks. These tasks have been carefully matched to allow comparison.

The analysis of the Icon Palette Experiment data [5] revealed several points relevant to our Text Legibility Experiment. The type of icon, type of background, and transparency level were all statistically significant ($p<.0001$), as were the interactions between these factors. Graphs 2 and 3 summarize some of these interactions. Briefly, solid icons and solid image backgrounds are significantly more interference resistant than line art or text, resulting in the best performance. Line art icons and text icons perform equivalently, as do wire frame backgrounds and text page backgrounds. There is no significant performance degradation between 0% (opaque) and 50% transparent.

Levels over 75% are error prone. In total 18% of the experimental trials were marked illegible. However, most of these errors occurred at 90% where more than half (55%) of the trials were marked illegible. *All* icon types over wire frame backgrounds or text pages were illegible at 90%. Finally, we determined the "threshold of frustration", the point at which subjects give up because the effort seems excessive. At 90% subjects marked trials illegible after attempting them for an average of 2.6 seconds, roughly twice the average trial time.

EXPERIMENT - TRANSPARENCY & TEXT LEGIBILITY

This experiment explores the issue of focused attention and interference in the context of text legibility and item selection. As in the Icon Palette Experiment, this experiment also represents an extension to the Stroop studies. The text menu replaced the Stroop color patch, while the image files replaced the simple Stroop word (e.g., Figures 1, 2). The transparency level varied randomly from 0% (completely opaque) to 100% transparent or clear. We used a "regular" Motif style font (Helvetica, bold, 14 point, italic) and our proposed Anti-Interference (AI) font, which uses luminance values to create a contrasting outline (e.g., Figure 4). All combinations of font styles X background types X transparency levels were run.

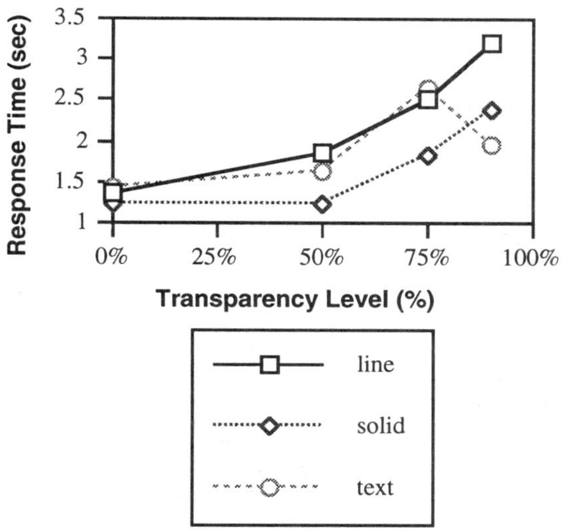

GRAPH 2. Mean Response Times – *Icon* Type

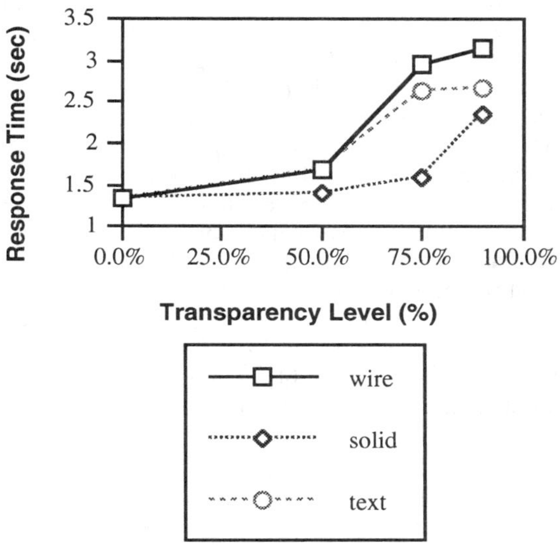

GRAPH 3. Mean Response Times – *Bkgrnd* Types

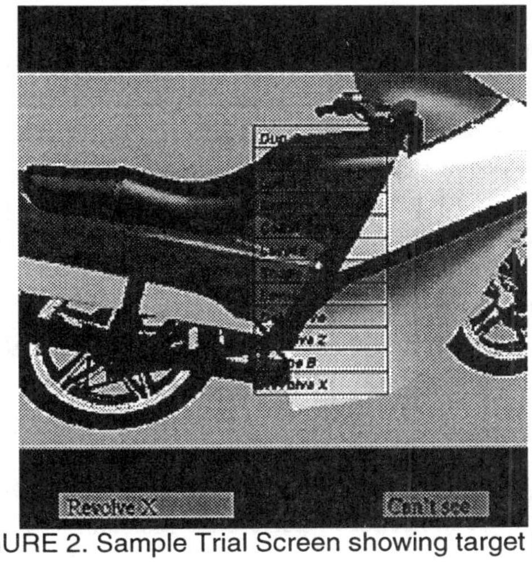

FIGURE 2. Sample Trial Screen showing target item.

Applying the Previous Experiments

The Text Selection Experiment represents a *foreground* focused attention task and, as such, we anticipate a performance curve which resembles those found in the Icon Palette Experiment (i.e., transparency increases should degrade performance) (Graphs 2 and 3). However, unlike the palette selection task where the *entire* icon was made transparent, the text label remains opaque – only the surface area *around* the label is made transparent (e.g., Figure 3). In the Icon Palette Experiment, our icons were solid objects (as many icons typically are). In order to achieve a transparency effect, the icon image itself must be made transparent. In the case of text labels however, the text occupies only a small percentage of the "selectable region", therefore we may leave the text opaque and still achieve reasonable transparency using the remainder of the selectable area around it (e.g., Figure 3b). (Both design alternatives are shown in Figure 3. We feel Figure 3b represents the more realistic design choice. This was the method used in our experiment.)

The text selection task itself is a legibility task suggesting cut-off points similar to those from the Stroop Word Naming Experiment [4] (Graph 1). Best performance is expected to be maintained from 0% (opaque) to 50% (i.e., interference is no longer an issue). Poor performance and high error rates should occur above 75% (i.e., 25% of the foreground shows, 75% of the background shows). We might anticipate that 90% will be difficult to use (as in the Stroop Experiment). However, note that these cut-off point estimates are based on experiments where the *entire* target object was transparent. The actual cut off points are more likely to shift right on the predicted curve, given the opaque text labels – implying more resistance to visual interference. This suggests that from 0% to some level > 50%, performance will be roughly equivalent. Opaque text labels might remain usable up to 100% transparent (clear menu area).

When applying the Anti-Interference (AI) fonts, we anticipate more interference–resistant images than regular font text (Figure 4). This would give us a flatter curve which is shifted towards better performance. (This is not unlike the effect shown in Graph 2 and 3 when the complexity of the image was simplified, for example, from text to solid).

Hypotheses

H1: As transparency level increases visual interference will increase. This will result in poorer performance (i.e., slower response times and increased error rates).

H2: Increased complexity or information density on the background will make text legibility decrease. Text backgrounds will have the worst performance, followed by wire-frame, then solid images.

H3: AI fonts will significantly improve performance by creating more interference resistant text.

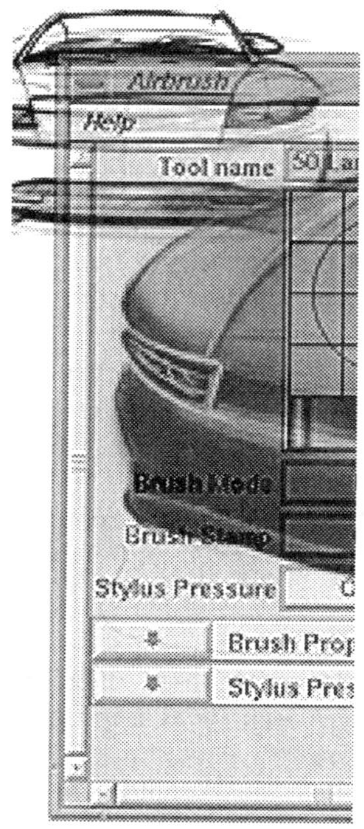

3 (a) labels & surface around labels are both transparent

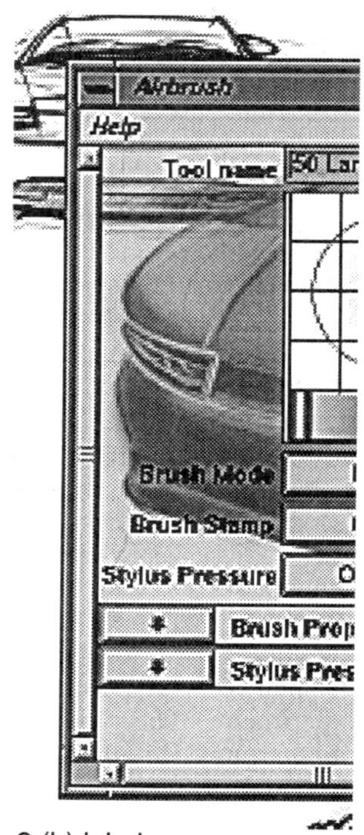

3 (b) labels are opaque, surface around labels is transparent

FIGURE 3. Comparison of design alternatives for transparent text items. (Image resolution degraded due to scaling.) Actual screen images were much higher quality.)

4 (a) Regular fonts, 100% transparent, wire bkgrnd

4 (b) AI fonts,100% transparent, wire bkgrnd

Experimental Design

A fully randomized, within subject, repeated measures design was used. There were three independent variables: type of font, type of background, and transparency level. A total of 540 trials were run for each subject. Trials were presented in random order. Each session lasted about 45 minutes. Dependent variables of selection response time (based on a mouse click) and errors were logged. Two error conditions were possible: the subject pressed the "can't see" button indicating that the item was not legible, or the subject selected the incorrect menu item. In the latter case, the item selected and it's location were logged. Error trials were removed from subsequent analysis of response time data. Error data were analyzed separately.

We used 2 groups of text items within the menu: each group was visually similar to ensure true legibility performance. The menu items were: Revolve X, Revolve Y, Revolve Z, and Dup Curve, Comb Curve, Del Curve. Six other menu items were randomly distributed with the target items. (A 12 item menu was felt to be representative of the average menu/menu size used within the actual product.) Items were randomly assigned positions within the menu for each trial. This was done to ensure the experiment was not confounded by subjects learning the position of items. (We were interested in testing true text legibility rather than menu usability. Randomly ordered menus will produce worst case data which overestimate performance degradation, versus standard menu usage. This gives us a conservative range of transparency levels.) The target item was presented to the subject throughout the trial as a reminder. This was to prevent memory errors (which were not pertinent to the goals of this study).

We randomly assigned background images of three types: text pages, wire frame images, and solid images. Three samples of each type were created. Images were 8-bit color rendered images. These backgrounds were aligned such that a major portion of the content was directly under the menu.

We randomly assigned the level of transparency to the menu. These levels were based on our previous experimental experience [4, 5] and test pilot results with this experiment. Levels of 0% (traditional opaque menus), 50%, 75%, 90% and 100% (clear) were used. The opaque level represented the baseline condition where the fastest performance was anticipated. Transparency levels were produced using alpha blending of the foreground and background images (as opposed to stippling or masking). A level of 75% transparent would mean that 75% of the background image was combined with 25% of the foreground image, producing the effect of a highly transparent menu.

Finally, we randomly assigned either regular font style or our AI font style to the items. Regular fonts were matched to the Motif style menus that appeared from windows on the SGI (Helvetica, 14 point, bold, italic was the best match). We developed Anti-Interference (AI) fonts as a potential interference resistant font technique (Figure 4b). Since an AI font has two opposing color components, it remains visible in any color background.

In AI fonts, the opposing outlines of the text are rendered in a color which has the maximal contrast to the color of the text. For any selected text color vector [R, G, B], our AI font algorithm calculates the luminance value Y according to the YIQ color model used in television broadcasting ([3], page 589). Note that the red, green and blue components are not equally weighted in contributing to luminance.

$$\begin{bmatrix} Y \\ I \\ Q \end{bmatrix} = \begin{bmatrix} 0.299 & 0.587 & 0.114 \\ 0.596 & -0.275 & -0.321 \\ 0.212 & -0.528 & 0.311 \end{bmatrix} \begin{bmatrix} R \\ G \\ B \end{bmatrix}$$

Based on the value of Y, our algorithm then determines the outline color with the maximal luminance contrast. In practice, only two color vectors can be the candidates for the solution: [0,0,0] (black) when $Y > Y_{max}/2$ or $[R_{max}, G_{max}, B_{max}]$ when $Y < Y_{max}/2$, where Y_{max} is the maximum luminance value and $R_{max}, G_{max}, B_{max}$ are the maximum red, green and blue value respectively.

Equipment

The experiments were conducted on an SGI Indy™ using a 20 inch color monitor. Subjects sat at a fixed distance of 60cm from the screen (average distance when working normally).

Procedure

Subjects were given 20 practice trials. These trials were randomly selected from the set of 540 possible combinations. For each trial, subjects were shown a target text item to study (lower left corner, Figure 2). When ready, subjects pressed a "next trial" button (not shown) which displayed the menu superimposed over the background at a randomly ordered transparency level. Items were randomly distributed on the menu. Subjects had to locate and click on the target item within the menu. If they could not see the item on the menu (i.e., illegible) they could press a "can't see" button. The target item remained on the screen throughout the trial for reference purposes. Subjects could take short rest breaks whenever necessary. Response times and errors were logged. Response selections were made using the mouse. Subjects were debriefed at the end of the experiment. Open ended comments were recorded.

Subjects

A total of 10 students from the University of Toronto served as subjects. They were pre-screened for color-blindness and for familiarity with the product from which the images and items were taken. Subjects were paid for their participation and could voluntarily withdraw without penalty at any time.

RESULTS

We have categorized our results by Response Time analysis, Error analysis, and comments from the interviews with subjects.

Quantitative Statistical Analysis - Response Time

Highly significant main effects were found for all of our major variables: background type, transparency level, and font type (Table 1). However, we are primarily interested in the transparency and font effects and their interactions with background type. Statistically significant interaction effects are reported in Table 1.

condition	df	F value	p<
background type	8, 72	1.06	.01
transparency level	4, 36	4.12	.0001
font type	1, 9	3.38	.0001
bkgrnd type X font type	8, 72	1.59	.001
bkgrnd type X transp	32, 288	2.44	.01
bkgrnd X font X transp	32, 287	3.76	.001

TABLE 1. Results for Main Effects and Interactions

The primary results of interest are plotted below (Graphs 4 and 5a, b, c)(across all subjects and menu items). Graph 4 depicts the interaction between font style and transparency level. Graph 5 a, b, c show the interaction between background types and transparency level.

To determine if the differences are significant between the individual lines plotted within each of the graphs, a Student-Newman-Keuls (SNK) test was conducted post-hoc as a comparison of means. (This determined the clustering of items within font type, background type, and transparency level and indicated which items are not statistically different from each other.)

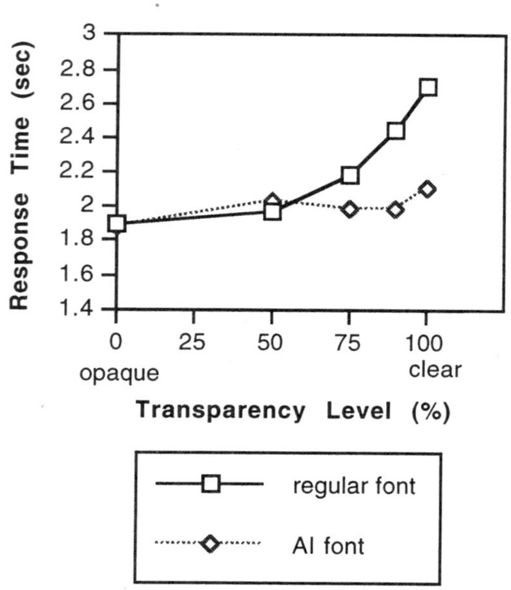

GRAPH 4. Mean Response Times for Transparency Levels X **Font Style** (across all background types)

We conducted subsequent analyses on the font style X background type interactions. Regular menu fonts showed strong interaction effects with the matched text page background and the dense wire frame backgrounds. The solid images with black components also performed poorly. Somewhat surprisingly, the best (most interference resistant) backgrounds were the non-matched text pages. For the regular font style, there were statistically significant differences between the following transparency levels: 100% - poorest, 90%, 75%, and 50%+0% (which performed equivalently well.). (This finding is consistent with our previous experimental results.) AI fonts were relatively insensitive to the type of background. Other background images were not significantly different. For AI fonts, there were statistically significant differences between the following transparency levels: 100% - poorest, 50%+75%+90% (not different), 0% - best.

We also conducted a finer grained analysis *at each transparency level.* At 0% and 50%, there were no statistical differences between background types or between font styles. At 75%, 90%, and 100% transparency the AI font performed significantly faster than the regular font (shown in Graph 4). There are significant differences *between backgrounds* at these levels, though these differences are not based on the type (text, wire, solid) but rather on the individual image properties. For example, the text pages each used a different font style, one of which was purposely matched to the menu item font style. This page performed significantly slower than the other pages (Graph 5a). The denser wire frame images (i.e., more complex meshes and therefore darker in color) performed significantly slower than the simpler wire frames (Graph 5b). The solid images with black components (the truck and the camcorder), performed significantly slower than the solid multi-colored motorcycle image (Graph 5c).

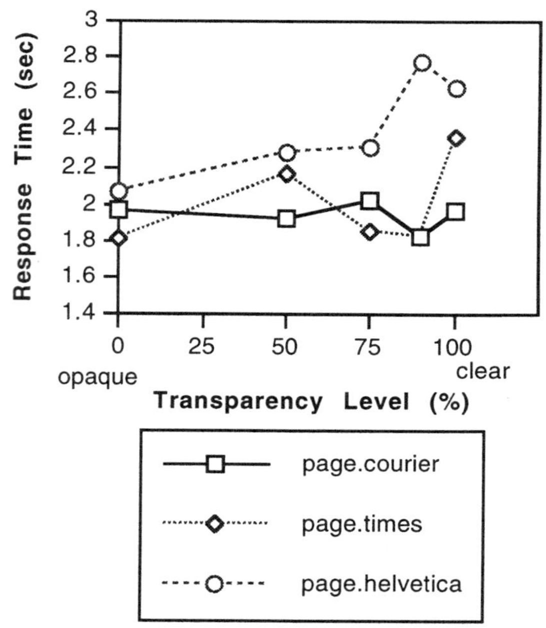

GRAPH 5a. Mean Response Times for Transparency Levels X **Page** Background Types (across font types).

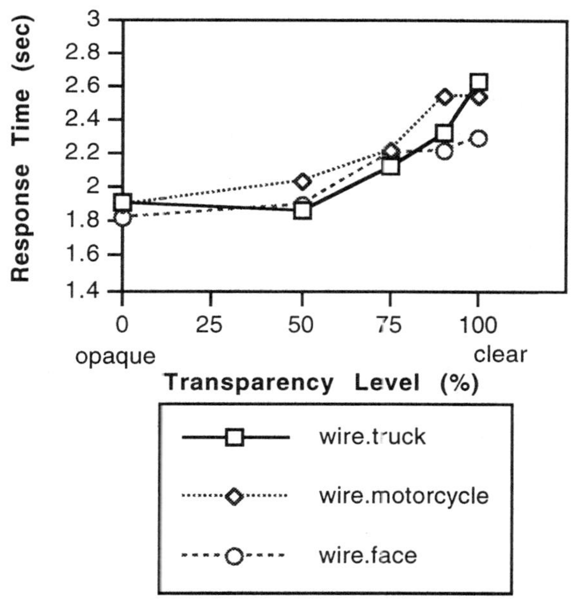

GRAPH 5b. Mean Response Times for Transparency Levels X **Wire** Background Types (across font types).

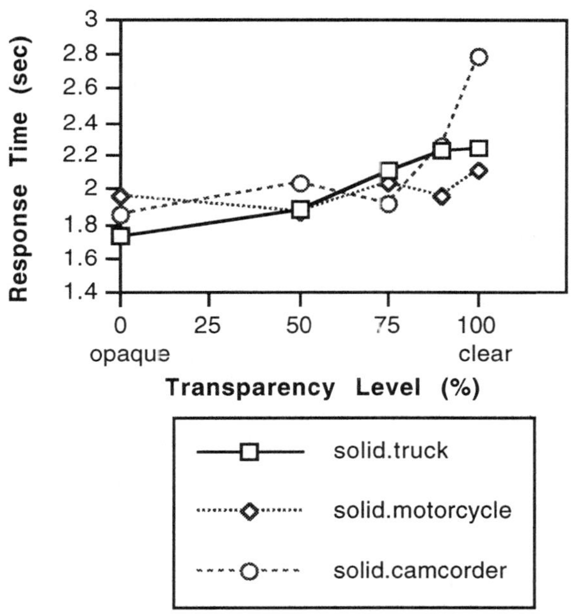

GRAPH 5c. Mean Response Times for Transparency Levels X **Solid** Background Types (across font types).

Targeting Error Results

In total, <1% of the trials resulted in *targeting errors* or misses. The low number of errors indicates that subjects did not tend to guess. There were two types of targeting error possible: accidental selection of an adjacent menu item (45% of total) and substitution of an incorrect menu item (55%). In the latter case, the user incorrectly identified the target item by replacing it with a similarly named item such as Revolve X instead of Revolve Y.

The adjacency item errors are most strongly influenced by the width of the target areas. Since this was designed to match standard Motif menu widths, we did not increase the width size to reduce these errors. However, we are most interested in substitution misses, since these are partially attributed to poor visibility of the target item. These errors were surprisingly evenly distributed across transparency levels. AI fonts made little difference in reducing these errors.

Legibility "Error" Results

Only about 1% of the experimental trials were marked illegible. Of these, 90% occurred at the 100% level (clear) and 10% occurred at the 90% level. All of these illegible trials were in the regular font condition (i.e., *no* AI font trials were marked illegible).

At the 90% level, mostly text items over the text pages or wire frame backgrounds were illegible. At the 100% level, the two solid backgrounds with black color components accounted for 70% of the illegible trials. (The menu font was black, therefore one would expect these trials to be illegible). Surprisingly, text pages accounted for only 3% of the errors made at 100% level.

The mean response time for legibility errors was 6.84 seconds (the "threshold of frustration"), almost 3 times the response time for other trials. This implies that subjects exerted substantial effort to respond to each trial before giving up. In effect, this figure represents the "tolerance threshold" beyond which it is too much effort to locate the target.

Subjective Comments

Subjects commented that wire frame backgrounds seem most difficult, the solid backgrounds were easiest, and highly transparent menus over black backgrounds were very hard. Most subjects commented that even a small change in the transparency level (from 100% clear to 90%), made a substantial difference in these black–on–black conditions. This change allowed subjects to see and select items where previously they marked the trial "can't see". Subjective preference seemed to favor changing the transparency level to improve visibility, as opposed to changing to the AI font. Several subjects commented that they did not like the "outline font" and if given a choice, preferred the 50% transparency level.

DISCUSSION

Transparency levels significantly affected response time and error rates (independent of font type or background). We found evidence to support our predictions about the relationship between regular font performance and AI font performance. The AI fonts produced a substantially flatter performance curve, shifted towards better (i.e., faster) performance, implying they are more interference resistant. The real advantage of using AI fonts was only realized at higher transparency levels (i.e., over 50%). In fact, AI fonts at 75% and 90% produce results similar to those of using regular fonts at 50%. This might be used as a design trade-off for text-based transparent interfaces.

Font type X background content interactions were most strongly affected at highly transparent levels. Performance differences are small between 0% to 50%. (This is consistent with results from our Stroop Experiment and the Icon Palette Experiment.) Surprisingly, the text backgrounds produced much better performance than expected. The most critical dimension of interference with text menu selection tasks was color conflict. The closer in shade and hue the background is to the text color, the higher the interference and the worse the resulting performance.

CONCLUSIONS

This experiment was designed as a text menu selection task. The results should generalize to text legibility in other UI contexts beyond menus. Performance is actually under estimated here for a menu usage scenario, since items did not appear in the same location each time and hence positional learning would not benefit performance. One variant of the experiment would be to run a fixed menu condition to address this.

Both this experiment and the Icon Palette Experiment assume priority is given to selecting items from the foreground and hence they measured this selection criterion only. Clearly to round out the research we need to measure the level of awareness the subjects preserve of the background content. In particular, how are background focused attention tasks affected by transparency? To this end, we have just completed a study which tests selection accuracy of features from background images while icon palettes and text menus are superimposed, varying the level of transparency of the palettes and menus. We believe that this latest experiment, which uses the same stimuli and methodology, provides us with a comparable background task. This measure of background visibility is particularly relevant for tasks like the ToolGlass work [1, 2, 10] or click-through tools which require alignment of the palette item with a specific background object or area.

While this paper presented results for using text superimposed over a variety of background images, this methodology can be generalized to other types of interfaces by incorporating images or backgrounds from *any* target application or working product. The idea is to capture realistic screens at a single moment in time. With these captured images, any sort of menu, window, or palette can be superimposed at varying transparency levels and tested. Using this approach, performance can be predicted and the most appropriate settings can be determined for a variety of target applications. These empirical results can be combined with subjective assessments to provide strong insights about the most and least preferred design solutions in a generalized way. Our long-term goal is in providing user interfaces which improve the fluency of work by more seamlessly integrating the tools with the task space.

ACKNOWLEDGMENTS

Primary support for this research is gratefully acknowledged from Alias|Wavefront. We also wish to particularly thank Bill Buxton for his substantial insights and contributions to this research program. We would also like to thank Hiroshi Ishii, Shumin Zhai, Gord Kurtenbach, the CHI reviewers, and members of the Graphics Lab and Cognitive Engineering Lab for their comments and contributions.

REFERENCES

1. Bier, E. A., Stone, M. C., Pier, K., Buxton, W., and DeRose, T. D. Toolglass and magic lenses: The see-through interface. *Proc.. of SIGGRAPH'93*. Anaheim, CA, 1993. 73-80.
2. Bier, E. A., Stone, M. C., Fishkin, K., Buxton, W., and Baudel, T. A Taxonomy of See-Through Tools *Proc. of CHI'94*, Boston, Mass. 1994, 358-364.
3. Foley, J.D., van Dam, A., Feiner, S.K., and Hughes, J.F. *Computer Graphics - Principles and Practice* (2nd ed), Reading, Mass.: Addison-Wesley, 1992.
4. Harrison, B. L., Ishii, H., Vicente, K. J., Buxton, B. Transparent Layered User Interfaces: An Evaluation of a Display Design Space to Enhance Focused and Divided Attention. *Proc. of CHI'95,* Denver, Colorado. 1995. 317-324.
5. Harrison, B. L., Kurtenbach, G., and Vicente, K. J. An Experimental Evaluation of Transparent User Interface Tools and Information Content. *Proc. of UIST'95*, November, 1995, 81-90.
6. Ishii, H. and Kobayashi, M. Clearboard: A seamless medium for shared drawing and conversation with eye contact. *Proc. of CHI'91*, Monterey, CA, 1991. 525-532.
7. Ishii, H. TeamWorkStation: Toward a Seamless Shared Workspace. *Proc.of CSCW'90* L.A., CA, 1990. 13-26
8. Knowlton, K. C. Computer displays optically superimposed on input devices. *Bell System Technical Journal*, Vol. 56, No. 3, March, 1977. 367-383.
9. Schmandt, C.. Spatial input/display correspondance in a stereoscopic computer graphic workstation. *Computer Graphics*, Vol. 17, No. 3., 1983, 253-259.
10. Stone, M. C., Fishkin, K., and Bier, E. A. The Movable Filter as a User Interface Tool. *Proc. of CHI'94*, Boston, Mass. 1994. 306-312.
11. Stroop, J. R. Factors affecting speed in serial verbal reactions. *Journal of Experimental Psychology,* 18, 1935, 643-662.
12. Wickens, C. D., Martin-Emerson, R., and Larish, I. Attentional tunneling and the Head-up Display. *Proc. of the 7th Annual Symposium on Aviation Psychology,* Ohio State University, Ohio, 1993. 865-870.
13. Zhai, S., Buxton, W., and Milgram, P. The "silk cursor": Investigating transparency for 3D target acquisition. *Proc. of CHI'94,* Boston, MA., 1994. 459-464.

Do Color Models Really Make a Difference?

Sarah Douglas and Ted Kirkpatrick
Department of Computer Science
University of Oregon
Eugene, OR 97403
douglas@cs.uoregon.edu, ted@cs.uoregon.edu

ABSTRACT

User interfaces for color selection are based upon an underlying color model. There is widespread belief, and some evidence, that color models produce significant differences in human performance. We performed a color-matching experiment using an interface with high levels of feedback. With this interface, we observed no differences in speed or accuracy between the RGB and HSV color models, but found that increasing feedback improved accuracy of matching. We suggest that feedback may be an important factor in usability of a color selection interface.

KEYWORDS

Color models, color selection, RGB, HSV, user interfaces.

INTRODUCTION

With the proliferation of color displays, color selection has become a common task. Color selection can be done in a variety of ways, but the most common method today is a direct-manipulation color selection tool. Both the Apple Macintosh and Microsoft Windows provide such tools as part of their system software. Color selection tools are typically organized around a *color model*: an organization of the range of displayable colors into a three-dimensional space. Many such color models have been proposed, each oriented towards a specific task. Table 1 lists several models, their intended usage, their axes, and citations to more detailed descriptions.

There is widespread belief that some models are more "natural" than others. For example, the standard reference work on computer graphics by Foley at al. [2] claims that:

> The RGB, CMY, and YIQ models are hardware-oriented. By contrast, Smith's HSV (hue, saturation, value) model ... is user-oriented, being based on the intuitive appeal of the artist's tint, shade, and tone. (p. 590)

Later, the same text states:

> There is a widespread belief that the HSV model is especially tractable, usually making it the model of choice. (p. 597)

One color model, TekHVC, has even been patented by Tektronix Corporation [9].

"Natural" and "intuitive" can be defined many ways. We could compare the effects of color models on user performance using any number of criteria. How quickly can an expert perform color selection? How accurately can an expert match? How much practice does it take to arrive at a specified level of proficiency, with proficiency defined in terms of time and accuracy? How well does a color model help a user select harmonious or functionally useful colors?

There is surprisingly little empirical data comparing color models. Schwarz, Cowan, and Beatty [6] performed the major experiment to date (referred to in the remainder of this paper as "the Schwarz study"). They compared five models and found many significant differences between them. In particular, they found the RGB model to be the fastest yet least accurate, while the HSV model was amongst the slowest and most accurate. The slower speed of the HSV model suggests it is not so "tractable" as commonly believed. This belief is so strongly rooted that the above quote from Foley immediately follows their description of the Schwarz results, yet the apparent contradiction is unremarked.

The arguments for or against a given color model are typically presented abstractly, without consideration of the interface which represents that model to the user. The model and the interface cannot be separated, because the factors affecting performance of a color model are complex and strongly affected by the interface: perception, screen representation, learning, and time vs. accuracy tradeoffs. The complexity of the issue and the perplexing nature of some of the Schwarz results make the area worth revisiting. We begin with a careful analysis of the empirical results to date.

Table 1: some commonly-used color models

Acronym (alternate)	Described in	Intended Use	Axis 1	Axis 2	Axis 3	Used in
RGB	[2]	Device-specific color specification	Intensity of red gun	Intensity of green gun	Intensity of blue gun	Macintosh, Windows
HSV (HSB)	[8]	Color mixing	Hue	Saturation	Value	Macintosh Color Picker
HLS (HSL)	[8]	Color mixing	Hue	Lightness	Saturation	Windows Custom Color dialog
LAB	[3]	Measuring color distance in accordance with human perception	Lightness	red/green balance	green/blue balance	
CMY	[2]	Color printing	Cyan	Magenta	Yellow	
YIQ	[6]	North American broadcast television	Luminance	blue-green / orange balance	yellow-green/ magenta	
Opponent*	[6]	Model of human color vision channels	Achromatic	red/green	yellow/blue	
TekHVC	[9]	Perceptually uniform color selection on electronic displays	Hue	Value	Chroma	Color selection for Tektronix terminals

* The Opponent "model" is in fact a family of related models derived from similar but slightly different theories of color perception.

PREVIOUS RESEARCH

There are only three published empirical studies exploring the influence of color models on the speed and accuracy of color selection. Berk, Brownston, and Kaufman [1] compared a color naming language of 627 distinct names versus specifying numerical coordinates in the RGB and HSV systems. They found that the naming system produced the most accurate results, with HSV coordinates next, and RGB coordinates worst of all. However, these results do not apply in the cases of interest to us, situations where the user can select from millions of potential colors rather than only 627.

Murch [5] summarizes a color-matching experiment comparing the number of steps subjects took to match colors using the RGB, HSL, and Swedish Natural Color System models. A mixture of experienced and inexperienced subjects was used. For inexperienced subjects the HSL system is reported to require the fewest steps. Unfortunately, no details of this experiment were ever published, so we can neither analyze his results nor attempt to replicate them.

As mentioned earlier, the Schwarz study is the current reference work for empirical data about color models. In this study, five different color models were compared: LAB, HSV, Opponent, YIQ, and RGB. Each color model was implemented with two input methods. The experimental design was five by two factorial, with color model and input method as the between-subjects variables.

While the experiment studied two methods of input, these were all limited in similar ways. In each case, the screen representation was identical. For each match, a "target" color was displayed in a rectangle on the screen and the subject used the interface to set the color of a second "controlled" rectangle to match the first one as closely as possible (Color Plate 1). The interfaces differed in how the subject used a puck on a graphics tablet to control the three parameters of the color model. In one interface, called "3*1d", the each parameter was controlled by horizontal motion (Figure 1). Three puck buttons selected which parameter was being actively controlled. In the second method, called "2d + 1d", horizontal motion controlled one parameter and vertical motion another. Pressing a button made horizontal motion control the third parameter.

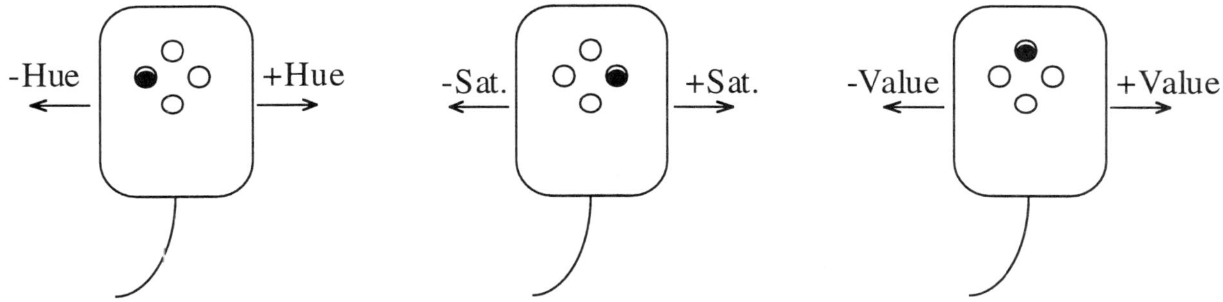

Figure 1: A "3*1d" input scheme. All parameters are controlled by horizontal puck movement, with three separate buttons selecting the active parameter. (Adapted from Fig. 6 of [6]).

A given subject used one color model / interface combination to match five colors six times. The authors analyzed the time required by the subjects to match, the accuracy of the final match, relationship of color model axes to accuracy in various perceptual attributes of the target, time to reach a given level of accuracy, and learning. Accuracy was measured in color distance units (cdus) of the LAB color space. The amount of data reported in their work is tremendous; the following two statistically significant results stand out:

1. Subjects matched most quickly with the Opponent and RGB models (means of 77 and 78 seconds), with HSV twenty-two percent slower (mean of 94 seconds).
2. Subjects matched most accurately with LAB, followed in decreasing order by HSV, Opponent, YIQ, and RGB. The best color model / interface pair, LAB with 2d+1d interface, had a mean accuracy of about 5 cdus, while RGB with a 2d+1d interface was ninety percent worse with a mean accuracy of about 9.5 cdus (these are geometric, not arithmetic, means).

While the experiment was done with due rigor, there were aspects of the experimental task which may have confounded the results. The experiment was done in 1985, at a time when interface design was in its infancy, and the interface used was rather primitive and not representative of contemporary systems. We wondered if the differences in performance they attributed to color models hold with modern interfaces. We located the following limitations in their interface:

1. No visual feedback of the location of the current color in the color space

In neither interface was the subject given any indication of the dimensions of each parameter of the space. Furthermore, they were given no indication of how close they were to the boundaries of each axis. The controlled color simply stopped changing without warning when the subject moved the puck outside the range of one of the coordinates. They refer to this process as "clipping". We conjecture the subjects may have been slower and less accurate because they had so little information available to orient themselves within the color space. This inadequate representation may even have affected some color models more than others, biasing the comparison of models.

2. No kinesthetic or visual feedback from puck position

The lack of visual representation was compounded by the use of relative coordinates for the puck. This meant there was no fixed mapping between the location of the puck on its tablet and the value of a given parameter, eliminating another means the subjects might have used to orient themselves in the space. For example, the puck location gave no indication of how close they were to being clipped. The subjects couldn't orient themselves by "feel" (the location of their arm) nor visually (by looking at the puck).

3. No feedback of the effects of each parameter

While the subjects were initially instructed in the effects of each parameter, they had no visible representation of what the parameters did. It is difficult to infer the effect of a parameter from simply moving the puck and observing the results, because the kind of change in the controlled color varies depending upon what color is currently displayed. For example, in the HSV model the saturation parameter will vary the amount of red if the controlled color has a red hue, but will increase the amount of blue if the controlled color is in that hue. Similar interactions between the parameters occur in the other color models.

The Schwarz interfaces are arguably not typical of the direct manipulation interfaces popular today. Ben Shneiderman's classic definition of direct manipulation [7] includes "continuous display of the object of interest" and "rapid, incremental, reversible operations whose impact on the object of interest is immediately visible." In other words, the user interface should provide rapid feedback of changes to the object of interest. In the case of color models the key question is “what is the object of interest?” While the Schwarz interface displays the current color, it does not display the color’s location within the space of all displayable colors. We believe that the location of the current color is as important to the user as the color itself—the real “object of interest” is not being displayed. Designers of current commercial systems have taken this into account: the Macintosh and Windows tools mentioned earlier both display the location of the current color.

In summary, the Schwarz study contradicts widely-held folklore about the superiority of the HSV color model. A question remains: Will these effects recur in an interface with higher feedback?

METHOD

We designed an experiment comparing the performance of color models in the high-feedback interfaces in use today. We were also interested in how screen representation affects subjects’ performance, and made interface feedback level a second controlled experimental factor.

Experimental Design

The experimental design was two-way factorial, with color models and interfaces as the two between-subject variables, for a total of four subject groups. We used two color models, RGB and HSV, and two interfaces with different kinds of feedback. Twelve subjects were in each group, randomly assigned to a particular color model x interface group. We selected the RGB and HSV models because they are commonly used in color selection tools, are frequently contrasted with one another in the graphics literature, and were two of the most extreme cases of the five used in the Schwarz study.

We were interested in how feedback in the interface affects the usage of color models; our experiment used two interfaces which had increasing levels of visual feedback. To address our first two concerns about representation of the color space, both of our interfaces displayed the location of the current color within the color model. Each of the three parameters of the model was represented by a slider, and an arrow indicated the current value of the associated parameter within its total range (see Color Plates 2 and 3). The user controlled the current color either by dragging the arrow along the slider with the mouse or by clicking directly on some row of the slider. Both of these methods were explicitly demonstrated to the user during the instructional phase.

We wanted to see if the interface, and in particular the visual representation of the *effects* of each parameter, measurably affected users’ performance with a color model. To compare the influence of such a representation, we used two different formats of sliders. One format, called "position-only" (Color Plate 2), gave no indication of what each parameter did: the interior of the sliders was a constant gray at all times. The second format, called "position+effect" (Color Plate 3), filled each slider with a range of colors. Each pixel row on the slider displayed the color that the controlled rectangle would take if the arrow were moved to that row. A user could look at the slider and know what effect it would have if it were moved to any point.

Subjects

We believed that the differences between color models would be most apparent while users were learning them, so only subjects with little to no prior experience with color usage and selection were used in the study. All subjects were given a screening questionnaire about their experience working with colors in both traditional artistic media and computer programs.. The selected subjects were forty-eight unpaid undergraduates. Most were from the first year of the computer science program, while others were enrolled in computer literacy courses. Subjects were also screened with an Ishihara color plates test to ensure that they had normal color vision.

Experimental Environment

The experiments were conducted in a room with controlled lighting Due to memory limitations in the graphics card, the display was functioning at a lower than normal resolution, so subjects sat eight feet away from the screen so that individual pixels would be indistinguishable. The components of the interface were sized for comfortable viewing at that distance.

The experiment was run on an Apple Macintosh IIfx with an Apple 8.24GC accelerated graphics card capable of representing 16 million colors. A SuperMac PressView 21 display was used, set to a whitepoint of D65. This monitor is designed to be used in color-critical applications, has stable color rendition characteristics, and can be set for various calibrated white point and gamma values. We recalibrated the monitor using the SuperMatch calibration tool several times during the experiment to maintain the chromaticities of our target colors. All of our target colors were represented in the RGB space of the standard EBU phosphor chromaticities used in this monitor, and our RGB and HSV models used these phosphor chromaticities as the basis of their axes.

We selected thirty colors. Six of these were from the original Schwarz experiment. The remaining twenty-four were taken from the MacBeth ColorChecker chart [4], a standard reference chart for tests of color rendition. Twelve of these are representative of colors commonly found in natural and office environments (flesh tones, sky blue, and common office colors), six are the additive and subtractive color primaries, and the final six are an achromatic ramp from black to white.

Our data collection program logged the current slider positions and the value of the controlled color every tenth of a second. In particular, the final reading of each match indicated the total time and distance between the controlled and target colors.

Experimental Task

We used a color-matching task: subjects adjusted a controlled color until it matched a target color. Both controlled and target colors subtended just less than two degrees of visual arc of the subject's field of view, allowing us to calculate chromaticities using the 1931 CIE 2° standard observer functions [3]. Each subject used a single color model x interface combination to match the same sequence of thirty different colors. All interaction with the program was done using the standard Macintosh mouse to move three sliders on the screen.

The experimenter demonstrated how to manipulate the sliders using the mouse. To replicate a situation of use similar to what most users typically encounter, no abstract explanation of the color model was given to subjects. They were not explicitly told what the three parameters of their color model were, nor were the parameters named on the screen. In the instructions, subjects were asked to learn how the different sliders affected the color during the course of the experiment. We used Schwarz' wording to describe how closely the subjects should try to match the target color: "continue to refine the match until you think they are the same color or until it becomes *extremely* difficult to get the colors any closer to each other."

After the instruction period, subjects were given ten minutes to practice using the system. The experimenter was present for the first match and then left them alone for the remainder of their practice. The colors used during the practice time were different from those used in the actual experiment. After the practice period, the experimenter returned and started the sequence of thirty experimental colors. Subjects had three minutes to complete a single match. If they did not finish in three minutes, the match was ended by the program and the subjects moved on to the next color. Subjects performed this sequence alone and at their own pace. Times for this phase of the experiment ranged from twenty minutes to an hour and a half, with most subjects taking about forty-five minutes. A concluding questionnaire asked about the subjects' satisfaction and comfort with the experiment.

RESULTS

The average times and accuracies for the four experimental conditions are given in Table 2. With a significance level of $p \leq .05$, analysis of variance revealed no significant differences in time or accuracy measured in LAB color distance units (cdus) between the models. The feedback factor (Table 3) had no significant effect on time, but did significantly affect accuracy ($F_{1,44} = 6.76$, $p = .013$). The mean distance from the target was 2.16 cdus (26%) lower when the subjects were given feedback about the effects of each slider. Note that since there was no significant difference in time between the two feedback conditions, subjects were matching more accurately in the same amount of time and not simply trading off speed for accuracy.

DISCUSSION

The color model is widely presumed to be fundamental to the usability of a color selection tool, yet even with two different interfaces we could find no significant difference in time or accuracy between the RGB and HSV color models. In fact, this is the second experiment we have run using this protocol. The earlier experiment had technical difficulties which prevented us from being able to use all of its data, but the twenty-four data points which are usable also show no significant difference between RGB and HSV. Finally, in a similar experiment, Wells [10] could find no difference in time or accuracy between these two color models. We are not aware of any measured differences between color models when their interfaces provide strong visual feedback.

The high variance of this population may have masked some effects of color model and feedback. With twenty-four subjects in each color model or feedback condition, we have a 95% chance, i.e., $\beta = .05$, of detecting differences of 25 seconds or more between the mean times of the two color models. To accurately detect differences of, say, 10 seconds, would have required over 100 subjects in each condition—far more than was practically possible Considering accuracy of final match, our experiment could detect differences of 3 cdus or more between the mean accuracies of the two color models. While our sample size may not be large enough to detect moderate differences in time and accuracy between the models, we feel it is sufficient to detect the kind of major differences which folklore ascribes to color model.

Comparing the conclusions of the Schwarz study and our own suggests which factors determine the influence of color model on a color matching task. We consider three factors: practice effects, levels of visual feedback of the interfaces, and user selection strategies.

Practice Effects

It takes time to learn a color model. Perhaps differences between color model would emerge after the subjects had more practice. Although in both Schwarz and our present study subjects completed thirty trials, the Schwarz study used the same five colors repeated six times. Our study used thirty different colors to more nearly represent the wide variety that users typically select. We observed that in all our conditions subjects had high variance, suggesting that they were still in early stages of learning. Reducing variance with more practice would perhaps create significant differences in our experiment. For example, RGB with high feedback, which has a mean nearly ten seconds less than the other conditions, might be significantly faster (see Table 2).

Visual Feedback

Our study had significant visual feedback, whereas the Schwarz study had little. This suggests that the Schwarz results may apply only to very low-feedback interfaces. Our data show that feedback does affect performance in a color-matching task, improving accuracy of the match. The data suggest that it makes very little difference which color model is presented to the user for color selection, *provided the location of the current color within the color space is represented*. Users may adapt to whichever model they are given and the model doesn't make a difference.

Selection Strategy

If they are not using the conceptual map provided by the color model, how did our users orient themselves in the color space? They may have adopted a simpler strategy which was independent of the color model. For example, they might have used the following hill-climbing strategy: "Move in a direction. If you are closer to your target, continue moving. If you are further away from the target, backtrack and pick another direction."

To discover user strategies we must look at the paths individual users took through the color space from the initial gray towards the target color. A color model is supposed to help a user predict which adjustments to the sliders will take the controlled color closer to the target. We sought a measure of how *directed* a subject's activity was. We define a *move* to be a single adjustment to a slider, from the time the mouse button was pressed inside the slider to the time the button was released. We characterize a move by its final color, the value of the controlled color at the time the button was released.

If a user has learned a color model and is actively using it to plan a path towards the target color, most of the moves will end with the controlled color closer to the target. We used the notion of moves to quantify how much backtracking the subjects did. If most of the subjects' moves took them closer to the target, it provides evidence that they are actively using the color model.

We broke every trial down into its constituent moves and computed the distance of the ending color from the target. Table 4 lists the percentage of total moves which ended with the subject closer to the target.

Table 2: times and accuracies for each condition.

Model	Feedback Type	Mean Secs.	Std. Dev.	Mean LAB cdus*	Std. Dev.
RGB	position-only	61.9	19.5	8.3	3.15
RGB	position+effect	50.3	18.7	6.1	3.26
HSV	position-only	59.9	27.3	8.0	2.17
HSV	position+effect	59.3	26.1	5.9	1.87

* The cdu data were positively skewed. For analysis of variance, the natural log of the distances was used.

Table 3: times and accuracies for feedback types.

Feedback Type	Mean Secs.	Std. Dev.	Mean LAB cdus[1].	Std. Dev.
position-only	60.9	23.2	8.23	2.89
position+effect	54.8	22.7	6.07	2.74
Percent Change	not. sig.		26%[2]	

1. The cdu data were positively skewed. For analysis of variance, the natural log of the distances was used.
2. Significant at p=.013.

Table 4: proportion of moves ending closer to the target

Color Model	Feedback Level	Percent Closer
RGB	position-only	57%
RGB	position+effect	60%
HSV	position-only	61%
HSV	position+effect	62%

The subjects only moved closer to their target on a little more than half of their moves. This admittedly crude measure suggests that the subjects were not using the color model to predict where their moves were going but instead adopted some sort of simple hill-climbing strategy. This hypothesis is also supported by the significant improvement in accuracy for the "position+effect" interface, which allows the subject to predict the effect of the next move by looking at the screen display rather than reasoning based upon the color model. The subjects were more accurate when they could better predict their next move.

Color Selection in Actual Practice

How applicable are our results to actual conditions of color selection? In the field, users typically perform a color *selection* task, picking a "suitable" or "harmonious" color for an image, rather than the color *matching* task of our experiment. We chose a color matching task for two reasons. First, it is a procedure with a long history in color science, allowing us to use a well-established experimental protocol. Second, the task gives us well-defined objective measures of performance, consistently applied for all subjects. By contrast, an experimental task of selecting "suitable" colors would introduce many uncontrolled variables, confounding our factors of color model and feedback.

Our research explores the precise effects of these two factors and their interactions. While color selection is different from color matching, the tasks both involve navigation through a color space, and we believe that the role of color model and feedback in navigation are comparable in both tasks. Once controlled experiments have clarified the relationships between color model and feedback, more qualitative field studies can be used to examine their effects in actual contexts of use.

CONCLUSIONS

This experiment explored the relationship between the color model and the interface which presented it to the user. We considered the effect of differing levels of feedback in the user interface. We performed a color-matching experiment with two interfaces with differing feedback levels: one interface that visually represented the user's current location and a second which supplemented that location information with an indication of the function of each color model parameter. With these interfaces we could not find a significant difference between the accuracy and speed of the RGB and HSV models, but found that higher levels of feedback resulted in more accurate matches. We recommend that designers of color selection interfaces pay careful attention to the amount and kind of feedback they provide—it may be as important as the color model.

Future Work

We would like to extend the work by looking in greater detail at the paths taken by the various users and determine whether they were using the color model or not. The approach of counting the proportion of moves closer to the target can be refined. We would like to see if the details of the traces are follow a pattern of systematic use of the axes of the color models or instead have the quasi-random character of a hill-climbing approach. As a further extension, we would like to run a longitudinal experiment to reduce the variance over a longer period of time and see what learning effects occur as the subjects become more practiced.

ACKNOWLEDGMENTS

The research work reported here was started by Don Hubbard and greatly assisted by Professor Gary Meyer. Bonnie John and Eckehard Doerry provided many useful comments on drafts of this paper.

REFERENCES

1. Berk, T., Brownston L. and Kaufman, A. A human factors study of color notation systems for computer graphics. *Communications of the ACM 25*, 8 (Aug. 1982), 547-550.
2. Foley, J., van Dam, A., Feiner, S. and Hughes, J. *Computer Graphics: Principles and Practice*, 2nd. ed. Addison Wesley, Reading, MA, 1990.
3. Hunt, R. W. G. *Measuring Color*, 2d. ed. Ellis Horwood, 1991.
4. Macbeth. *ColorChecker chart* (1990 ed.). Munsell Color, Baltimore, MD, 1990.
5. Murch, G. The effective use of color: cognitive principles. *TEKniques* 8, 2 (1984), 25-31.
6. Schwarz, M., Cowan, W. and Beatty, J. An experimental comparison of RGB, YIQ, LAB, HSV, and opponent color models. *ACM Transactions on Graphics 6*, 2 (April 1987) 123-158.
7. Shneiderman, B. Direct Manipulation: A Step Beyond Programming Languages. *IEEE Computer 16*, 8 (Aug. 1983) 57–69.
8. Smith, A. R. Color Gamut Transform Pairs. *Computer Graphics 12*, 3 (Aug. 1978), 12–19.
9. Tektronix, Inc. U. S. Patent number 4,985,853.
10. Wells, E. *A Comparison of Interactive Color Specification Systems for Human-Computer Interfaces.* M.S. Thesis in Visualization Sciences, Texas A and M University, 1994.

Externalising Abstract Mathematical Models

Lisa Tweedie, Robert Spence, Huw Dawkes and Hua Su

Department of Electrical Engineering,
Imperial College of Science, Technology and Medicine
South Kensington, London, SW7 2BT
Tel: +44 171 594 6261
l.tweedie@ic.ac.uk

ABSTRACT
Abstract mathematical models play an important part in engineering design, economic decision making and other activities. Such models can be externalised in the form of Interactive Visualisation Artifacts (IVAs). These IVAs display the data generated by mathematical models in simple graphs which are interactively linked. Visual examination of these graphs enables users to acquire insight into the complex relations embodied in the model. In the engineering context this insight can be exploited to aid design. The paper describes two IVAs for engineering design: The Influence Explorer and The Prosection Matrix. Formative evaluation studies are briefly discussed.

KEYWORDS: Interactive Graphics, Visualization

INTRODUCTION

Many mathematical problems can benefit from being examined visually. Indeed most spreadsheets and statistical packages enable users to quickly create static representations of their data. These graphs have an accepted role as tools for mathematical problem solving. However the value of adding interactivity to such representations has yet to gain widespread recognition.

Responsive (i.e. rapid) interaction can facilitate active exploration of problems in a manner that is inconceivable with static displays. For example users can start to pose "What if" queries spontaneously as they work through a task. Such exploration can enormously facilitate the acquisition of qualitative insight into the nature of the task at hand, as well as revealing direct quantitative results.

In this paper we describe what we call Interactive Visualisation Artifacts (IVAs). These are environments developed to enable users to solve a particular task - in this case within the field of engineering design.

The IVAs we will discuss here differ from much existing work principally because we are not attempting to visualise

CHI 96 Vancouver, BC Canada
© 1996 ACM 0-89791-777-4/96/04..$3.50

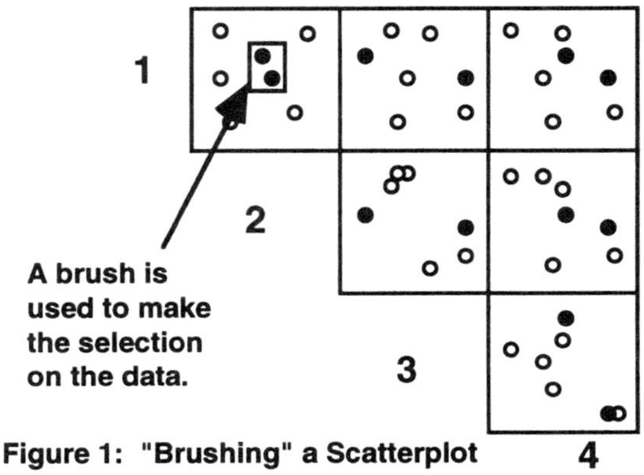

Figure 1: "Brushing" a Scatterplot

raw data but, rather, data which is precalculated or generated on demand from mathematical models. We also exclude data which maps comfortably onto natural representations e.g. 3D volumetric models of flow through a pipe. Instead we focus on more *abstract* mathematical models which have no obvious representation.

We can take as an example the design of an engineering artifact. Mathematical models (equations) exist which relate the artifact's performance to the parameters that describe the physical nature of that artifact. Thus, for a bridge, performances such as traffic capacity and cost can be calculated from a knowledge of parameters such as cable diameters and foundation depth. A designer needs to explore the relationships between parameters and performances in order to elicit a useful design.

The development of IVAs for such applications requires the creation of new representations that externalise pertinent aspects of the model. The IVAs we describe in this paper show how such novel representations can be created by **interactively linking simple graphs in several ways**. On a simple level we can link many similar graphs, as Becker et al [3] did with their "brushed" scatterplots (Figure 1). We can also link different *types* of representations together. For example, by selecting a subset of data on a histogram and colour encoding the same subset on a scatterplot. These links can also perform different functions - for example the selected subset could be colour encoded or it could be hidden from view.

Two IVAs for engineering design are described in this paper: the Influence Explorer and the Prosection Matrix. They exhibit powerful and effective linking both within and between IVAs.

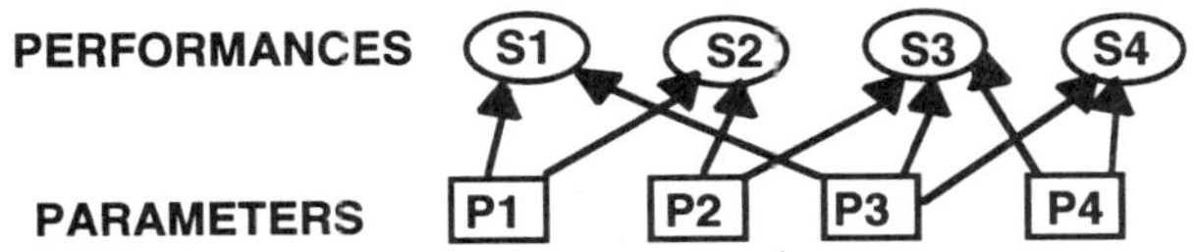

Figure 2: The Parameter->Performance relationship

Previous Work

The idea of linking graphical representations is not new. As early as 1978 Newton [12] was linking several scatterplots and colour encoding selections to discover trends in data. Many others have developed simple linking IVAs e.g. IVEE [1], Permutation Matrices [4], BEAD [5], SeeSoft ™[6], AutoVisual [7], VisDB [10], Nested Histograms [13], The Table Lens [14], Visulab [15], The InfoCrystal [17], The Attribute Explorer [18] and The Dynamic HouseFinder [20].

Most of these IVAs only use one type of representation to display data. However a combination of representations may also be beneficial, since the user is then able to consider the problem from several different perspectives. Schmid and Hinterberger [15] have called this "Comparative Multivariate Visualisation" and embodied the concept in their "Visulab" software. Here four different representations (Parallel Coordinates [9], Andrews Plots [2], Permutation Matrices [4] and Multiple Scatterplots [3]) can be linked in several ways : encoding with colour, hiding part of the data and reordering the data. The use of several different representations of data, and the manner of their linking, is a key issue in the development of IVAs.

Visual Design Issues

The design of any IVA should proceed with various characteristics of visual problem solving in mind (Tweedie [19]). As Nardi and Zarmer [11] point out, IVAs are external representations of the users problem which "*stimulate and initiate cognitive activity*". Zhang and Norman [21] identify that such external representations act as memory aids; provide information perceptually without need for interpretation; anchor and structure cognitive behaviour; and change the task.

Suchman [18] emphasises that "*it is frequently only on acting in a present situation that its possibilities become clear*". In other words users will often pick up information opportunistically from their environment. It is partly this tendency to stimulate opportunistic behaviour that makes IVAs interesting. Consequently, the visual cues provided must be designed to support this opportunistic process.

DESIGN FOR MANUFACTURABILITY

A typical task that has a mathematical model associated with it is that of engineering design. For a given product such as a light bulb, a model can be formed of the way the parameters (whose value is open to choice by the designer) influence performances (Figure 2). In the light bulb example, performances such as a bulb's brightness and its lifetime will partly be determined by parameters such as the number of coils in its filament and the thickness of that filament. The mathematical model is a set of equations, each relating a performance to a number of parameters.

The designer must choose numerical values for parameters in such a way that the performances they influence, usually in a very complex fashion, take on values acceptable to a customer. In other words, when designing a light bulb, the designer has to keep a specification in mind. If for example they are asked to design a light bulb that will be very bright and last for at least 6 months then they need to find the set of parameters values that will satisfy this specification.

The traditional design process

Given a set of parameters, an engineering artifact can be simulated to establish the corresponding performances. Unfortunately the reverse is not true: a designer cannot choose a performance value and calculate the parameters needed to achieve it. For this reason traditional design is characterised by a series of iterations in which the designer selects a set of parameters and then simulates the artifact to find out what the performances are. Design proceeds through the gradual adjustment of parameters until a satisfactory set of performance values is found. This design process is illustrated in figure 3a for an artifact defined by two parameters and influencing two performances. The design is represented by a single point moving in parameter and performance space. This "trial and error" approach can be tedious and time-consuming and is heavily dependent on a designer's expertise.

Precalculation

The design process can be immensely simplified if one has mathematical models of the relationship between parameters and performances. Figure 3b shows how such models can be used to create a precalculated exploration database. The designer selects a wide "Region of Exploration" in parameter space within which the final design might well be expected to lie. Within this region a large number of points (e.g. over 500) are generated randomly, each point representing a design. For each of these sets of parameter values the corresponding point in performance space is computed using the artifact's mathematical model. In our light bulb example, a dataset generated in this way would describe a variety of light bulbs each having randomly different parameter values and associated performances. The benefit of creating such a dataset is also illustrated in figure 3b. The designer can now readily select their desired performance values and "look up" which parameter sets give them those values.

Designing in the real world

Unfortunately the aim of engineering design is not simply that of finding a single set of parameter values that satisfies

Figure 3

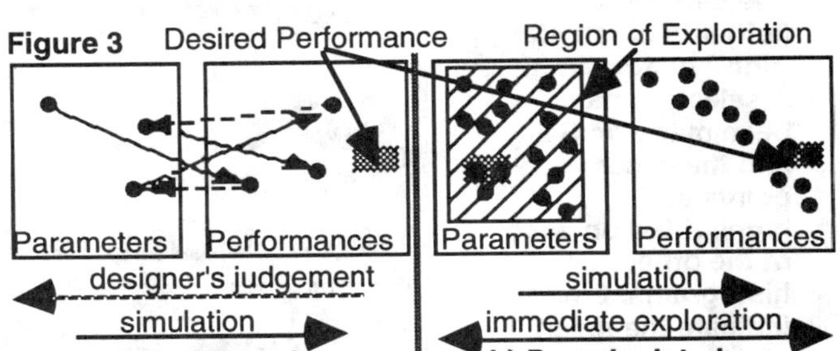

a) Traditional iterative simulation

b) Precalculated simulation

a specification. Inevitable fluctuations in manufacturing processes mean that parameter values can only be guaranteed to lie within a so-called tolerance *range*. For example the filament width of our light bulb might vary slightly during manufacture, and this variation could have a crucial effect on a performance. We therefore need to define exactly how much each parameter can vary. The combined set of parameter tolerance ranges defines a *tolerance region* in parameter space. These are the bulbs that will be manufactured.

Figure 4 shows the rectangular tolerance region for the simple case of two parameters. In the same space, an irregularly shaped "Region of Acceptability" defines the location of all the artifacts that satisfy the performance requirements. Achieving a good design is a matter of fitting these two regions to each other with maximum overlap

Overall Design Objectives

As well as satisfying the customer's requirements on performance, it is usually the case that there is also some overall objective that must be achieved. One such objective is that of maximising the manufacturing yield, which is the percentage of mass-produced bulbs that satisfy the customer's requirements on performance. With reference to Figure 4, yield is that percentage of the tolerance region which lies within the region of acceptability.

Another such design objective might be the unit manufacturing cost of each bulb that is shipped to the customer. Usually the wider the tolerances are on the parameters the cheaper the bulb will be to manufacture.

THE INFLUENCE EXPLORER

Precalculation forms the backbone of the Influence Explorer. Once the data has been precalculated (as described earlier), it provides an exploration database on which to start an investigation. Figure 5 shows how the population of 600 precalculated designs is displayed in the form of histograms. All performance histograms are plotted horizontally to the left of the screen and the parameter histograms vertically to the right. An artifact is represented once on each plot in the appropriate bin. Each column in the histogram represents the number of designs that fall within that bin. In other words, the histograms are frequency plots.

Qualitative Exploration

In order to form an effective external representation of the task the Influence Explorer must allow the user to gradually

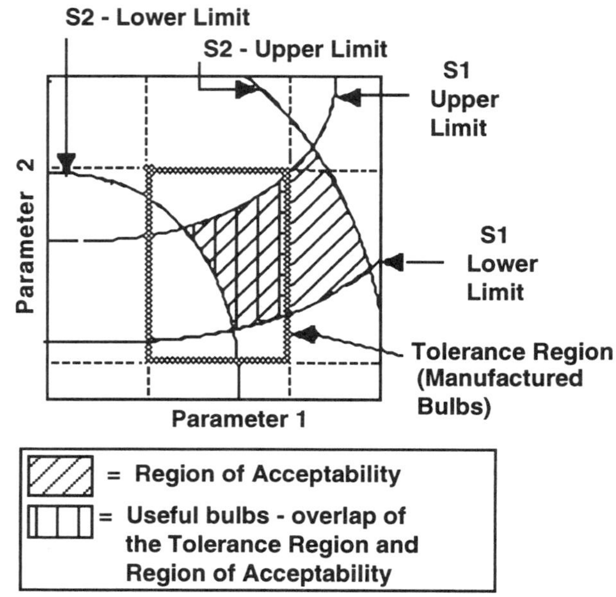

Figure 4: In 2-parameter space, two performances F1 and F2 define upper and lower limits for acceptable performance. Manufactured bulbs lie within the tolerance region.

build up a coherent picture of their problem, in other words the complexity must be introduced in stages.

In the initial stages of design the user will want to gain a *qualitative* understanding of the problem. The designer can place exploratory limits on parameters and performances, thereby defining ranges of those quantities. In Figure 5 a range of performance on S4 has been defined with a slider. This action leads to the colour linking (black) of those bulbs that lie within the selected range on the S4 histogram and all the other histograms, so that the selected subset can be viewed across all the histograms. The potential for exploring the inter-relation between parameters and performances is now apparent. Confidence in these perceived relations can be sought by interactively moving the selected range of S4 up and down its scale and observing the corresponding movement of the highlighted bulbs on the other scales. The power of such a dynamic action to generate insight is difficult to convey in static words and diagrams, but is *strikingly* obvious in actual use.

It is worth emphasising that the discovery of a "trade-off" relation between two performances is immensely important

Figure 5: The performance (left) and parameter (right) histograms. A selection has been made on S4 and these same points are highlighted on each of the other histograms. Circles indicate the mean of the selected points.

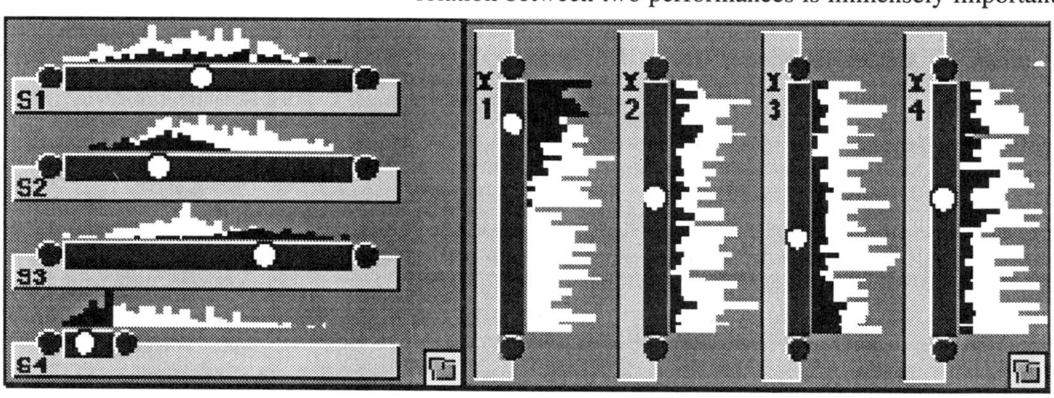

in engineering design. In the Influence Explorer this discovery is virtually immediate, whereas in conventional design practice such a trade-off might be discovered only after tedious search or, at worst, not at all.

Additional tools enhance the functionality of the Influence Explorer. A mouse-click on a bulb in one histogram highlights that same bulb, and displays corresponding values, in all the other histograms. Another option connects these points with a line and allows the comparison of several different bulbs. These lines are known as "parallel coordinate" plots [9]. Yet another option places a circle on each of the histogram scales indicating the mean of the currently selected bulbs (see figure 5). This is useful when a range is being moved as it eases detection of trends.

Quantitative Design decisions

As well as indulging in *qualitative* exploration, the designer must at some stage take note of the *quantitative* detail associated with a customer's requirements on performance. To do so a "specification option" is selected (Figure 6 - colour plate).

The placement of upper and lower limits on the performance scales invokes another linking mechanism. Red colour coding identifies bulbs that lie within all the performance limits, those bulbs which fail one limit are colour coded black, while dark and light grey denotes two and three failed limits respectively. Such colour coding provides valuable sensitivity information. For example, it is immediately noticed (Figure 6 - colour plate) that a relaxation of the upper limit on S4 would turn some black bulbs into (acceptable) red bulbs, knowledge which might well lead to a discussion about the wisdom of that particular upper limit. Negotiations concerning performance specifications are common to engineering and could be considerably clarified using this information.

Design for Manufacture

As already explained, inevitable variations in the manufacturing process are such that, in the design of a *mass-produced* artifact such as a light bulb, the designer must be concerned with the selection of parameter *ranges* rather than specific values. It is the combination of all these selected parameter ranges that must satisfy the performance limits defined by the customer.

Parameter ranges are defined by the selection of upper and lower limits (Figure 7 - colour plate), in exactly the same manner as for the performances. Again, the selection of parameter limits invokes a linking mechanism, once more leading to additional colour encoding. Though at first sight complex, the coding is, we suggest, matched to an engineering designer's real needs and, given the motivation provided by a tool offering responsive exploration, is readily, even eagerly learned. Figure 8 (colour plate) is a replica of Figure 4 with the relevant colour codings shown. Figure 8 and the table attached to figure 7 may help clarify the rationale behind this coding:

- **Red** denotes bulbs that satisfy all limits. They lie within parameter limits (and are therefore manufactured) and they satisfy the customer's performance limits.
- **Black** denotes a bulb that satisfies all the performance limits but lies outside one parameter limit , and is therefore not manufactured. Thus it will turn red if one parameter limit is adjusted to include it.
- **Blue** bulbs are those which are manufactured (and hence lie within parameter limits) but fail one or more performances. These are the bulbs which cause a reduction in yield. Tightening a parameter limit to eliminate blue bulbs (for example raising the lower limit of X1 in Figure 7) will reduce the number of manufactured artifacts which violate a customer's requirements, hence raising the yield. The Blue bulbs are coded in two shades of blue - **Dark Blue** indicates those bulbs that are manufactured and only violate one performance limit; relaxation of that performance limit will turn those bulbs into red ones (e.g. in figure 7 expanding the lower limit on S1 will turn the dark blue bulbs red). **Light Blue** indicates those bulbs which are manufactured and violate more than one performance limit.
- **Grey** bulbs are those which fail one parameter range and one or more performance limits. They would therefore turn blue if they were to be enclosed within the tolerance region. Thus in Figure 7 if the upper limit on X2 is extended to turn the black bulbs into red ones, this gain in the number of (red) acceptable bulbs would be offset by the number of grey bulbs turning blue and, thereby, adding unsatisfactory bulbs to the manufacturing process.

The principal advantage of such colour coding is that it indicates how *altering* the parameter or performance limits will effect the overall usefulness of the design.

Yield Enhancement

To facilitate design for maximum yield the Influence Explorer continuously computes, and displays in numerical form, the value of the yield. The designer may well begin by attempting to select parameter ranges that maximise the yield, hopefully to a value of 100%. In order to achieve such a high yield the user needs to adjust the tolerances taking account of where the red and therefore "useful" points lie and trying to reduce the number of blue points. By keeping an eye on the yield the user can slowly optimise their solution until they have found an optimum yield.

100% yield can obviously be achieved by making the parameter ranges sufficiently small (Figure 14 - colour plate), but another overall objective - the minimisation of manufacturing cost - militates against such a solution. It is normally the case that the wider the parameter ranges, the lower the cost of the artifact. There is therefore a strong incentive to select parameter ranges that are as wide as possible commensurate with an acceptably high yield (see Figure 15 - colour plate).

Focused Sampling

Unfortunately when interacting with tolerances limits the precalculated data set becomes a constraining factor in the Influence Explorer. Since the requirements are now becoming specific, it is unlikely that many of the original 600 points will fall within *all* the performance and parameter requirements. This curse of dimensionality results in very few colour coded points. To overcome this problem the Influence Explorer is programmed to

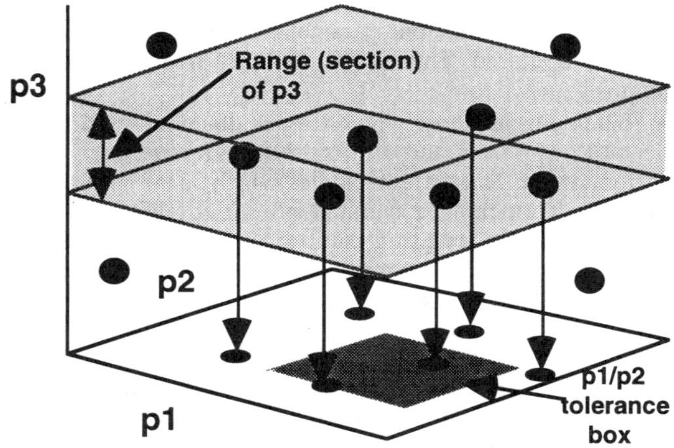

Figure 9: A section of p3 is projected onto a p1/p2 scatterplot

dynamically resample the model so that a number of points always fall within and close to the tolerance region. Evidence of this process can be seen in Figure 7 where the column heights within the tolerance limits are higher than column heights on the rest of each parameter histogram.

THE PROSECTION MATRIX

The Prosection Matrix provides an alternative perspective of the model. It is a set of scatterplots (Figure 10) arranged in a matrix, as suggested by Becker et al [3]. Each scatterplot corresponds to a different pair of parameters, and all possible parameter pairs are represented. Thus, for the bulb's four parameters there are six scatterplots.

The construction of each scatterplot is illustrated conceptually in Figure 9 for the simple case of a 3-parameter system. p1 and p2 are the scatterplot's two parameters. p3 is a third parameter on which a parameter range has been set. Only data that falls within p3's chosen parameter range is projected down onto the p1p2 plane. This is a **pro**jection of a **section** of parameter space, hence the name 'Prosection' (the term came from by a paper by Furnas and Buja [8]). This prosection process is repeated for every pair of parameters so that each scatterplot is displaying different data. The tolerance ranges for the scatterplots two parameters (p1 and p2 in figure 9) can also be projected on to the plot in the form of a tolerance box.

The Prosection Matrix shown in Figure 10 actually refers to a situation in which each parameter range is very small, leading to a small tolerance region (the small grey dot in the centre of each scatterplot). Because the parameter ranges are small, they define a very thin 'slice' through multi-dimensional parameter space, and therefore the resulting scatterplots show well-defined boundaries associated with the different performance limits of Figure 10. The colour coding used defines how well designs satisfy these performance limits. In Figure 10 designs that are acceptable are black, those that failed only one performance limit are dark grey and those that fail two are medium grey etc. One of the benefits of this colour coding is that the designer can explore the effect of moving the boundaries in the scatterplot. Thus, in Figure 11, the designer has moved the lower limit of performance S3 even lower. A comparison of Figure 10 and 11 reveals how the corresponding boundary has moved, increasing the area of the (here, black) acceptable region. Exploration of this kind allows a designer to form a strategy for combining and trading off different performance requirements.

Though Figure 9 provides a conceptual illustration of the formation of each scatterplot within the Prosection Matrix it is actually unsuitable for implementation because it would result in a very grainy representation. Instead, each scatterplot is filled using a matrix of small coloured squares. For example if we consider the (top left) X1X2 scatterplot in Figure 11 its area is divided in 44^2 squares, The Cartesian coordinates of each square's midpoint defines values of X1 and X2. Values of X3 and X4 are then

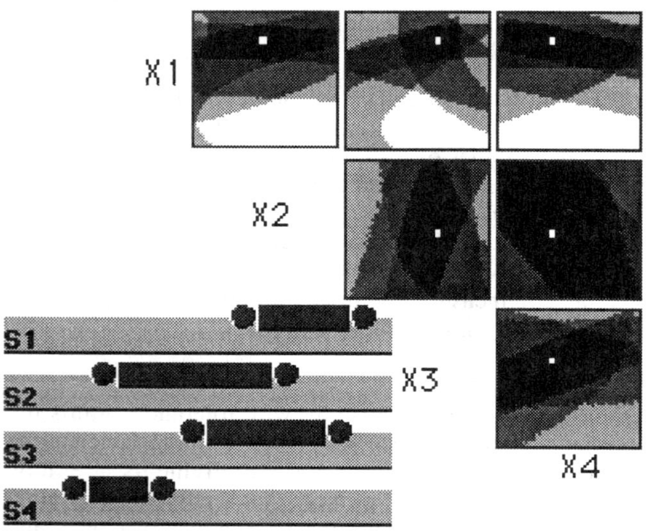

Figure 10: This Prosection Matrix represents 'slices' through parameter space. The grey scaling show how the data satisfies the performance requirements.

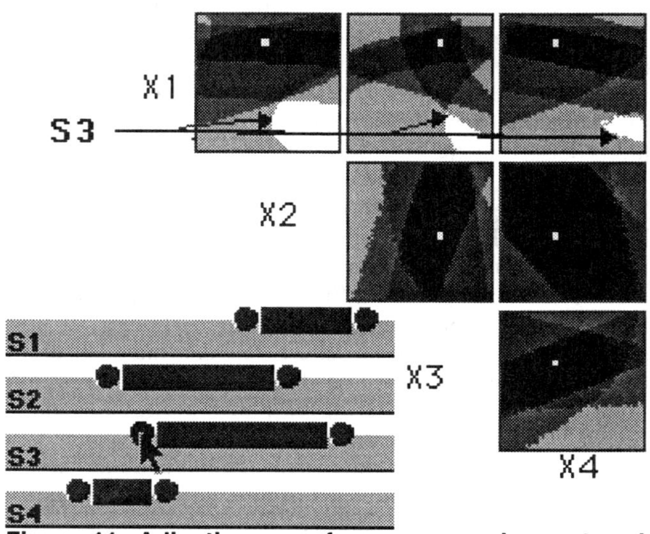

Figure 11: Adjusting a performance requirement and viewing how the related boundary moves in parameter space

selected randomly from within their tolerance range for each square. The corresponding values of the performances S1 to S4 are then computed from the model and compared with their respective limits. The square is then coloured according to the scheme already defined. For clarity, in the case of Figure 11 the X3 and X4 ranges are actually set to a single point so no randomisation occurs.

The existence of significant parameter *ranges* rather than single parameter values changes the detailed appearance of the Prosection Matrix but not its general character (Figure 12). Again consider the X1X2 scatterplot (top left). The original value of X1 has been replaced by a range of X1 as indicated by the yellow line. The immediate effect is that for all the scatterplots that don't have X1 as an axis, X1 is now randomly chosen within the selected *range* of X1 values rather than set at a single value. The increased fuzziness of these plots reflects this process. The rest of Figure 12 shows the effect of additionally assigning ranges to X2, X3 and X4.

Figure 13 (colour plate) shows how the Prosection Matrix looks when the performance and parameter limits are set as in Figure 7. The red regions now correspond to acceptable bulbs, whereas those that are manufactured lie within the yellow tolerance regions. The small percentage of red points within this region indicate a low yield (19%). In Figure 14 (colour plate) the user has set the tolerances to very narrow ranges to find a high yield (100%). Since wider tolerance ranges are normally associated with lower cost, the designer will endeavour to make the yellow -bounded tolerance region as large as possible, perhaps even trading off manufacturing yield against cost. Figure 15 (colour plate) shows how the user has adjusted the parameter ranges so that they just fit inside the red region, resulting in much wider tolerances (potentially cheaper components) whilst maintaining a reasonably high yield (96%)

FORMATIVE EVALUATION STUDIES

The design of IVAs is difficult - it is often hard to judge what users will find intuitive and how an IVA will support a particular task. We have therefore carried out a number of formative evaluation studies at different stages of the IVA's development. Ten pairs of subjects were tested. They were all graduate engineers/ scientists enrolled on PhD programs. The pairs worked together, first with the Influence Explorer, then the Prosection Matrix and finally both tools together. Reassuringly, each pair of subjects were able to complete a tolerance design task in about 30 minutes.

We learnt some very simple lessons from these evaluations:
a) *Maximise the directness of the interactivity.* For example one version of the Prosection Matrix forced users to map their interaction from the sliders. However users preferred to select and drag the tolerance box directly .
b) *Seek out the most crucial information and then represent it appropriately and simply.* The most obvious example of

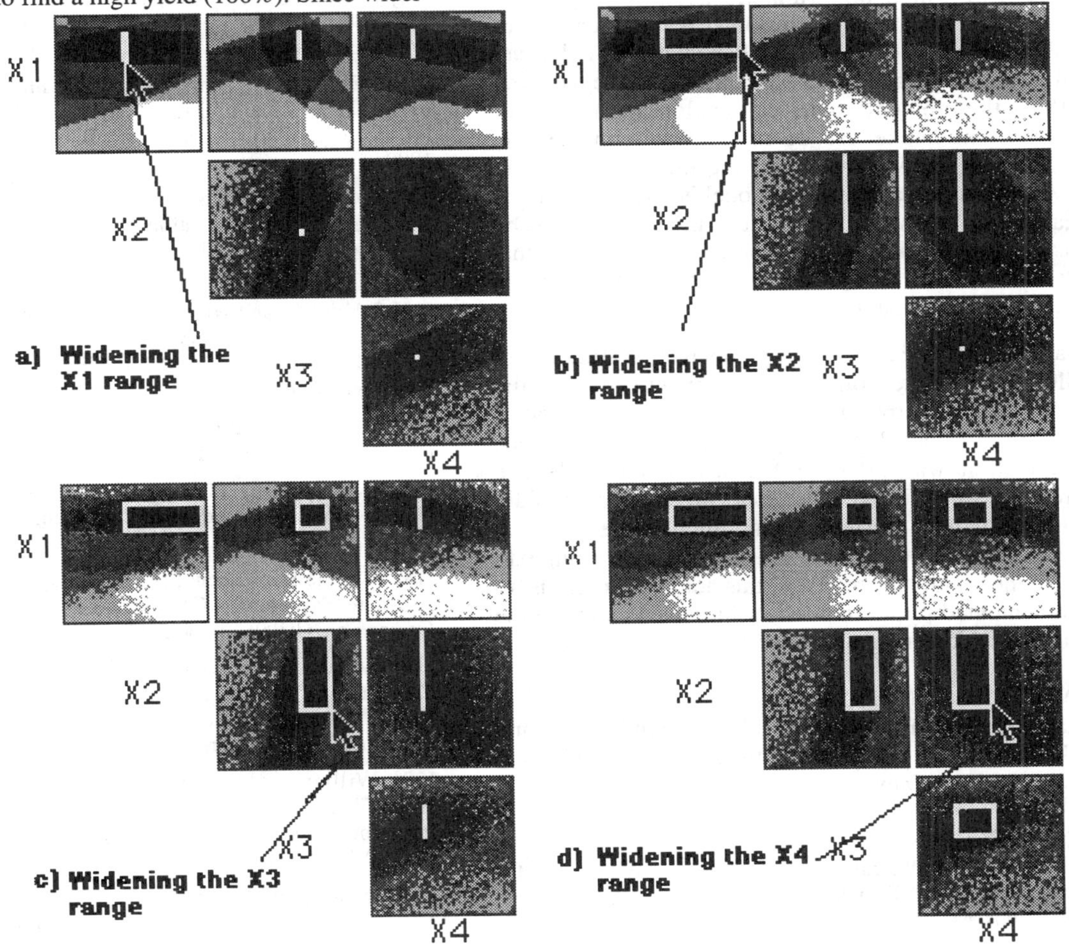

Figure 12: Gradually increasing the tolerance region so that sections of the data are projected. The boundaries become fuzzier as the ranges are adjusted.

this was the colour coding. Initially when considering the interface for setting up a performance specifications we attempted to colour code all the different variations of failure. Then we realised that this coding could be considerably simplified if we focused on encoding data that satisfied the performance limits and perhaps more importantly data that *almost* satisfied those limits. Colour coding the influence explorer for tolerance design was more difficult. The solution presented in this paper (Figure 8) has attempted to reduce the colour coded information to that which will provide immediate and useful information.
c) *There is a trade-off between the amount of information, simplicity and accuracy.* Ensuring that there is sufficient information to complete a task was an important issue. This emerged in the Influence Explorer when we tried adding tolerances with the original precalculated dataset. Using dynamic focused sampling overcame this problem.

CONCLUSIONS

The Influence Explorer and Prosection Matrix have now be utilised in a wide variety of industrial collaborations in electronic, structural and mechanotronic domains. The enthusiastic reaction of those who have observed and experimented with these IVAs suggests that the potential offered by immediately available and responsive interaction is considerable.

There are many reasons for this enthusiasm. One is the readiness with which opportunistic as well as planned exploration can be carried out. Another is the directness of external representations. Abstract Mathematical Models are difficult for the untrained user to interpret. However using these IVAs the problem holder can explore the model for themselves, and make use of their own considerable experience and knowledge to test the models validity in their own terms. A mathematical model is one thing, but an externalisation of that mathematical model that can be responsively explored is quite another. A third reason is that these tools transform a very difficult cognitive problem into a much easier perceptual task.

Many avenues of research and experimentation still need to be followed up. One concerns the enhancement of the designer's expertise by some of the automated tolerance design algorithms developed over the last two decades. One such algorithm was incorporated within the Influence Explorer and, when invoked, automatically and very rapidly (e.g. 10 seconds) adjusted the 'nominal value' of each parameter (the mid-point of the selected parameter range) to maximise the yield. Nevertheless, this automation needs to be complemented by an interface which will facilitate the human observation and guidance of automated design.

ACKNOWLEDGEMENTS

We thank Aarnout Brombacher (Philips, Eindhoven) and John Nelder. This work was implemented in C on a Macintosh by Huw Dawkes.

REFERENCES

[1] Ahlberg C. and Wistrand E., "IVEE: An Environment for Automatic Creation of Dynamic Queries Applications," CHI'95 Demonstrations, May 1995.

[2] Andrews D.F. "Plots of High-Dimensional Data" Biometrics, March 1972, pp 69-97

[3] Becker R.A., Huber P.J., Cleveland W.S. and Wilks A.R., "Dynamic Graphics for Data Analysis", Stat. Science 2, 1987.

[4] Bertin J., "Graphics and Graphic Information Processing", deGruyter Press, Berlin, 1977.

[5] Chalmers M., "Using a Landscape to represent a corpus of documents", Springer-Verlag Proceedings of COSIT '93, Elba, pp. 377-390, September 1993.

[6] Eick S.G., Steffen J.L. and Sumner E.E., " SeeSoft ™ - A Tool for Visualizing Line Oriented Software", IEEE Transactions on Software Engineering, pp. 11-18, 1992.

[7] Feiner S. and Beshers C."Worlds within Worlds: Metaphors for Exploring n-Dimensional Virtual Worlds", ACM Proceeings 1990 Conference on User Interface Software Design, pp 76-83

[8] Furnas G.W. and Buja A., "Prosection Views: Dimensional Inference through Sections and Projections", Journal of Computational and Graphic Statistics 3 (4), pp. 323-353, 1994.

[9] Inselberg A., "The plane with parallel co-ordinates", The Visual Computer 1, pp. 69-91, 1985.

[10] Keim D.A. and Kriegal H., "VisDB: Database Exploration using Multidimensional Visualization", IEEE Computer Graphics and Applications September, pp. 40-49, 1994.

[11] Nardi B.A. and Zarmer C.L., "Beyond Models and Metaphors: Visual Formalisms in User Interface Design", Journal of Visual Languages and Computing 4, pp. 5- 33, 1993.

[12] Newton C.M., " Graphics: from alpha to omega in data analysis", Graphical Representation of Multivariate Data, P.C.C. Wang (Ed) New York: Academic Press, pp. 59-92, 1978.

[13] Mihalisin T., Gawlinski E., Timlin J. and Schwegler J., "Visualizing Scalar Field on an N-dimensional Lattice", Proceedings of Visualization 90, IEEE CS Press, pp. 255-262, 1990.

[14] Rao R. and Card S.K., "The Table Lens: Merging Graphical and Symbolic Representations in an Interactive Focus + Context Visualization for Tabular Information", Proceedings of CHI'94, Boston, ACM Press, pp. 318-322, 1994.

[15] Schmid C. and Hinterberger H., "Comparative Multivariate Visualization Across Conceptually Different Graphic Displays", Proceedings of the SSDBM VII, IEEE Computer Society Press, September 1994.

[16] Spoerri A., "InfoCrystal: A visual tool for Information retrieval" Proceedings of Visualization '93 pp150-157.

[17] Suchman L.A., "Plans and Situated Actions - The Problem of Human-Machine Communication", Cambridge University Press, 1987.

[18] Tweedie L.A., Spence R., Bhoghal R. and Williams D., "The Attribute Explorer", ACM, Video Proceedings and Conference Companion, CHI'94, pp. 435-436, April 1994.

[19] Tweedie L.A., "Interactive Visualisation Artifacts: how can abstractions inform design?", People and Computers X : Proc. of HCI'95 Huddersfield, (Eds) Kirby M.A.R., Dix A.J. and Finlay J.E., Cambridge University Press, pp. 247-265, 1995.

[20] Williamson C. and Shneiderman B., "The Dynamic HomeFinder: Evaluating dynamic queries in a real estate information exploration system", ACM, Proceedings SIGIR'92, pp. 339-346, 1992.

[21] Zhang J. and Norman D.A., "Representations in Distributed Cognitive Tasks", Cognitive Science 18, pp. 87-122, 1994.

Structuring Information With Mental Models: A Tour of Boston

Ishantha Lokuge
MIT Media Lab
20 Ames Street
Cambridge, MA 02139
ishi@media.mit.edu

Stephen A. Gilbert
Brain & Cognitive Sciences
MIT, E10-120
Cambridge, MA 02139
stephen@psyche.mit.edu

Whitman Richards
MIT Media Lab
20 Ames Street
Cambridge, MA 02139
whit@media.mit.edu

ABSTRACT
We present a new systematic method of structuring information using mental models. This method can be used both to evaluate the efficiency of an information structure and to build user-centered information structures. In this paper we present the method using Boston tourist attractions as an example domain. We describe several interfaces that take advantage of our mental models with an activation spreading network. Multidimensional Scaling and Trajectory Mapping are used to build our mental models. Because of the robustness of the technique, it is easy to compare individual difference in mental models and to customize interfaces for individual models.

Keywords
Cognitive models, multidimensional scaling, visualization, interaction design, evaluation.

INTRODUCTION
We all know that a curious person can more efficiently absorb information when it is well structured than when it is arbitrarily scattered. The question that every information architect then asks is, "How might I best organize the information for that person?" This question contains three issues: what structures are useful for organizing information in general, what structures are useful for organizing *that* information, and what structures are useful for organizing information for *that* person.

To answer these above questions, we propose (i) collecting experimental data from a number of subjects, (ii) analyzing the mental models of those subjects with Multidimensional Scaling (MDS) [7, 15, 16] and Trajectory Mapping (TM) [4, 9, 13], and then (iii) using those models to design information structures. Such models should lead more quickly to suitable interfaces rather than beginning with trial and error explorations.

CHI 96 Vancouver, BC Canada
© 1996 ACM 0-89791-777-4/96/04..$3.50

Before continuing on to details, we offer definitions of "information structure" and "mental model." By "information structure" we mean an arrangement of pieces of information. The arrangement might be a 2-D array on a table or a screen, as in a card game or a spreadsheet. It might also be a 1-D ordering of items, like a shopping list. It could also consist of a set of information nodes with connecting association links, such as a hypertext. All the pieces of information should belong to the same conceptual type category, such as numbers to add, tasks to do, or words to remember. By "mental model" we mean not the explanatory model offered by Johnson-Laird [5], but rather a more general definition: the cognitive layout that a person uses to organize information in his or her memory.

THE EXAMPLE DOMAIN
Consider the map of Boston shown in Figure 1a. We have chosen fifteen different sites of activity taken from a tour guide book (listed in Figure 1b). This set of information pieces (or "stimuli," as we will call them) is a very high-dimensional in feature space, and it has a relatively large variance across people. That is, there are many features

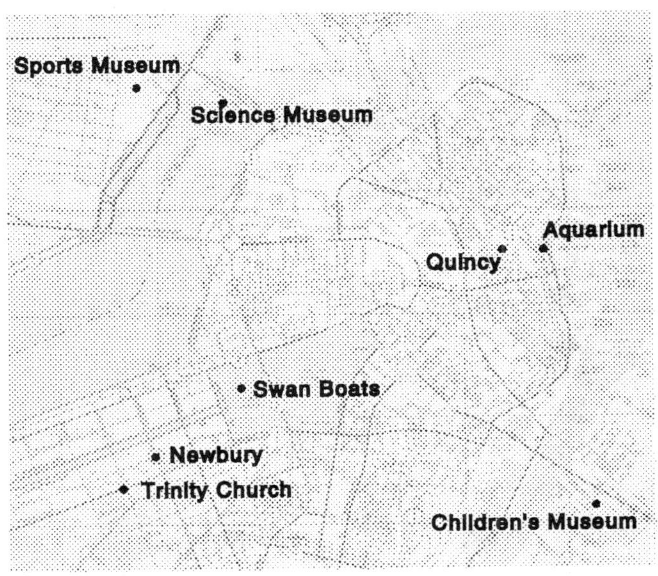

Figure 1a: Geographic layout of activities

Stimulus Set: Boston Tourist Attractions

1. Sports Museum
2. Children's Museum
3. Science Museum
4. Aquarium
5. Swan Boats (boat tour of garden)
6. Newbury Street (elegant shopping)
7. Quincy Market (outdoor mall)
8. Trinity Church (historic site)
9. Magic Show
10. Salem (nearby historic town)
11. Harvard University
12. Museum of Fine Arts
13. Zoo
14. Fenway Park (baseball stadium)
15. Arboretum (nature preserve)

Note: Activities 9-15 are outside the scale of the map.

Figure 1b: The stimuli for the MDS and TM experiments.

that can be used to describe the stimuli, and people do so in significantly different ways. As a contrasting example, a deck of playing cards contains very few features, namely the number of a card, its suit, and perhaps its color, and different people describe playing cards similarly.

MDS AND TM METHODS

A person who lives in Boston and knows the sites will have at least two mental models of them, one based on their geographic locations, and one based on their content. In order to illustrate the capabilities of Multidimensional Scaling (MDS), first used by Torgerson [16], Shepard [15], and Kruskal [7], we collected data from two subjects for each of these mental models (Figure 3). Note that the judgments based on geographic similarity (3a) are completely different from judgments based on content (3b). The input data for MDS takes the form of pairwise similarity judgments, and the output is an arrangement of the stimuli in a metric space.

To clarify the procedure for obtaining these MDS plots, we offer a simple example; consider a collection of seven black and white circles of different sizes. In Figure 2a, these circles are arranged randomly along the edges of a similarity matrix. The numbers show a subject's similarity rating on a scale of 1 to 7. From these numbers the MDS algorithm arranges the circles as shown in Figure 4, with neighboring circles being the most similar.

The distances between the points in the output is usually a non-linear transformation of the values in the similarity matrix. For Figure 3a, we asked the subjects for every pair of stimuli, "On a scale from 1 to 7, how similar are stimuli X and Y in terms of their **distance** from each other?" For Figure 3b, we asked, "How similar are stimuli X and Y in terms of their **content or theme**?" We then used KYST2 [6] to run the MDS and generate the graphs shown.

As one might expect, the distance-based MDS plot is similar to the actual map of Boston, though somewhat warped; the warping could stem from differing familiarity with the sites [11] or from thinking of distance as travel time instead of geographic distance. In the content-based MDS plot,

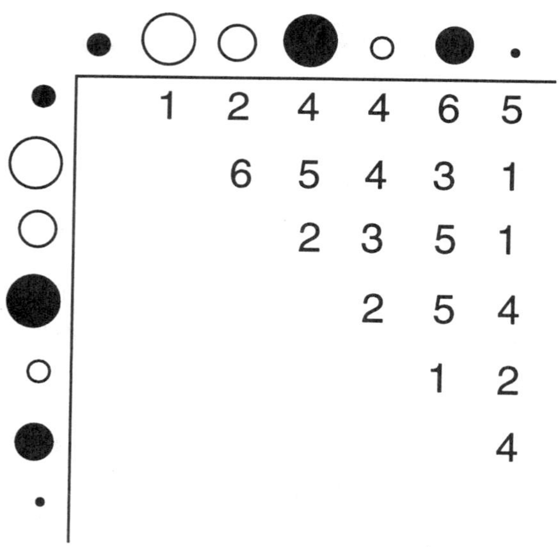

Figure 2a: Typical input data for the MDS algorithm; similarity data for black and white circles of different sizes. 7 = very similar; 1 = very dissimilar.

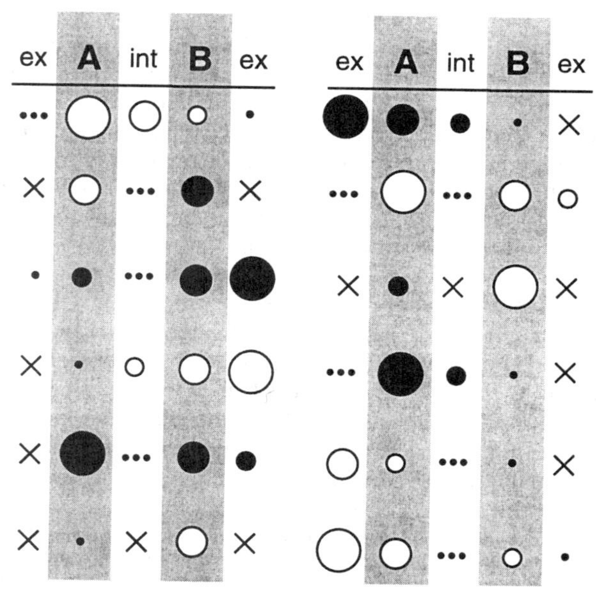

Figure 2b: Typical input data for the TM algorithm; extrapolations and interpolations for black and white circles of different sizes. Here are 12 of 21 possible pairs.

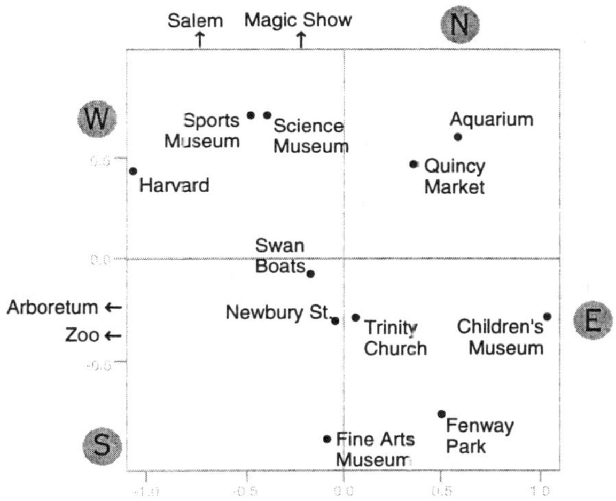

Figure 3a: MDS plot based on geographic similarity

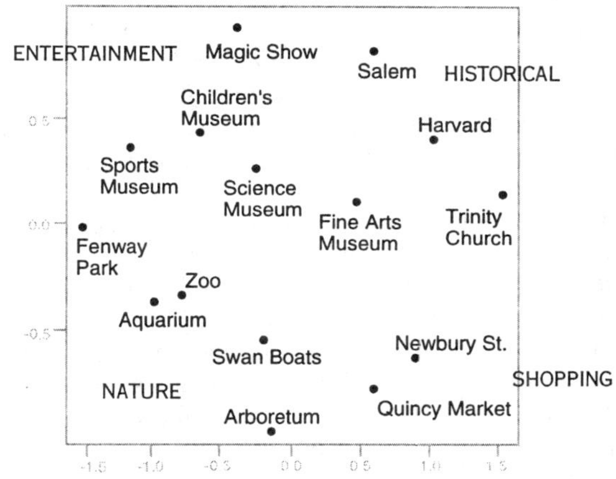

Figure 3b: MDS plot based on content similarity

similar activity sites like the Aquarium and the Zoo appear near each other, as do shopping areas Newbury Street and Quincy Market. One can use the groupings of points in an MDS plot to assign features to clusters of points, as we have done in Figure 3b with the features, "historical," etc. Likewise, many researchers who use MDS would attempt to assign meaning to the axes of the plot, suggesting perhaps that the X-axis runs from "playful to serious" and Y-axis runs from "outdoors to indoors". Such labels or category assignments must be done carefully and should be verified with separate experiments, however, because they are often biased by the experimenter's a priori knowledge of the data.

The reader might wonder what would be the outcome if we had asked subjects to give general similarity ratings without specifying what type of similarity. Would the resulting MDS plot have been an unfortunate mixture of the two plots in Figure 3? This issue raises the question of how we could have known what types of similarity to separate if we knew nothing about the data to begin with. To answer this question, we introduce the relatively new Trajectory Mapping (TM) procedure [4, 13, 14].

For high-dimensional feature spaces, often TM can better delineate the features of the data than MDS. Instead of giving similarity judgements as in MDS, the subject's task in TM is to imagine a conceptual feature or property that links a given pair of stimuli. The subject then extrapolates that feature in both directions to pick two stimuli from the remaining set that would be appropriate. The subject also picks an interpolant, i.e. a stimulus that would fit well within the pair.

Returning to our black and white circle example, a TM set of input data might appear as in Figure 2b. The members of the original pair are in columns A and B; the extrapolants are

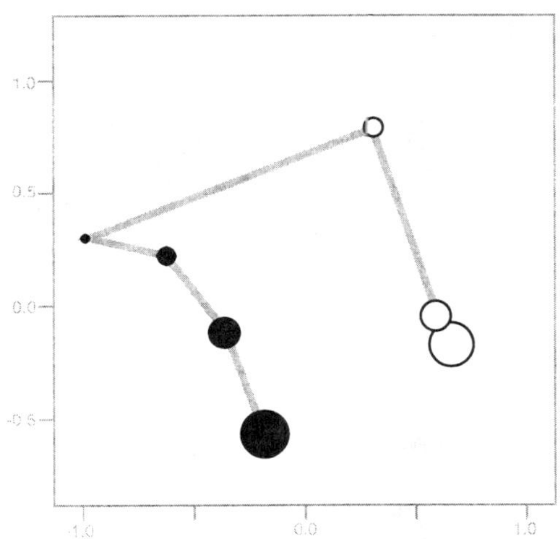

Figure 4: MDS and TM output for black and white circles.

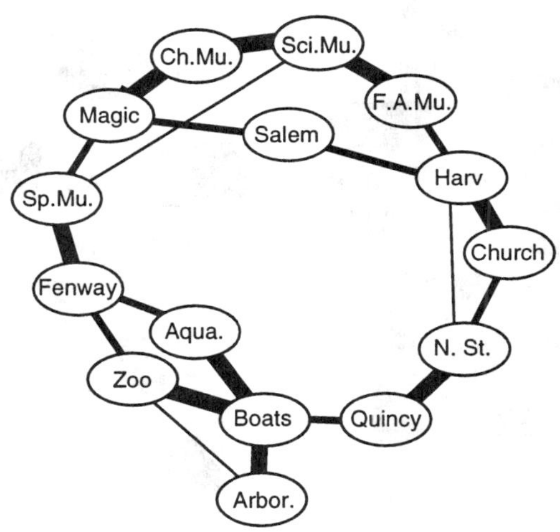

Figure 5: Trajectory map for the tourist site data

in the two "ex" columns, and the interpolant in the "int" column. As well as using a stimulus for each slot, the subject may also enter an "X" or a "...". An "X" indicates that the subject did not feel comfortable choosing a stimulus for that spot, and the "..." indicates that the subject could imagine a stimulus that would fit there, but that such a stimulus was not present in the given data set to choose from.

From this set of quintuples, we can now extract a connected graph of the stimuli in which the maximum number of quintuples fit. For example, in the top row of Figure 2b, we have an ordered set of white circles ending in a small dot in one column, and a set of black circles ending in the same small dot in the other column. If these quintuples are equally considered as constraints on the graph, the ending trajectory map will contain a path from the large white circle to the large black circle, going through the small dot, as shown in Figure 4.

BOSTON DATA

Figure 5 shows a trajectory map for tourist site data gathered from the authors. Note here that the positions of the nodes are not important; the mental model lies in the connections between the nodes, i.e. the topology of the graph. The weights on the links are based not on similarity, but rather on the robustness of that link across a gamut of parameters within the TM algorithm. The weight on a link can thus be thought of as the strength of the connection in the mental model. (A TM algorithm is being fine-tuned for release by Gilbert.)

By pruning the trajectory map to only its strongest links, one can see rough feature clusters emerge (see the heavier links

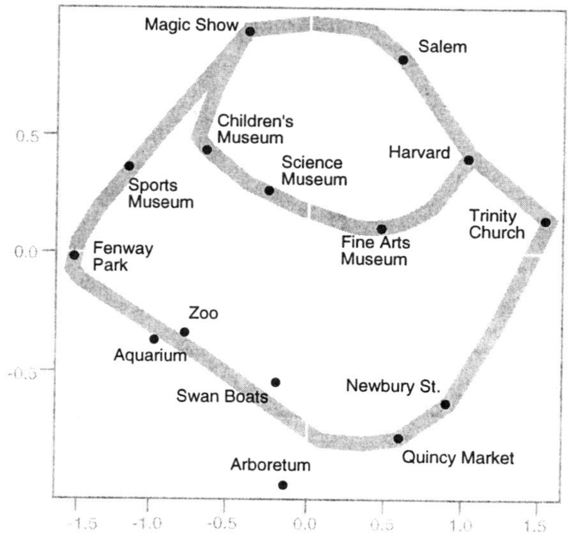

Figure 6: The mental models combined: a rough TM path superimposed over the MDS content plot.

in Figure 5). In our example, the clusters are roughly similar to the estimated clusters in the MDS plot (Figure 2b). In a trajectory map, however, the stimuli are ordered within each cluster, e.g. Arboretum, Swan Boats, Aquarium/Zoo. Figure 6 shows the combined mental models, a rough TM path drawn over the MDS content-based plot.

Because the tourist sites have several possible features that could be used by subjects to report their TM extrapolations and interpolations, one can discover the most salient features of the data set by running the algorithm across many

Figure 7a: Children's activities energized by the regional activation spreading network.

Figure 7b: Adults' activities energized by the regional activation spreading network.

Figure 8: The network activates the path segments when the user examines the sites Sports Museum, Fenway Park and Aquarium. The activation levels are mapped to image and typographic size, enabling the system to suggest to the user an appropriate next step based on the MDS and TM results.

subjects. It is likely with this tourist site information, for example, that some subjects would do the TM based on geographic distance, while others would do it based on the content of the sites. This feature difference would eventually manifest itself from obviously disparate trajectory maps, and lead to the phrasing of the MDS questions described earlier: similarity in terms of distance and similarity in terms of content. Examples of different trajectory maps for the same domain can be seen in [12].

EXPERIMENTATION

The mental models from TM and MDS provide an excellent basis for measuring the efficiency of an information structure that has been built from the models. One might arrange the stimuli serially according to the TM paths or distribute them according to the MDS plot. After collecting data from a new pool of subjects for measures of readability, ease of remembering, etc. (see [2, 3] for a typical array of memory measures), the information structure can be systematically varied by changing the parameters that produce the MDS and TM models.

EXAMPLE INTERFACES

If one considers the set of tourist attractions as an information space to be explored, we can also use the mental models to give the user well-founded suggestions as to his or her next step of exploration. As a demonstration of feasibility, we have designed a visualization system that allows the exploration of the Boston tourist attractions. Since we are no longer restrained to the geography of Boston, as an actual tourist would be, we must now answer the question, “How should we order the various sites?” To explore the different possible answers, we have built three different interfaces for the system, each of which defines an "attentional window" as the current region of interest in the information space. An activation spreading network based on the mental models defines the size of the attentional window as the user explores. Thus, if the aquarium node of the network is currently activated, and the models suggest that the swan boats node is closely related, then the activation will spread to swan boats, leading the attentional window to include swan boats as a potential next focus.

In the first two interfaces, the 15 sites are arranged two-dimensionally according to the MDS plot in Figure 3b. Whichever sites fall within the attentional window are rendered larger than the others. In one interface, the attentional window envelops MDS regions (Figure 7), and in the other, the window spreads across TM paths (Figure 8). Figure 7a shows the display of regional activation with emphasis on children's activities. Figure 7b shows the activities in an adult context. In contrast, Figure 8 shows several successive frames of path activation: when the user investigates the Sports Museum, the network suggests that Fenway Park or the Children's Museum might be a good next choice (those two sites are slightly enlarged in Figure 8a). As the user shifts attention to the next event, past activities fade away and activities further along the path become more conspicuous.

The difference between these two styles of exploration can be characterized by the width of the attentional window: narrow in the case of paths, and wide in the case of regions. By smoothly varying the width, one might change smoothly between modes of exploration.

The third interface attempts to combine the path and region following ideas of the first two. This interface depicts the sites as semitransparent multimedia cubes in a 3-D space (Figure 9). The cubes are arranged along the TM paths, but at each cube, other cubes within the same region can be seen orbiting the current cube nearby. Thus, the user can "fly" smoothly through the space along the TM routes, or branch off to a similar site within the current region. Also, the floor of each cube displays a geographic map with the site’s location high-lighted, thus incorporating all of the features that we have discussed thus far.

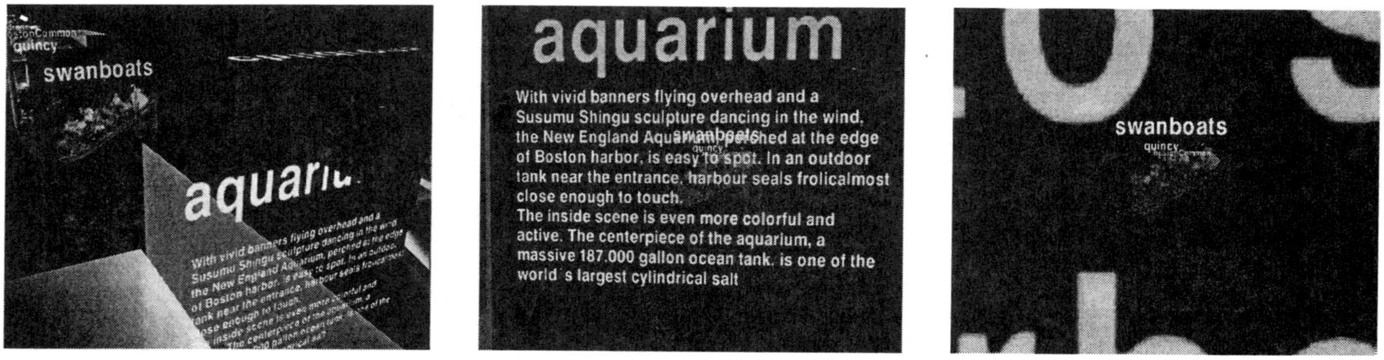

Figure 9: An interface that combines path and region following; the sites are represented by cubes in a 3-D space. The cubes lie along the TM paths, and the other sites from the MDS region encircle the cube within the attentional window.

The activation spreading network was designed by Lokuge and Ishizaki [10], and the visualization system is implemented on a Silicon Graphics Onyx workstation. This network links nodes in a space (Figure 10) and uses the ordering in the space to control the activation level of a node [1, 12]. When attention "jumps" to a new node, the network partially reduces the activation levels in the original set of nodes, leaving a faint trace as a history of the attentional sequence.

DISCUSSION

We have designed this visualization system with its various interfaces both as an existence proof that such a system could be devised and as an illustration of our proposed methodology for structuring information. We mentioned above the fact that a variety of mental maps exist for each data set, both within and across individuals. A further development would be an intelligent activation spreading network, i.e. one which contained the full repertoire of different mental models for a given data set and chose the best model based on the user's behavior. Such a repertoire could be described as a "hyper-mental-map" and could likely formed by gathering MDS and TM data on the mental models as stimuli themselves.

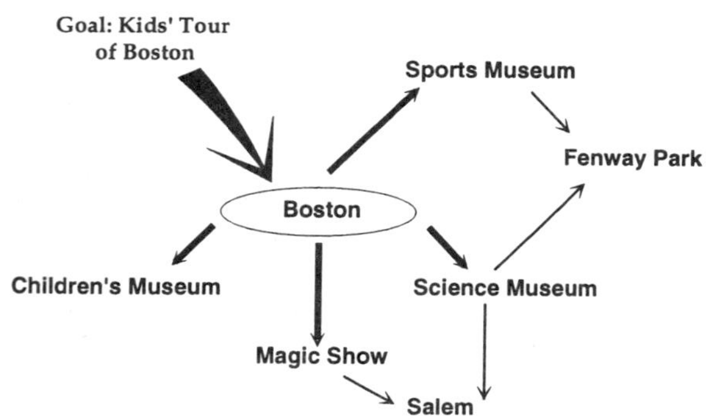

Figure 10: Schematic diagram of a regional activation spreading network. Activation energy spreads in the direction of the arrows initiated by the Goal: Kids' Tour of Boston.

We have proposed and implemented a method of organizing information space around cognitive maps. We plan next to explore the degree to which this method can be used with more generalized domains of knowledge, but examples from previous MDS and TM papers lends us hope that the method could become generally applicable. By accommodating an individual's search context (e.g. through paths or regions) and his or her particular model of a domain (e.g. a particular MDS or TM model), one can offer both a more personalized tour of the information space and a more easily absorbable mass of information.

ACKNOWLEDGMENTS

This work was in part sponsored by ARPA, JNIDS, NYNEX and Alenia. However, the views and conclusions expressed here are those of the authors and do not necessarily represent that of the sponsors.

REFERENCES

1. Anderson, J. A. Spreading activation theory of memory. *Journal of Learning and Verbal Behavior 22*, 261-295, 1983.

2. Atkinson, R.C. & Shiffrin, R.M. The control of short-term memory. *Scientific American, 225*, 82-90, 1971.

3. Craik, F.I.M. & Lockhart, R.S. Levels of processing: A framework for memory research. *Journal of Verbal Learning and Verbal Behavior, 11*, 671-684, 1972.

4. Gilbert, S. A. & Richards, W. Using trajectory mapping to analyze musical intervals. *Proceedings of the Sixteenth Annual Conference of the Cognitive Science Society.* 1994.

5. Johnson-Laird, P.N. *Mental models.* Cambridge, MA: Harvard University Press, 1983.

6. Kruskal, J.B. kyst2a. AT&T Bell Laboratories, Computing Science Research Center, Netlib repository of software. http://plan9.att.com/netlib/mds/index.html.

7. Kruskal, J.B. Nonmetric multidimensional scaling: A numerical approach. *Psychometrika. 29,* 28-42, 1964.

8. Lokuge, I. *Dynamic magical environments: Engaging interaction based on the art of illusion.* Masters Thesis, MIT Media Lab, 1995. To receive a copy email `docs@mit.edu` or call MIT Document Services at 617/253-5650.

9. Lokuge, I., Gilbert, S.A. & Richards, W. *Visualizing information spaces: A tour through Boston.* Presented at European Conference on Visual Perception '95, Tübingen. Abstract in *Perception, 24 Supplement*, p. 76.

10. Lokuge, I. & Ishizaki, S. GeoSpace: An interactive visualization system for exploring complex information spaces. *Proceedings of ACM SIGCHI'95*, Denver, Colorado, 1994.

11. Lynch, K. *Image of the City.* Cambridge, MA: MIT Press, 1960.

12. Maes, P. Situated agents can have goals in *Designing Autonomous Agents: Theory and Practice from Biology to Engineering and Back*, ed. P. Maes, MIT Press/Bradford Books, 1992.

13. Richards, W. & Koenderink, J.J. Trajectory mapping ("TM"): A new non-metric scaling technique. *Proceedings of European Conference on Visual Perception, Edinburgh (Abstract),* 1993. In press *Perception.*

14. Saint-Arnaud, N. *Classification of Sound Textures.* Masters Thesis, MIT Media Lab, 1995. To receive a copy email `docs@mit.edu` or call MIT Document Services at 617/253-5650.

15. Shepard, R.N. The analysis of proximities: Multidimensional scaling with an unknown distance function. I. & II. *Psychometrika*, 27, 125-140, 219-246, 1962.

16. Torgerson, W.S. Multidimensional scaling: I. Theory and method. *Psychometrika*, 4, 401-419, 1952.

Embed User Values in System Architecture:

The Declaration of System Usability

Elizabeth M. Comstock
Consultant Usability Engineer
Digital Equipment Corporation
550 King Street
Littleton MA 01460-1289 USA
+1 508 486 6275
comstock@delni.enet.dec.com

William M. Duane
PATHWORKS Technical Director
Digital Equipment Corporation
550 King Street
Littleton MA 01460-1289 USA
+1 508 486 7581
duane@ranger.enet.dec.com

ABSTRACT
The underlying architecture of complex software products profoundly influences their direction and usability. This paper shares an effort to embed usability within the architecture of complex network products. We began by attempting to build a conceptual model, but we ended by representing customers' and users' values in a *Declaration of System Usability* to guide product direction and system architecture decisions.

Keywords
System usability, complexity, system architecture, software architecture, design techniques, networks

PURPOSE

In this paper, we share how a group of usability engineers and technical directors at Digital Equipment Corporation embed usability within software system architecture.

We begin with a description of the context for this work – a large, complex family of networking products. We describe traditional approaches to achieving cross-product usability and relate usability to system architecture. We then describe our search for usability design principles based on users' experiences with networked computing. We initially thought a conceptual model would encapsulate the design principles in a way that would allow system architects to embed usability across the product family. Instead, we found a different device, a *Declaration of System Usability*. The Declaration does not replace other usability approaches; it is a companion or precursor to other approaches. It establishes a usability policy that guides high-level product design decisions, tuned to a specific set of customer uses. The paper closes with a description of how developing the Declaration changed the culture and products developed in our organization.

We hope our experience will motivate others to examine the relationship between usability and system architecture.

THE NETWORK COMPLEXITY PROBLEM

The Network Integration Software (NIS) group within Digital is the setting for the events related in this paper. NIS products like PATHWORKS™ aim to make it easier for people to productively use and manage their personal computers in a network environment.

Producing software for the PC LAN integration market is a major undertaking because computer networks are inherently very complex. They are a mixture of devices developed by many different vendors, different networking protocols and standards, different operating systems, and different computer types. They serve applications ranging from simple mail exchange to complex synchronization of distributed directories. In NIS, over 200 developers design and build thousands of software modules that control everything from network hardware to applications for software developers, PC LAN administrators, and end users.

Usability is a central theme in the design and development of NIS products. Similar to Nielsen [8], we use a broad definition of usability, including learnability, efficiency, memorability, few errors, and user satisfaction. We consider the usability of all aspects of NIS products with which users may interact, and we consider the system's utility to be a precondition of its usability.

Usability work is generally well integrated into the development of individual NIS products, and members of the NIS Usability Team work at all stages of product development, from product requirements determination through product design, development, and release [2]. Nevertheless, in spite of persistent usability work, users were not satisfied with the usability of NIS products. They reported that the products were complex and somewhat inconsistent. Using and managing computer networks required too much knowledge of the underlying technology.

TEXTBOOK APPROACHES

The NIS Usability Team began to look for additional approaches to ensuring usability across complex product sets. There is a large professional literature offering excellent advice on effective customer engagement, participatory design, usability engineering, and user interface design processes [11, 12]. These processes form the foundation for product usability. They are generally well-accepted and widely practiced in Digital [15].

One shortcoming of most usability methods is that they apply best during the development of *individual* software applications. As Nielsen [8, p. 71] says, "Usability cannot be seen in isolation from the broader corporate product development context where one-shot projects are fairly rare. Indeed, usability applies to the development of entire product families and extended projects where products are released in several versions over time."

What approach might help bring usability to a complex family of products like that produced by NIS? Advice on achieving system-wide usability falls into three categories.

First, many people recommend process mandates or "institutionalizing" good usability practices within an organization's product development. The idea is that what works for one product should be done on all products; the result will be overall usability. For example, Bellcore has a user-centered design policy focused on the methods developers will use. It states, "All producers of software products will apply user-centered design methods: task analysis, usability objectives, early prototyping, usability testing, and iterative design." [9, p. 493] Software development organizations in Digital have applied usability methods relatively effectively, and usability is represented in both formal and informal development practices [2,15].

A second general approach is to provide tools that allow individual developers to incorporate usability more easily and develop more consistent user interfaces. For example, Gould, Boies, and Lewis [5] describe a method of rapid prototyping that builds in guideline compliance. Other examples of this general approach are style guides [13], user interface standards, and terminology dictionaries [8]. The NIS group also recognizes the importance of consistency in achieving overall usability. As a parallel effort to the work described here, the NIS *User Interface Style Guide* was developed. It is now in use throughout NIS.

A third approach to system-wide usability is to find a unifying theme or conceptual model that provides developers with a common set of expectations about how final products should behave. Mayhew [7, p. 80] defines a conceptual model as "the general conceptual framework through which the functionality is presented." Conceptual models are best if they match users' internal representation or mental models. Following the conceptual model will then unify the interfaces of the separate components.

An explicit metaphor can help users understand the conceptual model by providing a mapping or analogy between a familiar domain, such as "the desktop," and the new domain, such as "networked computers" [1].

The third general approach, defining a conceptual model, is the one we considered most promising for addressing NIS system-wide usability issues. We set out to understand users' mental models and expectations for networked computing, intending to construct a conceptual model, and possibly an explicit metaphor, to guide design choices.

SYSTEM ARCHITECTURE AND USABILITY

In analyzing the network complexity problem, we realized that how usable a product set will be depends strongly on the system architecture that underlies the products.

By "system architecture" we mean the top-level design of software solutions. System architecture is often described using the analogy of blueprints for a house. The analogy we like better compares system architecture to city planning, – "there are multiple, relatively independent structures connected into a network over which people, goods (information), and services (utilities) flow. The structures are far from uniform and are at different points in their life cycle." The architecture activity is a "coordination activity" rather than a design blueprint [6, pp. xii-xiii].

System architectures typically persist far longer than the specific products designed with them. For example, the PATHWORKS architecture that was established in 1986 was replaced in 1995, but in that time span there were five major releases of the products based on that architecture.

At Digital, "technical directors" are responsible for system architecture. During the design of network products, technical directors make decisions that impact virtually every area. Starting with requirements gathering, technical directors look beyond the specific request the customer articulates and try to determine the underlying problem or opportunity. They use their understanding of how the technologies are evolving within the market to project which problems or opportunities will arise.

Once an opportunity has been identified, technical directors evaluate the wide spectrum of possible solutions to the problem. Each solution brings with it a series of tradeoffs that must be evaluated on a number of dimensions simultaneously in order to select an optimal solution. If the system architecture does not address usability in any form, the product components, each on a different schedule, and with different constraints, will be locally optimized around assumptions of the individual component developers. But the system as a whole will be chaotic and inconsistent.

Based on this understanding of the broad scope and long life of system architecture, we recognized that the NIS architecture should provide a rationale for making decisions that trade off usability against other considerations in product development. We expected that representing NIS-specific usability principles in the form of a conceptual model would form the basis of our "usability architecture," and that it would be a useful tool for technical directors as they made architectural decisions.

OUR EXPERIENCE

In the spring of 1994, Betsy Comstock, with support of several development managers and the NIS Usability Team, recruited a cross-functional team of seven senior contributors to serve on the "Usability Architecture Team." The team consisted of four engineers and technical directors, including Bill Duane, two usability specialists, and a product business manager. Members were chosen for their passion around usability issues and their broad influence on product development.

From the beginning, it was clear that the Usability Architecture Team shared a strong sense of the usability problems faced by NIS. We readily agreed on many anecdotes from our own experiences, from customers reports, and from internal development practices. We agreed that we needed a high-leverage approach to ensuring product usability, and we described the need with words like, "whole system," "top down," "strategic," and "usability architecture." The team crafted a mission statement containing the goal, "to develop, communicate, and ensure implementation of a usability architecture for future end user and system administration tasks." We expected to create a new conceptual model for computing in the network integration space, perhaps the next "desktop metaphor."

Goal of the Usability Architecture

Here's how the Usability Architecture Team summarized the characteristics of the conceptual model we were seeking: *The conceptual model is a set of design principles based on users' tasks and thought processes. When the conceptual model is used as the cornerstone of development, users will clearly experience an appropriate organization of functionality and a demonstrable reduction in the time it takes to learn and use the product family. The conceptual model aids high-level business and development decision-making by specifying how product components must appear to users to function and interrelate. The conceptual model is simple to communicate. It works like a "magnet" to provide a sense of development direction and to pull components toward a coherent whole for users.*

Two beliefs about our work were particularly salient – it needed to be based on users' tasks and thoughts, and it would influence product development over time, rather than all at once. Our primary criterion for success was that product development would move "in the right direction."

Developers' Assumptions

The Usability Architecture Team recognized that it was crucial to understand our own beliefs (as developers) about our customers and their requirements for our products. Therefore, at an early meeting, we conducted an extensive and humbling brainstorm session in which we discovered a number of "tensions" between the ideal and what we were actually doing. Here are a few examples:

- We develop as if we are like our customers, but we know they are more diverse.
- We develop for roles or levels of users, but we know it over-simplifies actual customer use.
- We integrate product technologies, but integration of users' tasks may be more important to customers.

The developers' assumptions contributed to the team's work by making us aware of the magnitude of the changes we were trying to cause, and our own roles in perpetuating certain less-effective beliefs and practices.

Immersion in User Data

The bulk of the work of the Usability Architecture Team can be characterized as immersion in user data, followed by a series of steps to abstract and distill the data. The beginning steps were very close to the users' statements, and the later steps were closer to users' core values.

We did not generate new data for this work. Instead, we collected and "re-used" customer data that NIS had recently collected for other purposes. Most of the data came from direct customer and user studies conducted within the previous year, including usability tests, field test reports, quality assurance reports from recently-developed NIS products, and transcripts from three large sets of visits to customer sites to understand their work. Other sources were published reports by industry analysts, press articles, and Digital Equipment Computer Users Society reports.

The team scoured the data, picking out what we called "customer assumptions," ideas and expectations in customer terms about what their networked environment should be like. We did *not* mean features or technologies, but rather how people wanted to think about and use their networked environment in the future. We found 231 customer assumptions such as the following:

- I want to print to anywhere from anywhere.
- I don't always work from the same location.
- I should have one user name and password to give me automatic access to everything I am entitled to use.
- I work on projects across departments.

- I want more meaningful names for network resources.
- Don't make me restart my machine when I want to rename something, move a user, or move a share.
- I rely on my knowledge of the current version to complete tasks on the new version.

From these we created 24 affinity groupings. They encapsulated the Usability Architecture Team's shared understanding of what we heard from customers and users about networked computing. Here are a few examples:

- Customers expect productivity improvements.
- Users come and go.
- Users expect to easily find anything connected to the network.
- Customers expect to be able to manage collections of similar objects as one object.
- Distributed resources should behave as personal resources.
- The administrator and user need to be insulated from changes in the network resources (such as their location, or which network operating system they use).
- Customers expect visual and behavioral consistency in user interfaces.

Themes

The next stage in the usability architecture work involved identifying core themes in what we were learning from the customer assumptions and our own assumptions. We expected to use the themes as "building blocks" for the conceptual model. Themes such as the following emerged:

- Users need universal access, information on demand.
- Networks are chaotic, dynamic environments.
- Tasks should be performed independent of technology and physical location.
- Networked systems should behave "naturally."
- Tasks should accommodate the concept of groupings treated as an individual item (groups of users, groups of systems, groups of tasks).

Metaphors

Next, each team member chose metaphors for networked computing that they thought represented significant aspects of the customer assumptions and themes. Some of the metaphors we considered were the US highway system ("See the USA in your Chevrolet™"), cable TV boxes and remote control devices, building a house with a general contractor, Federal Express™, town government, musical scores and an orchestra, Amish barn-raising, family life in Eastern and native American cultures, baseball teams, and mitochondria in human cells.

The metaphor exercises were enjoyable, but the team was beginning to see that an explicit metaphor was not what we needed. Each metaphor had major flaws, and we couldn't imagine designing a system with these metaphors in mind. We realized that most NIS products were used in environments where other end-user products set the metaphor. Our products should not call attention to themselves with their own metaphor, but invisibly blend into the fabric of the users' work. A visible conceptual model no longer seemed appropriate.

Essences

We made one additional step toward finding a conceptual model. We felt that each metaphor captured something of the *essence* of what networked computing should be like. Taken together, ideal network computing and all the metaphors shared significant characteristics. We identified 19 such characteristics that we called "essences." Here are some examples:

- There is primacy of user intentions.
- Underlying complexity provides value to users without being difficult to use.
- Benefits outweigh the costs of system membership.
- Change is a natural part of the system. Throughout change, the system continues to provide benefit to group members.
- Resources exist for the benefit of all, with varying degrees of utilization.

The Crisis

The previous steps occurred during about three months of weekly meetings. Frustration with the slow pace was rising. The team agreed, "We are *done* brainstorming." We had exhausted our motivation for the current direction, but we had not arrived at a conceptual model or metaphor for our products, and it didn't look like we would. Nevertheless, the team strongly agreed that we had distilled something very important. If it wasn't a conceptual model we needed, then what *was* it?

The Breakthrough to Declaration

We consulted with Dennis Wixon, Program Manager for Usability at Digital, who reviewed the work we had done and listened as we said we felt that a conceptual model was not emerging. We described how we were steeped in a set of beliefs about what our products needed to be to maximize usability, and that we had a sense of the higher-order principles that should guide product design. We felt we had uncovered something beyond users' expectations, something like users' values, or the ethical principles the products should embody. But we didn't see how to encapsulate our learning, to impel action, to fill the role we had intended for the conceptual model.

Dennis said, "Perhaps you need to think of this knowledge in a different form. I think you are making a declaration."

The sense of a "declaration" is that it brings about a new state, or new behavior. Winograd and Flores [14, p. 59], defining the categories of speech act, say, "Declarations bring about the correspondence between the propositional content of the speech act and reality, as illustrated by the example of pronouncing a couple married." The definition we like best is what Whiteside [10, p. 91] calls a transformational proclamation: "...an expression in language that creates the possibility of a new future by virtue of its being expressed powerfully within a befitting context."

This was the breakthrough we needed! It wasn't a conceptual model, but rather a declaration. We were ready to *declare* that our organization would move its products in a direction in accordance with the customer values and principles we'd uncovered.

THE *DECLARATION OF SYSTEM USABILITY*

We modeled the *Declaration of System Usability* on the United States Declaration of Independence [3]. This was a convenient, memorable vehicle for our declaration, and it provided a format. We began with the "truths," the essential characteristics of the users, their environments, and Digital's NIS business. We then abstracted six separate declaration points, listed in the second half of Figure 1.

The first declaration point states that we will integrate people's tasks and intentions, not underlying technology. This point should be familiar to usability professionals [c.f., 4]. It states the primacy of a task-based approach to system design that was clearly requested by our customers.

The second declaration point states that we will recognize the primacy of the person. People are not represented in today's networking; only their accounts or access points to the system are represented. One of the major sources of network complexity is that people use multiple machines, multiple accounts, multiple passwords, and multiple roles in their organizations. We believe that network system use and management will be simpler if the system "understands" the concept of a person, regardless of where they are and what resources they are trying to use.

The third declaration point recognizes that people use networked computers to work *with* other people. We pledge to facilitate group operations in the broadest sense, allowing groups of people to be treated as single entities, without requiring individuals to separately manage the groups. Similar to the second declaration point, we believe that network system use and management will be simpler if the system "understands" the concept of groups.

The fourth declaration point relates to the first. It recognizes that taking a task-based approach means *not* requiring knowledge of the underlying network technology.

The fifth declaration point establishes a new way to think about change in network environments. It recognizes that in most network environments, change is feared and avoided because it causes so many problems. We pledge to build products that recognize that change is the norm, in fact, often initiated for positive reasons, and we pledge to hide changes that are irrelevant to users' tasks.

The final declaration point recognizes the importance of cross-component user interface consistency and establishes the basis for the use of the NIS *User Interface Style Guide* described previously.

Since it is critical that the NIS technical directors support the Declaration at a fundamental level, we decided that its ongoing ownership did not belong with the team that created it, but rather with the technical directors themselves. We revised the Declaration until the following people were willing to sign it: every member of the Usability Architecture Team, every technical director, key development managers, and representatives of product management and marketing. Over the course of 3 months and dozens of meetings, the Declaration went through 10 major drafts. The final *Declaration of System Usability* was printed on parchment-like paper, made available in both Postscript and World-Wide Web formats on Digital's internal network, and distributed with each copy of the NIS *User Interface Style Guide*.

EFFECTS OF THE DECLARATION

The Declaration has had a significant impact on the design and development of NIS products. Here are a few specific examples from the new architecture, of which the first product is the recently-released PATHWORKS V6.0:

Today, when multiple network operating systems (NOSs) are present in the same PC LAN environment, administrators use separate applications to perform the same task on different NOSs. For example, if an administrator needs to modify the password to the accounts of a particular user, the administrator will use a different tool to change the password for each NOS. This requires the administrator to know what type of NOS is supporting the various user accounts, and to do the same task in different ways in each of the NOS environments.

Based on the first declaration point, PATHWORKS realigned the administrative model of account management with the task the administrator is performing. The administrator can perform account maintenance without seeing the boundaries between the various NOS environments. For example, to manage passwords, the administrator need only select "account maintenance" for a particular user and then select "change password." The system performs all the NOS specific functions needed to change the password. This task-based redesign of the management approach was driven by the Declaration.

A second example is the design of PATHWORKS Single Login, the ability for one password to give a person access to all their network resources. We were having difficulty deciding how far we should go to address the security issues in heterogeneous NOS environments. One option was

The Declaration of System Usability

IN DIGITAL, JANUARY 9, 1995

The Unanimous Declaration of the Network Integration Software System Architects

When in the course of human events, it becomes necessary to establish a new direction for product usability, it is imperative to state the foundation for the new approach.

For Network Integration Software, we hold these truths to be self-evident, that

- *Communities* of people are a fundamental structure of working.
- The innate diversity in communities and environments results in heterogeneous, distributed computing solutions.
- Change is a natural part of those communities and environments.
- Community productivity and cost of ownership are primary purchase criteria.
- Usability of software, both within and across components, is a critical market success factor.
- Usability depends on designing from a common set of system assumptions.
- A highly usable product set is easy for people to learn and remember, it is efficient and satisfying to use, and few errors occur. People fulfill their intentions in a way that feels integrated, graceful, enjoyable, and aesthetically pleasing.

We, therefore, the Usability Architecture Team and the System Architects, representing the Network Integration Software development organizations of Digital Equipment Corporation, do solemnly publish and declare that *all* future products we develop will treat usability as a critical system attribute and will strive to:

- Integrate people's tasks and intentions, not underlying technology.

- Preserve a person's unique identity, regardless of the location from which they enter the network, the technology they use, the communities to which they belong, and the tasks they perform. Allow people to perform any task called for by their role in their organization.

- Treat a group as a single entity, independent of its changing members, their locations, and the technologies they use. Enhance the effectiveness of these communities of people by making group membership automatically provide all the shared resources and capabilities of the group.

- Enable people to view, organize, use, and manage the rich distributed environment without having to know about its underlying technology or location.

- Make the distributed system robust in an ever-changing environment. Reveal changes in the distributed environment only when those changes are relevant to people's ability to achieve their desired goals.

- Build user interfaces that are consistent in appearance and behavior with people's expectations, industry standards, and other Network Integration Software products.

And for the support of this Declaration, we mutually pledge to each other our work, our fortunes, and our honor.

Alan Abrahams John Adams Kim Burton Danny Cobb Betsy Comstock
Bill Duane Dennis Giokas Patti Meara Paul Messier Neil Murray
Cathy Smith Marlene Steger Chris Strutt Colin Strutt Ben Thomas
Anita Uhler Michelle Waugh Sarah Webber Phil Wells Kathrin Winkler

a complex and comprehensive security solution including access control lists and encryption key administration policies. Another option was to abandon the entire strategy for Single Login. What was missing was guidance to help us bound what we wanted to achieve.

As the complete system architecture became better defined, we used the second declaration point to bound the design for Single Login. As a result, PATHWORKS decided to address the ease-of-use and location-independence problems associated with logging in to NOS environments, and to preserve the security from the existing NOS environments rather than create a new security solution.

Perhaps one of the most important impacts of the Declaration was on the design of Directory Assistant, our underlying distributed directory, and how it integrates with the Microsoft Windows™ and Windows 95™ operating systems. When introducing a new technology, there is a pull to directly expose the new technology to the user. As PATHWORKS worked through the various alternatives for the distributed directory solution, we relied heavily on the Declaration to help prune the space of options for the system design. In particular, the third, fifth, and sixth declaration points had impact in this area.

PATHWORKS decided to develop a directory solution that was not visible directly to the user, but rather enhanced existing services to make them more robust, more scaleable, and NOS independent. PATHWORKS built the concepts of teams and groups into the system architecture from the start so that we can now address large and small collections of people and network resources as a single item. PATHWORKS also designed a solution that used existing distributed directories in the customer environment rather than require the customer to deploy a new directory. Lastly, PATHWORKS leveraged the fact that distributed directories create a level of indirection between the end user and the administrator so that administrators can change the underlying NOS environment and distributed services without impacting end users.

A final example from a different perspective is the way in which NIS technical directors present PATHWORKS V6.0 to customers. Initial presentations focused on the new technologies in the product and example applications. From an engineering point of view, the attempt was to educate customers on the benefits of the new technologies. The typical presentation assumed that customers would map the technologies into their environment and see the value for themselves. This approach did not work.

Based on the fourth declaration point, the presentation was inverted. It began with customer configurations and problems, and contrasted the way in which the customers are dealing with the problems now against the way in which they would deal with the problems when PATHWORKS was deployed. The scope was then expanded to give brief examples of how the same approach works for other problems. All discussion of the technical mechanisms used to effect this change in the work environment was deleted from the talk, and a set of backup slides was produced to address technical details in case questions arose. The presentation is now extremely well received, and the backup slides are rarely used.

As we have illustrated, the Declaration provides a clear user-centered product focus and everyday guidance for NIS technical directors as they consider questions such as: Are our products being developed in the "right" direction? Do the components interact properly? Does our system architecture support ("afford") usability? In support of the notion that the Declaration is for architects is our observation that it doesn't mean much to line engineers, many of whom consider it "gimmicky," not specific enough to their work tasks, and not clear enough about what the exact implications are for their work.

In addition to focusing the work of technical directors, the Declaration has subtly altered the work of usability specialists in NIS. It has established the role of usability in decisions about product family directions. And it has shifted the emphasis of our work toward the early conceptual stages of product development.

The success of the Declaration lies in its conceptual value to the participants -- it helps organize our experience in a meaningful way, somewhat like a theory does. Different from a theory, however, the Declaration also impels action, changing both products and behavior.

CONCLUSION

In summary, we believe that a fundamental determinant of the usability of a set of products is its underlying system architecture. But system architects and other technical leaders have few tools or examples of ways that usability can be embedded in system design at the architecture level. We created a powerful declaration, driven by user data, as a new way to embed usability in system architecture.

The method we used to generate the Declaration contains elements of all the categories of textbook advice described above. Like the methods suited to the development of specific products, the Declaration is tied to users' real work and expectations. Like usability mandates, the Declaration sets a policy for product development, based on product content and values rather than usability processes. Like other tools for developers, the Declaration functions as a tool for system architects to use in their high-level decision-making. And, like a conceptual model, the Declaration identifies principles in users' expectations that must be represented in the products.

What is perhaps most different about the Declaration is the *level* at which it operates. As described in the previous section, the Declaration provides a clear product focus and everyday guidance for NIS technical directors.

What Made this Approach Work

There were many aspects of the Usability Architecture Team that we believe made it function exceptionally well and that we'd recommend to others who consider a similar venture. First, the team was very diverse. About the only thing shared by all members was a passion for usability.

Second, the team became immersed in vast amounts of customer data from diverse sources in our business. We believe in the Declaration partly because it is so well-grounded and we spent so much time digesting the data.

Third, we continued abstracting and reconsidering the data long enough to allow the important ideas to emerge. This was very difficult, especially considering our busy, deliverable-driven schedules outside the team. But as we began to see that there was value in what we were finding, our impatience turned into recognition that we were generating a mind shift, a change in attitudes and beliefs. Change like this takes time.

And finally, we generated the support of the technical directors and managers. Without their support, the Declaration would not influence product development.

In searching for new ways to improve product development and enhance usability, we invite usability professionals to explore the form and level of the recommendations they make about usability. We urge other organizations to search for and share ways that fundamental user values can be embedded in the architectures of the systems we build.

ACKNOWLEDGMENTS

The Declaration depended on gracious, thoughtful contributions of many people. Jean Proulx, NIS Vice President, sponsored the Usability Architecture Team and ensured its committed membership. John Adams, Networking Technical Director, sponsored the Declaration in the technical community. Michelle Chambers, Dennis Giokas, Neil Murray, Marlene Steger, Colin Strutt, and Sarah Webber were crucial to the work of the team. Minette Beabes helped define the team's process. Rick Frankosky and Nancy Clark headed the style guide effort. All the signers of the Declaration contributed wise comments in mapping it to their work. Pat Billingsley contributed insights based on her "usability policy statements." George Casaday, Michael Good, Tom Graefe, Deborah Mayhew, Anne Parshall, Mary Beth Raven, Colin Strutt, Dennis Wixon, and Sarah Webber made valuable comments on an earlier draft of this paper. And most significantly, Dennis Wixon enabled our breakthrough with the concept of a declaration and inspired the work described in this paper.

REFERENCES

1. Carroll, J. M., Mack, R. L., and Kellogg, W. A. Interface metaphors and user interface design. In M. Helander, Ed., *Handbook of Human-Computer Interaction*, North Holland, Amsterdam, The Netherlands, 1988, 67-85.
2. Comstock, E. M., and Wixon, D. R. Usability at Digital after 15 years: Principles and pitfalls. In *CHI '94 Conference Companion*, ACM, New York, NY, 1994, 157-158.
3. The Declaration of Independence. In *Encyclopaedia Britannica*, 6, Chicago, IL, 1989, 282-284.
4. Gentner, D. R., and Grudin, J. Why good engineers (sometimes) create bad interfaces. In *CHI '90 Proceedings*, ACM, New York, NY, 1990, 277-282.
5. Gould, J. D., Boies, S. J., and Lewis, C. Making usable, useful, productivity-enhancing computer applications. *Commun. ACM 34*, 1 (January, 1991), 74-85.
6. Laverdure, L., Srite, P., and Colonna-Romano, J. *NAS Architecture Reference Manual*. Digital Press, Maynard, MA, 1993.
7. Mayhew, D. J. *Principles and Guidelines in Software User Interface Design*. Prentice-Hall, Englewood Cliffs, NJ, 1992.
8. Nielsen, J. *Usability Engineering*. Academic Press, Boston, MA, 1993.
9. Salasoo, A., White, E. A., Dayton, T., Burkhart, B. J., and Root, R. W. Bellcore's user-centered design approach. In M. E. Wiklund, Ed, *Usability in Practice*. Academic Press, Cambridge, MA, 1994, 489-515.
10. Whiteside, J. *The Phoenix Agenda*. Oliver Wright Publications, Essex Junction, VT, 1993.
11. Whiteside, J., Bennett, J., and Holtzblatt, K. Usability engineering: Our experience and evolution. In M. Helander, Ed., *Handbook of Human-Computer Interaction*, North Holland, Amsterdam, The Netherlands, 1988, 791-817.
12. Wiklund, M. E., Ed., *Usability in Practice*. Academic Press, Cambridge, MA, 1994.
13. Wilson, C. E., Loring, B. A., Conte, L., and Stanley, K. Usability engineering at Dun & Bradstreet Software. In Wiklund, M. E., Ed., *Usability in Practice*. Academic Press, Cambridge, MA, 1994,389-425.
14. Winograd, T., and Flores, F. *Understanding Computers and Cognition*. Ablex Publishing Corporation, Norwood, NJ, 1986.
15. Wixon, D. R., and Comstock, E. M. Evolution of usability at Digital Equipment Corporation. In Wiklund, M. E., Ed., *Usability in Practice*. Academic Press, Cambridge, MA, 1994, 147-193.

Sensuality in Product Design: a Structured Approach

G.H. Hofmeester
Philips Corporate Design
PO. Box 218
5600 MD Eindhoven
The Netherlands
+31 40 732302
c896412@
nlccmail.snads.philips.nl

J.A.M. Kemp
Philips Research
Institute of Perception Research /
IPO
PO. Box 513
5600 MB Eindhoven
The Netherlands

A.C.M. Blankendaal
Delft University of Technology
Faculty of Industrial Design
Engineering
Jaffalaan 9
2628 BX Delft
The Netherlands

ABSTRACT

This paper describes a user-centred process for designing a product which induces a sensual feeling. It is assumed that in the design of consumer products feelings are an essential part of human-product interaction. The objective of the project discussed here was to pro-actively design a pager which the target user group (women aged 18-30 years) perceived as sensual.

Users were involved at an early stage of the design process. Based on information gathered in a series of interviews two pagers were designed. In an evaluation both models were perceived as significantly more sensual than a reference model.

Keywords

Sensuality, eroticism, product design, pager, communication, pleasure, emotion, market research, early user involvement.

INTRODUCTION

In this paper it is assumed that feelings play an important role in the human-product interaction with consumer products. In this respect, Logan [2], mentions that "for certain product categories such as consumer electronics, an expanded definition of usability is required. This expanded definition includes emotional elements of product design". Nass [3] mentions social behaviour towards computers: users "exhibit behaviours and make attributions toward computers that are nonsensical when applied to computers but appropriate when directed at other humans".

The way users experience interaction with a product has many dimensions. It is assumed that sensuality is one of the positive feelings influencing our perception. Therefore, we think sensuality can play a role in the experience of a product. Since it is assumed that this feeling is positive, it can increase the pleasure involved in using the product.

CHI 96 Vancouver, BC Canada
© 1996 ACM 0-89791-777-4/96/04..$3.50

The designer can influence the way feelings are induced by a product. The designer "has powerful abilities to convey complex, non-obvious information using shape and colour" [4].

The method used in this project can help the designer to create a product which induces a particular feeling for a specified target group. This was done by involving potential users at an early stage in the design process and by keeping them involved during the evaluation phase. When used in an iterative process, this early user involvement provides the designer with a tool to monitor feedback on the design as it progresses. Research done at Philips Corporate Design to investigate pleasure in the use of products provided the background for the research methods.

A pager was chosen as a carrier for developing our approach for two reasons:

1. A pager is a device you wear close to your body, and the body is an important factor in relation to sensuality.
2. A pager allows communication with other people. Action and reaction are important aspects of a sensual interaction.

A pager is a portable communication device, which can receive personal messages through radio broadcast. Pagers for personal use are thought to be an emerging market. Form-giving can play an important role in user interface design [4]. In the design of a pager, the product's shape and colour is seen as part of the interaction design. In a small personal product like a pager, the interaction isn't limited to the retrieval of messages, but extends to the complete handling of the product and the feelings that are involved in that.

The target group chosen was women aged 18 to 30 years. This group was interesting for two reasons:

1. We were interested in designing for private as opposed to professional use (a younger audience was thought to be more appropriate for this type of use).
2. Women were chosen because current pagers are targeted at a male audience.

Thus, the objective of this project was to design a pager for women aged 18 to 30 years, which induces a sensual feeling. For Philips this was an exploration (it was a graduation project) to learn about how to design products that induce particular emotions.

Sensuality
Literature surveys focusing on the relation between design and sensuality indicated that little information is available about this topic.

Even though sensuality has been described in many ways, a clear definition could not be found in these surveys. Frijda [1] for example, describes sensuality as being charmed or fascinated, being in love, feeling desire, lustful, excited, feeling pleasure and satisfaction. Because there are so many ways of describing sensuality, it was decided not to define this term for the first series of interviews. The subjects in these investigations were presented only with the term 'sensuality'[1], thus leaving it open for their own interpretation. The terms that came up in the first series interviews were used to investigate how sensual the final design concepts were perceived to be.

Set-up
Figure 1 shows an overview of the design process. In the exploration phase we interviewed people from the target user group to find product properties which induce a sensual feeling. The results were translated into two design concepts in the design phase. Finally these concepts were evaluated by comparing their sensual properties to a reference model.

Figure 1 Overview of the design process.

PHASE 1: EXPLORATION
A series of interviews was set up to discover which product properties may cause a sensual feeling.

Method
Subjects were twelve women recruited from design schools. It was assumed that designers would have a richer language for describing sensual aspects of products and would be more at ease talking about feelings in relation to products. A disadvantage could be that these subjects are biased compared to the whole target group. Their age varied from 18 to 29. The interviewer was female.

The subjects were asked to bring objects they experienced as being sensual. The interview was divided into two parts. In the first part the subjects were asked to name, as precisely as possible, product properties that could induce a sensual feeling inspired by the objects they brought with them. In the second part of the interview the interviewer explained the functionality of an alphanumerical pager without showing the device or naming it. The subject was asked to imagine a pager that can bring about a sensual feeling. Finally the subjects were asked to rate the properties they had named according to their importance.

[1] In Dutch the term 'erotiek' was used, but this was not translated into the English word 'eroticism' because, according to us, 'sensuality' comes closer to the Dutch meaning of 'erotiek'.

Figure 2 A candelabra that was brought to one of the interviews.

Results and analysis
This paragraph describes the analysed results from the interviews. To be able to give a representation of the interviews that was appropriate for input in the design process, product properties were taken from the transcriptions of the interviews. Some properties were grouped in categories, according to the interpretation of the designer. This analysis resulted in a number of categories of product properties that can induce a sensual feeling according to the subjects. Figure 3 shows a frequency table with the properties that were mentioned most often. Figures 4 and 5 show the results of a rating by the subjects, according to the importance of the properties for a sensual product.

properties	frequency
organic, human, body	14
smooth	13
handsize, fitting comfortably in the hand	12
warmth	12
caress, skin close	12
flow, swell, rise, expand	11
nice feeling, protuberance, lumpy, irregular, hole	11
rounding, curve	11
soft	10
flexible, malleable, elastic	10
pleasure, nice, enjoying	6
wearing on the chest	7
wearing in the pocket	5

Figure 3 The properties causing a sensual feeling that were most often mentioned. The right column shows the number of times the properties from that category were mentioned in all the interviews.

objects	score
soft	74
caress, skin close	55
smooth	54
slope, slightly curved, firm line, thick-thin	47
rounding, curve	46
shiny, glossy, reflection	35
flexible, malleable, elastic	34
warmth	31
heavy, sagged shape	26
contrast in colour	23

Figure 4 The 10 object properties causing a sensual feeling that were rated highest. Score refers to the total sum of the ratings. The ratings per property range from 12 to 1 (12 for the most important).

pager	score
organic, human, body	54
warmth	54
wearing on the chest	53
handsize, fitting comfortably in the hand	48
smooth	40
hard	34
heavy, sagged shape	32
flow, swell, rise, expand	30
nice feeling, protuberance, lumpy, irregular, hole	29
warm light colour, red	24

Figure 5 The 10 pager properties causing a sensual feeling that were rated highest. Score refers to the total sum of the ratings.

Because 'sensuality' can be seen in so many different ways, it was necessary to form groups of properties that indicate different preferences. To indicate this differentiation a correspondence analysis was performed on the data. The analysis produced three factors. Factors can be seen as axises in a 3-dimensional space in which all the properties are mapped (figure 6). The properties that all the subjects thought to be important are in the middle. The more extreme properties have more distance from the centre. We defined each of the factors by two clusters of properties that represent the extremes of each factor. Thus this analysis resulted in three pairs of clusters of product properties (figure 7).

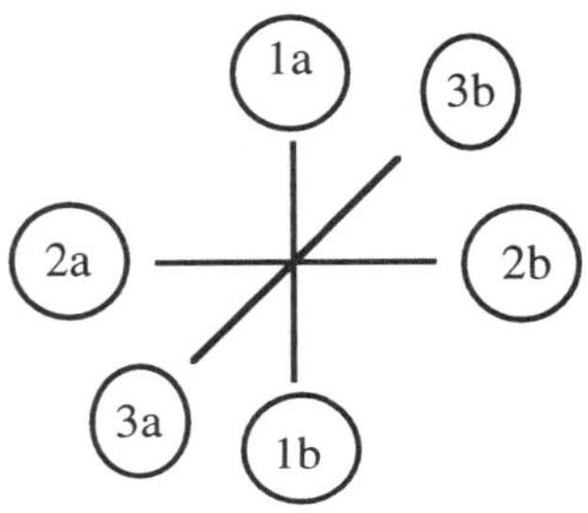

Figure 6 The six clusters of product properties in the 3-dimensional space.

cluster 1a	cluster 1b
• vibration • flexible, malleable, elastic • caress, skin close • soft • handsize, fitting comfortably in the hand	• wearing on the arm • slope, slightly curved, firm line, thick-thin • flow, swell, rise, expand • shiny, glossy, reflection

cluster 2a	cluster 2b
• flow, swell, rise, expand • wearing on the chest • inwards, alone • secretly, mysterious, unnoticeable	• heavy, sagged shape • fabric, satin, plush, velvet • scent • warmth

cluster 3a	cluster 3b
• wearing on the arm • wearing on the neck • nice feeling, protuberance, lumpy, irregular, hole	• countersunk keys • slope, slightly curved, firm line, thick-thin • warm light colours, red • shiny, glossy, reflection • scent • rounding, curve

Figure 7 The properties that form the three pairs of clusters.

Conclusions

A brief representation of the results of the interview was needed as starting point for the design process. This was done in two categories: 'basic' properties and 'extreme' properties. For 'basic' the six properties with the highest ratings were chosen from the tables in figures 3 and 4. These were:

- Organic, human, body
- Warm
- Smooth
- Soft
- Touch, skin close
- Wearing on the chest

For 'extreme' the six clusters from the correspondence analysis were used. The 'basic' properties represent elements that always have to be in the design for a sensual pager. The 'extreme' properties represent different preferences that different groups of users might have.

In this phase of the design process the definition of 'sensuality' proved to be a major obstacle. It is hard to explain this concept to subjects without being too specific.

PHASE II: DESIGN

In this phase the results from the interviews were translated into collages. The collages, the 'basic' and 'extreme' properties and the transcriptions from the interviews were used as design input. Two design concepts were created.

Twelve collages were made. They represent the six 'basic and six 'extreme' elements mentioned in the previous paragraph. Input for the collages were the transcriptions of the interviews and the objects the subjects brought with them. The goal was to make the results of the interviews more appropriate for design input by defining atmosphere, colours, shapes, textures and materials. The collages were boards (100x70 centimetres) with full colour images of the objects the subjects brought and images, 3-dimensional shapes and materials the designer related to the properties mentioned.

One factor, representing two pairs of clusters, that seemed to be most appropriate for developing two different concepts, was chosen. This was factor 2 (see figure 7). Two designs were developed on the basis of the two collages of that factor. The collages of the six 'basic' properties were used as a reference.

Description of the 'Basic' Properties

The comments the subjects made in the interviews concerning these 'basic' properties are described below.

Organic, Human, Body

Most of the subjects mentioned organic shapes. According to them, these refer to body shapes. This "human side" of a pager is associated with intimacy. One of the subjects related organic shapes with a "female feeling". Organic can mean that the shape has protrusions which are interesting to play with. The transitions from one shape to another should never be sharp though. It can also mean that the shape is convex, or bulging.

Warmth
The colour red was mentioned in the interviews as sensual, because it suggests warmth and that makes you feel good. Fabric was seen as a warm material. Several subjects said the pager should be at body (or skin) temperature, but not be sweaty (This was said in combination with wearing the pager close to your body).

Smooth
The surface should be smooth, but also have some texture. The surface should be nice to run your finger over. Surfaces that were mentioned in this respect were: skin, fabric, chestnut skin, the surface of a shell and wood.

Soft
According to the subjects, softness refers to giving way of the surface or to the structure of the surface itself. When the surface can give way a little, it should not be too flexible. When the surface always returns to it's original shape, it was associated with skin. It makes an object nice to play with, when you can pinch it a little. Soft flexible rubber and velvet were mentioned in this context. When the surface itself is soft, it makes one want to touch it. This was associated with skin. The skin of a peach was mentioned in this context. A surface that is smooth and warm or a matte surface was also experienced as soft.

Touch, skin close
The shape should invite one to touch, by fitting close to the hand, so that the fingers fit around it. There should be different ways to hold the device. The shape should be round, with smooth transitions, like a body, so that when you run over the surface with your finger, it is "enjoyable without interruption". The device should be worn close to the body. Touching can be more interesting, or exciting, when your finger sometimes feels a little bump in the surface. It is also exciting when you almost don't feel the touch of the surface on your hand, like when you move your fingertips over the palm of your hand. One of the subjects mentioned that something could happen when you touch certain spots on the surface. These spots should not be obvious. She thought it was an exciting idea that you are the only one who knows how the device works. You must be able to play with the device, finger it, for instance when it is in your pocket. The device can also be malleable. Pinching and massaging is associated with sensuality. The shape could grow when a message comes in or a key could move outward. When the device is worn in the pocket, the user will be the only one who feels the device pushing against her skin.

Wearing on the chest
Several subjects mentioned wearing on the chest as the most sensual place. It was seen as a nice place, it is easy to touch the device whenever you want. It was also seen as a hidden and special place.

Design Concept 1
This design is based on the cluster from factor 2 that includes the properties 'flow, swell, rise, expand', 'wearing on the chest', 'inwards, alone' and 'secretly, mysterious, unnoticeable'. Figure 8 shows an image of the collage.

On the basis of these properties and the collages a design was developed. Following is a description of the 'extreme' properties and a description of the design. Figure 9 shows a picture of the resulting design.

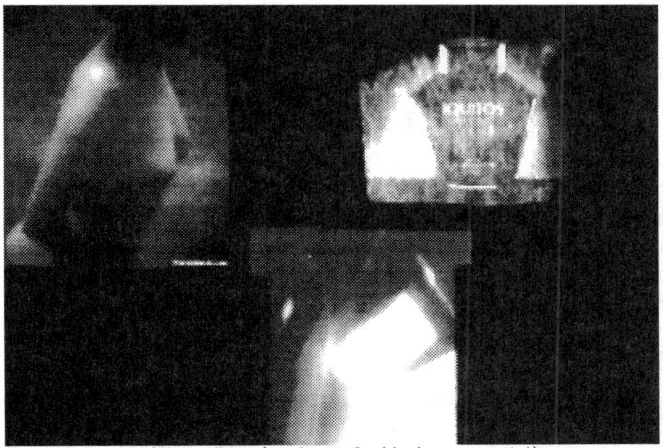

Figure 8 A part of the collage for cluster 2a (design concept 1).

Description of the 'Extreme' Properties of Concept 1
In this paragraph the comments by the subjects for the properties from cluster 2a are described. The property 'wearing on the chest' is described in the previous paragraph.

Flow, Swell, Rise, Expand
One subject in the interviews mentioned the subtle rising of a Citroen car when it is started. This is an almost unnoticeable motion. For a pager this could be translated in the pager slowly starting to glow when a message is detected, like a 'cloud of ink spreads in water'. It could also slowly change colour, like 'milk in your coffee'. Other subjects mentioned the pager becoming warmer and lighting up, like 'a subtle glittering'. A sensual pager should be 'intimate, calm and slow'.

Inwards, Alone
Intimacy was often mentioned in relation to sensuality. The pager should be small, implying that it is only for the owner. Wearing on the chest relates to this. The device should be inconspicuous. When other people are around, they shouldn't notice the pager. According to one of the subjects, a sensual feeling lets you forget everything for a little while, distracts you from what you were doing. The user should be the only one who notices the alert signal, when a message is detected. The signal could be a whispering sound or a soft vibration, as long as other people are not disturbed.

Secret, Mysterious, Unnoticeable
Several subjects mentioned semi-transparency. "You want to see what it is, but you can't." This was compared with semi-transparent clothing. Because of the vagueness of the details, everything seems to be more beautiful. It can be exciting when the pager is hidden. One subject mentioned

that the pager could beat like a heart, allowing only the user to feel it. Another subject mentioned that the user should be the only one who can see or hear the message.

Description of Design Concept 1

The device measures 70x45x20 millimetres. It is shaped in the form of a drop, with a hole going though it on an angle. The shape of the pager and the hole, make it possible to wear it on the chest, like a pendant. It is made out of plastic, which is semi-transparent. The colour is blue. The finish is a matte soft-touch paint. The parting line, going all around the side of the product, is filled with a silicon rubber. The controls are a small high-gloss metal key on the front, which feels like a little bump on the surface, and two touch areas on the back. The touch-areas are distinguishable because they are slightly sunken into the surface. The output is formed by six symbols and twelve digits. These are light images that are projected on the front surface of the product. When they are not lit, they are almost invisible.

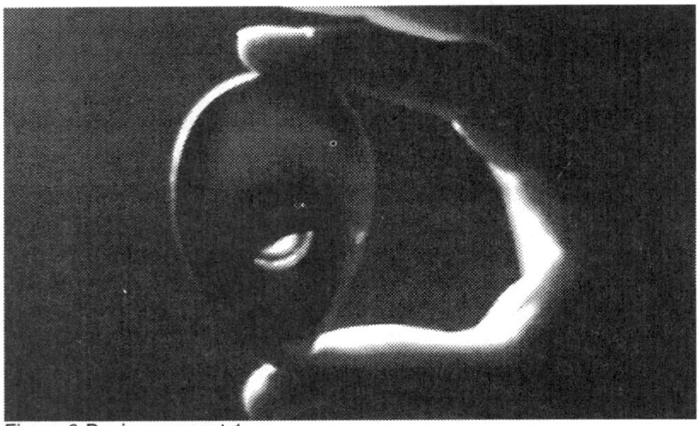

Figure 9 Design concept 1.

When a message is received, the device slowly starts to glow. The user can activate the pager by pressing the metal key on the front of the device. Subsequently, several symbols and numbers will appear on the surface of the pager, depending on the content of the message.

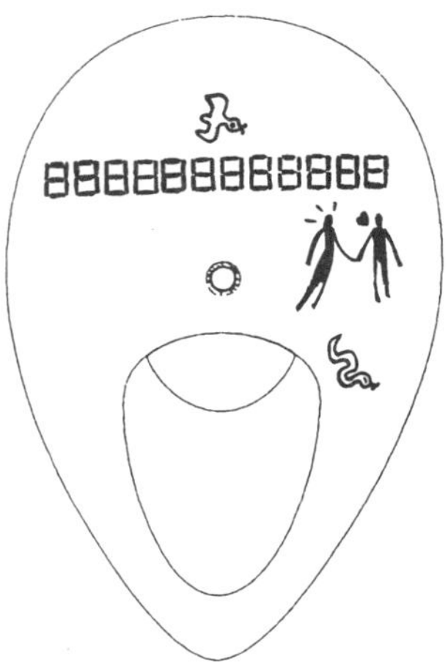

Figure 10 Front view of design concept 1 including the six graphic symbols and twelve digits.

Figure 10 shows the graphic symbols that can represent a message. There are six symbols:

- a bird, which can represent positive, affirmative or happy
- a snake, which can represent negative, or sad
- two human figures, which can light up separately or together, which can represent alone or together, you or me
- a heart, which can represent feeling or leisure
- some lines, which can represent thinking or business.

These symbols are not pretending to be universal, they present an exploration of a non-verbal interface. The user can give them meaning by the way she uses them, the presented meanings are a suggestion from the designer. In addition to these symbols a 12-digit number can be displayed, representing for instance a telephone number or a time for a suggested appointment. By combining these symbols, messages can be composed. For instance, the bird, the two human figures, the heart and a telephone number can mean something like "me and you, happy feeling", or it can mean "Can you call me back to make an appointment in our free time?". In this way, the sender is given the possibility to convey messages with an emotional character and gives the sender the opportunity to use his or her creativity more, compared to a purely numeric interface. The user can scroll through the messages in the memory of the pager by moving her finger over one of the touch areas on the back of the pager. The other touch area can be used to set the alert signals.

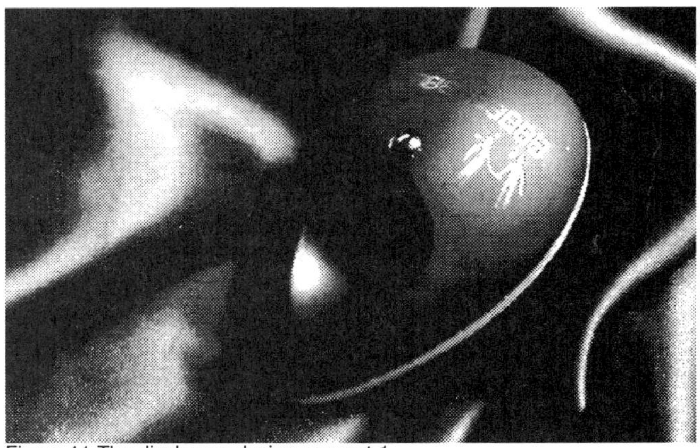

Figure 11 The display on design concept 1.

Design Rationale for Concept 1

The organic shape (including the hole) of the pager refers to the body. The curved lines create a tension, which was often mentioned in the interviews. The symbols used in the display enhance this organic character (see figure 11).

The finish of the pager is a soft-touch paint. Stroking the device as a way of scrolling instead of clicking a key, is a way of trying to enhance this softness.

The alert signal, a light which rises slowly to a maximum, is a characteristic emphasising the 'flowing' transition. The glowing of the alert light suggests warmth.

The pager normally hangs upside down on the cord. When the user wants to see the messages, she is likely to hold it in the cup of her hand, close to her. This emphasises an atmosphere of intimacy, relating to 'inward, alone'. The user can wear the pager close to her body, making it a very personal device. It can be further personalised by using a cord or ribbon to hang the pager on. The pager fits smoothly in the hand of the user, making it personal and also enabling the user to "forget the outside world". The symbols used in the display make it possible to communicate personal messages.

Semi-transparency and a blue colour emphasise the aspect of mystery, according to the subjects. The display is hardly visible when the device is not active. Only the user will know the device is activated by touching the small metal button on the front. The messages, which appear as symbols on the surface of the device, have a meaning connected to the person sending them. They don't have a prescribed meaning. Because of this, the sender and the user will be the only people able to understand the message.

Design Concept 2

The second design concept is based on the properties 'heavy, bulging shape', 'fabric, satin, plush, velvet', 'scent' and 'warmth'. A part of the collage made on the basis of these properties, is shown below (figure 12).

Figure 12 A part of the collage for factor 2b (design concept 2).

Description of the 'Extreme' Properties of Concept 2

Heavy Bulging Shape

Most of the subjects who were interviewed, mentioned that the pager should have round convex shapes. A heavy, bulging shape would be "peaceful"; "you can give yourself to it, without thinking you will break it".

Fabric

Several subjects mentioned fabric being a warm, soft and strong material. It feels nice to touch it. The temperature also feels nice, it immediately has your skin temperature. Fabric was associated with skin. The gloss of fabric can be attractive. The soft surface can tickle, and it makes you want to touch it. The combination of softness and strength was seen as sensual; it takes some force to push in a soft fabric.

The property 'warmth' is described in the beginning of this chapter. Scent was not addressed in this concept, because it was technically not feasible.

Description of the Design

This device measures 65x45x35 millimetres. It is wedge-shaped, bulging. A hard plastic casing, containing the electronic parts, is covered by a silicon rubber coating. The colour is dark red. The silicon coating encloses a silicon gel. Because of the gel filling, the coating is under tension. The coating can be pushed in a few millimetres. The shape is malleable but, because of the tension it will always return to its original form. The device has a fabric cover. One side of the device has a hard plastic finishing. This part has holes to let the sound from the loudspeaker out. The device has a small triangular black joystick. When a message is detected by the pager, the joystick moves out slowly. The joystick can then be used to step through the messages and to set the alert signal.

The pager can be clipped to clothes or worn in the pocket or a bag. The gel layer around the hard casing, allows the temperature of the pager to change. The little joystick will move out when a message is detected. It will push against the user's skin, if the pager is worn on the body. The joystick is used to step through the messages and to select the alert signal.

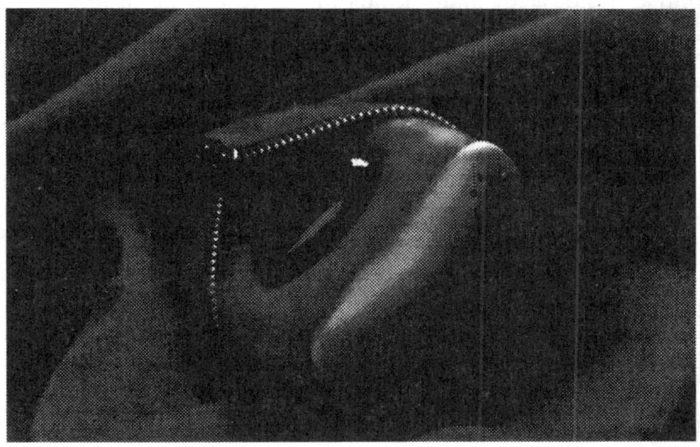

Figure 13 Design concept 2 with a fabric cover with a zipper..

The interface is auditory, there is no visual display. Basically, it has the same principle as the interface described in concept 1. The graphical icons are replaced by auditory icons, and the twelve digits are replaced by spoken numbers. The auditory icons are based on three instruments:

- a clarinet, which is a neutral sound in this case
- a cello, representing sad or negative
- a flute, representing happy or affirmative.

These instruments are played in ascending or descending tones, representing respectively 'you' and 'me'. The sounds can be modified, representing 'business' and 'leisure'. To be able to hear the messages, the user has to hold the pager close to her ear. Other people won't be able to hear the sounds.

Design Rationale for Concept 2
The organic shape of the pager is bulging, which was mentioned by some of the subjects as being sensual. The joystick can function as a playful element, referring to the protrusions some subjects mentioned.

The silicon gel can store and dissipate warmth. When it has not been worn for some time, the pager will feel cold. When wearing it, the pager will become warm and stay warm for some time. This refers to the pager being at body temperature, which was mentioned by several subjects. The colour of the pager is dark red, which was mentioned as a warm and sensual colour.

The pager is covered by fabric, referring to the smooth and skin-like qualities mentioned in the interviews. The cover is made out of two different fabrics, with different textures, making it more interesting to feel. Softness in this pager is a combination of giving way of the surface and a soft surface texture. The gel has the skin-like qualities that were mentioned in the interviews.

The whole pager is designed to be an object that is interesting to touch and play with. The silicon coating, filled with gel, gives it a heavy, bulging shape. The joystick, used as an input method, also has a more sturdy character then the keys that are normally used on pagers. To give the pager a finish which provides a good tactile sensation, it has a fabric cover. This cover can also be used to customise the device; many kinds of fabric can be used.

PHASE 3: EVALUATION
The objective of the evaluation was twofold:
1 To investigate whether the designed pagers would induce a sensual feeling.
2 To find out if the clusters from the correspondence analysis were related to the concept designs that were designed on the basis of those clusters.

Method
Subjects were 27 women, aged 18-30. The subjects from the first series of interviews were not part of this group, because they were already biased. The stimuli in this evaluation study were the two concept pager models and a reference pager model (an alphanumerical pager, called 'The Informer') currently available on the consumer market, but originally designed for professional use. Because no interactive prototypes were available for the design concepts, hard models served as test objects. The reference pager was also represented by a hard model, to pursue an equal level of detail. The subjects were asked to rate the models on semantic differential scales, using the properties derived from the interviews.

An instruction sheet explained the set-up of the study and the kind of models that were evaluated. An interviewer introduced the subject and explained how the semantic differentials should be used. Each subject then read a short explanation about what pagers are. Each pager was accompanied by another sheet, explaining the user interface. The pagers were then rated one by one in a random order. A short debriefing ended the session.

Results
The results from the evaluation study are shown in figures 14, 15 and 16. These figures are graphical profiles showing the means of the scores per item.

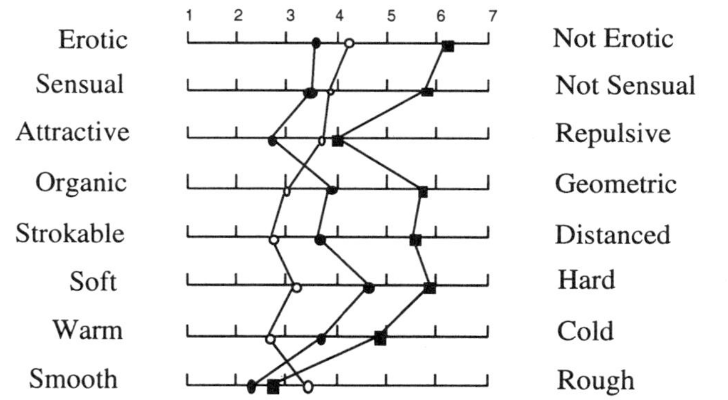

Figure 14 The means for the semantic differentials referring to sensuality.

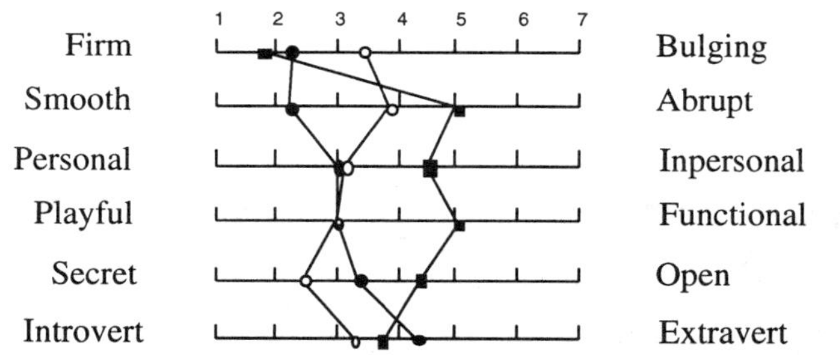

Figure 15 The means for the semantic differentials referring to cluster 2a (design concept 1).

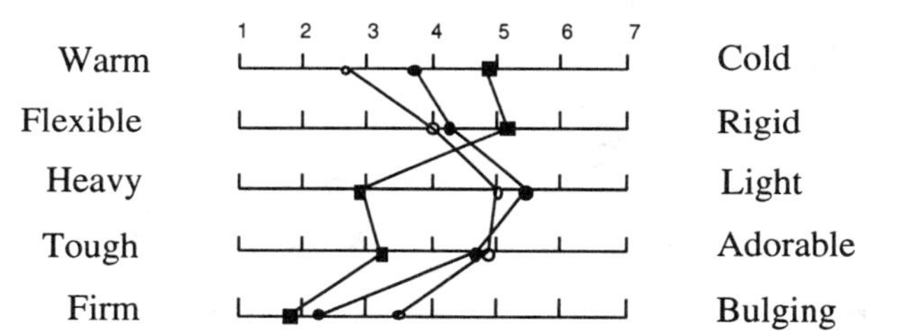

Figure 16 The means for the semantic differentials referring to cluster 2b (design concept 2b).

● Design Concept 1 ○ Design Concept 2 ■ Reference Model

Conclusions from the Evaluation Study
In the group with general sensual properties (figure 14) a clear distinction is visible between design concept 1 and design concept 2 on the one side and the reference model on the other. The two concept designs were rated significantly higher on the terms 'erotic', 'sensual', 'organic', 'strokable', 'soft' and 'warm' than the reference model (a t-test was performed on the results). Two terms are rated differently from what was expected: concept 1 was perceived as significantly more 'attractive' than both concept 2 and the reference model. Concerning the item 'smooth' only concept 1 and concept 2 were perceived significantly different, concept 1 was seen as smoother.

In the two categories where we expected a distinction between two concept designs (figures 15 and 16), the difference is less obvious. Four of the six items attributed to concept 1 show a significant distinction between the two models. Two of them, 'firm' and 'smooth', show the anticipated result. The results for the items 'secret' and 'introvert' however are reversed from the expected result. For the items attributed to concept 2, two out of five show the expected result significantly; 'soft' and 'bulging'.

Figure 17 The user has to hold the pager close to her ear to hear the messages.

CONCLUSIONS AND DISCUSSION

The objective of this project was to design a product that induces a sensual feeling. The resulting designs were perceived as significantly more sensual than a reference model.

Further conclusions from this project are divided into two areas: the process for designing a product that can induce a sensual feeling and observations about the designs.

Process

There are a number of factors that were essential for the process. The interviews were useful for gathering information about product properties. They also gave clues for the relative importance of these properties. Secondly, collages were necessary to make the step from the results of the interviews, which were mainly verbal, to the design phase. Finally the intuition of the designer played an important role. The results of the interviews had to be interpreted. The designer carried out this interpretation. It is impossible to conceive a basic form for the design without this subjective interpretation of the results.

Using semantic differentials, quick investigations can be conducted to obtain an overview of the rate of success in regard to the items that were used as input for the product design. Only small subject samples are needed to obtain significant results.

Design

The user interface was designed to enable the sender of a message to express feelings in a non-verbal way. Because of the spontaneous development of Emoticons, typographic symbols used in E-mail communication, it is assumed there is a need to communicate messages with an emotional content. The user interface has to be tested however to deter-mine its possibilities. The user interface in concept 1 shows the possibilities of integrating a display and controls in a product in a way that is more integrated in the whole product concept than currently used LCD's and keys. The user interface in concept 2 shows an example of an auditory interface, which uses the same symbolic language. This approach also needs to be evaluated.

Design processes and evaluations are often visually oriented. From the results of the interviews, it can be concluded that attention should be given to tactile and auditory qualities of products to make a design complete and coherent .

Lessons Learned

A process like the one presented in this report can support design decisions related to the feelings that are induced by a consumer product. It is important for a company like Philips, that is changing to become more consumer oriented, to take feelings induced by design seriously. An additional advantage is that new product designs can be created by understanding the needs of potential users and their feelings, rather than starting from on technical innovation. New kinds of products might evolve from such a process.

Involving users at an early stage of the process can increase the chance that consumer products will induce particular feelings for their users. It can clarify and deepen design briefs, so that a commissioner can define what he wants in a better way and the designer has a broad range of information and input regarding users and their feelings. To fully use this user input, the process of investigation and design should be iterative.

(The design models are protected and the user interface is patented.)

REFERENCES

1. Frijda, N. H. De Seksuele Emoties. *De Psycholoog.* (July, 1993), 278-284.

2. Logan, Robert J., Augaitis, S. & Renk, T. Design of Simplified Television Remote Controls: a Case for Behavioral and Emotional Usability, in Proc. Human Factors and Ergonomics Society (1994), 365-369.

3. Nass, C., Steuer, J. & Tauber, Ellen R. Computers are Social Actors, in Proc. Chi'94 Human Factors in Computing Systems (Boston, April 24-28, 1994) ACM Press, 72-78.

4. Smets, G., Overbeeke K. & Gaver, W. Formgiving: expressing the Nonobvious, in Proc. Chi'94 Human Factors in Computing Systems (Boston, April 24-28, 1994) ACM Press, 79-84.

Designing the muse: A Digital Music Stand for the Symphony Musician

Christopher Graefe, Derek Wahila, Justin Maguire, Orya Dasna
1322 Wightman Street
Pittsburgh, PA 15217
(412)421-4158
derek@andrew.cmu.edu

ABSTRACT

As part of the 1995 Apple Design Project, we designed and prototyped the muse, a digital music stand for the symphony musician. Our group consisted of four students from Carnegie Mellon University. We worked closely with members of the Pittsburgh Symphony Orchestra during the development of our product. By observing their practice, rehearsal, and performance habits, we studied the symphony culture and generated the concept of a product that would replace a number of conventional tools and processes with a single digital device. The integration of the interface and industrial design resulted in a cohesive look and feel to the muse. The muse contains a metronome with audio and visual feedback, a pitch-generating tuner, stylus-based-on-screen annotation, inter-symphony communication capabilities, a music library, and manual or automatic page turning with indexing. The muse is fashioned from mahogany, aluminum, and steel to reflect the timeless beauty of the instruments with which it shares the stage.

KEYWORDS:

Iterative design process, music stand, industrial design, interaction design, coordination support, annotation, tuning

INTRODUCTION

During the Spring of 1995, Carnegie Mellon University participated in the Apple Design Project. Our group, consisting of four members, combined varied academic talents and generated a product idea for a digital music stand for the symphony musician. Our areas of academic pursuits included graphic design, industrial design, professional writing, computer science, fine art, theater set design, and anthropology. Perhaps our greatest challenge was overcoming the lack of musical performance experience that plagued all of us.

CHI 96 Vancouver, BC Canada
© 1996 ACM 0-89791-777-4/96/04..$3.50

Our goal was to create a product that reflected the culture and practice of symphony musicians. In order to understand fully the needs of the symphony musician, we observed, studied, researched, and interviewed members of the Pittsburgh Symphony Orchestra. The resulting product concept was the muse.

The muse facilitates the individual practice, group rehearsal, and formal performance needs of symphony musicians. The muse consists of a portable digital display and matching stand. The features of the muse include a metronome with audio and visual feedback, a pitch-generating tuner, stylus-based-on-screen annotation, inter-symphony communication capabilities, a music library, and manual or automatic page turning with indexing.

DEFINING OUR PROBLEM AND APPROACH

Our research began with a survey, distributed over twenty Internet newsgroups. It queried musicians on practice and rehearsal habits, preferences, and problems. We received over 100 responses from musicians of all types—rock, jazz, classical, amateur, student, and professional. Some of the ideas introduced as a result of survey responses included automatic page turning, computer accompaniment, score arrangement, and self-generating music.

Given our decision to work with professional symphony musicians, we compiled the responses which were appropriate for that setting and developed a follow-up survey to send out to classical musicians who had responded to the first survey. We received approximately forty responses to this second survey which provided us with the perspectives of many different musicians and the seeds for many of the ideas we eventually incorporated into the muse. An even more beneficial outcome of the survey were the personal contacts we made, most significantly Harold Smoliar, the English Horn player for the Pittsburgh Symphony Orchestra (PSO).

We were very cautious in our initial dealings with the PSO. We anticipated much resistance from the symphony, whom we believed would be a "socially sophisticated and technophobic" audience. Although these stereotypes were quite strong and seemingly justified, they were wrong.

The PSO is a professional orchestra rooted in centuries-old traditions. We feared that trying to change the methods and habits of these musicians might prove futile. We knew that we needed to present our ideas to them with reserve and in incremental steps. If we had brought a finished prototype to our first focus group, the group might have viewed us as too forceful and close-mined. We did not have a predetermined solution before we began this project, and we wanted to make sure the PSO understood that. Our design process relied heavily on the musicians' input.

GATHERING DATA

Background Research

Before attending our first rehearsal, we researched the workings and practices of symphony orchestras. We purchased literature of the trade, studied seating charts, conductors' movements, and each musician's seating and body positions in relation to that musician's instrument. Using this information we were able to familiarize ourselves with the musicians' vocabulary and acquire the basic information necessary for making future decisions. We also used this research to define industrial design constraints, such as the size and weight of our product based on existing limitations like storage space and maximum transportation weights.

Expert Informant

Harold, our symphony contact, became an invaluable advisor. He answered our (almost daily) barrage of questions, acted as a sounding-board for untested product ideas before we presented them to a focus group, introduced us to visiting conductors and other PSO musicians, and most importantly, arranged our many visits to Heinz Hall, the home of the PSO.

Symphony Observations

By attending a number of rehearsals and performances at Heinz Hall, we began to understand the routines and roles of the musicians and the conductor. We documented these behaviors on video and later used them to pinpoint areas of communication concerns between the conductor and musicians, musicians in the same section, or musicians in different sections. Rehearsals were our first exposure to the symphony "backstage." Understanding what musicians did with their music when they were not on stage was equally as important since the muse would replace their printed music in all situations. We needed to thoroughly understand the environment before we could design a suitable product for our intended audience.

Interviews with Others

In addition to our meetings with the PSO musicians, we spoke with music students on the Carnegie Mellon campus and faculty in the music and computer science departments. Specifically, we consulted with a Computer Science faculty member to discuss the feasibility of the technology we intended to use. He critiqued the methods and hardware we were proposing and offered some alternate methods which were adopted. Although the PSO was our audience, we utilized other resources which could provide technical feedback and opinions on the functionality of the muse.

NEEDS AND PRACTICES

The Three Situations for Use of the muse

After gathering data and speaking with our various contacts, we were able to define three distinct situations for using the muse: practice, rehearsal, and performance. At home, musicians learn their music, practicing it to the point that they are competent and can recognize where special attention is needed. Rehearsal is where the conductor and the musicians work to bring the piece together. The focus is on cues and the 'sound of the symphony' — not on the individuals. Performance is the culmination of practice and rehearsal; after weeks of practice and one week of rehearsal, the piece is performed for an audience, and the cycle begins again.

Communications on the Stage

We could see that communication problems existed once the rehearsal began. The orchestra's apparent lack of organization and order while "tuning up" before the maestro arrived on stage was unexpected — a significant contrast to a symphony performance. Often the maestro would have trouble conveying which note in the score he was referring to. Several times when musicians tried to describe something to him communication broke down.

When a musician has a concern, that musician consults a peer, the first chair of the section, or the conductor. While speaking with a "neighbor," it is common for the musician to rotate their own stand and point at the music in question. When the communication spans the stage, such as to the conductor, it is impossible to indicate where the area of concern is on the printed music — it must be described verbally. This in turn causes problems of audibility. For instance, when the first chair violin gives a directive to the violin section, the musicians sitting in the last row often have difficulty hearing them. All of these competing conversations and communications create a complex web of interactions among musicians on the stage.

Annotation

Annotation is a large part of the symphony rehearsal: Musicians make notes on their printed music based on personal observations or feedback from their first chair, conductor, or peers. Musicians also mark up their music in practice, but only with notes specific to their needs.

Page Turning

While musicians in some sections of the symphony have the luxury of individual music stands, string musicians must share stands. When two musicians share a stand, the individual sitting on the inside of the orchestra (away from the audience) must turn the page. In most cases, a page break occurs during a rest for the particular instrument. When it is does not, the musician who is required to turn the page must stop playing. Thus, in a performance, page turning actually results in perceptible "dips" in the music's volume. In rehearsal, page turns may occur in both directions since the conductor may choose to focus on a part of the composition and rehearse it over and over. We needed to address both types of page turning.

Tuning

Whether for a rehearsal or performance, each time a musician comes on to stage, they tune their instruments. Different symphonies tune to different A pitches. The most common pitch used is the 'concert A' (440 Hertz). Some symphonies tune to A444 or even A415. This discrepancy is not common, but without it, the muse would be unusable to some symphonies.

Music Management

We discussed with the Heinz Hall music librarians the problems associated with current methods of music distribution. Only a few musical scores are not copyrighted — it is those pieces that PSO owns and can to play free of charge. We learned that the majority of the music the symphony plays is laden with copyrights. For pieces that the Symphony rents, there are performance licensing terms. The terms of the rental contract depend on whom the symphony is performing the piece for, as well as, the percentage of the composition that they will be playing.

FUNCTIONALITY AND ENABLING TECHNOLOGY

As a result of our visits to PSO rehearsals, and our meetings with Carnegie Mellon faculty, staff, and students, the features of the muse began to take shape. We compiled our observations, focused our ideas, decided on the final functionality of the muse, and determined how that functionality would be conveyed to the musicians (i.e. what tools we would provide). However, we did not decide at this point which functions would have a hard interface (buttons, switches, stylus) and which would be completely embodied in the software interface.

Functionality

After reviewing the information gathered, we decided on the "tools" and functions to include in the muse: (1) Musicians were delighted with the prospect of eliminating manual page turning from the symphony performance and letting the muse control it. However, page turning still needed to be under the musician's control, since automatic page turning would not be helpful in all rehearsal situations. (2) Since musicians are constantly writing on their scores, we wanted to provide a function for annotation — one that allowed for the marks from the conductor and first chair of each section could be distributed to the rest of the symphony, eliminating the arduous task of copying notations by hand. (3) Nearly every musician owned a metronome and a tuner. Including these devices in the muse would reduce the number of devices musicians carried onto stage. This feature could be integrated with other muse functions like annotated tempo changes. (4) A method was needed for musicians to access other instruments' parts and allow them to view select parts of the entire symphonic score as the piece is played — creating a redundant system of cueing. (5) By including a library tool, musicians would be able to download music from the Heinz Hall Collection, store it locally, and display it on the muse.

In addition to these functions, we needed an area reserved for setting preferences that controlled how the features of the muse behaved for each musician (such as the size of music displayed, the tonal range of each instrument, page turning settings, etc.).

Enabling Technologies

Batteries

The muse had to be able to operate at locations outside of Heinz Hall, such as, at other music halls or at home. Batteries were necessary to afford this portability. Because it would be impractical for a musician to carry the stand around with the display each time they moved, the display must be able to run independent of the base. Hence, the display needed its own power supply. These battery requirements impacted the industrial design, so it was important to identify these needs and find solutions early in the design process. We researched compact rechargeable batteries with long-lasting power and a short recharge time which matched our needs.

Wireless

In order for the muse to receive music from the Heinz Hall Collection, some sort of data communication must be possible. To avoid wires strung around the stage during a rehearsal or performance which would impede musicians walking on stage, wireless connections would be used. This network would increase security and prevent potential copying of musical scores through the use of data compression and encryption.

Microphones

To include a tuner and automatic page turning in the muse we needed a small, accurate microphone with low power consumption. When a musician is using the tuner to tune an instrument during rehearsal, the microphone must discern that instrument's tones from those of the surrounding instruments.

Software

In the early stages of the design process, it was necessary to confirm that we were not replicating any existing products. Speaking to personal computer software distributors, we discovered products that support arrangement and notation of music, and allow for electronic composition and publishing of music. We realized that much of the current technology could be used in our product. One package's scanning ability could be used by music distributors to transform sheet music into digital form, and a derivative of Vivace's[1] real-time accompaniment technology could be used to facilitate automatic page turning.

INDUSTRIAL DESIGN AND INTERFACE DESIGN

Our design process was iterative — not only in the software interface, but also in the industrial design. The research we performed and the interviews we conducted also had an iterative flavor; as the product definition grew in detail, we refined our research techniques and in turn yielded better feedback from the musicians.

As we learned more about symphony musicians, our initial concepts changed, along with the features of the product. We first believed that classical symphony musicians would be resistant to change — that they would not be interested in the advantages that the muse had to offer.

First Iteration

The first designs showed our initial hesitation to break away from convention. The stand still reflected the traditional music stand, and the interface widgets visually mimicked conventional devices. While we were exploring new ideas and approaches we tended to keep looking to the past for inspiration and guidance.

Industrial Design

Our first step was to build a display sketch model to understand better the scale that we were proposing. We decided early in the process to use screen sizes of 9 by 12 inches per page (see Figure 1) — slightly larger than the conventional printed music that the PSO uses. Since this is a rather large finished size and we wanted the display portion to be portable, it needed to fold in half.

Our first stands (see Figure 2) were part of a series of semantic studies to see how we could improve on the traditional music stand. The issues that we were concerned with were mobility, flexibility, weight, location of the power source, and how the stand would support the display.

Interface

We began prototyping the interface with only two tools: the tuner and the metronome. We believed that using a metronome modeled after a conventional metronome would be a logical extension of the musicians' knowledge (see Figure 3). For similar reasons, we modeled the tuner design after a conventional analog tuner (see Figure 4). Again, we planned to use the musicians' familiarity with a physical tool to teach them how to use a digital tool.

Feedback

We presented the first iteration informally to PSO musicians, CMU faculty, and students. From responses to the presentations, we learned that digital metronomes were used instead of the analog type we had modeled our interface after. The tuner was described as awkward and visually confusing, almost more of a display then a tool for tuning. The symphony musicians commented that the bases for the stand were too long and potentially obtrusive for some musicians such as the harpist or basist (see Figure 5).

Second Iteration

After reevaluating our interface designs, we noticed that they seemed very disjointed from the industrial design of the product. Furthermore, as we tried to design tools such as the library that could not be represented as literal as a tuner and a metronome, we realized that the metaphors we were clinging to could potentially confuse the musicians and create uglier, jumbled screens.

Industrial Design

Realizing that the stand would be sharing the stage with million dollar instruments, we experimented with more graceful forms and materials that reflected those in the instruments on stage. Mahogany, aluminum, and steel became our materials of choice, and the form began to diverge from the conventional look of a music stand. Creating a wooden support arm that came out of the base not only gave the shaft more support, but allowed a beautiful contrast of materials. In addition, we refined ideas about where the power sources within the stand and display should be placed and how they would work together (see Figure 6).

Interface

As the industrial design progressed, we were very intrigued by its graceful form. We experimented with bent steel for the tube that supported the stand. Inspired by the basic form and gesture of the industrial design, we returned to the drawing board and generated new sketches of the interface tools.

We found that by trading the metaphors we had been working with for a new, non-representational design language and a limited color palette, we were able to design the tools with a cohesive form language that reflected the industrial design and worked together as a family. Each tool had a linear element that surrounded areas of colors (see Figures 7,8,9 for examples). The functionality of each tool was contained in the colored area, with different colors establishing a hierarchy within each tool. By keeping the tools simple, all the interactions with the muse could be achieved through a small set of interface widgets.

The challenge we faced in designing these tools was how to lead the musicians through the information space effectively. This was extremely difficult in the library tool, where there are potentially two libraries displayed at once and music needs to be moved from one collection to the other. To solve this issue, we employed the notion of progressive disclosure, first displaying the local library and then after an additional action by the musician, revealing the symphony's collection. Despite these challenges, we were able to communicate our intentions and the tools' functionality through scaleable interface elements.

Feedback

When we presented the second iteration prototype to a focus group of ten symphony musicians, we received positive feedback concerning both the industrial design and the interface. They felt the selection of tools was appropriate and including devices like the tuner and metronome would reduce stage clutter if they were integrated into a single device. However, the musicians still had some concerns. They felt that the microphone was too far away to pick up the sound of an instrument, especially in a loud rehearsal. Many shared ideas about alternative ways to navigate manually through the music. The musicians also felt that navigation in the music should be facilitated by adding functions to reduce the possibility of "getting lost" during a rehearsal or performance: Certain pages could be marked, a small screen could display the previous page, or a moving staff might show the measure being played.

Despite the musicians' positive feedback, we were careful not to implement any of their ideas without careful consideration. After analyzing their suggestions and compiling our own observations we began the final iteration. Simplicity was the key to making sure that all musicians could use the product without difficulty, and this drove our final design.

FINAL PRODUCT

Physical Features

The muse is comprised of a portable digital music display and a matching stand to which the display attaches during rehearsals and performances. The display is foldable with two 9"x 12" high resolution flat panel touch-sensitive displays, a built-in microphone, and two speakers. Inside the display is a hard drive for storage of musical scores and a wireless modem for inter-orchestral communication. The muse is powered by rechargeable batteries inside the display. These batteries are charged every time the musician uses the product on its stand — which has its own rechargeable batteries. The stand and display are built from mahogany, aluminum, and steel to reflect the timeless beauty of the instruments with which they share the stage (see Figure 10).

Interface Features

Automatic Page Turning

To facilitate a symphony performance, the muse listens to the musician and is constantly aware of that musician's location within the music being played. The musician sets a position on the page that, when reached, cues the muse to turn the page. The pages are replaced individually, first on the left, and then on the right — so there is never a break in the music. This eliminates the need for the musician to stop playing and interrupt concentration; the page turn is automatic. Alternatively, the musician can use a manual method to turn pages through two buttons located on the top corners of the display. These buttons turn one page forward or backwards when pressed with a hand, bow, or other device.

Annotation

The musicians can mark up their music using the touch sensitive display and stylus. In addition to seeing their own markings, musicians can view the markings distributed across the orchestra by the conductor or the first chair of their section. This saves musicians the time and labor of copying the notation of several different people onto their own music. It also grants musicians the ability, during practice, to start with a "clean slate" by turning off all of their markings and focus on the music without any interpretations.

By allowing immediate annotation from a first chair or conductor to the musicians, a number of the communication problems normally associated with a symphony rehearsal can be alleviated. By sending the markings electronically, there is no confusion with the changes or to what they apply.

Metronome

The metronome (see Figure 11) allows musicians to set tempos and preview them as sound clicks or a blinking light during practice and rehearsal. The metronome can be used to place multiple tempos in the score where the beat changes, so the feedback from the muse can automatically adjust as the musician plays the piece. This feedback can be turned on and off without deleting the tempo settings.

Tuner

The tuner (see figure 12) allows a musician to select a note in an instrument's range for tuning. The musician's instrument is set in the preferences menu of the muse, so that the appropriate scale is displayed for the musician to choose from. After the musician selects the desired note (generally the concert A), the tuner will play that pitch for the musician to match. As the musician plays the tone, the muse listens to the instrument and displays how sharp or flat the note is. Once the pitch matches the muse's tone, the tuner is automatically closed so the musician can immediately begin playing without having to release the instrument.

Views

The views feature gives musicians access to the parts of any other instrument in a given score. This allows musicians to see their location in the score in relation to other instruments that they may be listening to for cues — it gives them a visual cue in addition to an audio one. The pages are then repaginated on the muse to reflect the new staff(s) of music added to the display and will turn accordingly with automatic progression.

Library

Music is downloaded to the muse via wireless communication from the symphony's digital music library. Because of strict copyright laws surrounding music distribution and performance, permission would still need to be granted by the music librarians for personal requests. Musicians would have the ability to sort through the symphony library by composer, title, or performance date (see Figure 13). After selecting a piece, a musician can download it to the personal collection on the hard drive in the muse, which has the capability to store 100 pieces of music. If the piece has certain copyright restrictions, the musician may have to wait for the request to be processed by one of the music librarians. Once downloaded to the muse, any of the music can be selected for display.

Preferences

Every muse can be customized through preferences to meet the needs of individual musicians. The preferences include the musician's name, symphony name, instrument, page turning options, size of music displayed, etc. Once these preferences are set, their values affect the other six functions of the muse, allowing it to work with any musician playing any instrument.

Notes

When the musician turns on the muse, a screen displays that musician's name, instrument, and orchestra. Layered on top of this text are personal notes and important symphony announcements from the personnel manager and symphony staff. After reading the notes the musician can close them by tapping on them with the stylus. These notes complement or replace the verbal announcements made at the start of every symphony rehearsal.

CONCLUSION

The iterative process must be central to an effective design methodology. When choosing a potentially resistant audience, it is necessary to present concepts at a basic level. Once an audience has accepted these ideas, more complex issues can be introduced. These cycles allow for the constant modification of previous work, and keep an audience engaged in the development.

By maintaining cohesive industrial and interface designs, accompanied by a strategic design process, we were able to introduce new technology to, and spark the imagination of, the Pittsburgh Symphony Orchestra.

ACKNOWLEDGMENTS

We would like to thank Roy McKelvey (our trusted advisor), Harold Smoliar, Roger Dannenberg, Riccardo Schultz, Apple Computer, Tom Erickson, the Pittsburgh Symphony Society, Christina Farrell, and Sharahn McClung.

REFERENCES

[1] *Vivace*, real-time MIDI accompaniment hardware, copyright 1994 Coda Music Technologies

Rapid Scout: Bridging the Gulf Between Physical and Virtual Environments

David S. Ranson, Emily S. Patterson, Daniel L. Kidwell, Gavin A. Renner, Mike L. Matthews, Jim M. Corban, Emil Seculov, and Constantine S. Souhleris
Cognitive Systems Engineering Laboratory
The Ohio State University
Columbus OH 43210 USA
+1 614 292 6287
ranson@csel.eng.ohio-state.edu

ABSTRACT
We explored how to bridge the gulf between physical and virtual environments for the sport of whitewater paddling. Field observations, critical incident analysis, exploratory prototyping, and field and lab evaluations were used to make discoveries. Lessons learned in this ethnographic process led to the design of a guiding, communication, and navigation aid for kayakers and canoeists. In designing "Rapid Scout", we gained insights on making virtual representations context-sensitive, coupling multiple perspectives, dealing with uncertainty, and extending human views. Ways to facilitate collaboration through shared graphic frames of reference were also explored.

Keywords
Visualization, representation aiding, groupware, decision support, portable computing, and ethnography.

BACKGROUND
Our senses are exposed to an ocean of information in the physical world. Computers allow us to add to what is naturally available. Yet a gulf often exists between the physical world and the virtual worlds we create on computers. Not only do we have trouble finding relevant information, but we often find that virtual representations are disconnected from the "real world" entities to which they refer. For instance, virtual representations may fail to highlight changes, or their level of abstraction may be irrelevant to user tasks. Given problems like these, better mappings between the virtual and physical are needed. †

Bridging the gulf between the physical and the virtual requires discoveries on several fronts. More knowledge is needed about coordinating multiple virtual perspectives with existing physical views. Issues also arise in putting data into context, choosing frames of reference, and indicating limits [1]. Moreover, means to enhance cooperation between people must be explored because virtual artifacts are inevitably used in group settings.

The Natural Lab of Whitewater Paddling
We chose the whitewater domain to serve as our natural laboratory, because it contains challenges and constraints relevant to coupling virtual and physical worlds (Figure 1). Critical characteristics inherent in other complex domains include a dynamic noisy environment, high stakes, uncertainty, multiple players, as well as varying tempos and demands [2]. Due to the extreme nature of this risky environment, these characteristics take on forms that create significant challenges and opportunities.

Figure 1. The domain of whitewater paddling. Kayaker paddling over a ledge on the New River in West Virginia.

In particular, the complexity of the hydrotopography of rapids offers fertile ground for representation aiding. The dynamic flow, river bed shape, and obstacles combine to challenge a paddler's judgment and maneuvering ability (see rapid in Figure 2). It takes years to learn how to observe, abstract, and judge what the subtle signs mean at different water levels (i.e., the process of "reading water"). Paddlers rely heavily on scouting and communicating with others to

† Apple Computer, Inc. organizes an annual design project to provide students with user-interface design experience. In 1995, the theme was integrating physical and virtual worlds.

manage risk. Novices and experts alike actively seek and share information.

Figure 2. Aerial photo showing rapid hydrotopography.

What are the challenges that make bridging the gulf between the virtual and the physical in this domain difficult? Of most importance, representations must complement what paddlers see in the physical world. How did we achieve this? We explored means to extend views by showing what is hidden, obscure, or impossible to scout. We learned how to teach paddlers to read water by highlighting the relationships which matter to them. We discovered new techniques for showing contrasts and abstractions. And, we explored new ways to enhance collaborative activity. The lessons learned from tackling challenges like these can be generalized to other domains in which close virtual and physical coupling is important.

Overview of the Design Process

Our design process can best be characterized by an analogy to the domain we studied. Designing Rapid Scout was comparable to running a river with many hazards, channels, tributaries, pushy currents, and possible routes. We faced diverse obstacles that formed a constraint space in which we had to maneuver. In the beginning of the ten-week project, we selected a user group which we felt could benefit by a closer coupling of physical and virtual environments. We then immersed ourselves in field investigations, where we discovered that our initial model of activity in whitewater paddling was incorrect and that there were significant opportunities for providing guidance through an on-the-river device. Once the general Rapid Scout concept was selected, we produced and evaluated in parallel exploratory prototypes for the representation, communication, and hardware elements in order to discover further requirements.

A map of our design process is represented in Figure 3. There are three main sections in our design process: (1) our initial model of the domain, (2) field investigations to revise our model, and (3) continuous exploratory prototyping and evaluation. The map summarizes our methods, findings, challenges, and their implications for the design of Rapid Scout.

The Rapid Scout Design Process

Starting with a folk model of the domain

We had doubts that an on-the-river aid would be successful due to several assumptions which we overturned

- Thrill seekers intent on pushing their limits would avoid decision aids
- Naturalists would resist computerized devices
- Paddlers depend on their own skills and judgment
- On-the-river aid would distract the paddler

Studying cognition in the wild

We developed a model of domain demands, artifact functions, and user requirements through ethnographic investigations.

Methods

- Domain artifact examination
- Field observation
- Incident interviews
- Newsgroup probes and surveys
- Knowledge elicitation
- Task analysis
- Sport participation

Field study findings

- Noisy, complex waterscape
- Water level greatly changes difficulty
- Even experts are information hungry
- Available physical views are limited
- Information is frequently incorrect, missing, or stale
- Class rating system is insufficient
- Communication breakdowns due to ambiguity and under-specification
- Safety and temporal constraints on use

Design implications

- Highlight important relationships
- Tailor representations to flow context
- Highlight change and events
- Extend user perspectives with virtual views and abstractions
- Allow users to annotate, update, and share information
- Provide basis of class ratings for rapids
- Provide shared frame of reference
- Don't interfere with swims or wet exits

Developing the Rapid Scout concept

During design, we used exploratory prototypes and several evaluations to discover new requirements while refining the product concept.

Methods

- Interviews
- Scenario-driven development
- Cognitive walkthroughs
- Flip book evaluation on the river
- Usability testing in the lab
- Observation of similar domains
- Physical mock-ups

Design challenges

- Selecting and coordinating views
- Showing relationships and limits
- Layering advice and its information basis
- Coordinating frames of reference
- Filtering out noise
- Extending views to show what is hidden
- Creating micro/macro representations
- Supporting route planning / decisions
- Portable computing in a "rough" world

Evaluation findings

- Tailoring representations to current flow reduced confusion
- Representations captured essential relationships
- Targeted and open communication means are warranted
- Texture maps should better denote flow aspects
- Transitions between views should be streamlined
- Five new hardware constraints discovered

Figure 3. Overview of design process.

STARTING WITH A NAIVE FOLK MODEL

All designers begin with an implicit or explicit model of cognitive activity in a domain. Generally, this model should be viewed as tentative and should be tested by ethnographic investigations. We discovered through field observation that our initial model of whitewater paddling was incorrect. First, we considered paddlers to be either in a thrill-seeking or a back-to-nature camp. We were concerned that individuals intent on pushing their limits would not want any decision aids. Likewise, we were concerned that the back-to-nature contingent would be resistant to computer technology on the river. We also believed that the sport was not team-oriented in that paddlers depended on their individual skills and judgment. Lastly, we were concerned that the paddlers would be preoccupied with the activity of paddling. The tempo would be too high to permit any motor, perceptual, or cognitive interaction with a computer aid.

Through field research, we found that these assumptions were simply not true. Paddlers tended to be cautious decision makers, information hungry, and very reliant on others. Their desire for more accurate information due to risks already led them share information using technology (e.g., the World Wide Web). We also discovered that significant opportunities for interaction with a device do arise. A paddler's hands, eyes, and mind are free at many times (e.g., on flat water sections between rapids, scouting on shore, and resting in the eddies/pools within the rapids). The distribution of these locations still place severe constraints on when a paddler can use a portable computer, but designing around these constraints offers new insights on how to simplify interaction in virtual worlds.

STUDYING COGNITION IN THE WILD

Comparing Artifacts and Analyzing Tasks

We began our exploration by comparing existing domain artifacts to see how they functioned as cognitive tools and supported collaboration. We looked at formal media such as guidebooks and instructional videos as well as the user-created forums on the World Wide Web. The lively web exchange of advice and stories stressed that paddlers actively seek information. Advice tailored to different river levels and complaints about guidebook inaccuracy stood out. This finding pointed to the need for context-sensitivity.

While examining these artifacts, we also developed a model of the tasks involved. At the highest-level, running a river can be broken into five stages: putting in, paddling flat water sections, scouting rapids, running rapids, and taking out. The detailed cognitive models of these stages prepared us for observing and asking questions.

Field Observation and Corpus Building

Our strategy was to ensure usefulness by grounding ourselves in the domain and by not committing to one design direction too early. Paddlers were observed during three field trips to the New River Gorge in West Virginia. We rafted the river to gain first-hand knowledge of its features so that we could ask relevant questions. We also watched guides teaching others about the river. Over 30 interviews were conducted in which we adopted an incident-based approach to elicit what paddlers know best (i.e., their experiences with close calls and accidents). Using the critical decision method, we asked paddlers to tell an entire story and then we followed up with questions to clarify critical decision-making points [3]. This corpus of incidents was used to identify ways to aid paddlers.

In the interviews, paddlers were encouraged to draw or annotate diagrams of rapids to help recall and explain the situations. In the example shown in Figure 4, the kayaker did not make a turn in time and was temporarily pinned by an undercut rock. He had not realized how much harder a previous day's route would be at a lower level. This pointed to the need for route recommendations that are tailored to different water levels. His story also indicated the need to show boat angle and size on recommended routes as well the relation of the route to flow strength and direction. In general, incidents like this one emphasized the need to put data into context and highlight relationships.

To further build our corpus of critical incidents, we found the Internet to be a fruitful source. In the paddlers' newsgroup, we monitored postings and sent out probe messages to see what information people share. A critical incident survey was also posted. Many stories of mishaps were described in the posts. Advice on running specific rapids abounded. We also came across postings warning others about new hazards which unpredictably arise in this dynamic physical world. For example, boaters warned others about trees that fell over into the river creating lethal strainers. These warnings showed us that paddlers need to update each other after their trips to keep the virtual world synchronized with the physical world.

Figure 4. A paddler's sketch of a critical incident in which he was temporarily pinned by an undercut rock.

Context-Sensitive Needs Due to Flow Changes

Before deciding to run a river, paddlers need to know the difficulty of rapids at the projected level. The nature of rapids changes drastically depending on the volume of water indicating the need for putting data into context. As the flow changes, some hydraulics, known as holes, can be transformed from friendly surfing spots to deadly keepers which will recirculate an unwary paddler forever (Figure 5). The degree and pattern of recirculation for any hole indicates the level of threat. Flow changes also expose rocks that may pin a boat, drowning a paddler who flips. Other types of dangers exist (e.g., rock sieves, whirlpool eddies, and pourovers). The threat posed by each hazard depends on its shape, size, location, and the flow amount. The implication is that virtual representations need to show how flow relates to these aspects of each feature. Merely labeling hazards with icons or words would be insufficient.

Figure 5. Keeper holes are one river hazard because at certain levels the recirculating flow can fatally trap a boater.

Decision Making Challenges
As in many activities, paddlers manage risk by judging their ability, the difficulty, and the safety consequences for a particular run. Decision making dilemmas arise due to the difficulty of knowing these relative limits in an environment filled with uncertainties (e.g., gaps in knowledge, misrepresentations, or hidden obstacles). Most accidents occur when paddlers are completely surprised by hazards. They may miss hazards because their water reading skills are not sufficiently developed. In other cases, they may be misled by inaccurate or superficial descriptions of rapids. For instance, several kayakers have been fatally pinned by a small undercut rock on a seemingly innocuous rapid on the New River because this rock only becomes a hazard at low levels and is not mentioned in any guidebook. Decision making is further complicated by the fact that heuristics break down. For example, paddlers cannot always assume that a rapid becomes more difficult at greater flows. Hazards may be completely washed out at high flows. Low or intermediate flows may in fact be more dangerous. Knowing what changes mean is critical. Computers as decision aids are very well-suited to tailoring representations to changes in an environment.

Problems Due to Over-Generalized Ratings
Boaters check gauge readings to find out river levels. However, a number from a gauge is a poor indicator of rapid difficulty. One number fails to capture what flow means. For example, in attempting to interpret 1500 cubic feet per second, a paddler must know the difficulty rating which others assign the rapid at that level (on a scale from Class I to VI). The rating assigned to the rapid generalizes over many factors, and consequently it fails to tell the entire story. A rapid rating of Class IV does not indicate the types, locations, and number of hazards. It also fails to mention the recommended lines and whether the high rating is due to technical difficulty or safety threats. Abstractions like expert ratings are useful heuristics, but decision making uncertainty is increased when their basis is hidden. Visualizations are needed that abstract out the meaning of flow changes to paddlers. The relations between expert interpretations and the physical world must be shown.

Communication Problems and Needs
Several incidents pointed to the need for shared frames of reference and extended communication abilities. The following two examples provide some insight:

- *Underspecified instructions.* One canoeist did not adequately explain how to avoid a large hole so a novice became trapped in it. Her advice was to "go left" instead of "you need to go within ten feet of the left bank and then ferry hard across strong current which is about 100 yards wide. "
- *Ambiguous gestures.* A private rafter gestured by raising his hands in parallel. A companion assumed that meant "river clear". It really meant to follow along either bank to avoid a pourover in the middle of the river. This boater ended up in the pourover.

These two examples show the communication limitations in this physical setting. Virtual representations provide a new means for joint reference. Paddlers may more precisely specify plans to others by annotating graphics with marks or gestures and then pointing to features in the real world. Moreover, communication can be extended over a greater distance and over the noise of the rapids.

The Main Insights from the Field Studies
The principle conclusions include the following:

- *Reading water is a knowledge-intensive skill.* It takes many years to learn how to interpret complex, noisy hydrotopography to identify safe routes and hazards. Representation aiding offers a way to speed up and improve the learning process.
- *Current representations are not context-sensitive.* Guidebooks are incomplete and inaccurate, because they generally describe rapids for an average water level.
- *Cognitive activity is distributed.* Knowledge is spread out across artifacts and people [4]. Facilitating the sharing of knowledge is a key leverage point.
- *Communication breakdowns occur.* Paddlers consult others when making decisions more than we expected . In most of the incidents, mishaps occurred due to underspecified or ambiguous instructions.

DEVELOPING THE RAPID SCOUT CONCEPT

In our field research, we discovered many on-the-river needs. Significant opportunities existed for improving communication over people, time, and distance using computers. With a down-the-river guide, we sought to use graphic representations to provide a shared virtual frame of reference. Prototyping this Rapid Scout concept enabled us to explore issues relevant to integrating virtual and physical environments. We needed to put data into context, show relationships, highlight change and events, and draw contrasts. In creating it, we also would have to determine how multiple virtual perspectives can be coupled with the physical views to enhance and extend our senses. Representations would also have to be tailored to a specific water level to satisfy the requirement for context-sensitive information. Once we converged on these goals, we divided the design into three parts: representation, communication, and hardware aspects of the prototype.

Virtual Representation Design

A key goal was to facilitate the sharing of knowledge across many distributed cognitive agents both on and off the river. These agents included kayakers, canoeists, raft guides, rescue squads, and park rangers. Information needs and agent interactions were characterized based on rapid- and group-specific scenarios. Five expert paddlers familiar with the New River Gorge were consulted to identify rapid-specific scenarios and representation needs.

Designing Views, Structure, and Transitions

Our team, which included one kayaker, then identified possible views of the river, and compared their strengths and weaknesses. Physically-available views are often very limited (e.g., where steep canyon walls make it impossible to scout from the shore). Virtual views which are not limited by physical constraints provide new ways to expand what paddlers can see. Paddlers can be shown an overview of an entire rapid, an otherwise inaccessible side view, or overviews which show what is just around the bend. From our analysis, we chose the views that would give paddlers the most appropriate information for the selected scenarios. We avoided the garden path tendency to provide every single possible view of a rapid. Such a default approach only increases user input, navigation, and tailoring burdens.

By showing view sketches and scenario-based storyboards to users, we determined that the following views would be prototyped: a full map view of the river, half-mile overviews, a top-of-the-rapid view, a Triptik, bird's eye overviews of each rapid, and video close-ups of particularly dangerous hazards or difficult drops. In addition, we planned screens for rating personal ability, depicting the basis for rapid ratings, as well as saving and sharing annotations and stories.

In using Rapid Scout, a boater first would download or buy information about a specific river or region. Links to automated river level gauges could then be made to download flow readings to tailor the representations to the current level. Upon arriving at the river put-in, a paddler would call up the full-map view of the river. This view shows the river layout with all rapids, access points, and other geographical information. A guide's narrative with introductory video clips can also be played to learn about highlights and the most difficult rapids.

Half-Mile and Triptik Overviews

While paddling downstream, the user can transition to successive half-mile views (see Figure 6). At this scale, these overviews encompass flat water sections and a few of the upcoming rapids. The location of the user and other paddlers with the device is shown within the 10-meter accuracy enabled by global positioning systems. Major river features such as wave trains also become visible in these views. Virtual landmarks are highlighted that can serve as points of reference to deal with uncertain data. For instance, two rocks which form a saddle on the New River are shown as a virtual reference point for verifying river level. When the saddle is filled, the user can confirm that river is indeed over three feet. The half-mile views serve three main purposes: (a) showing what is around the bend to support anticipation; (b) tracking a paddler's location relative to friends, groups, landmarks, and rapids; as well as (c) supporting targeted communication through the selection of boater symbols (discussed in the next section).

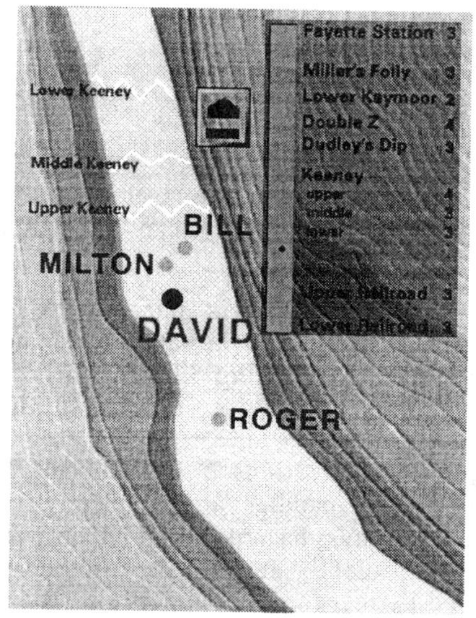

Figure 6. Half-mile and Triptik overview.

Two other mini-views are overlaid on the half-mile view. First, a top-of-the-rapid photo can be called up to facilitate recognition of rapids (providing another way to verify virtual-physical location). Secondly, a condensed and flattened Triptik showing the sequence of rapid names and a paddler's progress is provided on the right side of the half-mile view. Space limitations prevented the use of a full river map so we decided to provide this straightened-out view. The Triptik enables gauging the time left to complete the river. It also serves as a scrolling bar and menu providing a physical frame of reference for navigating to other views for communication and planning purposes.

Bird's Eye Overviews

When paddlers reach the top of a rapid, they can then switch to the bird's eye overview of that rapid (see Figure 7). It provides a big picture of a rapid's layout which is comparable to an aerial photo from 500 feet. It extends what a paddler can see in the physical world (e.g., showing the downstream side of a "blind drop"). It also shows them an undistorted layout of the rapid. In this view, we heavily use layering and separation techniques [5]. Given our exploratory prototyping approach, we separated layers of information so that we could discover useful combinations of layers (see Figure 8 for the layer model). We anticipated combining layers later on to simplify interaction.

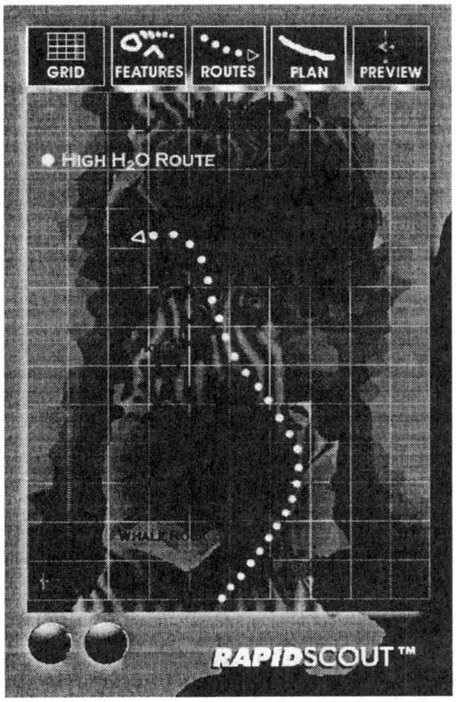

Figure 7. Bird's eye overview of a rapid.

Due to the importance of flow as a unifying factor, we chose to represent it in the base layer of the bird's eye view. Flow is shown in relation to other features by an animated texture map. This map is a micro-macro representation that uses tiny lines varying in length and direction to form meaningful flow patterns [5]. The patterns indicate relative sizes of features such as waves to indicate degrees of difficulty and danger. Safe limits are highlighted on the analogical representation of flow to provide meaningful alarms in context. For instance, we highlight when the a hole's recirculation turns it into a grabby keeper. Features below the surface which are hard to spot even with trained eyes are also shown on this base layer (e.g., undercut shapes of rocks). Showing these hidden features once again demonstrates how virtual representations provide unique capabilities for extending views into the physical world.

Additional layers include grid scales, recommended routes, and simulated previews (Figure 8). Video close-ups from shore side scouting locations also are available as options.. We chose to provide the recommended routes as optional layers because we maintain that users must have a basic understanding of the physical world before they are presented an expert's advice. Such an understanding allows them to better judge the validity of decision aid advice and teaches them the basis of recommendations [6]. Providing video close-ups of hazards as separate layers permitted access to more detail and different vantage points in a way that simplified navigation and reduced clutter.

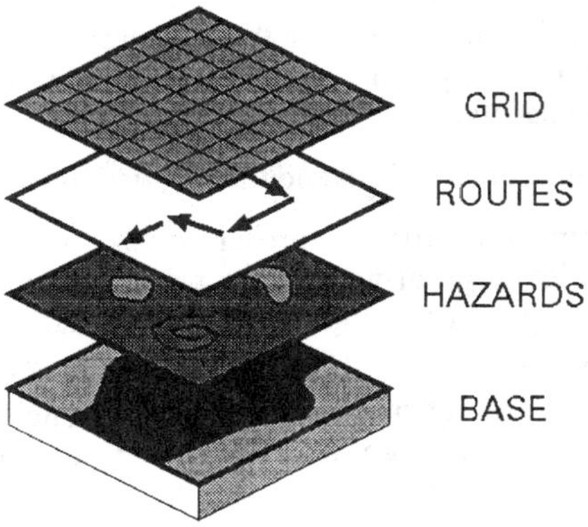

Figure 8. Layering of information model.

Evaluating the Prototype in the Field and Lab

Our river representations were evaluated iteratively at different stages using sketches, flip books, and computer prototypes. The emphasis was on discovering significant requirements (e.g., what layers should be combined) rather than on identifying minor glitches (e.g., font sizes need to be increased). We used simple as well as more functional prototypes in order to collect data early on. One such simple prototype was the laminated flip book that we used in field evaluations. The flip book included the full map, half-mile views, bird's eye overviews of two rapids, and layers which could be added to the overview (e.g., feature details, grid, and routes). Eight paddlers duct-taped these flip books to their spray skirts immediately before these two rapids to determine the usefulness of the representations in context (see Figure 9). Several insights for improving the representations were gained through this in situ testing. Ways to more accurately represent flow and the degree of hole recirculation were pointed out. Better layering schemes also became apparent leading us to combine the base water flow layer with the hazards layer.

Figure 9. Paddlers using the flip book prototype before a rapid during the field evaluation.

We also conducted user tests with an interactive prototype. We first provided a guidebook description of a rapid [7]. Then, we asked the user to explain how to run the rapid at 3.5 feet to an experimenter who role-played a novice who was not familiar with the rapid. We then asked each subject to perform the same task for two different rapids using a dynamic computer prototype. Natural verbal protocols were collected and analyzed.

Our findings from the field and lab evaluations included:

- Tailoring the virtual representations to the particular water level greatly reduced paddler confusion. In contrast, paddlers using the guidebook had to repeatedly re-read the description to see if the advice was relevant.
- The representations captured the essence of expert descriptions though we discovered several ways to improve them (e.g., by altering the flow texture map).
- Transitions between views and layers needed to be streamlined to improve navigation between displays.
- A shared frame of reference greatly reduced ambiguity in communication. Moreover, less effort was required to direct another person's attention to specific features.

Design for On-the-River Communication

Drawing from the corpus of cases, we developed several on-the-river communication scenarios which we used to specify requirements, design solutions, and evaluate the prototype. Routine scenarios included an expert explaining a route to a novice before and after the expert runs it, an instructor teaching a class how to run a rapid, and a 20 person paddling club with interchanging subgroups. Non-routine scenarios which expose brittleness were also considered (e.g., when people become separated, equipment is lost, parts of the device fails, or a person is injured).

Two types of communication appeared necessary; namely, an open form and a targeted form of communication. The open form of communication is analogous to posting on newsgroups where preset groups are contacted. Whereas, the targeted communication is like e-mail which is directed to specific locations of people or groups. In designing the open communication means, many ideas came to us from our observations of the use of voice loops at NASA Mission Control. Based on their example and our requirements, we adopted a channel-based system that has two volume levels to support monitoring and talking on several channels at once. Channels being monitored are set at the lower volume to minimize distraction while still taking advantage of our divided attention ability. The scenarios helped us specify the number of channels needed and their function dedications. We included ten general-purpose channels, a "park ranger" channel, a “chatting” channel, and an option to broadcast simultaneously to all channels. Channels were monitored or talked on by pressing buttons on the edge of the device. The degree of button depression providing feedback about whether the channel was being monitored or talked on.

In addition to the channel metaphor, we allowed for targeted communication. By selecting boat symbols from the half-mile views of the river, a user could talk directly to that boater or group (see Figure 6). By directing messages to only those people for which they are intended, this means of communication promised to reduce nuisance broadcasts and improve privacy. It also provided a physical frame of reference for organizing the communication options.

Although both means of communication looked promising, we were unsure about which method would be the most useful in different circumstances. In keeping with the exploratory prototyping approach, the two communication paradigms were combined to discover in future user tests when each method is most appropriate. When combined with the graphic shared frame of reference, these open and targeted means of communication promised to extend the communication abilities of paddlers significantly.

Hardware Design

The most striking aspect of the hardware design process was our ability to discard prototypes when new requirements were discovered. Prototypes were used to explore the constraint space rather than to refine a single concept.

The primary consideration when exploring this space was the user’s safety. Many ideas were abandoned after interviews and testing with users showed that they could become entangled on river objects or impair swimming. Some of these discarded prototypes and additional requirements included:

- A hardback screen placed in a transparent pocket on the spray skirt was rejected because it could cause the skirt to implode under heavy water pressure.
- A hardback-pullout screen housed in a drawer on the front of the kayak was dropped because it would cover the safety quick-release loop on the spray skirt.
- A flexible pull-out screen attached to the spray skirt was a success with paddlers in our usability tests, but was judged to be too futuristic.

Eventually, the requirements that we met were that the device be waterproof, shockproof, compact, light, rigid, and glare-resistant. In addition, the device could not interfere with swimming, pulling off the spray skirt, paddling, or walking. It also had to be readily accessible and easy to use in relatively calm eddies. Furthermore, we decided that equipment alterations were undesirable to keep costs down and to make it easy to rent the device from outfitters, or to share it with fellow boaters.

The latest prototype is a PDA-sized device which will be encased in a rubber coating and attached to the front of the paddler by a neoprene belt (see Figure 10). Interaction with the magnetically-sensitive touch screen is conducted using a glove with magnetized finger tips (normal electrostatic touch screens had to be ruled out because of the water). This solution satisfies the above requirements though we still view it as an exploratory tool.

Similar portable hardware already is being introduced to such sports environments (e.g., PDAs with GPS links). However, these devices generally only provide user location coordinates. In the long run, these products should aim to incorporate more functionality and information as illustrated by the Rapid Scout concept.

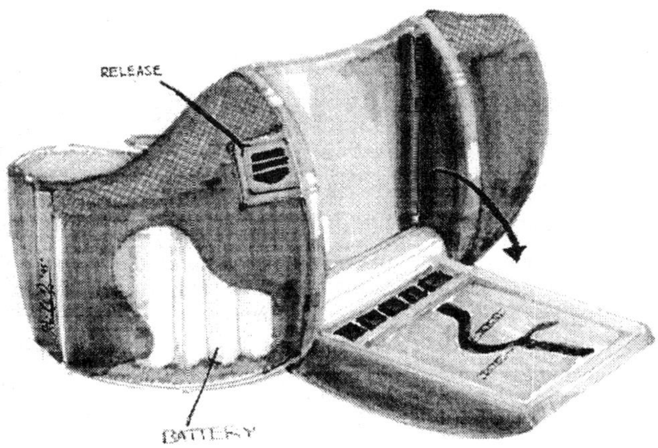

Figure 10. The Rapid Scout hardware.

CONCLUSION

Rapid Scout brings together scattered knowledge and expands paddler communication abilities on the river. In designing it, we have tackled challenges including:

- abstracting out critical relationships to show people what they need to look for in the physical world (e.g., analogical representations of the degree of threat),
- providing context-sensitive information (e.g., tailoring to flow changes),
- extending user perspectives with virtually-possible views and abstractions (e.g., bird's eye overview),
- highlighting important contrasts and change (e.g., micro-macro texture map),
- indicating safety-critical limits and hidden hazards (e.g., showing degrees of recirculation),
- dealing with an unpredictable environment (e.g., providing updating, annotation, and sharing abilities),
- coordinating multiple virtual perspectives with available views in the physical world (e.g., through navigation mechanisms),
- addressing severe constraints on portable computing in this rough environment (e.g., synchronizing interaction with paddling downtimes),
- improving communication (e.g., providing a shared frame of reference and supporting collaboration over a greater distance and the noise of the rapids).

Recent advances in technology (e.g., GPS, portable computing) have provided the designer with new opportunities for bridging the gulf between physical and virtual environments. The key to harnessing the power of virtuality and ensuring that a new design will function as a useful tool is to gain an in-depth understanding through user-centered methodologies such as field investigations and exploratory prototyping.

ACKNOWLEDGMENTS

We gratefully acknowledge the support of Apple Computer, Inc. Several people guided us, most notably, our Apple liaison, Matthew Holloway, and the course instructors, Dr. David Woods and Dr. Susan Roth. North American River Runners provided us with video footage of the New River Gorge. And, of course, we are grateful to the paddlers who provided us with valuable information at every design stage.

REFERENCES

1. Woods, D.D. *Visualizing Function: The Theory and Practice of Representation Design in the Computer Medium* (in preparation).
2. Orasanu, J. and Connolly, T. The Reinvention of Decision Making, in Klein, G.A., Orasanu, J., Calderwood, R. and Zsambok, C.E., eds., *Decision Making in Action.* Ablex, Norwood, NJ, 1993, 3-21.
3. Klein, G.A, Calderwood, R., and MacGregor, D. Critical decision method for eliciting knowledge. *IEEE Transactions on Systems, Man, and Cybernetics*, 19, 3 (May/June 1989), 462-472.
4. Hutchins, E. *Cognition in the Wild.* The MIT Press, Cambridge, MA, 1995.
5. Tufte, E. *Envisioning Information.* Graphics Press, Chesire, CT, 1992.
6. Woods, D.D. and Roth, E.M. Aiding human performance II: From cognitive analysis to support systems. *Le Travail Humain*, 51 (2), 139-171.
7. Nealy, W. *Whitewater Home Companion Vol I - II*; Menasha Ridge Press, Birmingham, AB, 1981.

Interaction design and human factors support in the development of a personal communicator for children

Ron Oosterholt, Mieko Kusano, Govert de Vries

Philips Corporate Design, P.O. Box 218, 5600 MD Eindhoven, The Netherlands

Internet e-mail: C887549@nlccmail.snads.philips.nl

ABSTRACT

Today's computer games for children are primarily focused on boys. Two years ago Philips started the development of a new 'personal communication' product that addresses the needs of young children and especially the needs of young girls. This article is focused on the interaction design and human factors support provided throughout the development of this product. It illustrates the involvement of the interaction design discipline, ranging from the initial generation and visualization of interface ideas to the final transfer to the software engineering team of detailed user interface specifications. The article also describes how human factors support ensured that potential users were involved on continuously in the design process, as well as how this involvement influenced the development of the final product. The article concludes with a discussion of the lessons learned in designing products for children.

Keywords

Children, communicator, user interface, interaction, design, development process, qualitative research, methods and techniques.

INTRODUCTION

Market studies indicated that within the electronic games industry, there is a potentially uncovered market niche for feminine-based functionality, especially in the teenage range. It appears that the video games of today do not attract girls, because of the nature of the games; where boys are focused on rules and winning, girls will use rules creatively or change them.

By focusing on this very particular target group, it was possible to develop new directions. However, we feel that the characteristics of the final product will address a much larger audience, including boys.

Philips Corporate Design contributed in all phases of the project with a multi-disciplinary team covering product design, interaction design, human factors support and graphic communication design.

PRODUCT DESCRIPTION

The product consists of a small handheld device that features a touch-sensitive liquid crystal display, pen input, infrared communication, and audio output (Figure 1). It has built-in software as well as external software available on separate cards. The functionality and interface of the product focuses on fun, creative, communicative, personal, and magical applications.

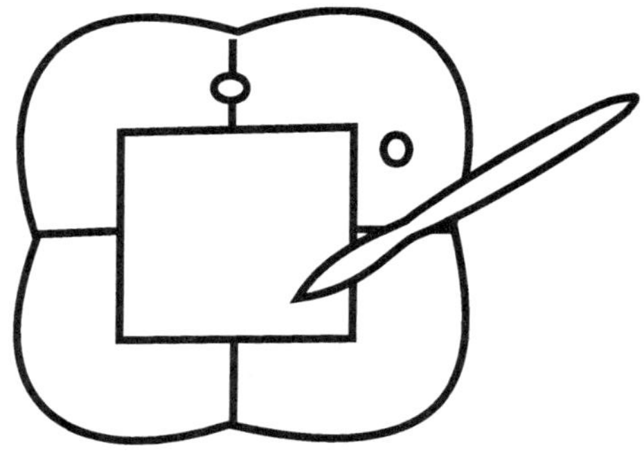

Figure 1: The communicator with pen

Figure 2: The product display showing the 'world ' .The world allows for navigation, access to specific applications, basic functions, and storage.

Interaction between child and product primarily takes place through pen and display. The interface uses the metaphor of a 'living world'† in which the user can freely move around (Figure 2).

The user can enter all kinds of 'applications' such as a weekly calendar/alarm clock, a photo album, a fortune teller, a communicator, as well as many others (Figure 3).

The user can use her product to create letters, tunes and drawings that can be stored within the product, onto cards or be sent by infra-red to another product.

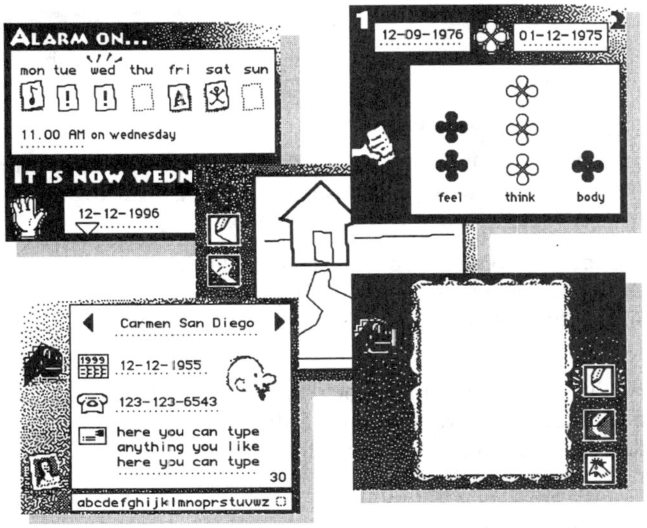

Figure 3: Some of the built-in applications: weekly alarm, matchmaker, communicator, photo album, and painter.

DEVELOPING THE PRODUCT

The following phases are used as a framework for describing the product development process: *initiation*, *concept creation*, *specification*, and *finalisation*.

INITIATION

The goal of the initiation phase was to translate an idea into a sensible combination of market opportunity, feasible technology and design direction determined by the target user needs; in other words 'the opportunity definition'.

The project started within 'Philips New Business Creation', a structure within the Philips organization dedicated to fast exploration of the viability of new product ideas. The idea in this case being a 'communicator for young girls'.

Co-design at an international primary school

The goals of the first co-design workshop held at an international primary school, were to get insight into the personal and social aspects of a 7 - 12 year old girl's daily life, and to obtain design directions by actively involving the youngsters in participatory design sessions.

Representatives of the whole design team were present at the sessions.

Children were visited at school where there is a familiar environment of peer interaction. We invited groups of 8 to 12 children at one time to avoid discomfort they would experience if interviewed alone. Group discussions were held, round-robin questionnaires were used and children were asked to make sketches of their 'ideal' product. During these sessions we gradually focused and revealed the intent of the product idea.

In order to obtain information about the actual setting in which the product would be used the children were also given photo cameras and asked to take pictures of, for example, computers they use, diaries they have, their room, etc. Furthermore, one group of children was asked to write a story in which the product would play a role (Figure 4).

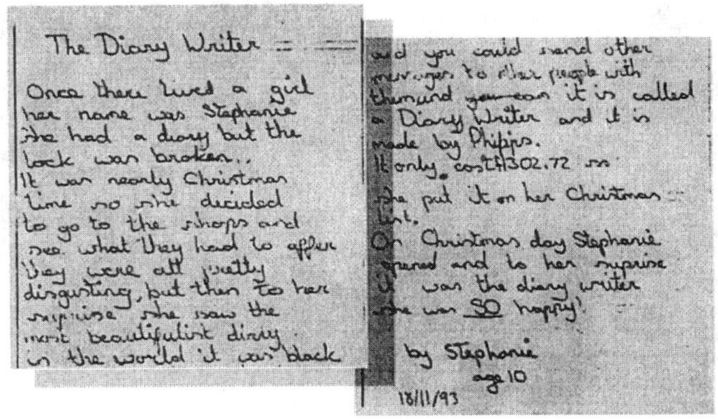
The Diary Writer
Once there lived a girl her name was Stephanie she had a diary but the lock was broken. It was nearly Christmas time so she decided to go to the shops and see what they had to offer they were all pretty disgusting, but then to her surprise she saw the most beautifulist diary in the world it was black and you could send other messages to other people with thousand you can it is called a Diary Writer and it is made by Philips. It only cost £302.72 so she put it on her Christmas list. On Christmas day Stephanie opened and to her surprise it was the diary writer she was SO happy!
by Stephanie age 10
18/11/93

Figure 4: Example of child's story

Results of the Co-Design Workshop.
Results of the workshop indicated that communication, the pen based interface and the multi-functionality were appreciated. The majority of youngsters was very positive about the concept.

Important differences were identified between boys and girls, both with respect to the games they are interested in and in the functionality of the device. Boys were interested in a device with a broader range of functionality, while girls were more interested in communication. Girls liked other type of games (e.g. Marioland™) than boys and mentioned frequently that they did not like fighting games.

Personalisation was also found to be important. Youngsters mentioned for example, that they would like the product to warn them about an incoming message differently, dependent on the circumstance one is in. For instance one girl mentioned that the product should 'cough' when a message was received so that the teacher would not notice that she was using her product.

Evaluation of First Set of Product Models

A second session at the same school provided feedback on the first set of product models (Figure 5).

The children were asked what they thought about several aspects of the models such as the colour, the shape, the styles, robustness, etc. Group discussion took place at

† all interface graphics as shown in this paper are pending registration.

the end of each session to assess and evaluate the details of the models.

Results of the Evaluation of the Models.
Results of the evaluation indicated that children liked the possibility to protect the screen when carrying the product. Different bags and cases for carrying the product should be provided. The stylus should be stored within the device to avoid loosing it. The pen should not be stored in the bottom of the device because that created the impression that it can fall out.

Figure 5: Set of product models

The children perceived the product as a personal product that should not be easily to access by others without their permission. The hardware should reflect therefor privacy and security.

The most negative aspect of the models was the colour. Most children suggested that the product should be dark just like their parents' hi-fi equipment. We interpreted and translated this finding as: the product is relatively expensive and therefore should communicate sophistication and quality which associated with the dark colours of hi-fi equipment.

Although the children were evaluating foam models that did not incorporate any functionality, they were capable of assessing a lot of aspects of the product directly related to the usability of the device. The participation of designers in the sessions showed clear benefits. The designers and human factors specialists could discuss the reasoning behind the concepts. An advantage hereby was that the designers got the opportunity to explain why they made certain decisions to which the participants could then respond.

The first user interface sketch
The first user involvement sessions provided not only feedback on models but also input for a first 'dynamic sketch' illustrating a possible user interface (Figure 6).

Using an animation tool, issues such as navigational metaphor, consequences of a pen-based dialogue, types of applications, and visual style were explored.

Figure 6: Some shots from the first visualization of the product idea using a computer animation tool.

CONCEPT CREATION
The goal of the concept creation phase was to come towards the definition of a clear concept with regard to the product design and user interface.

Children's Workshop on Product Metaphor
As input for this phase, workshops on product metaphors were conducted to provide input for possible interface concepts.

At this time it became clear that the product had to have a distinct set of values - in product as well as interface design. Those values were:

- to support communication by stimulating social interaction between children.
- to evoke creativity - instead of achieving 'hi-scores', the product had to stimulate the children's fantasy.
- to be alive - unexpected fun things should happen, surprising and pleasurable to the user that give the product more character.
- intimacy - the product is a personal asset, containing personal information.

Based on these values the design team created five different metaphors. Each metaphor was represented by a story (Figure 7). The girls were asked to 'translate' the metaphor into a collage, using a combination of drawings, essays and existing pictures.

The goal of the workshop was to get insight into how the girls appreciated the different metaphors, using collage techniques to visualize their ideas about the different metaphors.

Figure 7: Illustration explaining one of the metaphors: the wizard.

Results of the metaphor workshop.

Results indicated that girls preferred to have an interface and functionality where they were able to create, communicate and organize personal 'things'. The creativity of the girls showed different levels of abstraction, that made it impossible to compare the collages and therefor the metaphors with each other. The fact that the girls became so creative was a general positive feedback on the metaphors.

Designers' Workshop On Product Metaphor

The children's workshop was followed by another session with interaction designers in order to explore concepts of interaction and functionality (Figure 8).

Figure 8: Designers' workshop

Scenarios were used to describe the children's environment and the context of use of the product. This resulted in first sketches for the interface.

Interaction Prototyping

With the use of computer-based prototyping tools, a number of ideas from the workshop were illustrated dynamically (Figure 9) and an initial document was written that defined the product's interface and functionality.

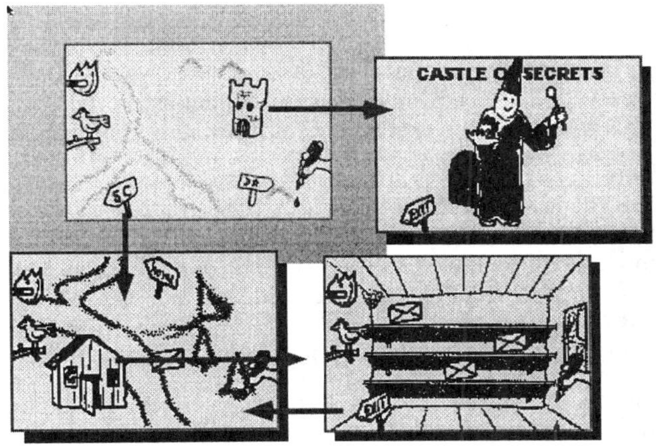

Figure 9: Illustrations from the first dynamic visualizations

SPECIFICATION

The goal of the specification phase was to produce a first draft of functional and user interface specifications agreed upon by the team, and to focus on one or two concepts for hardware design.

Display Workshop

A study was performed to investigate requirements for the size and resolution of the display. The children should be able to write or type messages on the touch screen using a pen.

We wanted to find an optimum between writability and portability, taking into account left & right handed writers and the motor & cognitive skills of children.

Foam models and Apple Newtons™ were used for this study. The foam models (Figure 10) were used to simulate different display formats, get feedback on how children would handle the product, and to test the writability of the product while users were standing. The validity of using the foam models to investigate children's writing behaviour was tested by comparing the children's writing capabilities while using the foam models and while using an Apple Newton™ (Figure 11).

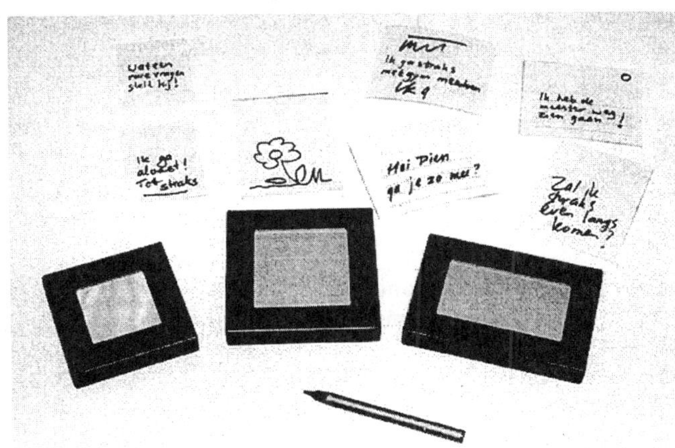

Figure 10: Foam models used in the workshop including children's writing examples.

Results of the Display Workshop.
No important differences between writing performance on the foam models and on the Apple Newtons™ were observed. The foam models were concluded to be useful tools to assess the writability and portability of different screens sizes.

Left handed children used the upper left part of the product as leaning place while writing, whereas the right handed children used the lower right part of the product. Based on this finding it was concluded that the top right and low left corner around the screen had to offer hand resting space to support both left and right handed users.

All the children chose writability over portability. Portability was not such an important issue because all children mentioned they would put the product in their backpacks.

Figure 11: Writing on the Display of a Foam Model

As expected, there were large differences between writing performance of children aged 7 and 12 years old. Therefor it was decided to build an optimal product for children of 10-12 year old.

User Interface Evaluation
The goal of the user interface evaluation was to obtain feedback on ideas and directions developed by the user interface design team. Two user interface concepts were presented to users at a fair for youngsters.

Both concepts contained exactly the same functions and shared the same hardware. They differed in the directness of accessing functions and the visual explicitness of their metaphors. Also the concept of storing information (the archiving function) was different for both concepts.

Concept A. This concept had one 'home screen' (Figure 12) that displayed almost all available functions of the device. The visual presentation and size of each function was limited to be able to fit all functions within one screen. The amount of objects that could be stored was limited to the space available on this screen.

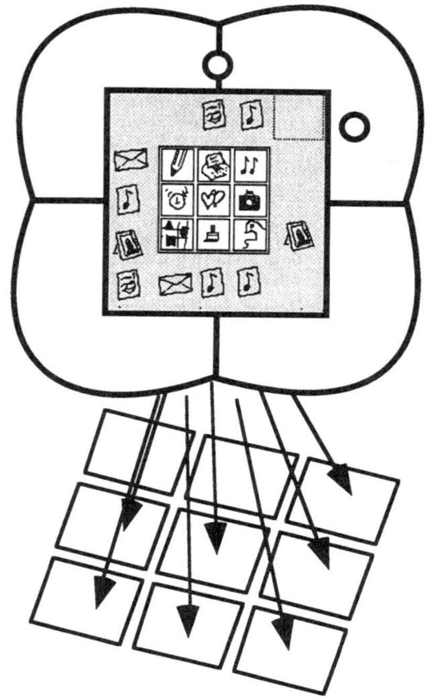

Figure 12: Concept A, direct access to all functions using a top-level overview screen.

Concept B. The second concept featured a 'world' that consisted of several screens (Figure 13). Applications were distributed over the screens and thus not always directly accessible. Applications were visualized by a large icon in the center of the screen. A number of basic tools were represented by detailed animated figures that were always present at the sides of the screen.

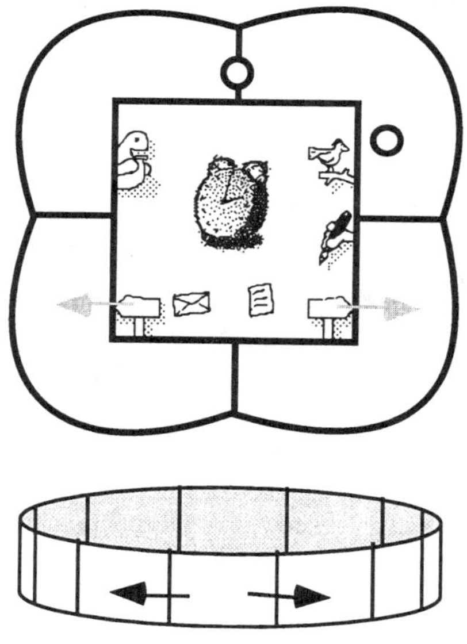

Figure 13: Concept B, indirect access through a 'linked list' navigational model

All participants were shown both concepts. The order in which they were was randomized. After they had been shown both concepts, a number of questions were asked about the interaction.

Results of the User Interface Evaluation.
Most participants mentioned that concept B was more fun because more space was available to do interesting things. Positive comments were made about the objects moving on the screen and the bigger size of the graphic elements representing the applications. Some participants mentioned that although concept A appeared to be easier and more efficient to use, this benefit would only be temporary. The children expected that after a short learning period, both concepts would be equally easy to use.

It was striking that many of the arguments the design team had used when discussing the interface concepts internally were recognized by the children.

Concept Interaction Design

A metaphor that suits the user as well as the technology
The paradigm of an interface metaphor has a user as well as a technology side. A metaphor may seem to fit to the user expectations and needs nicely until another technological idiosyncrasy appears and has to be incorporated within that same metaphor.

For instance the idea of using a little animated battery to display the power level of the batteries (Figure 14) at a later stage proved not to be feasible because of difficulties in measuring the power level of rechargeable batteries.

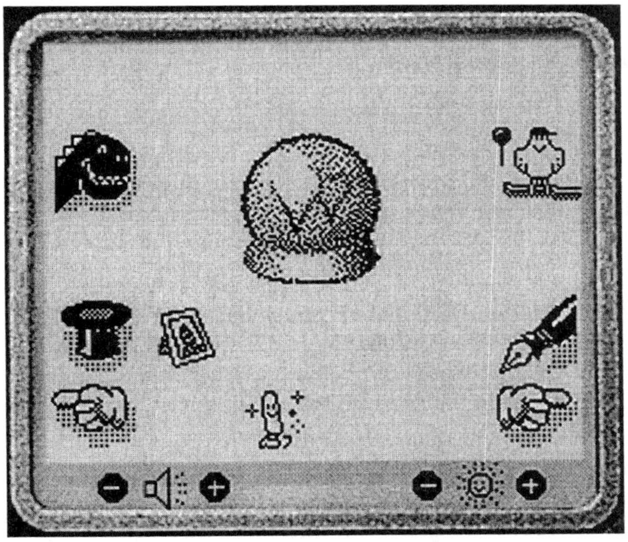

Figure 14: Screen showing an animated battery (bottom center)

Another example were the 'vector' based drawings that the interface initially allowed for. These drawings were internally described by vectors as opposed to bitmaps. As each drawing is allocated a fixed amount of memory it can only hold a limited number of lines. We tried to explain this concept to the user by using an 'inkpot' tool that indicates the amount of ink left (Figure 15); if it runs out of ink you cannot draw any further. You can 'recycle' the ink by erasing lines which refills the inkpot.

Figure 15: An inkpot (at the left in each screen) was used to explain memory usage for vector based drawings

In user tests it became clear that the concept of vector based drawing caused such misunderstanding and frustration that we left it out of the interface.

Designing in the Dark.
In the detailed concept phase many hardware and software decisions were uncertain for a long time. Issues such as the type of microprocessor, display size, using standard or proprietary software made it difficult to provide clear boundaries for the 'design space'. Equally difficult was to decide on hard- and software requirements with no clearly specified user interface design!

Who Is Our User?
Though we adopted a user centered approach from the start, we did not have a formal structure for recording the information generated. Having no clear understanding and definition of user requirements hampered progress as many user-related issues were repeated over and over in discussions.

FINALISATION

The goal of the finalisation phase is to engineer the product and get it out! Typically this phase is the most intensive and time consuming of the entire development process. More people are added to the team, putting more pressure on communication overhead and requiring more formalized procedures for transferring information.

Usability evaluation

Various usability evaluations were performed to provide answers to general user interface issues (such as consistency of interface mechanisms) as well as to specific questions. Examples of issues that were investigated were ideas for games, children's writing and drawing performance, and the understanding of specific applications.

The approach taken in most sessions was that the children were asked to play with a game or an application for a certain period of time (Figure 16).

In order to simulate more expert use, some test participants took part on several occasions. They were asked to use applications and games repeatedly.

Figure 16: Children using infrared communication on a during a usability evaluation

The Results.
Many opportunities concerning the improvement of specific applications were suggested. For example drawing and especially writing performance with 'vector drawing' was difficult for the children and found to be unacceptable to be added to the device.

During the development process we discovered the importance of always communicating the validity and limitations of our investigations to the development team. For example, the designers were told that it was impossible to draw firm conclusions based on our tests about the 'playability' of the games that we tested.

Since the product-market combination was new for Philips, the marketing of the product was considered to be an important and difficult issue. The results of the qualitative user involvement sessions were sometimes used in discussions about marketing issues. The human factors people had to ensure that usability data should not be interpreted as marketing data.

Engineering Interaction Design
The development of a detailed design of the user interface is a process of iterative refinement. As constraints in hardware and software become clearer (e.g. display size and quality, memory and computational speed requirements) the design can be adjusted accordingly.

Not Having the Final Hardware
Though in this phase most hardware decisions were specified, actual sample components were not available until the very end of this phase. That made the specification of interface graphics and sound very difficult as we could only approximate how they would work out within the final product.

Prototyping
The use of prototyping played an important role in this final phase. Simulations of the interface were used as part of the market evaluations. More functional and detailed prototypes were used to obtain more specific feedback. When prototyping you have to clearly keep in mind the law of diminishing returns, as it takes more and more time to prototype more detailed issues, while at the same time it does not add much more quality.

Transfer of User Interface Specifications
Through many discussions with hardware and especially software people we tried to get to a mutually acceptable method of specifying the user interface.

Here designers and engineers had a clear conflict of interests: software engineers required a complete and formal specifications document, while designers wanted to combine formal as well as informal methods (such as simulations using an animation tool) to explain and illustrate general concepts and rules. This was quite a struggle and at one point the software team was not even allowed to look at the simulations the interaction designers had made as those were considered 'inaccurate and only adding confusion'.

Freeze Functionality Before It Freezes You
Well into the finalisation phase, the functionality changed or new functions were being added, making it more difficult to produce a realistic planning. It is important to fully use the creative forces in the project team. However it is more important to realize when to stop the addition of new functions may at one point only result in delays without any improvements to the product. Ideas on additional products as well as services started also to develop in this phase. It was difficult to decide whether or not to adapt the current product to these 'future' uses.

LESSONS LEARNED

General Lessons On The Design Process

Specify Your User Requirements And Define Milestones
The rationale behind specifying user requirements is not just to develop them, but to make sure that the team agrees on the assumptions and realizes how and when they have and can be changed.

A Product Is Not Designed In A Vacuum.
Start thinking on additional and follow-up products in an early stage, so one does not have to suddenly change or add extra functionality in a later phase .

Users Are Not Designers.
Not all answers can be generated by user or market tests. Users will generally relate any new product concept to existing products. The pen interface for instance was regarded as 'old fashioned' by parents because for them a keyboard was the most sophisticated input device. They had only just 'accepted' computer keyboards in their lives and could not understand that pen input would be the next step.

Act Quick And Dirty If Necessary.
Often, the purpose of our tests was not to decide whether one interface concept was more usable than an alternative concept, but to discover issues that are important to the children. Small qualitative user involvement sessions are therefore often appropriate. Furthermore such sessions provided an opportunity for designers to 'enter' the children's world.

What Is Specific About The Design Process When Designing For Children?

Let The Team Participate In Testing With Youngsters.
Provide situations where the whole development team has close contact and interaction with the target group. Especially in the first stages these sessions are most fruitful.

Children Can Use Their Imagination.
Children appear to be more imaginative than adults as well as are more capable of expressing their imagination. This can be very useful in discussing a new inventive product as well as in testing a prototype that presents only a small representation of the total product. Actively involving children in the concept phase of the product creation process can be extremely valuable.

Sensitivity About The Purpose Of Sessions.
Explaining to children that not they but the product is being tested is sometimes difficult. For instance, when performing product testing at schools, where children frequently have exams and tests, it can be difficult for them to change their attitude towards the "official visitors." In addition, children can be very direct and tough towards their peers and having group discussions therefore can lead to severe altercations.

Limited Powers Of Expression.
Since children, compared to adults, have limited experience in expressing their feelings and thoughts, it is very common that one group of children may feel more comfortable communicating verbally while others may prefer to use pen and paper. It is important for the human factors specialist to cater to these differences in communication.

Enter Their World; The Media Generation.
The children of today are sometimes referred to as the 'media generation'. Watching television, movies and reading flashy magazines with lots and lots of images are important activities within their daily lives. We can relatively easily gain access to the information available to the children. However, we do not know how they perceive the stimuli unless we "enter their world" and discuss the topics with them.

Avoid The Second Childhood Fallacy.
A common mistake is to think that adults can explain why a child likes a particular game without talking directly to the child. It has been the experience that the reason why adults like a certain product as well a why they think a child would like a certain product is frequently completely different from why children actually like it. One of the most common examples of this are Disney's animated movies. Children often appreciate completely different aspects of these movies than adults.

What Is Specific About The Product When Designing For Children?

Quick change of Interest and Fashion.
The interests of children as well as their perception of things change rapidly. This is one of the most important difficulties that designers of products for children are confronted with. Products, television series, celebrities, etc. can be trendy and 'cool' today and considered to be boring, old fashioned and ugly tomorrow. Therefore, one of the most important design guidelines is not to try to be fashionable.

Designing For Children Means Designing For Pleasure.
Human factors specialists are trained to focus on product usability. This may be one of the most important aspect for a fax machine. However, an important aspect of most children's products is entertainment; providing pleasure is therefore a primary goal. Human factors engineers therefore, need to make "pleasure-of-use" measurable and provide more feedback of this dimension to the product team.

Importance Of Designing For Product Usage Over Time.
Products should be able to 'grow' with the users and be efficient and effective as well as be a "pleasure to use" in the initial learning phase well as in ensuing stages of product employment.

Importance Of Sophistication In Design And Interaction.
Children are very skilled and experienced users of technology. In many families, only the children can perform a timer recording with the VCR. As a result of this they have high expectations for new products. Children will automatically compare 'their' products with products that their parents have at home.

Limit Target User Group.
Children in the age-range of our product are developing at an incredible speed, physically as well as mentally. It is important to focus on a very specific range, as widening the concept to fit a larger group will more probably make it suitable for no-one.

THE FUTURE...

The product is expected to be launched in the United States and Europe in September 1996. Currently Philips is putting effort in expanding the product range as to address other age groups as well.

INFORMATION AND QUESTIONS

For more information contact the authors, or I.Boots at +31 40 27 33 621

ACKNOWLEDGMENTS

The authors would like to thank Leo Beuk, Anneko van Dorssen, Khodi Feiz, Lorna Goulden, Gerard Jorna, Raghu Kolli, Rob Lambourne, Ian McClelland, Irene McWilliam, and Bruce Thomas for their support and advice.

Demo or Die: User Interface as Marketing Theatre

Annette Wagner and Maria Capucciati
SunSoft, Inc.
2550 Garcia Ave., MTV 21-225
Mountain View, CA 94043-1100, USA
(415) 336-5427, (415) 336-5358
Email: annette.wagner@sun.com, maria.capucciati@sun.com

ABSTRACT

This design briefing describes the design and development of a demonstration which simultaneously utilizes and illustrates the use of SunSoft's distributed object technology, NEO. The design is notable in that the demo is primarily a marketing tool, not a product. We discuss the factors that made the NEO demo different from a typical project, and how we created a successful user experience through the visual design and story of the NEO demo.

Keywords

Human interface design, objects, NEO, NeXT, demonstration, presentation, visual language, storyboards, graphic design, theatre.

BACKGROUND

In 1991, SunSoft began working on an application framework called NEO (Network Enterprise Objects). The intent of NEO is to provide customers with an object-oriented technology that will enable developers to construct applications using distributed, reusable components.

In 1993, SunSoft purchased existing software technology from the NeXT Corporation. The NeXTStep environment is being evolved into OpenStep.

As part of the marketing effort for NEO, an engineering team called DOVE (Distributed Objects Vision Engineering) was created. The focus of the team is to create demonstration applications which simultaneously utilize and illustrate distributed object technology. The demo is used by NEO upper management in various public forums to present a packaged vision of the development possibilities available with NEO objects.

The audience for the NEO demo included a broad collection of developers, business people, analysts, and press. Each segment of the audience needed the demo to be convincing. In addition to being credible from a technical and business perspective, the demo had to have high production values and a dramatic impact on the audience. We wanted to capture the audience's interest and impress them with a quality presentation.

Why is This Interface Notable?

This interface was quite a departure from the usual projects we work on at SunSoft. The most obvious difference was that the NEO demo (as we will refer to the project) was not a product and did not have a typical product schedule. The schedule was heavily tied into marketing events, most notably the product announcement.

The interface had to illustrate the advantages of a technology under construction, while presenting something exciting and valuable to the audience, yet not give a false impression of the future product's capabilities. We knew that reality would not be as important as perception in the presentation. As Brenda Laurel writes, "The magic is created by both people and machines, but who, what, and where they are *do not matter* to the audience." [1]

Finally, the project had a significant level of involvement from NEO upper management. While all projects have some management involvement, on this project, management had to feel comfortable with the presentation scenario, as they would be presenting it often and using it to promote the NEO technologies.

The Goals

The project had two main goals: to show examples of certain key technologies through the content of the demo and to reflect the process of building applications with NEO technology. Since this was not a hands-on demo, we were not necessarily concerned with total fidelity to usability. Instead, a key goal of the project was to present a theatrical experience for the audience.

To meet these goals we had to have a believable business story to tell. Writing this story was our first milestone and the story became our script. As in theatrical productions, we asked the audience to suspend disbelief and involve themselves in the story even though some parts of the demo were not happening in reality.

As UI designers we had a personal goal of making sure the demo was an example of a great human interface. The entire demo had to be as visually clear and dazzling as possible.

The demo is shown to customers at close range in a demo booth, but it is also presented on huge video screens to hundreds of people in large halls. Displaying a complex technology in a simple, understandable yet dramatic fashion on both types of "stages" was one of our challenges.

The Team

The team consisted of a manager, a team of software engineers, and at varying stages, two human interface designers and two graphic artists. Annette Wagner was the human interface designer and art director at the start of the NEO demo project (February 1995) and took the demo through its first implementation and presentation at SunSoft's annual developers' conference. Maria Capucciati took on the project in June 1995 and made the revisions for the NEO product announcement in September 1995.

The authors had multiple roles on the project team. We acted as art directors in making certain the visuals were consistently high quality and the story was clearly presented. We provided UI design expertise for the GUI development to make the human interface of the demo realistic enough that viewers could see how the NEO technology could be applied to their own business contexts.

We played a crucial role as theatrical directors. Many times the software team felt they were too close to the demo to be able to tell if the story was working from a dramatic viewpoint, and used us as reviewers. We dealt with the projection and color issues much as a stage manager or lighting designer would, and we worked as usability engineers by tracking and evaluating the feedback the team got on the demo.

MAJOR DESIGN ISSUES

Constraints

The biggest constraint we faced as a team was our unfamiliarity with the capabilities of the NeXTStep and OpenStep technologies and the fact that all the technology was under construction and therefore a moving target.

We created the GUI for the NEO demo using the NeXT Interface Builder. Interface Builder turned out to be more developer-oriented than we would have liked. It was easy for us to create simple windows and panels, but not to create custom widgets. Nor was it straightforward to connect and run the application to test if it worked.

The demo was written using distributed objects and other NEO technology to process information. Fakery was used only for expediency during crunch times or to compensate for slow performance or missing functionality resulting from building on a constantly evolving software platform.

As designers, we were constrained by the unorthodox color mapping used in NeXTStep. NeXTStep runs with 12-bit color plus 4 bits alpha channel. Moving back and forth between Solaris, NeXTStep and the Macintosh to do visuals meant that we could not trust the colors we saw on any one screen.

The "main event" style presentations of the demo at the conferences utilized a Barco projector to display the demo on huge video screens. The Barco can have unpredictable effects on the saturation level of colors which required us to run special tests with Barco projectors, not a common piece of equipment for most companies. The Barco has a softer focus and requires the graphics and type to be quite large. Small type and complicated icons become unreadable at a viewing distance of 20 feet. In the second version of the NEO demo, we focused on how much text we could reasonably replace with graphic elements to better convey the message to the audience.

Other constraints included having to support running a large and small version of the demo: the large for the Barco presentations and the small for a 17" screen for booths. We had to coordinate where windows came up on the screen relative to each other so that critical information was always visible as the demo progressed.

Design Process

The team working on the NEO demo lived in two separate buildings at Sun. Meetings usually took place in the engineers' building. The team would meet around a whiteboard and work out the details of the demo with regard to software and story.

A central focus of all our design meetings was whether the design under discussion would be believable to the audience. If we didn't think it necessarily represented reality, our next priority was how to make it **look** as real as possible. For example, at one point in the story the presenter "wires" in a new NEO object. In reality, a user would probably employ a development tool to wire in a new object. That kind of tool would have complicated the demo unnecessarily. We simplified the concept down to a dialog which looked realistic while intimating complexity.

Schedules were very tight and ideas had to be prototyped and implemented as quickly as possible to see if they fit in with the overall presentation. The designers would prototype the screens in NeXT Interface Builder or on the Macintosh, then send them to the engineers along with a written interaction scenario. The engineers would build and run the application and the entire group would review it.

When we worked in Interface Builder, we tried to do as much up-front visual work for the engineers as possible, including the placement of icons. The Interface Builder files were passed back and forth as much as possible so that we did not get "out of sync" on the human interface design. We also printed and hung up screenshots in the offices of the engineers to keep everyone up to date on the latest design.

Building a Story

Initially, the project was kicked off with a series of meetings with marketing, NEO managers, and customers to determine

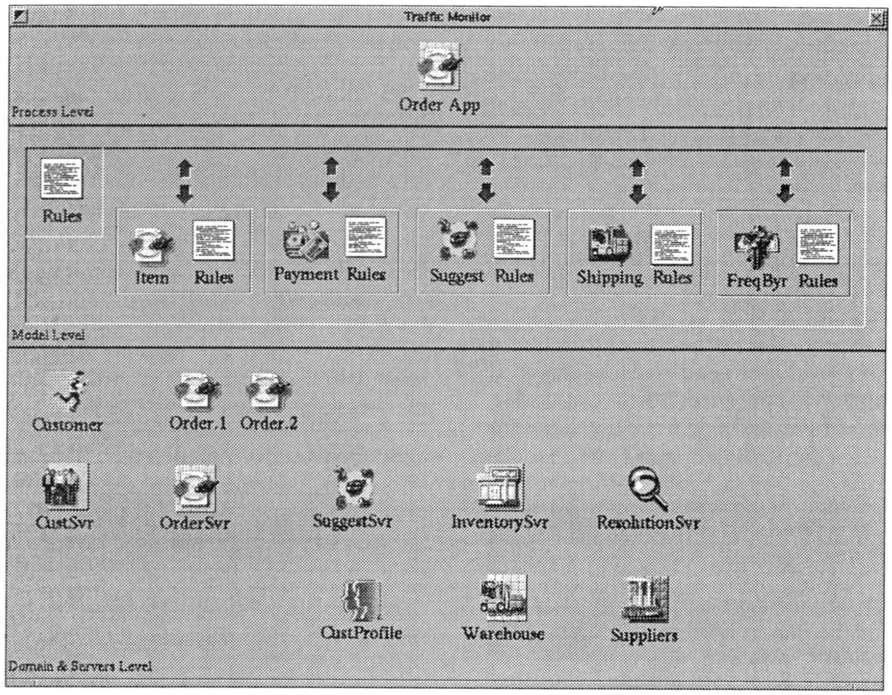

Figure 1: This was one of the original "Locator" shots. It shows an early attempt to encapsulate business rules into NEO objects.

a story or set of stories that we could base the demo on. We wanted stories about business problems that could be solved with the NEO technology. We encouraged people to tell us war stories about things that worked or not for customers they knew. The gist of these war stories was captured on white boards and big drawing pads.

The role of the art director was to take the story ideas and turn them into rough storyboards. We started by taking the story idea and writing a scenario around it. Scenarios were made as realistic as possible. They contained context on the company, the people, and their business problems. The scenarios were then reviewed and the ones that had the most potential were then merged into one story which was the basis for the NEO demo. The story line we finalized on revolved around an order entry system that needed to have certain critical changes made to it to reflect current business opportunities.

The story was turned into a script and storyboard to aid everyone in visualizing the demo. The storyboard showed frames in which critical interactions took place. Originally, the storyboards were hand drawn, and evolved into reality as screen shots and then code was developed. Eventually the storyboard was completely superseded by the actual demo.

The Traffic Monitor: Making the Invisible Visible

One can think of NEO as an intermediate layer between the traditional client layer (the application GUI) and the server layer (the legacy databases). (This architecture can be seen in Figure 4.) The NEO objects can be set up to talk to either layer. Adding new functionality can be as simple as dropping in a new object and wiring it up.

The NEO demo is targeted at business customers who would use NEO to run their business software and its associated business processes. Each business process has a clearly defined set of steps and rules that have to take place for the process to be completed. For example, for an order to be placed, there are a set of constraints that must be met. The steps and rules for a business process can be encapsulated into a NEO object.

The British director Peter Brook believes that "the notion that the stage is a place where the invisible can appear has a deep hold on our thoughts."[2] As our demo story developed, we realized we really needed a stage on which to *show* people the invisible: how the business process objects were working with each other and with the other layers of the system. We also wanted to demonstrate how a change would affect the whole system or not, as the case may be.

This "viewer" started out life as the "Locator"; the place where you could see NEO objects sending messages to each other and to servers, etc. Initially no one had a very clear vision of what this window might look like or what it might show. Ideas ranged from icons for each application to icons for each object. Maybe icons could show the underlying rules for how objects interacted with each other. Maybe icons show status, or lines are drawn to show which objects are talking to each other. Some icons could be drawn differently to show they are remote versus local.

Figure 1 shows an initial layout where we toyed with the idea of showing how rules might be encapsulated in NEO objects. We abandoned that as being too confusing and developed several versions (Figures 2 and 3) before ending up with the layout we have now. Figure 4, the final layout,

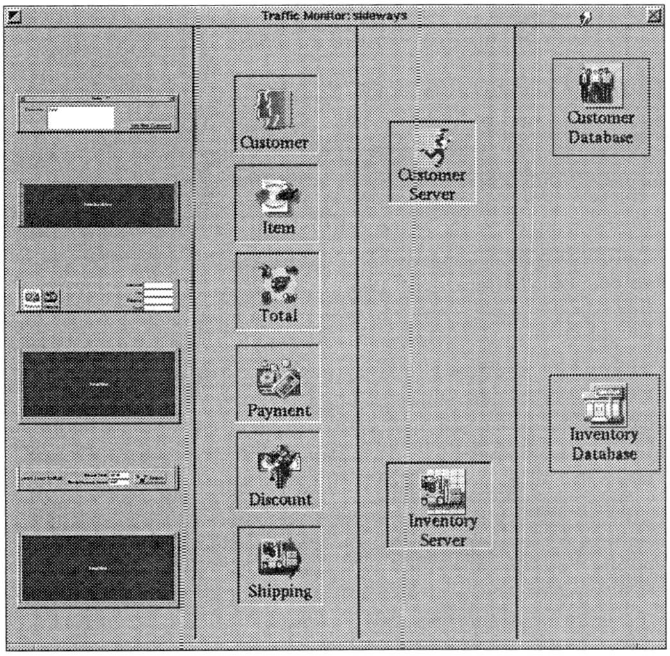

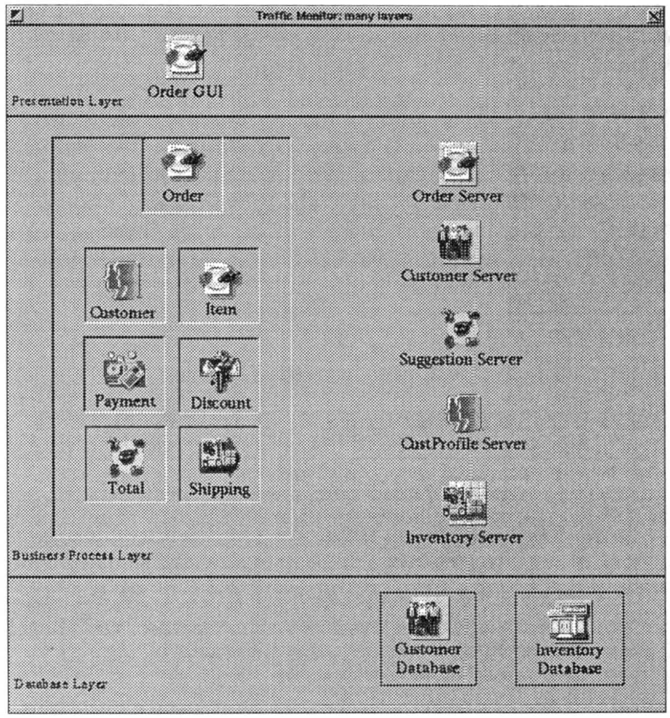

Figures 2 and 3. Early layouts of the Traffic Monitor.

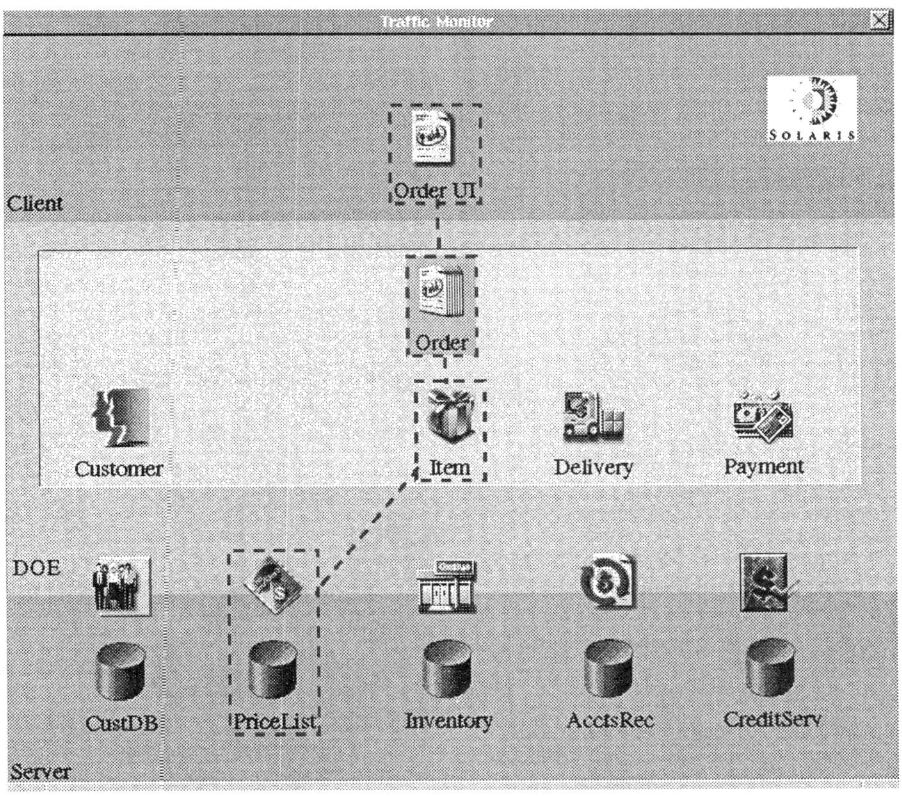

Figure 4: This shows the final layout of the Traffic Monitor for the first version of the NEO demo. It also shows an example of the animation that appeared when objects were sending information to each other.

shows three layers: the client layer at the top, the NEO objects layer in the center and the server/legacy layer at the bottom. We called it the "Traffic Monitor".

When a presenter is running the NEO demo, the Traffic Monitor uses animation (Figure 4) to show the interaction between the system layers as actions are performed by the presenter. In that respect it sits in the background as a sort of onstage narrator for events that are taking place elsewhere in the demo. However, it is also used in the foreground of the demo script to show how adding a NEO object affects the business process.

Adding Objects: Building Up to the Change

One major marketing thrust for the NEO demo was to demonstrate the ease of changing a system by adding a NEO object transparently. Our story line involved a large retail store chain that needed to respond quickly to business decisions made by competitors. The retail chain, called the "Good Buys", wanted to counter aggressive marketing strategies from the competition by running its own sales promotion. In real life, sales of promotional items would need to be tracked in the store's order entry system.

This piece of the demo was very hard to get consensus on. Management kept reiterating that the change had to be obvious, but were unable to articulate clearly how they wanted to see that happen and many times contradicted themselves. The team went through several iterations on basic ideas before settling on the idea used in the demo. The first version of the demo was limited by the fact that we did not have drag-and-drop functionality working.

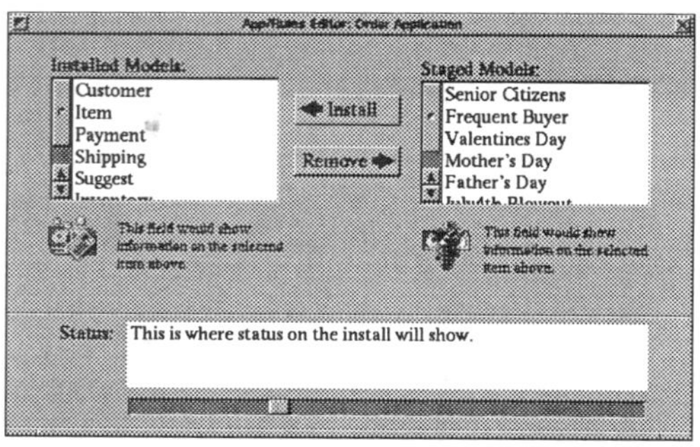

Figure 5. An early screen design for the "Installer" concept.

Some people thought the change should be shown in the form of an installation (Figure 5), others thought it should happen from some kind of programming view. Some of the ideas required a context shift during the demo from the store to a developer's office. Audiences usually require the context of changing scenery, costumes or props to realize they are in another space. Because the stage demo had to move rapidly, we had no time to set up a new context; but without a discernible shift we could lose people. We kept coming up with ideas until we found one that worked without a major context shift. This design work was happening in parallel to the Traffic Monitor work. As the Traffic Monitor took on more substance we were able to see how we could use it to show the change.

For the first version of the demo, the change was accomplished by adding a pre-existing NEO object called "Promo", which contained all the business rules for tracking promotional items in addition to regular sales.

In the first version of the NEO demo, we wanted to show some kind of NEO object collection where the user could select the Promo object and then add it, but we ran out of time. Instead the Promo object was selected by bringing up a "Load Module" dialog. Unfortunately, selections in the dialog box were made so quickly that very few audience members realized that anything had changed.

Once the Promo object is added to the Traffic Monitor, we show it being wired into the NEO object layer. Once the wiring is done, the GUI for the Promo object shows up in the Order Entry GUI and the salesperson can determine the additional benefit for the customer (Figure 6). Interestingly, this part of the demo introduced certain tensions. The technical audience needed to see all the steps to make the demo believable for them. The analyst audience thought it was far too detailed.

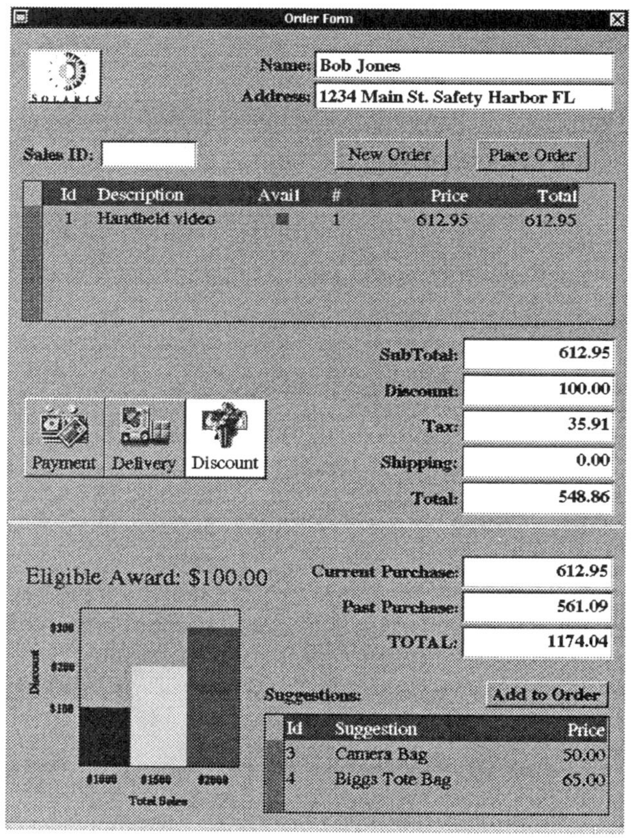

Figure 6. This is the Order Entry GUI. In this screenshot the Promotion GUI panel is displayed at the bottom of the order form.

For the second version of the demo, we decided to illustrate the assumption that customers using NEO could purchase or build their own object "libraries" from which they can pull objects as needed. (This was implied in the first version.) We designed a window called the "Object Catalog", which showed a collection of objects ready for use (Figure 7). To further accent the change, we used the drag and drop capabilities of OpenStep to show the object being dragged into the system rather than being added through a dialog box.

Object Sharing: Be Nice to Your Neighbors

Another scenario we wanted to visualize in the NEO demo was that of two GUIs sharing information from the same NEO object at different times. The first version of the NEO demo focused on one GUI, the Order Entry GUI. Everyone agreed that including object sharing, or shared services, was a high priority for the subsequent version. It required adding one more GUI which would be a view onto a set of services shared with the Order Entry GUI.

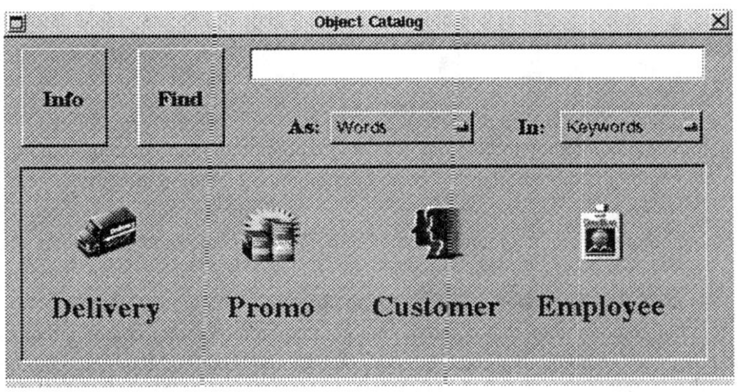

Figure 7: The Object Catalog as used in the final demo.

We needed a way to work the new GUI into the existing story. The original story premise is that the presenter plays a salesperson in a retail store. We added to this scenario by creating a new GUI for commissions and rewards. The presenter could now drag his sales ID from the Order Entry GUI into the Commission GUI. This GUI showed not only the salesperson's cumulative commission, but how close he was to earning a sales prize such as a television set or a trip (Figure 8).

At first, we thought that the Commission GUI should somehow appear when the Promo object was added to the system. It seemed logical that a sales contest of some kind should be associated with a promotional campaign. We concluded, however, that commission is a standard fact of a salesperson's life. It made more sense to say that every sale entered through the Order Entry GUI would have a commission associated with it, and that the introduction of the Promo object would simply change the policy by which commission was paid. So, instead of the Promo object introducing the Commission GUI, the Commission GUI is simply shown as a standard part of the system. Then when the Promo object is added, it changes the set of rules used by the Commission GUI. The two GUIs, Order and Commission, are then shown to share a new "Promo" object in the NEO layer.

Figure 8: The Commission GUI as used in the final demo.

We also added another new object representing the salesperson ("Employee"). Integrating these objects into an already crowded Traffic Monitor while keeping them all readable proved quite challenging (Figure 9). We discussed several ideas, such as adding a new GUI layer above the client layer, displaying each GUI's set of objects one at a time, and duplicating objects in two places on screen. We were finally constrained by the simple fact that there just wasn't enough room and we needed to reduce clutter, not add to it.

Anecdotal Data: Now Do This...

Since the NEO demo wasn't a product, we performed no formal usability testing on it. This didn't mean that we didn't receive plenty of feedback from a variety of sources. We received notes from the presenters themselves, from the audiences and from the development team. We attended as many of the demo presentations as possible and took copious notes on what worked or didn't work. In this section we will step through the different kinds of feedback and how it affected the final demo.

One of our most pervasive challenges with the NEO demo was making changes to the system more visually obvious. A basic tenet of stage work is that if the audience can't see what the performer just did, they haven't experienced it. Subtlety was not going to serve us well on such a large scale as a conference stage. We needed to find ways of pointing up aspects of the interaction we wanted the audience to notice. Sometimes we were able to accomplish this with big visual cues, such as the Traffic Monitor animation. Other times we worked the change into the verbal parts of story line so the audience would walk through it with us. This was quite different than the usual approach in which the

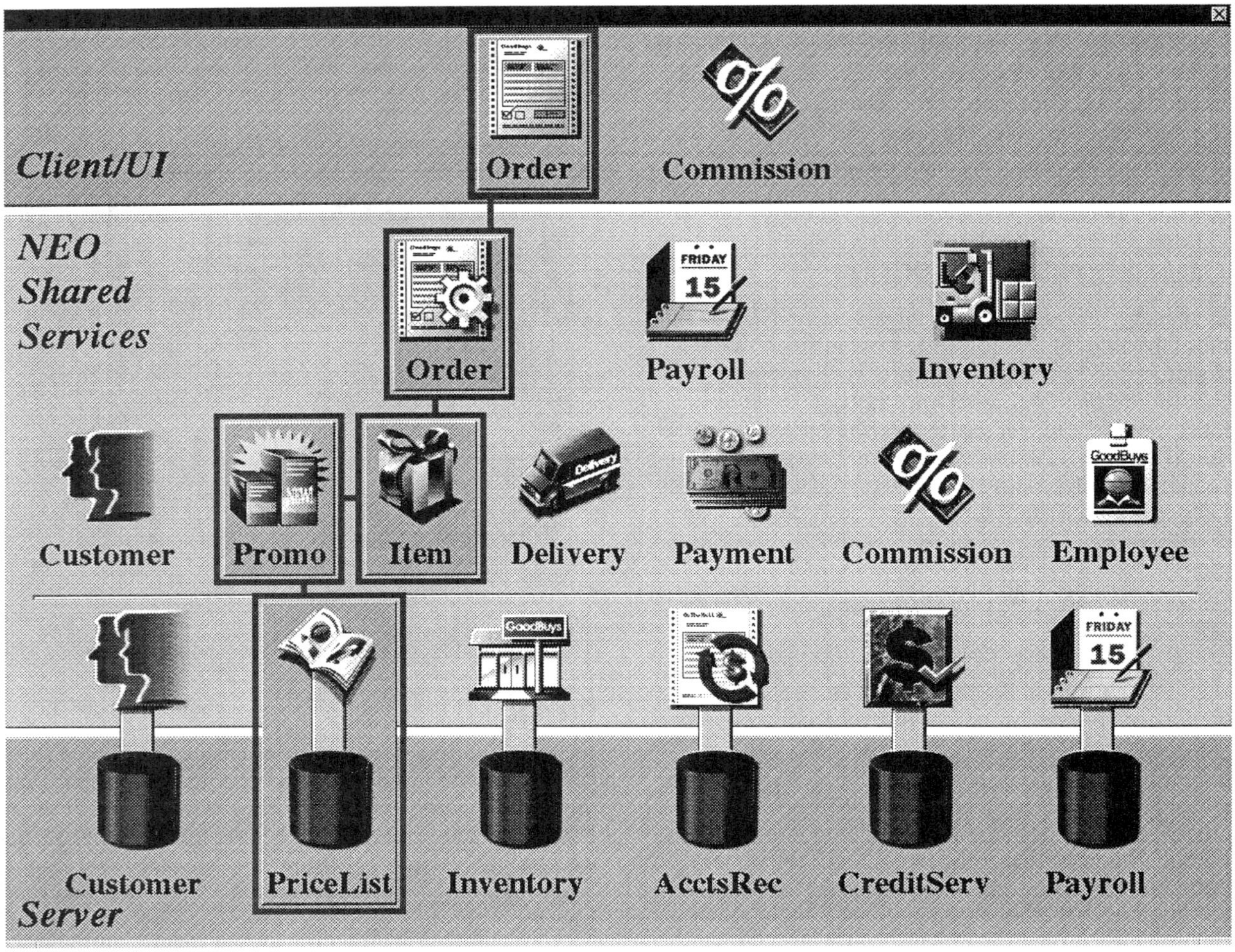

Figure 9: The final layout of the Traffic Monitor for the product announcement.

successful human interface is the one that integrates so well into the task as to be transparent to the user.

A good example of a story line change was the section of the demo where the presenter adds the Promo object to the system. As we discussed in the section "Adding Objects", one tactic we used to make the object addition more obvious was to have the presenter actually drag and drop the Promo icon rather than finding the file name in a dialog box. In the first version of the NEO demo, the object was added to the Traffic Monitor and wired up there. We decided to add a twist by having the presenter drag the Promo object to the Order Entry GUI instead. The ability to add an object directly to an open, running application made it more interesting from a technical viewpoint, too.

To further point up the change, the script than called for the presenter to attempt to place an order for a promotional item. It wouldn't work - because the NEO object hadn't been wired up yet. The presenter would then connect the object with the rest of the system and proceed.

In general, as major pieces of the demo were built we would notify the various critical people from NEO management who needed to review the demo. They would show up, we would walk through the demo and story in whatever state it existed, and they would give us feedback. Often we found a certain tension between the requirements of the presenter running the demo, and those of the audience viewing the demo. Many times we received conflicting feedback; for example, they'd tell us to make everything bigger on screen and add more functionality. Obviously, if we added more features then we had no room to make things bigger. The DOVE team manager was tasked with sorting through this feedback and worked with people to clarify their thoughts. The best approach was to do a storyboard or screen shot and simply ask, is this what you meant by X?

However, taking this approach didn't always work. During the demo we use a map to show where the "Good Buys" stores are relative to the competitors' stores. The color had been chosen by the designer to provide the best contrast for the icons that needed to appear on the map. At the last minute before the SunSoft Developers' Conference, management decided it was too bright and should be a lighter color. The engineer went ahead and changed it without mentioning it to the designers.

The result was a map with exceptionally poor contrast on which the icons used to show the stores were completely washed out. We learned not to make last minute changes without testing, and confirmed the color saturation problems inherent with Barco projection systems. In fact, the demo presentation at the conference confirmed many concerns we had with regard to the complexity of icons, color saturation, and type face size. These notes went straight into the next revision of the demo.

Conclusions

The NEO demo project provided many ways for us to stretch our human interface skills and to use skills from other areas of expertise like play writing, storyboarding, acting and art direction.

The theatrical experience is always incomplete without the presence and reaction of an audience. We designed and built a production, and really did not know if we would be successful until we presented it to a live audience. Our measure of success would be if the demo communicated the concepts and ideas that management wanted to convey.

During the first demo at the SunSoft Developers Conference, the authors were sitting behind two conference attendees who closely followed the demo, pulled out the demo white paper, and proceeded to discuss the possible capabilities this might offer them. When they walked away considering ideas on how to use NEO object technology back home, we felt we had accomplished our task successfully.

ACKNOWLEDGMENTS

We would like to acknowledge the DOVE team at SunSoft: Amy Pearl, Pierre Delisle, Malini Minasandram, and Payam Mirrashidi. Thanks also to Michael Quillman of SunSoft and Marsh Chamberlain for their graphic design work, and to Alan Eyzaguierre and Dan Fish for NextStep help.

REFERENCES

1. Laurel, Brenda. *Computers as Theatre.* Addison-Wesley, Reading, Massachusetts, 1991

2. Brook, Peter. *The Empty Space.* Atheneum Publishers, New York, 1968.

3. NeXT Computer, Inc. *NeXtStep User Interface Guidelines.* Addison-Wesley, Reading, Massachusetts, 1992

4. SunSoft. *The SunSoft NEO "Good Buys" Demonstration Technical Report*, Part Number 95394-001. SunSoft, 2550 Garcia Avenue, Mountain View, CA, 94043

A User Interface for Accessing 3D Content on the World Wide Web

Mike Mohageg, Rob Myers, Chris Marrin, Jim Kent, David Mott, and Paul Isaacs

Silicon Graphics, Inc.
2011 N. Shoreline Blvd.
Mountain View, CA 94039-7311
(415) 960-1980
{michaelm,rob,cmarrin,jkent,mott,pauli}@sgi.com

ABSTRACT

A strategy for accessing and viewing three dimensional data on the World Wide Web is introduced. Factors driving the user interface design of a 3D web browser are presented. The interface for the initial implementation of Silicon Graphics' WebSpace™ Navigator, the first commercially available 3D Web browser, is given. Close attention is paid to design issues. Usability lessons learned from this interface are described and it is shown how they affected the second generation browser interface design.

Keywords

User interface design, three dimensional (3D) navigation, World Wide Web (WWW), Virtual Reality Modeling Language (VRML)

INTRODUCTION

Users of the World Wide Web typically access documents comprised of text and images, with access to audio and video. We believe that 3D environments are equally viable and compelling "documents" of interest on the web, with applicability to architecture, education, engineering, advertising, entertainment, and more. For instance, web-based 3D allows a web user to enter 3D models of places that are too dangerous to visit physically, or historical locations that no longer exist (e.g., Pompeii), or remote and/or physically restricted locations. A user might enter a re-creation of an ancient Aztec city, for example, and walk through it to investigate this historic site. The site could establish links between objects in the 3D environment and multi-media content describing the objects role in Aztec culture.

In a more commercial application, a 3D museum model allows users to walk through the rooms of the museum and view art exhibitions. The user can click on a piece of art to hear information about the piece, or be taken to a Hyper Text Markup Language (HTML) page that provides textual information and a movie about the piece. Conversely, standard HTML pages can contain links to 3D content. Users can investigate a 3D world then return to their HTML documents.

For more detailed discussion and motivation for using 3D data on the web, see [7,10].

Viewing and interacting with 3D data can be significantly more complicated than viewing 2D text and graphics. Users need to examine 3D objects from different viewpoints and navigate through scenes to gain a better understanding of the data. An interface for the exploration of 3D data must provide adequate controls for the user to inspect objects and scenes. We have developed a user interface for this purpose.

WebSpace is a viewer for 3D content delivered over the web [3]. An emerging standard for web-based 3D content is the Virtual Reality Modeling Language (VRML) [8]. WebSpace is a viewer for VRML data as Netscape, for instance, is a viewer for HTML data.

WebSpace 1.0 is the first commercially available VRML viewer. Designing the user interface presented some interesting challenges; in particular, we needed to combine 3D user interface know-how with emerging conventions on the web. This paper will present the initial design of WebSpace 1.0, with emphasis on what we learned about web-based 3D user interfaces, and how we incorporated these lessons into the WebSpace 1.1 user interface.

FACTORS DRIVING THE DESIGN

There were 4 main driving factors in designing the UI for WebSpace 1.0.

1. The user's primary tasks

2. Existing body of design work for 3D
3. Burgeoning conventions for the web
4. Meeting the needs of both novice and experienced users

The User's Primary Tasks

The two main tasks for users surfing the web are content retrieval and content viewing.

The popularity of HTML browsers is due to the ability to follow links quickly and easily retrieving information with a single mouse click. We wanted linking to be the primary task afforded the user in WebSpace. Links constitute not only a mechanism for retrieving information of interest, but also for navigation among 3D scenes and perhaps within scenes. Users, we surmised, would be busy linking from one cyber–place to another. Mouse clicks in the main viewing area of WebSpace were thus reserved for following links.

The other main task for 3D users is viewing data from different points of view. In contrast to the passive activity of reading text in an HTML browser, possibly using a scrollbar to display information that exceeds the window size, 3D content is often best understood when the data can be viewed interactively from different points of view. Viewing controls had to be easily accessible in the WebSpace interface.

In general, two viewing paradigms are used to view 3D data: navigation and examination. In navigation, the interaction dynamics are as though the 3D scene is a fixed, immovable world, and the user maneuvers through the world by walking, flying, or similar means. Conversely, with examination, the dynamics of the user interaction are as though the user is stationary and at a certain distance away from the center of an object. The user can tumble the object to view different sides. This type of viewer is best suited for tasks where the user's objective is to view an object as though s/he were holding it, such as viewing a model of a coffee mug. Because of the varied 3D content on the Web, WebSpace would need to provide user interfaces for both viewing paradigms.

Existing Body of 3D UI Design

A source of design concepts was existing 3D user interface work [2,11,12]. Our previous experience in 3D applications allowed for direct transfer of many UI elements [4,5,6]. For instance, we had a good understanding of the basic functionality needed to navigate and view in 3D. Our challenge was to make these functions accessible and usable to web users with little 3D user interface experience.

We were also able to draw from the interfaces of popular 3D games, such as Doom. Many computer users move through 3D worlds on a daily basis and have attained a certain savvy for navigating with simple keypad commands and mouse gestures. We wanted to incorporate aspects of these interfaces to meet expectations and facilitate the transition from 3D in a game to 3D on the web.

Burgeoning Conventions From the Web

Despite the web's infancy, a few de–facto conventions have emerged. Links embedded in content are a mainstay of HTML web pages, as is single clicking to follow a link. Presenting the Universal Resource Locator (URL) of a link destination when the cursor is over an anchor is another useful convention. Users can quickly get more information about the destination before they traverse a link. Our goal was to replicate the most useful features and conventions of HTML browsers into our VRML viewer where appropriate.

Varying User Experience Levels

Providing a modeless interface that met the needs of both novice and experienced users was a major goal for WebSpace 1.0. We presumed that most users would be novices at 3D navigation and that we would "bias" our UI in favor of novices. This meant making all important functions easily accessible and usable. With novices there was also an element of enticement. A subgoal was to provide a UI that would encourage first–time users to "try out" our product. We wanted users to experiment with WebSpace and eventually become immersed in a 3D world.

Conversely, there are 3D knowledgeable users who find the trappings of a novice interface too cumbersome. We did not want to diminish the 3D experience in any way for these expert users; thus, we needed to provide the same functionality in a fashion that was less obtrusive, but still easy to use.

DESIGN OF WebSpace 1.0

Figure 1 presents the user interface for WebSpace 1.0. The areas of most interest are the viewing window, where the 3D content appears, and a dashboard to manage interactive viewing.

Viewing Window

All 3D scenes appear in the viewing window. We believed that finding and following links would be the most critical tasks performed in this window. We tailored our design accordingly, by reserving clicking in the viewing window while the cursor was over a linked object for following links (as in HTML browsers). Where HTML allows for text and images to be link anchors, VRML allows 3D objects in the scene to be link anchors.

HTML browsers often draw link objects in a different color so that the user can easily find them, and we provided two functions to make certain that users could find links in a VRML world. First, when the cursor passes over a link anchor, we automatically highlight the object by brightening its appearance. Following the lead of HTML browsers, we also display the URL for the link at the bottom of the WebSpace window. Additionally, we provided a function to highlight all the links, allowing users

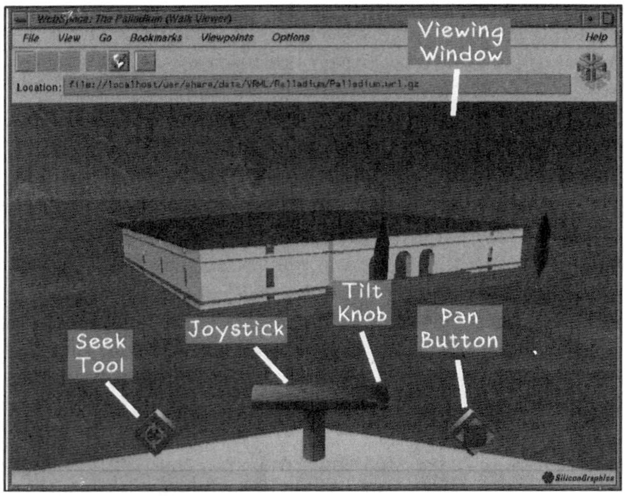

Figure 1 – WebSpace 1.0

to immediately view all links in the visible area of the 3D scene.

Dashboard

WebSpace 1.0 presents a graphical dashboard across the bottom of the viewing window, to provide ready access to the most important navigation tools. The dashboard contains 3 fixtures: the joystick, the pan control, and the seek tool, as shown in Figure 1. A similar dashboard was created for the examination paradigm with the joystick replaced by a virtual trackball.

The paradigm for the navigation tool is that of a user "walking" around a virtual world. The walk paradigm constrains the up direction of the scene and the height of the camera above a plane perpendicular to that direction. The primary functions needed for this walk paradigm are:

- the ability to move forward and backward
- the ability to turn left and right
- the ability to tilt the camera up and down

All of this functionality is mapped onto a single affordance on the dashboard. The joystick was selected as it is representative of devices with which the naive user would be familiar. Since it supports all of the primary functions, it is positioned in the center of the dashboard. As the user interacts with it, it gives feedback by moving/turning in the direction of motion.

The primary viewing functions map to the joystick as follows:

- Clicking on the joystick and "pushing" it forward (backward) by moving the cursor toward the top (bottom) of the window causes forward (backward) motion. The further the cursor moves from the initial click location, the faster the motion.

- Clicking on the joystick and "rotating" it by moving the cursor to the right (left) causes the camera to turn right (left). The further the cursor moves from the initial click location, the faster the rotation.

- Clicking and moving both up/down and right/left causes a composition of these two motions.

- A small "knob" on the right side of the joystick rotates to tilt the camera up and down.

Also to assist navigational,, "dead" zones were added around the initial mouse click point. These zones consist of a narrow vertical and horizontal stripe of pixels centered at the click point. If the mouse remains in the vertical zone while moving toward the top/bottom of the window, the camera moves forward/backward with no turning. If the mouse remains in the horizontal zone while moving toward the left/right of the window, the camera rotates with no forward/backward motion.

In addition to the primary functions, additional capabilities are provided by the other two dashboard affordances. The pan control on the right side of the dashboard allows the user to move the camera in the plane perpendicular to the viewing direction, providing sidling and height adjustment functionality. The control is oriented in the plane of the window and pivots about its center up/down and left/right. Like the joystick, there are dead zones about the initial click point that allow the camera to be moved straight up (down) by moving the mouse toward the top (bottom) of the window and staying in the vertical dead zone. Similarly, moving the mouse toward the right (left) of the window while staying in the horizontal dead zone causes the camera to move directly right (left). Straying outside of the dead zone allows for compound up/down, left/right movement. The speed of movement is controlled by the distance the mouse is moved away from the initial click point.

The seek tool provides an alternate "click and go" navigation method. In this paradigm, the user clicks the mouse on an object of interest and the camera is smoothly moved toward that object. In WebSpace 1.0, clicking on the seek tool puts the interface into a temporary mode where the next mouse click in the viewing window causes the camera to move toward the point clicked. The camera is moved half the distance to the object and tilts so that the point clicked is in the center of the viewing window. A modal approach was used to preserve the primary interpretation of clicking in the viewing window as following a link.

Other Relevant Interface Items

VRML allows content authors to create specific interesting vantage points in the world, and providing a descriptive name for each. These vantage points are accessed via the Viewpoints menus. Selecting a viewpoint from the menu smoothly animates the camera from its current position to the selected vantage point.

Various mouse and keyboard shortcuts are provided to allow 3D knowledgeable users to bypass the dashboard. For example, the primary functions of moving forward and back, and turning left and right, can be initiated by pressing the keyboard arrow keys.

The buttons along the top of the window are similar to those found in most HTML browsers. These buttons provide for moving forward and backward between scenes, going to the user's home scene, reloading content, and other common web browser functionality. Our intent was to foster transfer of learning from HTML browsers to WebSpace.

To provide additional feedback concerning the destination of a link, author-supplied descriptions of link destinations are displayed above the viewing area. The descriptions are significantly less cryptic than a URL, and can be useful in determining whether to follow a link.

EVALUATIONS AND WHAT WE LEARNED

We performed evaluations before and after releasing WebSpace 1.0. Informal usability testing was conducted prior to the release and user observations were completed after the release. The informal usability testing intended to investigate specific navigation issues; we were confident that the examining user interface was simple and clear. So we chose to use our limited time in evaluating navigation.

Informal Usability Testing

One of our biggest concerns during the design process was making certain that users could use the dashboard to navigate through a scene. It was unclear whether users would be able to easily maneuver to get to a location of interest in a scene. We were also interested in identifying whether users understood the controls we had provided on the dashboard (seen in Figure 1).

Therefore, the usability evaluation was designed to collect information on:

- ease/difficulty of users navigation through a scene
- users' explanations and expectations of dashboard controls.

Procedure and Results

Users were presented with two scenes: a 3D model of an exhibition booth (with many stations to visit), and a scene with more abstract content, containing an island with irregular surfaces and structures emanating from it.

Testing was performed in an informal fashion. Six 3D inexperienced users used WebSpace to perform the navigation and "explanation" tasks. The tasks were given to the participants by the experimenter. Verbal protocols were used to collect user feedback. For instance, the experimenter asked participants to navigate to a particular location in the booth. The participant would then describe and verbalize thoughts on the process and aspects of the navigation UI that s/he found confusing, problematic, or useful. The experimenter also monitored the participants' actions closely and recorded any subtle problems and issues.

The usability testing uncovered 3 major issues: poor control/display relationship, the need for an overview, and the need for navigation speed controls.

Control/Display Relationship

The control/display relationship between mouse input and movement through the scene was very poor for the typical frame rate average workstations could achieve (in rendering complex 3D scenes). The original control/display relationship was linear; that is, there was a constantly increasing relationship between joystick (mouse) movement and the speed of navigation through the scene. This relationship lead to considerable navigational difficulty because users, especially novices, tend to make gross gestures with the mouse during navigation. For example, a user who is headed to the left of the intended target will move the mouse to the right to correct her course. However, the mouse drag to the right often has a high amplitude. With a linear relationship the mouse drag to the right leads to a sudden and large over-correction to the right. The user then corrects back to the left, but again over-corrects. This pattern continues and users become quite frustrated since they "can't even move in a straight line." With a workstation that can render the scene at 30 fps, the linear relationship will work well; however, with typical rates of 8-12 fps the linear relationship leads to significant navigational difficulty.

The solution was to introduce damping by using an exponential control/display relationship rather than linear. With an exponential relationship the user was free to move the mouse with fairly large gestures without having very large impact on the speed and direction of movement. The exact nature of the curve was fine tuned to create a relationship that was responsive but not difficult to control.

Need For an Overview

As realistic as computing technology can make it seem, navigating a computer-based 3D scene does not provide all the cues that navigating in the real world provides. In particular, the overall context available in real world navigation (or "wayfinding") is not available in computer-based navigation [1,9]. Therefore, it can be difficult for users to develop an overall mental model of a computer-based scene, unless they have prolonged exposure. Our testing showed this to be an issue in WebSpace as well.

While participants could navigate to desired locations, they often commented on not being completely sure of their current location in relation to other locales/landmarks in the scene.

The standard solution to the "lost in space" problem is to provide a map or "bird's eye view" of the world to help users orient themselves. However, we could not automatically create such maps based on the 3D scene information alone. Providing such an aid seemed to be the responsibility of the content creator. Therefore, we took no special measures to handle this issue, except to encourage content developers to provide such navigational aids.

Controlling Speed

3D scenes are of different sizes and shapes; there are no restrictions on how large/small they can be. It is part of the content creator's responsibility to set a travel speed appropriate for the size of the scene being created. For instance, users will want to move very quickly through a model of New York City, but much slower when navigating a studio in Greenwich Village.

VRML allows content creators to set the speed for the scenes they create. However, our test participants helped uncover two situations where the speed was not what they were expecting:

1. The user wanted to travel slower/faster than the author defined speed (even though the author has specified a reasonable speed)

2. The author had failed to provide a speed or specified an inappropriate speed.

In both cases users need to have a degree of control over the speed of their movement in the scene. We provided 3 menu items to set speed. One was used to increase speed while the other was used to decrease it. A third was used to return the speed to that originally specified by the author (the "default" speed).

User Observations

We had several opportunities to observe novices using WebSpace 1.0. Most observations were made at ACM SIGGRAPH '95 where attendees used the viewer at kiosks dispersed throughout the convention center. There was a VRML model of the SIGGRAPH exhibition floor with all the booths. Users could use WebSpace to move through the show floor and access information on any booth of interest. Also, chat rooms were created where users could enter and see others (represented as avitars) as well as interact with them.

We also observed individual users at their personal workstations (mostly at Silicon Graphics' Mountain View, CA campus). These users were free to access and navigate any content they preferred and provide us with feedback on the positives and negatives of the product.

User Expectations

The most interesting discovery was that users were not very motivated to employ UI fixtures to navigate a scene. Users expected to simply click in the viewing window and have some sort of navigation take place automatically. Note that this is in direct conflict with our intent to be consistent with web conventions by reserving clicking in the viewing window for traversing links. It was very clear, however, that many novices expected to click on an object or area of interest and be taken there. They seemed to want to use the cursor as a pointer that would whisk them to their location of interest within the scene. This is the functionality we had defined for the Seek Tool, but many users wanted this behavior to be a primary navigation mechanism. Our challenge now was to support this seeking behavior without violating the link following convention.

For those users who were interested in using the dashboard for navigation, most were unable to easily determine how to use the joystick. The intent of the joystick was to offer users a fixture with an inviting physical quality that would compel users to "grab" and push. However, most novice users expected a single click on navigation affordances to result in some form of navigation. We were confident that the interaction dynamics of grabbing and pushing a control forward was the correct approach, but it seemed that we needed to also support the expectation of clicking to invoke behavior.

Impact of Content Attributes

A common mechanism for navigating within an HTML document is following internal links. These are links that position the browser at a different part of the current document. Following internal links is commonly used for coarse navigation, such as accessing the general topic the user is interested in. Once there, users rely on the scroll bar (or potentially text searching) to perform fine navigation to access the exact information they seek. Most users of WebSpace 1.0 drew on this model in interacting with 3D worlds as well. Many anticipated being able to click on an in-scene object to take them to places of interest. The viewpoints menu contains points of interest; however, users prefer to maintain focus on the content rather than access a menu outside the main viewing window. This was a direct instance where content attributes, which were beyond the control of the WebSpace UI, had significant impact on the usability of the product. Most scenes contain links all of which lead to other 3D scenes or HTML documents. Therefore, the user expectation of being able to click on an in-scene object to move to a location of interest in the scene was not commonly supported by content developers.

Another aspect of content attributes was a subtle, yet important, issue of setting user's navigational expectations. Every scene has an entry point, which authors are free to define. Many scenes defined the entry view to be a point above the content, a "bird's eye" view of sorts. While these views help to orient users, they also suggest a flying navigational paradigm. That is, if users enter a scene in the sky (or at some high elevation), they will immediately assume that they can fly around a scene in order to navigate.

However, WebSpace 1.0 supports walk navigation, where the users can move freely through a scene, but their elevation is fixed. The sidling fixture can be used to change elevation, but once the user starts to move forward the elevation is fixed. This is the most common type of navigation paradigm and is the correct functionality for WebSpace. Nonetheless, content often set users expectations that they were flying. Thus their interaction with the navigation dashboard could lead to dissonance since they believed they were controlling a flying, rather than walking, user interface.

DESIGN CHANGES FOR WebSpace 1.1

After observing the problems encountered with the initial user interface, we redesigned it to both overcome the shortcomings and to improve the look of the UI (See Figure 2). We moved the dashboard from the scene into a separate area below the viewing window to keep it from obscuring portions of the scene, while maintaining the illusion that the user is looking over the dashboard into the scene. A separate window also allowed us to photorealistically render components of the dashboard while not interfering with rendering performance of the main viewing window. This increases the association to real world devices for the user.

The importance of navigation, especially seek, was underestimated in WebSpace 1.0. But to allow the novice to follow links and to keep consistency with HTML browsers, we needed to maintain the simple "click to link" behavior. We decided to allow users to indicate their preference for single clicking in the scene: seeking or following links. Buttons on the dashboard allow users to select the current preference. Note that these are not modes; the user always has access to navigating and following links. The preference simply sets the primary functionality of the cursor.

With the "click to link" preference, the user clicks on a linked object to go to that destination, as in an HTML browser. Navigation is done with the dashboard or in the viewing window with keyboard modifiers. The novice starts with this preference since all functions are obvious.

With the "click to navigate" preference, the user can hold down one or more mouse buttons and drag in scene to navigate (walk, pan, or tilt in the Walk Viewer, spin, pan, or dolly in the Examiner Viewer). Clicking in scene seeks to the object clicked on, moving close enough so that the object fills the viewing window (rather than moving half way to the object, as in WebSpace 1.0). Double clicking on a linked object follows that link. This gives a very powerful navigation model to experienced users allowing modeless navigation and link following.

Our observations of WebSpace 1.0 caused us to place one

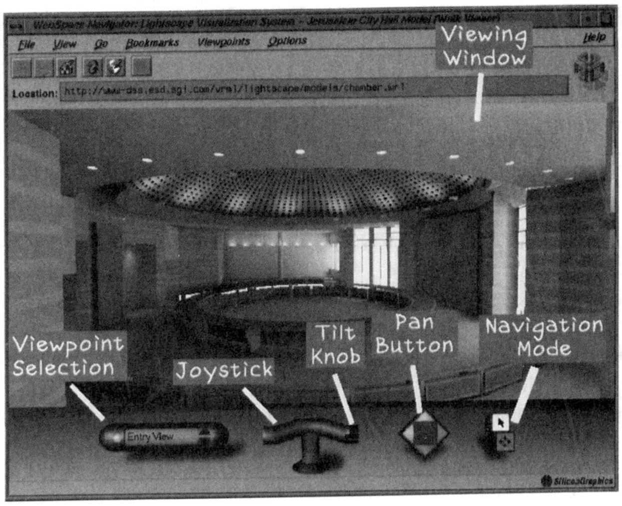

Figure 2 – WebSpace 1.1

additional component on the dashboard. The Viewpoint menu had proven to be a very effective navigation tool so we put it on the dashboard to make it more accessible. The current viewpoint is displayed, with controls for stepping through the viewpoints, and a lighted button tells the user if s/he is currently at the displayed viewpoint.

All functions on the dashboard have a prompt message displayed when the cursor is over them. These prompts provide information about the behavior of the control (e.g. – "Joystick: drag to walk or turn"). Cursor shapes appropriate to the function are shown as well. In "click to navigate" the seek cursor is normally shown. Clicking in the main window to seek changes this to a "seek in progress" cursor, while clicking and dragging changes it to a walk cursor. In "click to link" the cursor is a pointing finger (chosen to match HTML browsers) when the user is over a link.

REFLECTIONS ON THE DESIGN PROCESS

There are two main items to share concerning UI design/development for WebSpace 1.0 and 1.1. First, it would have been useful to perform more rigorous usability testing with a wider range of users and more varied scenes prior to the 1.0 release. However, the requirements of an extremely tight delivery schedule and our naivete concerning the types of scenes that would be available in the future restricted our ability to do rigorous testing. Nonetheless, it is clear that obtaining feedback from a representative sample of users would have positively influenced the UI or at least better prepared us to anticipate our post–1.0 findings.

Secondly, UI practitioners must always temper their passions for the user interface with the fact that other factors *also* contribute to the success of a product. In the case of WebSpace, factors such as rendering performance, full support for the VRML specification, and "peaceful" coexistence with HTML browsers were also critical. Given limited development resources, all of these success factors needed to receive attention and the UI is but one of these factors. As a result, not all of the UI changes suggested from post-1.0 evaluations were implemented in 1.1. The next release of the product will incorporate more of the UI enhancements. This is yet more data suggesting that it is very difficult to have a perfectly well balanced and complete UI in the first release of a product.

ACKNOWLEDGEMENTS

Our thanks to Rikk Carey, under whose direction this project was developed. Thanks to Gavin Bell, who spearheaded the technical specification of VRML. Thanks to Delle Maxwell for her artistic talents and help in creating the WebSpace user interface. And thanks to the entire Silicon Graphics Open Inventor team for their technical expertise and support.

REFERENCES

1. L. T. Kozlowski, and J.B. Kendall. *Sense of Direction, spatial orientation, and cognitive maps.* Journal of Experimental Psychology: Human Perception and Performance (1977). Vol 3, No. 4, 590-598.

2. J. D. Mackinlay, S. K. Card, and G. G. Robertson. *Rapid controlled movement through a virtual 3D workspace.* Computer Graphics (SIGGRAPH '90 Proceedings) (Aug. 1990), F. Baskett, Ed. vol. 24, 171-176.

3. J. Muchowski. *WebSpace User's Guide*, 1995, Silicon Graphics http://www.sgi.com/Products/WebFORCE/WebSpace/help/help.html

4. J. Muchowski, D. Myers. *IRIS Annotator 1.0 User's Guide*, 1995, Silicon Graphics.

5. D. Myers. *IRIS Showcase 3.0 User's Guide*, 1993, Silicon Graphics.

6. D.Myers, E. Deeth. *InPerson 2.0 User's Guide*, 1995, Silicon Graphics.

7. M. Pesce. *Building and Browsing Cyberspace.* New Riders Publishing, Indianapolis, IN, 1995.

8. M. Pesce, G. Bell, A. Parisi, *VRML 1.0 Specification*, August 26, 1995 http://vrml.wired.com/vrml.tech/vrml10-3.html

9. E. K. Sadalla, W. J. Burroughs, and L.J. Staplin. *Reference points in spatial cognition.* Journal of Experimental Psychology: Human Learning and Memory (1980) . Vol. 6, No. 5, 516-528.

10. Silicon Graphics. *VRML Library Archive* http://webspace.sgi.com/Archive/Scenarios/

11. P. S. Strauss and R. Carey. *An object-oriented 3D graphics toolkit.* Computer Graphics (SIGGRAPH '92 Proceedings) (July 1992), E. E. Catmull, Ed., vol. 26, 341-349.

12. R. C. Zeleznik, K. P. Herndon, D. C. Robbins, N. Huang, T. Meyer, N. Parker, and J. F. Hughes. *An interactive 3D toolkit for constructing 3D widgets.* Computer Graphics (SIGGRAPH '93 Proceedings) (Aug. 1993), J. T. Kajiya, Ed., vol. 27, 81-84.

The Windows® 95 User Interface: A Case Study in Usability Engineering

Kent Sullivan
Microsoft Corporation
One Microsoft Way
Redmond, WA 98052-6399
+1 206 936 3568
kentsu@microsoft.com

ABSTRACT
The development of the user interface for a large commercial software product like Microsoft® Windows 95 involves many people, broad design goals, and an aggressive work schedule. This design briefing describes how the usability engineering principles of iterative design and problem tracking were successfully applied to make the development of the UI more manageable. Specific design problems and their solutions are also discussed.

Keywords
Iterative design, Microsoft Windows, problem tracking, rapid prototyping, usability engineering, usability testing.

INTRODUCTION
Windows 95 is a comprehensive upgrade to the Windows 3.1 and Windows for Workgroups 3.11 products. Many changes have been made in almost every area of Windows, with the user interface being no exception. This paper discusses the design team, its goals and process then explains how usability engineering principles such as iterative design and problem tracking were applied to the project, using specific design problems and their solutions as examples.

Design Team
The Windows 95 user interface design team was formed in October, 1992 during the early stages of the project. I joined the team as an adjunct member, to provide usability services, in December 1992. The design team was truly interdisciplinary, with people trained in product design, graphic design, usability testing, and computer science. The number of people oscillated during the project but was approximately twelve. The software developers dedicated to implementing the user interface accounted for another twelve or so people.

Design Goals
The design team was chartered with two very broad goals:

- Make Windows easier to *learn* for people just getting started with computers and Windows.
- Make Windows easier to *use* for people who already use computers—both the typical Windows 3.1 user and the advanced, or "power", Windows 3.1 user.

With over 50 million units of Windows 3.1 and 3.11 installed plus a largely-untapped home market, it was clear from the outset that the task of making a better product was not going to be a trivial exercise. Without careful design and testing, we were likely to make a product that improved usability for some users and worsened it for millions of other users (existing or potential). We understood fairly well the problems that intermediate and advanced users had but we knew little about problems beginning users had.

Design Process
Given very broad design goals and an aggressive schedule for shipping the product (approximately 18 months to design and code the user interface) we knew from the outset that a traditional "waterfall" style development process would not allow us sufficient flexibility to attain the best-possible solution. In fact, we were concerned that the traditional approach would yield a very unusable system.

In the "waterfall" approach, the design of the system is compartmentalized (usually limited to a specification writing phase) and usability testing typically occurs near the end of the process, during quality assurance activities. We recognized that we needed much more opportunity to create a design, try it out with users (perhaps comparing it to other designs), make changes, and gather more user feedback. Our desire to abandon the waterfall model and opt for iterative design fortunately followed similar efforts in other areas of the company, so we had concrete examples of its benefits and feasibility.

ITERATIVE DESIGN IN PRACTICE
Figure 1 outlines the process that we used. The process was typical of most products designed iteratively: paper or computer-based prototypes were used to try out design ideas and to gather usability data in the lab. Once a design had been coded, it was refined in the usability lab. When enough of the product had been coded and refined, it was examined more broadly, over time, in the field. Minor usability problems identified in the field were fixed before shipping the product. More importantly, the data gathered in the field is being used to guide work on the next version.

CHI 96 Vancouver, BC Canada
© 1996 ACM 0-89791-777-4/96/04..$3.50

Our iterative design process was divided into three major phases: exploration, rapid prototyping, and fine tuning.

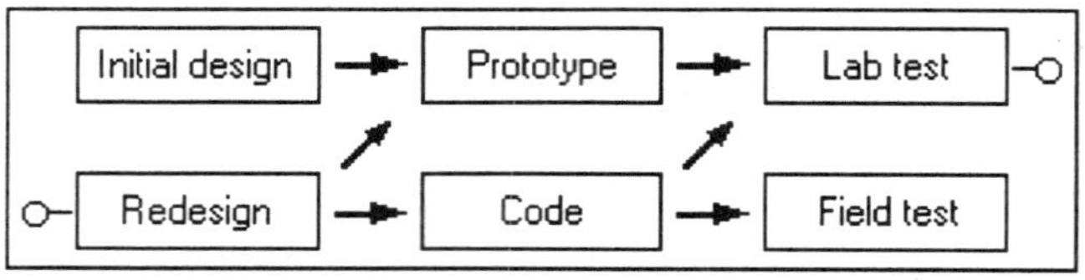

Figure 1: Windows 95 iterative design process.

Exploration Phase

In this first phase we experimented with design directions and gathered initial user data. We began with a solid foundation for the visual design of the user interface by leveraging work done by the "Cairo"[1] team. We inherited from them much of the fundamental UI and interaction design (the desktop, the "Tray", context menus, three-dimensional look and feel, etc.). We also collected data from product support about users' top twenty problems with Windows 3.1.

Figure 2 shows a prototype Windows 95 desktop design that we usability tested in January 1993[2]. This design was based on Cairo and incorporated a first pass at fixing some of the known problems with Windows 3.1 (window management in particular).

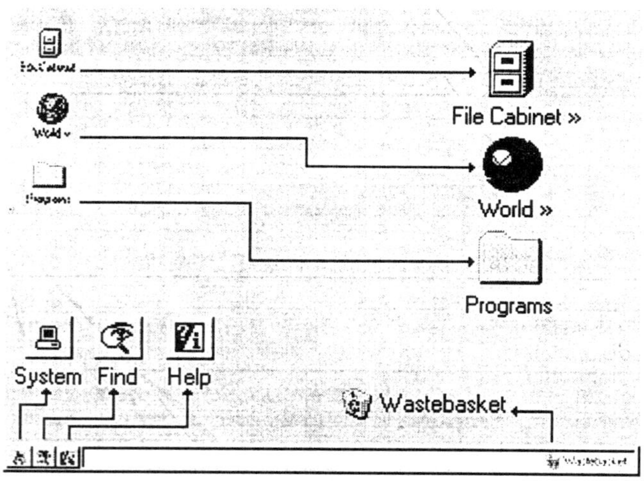

Figure 2: Early Windows 95 desktop (with callouts to enhance clarity).

The top icon, File Cabinet, showed a Windows 3.1 File Manager-type view (left pane shows hierarchy, right pane show contents). The second icon, World, showed items on the network. The third icon, Programs, was a folder which contained other folders full of links to programs on the computer. Along the bottom was the "Tray", which featured three buttons (System, Find, and Help) and a file storage area. Another icon, Wastebasket, was a container for deleted files.

[1] A future version of Microsoft Windows NT™. Initial design work for the Cairo UI began in 1990.

[2] Using a mixture of paper, Microsoft Visual Basic™, and code (C language).

The usability studies of the prototype desktop were conducted in the Microsoft usability lab, as were later tests.[3] We conducted typical iterative usability studies. Three to four users representing each distinct group of interest (typically beginning and intermediate Windows 3.1 users) completed tasks which exercised the prototype. Questions we addressed in testing were sometimes very broad (e.g., "Do users like it?") and sometimes very specific (e.g., "After ten minutes of use, do users discover drag and drop to copy a file?"). We collected data typical for iterative studies: verbal protocols, time per task, number of errors, types of errors, and rating information.

Early Findings

Our usability testing of this prototype revealed much including several surprises:

- Beginning users and many intermediates were confused by the two-pane view of File Cabinet. (See Figure 3.) They were unsure of the relationship between the panes and how to navigate between folders. Beginners were often overwhelmed by the visual complexity of the File Cabinet and had more basic problems, such as not understanding how folders could exist inside of other folders. Many users were also confused by the Parent Folder icon. It appeared in every folder and looked like a file, yet was really a navigation control for moving up the hierarchy one level.

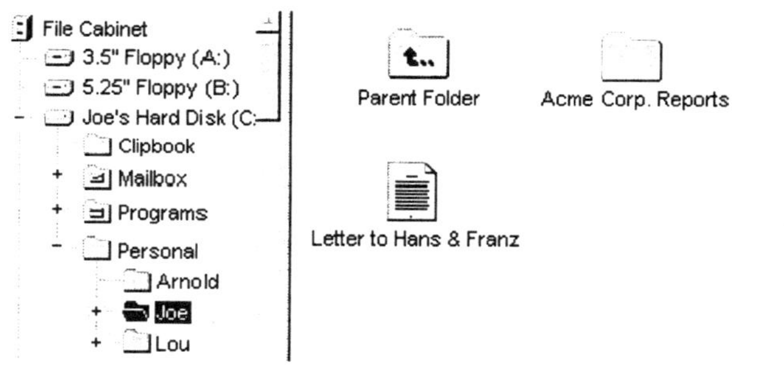

Figure 3: File Cabinet, an early file system viewer.

- Users of every type were confused by the Programs folder. We thought that having a folder on the desktop with other folders and links to programs inside it would be a natural transition for Windows 3.1 users accustomed to Program Manager, while being relatively easy to learn for beginners. We were wrong! Beginners quickly got lost in all of the folders (unlike File Cabinet, each folder opened into a different window) and other users had a lot of trouble deciding whether they were looking at the actual file system and its files or just links to actual files.

- Users had considerable difficulty deciding what each of the three buttons on the Tray was for and later had trouble remembering where to go for a particular command because their functions overlapped in certain

[3] For a summary of the usability lab facilities, see chapter 11 of [5].

contexts (e.g., to find something in Help, do you go to Find or to Help?).

Comparison to Windows 3.1

From the first lab studies it became clear that we needed a baseline with Windows 3.1, to better understand what problems existed prior to Windows 95 and what problems were unique to the new design. First, we gathered market research data about Windows 3.1 users' twenty most-frequent tasks. We then conducted several lab studies comparing Windows 3.1 and Windows 95, focusing on the top twenty tasks derived from the market research data. We also interviewed professional Windows 3.1 (and Macintosh, for comparison) educators, to learn what they found easy and difficult to teach about the operating system.

The key findings were:

- In Windows 3.1, beginning users took over 9 ½ minutes, on average, to locate and open a program that was not immediately visible. Results were not much better for our Windows 95 prototype. These results were clearly unacceptable, given that our market research data (and common sense) told us that starting a program was users' number one task.
- Beginning users and some intermediates had a lot of trouble using the mouse, especially double-clicking. As a result, they often failed to find things in containers when the only way to open them was double-clicking.
- Beginning users and many intermediates relied almost exclusively on visible cues for finding commands. They relied on (and found intuitive) menu bars and tool bars, but did not use pop-up (or "context") menus, even after training.
- All but the most advanced users did not understand how to manage overlapping windows efficiently. Beginners had the most trouble—when they minimized a window, they considered it "gone" if it was obscured by another window. We heard many stories from educators (and witnessed in the lab) how users caused the computer to run out of RAM by starting multiple copies of a program instead of switching back to the first copy. Intermediate users were more proficient but still had trouble, especially with Multiple-Document-Interface (MDI) applications such as Program Manager and Microsoft Word. Market research data confirmed the problem by revealing that 40% of intermediate Windows users didn't run more than one program at a time because they had some kind of trouble with the process.[4]
- Beginning users were bewildered by the hierarchical file system. Intermediate users could get around in the hierarchy, but often just barely, and usually saved all of their documents in the default directory for the program they were using. This problem (especially the novice case) was also observed with Macintosh users.

A Change of Direction

The results from these studies and interviews greatly changed the design of the Windows 95 UI. In the early Windows 95 prototype, we had purposefully changed some things from Windows 3.1 (e.g., the desktop was now a real container) but not others (e.g., File Manager and Program Manager-like icons on desktop) because we were afraid of going too far with the design. We were aware that creating a product which was radically different from Windows 3.1 could confuse and disappoint millions of existing users, which would clearly be unacceptable.

However, the data we collected with the Windows 95 prototype and with Windows 3.1 showed us that we couldn't continue down the current path. The results with beginning users on basic tasks were unacceptably poor and many intermediate users thought that Windows 95 was just different, not better.

We decided to step back and take a few days to think about the situation. The design team held an offsite retreat and reviewed all the data collected to date: baseline usability studies, interviews, market research, and product support information. As we discussed the data, we realized that we needed to focus on users' most-frequent tasks. We also realized that we had been focusing too much on consistency with Windows 3.1.

Essentially, we realized that a viable solution might not look or act like Windows 3.1 but would definitely provide enough value to be attractive for users of all levels, for potentially different reasons. We realized that a truly usable system would *scale* to the needs of different users: it would be easy to discover and learn yet would provide efficiency (through shortcuts and alternate methods) for more-experienced users.

Rapid Iteration Phase

As we started working on new designs, we hoped to avoid the classic "easy to learn but hard to use" paradox by always keeping in mind that the basic features of the UI must scale. To achieve this goal, we knew we needed to try many different ideas quickly, compare them, and iterate those which seemed most promising. To do this, we needed to make our design and evaluation processes very efficient.

UI Specification Process Evolution

Although we had opted for an iterative design approach from the beginning, one legacy of the waterfall design approach remained: the monolithic design specification ("spec"). During the first few months of the project, the spec had grown by leaps and bounds and reflected hundreds of person-hours of effort. However, due to the problems we found via user testing, the design documented in the spec was suddenly out of date. The team faced a major decision: spend weeks changing the spec to reflect the new ideas and lose valuable time for iterating or stop

[4] Interestingly, educators told us this problem also existed on the Macintosh, even though the UI for switching among programs was totally different.

updating the spec and let the prototypes and code serve as a "living" spec.

After some debate, the team decided to take the latter approach. While this change made it somewhat more difficult for outside groups to keep track of what we were doing, it allowed us to iterate at top speed. The change also had an unexpected effect: it brought the whole team closer together because much of the spec existed in conversations and on white boards in people's offices. Many "hallway" conversations ensued and continued for the duration of the project.

To ensure that interested parties stayed informed about the design, we:

1. Held regular staff meetings for the design team. These weekly (sometimes more often) meetings allowed each of us to check in about what we were doing and to efficiently discuss how what one person was working on affected other work.

2. Broadcasted usability test schedules and results via electronic mail. Design team members received regular notification of upcoming usability tests and results from completed tests so they could more easily keep abreast of the usability information and how the design was evolving.

3. Formally tracked usability issues. With a project the size of Windows 95, we knew we needed a standard way to note all of the usability issues identified, record when and how they were to be fixed, and then close them once the fix was implemented and tested successfully with users. This process is discussed more in the "Keeping Track of Open Issues" section.

4. Held regular design presentations for outside groups. As the project progressed, more and more groups (inside and outside Microsoft) wanted to know what we were doing, so we showed them and demonstrated what we were working on. These presentations were more effective than a written document, because the presentations were easier to keep up-to-date and allowed timely design discussions.

Separate UI for Beginners

The first major design direction we investigated was a separate UI ("shell") for beginning users. The design was quickly mocked up in Visual Basic and tested in the usability lab. (See Figure 4.) While the design tested well, because it successfully constrained user actions to a very small set, we quickly began to see the limitations as more users were tested:

1. If just one function a user needed was not supported in the beginner shell, s/he would have to abandon it (at least temporarily).

2. Assuming that most users would gain experience and want to leave the beginner shell eventually, the learning they had done would not necessarily transfer well to the standard shell.

3. The beginner shell was not at all like the programs users would run (word processors, spreadsheets, etc.). As a result, users had to learn two ways of interacting with the computer, which was confusing.

For these reasons and others, we abandoned the idea. Importantly, because we used a prototyping tool and tested immediately in the usability lab, we still had plenty of time to investigate other directions.

Rapid Iteration Examples

Below are overviews of five areas where we designed and tested three or more major design iterations. There are many more areas for which there is not adequate space to discuss.

1. Launching Programs: Start Menu. Although we abandoned the idea of a separate shell for beginners, we salvaged its most useful features: single-click access, high visibility, and menu-based interaction. We mocked up a number of representations in Visual Basic and tested them with users of all experience levels, not

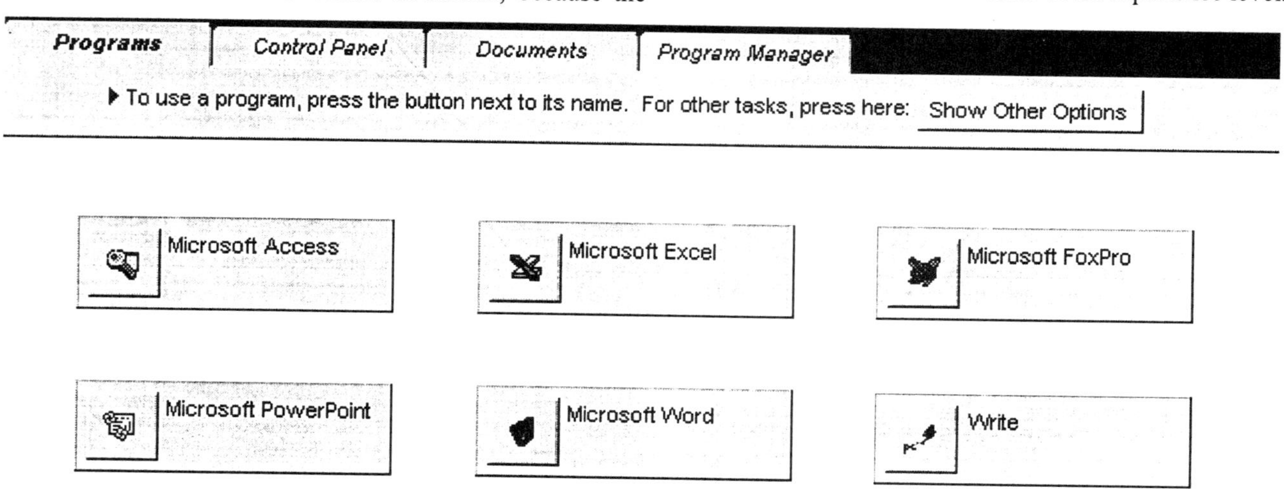

Figure 4: Partial view of separate shell for beginners.

just beginners, because we knew that the design solution would need to work well for users of varying experience levels. Figure 5 shows the final Start Menu, with the Programs sub-menu open. The final Start Menu integrated functions other than starting programs, to give users a single-button home base in the UI.

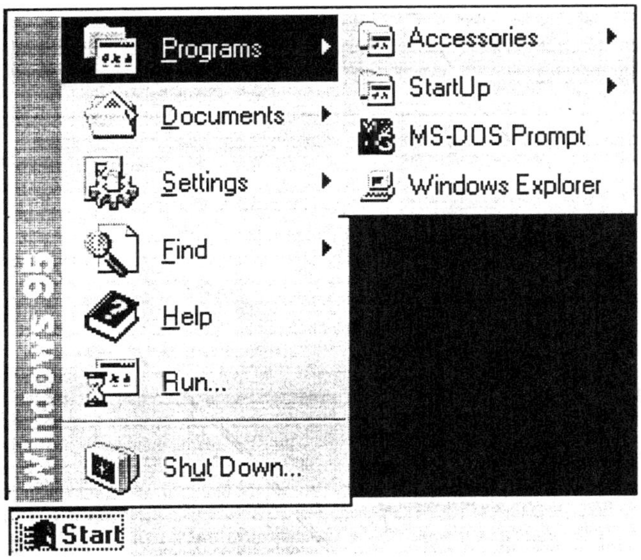

Figure 5: Start menu with Programs item open.

2. Managing Windows: Task Bar. Our first design idea for making window management easier was not very ambitious, but we weren't sure how much work was needed to solve the problem. The first design was to change the look of minimized windows from icons to "plates". (See Figure 6.) We hoped that the problem would be solved by giving minimized windows a distinctive look and by making them larger. We were wrong! Users had almost exactly the same amount of trouble as with Windows 3.1. Our testing data told us that the main problem was windows not being visible at all times, so users couldn't see what they had open or access tasks quickly. This realization led us fairly quickly to the task bar design, shown in Figure 9. Every task has its own entry in the task bar and the bar stays on top of other windows. User testing confirmed that this was a feasible solution to the problem.

Figure 6: "Plate" visualization for minimized windows.

3. Working with Files: "Open" and "Save As" dialogs. Information from product support plus lab testing told us that beginners and intermediates had a lot of trouble using the system-provided dialogs for opening and saving files. (See Figure 7.) The problems stemmed from the fields in the dialog not being in a logical order and having a complex selection methodology. The Cairo team took the lead on this problem and constructed a comprehensive Visual Basic prototype that included a mock file system. We tested many variations until we arrived at the final design shown in Figure 8.

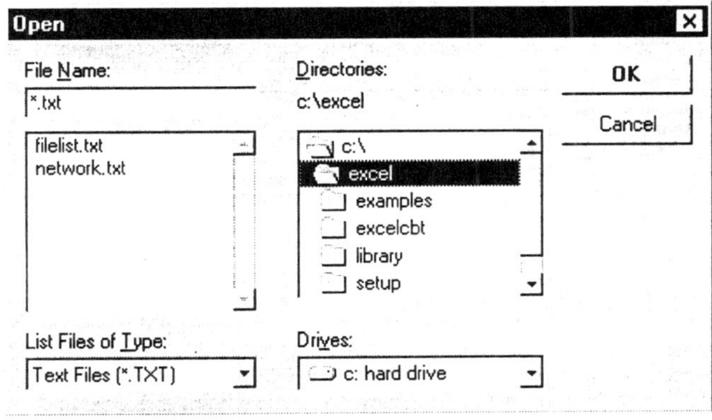

Figure 7: Windows 3.1 File•Open dialog box.

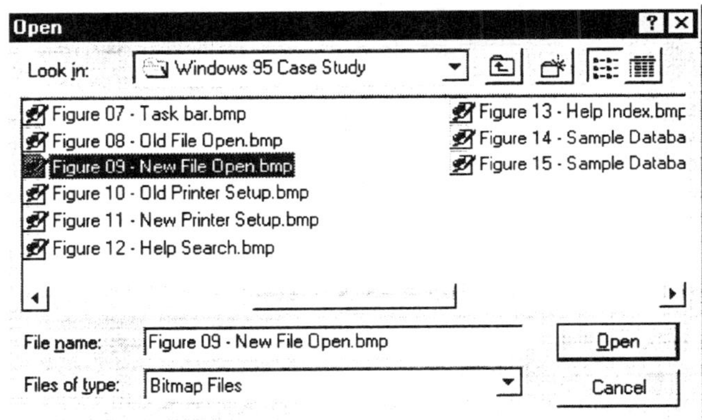

Figure 8: Windows 95 File•Open dialog box.

4. Printing: Setup Wizard. Product support information told us that printer setup and configuration was the number one call-generator in Windows 3.1. Many of the problems stemmed from the printer setup UI. (See Figure 10.) Searching for a printer was difficult because all printers were in one long list. Choosing a port for the printer, especially in a networked environment, required tunneling down 4-5 levels and featured non-standard and complicated selection behavior. About the time we started work on this problem, members of the design team began investigating wizards as a solution to multi-step, infrequent tasks. Printer setup fit this definition nicely and the resulting wizard tested very well with users. The printer selection screen from the final wizard is shown in Figure 11.

Figure 9: Task bar with Start button, programs, and clock.

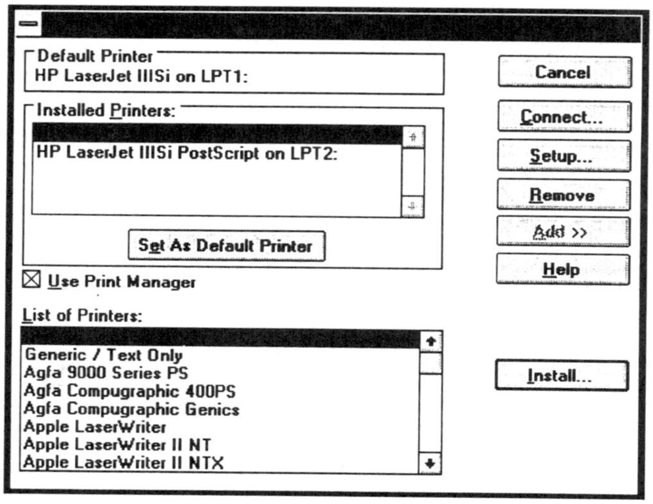

Figure 10: Main Windows 3.1 printer setup dialog box.

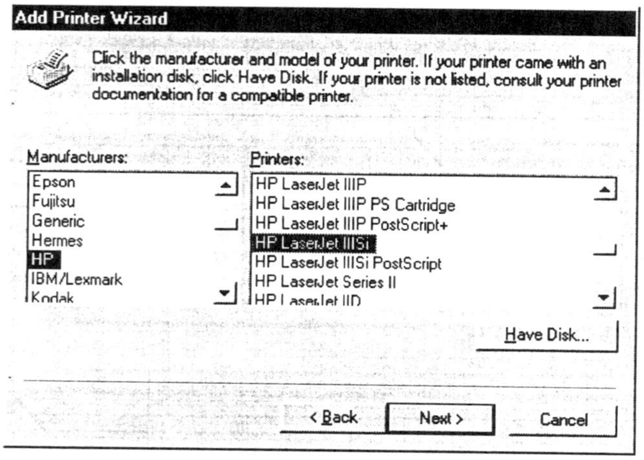

Figure 11: Screen from Windows 95 Add Printer wizard.

5. Getting Help: Search dialog/Index tab. Lab testing of Windows 3.1 showed that users had trouble with the Search dialog in Help. (See Figure 12.) Users had difficulty understanding that the dialog was essentially two parts and that they needed to choose something from the first list and then from the second list, using different buttons. We tried several ideas before arriving at the final Index tab. (See Figure 13.) The Index tab only has one list, and keywords with more than one topic generate a pop-up dialog that users have no trouble noticing.

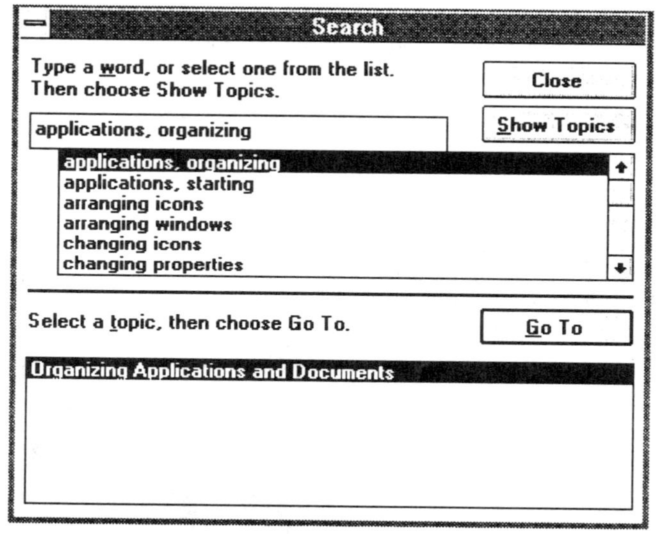

Figure 12: Windows 3.1 Help•Search dialog.

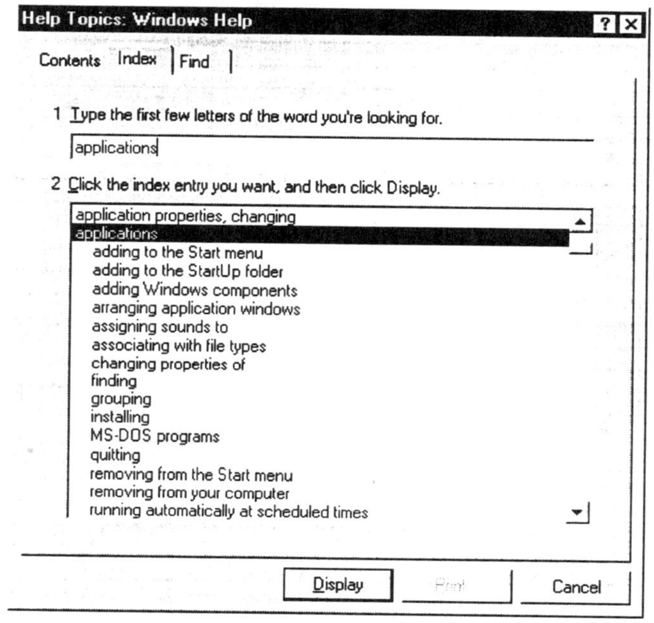

Figure 13: Windows 95 Help•Index tab.

Fine Tuning Phase

Once we had designed all of the major areas of the product, we realized that we had to take a step back and see how all of the pieces fit together. To accomplish this, we conducted summative lab tests and a longitudinal field study.

- Summative lab testing. Using the top twenty tasks identified from market research, we conducted holistic tests of the entire UI. Users of different experience levels completed isomorphic sets of tasks, to measure ease of learning and ease of use once learned. We compared performance with Windows 3.1 as a baseline. After piloting the test in-house to work out problems with the procedure, the test was conducted by an outside vendor, so that the results could be used in a white paper [3]. The results were very encouraging—users finished the tasks in about half the time it took them in Windows 3.1 and they were more satisfied with Windows 95 in 20 of the 21 categories surveyed.

- Longitudinal field study. Using the final beta of Windows 95, we conducted a 20-person field study. We first examined how users worked with Windows 3.1 then watched them set up Windows 95. We returned after a week and after a month to measure learning and changes in use over time. We did not find any major usability holes in the product but did tweak wording in the UI and in Help topics. Some of the data collected is being used by product planners for the next version of Windows and also by product support, as a concise list of things to watch out for when taking support calls.

KEEPING TRACK OF OPEN ISSUES

Throughout the course of designing and testing the Windows 95 UI, we applied various usability engineering principles and practices [2] [4]. With a project the size of Windows 95, we knew we needed a standard way to note all of the usability issues identified, record when and how they were to be fixed, and then close them once the fix was implemented and tested successfully with users.

We designed a relational database to meet this need. (See Figure 14.) After every phase of lab testing, I entered new problems as well as positive findings and assigned them to the appropriate owners—usually a designer and a user education person together. The status of existing problems was also updated—either left open if more work was needed or closed if solved. Every couple of weeks I ran a series of reports that printed all of the remaining problems, by owner, and distributed them to the team members. (See Figure 15.) We met to discuss progress on solutions and when the changed designs would be ready to test with users.

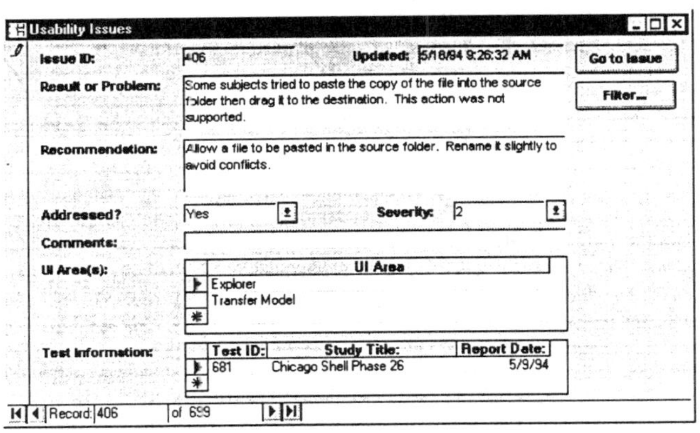

Figure 14: Sample tracking database record.

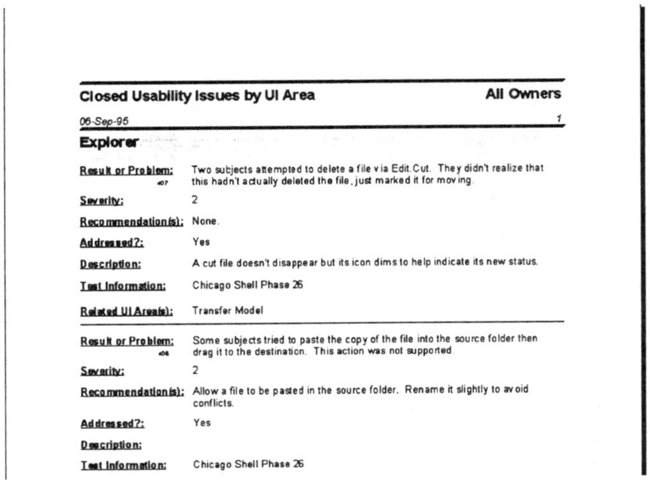

Figure 15: Sample tracking database report.

Report Card

As with any project, the "proof is in the pudding" so sharing some summary statistics is in order.

Lab Testing

We conducted sixty-four phases of lab testing, using 560 subjects. Fifty percent of the users were intermediate Windows 3.1 users; the rest were beginners, advanced users, and users of other operating systems. These numbers do not include testing done on components delivered to us by other teams (Exchange email client, fax software, etc.) Testing on those components accounts for approximately 25 phases and 175 users.

Problem Identification

For the core shell components[5], 699 different "usability statements" were entered into the database during the project. Of that number, 148 were positive findings and 551 were problems. The problems were rated with one of three levels of severity:[6]

- Level 1: Users were unable to continue with a task or series of tasks due to the problem.
- Level 2: Users had considerable difficulty completing a task or series of tasks but were eventually able to continue.
- Level 3: Users had minor difficulty completing a task or series of tasks.

Of the 551 problems identified, 15% were judged to be level 1, 43% level 2, and 42% level 3.

Problem Resolution

During the project, there were five types of resolution:

1. Addressed. The team fixed the problem and it tested successfully with users.

---

5 Does not include components delivered by other teams.

6 Based on a rating scale defined in [1].

2. Planned. The team designed a fix for the problem and we are waiting for it to be implemented.

3. Undecided. The team is not sure whether to fix the problem or is unsure if a fix is feasible.

4. Somewhat. The team designed a fix and it was tested with users, and the results were satisfactory but some issues remain.

5. Not Addressed. The team is not going to fix the problem.

By the end of the project, all problems with resolution "planned" or "undecided" had migrated to one of the other categories. Eighty-one percent of the problems were resolved "Addressed", 8% were resolved "Somewhat", and 11% were resolved "Not Addressed". Most of the issues that were not addressed were due to a technical limitation, or sometimes a scheduling limitation.

CONCLUSIONS

The Windows 95 project was the first experience for many of the team members for doing iterative design, usability testing, and problem tracking.

Iterative Design

Perhaps the best testament to our belief in iterative design is that literally no detail of the initial UI design for Windows 95 survived unchanged in the final product. At the beginning of the design process, we didn't envision the scope and volume of changes that we ended up making. Iterative design, using prototypes and the product as the spec, and our constant testing with users allowed us to explore many different solutions to problems quickly.

The design team became so used to iterating on a design that we felt rushed when, near the end of the project, we had to do some last-minute design work. There wasn't sufficient time to iterate more than once. We were disappointed that we didn't have time to continue fine tuning and re-testing the design.

Specification Process

The "prototype or code are the spec" approach overall worked well, although we naturally have refined the process over time. For example, all the prototypes for a given release of the product now reside in a common location on the network and include instructions for installing and running them.

The design team continues to write initial specification documents and circulate them for early feedback. Once prototyping and usability testing has begun, however, the spec often refers readers to the prototype for details. We have essentially found that the prototype is a richer type of specification, for less work, since it has other uses (usability testing, demos, etc.). A prototype also invites richer feedback, because the reviewer has to imagine less about how the system would work.

Usability Testing

Although doing design and user testing iteratively allowed us to create usable task areas or features of the product, user testing the product holistically was key to polishing the fit between the pieces. As discussed previously, we made changes to wording in the UI and in Help topics based on the data collected. If we had not done this testing, users' overall experience with the product would have been less productive and enjoyable.

Problem Tracking

The high fix rate for usability problems would not have been possible without the intense dedication of all the team members. The tracking database made the whole process more manageable and ensured that issues didn't slip between the cracks. However, the fixes would not have been made if the team had not believed in making the most-usable product possible. Key to this belief was our understanding that we probably weren't going to get it right the first time and that *not* getting it right was as useful and interesting to creating a product as getting it right was.

In the tracking database, all of the issues marked "Somewhat" or "Not Addressed" were rolled over into a new database, as a starting point for design work on the next version of Windows. Product planners and designers worked with the information on a daily basis, as well as processing reports from product support.

ACKNOWLEDGMENTS

Thanks to Jane Dailey, Chris Guzak, Francis Hogle, Marshall McClintock, Mark Malamud, Suzan Marashi, and Mark Simpson for reviewing this design briefing and providing comments. Thanks to Lauren Gallagher, Shawna Sandeno, and Jennifer Shetterly for graphic design assistance.

REFERENCES

1. Dumas, J. S. and Redish, J. C. (1993). *A Practical Guide to Usability Testing* (pp. 324-325). Norwood, NJ: Ablex Publishing Company.

2. Nielsen, J. (1993). *Usability Engineering*. San Diego, CA: Academic Press, Inc.

3. Usability Sciences Corporation. (1994). *Windows 3.1 and Windows 95 Quantification of Learning Time & Productivity*. (Available from http://www.microsoft.com/windows/product/usability.htm.)

4. Whiteside, J. L., Bennett, J, & Holtzblatt, K. (1988). Usability Engineering: Our Experience and Evolution. In M. Helander (Ed.), *Handbook of Human-Computer Interaction* (pp. 791-817). Amsterdam: Elsevier Science Publishers, B. V.

5. Wiklund, M. E. (1994). *Usability in Practice: How Companies Develop User-Friendly Products*. Cambridge, MA: Academic Press, Inc.

Usability Improvements in Lotus cc:Mail for Windows

Stacey L. Ashlund
Lotus Development Corporation
800 El Camino Real West
Mountain View, CA 94040 USA
+1 415 335 6593
sashlund@ccmail.com

Karen J. Horwitz
Lotus Development Corporation
800 El Camino Real West
Mountain View, CA 94040 USA
+1 415 335 6771
khorwitz@ccmail.com

ABSTRACT

This is a case study about a commercial software design and development process. The highly successful product contained some usability problems that were apparent from a usability perspective, but were to be delayed in the upcoming release. A Lotus Notes database was used to record usability issues, UI design recommendations, and decision rationale. This database was the key strategy that helped convince the team to make changes. The processes and UI design solutions described are not new; rather this design briefing focuses on how they were deployed to effect change that wouldn't have happened otherwise. "Before" and "After" screen shots illustrate this success story.

Keywords

User Interface Design, User-Centered Design, Design Process, Usability Engineering, Usability Testing, E-mail.

INTRODUCTION

When the first usability engineer joined Lotus cc:Mail in the fall of 1993, the popular award-winning LAN e-mail product had 6 million users. At the time of this writing, two years later, the number is over 8 million. cc:Mail runs (or is being developed) on Windows, Mac, OS/2 WPS, DOS, Unix OPEN LOOK, Windows 95, and the World Wide Web. With such a significant installed base and multiple platforms, any user interface change faces considerable coordination and discussion.

This design briefing describes the usability efforts on the immediate successor to Lotus cc:Mail for Windows V2 that were directed towards improving its usability for end-users.

The Usability and Design Team

The usability and UI design work described in this briefing was a collaborative effort among two usability engineers, one UI designer, and several developers, technical writers, and product managers. Quality engineers and technical support also contributed to the process.

CHI 96 Vancouver, BC Canada
© 1996 ACM 0-89791-777-4/96/04..$3.50

Until this point in time, cc:Mail had gathered considerable feedback from its customers, but mainly from two types of customers: high-level decision makers with purchasing authority for a corporate-wide e-mail system, and cc:Mail LAN administrators. The usability group was formed to get in touch with the end-users, and to improve and evolve the product from this perspective.

Phases of the Design Process

This design briefing summarizes four overlapping phases of the design process. Note that this is how the process actually happened, not how it was originally intended.

The first phase is referred to as "The Next Major Release" in this briefing. Design and development was already in progress on this release by the time the usability lab was constructed in early 1994. There was already a strong usability group at Lotus headquarters, but the effort was new to the cc:Mail division until this time. The second phase, "Usability Testing", began in April, 1994. The third phase, "Usability Tracking", began in the summer of 1994. A fourth phase, referred to internally as "The Food and Shelter Release", began in the fall of 1994. Iterative UI design work was taking place throughout all four of these overlapping phases, so is not explicitly called out. Some "Before" and "After" screen shots are included to demonstrate the kinds of usability improvements made.

PHASE 1: THE NEXT MAJOR RELEASE

By the time the usability lab and team were created, the decision had been made that the next release of Lotus cc:Mail was to be a major release, not a point release. The plan was to produce an entirely new and improved version of cc:Mail, including many new features. From a usability perspective, the ideal goal for a product with such a significant installed base would have been to retain the good aspects of the UI and improve the bad. Instead, the development plan was to throw it all out and start over fresh. Since the underlying functionality was to be significantly different, this fact was to be reflected in a brand new cc:Mail UI.

A committee called UA/UI (User Agent/User Interface) was in existence at this point in the process. The User Agent referred to the "client", or the code that presented the UI of cc:Mail. The members of the UA/UI committee included development representatives from the five cc:Mail platform teams (Windows, Mac, OS/2, DOS, and OPEN LOOK), managers, technical writers, product management, and the one usability engineer. Approximately nine people attended a typical UA/UI meeting. One person was designated to take minutes, but no other roles were established. For several weeks, the committee met eight hours a day, four or five days a week, gradually reducing to half- or full-day meetings once or twice a week.

The UA/UI committee was planning the next major release to be the first version to run on Windows 95 (still called V4 or Chicago then). This new environment meant designing for SDI (Single Document Interface), instead of MDI (Multiple Document Interface). It also meant a new focus on "objects" (OLE2). Since the UA/UI meetings focused on these technologies, they were heavily system-centered, as opposed to task-oriented or user-centered.

A typical UA/UI discussion revolved around types of message lists and storage methods. Whenever a visual or behavioral UI design issue was raised, it was postponed, as the developers could rarely agree on a cross-platform UI solution. For example, if a graphical representation proposed for Windows did not have an obvious DOS alternative, or had a conflicting meaning in OS/2, the discussion was noted in the minutes and put on hold indefinitely.

UA/UI meeting minutes, mainly questions, open issues, and investigative action item assignments, were typed and distributed, read, revised, and redistributed. Additional UI design and development discussions took place via e-mail and in hallway discussions. The modal of the UA/UI meetings was clearly "design by committee". After a while, the usability engineer was asked to run these meetings. Due to this intensive time commitment, usability testing was not yet taking place in the new lab.

PHASE 2: USABILITY TESTING

While the work on the next major release progressed from an architectural standpoint, the lengthy UA/UI discussions eventually faded out. It became clear to the committee that it was too early to agree on UI designs. The usability team grew to include two student interns and then began conducting testing. Initial usability testing focused on the currently released versions of cc:Mail for LAN and Mobile across platforms.

User-Centered E-Mail Tasks

Based on the first few rounds of user analysis and task analysis, the usability team created and refined the following "Top 10 list" of the most basic e-mail tasks:

1 **Read.** (Differentiate new mail from old; distinguish high priority messages from normal or low; identify the sender, other recipients, date and time sent, etc.)

2 **Write & Send.** (Create a message; address it; write it; set priority; optionally save a copy; send it.)

3 **Reply.** (Reply to sender, some, or all recipients; keep none, some, or all file attachments.)

4 **Forward.** (Recognize a forwarded message; view forwarding information; forward one or more messages with or without forwarding information.)

5 **Delete.** (Delete one or more messages; put a message in the Trash or permanently delete it; know if Trash is enabled or how to enable it; set when to empty the Trash; retrieve a deleted message.)

6 **Print.** (Print one or more messages and any or all attachments, with or without the header; print a list of messages, e.g., just author, subject, and date.)

7 **Attachments.** (Read an attached file, view or launch it; attach one or more files; save attached files to disk.)

8 **Folders.** (Create a folder; store one or more messages in a folder; access messages in folders.)

9 **Mailing Lists.** (Create a mailing list; address a message to a mailing list.)

10 **Search.** (Find a message given the author, subject, date, word in the body of the message, etc.)

This list does not include implicit navigational tasks, such as going back to an open message, getting back to the Inbox, reading next and previous messages, or closing a window. It also does not include all the possible advanced tasks, such as finding copies of messages already sent, saving messages in progress, automating message storage by creating and running rules, etc. This list stood the test of time. The one thing everyone always agreed to is that these are the most commonly performed e-mail tasks and so should be the primary focus of UI design and usability efforts. This was an essential first step that helped the usability team eventually get buy-in on UI changes from the rest of the product team.

Prototype Testing

In addition to testing released versions of cc:Mail, paper, Visual Basic, and Visual C++ prototypes were also tested. These prototypes were primarily designed by development, with contributions from the usability team and the UI designer. Prototype testing was valuable because it provided feedback on non-trivial UI variations without taking as much time as full implementation.

Competitive Testing

The usability team also tested competitive products, such as Microsoft Mail, according to the same user population and the basic tasks. Developers often justified some of the known usability problems in cc:Mail for Windows by placing the blame on the environment, e.g., "That's just the way Microsoft Windows works." Testing competitive products afforded an opportunity to gather usability feedback on alternative design solutions without requiring any additional prototyping or implementation. Competitive testing revealed design ideas of how to do things better as well as what not to do. This testing proved to be a highly valuable source of motivation for change, particularly when a common feature was easier to use in another Windows product.

PHASE 3: USABILITY TRACKING IN NOTES

In addition to conducting testing, the usability team designed and developed a Lotus Notes database. The primary purpose of the database was to serve as a mechanism for tracking usability issues identified in testing. Each issue was put into a separate Notes "document" which included a description of the problem, which platforms it applied to, and any cross-platform consistency issues. Issues in cc:Mail on one platform frequently related to other platforms as well, as well as to issues in competitive products. To manage this information, Notes "views" were created for each product. Then, the issues could be viewed by priority, functional category, or status.

Priority levels ranged from one to five and were assigned by the usability team based on frequency of the task and severity of the consequences. The number of people who experienced a problem in a test was also a contributing factor. For example, a problem experienced by eight of eight users in a test was assigned the highest priority. Categories included areas of e-mail determined by development, such as addressing, folders, mailing lists, and search. Issues could either be "open", or assigned a status such as In Progress, Done, or Deferred, based on agreement between the usability team and development. This method was used for cc:Mail on all platforms.

With the creation of the database, developers and product managers no longer had to make assumptions about addressing issues in the current product, for example, as they could simply "query" the database to see all addressing usability problems by priority or status. The database provided an easy way to produce status reports for upper management, to assess the impact of a change in one area of the UI, and to compare against the usability of similar features in competitive products.

Encouraging Team Participation in Testing

The Lotus Notes database was also used to post reports and maintain the schedule of upcoming tests to encourage project team members (in all roles) to be involved. Team members could contribute by observing tests and giving the usability team their impressions. All teams within Lotus could access the database, but the views containing confidential customer information on test participants were restricted to the usability team only. This was helpful in that it made usability efforts visible to a broad range of people working on the product. In addition, it was part of the Lotus corporate culture to use Notes databases for project management, so it gave the usability group a tangible presence across the company.

PHASE 4: A "FOOD AND SHELTER" RELEASE

The next significant turn of events occurred when the major release was intercepted by plans to do a much sooner release. Work on the Next Major Release would continue, but a large portion of resources were temporarily rededicated to the urgent "Food and Shelter" release. The remainder of this briefing will focus on this "Food and Shelter" release. This release was to have back-end changes only, no UI changes and no new features. It was nicknamed "food and shelter" to indicate that it would contain only the essential underlying changes needed to ship it as soon as possible. Another popular phrase for referring to it internally was "low-hanging fruit", to give the analogy that the very apparent, easy, quick things were to be fixed, and nothing else (just as ripe, low-hanging, fruit is easy to grab). With this philosophy, the ever-growing number of usability issues in the database had little hope of getting reduced in the short term.

Reconciling Usability vs. Food and Shelter

To respond to this change in schedule, the persistent usability team also adopted the "low-hanging fruit" attitude and compiled a short list of usability issues based on testing and submitted this to product management and development. This list included only high priority issues that would be quick, easy, and low-risk to fix. When an issue was extremely high priority, but very difficult to fix, the usability team documented the ideal solution in the database and proposed one or more possible compromise solutions to development. If the list were too long, it was sure to be overwhelming and summarily rejected.

UI Specification, Refinements, and Iteration

Fortunately for the usability team (and the end-user), product management was concerned with finding ways to keep customers satisfied with improvements to the product without causing further delays. Some of the largest cc:Mail customer sites had voiced dissatisfaction about some of the same high priority usability problems observed in testing. Product management requested that the usability team work with development to find solutions to these problems.

At this time, the UI designer was still assigned 100% to the ongoing work on the Next Major Release. She acted in a consulting role to the usability team and communicated usability results to the developers on the major release. Due to the limited design resources, the usability team adopted multi-disciplinary responsibilities and began writing design specs for some of the highest priority issues in the usability database. Design rationales were recorded in the Notes database to ensure against backtracking on an issue in subsequent design iterations.

Although everyone understood and agreed with the usability issues, development didn't know what to do about most of them without making major implementation changes. As this was not possible, since all UI changes had been forbidden from this release, the usability team presented suggestions in a more manageable form. Instead of large-scale, ideal solutions to the biggest problems, multiple partial solutions were presented to development. Development could then pick the solutions that were most feasible.

THE RESULT: GOOD NEWS FOR THE USER

Before long, the developers had implemented several of these usability fixes. Usability testing was then conducted on the revised code. This testing revealed some necessary refinements to areas that had changed. By stressing the fact that these were refinements to existing problems, e.g., a change fixed a big problem but introduced several related smaller problems, not new problems, all but the most technically difficult problems were fixed. Subsequent usability testing convinced the team that the right changes had been made successfully.

Little by little, of the 350 usability issues logged against cc:Mail for Windows, almost one-third of the total got fixed in the "Food and Shelter" release. **Table 1** shows the numbers of usability issues that were deferred, and fixed, according to priority. These numbers show that the percentage of fixes increases as the priority increases, demonstrating that usability efforts were focused on improving the most important areas.

Table 1. Usability Issues

Priority	Deferred	Fixed	% Fixed
High	42	53	56%
Med-High	46	26	36%
Medium	68	19	22%
Med-Low	45	9	17%
Low	40	2	5%

EXAMPLES

This section shows a few "Before" and "After" examples of the kinds of UI changes implemented as a result of these usability efforts.

Example 1

Figure 1 shows the top portion of the main cc:Mail window in V2. It contains a title bar, menu bar, and SmartIcon bar above the Inbox (which displays the new messages). The visible SmartIcons can be customized by the user, but by default are displayed as shown and listed in this picture. It can be readily seen that some of the most basic tasks were not accessible from this default set of icons, such as Reply and Send, but many less-often needed icons were included, such as Rules, User Setup, and Empty Trash. The revised SmartIcon bar is shown in **Figure 2**.

The number of icons was only increased by two. Search was retained, but moved farther to the right, after the more common icons. Help was moved near the end to increase its visibility. Rules, User Setup, Rename, Cascade, Tile, Empty Trash, and Change Font were all removed from the default set. Reply, Send, Attach, Read Previous and Next Message, Save As, Save Draft, and Close Window were all added. The generic icon for Create was split up into two new icons to provide for its most often needed uses; Create Folder and Create Mailing List. In V2 there was no icon for Close Window, so an icon was created for this purpose. Prior to usability testing, it was not known that users had a difficult time with such a simple task as closing a window, as windows were maximized by default in cc:Mail V2. Icons removed and added are listed in *italics* below.

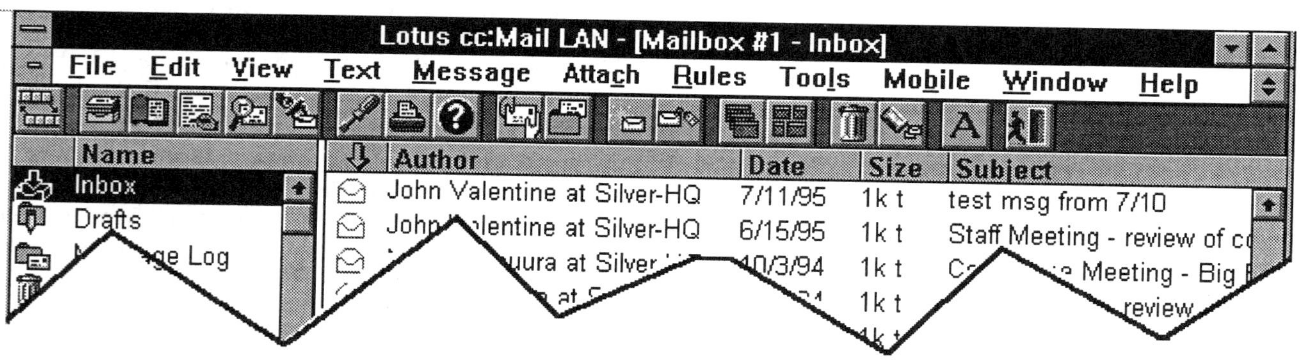

Switch, Inbox, Address Book, Prepare, Search, *Rules, User Setup,* Print, Help, Forward, Store, Create, *Rename, Cascade, Tile,* Delete, *Empty Trash, Change Font,* Exit

Figure 1. Before: Top Portion of cc:Mail for Windows V2 Main Window (icons listed in *italics* were removed)

Switch, Inbox, Address Book, Prepare, *Reply,* Forward, *Send, Attach, Read Previous Message, Read Next Message,* Print, Delete, Store, *Save As, Save Draft,* Search, Create Folder, Create Mailing List, *Close Window,* Help, Exit

Figure 2. After: Revised Set of SmartIcons (icons listed in *italics* were added)

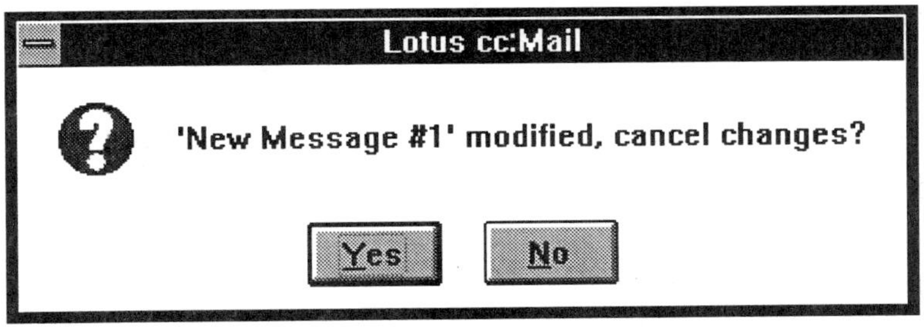

Figure 3. Before: Closing a New Message in Progress (or a Modified Existing Message)

Example 2

Figure 3 shows the dialog box from cc:Mail for Windows V2 that was displayed when a new message was started, and then the message window was closed. The dialog box was displayed to confirm whether the user really wanted to close the window and lose anything entered in the message so far. The problems with this dialog box may be obvious. The phrasing of the question was confusing, as it was the reverse of the common confirmation found in other applications, "Do you want to save your changes? Yes or No". Users expected that Yes would be the safe choice, and save their changes. But in reality Yes "canceled" the changes, or discarded them. In addition, there was no way to use this dialog box to save the changes at all. The only "choice" the user was given was to lose the changes or not close the window. Clicking No simply dismissed the dialog box and left the message window open. Usability testing revealed that this dialog box was difficult to use by novices as well as experts who had been using cc:Mail for years.

The redesigned dialog box is shown in **Figure 4.** With this new dialog box, the message can be saved "as is" in the Drafts folder for later completion (a "feature" added as part of this usability fix). The message can be sent if it is already addressed. Or the message can be closed and discarded. Clicking OK is a "safe" choice by default.

Similarly, if an existing message is modified (a message that the user has received, as opposed to a new message), and then closed, the dialog box shown in **Figure 3** was also displayed in V2. The revised dialog box is shown in **Figure 5.** Again, this time the user was given useful choices, instead of just the ability to discard the changes. The modified message can be converted into a reply or a forward, or discarded.

These changes did not require adding any new features to the application. cc:Mail already contained the functionality to save a draft or allow the user to forward or reply to a message. These features were just never before offered to the user upon closing a message window. It had not been anticipated that users would use the action of closing a window as a "fall back plan" or shortcut for completing a message. Note that the fact that a user can modify an existing message at all was not changed, as it was far to extensive and entrenched in the model. Rather, very simple UI design and implementation provided the user with useful choices when and where they needed them. Users tended not to recognize this as a change in usability testing, but were now able to answer their e-mail without having to think about what "cancel changes" would do.

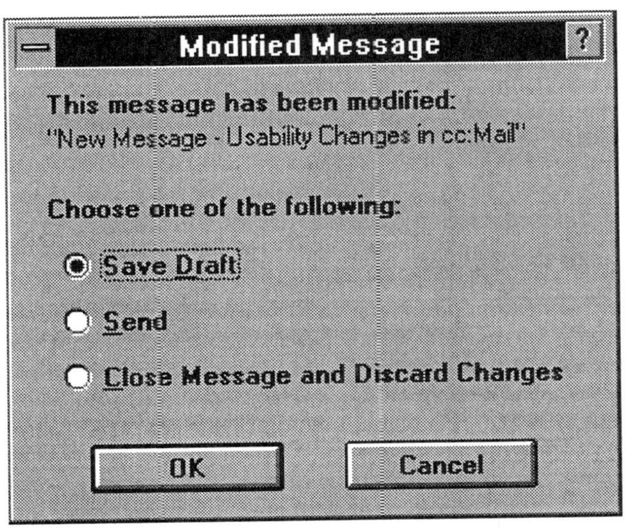

Figure 4. After: Closing a New Message in Progress

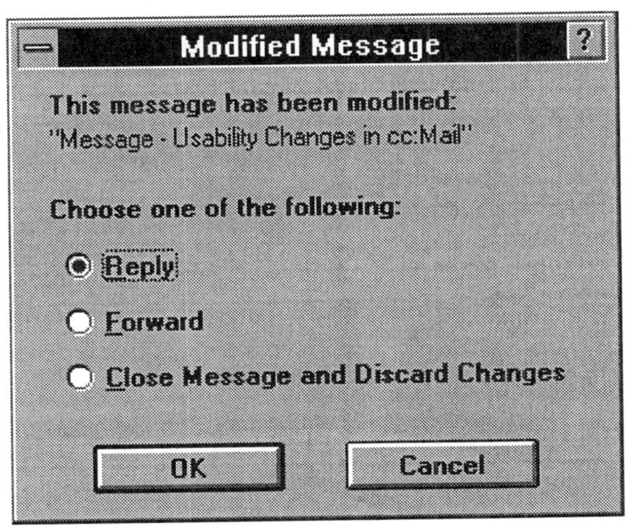

Figure 5. After: Closing a Modified Existing Message

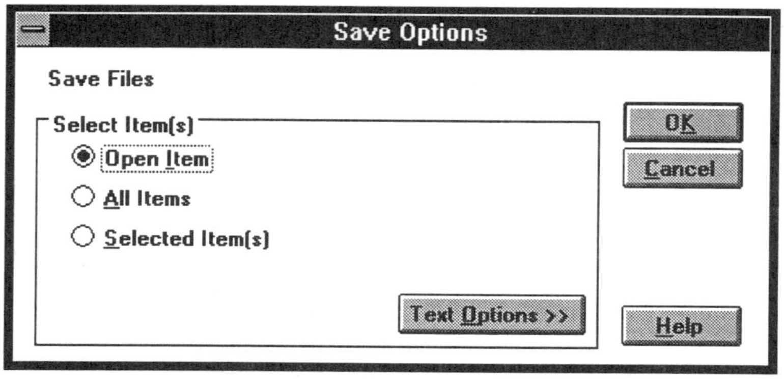

Figure 6. **Before:** Saving a Message and/or Attachment(s)

Example 3

Figure 6 shows the dialog box from cc:Mail for Windows V2 that was displayed when the user chose the Save command from the File menu. It could be used to save a message (and/or any or all of its file attachments) out to disk. Users were confused by the term "item" (as the term "attachment" was much more common in the UI). They also didn't like having to click OK before entering a file name, as they didn't know what the file would be called or where it would be saved by default. They had to click OK and hope that cc:Mail would save the file with an obvious name, not knowing that they would ever be prompted to enter a file name. When OK was clicked, the Save Options dialog box was dismissed and a secondary dialog box was displayed, allowing the user to then enter or change the file name and location.

The revised Save As dialog box is shown in **Figure 7.** The default file location and name is displayed in a field and can be changed. Alternatively, the Browse button displays an optional secondary dialog box as shown in

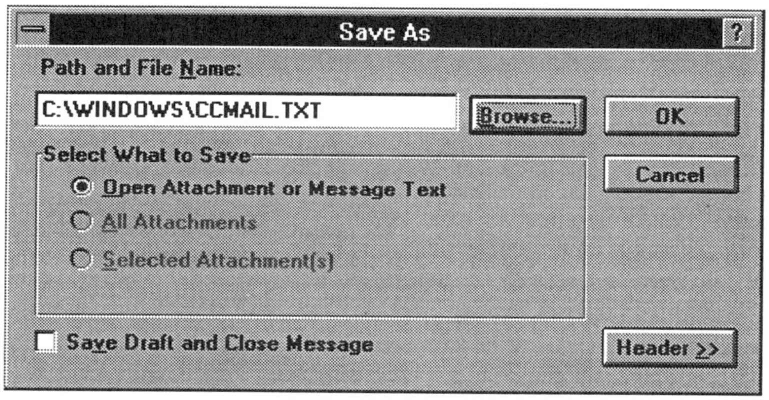

Figure 7. **After:** Saving a Message and/or Attachment(s)

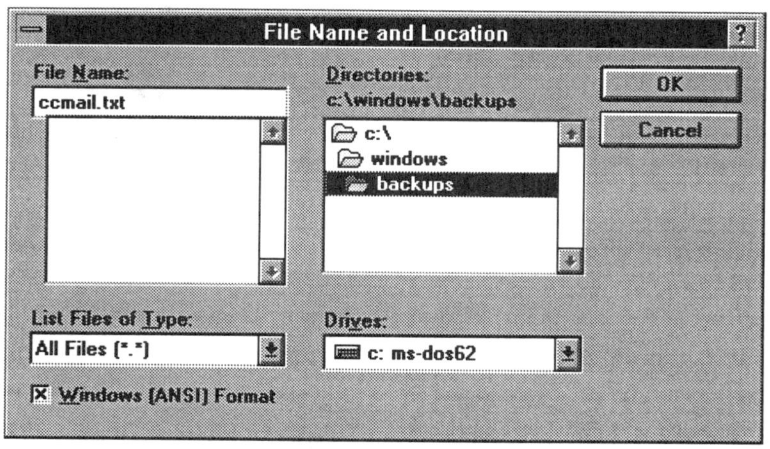

Figure 8. **After:** The Browse button displays this secondary (optional) dialog box

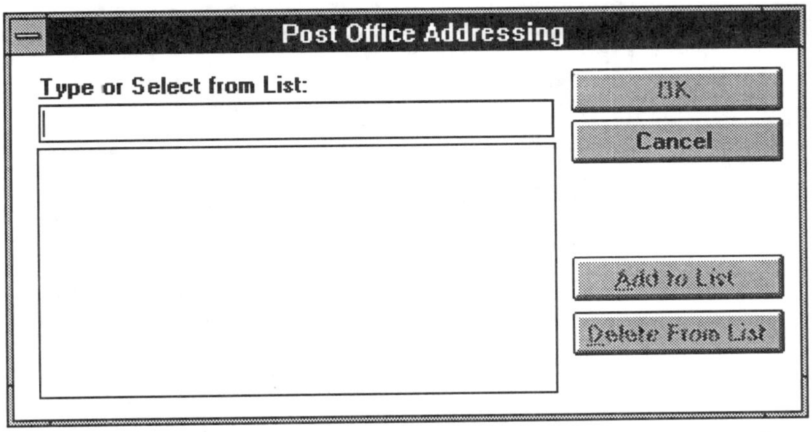

Figure 9. Before: Addressing via a Gateway, such as X400, Internet, or Fax

Figure 8. In addition, the wording of the radio buttons was clarified regarding attachments and message text. The "Text Options" button only contained settings related to the message header, so is renamed and regrouped appropriately. And finally, the Save Draft "feature" is made available here, where new users often expected to find it.

Example 4

cc:Mail was originally intended for users on a LAN within a single company to send e-mail to each other. This is very easy within cc:Mail. When the first few characters of the name of someone within the same company are typed into the address of a new message, cc:Mail "watches" and displays a name that matches the characters typed so far. Therefore, it is not straightforward to address to an external internet address. Names or addresses that do not appear in the cc:Mail directory cannot simply be entered into the address field of a new message.

To enter an internet address in cc:Mail V2, the user must first type the name of a gateway, such as "Internet" or "SMTP" (determined by the cc:Mail administrator), and then enter the address in a "Post Office Addressing" dialog box, as shown in **Figure 9.** Here, the user could enter any internet address, e.g., ashlund.chi@xerox.com, and optionally add it to the list so it could simply be selected for future use. The same model applied for X400 addresses or sending a fax from cc:Mail. Users had great difficulty with this dialog box; they didn't know what they could type in the field. The revised dialog box is shown in **Figure 10.** Simple buttons were added to display optional secondary dialog boxes containing "templates" to fill in for each of the three types of address formats (e.g., Name @ Domain for addressing via an Internet gateway). Clicking the Internet button displays a dialog box containing two fields, labeled Name and Domain, separated by an @.

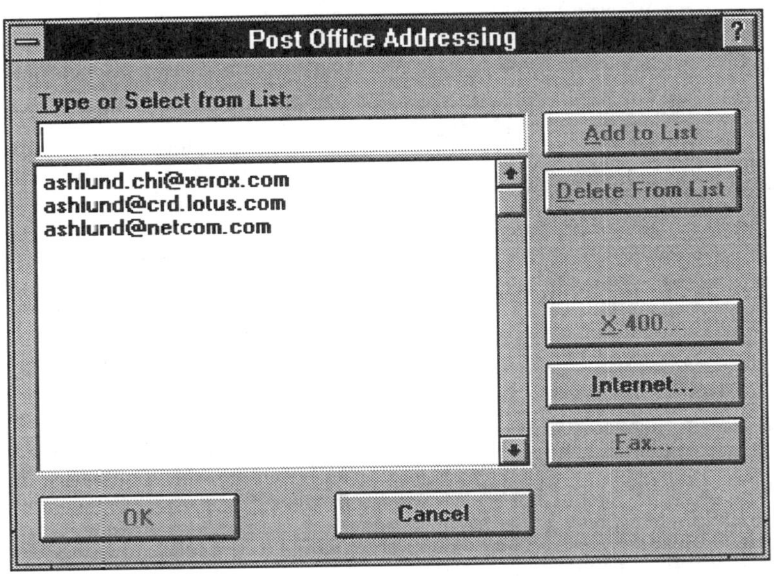

Figure 10. After: Addressing via a Gateway, such as X400, Internet, or Fax

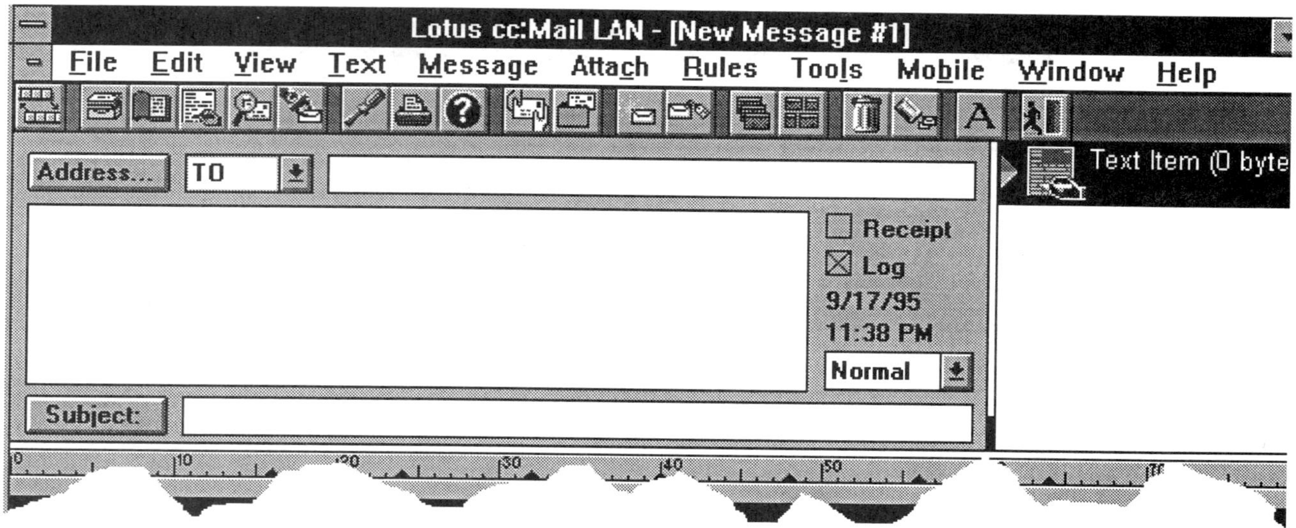

Figure 11. Before: Top Portion of cc:Mail for Windows V2 Message Window

Example 5
Figure 11 shows the top portion of a new message window in cc:Mail for Windows V2. To address a new message, a name from the cc:Mail directory is typed on the text entry field to the right of the "To" combo box. After typing the name, the user must press the Enter key to put the name into the blank list box below the field. If Enter is not pressed, the name is visible, but the Send command is inactive. The Send menu command is gray and the Send icon just beeps when clicked. The user receives no useful feedback as to the cause of the problem or how to correct it.

The problem of having two separate places for addresses (one to enter them and one to view them) couldn't be solved in the short term. Instead, the problem was essentially solved with a simple workaround; the Send command was enabled regardless of whether a name was simply typed or typed and entered. When a typed name is not entered and Send is chosen, a dialog box appears to prompt the user, e.g., "A name has been typed in but not entered into the address list. Do you want to send the message to this address? Ashlund, Stacey". By choosing the default button, Yes, the message can be sent. User confirmation was required because of the critical nature of accidentally sending a message to an unintended recipient.

Other Examples
Many of the other changes are not as visual. In cc:Mail for Windows V2 all windows started by default as maximized. This made it difficult for users to navigate within cc:Mail; they'd forget which message windows were open, and had difficulty getting back to windows hidden behind other maximized windows. The redesign changed the default window size to nearly full-size, but leaving just enough room to see if there was another open window behind the current one. If users could see it, they could click on it. Another change was enabling the use of the Escape key to close windows, in addition to the difficult Windows standard Control-F4 or double-clicking the hidden control menu (the lower of the two rectangles in the upper left corner of **Figure 11**). Lastly, many commands in V2 were modal, e.g., the user must first open and go to the Address Book Window before the Create Mailing List command is enabled. The redesign allows the user to choose the command from any window, and if the necessary window is not yet open or visible, it is automatically displayed.

CONCLUSIONS
These examples may seem very minor, but they added up to a significant difference for the user. The biggest reason for this success was that the usability team did not propose large-scale changes to the UI, only small changes, such things as rearranging icons and rewording dialog boxes. In usability testing throughout the development cycle, users found that cc:Mail behaved more like users expected it to than in the previous version. In most cases, changes were so subtle that users didn't know what had changed, only that it had changed for the better. They were now able to accomplish the basic tasks.

Creating the Notes database for tracking usability issues was the single most important strategy used to convince the team to make changes and accomplish these measurable usability successes. It provided a reliable source of quantitative results and was indispensable to this project.

The usability problems and processes described here are surely not novel to the CHI community. And yet such apparent usability problems actually existed in a highly successful best-selling end-user product. It was the judicious application of well-known UI design principles, combined with a software engineering tracking methodology, that finally got them fixed.

ACKNOWLEDGMENTS
Thanks to everyone at Lotus who worked on this product.

Real World Design in the Corporate Environment: Designing an Interface for the Technically Challenged

Susan Hopper
Merrill Lynch
User Interface Design
400 College Road East
Princeton, NJ 08540
(609) 282-4793
email:Susan_Hopper@ml.com

Harold Hambrose
Electronic Ink
President
401 S. Second Street Suite 304
Philadelphia, PA
email:Harold_Hambrose@ml.com

Paul Kanevsky
Merrill Lynch
Strategic Market Systems
400 College Road East
Princeton, NJ 08540
(609) 282-5747
email:Paul_Kanevsky@ml.com

ABSTRACT
The development of a graphical user interface for Merrill Lynch's Trusted Global Advisor (TGA) system is a major endeavor to bring enhanced information access and updated technology to the desktops of more than 15,000 financial consultants and industry professionals firmwide.

The TGA development team's goals and challenges are two-fold. The business goal is to create a comprehensive, integrated computing environment that is unique and would identify Merrill Lynch as the technology pioneer in the financial services industry.

The technological challenge included the design of a graphical user interface that could be easily learned and understood by all users in the Firm—the majority of which are PC illiterate. In order to have acceptance from the users, this new system has to appeal to both the first-time GUI user and mouse aficionados alike.

KEYWORDS
user interface, corporate environment, hierarchy, tab metaphor, iterative design, book, shell.

INTRODUCTION
The system being replaced is a 3270, character-based mainframe system. The current network is a usability nightmare, but contains an enormous amount of valuable information that has to be maintained and transferred to the new system. In addition, the old system forces the user to know three-letter function codes (more than 300 in all) for any task they wants to accomplish.

The new platform design is utilizing the Microsoft Windows NT™ operating system running under a graphical user interface in a TCP/IP networking environment. The interface has to allow

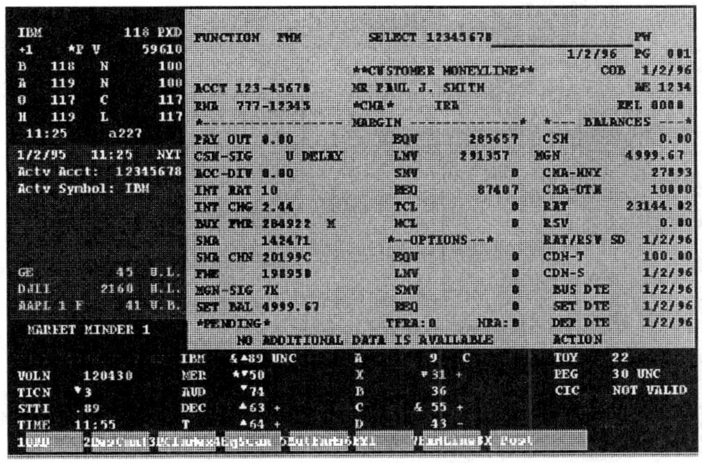

Figure 1. PRISM
Current 3270 Market Data Retrieval System

users to easily accomplish tasks in a minimal amount of time.

The challenge here is to make the technology as transparent to the user as possible. The team's directive: the user should only be concerned with what they need to do; how to do it on the new system should be obvious.

The team's challenges to date:

- How do you design a comprehensive system that seamlessly integrates 350 separate applications into one easy to learn and use business tool?
- How do you design an interface simple enough for even the most inexperienced of users, NONE of whom can afford to lose even one day of business for training?
- How do you introduce user interface design and usability concepts to a huge development community and make these processes work in an area traditionally resistant to change?

I - THE SHELL: A HISTORY OF THE DESIGN
When this project was originally started in 1993, there were many prototype iterations and opinions of what the "the Shell" should look like and how users would be expected to interact

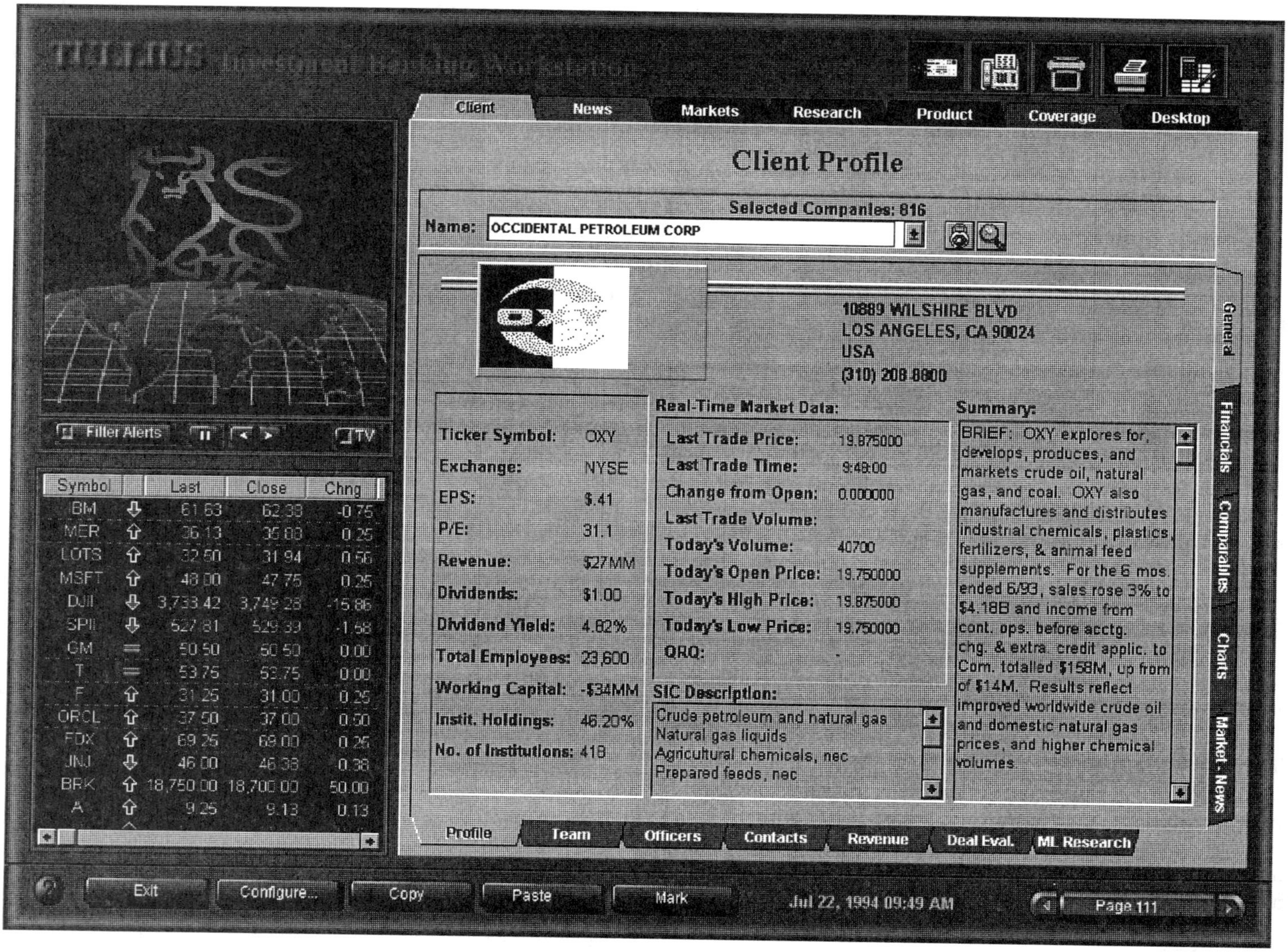

Figure 2. CICERO

The latest version of CICERO that was adopted for TGA. Drag and drop targets resided at the top of the screen.

with it. Multiple shell designs were produced, none of which seemed to work. Accurate evaluations of unsuccessful iterations didn't take place, as qualified Human Factors Engineers and User Interface Designers were not involved in the project. The team seemed to be designing in a vacuum—allowing only a select (and often unqualified) few to critique the design.

Eventually, the team was reorganized to include professionals who had already created a very successful shell-based design in another area of the company. This earlier product was created for a smaller-scale system, dubbed "CICERO." The user base was familiar with Windows™, and CICERO was to replace numerous off-the-shelf products that were being used to accomplish the user's tasks. No formal usability tests were done, however, informal testing provided positive feedback as to the ease-of-use of the CICERO system. With the infusion of much needed expertise and guidance, the TGA project was refocused and put on the right track.

The Shell needed to accomplish several things—it needed to be extremely powerful, in that all utilities and access to all information should be easy to find. Nothing could be buried. The time-on-task for a user was critical. This alone created a design challenge. How crowded could a 1024 x 768 screen be? We didn't want to overwhelm the user, but we wanted everything within easy reach.

The Shell design was based on the CICERO tab metaphor (shown above), whose Windows™ users found extremely easy to understand. Navigation to information was achieved through the use of up to three levels of tabs. The tabs were located clockwise around the application window. The primary level tabs were across the top of the space, the secondary tabs were positioned vertically on the right side of the space, and the tertiary tabs were located underneath the application window. Access to information was achieved by clicking on a top level tab, then on active secondary choices and tertiary tabs if necessary. By utilizing the tab metaphor from CICERO in the TGA shell design—segmenting the applications in a hierarchical format with which the users were familiar, we hoped to lessen the learning curve.

In addition to the application space, the TGA shell also needed to display real-time data at all times, such as stock quotes and other market information. These would be viewed in the InfoCenter, a panel located on the left-hand side of the application space. Users also indicated that they wanted to view company video broadcasts and TV news channels in the InfoCenter. A common set of functions across all applications such as print, fax, e-mail, on-line help and tutorials are also provided by the Shell via a set of buttons in an area known as the Action Bar.

II - DESIGN ITERATIONS

Once the CICERO model was adopted, we needed to refine it for the new user base. We created several versions, each iteration was based on a new requirement from management or users.

Initially the outgoing utilities such as print and fax were located at the top right, to keep them in view, however, we discovered through our own use that it was awkward to drag upwards, so they were moved to the lower right. Since our users need to be aware of many things at once, not all of equal importance, we developed a mechanism to alert users to incoming messages or alerts that they need to view or take action upon such as an opinion change or an incoming e-mail message. This message center consisted of buttons which appeared to have a light indicating the urgency of the alert. Red was critical, yellow was not critical but that there was a message or alert that was present, green indicated empty or no alert or message was present. We soon discovered that these colored buttons became distracting and were removed. This facility was replaced by a scrolling window which the user could configure to view only the alerts they were most concerned with.

As time passed, Shell real estate became quite valuable. The area known as the Device Bar was expanded to include Calendars, clocks, intelligent messengers and Go To and Return To controls.

Also our tastes had changed. We now preferred a flatter, sleeker look for the Shell. We maintained three-dimensionality, but lowered the height of buttons and frames—giving us a little more visual breathing room.

Behind the Screens

To achieve a truly integrated computing environment, all applications developed internally or purchased (e.g., Microsoft Office™) are subordinated and controlled by the shell. In effect, they become pages in the TGA book, and cannot be accessed as "stand-alone." The uncluttered layout and shell-managed display avoids the confusion caused by the floating or overlapped applications, while experienced Windows™ users are not hindered in the performance of their daily tasks.

Several methods were used to achieve this goal. All applications reside within the application space in the shell. The shell manages the process of showing and hiding application screens, and does not allow any portion of an application to become obscured. Intuitive bookmarking and navigational methods are implemented to give the user the feel of continuity and integration within the shell.

To reinforce this feeling of continuity, the shell provides a context management and sharing mechanism. Using context management, the user can pick the focus of interest once for various applications. For example, a user can select John Smith as the client context, and then navigate to the client profile application. With the same client in focus, the user can then switch to the asset allocation application to see John Smith's holdings. In the background, the shell delivers all the necessary information to each application as soon as a new client is selected. The context sharing can be as simple as passing an account number, or as complex as passing multiple database records from application to application.

The bookmarking capability in the shell simplifies the interrupt-driven day of a Financial Consultant. Using the same example, while the user is viewing John Smith's information his telephone rings. It's Mike Doe and he wants to buy a stock. The user clicks on the order book and places the order. To return to the unfinished task, the user simply clicks on the Client book and his other client and his profile are presented at exactly the point he left them.

III - A CRY FOR STANDARDS (OR PUTTING THE CART BEFORE THE HORSE) : THE DESIGN TEAM IS FORMED

With the Shell design firmly entrenched, we set out on our adventure to bring the Shell to the development community. True to corporate style, a committee was formed to quell the serious demand for some sort of user interface standards. We had no clear-cut objectives other than to go into seclusion and miraculously come out with UI standards for the Shell and as-yet-undeveloped applications.

The Design Team members represented the areas of technology, business, design and human factors. Each discipline was represented by at least two individuals.

After several months of brainstorming and brain-bashing, we came out with a set of half-baked, fairly useless standards. It didn't go beyond the UI guidelines already available from software manufacturers and industry experts, with a few exceptions. We created groups of controls such as the Finder, which handled context management. Although the standards reiterated what most GUI developers already knew, we recognized that a large portion of *our* development community had never been exposed to GUI development before (they were, until recently, COBOL mainframe programmers) and that we needed to educate them on the various controls. Although they could have read the guides, we wanted to create one comprehensive document that they could refer to for anything.

This attempt failed. Standards spoke of *what* a control was, but offered little assistance in *how* a control was to be used. All applications posed unique design challenges and the Standards document proved to be a poor cookbook for applications design. We were immediately sent back to try again by senior management. Realizing that the composition of this team was insufficient, the original team was reorganized to include new members with UI design skills and human factors experience. Still, we ran into the concern that we were putting the cart before the horse. But the demand grew and we complied. After several more weeks, a Standards document was published. It included more corporate standards to promote Merrill's look and feel such as color usage standards, fonts, spreadsheet controls, group box controls, "more detail" controls and language. It was a starting point that would assist developers in fulfilling their directive to create applications that had the same look and feel.

Even though the Design Team felt as if we were not completely comfortable with the standards we published, the exercise was not useless. We found that we needed to amend the Standards Guide or publish Updates on a relatively frequent basis. This not only aggravated the developers, but potentially pushed back their delivery dates.

When interface design began in earnest, the Standards could be amended. Now came the hard part—getting the standards to fit into the interface design of the applications—or vice versa depending on the developer or their manager.

IV - INTO THE TRENCHES

Upon general distribution of the first draft of the Design Standards and Guidelines, the Design Team re-evaluated its position in the development environment. Up to this point, the team had been a decision-making body responsible for the creation of a list of recommendations for the design of the TGA interface. The team had to now mobilize in order to affect change in an environment that had already progressed in the development effort without the benefit of interface design standards and guidelines.

In order to efficiently affect the most change within the many application groups developing end-user interfaces, the Design Team decided that it would be advantageous to divide and conquer. Sub-teams were formed from the members of the design team and assigned to various application development projects. These sub-teams consisted of four members—one member from each of the disciplines that comprised the original committee. There was a sub-team for each of the major development efforts, such as Client applications, Product applications, Research, Business Management, etc.. The design team as a whole would remain intact, but to service the development groups as smaller, more dynamic teams seemed to work best.

The sub-teams met on an as-needed basis, more in a consultative fashion at first. Usually the UI designers would venture out first to assist developers with standards questions and then UI design. Eventually an informal review of the application was scheduled with the whole sub-team. A document was to be produced to assist the developers in making any necessary changes, however, this seemed to infer a more formal approach and the document was abandoned. Verbal communication seemed to be enough. The developers also had input into the design of controls or variations in layout to accommodate any special needs that may have.

Cross Application Reviews were developed to assure that any function that may be common to other applications was being done consistently. These reviews were done by the entire Design Team. This was in addition to any formal reviews that were scheduled with the sub-teams.

The Up Side

With smaller, more accessible teams, developers were now encouraged to utilize these individuals as a resource for the definition of their user interface—not simply as a governing body bestowing a blessing (or not) on their UI design efforts. Individuals with a particular skill were now seen by developers as an aid—not a review checkpoint. Members of these smaller teams could now communicate rapidly to the whole design committee those decisions made while working with developers. Communication between the individual developers and the design team (as well as among the design team itself) was improved.

Because of the physical size of these sub-teams, members were able to sit in the developer's cubicle (their turf) to evaluate their user interfaces. This created a hands-on work session environment rather than the presentation-and-review scenario—the alternative with a large design committee. Developers no longer felt as if they were "going before the board" and interaction between them and the Design Team flourished. And since UI designers were able to assist any team (not just the sub-team to which they belonged) the sub-team's evaluations usually went more smoothly.

The Down Side

As a large committee, it was easy for individual members to leave certain areas of the guidelines and standards decision-making to others. Within smaller teams, however, it was critical for all individuals to be well versed in all design decisions documented in the Standards and Guidelines document and why they were made. It was important too, for sub-team members to support the design decisions recorded in the document, even though they may have disagreed when the decision was originally made. When members of the team responsible for a document contradict the statements recorded in the Standards document, this makes the team seem fragmented and unorganized. It is important for team members to voice disagreements and concerns about the documented guidelines and standards to the appropriate audience, but present a unified front.

Once out in the trenches in sub-teams, it was not difficult to forget the larger design committee to which we all belonged. It was critical to the survival of the Standards and Guidelines document (as well as the team), that design decisions and challenges that arose from sub-team work be communicated to other design team members. Without ties to the original team, we risked becoming as fragmented a development and design effort as the one that necessitated our creation.

It also became apparent that there weren't enough UI designers and Human Factors specialists to go around, so some applications fell through the cracks. They were discovered during formal Design Team Reviews and Cross Application Reviews. We are currently seeking to either streamline the process, or acquire more resources

V - BATTLE OF WILLS: PROCESS, STANDARDS AND APPLICATIONS DESIGN

Since all of the applications were to run under the shell, we needed the appearance of one big, consistent application. This presented another design challenge—introducing developers to the concept of user interface designers and usability engineers. Our entire development team for this project is more than 400 people. Although developers were familiar with a process, these new extra steps caused some anxiety among the community. Standards were welcomed; however, when it came time to follow a process, (which a project of this magnitude truly needs), there were some differences of opinion as to which process to follow and what to do when. As a result, no consistent process was followed for the most part.

As in most corporate environments, time is of the essence. Since no formal UI Design step was in place in the development lifecycle, developers forged ahead in order to meet their deadlines. And there were many of them—Beta 1, 2, and 3, Pilot, Release. Applications were developed rapidly, with little regard for usability. Usability Testing, however, was a formal step in the process. Most developers would go in on their scheduled usability lab day and promptly watch their application fail. A usability report was delivered and most changes would be made. Then the developers would parade in to usability and watch their application fail again. UI Design clearly needed to be a formal step in the process and the team campaigned for this. To date, it is now part of the process–however, the process is still being fine-tuned.

VI - A PAIN IN THE NECK: USABILITY TESTING ROUND-AN EXAMPLE

Now, we had our shell and some redesigned applications. We were ready to conduct our first formal Usability testing series. We brought in Financial Consultants from all over the country with different backgrounds and levels of PC experience. Our users were divided into three major groups, Administrative Assistants, Field Champions and FCSAC (Financial Consultants Systems Advisory Council).

Every user that was tested tilted their heads to the right to read the side or secondary tabs. We thought it might present a problem the first or second time through, but this problem persisted, even though the users were now familiar with the tab structure. We assumed the problem stemmed from the readability problems associated with rotating text vertically, since some letters would blend into each other and other letters would kern apart. We tried changing the font, the size, the color, we even anti-aliased the text—still the users tilted their heads and proclaimed they couldn't read the tabs. In addition, if the users found the correct side tab (after tilting their head), they missed the tertiary tabs because they were positioned at the bottom of the application area.

Another problem was that users didn't seem to understand the tab metaphor. The tab, tab, tab metaphor seemed alien to these users, they didn't understand the hierarchical structure. We also learned that part of the problem was one of language—which would have to be addressed separately. What *we* thought a tab should be called was foreign to the end user. So the business partners, who act as liaison to the end users, went out to talk to the Financial Consultants and their Administrative Assistants. Paper prototyping sessions were conducted to determine what the tabs should be named and what tasks would reside under them. Finally, users were influencing their product's form.

A secondary, but nagging complaint from users was the lack of color. After using PRISM for so long, they became accustomed to looking at a bright screen with large chunks or primary colors (blue, red, yellow and gray). TGA looked "depressing" and "too gray" to them. We had made a conscious effort to keep color to a minimum simply to not distract users and to use color only if was truly meaningful not just for aesthetic reasons. An understated and unobtrusive (not to mention not-blinding) interface was our goal. But it seemed our effort went unappreciated. They screamed for bright yellows and reds, greens and blues. Clearly we needed to make a compromise. So we went back to work.

VII - BACK TO THE DRAWING BOARD...AGAIN

After careful consideration of all usability issues, it was decided that we needed to take the design apart and strengthen the metaphor.

The interface was redesigned and the metaphor of a book shelf was introduced. The former four-level tab hierarchy was now

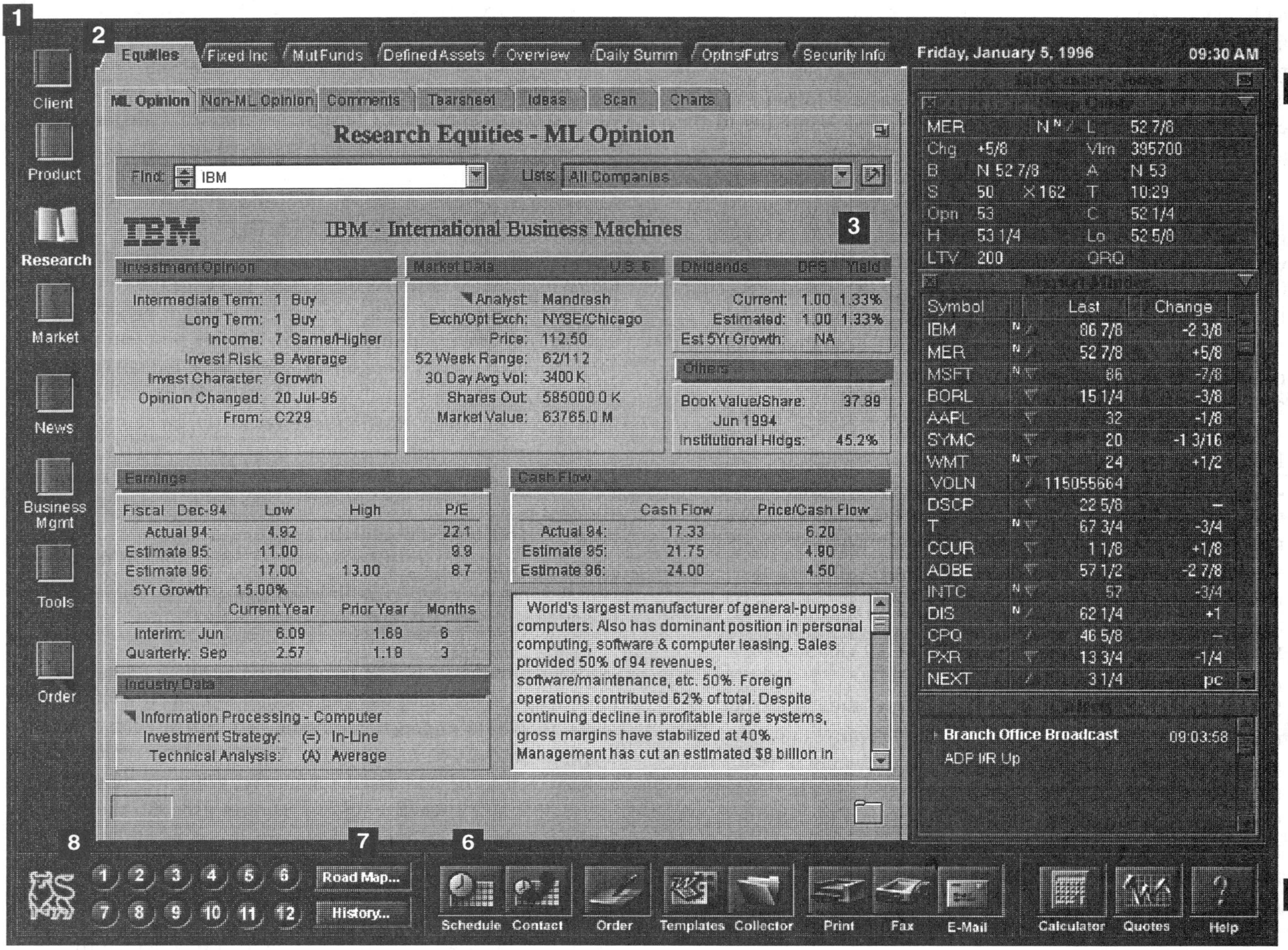

Figure 3. Current TGA

Latest version of TGA. 1. Books located on the left are primary means of navigation, highest level of hierarchy. 2. Tabs and chapters. 3. Application space. 4. InfoCenter. 5. Pop up utilities, such as Help, Snap Quote and Calculators. 6. Action Bar 7. Go To and Return To. 8. Predefined application buttons.

organized and presented on the screen as Books, Tabs, Chapters and Pages. The main benefit of this metaphor is that it hides the complexities of managing multiple applications from the user, while presenting a uniformly logical view of the data. For a novice user, opening a book is a simple as a single mouse click on the cover of the book. Flipping pages is just as simple, with a single click on the desired tab. The hierarchical organization, its dependencies and relationships are clear to the user through this presentation on the screen. For an advanced user, the shell provides short-cut keys to reduce the number of keystrokes and mouse clicks. To aid a novice user, the shell makes all of the transitions smoother and more apparent through extensive use of animation and sound effects.

The InfoCenter was moved to the right-hand side. Though this information was important, users felt it to be secondary to their task at hand. This put focus on the application area, where most of the work is performed.

The top-level tabs were replaced by the books which were placed vertically down the left side of the application area. They were color-coded, each book a different color. The secondary tabs, colored to coordinate with the active book, was moved to the top and the tertiary tabs were replaced by a tab-like control, called chapters, which also indicated if there was a fourth-level selection by an embossed down arrow. By placing all of these navigational controls closer together, we reduced mouse and eye movement greatly. The book, tab, chapter, page metaphor was something all the users could relate to. They could touch it and understand the underlying hierarchy-thereby reducing learning curve.

We increased the use of color in this design. Because we corresponded the color of the books to the associated tabs, at just a glance, users could quickly identify which book they were working in. Additionally we added color to the application space by using colored bars for group boxes and colored triangles for detail indicators, lessening the feeling of "grayness."

Usability Testing Round 2

We started with paper prototypes, taking them to different groups within the Firm. We showed user the old design and compared various versions of the new shell. This time we got a more positive reaction. They commented that the books looked more user-friendly, they were easier on the eye—"no more tilting your head." They liked the color coding of the books and they felt the interface itself was more pleasant to look at. So we proceeded with an electronic prototype. After a few weeks of tweaking the design, it was ready for another round of testing.

Again, we got positive results. Users no longer needed to tilt their heads, it was much easier to read, and they understood the hierarchy. Tertiary selections were easily located, and fourth-level functionality seemed to present no problems.

There were still a few issues to resolve, however. Readability was still clearly an issue. Users, having been used to reading 12 point Courier in all caps, found our 9 point Arial

WHERE WE ARE NOW

At the time of this writing, we are about halfway through our development effort. The shell and its applications are in the final revision stages, in preparation for the first round of Beta testing, which is looming on our calendars. Beta versions are going out in three offices (1 per month for 3 months). Then taking this feedback with us we will pilot TGA in select offices. Eventually a full rollout will commence in late 1996.

CONCLUSIONS

The ever-evolving design process on this project proved to be the biggest learning experience for most members of the team. When TGA was first conceived, this appeared to be a monumental project—one that would never see the light of a computer monitor. Seeing it take shape and was one of the most rewarding aspects of being on this project.

A few lessons learned ingrained in all future process: Prototypes come in all shapes and sizes. When you're still trying out concepts, use prototypes that don't require code. Use paper or multimedia tools to demonstrate your concepts.

We found that the shell was the furthest along in its development cycle (even though it had the fewest business requirements) because we continually prototyped with either still pictures (as in Photoshop) or scripting tools (Director). We could tweak and test until it was right, then we could build it. It doesn't have to "work" to get your ideas across. This way you can quickly mock up a conceptual model without worrying about coding, debugging and data.

Putting together a multidisciplinary Design Team was also an important factor. Once your objectives are clear, each member can contribute something valuable from their own perspective. It provides a more multidimensional design.

Recognize the iterative nature of the UI development process. Design solutions are seldom found at the start of any development project.

Another important lesson, especially in the corporate environment, is compromise. Deadlines are mightier than the standard, or usability, or UI design. Accept incremental changes. Developers want to build the best system they can and if they accept you as part of the team, there's no better partnership.
When in a team that is responsible for making decisions that affect many development areas, always defer to the person with the expertise (not the highest ranking member) when no one agrees. This is the whole point of a multidisciplanry team.

Mobilizing a larger entity such as the Design Team into the trenches can prove to gain many allies, especially if there is initial resistance to the design process. Working sessions are much more productive than being viewed as a sign-off checkpoint.

Lessons learned from the development community: to never turn away a user interface designer who wants to help. Working in a vacuum is not user-centered design, and it can be a lot of time wasted going in the wrong direction. User Interface designers and human factors specialists should get in the process as early as possible. There's nothing less productive than telling developers that "their baby is ugly" two thirds of the way into the development effort.

ACKNOWLEDGEMENTS

The work presented in this design briefing represents the collaborative work of many talented, committed and hard-working individuals, inspiring visionaries and brave leaders. These people include Ritch Gaiti,Andy Williams, Tony Pizi, Paul Kanevsky, the members of the Design Team: Alan Amira, Laura Flannery, Phil Gilligan, Betty Greenberg, Paul Ilechko, Pat McAleavy, Janine Purcell, Nicole Speigel, Maury Weinberg, and Christine Zafiris. Members of the development team: Ashe Vashtare, Chris Cobb, Doug Breuninger, Rob Sterlacci, Pam Smith, and numerous others who made this project possible.

New Technological Windows into Mind: There is More in Eyes and Brains for Human-Computer Interaction

Boris M. Velichkovsky
Unit of Applied Cognitive Research
Dresden University of Technology
D-01062 Dresden, Germany
++49 351 4634221
velich@psych.tu-dresden.de

John Paulin Hansen
System Analysis Department
Risoe National Laboratory
Roskilde DK-4000, Denmark
++45 467 75155
paulin@risoe.dk

ABSTRACT
This is an overview of the recent progress leading towards a full subject-centered paradigm in human-computer interaction. At this new phase in the evolution of computer technologies it will be possible to take into account not just characteristics of average human beings, but create systems sensitive to the actual states of attention and intentions of interacting persons. We discuss some of these methods concentrating on the eye-tracking and brain imaging. The development is based on the use of eye movement data for a control of output devices, for gaze-contingent image processing and for disambiguating verbal as well as nonverbal information.

Keywords
Attention, eye movements, human-computer interaction (HCI), neuroinformatics, levels-of-processing, noncommand interfaces, computer supported cooperative work (CSCW)

INTRODUCTION
Profound technological changes are sometimes caused by events initially considered to be completely irrelevant. It seems that we may be well on the eve of such changes in human-computer interaction, and these changes will be brought about by the recent development in the research methods of cognitive neuroscience. The emerging perspective is that of "subjective age" in the development of telematics. At this new phase in the evolution of computer technologies it will be possible to take into account not just some statistical characteristics of human beings, but create technical systems sensitive to a broad spectrum of actual states and intentions of a person. We are going to discuss -- and to demonstrate -- some of these perspectives concentrating on the following domains: brain imaging methods and, particularly, eye movement research. At the end, we will shortly refer to some relevant issues in the interdisciplinary field of neuroinformatics.

CHI 96 Vancouver, BC Canada
© 1996 ACM 0-89791-777-4/96/04..$3.50

ADVANCED EYE-TRACKING
A remarkable development takes place in the eye movement research. The new generation of eye-trackers replaces the nightmare situation of former laboratory studies (with subject's immobilization, prohibited speech, darkness, re-calibration of the method after every blink, etc.) by ergonomically acceptable measurement of gaze direction in a head-free condition. The new methods are fast and increasingly non-invasive [1, 7, 8, 19]. This implies that the process of eye movement registration does not interfere with other activities a person is involved in. As the gaze-direction is the only reliable (albeit not ideal) indices of the locus of visual attention there is an almost open-end list of possible applications of this methodology.

Gaze direction for a control of user- interfaces
The first and most obvious application can be called "eye-mouse". Some previous attempts of the kind have not been very successful as they failed to recognize a difference between eye movements and attention (cf. the so-called "Midas touch problem" [8]). By building in temporal filters, introducing an explicit clutch and/or clustering the fixations resulting from fast search saccades it is possible to guaranty practically errorless use of gaze direction for operating virtual keyboards and managing graphical user interfaces (GUI) [7, 16]. The eye-mouse reduces selection time in general. Its primary application area is where it is difficult or impossible to use the hands. In particular, physically disable or elderly persons no longer in command of their limbs and speech mechanisms may improve their communication abilities with this type of system. Eye movements data can be used to control different electronic devices,

including e-mail, fax, telephones, videophones and speech generators.

In contrast to the manually-controlled computer-mouse, an eye-mouse does not need an explicit visual feedback. However to ensure a high degree of reliability it has been suggested to give a visual feedback on the so-called dwell-time activation of buttons [7]. Fig.1 shows how this idea of an „Eyecon" may be realized. A small animation is made up by playing the sequence of buttons within 500 ms, each time the button is activated by a dwell. Besides from giving the user an opportunity to regret the activation, the animation in itself holds attention of the user at a precise location, which makes it possible to re-calibrate the system each time a button is used. A study of users acceptance performed on the Eyecon system found a spontaneous positive attitude towards the principle [5]. In general more than 95% of responders evaluated the interaction as "exiting", about 70% expressed their believe that they expect "to see eye tracking in the future as an everyday thing".

Figure 1

A different approach to gaze-mediated interaction is simply to leave the idea of using eye-tracking as a substitute for a mouse. Instead, the raw data may be interpreted at a higher semantic level and used in a new type of *noncommand* multimedia applications, which continuously measure the amount of attention being paid to individual objects in the display (see e.g. [9, 17]). It has been proposed to term this noncommand interaction principle "interest and emotion sensitive media" (IES) [7]. The possibility of making a coupling of ocular measurements and the stimuli material allows for a quasi-passive user influence on electronic media. This can be achieved by measuring 1) the interest of the users by identification of the areas of attention on complex templates, and 2) their emotional reactions by evaluating the blink rate and changes in pupil size (cf. [7, 19]). IES may respond to these continuous measurements at narrative nodes by editing among the branches of a multiplex script board that will in turn influence the composition and development of events being watched.

Of course, several hybrid solutions for a combination of command and noncommand principles are possible. In Fig.2A traditional GUI-style buttons are used for gaze-pointing. In the next two pictures alternative selection objects are either explicitly delineated (2B) or their active areas are marked by a higher optical resolution (2C). Finally, in Fig.2D objects are functioning as implicit (non-visible) buttons of shifting size and location for the quasi-passive mode of operation.

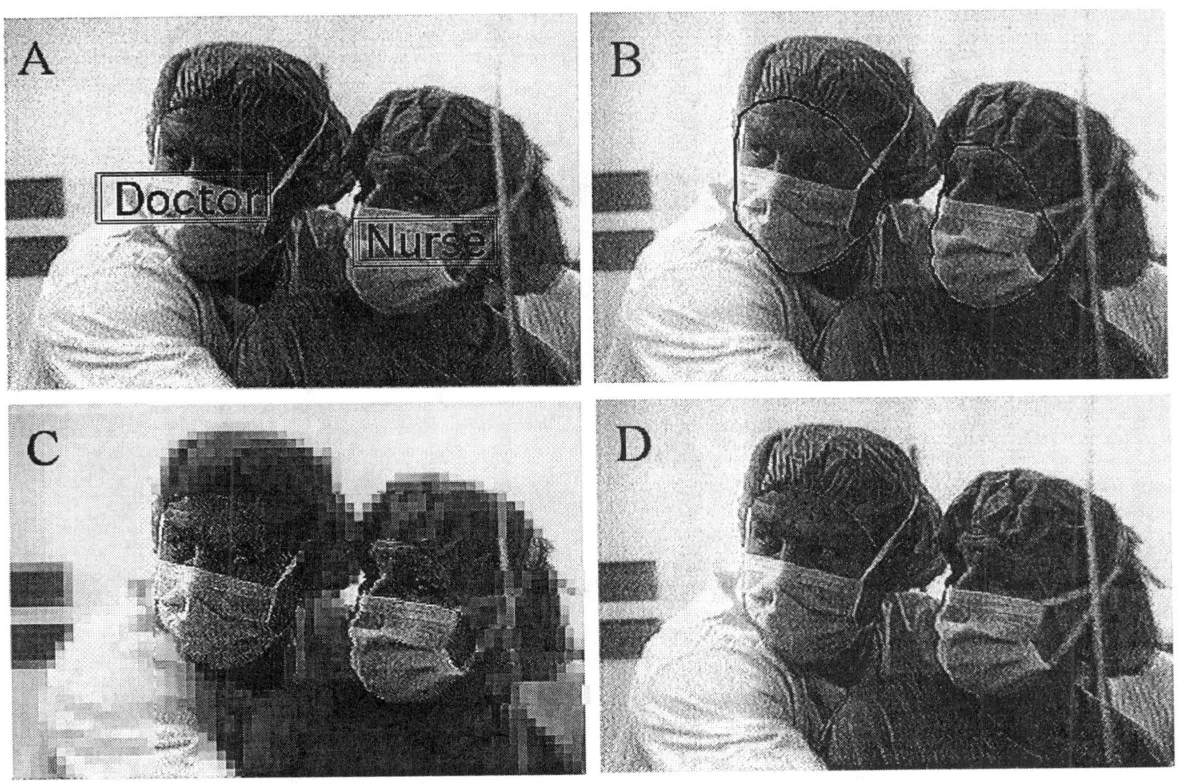

Figure 2

Towards a new generation of communication tools

Our next example is related to communication of intentions. It is well known that the efficiency of face-to-face interaction is higher than the efficiency of the most sophisticated multimedia forms of communication and CSCW tools, which are in turn better than email or voice communication [13]. There is a way to narrow (and even to overcome) this gape by appropriate management of attentional resources. This can be done on a modern technological level but in principle along the lines of organization of early mother-child communication: by supporting the "joint attention" state of the partners [2, 23]. Such a state implies that the partners are to be able to attend -- and therefore to fixate -- the same objects at the same time. In a series of experiments we succeeded to demonstrate that a transfer of the gaze direction data from an expert to a novice helps in the solution of a puzzle task [19, 20].

Closely related are tasks of interactive documentation and cooperative support: As a service engineer is performing maintenance or repair work on a device he or she might get advice from a human expert located at a remote site. Because eye-movement data reveal insights about the central aspects of problem solving, the technology allows us on the one hand to make an expert's way of performing available to novices (without having to formalize anybody's knowledge). On the other hand it gives the possibility to monitor and, if necessary, correct a novices performance (see [19], Experiment 2). Another currently relevant situation may be the so-called key-hole surgery: the eye fixations of a surgeon can be registered on-line when he or she examines the image provided by an endoscope camera. A colleague controlling the camera would then get a far better support to position the endoscope optimally by knowing from moment to moment what the surgeon is paying attention to.

The second large class of the telematic applications is connected with visualization of users non-verbal perception [14, 20]. Indeed, in real life we are often confronted with situations in which the knowledge needed to solve a problem is not present in an explicit and/or unambiguous form easily available for verbal communication. In order to reconstruct the current subjective interpretation of an ambiguous picture we propose, firstly, to build “attentional landscapes” describing (on the basis of spatial distribution of eye fixations) the resolution functions of visual details and, secondly, to use these attentional landscapes as filters to process the physical image. The usual results are illustrated by Fig.3 where an initial picture (3A) as well as both empirically reconstructed interpretations are shown.

Figure 3A

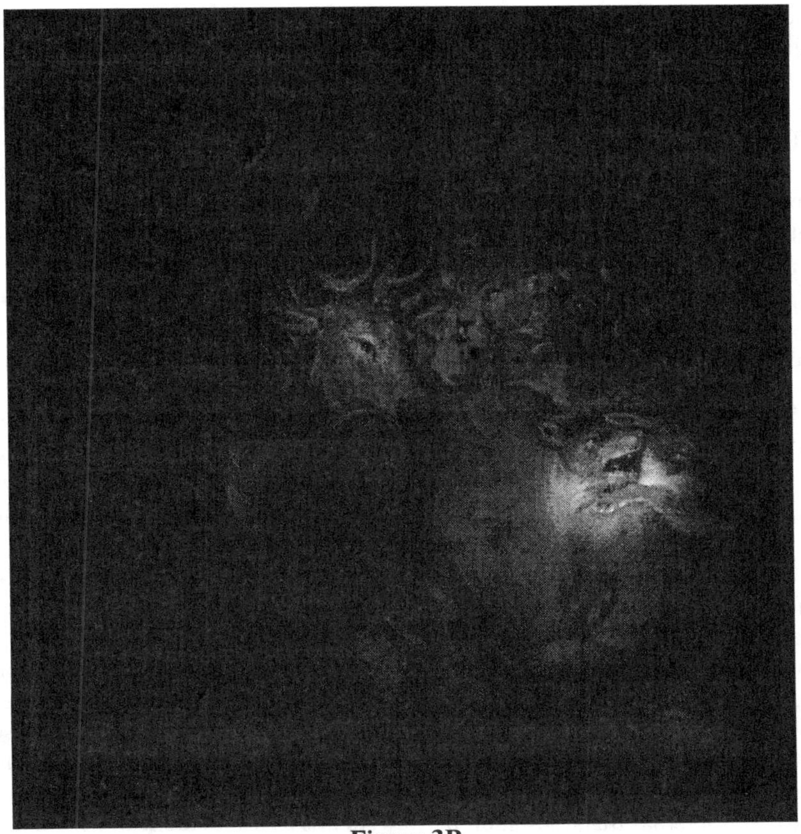

Figure 3B

Figure 3C

With the proposed technology of the gaze-contingent processing (see [11] for technical details) users will be able to exploit implicit knowledge for teaching, joint problem solving, or generally speaking for communicating of practical knowledge and skills. The goal of applying this technology to medical imaging is in particular to make the expertise that is implicit in how experts interpret complex and often ambiguous visual information (like computer tomography, magnetic resonance or X-ray images) available to others for a peer commentary and for training purposes. As the medical diagnostics is a costly and rather unreliable [10] endeavor any form of such a visualization is deserving a public attention.

The basic idea behind these examples is not to simulate the face-to-face communication but enhance it [21]. Gaze-contingent processing can be used for several other purposes as well. One of them can be enhancing low-bandwidth communication, firstly, by an appropriate selection of information channels and, secondly, by transmission with high resolution of only those parts of an image which are at the focus of attention. In this way also low-bandwidth channels can be optimally exploited, e.g. in virtual reality (VR) applications. There is however a general problem on the way to realization of the most of these applications -- not every visual fixation is "filled with attention" because our attention can be directed "inward", on internal transformation of knowledge. This is why in many cases one has to think about a control of the *actual level* of human information processing [3, 18].

FUNCTIONAL BRAIN ANALYSIS

What could be expected from the neurophysiological methods in the present context is to provide some *global information* about modality and level of processing, not the detailed state of every potential "module" of such a processing. We use as a preliminary framework the scheme of the brain developmental gradients shown in Fig.4 (see [4] for a thoroughly analysis). The numbers signify here the coefficients of growth of corresponding regions during the transmission from higher primates to human beings. These gradients -- from mostly posterior (visual) to anterior (prefrontal) regions of the cortex -- demonstrate an increasing conceptually-driven character of human information processing which becomes (with a higher level) more independent from the physical parameters of an interface.

A half of dozen of the modern brain imaging methods, such as Positron Emission Tomography (PET) or Magnetic Resonance Imaging (MRI), belong to the most sophisticated tools of contemporary science. Though the data obtained with these methods are often difficult to interpret the dominating opinion is that they convey stable and in-depth analysis of physiological states and processes. However these methods are extremely expensive and cumbersome in use. Their temporal resolution is also usually very low. There is hardly a chance that the methods will be used during the next years for practical purposes outside medicine.

As an alternative one can think about a variety of simple algorithms of computing parameters of classical EEG data. Particularly, the new method of evoked coherence of EEG [22] allows to differentiate: 1) sensory modalities (e.g. visual or tactile) of information processing; 2) perceptual (data-driven) *versus* cognitive (conceptually-driven) modes of attention, 3) cognitive processing and metacognitive attitudes to the task, others and self. Three brain-coherence images of Fig.5 show how different tasks are performed by the same user with the same visually presented verbal information. One can easily see that the coherent areas of processing (which are darker in the picture) extend to prefrontal areas of cortex with the change of task from superficial visual analysis to semantic categorization and to an evaluation of the personal significance of the material.

The data are similar to those of conventional imaging methods and they are thoroughly comprehensive from the point of view of neuropsychological research. The big difference is that the method of evoked coherence analysis is cheap and easier to perform than the standard imaging procedures. As this new method is rather fast (300 to 500 ms summation time) it may be used for an on-line adaptation of interface characteristics, as it may be necessary for support of direct (data-driven) or indirect (conceptually-driven) modes of work. The second mode of processing have been largely neglected in the modern GUI (see [6] on the recent empirical evidence and implications for interface design). The perspective here is also a support of *multilevel interfaces* in telerobotics where a combination of the eye-mouse and the evoked coherence analysis to detect intentions gives promises of a truly new interaction principle: point with your eye and click with your mind!

A MULTIDISCIPLINARY AGENDA

In line with the vision that the ultimate goal of any technology is to optimally support human resources (knowledge, skills, expertise) we are focusing in our investigation on the technology for communication of practical knowledge and skills in geographically distributed environments. Many of the applications we describe in the paper would be impossible without combining of data and methods from two domains: computer science and cognitive neurophysiology. For instance, with the novel eye-tracker interfaces based on self-organizing maps it is possible to reach a degree of precision and speed that makes real-time VR's or telematics applications of gaze-contingent processing possible [12]. There are first reports on the completely non-intrusive solutions for eye-tracking based on neural networks [1].

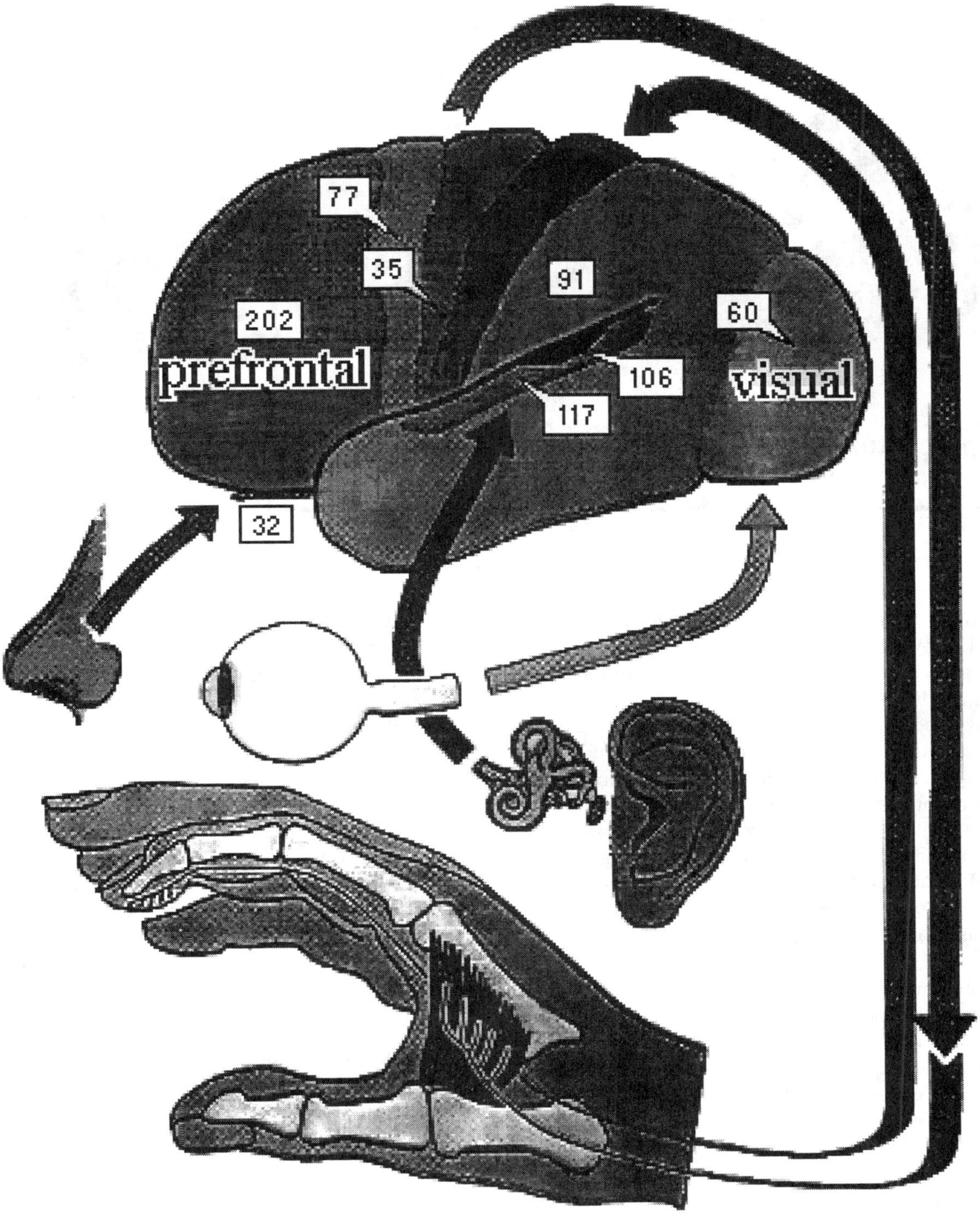

Figure 4

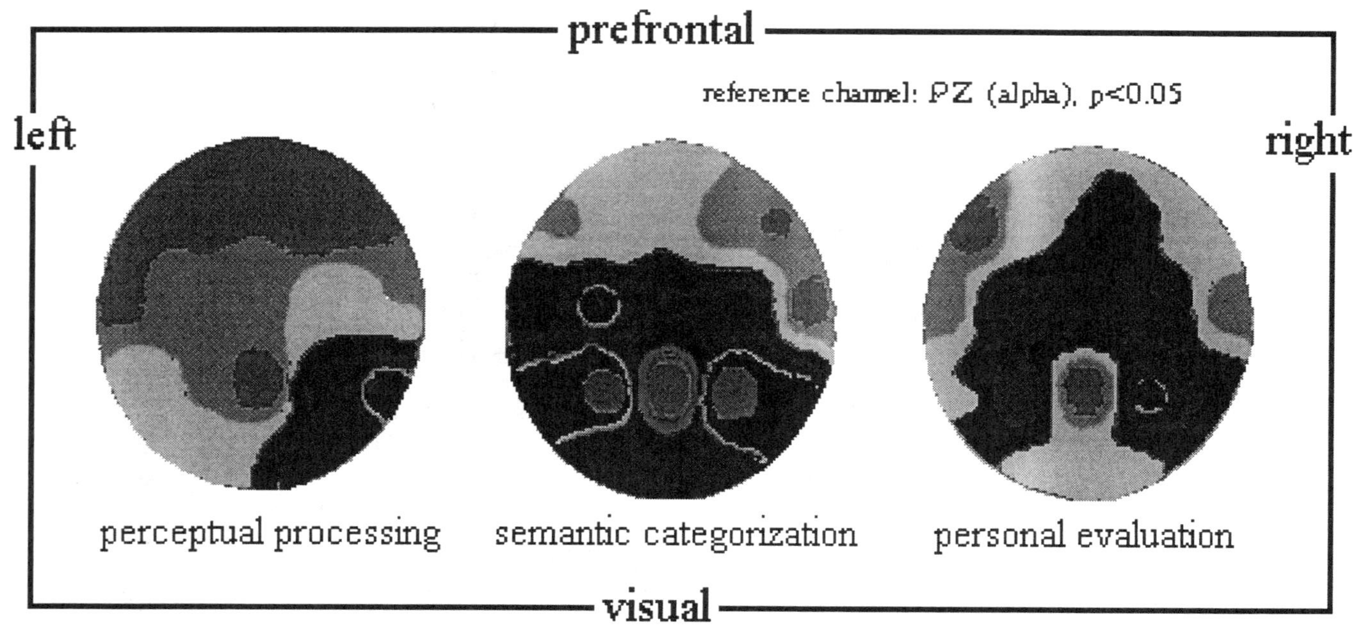

Figure 5

The message of neuroinformatics extends to the very core area of HCI by promising a new generation of flexible, learnable and, perhaps, emotionally responsive interfaces. Such multimodal and multilevel interfaces will connect us not only with computers but also with autonomous artificial agents. In a similar vein, an eclectic combination of location of fixations, their duration, pupil size and blink frequencies as indices of interests or different subjective interpretations of a scene can be recognized by neural networks, which may be individually pretuned in corresponding learning sessions. In addition, the notoriously low learning rate in neural networks can be speeded up by the recent development of the parametrized self-organizing maps [15].

As a whole, the proposed technologies represent a viable alternative to the more traditional (and unfortunately not very successful) approach of expert systems. This concerns in particular the availability of human expertise in remote geographical locations: from Vancouver to, at least, Vladivostok.

ACKNOWLEDGMENTS

We wish to thank Eyal Reingold and Dave Stampe (SR Research, Inc.) as well as Nancy and Dixon Cleveland (LC Technologies, Inc.) for their help in providing us with some of the modern eye-tracking methods. Thanks are due also to Marc Pomplun, Matthias Roetting, Andreas Sprenger, Gerrit van der Veer, Roel Vertigaal and Hans-Jurgen Volke who contributed in a very essential way to the described projects.

REFERENCES

1. Baluja, S., and Pomerleau, D. Non-intrusive gaze-tracking using artificial neural networks. *Neural information processing systems 6*, Morgan Kaufman Publishers, New York, 1994.

2. Bruner, J. The pragmatics of acquisition. In W.Deutsch (ed.), *The child's construction of language.* Plenum Press, New York, 1981.

3. Challis, B.H., Velichkovsky, B.M. and Craik, F.I.M. Levels-of-processing effects on a variety of memory tasks: New findings and theoretical implications. *Consciousness & Cognition, 5(1)*, 1996 .

4. Deacon, T.W. Prefrontal cortex and the high cost of symbolic learning. In B.M.Velichkovsky and D.M.Rumbaugh (eds.), *Communicating meaning: The evolution and development of language.* Lawrence Erlbaum Associates, Hillsdale NJ, 1996.

5. Engell-Nielsen, T., Glenstrup, A.J. and Hansen, J.P. Eye-gaze interaction: A new media -- not just a fast mouse. International *Journal of Human-Computer Interaction Studies*, 1995 (submitted).

6. Guilmore, D.J. Interface design: Have we got it wrong? *Human-computer interaction: Interact '95*, Chapman & Hall, London, 1995.

7. Hansen, J.P., Andersen, A.W. and Roed, P. Eye-gaze control of multimedia systems. In Y.Anzai, K.Ogawa and H.Mori (eds), *Symbiosis of human and artifact. Proceedings of the 6th international conference on*

human computer interaction. Elsevier Science Publisher, Amsterdam, 1995.

8. Jacob, R.J.K. Eye tracking in advanced interface design. In W.Barfield and T.Furness (eds.), *Advanced interface design and virtual environments*. Oxford University Press, Oxford, 1995.

9. Nielsen, J. Noncommand user interfaces. *Communications of the ACM*, 36(4), 83-99, 1993.

10. Norman, G.R., Coblentz, C.I., Brooks, L.R. and Babcock, C.J. Expertise in visual diagnostics: A review of the literature. *Academic Medicine Rime Supplement. 67*, 78-83, 1992.

11. Pomplun, M., Ritter, H. and Velichkovsky, B.M. Disambiguating complex visual information: Towards communication of personal views of a scene. *DFG/SFB360 Situated artificial communicators, Report 95/2*, University of Bielefeld, Bielefeld, 1995.

12. Pomplun, M., Velichkovsky, B.M. and Ritter, H. An artificial neural network for high precision eye movement tracking. In B.Nebel & L.Drescher-Fischer (eds.), *Lectures notes in artificial intelligence*. Springer Verlag, Berlin, 1994.

13. Prieto, F., Avin, C., Zornoza, A. and Peiro, H. Telematic communication support to work group functioning. In *Proceedings of the 7th European conference on work and organizational psychology*, Gyor, 19-22d of April, 1995.

14. Raeithel, A. and Velichkovsky, B.M. Joint attention and co-construction of tasks. B.Nardi (ed.), *Context and consciousness: Activity theory and human-computer interaction*. MIT Press, Cambridge MA, 1995.

15. Ritter, H. Parametrized self-organizing maps. In S.Gielen and B.Kappen (eds.), *ICANN93-Proceedings*, Springer Verlag, Berlin, 1993.

16. Stampe, D. M. and Reingold, E. Eye movement as a response modality in psychological research. In *Proceedings of the 7th European conference on eye movements*, Durham, University of Durham, 31st of August-3d of September, 1994.

17. Starker, I. and Bolt, R. A. A gaze-responsive self-disclosing display. In *CHI'90 Proceedings*, ACM Press, 1990.

18. Velichkovsky, B.M. The levels endeavour in psychology and cognitive science. In P.Bertelson, P.Eelen and G.d'Ydewalle (eds.), *International perspectives on psychological sciences: Leading themes*. Lawrence Erlbaum Associates, Howe UK, 1994.

19. Velichkovsky, B.M. Communicating attention: Gaze position transfer in cooperative problem solving. *Pragmatics and Cognition, 3(2)*, 199-222, 1995.

20. Velichkovsky, B.M., Pomplun, M. and Rieser. H. Attention and communication: Eye-movement-based research paradigms. In W.H.Zangemeister et al. (eds.), *Visual attention and cognition*. Elsevier Science Publisher, Amsterdam, 1996.

21. Vertegaal, R., Velichkovsky, B.M. and G. van der Veer. Catching the eye: Management of joint attention states in cooperative work. *SIGHI Bulletin*, 1996 (submitted).

22. Volke, H.-J. Evozierte Cohaerenzen des EEG I: Mathematische Grundlagen und methodische Voraussetzungen [Evoked coherence of EEG I: Mathematical foundations and methodical preconditions]. *Zeitschrift EEG-EMG*, *26(4)*, 215-221, 1995

23. Vygotsky, L.S. Thought and language, MIT Press, Cambridge MA, 1962 (1st Russian edition, 1934).

The American Library Association

Andrew Magpantay
American Library Association

ABSTRACT

The American Library Association (ALA), a nonprofit educational and service organization based in Chicago, Illinois is the world's oldest and largest professional library association. Founded in 1876, it currently has over 56,000 members – primarily librarians, but also trustees, publishers, and library supporters. Its mission is to provide leadership for the development, promotion, and improvement of library and information services and the profession of librarianship in order to enhance learning and ensure access to information for all.

In 1995, ALA embarked on a five year strategic initiative – ALA Goal 2000 – to advocate for the public's right to a free and open information society. As part of this initiative ALA has expanded its Washington Office, now celebrating its 50th anniversary, to increase its ability to influence national issues, policy and legislation. Additionally, ALA established an Office for Information Technology Policy, also in Washington, D.C., to address complex technology policy issues and promote the development and utilization of electronic access to information as a means to ensure the public's right to a free and open information society.

Common Ground: ALA and the information superhighway.

ALA, through its 11 divisions, 18 round tables, and 59 chapters, sponsors many educational programs related to developments on the information superhighway. Some of the topics covered at the 1995 annual conference in Chicago include: updates on library imaging projects; SGML; the virtual library; Internet access for children; intellectual freedom and privacy on the information superhighway; digital library projects; Internet developments in China and accessing Chinese resources on the Internet; electronic copyright; the World Wide Web; CD-ROM publishing; Internet GUIs; online classification systems; electronic data interchange (EDI); and advanced interfaces to information databases using probabilistic retrieval, classification, clustering, and query expansion.

CHI 96 Vancouver, BC Canada
© 1996 ACM 0-89791-777-4/96/04..$3.50

ALA is also involved in ongoing projects related to the development of the information superhighway.

ICONnect sponsored by the American Association of School Librarians, a division of ALA, is a program of online instruction, mentoring programs, mini-grants, and an Internet home page and gopher to help librarians and teachers teach information-age skills to students.

ALA has also partnered with private corporations to help bring the information super highway into communities. MCI Library LINK is a program sponsored by ALA and MCI to develop telecommunications projects in eight city libraries around the country. Libraries Online is a $3 million initiative with Microsoft to research and develop innovative approaches for extending information technologies to underserved populations.

Common Ground: Serving the information needs of all people.

By type of library there are approximately 15,946 public library facilities, 3,274 academic libraries, and 97,976 libraries in public and private schools, and 12,484 special libraries (i.e., corporate, medical, government libraries, etc.). The best available statistics to date show that approximately 20.9% of the public libraries are connected to the Internet and 67% of academic libraries (including 2-year public and private institutions) are connected, and about 35% of U.S. public schools (K-12) are connected.

Public libraries serve more than half of the adult population. Americans borrow more than 1.5 billion items per year from their public libraries including books and magazines, records, video and audio tapes, toys, games, computer software, and more; public librarians answered some 242 million reference questions in 1993.

Common Ground: Working with others for a free and open information society.

ALA has long been known as a vigorous defender of First Amendment rights. The Library Bill of Rights, adopted in 1939, continues to serve as a model for libraries and communities in defending against those who would censor the reading, viewing, or listening of others. In January 1996 ALA's council adopted 'Access to Electronic Information, Services, and Networks: an Interpretation of the Library Bill of Rights' to serve as a guide to librarians, library trustees, and others. In 1993 ALA, along with 15 other library groups and associations, developed 'Principles for the Development of the National Information Infrastructure' to serve as a guide to policy makers, the public, and industry. These principles offer guidelines for NII policy development in six broad areas: intellectual freedom, intellectual property, privacy, equity, ubiquity, and interoperability.

Currently, the American Library Association, through its membership, staff, and work with other organizations, continues to be active in key legislative and policy areas related to the development of the information superhighway including cybercensorhip, universal access, copyright, and the electronic distribution of government information.

More information about ALA, its policies, and other related documents can be found at *http://www.ala.org*. Questions or comments about the American Library Association can be e-mailed to ALA's Office for Information Technology Policy at `oitp@alawash.org`.

CHIkids: A Common Ground for Kids and Adults

Allison Druin
University of New Mexico
413 Montclaire Drive, NE
Albuquerque, NM 87107
505-256-0908
allisond@unm.edu

ABSTRACT
CHIkids challenges the traditional notion of childcare and rolls summer camp, technology, and CHI into a new hands-on experience for children. This is an opportunity for the next generation to explore computers, technology, and user interface design at the CHI 96 conference. Children (3-12 years of age) will have the opportunity to create multimedia stories, try the latest educational multimedia titles, test emerging software technologies with CHI researchers, and to be conference reporters using desktop publishing tools and the World Wide Web. These activities will be reported on and presented by CHIkids leaders at the close of the CHI 96 conference.

KEYWORDS
CHIkids, children, educational applications, desktop publishing, multimedia, World Wide Web, CD-ROMs, social impact, childcare.

THE CHIKIDS PROGRAM
Today children can interact with characters in age old fables or new original poetry. With computer technologies they can wander through animated reference materials that explain the scientific principles behind a light bulb or a nuclear reactor. With educational applications they can go out in space, back in time, or across the world and learn facts about science, history or geography. Children can also be authors of their own multimedia experiences. They can create World Wide Web pages that present music from around the world. They can design simulations that animate Arctic animals and the yearly snowfall in the North Pole [1] [2].

The games children play, the stories they read and create, and even who children meet, all have changed thanks to today's new computer technologies. It is critical therefore, that we as designers of future technologies stop and listen, observe and collaborate with children of all ages. It is only in this way that we will become sensitive to the needs and desires of one of the fastest growing population of technology users in the world: our children.

CHIkids is a new conference program that grew from its membership as a grassroots effort. Its purpose is to serve CHI researchers, children, and parents:

• For CHI researchers it can offer them the rare opportunity of working with and observing children of all ages enjoying new learning experiences with technology.

• For children it can offer them a creative, innovative program as challenging and exciting as the CHI 96 conference is for their parents.

• For parents it can offer the flexibility of managed childcare with the option of enjoying technology experiences with their children.

It is anticipated that this hands-on interactive program will serve up to 50 children of CHI participants per day, throughout the five days of the CHI 96 conference. Each day children will be grouped by age to explore four different areas of technology activities. This program will be led by KiddieCorp, an experienced childcare facilitator, and CHI volunteers with diverse backgrounds in teaching, graphic design, commercial multimedia development, curriculum and user interface design. What each of these professionals have in common is their interest in children and technology. Each has a strong desire to understand what can be done when lots of wonderful technology is put in the hands of young users. The following further describes the four different areas of technology exploration offered during CHI 96's CHIkids Program.

CD-ROM Field Trips
CHIkids Leader: Barbara Coppolla Jones, Albuquerque Public Schools

In this activity area children will use CD-ROMs and CDi as a way to learn about geography, history or science in an engaging and exciting way. For example, children can become "oceanographers", doing the things real oceanographers do. Or they may be master "sleuths", traveling the world to solve mysteries, learning geography and problem solving as they go. Part of each activity will be exploring these simulated worlds, While other activities will enable them to create multimedia presentations about their experiences, which may be published in the CHIKids Newsletter.

CHIkids Newsroom
CHIkids Leader: Vera Kark, Kark Art

Using current computer-based publishing tools, CHIkids will publish daily news about the CHI conference. Children will research and report on what is happening at the CHI conference's tutorials, panels, paper discussions, and upcoming events. Children may also review and write about various technology experiences that they have had during the CHIkids program. In collaboration with CHI Student Volunteers, CHIkids reporters will write, illustrate, and photograph news as they see it for their stories to be produced in print and electronic form. Both the printed and WWW versions will be distributed to the entire CHI community during the CHI 96 conference.

Multimedia Storytelling
CHIkids Leader: Michael Chanover, Disney Interactive

This area will offer children the chance to become multimedia storytellers. They will be given opportunities to draw, animate, create sounds, write content, use digital photographs all to develop their own interactive multimedia project. Children will come to understand what multimedia is, how it is developed by today's professionals, and what tools are available for children to use. Depending upon the children's interests, they may also be exposed to a range of authoring tools, scripting languages and debugging strategies. Children will come away from their multimedia storytelling experience with a finished multimedia project.

Technology Workouts
CHIkids Leader: Vineel Shah, RDA International

In this activity area children will examine the ways new technologies are tested for usability. Researchers from the CHI community will bring prototype and beta software for children to use. Together they will develop a usability test plan and execute it in a focus group situation. Older children will come to understand what it means to test software, and younger children will have fun playing with new technology experiences not yet available commercially. Researchers will receive valuable feedback from children on their work.

ACKNOWLEDGEMENTS
The CHIkids program gratefully acknowledges the support of all of its corporate sponsors, CHI volunteers, and child participants. In addition, the support of the CHI 96 conference committee, KiddieCorp, and the staff of the ACM have helped to define the scope and vision of CHIkids by donating extraordinary time and effort. Without this diverse and unique partnership the CHIkids program would never have become a reality.

REFERENCES
1. Druin, A. "A Place Called Childhood...". *interactions: New Visions of Human-Computer Interaction*. NY: ACM Press, 111.1 (January, 1996).

2. Druin, A., and Solomon, C. *Designing Multimedia Environments for Children: Computers, Creativity and Kids*. NY: John Wiley and Sons, In press.

Video Figures

The following five papers of the CHI 96 Conference Proceedings have video figures which can be found at the end of the CHI 96 Video Program:

Beating the Limitations of Camera-Monitor Mediated Telepresence with Extra Eyes
Kimiya Yamaashi, *Hitachi Ltd.*, Jeremy R. Cooperstock, Tracy Narine, *University of Toronto*, William Buxton, *University of Toronto and Alias|Waterfront*, (page 50)

A Palmtop Display for Dextrous Manipulation with Haptic Sensation
Haruo Noma, Tsutomu Miyasato, Fumio Kishino, *ATR Communications Systems Laboratories*, (page 126)

BrightBoard: A Video-Augmented Environment
Quentin Stafford-Fraser, *Rank Xerox Research Centre*, Peter Robinson, *University of Cambridge*, (page 134)

Wayfinding Strategies and Behaviors in Large Virtual Worlds
Rudolph P. Darken, *Naval Research Laboratory*, John L. Sibert, *The George Washington University*, (page 142)

Pavlov: Programming By Stimulus-Response Demonstration
David Wolber, *University of San Francisco*, (page 252)

In addition to these video figures, the CHI 96 Video Program includes the following technical videos, several of them also related to projects presented in other papers:

Visualization

Dynamic Timelines: Visualizing the History of Photography
Robin L. Kullberg, *MIT Media Laboratory*

Visualizing Large Trees Using the Hyperbolic Browser
John Lamping, Ramana Rao, *Xerox PARC*

The Influence Explorer–a Tool for Design
Lisa Tweedie, Bob Spence, Huw Dawkes and Hua Su, *Imperial College*

LifeLines: Visualizing Personal Histories
Brett Milash, Catherine Plaisant, Anne Rose, *University of Maryland*

Visualizing Information Retrieval Results: A Demonstration of the TileBar Interface
Marti A. Hearst, Jan O. Pedersen, *Xerox PARC*

Exploring Information With Visage
Peter Lucas, *MAYA Design Group, Inc.*, Steven F. Roth, *Carnegie Mellon University*

Design

SILK: Sketching Interfaces Like Krazy
James A. Landay, *Carnegie Mellon University*

TIME: Three-dimensional Input, Modification and Evaluation
Maarten Gribnau, Gert Pasman, *Delft University of Technology*

NEIMO, a Multiworkstation Usability Lab for Observing and Analyzing Multimodal Interaction
Joelle Coutaz, Daniel Salber, Eric Carraux, *CLIPS-IMAG*, Nathalie Portolan, *CCETT*

Light Switch Exploration Video 25th June 1995
Sam Hecht, *IDEO Product Development*

New Directions

Adaptative User Interfaces with Force Feedback
Christophe Ramstein, Jean-Francois Arcand, Martin Deveault, *Centre for Information Technology Innovation*

Temporal Typography: a Proposal to Enrich Written Expression
Yin Yin Wong, *MIT*

Lifestreams: an Alternative to the Desktop Metaphor
Scott Fertig, Eric Freeman, David Gelernter, *Yale University*

Improvisational Animation
Athomas Goldberg, Ken Perlin, *New York University*

World Wide Web

Browsing Anatomical Image Databases: A Case Study of the Visible Human
Chris North, Flip Korn, *University of Maryland*

The WebBook and the Web Forager: Video Use Scenarios for a World-Wide Web Information Workspache
Stuart K. Card, George G. Robertson, William York, *Xerox PARC*

The DeckScape Web Browser
Marc H. Brown, Digital *Equipment Corporation*, Robert A. Shillner, *Princeton University*

Copies of the Video Program are available in VHS (PAL or NTSC) and may be ordered prepaid from:

ACM Member Service Department
1515 Broadway
New York, NY 10257, USA

Telephone: +1 212 626 0500
Fax: +1 212 944 1318

E-mail: acmhelp@acm.org
ACM Order Number: 608962
ISBN Number: 0-89791-831-2

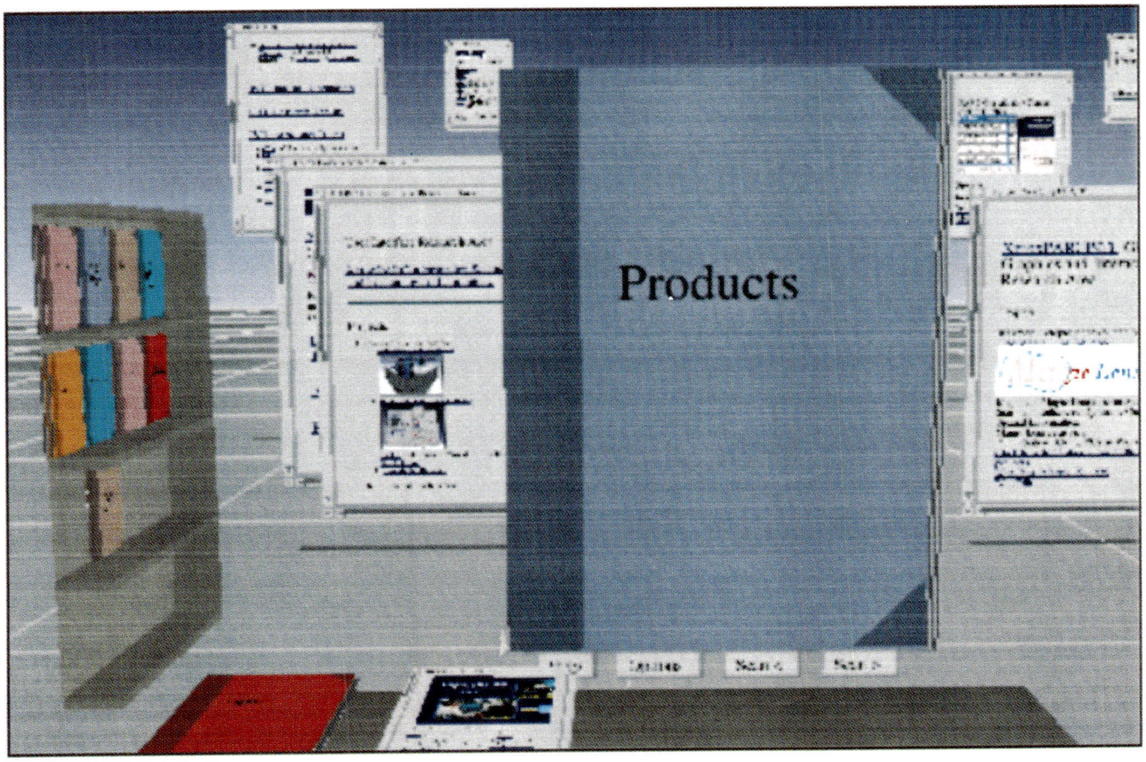

Card, Plate 1 (Fig. 5). The Web Forager.

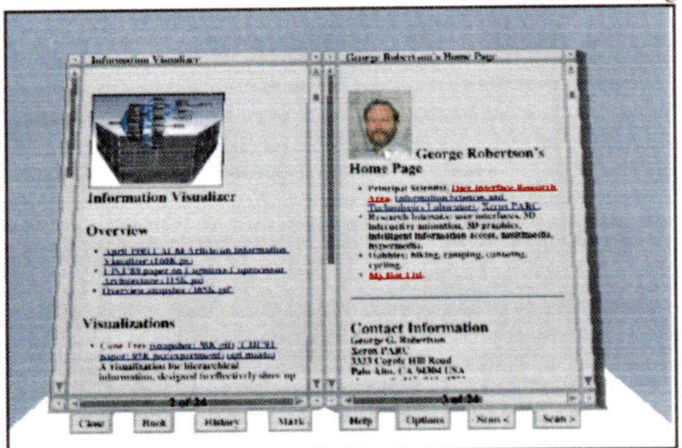

Card, Plate 2 (Fig. 2). Example of a WebBook.

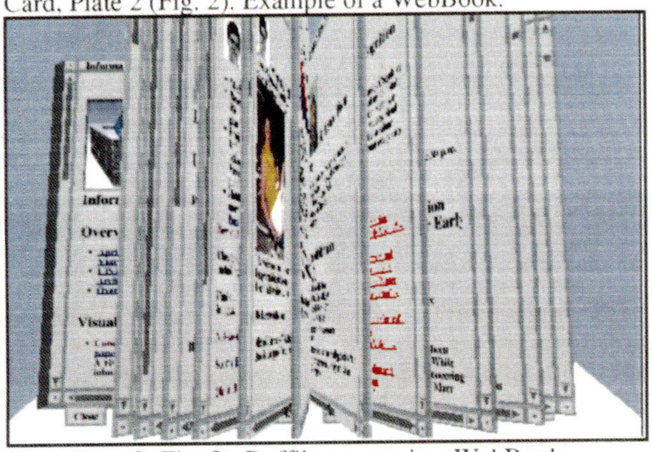

Card, Plate 3 (Fig. 3). Ruffling pages in a WebBook.

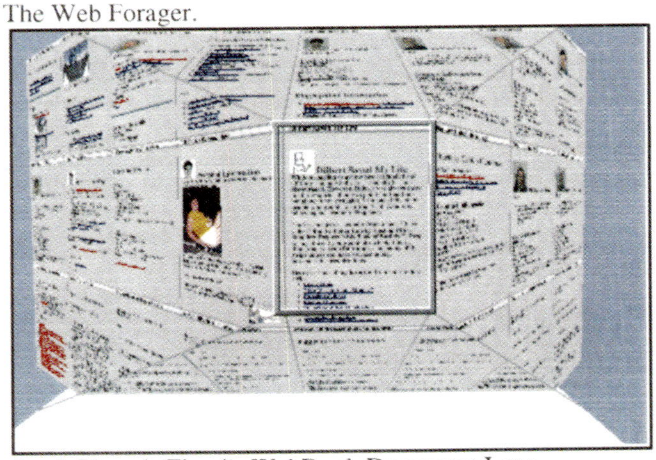

Card, Plate 4 (Fig. 4). WebBook Document Lens.

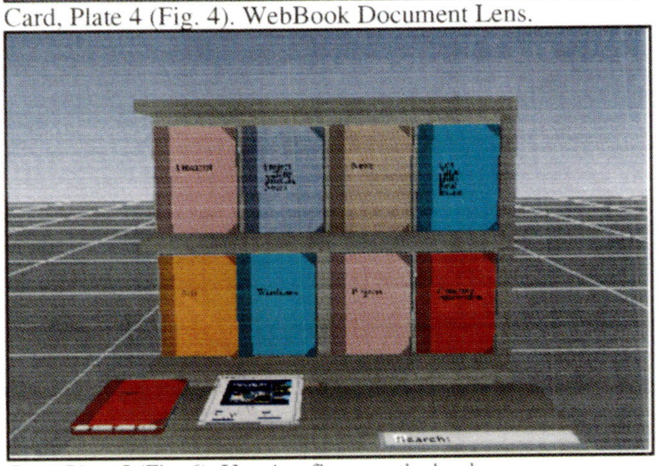

Card, Plate 5 (Fig. 6). User has flown to the bookcase

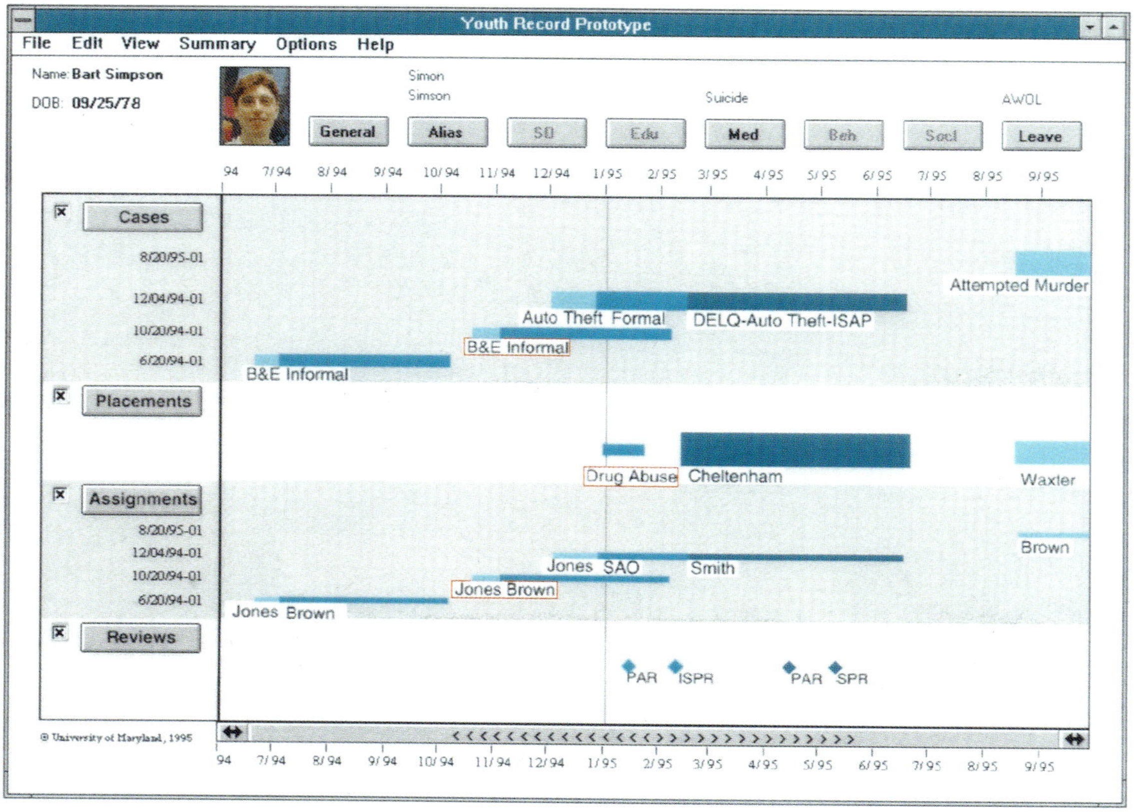

Plaisant, Color Plate 1 - Using LifeLines for Juvenile Justice records. This simple youth record shows cases, placements, assigned workers and available reviews. We can see a history of four cases, three already closed, one opened. A click on the "drug abuse" program highlights the labels of the associated breaking and entering case, and the workers who were assigned to the case (using red in this figure, but gray-out in the prototype).

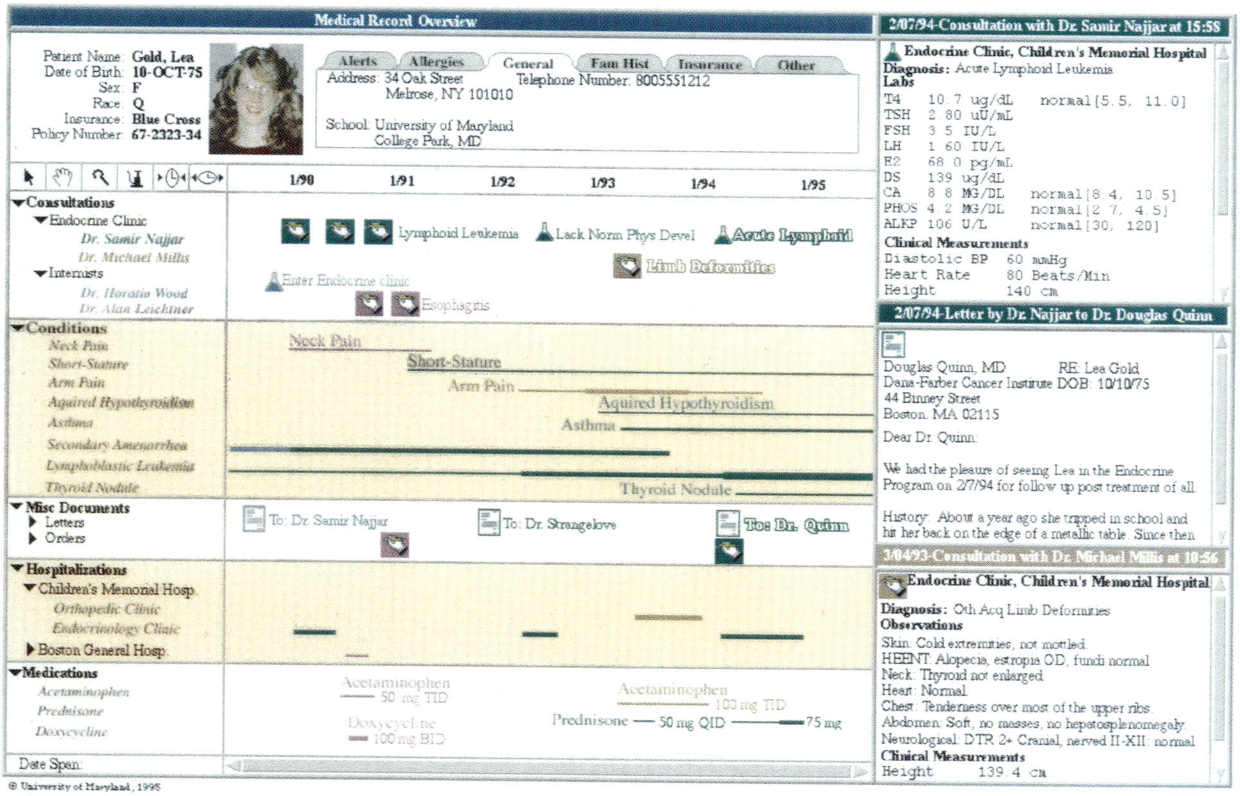

Plaisant, Color Plate 2 - Using LifeLines for medical records. Consultations, manifestations, documents, hospitalizations and treatments are shown in this record. Each doctor has a unique color. Line thickness shows severity and dosage. (Data partly based on a real case found in the literature.)

Douglas and Kirkpatrick Color Plates

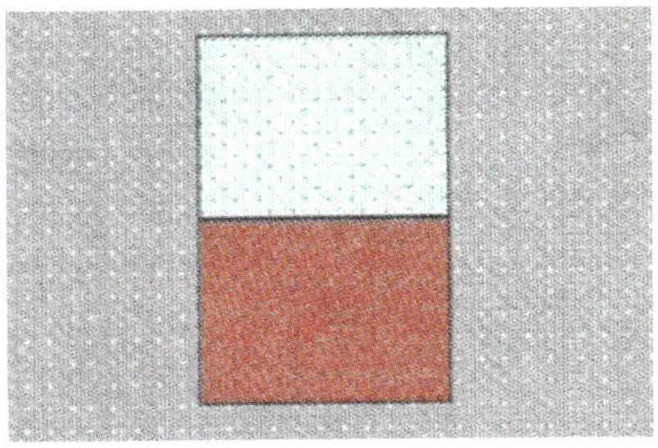

Color Plate 1: the style of display used in the Schwarz experiment. The top color is the "target" and the bottom color is the "controlled" color.

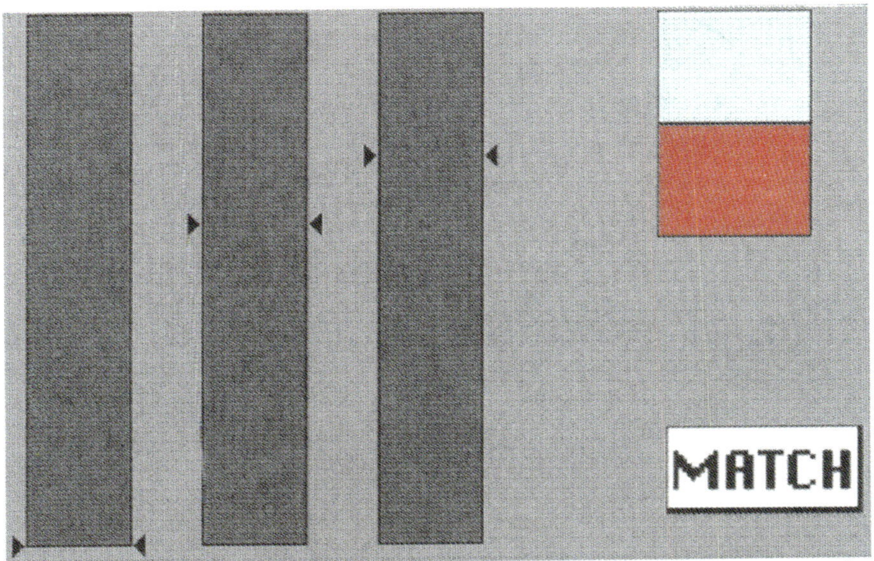

Color Plate 2: the "position-only" feedback level. The light green rectangle is the target color, while the color of the red rectangle is controlled by the positions of the arrows on the three sliders to the left.

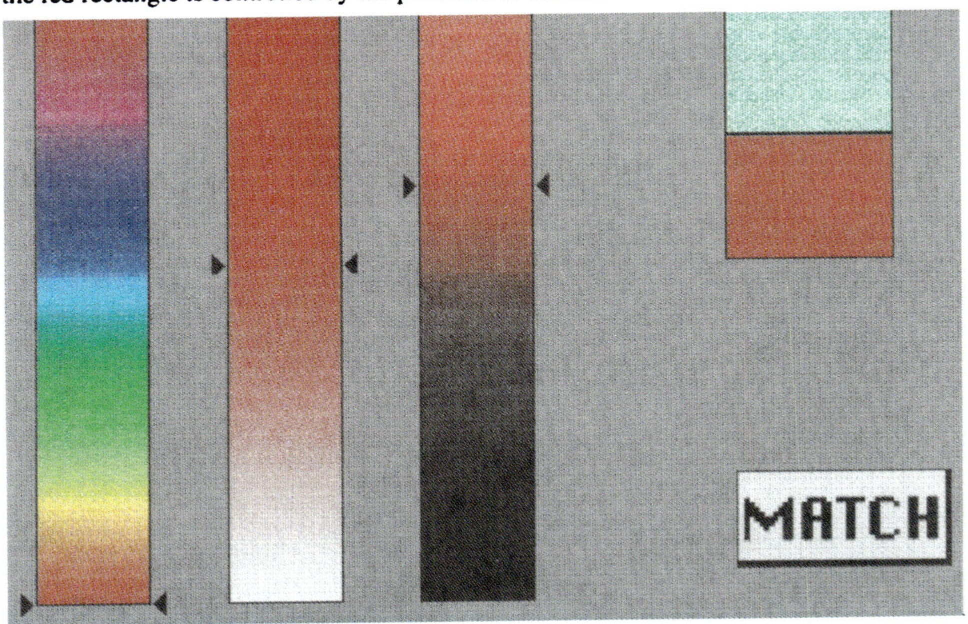

Color Plate 3: the "position+effect" feedback level. The interface components are the same, except now the sliders display the effects of the next move.

Figure 6: Setting up limits on the performance histograms (left)

Pass all limits
Fail 1 limit
Fail 2 limits
Fail 3 limits
Fails >3 limits

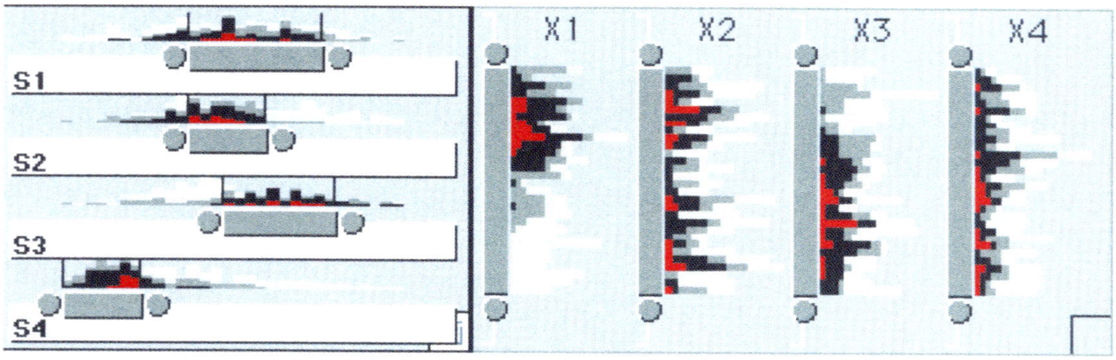

Figure 7: Setting up ranges on the parameter histograms.

Performances / Parameters: P, *, ** (colour matrix)

P = pass all perf. or para. limits
* = fail one perf. or para. limit
** = fail > one perf. or para. limit

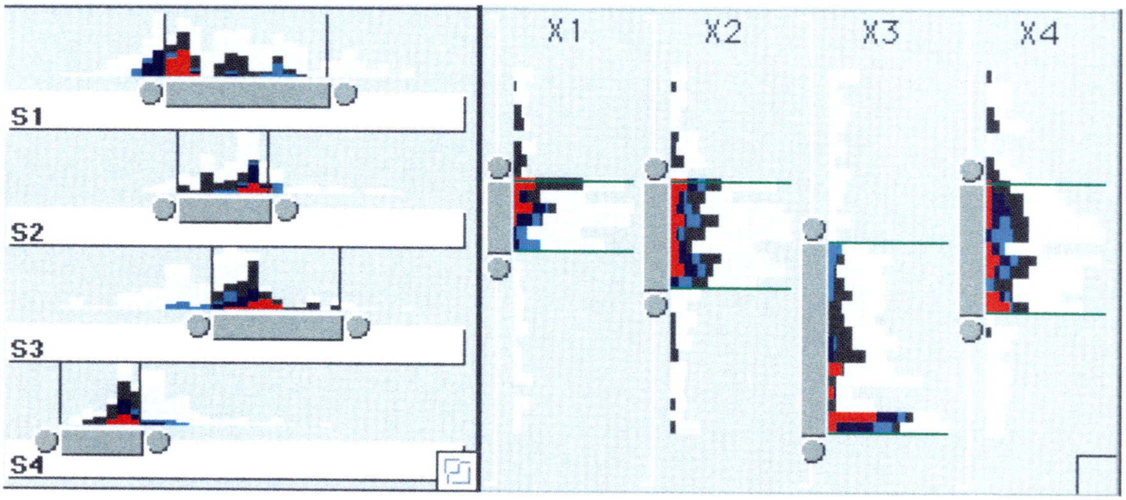

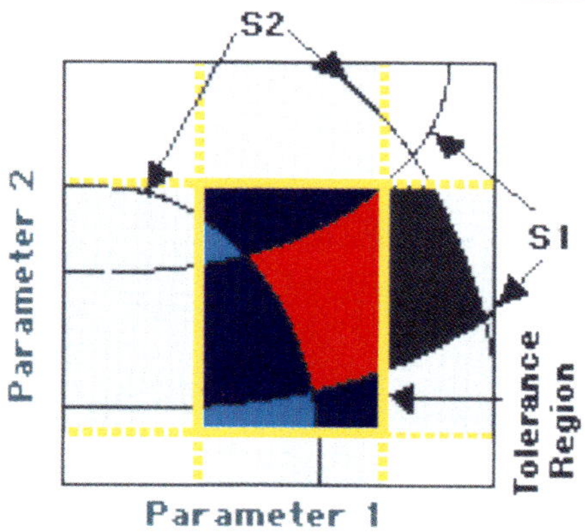

Figure 8: The colour coding for the tolerance setting (Figure 7) shown in 2 parameter space.

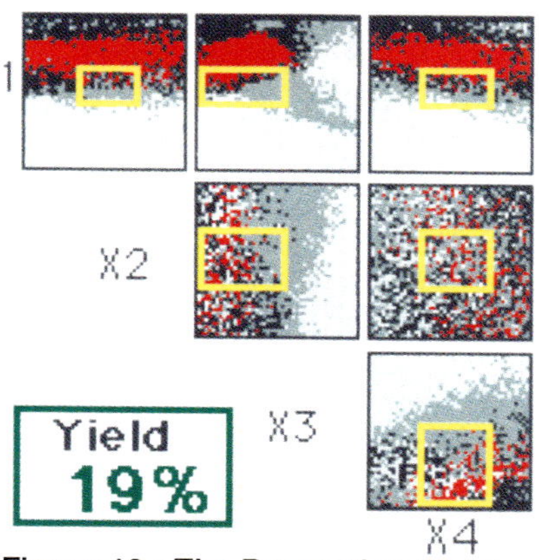

Figure 13 : The Prosection Matrix for the settings from figure 7.

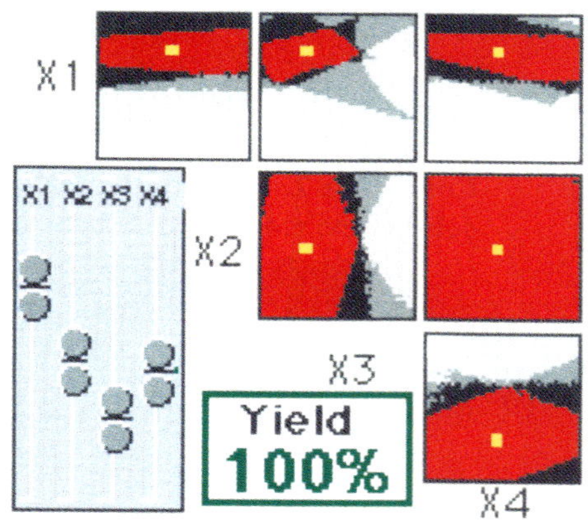

Figure 14: Here the parameter ranges are reduced to single values .

Figure 15: Maximising the widths of the parameter ranges to get high yield and minimum cost. (the same specification is used as in Figure 6). Note how the rectangular tolerance region just fits inside the red region of acceptability.

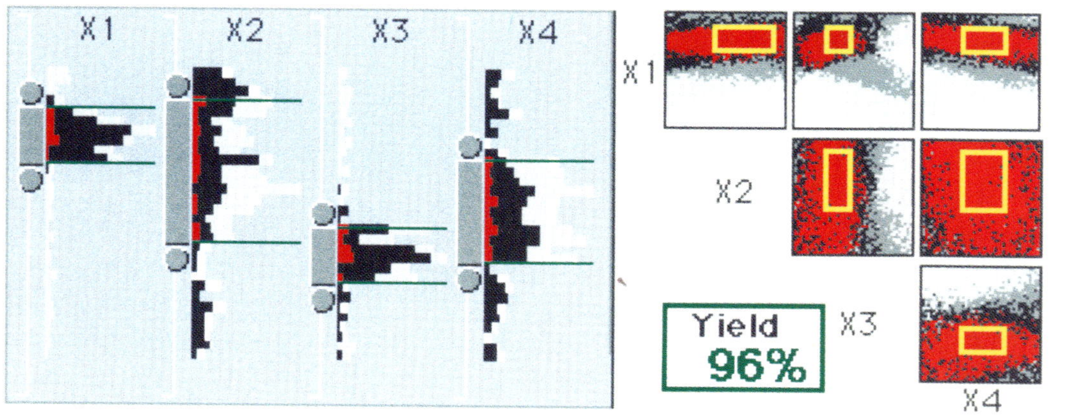

Figure 1 The first foam-core display model.

Figure 3 The original metronome interface.

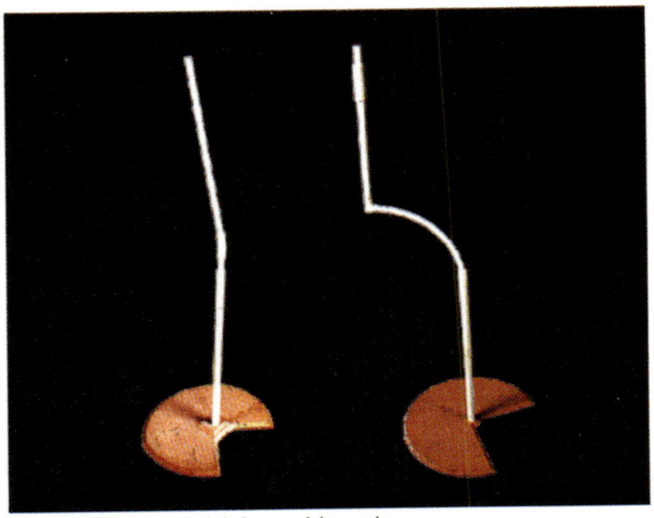

Figure 2 Some initial stand iterations.

Figure 4 The original tuner interface.

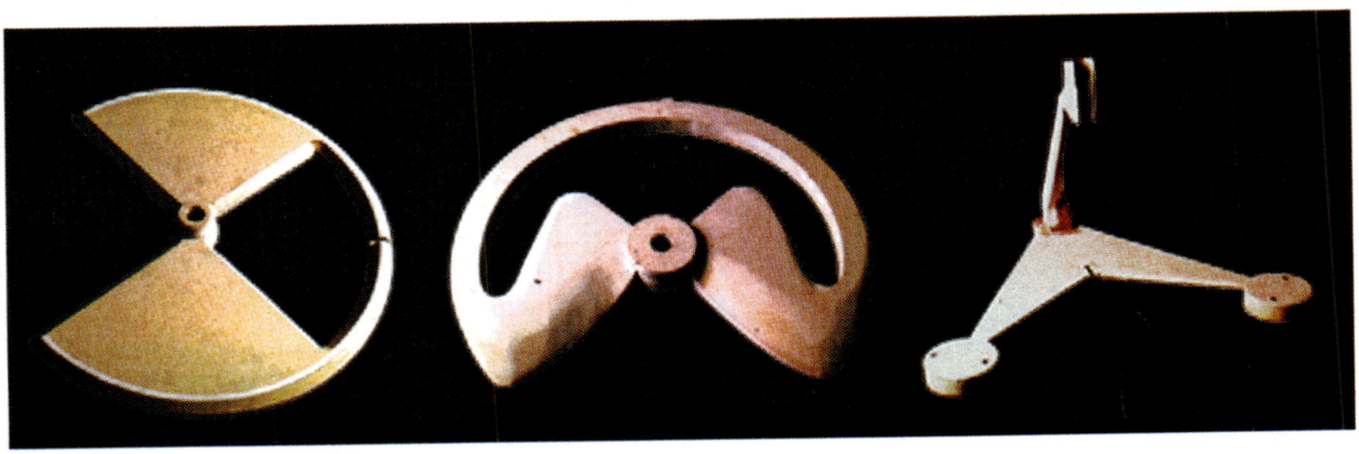

Figure 5 Early versions of the muse base.

Figure 6 The redesigned model, incorporating the new form language.

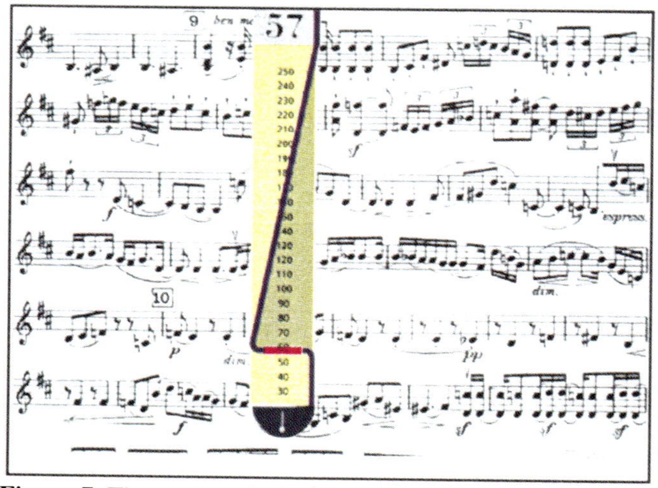

Figure 7 The metronome using the new palette.

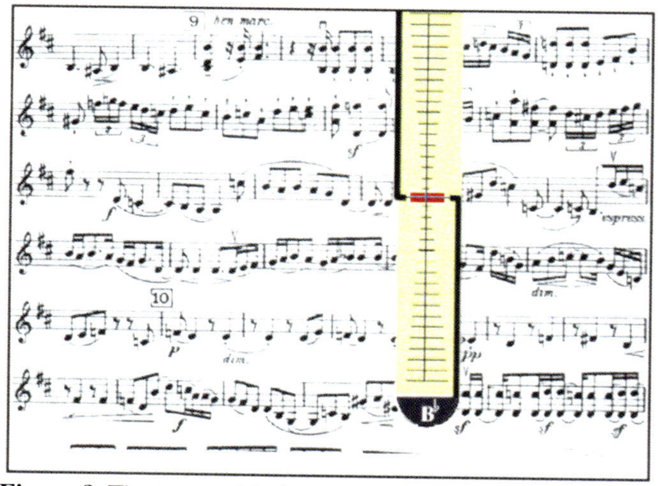

Figure 8 The tuner with the same design language.

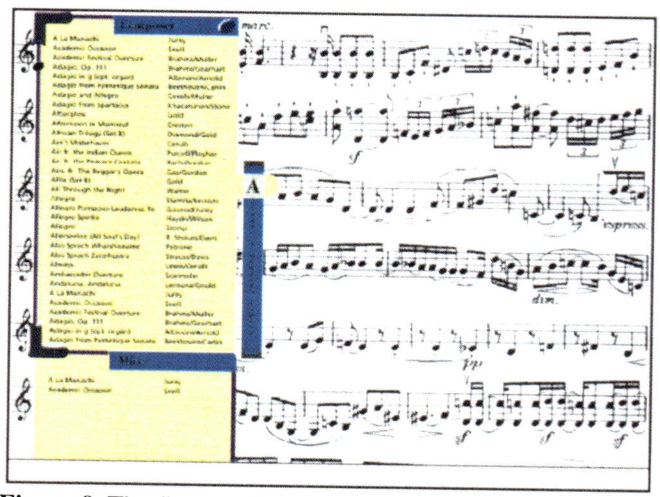

Figure 9 The first version of the library interface.

Figure 10 The final muse model.

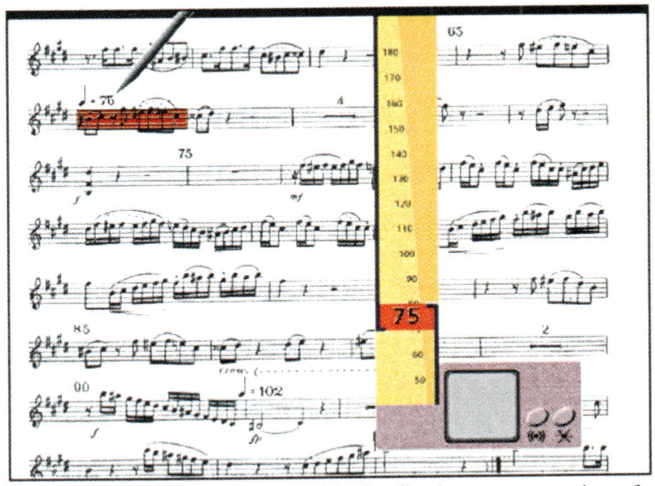

Figure 11 Setting a tempo with the final metronome interface.

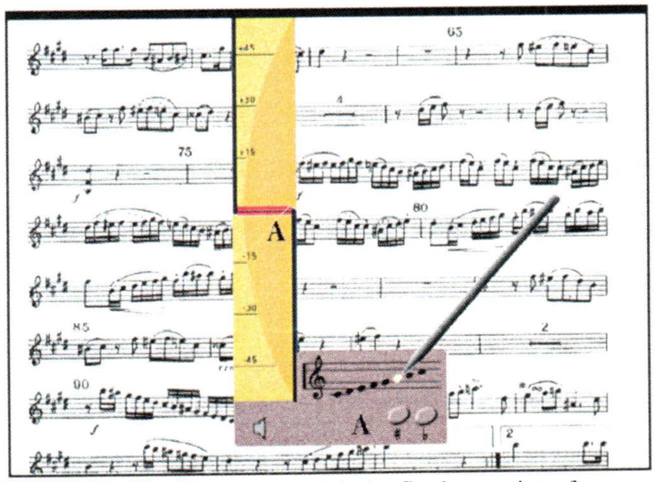

Figure 12 Choosing a note with the final tuner interface.

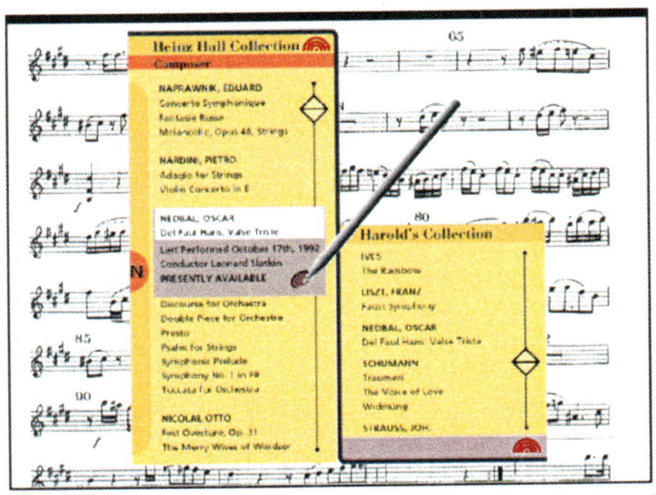

Figure 13 Using the final library interface to download music.

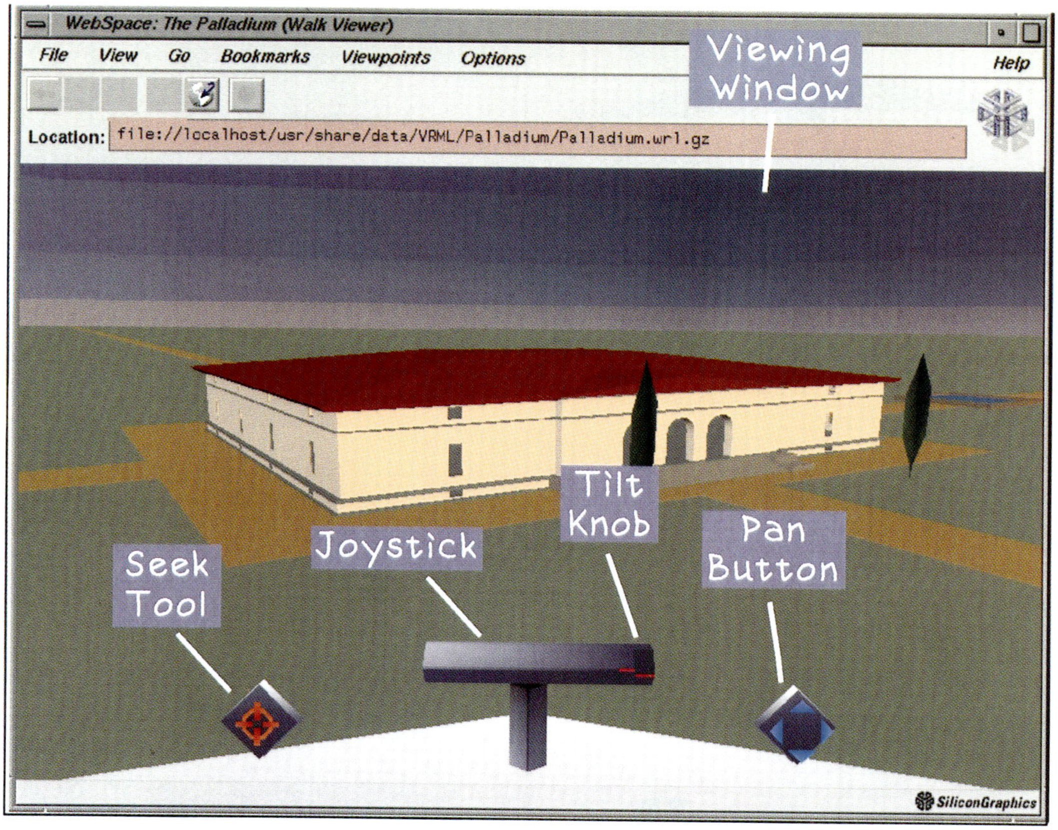

Figure 1 – WebSpace 1.0

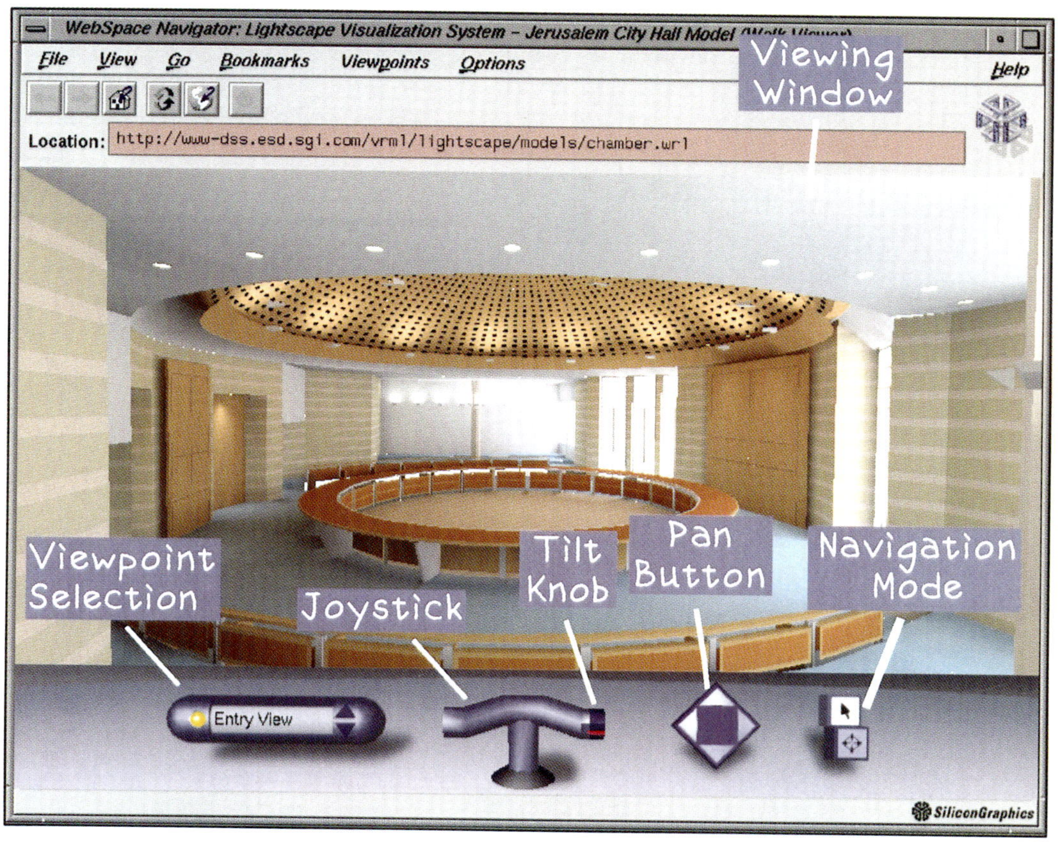

Figure 2 – WebSpace 1.1

ACM SIGCHI CONFERENCE PROCEEDINGS & VIDEOS

THE BEST IN MULTIMEDIA BOOKS

ACM Press Books

Current, insightful information at your fingertips is what you get with ACM Press Books. This collaborative effort between ACM and Addison-Wesley publishes the latest material in computer science and engineering.

Multimedia Programming

Object, Environments and Frameworks

Simon J. Gibbs, Dionysios C. Tsichritzis

As multimedia converges with communications, programmers are faced with the challenge of building increasingly complex interactive applications.

This book is an invaluable resource for programmers who may not be familiar with many of the techniques and terms associated with multimedia. It provides a conceptual foundation for multimedia programming based on object-oriented techniques, and explores software development environments including CD-i, QuickTime, and Multimedia PC, specifically designed for multimedia applications.

ISBN: 0-201-42282-4 ACM Order #: 704944 Members: ~~$31.95~~ **$26** Non-Members: ~~$35.50~~ **$28**

Multimedia Systems

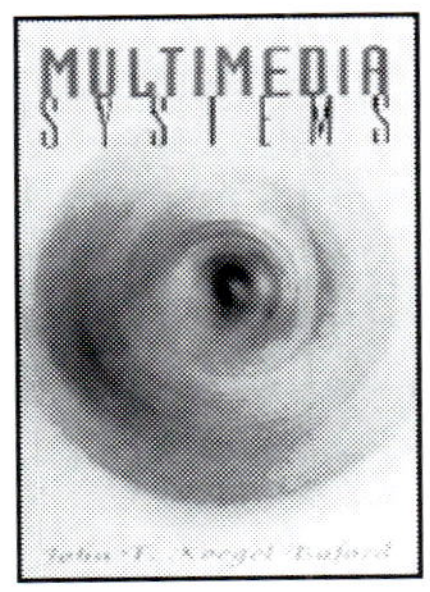

John F. Koegel Buford

"I like the Buford book because it's a timely compendium of many multimedia technologies, all of which are important to today'spractitioners ..."
Richard L. Phillips, *Los Alamos National Laboratories*
co-author, *Introduction to Computer Graphics*

With ongoing work in computing and communications driving new multimedia applications, designers and developers need convenient access to the latest ideas and experiences. Carefully edited by John F. Koegel Buford, *Multimedia Systems* brings such information together in one place and provides a coherent framework for understanding this rapidly changing field.

The book includes important interdisciplinary aspects of multimedia systems, among them, sound and video recording, television engineering, digital signal processing, systems architectures, user interfaces, and algorithms.

ISBN: 0-201-53258-1 ACM Order #: 704940 Members: ~~$40.75~~ **$33** Non-Members: ~~$45.25~~ **$36**

ALSO AVAILABLE

Multimedia Interface Design

Meera M. Blattner, Roger Dannenberg

ISBN: 0-201-54981-6 ACM Order #: 704920
Members: ~~$41.75~~ **$33** Non-Members: ~~$46.25~~ **$37**

ACM Press Books are available where technical books are sold. Or order directly from Addison-Wesley by calling 1-800-447-2226. ACM members should call 1-800-342-6626 (US and Canada) or +1-212-626-0500 (metro NY and outside the US) to receive member discount.

CHI96